John Walton
Northwestern University

Donald E. Carns
University of Nevada, Las Vegas

ALLYN AND BACON, INC.
Boston · London · Sydney · Toronto

Library of Congress Cataloging in Publication Data

Walton, John, 1937–   comp.
  Cities in change.

  Includes bibliographical references.
  1. Cities and towns—Addresses, essays, lectures.
I. Carns, Donald E. II. Title.
HT151.W32   1977   301.36′1   76–40193
ISBN 0–205–05579–6

Photo Credits:
p. 8 (upper), Talbot Lovering; p. 40 (right), A. Devaney, Inc.; p. 194, Metropolitan Life Insurance Company; p. 258, Arthur Grace, Stock, Boston; p. 580, Mike Mazzaschi, Stock, Boston.

79 009124

contents

CHAPTER
6 POLITICS AND CONTROL 259

CHAPTER
7 THE CHANGING CHARACTER OF URBAN POLITICS 355

PReface to first edition

A few years ago, due to the efforts of Scott Greer and David Minar, the departments of sociology and political science at Northwestern University initiated
a series of summer programs dealing with the urban phenomenon. These
annual sessions, which bear the name "Institute on Urbanism and Urbanization," typically attract a variety of undergraduate and graduate students
from colleges in the area as well as people from the local community.

During the summer of 1970, we found ourselves co-teaching one of these
institutes. We had individually offered such courses during the regular
school year, but team teaching and the variety of student interests allowed
the kind of interaction of ideas which suggested many interesting avenues
for improvement. Among these, we felt, was the possibility of bringing together under one cover a new and balanced set of materials that would better
reflect contemporary orientations to this field, which has changed so rapidly
in recent years.

Although notable exceptions exist, our survey of the literature on cities
suggests that most books, especially readers, are either too issue-oriented
(overly topical) or are heavyweight collections apparently designed for technical use by graduate students and practicing urban scholars. Many of these
books and readers tend to be static in their approach to cities; they are not
particularly oriented to change processes. Also, some of these offerings try
to touch all or most bases in the urban field rather than limiting themselves
to a manageable range of phenomena.

In our attempts to use other anthologies in the urban field, two problems
arise again and again. First, the compilers often include a great deal of older
or classical material. We are not suggesting that a careful reading of Georg
Simmel, Oswald Spengler, or Max Weber would not materially advance one's
understanding of cities. But these materials have appeared time and again,
and to put them into yet another anthology seemed to us a waste of time,
money, and the opportunity to present newer and equally interesting discussions of some perennial issues. Second, many editors do not put much of
themselves into their books. These collections often lack an explicit general plan, introductions to the readings, or an integration of themes, resulting in what the book trade calls a "nonbook."

We have tried to avoid these shortcomings in two ways. First, this collection contains an introductory chapter that provides a plan of the themes,
their integration, and suggested uses of the material. Following this general

orientation, each chapter is introduced by a brief discussion of the articles it contains and how they fit together. Second, we have included a number of essays prepared especially for this volume. This stems from the fact that our survey of the literature revealed an absence of high-quality discussions of several issue areas we felt should be included within our framework. Having identified these areas, we were then fortunate in successfully persuading colleagues with special expertise to write essays that appear here for the first time.

We feel we have improved upon existing books by eliminating or alleviating many of the problems mentioned above.

One of the organizing principles of this book is *change*. This is reflected in the overall organization, which progresses from general views of cities, especially the historical city, to the final chapter, some glimpses into possible futures of cities. We have concentrated on change in other ways, notably by pairing chapters 4 and 5 plus chapters 6 and 7 such that, in the first case, older and then emerging life styles and views of urbanity are presented, and in the second pair of chapters, politics and domination are followed by newer, change-oriented forms of political and social response. This kind of organization permits the reader to follow threads through thematic sections of the book and to appreciate the dynamic character of urban social and political life.

As an adjunct to our change orientation, we have also included articles which deal with a comparative focus on cities—specifically, portraits of urban patterns not customarily found in the western world and descriptions of urban life which help dispel the belief that the United States is unique in its possession of urban problems.

In summary, this volume has grown out of our endeavors to teach about the rapidly changing field of urban studies from a coherent contemporary perspective. The readings cover a broad, yet integrated, range of topics. In each selection we have tried to combine good scholarship with interesting reading. In addition to many recent articles not previously reprinted, we have included original material reflecting some of the most up-to-date thinking on the emerging city. More generally, the emphasis is on change: past to present and present to the foreseeable future. Our principal aim is to provide the student with some understanding of this change process and how it affects his or her city, society, and world. We hope our colleagues and students will find the materials as interesting as have we.

PREfACE TO SECOND EDITION

Judging from the comments we have received on the first edition of *Cities in Change*, instructors and their students in a variety of urban studies courses around the country have found the collection useful. We were gratified to learn that this audience agreed that our approach—based on concepts of the city, the process of urbanization, life styles, and politics, all woven together around the theme of change—provided at least one coherent perspective on this diverse field. While these reactions were generally quite favorable, we were also pleased to receive a number of suggestions on how the volume could be improved for classroom use and as a general reference work for more advanced students. These suggestions combined with the inevitable rapid change in the urban condition over the last few years have prompted us to bring out a largely revised edition.

In this second edition of *Cities in Change* nearly one-half of the selections are new, although the organization and approach remain the same. Several principles guided our efforts to improve upon the original volume. First, we endeavored to update the contents in areas where factual information or advances in research suggested some revision in earlier interpretations. By way of illustration, the new piece by Hermalin and Farley provides the most recent analysis of residential segregation in cities and suburbs. Second, we have provided more material related to the urban ecology tradition. Hoyt's paper introduces the classical models of the Chicago School and compares them with recent patterns of urban growth. Within that framework the reader may now regard the articles by Suttles on slums, Gans on suburbia, Zito on high-rise apartments, and others as portraits of different urban ways of life.

Third, a number of new inclusions touch on more contemporary urban problems. In a paper written especially for this volume, Hermalin, and Farley and Rubinowitz, discuss the problem of segregated housing and a variety of possible solutions from different standpoints. Gittell and Aronowitz provide two contrasting views on community control of education. McPherson's absorbing account of the organization of a group of ghetto homeowners to oppose their exploitation by real estate interests is suggestive of new political strategies to redress urban ills. Piven, Reeves, and Mollenkopf all deal with related facets of the fiscal crisis that now threatens the very survival of major cities. Still, while addressing these contemporary problems, the collection continues its emphasis on the general features of urban structure. Most of the topical articles operate from an interpretive frame-work and all of them are integrated with materials on basic trends and key concepts.

Finally, our first edition, like most collections, may have lacked sufficient integration or the drawing together of various themes. While this will always be a problem with efforts to portray a spectrum of issues and perspectives, we have attempted to reduce it by providing new introductions to each of the chapters and a new conclusion to the volume as a whole.

We are indebted to those who read and commented on the first edition, and we hope that their response to this set of materials is as active.

1
chapter

an approach to the city

During the approximately ten thousand years of human literate history on earth, and probably for a time before that, one ineluctable trend has characterized the organization of our lives: we have joined with larger and larger clusters of other people into what we call today *cities*. Our ability to leave the non-city is based, first of all, on society's capacity to produce agricultural surplus, for cities are not self-sufficient in that most basic of ways. Over the course of human history, cities have enlarged their food base through conquest and, later, mechanization and scientific discovery; in either case, larger and larger cities resulted. Living as we do in the last half of the twentieth century, we are experiencing a logarithmic growth of urban places not only in the more developed western countries, but also in newly developing nations of the world. Each year a greater proportion of all societies is urbanizing so that the urban life form is becoming overwhelmingly the modal one for man.

The systematic study of cities began not very long ago. It was initiated by Europeans and Americans who were in the main born and raised in non-urban environments. To many of them, the city represented chaos or the potential of chaos, a problem in social disorganization which either had to be wished out of existence or reorganized so that people, requiring the small face-to-face intimate group, could survive in such an alien setting as a fast-paced, impersonal city. Yet to the everlasting credit of these early urban students, many of them (especially the so-called Chicago school in this country) transcended their rural backgrounds, took a realistic look at cities, and started us on the way toward a disciplined study of the urban condition.

Today, most scholars who study cities have been lifelong urban residents—as are the students who read books like this one. Accustomed to this life form since birth, we are attuned, in many important ways, to appreciate its rich diversity. We cannot afford, except in our private moments of fantasy or when we drop out, to escape the realities of urban structures, cultures, and social problems. We may conclude, if we wish, that cities are inherently alien to the nature of man, but we cannot ignore the fact that more and more people in all societies are choosing, or are forced, to live in such conditions.

Over the past ten years, hundreds of books and articles have been published which deal with aspects of the urban environment. Many, if not most, of these publications appeared in response to rapidly shifting foci in urban studies, shifts frequently brought on by public moods, fancies, and the expediencies of practical urban and national politics. Seen in these terms, urban pollution, ghetto riots, and the form and function of the black family are good examples of areas where this responsiveness of social science and journalism to the ups and downs of public interest is apparent. And this is a good thing. For, among other benefits, these publications codify and frequently extend this public interest over time, help increase the probability that concerted and effective action may result, and certainly provide rich source materials for countless college classes which deal with the urban scene. What they do not do, in most cases, is address themselves to elements of cities which exist at the most basic level of conceptualization: how urban people view their world; how urban consciousness expands to nonurban environments; how city people adapt their styles of life to the exigencies of urban living, including their dependence upon networks of contacts rather than spatial arrangements; and how hierarchical power relations are organized in the city to produce efficiency and inefficiency, justice or injustice, and the like.

We have assembled these articles because these basic themes form an indispensable part of our approach to the city. The plethora of issue-oriented books now available provides a glimpse of only one side of the urban problem; it is equally important to approach urban phenomena on levels that transcend (or underpin) specific issues, events, or social problems. Indeed, to gain an adequate understanding of these issues, it is necessary to understand some of these broader principles of urban life. To be sure, we have included a considerable amount of material dealing with issues and events, for example, urban riots and the antipollution movement. But we have done our best to integrate these into broader frameworks, to contextualize them in the fabric of our urban imagination.

Further, this collection reflects a growing concern in social science, a comparative perspective on social phenomena. Comparisons are made among many of the articles appearing in this book and between articles and chapters; these relate elements of cities in time and space, and occasionally both, to seek those aspects of cities which transcend the immediate and the narrow and, occasionally, provide a view of causal processes at work.

Third, the book is oriented around the idea of *change*. The title suggests our orientation: cities, like most social facts, are ever-changing entities, growing or declining, rearranging themselves internally, and are intimately tied to the larger societies of which they are a significant part. To the greatest extent possible, we present two sides of many urban situations: "now" and "coming." When this is not done, nevertheless the student should think in those terms.

Fourth, we have tried to include only pieces written for this volume or those that have not yet received enough exposure to have achieved the status of classics. Obviously, some of the articles (for example, those by Childe and Greer) have been around for a while, but they are indispensable. On the other hand, many standard essays, such as those by Louis Wirth on urbanism as a way of life and by Robert E. Park, have been omitted. These are readily available from a number of sources; indeed, many readers which appeared in the 1960s are prefaced by some of these classics.

Finally, we have tried to conclude this anthology with a sense of the future. Not only do prediction and a view of future urban forms follow logically from our orientation toward change, but the last chapter also stimulates the student to exercise his or her own imagination about the future of cities.

For, as we have said, cities are here to stay; indeed, they may well represent, in broadest perspective, the only significant human life form for the next few hundred years.

HOW TO USE THIS BOOK

Let us begin with some general points about the book, then examine its organization in detail.

First of all, consider the size of this book. Some forty articles plus introductions comprise a formidable task for any student. We suggest you read the Table of Contents carefully, and then read the chapter introductions. Select those chapters or articles which fit your current interests and which best supplement other books you are using. The rest of the reader will always be there, ready for you to go back to, to browse through, when your interests shift or some new urban crisis springs up in this country.

Second, we have tried to balance the book in its level of technicality. Some of the articles are written in a journalistic style, others in a more technical way. The less technical pieces should increase your understanding and your urban vocabulary. We have avoided unduly specialized or esoteric articles, for our orientation is toward understanding basic processes in cities.

Carefully scan each introduction (including **this** one) before reading articles in a chapter.

This book is organized into four sections, each of which is discussed below in some detail.

I. Chapters 2 and 3 deal with the concept of *city* and the process of cities in the making, of people becoming urban in residence, and of whole societies urbanizing. Chapter 2 takes the student from the first cities, described by V. Gordon Childe, to what may be the last, Kenneth Boulding's view of cities in the international system of power politics and economics. On the way are selections on cities in newly developing and already developed parts of the world. Taken as a whole, this chapter is a logical introduction to the study of cities wherever or whenever they may exist. And Chapter 3 initiates our focus on change, although it is inherent in the progression of Chapter 2 also, for cities, their residents, and their surrounding societies are and have been in a state of flux, whether in the developed West or the developing Third World.

The introductions to chapters 2 and 3 summarize the contents and suggest salient approaches to the nature and emergence of cities. This unit of two chapters provides a take-off for several different points, among them an extensive study of new cities or cities in new states, the impact of becoming urban on migrants, and out of that a comparison of urban and nonurban milieus in terms of familism, human happiness and satisfaction, and the like. At this point, look at the next section on urban life styles, for many of these same themes are treated in detail there.

II. Chapters 4 and 5 concern urban living, first in terms of the styles and conditions found in cities, and, second, with relation to patterns of change

4

or trends which various writers feel are occurring in cities. The primary focus of this section is on cities in developed countries, especially the United States.

As noted above, themes which first emerge in section I can be picked up and traced in section II. In particular, the culture and ambience of cities receive some attention in both chapters 4 and 5, the central question being: Are cities unlivable? In Chapter 5, a city is discussed which *seems* to be civil, i.e., tolerant and habitable. Allied with this point, other articles discuss specific aspects of cities, pointing out how differentiated they are internally. Again, this theme, first stated in section I and now repeated, is to remind the student that it is not really valid to speak of "cities" as if they were homogeneous entities. A city is actually many cities—even many small towns in some cases—and certainly a great number of networks defined by mutual interests or conflicts. The richness found in diversity is a basic viewpoint of section II.

III. Chapters 6 and 7 shift the focus somewhat, for they concern power and social change in cities. Here again, the emphasis is on internal diversity, but the interaction among individuals and the polity and economy becomes one of the central points, along with various arrangements of power relations to be found in cities, especially in the United States. In recent years, riots, social movements, and general urban unrest have been in the headlines more and more often. In this section, we have tried to make these changes more intelligible by showing how they are the result of power relationships and socioeconomic deprivation in cities. Or, put differently, when men lack power, they realize it and their interests are both objectively and subjectively threatened or denied; if this continues long enough, something will happen. What that something is will, of course, vary. Again, the emphasis is on change Thus, Chapter 7 focuses on emerging processes of power and their effects.

If the student has followed the discussion to this point, he will realize that any number of themes were introduced in section I, described and analyzed in section II, and related to power and social change in section III. For example, recent urban migrants are discussed in Chapter 3, characterized in chapters 4 and 5, and related to broad patterns of unrest and political control in chapters 6 and 7. This reader will be most useful when the student adopts this kind of strategy: *follow points through the book as they are developed, discussed, analyzed, and shown to change.*

IV. Chapter 8 deals with the future of cities and urban societies. As mentioned before, it is a logical extension to the organization of the book as a whole. Thus, if the student is interested in minority groups who have only recently migrated to cities, he would first read about cities in general in Chapter 2; concentrate on the rural to urban shift in Chapter 3; read the characterizations of, for example, blacks in chapters 4 and 5; study the nature of powerlessness, power, and response in chapters 6 and 7; and conclude, in Chapter 8, with Downs's discussion of the future of the American ghetto. To be sure, not all themes can be threaded so neatly through the book, but the student will soon discover which can be traced in this way, and at the same time he may wish to stop off on the way to delve into some pocket of special interest to him.

Ultimately, any book is a personal statement, even an anthology. The selections in this book are our choice, of course, and we cannot please everyone. We have deemphasized some aspects of cities and emphasized others; for a book to cover everything would be an impossibility. But we feel the themes in this reader are some of the most fundamental and interesting for a clear and comprehensive understanding of modern cities. We hope the student will agree.

2
chapter

---

contents

ORIGINS OF CITIES

CITIES IN DEVELOPING COUNTRIES

CITIES IN DEVELOPED COUNTRIES

---

concepts of the city

the concept of "city" has not always meant what it does today, and probably will not mean the same thing in the future. As we use the term now, a city consists of a relatively dense population living off an agricultural hinterland, with or without manufacturing, but with some form of interdependence and specialization of functions. Cities have not been with us for long, especially when the entire sweep of man's existence is taken into account. It is this variability of viewpoints with which Chapter 2 deals, and the articles here are arranged in a logical progression of concepts of cities from preindustrial roots in the late Bronze Age to modern megalopoli intimately tied to worldwide systems of politics, economics, and warfare.

The first selection, V. Gordon Childe's "The Urban Revolution," deals with the origins of the first cities in the fertile crescent of the Tigris-Euphrates rivers. Childe's books, including *What Happened in History* and *Man Makes Himself*, deal with the same theme in more detail. The earliest cities were apparently concentrations of households in or near a river delta, organized around a ruler who invoked an urban deity (that is, a place god) in whose name he ruled. The growth of a priestly class also provided systems of continuing control, including counting schemes to deal with crops, labor, and the like. Keep in mind that pre-industrial cities—that is, cities before the sixteenth or seventeenth centuries in the West—were dependent on an agricultural system which was, itself, not mechanized. This gave rise to severe limitations on the size a city could attain, and if a city grew beyond the limits of its supporting agricultural hinterland, some form of military conquest was necessary to broaden the food base. Such was the case of Rome: it grew as its hinterland increased through conquest, and also while the area immediately around Rome was stripped bare. Athens in the so-called Golden Age, on the other hand, had a fairly small agricultural area to support it and was, by today's standards, a very small city.

We have come to equate certain concepts with our study of cities, especially the development of industrialization and urbanization. That is, we expect to find that the growth of cities into large metropolitan centers is a function of the increased scale of industrial production and its attendant control structures—bureaucracies. The article by Rhoads Murphey, "Urbanization in Asia," is a reminder that many different factors are important in the process of urbanization, among them the residue of colonial administration. A good part of Asia was colonized by European powers in the nineteenth and twentieth centuries. India is a prime example and is discussed by Murphey; others include Vietnam (French), Indonesia (Dutch), and China (various powers). In each case, cities developed without a wide-scale industrial base to support them. They exist today as monuments to the colonial planter or mercantile class, but they represent urban opportunities for the rural poor nonetheless. This has given rise to the concept of under-industrialization, or overurbanization—in either case the recognition that in newly developing nations there are more people in urban places than can be provided jobs, food, clothing, and shelter. And one should keep in mind that developed nations, such as the United States, share the same problem, largely stemming from patterns of systematic discrimination. Africa, Asia, and Latin America have, at the same time, the most accelerating rates of urbanization, the highest birth rates, and the lowest levels of industrialization in the world, and all this provides a very different view of urbanization than is found in the West.

The third article, "The Urban Pattern" by Hans Blumenfeld, analyzes the modern Western city. One of its central foci is concentration on post-industrial patterns, i.e., the movement of manufacturing to satellite cities within the larger metropolitan area and the concentration of service and control functions in the central city. Allied with this is a view of cities as metropolitan regions encompassing large urban and nonurban hinterlands. It is, in a sense, the city writ large, or, if one is inclined to the view, the end of the traditional city of factories and tenements and the development of the new city, a large, urbanized region tied together by a shrinking space-time ratio and by the electronics revolution in the media. These themes are repeated in some detail in articles in chapters 4 and 5, but it is Blumenfeld's treatment that ties them together into a coherent, predictive picture of the Western city.

1

V. GORDON CHILDE

The Urban Revolution

The concept of "city" is notoriously hard to define. The aim of the present essay is to present the city historically—or rather prehistorically—as the resultant and symbol of a "revolution" that initiated a new economic stage in the evolution of society. The word "revolution" must not of course be taken as denoting a sudden violent catastrophe; it is here used for the culmination of a progressive change in the economic structure and social organization of communities that caused, or was accompanied by, a dramatic increase in the population affected—an increase that would appear as an obvious bend in the population graph were vital statistics available. Just such a bend is observable at the time of the Industrial Revolution in England. Though not demonstrable statistically, comparable changes of direction must have occurred at two earlier points in the demographic history of Britain and other regions. Though perhaps less sharp and less durable, these too should indicate equally revolutionary changes in economy. They may then be regarded likewise as marking transitions between stages in economic and social development.

Sociologists and ethnographers last century classified existing pre-industrial societies in a hierarchy of three evolutionary stages, denominated respectively "savagery," "barbarism" and "civilization." If they be defined by suitable selected criteria, the logical hierarchy of stages can be transformed into a temporal sequence of ages, proved archaeologically to follow one another in the same order wherever they occur. Savagery and barbarism are conveniently recognized and appropriately defined by the methods adopted for procuring food. Savages live exclusively on wild food obtained by collecting, hunting, or fishing. Barbarians on the contrary at least supplement these natural resources by cultivating edible plants and—in the Old World north of the Tropics—also by breeding animals for food.

Throughout the Pleistocene Period—the Paleolithic Age of archaeologists—all known human societies were savage in the foregoing sense, and a few savage tribes have survived in out of the way parts to the present day. In the archaeological record barbarism began less than ten thousand years ago with the Neolithic Age of archaeologists. It thus represents a later, as well as a higher stage, than savagery. Civilization cannot be defined in quite such simple terms. Etymologically the word is connected with "city," and sure enough life in cities begins with this stage. But "city" is itself ambiguous so archaeologists like to use "writing" as a criterion of civilization; it should be easily recognizable and proves to be a reliable index to more profound characters. Note, however, that, because a people is said to be civilized or literate, it does not follow that all its members can read and write, nor that they all lived in cities. Now there is no recorded instance of a community of savages civilizing themselves, adopting urban life or inventing a script. Wherever cities have been built, villages of preliterate farmers existed previously (save perhaps where an already civilized people have colonized uninhabited tracts). So civilization, wherever and whenever it arose, succeeded barbarism.

We have seen that a revolution as here defined should be reflected in the population statistics. In the case of the Urban Revolution the increase was mainly accounted for by the multiplication of the numbers of persons living to-

V. Gordon Childe, "The Urban Revolution," *Town Planning Review*, vol. 21, no. 1 (April 1950), pp. 3–17. Reprinted by permission.

gether, i.e., in a single built-up area. The first cities represented settlement units of hitherto unprecedented size. Of course it was not just their size that constituted their distinctive character. We shall find that by modern standards they appeared ridiculously small and we might meet agglomerations of population today to which the name city would have to be refused. Yet a certain size of settlement and density of population is an essential feature of civilization.

Now the density of population is determined by the food supply which in turn is limited by natural resources, the techniques for their exploitation and the means of transport and food-preservation available. The last factors have proved to be variables in the course of human history, and the technique of obtaining food has already been used to distinguish the consecutive stages termed savagery and barbarism. Under the gathering economy of savagery, population was always exceedingly sparse. In aboriginal America the carrying capacity of normal unimproved land seems to have been from .05 to .10 per square mile. Only under exceptionally favorable conditions did the fishing tribes of the Northwest Pacific coast attain densities of over one human to the square mile. As far as we can guess from the extant remains, population densities of paleolithic and pre-neolithic Europe were less than the normal American. Moreover such hunters and collectors usually live in small roving bands. At best several bands may come together for quite brief periods on ceremonial occasions such as the Australian corroborrees. Only in exceptionally favored regions can fishing tribes establish anything like villages. Some settlements on the Pacific coasts comprised thirty or so substantial and durable houses, accommodating groups of several hundred persons. But even these villages were only occupied during the winter; for the rest of the year their inhabitants dispersed in smaller groups. Nothing comparable has been found in pre-neolithic times in the Old World.

The Neolithic Revolution certainly allowed an expansion of population and enormously increased the carrying capacity of suitable land. On the Pacific Islands neolithic societies today attain a density of thirty or more persons to the square mile. In pre-Columbian North America, however, where the land is not obviously restricted by surrounding seas, the maximum density recorded is just under two to the square mile.

Neolithic farmers could of course, and certainly did, live together in permanent villages, though owing to the extravagant rural economy generally practiced, unless the crops were watered by irrigation, the villages had to be shifted at least every twenty years. But on the whole the growth of population was not reflected so much in the enlargement of the settlement unit as in a multiplication of settlements. In ethnography neolithic villages can boast only a few hundred inhabitants (a couple of *pueblos* in New Mexico house over a thousand, but perhaps they cannot be regarded as neolithic). In prehistoric Europe the largest neolithic village yet known, Barkaer in Jutland, comprised fifty-two small, one-roomed dwellings, but sixteen to thirty houses was a more normal figure; so the average local group in neolithic times would average 200 to 400 members.

These low figures are of course the result of technical limitations. In the absence of wheeled vehicles and roads for the transport of bulky crops men had to live within easy walking distance of their cultivations. At the same time the normal rural economy of the Neolithic Age, what is now termed slash-and-burn or *jhumming*, condemns much more than half the arable land to lie fallow so that large areas were required. As soon as the population of a settlement rose above the numbers that could be supported from the accessible land, the excess had to hive off and found a new settlement.

The Neolithic Revolution had other consequences beside increasing the population, and their exploitation might in the end help to provide for the surplus increase. The new economy allowed, and indeed required, the farmer to produce every year more food than was needed to keep him and his family alive. In other words it made possible the regular production of a social surplus. Owing to the low efficiency of neolithic technique, the surplus produced was insignificant at first, but it could be increased till it demanded a reorganization of society.

Now in any Stone Age society, paleolithic or neolithic, savage or barbarian, everybody can at least in theory make at home the few indispensible tools, the modest cloths and the simple ornaments everyone requires. But every member of the local community, not disqualified by age, must contribute actively to the communal food supply by personally collecting, hunting, fishing, gardening or herding. As long as this holds good, there can be no full-time specialists, no persons nor class of persons who depend for their livelihood on food produced by others and secured in exchange for material or immaterial goods or services.

We find indeed today among Stone Age barbarians and even savages expert craftsmen (for instance flint-knappers among the Ona of Tierra del Fuego), men who claim to be experts in magic, and even chiefs. In paleolithic Europe too there is some evidence for magicians and indications of chieftainship in pre-neolithic times. But on closer observation we discover that today these experts are not full-time specialists. The Ona flintworker must spend most of his time hunting; he only adds to his diet and his prestige by making arrowheads for clients who reward him with presents. Similarly a pre-Columbian chief, though entitled to customary gifts and services from his followers, must still personally lead hunting and fishing expeditions and indeed could only maintain his authority by his industry and prowess in these pursuits. The same holds good of barbarian societies that are still in the neolithic stage, like the Polynesians where industry in gardening takes the place of prowess in hunting. The reason is that there simply will not be enough food to go round unless every member of the group contributes to the supply. The social surplus is not big enough to feed idle mouths.

Social division of labor, save those rudiments imposed by age and sex, is thus impossible. On the contrary community of employment, the common absorption in obtaining food by similar devices guarantees a certain solidarity to the group. For cooperation is essential to secure food and shelter and for defense against foes, human and subhuman. This identity of economic interests and pursuits is echoed and magnified by identity of language, custom and belief; rigid conformity is enforced as effectively as industry in the common quest for food. But conformity and industrious cooperation need no state organization to maintain them. The local group usually consists either of a single clan (persons who believe themselves descended from a common ancestor or who have earned a mystical claim to such descent by ceremonial adoption) or a group of clans related by habitual intermarriage. And the sentiment of kinship is reinforced or supplemented by common rites focused on some ancestral shrine or sacred place. Archaeology can provide no evidence for kinship organization, but shrines occupied the central place in preliterate villages in Mesopotamia, and the long barrow, a collective tomb that overlooks the presumed site of most neolithic villages in Britain, may well have been also the ancestral shrine on which converged the emotions and ceremonial activities of the villagers below. However, the solidarity thus idealized and concretely symbolized is really based on the same principles as that of a pack of wolves or a herd of sheep; Durkheim has called it "mechanical."

Now among some advanced barbarians (for instance tattooers or woodcarvers among the Maori) still technologically neolithic we find expert craftsmen tending towards the status of full-time professionals, but only at the cost of breaking away from the local community. If no single village can produce a surplus large enough to feed a full-time specialist all the year round, each should produce enough to keep him a week or so. By going round from village to village an expert might thus live entirely from his craft. Such itinerants will lose their membership of the sedentary kinship group. They may in the end form an analogous organization of their own—a craft clan, which, if it remains hereditary, may become a caste, or, if it recruits its members mainly by adoption (apprenticeship throughout Antiquity and the Middle Ages was just temporary adoption), may turn into a guild. But such specialists, by emancipation from kinship ties, have also forfeited the protection of the kinship organization which alone, under barbarism, guaranteed to its members security of person and property. Society must be reorganized to accommodate and protect them.

In pre-history specialization of labor presumably began with similar itinerant experts. Archaeological proof is hardly to be expected, but in ethnography metalworkers are nearly always full-time specialists. And in Europe at the beginning of the Bronze Age metal seems to have been worked and purveyed by perambulating smiths who seem to have functioned like tinkers and other itinerants of much more recent times. Though there is no such positive evidence, the same probably happened in Asia at the beginning of metallurgy. There must of course have been, in addition, other specialist craftsmen whom, as the Polynesian example warns us, archaeologists could not recognize because they worked in perishable materials. One result of the Urban Revolution will be to rescue such specialists from nomadism and to guarantee them security in a new social organization.

About 5,000 years ago irrigation cultivation (combined with stock-breeding and fishing) in the valleys of the Nile, the Tigris-Euphrates, and the Indus had begun to yield a social surplus, large enough to support a number of resident specialists who were themselves released from food-production. Water-transport, supplemented in Mesopotamia and the Indus valley by wheeled vehicles and even in Egypt by pack animals, made it easy to gather food stuffs at a few centers. At the same time dependence on river water for the irrigation of the crops restricted the cultivable areas while the necessity of canalizing the water and protecting habitations against annual floods encouraged the aggregation of population. Thus arose the first cities—units of settlement ten time as great as any known neolithic village. It can be argued that all cities in the old world are offshoots of those of Egypt, Mesopotamia and the Indus basin. So the latter need not be taken into account if a minimum definition of civilization is to be inferred from a comparison of its independent manifestations.

But some three millennia later cities arose in Central America, and it is impossible to prove that the Mayas owed anything directly to the urban civilizations of the Old World. Their achievements must therefore be taken into account in our comparison, and their inclusion seriously complicates the task of defining the essential preconditions for the Urban Revolution. In the Old World the rural economy which yielded the surplus was based on the cultivation of cereals combined with stock-breeding. But this economy had been made more efficient as a result of the adoption of irrigation (allowing cultivation without prolonged fallow periods) and of important inventions and discoveries—metallurgy, the plough, the sailing boat and the wheel. None of these devices was known to the Mayas; they bred no animals for milk or meat; though they cultivated the cereal maize, they used the same sort of slash-and-burn method as neolithic farmers in prehistoric Europe or in the Pacific Islands today. Hence the minimum definition of a city, the greatest factor common

to the Old World and the New, will be substantially reduced and impoverished by the inclusion of the Maya. Nevertheless, ten rather abstract criteria, all deducible from archaeological data, serve to distinguish even the earliest cities from any older or contemporary village.

1. In point of size the first cities must have been more extensive and more densely populated than any previous settlements, although considerably smaller than many villages today. It is indeed only in Mesopotamia and India that the first urban populations can be estimated with any confidence or precision. There excavation has been sufficiently extensive and intensive to reveal both the total area and the density of building in sample quarters and in both respects has disclosed significant agreement with the less industrialized Oriental cities today. The population of Sumerian cities, thus calculated, ranged between 7,000 and 20,000; Harappa and Mohenjo-daro in the Indus valley must have approximated to the higher figure. We can only infer that Egyptian and Maya cities were of comparable magnitude from the scale of public works, presumably executed by urban populations.

2. In composition and function the urban population already differed from that of any village. Very likely indeed most citizens were still also peasants, harvesting the lands and waters adjacent to the city. But all cities must have accommodated in addition classes who did not themselves procure their own food by agriculture, stock-breeding, fishing, or collecting—full-time specialist craftsmen, transport workers, merchants, officials, and priests. All these were of course supported by the surplus produced by the peasants living in the city and in dependent villages, but they did not secure their share directly by exchanging their products or services for grains or fish with individual peasants.

3. Each primary producer paid over the tiny surplus he could wring from the soil with his still very limited technical equipment as tithe or tax to an imaginary deity or a divine king who thus concentrated the surplus. Without this concentration, owing to the low productivity of the rural economy, no effective capital would have been available.

4. Truly monumental public buildings not only distinguish each known city from any village but also symbolize the concentration of the social surplus. Every Sumerian city was from

the first dominated by one or more stately temples, centrally situated on a brick platform raised above the surrounding dwellings and usually connected with an artificial mountain, the staged tower or ziggurat. But attached to the temples were workshops and magazines, and an important appurtenance of each principal temple was a great granary. Harappa, in the Indus basin, was dominated by an artificial citadel, girt with a massive rampart of kiln-baked bricks, containing presumably a palace and immediately overlooking an enormous granary and the barracks of artisans. No early temples nor palaces have been excavated in Egypt, but the whole Nile valley was dominated by the gigantic tombs of the divine pharoahs while royal granaries are attested from the literary record. Finally the Maya cities are known almost exclusively from the temples and pyramids of sculptured stone round which they grew up.

Hence in Sumer the social surplus was first effectively concentrated in the hands of a god and stored in his granary. That was probably true in Central America while in Egypt the pharoah (king) was himself a god. But of course the imaginary deities were served by quite real priests who, besides celebrating elaborate and often sanguinary rites in their honor, administered their divine masters' earthly estates. In Sumer indeed the god very soon, if not even before the revolution, shared his wealth and power with a mortal viceregent, the "City-King," who acted as civil ruler and leader in war. The divine pharoah was naturally assisted by a whole hierarchy of officials.

5. All those not engaged in food-production were of course supported in the first instance by the surplus accumulated in temple or royal granaries and were thus dependent on temple or court. But naturally priests, civil and military leaders and officials absorbed a major share of the concentrated surplus and thus formed a "ruling class." Unlike a paleolithic magician or a neolithic chief, they were, as an Egyptian scribe actually put it, "exempt from all manual tasks." On the other hand, the lower classes were not only guaranteed peace and security, but were relieved from intellectual tasks which many find more irksome than any physical labor. Besides reassuring the masses that the sun was going to rise next day and the river would flood again next year (people who have not five thousand years of recorded experience of natural uniformities be-

hind them are really worried about such matters!), the ruling classes did confer substantial benefits upon their subjects in the way of planning and organization.

6. They were in fact compelled to invent systems of recording and exact, but practically useful, sciences. The mere administration of the vest revenues of a Sumerian temple or an Egyptian pharaoh by a perpetual corporation of priests or officials obliged its members to devise conventional methods of recording that should be intelligible to all their colleagues and successors, that is, to invent systems of writing and numeral notation. Writing is thus a significant, as well as a convenient, mark of civilization. But while writing is a trait common to Egypt, Mesopotamia, the Indus valley and Central America, the characters themselves were different in each region and so were the normal writing materials—papyrus in Egypt, clay in Mesopotamia. The engraved seals or stelae that provide the sole extant evidence for early Indus and Maya writing no more represent the normal vehicles for the scripts than do the comparable documents from Egypt and Sumer.

7. The invention of writing—or shall we say the inventions of scripts—enabled the leisured clerks to proceed to the elaboration of exact and predictive sciences—arithmetic, geometry and astronomy. Obviously beneficial and explicitly attested by the Egyptian and Maya documents was the correct determination of the tropic year and the creation of a calendar, for it enabled the rulers to regulate successfully the cycle of agricultural operations. But once more the Egyptian, Maya and Babylonian calendars were as different as any systems based on a single natural unit could be. Calendrical and mathematical sciences are common features of the earliest civilizations and they too are corollaries of the archaeologists' criterion, writing.

8. Other specialists, supported by the concentrated social surplus, gave a new direction to artistic expression. Savages even in paleolithic times had tried, sometimes with astonishing success, to depict animals and even man as they saw them—concretely and naturalistically. Neolithic peasants never did that; they hardly ever tried to represent natural objects, but preferred to symbolize them by abstract geometrical patterns which at most may suggest by a few traits a fantastical man or beast or plant. But Egyptian, Sumerian, Indus and Maya artist-craftsmen

—full-time sculptors, painters, or seal-engravers —began once more to carve, model or draw likenesses of persons or things, but no longer with the naive naturalism of the hunter, but according to conceptualized and sophisticated styles which differ in each of the four urban centers.

9. A further part of the concentrated social surplus was used to pay for the importation of raw materials, needed for industry or cult and not available locally. Regular "foreign" trade over quite long distances was a feature of all early civilizations and, though common enough among barbarians later, is not certainly attested in the Old World before 3000 B.C. nor in the New before the Maya "empire." Thereafter regular trade extended from Egypt at least as far as Byblos on the Syrian coast while Mesopotamia was related by commerce with the Indus valley. While the objects of international trade were at first mainly "luxuries," they already included industrial materials, in the Old World notably metal the place of which in the New was perhaps taken by obsidian. To this extent the first cities were dependent for vital materials on long distance trade as no neolithic village ever was.

10. So in the city, specialist craftsmen were both provided with raw materials needed for the employment of their skill and also guaranteed security in a state organization based now on residence rather than kinship. Itinerancy was no longer obligatory. The city was a community to which a craftsman could belong politically as well as economically.

Yet in return for security they became dependent on temple or court and were relegated to the lower classes. The peasant masses gained even less material advantages; in Egypt for instance metal did not replace the old stone and wood tools for agricultural work. Yet, however imperfectly, even the earliest urban communities must have been held together by a sort of solidarity missing from any neolithic village. Peasants, craftsmen, priests and rulers form a community, not only by reason of identity of language and belief, but also because each performs mutually complementary functions, needed for the well-being (as redefined under civilization) of the whole. In fact the earliest cities illustrate a first approximation to an organic solidarity based upon a functional complementarity and interdependence between all its members such

as subsist between the constituent cells of an organism. Of course this was only a very distant approximation. However necessary the concentrations of the surplus really were with the existing forces of production, there seemed a glaring conflict of economic interests between the tiny ruling class, who annexed the bulk of the social surplus, and the vast majority who were left with a bare subsistence and effectively excluded from the spiritual benefits of civilization. So solidarity had still to be maintained by the ideological devices appropriate to the mechanical solidarity of barbarism as expressed in the preeminence of the temple or the sepulchral shrine, and now supplemented by the force of the new state organization. There could be no room for sceptics or sectaries in the oldest cities.

These ten traits exhaust the factors common to the oldest cities that archaeology, at best helped out with fragmentary and often ambiguous written sources, can detect. No specific elements of town planning for example can be proved characteristic of all such cities; for on the one hand the Egyptian and Maya cities have not yet been excavated; on the other neolithic villages were often walled, an elaborate system of sewers drained the Orcadian hamlet of Skara Brae; two-storeyed houses were built in preColumbian *pueblos*, and so on.

The common factors are quite abstract. Concretely Egyptian, Sumerian, Indus and Maya civilizations were as different as the plans of their temples, the signs of their scripts and their artistic conventions. In view of this divergence and because there is so far no evidence for a temporal priority of one Old World center (for instance, Egypt) over the rest nor yet for contact between Central America and any other urban center, the four revolutions just considered may be regarded as mutually independent. On the contrary, all later civilizations in the Old World may in a sense be regarded as lineal descendents of those of Egypt, Mesopotamia, or the Indus.

But this was not a case of like producing like. The maritime civilizations of Bronze Age Crete or classical Greece for example, to say nothing of our own, differ more from their reputed ancestors than these did among themselves. But the urban revolutions that gave them birth did not start from scratch. They could and probably did draw upon the capital accumulated in the three allegedly primary centers. That is most obvious in the case of cultural capital. Even today we use the Egyptians' calendar and the Sumerians' divisions of the day and the hour. Our European ancestors did not have to invent for themselves these divisions of time nor repeat the observations on which they are based; they took over—and very slightly improved—systems elaborated 5,000 years ago! But the same is in a sense true of material capital as well. The Egyptians, the Sumerians and the Indus people had accumulated vast reserves of surplus food.

At the same time they had to import from abroad necessary raw materials like metals and building timber as well as "luxuries." Communities controlling these natural resources could in exchange claim a slice of the urban surplus. They could use it as capital to support full-time specialists—craftsmen or rulers—until the latters' achievement in technique and organization had so enriched barbarian economics that they too could produce a substantial surplus in their turn.

2

RHOADS MURPHEY

Urbanization in Asia

Throughout most if not all of recorded history, there seems little question that there have been and still are more people living in cities, and more cities, in Asia than in any other continent. Until about 1750 or 1800, it seems likely that Asia (used throughout this paper to refer only to the area sometimes called "monsoon Asia," from Pakistan on the west to Indonesia and Japan on the east, but excluding Soviet Asia) contained more cities and more city-dwellers than the rest of the world combined, a position which it may have regained by the end of the present century if current rates of population growth and of urbanization continue. Indeed one of the primary reasons for distinguishing the area referred to as "monsoon Asia" from the Arab-Turkish-Persian world of the Middle East and from the areas now included in Soviet Asia is the density of its population and the importance of an urban-centered "great tradition," in Robert Redfield's phrase. Monsoon Asia has had so little common cultural ground with the rest of the Asian continent that it is both arbitrary and misleading to lump them together in almost any analysis of human institutions. This is so despite the fact that without much question the world's earliest true cities (as opposed to agricultural villages) arose in Asian Mesopotamia or in the Levantine uplands just west of it, and the probability that the rise of the first genuine cities in monsoon Asia owed something to direct or indirect contact with the earlier Mesopotamian model. But with the emergence of a civilized (literally city-based) tradition in monsoon Asia, culture contact with the Middle East appears to have dwindled into relative insignificance (with the qualified exception of India) and the "great traditions" of south and east Asia matured and endured largely in isolation from the rest of the world. When external contact finally became of major importance, it was with the probings, colonialism, and traders of Europe and America, and it is this impact which has left the greatest marks on contemporary south and east Asia, most strikingly and perhaps most importantly in its cities.

Our knowledge of Asian urbanization is far from being proportional to its importance on the world scale. We cannot even measure with any precision what the total Asian urban population is, let alone delineate with assurance the factors responsible for its past and present growth or project its likely future shape. We are hampered both by inadequate data, reflecting imperfect census systems, and by a relative paucity of published studies. Present knowledge is, however, grossly uneven. Japan, with relatively complete and accurate data and with a history of detailed study by Japanese scholars, is in a class by itself in this as in so many other respects. Urbanization in India is more accurately measured and better analyzed and understood than in most other Asian countries apart from Japan. But China, which may currently contain more cities and more city-dwellers than any country in the world, is plagued by gross shortages of hard data of every kind, and has been given very little attention by students of urbanization. The same is true of Indonesia, the third most populous nation in Asia with a total population well over 100 million—how much over

Rhoads Murphey, "Urbanization in Asia," *Ekistics*, vol. 21, no. 122 (January 1966), pp. 8–17. Reprinted by permission. This paper was delivered during a conference on International and Comparative Urban Studies held at Rutgers—The State University in June 1965, under the auspices of the Rutgers Committee on International Education and the Urban Studies Center.

and how much of the total should be regarded as urban are not accurately known. China and Indonesia, in fact, illustrate particularly pointedly the data limitations which confront the student of Asian urbanization, especially by contrast with the relative wealth and reliability of census information in the West. It is not merely that precise population totals are often lacking, but that the wide spread and variety of demographic information provided for at least the past several decades by many Western censuses is simply not available for most of Asia.

Nevertheless, it seems reasonably clear that at least a third of the present world total of urban population is now in Asia (as defined above), no matter how "urban" may be defined, but that the *degree* of urbanization in Asia is still considerably lower than in Europe or North America, since well over half of the world's total population is Asian. In neither respect—the total number of urban dwellers or the degree of urbanization—is there a reasonable correlation, by Western standards, with the absolute amount or the proportional share of industrialization, or with per capita incomes. This suggests two apparently contradictory conclusions: that most of Asia is "overurbanized," and that urbanization in Asia is still in its early stages, with a much higher degree of urbanization clearly in prospect as industrialization and commercialization gather momentum and as the presently very high rates of urbanization continue. Indeed perhaps the most striking feature of Asian cities in the two decades since the end of World War II is their uniquely rapid growth, a phenomenon which has understandably led to both of the above conclusions. Their contradictory nature can, unfortunately, be rationalized only by assuming (as there are ample grounds for doing) that in most Asian cities living conditions will continue to deteriorate before they can improve. It may well be true that Asian urbanization has outrun its industrial-commercial base, which is the essence of the "overurbanization" argument, but this is not sufficient grounds for assuming either that this process will not continue, or that there is somehow a better viable alternative open to societies and economies which we fervently hope are already engaged in the inevitably painful process of economic growth and transformation. These and other general considerations will be discussed more fully below.

Apart from the simple shortage of reliable census figures in many Asian countries, the student of urbanization is also plagued by varying census definitions of "urban." This is of course a familiar problem even in the Western world, but it does grossly hamper comparability, and even within a single national unit may give rise to perplexing ambiguity. The varying definitions of "urban" are not however purely arbitrary, but reflect real and important differences. Probably the most important of these revolves around the nature of agricultural land use and settlement in Asia, which for the most part follow patterns distinct from any in the West. Many Asian settlements with populations well over 2,000 (the lower limit of the "urban" category in the United States census) are almost exclusively agricultural in function and include or perform little or none of the functions commonly regarded as urban. In recognition of this, the Indian census sets the lower limit of the "urban" category in population terms at 5,000, although it is recognized that some genuinely urban settlements may thereby be excluded. The Chinese census, on the other hand, in an attempt to adjust to a similar reality, stresses function as well as population size, setting a lower limit numerically at 2,000 but including as urban many smaller settlements whose functions are clearly urban in nature— transport or small mining or manufacturing centers, for example—while excluding larger places which are primarily agricultural villages. But no census system except the Japanese takes account of another factor which also helps to distinguish Asian cities—the inclusion within the urban area—whether empirically or arbitrarily defined—of significant amounts of agricultural land and of agricultural workers. Such intra-urban land is, of course, worked extremely intensively and population densities associated with it may be at an urban or near-urban level, but it is nevertheless probably misleading to lump population figures from such areas with those from the functionally separate city.

There is the further problem of defining the spatial limits of a city for census purposes. Traditional Asian cities were relatively sharply distinct from surrounding rural areas in spatial terms, and in probably the majority of the Asian cities of the present the rural-urban line is easier to draw than in almost any present Western city. But the tremendously high rate of urbanization characteristic of Asia especially during the past two decades, the beginnings of the kind of "transport revolution" which helped to transform Western cities, and the rise or further expansion of nearly thirty Asian cities in the million class have meant that "urban sprawl" is no longer a Western monopoly. It is at least as difficult now to make a neat census delineation of the largest Asian cities as it is for large Western cities. Tokyo and Calcutta represent the extremes; "greater Calcutta" and "greater Tokyo" are both in fact megalopolises, each including within a single contiguous urban area what were once several separate cities and making it really impossible to draw an unambiguous line around the spatial limits of either conurbation, or even around the limits of the "urban sprawl" at the peripheries, which tends increasingly to melt gradually into a rural-urban continuum along the Hooghly or around the shores of Tokyo Bay and the edges of the Tokyo basin. Such problems may be appropriate enough for Tokyo, as indisputably the world's largest city, or for Calcutta as an acknowledged urban giant, but they are beginning to be apparent or are already far advanced in many other Asian cities, notably Bombay, Karachi, Madras, Delhi, Singapore, Kuala Lumpur, Djakarta, Manila, and Osaka. In general, "urban" must be taken as what each national census says it is, while recognizing that this is not a uniform or necessarily accurate or reliable guide to reality.

One final difficulty which hampers the search for accurate and complete urban data in Asia is the very large and continuing role played by rural-urban migration. Almost every large Asian city has apparently owed half or more of its recent rapid growth to migration. But even so general a statement must be qualified, since the nature of migration makes accurate counting difficult and since in most Asian cities it is clear that many if not most migrants continue to maintain close ties with their rural origins and periodically return there; apart from this, there appears to be a significant though largely unmeasured amount of attrition which means that *net permanent* migration is less, to an undetermined extent, than gross migration as it might be revealed by a census or sample taken at any one time. As one illustration of the indeterminate or perhaps the qualified nature, both of rural-urban migration in Asia and of the completeness and validity of available data on it, one may cite the common Indian (and traditional

Chinese) practice of giving one's ancestral village as place of origin or even of birth on the part of people who are unambiguously urban. At least in the Indian case, this is not entirely disingenuous since it is relatively common for urban women to go back to their villages to bear children and to return to the city domicile with their infants a few months after parturition. But uncertainties or ambiguities like these make it impossible to compile complete and accurate data on the role of migration in the growth of most Asian cities, and hence, given the admitted importance of that role, one is obliged to treat urban census figures with caution.

The reader should not, however, be left with the impression that there are no trustworthy data on Asian urbanization. Whatever their shortcomings, the data available afford students of urbanization ample opportunity to explore a field which Western scholars in particular have neglected in terms of its importance. The city has played an enormously significant role in both the traditional Asian societies of the past and in their current transformation, and any thorough understanding of the Asian half of the world must take full account of the urban factor. For students of urbanization per se, the Asian experience, past and present, offers an impressively wide and varied field which must be explored not merely for comparison with the Western experience but in order to understand the generic nature of cities. Through most of recorded history, Asia has bred more urbanism than the rest of the world. Its present rapid urbanization will not necessarily merely repeat the outlines of what has been called "the second urban revolution" in the West during the past two centuries; the urban revolution which now appears to be in progress in Asia is still in its early stages and will be shaped by Asian cultural and economic circumstances as well as by originally European innovations in manufacturing, trade, and transport.

The traditional Asian city was predominantly a political and cultural phenomenon rather than an economic one. The capitals and provincial administrative centers of the great Asian empires in China, India, Japan, and Southeast Asia functioned and were consciously intended as microcosms of the national policy—symbols of authority, legitimacy, and power, creators and molders of literate culture, seats of the dominant religious ideology, and resplendent thrones for the Great Tradition. Commercial and industrial functions were decidedly secondary, almost incidental, and were often in any case under varying degrees of control or manipulation by the state, whose chief monument was the city itself. Sites for such cities were chosen more with an eye to their administrative functions than to commercial advantage. Except for insular Japan (where productive and hence populous level land hugs the sea) and insular southeast Asia, traditional Asian cities were almost exclusively confined to inland locations from which they could best administer and control the territory of the state or best ensure its defense against incursion across what was regarded as the chief exposed frontier. Ch'ang An, Peking, and Delhi are classic examples of the former; Loyang, Nanking, Pataliputra, Ava, Ayuthia, Angkor, Polonnaruwa, and Jogjakarta of the latter. Cities were both sited and planned so as to ensure an appropriate symbolization of legitimate authority. In China and periodically in India the cities were walled (indeed the common Chinese word for *city* meant and still means also wall), not merely for protection but as a further mark of imperial or administrative sanction. City plans were in turn shaped by the great gates, one at each of the four cardinal points of the compass, from which major streets led to a center where some piece of monumental building—a drum tower, a temple, an array of government offices or troop barracks—further reinforced the symbol of authority. Commerce and manufacturing there certainly were, but although their absolute amounts were large, their relative importance rarely rivalled that of administration as the chief urban function, including the administration of trade; and commerce did not breed as in the West any significant group of independent entrepreneurs. In Japan, where cities were not walled, and in Southeast Asia where walling was at best inconsistent, the traditional city nevertheless functioned primarily as an administrative, ceremonial, and symbolic center rather than as a base for trade.

Cities of the sort described contrast forcibly with the urban type which has been dominant in the West for most of the past two or three millennia. At the beginning of the Western tradition, the cities of classical Greece were seaoriented and trade-oriented, as were the city colonies which the Greeks established elsewhere on the shores of the Mediterranean. Even Rome, although it became the capital of a huge empire and thus came to play both a real and a symbolic role as a center of authority and administration, was at best a hybrid in that trade remained one of its important functions through its maritime link with the port of Ostia and its incorporation of the commerce-centered Greek Mediterranean. But the greatest cities of medieval Europe were not the cathedral towns or the seats of royal power but the centers of trade— Venice, Genoa, Florence, Hamburg, Bruges—and London and Paris as commercial foci rather than as political capitals. The distinction has been preserved to the present in the case of London, where "the City," until the eighteenth century a geographically separate entity, is at least symbolically still set off from the seat of political authority at Westminster farther up the Thames. With the Age of the Discoveries, the accelerated revival of trade, and the coming of technological revolutions in agriculture, transport, and manufacturing, the Western city became and remains predominantly an economic phenomenon and with overwhelmingly economic functions.

In Asia, what was clearly a Western kind of city, derived directly from Western experience, was in effect imported by the expanding Europeans who moved eastward in the immediate wake of the discoveries in search of trade. Their early account of what they observed in Asia, and of their dealings with Asian powers, have left us in fact with some of our most valuable material on the traditional Asian city, as well as on the early growth of the new kind of city which they, as entrepreneurs par excellence, began to construct on the maritime fringes of the Asian empires. They chose sites with an eye to commercial advantage in terms of overseas trade, sites which could best tap the parts of each country most productive of goods for export and which could at the same time be reached by ocean-going ships. They were interested, in other words, in the kind of access which had been of little or no concern to the builders of most traditional Asian cities; and from the nucleus of originally small trading factories, often with forts to protect them, there grew up on these sites the great majority of Asia's present large cities outside of Japan. Even in Japan, however, the growth and nature of Kobe and Yokohama link them generically to some degree with Bombay, Calcutta, Singapore, and the other foreign-founded or foreign-dominated port cities where almost all of Asia's urban growth has been concentrated during the past three centuries. Tokyo, Nagoya, and Osaka too, Japan's three urban giants, grew in considerable part along similar lines and for the same reasons: as booming centers of an expanding trade between Asia and the West, and increasingly as little urban islands of Europe-in-Asia. For it was in these port cities, from Karachi to Batavia to Dairen, that the basic institutions of post-Renaissance Europe were planted: the sanctity and freedom of private property, the virtues of free enterprise, the power and self-satisfaction of capital, and the battery of techniques which had burgeoned in Europe to carry on the business of the new urban-centered world—stock companies, agency houses, bills of exchange, banking and insurance facilities, legal safeguards and sanctions for the protection of enterprise and property, and the vastly improved means of transport which were necessary for the expanding trade which gave these cities life.

The functions which these cities performed, and the institutional structure on which they rested, were largely new to Asia, which had traditionally lacked both the economic and the institutional infrastructure for the kind of commercial enterprise which Europeans built. Physically and in their morphology the new port cities clearly revealed their Western and colonial origins. In most of them Westerners and Asians were spatially segregated for housing, with accompanying differences not only in street development and architecture but in levels of living and their spatial manifestations. Urban skylines came to be dominated by larger buildings in almost purely European or American style, and although the populations of all of them rapidly became and remained predominantly Asian, the look of at least the cities' centers was and remains unmistakably Western. The principal business of these new urban concentrations was overseas trade, and they were virtually all therefore port cities; but since they also needed to maximize access to their commercial hinterlands they often arose on or near the lower courses of navigable rivers. This in turn created increasing problems for many of them as the size of ocean-going vessels increased and as deltaic harbors became less and less adequate. But so long as ocean-going ships could reach them, with the help of assiduous dredging, the advantage of combined landward and seaward access and the commercial productivity of the areas which relatively easy access by water made tributary to each city were strong enough to offset the difficulties of their immediate sites. Only Bombay, Singapore, Manila, Hong Kong, Tsingtao, and Dairen, blessed with excellent natural harbors, escaped from such site problems, although in the cases of Bombay and Tsingtao at the sacrifice of easy access to their hinterlands. River valleys and their deltas are commonly productive places, in Asia as elsewhere, and the commercial opportunities which they presented were powerful attractions despite the navigational hazards.

There were of course important differences between the different port cities which arose as a result of the Western impact, and the list is extensive. But there is enough common ground between them to suggest that they do in fact belong to a single generic type. The largest cities in each Asian country now belong in varying degrees to this type in that they grew out of Western-founded ports and trading factories or in that they owe the bulk of their modern growth not merely to trade with the West but to the successful transplanting onto Asian urban soil of Western institutions and techniques, producing a city which was and is far more Western than traditional Asian. In most of the smaller Asian countries, the single dominant port became and remains not simply primate but the only genuine city in the national unit, in terms both of size and of what Westerners at least would regard as major urban functions. China, India, and Japan continue of course to support a number of large older cities, once the seats of the Great Tradition, including their national capitals. But in most cases, the nature of these older indigenous cities has been transformed to such an extent that the past has been overwhelmed. So the city of Tokyo, in form and in function, has overwhelmed the old capital of Edo and its rather quaintly preserved castle in the middle of an exploding metropolis which is in many respects the heir of the Western impact rather than of the traditional *bakufu*. In all of the countries of Southeast Asia, sensitive new nationalism has still not prevented the originally colonial or foreign-influenced port city from becoming the national capital under independence. Not only was there no reasonable alternative, no other genuine city in any of these smaller countries with situational advantages and existing urban resources to rival those of the alien port, but the very origin and growth of nationalism took place in these foreign-dominated cities, where the Western model was planted for Asians to emulate.

There are now no Asian cities where the traditional form or function has been preserved unscathed. Indeed perhaps the major significance of the European-dominated port cities since the sixteenth century has been their role as centers of economic and institutional change which spread from them throughout the rest of each country and which has penetrated and altered even the urban citadels of the Great Tradition. Delhi and Peking are fully caught up in the process of revolutionary economic change, having abandoned their role as administrative guardians of the status quo. Ava, Pegu, Ayuthia, Polonnaruwa, Ch'ang An, and other inland capital cities of the past exist now only as archaeological sites. "The Asian city" is now a hybrid, part Asian and part Western, not merely in terms of its origins but in terms of its present functions, its physical character, and its morphology. Distinct functional types may of course be discerned, as among cities in the West, but just as Western cities have grown more and more alike as economic and technological change [has] accelerated, so Asian cities become more like one another and more like commercial-industrial cities everywhere else in the world. In general, then, the similarities between Asian and Western cities have during the past century or two become more striking than the differences. There are nevertheless some differences remaining, and some which seem likely to endure.

Some of these have already been touched on at the beginning of this essay. It is by no means clear, for example, that the West's experience with the process of urbanization will be duplicated in Asia, nor even that it will necessarily go as far, in terms of the proportion of the total population living in cities. If we take a population figure of 20,000 as a safe urban minimum in any area, about 15 percent of the present Asian population is urban, as against about 45 percent in the United States and about 40 percent in Europe. It is far from certain that most Asian economies (again with the exception of Japan) can produce or can tolerate the truly gargantuan urban population which would be represented by 40 percent of population totals as they will be by the end of the present century. On the other hand, there is also inadequate basis for assuming that urbanization in Asia can or will continue only in the same proportion to industrialization and commercialization as in the Western experience. It has already, in the view of many, dangerously exceeded that proportion, and yet there are still no significant signs of a major or permanent slowing of the urbanization rate. No one even superficially familiar with living conditions in large Asian cities can wholly disregard the argument that most of Asia is already seriously "overurbanized." But this perhaps over-glib term has never been more than vaguely defined, much less proven. Even the present frighteningly crowded cities, lacking in the bare minimum of what is referred to as "social overhead"—housing, water supplies, sanitation, public services—let alone amenities, represent what are probably the most dynamic forces in the process of economic development and exert critically important productive and catalytic effects. Less urbanization would probably be worse than more, either as a symptom of lesser vigor in the economy or as a cause. It is, after all, in cities that economic growth concentrates, especially of the kind which Asia is currently seeking—industrialization. There are no cost-free solutions to the problem of economic development, and short-run misery for some may be an inevitable prelude to longer-run improvement for others, in Asia as in the past experience of the West. With some obvious exceptions, there are probably not more productive uses for capital or for labor in most Asian countries than in the cities, and investment there probably yields quicker returns and with a greater multiplying effect.

Even in the West, the rate and pattern of urbanization and its correlation with industrialization varied widely as between different countries and at different periods, and it is clearly doing so in Asia at present. Urbanization has been most rapid since 1945 in Japan, where Tokyo for example added an average of 300,000 to its population in each of the eleven years following the end of the war. (Tokyo Metropolitan Government, "Problems of an Excessively Growing City and the Development of a Capital Region," Tokyo, 1957, p. 2). This represented to some extent a recovery from the abnormal loss of urban population, especially from Tokyo, during the last years of the war, but more importantly it reflects an unprecedented rapid rate of economic growth, including industrialization. Japan as a whole has probably experienced the most rapid rate of urbanization in the history of the world, especially in the period since 1920. Hong Kong is obviously a special case which is hardly comparable with national units, but as a single city (including Kowloon and contiguous urban areas) its rate of increase in population since 1945 undoubtedly tops the list, and it also represents the peak of urban population density. Its growth, however, has rested on an equally high rate of industrialization. Malaya (including Singapore but excluding the rest of Malaysia) has also been characterized by very rapid urbanization, again in relation to a high rate of economic growth, and the same has been true of Taiwan. Urbanization rates since 1945 have been to varying degrees lower in Indonesia, the Philippines, South Korea, Vietnam, Thailand, Laos, Cambodia, Burma, Ceylon, India and Pakistan, at least in part as a reflection of lower rates of economic growth than in Japan, Malaya, Hong Kong, and Taiwan, although with the possible exceptions of Laos and Cambodia urbanization rates for these countries were nevertheless high by world standards and especially in the cases of India, Pakistan, Thailand, and the Philippines. It is difficult or impossible to measure overall urbanization rates in China since 1945 or since 1949 in the absence of complete or accurate census figures, especially for city populations, even in the one modern census which has been taken in 1953. Reports in the Chinese press do, however, make clear that there has been a phenomenal growth of many cities, some of them virtually new, as a result of the government's policy of concentrating new industrial investment in areas previously neglected. Lanchow, Paotou, and Urumchi, for example, have grown exceptionally rapidly, while Shanghai, still the largest Chinese city, has had its growth controlled by government restrictions on in-migration and by forced removals of what were regarded as excess numbers for return to the countryside or for reassignment to new areas or urban construction and industrialization in the northwest or in Sinkiang.

Except for its larger scale, there does not seem to be anything about this process in Asia which differs significantly from the Western experience, where cities also grew, especially in the earlier stages of modern industrialization and urbanization, more through migration than through natural increase and where there was serious overcrowding ("overurbanization") before employment, housing, and municipal services began to catch up with booming city populations. The difference in Asia, in large part as a result of the much greater scale involved, may be that it will take longer for urban life to reach minimum acceptable standards, or that they may never attain current, let alone future, Western urban standards. Population densities in most Asian cities have already reached enormously high levels, and this may indeed be the most significant single respect in which Asian urbanism differs from urbanism in the West. In India, for example, there are an average of about 150,000 people per square mile in Old Delhi as a whole, at least three times the figure for the most crowded sections of American cities. The worst or most crowded wards of Delhi, Bombay, or Calcutta show almost incredible densities ranging from 300,000 per square mile to over 450,000. Such fantastic crowding of often illiterate city dwellers under slum conditions further increases the difficulties of accurate census taking.

BIBLIOGRAPHY

The foregoing article has attempted to summarize in very general terms some of the salient features of Asian urbanization, the general status of present knowledge of it, and some of the outstanding problems which confront the student. In what follows, an attempt will be made to summarize more specifically the work which has been done on and in the separate regions of Asia, principally from the geographical point of view.

Japan

Japan has been a relatively highly urbanized country for at least the past two centuries. Studies of Japanese urbanization have also been made both more appropriate and more fruitful by the relative abundance of reliable urban data, as one reflection of the sophistication of economic, educational, and technological growth in Japan. Unfortunately from the Western point of view, a great deal of the published material on Japanese urbanism is in Japanese, but some is also available in English and the total amount is rich and varied. The Association of Japanese Geographers established a Committee on Urban Studies in 1958, whose report titled *Research Materials on Urbanization* was published in 1959 (S. Yamaga, ed., *Toshika Kenyu Shiryo*, Tokyo, 1959). The report is primarily an inventory and bibliography, which has since been updated by S. Kiuchi, one of Japan's leading urban geographers, in an English-language article (S. Kiuchi, "Recent Developments in Japanese Urban Geography," *Annals*, Assoc. of Amer. Geographers, 1963, 93–102). All but a few of the studies mentioned in these two accounts are in Japanese. They include analyses of functional urban types, urbanization rates, rural-urban migration, "metropolitanization," economic base, land use, morphology, urban spread and absorption, urban influences on rural areas, inter-urban communications and flow, wage rates, and land prices. Considerable work has also been done in central place studies, the use of gravity models, densities and intensiveness, industrial location, historical studies of specific cities and city regions, and physical studies of urban sites. Some attention has also been paid by Japanese urban geographers to cross-culture comparison, and S. Kiuchi has in particular stressed the morphological differences between Japanese and Western cities (S. Kiuchi, "Problems of Comparative Urban Geography," in *Tsujimura Taro Sensei Koki Kinen, Chirigaku Rombonshu* ["Geographical Essays in Honor of Prof. Tsujimura's Seventieth Birthday"] Tokyo, 1961, pp. 557–73).

Urban planning has been increasingly emphasized in the literature on Japan, as a reflection of the virtual explosion of city populations and urbanized areas during the past two decades, and at least three Japanese journals are devoted to it: *Toshi Mondai, Toshi Mondai Kenkyu,* and *Shisei.* Most Japanese cities now have their own planning boards, many of which also carry out extensive studies of their own urban areas. (See for example the voluminous English-language report prepared for a U.N.T.A.B. mission to Japan titled *Basic Materials for the Comprehensive Development Plan of the Hanshin Metropolitan Region,* 2 vols., Osaka, 1960). The "castletown" origins of many of Japan's cities have been examined in a great variety of published studies, some primarily historical, others which focus on current urban morphology and structure as they have been influenced by earlier forms. (See for example J. W. Hall, "The Castle Town and Japan's Modern Urbanization," *Far Eastern Quarterly,* 1955, 37–56 [English]; K. Tanabe, "The Development of Spatial Structure in Japanese Cities with Regard to Castle Towns," *Science Reports of Tohoku University,* VIIth Series, Geography, no. 8, 1959, pp. 88–105 [English]; T. Matsumoto, "The Structure of Modern Castle Towns," *Geog. Review of Japan,* 1962, 97–112 [articles in this journal are in Japanese,

with short English summaries]. But the bulk of Japanese urban studies has been concentrated on contemporary problems, especially on what the Japanese literature refers to as "metropolitanization," the process of big-city expansion, suburbanization, regional concentration, changes in urban structure and morphology as a result of growth and of changes in transport and industrialization, and adjustments in the urban hierarchy. (For a recent review and some general conclusions, see T. Ishimizu, "The Present Status of Urbanization Studies among Japanese Academic Geographers," *Geog. Review of Japan,* 1962, 362–73. See also the forthcoming biographical essay by N. S. Ginsburg, "Urban Geography and Non-Western Areas," to appear in P. Hauser and L. Schnore, eds., *The Study of Urbanization;* I am indebted to Prof. Ginsburg for most of the inventory and bibliographical material presented here, especially on Japan, for which his forthcoming work gives much greater detail).

Western-language studies by geographers on Japanese urbanism are still discouragingly few, especially in proportion to the wealth of data and the impressive contributions of Japanese geographers. J. D. Eyre and J. H. Thompson have studied urban food supply problems and agricultural land use (J. D. Eyre, "Sources of Tokyo's Fresh Food Supply," *Geog. Review,* 1959, 455–76; J. H. Thompson, "Urban Agriculture in Southern Japan," *Economic Geography,* 1957, 224–37), and Eyre has also analyzed the sources of migrants to Tokyo, Osaka, and Nagoya in a series of revealing maps (Eyre, "Regional Variations in Japanese Internal Migration," *Papers of the Michigan Academy,* XLIX, 1964, 271–84). Older studies of urban origins, forms, and distribution by R. B. Hall and G. T. Trewartha are still valuable (R. B. Hall, "The Cities of Japan; Notes on Distribution and Inherited Forms," *Annals,* Assoc. of Amer. Geographers, 1934, 175–200; G. T. Trewartha, "Japanese Cities: Distribution and Morphology," *Geographical Review,* 1934, 407–17), and P. Scholler has more recently examined modern metropolitan growth (P. Scholler, "Wachstum und Wandlung Japanischer Stadtregionen," *Die Erde,* 1962, 202–34). But of all of the areas of Asia, Japan offers the greatest opportunity to Western students of urbanization, and the least realized. The China field is proportionately much less extensively worked, but Japan is not only more highly urbanized but is equipped with a wide range of dependable data and an impressive body of knowledge as a result of the efforts of Japanese scholars over many years. Western sociologists and anthropologists have begun to make major contributions to our knowledge of Japanese urban life (see most notably R. P. Dore, *City Life in Japan,* Berkeley, 1958; O. Shunsuke, "The Urban Phenomenon in Japan," *Journal of Asian Studies,* 1964, 122–29, and his many references; also T. O. Wilkinson, "A Functional Classification of Japanese Cities, 1920–1955," *Demography*, Spring, 1964), but for other Western students of urbanization this is still largely an untilled and potentially richly rewarding field.

China

While it is true that any study of modern urbanization in China must confront what amounts almost to a vast statistical void, traditional or pre-modern China accumulated without question the most immense body of detailed data on virtually every aspect of human experience that has ever been preserved from any culture. Much of traditional Chinese culture, and especially its literate aspects, centered in the city so that a great deal of the materials which have been preserved deal with urban phenomena. Very little use has yet been made of these data, and especially of the thousands of county (*hsien*) gazeteers. Some indication of their value for urban studies is provided by two revealing studies by S. D. Chang, which focus on the functions and distribution of the *hsien* (county) capitals as administrative centers through two thousand years of Chinese history (S. D. Chang, "Some Aspects of the Urban Geography of the Chinese Hsien Capital," *Annals*, Assoc. of Amer. Geographers, 1961, 23–45; and "Historical Trends in Chinese Urbanization," *Ibid.*, 1963, 109–43). Some limited attention has also been paid to the capital cities and their symbolic role, particularly Peking but also Ch'ang An. (See for example A. Wright, "Symbolism and Function: Reflections on Ch'ang An and Other Great Capitals," forthcoming in *Journal of Asian Studies*, August 1965; *ibid.*, "Ch'ang An, 583–904," in *Historic Ages of the Great Cities*, London, 1964.) The predominantly administrative consequences in institutional and locational terms are also considered and briefly contrasted with Western models, in an article by Murphey (R. Murphey, "The City as a Center of Change: Western Europe and China," *Annals*, Assoc. of Amer. Geographers, 1954, 349–62). In more general terms, the traditional Chinese city remains largely unstudied, as the representative of what was clearly the major urban tradition in the world until a century or two ago. (See however E. Balazs, "Les Villes Chinoises," *Receuils de la Soc. Jean Bodin*, vol. 6, 1954; W. Eberhard, "Data on the Structure of the Chinese City in the Preindustrial Period," *Ec. Dev. and Cultural Change*, April 1956.)

The treaty-ports have been given proportionately greater attention, but still relatively superficially, although for them as well there is a considerable body of data, principally in the records of the Maritime Customs, one of the oases in the statistical desert of modern China. Voluminous Western first-person and secondary accounts from the nineteenth and early twentieth centuries are also available. There is as yet only one book-length geographical or specifically urban study of any of the treaty-ports, although it does treat the largest and most important of them, Shanghai, and attempts to generalize from the Shanghai case (R. Murphey, *Shanghai: Key to Modern China*, Cambridge, Mass., 1953). Ginsburg, Spencer, and others have contributed smaller studies of other treaty-ports, including an example of those developed largely under the Japanese in Manchuria (N. S. Ginsberg, "Ch'ang Ch'un," *Economic Geography*, 1949, 290–307; N. S. Ginsburg, "Ch'ing Tao," *Economic Geography*, 1948, 181–200; J. E. Spencer, "Changing Chungking: The Rebuilding of an Old Chinese City," *Geographical Review*, 1939, 46–60; M. Hatch, "The Port of Tientsin," *Geographical Review*, 1935, 367–81; R. M. Hughes, "Hong Kong: An Urban Study," *Geogr. Journal*, 1951, 1–23; S. G. Davis, *Hong Kong in its Geographic Setting*, London, 1949). G. T. Trewartha's two articles on urban functions and distributions in pre-communist China are hampered by dependence on unreliable data and by superficial acquaintance with the Chinese setting (G. T. Trewartha, "Chinese Cities: Origins and Functions," *Annals*, Assoc. of Amer. Geographers, 1952, 69–93, and "Chinese Cities: Numbers and Distributions," *Ibid.*, 1951, 331–47).

The great acceleration of urban growth in China since 1949 has unfortunately not been accompanied by increased scholarly attention, primarily because of data shortages. On the basis of the incomplete data available, a few tentative analyses have been attempted. (The most useful of these is probably M. B. Ullman, "Cities of Mainland China: 1953 and 1958," International Population Reports, Series P-95, Washington, 1961, which suggests a classification of cities according to both size and function. See also T. Shabad, "The Population of Chinese Cities," *Geogr. Review*, 1959, 32–42, which relies mainly on Russian sources; J. S. Aird, "The Size, Composition, and Growth of the Population of Mainland China," International Population Reports, Series P-90, Washington, 1961; and J. P. Emerson, "Manpower Absorption in the Non-Agricultural Branches of the Economy of Communist China," *China Quarterly*, 1961, 69–84). But even the gross outlines of Chinese urbanization during the past decade are still largely unknown. Material available in enormous volume from the Chinese periodical and scholarly press, in Chinese and in selected translation, is seldom directly helpful, in part because accurate statistical data are not available domestically either, although there are frequent generalized references to new or rapidly growing cities, to migration patterns, to urban living conditions, and to the urban-related aspects of planned industrial location.

Contemporary Chinese geography concentrates virtually exclusively on regional resource development and on physical geography, and its journals publish almost nothing directly concerned with urban analysis. The relatively small volume of Chinese geographical publication before 1949 includes a small number of primarily descriptive accounts of individual cities, but their usefulness to Western scholars is further limited by the language barrier. In summary, our knowledge of urbanism and urbanization in China is extraordinarily slight, and especially so by contrast with the size of the problem and with its great historical depth. It seems particularly regrettable that we are at least for the present unable to see how in this outstandingly important case modern urbanization, with a significant industrial component, is grafted onto or transforms a pre-existing administrative urban structure of some completeness, and how the original treaty-ports are also to be integrated in what is already clearly becoming an expanded hierarchy heavily influenced by political considerations.

Southeast Asia

The existing geographical literature on urbanism in Southeast Asia appropriately reflects the relatively recent origin of any extensive urbanization, most of which has occurred during the last century and a half at most, and directly as a result of the colonial and commercial activities of Westerners and/or Chinese. The origins and nature of these cities which now in every case dominate each country in Southeast Asia are examined in three parallel articles which nevertheless duplicate one another surprisingly little (D. W. Fryer, "The Million City in Southeast Asia," *Geogr. Review*, 1953, 474–94; N. S. Ginsburg, "The Great City in Southeast Asia," *Amer. Journ. of Sociology*, 1955, 455–62; and R. Murphey, "New Capitals of Asia," *Econ. Dev. and Cultural Change*, 1957, 216–43). More detailed work is seriously hampered by the shortage of adequate or reliable statistical data, especially for Indonesia, Thailand, Vietnam, and Burma. An account of these handicaps is given in an article by R. J. Neville (R. J. W. Neville, "An Urban Study of Pontian Kechil, Southwest Malaya," *Journ. of Tropical Geog.*, 1962, 32–56), which is however based mainly on work in Malaya where census and other relevant data are comparatively more abundant and dependable. As an understandable consequence, and also as a result of the presence of at least two major universities in Malaya (at Singapore and at Kuala Lumpur) with extensive research staffs and facilities, a disproportionate share of the published literature on urbanization in Southeast Asia deals with Malaya (E. H. G. Dobby, "Settlement Patterns in Malaya," *Geogr. Review*, 1942, 211–32; *ibid.*, "Singapore, Town and Country," *Geogr. Review*, 1940, 84–109; D. F. Allen, *The Major Ports of Malaya*, Kuala Lumpur, 1951, and *The Minor Ports of Malaya*, Singapore, 1953; E. Cooper, "Urbanization

in Malaya," *Population Studies*, 1951, 117–31; H. Sendut, "Patterns of Urbanization in Malaya," *Journ. of Tropical Geog.*, 1962, 114–30; T. G. McGee, "The Cultural Role of Cities: A Case Study of Kuala Lumpur," *ibid.*, 1963, 178–96). Somewhat surprisingly, there has been relatively little attention paid by American geographers to urban phenomena in the Philippines, and in particular no adequate study of Manila, although one aspect of its commercial structure has been examined (W. E. McIntyre, "The Retail Pattern of Manila," *Geogr. Review*, 1955, 66–80). Two other Philippine studies attempt to establish a wider set of constructs. Ullman's examination of the urban hierarchy and of inter-island trade movements provides important comparative analysis with actual and theoretical hierarchies in other parts of the world (E. Ullman, "Trade Centers and Tributary Areas of the Philippines," *Geogr. Review*, 1960, 203–18), and Spencer attempts to supply a more reliable set of estimates for city sizes and for the structure of the urban hierarchy than the census figures alone suggest (J. E. Spencer, "The Cities of the Philippines," *Journ. of Geog.*, 1958, 288–94). Wernstedt has also examined the important Filipino commercial frame of inter-island trade in his study of Cebu (F. L. Wernstedt, "Cebu: Focus of Philippine Inter-Island Trade," *Econ. Geog.*, 1957, 336–46). One of the few geographical studies of urbanism in Indonesia is also concerned with city sizes, and with the rank-size rule, which the author finds does not appropriately fit his Indonesian data. The article attempts in addition to measure the proportions of non-Indonesian population (mainly Chinese) in each of the several cities considered, a matter which is of course especially relevant to all Southeast Asian cities (W. A. Withington, "The Kotapradja or 'King Cities' of Indonesia," *Pacific Viewpoint*, 1963, 87–91).

Urban structure and morphology are however probably the subjects of the largest single group of published studies on Southeast Asia, including the recent beginnings of a literature in the planning field, where attention has been focused in particular on Singapore (J. M. Frazer, "Town Planning and Housing in Singapore," *Town Planning Review*, 1953, 5–25; see also planning studies of Manila, Saigon, and Djakarta published in United Nations, *Public Administration Problems of New and Rapidly Growing Towns in Asia*, Bangkok, 1962). Earlier studies centering primarily on urban form include those by Spate and Trueblood on Rangoon (almost the only urban geographical study of Burma yet published in English), Dobby on Singapore (referred to above), and Withington on Medan (O. H. K. Spate and L. Trueblood, "Rangoon: A Study in Urban Geography," *Geog. Review*, 1942, 56–73; W. A. Withington, "Medan: Primary Regional Metropolis of Sumatra," *Journ. of Geog.*, 1962, 59–67).

The sociological/anthropological literature on the predominantly urban Chinese in Southeast Asia is relatively extensive, and a good deal of it deals directly with urbanism. (See for example G. W. Skinner, *Leadership and Power in the Chinese Community of Thailand*, Ithaca, 1958; Jacques Amyot, *The Chinese Community of Manila*, Chicago, 1960; D. Wilmot, *The Chinese of Semarang*, Ithaca, 1960; Barrington Kaye, *Upper Nankin Street, Singapore*, Singapore, 1960.) Other perceptive analyses of the sociological aspects of urbanization in southeast Asia include Geertz's recent study of the development of different forms of entrepreneurship in Javan towns, and Bruner's study of group identity (Clifford Geertz, *Peddlars and Princes: Social Development and Economic Change in Two Indonesian Towns*, Chicago, 1963; E. M. Bruner "Urbanization and Ethnic Identity in North Sumatra," *Amer. Anthropologist*, vol. 63, 508–21). The rapid mushrooming especially of Djakarta but also of Singapore, Kuala Lumpur, Manila, and Bangkok, accompanying urban sprawl, and the observable effects of local culture, national and political roles, and local economic realities on originally Western urban forms and functions have still to be examined in any detail.

India

Next to Japan, urbanization in India has received the greatest amount of research attention, but by both Indians and foreigners, and virtually all of the literature is in English. Probably its most important single theme is "overurbanization," in a variety of forms including the implications for economic planning and investment, schemes for urban development or re-development ("urban community development"), the dimensions and nature of rural-urban migration, surveys of living conditions in the cities, the debate over industrial "decentralization," and the problems of both urban and rural unemployment and underemployment. Discussions of Indian urbanization have also had to confront an essentially Gandhian anti-urban and pro-village sentiment which is still expressed, although it has had little or no apparent effect on the urbanization rate or in particular on the massive scale of rural-urban migration. The 1961 Census of India showed a slight slowing down of the rate of urbanization, as compared with the rate between 1941 and 1951, but this is not easy to account for beyond drawing attention to the possibility that living conditions and general economic opportunity in at least the larger cities may have been perceived by potential migrants from the rural areas as in balance slightly less favorable, a conclusion which almost certainly does accord with reality. Not only are the larger cities increasingly and dangerously overcrowded but the beginning of some improvement in levels of living, and perhaps of employment, are apparent in parts of the countryside. Continued concentration of industrial investment and of population growth in the already larger cities is however argued as rational, even though some new investment may also be allocated to other urban centers such as the new or expanded steel towns under the third five-year plan. The Bombay and Calcutta conurbations combined now contain about 40 percent of all Indian industrial plants, but such a degree of concentration is probably economic and does not necessarily distinguish India from industrial countries in the West. In any case, planning decisions for the regional allocation of urban investment should be governed by economic cost-benefit analysis rather than by sentiment or political considerations. The biggest cities will probably continue to grow relatively rapidly, and will continue to generate both more overcrowding and more urgent planning problems. The Calcutta conurbation alone may include eighty million people by the end of the present century.

The best single guide to Indian urbanization is the volume edited by Roy Turner which resulted from a 1960 seminar in Berkeley, California (Roy Turner, ed., *India's Urban Future*, Berkeley, 1962). Papers by Indians and Americans deal with urbanization rates and the role of migration, urban morphology and structure, sociological aspects of urban life, the economic implications of urbanization, the centralization-decentralization issue, and the role of the planner. A final paper by B. F. Hoselitz surveys the literature on urbanization in India and provides an excellent annotated bibliography. (An earlier version of the same paper appeared as "The Cities of India and Their Problems" in *Annals*, Assoc. of Amer. Geographers, 1959, 223–31.) As Hoselitz points out, there are a large number of socioeconomic studies of individual Indian cities, representing probably the largest single body of urban data, but fewer comprehensive analyses which succeed in providing an adequate spatial frame and which also consider urban structure and function, transport, hinterland relations, and planning problems. Outstanding among the latter are the two studies of R. L. Singh, on Banaras and Bangalore (R. L. Singh, *Banaras: A Study in Urban Geography*, Banaras, 1955, and *Bangalore: A Study in Urban Geography*, Banaras, 1964. See also J. M. Datta, "Urbanization in Bengal," *Geogr. Review of India*, 1956, 19–23; E. Ahmad, "Origins and Evolution of the Towns of Uttar Pradesh," *Geographical Outlook*, 1956, 38–58; O. H. K. Spate and E. Ahmad, "Five Cities of the Gangetic Plain," *Geogr. Review*, 1950, 260–78). John Brush has provided in his article in the Turner volume a good survey of Indian urban morphology, necessarily with considerable historical reference, an approach which also characterizes most of the many studies of urban form in Indian journals (John Brush, "The Morphology of Indian Cities," in Roy Turner, *op. cit.*, pp. 57–70; M. N. Nigam, "The Evolution of Lucknow," *Natl. Geographic Journ. of India*, 1960, 30–46; R. V. Joshi, "Urban Structure in Western India," *Geogr. Review* of *India*, 1956, 7–19; C. D. Deshpande, "Cities and Towns of Bombay Province: Aspects of Urban Geography," *Indian Geogr. Journal*, 1941, 284–97; P. P. Karan, "The Pattern of Indian Towns: A Study in Urban Morphology," *Journ. Amer. Inst. of Planners*, 1957, 70–75; V. R. Prabhu, "Dhawar: A Study in Indian Urban Landscapes," *Bombay Geogr. Magazine*, 1953, 56–63). The work of the geographer N. R. Kar is also notable for its comprehensive approach to the urban phenomenon especially of Calcutta, and for its use of statistical models, structural theory, and other recently developed analytic techniques as well as more traditional methods. His several studies are valuable not only because they help to illumine the nature and problems of India's largest city but also because they specifically delineate the differences and the similarities between Calcutta and Western cities, while at the same time stressing the controlling importance of the Western impact, in the case of Calcutta and of the Bengali and Indian urban hierarchy more generally (N. R. Kar, "Calcutta als Weltstadt," in J. M. Schultze, ed., *Zum Probleme der Weltstadt*, Berlin, 1959; *ibid.*, "Urban Characteristics of the City of Calcutta," *Indian Population Bulletin*, 1960, 34–67; *ibid.*, "Pattern of Urban Growth in Lower West Bengal, *Geogr. Review of India*, 1962, 42–59; *ibid.*, "Urban Hierarchy and Central Functions Around Calcutta, in Lower West Bengal, India, and Their Significance," in K. Norborg, ed., *Proceedings of the I.G.V. Symposium in Urban Geography, Lund, 1960*, Lund, 1962).

One of the few recent studies which also considers urban patterns before the British period is the paper by Robert Crane (R. I. Crane, "Urbanism in India," *Amer. Journ. of Sociology*, 1955, 107–14), but the British impact, especially on urban morphology, is treated in almost all of the analyses of contemporary city forms. The alien origins of the great port cities have been given relatively extensive historical treatment, but the geographic implications have been for the most part examined only incidentally. (For a specific geographic study of the Indian prototype of the treaty-ports, however, see R. Murphey, "The City in the Swamp: Aspects of the Site and Early Growth of Calcutta," *Geogr. Journal*, 1964, 241–56, which stresses the essentially Western nature of the city, the parallel with Bombay, Madras, and the port cities of Southeast Asia and China, and the role which Calcutta was the first to play in spreading economic change.) Bombay and Calcutta have been studied most extensively in the general urban literature, and especially in socioeconomic terms. Bombay has received particular attention as the chief center of the cotton textile industry, and a recent volume deals in great detail with the widespread implications of the recruitment of an urban industrial labor force (M. D. Morris, *The Emergence of an Industrial Labor Force in India: A Study of the Bombay Cotton Mills 1854–1947*, Berkeley, 1965). Socio-

economic work on Calcutta (see especially S. N. Sen, *The City of Calcutta: A Socio-Economic Survey*, Calcutta, 1960) has more recently been overshadowed by planning research on a very large scale as part of the project to produce a comprehensive metropolitan plan for Calcutta, still in its relatively early stages and for the most part not yet available in print. The similarly ambitious Delhi Planning Project is outlined at the pilot stage by B. Chatterjee, and dealt with in greater and more current detail by Clinard (B. Chatterjee, "Urban Community Development in India: The Delhi Pilot Project," in Roy Turner, *op. cit.*, pp. 71–73; M. B. Clinard, *Urban Community Development and Slums*, Glencoe, 1965—nine chapters of this work are devoted to the Delhi Project, and one to a similar but smaller project in Dacca, East Pakistan). The establishment in 1958 of an Indian journal devoted entirely to planning, *Urban and Rural Planning Thought* (Delhi), is a further indication of the rapid increase of planning research and activity in recent years.

Marketing systems and city hinterlands have been the subject of several smaller studies. (See for example Robert Mayfield, "The Range of a Good in the Indian Punjab," *Annals*, Assoc. of Amer. Geographers, 1963, 38–49; S. N. Reddy, "Vegetable Markets and Regional Relationships of Hyderabad City," *Geog. Review of India*, 1961, 24–40; W. C. Neale, H. Singh, and J. P. Singh, "Kurali Market: A Report on the Economic Geography of Marketing in Northern Punjab," *Ec. Dev. and Cultural Change*, 1965, 129–68; F. K. Khan and M. H. Khan, "Delimitation of Greater Dacca," *Oriental Geographer*, 1961, 95–120.) Functional classifications of cities, by employment, by size, and by population density have been attempted by Lal, Ahmad, and Learmonth (A. Lal, "Some Aspects of the Functional Classification of Cities and a Proposed Scheme for Classifying Indian Cities," *Natl. Geog. Journ. of India*, 1959, 12–24; N. Ahmad, "The Urban Pattern in East Pakistan," *Oriental Geographer*, 1957, 37–39; A. T. Learmonth *et al.*, *Mysore State: An Atlas of Resources*, Calcutta, 1960, and *Mysore State: A Regional Synthesis*, Calcutta, 1962), and P. P. Karan has related industrial changes to urban growth (P. P. Karan, "Changes in Indian Industrial Location," *Annals*, Assoc. of Amer. Geographers, 1964, 336–54).

India may present the clearest or at least the best known Asia example of the mixing of Asian and Western urban forms and of the long-term operation of Western-derived and Western-managed economic forces on existing and developing urban systems and on individual cities. What may make Indian cities particularly distinctive is their rapid growth at a time when the economy as a whole has not achieved substantial and permanent net gains of a self-perpetuating sort which can leave sufficient margin for basic "social investment," hence the arguments centering around "overurbanization." How far into the future such a pattern may extend, and to what degree Indian cities will become more reflective of Indian cultural and economic conditions and less reflective of Western influences are fruitful subjects for speculation. For the present, the amount and quality of published research on Indian urbanism, and its unique availability to Western scholars, plus the recent boost given to urban studies by the major planning efforts in Delhi, Calcutta, and elsewhere leave our understanding at a more satisfactory level than anywhere else in Asia outside of Japan, and suggest that it will continue to increase rapidly as the process of urbanization enters what may be a more distinctively Indian stage.

Asia

It remains to mention, and to acknowledge, some general works which deal with urban problems in Asia as a whole. By far the most valuable of these for the present essay is the long chapter by Norton Ginsburg titled "Urban Geography and Non-Western Areas," forthcoming in *The Study of Urbanization* and edited by Philip Hauser and Leo Schnore. Most of Ginsburg's chapter deals in fact with Asia and provides an excellent critical summary of the published literature. An earlier volume edited by Philip Hauser, *Urbanization in Asia and the Far East*, the proceedings of a joint UN/UNESCO/ILO Seminar on Urbanization in the ECAFE region in 1956 and published by UNESCO in Calcutta in 1957, is still useful both for its individual papers on a variety of social and economic aspects of urbanism and for the general summary by Hauser. "The City in the Asian Polity," Hugh Tinker's inaugural lecture of 1963 as Professor of Government and Politics at the School of Oriental and African Studies, University of London, published in pamphlet form in 1964, provides a graceful and stimulating survey of the character and significance of the traditional Asian city and contrasts it with the basically different kind of city which arose as a result of the Western impact. Gideon Sjoberg's *The Preindustrial City, Past and Present* (Glencoe, 1960) is an unreliable guide to traditional Asian urbanism, but the long critical review of Sjoberg's book by Paul Wheatley (*Pacific Viewpoint*, 1963, 163–88) titled "What the Greatness of a City Is Said To Be" helps to set the record straight and adds much additional material on the great Asian cities of the past.

In general, however, the study of urbanization in Asia must be regarded as only just begun, both in terms of the past and present scale of the problem and of its likely future dimensions. If, as seems probable, Asia and most of the rest of the world are still in the early stages of a process which may in the foreseeable future make them as urban-centered as Europe and the United States, this is one of the most urgent fields of research for all students of human society.

3

HANS BLUMENFELD

The Urban Pattern

The Latin word *urbs* is related to *orbis*, the circle. Like the English "town" and the Slavic *gorod*, related to "yard" and "girdle," it denotes as the basic characteristic of the urban phenomenon the enclosure which separates it from the open country. This is the city as it has existed through recorded history: a static unit, confined and defined by its enclosing boundary, and with a definite pattern of its internal organization, in which each part has a stable and defined relation to the whole.

But this volume deals, not accidentally, with "urban development." The static concept of the city is no longer valid. It is constantly changing and growing, and, as it grows, it bursts its girdle and overflows into the countryside. The result is universally viewed with alarm as "urban sprawl," as being "neither city nor country."

In this fluctuating mass, the old static patterns dissolve. If any pattern can be discerned, it can only be the pattern of flux. This apparent chaos can no longer be grasped as formation but only as transformation, as historical process.

Emergence of the Metropolis

For 5,000 years, two forms of human settlement predominated in all but the most scarcely populated areas of the globe: the city and the rural village. The vast majority lived in the latter, and most of the world's work was done there. The villages were largely self-sufficient, not only in agricultural products but also in such manu-

factured products and services as they required. The cities were the seat of the ruling elite—land-owning, political, military, religious, commercial—and those who supplied them with goods and services; these constituted a small minority, hardly ever exceeding 20 percent of the population. The "services" which, in exchange for food and raw materials, they supplied to the countryside were limited to military protection, dispensation of justice, and religious guidance. Urban trade was trading with other cities and with such other seats of the ruling elite as castles, manors, and monasteries, most of which, in the course of time, either disappeared or became the nuclei of cities.

This pattern changed radically only with what we rather narrowly call the Industrial Revolution, meaning the application of scientific methods to the processes of production and distribution. This resulted in two closely related and interacting processes: increasing division of labor and increasing productivity. Increasing productivity set more and more labor free for the production of manufactured goods and of services, and more and more productive activities were specialized out of the village economy and transformed into urban industries.

Increasing division and specialization of labor required increasing interaction and cooperation, both within and between establishments. This interaction required proximity. The presence of specialized workers attracted industrial and commercial establishments, and these in turn attracted other establishments and more workers. The process fed on itself. The great country-to-city migration began and is still continuing everywhere.

This great process of concentration was made

Hans Blumenfeld, "The Urban Pattern," *The Annals* of the American Academy of Political and Social Science, vol. 352 (March 1964), pp. 74–83. Reprinted by permission.

possible by the development of powerful means of long-distance transportation and communication, primarily the steamship, the railroad, and the electric telegraph, which, for the first time in history, made it possible to assemble at one point the food and raw materials required to support the life and work of millions of people.

Although technology had revolutionized long-distance transportation well before the middle of the nineteenth century, goods, persons, and messages within these huge agglomerations still moved almost exclusively by foot or by hoof. This limited their size to a radius of about one hour's walking time, or three miles. Within this narrow perimeter, houses, factories, docks, and railroad yards crowded together.

Almost half a century passed before new technology revolutionized internal transportation and communication: the bicycle, electric traction applied to streetcars and rapid-transit trains, the telephone, followed by the internal-combustion engine applied to passenger cars, trucks, and buses, and by radio and television. The city could expand. While the original inbound wave of the country-to-city migration continues in full force, it is now met by a new outbound city-to-suburb wave. This wave of expansion, which started about a century ago, is still gathering momentum. The result of the interaction of these two waves is a completely new form of human settlement which can no longer be understood in the traditional terms of town-and-country or of city-and-suburb. The concentrated nineteenth-century city with its separate suburbs was a short-lived transitional phenomenon. For the emerging new form of settlement we have as yet no word. For lack of a better term, I am calling it a metropolitan area or, for short, the metropolis.

The Metropolis and Its Region

For the purpose of this discussion I am defining the metropolis as an area in which at least half a million people live within a distance not exceeding forty-five minutes travel time from its center by means available to the majority of the population. With current North American technology, this means a radius of about thirty miles.

The essence and reason for existence of the metropolis is, as for its predecessor, the city, mutual accessibility—primarily, though by no means exclusively, mutual accessibility of place of residence and place of work. The metropolis extends as far as widespread daily commuting extends, and no farther.

However, its influence extends over a wider area which may be defined as the "metropolitan region," generally up to a time distance of about two hours from the center of the metropolis. Here the influence is twofold. Because the metropolis is easily accessible as a supplier of goods and of business and consumer services and also as a market for their products, establishments and households prefer to settle in towns within these regions rather than in those remote from metropolitan centers. While isolated towns are losing population relatively and often absolutely, each metropolis is typically surrounded by a number of active and growing "satellite" towns, based generally on manufacturing plants which are often branch plants of or migrants from the metropolis.

But the pattern of the region is determined not only by those functions which are served by the metropolis but also by those even more rapidly growing and wider ranging ones which serve the recreational needs of the metropolitan population: summer cottages, lodges, motels, camps, picnic grounds, parks, and facilities for a growing variety of land and water sports, with a host of services to their users. The Stockholm regional planners define a vast "summer Stockholm" surrounding the "winter" metropolis, and a similar "summer metropolis" can be identified everywhere in America.

A strange reversal is taking place. For thousands of years, the countryside has been the main locus of production, while the city was largely a place of consumption. Now, all activities but the immediate cultivation of the soil—even the raising and feeding of the new "animal" that draws the plow—have been specialized and transformed into "urban" activities. The same process, abetted by the same transportation technology which at one pole transformed the city into the giant metropolitan concentration, has, at the opposite pole, dissolved the village into ever fewer and more widely dispersed farms. But, over wide areas, though not everywhere, the dwindling farm population is being replaced by a different group, those who "retire" to the countryside. The vast majority of these retire only for short periods, weekends or a few weeks of vacation, but a growing number are permanent residents. This is true not only of the insignificant numbers of gentlemen-farmers but of many people of modest means, living on pensions, insurance, or other transfer payments, often supplemented by various services to tourists. No systematic research has explored this phenomenon, but casual observation indicates its growing significance. With increase in leisure time, it may ultimately influence the pattern of the metropolis itself.

For the present we are dealing only with the latter, the area of regular daily commuting, and only with its most frequent form, the "mononuclear" metropolis. There exist other metropolitan areas which are "polynuclear," resulting from a process for which Patrick Geddes coined the term "conurbation," the growing together of several important independent cities. This has occurred in areas of old and dense urban developments which had already expanded rapidly during the early phases of the Industrial Revolution. The English Midlands, the "Randstad Holland," and the Rhine-Ruhr concentration are the three major examples. In other areas of equally old and dense urban development which, however, started their transformation only at a later stage of the Industrial Revolution, one city increasingly assumes a dominant central role. Cases are Stuttgart for Württemberg, Zurich for northwestern Switzerland, and Milan for Lombardy. They become increasingly similar to the metropolitan areas in younger countries which started out from a single big city such as Chicago or Melbourne.

Many observers believe that the process of conurbation is now repeating itself on an enlarged scale in the United States, notably along the Atlantic seaboard from Boston to Washington. However, analysis of available data shows that daily commuting between the metropolitan centers located on this axis is quite insignificant and that intervening areas show densities which are, on the average, very low compared to those within the major metropolitan areas. The following discussion will therefore deal only with the single monocentric commuting areas as the "archetype" of the metropolis, recognizing, however, that its boundary with the region is fluid and tends to expand.

Characteristics of the Metropolis

The developing pattern of the transmutation of the traditional city into the metropolis can be understood best by identifying their essential differences.

1. The metropolis combines with the traditional city function of central leadership the traditional function of the countryside to provide the bulk of material production.

2. As a result, as a country reaches the "developed" level, the majority of its population is now, or soon will be, living in metropolitan areas or, at least, in metropolitan regions. The population of the individual metropolis is much larger than that of the city. The biggest metropolis, New York, contains ten times the population of the biggest pre-industrial city, Imperial Rome.

3. This larger population is dispersed over a much larger territory. With a radius of thirty miles it comprises a hundred times more land than the area determined by the three-mile radius of even the biggest foot-and-hoof cities.

4. This vast territory contains not only "urban-developed" land but also extensive "open" areas, parks, golf courses, country clubs, institutional campuses, even farms and forests.

5. Places of work and places of residence are located in separate areas.

6. Residential areas are segregated according to class or income of their residents.

This last-named difference calls for some comment. At first sight, it seems paradoxical that democratic capitalism should have produced a pattern so contrary to democratic ideology. In preindustrial societies, a large part of the "lower" classes lived on the premises of their masters, as slaves or domestic servants. The alley dwellings of Washington and other southern cities still reflect this older pattern. Elsewhere, as in Chinese cities, ambulant craftsmen worked and often slept in the compounds of their wealthy clients. Almost everywhere in preindustrial cities hovels are found next to or behind palaces. This did not disturb the "upper" classes. Their status was secured by family, title, rank, speech, manner, and clothing. In contemporary American society, these no longer determine status. Only financial status remains and is documented by conspicuous consumption. The decisive status symbol is the residence in the "good neighborhood," legally protected by zoning and fiercely defended against any intrusion of nonconforming elements, structural or human.

7. Finally, and only fairly recently, there is another reversal of an historical trend. Previously, as manufacturing specialized out of the peasant village and proliferated, the old elite-service city had become the industrial city, with industrial workers forming the majority of its population. Now, the same process of increasing productivity and specialization leads to a proliferation of mass services, business services specializing out of production for the market and consumer services specializing out of households. Now, industrial workers are predominant and growing in number primarily in the satellite towns of the metropolitan regions. In the metropolis itself, manufacturing employment is decreasing relatively and sometimes absolutely. Generally, two-thirds or more of the labor force works in a great variety of tertiary or service industries.

Pattern of Land Uses

As a result of these transformations, four basic types of "land use" can be identified: central business, industrial, residential, and open areas.

The historical core of the metropolis, the original "city," tends to remain its center. With the main lines of the transportation system oriented to it, this center remains the point most accessible to all parts of the metropolis and therefore attracts all those functions which serve the entire area. Partly attracted by these, partly for historical reasons, all those functions which require mutual contact also concentrate here, typically in office buildings. These two basic central functions attract others which serve them, such as eating and drinking places and parking facilities.

The resulting competition for space, both within the center and on the transportation facilities leading to it, leads to a displacement from the center of all those uses which require relatively much space and can also function elsewhere. These are primarily those dealing with goods, manufacturing, and warehouses, but also retail stores, consumer services, and residences.

As the metropolitan population grows and spreads out, outlying sectors accommodate sufficient population and purchasing power to support "second-order" services of their own, notably retail, but also most consumer and some business services. With continuing growth, the quality of the "second order" moves up, leaving a narrowing range of the "highest order" in the center. Similarly, second-order routine office functions also move out, leaving only the highest-order contact functions in the center. However, with the overall growth of the metropolis, both types of highest-order functions are growing and are being augmented by others of still higher order which can only exist when the size of the total market has reached a higher threshold.

Thus, the center is undergoing a process of continuous selective adaptation to those functions for which it is uniquely suited. Surprisingly, this unending change in quality seems to produce stability of quantity. The number of persons entering the central areas of major American cities has remained constant over the last thirty years. During the last twelve years, the same constancy has been observed in Toronto, a younger and smaller metropolis. Congestion acts as the selective agent which maintains the balance. The center is always "choked" but never "chokes itself to death."

From the center outward, density of population and of all activities decreases with amazing regularity. The curve, representing population density in concentric circles, falls constantly toward the periphery. Over time, this curve undergoes two typical modifications: it becomes flatter, and it becomes smoother. The increasing smoothness seems to indicate that the center, despite its relative decrease in quantity, increasingly dominates the entire area, superseding the influence of other, preexisting centers. The flattening results from a slow decrease of density in the inner and a rapid increase in the outer zones, each of which, however, finally stabilizes at a lower density than the previous one.

Modification by Transportation

Within this basic pattern, modifications are brought about by topography and by transportation. Whenever individual transportation predominates, time distances tend to be proportional to straight-line distances, and the overall form of the settlement tends to be circular. This was the case in the foot-and hoof city. The development of suburban railroads brought a change, because the trips made by their passengers were performed by two means of radically different speeds: a train at thirty miles an hour and walking at three miles per hour. As the technology of steam railroads dictated few and widely spaced stations, a pattern of small circular dots developed, strung out over a considerable length of railroad line, with a small commercial center at each station.

With the electric streetcar, stops were far more frequent, and the speed was only about three times walking speed. So the dots merged into solid and shorter lines, with commercial concentrations at their intersections.

When the automobile brought about a sudden and unpredictable reversal of the secular trend from individual to collective transportation, the use of one means of transportation for the entire trip and at fairly uniform speed reproduced, on a vastly larger scale, the circular form of the foot-and-hoof city. The structured pattern of developed and open land, which had begun to emerge in the railroad and streetcar areas, was submerged in universal sprawl. "Developments" were scattered all over the metropolitan area, cutting up the open space into smaller and oddly shaped remnants.

The developments are of two major types: industrial and residential. The former, used for manufacturing, warehousing, and transportation, select relatively large areas of level land with good access to transportation by water, air, rail, and road.

The Residential Pattern

Residential areas are practically unrestricted in their choice of location and cover much more extensive areas. They are patterned by two factors: family composition and income. Single adults and couples without children are more numerous in the inner zone, and families with children are more numerous in the outer zone. A recent survey of all nonsubsidized apartment houses in metropolitan Toronto showed that within each type—one-, two-, three-bedroom apartments—the percentage occupied by bachelors decreased and the percentage occupied by families with children increased from one concentric zone to the next one, from the center outward. This occurred despite the fact that, in the inner zones, the supply of one-bedroom apartments was higher and their vacancy rate lower than in the outer ones, and vice versa for the two and three bedroom apartments.

This is easy to understand: adults use the center city for work and many other purposes, but most of them have time and inclination for the use of open space only on weekends. Children hardly ever use the central city but use open space, private and public, at all hours of the day. The pattern of residential distribution by family type is entirely voluntary, deliberate, and rational. It is hard to find any sound reason for the fashionable outcry "to bring the middle-class family back into the city."

There are, of course, in the inner areas, families with children, many children indeed. But most of them live there not by choice but by economic compulsion, which, in part, limits their use of transportation but more generally and powerfully their choice of housing. Normally, a poor family has four choices: to build a shack, to double up with another family, to be subsidized, or to buy or rent secondhand—or twenty-secondhand—housing. The first choice has been completely barred and the second has been largely barred by the exercise of the police power. Subsidized housing, strictly limited-access, has, after a quarter century, accommodated barely one percent of American households. Only the last choice, constantly narrowed by slum clearance, remains.

At present, the pattern of segregation by income class is, in the United States, overlaid and obscured by race segregation. However, if and when colored citizens achieve full equality and the Negro middle class shares equally with the white middle class the right to segregate itself from the lower income groups, the pattern will stand out clearly. The lower income groups live exclusively in the inner zone, and most of the other income groups live in the outer zones.

Criteria

This is, in generalized terms, the "natural" pattern of the contemporary metropolis, as it develops without the benefit—or "malefit"—of planning. Is it "good"? In attempting to establish criteria of judgment, we have to resort to a series of pairs of contradictory desiderata.

1. *Minimize need and maximize opportunity for commuting to work.* As people come to the metropolis primarily "to make a living," it is important that they can find work close to their homes but also that they can avail themselves of the wide choice of jobs available in the metropolis. It is equally important to employers to be able to draw on the full range of skills available anywhere in the area.

2. *Access to center and to periphery.* As Ebenezer Howard put it, people are attracted by two magnets, "city" and "country." They want easy access both to central facilities and to open land.

3. *Separation and integration of functions.* Intermingling of different uses such as industry and housing tends to conflict. But complete isolation of different functions from each other threatens to narrow the horizon of the inhabitants of the metropolis and break it up into sterile and monotonous precincts.

4. *Identification with a part and identification with the whole.* People want to identify with and take part in the life of the community in which they live and which they can easily grasp and understand. But there is an equal if not greater need for understanding, interest, and pride in relation to the metropolis as a whole.

5. *Continuity and change.* Identification with any environment becomes impossible if it loses its identity. But change is the very nature of the metropolis and possibilities for change and growth must be kept open.

Finally, whatever demands may be derived from these or other criteria, they must be satisfied at the least possible cost.

Form of the Metropolis

In the light of these criteria, we may try to evaluate the developing form of the metropolis and proposals for its modification.

The need for commuting can be minimized by providing employment in every part of the metropolitan area. This requires the reservation, by zoning or by creation of industrial "districts" or "estates," of land for industry. But, with a growing majority of the labor force employed in services, the location of these assumes even greater importance. Service employment outside the central business district is growing, but it is scattered. Much could be gained by concentrating into major subcenters or "secondary downtowns" consumer, public, professional, and retail services. Probably, manufacturing plants of those labor-intensive industries which can operate on small lots might be located in their proximity. Around and possibly also within these centers, housing at relatively high densities could be developed. The concentration would, in turn, make possible the establishment of higher-order services.

Such centers would also satisfy the criteria of variety and of integration of functions and would be identifiable focal points, continuous as to location and basic arrangements but changing in detail, of the districts which they serve. There is no certainty about the most desirable size of such districts. However, it is pertinent to note that the estimates of the minimum population required for a self-contained urban unit have been steadily going up. Ebenezer Howard thought of 20–30,000 for his "garden cities." The English "New Town" program started with a limit of 50–60,000 but subsequently has raised it to 100,000 and more. American planners now talk of a quarter million. It may be that the half-million, which we specified as the minimum population of a metropolis, is required to support a really vital and attractive secondary downtown.

The concentration of many potential trip destinations would reduce the number of trips and also make it possible to provide good public transportation. This is likely to result in substantial economies in transportation costs.

While such centers would also, to some extent, increase the choice of jobs, maximization of opportunity requires primarily a relative compactness of the entire metropolis which can be effectively served by an economical transportation system.

Compactness also facilitates access to the metropolitan center. However, complete compactness would make access to open country very difficult. At the same time, the frequently advocated proposal to isolate each urban unit by a "green belt" would increase the distances to the center as well as to other units and would increase the cost of transportation and of public utilities. Increasing distances would also result from a "linear" scheme, which would line up its urban units along one axis.

It seems preferable to line up such units along a greater number of shorter lines, which would radiate from the metropolitan center. This would result in a "stellar" or "finger" scheme, with easily accessible wedges of open country between the fingers. It would, by its orientation to the metropolitan center, facilitate identification with the metropolis as a whole, while the centers of the districts, out of which the fingers are composed, would encourage identification with the district. Growth would be possible by adding new districts at the ends of the fingers, but it would be gradual, preserving continuity with the previous district.

Ends and Means

It appears that some modification of the "natural" pattern of the metropolis could make it "better." However, such modifications are hardly possible without some fairly substantial institutional changes.

Deliberate modification of the pattern of the metropolis presupposes that its area is brought under one jurisdiction, by annexation, federation, or any other means—if there are others. Separate municipalities, each hard-pressed to balance its budget and with the real estate tax as the main source of income, must of necessity, like the private real estate owner, attempt to get those land uses which produce the highest revenue and require the least operating cost— industry, commerce, and wealthy residents, preferably without children. They can hardly be expected to provide open space for the recreation of their neighbors nor to house and educate workers to produce added value in the factories and spend their money in the stores of the next municipality.

A metropolitan government could, legally, implement a land-use pattern by zoning. But zoning transfers development rights from some property owners to others. If a strong secondary downtown is to be created, values from other sites which might be chosen by its occupiers would be transferred to its area. If an area is to be kept open, its development value is transferred to all sites in the development fingers. The blatant inequity of such a procedure makes it unfeasible. Substantial development rights can be shifted around only within the same ownership, which, in this case, means ownership by a metropolitan authority.

Such an authority could become the owner of all or most of the land within its boundaries only if it could tap the very substantial income generated within its boundaries far more effectively than our present three-level tax structure permits.

These three measures would make it possible to modify the general metropolitan pattern. They could not, however, deal with the most serious inadequacy of the present pattern, the exclusion of the low-income groups from the expanding outer zones of the metropolis. This could be accomplished only by assumption of public financial responsibility for standard housing. It is self-deception to talk of "socially balanced" new neighborhoods or "New Towns" when one-third of the population cannot possibly afford to live in them.

Metropolitan-wide governments with commensurate financial resources, public land ownership, housing financed, though not necessarily owned or managed, by and for the public, not token ghettos for the poor—these are all "radical" innovations in terms of current American thinking. However, in different forms and degrees, all of them have been adopted, singly or jointly, within the framework of democratic capitalism by the countries of northwestern Europe.

The American and Canadian people are faced with a dilemma. They want, and want badly, two things. They want to live in an efficient, convenient, healthy, and pleasant environment, and they want, as individuals and collectively as municipalities, to be able to make an honest dollar out of every piece of property they happen to own. The two are basically incompatible. Sooner or later they will have to decide which one is more important to them.

3
chapter

contents

the process of urbanization

the purpose of this chapter is to describe from several standpoints the process by which localities grow into cities; what happens to individuals who participate in the process; what physical shapes and social forms emerge with urbanization.

But first things first. A seldom mentioned but fundamental dictum of social science states that we cannot know "what kind" of a phenomenon we have until we know "how much" of a phenomenon it is.

Accordingly, this chapter begins with a discussion of trends in world urbanization. In a paper written especially for this edition Parker Frisbie begins by marshalling a good deal of the evidence on the vast increase in the scale of world urbanization between 1920 and 1970. The evidence suggests that while there is a global trend toward urban life, nations and continents vary widely in the proportions of people living in cities. On a continuum, for example, the African nations are still predominantly rural, Latin American countries are roughly 50 percent urban, and the United States and Europe are predominantly urbanized. Beyond this factual description Frisbie goes on to consider some of the consequences of rapid urbanization for national life and development. We can infer from his analysis that there are many modes of urbanization and that its consequences vary across space and time.

The folk-urban or rural-urban continuum is a venerable concept in social scientific, not to mention popular, thinking about cities and the way they differ from the countryside. Where nineteenth century theorists had employed dichotomies such as "community and society," early students of urbanization substituted the idea of a continuum along which social organization and life styles changed from rural to urban settings. For example, they suggested that the organization of the family and neighborhood were more rational and specialized in the city while life styles were more individualistic. Oscar Lewis finds the concept to be a gross oversimplification. Lewis's classic study of migrants in Mexico City goes on to provide vivid detail on the complex process of adaptation to the urban environment. This work laid the foundation for a school of urban anthropology that continues to this day to elaborate on the ideas that Lewis set down here.

In the article that follows, Harley Prowning and Waltraut Feindt provide us with a detailed portrait of those people whose separate actions produce urbanization: the migrants. The study begins with data on a large group of migrants concerning their motives for journeying to the city. These complex motives entail, on the one hand, the declining opportunities for employment in the countryside and, on the other, perceived opportunities for work, education, and other amenities in the city. In ways that complement the Lewis study, they go on to show that urban migration is not necessarily a traumatic experience; migrants have visited the city before, know of potential jobs, have family and friends to assist them in adapting to the urban milieu. In short, these selections repudiate many of the classical myths about the harsh, impersonal life of the city; myths about urban social disorganization—a theme which will reappear often in this volume.

In the following section on social differentiation we get our first exposure to the urban ecology literature, an approach frequently identified with the "Chicago school" since many of its exponents taught at the University of Chicago in the 1920s and studied that city. Homer Hoyt's paper is particularly useful here since it first explicates the classical models of the Chicago school and then goes on to compare them to actual developments in the growth of U.S. and international cities. Naturally, many of the early models do not fit contemporary patterns of urban growth and Hoyt explains some of the reasons.

In its general organization, Chapter 3 seeks to build logically from basic population processes to higher levels of generalization concerning the variety of ways urban life is experienced by different sections of the population. A general theme among the separate selections is the need to evaluate commonsense intepretations through more careful scrutiny of the data generated in comparative studies. Clearly, any one group of selections cannot tap all important dimensions, but the articles presented here do give a strong flavor of how critical thinking about the process of urbanization should proceed.

4

W. PARKER FRISBIE

The Scale and Growth of World Urbanization

INTRODUCTION

Mankind's urban history is really quite brief. As Kingsley Davis (1955: 42) has so aptly put it:

> Compared to most other aspects of society—e.g., language, religion, stratification, or the family—cities appeared only yesterday, and urbanization, meaning that a sizable proportion of the population lives in cities, has developed only in the last few moments of man's existence.

From prehistoric times to the nineteenth century, urbanization was slow and uncertain in its development, with something of a regression occurring in the Dark Ages. Recent evidence suggests that even the largest of the ancient cities, Rome, can scarcely have exceeded 350,000 (cf. Hawley, 1971: 33). In fact, it seems safe to conclude that less than 3 percent of the world's population resided in cities of 20,000 or more at the beginning of the nineteenth century (Davis, 1955: 433). However, in the eighteenth century, the groundwork was being laid in Europe (and particularly in England) for rapid urbanization. Technological advances and social organizational changes occurred along a number of fronts which eventually gave rise to the development of commercial agriculture and improved transportation and communications facilities. With the coming of the Industrial Revolution, the great period of city building got underway in earnest.

An idea of just how swiftly urbanization has

The author is at the Department of Sociology and The Population Research Center at The University of Texas at Austin.

proceeded can be gathered from estimates of the world and urban populations across broad time intervals since 1800. The population of the world recorded almost a fourfold increase between 1800 and 1970. During the same period, the urban population (in places of 20,000 or more), as well as the population in cities of 100,000 or more, was multiplied fifty times over. Put differently, the urban population in 1970 was larger than the entire population of the world in the early decades of the nineteenth century (Davis, 1972: 55–57).

Such dramatic growth would produce alterations in the social structure of human existence simply by the sheer force of numbers. But the implications of this remarkable development go well beyond the mere concentration of people. As Amos Hawley's incisive comment indicates: "Urbanization, far from being merely a process of segregating in a few localities the part of a society's population engaged in non-extractive industries, is rather a comprehensive reorganization of the entire structure of society leaving no sector or sphere untouched" (1971: 219).

Small wonder then, given the significance that attaches to urbanization, that the phenomenon has been, and remains, a subject of intense interest to scholars and policymakers alike. And since the positive and negative effects of urbanization must be greater or less depending on the scale and rate of its development, the latter topics constitute a logical and necessary point of departure in the study of urbanization. The purpose of this article is to summarize a portion of the literature that describes the growth of urbanization in the world from 1920 to the present. In addition, the possible future course of world urbanization is explored by making use of projections to the year 2000. As with any other attempt to provide a broad, yet brief overview of a complex subject, the information presented must be highly selective, and some of the enormous, often exciting, and sometimes bewildering, complexities of reality must be sacrificed. However, description alone is by no means the goal. What are regarded as particularly crucial implications of urbanization are highlighted.

DATA AND METHOD

Different countries apply different criteria in identifying urban places, and definitions themselves may be changed over time. Obviously the number of people classified as urban will vary with the definition. Most, but not all, countries employ some minimal level of population size that must be met if a locality is to be classified as urban (e.g., see Hawley, 1971: 7; U.N., 1969: 7–10). To illustrate, the minimum size requirement in the United States is 2,500 persons. However, many places, in both less developed and more developed countries, may be designated as "urban" according to size, but possess few other features of urbanization. For example, there are villages with 5,000 or 10,000 inhabitants that are essentially concentrations of agriculturalists. Additional problems of data quality and comparability arise due to (a) the failure of nation-states to comply with international recommendations regarding the frequency of censuses; (b) the lack of consistency in the application of classificatory criteria; and (c) errors in census enumerations.

Although there may be little consensus with respect to whether certain places with 2,500 or even 10,000 residents are "really urban," there appears to be considerable agreement that localities with 20,000 or more inhabitants may be appropriately conceived as urban places (Davis, 1972: 35; U.N., 1969). This minimum size definition has been regularly employed by the United Nations because:

the available data suggest that the most extensive estimates can be made, with at least tolerable approximation, for the populations of localities with 20,000 or more inhabitants. To extend estimates to smaller localities would involve too much conjecture; to confine them

to larger localities would leave large urban populations out of account (U.N., 1969: 19).

Throughout the present analysis, the term "urban" refers to the population residing in places of 20,000 or more inhabitants, and the tabulations of data presented in this chapter are based, for the most part, on United Nations estimates or projections which employ the 20,000-plus criterion. While the data are subject to error on several counts, the broad trends seem clear and unchallengeable.

CURRENT SCALE AND DISTRIBUTION OF THE WORLD'S POPULATION

We shall soon have occasion to consider in detail the rapid increase in the urban population of the world. However, figures on the total, urban, and rural populations of the world and major world regions (Table 1) make abundantly clear the fact that "the world is still overwhelmingly a rural and village affair" (Davis, 1972: 43). United Nations data indicate that slightly over 70 percent of the world's population in 1970 was to be found in places with less than 20,000 persons. Other projections, arrived at separately from those provided by the U.N.,[1] show approximately 68 percent in places smaller than 20,000 (Davis, 1972: 40).

Among the more interesting points to be gleaned from inspection of Table 1 are the following: (1) The more developed areas of the world (such as Europe, Northern America, Oceania, and the Soviet Union), which contain less than one-third of the world's total population, have about 54 percent of the world's urban population. (See the last two rows of Table 1 which describe a somewhat more precise subdivision into more developed and less developed regions.) (2) Europe and Northern America, which together have about 19 percent of the total population of the globe, account for over 35 percent of all urban persons. (3) Any one of the world's developed areas is more urbanized than any of the less developed areas. The range in the developed areas is from 43 percent (Soviet Union) to 63 percent (North America), while among the less developed, the urban percentage varies from 16 percent (South Asia, Africa) to 38 percent (Latin America). There is of course considerable variation within categories.

Table 1. *The Current Scale and Distribution of World Urbanization: Total World Population, Urban Population, and Rural or Small-Town Population: 1970*

Areal Units	TOTAL POPULATION		URBAN POPULATION†			RURAL POPULATION‡		
	Absolute No. (in millions)	Percent of World Total	Absolute No. (in millions)	Percent of World Total	Percent of Areal Unit Urban	Absolute No. (in millions)	Percent of World Total	Percent of Areal Unit Rural
World Total	3,584	100.0	1,010	100.0	(28.2)	2,574	100.0	(71.8)
More Developed Major Areas	946	26.4	472	46.7	(49.9)	474	18.4	(50.1)
Europe	454	12.7	214	21.2	(47.1)	240	9.3	(52.9)
Northern America	227	6.3	142	14.1	(62.6)	85	3.3	(37.4)
Soviet Union	246	6.9	105	10.4	(42.7)	141	5.5	(57.3)
Oceania	19	0.5	11	1.1	(57.9)	8	0.3	(42.1)
Less Developed Major Areas	2,638	73.6	538	53.3	(20.4)	2,100	81.6	(79.6)
East Asia	911	25.4	198	19.6	(21.7)	713	27.7	(78.3)
South Asia	1,098	30.6	176	17.4	(16.0)	922	35.8	(84.0)
Latin America	283	7.9	107	10.6	(37.8)	176	6.8	(62.2)
Africa	346	9.6	57	5.6	(16.5)	289	11.2	(83.5)
MORE DEVELOPED REGIONS[a]	1,082	30.2	546	54.1	(50.5)	536	20.8	(49.5)
LESS DEVELOPED REGIONS[b]	2,502	69.8	464	45.9	(18.5)	2,039	79.2	(81.5)

[a] More developed regions refers to Europe, Northern America, Soviet Union, Japan, Temperate South America, Australia, and New Zealand.

[b] Less developed regions refers to East Asia without Japan, South Asia, Latin America without Temperate South America, Africa, and Oceania without Australia and New Zealand.

† In places with 20,000 or more population

‡ In places of less than 20,000 population

Source: Adapted and computed from United Nations, *Growth of the World's Urban and Rural Population, 1920–2000.* Population Studies, No. 44 (New York: UN, 1969). Table 31.

Table 2. *The World's Urban Population by Size of Place: 1970*

Size Class	Cumulative Population by Size Class	Cumulative Percentage of World Total	Cumulative Percentage of Urban Total
	(In millions)		
20,000+	1,169	32.2	100.0
100,000+	864	23.8	73.9
500,000+	572	15.8	48.9
2,000,000+	302	8.3	25.8

Source: Adapted from Kingsley Davis, *World Urbanization 1950–1970: Vol. II.* (Berkeley: Institute of International Studies, Population Monograph Series, No. 9, 1972). Table 12.

Size of Place

Human beings are currently concentrated in cities on a scale unprecedented in human history. Davis (1972: 27–28) estimates that the number of city dwellers in places of 100,000 or more reached 864 million in 1970. This figure represents nearly one-fourth of the world's population and close to three-fourths of all urbanites (based on the 20,000-plus standard; see Table 2). In the same year, the population in places of 2,000,000 or more (43 cities) exceeded 300 million—8 percent of the total and more than one-fourth of the urban population. As least as early as 1960, there were two metropolitan areas (New York and Tokyo) with a population above 12 million, a number larger than the entire urban population of Africa in 1930 and greater than the urban population of Oceania in 1960.

RECENT GROWTH BY WORLD REGION: 1920–1975

In Table 3, data are presented on the absolute size of the urban and total populations of several major regions of the world at ten-year intervals from 1920 to 1970, as well as recent projections to 1975. Percentage distributions, covering the same time intervals, appear in Table 4. The latter indicate (a) the proportion of the world's urban population found in each major region or group of regions and (b) the percent-

age of the population of each particular area that is urban.[2]

We can see that the total world population has expanded quite rapidly. In fact, it is estimated to have more than doubled in size in the 1920–1975 interval—an increase of about 2,000 million. But the acceleration in urban growth has overshadowed world growth. The urban population apparently doubled between 1920 and 1950, and *doubled again* from 1950 to 1975.

In recent times, both overall increase and urban growth have proceeded more swiftly in the less developed countries than in the more developed nations.[3] For example, in 1920, the total population of the less developed regions was about double that in the more developed regions, while the number of urban inhabitants of the less developed areas was only about half the number found in the developed areas. By 1970, the population of the less developed countries was three times larger than that of the developed nations, and the urban populations of the two sets of countries were approaching parity. In absolute terms, this means that the increment to the urban populations in the more developed areas of the world was about 400 million, while the less developed regions added 500 million urban residents.

The percentage distributions displayed in Table 4 are also informative. In the first (A) part of Table 4, it is demonstrated that the share of the world urban population found in the developed societies has continually declined from three-fourths of the total in 1920 to an estimated one-half of the total in 1975. In an earlier section it was noted that the era of rapid city building gained its initial impetus in the countries of western Europe, particularly in England. Europe's "head-start" is clearly reflected in Table 4A which shows that over 40 percent of the world's urban population was concentrated in that area in 1920—a proportion considerably greater than the sum total of all the percentages of the less developed major areas. However, Europe was unable to maintain such a lead as the pace of urbanization quickened elsewhere. By the 1970s, the proportion of the urban population claimed by each of three areas (East Asia, South Asia, in addition to Europe) was in the neighborhood of 20 percent.

Another useful way of partitioning the urban population is to consider the percentage urban in each individual area or region. Viewed in

Table 3. *Growth of the World Population and the World Urban Population by Region: 1920–1975*

A. Estimates and Projections of the Population in Urban Places (20,000 or more inhabitants) for the World and World Regions

URBAN POPULATION (in millions)

Areal Units	1920	1930	1940	1950	1960	1970[a]	1975[a]
World Total	266.4	338.2	431.5	533.0	760.3	1,010	1,169
More Developed Major Areas	179.9	222.0	267.9	299.6	389.5	472	517
Europe	112.9	131.8	149.8	159.5	187.9	214	225
Northern America	47.9	62.4	66.6	84.3	115.3	142	159
Soviet Union	16.0	24.0	47.0	50.0	78.0	105	121
Oceania	3.1	3.8	4.5	5.8	8.3	11	12
Less Developed Major Areas	86.5	116.2	163.6	233.4	370.8	538	652
East Asia	39.8	53.9	73.7	94.1	147.1	198	231
South Asia	26.9	34.5	50.6	77.1	117.5	176	217
Latin America	12.9	18.1	25.5	40.7	69.7	107	133
Africa	6.9	9.7	13.8	21.5	36.5	57	71
More Developed Regions[b]	197.7	247.1	303.9	343.2	449.6	546	600
Less Developed Regions[c]	68.7	91.1	127.6	189.8	310.7	464	569

B. Estimates and Projections of the Total Population of the World and World Regions

TOTAL POPULATION (in millions)

Areal Units	1920	1930	1940	1950	1960	1970[a]	1975[a]
World Total	1860.0	2068.6	2295.1	2515.5	2990.8	3584.0	3935.0
More Developed Major Areas	604.4	677.1	729.2	750.6	853.5	946.0	992.0
Europe	324.9	353.9	378.9	391.8	424.7	454.0	467.0
North America	115.7	134.2	144.3	166.1	198.7	227.0	243.0
Soviet Union	155.3	179.0	195.0	180.0	214.4	246.0	261.0
Oceania	8.5	10.0	11.0	12.7	15.7	19.0	21.0
Less Developed Major Areas	1255.6	1391.5	1565.9	1764.9	2137.3	2638.0	2943.0
East Asia	553.4	591.2	634.4	684.3	794.1	911.0	976.0
South Asia	469.8	529.0	610.1	696.7	857.9	1093.0	1246.0
Latin America	89.5	107.5	129.9	162.4	212.4	283.0	328.0
Africa	142.9	163.8	191.5	221.5	272.9	346.0	393.0
More Developed Regions[b]	672.7	757.9	820.6	857.8	976.5	1082.0	1136.0
Less Developed Regions[c]	1187.3	1310.7	1474.5	1657.7	2014.1	2502.0	2799.0

[a] Rounded to indicate greater roughness of projections.

[b] See Note a, Table 1.

[c] See Note b, Table 1.

Source: Adapted and computed from United Nations, *Growth of the World's Urban and Rural Population, 1920–2000.* Tables 8 and 31.

Table 4. *Percentage Distributions of the Urban Population of the World and of World Regions: 1920–1975*

A. Percentage Distribution, by Region, of the World Urban Population (in places of 20,000 or more)

	1920	1930	1940	1950	1960	1970	1975
	(Percentages)						
World Total	100.0	100.0	100.0	100.0	100.0	100.0	100.0
More Developed Major Areas	67.5	65.6	62.1	56.2	51.2	46.7	44.2
Europe	42.4	39.0	34.7	29.9	24.7	21.2	19.2
Northern America	18.0	18.4	15.4	15.8	15.2	14.1	13.6
Soviet Union	6.0	7.1	10.9	9.4	10.3	10.4	10.4
Oceania	1.2	1.1	1.0	1.1	1.1	1.1	1.0
Less Developed Major Areas	32.5	34.3	37.9	43.8	48.8	53.3	55.8
East Asia	14.9	15.9	17.1	17.6	19.4	19.6	19.8
South Asia	10.1	10.2	11.7	14.5	15.4	17.4	18.6
Latin America	4.8	5.4	5.9	7.6	9.2	10.6	11.4
Africa	2.6	2.9	3.2	4.0	4.8	5.6	6.1
More Developed Regions[a]	74.2	73.1	70.4	64.4	59.1	54.1	51.3
Less Developed Regions[b]	25.8	26.9	29.6	35.6	40.9	45.9	48.7

B. Percent of the Population of the World and of Each World Region that Is Urban (in places of 20,000 or more)

	1920	1930	1940	1950	1960	1970	1975
	(Percentages)						
World Total	14.3	16.3	18.8	21.2	25.4	28.2	29.7
More Developed Major Areas	29.8	32.8	36.7	39.9	45.6	49.9	52.1
Europe	34.7	37.2	39.5	40.7	44.2	47.1	48.2
Northern America	41.4	46.5	46.2	50.8	58.0	62.6	65.4
Soviet Union	10.3	13.4	24.1	27.8	36.4	42.7	46.4
Oceania	36.5	38.0	40.9	45.7	52.9	57.9	57.1
Less Developed Major Areas	6.9	8.4	10.4	13.2	17.3	20.4	22.2
East Asia	7.2	9.1	11.6	13.8	18.5	21.7	23.7
South Asia	5.7	6.5	8.3	11.1	13.7	16.0	17.4
Latin America	14.4	16.8	19.6	25.1	32.8	37.8	40.5
Africa	4.8	5.9	7.2	9.7	13.4	16.5	18.1
More Developed Regions[a]	29.4	32.6	37.0	40.0	46.0	50.5	52.8
Less Developed Regions[b]	5.8	7.0	8.6	11.4	15.4	18.5	20.3

[a] See Note a, Table 1.
[b] See Note b, Table 1.

Source: Computed from Table 3.

this way, it is evident that, in 1920, the world itself was less than 15 percent urbanized; by 1975, the figure was close to 30 percent (Table 4B). In the less developed regions, only 6 percent of the population was urban in 1920, compared to 30 percent in the more developed category. By the 1970s, these figures had risen to 20 percent and 50 percent respectively.

The urban proportion is generally smaller in the less developed areas today (1970s) than it was in the more developed countries in 1920. And all of the latter areas now have populations that are at least two-fifths urban (over 60 percent for Northern America), while the proportions in the less developed category tend to vary around 20 percent. Only Latin America is currently approaching the level of urbanization of the more developed world. This does *not* mean that the urban populations in less developed countries (LDCs) have not been expanding at a rapid rate. Indeed, it has already been demonstrated that the absolute increase in the number of urban residents has been spectacular. What it does mean is that the *rural* population of many LDCs has also recorded staggering increases. Overall, it is estimated by the U.N. that more than half of the gain in world population between 1920 and 1975 (over two billion persons) occurred in rural and small town places. The less developed regions accounted for approximately 1.6 billion of the 2 billion increment, and of that 1.6 billion, two-thirds was rural and small town growth.

Here one begins to get an idea of the problems currently being faced by developing countries. Asia (South and East Asia combined) has far and away the largest number and percentage of the world's urban population. Together, East and South Asia account for almost 450 million, or close to 40 percent of the urban population. At the same time, the rural or small town/village population of Asia is estimated to be in excess of 1.7 billion and growing, so that the degree of urbanization is only about 20 percent—lower than that for any other region, except for Africa's 18 percent. Thus, the heavily agrarian character of many third world countries, especially in Asia, is readily apparent. Not all of the rural population of Asia is agrarian, but the U.N. has estimated that 1.4 billion of the total are in agriculture—a figure that is 62 percent of the Asian, and 35 percent of the world's, population (Davis, 1975: 80).

Growth in the Urban Fraction Compared to the Urban Growth Rate

In the analysis of urban growth, it is necessary to make a distinction between changes that occur in the urban fraction, i.e., in the ratio of the urban population to the total population (urban + rural) on the one hand, and alterations in the urban growth rate per se on the other.[4] (See Davis, 1972, for an excellent discussion of this distinction.) In general, the reason such a distinction is necessary is that the urban fraction may remain unchanged from one time period to the next, not because urbanization has faltered, but simply because the rural population has increased apace. Enormous growth in urban populations may produce comparatively slight alterations in the urban fraction if the rural population is also increasing rapidly. A good example is to be found in the data shown in Table 5. Between 1930 and 1940 in Europe, the rate of growth of the urban fraction was approximately zero, a situation that may partially have resulted from actions leading to the outbreak of World War II. However, the urban population of Europe grew by 19 million during the 1930s (see Table 3), and the urban growth rate for the interval approached 14 percent.

Both types of rates are employed in Table 5 to describe the urban growth that took place between 1920 and 1970 in the same major world areas on which we have focused throughout. The rise in urbanization levels has, for the most part, been dramatic only in terms of the urban growth rate per se, not with respect to the urban fraction. (It should be remembered, however, that population growth overall has been so great that even a rather small increment in the urban fraction means the addition of massive numbers of urban residents.) For the five ten-year intervals covered, the rate of increase in the urban fraction has ranged between 10 and 20 percent, while absolute urban growth rates of 25 to 40 percent were common (Table 5).

Patterns observable in the two sets of rates are rather similar. For example, in both, the most rapid increase was in the less developed regions. In the latter areas, the rule (with some exceptions to be sure) is accelerating growth, i.e., an increase in the rate of growth, until the 1960–70 interval when some dampening seems to

Table 5. *Rate of Increase in the Urban Fraction and Absolute Rate of Increase of the Urban Population, 1920–1970*

(percentages)

Areal Units	GROWTH IN THE URBAN FRACTION				
	1920–30	1930–40	1940–50	1950–60	1960–70
World Total	14.0	15.3	12.8'	19.8	11.0
More Developed Major Areas	10.1	11.9	8.7	14.3	9.4
Europe	7.2	6.2	3.0	8.6	6.6
Northern America	12.3	0.0	10.0	14.2	7.9
Soviet Union	30.1	79.8	15.4	30.9	17.3
Oceania	4.1	7.6	11.7	15.8	9.4
Less Developed Major Areas	21.7	23.8	26.9	31.1	17.9
East Asia	26.4	27.5	19.0	34.1	17.3
South Asia	14.0	27.7	33.7	23.4	16.8
Latin America	16.7	16.7	28.1	30.7	15.2
Africa	22.9	22.0	34.7	38.1	23.1
More Developed Regions[a]	10.9	13.5	8.1	15.0	9.8
Less Developed Regions[b]	20.7	22.9	32.6	35.1	20.1

	ABSOLUTE GROWTH RATE OF THE URBAN POPULATION				
	1920–30	1930–40	1940–50	1950–60	1960–70
World Total	27.0	27.6	23.5	42.6	32.8
More Developed Major Areas	23.4	20.7	11.8	30.0	21.2
Europe	16.7	13.7	6.5	17.8	13.9
Northern America	30.3	6.7	26.6	36.8	23.2
Soviet Union	50.0	95.8	6.4	56.0	34.6
Oceania	22.6	18.4	28.9	43.1	32.5
Less Developed Major Areas	34.3	40.8	42.7	58.9	45.1
East Asia	35.4	36.7	27.7	56.3	34.6
South Asia	28.2	46.7	52.4	52.4	49.8
Latin America	40.3	40.9	59.6	71.2	53.5
Africa	40.6	42.3	55.8	69.8	56.2
More Developed Regions[a]	25.0	23.0	12.9	31.0	21.4
Less Developed Regions[b]	32.6	40.1	48.7	63.7	49.3

[a] See Note a, Table 1.

[b] See Note b, Table 1.

Source: Computed from Table 3.

have occurred. In the developed regions, the rate of change is more muted, and shows a tendency to taper off during the war years, to accelerate during the 1950s, only to recede again during the 1960s.

Growth of the Big City Population

Interesting estimates prepared by Kingsley Davis (1972) showing the absolute and percentage increase in the populations of cities by size

Table 6. *Growth of Cities, by Size Class, According to Their Size at the Beginning of Each Decade: 1950–60 and 1960–1970*

Lower Limit of Class	1950		1960	POPULATION GROWTH	
	Number of Cities	Population (millions)	Population (millions)	Absolute (millions)	Relative (Per Cent)
8,000,000+	2	22.7	25.1	2.4	10.3
4,000,000	9	47.0	61.4	14.4	30.7
2,000,000	15	38.9	54.5	15.6	40.0
1,000,000	53	73.0	97.9	24.9	34.1
500,000	108	73.0	99.8	26.8	36.7
250,000	189	63.2	88.6	25.4	40.2
125,000	381	65.5	89.3	23.8	36.3
100,000	205	22.7	31.0	8.3	36.9
Total	962	406.0	547.6	141.6	34.9
	1960		1970[a]		
8,000,000+	3	34.8	39.8	5.0	14.6
4,000,000	13	76.1	102.0	25.9	34.0
2,000,000	27	71.1	95.5	24.4	34.2
1,000,000	71	100.8	135.6	34.8	34.5
500,000	138	98.6	136.8	38.2	38.7
250,000	266	91.1	125.1	34.0	37.3
125,000	550	94.7	132.1	37.4	39.5
100,000	226	25.0	34.6	9.6	38.5
Total	1,294	592.2	801.5	209.3	35.3

[a] Davis's "A" estimate for 1970 (see source below)

Source: Kingsley Davis, World Urbanization 1950–1970, Volume II: Analysis of Trends, Relationships, and Development. (Berkeley: Institute of International Studies, Population Monograph Series, No. 9, 1972). Table 25.

class from 1950 to 1970 appear in Table 6. Although there is some fluctuation, it appears that the secondary, or medium-sized, cities are growing as fast, or faster, than the largest places. It is important to note that Table 6 shows growth in cities according to their size at the beginning of each decade. The question being asked is essentially this: "If a city is of size X (say, 1,000,000) at the start of a time interval, will it tend to grow faster or slower than a city of size Y (say, 500,000) during the interval?" Classifying according to size class at the beginning of each decade avoids the inflation of numbers due simply to cities being reclassified upwards as their populations increase. For example, in Table 6, we see that in 1960 there were 27 cities

of size 2,000,000, as compared to only 15 in that size class in 1950. If attention were not confined to the growth of the 15 cities which began the 1950s in that size class, a large part of the increase in population would have come merely from the addition of 12 "new cities," and the relative increase would have been over 80 percent instead of the 40 percent shown. Both types of information are useful. The point to be made is that one must be careful when employing such data that no distortion of interpretation arises due to a lack of clarity concerning the type of information being analyzed.

Substantively, the major conclusions are: (1) the *number* of large cities is increasing, which, in turn, means that (2) the proportion of the population residing in great cities is also increasing. (3) Secondary or intermediate-sized cities are growing at least as fast, and perhaps faster, than the very large agglomerations. The qualification expressed ("perhaps faster") is necessary because of the possibility that the muted relative increase of the larger cities may be more apparent than real. That is, it is more difficult to keep track of the populations at the periphery of huge agglomerations, since their growth may outrun the expansion of the political and/or statistical boundaries designed to take it into account. To illustrate, large numbers of people may be found in the vicinity of urban centers, who are very much a functional part of the city with respect to their place of work, business dealings, recreational patterns, etc., but who are not counted as part of the city's population because they live outside the "city limits" (or outside the boundaries demarcating metropolitan areas).[5]

Summary of Recent Growth Patterns

Several aspects of the scale and growth of modern urbanization deserve reiteration. (1) By 1970, approximately 30 percent of the world's people were in places of 20,000 or more inhabitants (compared to between 2 and 3 percent in 1800, and less than 10 percent in 1900). (2) Urban growth, in both absolute and relative terms, has in the less developed regions far surpassed that in the more developed world. (3) With the extremely large populations in the former areas, their share of the world's urban population has recently come to parallel that of the developed regions, even though on an individual basis, the less developed areas remain heavily rural. Put differently, the population of the less developed regions was about 20 percent urban by 1975, but this figure represents approximately one-half of the world's urban population. (4) Regardless of the fluctuations in the rate of increase, the absolute numbers involved in urbanization are immense. The number of people in places of 20,000 or more doubled between 1950 and 1975 (an increase of 500 million), so that by the latter date, an estimated 1.2 billion persons were in urban places. By 1975, the less developed regions had almost as many persons in cities as the more developed had in their total populations in 1920. (5) The

populations of cities of intermediate size are expanding at least as fast as the populations of very large cities.

THE FUTURE OF URBAN GROWTH

Growth to the Year 2000

The incalculable impact on human existence occasioned by the growth of urbanization in the world requires consideration of the future course of the phenomenon. Unfortunately, we have no foreknowledge as such. There are an indefinite number of factors (some known, others as yet unknown) which may affect future trends. The impossibility of taking all of these into account (or even of discovering what they all are), as well as the problems of impreciseness in the data, make forecasting a hazardous undertaking. But, although we cannot "predict," we can "project"; i.e., we can engage in informed speculation based on what we know about past trends and by making reasonable assumptions about the future.

The closer to the present our projections are, the better the chance that they will be reasonably accurate. Accordingly, projections made by the United Nations usually encompass only a few decades. While the extrapolation of urbanization trends is even more subject to error than the projection of overall population change, it is at least possible to specify the implications of urban growth if it continues in a manner similar to that recently encountered.

The data utilized in Tables 7 and 8 are based on United Nations "medium" population projections. (For our purposes, it is only necessary to recognize that numbers both higher and lower than those appearing in Tables 7 and 8 are within the realm of plausibility.) Let us briefly observe some of the more striking features of the projections and then turn to the implications of the envisioned growth.

The world's population is projected to grow to 6 billion by the year 2000 (Table 7). This represents an increase of 3 billion or a doubling of the 1960 figure. The urban population may more than triple in the same interval, from 760 million in 1960 to 2.3 billion by 2000, with the lion's share (over 70 percent, or 1.6 billion) allocated to the less developed regions. For the sake of completeness, Table 8 is included to show the pro-

Table 7. *Projected Growth of the World and the World Urban Population by Region: 1960–2000*

(in millions)

Areal Units	1960	1980	2000
Total Population:			
World Total	2991	4318	6112
More Developed Major Areas	854	1042	1266
Europe	425	479	527
Northern America	199	262	354
Soviet Union	214	278	353
Oceania	16	23	32
Less Developed Major Areas	2137	3276	4846
East Asia	794	1041	1287
South Asia	858	1408	2153
Latin America	212	378	638
Africa	273	449	768
More Developed Regions[a]	976	1194	1441
Less Developed Regions[b]	2015	3125	4671
Urban Population (localities of 20,000 inhabitants and over):			
World Total	760	1354	2337
More Developed Major Areas	389	567	784
Europe	188	237	290
Northern America	115	177	253
Soviet Union	78	141	222
Oceania	8	13	19
Less Developed Areas	371	786	1553
East Asia	147	267	425
South Asia	118	266	568
Latin America	69	163	342
Africa	37	90	218
More Developed Regions[a]	450	661	901
Less Developed Regions[b]	310	693	1436

[a] See note a, Table 1.

[b] See note b, Table 1.

Source: Adapted from United Nations, *Growth of the World's Urban and Rural Population, 1920–2000.* Table 32.

Table 8. *Total, Urban, and Big-City Populations of the World: 1960 and 1980*

(in millions)

Areal Units	1960	1980
Total Population:		
World Total	2991	4318
Europe	425	479
Other more developed regions[a]	551	715
Less developed regions[b]	2015	3124
Urban Population (20,000 inhabitants and over):		
World Total	761	1354
Europe	188	237
Other more developed regions	262	424
Less developed regions	311	693
Cities of 500,000 inhabitants and over:		
World Total	352	665
Europe	81	106
Other more developed regions	140	237
Less developed regions	131	322
Cities of 2,500,000 inhabitants and over:		
World Total	142	351
Europe	24	40
Other more developed regions	74	146
Less developed regions	44	165

[a] See note a, Table 1.

[b] See note b, Table 1.

Source: Adapted from United Nations, *Growth of the World's Urban and Rural Population, 1920–2000.* Table 35.

jected growth by size class of cities for the world, Europe and other developed regions, and the less developed regions. These projections extend only to 1980, the farthest point to which the U.N. considered it reasonable to make size-class forecasts. The only facet of Table 8 that requires comment, beyond remarks which also pertain to Table 7, is that Table 8 shows larger cities growing somewhat more rapidly than smaller ones. However, these figures do not make adjustment for the upward reclassification of cities, so that it remains appropriate to conclude that moderate-sized places are growing as fast as the larger cities.

The urban population of Asia (both East and South Asia taken together) is projected to increase by over 700 million from 1960 to 2000. This would mean a grand total of almost 1 billion Asians in cities by 2000, a figure near the total urban population of the *entire world* in 1970, and greater by far than the world urban total of 760 million in 1960! Such figures are little short of incredible. What such trends mean in terms of individual cities has been graphically demonstrated by Fox (1975) who has made projections, based on somewhat different assumptions than those employed by the U.N., for various cities in Latin America. To illustrate, Fox (1975) shows Caracas with 6.5 million inhabitants in the year 2000, Lima-Callao with 9.8 million, and Mexico City (total Urbanized Area) with a mind-boggling 31.7 million. Such figures, as Fox indicates, are not offered as predictions of what will happen, but as indicators of the magnitude of the problems that may be encountered if present growth trends continue for very long.

Before moving to a consideration of additional implications, let us note a few more of the striking pieces of information to be found in Table 7. In comparison with the less developed regions, the total and urban increases projected for the more developed areas of the world seem almost slight. Yet the urban population of the latter regions is expected to more than double in the 1960–2000 interval with the addition of 450 million persons.

Although no percentages are shown, a simple calculation will demonstrate that the proportion of the world's urban population in the less developed category will have increased from near 30 percent in 1920 to well over 60 percent by the turn of the century. Asia alone may have over 40 percent of the total urban population, which, when added to Latin America's 15 percent, makes up over half the total.

Finally, despite the massive urban expansion that is indicated, large areas of the world will continue to be highly rural. If the projections approach accuracy, two-thirds or more of the populations of East Asia, South Asia, and Africa will be rural in the year 2000.

Implications of the Continuation of Recent Trends in Urban Growth

The first major implication is obviously that, while current trends may continue until the turn of the century, or slightly beyond, they cannot, by any stretch of the imagination, continue indefinitely. "If the proportion urban were to continue to rise at the 1950–1970 rates . . . 100 percent would be living in [urban] places by 2031" (Davis, 1972: 52). Although the preceding statement refers to the urban population as nationally defined, and not to our 20,000-plus criterion, it is also the case that if the 1950–70 rate of increase in the population living in places of 100,000 or more were to continue unabated, 50 percent of the world would be in places of 100,000 or larger by 2009 and 100 percent by 2045 (Davis, 1975: 52).

On the other hand, it should be recognized that increments of the sort projected in Tables 7 and 8 are perfectly possible and that, in most of the world, the momentum of urban growth shows no immediate signs of subsiding. Indeed, a tremendous enlargement of the urban population seems a virtual certainty between now and the turn of the century.

A second and related implication concerns the relationship between urbanization and economic development in the lesser developed countries (LDCs). If the vast accumulation of urban population in these areas were to be accompanied by a decline in the rural population, or even a sharp reduction in the rural growth rate, the prognosis for development would not appear quite so bleak. In the past, in developed countries, there has been a strong correlation between urbanization and economic development (Schnore, 1969: 91–106), as there occurred large-scale movements out of rural areas and small-scale agricultural production into an urban/industrial milieu. This process not only relieved population pressure in rural areas at the same time that the labor force was being concentrated in places more accessible to industrial activities, but it also facilitated the transition to a mechanized and more productive form of agriculture enterprise (e.g., see Higgins, 1967: 120–123). This, in capsule version, is the way it went in the now developed countries. But, unless far-reaching modifications are made in current trends, this is *not* the way it will go for much of the developing world. The reason is that the LDCs find themselves in a different and, in many ways, less advantageous position than that enjoyed earlier by the developed countries.

Compared to the situation in the more developed countries at an earlier stage, today's LDCs have a higher rate of natural increase (births minus deaths). No longer are there open or sparsely settled places to which surplus population can be "exported." Further, technology in the nineteenth century was such that the skills developed in cottage industry and rural handicrafts were easily transferable to urban industrial activities. Such a facile transference is not possible in this era of advanced technology. Finally, LDCs find themselves engaged in an effort to develop economically while, at the same time, competing on an international scale with *already developed* nations.[6]

A third implication relates to available options. If burgeoning urban populations create ever-greater difficulties, what alternatives are available to the less developed countries? In most cases, it will not be possible to reduce the burden of rapid urban growth by redirecting population from the largest to the more moderately sized cities. As we have seen, the latter are growing at least as fast as the largest places and are themselves experiencing difficulty in providing adequate housing and employment opportunities for their residents (see Fox, 1975, on the Latin American case). Likewise, attempts to shut off rural-to-urban migration, or to send significant numbers of urban dwellers back to rural hinterlands, will be of little help in situations where rural poverty and population pressure have coincided to produce a major impetus for movement to urban areas in the first place.

A third option, increasing mortality, should not be regarded as an alternative solution, but as a possibility to be avoided.

The point that most needs to be emphasized is neatly summarized in the phrase: "The urban explosion is the population explosion" (Fox, 1975: 8). That is to say, the reasons underlying the rapid augmentation of urban populations are much the same as those which explain the growth of the world's population as a whole. The fallacy of assuming urban growth to be simply a function of rural-to-urban migration needs to be dispelled. Because cities are growing rapidly by natural increase (i.e., an excess of births over deaths), as well as by in-migration, policies designed to slow rural-to-urban movement will not stop the expansion of city populations. Further, any notion of slowing or stopping city growth without a similar contraction of total growth cannot be seen as reasonable. It has been convincingly argued that such a policy

would eventuate in an enormous concentration in rural areas, the likely outcome of which would be to "completely reverse the path of modernization" (Davis, 1972: 72). Thus, the most promising alternative seems to be a reduction in birth rates, thereby slowing population increase in both rural and urban areas. But lower fertility can improve matters only very slowly. For example, even in the United States, if fertility remains at, or near, bare replacement levels (about 2.11 children per woman) as it has in the 1970s, zero population growth will not be reached until well into the twenty-first century owing to the fact that the number of persons of childbearing age will continue to be proportionately great. As Frejka (1973) has demonstrated:

> Practically all countries with currently low fertility are not likely to experience a reduction of their population even if fertility should be somewhat below replacement. Countries with currently high fertility can expect quite substantial growth even if they manage to decrease their fertility rather rapidly (quoted in Peck, 1974: 26).

What is to be the outcome for the less developed countries, then? It may be, as Kingsley Davis suggests in regard to Asia, that "'development' and 'personal consumption' will part company." With tight, centralized control, urbanization and development might be accomplished, but it would be "development without prosperity, urbanization . . . without urbanity" (1975: 85).

Another somewhat more optimistic scenario arises out of a fact that we have until this juncture tended to regard as unfortunate, viz., that urbanization is not the same thing as industrialization. Nor is industrialization, for that matter, synonymous with economic development, though the former, in developed countries, seems to lead to the latter. (On these interrelationships, see Higgins, 1967: 117–154.) It has been argued that it is possible to take economic advantage of high growth rates and concentration of population through efficient labor-intensive modes of production (Hawley, 1971: 283–284). Such a potential is perhaps most apt to be realized in extractive industry (agriculture, mining, etc.) and in certain kinds of service functions. This strategy might not lead to "industrial development" as it is conventionally conceived, but it could well lead to economic development, especially if coupled with a slackening of the fertility rate. Frejka's models (1973) showing rapid and slow paths to non-growing populations sharply focus our attention on alternatives for the future. A slow move toward zero population growth would result in a world population of over 15 billion by the year 2150. However, a rapid move toward ZPG implies a population of only 8.4 billion at the same future point in time. Both paths would, no doubt, require that much of the growth be absorbed by cities, but clearly the lower numbers may be manageable, while the larger numbers probably are not—at least not in any fashion that would be seen as acceptable by the populations involved.

Finally, in spite of the numerous problems that have been suggested by the foregoing, there is no inclination to close this examination of the scale and growth of world urbanization on an unduly pessimistic note. Hawley asserts correctly that "the overgrown city in the developing countries is in a favorable position for the facilitation of modernization and economic growth" (1971: 284). In many areas of the world, there has occurred a "metropolitanization of society" in which the economic, social, political, and cultural dynamism of cities has expanded the sphere of urban organization in a complex web of interdependencies until it comprehends an entire society, thereby promoting greater social cohesion and enhancing the potential for economic development. As urbanization develops, certain feedback mechanisms appear to operate that work to the mutual benefit of both urban and rural populations. It is possible, as was hopefully expressed in an earlier effort to describe world urbanization, that "complementarity and mutual benefits may be generated among areas where at present only a conflict of local interests is most in evidence" (U.N., 1973: 88).

Notes

1. It has been suggested (Davis, 1972: 1–8) that the Population Division of the United Nations was at least aware of the work being carried on by Davis and his colleagues, and may well have employed similar methods of estimation.

2. In other words, in the first instance, the denominator is the total *urban* population of the world and numerators are the numbers of persons in urban places in each of the areal unit categories. The second set of percentages was arrived at by dividing the urban population of each individual region or world area by the total population (urban plus rural) of the same region or world area.

3. On the other hand, the speed with which urban populations are being incremented in the former category of countries probably exceeds only slightly, if at all, the urban growth of today's developed countries at an earlier stage, i.e., in the nineteenth century.

4. The urban fraction may be designated by the formula $POP_u/(POP_u + POP_r)$ with changes over time computed on the basis of the value of the ratio at one point in time compared to the value at a later point in time. By contrast, the absolute urban growth rate as employed here involves dividing the actual increase during an interval by the size of the population at the beginning of the interval, or symbolically

$$\frac{POP_u^{t+k} - POP_u^t}{POP_u^t}$$

5. For example, Standard Metropolitan Statistical Areas (SMSAs) may be "underbounded" in the sense that growth may occur at the periphery in the intercensal period which will not be included in the count of the SMSA population until a subsequent enumeration.

6. Much of the discussion in this and the preceding paragraph is based on an earlier exposition by Hawley (1971: Chap. 12).

References

Davis, Kingsley. "Asia's Cities: Problems and Options." *Population and Development Review* 1 (September, 1975): 71–86.

Davis, Kingsley. "The Origin and Growth of Urbanization in the World." *American Journal of Sociology* 60 (March, 1955): 429–437.

Davis, Kingsley. *World Urbanization 1950–1970: Vol. II: Analysis of Trends, Relationships, and Development* (Berkeley: Institute of International Studies, Population Monograph Series, No. 9, 1972).

Fox, Robert W. *Urban Population Growth Trends in Latin America* (Washington, D.C.: Inter-American Development Bank, 1975).

Frejka, Tomas. *The Future of Population Growth: Alternative Paths to Equilibrium* (New York: Wiley, 1973).

Hawley, Amos H. *Urban Society: An Ecological Approach* (New York: Ronald Press, 1971).

Higgins, Benjamin. "Urbanization, Industrialization,

and Economic Development." Pp. 117–155 in Glenn H. Beyer (ed.), *The Urban Explosion in Latin America: A Continent in Process of Modernization* (Ithaca, N.Y.: Cornell University Press: 1967).

Keyfitz, Nathan. "Political-Economic Effects of Urbanization in South and Southeast Asia." Chapter 8 in P. M. Hauser and Leo F. Schnore (eds.), *The Study of Urbanization* (New York: Wiley, 1967).

Peck, Jennifer M. *Population Bulletin: World Population Projections: Alternative Paths to Zero Growth* (Washington, D.C.: Population Reference Bureau, 1974).

Schnore, Leo F. "The Statistical Measurement of Urbanization and Economic Development." Chapter 5 in W. A. Faunce and W. H. Form (eds.), *Comparative Perspectives on Industrial Society* (Boston: Little, Brown, 1969).

United Nations. *Growth of the World's Urban and Rural Population, 1920–2000* (New York: Department of Economic and Social Affairs, Population Studies No. 44, 1969).

United Nations. "World Urbanization Trends, 1920–1960." Chapter 5 in John Walton and Donald E. Carns (eds.), *Cities in Change: Studies in Urban Condition*, 1st Edition (Boston: Allyn and Bacon, 1973).

5

OSCAR LEWIS

Further Observations on the Folk-Urban Continuum and Urbanization with Special Reference to Mexico City

My interest in studies of urbanism and the urbanization process in Mexico City has been a direct outgrowth of my earlier study of Tepoztlan. In that work I suggested that the folk-urban continuum was an inadequate theoretical model for the study of culture change and that it needed drastic revision.[1] Later, in my follow-up study of Tepoztecans who had migrated to Mexico City, I found evidence which strengthened this conviction, this time viewing the problem from the urban pole.[2]

Each of the terms folk, rural, and urban encompasses a wide range of phenomena with multiple variables which have to be carefully sorted out, ordered, dissected, and perhaps redefined if we are to establish meaningful, causal relationships among them. Each of these terms implies relatively high-level abstractions intended for the characterization of whole societies or large segments thereof. Although such characterizations are attractive because of their simplicity and may be useful in distinguishing gross stages or types in societal evolution, they confuse issues in the study of short-run

changes, and their heuristic value as research tools has never been proven.

Hauser has put this criticism admirably. He writes,

> There is evidence, by no means conclusive as yet, that both parts of these dichotomies [i.e., folk-urban and rural-urban] represent confounded variables and, in fact, complex systems of variables which have yet to be unscrambled. The dichotomizations perhaps represent all too hasty efforts to synthesize and integrate what little knowledge has been acquired in empirical research. The widespread acceptance of these ideal-type constructs as generalizations, without benefit of adequate research, well illustrates the dangers of catchy neologisms which often get confused with knowledge.[3]

In his elaboration of the folk-urban continuum, Redfield sought to achieve greater sophistication than earlier societal typologies by utilizing traits or variables that were of a general, more abstract nature. For example, whereas Hobhouse, Wheeler, and Ginsburg distinguished among food-gathering, hunting and fishing, agricultural, and pastoral economies, and sought to establish their social and juridical correlates, Redfield's definition of the folk society as an ideal type never specified a type of technology or economy beyond stating that it was simple, subsistence motivated, without money, familial, and so on.

In his later work Redfield showed some im-

Oscar Lewis, "The Folk-Urban Ideal Types: A. Further Observations on the Folk-Urban Continuum and Urbanization with Special Reference to Mexico City," in Philip M. Hauser and L. F. Schnore (eds.), *The Study of Urbanization* (New York: John Wiley & Sons, Inc., 1965), pp. 491–503. Reprinted by permission.

portant but subtle changes in his thinking which have not been given sufficient emphasis by his followers and disciples, many of whom suffer from fixation or culture lag. Here I should like to mention two such changes. First, he seemed to be less sanguine about the possibility of deriving sound general propositions concerning social and cultural change and gave more stress to descriptive integration, "understanding," and the element of art in the social sciences. Compare, for example, his *Folk Culture of Yucatán* with *The Village That Chose Progress*. In the former, he was still optimistic about finding regularities in culture change. In the latter, he gave us a brilliant description of changes in Chan Kom but made no attempt to relate these changes to the theoretical framework of the folk-urban continuum.

A second change is to be seen in *The Primitive World and Its Transformations*, where he no longer conceives of the folk society exclusively as an ideal type. Rather, he treats it as a type of real society. In this book Redfield takes a frank neo-evolutionary stance, identifying the folk society with the preagricultural or preneolithic period and with the tribal (and I would add pretribal) level. In an effort to find common elements he paints with a big brush, lumping together all the peoples of the world prior to the neolithic, irrespective of whether they were food-gatherers, fishers, or hunters, whether they had rich or poor resources, whether they were starving or produced some surplus. In the very nature of the case, this approach glosses over the more refined archeological distinctions, between the Lower and Upper Paleolithic, each with subdivisions based upon new technologies and inventions.

True, we have little evidence about societal types for the prehistoric periods. However, a theoretical scheme must somehow take into account many levels and types of societal development prior to the rise of cities. Otherwise, there are unexplained and sudden breaks in the postulated evolutionary sequence from folk to urban. Indeed, if one had to choose between evolutionary schemes, there is still a good deal to be said in favor of Morgan's *Ancient Society* despite its many factual errors and crude technological determinism. Fortunately, we have other and more sophisticated alternatives, such as the multilinear evolution of Julian Steward and the recent work of Irving Goldman.[4]

The identification of the folk society with the preneolithic seems to me to invalidate or, at least, to raise serious questions about Redfield's work in *The Folk Cultures of Yucatán*, since all of the Yucatán communities were agricultural peasant societies, which, by his own definition, are part societies subject in varying degree to urban influences. Even his most "folk-like" community of Quintana Roo was producing hennequin for the world market!

Similarly, some of my own criticism of his Tepoztlan work, as well as Sol Tax's criticism based on the Guatemalan studies, would seem to be beside the point since both Tax and I were dealing with communities which had left the folk stage (if they were ever in it) for at least a few thousand years. To this extent, Ralph Beals's comment that Tepoztlan was not a crucial case for evaluating the transition from folk to peasant to urban has considerable merit, because Tepoztlan was already a well-advanced peasant society in pre-Hispanic days. But by the same token, I know of no other contemporary community study in Meso-America which would serve this purpose any better. Actually, Redfield had assumed a survival of folk, that is, paleolithic, elements in Tepoztlan, a period for which we have no evidence in that village.

The traditional contrast between societies based on kinship versus those based on nonkinship or contract is not only inaccurate but of so broad and general a nature as to be of little help in the analysis of the process of change. To say of a society that it is organized on a kinship basis does not tell us enough for purposes of comparative analysis. It may be a nuclear family system as among the Shoshone Indians, a lineage system as in Tikopia, or a clan system as among the Zuni Indians. We still have a lot to learn about the more modest problem of how and under what conditions in a given society, a simple nuclear, bilateral system turns into a unilateral clan system, and the social, economic, and psychological concomitants thereof. As a general proposition I would like to suggest that we may learn more about the processes of change by studying relatively short-run sequential modifications in particular aspects of institutions in both the so-called folk and urban societies, than by global comparisons between folk and urban.

Preurban and preindustrial societies have been capable of developing class stratification, elaborate priesthoods, status rivalry, and many other phenomena that are implicitly and unilaterally attributed to the growth of cities, according to the folk-urban conception of social change. Tonga, the Maori, and native Hawaii are good examples of this. Even among a fishing and hunting people like the Kwakiutl Indians, we find class stratification, slavery, and war. The Kwakiutl case illustrates the importance of including natural resources as a significant variable in evolutionary schemes. I find no such variable in the folk-urban continuum.

In place of, or in addition to, the handy designations, folk society, peasant society, urban society, we need a large number of subtypes based on better defined variables and perhaps the addition of new ones.[5] Hauser's observation on the western ethnocentrism implicit in the folk-urban and rural-urban dichotomies is well taken. Redfield's firsthand research experience in Mexican communities, which were essentially endogamous, tended to confirm his preconception of the folk society as "inward-looking." The thinking of Simmel, Tönnies, Durkheim, and others, which influenced Redfield, was also based on experience with the endogamous peasant communities of Europe. Had these men done field work with the Nuer of Africa, with the Australian aborigines, or with the north Indian peasants, it is quite possible that Redfield's ideal-type model of the folk society might have been somewhat different.

Before turning to an examination of some of the assumptions of the Simmel-Wirth-Redfield axis regarding urbanism, I would like to present in brief some of my own research findings in Mexico which can serve as a starting point for the discussion. The relevant findings of my first Mexico City study of 1951 can be summarized as follows: (1) Peasants in Mexico City adapted to city life with far greater ease than one would have expected judging from comparable studies in the United States and from folk-urban theory. (2) Family life remained quite stable and extended family ties increased rather than decreased. (3) Religious life became more Catholic and disciplined, indicating the reverse of the anticipated secularization process. (4) The system of *compadrazgo* continued to be strong, albeit with some modifications. (5) The use of village remedies and beliefs persisted.

In the light of these findings I wrote at the time, ". . . this study provides evidence that

urbanization is not a single, unitary, universally similar process but assumes different forms and meanings, depending upon the prevailing historic, economic, social, and cultural conditions."[6]

Because of the unusual nature of my findings, I decided to test them in 1956–1957 against a much wider sample of non-Tepoztecan city families. I selected two lower-class housing settlements or *vecindades*, both located in the same neighborhood within a few blocks of the Tepito market and only a short walk from the central square of Mexico City. In contrast with the Tepoztecan city families who represented a wide range of socioeconomic levels and were scattered in twenty-two *colonias* throughout the city, my new sample was limited to two settlements whose residents came from twenty-four of the thirty-two states and territories of the Mexican nation.[7]

On the whole, my research findings tended to support those of the earlier study. The findings suggested that the lower-class residents of Mexico City showed much less of the personal anonymity and isolation of the individual which had been postulated by Wirth as characteristic of urbanism as a way of life. The *vecindad* and the neighborhood tended to break up the city into small communities that acted as cohesive and personalizing factors. I found that many people spent most of their lives within a single *colonia* or district, and even when there were frequent changes of residence, they were usually within a restricted geographical area determined by low rentals. Lifetime friendships and daily fact-to-face relations with the same people were common, and resembled a village situation. Most marriages also occurred within the *colonia* or adjoining *colonias*. Again, I found that extended family ties were quite strong, as measured by visiting, especially in times of emergency, and that a relatively high proportion of the residents of the *vecindades* were related by kinship and *compadrazgo* ties.

In spite of the cult of *machismo* and the overall cultural emphasis upon male superiority and dominance, I found a strong tendency toward matricentered families, in which the mother played a crucial role in parent-child relations even after the children were married. In genealogical studies I found that most people recalled a much larger number of relatives on the mother's side than on the father's side.

I also found that the *vecindad* acted as a

shock absorber for the rural migrants to the city because of the similarity between its culture and that of rural communities. Both shared many of the traits which I have elsewhere designated as "the culture of poverty." Indeed, I found no sharp differences in family structure, diet, dress, and belief systems of the *vecindad* tenants according to their rural-urban origins. The use of herbs for curing, the raising of animals, the belief in sorcery and spiritualism, the celebration of the Day of the Dead, illiteracy and low level of education, political apathy and cynicism about government, and the very limited membership and participation in both formal and informal associations, were just as common among persons who had been in the city for over thirty years as among recent arrivals. Indeed, I found that *vecindad* residents of peasant background who came from small land-holding families showed more middle-class aspirations in their desire for a higher standard of living, home ownership, and education for their children than did city-born residents of the lower-income group.

These findings suggest the need for a reexamination of some aspects of urban theory and for modifications which would help explain the findings from Mexico City and other cities in underdeveloped countries, as well as those from Chicago.

Wirth defines a city as "a relatively large, dense, and permanent settlement of socially heterogeneous individuals." By "socially heterogeneous" he had in mind primarily distinctive ethnic groups rather than class differences. Wirth defines urbanism as the mode of life of people who live in cities or who are subject to their influence. Because Wirth thinks of the city as a whole, as a community (and here, I believe, is one of his errors), he assumes that all people who live in cities are affected by this experience in profound and similar ways, namely, the weakening of kindship bonds, family life, and neighborliness, and the development of impersonality, superficiality, anonymity, and transitoriness in personal relations. For Wirth the process of urbanization is essentially a process of disorganization.[8]

This approach leads to some difficulties. For one thing, as Sjoberg has pointed out, ". . . their interpretations [i.e., those of Park, Wirth and Redfield] involving ecology have not articulated well with their efforts to explain social activi-

ties."[9] Wirth himself showed some of the contradictory aspects of city life without relating them to his theory of urbanism. He writes of the city as the historic center of progress, of learning, of higher standards of living, and all that is hopeful for the future of mankind, but he also points to the city as the locus of slums, poverty, crime, and disorganization. According to Wirth's theory both the carriers of knowledge and progress (the elite and the intellectuals) and the ignorant slum dwellers have a similar urban personality, since presumably they share in the postulated urban anonymity and so on.

It is in the evaluation of the personality of the urban dweller that urban theory has gone furthest afield. It leaps from the analysis of the social system to conjecture about individual personality; it is based not on solid psychological theory but on personal values, analogies, and outmoded physiopsychological concepts. Some of the description of the modern urbanite reads like another version of the fall of man. The delineation of the urbanite as blasé, indifferent, calculating, utilitarian, and rational (presumably as a defensive reaction to preserve his nervous system from the excessive shocks and stimuli of city life), suffering from anonymity and anomie, being more conscious and intellectual than his country brother yet feeling less deeply, remain mere statements of faith.[10]

Besides the lack of an adequate personality theory, it seems to me that some of the difficulty stems from the attempt to make individual psychological deductions from conditions prevailing in the city as a whole. The city is not the proper unit of comparison or discussion for the study of social life because the variables of number, density, and heterogeneity as used by Wirth are not the crucial determinants of social life or of personality.[11] There are many intervening variables. Social life is not a mass phenomenon. It occurs for the most part in small groups, within the family, within households, within neighborhoods, within the church, formal and informal groups, and so on.

Any generalizations about the nature of social life in the city must be based on careful studies of these smaller universes rather than on a priori statements about the city as a whole. Similarly, generalizations about urban personality must be based on careful personality studies. The delineation of social areas within cities and a careful analysis of their characteristics would take us a long way beyond the overgeneralized formulations of "urbanism as a way of life."

Basic to this Simmel-Wirth-Redfield approach are the supposed consequences of the predominance of primary relations in small rural communities versus the predominance of secondary relations in large cities. It seems to me that the psychological and social consequences of primary versus secondary relations have been misunderstood and exaggerated for both the country and the city. I know of no experimental or other good evidence to indicate that exposure to large numbers of people per se makes for anxiety and nervous strain or that the existence of secondary relations diminishes the strength and importance of primary ones. Primary group relations are just as important psychologically for city people as they are for country people, and sometimes they are more satisfying and of a more profound nature. And although the sheer number of secondary relations in the city is much greater than in the country, these relations can also be said to be secondary in the sense that their psychological consequences are minor.

The number of profound warm and understanding human relationships or attachments is probably limited in any society, rural or urban, modern or backward. Such attachments are not necessarily or exclusively a function of frequency of contact and fewness of numbers. They are influenced by cultural traditions which may demand reserve, a mind-your-own-business attitude, a distrust of neighbors, fear of sorcery and gossip, and the absence of a psychology of introspection.

George Foster's recent comparative analysis of the quality of interpersonal relations in small peasant societies, based on anthropological monographs, shows that they are characterized by distrust, suspicion, envy, violence, reserve, and withdrawal.[12] His paper confirms my earlier findings on Tepoztlan.

In some villages, peasants can live out their lives without any deep knowledge or understanding of the people whom they "know" in face-to-face relationships. By contrast, in modern Western cities, there may be more give and take about one's private, intimate life at a single "sophisticated" cocktail party than would occur in years in a peasant village. I suspect there are deeper, more mature human relationships among sympathetic, highly educated, cosmopolitan individuals who have chosen each other in friendship, than

are possible among sorcery-ridden, superstitious, ignorant peasants, who are daily thrown together because of kinship or residential proximity.

It is a common assumption in social science literature that the process of urbanization for both tribal and peasant peoples is accompanied by a change in the structure of the family, from an extended to a nuclear family. It is assumed that the rural family is extended and the urban, nuclear. It must be pointed out that not even all primitive or preliterate people are characterized by a preponderance of the extended family as the residential unit. The Eskimo is a good example. Among peasantry, also, one finds a wide range of conditions in this regard. In most highland Mexican villages the nuclear family predominates as the residence unit. Very often and without any evidence, this fact is interpreted as a symptom of change from an earlier condition. In India, one finds a remarkable difference in family composition by castes within a single village. For example, in Rampur village in the state of Delhi, the Jats and Brahmans, both of whom own and work the land, have large, extended families, whereas the lower-caste Sweepers and Leatherworkers have small nuclear families.

I suggest that we must distinguish much more carefully between the existence of the extended family as a residence unit and as a social group. In Mexico the extended family is important as a social group in both rural and urban areas where the nuclear family predominates as the residence unit. In Mexico the persistence of extended family bonds seems compatible with urban life and increased industrialization. Moreover, the *compadre* system, with its extension of adoptive kinship ties, is operative, though in somewhat distinctive ways, on all class levels. I suspect that increased communication facilities in Mexico, especially the telephone and the car, may strengthen rather than weaken extended family ties.

One of the most distinctive characteristics of cities, whether in the industrial or preindustrial age, is that they provide, at least potentially, a wider range of alternatives for individuals in most aspects of living than is provided by the nonurban areas of the given nation or total society at a given time. Urbanism and urbanization involve the availability of a wide range of services and alternatives in terms of types of work, housing, food, clothing, educational facilities, medical facilities, modes of travel, voluntary organizations, types of people, and so on.

If we were to accept these criteria as definitive traits we could then develop indices of the degree of urbanization of different sectors of the population within cities. For example, if the population of any subsector of a city had fewer alternatives in types of clothing, foods, and so on, either because of traditional ethnic sanctions or lack of economic resources, we could designate this population sector as showing a lower degree of urbanization than some other sector. This does not apply to the city alone; the scale of urbanization can also be applied to villages, towns, and to their respective populations.

As I see it, therefore, there are two sides to the urbanization coin: one, the amount and variety of services and the like to be found in any city, and two, the extent to which different sectors of the city residents can partake of these services. From this distinction it follows that two cities may show the same urbanization index in terms of the number and variety of services per capita but may be very different in terms of the degree of urbanization (cosmopolitanism) of the various sectors of its inhabitants.

It also follows that there are many ways of life which coexist within a single city. This is particularly evident in the underdeveloped countries where class or caste differences are sharp. In Mexico City, for example, there are approximately a million and a half people who live in one-room *vecindades* or in primitive *jacales*, with little opportunity to partake of the great variety of housing facilities available for the tourists and the native bourgeoisie. Most of this large mass still have a low level of education and literacy, do not belong to labor unions, do not participate in the benefits of the social security system, make very little use of the city's museums, art galleries, banks, hospitals, department stores, concerts, airports, and so on. These people live in cities, indeed, a considerable portion were born in the city, but they are not highly urbanized. From this point of view, then, the poor in all cities of the world are less urbanized, that is, less cosmopolitan, than the wealthy.

The "culture of poverty" is a provincial, locally oriented culture, both in the city and in the country. In Mexico it is characterized by a relatively higher death rate, a higher proportion of the population in the younger age groups (less than 15 years), a higher proportion of gainfully employed in the total population, including child labor and working women. Some of these indices for poor *colonias* (districts) of Mexico City are much higher than for rural Mexico as a whole.

On another level the "culture of poverty" in Mexico, cutting across the rural and the urban, is characterized by the absence of food reserves in the home, the pattern of frequent buying of small quantities of food many times a day as the need occurs, borrowing money from money lenders at usurious interest rates, the pawning of goods, spontaneous informal credit devices among neighbors, the use of secondhand clothing and furniture, particularly in the city which has the largest secondhand market in Mexico, a higher incidence of free unions or consensual marriages, a strong present-time orientation, and a higher proportion of pre-Hispanic folk beliefs and practices.

In the preoccupation with the study of rural-urban differences, there has been a tendency to overlook or neglect basic similarities of people everywhere. In a recent paper Bruner[13] has illustrated this point for Indonesia where he found that the urban and rural Toba Batak are essentially part of a single social and economic ceremonial system.

Mexico-India contrasts also illustrate his point. In Mexico, Catholicism gives a similar stamp to many aspects of life in both rural and urban areas. The nucleated settlement pattern of most Mexican villages with the central church and plaza and the barrio-subdivisions, each in turn with its respective chapel, makes for a distinctive design which is in marked contrast to the north Indian villages where Hinduism and the caste system have made for a much more segmented and heterogeneously organized type of settlement pattern. It is my impression that a similar contrast is to be seen in some of the cities of these two countries and I believe this merits further study. Taking another example from India, we find that the way of life of the urban and rural lower castes, such as Washermen and Sweepers, have much more in common with each other than with the higher caste Brahmans in their respective urban and rural contexts.

Although I agree that number, density, permanence of settlement and heterogeneity of population is a workable definition of a city, I believe we need an additional, more elementary set of variables, with a narrower focus, to explain what goes on within cities. The sheer physical conditions of living have a considerable influence on social life, and I would include, among the variables, such factors as stability of residence, the settlement pattern, types of housing, the number of rooms to a family, and property concepts.

A type of housing settlement like the *vecindad*, which brings people into daily face-to-face contact, in which people do most of their work in a common patio, share a common toilet and a common washstand, encourages intensive interaction, not all of which is necessarily friendly. It makes little difference whether this housing and settlement pattern is in the city or the country, indeed whether it occurs among the tribal peoples of Borneo or the Iroquois Indians. In all cases it produces intense interaction, problems of privacy, quarrels among children, and among their parents.

Stability of residence too has many similar social consequences wherever it occurs. As I have already shown, in Mexico City the *vecindades* make for a kind of community life which has greater resemblance to our stereotyped notions of village life than to Wirth's description of urbanism. Stability of residence may result from a wide variety of factors, both in rural and urban areas. Nor can we assume that it is a necessary concomitant of nonurban societies; witness the nomadism of the Plains Indians or of agricultural workers in parts of the Caribbean.

Certain aspects of the division of labor stand up well as an elementary narrow-focus variable. When the family is the unit of production and the home and the work place are one, certain similar consequences follow for family life, both in the country and the city. I have in mind similarities in family life of small artisans in Mexico City and rural villages. In both, husband and wife spend most of the day together, children are early recruited into useful work, and there is much interaction among family members. Thus, in terms of the amount of time husbands spend away from home, there is much more similarity between a peasant and a factory worker than between either of these and an artisan.

What we need in comparative urban studies as well as in rural-urban comparisons, within a single culture and crossculturally, are carefully controlled, narrow-focus comparisons of subunits. Here I shall list what seem to be to be priorities in research, with special reference to the underdeveloped countries.

1. The delineation of distinctive regions within cities in terms of their demographic, ecological, economic, and social characteristics with the objective of developing measures of urbanization for distinctive population sectors as well as for the city as a whole.
2. Crosscultural studies of comparable population sectors within cities. For example, we might compare lower-class areas in cities of Japan, India, England, and Mexico, utilizing a common research methodology, so that we could check the role of distinctive cultural factors on comparable urban sectors.
3. Comparisons of the economic, social, and psychological aspects of an equal number of families with the same full-time nonagricultural occupations in a village and in the city within a single country. One objective would be to test the influence of the rural versus the urban milieu and the many theories associated with the presumed differences between them.
4. Studies of the socioeconomic and psychological consequences of the introduction of factories in villages and towns in predominantly peasant countries. A crucial methodological point in such studies would be to select communities prior to the introduction of the factory so that we could have a solid baseline against which changes can be measured. One of the weaknesses of practically all studies to date is that they have had to reconstruct the prefactory conditions of the community. For example, the otherwise excellent study of a Guatemalan community by Manning Nash had to reconstruct the village culture as it was seventy years before, when the factory was first introduced.
5. Most studies of the influence of factories have dealt with light industries such as textiles or rayons. It would be good to have studies on the effects of heavy industries such as steel or mining, or chemical plants which demand more skilled labor and continuous operation.
6. Intensive case studies of individuals and families who have moved from tribal communities to urban centers, focusing on the problems of adjustment and the process of acculturation. In terms of method, it would be important to select families from communities which have been carefully studied.
7. Similar studies should be done for peasants and plantation workers who move to the city. The objective of studying subjects

from different backgrounds is to learn what differences, if any, this will have upon the urbanization process. I suspect that the greater disorganization reported by Joseph A. Kahl in his review of African materials as compared to Mexican data can be explained by the fact that the African studies reported on tribal peoples moving to the city whereas in Mexico we are dealing with peasants. On purely theoretical grounds I would expect that culture shock would be greater for tribal peoples.

Notes

1. Oscar Lewis, *Life in a Mexican Village: Tepoztlan Restudied* (Urbana, Ill.: University of Illinois Press, 1951).
2. There has been a growing literature of criticism of the folk-urban and rural-urban dichotomies by urban sociologists. See, for example, Theodore Caplow, "The Social Ecology of Guatemala City," *Social Forces*, 28 (December 1949); Philip M. Hauser, "Observations on the Urban-Folk and Urban-Rural Dichotomies as Forms of Western Ethnocentrism," in Philip M. Hauser and L. F. Schnore (eds.), *The Study of Urbanization* (New York: Wiley, 1965), pp. 503–517; William L. Kolb, "The Social Structure and Function of Cities," *Economic Development and Culture Change* (October 1954); O. D. Duncan and Albert J. Reiss, Jr., *Social Characteristics of Urban and Rural Communities, 1950* (New York: Wiley, 1956), part 4; Gideon Sjoberg, "Comparative Urban Sociology," *Sociology Today* (New York: Basic Books, 1959), pp. 334–359. Horace Miner has attempted to defend the Redfield position in what seems to me to be a rather apologetic article. A careful reading will show that he accepts most of the criticism although he swallows hard. See his "The Folk-Urban Continuum" in Paul K. Hatt and Albert J. Reiss, Jr. (eds.), *Cities and Society* (Glencoe, Ill.: The Free Press, 1957), pp. 22–34.
3. Hauser, *op. cit.*, p. 514.
4. Julian H. Steward, *Theory of Culture Change* (Urbana, Ill.: University of Illinois Press, 1955); Irving Goldman, "Status Rivalry and Cultural Evolution in Polynesia," *American Anthropologist*, 57, No. 4 (August 1955), pp. 680–697; Irving Goldman, "Cultural Evolution in Polynesia: A Reply to Criticism," *Journal of the Polynesian Society*, 66, no. 2 (June 1957), pp. 156–164; Irving Goldman, "The Evolution of Status Systems in Polynesia," in A. F. C. Wallace (ed.), *Men and Cultures* (Philadelphia, 1960), pp. 255–260.
5. I have made this point in an earlier paper, "Peasant Culture In India and Mexico," in McKim Marriott (ed.), *Village India, American Anthropologist*, vol. 57, no. 3, part 2. Memoir No. 83, June 1955: "For both applied and theoretical anthropology we need typologies of peasantry for the major culture areas of the world. . . . Moreover, within each area we need more refined subclassifications. Only after such studies are available will we be in a position to formulate broad generalizations about the dynamics of peasant culture as a whole." P. 165.
6. Oscar Lewis, "Urbanization Without Breakdown: A Case Study," in *The Scientific Monthly*, 75, no. 1 (July 1952). In this article I have suggested a number of specific Mexican conditions which might explain the special findings. More recently, Joseph A. Kahl has restated and elaborated upon some of these points in his article "Some Social Concomitants of Industrialization and Urbanization: A Research Review," *Human Organization*, 18 (Summer 1959), pp. 53–74.
7. Oscar Lewis, "The Culture of the Vecindad in Mexico City: Two Case Studies," *Actas del III Congreso Internacional de Americanistas*, tomo I, San Jose, Costa Rica, 1959, pp. 387–402.
8. Louis Wirth, "Urbanism as a Way of Life," *American Journal of Sociology*, 44 (July 1938), pp. 1–24.
9. Sjoberg, *op. cit.*, p. 340.
10. Wirth, "Urbanism as a Way of Life," in *Community Life and Social Policy* (Chicago: University of Chicago Press, 1956), pp. 119–120.
11. Sjoberg has correctly criticized the logic of comparison inherent in the writings of Redfield and Wirth on folk-urban theory on the ground that they were comparing a whole society with a part society. Here my criticism is that Wirth treated the city as a whole society for purposes of social relations and personality.
12. George Foster, "The Personality of the Peasant," paper read at the 58th Annual Meeting of the American Anthropological Association, Mexico City, 1959.
13. Edward M. Bruner, "Urbanization and Culture Change: Indonesia," paper read at the 58th Annual Meeting of the American Anthropological Association in Mexico City, December 28, 1959.

6

HARLEY L. BROWNING · WALTRAUT FEINDT

The Social and Economic Context of Migration to Monterrey, Mexico

This study is a report of 904 men aged 21–60 and their last migration to Monterrey, Mexico. It provides a descriptive account of this migration, including conditions (primarily economic) leading to departure from community of origin, the composition of the migratory group, and the conditions attending arrival in Monterrey. It also addresses itself to a problem of more general concern; namely, the appropriateness of some current conceptions of the rural-urban migratory process as it occurs in developing countries today.[1]

THE CHRONOLOGY OF MIGRATION TO MONTERREY

Adequate accounts of what actually takes place in the course of migration from one place to another are uncommon, whether in developed or developing countries. Census-based reports, while useful in plotting migration streams and

Reprinted from *Latin American Urban Research* Vol. 1, F. F. Rabinovitz and F. M. Trueblood editors, © 1971, pp. 45–70 by permission of the Publisher, Sage Publications, Inc.

Author's Note: This research is based on a project jointly sponsored by the Centro de Investigaciones Económicas of the Facultad de Economía, Universidad de Nuevo León and the Population Research Center of the Department of Sociology at The University of Texas at Austin. The research at both institutions was facilitated in part by grants from the Ford Foundation. The directors of the project are Jorge Balán and Elizabeth Jelín (formerly of the Universidad de Nuevo León) and Harley L. Browning.

in comparing socioeconomic characteristics of migrants and natives, provide little if any information on the social and economic context of migration. This means that sample surveys are the one source of information that we can turn to. Although a number of recent survey studies provide some information on the migratory process,[2] it is rare that we can construct in adequate detail the chronology of the move, from its beginnings in the community of departure, during the move itself, to the initial accommodation in the community of destination.

Since the Monterrey mobility study represents a deliberate effort to obtain such a chronology of migration to a large city, it is well at this point to consider both the choice of Monterrey for such a study and the relevant technical details in the execution of the survey. Monterrey is a large, rapidly-growing metropolitan center in Mexico, a country that has experienced sustained economic development over the last generation. Since 1940, the city grew from 186,000 to an estimated 950,000 at the time of the survey in 1965. Given such rapid growth, it comes as no surprise that more than two-thirds of the adult population was born outside of Monterrey. Another important characteristic of Monterrey is its prominence as the second leading industrial center of Mexico. As the iron and steel center of the nation, to a degree not encountered in the other large cities of Mexico, it is a city with large, modern factories. Monterrey is still very much a blue-collar city, there being less than a quarter of the male labor force in white-collar employment. At the same time, however, an important sector of the labor force is still employed in such marginal occupations as street vendors, construction workers, and so on. Thus the "duality" often encountered in cities of developing countries is also present in Monterrey, although to a lesser degree. What is important is that Monterrey has had impressive economic growth in the last twenty-five years or so and, because of this fact, has exercised a strong attraction for migrants.

Turning to the survey design itself, the sample is of 1,640 men aged 21–60 and resident in the metropolitan area of Monterrey during the summer of 1965. It is a two-stage stratified cluster design, in which older men (41–60) and those living in areas with higher incomes are over-represented. Although it is possible to convert the weighted sample into a representative one, the actual sample is used in this essay because our concern is not primarily with migration rates, but with the migratory process itself. In any event the distributions of the representative and actual samples generally do not differ greatly.[3]

In this essay we deal with migrants only. The distinction between natives and migrants is based not upon where the respondent was born, but on a sociologically more relevant unit, his "community of origin." This is defined as that place where the respondent spent the most time between the ages five through fifteen. Of our 1,640 men, 56 percent (904) were born outside of Monterrey and their community of origin was not Monterrey. Fourteen percent (228) were born outside of Monterrey but migrated there in childhood and spent their formative years in Monterrey.

To determine the social and economic environment in which migration took place, we asked our migrant respondents a series of temporally sequential questions that served to recreate for us the circumstances of their final move to Monterrey. Although 18 percent of the migrants (165 out of 904) had one or more previous migrations to Monterrey with a duration of at least six months, we asked the battery of questions only for last migration to Monterrey because it would have been impractical to do so for all migrations, not to mention the greater unreliability of response for the earlier moves.

In ordering this essay we follow closely the temporal sequence of last migration to Monterrey. The various specific questions were subsumed under the following three headings:

(1) *Factors Influencing the Decision to Come to Monterrey.* Kind of last employment before coming to Monterrey and satisfaction with it; relative importance of work, family, education and community; consideration of alternate destinations; acquaintance with Monterrey by means of prior visits or residence; concreteness of work plans before coming to Monterrey and planned duration of stay; and degree of satisfaction with decision to migrate at the time of the interview.

(2) *Composition of the Migratory Group.* Marital status at time of migration; whether journey was made alone or with relatives or friends; in case of "split" migration (when members of family came at different times) who came with whom, in what order, and at what time.

(3) *Kinds of Contacts and Forms of Assistance in Settling in Upon Arrival to Monterrey.* Who migrants knew in Monterrey prior to arrival; forms of assistance received, if any; presence of relatives and friends in same neighborhood; contact with persons in communities lived in prior to Monterrey.

CONCEPTIONS OF THE MIGRATORY PROCESS

Beyond the descriptive and chronological account of migration lie questions concerning appropriate models of the migratory process as it occurs in developing countries. We are now in a stage when certain older conceptions, mainly deductive in character and derived from European and U.S. theorists, are being challenged by other conceptions that have emerged largely from empirical field investigations of the migratory process. The older conceptions had erected the myth of "migrant man" that shared many of the limitations of "economic man" as created by the economists and "political man" or more narrowly "voter" of the political scientists. All three were based upon two faulty premises: (1) that the individual acted in social isolation; (2) that the decision-making process was a rational one.

Economic man weighed the pecuniary advantages and disadvantages of a given course of action, while political man carefully reviewed all available information provided by competing candidates before casting his ballot. In like manner, migrant man carefully balanced the advantages and disadvantages of remaining in a place and when the scales tipped toward the unfavorable he migrated to that place offering the best prospects for one of his background. The obvious fact that men are attached to social groups, which affect them in ways not maximal for individual self interest, was excluded from consideration. Much of the recent history of economics and political science has reflected the "discovery" of man as a social animal.

The same thing seems to be happening with respect to migration. Probably the most glaring deficiency of older conceptions of migrant man was their neglect of the importance of family and kinship relationships at all stages of the migratory process. Ironically enough, family and kinship were assigned great prominence in the depiction of the social fabric in the community of origin, particularly in rural and village environments. Here we encounter what may be called "the great dichotomy," a powerful theme that has recurred continually in the history of sociology. Its lineage is impressive: from Maine's "status" and "contract," Tönnies's "Gemeinschaft" and "Gesellschaft," Spencer's "military" and "industrial," Durkheim's "mechanical" and "organic," Redfield's "folk" and "urban" down to contemporary variations on "traditional" and "modern."

However useful the great dichotomy may have been in other contexts, its application to migration has had deleterious effects. The reification of the dichotomy, unfettered by any empirical support, led to a conception of the community of origin, the village, that was idealized in terms of the extent, warmth and solidarity of familial and communal interpersonal relations. By definition, therefore, the community of destination, the city, must display opposite characteristics. The migrant is seen as wrenched from his community of origin of which he was an organic part, embarking alone on a lonely journey to the great city. There, unshielded by any sort of social protection, he is exposed to the full force of an impersonal, even hostile, environment. Is it any wonder that migration, from this perspective, can be anything but a traumatic experience where individuals are torn from the deep sociological roots of their community of origin and then exposed, in vulnerable isolation, to all the forms of disorganization and anomie endemic in the urban environment?

Inexplicably, it rarely seems to have occurred to the authors of the above conception of migrant man that family and kin ties need *not* be severed either during the migration itself or when the migrant had arrived in the city. One of the main objectives of this study is to explicitly show how family relationships and kinship networks function at all stages of the migratory process. The former is considered by reference to stage in the family life cycle. We classify our migrants into three groups:

- *Young Bachelors* (*A*). Men aged 16–25 who were unmarried at last arrival to Monterrey (274 respondents).
- *Young Family Men* (*B*). Men aged 26–35 who were married and with children upon last arrival (183 respondents; included are 42 men aged 21–25).
- *Older Family Men* (*C*). Married men with children who were age 36 or older upon last arrival to Monterrey (205 respondents).

The broader kinship networks are taken up wherever appropriate.

Two other characteristics of the migrants besides their family and kin relationships will warrant attention. We have already alluded to the particular importance of rural-urban migration in the earlier conceptions. One mode of presentation of the results will be to separate migrants engaged in farm unemployment from migrants in nonfarm employment immediately prior to last migration to Monterrey. Since 141 men did not work immediately before coming to Monterrey, there are 303 men with farm and 460 with nonfarm backgrounds.

Finally, we want to introduce a temporal dimension into the discussion, for we cannot assume that in a fast-changing society such as Mexico the patterns we find for one particular time will be present in another. Consequently, we shall introduce time-of-arrival cohorts (always to be understood as last arrival) made up of those who arrived prior to 1941 (159); those between 1941–50 (211); those between 1951–60 (354); and the last arrivals between 1961–65 (180).

THE DECISION TO MOVE

Why do men migrate? More concretely, why did our respondents decide to go to Monterrey? Many factors impinge upon the decision to migrate, ranging from those more remote in a person's past (i.e., level of educational attainment) to those intermediate (i.e., drought conditions over the past several years) down to the immediate precipitant of the move (i.e., loss of job, word from a relative of a good job opening in the city). Most people are scarcely aware themselves of all the considerations that enter into their decision to migrate.

One point has been reasonably well established in a number of studies, however. When men are asked to explain why they migrated, economic factors related to their work invariably are selected as most important.[4] This generalization holds for the Monterrey migrants as well. We first asked our respondents the open question, "What influenced your decision to move?" and then we asked them to select the most important reason. As shown in Table 1, 70 percent of the migrants to Monterrey mentioned work as the most important factor influencing their decision to move. This figure is very close to the 65 percent of male migrants who reported reasons related to work as primary in a national survey conducted by the U.S. Bureau of the Census for the year March, 1962, to March, 1963 (1966) and also similar to the 62.0 percent reported for males migrating to Santiago, Chile by Elizaga (1966).

Next in importance are family reasons. The 17 percent for Monterrey compares with 13.6 for the U.S. sample and 7.6 percent for Santi-

ago. Family reasons are difficult to interpret because of the diversity of situations subsumed under the family label. It is obviously related to stages in the family life cycle. In Table 1 Young Bachelors have the highest percentage, reflecting the fact that some come to Monterrey not on their own initiative but rather that of their parents'. In contrast, the Young Family Men have their own families and are primarily work oriented. Some family moves are occasioned by a sense of family responsibility, as when a young man comes to assist aging or ailing parents, a move that may be to his own economic detriment.

Interestingly enough, education is far more important for Older Family Men than for the other groups; one of every seven of these men migrated primarily for that reason. Clearly the education is not for themselves but for their children. In Mexico, educational facilities in rural areas and small urban places are likely to be lacking or deficient, even on the primary level. If a student is to go on to secondary school and then to university, he must do so in the larger urban centers. Monterrey overall has the best facilities for higher education (a public and a private university) outside of Mexico City. Thus the older migrant, while not regarding migration as a means of directly bettering his own lot, sees it as an opportunity for materially improving the chances of his children.

It is worth mentioning that only three percent of the migrant men select "community" as a principal reason for migrating. They must respond in some degree favorably or unfavorably to Monterrey itself, but it is quite clear that this factor alone only rarely is considered to be decisive in bringing about migration.

Table 1. *Major Reason for Migrating by Family Life Cycle (in percent)*

Major Reason	All Migrants	Young Bachelors	Young Family Men	Older Family Men
Work	70	70	78	68
Family	17	18	11	14
Education	7	6	3	14
Community	3	4	4	1
Other	3	3	4	3
Total	100	101	100	100
N =	(810)[a]	(250)	(183)	(204)

[a] This total is not the addition of the Life Cycle Groups A + B + C, but contains all migrants to Monterrey, less the 94 who did not work immediately before coming to Monterrey or who did not work the first year there.

THE RELATIONSHIP OF WORK EXPERIENCE TO MIGRATION

We have established that work-related factors are by far the most important ones influencing the decision to move to Monterrey. Let us therefore first consider the work situation of migrants prior to migration. Table 2 presents the major industry categories in which the men were employed just before coming to Monterrey by time of arrival. Agricultural employment is most important for each time period but what is unusual and perhaps unexpected is that changes

Table 2. *Last Work Before Migration by Time of Last Arrival (in percent)*

| | TIME OF LAST ARRIVAL | | | | |
Major Industry	1961–65	1951–60	1941–50	Before 1941	Total
Agriculture	37	46	39	29	40
Mining	4	4	9	8	6
Manufacturing	25	19	16	20	20
Construction	3	9	6	10	7
Commerce	10	9	12	17	11
Transportation, Communications	9	4	6	7	6
Services	12	9	13	9	11
Total	100	100	101	100	101
N =	(172)	(304)	(172)	(115)	(763)[a]

[a] This table excludes 141 migrants who either did not work before migrating to Monterrey, or who were already commuting to work in Monterrey, or where industry was insufficiently specified.

in its importance over time do not correspond to the national trends in agricultural employment, during which there has been a steady proportional decline throughout most of the last 35 years.[5] For our sample, the proportion of the total employed in agriculture is at its lowest point in the years before 1941 and then it gradually builds to a high of 52 percent in the 1951–55 period, only to decline to 37 percent in the 1961–65 period. How are we to account for this U-shaped curve? As urged elsewhere (Browning and Feindt, 1969), migrants to Monterrey before 1941 were positively selective of the populations from which they originated. They were more likely to have higher educational attainment and to be in nonagricultural employment. More recent migrants to Monterrey, however, are much less selective as a group. This selectivity interpretation also accounts for the elevated proportion we find in manufacturing before 1941, for it will be remembered that this was before the major thrust of industrialization occurred in Mexico. Only for the 1961–65 period did the proportion in manufacturing rise to match that of the earlier period. The other industrial categories generally show little variation over time. Mining declined, but this is consistent with the decline in mining activity in general over the last several decades.

Since work is the most important factor influencing the decision to migrate to Monterrey, it may be assumed that it was the men's dissatisfaction with the conditions of their work that set off the whole migratory process. We asked our respondents, "Were you satisfied with your last job before coming to Monterrey?" Rather surprisingly, well over one-half (56 percent) reported themselves satisfied, 14 percent were partly satisfied, and only 30 percent unequivocally expressed dissatisfaction with their job.

If most of the men were satisfied with their job, why did they quit? We asked our men to select the single most important reason for leaving their last work and this is given by major industry in Table 3. We distinguish between those who reported specific reasons related to work (34 percent for all migrants) and those who only reported a vague desire for better work (10 percent). There appears, within the context of this table, to be an approximate balance between those who left their work because of forces of attraction as compared to forces of repulsion. Twenty-seven percent reported they wanted more pay or the possibility for advancement while 28 percent left because their work terminated or went badly, "se iba mal." There are considerable differences within

Table 3. *Principal Reason for Leaving Last Work by Major Industry (in percent)*

Principal Reason	MAJOR INDUSTRY						
	Agriculture	Mining	Manufacturing	Transp. and Constr.	Commerce	Services	Total
More salary, advancement, etc.	22	17	31	31	36	31	27
More stability	4	5	1	3	1	6	3
Better working conditions	2	21	2	1	3	8	4
More independence	0	0	1	0	0	2	0
Total specific work reasons	(28)	(43)	(35)	(35)	(40)	(47)	(34)
Wanted better work	12	2	10	13	4	10	10
Work discontinued	39	33	20	16	19	13	28
Family reasons	10	10	15	16	21	11	13
Other reasons	11	10	19	21	16	21	15
Total	100	98	99	101	100	102	100
N =	(284)	(42)	(124)	(77)	(75)	(52)	(654)[a]

[a] Excluded from this table are 250 migrants who either did not work before migrating to Monterrey or who were transferred, or who did not state reasons.

industries. Nearly four of ten men in agriculture left because they were "forced" off the land. Only mining approached this figure, doubtless reflecting the decline of mining in northeastern Mexico. Specific work-related reasons other than pay and advancement (more stability, better working conditions and more independence) were of minimal importance save for mining, where a fifth said they left because they wanted better working conditions. The fact that "more independence" receives almost no mention is not because the men are ignorant of its significance; when asked elsewhere in the interview to compare their jobs with those of their fathers, the 26 percent of those in the representative sample who reported themselves worse off than their fathers gave less independence as the main reason.

Once the migrant has made a decision to ter-minate his employment or had this decision made for him by others or by natural factors, the question arises as to how long an interval exists between leaving work and the move to Monterrey. One might think that the respondents would stay in the community for considerable periods of time after their last employment, hoping to find something else before finally moving on to Monterrey. To get at this point we asked the question, "How long after terminating your last employment was it until you moved to Monterrey?" Sixty percent reported coming immediately to Monterrey and 87 percent made the journey within one month. While the results indicate that the men do not generally "hang around" after their last job, it is likely in many cases that the decision to move began to form in the minds of respondents long before actual termination of work and that preparations were made in advance of leaving the job.

Another point of interest in tracing the migratory progress is the number of alternatives regarding place of destination. Of course, we know that our respondents came to Monterrey, but did they consider other destinations before making their choice? Eighty-nine percent said they did not. For the eleven percent who did entertain an alternate destination it was preponderantly a large urban place. Rural or small urban centers had very little attraction for the migrants. About equal proportions considered other urban centers in northeastern Mexico, Mexico City, urban places in other parts of Mexico, and the U.S.A. What tipped the scales in favor of Monterrey? Family and work reasons each are mentioned by about a third, with the other third involving idiosyncratic factors.

The decision to move to Monterrey no doubt was influenced to some extent by direct acquaintance with the city. Nearly two-thirds (63 percent) of the migrants had been to Monterrey prior to the final migration. Even for migrants who arrived before 1941, more than one-half (52 percent) had been to Monterrey. The figure rises to 75 percent for the latest arrivals (1961–65). Clearly, for most migrants, and especially those of recent arrival, the move to Monterrey was no perilous voyage into unknown and uncharted seas. In addition, not all migrations to Monterrey were considered at the time to be permanent changes of residence. We asked our respondents whether their plans had been to remain in Monterrey or eventually to return to their place of origin. Two-thirds (65 percent) reported that they had come to Monterrey with definite expectations of staying; that is, they had sold everything before coming. Twenty percent were more tentative and had come to see what would happen. If they liked Monterrey, they had planned to remain. The rest (16 percent) came with the idea of staying only for a time and then returning to their place of origin.

This figure is a good deal higher for those arriving after 1960 (25 percent) than for the earlier arrivals. The percentage declines to a low of nine percent for those arriving before 1941. Doubtless some part of the 1961–65 arrival cohort will leave Monterrey in the near future. That this group contains a substantial number of transient men (military, business and government) assigned to Monterrey is attested to by the fact that there is a high proportion (11 percent) who arrived with a signed work contract. A substantial part of this group will be gone by the end of a five-year interval, hence their effect is concentrated mainly in the 1961–65 arrival cohort.

Most of the migrants (58 percent) came to Monterrey with nothing more than the hope of finding a satisfactory job. Only 23 percent arrived either with a signed contract or with a definite job promised to them. Another eight percent had a fairly concrete plan for obtaining work. Ten percent did not come to Monterrey to seek work and they are concentrated in the youngest (11–15) and oldest (45–60) age categories. If the major industries in which the migrants were employed before they came to Monterrey are considered, we find that only ten percent of those in agriculture had either a contract or a specific job lined up. By contrast, 27 percent in manufacturing and 41 percent in services had made such an arrangement. This clearly is linked to the marketable skills the migrants can bring to a metropolitan environment.

OVERALL EVALUATION OF THE MOVE TO MONTERREY

At the end of the series of questions dealing with reasons for leaving their job and for coming to Monterrey we asked the question, "Finally, are you satisfied with having come to Monterrey?" The overwhelmingly positive response (92 percent reported themselves satisfied) to this question was unexpected. (Only three percent gave an unqualified no, while five percent said they were satisfied in part.) That nine of every ten men said they were satisfied with the move no doubt overstates the positive response, for it is well known that people have a tendency to report themselves satisfied with their present situation, no matter what it is. And, of course, although data are lacking, it is undeniable that many of the most dissatisfied migrants had left Monterrey by the time of the survey.

But even if we acknowledge that 92 percent is too high, it still is indisputable that the great majority of migrants were satisfied with their decision to migrate to Monterrey. When asked why they were satisfied, the answers were illuminating. Nine percent expressed general satisfaction. Eighteen percent said in effect that they were content because in Monterrey they were able to satisfy at least the minimal conditions for livelihood ("I have **work**," "I'm not hungry"). Of those employed in agriculture, mining, and construction before migrating, about a third responded in this manner. This background generally involves risky and undependable work. Moreover, these migrants do not bring skills that have a high value in the urban environment, so it may be that they simply do not have high aspirations.

Although most of our men said they migrated because of work-related reasons, only 19 percent specifically mentioned their work as the reason for their satisfaction in moving. One-fourth (25 percent) said they enjoyed a higher level of living in Monterrey ("earn more," "live better"). Fifteen percent report family reasons and ten percent satisfaction with the community, the latter reason being over-represented among the higher-status migrants.

Since there are only a few cases of expressed dissatisfaction with the decision to migrate to Monterrey, they cannot be analyzed in detail. These men are mainly disappointed with income and level of living (32 percent) and with the community (25 percent). Only 16 percent report dissatisfaction with work itself.

MARITAL STATUS AND COMPOSITION OF THE MIGRANT GROUP

In this section we will first consider the marital status of the men upon arrival to Monterrey. Then we will deal with the actual migratory act itself in relation to the family group involved. While marital status restricts the possible combinations of the migratory act, it does not permit us to predict who will migrate with whom. For instance, a Young Bachelor obviously cannot migrate with his family of procreation, but he may come alone, with his family of origin, or with other relatives or friends. A married man with children may make it a three-generational group by bringing his parents along. The timing of such a move may even be in three parts: first the father comes alone, then he sends for his wife and children, and finally the parents are called. The patterns of movement can become complex.

Marital status is linked closely to age. Not unexpectedly, men who migrate to Monterrey between ages 16 and 20 are nearly all single, while those 31 and over are nearly all married. There is an even balance between single and married in the 21–30 age group.

Considering marital status by time-of-arrival cohorts, we find a pronounced trend toward a married state from the oldest to the most recent arrivals:

	TIME OF LAST ARRIVAL				
	1961–65	1951–60	1941–50	Before 1941	Total
Single	23	42	59	79	49
Married	72	55	38	20	48
Widowed, divorced or separated	4	3	3	1	3
Total	99	100	100	100	100
N =	(180)	(354)	(211)	(159)	(904)

This trend is affected by the fact that as a group the men who migrated earlier to Monterrey were younger. There are insufficient cases to present all arrival cohorts by age, but for the men who were aged 21–30 at time of arrival we find that

59 percent of those arriving before 1941 were single. This declines to 43 percent for the 1961–65 period.

Not only are the recent migrants more likely to arrive married, they are also more likely to

Table 4. *Married Men by Number of Dependent Children by Time of Last Arrival to Monterrey (in percent)*

| Dependent Children | TIME OF LAST ARRIVAL | | | | |
	1961–61	1951–60	1941–50	Before 1941	Total
None	22	23	21	42	24
One	19	14	19	32	18
Two	27	22	21	6	22
Three	12	16	19	13	15
Four	11	17	10	7	13
Five or more	9	8	10	0	8
Total	100	100	100	100	100
N =	(130)	(196)	(80)	(31)	(437)ᵃ

ᵃ Married men include only those 21 years or older upon arrival to Monterrey. Dependent children are all those ten years or under.

arrive with children. Table 4 presents those who were at least 21 years upon last arrival to Monterrey and who were married. The proportion arriving with three or more children rises from 19 percent in the earliest period to a peak of 41 in the 1951–60 interval. This pattern is consistent with the declining selectivity hypothesis advanced earlier.

We can now relate marital status, in the form of the Family Life Cycle Groups, to the actual migration itself. Table 5 shows the composition of the migratory group. Note that only one-

fifth of the migrants come alone. Does this fit the image of the lone and lonely migrant? Even among the Young Bachelors only a third come alone. Young Family Men are more likely to arrive in three-generational groups, but such an arrangement is not common in any of the groups.

It is worthy of note that when respondents are examined by time of arrival, 44 percent of the Young Bachelors (and 56 percent of all single men) who arrived in the 1961–65 period came alone. No doubt this reflects the transient status

Table 5. *Composition of Migratory Group by Family Life Cycle (in percent)*

Migratory Group	All Migrants	Young Bachelors	Young Family Men	Older Family Men
Respondent alone	19	31	8	9
With family of procreation	39	—	72	83
With family of origin	34	66	2	1
With family of origin & procreation	6	—	15	5
Other combinations	2	3	3	1
Total	100	100	100	99
N =	(891)ᵃ	(274)	(184)	(208)

ᵃ Thirteen cases with no information are excluded.

75

Table 6. *Type of Migration by Family Life Cycle and Farm-Nonfarm Background (in percent)*

Type of Migration	All Migrants	YOUNG BACHELORS (A)			YOUNG FAMILY MEN (B)			OLDER FAMILY MEN (C)		
		Farm	Non-farm	Total Group A	Farm	Non-farm	Total Group B	Farm	Non-farm	Total Group C
Solitary	20	24	34	31	15	4	8	10	9	9
Simultaneous	38	15	20	18	44	73	62	50	53	52
Split	42	61	46	51	41	23	30	40	38	39
Total	100	100	100	100	100	100	100	100	100	100
N =	(884)[a]	(88)[b]	(146)[b]	(274)	(71)[b]	(112)[b]	(183)	(91)[b]	(110)[b]	(205)

[a] Excluded are 20 cases with no information.
[b] Based only on migrants who worked before coming to Monterrey.

of some of these men in military, industry, and government employment. Otherwise, there are no significant changes in this migratory pattern over time.

The dimension of migration we have not yet tapped is the sequence and timing of movement when persons other than the respondent are involved. Logically we may identify: (1) *solitary migration,* when the man comes alone and no one precedes or follows him; (2) *simultaneous migration,* when everyone in the migratory group, however it is made up, comes together; or (3) *split migration,* when the migratory group comes at different intervals. The respondent may be in the avant-garde or rear guard of the group. For example, as a son he may go first to find a job and then prepare for the arrival of his parents and siblings. The possible combinations are many.

Table 6 gives the three types of migration by Family Life Cycle Groups and Farm-Nonfarm background of the migrants. Predictably, it is the Young Bachelors who are most likely to come alone, but nine percent of the Older Family Men come alone. This would include some of the transient 1961–65 migrants or men abandoning their families. Young Family Men understandably travel to Monterrey as part of a group. Migrants who worked in agriculture before coming to Monterrey are less likely to come as a group and more likely to be part of the "bridging" process that is characteristic of split migrations. Among the Young Family Men the difference between those with farm and non-farm background is particularly strong (44 and

73 percent respectively for simultaneous migration and 41 and 23 percent for split migrations). About the same number of respondents in the split migration category came in the avant-garde as in the rear guard (41 and 42 percent respectively).

Finally, there is the time interval within split migration between the first and last arrival. What is striking is the considerable length of time that is sometimes needed to complete the split migration pattern. Over forty percent of all Young Bachelors with split migration are involved in a sequence that takes more than three years to work itself out. Among Young Family Men this time period is reduced: forty-six percent reunite with their families within six months. Even here, however, almost an equal proportion (44 percent) require more than a year to bring the family together.

This brief survey of split migration patterns touches upon an aspect of migration that is sometimes overlooked. Migration, in this perspective of family units and kinship networks, is properly seen as a continuous process, not a movement restricted only to the number of days a person, with or without companions, needs to journey to Monterrey. As we have seen, a sizeable part of the migration extends over a period of years. It is a relatively stable pattern for it does not vary greatly when examined by time-of-arrival cohorts. This suggests that for any specific date we can confidently predict for Monterrey a fair volume of subsequent migration simply as a result of the split migration pattern. This is but another way of saying that migration to Monterrey generates its own momentum and, to a certain extent, becomes independent of economic opportunity.

MIGRATION TO MONTERREY AND FORMS OF ASSISTANCE

It has been established that most migrants were acquainted with the city prior to last arrival. But did they know anyone there and, if so, did this mean they had an easier time of it? Is assistance made available to the migrants and, if so, in what form? How does this assistance ease the adjustment to life in Monterrey?

The first question is whether the migrants had relatives or friends living in Monterrey at the time of the last migration. A very large proportion (84 percent) had. Because of the heavy flow of migrants into Monterrey during the last decades, the probability of having relatives or friends in Monterrey should be greatest for the more recent arrivals. This is true to the extent that the figure rises from 77 percent for those arriving before 1941 to 86 percent in the 1961–65 cohort. What is striking is how narrow the range is. Evidently, the familial and kinship networks in Monterrey were established well before the migratory surge reached its highest intensity after 1940.

Of course, the mere presence of relatives or friends does not insure that help will be forthcoming. How many of the migrants with these relationships actually received assistance? Two-thirds of those who had friends or relatives living in Monterrey obtained help in some form. Unfortunately, since there were no questions on this point, we do not know what part of the 32 percent who were not aided asked for assistance but were denied it.

The most common form of assistance (70 percent of all aid) is the provision of food and shelter—a highly personal and family-related form of assistance. Our Monterrey data suggest that the kinship network is rather effective in taking care of the basic needs of the migrants immediately after arrival to the metropolis. This pattern is quite stable by time of arrival. All other kinds of aid are much less common. Help in finding a job is of a certain importance (14 percent), especially for the more recent bachelor arrivals. Assistance in finding housing for those families who did not stay

with relatives accounted for ten percent of all aid. Direct financial assistance, either by paying for the trip or lending money is rare (seven percent). Migrants cannot expect much help from those "back home." Only thirteen percent of the migrants received any kind of assistance. Most of it takes the form of a one-way bus ticket, predominantly to young, single migrants under 20 years of age. Unquestionably this is related to the forces that bring about migration in the first place—poor economic conditions that generate only little cash income.

At this point, let us consider again the phenomenon of split migration introduced in the last section. Help can flow in two directions: from the arrival(s) in Monterrey to the remaining member(s) of the group in the community of departure and vice versa. For example, a family may send a son to school in Monterrey and pay his expenses. After he has finished schooling and obtained a job he may help the rest of his family to come to Monterrey, or perhaps to assist in the education of his younger brothers and sisters in the city.

In those cases of split migration in which there was at least a six-month interval between the first and last arrivals we inquired as to whether those who remained behind sent money to the avant-garde in Monterrey. Only 19 percent did. A much greater flow of money went from Monterrey to the prior community of residence. Forty-seven percent of the first arrivals reported sending money back to those remaining, a figure showing relatively little variation through time. Given the importance of rural-urban migration and the fact that Monterrey generally provides better economic opportunities (especially in generating cash income) than the previous communities of residence (mainly rural), it is not surprising that such a pattern exists. But there also are forms of aid other than money. Those of the avant-garde who could or did not send money (53 percent) helped the latecomers in various other ways. Finding housing for the latecomers was by far the most common way (78 percent of all non-monetary aid). It may be puzzling that only ten percent of all non-monetary aid is help in finding work until we remember that the latecomers are often wives and children who normally would not be part of the labor force. This relationship shows up too in the category "went to get them" (nine percent of all non-monetary aid). We had not anticipated such a response but the men consider it a type of help and doubtless it is, especially for those unaccustomed to travel, such as women with children or older people.

LIVING ARRANGEMENTS UPON ARRIVAL

Looking at the circumstances surrounding arrival to Monterrey and how it might affect the migrants—particularly those coming directly to Monterrey from small villages—we singled out housing arrangements for closer analysis. Migrants who first live with relatives or friends are more likely to be introduced to the city gradually and by guides they know and trust, while those living independently presumably have to fend for themselves in the new environment. Table 7 shows that more than half of the migrants first lived with relatives or friends already established in Monterrey. This holds not only for the Young Bachelors, but for men with families which, considering the restricted housing space in Monterrey for the great mass of population, certainly entails considerable crowding.

Migrants from farm backgrounds are more likely to receive protection and shelter from relatives than those originating from nonfarm backgrounds. Those most in need of primary group contacts are most likely to experience the city first through a familial context. An interesting sidelight reflecting the male dominance

pattern of the Mexican family structure is the fact that of the married migrants who lived with relatives 71 percent resided with relatives of the husband, while only 21 percent lived with relatives of the wife. (Eight percent lived with friends.) It is unlikely that these percentages reflect the lesser availability of wife's relatives in Monterrey. It is more reasonable to assume that the husband will generally avoid a form of dependence upon his wife's relatives for fear that it will weaken his authority within his own nuclear family.

What about those migrants who live independently of established relatives or friends upon their arrival to the metropolis? Did they live independently because they did not know anybody? Table 8 shows that this is true for 41 percent of the migrants who lived independently (18 percent of all migrants). There are significant differences between the family life cycle groups: 53 percent of the Young Bachelors lived independently as compared with 25 percent of the Young Family Men. Most Young Family Men living independently evidently did so by their own choosing; 43 percent of them were aided in finding housing by relatives or friends or by the company employing them.

Looking at Table 8 it appears that the Young Bachelors are the group conforming most closely to the stereotyped image of the migrant alone in the big city. Thirty-eight percent of the Young Bachelors living independently (15 percent of

Table 7. *Living Arrangement upon Arrival to Monterrey by Family Life Cycle and Farm-Nonfarm Background (in percent)*

Living Arrangement	All Migrants	YOUNG BACHELORS (A)			YOUNG FAMILY MEN (B)			OLDER FAMILY MEN (C)		
		Farm	Non-farm	Total Group A	Farm	Non-farm	Total Group B	Farm	Non-farm	Total Group C
Lived with relatives or friends already in Monterrey	58	76	57	62	74	42	55	67	51	58
Lived independently	42	24	43	38	26	58	45	33	49	42
Total	100	100	100	100	100	100	100	100	100	100
N =	(881)[a]	(87)[b]	(143)[b]	(270)	(70)[b]	(111)[b]	(181)	(91)[b]	(111)[b]	(206)

[a] Excluded are 23 cases with no information.
[b] Based only on migrants who worked before coming to Monterrey.

Table 8. *Forms of Assistance to Those Living Independently upon Last Arrival to Monterrey by Family Life Cycle*

Forms of Assistance	All Migrants Living Independently	Young Bachelors	Young Family Men	Older Family Men
Did not know anyone in Monterrey	41	53	25	35
Knew someone but received no help	32	28	31	40
Relatives or friends prepared housing	7	7	11	6
Relatives or friends helped find housing	10	6	14	11
Company helped find housing	11	6	18	8
Total	101	100	99	100
N =	(384)	(107)	(83)	(95)

all migrants) were to be found in *pensiones* or similar arrangements. But a Mexican *pensión* is a far cry from an impersonal hotel; it is usually run by a *señora* who provides meals and a certain amount of motherly supervision and the young lodgers more often than not share rooms. Whatever the lot of these Young Bachelors, there is a larger proportion of Young Bachelors (42 percent) who do not lack for family living; they migrated with their family of origin and live with their parents independent of other relatives or friends in the city. Another 20 percent live with their employers, i.e., heads of private households, masters for apprentices, small shopkeepers, the military. Most of the family men (over 90 percent) who do not move in with relatives or friends already in Monterrey live with their own migratory group, that is, their family of procreation.

This discussion of the extent of kinship contacts of migrants upon arrival to Monterrey can be summarized in the following table whereby the migrants are grouped in five categories according to the amount of kin interaction:

		Percent	N
Category 1	Lived with relatives, had additional relatives in neighborhood	20	(171)
Category 2	Lived with relatives, but no additional relatives in neighborhood	38	(337)
Category 3	Lived independently, had relatives in neighborhood	11	(100)
Category 4	Lived independently, no relatives in neighborhood but elsewhere in the city	17	(145)
Category 5	Lived independently, no relatives in neighborhood or in the rest of the city	14	(124)
Total		100	(877)ᵃ

ᵃ Excluded are 27 cases with no information on one or more of the three questions used to make up the index.

Migrants in Category 1 are most deeply involved in a network of family relations in Monterrey. Not only do they live with relatives, but they are in close contact with other relatives who live in the same neighborhood. When asked how often they visited these relatives during the first year in Monterrey, 60 percent answered "more than once a week," 26 percent "once a week or every 15 days," ten percent "once a month or less," and only four percent "never visited." Migrants in Category 3 visit to a similar extent. We can say, therefore, that migrants in the first three categories (69 percent of all migrants), are members of close-knit family networks. We cannot say that those in Category 4 do not interact with kin, since we do not have information on contacts with relatives in Monterrey who live outside the neighborhood. The migrants in Category 5 (representing one of every seven men) are the ones who had to make their start in the city without the presumed benefit of family relations.

We say "presumed" benefit, for we should not jump to the conclusion that those migrants without extensive kinship contacts in a metropolis necessarily are worse off than those who have them. The benefit derived from kinship networks depends upon the background of the migrants. If they originate from rural or small urban places the kinship network is the only

buffer between the migrant and his new environment. It has been shown (Browning and Feindt, n.d.) that of those migrants to Monterey whose community of origin was rural—and they make up more than one-half of all migrants—59 percent came directly to Monterrey. For these men there is no possibility of prior socialization to the ways of metropolitan Monterrey by virtue of residence in some other urban place. Those coming to Monterrey from metropolitan or large urban places will be less in need of kinship networks to ease the transition.

In Table 9 one finds the larger the community of origin (where respondents grew up) the more likely it is that in-migrants will not be part of neighborhood kinship networks. In every case, however, well over one-half are part of such primary groups. Much the same pattern is observed for farm-nonfarm employment immediately prior to last arrival in Monterrey and education. Since we are not concerned in this essay with the long-term adjustment of migrants to the occupational milieu of Monterrey, we will only suggest that, of itself, participation in kinship networks is not requisite for socioeconomic success. It may be, however, that *within* major socioeconomic categories (less than primary school, farm background, etc.) those with kinship networks will do better than those without.

Table 9. *Membership in Kinship Networks by Size Class of Community of Origin, Farm-Nonfarm Background, and Education (in percent)*

Size Class of Community of Origin	NEIGHBORHOOD KINSHIP NETWORK			N
	Yes[a]	No[a]	Total	
Rural (–5,000)	73	27	100	(479)
Small urban (5,000–19,999)	70	30	100	(182)
Medium urban (20,000–99,999)	62	38	100	(161)
Large urban (100,000+)	56	44	100	(43)
Last employment before arrival to Monterrey				
Farm	82	18	100	(292)
Nonfarm	62	38	100	(447)
Education				
Primary education or less	73	27	100	86)
Beyond primary	55	45	100	90)

[a] Social Contact Categories 1, 2, and 3 are YES; 4 and 5 are NO.

Table 10. *Kind of Contact with Relatives or Friends in Place Lived in Longest by Time of Arrival to Monterrey (in percent)*

Presence of Relatives	TIME OF LAST ARRIVAL				
	1961–65	1951–60	1941–50	Before 1941	Total
Respondent has relatives in other place	93	90	85	77	88
Respondent no relatives in other place	7	10	15	23	12
Total	100	100	100	100	100
N =	(179)	(350)	(206)	(155)	(890)ª
If Relatives, King of Contact					
Send money, write and visit	9	5	7	5	6
Write and visit	37	35	35	27	34
Visit only	17	27	32	36	27
Write only	19	13	10	4	12
Other	4	2	1	3	2
No contact	15	18	15	26	18
Total	101	100	100	101	99
N =	(167)	(316)	(176)	(120)	(779)

ª Excluded are 14 cases with no information.

THE MIGRANT'S MAINTENANCE OF CONTACTS WITH PERSONS IN COMMUNITIES OF PREVIOUS RESIDENCE

Most of the migrants to Monterrey had friends or relatives living there before they arrived. But once in Monterrey how close are the ties they maintain to people in communities they have lived in before? Some 88 percent still have relatives and friends there and the more recent the arrival to Monterrey the more likely they are to have relatives or friends in these places (see Table 10). The figure rises from 77 percent in the earliest arrival cohort to 93 percent in the latest (1961–65). That is, about three of every four migrants identified friends and relatives in places of previous residence even after the passage of 25 or more years since migrating. Of all respondents who reported affirmatively, 69 percent had relatives or friends only in their community of origin, 18 percent in both community of origin and one or more other places, and 13 percent had relatives and friends only in communities other than their community of origin.

The question remains whether or not our respondents actually maintained contact, and in what form, with their relatives and friends. As Table 10 reveals, of those with relatives or friends still living in communities the respondent had resided in, four out of every five migrants maintain relations of some kind. The most frequent way of maintaining contact is a combination of writing and occasional visits (34 percent), followed by those who visit only (28 percent). The forms which the contacts with relatives or friends in previously lived in communities assume vary by time of arrival. When we consider all forms of contact, those which involve writing occur to a much higher degree among later arrivals. On the other hand, visiting is mentioned significantly more often by the earlier arrivals than by the later ones.

CONCLUSION

The reader who has followed us through the many descriptive details of the chronology of last migration to Monterrey should not require much convincing on the importance of social, particularly familial, factors in the process of migration. The concept of "process" needs to be emphasized. Over many years of sustained heavy in-migration to Monterrey, a relation with other communities, via the kinship and friendship network, has developed so that migration rightfully is seen as a continuous process, nearly always involving simultaneously many people in at least two localities.

Within this perspective the migratory pattern is quite stable; it is the individuals who change positions in the process. At any given point in time a person may be labelled differently from the way he would be at another point.[9] Migrants depend upon earlier arrivals for help in establishing themselves and they in turn assist in the accommodation of later arrivals. Migration begets migration in a way not directly related to the economic allure of Monterrey and tends to be self-perpetuating.

Our findings, taken in their totality, lend very little support to some common impressions of migration in Latin America. People are not uprooted from their communities of origin to be driven into a great, grey, hostile, metropolitan environment where they, in vulnerable isolation, are exposed to all forms of disorganization. The great majority of men reported themselves glad they made the change. The experience is not nearly as disruptive or traumatic as it sometimes is portrayed. Only a few of the migrants come alone, and most of them have relatives or friends awaiting them in Monterrey to help ease the period of adjustment.

These conclusions are not novel. For Mexico at least, Oscar Lewis (1952) had suggested some time ago a pattern similar to the one presented here. And we may anticipate that as empirical studies of migration increase in number and as more countries are represented, the older speculative conceptions of migration will be superseded. Cornelius has performed a valuable service in his comprehensive comparison of "developmental theorists and Latin Americanists" with "empirically-based studies." His interest is not with the migratory process as such but the consequences of urban environment upon migrants. He is able to demonstrate quite effectively that the "theorists" had posited many negative consequences for migrants (felt deprivation, frustration of socioeconomic expecta-

tions, personal and/or social disorganization, alienation, etc.) that were only rarely substantiated in the empirical studies. His finding is also supported by the Monterrey data. In the United States, to cite but one example, Brown, *et al.* (1963) found that migration from a Kentucky locale occurs within a kinship context no doubt similar to that of many migrants to Monterrey. And, of course, African studies of migration, Little (1966) for example, have always placed great emphasis upon the social context of migration.

We should not like to leave the impression that migration to cities in Latin America involves no strain, or that it is always successful. Given the great differences in environments between rural and metropolitan areas, there have to be adjustments, not all of them pleasant. And it must be remembered that our findings are for Monterrey, a city with better than average economic growth. Other urban centers, particularly the stagnant ones, may display somewhat different patterns. We are, however, of the belief that the Monterrey pattern is not atypical in Latin America and that the adaptation of migrants is fairly successful. Man is a far more adaptable animal than he is sometimes given credit for!

Notes

1. Certain restrictions on the scope of this essay should be seen within the context of the larger project, the Monterrey Mobility Study, from which the data are taken. We do not concern ourselves with the geographic origins of the migrants, the number of moves, conformity to the stage migration hypothesis and the phenomenon of return migration. These features are taken up in another article, "Patterns of Migration to Monterrey, Mexico" (Browning and Feindt, n.d.). The important question of the extent to which migrants differ from comparable populations in their community of origin for such characteristics as education and occupation is considered in "Selectivity of Migrants to a Metropolis in a Developing Country: A Mexican Case Study" (Browning and Feindt, 1969). The problem of how well the migrants fare in the occupational structure of Monterrey when compared with the natives is analyzed elsewhere (Browning and Feindt, 1968). Jorge Balán, "Are Farmers' Sons Handicapped in the City?" (1968) uses Monterrey data to relate social origin to occupational achievement in the city. Finally, the matter of value orientations and attitudes of migrants toward work, family,

and so forth, is the subject of a study in progress by Richard Rockwell.

2. Within Latin America, an incomplete listing would include studies sponsored by the Centro Latinoamericano de Demografía (CELADE) for Santiago, Chile (Elizaga, 1966), and Lima, Peru, that have yet to be reported in detail. There is also the work of Germani (1961) for Buenos Aires, Hutchinson (1963) in Brazil, the MacDonalds (1968) in Venezuela, and Butterworth (1962) for Mexico City, among others.

3. For further details on the Monterrey study see Balán, et al. (1967) or an unpublished translation, "Technical Procedures in the Execution of the Monterrey Mobility Survey," available upon request from the Population Research Center, University of Texas at Austin.

4. Henry Shyrock (1969) reviews surveys in the United States, Canada, Chile, Turkey, India, Japan, and Korea relevant to this point. He points out that comparability is still limited due to differences in survey design, especially in classification schemes of reasons for moving.

5. Mexican census data on the labor force present problems of comparability from one census date to another, but in 1930, 72 percent of the economically active male population of Mexico was reported in agriculture and other primary activities. This declined to 59 percent for the 1960 census and, no doubt, it had dropped two or three more percentage points by 1965.

6. For example, a Young Bachelor may have come to Monterrey alone at the time of the survey with no intention of bringing any other members of his family. He is classified in the "solitary" category. Five years later he changes his mind and calls for his parents to come. At that time he would be reclassified as a "split" migrant.

References

Balán, Jorge, E. J. Balán and H. L. Browning (1967) *Movilidad Social, Migración, y Fecundidad en Monterrey Metropolitano*. Monterrey, Mexico: Centro de Investigaciones Económicas, Universidad de Nuevo León.

Balán, Jorge (1968) "Are farmers' sons handicapped in the city?" *Rural Sociology* 33 (June): 160–174.

Brown, James S., H. K. Schwarzweller and J. J. Mangalam (1933) "Kentucky mountain migration and the stem-family: an American variation on a theme by LePlay." *Rural Sociology* 28 (March): 48–69.

Browning, Harley and W. Feindt (1968) "Diferencias entre la población nativa y la migrante en Monterrey." *Demografía y Economía* (México) 2, No. 2, 183–204.

——— (1969) "Selectivity of migrants to a metropolis in a developing country: a Mexican case study." *Demography.*

——— (n.d.) "Patterns of Migration to Monterrey, Mexico." Austin: Population Research Center (mimeo.).

Butterworth, Douglas S. (1962) "A study of the urbanization process among Mixtec migrants from Tilaltongo in Mexico City." *América Indígena* 22 (July): 257–74.

Cornelius, Wayne Jr. (1970) "The political sociology of cityward migration in Latin America: toward empirical theory."

Elizaga, Juan C. (1966) "A study of migration to greater Santiago [Chile]." *Demography* 3, No. 2: 352–377.

Germani, Gino (1961) "Inquiry into the social effects of urbanization in a working-class sector of Buenos Aires." Pp. 206–233 in P. M. Hauser (ed.) *Urbanization in Latin America.* New York: International Documents Service.

Hutchison, Bertram (1963) "The migrant population of urban Brazil." *América Latina* 6 (April-June): 41–71.

Lansing, John B. and E. Mueller (1967) *The Geographic Mobility of Labor.* Ann Arbor, Mich.: Institute for Social Research.

Lewis, Oscar (1952) "Urbanization without breakdown: a case study." *Scientific Monthly*, 75 (July): 31–41.

Little, Kenneth (1966) *West African Urbanization: A Study of Voluntary Associations in Social Change.* London: Cambridge University Press.

MacDonald, Leatrice D. and J. S. MacDonald (1968) "Motives and objectives of migration: selective migration and preferences toward rural and urban life." *Social and Economic Studies* 17 (December): 417–434.

Shryock, Henry (1969) "Survey statistics on reasons for moving." Paper presented at the meetings of the International Union for the Scientific Study of Population, London (September 3–11).

U.S. Bureau of the Census (1960) "Reasons for Moving: March 1962 to March 1963." *Current Population Reports, Population Characteristics*, P-20, No. 154 (August 22).

7

HOMER HOYT

Recent Distortions of the Classical Models of Urban Structure

Since the general patterns of city structure were described by Burgess in 1925[1] and 1929[2] and by myself in 1939[3] there has been a tremendous growth of urban population, not only in the United States, but throughout the world. To what extent has this factor of growth changed the form or shape of urban communities?

While the Burgess concentric circle theory was based on a study of Chicago—a city on a flat prairie, cut off on the east by Lake Michigan—and patterns of growth in other cities would be influenced by their unique topography, his formulation had a widespread application to American cities of 1929. Burgess made a brilliant and vivid contribution to urban sociology and urban geography which inspired the present writer as well as the sociologists and geographers who made subsequent studies of city patterns.

In the era of the Greek cities in the fifth century B.C. a city was considered an artistic creation which should maintain its static form without change. To take care of population growth, the Greeks sent out colonies, like swarms of bees, to found new cities on the ideal model. Plato said that the ideal city should not contain over 5,000 inhabitants although he himself was the product of an Athens with a 250,000 population. In the Middle Ages most continental European cities were surrounded by walls and many, like Milan, Italy preserved an unaltered form for hundreds of years.

In the United States, however, there has been a tremendous growth of metropolitan areas since

1930. The number of large urban concentrations with a population of a million or more has increased from 10 to 22. The population in the 140 metropolitan districts was 57,602,865 in 1930, of which 40,343,442 were in central cities and 17,259,423 were outside these cities. In 1940 in these 140 metropolitan districts the population was 62,965,773 of which 42,796,170 were in central cities and 20,169,603 were outside these cities.[4] After World War II, in the rapidly growing decade from 1950 to 1960, the population of 216 Standard Metropolitan Areas grew from 91,568,113 to 115,796,265. Most of the growth in the past census decade was in the suburbs, but central city population grew from 52,648,185 to 58,441,995, a gain of only 11 percent, while the population outside the central cities increased from 38,919,928 to 57,354,270, a rise of 47.4 percent.[5] The population in the central areas of 12 of the largest American metropolitan regions actually declined in this decade from 22,694,799 to 21,843,214, a loss of 3.8 percent.[6] The population loss in the central cores of these cities was much greater, since some central cities still had room for new growth within the other edges of their boundaries. There was also a displacement of white population by non-white population. From 1930 to 1950 the non-white population in 168 SMA's increased from 4,913,703 to 8,250,210.[7] The chief gain was in the central cities where the non-white population rose from 3,624,504 in 1930 to 6,411,158 in 1950. From 1950 to 1960 the non-white population in central cities increased to 10,030,314. The non-white population in SMA's outside central cities was only 2,720,513 in 1960. On the other hand while 43,142,399 white persons lived in central cities of SMA's in 1960, 49,081,533 white persons lived in

From *Land Economics*, Vol. XL, No. 2 (May 1964) (© 1964 by the Regents of the University of Wisconsin), pp. 199–212.

SMA's outside the central cities. While the central city population in these 12 SMA's was declining, population outside these central cities rose from 13,076,711 in 1950 to 20,534,833 in 1960, a gain of 57 percent.

In 1960 the population of the areas outside the central cities in these 12 great metropolitan areas almost equalled the population in the central areas and by 1964 the population in the areas outside the central cities has certainly surpassed the number in the central city.

While the cities of 50,000 population and over have been growing at a rapid rate in the past decade, the smaller cities with less than 50,000 population have been increasing in numbers at a slower pace, or from 27.4 million in 1950 to 29.4 million in 1960.[8] The smaller cities thus would be enabled to maintain their static form with the growth element chiefly affecting the larger metropolitan areas as a result of the shift in population growth from the center to the suburbs and a change in the racial composition of many central cities.

Not merely population growth, but a rise in per capita national income from $757 in 1940 to $2,500 in 1963, with a greater proportionate increase in the middle class incomes, an increase in the number of private passenger automobiles from 22,793,000 in 1933 to 70 million in 1963, and the building of expressways connecting cities and belt highways around cities, were all dynamic factors changing the shape and form of cities since the description of city patterns in 1925 and 1939. Let us examine the different concentric circles or zones or sectors described in the books over a quarter of a century ago and see how the principles then enunciated have been changed by the growth factors.

THE CENTRAL BUSINESS DISTRICT: FINANCIAL AND OFFICE ZONE AND THE RETAIL SHOPPING ZONE

In 1929 Burgess wrote: "Zone I: The Central Business District. At the center of the city as the focus of its commercial, social and civic life is situated the Central Business District. The heart of this district is the downtown retail district with its department stores, its smart shops, its office buildings, its clubs, its banks, its hotels, its theatres, its museums, and its headquarters of economic, social, civic and political life."[9]

Burgess thus accurately described the central business district of Chicago and most large American cities as of the date he was writing (1929), a description which would hold true in the main to the end of World War II. Since 1946, extraordinary changes in the American economy have occurred which have had a pronounced effect on the structure of the downtown business districts of American cities.

Burgess had noted in 1929 the existence of local business centers, or satellite "loops" in the zone of better residences: "The typical constellation of business and recreation areas includes a bank, one or more United Cigar Stores, a drug store, a high class restaurant, an automobile display row, and a so-called 'wonder' motion picture theatre."[10] I also had noted, in 1939, the extensions of stringlike commercial developments beyond the central business districts, and the rise of satellite business centers: "Again, satellite business centers have developed independently beyond the central business district, or on the city's periphery. These are usually located at or near suburban railway stations, elevated or subway stations, intersecting points between radial and crosstown street car lines, or intersecting points of main automobile highways."[11]

In 1964, the central retail district, with its large department stores, still remains the largest shopping district in its metropolitan area, and all the outlying business districts at street car intersections, subway or suburban railway stations are still operating, but their dominating position has been greatly weakened by the construction, since 1946, of an estimated 8,300 planned shopping districts, with free automobile parking, in the suburbs or on the periphery of the central city mass. The tremendous growth of the suburban population, which moved to areas beyond mass transit lines, facilitated by the universal ownership of the automobile, and decline in the numbers and relative incomes of the central city population, invited and made possible this new development in retail shopping.

The regional shopping center—with major department stores, variety, apparel and local convenience stores, practically duplicating the stores in the downtown retail area and built on large tracts of land entirely away from street cars, subways, elevated or railroad stations—was virtually unknown prior to World War II. The first of these centers, Country Club Plaza in Kansas City, had been established in 1925 and there were a few others with department stores and a number of neighborhood centers on commercial streets, with parking areas in front of the stores, but the wave of the future was not discerned by planners or land economists before 1946.

There are many types of these new planned centers; the regional center on 50 to 100 acres of land with at least one major department store; the community center on 20 to 30 acres of land with a junior department store as the leading tenant; and the neighborhood center with a supermarket, drug store and local convenience shops on five to 10 acres of land. But the type having the greatest impact on the downtown stores is the regional center which directly competes with downtown in the sale of general merchandise.

General merchandise stores, that is, department and variety stores, had long been the dominating magnets and attractions of the central retail areas. In this field the CBD stores had almost a monopoly in most cities prior to 1920 and even held a dominating position after the establishment of some outlying department stores at street car intersections or subway stations in Chicago and New York. There had been for years neighborhood grocery stores, drug stores and even small apparel and dry goods stores and some variety stores outside the central business district but the department store sales of the CBD's were probably 90 percent or more of the total department store volume of the entire metropolitan area.

In 1958 the central general merchandise stores, chiefly department stores, in the largest cities of a million population and over, had a lower sales volume than the aggregate of the sales of department stores in all the shopping centers outside of the CBD, or $3.6 billion compared to $5.65 billion, as Table 1 shows. There were 125 regional shopping centers in 1958 but many more have been completed since that date and the 1963 United States Retail Census of Shopping Districts will undoubtedly show a still greater increase in the department store sales outside of the CBD.

In 94 metropolitan areas with a population of 100,000 and over and total population of 91,937,103 in 1960, dollar sales outside the CBD's had increased by 53.8 percent, but in the CBD's only 3.4 percent. There was an actual decline in general merchandise sales from 1954 to 1958 in the CBD's of Los Angeles, Chicago, Philadelphia, Detroit, Boston, St. Louis, Washington, D.C., Cleveland, Baltimore, Milwaukee and Kansas City.

These new planned shopping districts, with their ample parking areas, cover more ground than the combined areas of the CBD's in all American cities. I have calculated that there were 30,460 acres or 47.5 square miles in the central business districts of the standard metropolitan areas in the United States in 1960, compared with 33,600 acres or 52.5 square miles in all types of new planned centers.[12] Since 1960, however, many new planned centers have been built and there are now probably 150 regional shopping centers. In 1964 the ground space occupied by these centers, as well as that of the

Table 1. *General Merchandise Sales in CBD's by Metropolitan Area Size Groups*

Metropolitan Area Size	Population	(Thousands of Dollars)				Percent Increase 1954–1958	
		1958		1954		In CBD	Outside CBD
		In CBD	Outside CBD	In CBD	Outside CBD		
1,000,000 and Over	61,582,070	$3,577,169	$5,652,995	$3,522,089	$3,837,350	1.6	47.3
500,000–999,000	17,021,848	1,422,369	1,151,601	1,387,056	618,203	4.0	86.3
250,000–499,000	10,491,540	928,358	513,668	849,474	311,573	9.3	64.9
100,000–249,000	2,841,645	279,452	111,774	263,530	62,817	6.0	77.9
Total	91,937,103	$6,227,348	$7,430,038	$6,022,149	$4,829,943	3.4	53.8

many new discount houses with large parking areas, has considerably increased the space occupied by shopping centers as compared with 1960.

In contrast to the tremendous growth of the planned shopping districts, there has been very limited building of new retail stores in downtown areas; the notable exceptions being Midtown Plaza in Rochester, New York; the redevelopment of the business center of New Haven, Connecticut with new department stores, offices and garages, connected by a new highway to the existing expressway; the location of new Sears Roebuck and Dayton department stores in central St. Paul; and the erection of garages for department stores in other cities.

Office Buildings

Office building expansion, unlike retail stores, bears no direct relation to population growth but depends entirely on the extent to which a city becomes an international or regional office management or financial center. Generalization therefore cannot be made about office buildings which would apply to all cities since the number of square feet of office space per capita in the metropolitan area varies from 2.2 square feet in San Diego to 7.5 square feet in Chicago, 16 square feet in New York and 25 square feet in Midland, Texas.

New York City has become the outstanding headquarters center of the United States, with an estimated 171,300,000 square feet of office space. It has had a tremendous growth since 1946, with 55 million square feet added since World War II. The trend has been uptown, away from downtown Wall Street to Park Avenue, 42nd Street and Third Avenue near Grand Central Station. The world's greatest concentration of office buildings is in the Grand Central and Plaza districts of New York City. From 1947 to 1962 inclusive, there was a total increase of 50,632,000 square feet of rentable office area in Manhattan, of which 33,839,000 square feet, or 66.8 percent, was in the Grand Central and Plaza areas. In the same period, in the lower Manhattan area, or the combined financial, city hall and insurance districts, 10,935,000 square feet or 21.6 percent of the total were constructed. A partial reversal of the uptown trend in Manhattan will result from the proposed

building of the World Trade Center with 10 million square feet of office space, in twin towers 1350 feet high, on the Lower West Side. This development, by the Port of New York Authority, will be started in 1965 and is scheduled for completion by 1970.[13]

In Washington, D.C. there is approximately 16 million square feet of office space. An estimated 11 million square feet have been built since 1946, of which 9 million square feet are in the area west of 15th Street, in the direction of the high grade residential growth.

The location of new office buildings in central city areas has been determined in part by the slum or blighted areas, with old buildings which could be cleared away, such as in the Golden Triangle of Pittsburgh or Penn Center in Philadelphia, or location in air rights over railroad tracks as the Merchandise Mart and Prudential buildings in Chicago, the Pan Am Building and other buildings on Park Avenue in New York and the Prudential Building in Boston. The ability to secure land at a relatively low cost on West Wacker Drive in Chicago caused insurance companies to build there.

Sometimes these new office districts are not at the center of transportation. In Los Angeles new office building has moved away from the central business districts toward the high grade residential areas. From 1948 to 1960 15,500,000 square feet of office floor space was constructed in Los Angeles, of which only 1,500,000 square feet was built in the 400-acre area of the central business district, although 1,000,000 square feet were erected in the southwesterly and western fringe areas of the central business district.[14] This decentralization is in marked contrast to the concentration of offices in New York City.

There has also been a tendency for large office buildings of insurance companies, which conduct a self-sufficient operation not dependent on contact with other agencies, to locate on large tracts of land several miles from the center of the city as the Prudential regional office buildings in Houston and Minneapolis in 1951, and the Connecticut General Insurance Company in Hartford. Office centers are also developing around some of the regional shopping centers, as at Northland in Detroit, Ward Parkway in Kansas City and Lenox Square in Atlanta.

In Houston more than 6 million square feet of new office space has been added to downtown areas in the past three years, the growth proceeding westerly in the direction of the high income areas. While the main office building district of most cities is still within the confines of the central area, the office center is not fixed but is moving in the direction of high income areas, as in New York City, Washington, D.C., Los Angeles and Houston. This conforms to the statement I made in 1939.[15]

A tall office building that looms in the sky as a beacon or landmark has been built in many cities of moderate size by banks, oil companies or insurance companies for the sake of prestige, regardless of cost or rental demand. In many cities of growing population few new office buildings have been erected. Thus, generalizations can no longer be made about office building locations which will apply to all cities in the United States.

Hotels and Motels

There is a concentration of hotels near each other in large cities so that they can accommodate conventions but central hotels have declined in importance because of the new motels and motor hotels (with parking) on the periphery of the central business district or on the outskirts of the city. This rapid growth in both intown motels and those on the periphery is a use not anticipated in 1939.

Apartments in Central Areas

There is a trend to the building of new apartments in or near central business districts, such as the Marina Towers in Chicago, the apartments in redeveloped areas in Southwest Washington, D.C. and as proposed for the Bunker Hill redevelopment in downtown Los Angeles. Hence the statement by Burgess that: "Beyond the workingmen's homes lies the residential district, a zone in which the better grade of apartments and single family residences predominate" must be qualified now, as it was in 1939, when I pointed to the Gold Coast of Chicago and Park Avenue in New York City.[16]

Thus, in view of the shifting of uses in the central business districts, the overall decline in the predominance of central retail areas, the rapid growth of office centers in a few cities compared to a static situation in others, the emergence of redeveloped areas, and intown motels, the former descriptions of patterns in American cities must be revised to conform to the realities of 1964.

THE WHOLESALE AND LIGHT MANUFACTURING ZONE

Burgess described the zone next to the central business district as: "Clinging close to the skirts of the retail district lies the wholesale and light manufacturing zone. Scattered through this zone and surrounding it, old dilapidated buildings form the homes of the lower working classes, hoboes, and disreputable characters. Here the slums are harbored. Cheap second hand stores are numerous, and low prices 'men only' moving picture and burlesque shows flourish."[17] This is a vivid description of West Madison Street and South State Street in Chicago in the 1920's. Since that time the wholesale function has greatly declined and with the direct sale by manufacturers to merchants the 4-million-square-foot Merchandise Mart, across the Chicago River north of the Loop, absorbed most of the functions formerly performed by wholesalers. The intermixture of slums and old dilapidated buildings with light industry is being cleared away in redevelopment projects and the West Side Industrial District in Chicago has been created immediately west of the Loop on cleared land.

Light manufacturing, in the garment industry particularly, still clings close to the retail and financial center in New York City because the garment industry depends on fashion and the entertainment of out-of-town buyers.

Other light manufacturing industries have tended to move away from the center of the city to the suburbs where they can secure ample land areas for one-story plants, storage, and parking for their employees' cars. These new modern plants, in park-like surroundings, which emit no loud noise or offensive odors, are not objectionable even in middle-class residential areas, and workers can avoid city traffic in driving to their place of employment, or they can live nearby.

THE FACTORY OR HEAVY INDUSTRIAL DISTRICT

In 1929 Burgess placed the wholesale district in Zone I, the central business district, and described Zone II as the zone in transition, which included the factory district in its inner belt as follows:

Zone II: The Zone in transition. Surrounding the Central Business District are areas of residential deterioration caused by the encroaching of business and industry from Zone I. This may therefore be called the Zone in Transition, with a factory district for its inner belt and an outer ring of retrogressing neighborhoods, of first-settlement immigrant colonies, of rooming-house districts, of homeless-men areas, of resorts of gambling, bootlegging, sexual vice, and of breeding-places of crime. In this area of physical deterioration and social disorganization our studies show the greatest concentration of cases of poverty, bad housing, juvenile delinquency, family disintegration, physical and mental disease. As families and individuals prosper, they escape from this area in Zone III beyond, leaving behind as marooned a residuum of the defeated, leaderless, and helpless.[18]

In 1939 I pointed out tendencies of heavy industries to move away from close-in locations in the "transition zone."[19] Since that time heavy manufacturing has tended more and more to seek suburban locations or rural areas, as nearly all workers now come in their own automobiles and for the most part live in the suburban areas themselves. Factory location in slum areas is not now desired for the clerks and factory workers no longer live there. All of the reasons I cited in 1939 for industries moving to suburban areas apply with greater force in 1964.

In regard to residential uses, this zone in transition was defined as the slum and blighted area of Chicago in 1943[20] and under the slum clearance and redevelopment laws which enabled federal authorities to acquire by condemnation, properties in blighted areas, it has been extensively cleared and rebuilt with modern apartments, both private and public. The remnants of this area which have not been cleared away still retain the characteristics Burgess described in 1929, and the problems of juvenile delinquency and overcrowding have been accentuated in the last 35 years by the in-migration of low income Negro families to Chicago as well as to other northern cities.

ZONE OF WORKINGMEN'S HOMES

Encircling the zone of transition, now the slum and blighted area, is Zone III, described by Burgess as follows:

Zone III: The Zone of Independent Workingmen's Homes. This third broad urban ring is in Chicago, as well as in other northern industrial cities, largely constituted by neighborhoods of second immigrant settlement. Its residents are those who desire to live near but not too close to their work. In Chicago, it is a housing area neither of tenements, apartments, nor of single dwellings; its boundaries have been roughly determined by the plotting of the two-flat dwelling, generally of frame construction, with the owner living on the lower floor with a tenant on the other.[21]

The buildings in this zone, now 35 years older than when Burgess wrote in 1929, were in general classified in The Master Plan of Residential Land Use of Chicago as "conservation."[22] This area is not yet a slum but next in order of priority to be cleared away. In some blocks older structures can be razed and the newer ones rehabilitated. A large proportion of its former occupants, white families with children of school age, have moved to the suburbs and it is now occupied mainly by single white persons, older white families or by Negro families in all age groups.

In some cases these older close-in residential sections may be rehabilitated and become fashionable, as in the Georgetown area of Washington, D.C., Rittenhouse Square in Philadelphia and the Near North Side of Chicago; and this is an exception to be noted to Burgess' theory.

BETTER RESIDENTIAL AREA

Zone IV: The Zone of Better Residences. Extending beyond the neighborhoods of second immigrant settlements, we come to the Zone of Better Residences in which the great middle-class of native-born Americans live, small business men, professional people, clerks, and salesmen. Once communities of single homes, they are becoming, in Chicago, apartment-house and residential-hotel areas.[23]

This zone was classified in the Master Plan of Residential Land Use of Chicago in 1943 as "stable," indicating that the residences were still of sound construction and had many remaining years of useful life. As the second immigrant settlers, now indistinguishable from the native born population, once moved from Zone III into this area, so now many of the former residents of this area have moved mainly from this area into the new areas near the periphery of the city or into the suburbs. Some of the areas vacated by them are now occupied by the non-white population.

THE COMMUTERS ZONE

Burgess described the commuters zone as follows:

Zone V. The Commuters Zone. Out beyond the areas of better residence is a ring of encircling small cities, towns, and hamlets, which, taken together, constitute the Commuters Zone. These are also, in the main, dormitory suburbs, because the majority of men residing there spend the day at work in the Loop (Central Business District), returning only for the night.[24]

Burgess thus took into account in his fifth zone the existence of suburban towns. However, he refers to them as a "ring" implying that they formed a circular belt around Chicago. However, at the time Burgess wrote in 1929, there was no circle of towns around Chicago but a pattern of settlement along the railroads with six great bands of suburban settlement radiating out from the central mass of Chicago like spokes of a wheel and with large vacant areas in between.[25] Chicago's early growth had taken the form first of starfish extensions of settlement along the principal highways and street car line.[26] By 1929 the vacant areas in the city between these prongs had been filled in with homes so that there were then in fact belts or concentric circles of settled areas within the City of Chicago. At that time, however, the suburban area of Chicago conformed to the axial pattern of growth with the highest income sector located on one of the six radial bands—the North Shore, along Lake Michigan. There were other high income areas in the other bands of growth but no continuous belt of high income areas around Chicago. Since 1929 the vacant areas between these radial extensions of settlement along suburban railroads have been filled in largely with homes of middle income residents. Many of the new planned shopping districts are now located in between these bands of original settlement along railroads, where large vacant tracts could be secured.

Beyond his five zones, Burgess later identified two additional zones lying beyond the built-up area of the city: "The sixth zone is constituted by the agricultural districts lying within the circle of commutation . . . The seventh zone is the hinterland of the metropolis."[27]

Richard M. Hurd, in his classic *Principles of City Land Values*[28] had, as early as 1903 developed the central and axial principles of city growth; yet to many persons, before Burgess formulated his theory many years later, cities appeared to be a chaotic mixture of structures with no law governing their growth. Burgess, with acute powers of observation and without all of the great body of census and planning data that has been made available since he wrote, made a remarkable formulation of principles that were governing American city growth in 1929 and he related these principles to the basic facts of human society. Since 1929, however, not only have the vest detailed city data of the United States censuses been made available for study and analysis, but dynamic changes have occurred in our economy which have had a profound influence on the structure of our cities. Since 1929 over 10 million new houses have been constructed on the suburban fringes of American cities, beyond the old central mass, in areas made available for residential occupancy by the increase in the number of private passenger automobiles in the United States from 8 million in 1920 to 66 million in 1964, and the highways subsequently built to accommodate them.

Apartment buildings, once confined to locations along subways, elevated lines or near suburban railroad stations, are now springing up in the suburbs, far from mass transit. Many families without children of school age desire the convenience of an apartment, involving no work of mowing lawns, painting and repairing, and with the comforts of air conditioning and often a community swimming pool. Complete communities are now being developed in the suburbs, with a mixture of single family homes, town houses and apartments, and with their own churches, schools, shopping centers and light industries, some even with a golf course and bridle paths, of which the 7,000-acre Reston development near the Dulles Airport in the Washington, D.C. area is an outstanding example. Thus the dynamic changes of the past quarter century make it necessary to review concepts developed from studies of American cities in 1925 and 1939.

THE SECTOR THEORY

One concept needs to be examined again—the sector theory of residential development. In 1939 I formulated the sector theory, which was to the effect that the high income areas of cities were in one or more sectors of the city, and not, as Burgess seemed to imply when he said: "beyond the workingmen's homes lies the residential district, a zone in which the better grade of apartment houses and single family residences predominate."

In a study of 64 American cities, block by block, based on the federal government's Work Project Administration's basic surveys of 1934, and studies of a number of large metropolitan areas, I prepared maps showing that high rent areas were located in one or more sectors of the city, and did not form a circle completely around it. Has this changed since 1939? In a survey of the entire Washington, D.C. metropolitan area in 1954 it was found that the main concentration of high-income families was in the District area west of Rock Creek Park, continuing into the Bethesda area of Montgomery County, Maryland. There were other scattered high income clusters in the Washington area. In surveys of other metropolitan areas it was discovered that the main concentration of high income families is on the north side of Dallas, west and southwest sides of Houston, northward along the Lake Shore of Chicago, the south side of Kansas City, in the Beverly Hills area of Los Angeles, on the south side of Tulsa, the north side of Oklahoma City, the west side of Philadelphia, and the southwest side of Minneapolis. In the New York metropolitan area there are a number of nodules of high income in Westchester County, Nassau County, Bergen and Essex Counties in New Jersey, but the predominant movement was northward and eastward.

In a trip to Latin America cities in the summer of 1963 I found that the finest single family homes and apartments in Guatemala City, Bogota, Lima, La Paz, Quito, Santiago, Buenos Aires, Montevideo, Rio de Janeiro, Sao Paulo and Caracas were located on one side of the city only.[29]

The automobile and the resultant belt highways encircling American cities have opened up large regions beyond existing settled areas, and future high grade residential growth will probably not be confined entirely to rigidly defined sectors. As a result of the greater flexibility in urban growth patterns resulting from these radial expressways and belt highways, some higher income communities are being developed beyond low income sectors but these communities usually do not enjoy as high a social rating as new neighborhoods located in the high income sector.

CHANGES IN POPULATION GROWTH IN METROPOLITAN AREAS OUTSIDE THE UNITED STATES

Since the rate of population growth, particularly of the great cities of one million population and over, is a most important element in changing city structure, let us examine these differential rates of growth.[30] There has in fact, been a wide variation in the rate of population growth in the great metropolitan areas throughout the world since 1940. In England, in London and the other large metropolitan areas, the population has remained stationary; on the Continent of Europe outside Russia, the growth rate of the great metropolitan areas has slowed down to 20 percent in the decade from 1950 to 1960. In Russia, eight of the largest older metropolitan areas increased in population only 15 percent from 1939 to 1962 but in this period many entirely new cities were built and other smaller cities grew in size until Russia now has 176 metropolitan areas with a population of 100,000 or more. China has had a great urban surge since 1945 to 1950 and reports a gain of 91 percent in the population of 18 great metropolitan areas as a result of its enforced industrialization process. This was reportedly carried too far and city dwellers had to be ordered back to the farms to raise food. Japan's five largest metropolitan area concentrations increased in numbers by 41 percent from 1951 to 1961. Fast suburban trains carry workers to and from downtown places of employment. In India, Delhi and New Delhi have more than doubled in population from 1951 to 1961 as a result of greatly expanded government and manufacturing activity. Other great Indian cities have grown rapidly, with 300,000 or more sleeping in the streets of Calcutta. In Australia, Sydney and Melbourne increased by 32 percent from 1951 to 1961. In Egypt, Cairo has gained 155 percent in numbers since 1940 as a result of being the chief headquarters of the Arab world. African cities like

Nairobi and Leopoldville have gained rapidly. In Latin America, the urban population has exploded, with eight of its largest metropolitan areas gaining 166 percent from 1940 to 1962. The Sao Paulo metropolitan area, jumping from 1,380,000 to 4,374,000, gained 217 percent. Mexico City shot up from 1,754,000 to 4,666,000, a rise of 166 percent, in the same period of time.

CHANGES IN STRUCTURE OF CITIES OUTSIDE THE UNITED STATES

While there are some similarities in the patterns of urban growth in the United States and foreign cities, as for example, in the sector theory, there are also some marked differences, as a result of the following five factors:

1. Ownership of automobiles. The chief factor in enabling city populations to spread out, to develop vast areas of single family homes on wide lots far from main transit facilities, to develop so many new shopping centers and so many dispersed factories, has been the almost universal ownership of the private automobile. Only the United States, New Zealand, Australia and Canada, which have developed city patterns similar to ours, had a high rate of auto ownership to population in 1955, or from 181 per 1,000 in Canada and 183 in Australia to 339 per 1,000 in the United States.[31] Northern European nations had from 58 to 111 cars per thousand of population but most Asiatic and African nations and most of the South American countries had less than 15 cars per 1,000 population. Argentina and Uruguay had 32 cars per 1,000 population in 1955.

The number of automobiles in northwestern Europe has shown marked gains recently: in West Germany from 1955 to 1963 the rate increased from 58 to 122 per 1,000 persons; in the United Kingdom for the same period the rate increased from 92 to 120 per 1,000 persons; and for the same period in Belgium the rate increased from 60 to 106 per 1,000 persons.

Obviously, in most of the world the urban population must depend upon busses or bicycles and live in apartments which can be economically served by subways, street cars or busses. Hence the great expansion into rural areas can take place only when there are suburban railroads as in Buenos Aires, Rio de Janeiro, Delhi and Tokyo, or subways as in London, Moscow, Tokyo, Madrid, Barcelona and Paris. Poor families live in central areas on steep mountainsides in Rio de Janeiro and Caracas, in shacks built by themselves; they live in blocks of tenements in central Hong Kong; sleep on the streets in downtown Calcutta, and build mud huts in central Nairobi.

2. Private ownership of property. The pattern of American cities is the result of private ownership of property, which cannot be taken by condemnation except for a public use or in a blighted area and for which compensation must be paid when appropriated. There is now almost universal zoning control which regulates types of use, density of use and height of buildings; but these controls, first adopted in New York in 1916, had no effect upon early city growth and they have been modified or changed thousands of times. Otherwise it would not have been possible to develop the 8,300 new shopping centers nearly all of which required zoning in depth rather than strip zoning, nor could thousands of apartment buildings have been constructed in suburban areas.

Consequently, it is impossible to preserve green areas and open spaces without paying for the right. While the public cannot prevent the private owner from building on his land, zoning ordinances in some communities requiring one to five acres of land for each house have practically limited the utilization to occupancy by wealthy families because the high cost of sewer and water lines and street pavements in such low density areas virtually prevents building of houses for middle- or low-income family occupancy. Urban sprawl, or the filling in of all vacant areas, has been the bane of planners who would like to restore the early star-shaped pattern. Where the State owns all of the land, as in Russia, or controls it rigidly, as in Finland, dense apartment clusters can be built along subway lines and the areas in between kept vacant.

3. Central Area Attractions. The central retail areas of foreign cities have not deteriorated as a result of outlying shopping center competition for there are few such centers because very few people own cars. Crowds throng the shops on Florida Street in Buenos Aires and Union Street in Lima, which are closed to automobile traffic in shopping hours. Galerias, an elaborate expansion of the arcade, often extending up to five or six levels, have recently been built in downtown Santiago, Sao Paulo and Rio de Janeiro. Rotterdam has its new central retail area; Cologne its shopping street, a pedestrian thoroughfare. In these foreign cities, residents find the downtown area the chief attraction. The parks of Tokyo, London, Paris, Buenos Aires and Rio de Janeiro are downtown; so are the palaces and government offices, the great cathedrals, the museums, theatres, restaurants and night life of many foreign cities. The Forum and Colosseum in Rome, the Acropolis in Athens, Notre Dame in Paris, Westminster Abbey and the Tower of London are all in or near central areas.[32]

One change is occurring which is altering the skyline of many foreign cities—the advent of the tall office building. Formerly, cities outside the United States prized their uniform skyline broken only by the spire of a great cathedral or an Eiffel Tower. But now tall office buildings loom above London and Milan; they are planned for Paris. Caracas has its 30-story Twin Towers; Rio de Janeiro a new 35-story office building, El Centro; Mexico City its 32-story office building; and Sao Paulo has a great concentration of tall buildings in its downtown area.

4. *Stability of the currency.* The great building boom in the United States has been financed on money borrowed from banks and insurance companies. Despite gradual inflation, most people have confidence in the American dollar. The volume of mortgage credit for building in 1 to 4 family units increased from $17.4 billion in 1940 to $182.4 billion in December 1963. Shopping centers are financed on the basis of guaranteed leases by national chain store tenants which afford sufficient funds to construct the center. In nations like Brazil, however, where the interest rates are 3 to 5 percent a month and the cruzeiro has dropped from 384 to 1300 to the dollar in a year's time, it is impossible to secure long term loans. New buildings can be effected only by paying all cash as the work proceeds. An inflation of any marked extent in the United States would drastically curtail the supply of mortgage funds available for new building.

5. *Redevelopment laws.* The federal government in 1952 was authorized by Congress to pay two-thirds of the difference between the cost of acquiring sites in blighted areas and the resale price for new development. This has made possible the clearing and rebuilding of central areas which could not be done without both the power of condemnation and the write-down of the difference between the acquisition cost and the re-use value.

The principles of city growth and structure, formulated on the basis of experience in cities in the United States prior to 1930, are thus subject to modification not only as a result of dynamic changes in the United States in the last few decades but these principles, originating here, are subject to further revisions when it is sought to apply them to foreign cities.

Notes

1. R. E. Park and E. W. Burgess, *The City* (Chicago: University of Chicago Press, 1925), pp. 47–62.
2. E. W. Burgess, "Urban Areas," in T. V. Smith and L. D. White (eds.), *Chicago: An Experiment in Social Science Research* (Chicago: University of Chicago Press, 1929), pp. 114–123.
3. Homer Hoyt, *The Structure and Growth of Residential Neighborhoods in American Cities* (Washington, D.C.: Federal Housing Administration, 1939).
4. United States Census of Population 1940, Vol. 1, Table 18, p. 61.
5. United States Department of Commerce, Bureau of the Census, *Standard Metropolitan Areas in the United States as Defined October 18, 1963*, Series P-23, No. 10, December 5, 1963. (Newark, New Jersey is included in New York Metropolitan Area.)
6. Baltimore, Boston, Chicago, Cincinnati, Cleveland, Detroit, Minneapolis-St. Paul, New York, Philadelphia, St. Louis, San Francisco-Oakland and Washington. D.C.
7. United States Census of Population, 1930, 1940, 1950.
8. Harold M. Mayer, "Economic Prospects for the Smaller City," *Public Management* (August 1963).
9. Ernest W. Burgess, "Urban Areas," op. cit.
10. Ibid.
11. Hoyt, op. cit., p. 20.
12. Homer Hoyt, "Changing Patterns of Land Values," *Land Economics* (May 1960), p. 115.
13. *The New York Times* (January 19, 1964).
14. *Los Angeles Centropolis 1980, Economic Survey*, Los Angeles Central City Committee and Los

93

Angeles City Planning Department (December 12, 1960), p. 19.

15. Hoyt, *Structure and Growth*, op. cit., p. 108.
16. Ibid., p. 23.
17. Ernest M. Fisher, *Advanced Principles of Real Estate Practice* (New York: The Macmillan Co., 1930), p. 126, citing R. E. Park and E. W. Burgess, *The City*, op. cit., Ch. 11.
18. Burgess, "Urban Areas," op. cit.
19. Hoyt, op. cit., p. 20.
20. Chicago Plan Commission, *Master Plan of Residential Land Use of Chicago*, Homer Hoyt, Director of Research (1943), Fig. 89, p. 68.
21. Burgess, "Urban Areas," op cit.
22. Chicago Plan Commission, op. cit.
23. Burgess, "Urban Areas," op cit.
24. Ibid.
25. Chicago Plan Commission, op. cit., frontispiece, p. 2.
26. Ibid., Fig. 3, p. 22.
27. E. W. Burgess, "The New Community and Its Future," *Annals of the American Academy of Political and Social Science*, 149 (May 1930): 161, 162.
28. Richard M. Hurd, *Principles of City Land Values* (1st edition 1903, republished by *The Record and Guide*, New York, 1924).
29. "The Residential and Retail Patterns of Leading Latin American Cities," *Land Economics* (November 1963).
30. Homer Hoyt, *World Urbanization—Expanding Population in a Shrinking World*, Washington, D.C.: Urban Land Institute Technical Bulletin 43 (April 1962). See also "The Growth of Cities from 1800 to 1960 and Forecasts to Year 2000," *Land Economics* (May 1963), pp. 167–173.
31. Morton Ginsburg, *Atlas of Economic Development* (Chicago: University of Chicago Press, 1961), p. 74.
32. Homer Hoyt, "The Structure and Growth of American Cities Contrasted With the Structure of European and Asiatic Cities," *Urban Land* (Washington, D.C.: Urban Land Institute, September 1959).

4
chapter

contents

urban life styles

Reactions to urbanism have tended to take certain well-defined paths in scholarly circles. One significant viewpoint has centered on the "rural-urban continuum" discussed in the last chapter. In the nineteenth century, one of the first critiques of cities arose out of the German tradition characterized by a sense of totalities or "Gestalten." Writers like Tonnies and Spengler saw in cities evidence of the decline of man's communal nature, his sense of rootedness in the small face-to-face group, and the growth of alienation, unhappiness, social dislocation, and the like. This point of view has always been a part of American social science too and, in fact, has been deeply imbedded in the American consciousness. Thus, it is probably safe to say that Americans are not really an urban people, for their ideal culture—that is, those images to which they respond and which form their fantasies—have always been nonurban. We have gone so far as to create a fictive American past, a Currier-and-Ives sense of the good life on the farm, which has helped us cope with an essentially alien existence: the realities of life in big cities.

The first section of Chapter 4 states two points of view about urban man that are not necessarily contradictory. Stanley Milgram begins by reviewing the "urbanism as alien to man" argument sketched above. He reasons that some link must be established between the conditions of urban life—crowds, secondary relations, speed—and individual reactions; he introduces the concept of "overload" and uses it to analyze urban peoples. The conclusion that is significant for a sociology of urbanism is the fact that norms arise that are geared to promote privacy and to deal with impersonality and distrust. Thus, life in Manhattan is a quite different experience from life in a small town, and the difference is not merely quantitative but qualitative as well.

Joe Feagin's notes on community disorganization approach the problem from an entirely different direction. Noting a general tendency that regards certain segments of the urban community as disorganized, chaotic, or normless—characterizations parallel to Milgram's depiction of impersonality and distrust at the individual level—Feagin sets out to evaluate this view on the basis of evidence from several areas. Research on topics such as migration, community behavior during disasters, collective violence, and life among the urban poor all suggest that community organization prevails, albeit in forms that vary from those of the dominant society in normal times. By treating the question of migration in the broader context of community organization this discussion provides a natural bridge with Chapter 3 and begins to generalize urban processes. Of particular note is Feagin's discussion of the policy implications of the fact of indigenous organization and the problems that are created when policy makers act on the ill-informed stereotype of community disorganization, as in the case of the black family. As we said,

Milgram's and Feagin's views are not necessarily contradictory. At some points they engage one another and at others they depart. It may be useful to think about senses in which they may both be right and, alternatively, points on which either one or the other is right.

The next section, "Alienation: White and Black," concentrates on two urban subpopulations, each of which comprises a significant portion of central cities, and, in the case of whites, suburbs also. The concept of "alienation" has undergone some curious changes of meaning since Marx, but in the sense used here it refers to powerlessness, being trapped in a system that has increasingly less meaning and offers fewer and fewer rewards. The Peter Schrag article deals with the middle "majority" of American urbanites or the "silent majority." These are the people who have been described as loyal supporters of the System, but now we see the other side of their character: frustration with high taxation, with neighborhood instability, with encroachments of the black man. But despite their frustrations and fears, the American Dream seems to be still viable among these white middle-Americans; indeed, their revolt, if one can call it that, is certainly done in the name of many of the values associated with Americanism. As Robert Coles shows us, for the black child growing up in the rotting and rotten ghettos of American cities, belief in that dream is becomingly increasingly impossible. The only recourses exist in fantasy, tough coping behavior, or revolution; and the techniques for success in the demanding (or impossible) environment of the black ghetto cannot function to help the black child get out. It is the impossibility of escape that strikes us most forcibly and makes the tortured sounds of the middle-American seem hollow, even if they are well meant and valid within their frame of reference.

The final section contrasts social organization and ways of life in the city and suburb. In different ways both Gerald Suttles and Herbert Gans call into serious question many of the prevailing myths about urban life. Yet, at the same time these paired descriptions suggest vast differences in the urban world of the slum dweller and suburbanite. Suttles' description of Chicago's West Side prior to urban renewal portrays a community closely organized around ethnicity, territory, and the hard demands of slum life. Gans shows us that the new community suburb of Levittown is not a kind of overconforming cultural wasteland as suburbs are often described. Rather, this is a community of former city dwellers actively seeking what they regard as a better environment. Within close proximity they are good neighbors, engage in civic life, and attend to events in the wider world. If their life styles are more homogeneous than urbanites' it is because they have actively sought them out and not because they are regimented by some vague demands of suburban conformity.

After we have seen these two urban worlds typified, the Hermalin and Farley article gives us a sense of the gulf between them. Their discussion begins with some essential data on trends toward the social, economic, and racial polarization of city and suburb, a problem that underlies the controversy over segregated schools and busing. Interestingly, however, they go on to provide evidence from national opinion surveys suggesting that suburbanites may be more disposed to integrated housing than is commonly believed if we judge only from scattered resistance to busing. Or, perhaps, suburbanites find integration a lesser evil than busing. In any event, the evidence is surprising and suggests possible solutions to this most fundamental of urban problems. The student interested in pursuing the question might turn from here to the article by Rubinowitz in Chapter 7.

This chapter provides a cross-section of the ways of life of several important segments of the urban community. Four themes tie the articles together. First, these studies serve to demythologize the nature of urban life; to dispel stereotypical ideas whether these relate to disorganization within the inner city or hyperconformity in the suburbs. Second, they provide detailed pictures of the world as experienced by different segments of the urban population. Third, they corroborate the fact that however much these communities differ, they are all organized on the basis of particular norms and complex social networks in which individuals are embedded. Finally, and of greatest importance, the selections demonstrate that the principles upon which these communities are organized vary widely from ethnicity, territory, and poverty in the slum to social class, relative affluence, and the enactment of new life styles in the suburb. If we understand these principles, their material foundation and contextual logic, then we may understand the nature of urban social differentiation—the nature of the "parts" and how they fit together.

8

STANLEY MILGRAM

The Experience of Living in Cities

When I first came to New York it seemed like a nightmare. As soon as I got off the train at Grand Central I was caught up in pushing, shoving crowds on 42nd Street. Sometimes people bumped into me without apology; what really frightened me was to see two people literally engaged in combat for possession of a cab. Why were they so rushed? Even drunks on the street were bypassed without a glance. People didn't seem to care about each other at all.

This statement represents a common reaction to a great city, but it does not tell the whole story. Obviously cities have great appeal because of their variety, eventfulness, possibility of choice, and the stimulation of an intense atmosphere that many individuals find a desirable background to their lives. Where face-to-face contacts are important, the city offers unparalleled possibilities. It has been calculated by the Regional Plan Association (1) that in Nassau County, a suburb of New York City, an individual can meet 11,000 others within a ten-minute radius of his office by foot or car. In Newark, a moderate-sized city, he can meet more than 20,000 persons within this radius. But in midtown Manhattan he can meet fully 220,000. So there is an order-of-magnitude increment in the communication possibilities offered by a great city. That is one of the bases of its appeal and, indeed, of its functional necessity. The city provides options that no other social arrangement permits. But there is a negative side also, as we shall see.

Granted that cities are indispensable in complex society, we may still ask what contribution psychology can make to understanding the experience of living in them. What theories are relevant? How can we extend our knowledge of the psychological aspects of life in cities through empirical inquiry? If empirical inquiry is possible, along what lines should it proceed? In short, where do we start in constructing urban theory and in laying out lines of research?

Observation is the indispensable starting point. Any observer in the streets of midtown Manhattan will see (i) large numbers of people, (ii) a high population density, and (iii) heterogeneity of population. These three factors need to be at the root of any sociopsychological theory of city life, for they condition all aspects of our experience in the metropolis. Louis Wirth (2), if not the first to point to these factors, is nonetheless the sociologist who relied most heavily on them in his analysis of the city. Yet, for a psychologist, there is something unsatisfactory about Wirth's theoretical variables. Numbers, density, and heterogeneity are demographic facts but they are not yet psychological facts. They are external to the individual. Psychology needs an idea that links the individual's *experience* to the demographic circumstances of urban life.

Stanley Milgram, "The Experience of Living in Cities," *Science*, vol. 167 (March 13, 1970), pp. 1461–1468. Copyright © 1970 by the American Association for the Advancement of Science. Reprinted by permission.

This article is based on an address of September 2, 1969, to the 77th annual meeting of the American Psychological Association in Washington, D.C.

One link is provided by the concept of overload. This term, drawn from systems analysis, refers to a system's inability to process inputs from the environment because there are too many inputs for the system to cope with, or because successive inputs come so fast that input *A* cannot be processed when input *B* is presented. When overload is present, adaptations occur. The system must set priorities and make choices. *A* may be processed first while *B* is kept in abeyance, or one input may be sacrificed altogether. City life, as we experience it, constitutes a continuous set of encounters with overload, and of resultant adaptations. Overload characteristically deforms daily life on several levels, impinging on role performance, the evolution of social norms, cognitive functioning, and the use of facilities.

The concept has been implicit in several theories of urban experience. In 1903 Georg Simmel (3) pointed out that, since urban dwellers come into contact with vast numbers of people each day, they conserve psychic energy by becoming acquainted with a far smaller proportion of people than their rural counterparts do, and by maintaining more superficial relationships even with these acquaintances. Wirth (2) points specifically to "the superficiality, the anonymity, and the transitory character of urban social relations."

One adaptive response to overload, therefore, is the allocation of less time to each input. A second adaptive mechanism is disregard of low-priority inputs. Principles of selectivity are formulated such that investment of time and energy are reserved for carefully defined inputs (the urbanite disregards the drunk sick on the street as he purposefully navigates through the crowd). Third, boundaries are redrawn in certain social transactions so that the overloaded system can shift the burden to the other party in the exchange; thus, harried New York bus drivers once made change for customers, but now this responsibility has been shifted to the client, who must have the exact fare ready. Fourth, reception is blocked off prior to entrance into a system; city dwellers increasingly use unlisted telephone numbers to prevent individuals from calling them, and a small but growing number resort to keeping the telephone off the hook to prevent incoming calls. More subtly, a city dweller blocks inputs by assuming an unfriendly countenance, which dis-

courages others from initiating contact. Additionally, social screening devices are interposed between the individual and environmental inputs (in a town of 5000 anyone can drop in to chat with the mayor, but in the metropolis organizational screening devices deflect inputs to other destinations). Fifth, the intensity of inputs is diminished by filtering devices, so that only weak and relatively superficial forms of involvement with others are allowed. Sixth, specialized institutions are created to absorb inputs that would otherwise swamp the individual (welfare departments handle the financial needs of a million individuals in New York City, who would otherwise create an army of mendicants continuously importuning the pedestrian). The interposition of institutions between the individual and the social world, a characteristic of all modern society, and most notably of the large metropolis, has its negative side. It deprives the individual of a sense of direct contact and spontaneous integration in the life around him. It simultaneously protects and estranges the individual from his social environment.

Many of these adaptive mechanisms apply not only to individuals but to institutional systems as well, as Meier (4) has so brilliantly shown in connection with the library and the stock exchange.

In sum, the observed behavior of the urbanite in a wide range of situations appears to be determined largely by a variety of adaptations to overload. I now deal with several specific consequences of responses to overload, which make for differences in the tone of city and town.

Social Responsibility

The principal point of interest for a social psychology of the city is that moral and social involvement with individuals is necessarily restricted. This is a direct and necessary function of excess of input over capacity to process. Such restriction of involvement runs a broad spectrum from refusal to become involved in the needs of another person, even when the person desperately needs assistance, through refusal to do favors, to the simple withdrawal of courtesies (such as offering a lady a seat, or saying "sorry" when a pedestrian collision occurs). In any transaction more and more details need to be dropped as the total number of units to be processed increases and assaults an instrument of limited processing capacity.

The ultimate adaptation to an overloaded social environment is to totally disregard the needs, interests, and demands of those whom one does not define as relevant to the satisfaction of personal needs, and to develop highly efficient perceptual means of determining whether an individual falls into the category of friend or stranger. The disparity in the treatment of friends and strangers ought to be greater in cities than in towns; the time allotment and willingness to become involved with those who have no personal claim on one's time is likely to be less in cities than in towns.

Bystander intervention in crises. The most striking deficiencies in social responsibility in cities occur in crisis situations, such as the Genovese murder in Queens. In 1964, Catherine Genovese, coming home from a night job in the early hours of an April morning, was stabbed repeatedly, over an extended period of time. Thirty-eight residents of a respectable New York City neighborhood admit to having witnessed at least a part of the attack, but none went to her aid or called the police until after she was dead. Milgram and Hollander, writing in *The Nation* (5), analyzed the event in these terms.

Urban friendships and associations are not primarily formed on the basis of physical proximity. A person with numerous close friends in different parts of the city may not know the occupant of an adjacent apartment. This does not mean that a city dweller has fewer friends than does a villager, or knows fewer persons who will come to his aid; however, it does mean that his allies are not constantly at hand. Miss Genovese required immediate aid from those physically present. There is no evidence that the city had deprived Miss Genovese of human associations, but the friends who might have rushed to her side were miles from the scene of her tragedy.

Further, it is known that her cries for help were not directed to a specific person; they were general. But only individuals can act, and as the cries were not specifically directed, no particular person felt a special responsibility. The crime and the failure of community response seem absurd to us. At the time, it may well have seemed equally absurd to the Kew Gardens residents that not one of the neighbors would have called the police. A collective paralysis may have developed from the belief of each of the witnesses that someone else must surely have taken that obvious step.

Latané and Darley (6) have reported laboratory approaches to the study of bystander intervention and have established experimentally the following principle: the larger the number of bystanders, the less the likelihood that any one of them will intervene in an emergency. Gaertner and Bickman (7) of The City University of New York have extended the bystander studies to an examination of help across ethnic lines. Blacks and whites, with clearly identifiable accents, called strangers (through what the caller represented as an error in telephone dialing), gave them a plausible story of being stranded on an outlying highway without more dimes, and asked the stranger to call a garage. The experimenters found that the white callers had a significantly better chance of obtaining assistance than the black callers. This suggests that ethnic allegiance may well be another means of coping with overload: the city dweller can reduce excessive demands and screen out urban heterogeneity by responding along ethnic lines; overload is made more manageable by limiting the "span of sympathy."

In any quantitative characterization of the social texture of city life, a necessary first step is the application of such experimental methods as these to field situations in large cities and small towns. Theorists argue that the indifference shown in the Genovese case would not be found in a small town, but in the absence of solid experimental evidence the question remains an open one.

More than just callousness prevents bystanders from participating in altercations between people. A rule of urban life is respect for other people's emotional and social privacy, perhaps because physical privacy is so hard to achieve. And in situations for which the standards are heterogeneous, it is much harder to know whether taking an active role is unwarranted meddling or an appropriate response to a critical situation. If a husband and wife are quarreling in public, at what point should a bystander step in? On the one hand, the heterogeneity of the city produces substantially greater tolerance about behavior, dress, and codes of ethics than is generally found in the small town, but this diversity also encourages people to withhold aid for fear of antagonizing the participants or crossing an inappropriate and difficult-to-define line.

Moreover, the frequency of demands present in the city gives rise to norms of noninvolvement. There are practical limitations to the Samaritan impulse in a major city. If a citizen attended to every needy person, if he were sensitive to and acted on every altruistic impulse that was evoked in the city, he could scarcely keep his own affairs in order.

Willingness to trust and assist strangers. We now move away from crisis situations to less urgent examples of social responsibility. For it is not only in situations of dramatic need but in the ordinary, everyday willingness to lend a hand that the city dweller is said to be deficient relative to his small-town cousin. The comparative method must be used in any empirical examination of this question. A commonplace social situation is staged in an urban setting and in a small town—a situation to which a subject can respond by either extending help or withholding it. The responses in town and city are compared.

One factor in the purported unwillingness of urbanites to be helpful to strangers may well be their heightened sense of physical (and emotional) vulnerability—a feeling that is supported by urban crime statistics. A key test for distinguishing between city and town behavior, therefore, is determining how city dwellers compare with town dwellers in offering aid that increases their personal vulnerability and requires some trust of strangers. Altman, Levine, Nadien, and Villena (8) of The City University of New York devised a study to compare the behaviors of city and town dwellers in this respect. The criterion used in this study was the willingness of householders to allow strangers to enter their home to use the telephone. The student investigators individually rang doorbells, explained that they had misplaced the address of a friend nearby, and asked to use the phone. The investigators (two males and two females) made 100 requests for entry into homes in the city and 60 requests in the small towns. The results for middle-income housing developments in Manhattan were compared with data for several small towns (Stony Point, Spring Valley, Ramapo, Nyack, New City, and West Clarkstown) in

Table 1. *Percentage of entries achieved by investigators for city and town dwellings (see text).*

	Entries achieved (%)	
Experimenter	City*	Small town†
Male		
No. 1	16	40
No. 2	12	60
Female		
No. 3	40	87
No. 4	40	100

* Number of requests for entry, 100.
† Number of requests for entry, 60.

Rockland County, outside of New York City. As Table 1 shows, in all cases there was a sharp increase in the proportion of entries achieved by an experimenter when he moved from the city to a small town. In the most extreme case the experimenter was five times as likely to gain admission to homes in a small town as to homes in Manhattan. Although the female experimenters had notably greater success both in cities and towns than the male experimenters had, each of the four students did at least twice as well in towns as in cities. This suggests that the city-town distinction overrides even the predictably greater fear of male strangers than of female ones.

The lower level of helpfulness by city dwellers seems due in part to recognition of the dangers of living in Manhattan, rather than to mere indifference or coldness. It is significant that 75 percent of all the city respondents received and answered messages by shouting through closed doors and by peering out through peepholes; in the towns, by contrast, about 75 percent of the respondents opened the door.

Supporting the experimenters' quantitative results was their general observation that the town dwellers were noticeably more friendly and less suspicious than the city dwellers. In seeking to explain the reasons for the greater sense of psychological vulnerability city dwellers feel, above and beyond the differences in crime statistics, Villena (8) points out that, if a crime is committed in a village, a resident of a neighboring village may not perceive the crime as personally relevant, though the geographic distance may be small, whereas a criminal act committed anywhere in the city, though miles from the city-dweller's home, is still verbally located within the city; thus, Villena says, "the inhabitant of the city possesses a larger vulnerable space."

Civilities. Even at the most superficial level of involvement—the exercise of everyday civilities —urbanites are reputedly deficient. People bump into each other and often do not apologize. They knock over another person's packages and, as often as not, proceed on their way with a grumpy exclamation instead of an offer of assistance. Such behavior, which many visitors to great cities find distasteful, is less common, we are told, in smaller communities, where traditional courtesies are more likely to be observed.

In some instances it is not simply that, in the city, traditional courtesies are violated; rather, the cities develop new norms of noninvolvement. These are so well defined and so deeply a part of city life that *they* constitute the norms people are reluctant to violate. Men are actually embarrassed to give up a seat on the subway to an old woman; they mumble "I was getting off anyway," instead of making the gesture in a straightforward and gracious way. These norms develop because everyone realizes that, in situations of high population density, people cannot implicate themselves in each other's affairs, for to do so would create conditions of continual distraction which would frustrate purposeful action.

In discussing the effects of overload I do not imply that every instant the city dweller is bombarded with an unmanageable number of inputs, and that his responses are determined by the excess of input at any given instant. Rather, adaptation occurs in the form of gradual evolution of norms of behavior. Norms are evolved in response to frequent discrete experiences of overload; they persist and become generalized modes of responding.

Overload on cognitive capacities: anonymity. That we respond differently toward those whom we know and those who are strangers to us is a truism. An eager patron aggressively cuts in front of someone in a long movie line to save time only to confront a friend; he then behaves sheepishly. A man is involved in an automobile

accident caused by another driver, emerges from his car shouting in rage, then moderates his behavior on discovering a friend driving the other car. The city dweller, when walking through the midtown streets, is in a state of continual anonymity vis-à-vis the other pedestrians.

Anonymity is part of a continuous spectrum ranging from total anonymity to full acquaintance, and it may well be that measurement of the precise degrees of anonymity in cities and towns would help to explain important distinctions between the quality of life in each. Conditions of full acquaintance, for example, offer security and familiarity, but they may also be stifling, because the individual is caught in a web of established relationships. Conditions of complete anonymity, by contrast, provide freedom from routinized social ties, but they may also create feelings of alienation and detachment.

Empirically one could investigate the proportion of activities in which the city dweller or the town dweller is known by others at given times in his daily life, and the proportion of activities in the course of which he interacts with individuals who know him. At his job, for instance, the city dweller may be known to as many people as his rural counterpart. However, when he is not fulfilling his occupational role—say, when merely traveling about the city—the urbanite is doubtless more anonymous than his rural counterpart.

Limited empirical work on anonymity has begun. Zimbardo (9) has tested whether the social anonymity and impersonality of the big city encourage greater vandalism than do small towns. Zimbardo arranged for one automobile to be left for 64 hours near the Bronx campus of New York University and for a counterpart to be left for the same number of hours near Stanford University in Palo Alto. The license plates on the two cars were removed and the hoods were opened, to provide "releaser clues" for potential vandals. The New York car was stripped of all movable parts within the first 24 hours, and by the end of 3 days was only a hunk of metal rubble. Unexpectedly, however, most of the destruction occurred during daylight hours, usually under the scrutiny of observers, and the leaders in the vandalism were well-dressed, white adults. The Palo Alto car was left untouched.

Zimbardo attributes the difference in the treatment accorded the two cars to the "acquired feelings of social anonymity provided by life in a city like New York," and he supports his conclusions with several other anecdotes illustrating casual, wanton vandalism in the city. In any comparative study of the effects of anonymity in city and town, however, there must be satisfactory control for other confounding factors: the large number of drug addicts in a city like New York; the high proportion of slum-dwellers in the city; and so on.

Another direction for empirical study is investigation of the beneficial effects of anonymity. The impersonality of city life breeds its own tolerance for the private lives of the inhabitants. Individuality and even eccentricity, we may assume, can flourish more readily in the metropolis than in the small town. Stigmatized persons may find it easier to lead comfortable lives in the city, free of the constant scrutiny of neighbors. To what degree can this assumed difference between city and town be shown empirically? Judith Waters (10), at The City University of New York, hypothesized that avowed homosexuals would be more likely to be accepted as tenants in a large city than in small towns, and she dispatched letters from homosexuals and from [other] individuals to real estate agents in cities and towns across the country. The results of her study were inconclusive. But the general idea of examining the protective benefits of city life to the stigmatized ought to be pursued.

Role behavior in cities and towns. Another product of urban overload is the adjustment in roles made by urbanites in daily interactions. As Wirth has said (2): "Urbanites meet one another in highly segmental roles. . . . They are less dependent upon particular persons, and their dependence upon others is confined to a highly fractionalized aspect of the other's round of activity." This tendency is particularly noticeable in transactions between customers and individuals offering professional or sales services. The owner of a country store has time to become well acquainted with his dozen-or-so daily customers, but the girl at the checkout counter of a busy A&P, serving hundreds of customers a day, barely has time to toss the green stamps into one customer's shopping bag before the next

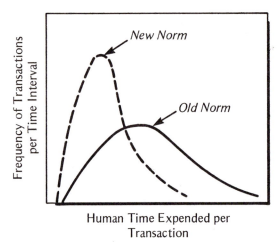

Figure 1. *Changes in the demand for time for a given task when the overall transaction frequency increases in a social system. [Reprinted with permission from R. L. Meier,* A Communications Theory of Urban Growth, *1962. Copyrighted by M.I.T. Press, 1962]*

customer confronts her with his pile of groceries.

Meier, in his stimulating analysis of the city (4), discusses several adaptations a system may make when confronted by inputs that exceed its capacity to process them. Meier argues that, according to the principle of competition for scarce resources, the scope and time of the transaction shrink as customer volume and daily turnover rise. This, in fact, is what is meant by the "brusque" quality of city life. New standards have developed in cities concerning what levels of services are appropriate in business transactions (see Figure 1).

McKenna and Morgenthau (11), in a seminar at The City University of New York, devised a study (i) to compare the willingness of city dwellers and smalltown dwellers to do favors for strangers that entailed expenditure of a small amount of time and slight inconvenience but no personal vulnerability, and (ii) to determine whether the more compartmentalized, transitory relationships of the city would make urban salesgirls less likely than small-town salesgirls to carry out, for strangers, tasks not related to their customary roles.

To test for differences between city dwellers and small-town dwellers, a simple experiment was devised in which persons from both settings were asked (by telephone) to perform increasingly onerous favors for anonymous strangers.

Within the cities (Chicago, New York, and Philadelphia), half the calls were to housewives and the other half to salesgirls in women's apparel shops; the division was the same for the 37 small towns of the study, which were in the same states as the cities. Each experimenter represented herself as a long-distance caller who had, through error, been connected with the respondent by the operator. The experimenter began by asking for simple information about the weather for purposes of travel. Next the experimenter excused herself on some pretext (asking the respondent to "please hold on"), put the phone down for almost a full minute, and then picked it up again and asked the respondent to provide the phone number of a hotel or motel in her vicinity at which the experimenter might stay during a forthcoming visit. Scores were assigned the subjects on the basis of how helpful they had been. McKenna summarizes her results in this manner:

> People in the city, whether they are engaged in a specific job or not, are less helpful and informative than people in small towns; ... People at home, regardless of where they live, are less helpful and informative than people working in shops.

However, the absolute level of cooperativeness for urban subjects was found to be quite high, and does not accord with the stereotype of the urbanite as aloof, self-centered, and unwilling to help strangers. The quantitative differences obtained by McKenna and Morgenthau are less great than one might have expected. This again points up the need for extensive empirical research in rural-urban differences, research that goes far beyond that provided in the few illustrative pilot studies presented here. At this point we have very limited objective evidence on differences in the quality of social encounters in city and small town.

But the research needs to be guided by unifying theoretical concepts. As I have tried to demonstrate, the concept of overload helps to explain a wide variety of contrasts between city behavior and town behavior: (i) the differences in role enactment (the tendency of urban dwellers to deal with one another in highly segmented, functional terms, and of urban sales personnel to devote limited time and attention to their customers): (ii) the evolution of urban norms quite different from traditional town values (such as the acceptance of noninvolvement, impersonality, and aloofness in urban life); (iii) the adaptation of the urban dweller's cognitive processes (his inability to identify most of the people he sees daily, his screening of sensory stimuli, his development of blasé attitudes toward deviant or bizarre behavior, and his selectivity in responding to human demands); and (iv) the competition for scarce facilities in the city (the subway rush; the fight for taxis; traffic jams; standing in line to await services). I suggest that contrasts between city and rural behavior probably reflect the responses of similar people to very different situations, rather than intrinsic differences in the personalities of rural and city dwellers. The city is a situation to which individuals respond adaptively.

Further Aspects of Urban Experience

Some features of urban experience do not fit neatly into the system of analysis presented thus far. They are no less important for that reason. The issues raised next are difficult to treat in quantitative fashion. Yet I prefer discussing them in a loose way to excluding them because appropriate language and data have not yet been developed. My aim is to suggest how phenomena such as "urban atmosphere" can be pinned down through techniques of measurement.

The "atmosphere" of great cities. The contrast in the behavior of city and town dwellers has been a natural starting point for urban social scientists. But even among great cities there are marked differences in "atmosphere." The tone, pacing, and texture of social encounters are different in London and New York, and many persons willingly make financial sacrifices for the privilege of living within a specific urban atmosphere which they find pleasing or stimulating. A second perspective in the study of cities, therefore, is to define exactly what is meant by the atmosphere of a city and to pinpoint the factors that give rise to it. It may seem that urban atmosphere is too evanescent a quality to be reduced to a set of measurable variables, but I do not believe the matter can be judged before substantial effort has been made in this direction. It is obvious that any such approach must be comparative. It makes no sense at all to say that New York is "vibrant" and "frenetic" unless one has some specific city in mind as a basis of comparison.

In an undergraduate tutorial that I conducted at Harvard University some years ago, New York, London, and Paris were selected as reference points for attempts to measure urban atmosphere. We began with a simple question: Does any consensus exist about the qualities that typify given cities? To answer this question one could undertake a content analysis of travel-book, literary, and journalistic accounts of cities. A second approach, which we adopted, is to ask people to characterize (with descriptive terms and accounts of typical experiences) cities they have lived in or visited. In advertisements placed in the *New York Times* and the *Harvard Crimson* we asked people to give us accounts of specific incidents in London, Paris, or New York that best illuminated the character of that particular city. Questionnaires were then developed, and administered to persons who were familiar with at least two of the three cities.

Some distinctive patterns emerged (12). The distinguishing themes concerning New York, for example, dealt with its diversity, its great size, its pace and level of activity, its cultural and entertainment opportunities, and the heterogeneity and segmentation ("ghettoization") of its population. New York elicited more descriptions in terms of physical qualities, pace, and emotional impact than Paris or London did, a fact which suggests that these are particularly important aspects of New York's ambiance.

A contrasting profile emerges for London; in this case respondents placed far greater emphasis on their interactions with the inhabitants than on physical surroundings. There was near unanimity on certain themes: those dealing with the tolerance and courtesy of London's inhabitants. One respondent said:

When I was 12, my grandfather took me to the British Museum . . . one day by tube and recited the *Aeneid* in Latin for my benefit. . . .

He is rather deaf, speaks very loudly and it embarrassed the hell out of me, until I realized that nobody was paying any attention. Londoners are extremely worldly and tolerant.

In contrast, respondents who described New Yorkers as aloof, cold, and rude referred to such incidents as the following:

I saw a boy of 19 passing out anti-war leaflets to passersby. When he stopped at a corner, a man dressed in a business suit walked by him at a brisk pace, hit the boy's arm, and scattered the leaflets all over the street. The man kept walking at the same pace down the block.

We need to obtain many more such descriptions of incidents, using careful methods of sampling. By the application of factor-analytic techniques, relevant dimensions for each city can be discerned.

The responses for Paris were about equally divided between responses concerning its inhabitants and those regarding its physical and sensory attributes. Cafes and parks were often mentioned as contributing to the sense that Paris is a city of amenities, but many respondents complained that Parisians were inhospitable, nasty, and cold.

We cannot be certain, of course, to what degree these statements reflect actual characteristics of the cities in question and to what degree they simply tap the respondents' knowledge of widely held preconceptions. Indeed, one may point to three factors, apart from the actual atmospheres of the cities, that determine the subjects' responses.

1. A person's impression of a given city depends on his implicit standard of comparison. A New Yorker who visits Paris may well describe that city as "leisurely," whereas a compatriot from Richmond, Virginia, may consider Paris too "hectic." Obtaining reciprocal judgment, in which New Yorkers judge Londoners, and Londoners judge New Yorkers, seems a useful way to take into account not only the city being judged but also the home city that serves as the visitor's base line.

2. Perceptions of a city are also affected by whether the observer is a tourist, a newcomer, or a longer-term resident. First, a tourist will be exposed to features of the city different from those familiar to a long-time resident. Sec-

ond, a prerequisite for adapting to continuing life in a given city seems to be the filtering out of many observations about the city that the newcomer or tourist finds particularly arresting; this selective process seems to be part of the long-term resident's mechanism for coping with overload. In the interest of psychic economy, the resident simply learns to tune out many aspects of daily life. One method for studying the specific impact of adaptation on perception of the city is to ask several pairs of newcomers and old-timers (one newcomer and one old-timer to a pair) to walk down certain city blocks and then report separately what each has observed.

Additionally, many persons have noted that when travelers return to New York from an extended sojourn abroad they often feel themselves confronted with "brutal ugliness" (13) and a distinctive, frenetic atmosphere whose contributing details are, for a few hours or days, remarkably sharp and clear. This period of fresh perception should receive special attention in the study of city atmosphere. For, in a few days, details which are initially arresting become less easy to specify. They are assimilated into an increasingly familiar background atmosphere which, though important in setting the tone of things, is difficult to analyze. There is no better point at which to begin the study of city atmosphere than at the moment when a traveler returns from abroad.

3. The popular myths and expectations each visitor brings to the city will also affect the way in which he perceives it (see 14). Sometimes a person's preconceptions about a city are relatively accurate distillations of its character, but preconceptions may also reinforce myths by filtering the visitor's perceptions to conform with his expectations. Preconceptions affect not only a person's perceptions of a city but what he reports about it.

The influence of a person's urban base line on his perceptions of a given city, the differences between the observations of the long-time inhabitant and those of the newcomer, and the filtering effect of personal expectations and stereotypes raise serious questions about the validity of travelers' reports. Moreover, no social psychologist wants to rely exclusively on verbal accounts if he is attempting to obtain an accurate and objective description of the cities' social texture, pace, and general atmosphere. What he needs to do is to devise means of embedding objective experimental measures in the daily flux of city life, measures that can accurately index the qualities of a given urban atmosphere.

Experimental Comparisons of Behavior

Roy Feldman (15) incorporated these principles in a comparative study of behavior toward compatriots and foreigners in Paris, Athens, and Boston. Feldman wanted to see (i) whether absolute levels and patterns of helpfulness varied significantly from city to city, and (ii) whether inhabitants in each city tended to treat compatriots differently from foreigners. He examined five concrete behavioral episodes, each carried out by a team of native experimenters and a team of American experimenters in the three cities. The episodes involved (i) asking natives of the city for street directions; (ii) asking natives to mail a letter for the experimenter; (iii) asking natives if they had just dropped a dollar bill (or the Greek or French equivalent) when the money actually belonged to the experimenter himself, (iv) deliberately overpaying for goods in a store to see if the cashier would correct the mistake and return the excess money; and (v) determining whether taxicab drivers overcharged strangers and whether they took the most direct route available.

Feldman's results suggest some interesting contrasts in the profiles of the three cities. In Paris, for instance, certain stereotypes were borne out. Parisian cab drivers overcharged foreigners significantly more often than they overcharged compatriots. But other aspects of the Parisians' behavior were not in accord with American preconceptions: in mailing a letter for a stranger, Parisians treated foreigners significantly better than Athenians or Bostonians did, and, when asked to mail letters that were already stamped, Parisians actually treated foreigners better than they treated compatriots. Similarly, Parisians were significantly more honest than Athenians or Bostonians in resisting the temptation to claim money that was not theirs, and Parisians were the only citizens who were more honest with foreigners than with compatriots in this experiment.

Feldman's studies not only begin to quantify some of the variables that give a city its distinctive texture but they also provide a methodological model for other comparative research. His most important contribution is his successful application of objective, experimental measures to everyday situations, a mode of study which provides conclusions about urban life that are more pertinent than those achieved through laboratory experiments.

Tempo and Pace

Another important component of a city's atmosphere is its tempo or pace, an attribute frequently remarked on but less often studied. Does a city have a frenetic, hectic quality, or is it easygoing and leisurely? In any empirical treatment of this question, it is best to start in a very simple way. Walking speeds of pedestrians in different cities and in cities and towns should be measured and compared. William Berkowitz (16) of Lafayette College has undertaken an extensive series of studies of walking speeds in Philadelphia, New York, and Boston, as well as in small and moderate-sized towns. Berkowitz writes that "there does appear to be a significant linear relation between walking speed and size of municipality, but the absolute size of the difference varies by less than ten percent."

Perhaps the feeling of rapid tempo is due not so much to absolute pedestrian speeds as to the constant need to dodge others in a large city to avoid collisions with other pedestrians. (One basis for computing the adjustments needed to avoid collisions is to hypothesize a set of mechanical manikins sent walking along a city street and to calculate the number of collisions when no adjustments are made. Clearly, the higher the density of manikins the greater the number of collisions per unit of time, or, conversely, the greater the frequency of adjustments needed in higher population densities to avoid collisions.)

Patterns of automobile traffic contribute to a city's tempo. Driving an automobile provides a direct means of translating feelings about tempo into measurable acceleration, and a city's pace should be particularly evident in vehicular velocities, patterns of acceleration, and latency of response to traffic signals. The inexorable tempo of New York is expressed, further, in the manner in which pedestrians stand at busy intersections, impatiently awaiting a change in traffic light, making tentative excursions into the intersection, and frequently surging into the street even before the green light appears.

Visual Components

Hall has remarked (17) that the physical layout of the city also affects its atmosphere. A grid-iron pattern of streets gives the visitor a feeling of rationality, orderliness, and predictability but is sometimes monotonous. Winding lanes or streets branching off at strange angles, with many forks (as in Paris or Greenwich Village), create feelings of surprise and esthetic pleasure, while forcing greater decision-making in plotting one's course. Some would argue that the visual component is all-important—that the "look" of Paris or New York can almost be equated with its atmosphere. To investigate this hypothesis, we might conduct studies in which only blind, or at least blindfolded, respondents were used. We would no doubt discover that each city has a distinctive texture even when the visual component is eliminated.

Sources of Ambiance

Thus far we have tried to pinpoint and measure some of the factors that contribute to the distinctive atmosphere of a great city. But we may also ask, Why do differences in urban atmosphere exist? How did they come about, and are they in any way related to the factors of density, large numbers, and heterogeneity discussed above?

First, there is the obvious factor that, even among great cities, populations and densities differ. The metropolitan areas of New York, London, and Paris, for example, contain 15 million, 12 million, and 8 million persons, respectively. London has average densities of 43 persons per acre, while Paris is more congested, with average densities of 114 persons per acre (18). Whatever characteristics are specifically attributable to density are more likely to be pronounced in Paris than in London.

A second factor affecting the atmosphere of cities is the source from which the populations are drawn (19). It is a characteristic of great cities that they do not reproduce their own populations, but that their numbers are constantly maintained and augmented by the influx of residents from other parts of the country. This can have a determining effect on the city's atmosphere. For example, Oslo is a city in which almost all of the residents are only one or two generations removed from a purely rural existence, and this contributes to its almost agricultural norms.

A third source of atmosphere is the general national culture. Paris combines adaptations to the demography of cities and certain values specific to French culture. New York is an admixture of American values and values that arise as a result of extraordinarily high density and large population.

Finally, one could speculate that the atmosphere of a great city is traceable to the specific historical conditions under which adaptations to urban overload occurred. For example, a city which acquired its mass and density during a period of commercial expansion will respond to new demographic conditions by adaptations designed to serve purely commercial needs. Thus, Chicago, which grew and became a great city under a purely commercial stimulus, adapted in a manner that emphasizes business needs. European capitals, on the other hand, incorporate many of the adaptations which were appropriate to the period of their increasing numbers and density. Because aristocratic values were prevalent at the time of the growth of these cities, the mechanisms developed for coping with overload were based on considerations other than pure efficiency. Thus, the manners, norms, and facilities of Paris and Vienna continue to reflect esthetic values and the idealization of leisure.

Cognitive Maps of Cities

When we speak of "behavioral comparisons" among cities, we must specify which parts of the city are most relevant for sampling purposes. In a sampling of "New Yorkers," should we include residents of Bay Ridge or Flatbush as well as inhabitants of Manhattan? And, if so, how should we weight our sample distribution? One approach to defining relevant boundaries in sampling is to determine which areas form the psychological or cognitive core of the city. We weight our samples most heavily in the areas considered by most people to represent the "essence" of the city.

The psychologist is less interested in the geographical layout of a city or in its political boundaries than in the cognitive representation of the city. Hans Blumenfeld (20) points out that the perceptual structure of a modern city can be expressed by the "silhouette" of the group of skyscrapers at its center and of smaller groups of office building at its "subcenters" but that urban areas can no longer, because of their vast extent, be experienced as fully articulated sets of streets, squares, and space.

In *The Image of the City* (21), Kevin Lynch created a cognitive map of Boston by interviewing Bostonians. Perhaps his most significant finding was that, while certain landmarks, such as Paul Revere's house and the Boston Common, as well as the paths linking them, are known to almost all Bostonians, vast areas of the city are simply unknown to its inhabitants.

Using Lynch's technique, Donald Hooper (22) created a psychological map of New York from the answers to the study questionnaire on Paris, London, and New York. Hooper's results were similar to those of Lynch: New York appears to have a dense core of well-known landmarks in midtown Manhattan, surrounded by the vast unknown reaches of Queens, Brooklyn, and the Bronx. Times Square, Rockefeller Center, and the Fifth Avenue department stores alone comprise half the places specifically cited by respondents as the haunts in which they spent most of their time. However, outside the midtown area, only scattered landmarks were recognized. Another interesting pattern is evident: even the best-known symbols of New York are relatively self-contained, and the pathways joining them appear to be insignificant on the map.

The psychological map can be used for more than just sampling techniques. Lynch (21) argues, for instance, that a good city is highly "imageable," having many known symbols joined by widely known pathways, whereas dull cities are gray and nondescript. We might test the relative "imagibility" of several cities by determining the proportion of residents who recognize sampled geographic points and their accompanying pathways.

If we wanted to be even more precise we could construct a cognitive map that would not only show the symbols of the city but would measure the precise degree of cognitive significance of any given point in the city relative to

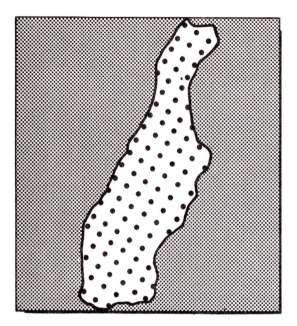

Figure 2. *To create a psychological map of Manhattan, geographic points are sampled, and, from photographs, the subjects attempt to identify the location of each point. To each point a numerical index is assigned indicating the proportion of persons able to identify its location.*

comes to see himself as functioning in a larger urban field. But the process of ghettoization, to which the black teen-ager is subjected, may well hamper the expansion of his sense of the city. These are speculative notions, but they are readily subject to precise test.

Conclusion

I have tried to indicate some organizing theory that starts with the basic facts of city life: large numbers, density, and heterogeneity. These are external to the individual. He experiences these factors as overloads at the level of roles, norms, cognitive functions, and facilities. These overloads lead to adaptive mechanisms which create the distinctive tone and behaviors of city life. These notions, of course, need to be examined by objective comparative studies of cities and towns.

A second perspective concerns the differing atmospheres of great cities, such as Paris, London, and New York. Each has a distinctive flavor, offering a differentiable quality of experience. More precise knowledge of urban atmosphere seems attainable through application of the tools of experimental inquiry.

any other. By applying a pattern of points to a map of New York City, for example, and taking photographs from each point, we could determine what proportion of a sample of the city's inhabitants could identify the locale specified by each point (see Figure 2). We might even take the subjects blindfolded to a point represented on the map, then remove the blindfold and ask them to identify their location from the view around them.

One might also use psychological maps to gain insight into the differing perceptions of a given city that are held by members of its cultural subgroups, and into the manner in which their perceptions may change. In the earlier stages of life, whites and Negroes alike probably have only a limited view of the city, centering on the immediate neighborhood in which they are raised. In adolescence, however, the field of knowledge of the white teen-ager probably undergoes rapid enlargement; he learns of opportunities in midtown and outlying sections and

References and Notes

1. *New York Times* (15 June 1969).
2. L. Wirth, *Amer. J. Soc.* 44, 1 (1938). Wirth's ideas have come under heavy criticism by contemporary city planners, who point out that the city is broken down into neighborhoods, which fulfill many of the functions of small towns. See, for example, H. J. Gans, *People and Plans: Essays on Urban Problems and Solutions* (Basic Books, New York, 1968); J. Jacobs, *The Death and Life of Great American Cities* (Random House, New York, 1961); G. D. Suttles, *The Social Order of the Slum* (Univ. of Chicago Press, Chicago, 1968).
3. G. Simmel, *The Sociology of Georg Simmel*, K. H. Wolff, Ed. (Macmillan, New York, 1950) [English translation of G. Simmel, *Die Grosstadte und das Geistesleben Die Grosstadt* (Jansch, Dresden, 1903)].
4. R. L. Meier, *A Communications Theory of Urban Growth* (M.I.T. Press, Cambridge, Mass., 1962).
5. S. Milgram and P. Hollander, *Nation* 25, 602 (1964).

6. B. Latané and J. Darley, *Amer. Sci.* 57, 244 (1969).
7. S. Gaertner and L. Bickman (Graduate Center, The City University of New York), unpublished research.
8. D. Altman, M. Levine, M. Nadien, J. Villena (Graduate Center, The City University of New York), unpublished research.
9. P. G. Zimbardo, paper presented at the Nebraska Symposium on Motivation (1969).
10. J. Waters (Graduate Center, The City University of New York), unpublished research.
11. W. McKenna and S. Morgenthau (Graduate Center, The City University of New York), unpublished research.
12. N. Abuza (Harvard University), "The Paris-London-New York Questionnaires," unpublished.
13. P. Abelson, *Science* 165, 853 (1969).
14. A. L. Strauss, ed., *The American City: A Sourcebook of Urban Imagery* (Aldine, Chicago, 1968).
15. R. E. Feldman, *J. Personality Soc. Psychol.* 10, 202 (1968).
16. W. Berkowitz, personal communication.
17. E. T. Hall, *The Hidden Dimension* (Doubleday, New York, 1966).
18. P. Hall, *The World Cities* (McGraw-Hill, New York, 1966).
19. R. E. Park, E. W. Burgess, R. D. McKenzie, *The City* (Univ. of Chicago Press, Chicago, 1967), pp. 1–45.
20. H. Blumenfeld, in *The Quality of Urban Life* (Sage, Beverly Hills, Calif., 1969).
21. K. Lynch, *The Image of the City* (M.I.T. and Harvard Univ. Press, Cambridge, Mass., 1960).
22. D. Hooper (Harvard University), unpublished.
23. Barbara Bengen worked closely with me in preparing the present version of this article. I thank Dr. Gary Winkel, editor of *Environment and Behavior*, for useful suggestions and advice.

9

JOE R. FEAGIN

Community Disorganization: Some Critical Notes*

In recent years numerous discussions of urban communities have given great weight to themes of disorganization and disorder. This paper critically examines several important conceptual, procedural, and substantive issues inherent in most treatments of community disorganization. To illustrate such fundamental problems as "overgeneralization" and dominant group bias five specific topics—migration, disasters, slums, ghettos, and collective violence—were selected for intensive analysis.

In recent years most popular and many scholarly discussions of urban communities have given great weight to themes of disorganization and disorder. Stress on community problems often seems to be the order of the day, whether the "community" being discussed is a few hundred black families in a ghetto setting, a large white-collar suburb, or an entire metropolitan area. Yet in spite of this growing emphasis social science analysts have not spent as much time as one might have expected grappling with the important conceptual and empirical issues involved in discussions of disorganization. It is my intention in this exploratory paper to point up a few of these critical issues, providing some

Reprinted with permission of Macmillan Publishing Co., Inc. from *Sociological Inquiry*, Vol. 43, Nos. 3–4 (1973), pp. 123–146. Copyright © 1974 by Sociological Inquiry.
* This paper is a revised version of a paper presented at the 1972 American Sociological Association meetings in New Orleans, Louisiana. I would particularly like to thank Charles Tilly, Robert Perrin, S. Dale McLemore, David Perry, Charles Bonjean, Alejandro Portes, Marcia Effrat, and Andy Effrat for their useful comments on an earlier version of this paper.

preliminary spadework for future conceptual and empirical analysis.

Although it is not the purpose of this paper to develop a comprehensive conceptual framework for the analysis of community, a few comments on definitions will provide a useful starting point. With only mild exaggeration Bell and Newby (1972: 27) have argued that every sociologist "has possessed his own notion of what community consists of, frequently reflecting his ideas of what it *should* consist of." Indeed, Hillery's (1955) review of nearly one hundred definitions of community still stands as the only systematic attempt to sift out essential characteristics. In spite of the fact that an incredibly diverse assortment of characteristics was found to be associated with the term "community," Hillery's elaborate classification indicated that three basic defining characteristics have often been distinguished: a limited geographical area, normative sharing, and social interaction. While the delineation of community in these terms is little more than a beginning, particularly because of the vagueness of notions like "limited geographical area," it is already in advance of definitional analysis in regard to community disorganization. Apparently, only two or three analysts have recently sketched out the critical aspects or characteristics of community disorganization. Working at a rather abstract level, Bernard (1968: 163) has suggested that the disorganization of a community be viewed as "a state in which one or more of the several subsystems, for whatever reason, fail to function at some specified expected level of effectiveness, or it may be defined as the processes that lead to such a state, or it may refer both to the processes and to the state." Basic to this view is the idea that disorganization entails a serious malfunction in a subsystem of a community's social system. Of importance too is the emphasis on disorganization as both a process and as a state.

Coleman (1971), on the other hand, seems to have developed his view of community disorganization in a less abstract way, by reviewing how the concept of community disorganization has actually been used by students of society and by examining examples often cited. Coleman (1971: 659) has distilled "the two elements of community disorganization pointed to by many authors." He terms the two types "distintegration" and "conflict." First, there is the category of phenomena which involve a lack or deterioration of social norms or consensus. By implication the lack or deterioration of social ties or orderly social arrangements emphasized by other authors would also fall under this rubric. "Disintegration" is a term often used to denote this type of community disorganization. Yet other phenomena are described in the language of disorganization because the collective patterns of behavior involved (e.g., collective violence) are regarded as challenging established structures of power and resources in communities, disorderly behavior which makes evident divergent values and perspectives. "Conflict" is a term often used to describe this type of community disorganization. Yet value or perspective conflict is not the main characteristic of collective violence which leads many to view it in disorganization terms. For many, collective violence on the part of dissenting minorities is seen as distinctively irrational and abnormal and thus, as a very serious example of community disorganization; and many also link disintegration of social ties and norms among minorities, seen as an earlier phase, to the emergence of radicalism and collective violence. The relevance of these two perspectives to the general definitions of community which were reviewed

by Hillery seems fairly clear. Those typical definitions depicted community organization in terms of normative consensus and social interaction. And many authors, including those reviewed by Coleman, have assessed community disorganization in terms of a breakdown in normative and social integration.

In addition, some observers of community life have used disorganization terminology not only where they see social disintegration or conflict, but also where they note deviant organization. Certain behavior patterns found in some segments of urban communities have been regarded as radically different from conventional behavior and thus, as examples of pathological organization. In his critical review of the cultural and family disorganization literature Valentine (1968: 23) noted the tendency for social scientists to leap "from social statistics, which are deviant in terms of middle-class norms, to a model of disorder and instability." This has particularly been true in the case of conventional portraits of slum and ghetto communities, with combinations of the disintegration and deviant organization perspectives being common. Of course, technically speaking, there is a certain contradiction in the terms used by many analysts, since, as Nisbet (1970: 263) has pointed out with regard to such frequency cited examples of disorganization as prostitution and organized crime, "a great deal of so-called disorganization in society is anything but that."

Thus, it seems that there are three broad reasons the language of community disorganization has been used in the analysis of community phenomena reflecting concern with disintegration, conflict, and deviant organization. The conventional approach to community disorganization, particularly the approach which deals with concrete community problems, assesses to what extent certain presumptively pathological conditions exist in a particular geographical area, and if they seem serious, depicts that situation in the terminology of community disorganization. Analysts of community change have been particularly captivated by the widely used language of disorganization.

There are several important procedural, conceptual, and substantive issues inherent in most treatments of community topics using this language, including such issues as generalizing from a part to the whole, dominant group bias in interpretation, overlays or layers of organization and disorganization, and the tendency to gloss over or to be unaware of empirical counter-evidence. I will return to these issues in a general way in the concluding section, but first I would like to examine the way in which these issues arise in regard to a number of specific community problems often discussed in terms of disorganization. Given the diverse assortment of phenomena depicted in these terms, it has been necessary to be selective. Somewhat arbitrarily, thus, I have chosen to limit the discussion which follows to urban communities and to examine migration, disasters, slums, ghettos, and collective violence in order to illustrate some important procedural, conceptual, and substantive issues.

The topics of migration and disasters have been chosen to illustrate primarily (but not exclusively) the disintegration perspective; in the literature the "community" of interest here has often been of town or city size, although the impact of these factors has also been assessed frequently in regard to subareas of cities. The topics of slums and ghettos will be reviewed in order to illustrate both the disintegration and deviant organization perspectives, with the "community" of interest usually being a subarea of a city. Collective violence has been selected to illustrate primarily the conflict aspect of disorganization theorizing, with "community" in the literature referring sometimes to subareas of cities and sometimes to the larger context. As will be seen, however, it is not impossible to make rigid distinctions between these three disorganization perspectives, since many social analysts have blended all three perspectives in developing interpretations.

DISORGANIZATION: DISINTEGRATION

Disintegration of orderly social arrangements and the weakening of social norms by a variety of disruptive factors have been of paramount interest to many recent observers of the urban scene, including some who would go so far as to characterize urban society as chaotic and exploding (e.g. Hauser 1969). Take, for example, urban migration, often seen as the culprit lying behind much community disintegration and disorganization. The image of the migrant to urban areas who has a severely disruptive effect on community order and plays a significant role

in the weakening or disappearance of norms and orderly social arrangements at the point of destination is still a powerful one in evaluations of community problems. Cornelius (1970: 98) has underlined the importance of Louis Wirth, the "Chicago School" or urban sociology, and folk-urban analysts such as Redfield in generating views of urban life and of migrant assimilation which emphasize disorganization:

> The resulting description emphasized the anomic, disintegrative, disorienting, depersonalizing features of urban life and entry into the urban environment, manifested in psychological maladjustment, poorly defined social roles, breakdown of traditional value systems and controls on deviant behavior, the weakening of family and kinship ties, and the decline of religious life. . . . Such conditions are assumed necessarily to accompany exposure to the urban environment, and then incidences of various forms of personal and social pathology in areas heavily settled with in-migrants . . . are listed as indicators.

After tracing the origin and character of disorganization theories in North American sociology, Cornelius demonstrates the use of similar disorganization theories in assessing the adaptation and political behavior of migrants to Latin American cities. Similarly, Nelson (1970: 396) has documented the disintegration assumptions in research on migration to Latin American cities:

> It is often assumed that many or most of the newcomers have been torn from a tightly structured rural society and plunged into a bewildering, impersonal, and harsh environment with few or no sources of support and guidance. Shock and isolation produce personal disorientation and political anomie.

With regard to migration to North American cities specific emphasis has been placed on deviant organization and conflict effects as well as on disintegrating effects. The impact of migration on urban crime and collective violence, as well as on the evolution of family organization in areas settled by migrants, has been stressed. For example, Coleman (1971: 703) seems to accept a combined interpretation of the disorganizing tendencies of migration: "The flow of blacks and Puerto Ricans into large cities is great, and these migrants initially have no stake in the city, no reason for not committing crime other than the fear of getting caught." For some it has been an easy step from this view of crime and migration to the parallel view that normless and tieless migrants contributed greatly to the collective violence in urban ghettos during the last decade (see Skolnick 1969; Fogelson and Hill 1968; Lupsha 1969). Moreover, Frazier's (1957: 630ff) view of the disintegrating effects of migration on typical black families—the breakup in urban areas of family patterns adapted to rural areas—has been widely influential. Referring to the breakup of migrating black families, Moynihan and Glazer (1963: 52) have underlined the cataclysmic effects of migration:

> Migration, uprooting, urbanization always create problems. Even the best organized and best integrated groups suffer under such circumstances. But when the fundamental core of organization, the family, is already weak, the magnitude of these problems may be staggering.

Other writers (Moynihan 1965; Forman 1971) have similarly accepted or developed this line of argument, and some have suggested that one negative result of continuing migration was the development of a pathological type of family organization, female-headed families, thus combining disintegration and deviant organization perspectives.

Yet conventional wisdom about the comprehensive disintegrating and disorganizing effects of migration per se has been brought into question in recent years by the evidence and analysis of a number of researchers. Reviewing the literature relevant to U.S. cities, Tilly (1968: 155) has recently made a convincing case for questioning many of the misconceptions which pass for wisdom in regard to migration:

> As for problems directly produced by migration, my main message has been that they have been seriously misunderstood and exaggerated. Migrants as a group do not notably disturb public order, their arrival does not lower the quality of the city's population, they place no extraordinary demands on public services, and they do not arrive exceptionally burdened with personal problems.

For example, looking at the available literature on crime and migration, Tilly found that black migrants had lower delinquency rates and imprisonment rates than native residents of the area studied. Moreover, examination of family disorganization revealed that recent migrants "were less likely than the rest to have broken families, and this is especially true within the nonwhite population" (Tilly 1968: 148). In addition, conventional assumptions about recent migrants fueling ghetto revolts in the United States have been contradicted by empirical evidence on the characteristics of rioters indicating native birth or long-term residence (Tilly 1968; Fogelson and Hill 1968; Lupsha 1969).

Nor was Tilly the first to question conventional views of disorganization and migration; a few years before, in a brief but neglected assessment, Wilensky and Lebeaux (1965: 123–124) had questioned the presumed disruptive effects of migration. Citing a few scattered pieces of empirical research, they suggested that geographical mobility was central to the urban scene, but "not necessarily disruptive." Both Tilly (1965) and Wilensky and Lebeaux have noted the critical importance of kinship and friendship networks in the assimilation of migrants into a new urban milieu. The great importance of informal and formal social networks, aspects of social organization, in the period between migrant departure and complete urban adjustment has frequently been neglected in studies of migrants and urban problems.

With regard to disorganization theories of urban migration as applied to Third World countries, particularly Latin American countries, a number of analysts have begun to piece together data which raise serious questions about images of disintegration and disorder. Mangin (1970: xvi) has suggested that, while much literature has focused on the destructive effects of migration, "the remarkable thing is the efficient way so many peasants have adapted and contributed to city development." In the first systematic review of several dozen empirically based studies bearing in some way on cityward migration, with emphasis on Latin American cities, Cornelius (1970: 103ff) concluded that the evidence did not support the view of urban migration as severely frustrating, socially disorganizing, or politically alienating. Cornelius (1970: 106) also noted that several studies indicated significant political (organization) activity among in-migrants, although not of the revolutionary kind many disorganization theorists would expect. Reviewing Third World urban migration, Nelson (1970: 396) came to the similar conclusion that there was virtually no evidence that recent migrants tend to be distinctively "radical or violence-prone" and that disorganization-revolution theories have gone wrong by neglecting data indicating that many or most urban migrants have prior urban exposure and receive extensive settling-in help from family, friends, and employers.

In sum, then, recent reviews of the evidence raise serious questions about disorganization theories of urban migration. The assumed disintegrating and disorganizing effects of migration, especially with regard to social isolation, weakening of norms, family character, crime, collective violence, and political radicalism, need much further examination. The supposed connections between migration and community disorganization are actually not well established, although one needs to exercise caution in generalizing from the limited data available. At the very least, firm conclusions about migration as disorganizing to communities should be avoided; much research yet remains to be done.

While I am most conversant with urban migration as an example of growing research evidence contradicting conventional perspectives on community disintegration, other topics which have commonly been discussed in the language of disintegration also seem to be attracting revisionists. For example, recent disaster research reports have taken issue with conventional notions about the impact of external factors such as disasters on urban communities. In a fashion similar to discussions of urban migration, disasters have been cited as major examples of cataclysmic events precipitating panic, a breakdown in orderly social arrangements and law and order, a lack of family and other co-ordinated action, and the disappearance of goal-oriented behavior. For example, Bernard (1962: 349), who seems aware of some of the contradictory evidence cited below, has depicted disasters as important examples of community disintegration and disorganization. Dynes (1970: 7–8) has summarized popular and scholarly disaster perspectives which at the community level include the image of a social jungle:

People, hysterical and helpless, gradually shed the veneer of civilization and exploit others. It is said that looting is common,

and that outside authority is perhaps necessary in order to inhibit these resurgent primitive urges. It is assumed that many will flee from the disaster area in mass panic, leaving the community stripped of its human and natural resources.

However, in recent monographs Quarantelli and Dynes have summarized research on disasters, much of it conducted by the Disaster Research Center at Ohio State University, which seems to contradict the exaggerated emphasis in conventional wisdom on community disintegration. Thus, Quarantelli and Dynes (1972: 67–70) found little evidence of irrational panic in face of impending hurricanes and similar disasters: "It appears that the major problem in an emergency is getting people to move, rather than preventing panic and disorderly flight."

The image of random or uncoordinated behavior in communities where disasters occur is also contradicted by the evidence. Quarantelli and Dynes (1972: 68) conclude from their data that:

In general, disaster victims react immediately to their plight. Individuals first seek help from family and friends, then from larger groups such as churches. . . . The pattern of self-reliance and informal mutual help covers all forms of disaster behavior.

Informal social networks and channels continued to play a critical role in such situations; Dynes (1970: 8) concluded that "what people have learned about social life in the past is not suddenly discarded as a result of such events."

In addition to this meaningfully patterned behavior, researchers have found little in the way of serious breakdowns in social norms. Looting or other criminal behavior during disasters has been remarkably infrequent. Quarantelli and Dynes (1972: 68) found no declarations of martial law and no "instance in which a person left an important emergency post out of anxiety." In sum, then, the image of extensive disintegration in the wake of disaster has not been substantiated by field research.

DISORGANIZATION: DISINTEGRATION AND DEVIANT ORGANIZATION

Yet another example of inaccuracy and exaggeration in conventional wisdom about the urban scene can be seen in the numerous discussions of the disintegrating and disorganized character of social life in "slum" communities: the breakdown of traditional norms and values, the lawlessness, the quest for immediate gratification, the deterioration of family and kinship ties, the social isolation and anonymity. For many conventional observers a major example of disintegration, viewed both in continuing process and present structure terms, has been the urban slum community. For many, too, the slum has been the repository of deviant and undesirable types of social organization, such as prostitution and organized crime. More often than not, these two somewhat distinctive disorganization perspectives have been conjoined in slum analyses.

Essentially negative portraits of the poor, especially of the poor in United States cities, have been part of the lore of social scientists for a number of decades:

The slum is a distinctive area of disintegration and disorganization.

Over large stretches of the slum men neither know nor trust their neighbors. Aside from a few marooned families, a large part of the native population is transient: prostitutes, criminals, outlaws, hobos.

The slum gradually acquires a character distinctively different from that of other areas of the city through a cumulative process of natural selection that is continually going on as the more ambitious and energetic keep moving out and the unadjusted, the dregs, and the outlaws accumulate (Zorbaugh 1929: 128–129).

Although several decades have elapsed since Zorbaugh wrote these sentences, crucial elements of this perspective have persisted into the present period. Thus, Forman (1971: 103, 127ff) adopts a perspective which virtually equates the slum and its inhabitants with pathology and disorganization, stressing family disorganization, gambling, prostitution, drugs, and psychological abnormality. And Hunter (1968: 20–93) seems to be more or less in the Zorbaugh tradition when he accents the key elements of the slum problem: social isolation, alienation, run-down housing, cultural limitation, migration, crime, and broken families.

Views of poor communities which accentuate negative or pathological traits have been particularly influenced by the culture-of-poverty generalizations of anthropologist Oscar Lewis (1965). The culture-of-poverty perspective emphasizes the transgenerational character of the defective subculture of those residing in slum areas, particularly in Latin America and in the United States, and fits nicely with other approaches viewing the slum in disorganization terms. The widespread acceptance of this view can be seen in the legitimacy given to it even in the government publications. A recent scholarly publication, *Growing Up Poor* (Chilman 1966), has in effect given United States government sanction to the culture-of-poverty portrait, with its special emphasis on personal disorganization and sociopsychological issues: superstitious and rigid thinking, impulsive parental behavior, inadequate childrearing practices, lack of ability to defer gratification, little emphasis on educational achievement, poor impulse control, little value placed on neatness, little expressed affection. For many observers enumeration of characteristics such as these has served to sum up in a general way the character of slum life.

In spite of this dominant emphasis on disorganization and defective subcultures, from time to time a few social scientists have challenged key aspects of the conventional wisdom. Some time ago, Whyte tried to stem the rush to judgment among those writing in the Zorbaugh tradition. Linking conventional wisdom about the disorganizing effects of urbanization in general, as expressed by Louis Wirth and others, to these views of the slum, Whyte noted:

If the city represents the highest development of individualization and hence of social disorganization, some scholars have thought to find in the slums the most striking manifestations of these phenomena that exist in the city (Whyte, 1943: 34).

Whyte (1943: 37) continued by arguing that his field study of the poor in Boston revealed substantial evidence of extensive and meaningful social organization, particularly primary organization, among the families he studied: "Here people live in family groups and have built up an elaborate social organization." Moreover, Whyte concluded by questioning the conventional view of non-middle-class organization (e.g., political machines and organized crime) as community disorganization.

Whyte's call for serious consideration of social networks and organization among the poor went virtually unheeded for several decades. It was not until the 1960s that a number of research studies began to demonstrate the existence of meaningful social integration and organization among the poor, studies moving away from the dominant concern with pathology. More has been found among the poor than disintegration and crime-oriented organization. In *The Urban Villagers* (1962) Gans reported finding an urban village among the Italian poor in Boston. Complex and intimate social networks were quite important in the integration of the West End of Boston, extensive social organization that put meaning into day-to-day existence. Similarly Fried and Gleicher (1961) have pointed to the significance of informal networks and internal social structure in providing residential satisfaction for poor urbanites. More recently, in his study of a complex Chicago slum area, Suttles (1968: 3) rejected the labels of "disorganization" and "value rejection," concluding that the area studied was "intricately organized" and that the overwhelming majority of the residents were "quite conventional people." While Suttles' analysis is limited by its focus on street life and adolescent males, it provides additional evidence of the integrative importance of peer groups and social networks among the urban poor.

Moreover, a few recent studies (e.g., Lane 1968) have shown that the number of secondary organizations, particularly voluntary associations, in urban areas of extreme poverty in the United States is more substantial than disintegration theorists might expect. Indeed, those operating from an extreme disintegration point of view might be hard pressed to explain the emergence of the substantial number of protest organizations, including tenants' group and welfare rights organizations, during the last decade in the United States.

A number of analysts have recently questioned the conventional wisdom which exaggerates disintegration and deviant organization in the slum areas of Latin American cities. Cornelius (1970: 114–115) has argued that the traditional emphasis on disorganization has caused Latin American researchers to overlook the critical informal associational activity in poor areas, including areas settled by poor in-migrants. Squatter settlements in Latin American cities

have shown a considerable amount of informal interaction and nonassociational groupings:

> This pattern appears to have developed most strongly in the Brazilian *favelas*, where numerous forms of *both* associational and nonassociational group activity have been observed, including mutual aid networks, credit cooperatives, *ad hoc* systems for distribution of water and electricity, cooperative marketing arrangements, group activity to raise money to buy illegally occupied land, and a variety of recreational groupings (Cornelius, 1970: 115).

This richness of social organization has been documented not only for Brazil but also for other Latin American slum areas, including those in Venezuela and Guatemala. Mangin (1970: xxix) reported that research in Peru revealed the readiness and ability with which residents of poor communities responded to new opportunities for gaining political power, including providing participants in and leadership for political organization. Pointing to the widespread organization found in a number of recent studies, Mangin (1970: xxvii) argued that perspectives such as those emphasizing a culture of poverty overemphasized "internal conditions, personality factors, and the like" and underemphasized "external economic conditions." Valentine's (1968: 55–60) argument in regard to culture-of-poverty perspectives such as that of Oscar Lewis was even more direct, since Valentine found in Lewis's own research evidence of substantial community organization and cosmopolitanism in poor areas, rather than overwhelming disorganization and pathology.

This research on urban slums in the United States and Latin America, taken together with studies of social integration among the working-class poor in European cities (e.g., Young and Wilmott 1957), points up an important difference between (1) a perspective which shows awareness of the physical, economic, and psychological difficulties faced by poor urbanites and at the same time seriously recognizes the presence of integrative norms, social networks, and other "positive" social phenomena (strengths) to be found among poor urbanites, and (2) a perspective which views the *typical* poor urbanite as a malintegrated isolate, criminal, or moral derelict, a person so caught up in social or personal disorganization that he or she cannot cope with everyday life or respond to economic and political opportunities if these appear. Lest the reader misconstrue this as a Pollyanna-type argument and jump to the opposite conclusion that all is well among the poor, I would hasten to add that much research (e.g., Gans 1962; Ryan 1971) indicates that economic and political deprivation, shaped in the main by factors outside the slum, is also a fact of life for most slum residents. Yet these critical environmental aspects of slum existence have received much less attention than they deserve. As with migration and disasters, much additional research is needed before we can accurately generalize about the complexity and overlays of life in slum communities.

At a time when a number of scholars have begun to look beyond the conventional portrait of slum disorganization, most are still writing one-sided accounts of life in black communities in the United States. Until recently few had raised questions about the widespread use of the language of disorganization in regard to ghetto dwellers. Authors as diverse as Frazier (1957), Myrdal (1964), Clark (1965), Rainwater (1966), and Moynihan (1965) have given emphasis to disintegration and deviant organization themes (e.g., social isolation, widespread family disorganization, lack of integration, nondeferred gratification, fleeting friendships, anomie) in regard to black ghettos. Some inclination toward black pathology and disintegration themes can be found even among some scholars who have been skeptical about the general slum-as-disorganization perspective. Fried and Levin (1968) have questioned whether black ghettos have the same patterns of community and family cohesiveness as other working-class slums; and Clinard (1966: 60) has suggested that the outstanding characteristic of the typical black slum resident "is the high degree of instability in his family life."

Indeed, one of the most prominent social science discussions in recent years has focused on the lack of social integration, normative consensus, and cohesion in black ghetto areas. Central in discussions of community disintegration or deviant organization have been the character and structure of black families. Influenced by Frazier (1957), Moynihan, in his now-famous *The Negro Family* (1965: 5), argued that "at the heart of the deterioration of the fabric of Negro society is the deterioration of the Negro family. It is the fundamental source of the weakness of the Negro community at the present time." He then proceeded to suggest that the typical black American family was a broken or disintegrated family, and in turn tied that disintegration to other problems of black communities. Moynihan dramatically accentuated the "tangle" of pathology and crumbling social relations which in his view characterized black communities. In a fashion similar to many writing in the Frazier-Moynihan tradition, Coleman (1971: 703) has also accented in passing the "abnormality" of black areas, "the absence of integration, the absence of any processes that produce a common bond of identity."

The policy impact of this disintegration and pathology emphasis in the social science literature on ghettos can be traced in prominent government reports, such as the *Report of the National Advisory Commission on Civil Disorders*. Under a conventional heading of "Unemployment, Family Structure, and Social Disorganization," this report (National Advisory Commission on Civil Disorders, 1968: 7) used a variety of disorganization codewords:

> The culture of poverty that results from unemployment and family breakup generates a system of ruthless, exploitative relationships within the ghetto. Prostitution, dope addiction, and crime create an environmental "jungle" characterized by personal insecurity and tension.

In examining the conventional ghetto portrait it becomes clear that must of what has been asserted about slum life in general has also been applied to black ghetto life. As with the case of the more general slum discussions, a major difficulty with this portrait is that there is a growing amount of contradictory evidence. At best, images of ghettos depicting life and people there solely in term of pathology and disintegration are gross exaggerations. Increasingly, research in the 1960s and 1970s has raised serious questions about these conventional images. Elsewhere Perry and I (1972: 460) have reviewed the small but expanding literature on ghetto family life and social structure and have suggested, in regard to *typical* ghetto residents and relative to dominant group patterns,

> that there is a socially significant, healthy, and diverse primary family structure, there is a high level of kinship interaction which is

also quite intense, and there is a high level of friendship and neighboring [in ghetto communities]. Hence, there is evidence which suggests that the internal structure . . . of the ghetto is not necessarily an environment which atomizes the person in an alienated state with no friends or organizational support from family or relatives.

Reviewing the literature on secondary organization, participation, and cosmopolitanism, we have also averred (1972: 460) that the typical black ghetto resident's everyday work is probably not one in which he,

like the turtle, is encapsulated and, when threatened, will not leave his shell. We discovered that he has as much, if not more contact with the news media than white urbanites; he participates as much [as] if not more than white urbanites in voluntary organization; and he can be as cosmopolitan [as] if not more cosmopolitan than white urbanites when it comes to traveling around the city and interacting with persons of other social identities.

Documentation for these arguments can be found in monographs by Meadow (1962), Babchuk and Thompson (1962), Feagin (1966), Podell (1968), and Wellman (1971).

To take the widely discussed issue of the black family, we have seen recently a significant expansion of research efforts directed at a better understanding of the strengths and weaknesses of black families, research efforts triggered by the public debate. Moynihan fostered the view that the typical black family was disorganized, that female-headed or matriarchal families predominated, and that black males did not contribute greatly to the support of their families. However, the argument that discussions of ghetto family life focusing on disorganization are replete with misconceptions has received support in a number of recent studies. For example, Hill (1971), drawing on government statistics and a few other sources, reached some provocative conclusions: (1) that most black families were male-headed; (2) that most intact black families were not matriarchal, but egalitarian or patriarchal in decision-making structure; (3) that black husbands were not peripheral wage earners, but the main providers in most families; (4) that the extent of family desertion had been greatly exaggerated; and

(5) that there was surprising emphasis on the importance of education among low-income black families. Other recent research studies have corroborated this image of the average black family as male-headed and egalitarian (or patriarchal), rather than as female-headed and matriarchal (Billingsley 1968; Hyman and Reed 1969; Mack 1972).

In addition to themes of social disintegration and family disorganization, one also finds a special emphasis in many ghetto analyses on a variety of types of pathological or deviant organization, as can be seen in the references of the National Advisory Commission on Civil Disorders (1968: 7) to prostitution, narcotics, and crime. This type of disorganization emphasis can be found not only in discussions of black ghettos but also in discussions of other types of slums as well, so much so that the "jungle" portraits of these areas often blend together discussions of disintegration with discussions of types of organization deviant from conventional or dominant group standards. Indeed, social phenomena such as family disorganization have been examined by analysts using both the disintegration and pathological organization perspectives.

While I do not have the space here to consider all the ramifications of this pathological organization issue, several points are important to note. In the first place, while criminal behavior and organization may exist to a disproportionate degree in slum and ghetto areas (a conclusion which may be shaky in light of recent research on white-collar crime), it seems to be exaggerated in many assessments of day-to-day life in these areas. It is too easy to move from characteristics of a minority of residents of a given urban community, however unconventional and colorful, to ungrounded generalizations about areas in general. Second, the quick typification of slum and ghetto areas in pathological organization terminology, with its frequently accompanying overtones of character flaws and individual blame, tends to play down the intimate relationship between non-middle-class social organization in these areas and the larger social system surrounding them. In most cases it remains to be demonstrated in what ways a given type of non-middle-class organization or pattern of behavior is pathological, nor is the standard of reference (i.e., what is normal and why) clearly specified. While I do not mean to suggest that one could not specify meaningful standards for social pathology (e.g., phenomena demonstrably harmful to the residents of a given community), it would be relatively difficult to demonstrate that the patterns of behavior commonly viewed as disorganized or pathological are not in fact adaptive-functional sociocultural arrangements. We still have a great need for additional (and preferably comparative) research along the lines of Merton (1957: 72), who, in a pioneering research study, showed the "functional equivalence" of certain types of quasi-legal behavior in poor areas. As Nisbet (1970: 263) has recently asserted, "there may in fact be no disorganization at all, in any empirical sense of the term, behind the rise of delinquent, criminal, or other problem behavior."

DISORGANIZATION AND CONFLICT

In addition to social disintegration, the other major type of disorganization which Coleman (1971) differentiated was community conflict. For Coleman the accent seemed to be on the divergent norms, values, or perspectives which open conflict made evident, leading to situations of community disorder and "paralysis." Not surprisingly, recent developments in United States cities, particularly the collective violence of black Americans and college students, have catapulted violent conflict into many discussions of disorganization and community problems. That urban violence here, as well as that in urban areas of other countries, has reflected divergent values and perspectives seems undeniable on the basis of existing data. However, many who have viewed collective violence in negatively toned disorganization terms have had more in mind than a clash of perspectives frustrating unified community effort. Many have viewed collective violence as a stage of community disorganization flowing from an earlier stage of disintegration, which in turn resulted from social change such as cityward migration; and many have expressed the view that open attacks on established arrangements can be consigned to the category of uniquely pathological, abnormal, or irrational behavior.

However, a few researchers—particularly those recently engaged in empirical research

on collective violence—have begun to question conventional views of violent conflict. In discussing migration I referred to a few researchers who had queestioned the common model: change → disintegration → violent conflict. This model views violent conflict or political radicalism as a developmental stage flowing from an earlier stage of community disintegration. Among the change factors often seen as underlying disintegration would be migration. Yet in regard to ghetto violence in United States cities, we have already seen that research on rioters indicated recent migrants played a minor role in the development of rioting (Fogelson and Hill 1968; Feagin and Hahn 1973). Cornelius (1970) and Nelson (1970), reviewing the scattered empirical data on Third World cities, similarly concluded that weight of evidence was against theories linking migrants, disintegration, and radical political action. Problematic too in some disintegration → violent conflict linkages are assumptions about the disintegrating and disorienting world of the slum, questionable assumptions in light of the evidence previously considered.

In addition, the change → disintegration → violent conflict model seems to have provided the backdrop for much traditional analysis depicting collective violence in terms of abnormality, pathology, and irrationality. Criticizing theories of Le Bon (1952), Smelser (1962), and Brown (1965), Skolnick (1969: 332) and his associates summed up elements of the traditional social science view:

> Under this conception, the routine processes of any given society are seen as stable, orderly, and predictable, operating under the normative constraints and cumulative rationality of tradition. The instability, disorder, and irrationality of collective behavior, therefore, are characteristic of those groups that are experiencing 'social strain'—for example, the unemployed, the recent migrant, the adolescent.

Skolnick (1969) and his associates were among the first to question the contrast between the rational-normal state and irrational-pathological dissidents. They argued that conventional popular and social science approaches were less than adequate because of the inconsistency of the terminology (not viewing the violent behavior of authorities as such), because of such lack of attention to recurrent patterns (viewing collective violence of dissidents as irrational and formless, when in fact there has been a good bit of structure and pattern), and because of inadequate attention to the power-authority context of collective action. Moreover, critically assessing the influential perspectives of Smelser (1962) and Gurr (1970), Nardin (1971) underscored the ideological character of much social science theorizing. Referring to the influential work of Smelser, he noted that "the policy implications of the theory of collective behavior, where drawn, are never in the form of advice to reformers or the discontented, but only to the 'agents of social control'" (Nardin 1971: 28). Objecting to social science vocabularies with no provision for irrational social control by the state or rational violence by dissidents, Nardin (1971: 29) argued that

Like Smelser's, Gurr's theory begins with the distinction between legitimate or normal and illegitimate or abnormal political behavior. As does Smelser, Gurr tends to associate the behavior of political authorities with the former category and the behavior of partisans with the latter. Given this conceptualization of the nature of political violence, Gurr, like Smelser, writes largely from the point of view of the authorities.

Because of this dissatisfaction with the traditional perspective, Skolnick, Nardin, Tilly, and a number of others engaged in empirical research on collective violence have begun to move away from the common (change → disintegration or strain → collective violence) model to a new (power-political process → collective violence) model. Drawing on empirical data on violence in European cities, Tilly (1969) has been one of the most articulate advocates of this latter model. Tilly has argued that the weight of evidence points toward the normality of collective violence in the life histories of Western societies. Arguing that neither a universal aggressive instinct nor pathological moments or men was necessary to explain the occurrence of collective acts of destruction, Tilly suggested that "historically, collective violence has flowed regularly out of the central political processes of Western countries" (1969: 4). An essential point in Tilly's analysis is that

collective violence has often emerged in the history of societies where social groups found themselves locked into a struggle for power. Groups moving up in the structure of power have engaged in various collective actions, including violence, in an attempt to gain power, while other groups already in power have fought by whatever means necessary—including particularly the use of the established police forces —to maintain their advantage in power and resources. Nardin (1971: 36) has also developed a political process perspective, arguing that collective violence of dissidents has arisen not out of the failure of the state to control those enduring strain but out of real conflicts of only partly reconcilable interests. From this perspective government is a party to community conflict.

A more adequate approach to violent conflict in urban communities might bring organization, rather than disorganization or disintegration, to the center of the explanatory framework. Within cities there have always been unequal distributions of power, wealth, and other resources; these distributions have been a fundamental component of community organization. Obserschall (1973: 33) underscored this crucial point:

Social conflict arises from the structured arrangement of individuals and groups in a social system—from the very fact of social organization. . . . Some are better off, and others are worse off. Those who are favored have a vested interest in conserving and consolidating their existing share; those who are negatively privileged seek to increase theirs, individually or collectively.

Not only has violent conflict flowed out of this distributional structure, but much collective violence has also been characterized by other social patterns—by goal-oriented activity, by normative consensus among dissidents (and police forces), and by the use of preexisting social networks (Nardin 1971; Feagin and Hahn 1973). While many problems in the character and structure of community conflict of a violent type can be resolved only by further research, the proponents of the political process → collective violence model have already raised very basic questions about traditional popular and social science conceptualizations.

CONCLUSION

Even this brief review of a few topics often discussed in the language of disorganization and disorder points up a number of persisting conceptual and empirical dilemmas recurring in the analyses of those concerned with community issues. One important analytical problem is the tendency to overgeneralize. The inclination to depict whole communities as disorganized or disintegrating may be partially explained by the tendency to jump from characteristics of a part to characteristics of the whole. A conspicuous example of this leap can be seen in the conventional discussion of widespread family disorganization in black communities. Even if one accepts the common (if yet to be demonstrated) view that female-headed families are distinctively pathological, a view used to buttress general images of ghetto deterioration, one cannot accurately generalize from statistics which show a minority of ghetto families to be female-headed to the conclusion that *the* black family is unstable or disorganized or that family disintegration is a defining characteristic of black ghettos. Thus the black family might more accurately be viewed, even from a middle-class point of view, as integrated or "healthy." This tendency to overgeneralization and exaggeration is not limited to discussions of black ghettos; it is sometimes characteristic of discussions of slums, migration, and disasters too. A careful analyst should not jump from the characteristics of limited segments of communities under analysis—even characteristics which might plausibly be demonstrated to be pathological—to a characterization of entire communities in pathological terms.

Yet another problem in numerous discussions of disorder and disorganization is the problem of class or dominant group bias. Valentine has underlined the point that even where it is empirically verified for segments of communities, *different* organization in urban communities should not be regarded as *disorganization*. Too often there has been a leap

from social statistics, which are deviant in terms of middle-class norms, to a model of disorder and instability . Such reasoning effectively eliminates consideration of possible cultural forms that . . . might have their

own order and functions (Valentine, 1968: 23).

This general point about middle-class or dominant group bias in popular and social science treatments of social pathology and disorganization is not new. Several decades ago, Mills (1963) made a similar argument in his article on the ideology of social pathologists. While Mills's critique may apply somewhat more directly to those who work in a relatively unsophisticated way with community problems and less to many social science analysts working with community disorganization, his argument that analysts of pathological organization and behavior patterns are inclined to accept the norms of dominant groups as standards for evaluation is still quite relevant.

Indeed, if terms like "disorganized" and "pathological" are to retain any social science utility, much conceptual and definitional work remains to be done. The ideological use of pathological terms to characterize disliked or non-middle-class patterns of social behavior will no longer suffice. Thus, in order to designate certain patterns or organizations as pathological, one might reasonably be required to demonstrate that they are in fact harmful to, or dysfunctional for, the community in question. If this operation were further specified and applied to commonly cited examples of social pathology such as broken families or the "rackets," it might well turn out that these cases were not pathological, but rather adaptive-functional (albeit different) structures. Indeed, many decades ago Durkheim (1966) emphasized the problem of defining social pathology and concluded that one could not talk of pathology until one had a clear idea of what normalcy was for a given set of social units.

By way of conclusion, I would like to emphasize three of the more serious consequences of the tendency among popular and social science analysts to leap too quickly to the rhetoric of disorganization and abnormality in discussing community issues such as those reviewed in this paper. In the first place, much social analysis has been so preoccupied with disorganization that the order and integration of the communities or subcommunities being examined has been neglected or unrecognized, even though there may have been important similarities between that order (networks, families, goals, norms, values, etc.) and that which can be found elsewhere. This neglect of internal organization needs to be remedied by much additional research, whether the concern is with slums, ghettos, or communities hit by disasters. Moreover, the central theme of a more adequate conceptual approach might well be *organization,* with (1) continuity of social structure (as in the case of migration), (2) normative and organizational similarities between various socioeconomic groups, (3) different (but adaptive-functional) sociocultural structures, and (4) overlap of similar-different sociocultural structures being crucial topics for analysis.

Secondly, the conventional terminology tends to play down external factors. A number of researchers have recently accentuated the importance of the external structural and organizational terms. In evaluating the deficiencies of disintegration theories of migration, Cornelius (1970: 115–116) questioned the traditional neglect of certain theoretically critical variables external to the migrants. Noting the absence of research on the governmental context, a major environmental variable, he called for more extensive research on the actions of established elites, government administrators, and power holding groups in shaping the circumstances and adaptive responses for urban migrants. And both Tilly (1969) and Nardin (1971) raised this issue of the broader sociopolitical context in reviewing the topic of collective violence by dissidents.

One of the most serious consequences of the rather pervasive disorganization pathology perspective, and the community analysis flowing from it, has been the effect on policy making and public action. The operation of the bias can often be seen in the process of definition of community problems. Skolnick and Currie (1970: 1–16) emphasized this selectivity issue by suggesting the question, "Why have certain community problems been given far more attention than others?" They further criticized the tendency to accept dominant values and power structures as given and to select as community problems only those social maladjustments recognized as such by dominant groups. The research studies by Gans (1962) and Fried (1963) on the grief which city officials brought into the lives of poor Italian Americans as a result of

defining (inaccurately) their area of the city as a disorganized, pathological slum area, and subsequently bulldozing it in the name of urban renewal, remain as major examples of research illustrating the serious policy consequences of the disorganization perspective.

While it is the case that many researchers working in the area of community studies are aware of the intrusion of dominant group bias into conceptual analysis, critical arguments such as those made by the revisionists discussed in this paper have not affected research operations as much as one might have expected. Most analysts of community problems are still more likely to focus on the characteristics and behavior of victims of society, rather than on the perhaps more critical problem of the surrounding sociopolitical system. I would like to stress that many of the disorganization topics discussed here seem to cry out for more thorough empirical research, including solid (if not prestigious) descriptive analysis, as well as new conceptual approaches. Beyond that, there is the need to pay more attention to those who have admonished us to look beyond the relatively unresistant and easily researched units of communities to the problematic character of dominant values and power structures.

References

Babchuk, Nicholas, and Ralph V. Thompson. 1962. "The Voluntary Association of Negroes," *American Sociological Review* 27 (October): 647–655.

Bell, Colin, and Howard Newby. 1972. *Community Studies.* New York: Praeger.

Bernard, Jessie. 1962. *American Community Behavior,* rev. ed. New York: Holt, Rinehart, and Winston.

———. 1968. "Community Disorganization," in David Sills (ed.), *Encyclopedia of the Social Sciences,* Vol. III. New York: Macmillan, 163–168.

Billingsley, Andrew. 1968. *Black Families in White America.* Englewood Cliffs, N.J.: Prentice-Hall.

Brown, Roger. 1965. *Social Psychology.* New York: The Free Press.

Chilman, Catherine S. 1966. *Growing Up Poor.* Washington, D.C.: U.S. Government Printing Office.

Clark, Kenneth B. 1965. *Dark Ghetto.* New York: Harper and Row.

Clark, S. D. 1962. *The Developing Canadian Community*, 2nd ed. Toronto: University of Toronto Press.

Clinard, Marshall B. 1966. *Slums and Community Development*. New York: The Free Press.

Coleman, James S. 1971. "Community Disorganization and Conflict," in Robert K. Merton and Robert A. Nisbet (eds.), *Contemporary Social Problems*, 3rd ed. New York: Harcourt, Brace, Jovanovich, 657–708.

Cornelius, Wayne A. 1970. "The Political Sociology of Cityward Migration in Latin America: Toward Empirical Theory," in Francine M. Rabinowitz and Felicity M. Trueblood (eds.), *Latin American Urban Annual*. Beverly Hills, Cal.: Sage Publications, 95–147.

Durkheim, Emile. 1966. *The Rules of Sociological Method*, 8th ed. Trans. by Sarah A. Solovay and John H. Mueller. New York: The Free Press.

Dynes, Russell R. 1970. *Organized Behavior in Disaster*. Lexington, Mass.: D. C. Heath.

Feagin, Joe R. 1966. *The Social Ties of Negroes in an Urban Environment*. Cambridge, Mass.: Harvard University. Unpublished Ph.D. dissertation.

———, and Harlan Hahn. 1973. *Ghetto Revolts*. New York: Macmillan.

Fogelson, Robert M., and Robert B. Hill. 1968. "Who Riots?" in *Supplemental Studies for the National Advisory Commission on Civil Disorders*. Washington, D.C.: U.S. Government Printing Office, 217–248.

Forman, Robert E. 1971. *Black Ghettos, White Ghettos, and Slums*. Englewood Cliffs, N.J.: Prentice-Hall.

Frazier, E. Franklin. 1957. *The Negro in the United States*, rev. ed. New York: Macmillan.

Fried, Marc. 1963. "Grieving for a Lost Home," in Leonard J. Duhl (ed.), *The Urban Condition*. New York: Basic Books, 151–171.

———, and P. Gleicher. 1961. "Some Sources of Residential Satisfaction in an Urban Slum," *Journal of the American Institute of Planners* 27:305–315.

———, and Joan Levin. 1968. "Some Social Functions of the Urban Slum," in Bernard J. Frieden and Robert Morris (eds.), *Urban Planning and Social Policy*. New York: Basic Books, 60–83.

Gans, Herbert J. 1962. *The Urban Villagers*. New York: The Free Press.

Glazer, Nathan, and Daniel P. Moynihan. 1963. *Beyond the Melting Pot*. Cambridge, Mass.: Harvard University Press.

Gurr, Ted R. 1970. *Why Men Rebel*. Princeton: Princeton University Press.

Hauser, Philip M. 1969. "The Chaotic Society: Product of the Social Morphological Revolution," *American Sociological Review* 34 (February): 1–18.

Hill, Robert B. 1971. *The Strengths of Black Families*. New York: Emerson Hall Publishers.

Hillery, George A. 1955. "Definitions of Community: Areas of Agreement," *Rural Sociology* 20 (June): 111–123.

Hunter, David R. 1968. *The Slums*. New York: The Free Press.

Hyman, Herbert H., and John S. Reed. 1969. "Black Matriarchy Reconsidered: Evidence from Secondary Analysis of Sample Surveys," *Public Opinion Quarterly* 33 (Fall): 346–354.

Lane, John. 1968. "Voluntary Associations Among Mexican Americans in San Antonio, Texas." Austin, Texas: University of Texas. Unpublished Ph.D. dissertation.

Le Bon, Gustave. 1952. *The Crowd*. London: Ernest Benn.

Lewis, Oscar. 1965. *La Vida*. New York: Random House.

Lupsha, Peter A. 1969. "On Theories of Urban Violence," *Urban Affairs Quarterly* 4:273–295.

Mack, Delores E. 1971. "Where the Black-Matriarchy Theorists Went Wrong," *Psychology Today* 4 (January): 24, 86–87.

Mangin, William. 1970. "Introduction," in William Mangin (ed.), *Peasants in Cities*. Boston: Houghton Mifflin Co., xiii-xxxix.

Meadow, Kathryn P. 1962. "Negro-White Differences Among Newcomers to a Transitional Urban Area," *The Journal of Intergroup Relations* 3: 320–330.

Merton, Robert K. 1957. *Social Theory and Social Structure*, rev. ed. Glencoe: The Free Press.

Mills, C. Wright. 1963. "The Professional Ideology of Social Pathologists," in Irving L. Horowitz (ed.), *Power, Politics and People: The Collected Essays of C. Wright Mills*. New York: Ballantine Books, 525–552.

Moynihan, Daniel P. 1965. *The Negro Family: The Case for National Action*. Washington, D.C.: U.S. Government Printing Office.

Myrdal, Gunnar. 1964. *An American Dilemma*, Vol. 2. New York: McGraw-Hill.

Nardin, Terry. 1971. "Theories of Conflict Management," *Peace Research Reviews* 4 (April): 1–93.

National Advisory Commission on Civil Disorders. 1968. Report of the National Advisory Commission on Civil Disorders. Washington, D.C.: U.S. Government Printing Office.

Nelson, Joan. 1970. "The Urban Poor: Disruption or Political Integration in Third World Cities?" *World Politics* 22: 393–414.

Nisbet, Robert A. 1970. *The Social Bond*. New York: Knopf.

Oberschall, Anthony. 1973. *Social Conflict and Social*

Movements. Englewood Cliffs, N.J.: Prentice-Hall.

Perry, David C., and Joe R. Feagin. 1972. "Stereotyping in Black and White," in Harlan Hahn (ed.), *People and Politics in Urban Society.* Beverly Hills, Cal.: Sage Publications, 433–463.

Podell, Lawrence. 1968. *Families on Welfare in New York City.* New York: Center for the Study of Urban Problems, City University of New York.

Price, Daniel O. 1971. "Rural-Urban Migration and Poverty: A Synthesis of Research Findings, With a Look at the Literature." Austin, Tex.: Report submitted to Office of Economic Opportunity.

Quarantelli, E. L., and Russell R. Dynes. 1972. "When Disaster Strikes It Isn't Much Like What You've Heard About," *Psychology Today* 5 (February): 67–70.

Rainwater, Lee. 1966. "The Crucible of Identity: The Negro Lower-Class Family," *Daedalus* 95: 172–216.

Ryan, William. 1971. *Blaming the Victim.* New York. Random House Vintage Books.

Skolnick, Jerome. 1969. *The Politics of Protest.* New York: Simon and Schuster.

———, and Elliott Currie (eds.). 1970. *Crisis in American Institutions.* Boston: Little Brown and Co.

Smelser, Neil J. 1963. *Theory of Collective Behavior.* New York: The Free Press.

Suttles, Gerald D. 1968. *The Social Order of the Slum.* Chicago: University of Chicago Press.

Tilly, Charles. 1965. *Migration to an American City.* Wilmington, Del.: Agricultural Experiment Station and Division of Urban Affairs. University of Delaware.

———. 1968. "Race and Migration to the American City," in James Q. Wilson (ed.), *The Metropolitan Enigma.* Cambridge, Mass.: Harvard University Press, 136–157.

———. 1969. "Collective Violence in European Perspective," in Hugh D. Graham and Ted R. Gurr (eds.), *Violence in America.* New York: Bantam Books, 4–44.

Valentine, Charles A. 1968. *Culture and Poverty.* Chicago: University of Chicago Press.

Wellman, Barry. 1971. "Crossing Social Boundaries: Cosmopolitanism among Black and White Adolescents," *Social Science Quarterly* 52 (December): 602–624.

Whyte, William F. 1943. "Social Organization in the Slums," *American Sociological Review* 8 (February): 34–39.

Wilensky, Harold L., and Charles N. Lebeaux. 1965. *Industrial Society and Social Welfare.* New York: The Free Press. Paperback.

Young, Michael, and Peter Willmott. 1957. *Family and Kinship in East London.* Baltimore: Penguin Books.

Zorbaugh, Harvey W. 1929. *The Gold Coast and the Slum.* Chicago: University of Chicago Press.

10

PETER SCHRAG

The Forgotten American

There is hardly a language to describe him, or even a set of social statistics. Just names: racist-bigot-redneck-ethnic-Irish-Italian-Pole-Hunkie-Yahoo. The lower middle class. A blank. The man under whose hat lies the great American desert. Who watches the tube, plays the horses, and keeps the niggers out of his union and his neighborhood. Who might vote for Wallace (but didn't). Who cheers when the cops beat up on demonstrators. Who is free, white and twenty-one, has a job, a home, a family, and is up to his eyeballs in credit. In the guise of the working class—or the American yeoman or John Smith—he was once the hero of the civics book, the man that Andrew Jackson called "the bone and sinew of the country." Now he is "the forgotten man," perhaps the most alienated person in America.

Nothing quite fits, except perhaps omission and semi-visibility. America is supposed to be divided between affluence and poverty, between slums and suburbs. John Kenneth Galbraith begins the foreword to *The Affluent Society* with the phrase, "Since I sailed for Switzerland in the early summer of 1955 to begin work on this book . . ." But *between* slums and suburbs, between Scarsdale and Harlem, between Wellesley and Roxbury, between Shaker Heights and Hough, there are some eighty million people (depending on how you count them) who didn't sail for Switzerland in the summer of 1955, or at any other time, and who never expect to. Between slums and suburbs: South Boston and South San Francisco, Bell and Parma, Astoria and Bay Ridge, Newark, Cicero, Downey, Daly City, Charlestown, Flatbush. Union halls,

American Legion posts, neighborhood bars and bowling leagues, the Ukrainian Club and the Holy Name. Main Street. To try to describe all this is like trying to describe America itself. If you look for it, you find it everywhere: the rows of frame houses overlooking the belching steel mills in Bethlehem, Pennsylvania, two-family brick houses in Canarsie (where the most common slogan, even in the middle of a political campaign, is "curb your dog"); the Fords and Chevies with a decal American flag on the rear window (usually a cut-out from the *Reader's Digest*, and displayed in counter-protest against peaceniks and "those bastards who carry Vietcong flags in demonstrations"); the bunting on the porch rail with the inscription, "Welcome Home, Pete." The gold star in the window.

When he was Under Secretary of Housing and Urban Development, Robert C. Wood tried a definition. It is not good, but it's the best we have:

He is a white employed male . . . earning between $5,000 and $10,000. He works regularly, steadily, dependably, wearing a blue collar or white collar. Yet the frontiers of his career expectations have been fixed since he reached the age of thirty-five, when he found that he had too many obligations, too much family, and too few skills to match opportunities with aspirations.

This definition of the "working American" involves almost 23 million American families.

The working American lives in the gray area fringes of a central city or in a close-in or very far-out cheaper suburban subdivision of a large metropolitan area. He is likely to own a home and a car, especially as his income begins to rise. Of those earning between $6,000 and $7,500, 70 percent own their own homes and 94 percent drive their own cars.

94 percent have no education beyond high school and 43 percent have only completed the eighth grade.

He does all the right things, obeys the law, goes to church and insists—usually—that his kids get a better education than he had. But the right things don't seem to be paying off. While he is making more than he ever made—perhaps more than he'd ever dreamed—he's still struggling while a lot of others—"them" (on welfare, in demonstrations, in the ghettos) are getting most of the attention. "I'm working my ass off," a guy tells you on a stoop in South Boston. "My kids don't have a place to swim, my parks are full of glass, and I'm supposed to bleed for a bunch of people on relief." In New York a man who drives a Post Office trailer truck at night (4:00 p.m. to midnight) and a cab during the day (7:00 a.m. to 2:00 p.m.), and who hustles radios for his Post Office buddies on the side, is ready, as he says, to "knock somebody's ass." "The colored guys work when they feel like it. Sometimes they show up and sometimes they don't. One guy tore up all the time cards. I'd like to see a white guy do that and get away with it."

What Counts

Nobody knows how many people in America moonlight (half of the eighteen million families in the $5,000 to $10,000 bracket have two or more wage earners) or how many have to hustle on the side. "I don't think anybody has a single job anymore," said Nicholas Kisburg, the research director for a Teamsters Union Council in New York. "All the cops are moonlighting, and the teachers; and there's a million guys who are hustling, guys with phony social-security numbers who are hiding part of what they make so they don't get kicked out of a housing project, or guys who work as guards at sports events and get free meals that they don't want to pay taxes on. Every one of them is cheating. They are underground people— *Untermenschen*. . . . We really have no systematic data on any of this. We have no ideas of the attitudes of the white worker. (We've been too busy studying the black worker.) And

yet he's the source of most of the reaction in this country."

The reaction is directed at almost every visible target: at integration and welfare, taxes and sex education, at the rich and the poor, the foundations and students, at the "smart people in the suburbs." In New York State the legislature cuts the welfare budget; in Los Angeles, the voters reelect Yorty after a whispered racial campaign against the Negro favorite. In Minneapolis a police detective named Charles Stenvig, promising "to take the handcuffs off the police," wins by a margin stunning even to his supporters; in Massachusetts the voters mail tea bags to their representatives in protest against new taxes, and in state after state legislatures are passing bills to punish student demonstrators. ("We keep talking about permissiveness in training kids," said a Los Angeles labor official, "but we forget that these are our kids.")

And yet all these things are side manifestations of a malaise that lacks a language. Whatever law and order means, for example, to a man who feels his wife is unsafe on the street after dark or in the park at any time, or whose kids get shaken down in the school yard, it also means something like normality—the demand that everybody play it by the book, that cultural and social standards be somehow restored to their civics-book simplicity, that things shouldn't be as they are but as they were supposed to be. If there is a revolution in this country—a revolt in manners, standards of dress and obscenity, and, more importantly, in our official sense of what America is—there is also a counter-revolt. Sometimes it is inarticulate, and sometimes (perhaps most of the time) people are either too confused or apathetic—or simply too polite and too decent—to declare themselves. In Astoria, Queens, a white working-class district of New York, people who make $7,000 or $8,000 a year (sometimes in two jobs) call themselves affluent, even though the Bureau of Labor Statistics regards an income of less than $9,500 in New York inadequate to a moderate standard of living. And in a similar neighborhood in Brooklyn a truck driver who earns $151 a week tells you he's doing well, living in a two-story frame house separated by a narrow driveway from similar houses, thousands of them in block after block. This year, for the first time, he will go on a cruise—he and his wife and two other couples—two weeks in the Caribbean. He went to work after World War II ($57 a week) and he has lived in the same house for twenty years, accumulating two television sets, wall-to-wall carpeting in a small living room, and a basement that he recently remodeled into a recreation room with the help of two moonlighting firemen. "We get fairly good salaries, and this is a good neighborhood, one of the few good ones left. We have no smoked Irishmen around."

Stability is what counts, stability in job and home and neighborhood, stability in the church and in friends. At night you watch television and sometimes on a weekend you go to a nice place—maybe a downtown hotel—for dinner with another couple. (Or maybe your sister, or maybe bowling, or maybe, if you're defeated, a night at the track.) The wife has the necessary appliances, often still being paid off, and the money you save goes for your daughter's orthodontist, and later for her wedding. The smoked Irishmen—the colored (no one says black; few even say Negro)—represent change and instability, kids who cause trouble in school, who get treatment that your kids never got, that you never got. ("Those fucking kids," they tell you in South Boston, "raising hell, and not one of 'em paying his own way. Their fucking mothers are all on welfare.") The black kids mean a change in the rules, a double standard in grades and discipline, and—vaguely—a challenge to all you believed right. Law and order is the stability and predictability of established ways. Law and order is equal treatment —in school, in jobs, in the courts—even if you're cheating a little yourself. The Forgotten Man is Jackson's man. He is the vestigial American democrat of 1840: "They all know that their success depends upon their own industry and economy and that they must not expect to become suddenly rich by the fruits of their toil." He is also Franklin Roosevelt's man—the man whose vote (or whose father's vote) sustained the New Deal.

There are other considerations, other styles, other problems. A postman in a Charlestown (Boston) housing project: eight children and a ninth on the way. Last year, by working overtime, his income went over $7,000. This year, because he reported it, the Housing Authority is raising his rent from $78 to $106 a month, a catastrophe for a family that pays $2.20 a day for milk, has never had a vacation, and for

which an excursion is "going out for ice cream." "You try and save for something better; we hope to get out of here to someplace where the kids can play, where there's no broken glass, and then something always comes along that knocks you right back. It's like being at the bottom of the well waiting for a guy to throw you a rope." The description becomes almost Chaplinesque. Life is humble but not simple; the terrors of insolent bureaucracies and contemptuous officials produce a demonology that loses little of its horror for being partly misunderstood. You want to get a sink fixed but don't want to offend the manager; want to get an eye operation that may (or may not) have been necessitated by a military injury five years earlier, "but the Veterans Administration says I signed away my benefits"; want to complain to someone about the teenagers who run around breaking windows and harassing women but get no response either from the management or the police. "You're afraid to complain because if they don't get you during the day they'll get you at night." Automobiles, windows, children, all become hostages to the vague terrors of everyday life; everything is vulnerable. Liabilities that began long ago cannot possibly be liquidated: "I never learned anything in that school except how to fight. I got tired of being caned by the teachers so at sixteen I quit and joined the Marines. I still don't know anything."

At the Bottom of the Well

American culture? Wealth is visible, and so, now, is poverty. Both have become intimidating clichés. But the rest? A vast, complex, and disregarded world that was once—in belief, and in fact—the American middle: Greyhound and Trailways bus terminals in little cities at midnight, each of them with its neon lights and its cardboard hamburgers; acres of tar-paper beach bungalows in places like Revere and Rockaway; the hair curlers in the supermarket on Saturday, and the little girls in the communion dresses the next morning; pinball machines and the *Daily News*, the *Reader's Digest* and Ed Sullivan; houses with tiny front lawns (or even large ones) adorned with statues of the Virgin or of Sambo welcomin' de folks home; Clint Eastwood or Julie Andrews at the Palace; the trotting tracks and the dog tracks—Aurora Downs, Connaught Park, Roosevelt, Yonkers, Rockingham, and forty others—where gray men come not for sport and beauty, but to read numbers, to study and dope. (If you win you have figured something, have in a small way controlled your world, have surmounted your impotence. If you lose, bad luck, shit. "I'll break his goddamned head.") Baseball is not the national pastime; racing is. For every man who goes to a major-league baseball game there are four who go to the track and probably four more who go to the candy store or the barbershop to make their bets. (Total track attendance in 1965: 62 million plus another 10 million who went to the dogs.)

There are places, and styles, and attitudes. If there are neighborhoods of aspiration, suburban enclaves for the mobile young executive and the aspiring worker, there are also places of limited expectation and dead-end districts where mobility is finished. But even there you can often find, however vestigial, a sense of place, the roots of old ethnic loyalties, and a passionate, if often futile, battle against intrusion and change. "Everybody around here," you are told, "pays his own way." In this world the problems are not the ABM or air pollution (have they heard of Biafra?) or the international population crisis; the problem is to get your street cleaned, your garbage collected, to get your husband home from Vietnam alive; to negotiate installment payments and to keep the schools orderly. Ask anyone in Scarsdale or Winnetka about the schools and they'll tell you about new programs, or about how many are getting into Harvard, or about the teachers; ask in Oakland or the North Side of Chicago, and they'll tell you that they have (or haven't) had trouble. Somewhere in his gut the man in those communities knows that mobility and choice in this society are limited. He cannot imagine any major chance for the better; but he can imagine change for the worse. And yet for a decade he is the one who has been asked to carry the burden of social reform, to integrate his schools and his neighborhood, has been asked by comfortable people to pay the social debts due to the poor and the black. In Boston, in San Francisco, in Chicago (not to mention Newark or Oakland) he has been telling the reformers to go to hell. The Jewish schoolteachers of New York and the Irish par-

ents of Dorchester have asked the same question: "What the hell did Lindsay (or the Beacon Hill Establishment) ever do for us?"

The ambiguities and changes in American life that occupy discussions in university seminars and policy debates in Washington, and that form the backbone of contemporary popular sociology, become increasingly the conditions of trauma and frustration in the middle. Although the New Frontier and Great Society contained some programs for those not already on the rolls of social pathology—federal aid for higher education, for example—the public priorities and the rhetoric contained little. The emphasis, properly, was on the poor, on the inner cities (e.g., Negroes) and the unemployed. But in Chicago a widow with three children who earns $7,000 a year can't get them college loans because she makes too much; the money is reserved for people on relief. New schools are built in the ghetto but not in the white working-class neighborhoods where they are just as dilapidated. In Newark the head of a white vigilante group (now a city councilman) runs, among other things, on a platform opposing pro-Negro discrimination. "When pools are being built in the Central Ward—don't they think white kids have got frustration? The white can't get a job; we have to hire Negroes first." The middle class, said Congressman Roman Pucinski of Illinois, who represents a lot of it, "is in revolt. Everyone has been generous in supporting anti-poverty. Now the middle-class American is disqualified from most of the programs."

"Somebody has to say no . . ."

The frustrated middle. The liberal wisdom about welfare, ghettos, student revolt, and Vietnam has only a marginal place, if any, for the values and life of the working man. It flies in the face of most of what he was taught to cherish and respect: hard work, order, authority, self-reliance. He fought, either alone or through labor organizations, to establish the precincts he now considers his own. Union seniority, the civil-service bureaucracy, and the petty professionalism established by the merit system in the public schools become sinecures of particular ethnic groups or of those who have learned to negotiate and master the system. A man who worked all his life to accumulate the points and grades and paraphernalia to become an assistant school principal (no matter how silly the requirements) is not likely to relinquish his position with equanimity. Nor is a dock worker whose only estate is his longshoreman's card. The job, the points, the credits become property:

Some men leave their sons money [wrote a union member to the *New York Times*], some large investments, some business connections, and some a profession. I have only one worthwhile thing to give: my trade. I hope to follow a centuries-old tradition and sponsor my sons for an apprenticeship. For this simple father's wish it is said that I discriminate against Negroes. Don't all of us discriminate? Which of us . . . will not choose a son over all others?

Suddenly the rules are changing—all the rules. If you protect your job to your own you may be called a bigot. At the same time it's perfectly acceptable to shout black power and to endorse it. What does it take to be a good American? *Give the black man a position because he is black, not because he necessarily works harder or does the job better.* What does it take to be a good American? Dress nicely, hold a job, be clean-cut, don't judge a man by the color of his skin or the country of his origin. What about the demands of Negroes, the long hair of the students, the dirty movies, the people who burn draft cards and American flags? Do you have to go out in the street with picket signs, do you have to burn the place down to get what you want? What does it take to be a good American? *This is a sick society, a racist society, we are fighting an immoral war.* ("I'm against the Vietnam war, too," says the truck driver in Brooklyn. "I see a good kid come home with half an arm and a leg in a brace up to here, and what's it all for? I was glad to see *my kid* flunk the Army physical. Still, somebody has to say no to these demonstrators and enforce the law.") What does it take to be a good American?

The conditions of trauma and frustration in the middle. What does it take to be a good American? Suddenly there are demands for Italian power and Polish power and Ukrainian power. In Cleveland the Poles demand a seat on the school board, and get it, and in Pitts-

burgh John Pankuch, the seventy-three-year-old president of the National Slovak Society demands "action, plenty of it to make up for lost time." Black power is supposed to be nothing but emulation of the ways in which other ethnic groups made it. But have they made it? In Reardon's Bar on East Eighth Street in South Boston, where the workmen come for their fish-chowder lunch and for their rye and ginger, they still identify themselves as Galway men and Kilkenny men; in the newsstand in Astoria you can buy *Il Progresso*, *El Tiempo*, the *Staats-Zeitung*, the *Irish World*, plus papers in Greek, Hungarian, and Polish. At the parish of Our Lady of Mount Carmel the priests hear confession in English, Italian, and Spanish and, nearby, the biggest attraction is not the stickball game, but the *bocce* court. Some of the poorest people in America are white, native, and have lived all of their lives in the same place as their fathers and grandfathers. The problems that were presumably solved in some distant past, in that prehistoric era before the textbooks were written—problems of assimilation, of upward mobility—now turn out to be very much unsolved. The melting pot and all: millions made it, millions moved to the affluent suburbs; several million—no one knows how many—did not. The median income in Irish South Boston is $5,100 a year but the community-action workers have a hard time convincing the local citizens that any white man who is not stupid or irresponsible can be poor. Pride still keeps them from applying for income supplements or Medicaid, but it does not keep them from resenting those who do. In Pittsburgh, where the members of Polish-American organizations earn an estimated $5,000 to $6,000 (and some fall below the poverty line), the Poverty Programs are nonetheless directed primarily to Negroes, and almost everywhere the thing called urban backlash associates itself in some fashion with ethnic groups whose members have themselves only a precarious hold on the security of affluence. Almost everywhere in the old cities, tribal neighborhoods and their styles are under assault by masscult. The Italian grocery gives way to the supermarket, the ma-and-pa store and the walk-up are attacked by urban renewal. And almost everywhere, that assault tends to depersonalize and to alienate. It has always been this way, but with time the brave new world that replaces old patterns becomes increasingly bureaucratized, distant, and hard to control.

Yet beyond the problems of ethnic identity, beyond the problems of Poles and Irishmen left behind, there are others more pervasive and more dangerous. For every Greek or Hungarian there are a dozen American-Americans who are past ethnic consciousness and who are as alienated, as confused, and as angry as the rest. The obvious manifestations are the same everywhere—race, taxes, welfare, students—but the threat seems invariably more cultural and psychological than economic or social. What upset the police at the Chicago convention most was not so much the politics of the demonstrators as their manners and their hair. (The barbershops in their neighborhoods don't advertise Beatle Cuts but the Flat Top and the Chicago Box.) The affront comes from middle-class people—and their children—who had been cast in the role of social exemplars (and from those cast as unfortunates worthy of public charity) who offend all the things on which working class identity is built: "hippies [said a San Francisco longshoreman] who fart around the streets and don't work"; welfare recipients who strike and march for better treatment; "all those [said a California labor official] who challenge the precepts that these people live on." If ethnic groups are beginning to organize to get theirs, so are others: police and firemen ("The cop is the new nigger"); schoolteachers; lower-middle-class housewives fighting sex education and busing; small property owners who have no ethnic communion but a passionate interest in lower taxes, more policemen, and stiffer penalties for criminals. In San Francisco the Teamsters, who had never been known for such interests before, recently demonstrated in support of the police and law enforcement and, on another occasion, joined a group called Mothers Support Neighborhood Schools at a school-board meeting to oppose—with their presence and later, apparently, with their fists —a proposal to integrate the schools through busing. ("These people," someone said at the meeting, "do not look like mothers.")

Which is not to say that all is frustration and anger, that anybody is ready "to burn the country down." They are not even ready to elect standard model demagogues. "A lot of labor people who thought of voting for Wallace were ashamed of themselves when they realized what they were about to do," said Morris Iushewitz, an officer of New York's Central Labor Council. Because of a massive last-minute union campaign, and perhaps for other reasons, the blue-collar vote for Wallace fell far below the figures predicted by the early polls last fall. Any number of people, moreover, who are not doing well by any set of official statistics, who are earning well below the national mean ($8,000 a year), or who hold two jobs to stay above it, think of themselves as affluent, and often use that word. It is almost as if not to be affluent is to be un-American. People who can't use the word tend to be angry; people who come too close to those who can't become frightened. The definition of affluence is generally pinned to what comes in, not to the quality of life as it's lived. The $8,000 son of a man who never earned more than $4,500 may, for that reason alone, believe that he's "doing all right." If life is not all right, if he can't get his curbs fixed, or his streets patrolled, if the highways are crowded and the beaches polluted, if the schools are ineffectual he is still able to call himself affluent, feels, perhaps, a social compulsion to do so. His anger, if he is angry, is not that of the wage earner resenting management—and certainly not that of the socialist ideologue asking for redistribution of wealth—but that of the consumer, the taxpayer, and the family man. (Inflation and taxes are wiping out most of the wage gains made in labor contracts signed during the past three years.) Thus he will vote for a Louise Day Hicks in Boston who promises to hold the color line in the schools or for a Charles Stenvig calling for law enforcement in Minneapolis but reject a George Wallace who seems to threaten his pocketbook. The danger is that he will identify with the politics of the Birchers and other middle-class reactionaries (who often pretend to speak for him) even though his income and style of life are far removed from theirs; that taxes, for example, will be identified with welfare rather than war; and that he will blame his limited means on the small slice of the poor rather than the fat slice of the rich.

If you sit and talk to people like Marjorie Lemlow, who heads Mothers Support Neighborhood Schools in San Francisco, or Joe Owens, a house painter who is president of a community-action organization in Boston, you quickly discover that the roots of reaction and the roots of reform are often identical, and that the response to particular situations is more often contingent on the politics of the politicians and leaders who appear to care than on the conditions of life or the ideology of the victims. Mrs. Lemlow wants to return the schools to some virtuous past; she worries about disintegration of the family and she speaks vaguely about something that she can't bring herself to call a conspiracy against Americanism. She has been accused of leading a bunch of Birchers, and she sometimes talks Birch language. But whatever the form, her sense of things comes from a small-town vision of national virtues, and her unhappiness from the assaults of urban sophistication. It just so happens that a lot of reactionaries now sing that tune, and that the liberals are indifferent.

Joe Owens—probably because of his experience as a Head Start parent, and because of his association with an effective community-action program—talks a different language. He knows, somehow, that no simple past can be restored. In his world the villains are not conspirators but bureaucrats and politicians, and he is beginning to discover that in a struggle with officials the black man in the ghetto and the working man (black or white) have the same problems. "Every time you ask for something from the politicians they treat you like a beggar, like you ought to be grateful for what you have. They try to make you feel ashamed."

When Hope Becomes a Threat

The imponderables are youth and tradition and change. The civics book and the institution it celebrates—however passé—still hold the world together. The revolt is in their name, not against them. And there is simple decency, the language and practice of the folksy cliché, the small town, the Boy Scout virtues, the neighborhood charity, the obligation to support the church, the rhetoric of open opportunity: "They can keep Wallace and they can keep Alabama. We didn't fight a dictator for four years so we could elect one over here." What happens when all that becomes Mickey Mouse? Is there an urban ethic to replace the values of the small town? Is there a coherent public philosophy, a consistent set of beliefs to replace family, home, and hard work? What happens when the hang-ups of upper-middle-class kids are in fashion and those of blue-collar kids are not? What happens when

Doing Your Own Thing becomes not the slogan of the solitary deviant but the norm? Is it possible that as the institutions and beliefs of tradition are fashionably denigrated a blue-collar generation gap will open to the Right as well as to the Left? (There is statistical evidence, for example, that Wallace's greatest support within the unions came from people who are between twenty-one and twenty-nine, those, that is, who have the most tenuous association with the liberalism of labor.) Most are politically silent; although SDS has been trying to organize blue-collar high-school students, there are no Mario Savios or Mark Rudds—either of the Right or the Left—among them. At the same time the union leaders, some of them old hands from the Thirties, aren't sure that the kids are following them either. Who speaks for the son of the longshoreman or the Detroit auto worker? What happens if he doesn't get to college? What, indeed, happens when he does?

Vaguely but unmistakably the hopes that a youth-worshiping nation historically invested in its young are becoming threats. We have never been unequivocal about the symbolic patricide of Americanization and upward mobility, but if at one time mobility meant rejection of older (or European) styles it was, at least, done in the name of America. Now the labels are blurred and the objectives indistinct. Just at the moment when a tradition-bound Italian father is persuaded that he should send his sons to college—that education is the only future—the college blows up. At the moment when a parsimonious taxpayer begins to shell out for what he considers an extravagant state university system the students go on strike. Marijuana, sexual liberation, dress styles, draft resistance, even the rhetoric of change become monsters and demons in a world that appears to turn old virtues upside down. The paranoia that fastened on Communism twenty years ago (and sometimes still does) is increasingly directed to vague conspiracies undermining the schools, the family, order and discipline. "They're feeding the kids this generation-gap business," says a Chicago housewife who grinds out a campaign against sex education on a duplicating machine in her living room. "The kids are told to make their own decisions. They're all mixed up by situation ethics and open-ended questions. They're alienating children from their own parents." They? The churches, the schools, even the YMCA and the Girl Scouts, are implicated. But a major share of the villainy is now also attributed to "the social science centers," to the apostles of sensitivity training, and to what one California lady, with some embarrassment, called "nude therapy." "People with sane minds are being altered by psychological methods." The current major campaign of the John Birch Society is not directed against Communists in government or the Supreme Court, but against sex education.

(There is, of course, also sympathy with the young, especially in poorer areas where kids have no place to play. "Everybody's got to have a hobby," a South Boston adolescent told a youth worker. "Ours is throwing rocks." If people will join reactionary organizations to protect their children, they will also support others: community-action agencies which help kids get jobs; Head Start parent groups, Boys Clubs. "Getting this place cleaned up" sometimes refers to a fear of young hoods; sometimes it points to the day when there is a park or a playground or when the existing park can be used. "I want to see them grow up to have a little fun.")

Can the Common Man Come Back?

Beneath it all there is a more fundamental ambivalence, not only about the young, but about institutions—the schools, the churches, the Establishment—and about the future itself. In the major cities of the East (though perhaps not in the West) there is a sense that time is against you, that one is living "in one of the few decent neighborhoods left," that "if I can get $125 a week upstate (or downstate) I'll move." The institutions that were supposed to mediate social change and which, more than ever, are becoming priesthoods of information and conglomerates of social engineers, are increasingly suspect. To attack the Ford Foundation (as Wright Patman has done) is not only to fan the embers of historic populism against wealth and power, but also to arouse those who feel that they are trapped by an alliance of upper-class Wasps and lower-class Negroes. If the foundations have done anything for the blue-collar worker he doesn't seem to be aware of it. At the same time the distrust of professional educators that characterizes the black militants is becoming increasingly prevalent among a minority of lower-middle-class whites who are beginning to discover that the schools aren't working for them either. ("Are all those new programs just a cover-up for failure?") And if the Catholic Church is under attack from its liberal members (on birth control, for example) it is also alienating the traditionalists who liked their minor saints (even if they didn't actually exist) and were perfectly content with the Latin Mass. For the alienated Catholic liberal there are other places to go; for the lower-middle-class parishioner in Chicago or Boston there are none.

Perhaps, in some measure, it has always been this way. Perhaps none of this is new. And perhaps it is also true that the American lower middle has never had it so good. And yet surely there is a difference, and that is that the common man has lost his visibility and, somehow, his claim on public attention. There are old liberals and socialists—men like Michael Harrington—who believe that a new alliance can be forged for progressive social action:

> From Marx to Mills, the Left regarded the middle class as a stratum of hypocritical, vacillating rear-guarders. There was often sound reason for this contempt. But is it not possible that a new class is coming into being? It is not the old middle class of small property owners and entrepreneurs, nor the new middle class of managers. It is composed of scientists, technicians, teachers, and professionals in the public sector of the society. By education and work experience it is predisposed toward planning. It could be an ally of the poor and the organized workers—or their sophisticated enemy. In other words, an unprecedented social and political variable seems to be taking shape in America.
>
> The American worker, even when he waits on a table or holds open a door, is not servile; he does not carry himself like an inferior. The openness, frankness, and democratic manner which Tocqueville described in the last century persists to this very day. They have been a source of rudeness, contemptuous ignorance, violence—and of a creative self-confidence among great masses of people. It was in this latter spirit that the CIO was organized and the black freedom movement marched.

There are recent indications that the white lower middle class is coming back on the roster of public priorities. Pucinski tells you that liberals in Congress are privately discussing the pressure from the middle class. There are proposals now to increase personal income-tax exemptions from $600 to $1,000 (or $1,200) for each dependent, to protect all Americans with a national insurance system covering catastrophic medical expenses, and to put a floor under all incomes. Yet these things by themselves are insufficient. Nothing is sufficient without a national sense of restoration. What Pucinski means by the middle class has, in some measure, always been represented. A physician earning $75,000 a year is also a working man but he is hardly a victim of the welfare system. Nor, by and large, are the stockholders of the Standard Oil Company or U.S. Steel. The fact that American ideals have often been corrupted in the cause of self-aggrandizement does not make them any less important for the cause of social reform and justice. "As a movement with the conviction that there is more to people than greed and fear," Harrington said, "the Left must . . . also speak in the name of the historic idealism of the United States."

The issue, finally, is not *the program* but the vision, the angle of view. A huge constituency may be coming up for grabs, and there is considerable evidence that its political mobility is more sensitive than anyone can imagine, that all the sociological determinants are not as significant as the simple facts of concern and leadership. When Robert Kennedy was killed last year, thousands of working-class people who had expected to vote for him—if not hundreds of thousands—shifted their loyalties to Wallace. A man who can change from a progressive democrat into a bigot overnight deserves attention.

11

ROBERT COLES

Like It Is in the Alley

"In the alley it's mostly dark, even if the sun is out. But if you look around, you can find things. I know how to get into every building, except that it's like night once you're inside them, because they don't have lights. So, I stay here. You're better off. It's no good on the street. You can get hurt all the time, one way or the other. And in buildings, like I told you, it's bad in them, too. But here it's o.k. You can find your own corner, and if someone tries to move in you fight him off. We meet here all the time, and figure out what we'll do next. It might be a game, or over for some pool, or a coke or something. You need to have a place to start out from, and that's like it is in the alley; you can always know your buddy will be there, provided it's the right time. So you go there, and you're on your way, man."

Like all children of nine, Peter is always on his way—to a person, a place, a "thing" he wants to do. *"There's this here thing we thought we'd try tomorrow,"* he'll say; and eventually I'll find out that he means there's to be a race. He and his friends will compete with another gang to see who can wash a car faster and better. The cars belong to four youths who make their money taking bets, and selling liquor that I don't believe was ever purchased, and pushing a few of those pills that *"go classy with beer."* I am not completely sure, but I think they also have something to do with other drugs; and again, I can't quite be sure what their connection is with a "residence" I've seen not too far from the alley Peter describes so possessively. The women come and go—from that residence and along the street Peter's alley leaves.

Peter lives in the heart of what we in con-

temporary America have chosen (ironically, so far as history goes) to call an "urban ghetto." The area was a slum before it became a ghetto, and there still are some very poor white people on its edges and increasing numbers of Puerto Ricans in several of its blocks. Peter was not born in the ghetto, nor was his family told to go there. They are Americans and have been here *"since way back before anyone can remember."* That is the way Peter's mother talks about Alabama, about the length of time she and her ancestors have lived there. She and Peter's father came north *"for freedom."* They did not seek out a ghetto, an old quarter of Boston where they were expected to live and where they would be confined, yet at least some of the time solidly at rest, with kin, and reasonably safe.

No, they sought freedom. Americans, they moved on when the going got *"real bad,"* and Americans, they expected something better someplace, some other place. They left Alabama on impulse. They found Peter's alley by accident. And they do not fear pogroms. They are Americans, and in Peter's words: *"There's likely to be another riot here soon. That's what I heard today. You hear it a lot, but one day you know it'll happen."*

Peter's mother fears riots too—among other things. The Jews of Eastern Europe huddled together in their ghettos, afraid of the barbarians, afraid of the *Goyim*, but always sure of one thing, their God-given destiny. Peter's mother has no such faith. She believes that *"something will work out one of these days."* She believes that *"you have to keep on going, and things can get better, but don't ask me how."* She believes that *"God wants us to have a bad spell here, and so maybe it'll get better the next time—you know in Heaven, and I hope that's where we'll be going."* Peter's mother, in other words, is a

Robert Coles, "Like It Is in the Alley," *Daedalus*, vol. 97, no. 4 (Fall 1968), pp. 1315–1330. Reprinted by permission.

pragmatist, an optimist, and a Christian. Above all she is American: *"Yes, I hear them talk about Africa, but it don't mean anything to us. All I know is Alabama and now it's in Massachusetts that we are. It was a long trip coming up here, and sometimes I wish we were back there, and sometimes I'd just as soon be here, for all that's no good about it. But I'm not going to take any more trips, no sir. And like Peter said, this is the only country we've got. If you come from a country, you come from it, and we're from it, I'd say, and there isn't much we can do but try to live as best we can. I mean, live here."*

What is "life" like for her over there, where she lives, in the neighborhood she refers to as "here"? A question like that cannot be answered by the likes of me, and even her answer provides only the beginning of a reply: *"Well, we does o.k., I guess. Peter here, he has it better than I did, or his daddy. I can say that. I tell myself that a lot. He can turn on the faucet over there, and a lot of the time, he just gets the water, right away. And when I tell him what it was like for us, to go fetch that water—we'd walk three miles, yes sir, and we'd be lucky it wasn't ten—well, Peter, it doesn't register on him. He thinks I'm trying to fool him, and the more serious I get, the more he laughs, so I've stopped.*

"Of course it's not all so good, I have to admit. We're still where we were, so far as knowing where your next meal is coming from. When I go to bed at night I tell myself I've done good, to stay alive and keep the kids alive, and if they'll just wake up in the morning, and me too, well then, we can worry about that, all the rest, come tomorrow. So there you go. We do our best, and that's all you can do."

She may sound fantastic, but she appears to be a nervous, hard-working, even hard-driven woman—thin, short, constantly on the move. I may not know what she "really" thinks and believes, because like the rest of us she has her contradictions and her mixed feelings. I think it is fair to say that there are some things that she can't say to me—or to herself. She is a Negro, and I am white. She is poor, and I am fairly well off. She is very near to illiterate, and I put in a lot of time worrying about how to say things. But she and I are both human beings, and we both have trouble—to use that word—"communicating," not only with each other, but with ourselves. Sometimes she doesn't tell me something she really wants me to know. She

has forgotten, pure and simple. More is on her mind than information I might want. And sometimes I forget too: *"Remember you asked the other day about Peter, if he was ever real sick. And I told you he was a weak child, and I feared for his life, and I've lost five children, three that was born and two that wasn't. Well, I forgot to tell you that he got real sick up here, just after we came. He was three, and I didn't know what to do. You see, I didn't have any mother to help out. She always knew what to do. She could hold a child and get him to stop crying, no matter how sick he was, and no matter how much he wanted food, and we didn't have it. But she was gone—and that's when we left to come up here, and I never would have left her, not for anything in the world. But suddenly she took a seizure of something and went in a half hour, I'd say. And Peter, he was so hot and sick, I thought he had the same thing as his grandmother did and he was going to die. I thought maybe she's calling him. She always liked Peter. She helped him be born, she and my cousin, they did."*

Actually, Peter's mother remembers quite a lot of things. She remembers the "old days" back South, sometimes with a shudder, but sometimes with the same nostalgia that the region is famous for generating in its white exiles. She also notices a lot of things. She notices, and from time to time will remark upon, the various changes in her life. She has moved from the country to the city. Her father was a sharecropper and her son wants to be a pilot (sometimes), a policeman (sometimes), a racing-car driver (sometimes), and a baseball player (most of the time). Her husband is not alive. He died one year after they all came to Boston. He woke up vomiting in the middle of the night —vomiting blood. He bled and bled and vomited and vomited and then he died. The doctor does not have to press very hard for "the facts." Whatever is known gets spoken vividly and (still) emotionally: *"I didn't know what to do. I was beside myself. I prayed and I prayed, and in between I held his head and wiped his forehead. It was the middle of the night. I woke up my oldest girl and I told her to go knocking on the doors. But no one would answer. They must have been scared, or have suspected something bad. I thought if only he'd be able to last into the morning, then we could get some help. I was caught between things. I couldn't leave him to go get a policeman. And my girl, she was* afraid to go out. And besides, there was no one outside, and I thought we'd just stay at his side, and somehow he'd be o.k., because he was a strong man, you know. His muscles, they were big all his life. Even with the blood coming up, he looked too big and strong to die, I thought. But I knew he was sick. He was real bad sick. There wasn't anything else, no sir, to do. We didn't have no phone and even if there was a car, I never could have used it. Nor my daughter. And then he took a big breath and that was his last one."

When I first met Peter and his mother, I wanted to know how they lived, what they did with their time, what they liked to do or disliked doing, what they believed. In the back of my mind were large subjects like "the connection between a person's moods and the environment in which he lives." Once I was told I was studying "the psychology of the ghetto," and another time the subject of "urban poverty and mental health." It is hoped that at some point large issues like those submit themselves to lives; and when that is done, when particular but not unrepresentative or unusual human beings are called in witness, their concrete medical history becomes extremely revealing. I cannot think of a better way to begin knowing what life is like for Peter and his mother than to hear the following and hear it again and think about its implications: *"No sir, Peter has never been to a doctor, not unless you count the one at school, and she's a nurse I believe. He was his sickest back home before we came here, and you know there was no doctor for us in the country. In Alabama you have to pay a white doctor first, before he'll go near you. And we don't have but a few colored ones. (I've never seen a one.) There was this woman we'd go to, and she had gotten some nursing education in Mobile. (No, I don't know if she was a nurse or not, or a helper to the nurses, maybe.) Well, she would come to help us. With the convulsions, she'd show you how to hold the child, and make sure he doesn't hurt himself. They can bite their tongues, real, real bad.*

"Here, I don't know what to do. There's the city hospital, but it's no good for us. I went there with my husband, no sooner than a month or so after we came up here. We waited and waited, and finally the day was almost over. We left the kids with a neighbor, and we barely knew her. I said it would take the morning, but I never thought we'd get home near suppertime. And they wanted us to come back and come back, because it was something they couldn't do all at once—though for most of the time we just sat there and did nothing. And my husband, he said his stomach was the worse for going there, and he'd take care of himself from now on, rather than go there.

"Maybe they could have saved him. But they're far away, and I didn't have money to get a cab, even if there was one around here, and I thought to myself it'll make him worse, to take him there.

"My kids, they get sick. The welfare worker, she sends a nurse here, and she tells me we should be on vitamins and the kids need all kinds of check-ups. Once she took my daughter and told her she had to have her teeth looked at, and the same with Peter. So, I went with my daughter, and they didn't see me that day, but said they could in a couple of weeks. And I had to pay the woman next door to mind the little ones, and there was the carfare, and we sat and sat, like before. So, I figured, it would take more than we've got to see that dentist. And when the nurse told us we'd have to come back a few times—that's how many, a few—I thought that no one ever looked at my teeth, and they're not good, I'll admit, but you can't have everything, that's what I say, and that's what my kids have to know, I guess."

What *does* she have? And what belongs to Peter? For one thing, there is the apartment, three rooms for six people, a mother and five children. Peter is a middle child with two older girls on one side and a younger sister and still younger brother on the other side. The smallest child was born in Boston: *"It's the only time I ever spent in a hospital. He's the only one to be born there. My neighbor got the police. I was in the hall, crying I guess. We almost didn't make it. They told me I had bad blood pressure, and I should have been on pills, and I should come back, but I didn't. It was the worst time I've ever had, because I was alone. My husband had to stay with the kids, and no one was there to visit me."*

Peter sleeps with his brother in one bedroom. The three girls sleep in the living room, which is a bedroom. And, of course, there is a small kitchen. There is not very much furniture about. The kitchen has a table with four chairs, only two of which are sturdy. Thee girls sleep in one big bed. Peter shares his bed with his brother. The mother sleeps on a couch. There is one more chair and a table in the living room. Jesus looks down from the living room wall, and an undertaker's calendar hangs on the kitchen wall. The apartment has no books, no records. There is a television set in the living room, and I have never seen it off.

Peter in many respects is his father's successor. His mother talks things over with him. She even defers to him at times. She will say something; he will disagree; she will nod and let him have the last word. He knows the city. She still feels a stranger to the city. "*If you want to know about anything around here, just ask Peter,*" she once said to me. That was three years ago, when Peter was six. Peter continues to do very poorly at school, but I find him a very good teacher. He notices a lot, makes a lot of sense when he talks, and has a shrewd eye for the ironic detail. He is very intelligent, for all the trouble he gives his teachers. He recently summed up a lot of American history for me: "*I wasn't made for that school, and that school wasn't made for me.*" It is an old school, filled with memories. The name of the school evokes Boston's Puritan past. Pictures and statues adorn the corridors— reminders of the soldiers and statesmen and writers who made New England so influential in the nineteenth centry. And naturally one finds slogans on the walls, about freedom and democracy and the rights of the people. Peter can be surly and cynical when he points all that out to the visitor. If he is asked what kind of school he would *like,* he laughs incredulously. "*Are you kidding? No school would be my first choice. They should leave us alone, and let us help out at home, and maybe let some of our own people teach us. The other day the teacher admitted she was no good. She said maybe a Negro should come in and give us the discipline, because she was scared. She said all she wanted from us was that we keep quiet and stop wearing her nerves down, and she'd be grateful, because she would retire soon. She said we were becoming too much for her, and she didn't understand why. But when one kid wanted to say something, tell her why, she told us to keep still, and write something. You know what? She whipped out a book and told us to copy a whole page from it, so we'd learn it. A stupid waste of time. I didn't even try; and she didn't care. She just wanted an excuse not to talk with us. They're all alike.*"

Actually, they're all *not* alike, and Peter knows it. He has met up with two fine teachers, and in mellow moments he can say so: "*They're trying hard, but me and my friends, I don't think we're cut out for school. To tell the truth, that's what I think. My mother says we should try, anyway, but it doesn't seem to help, trying. The teacher can't understand a lot of us, but he does all these new things, and you can see he's excited. Some kids are really with him, and I am, too. But I can't take all his stuff very serious. He's a nice man, and he says he wants to come and visit every one of our homes; but my mother says no, she wouldn't know what to do with him, when he came here. We'd just stand and have nothing to talk about. So she said tell him not to come; and I don't think he will, anyway. I think he's getting to know.*"

What is that teacher getting to know? What *is* there to know about Peter and all the others like him in our American cities? Of course Peter and his friends who play in the alley need better schools, schools they can feel to be theirs, and better teachers, like the ones they *have* in fact met on occasion. But I do not feel that a reasonably good teacher in the finest school building in America would reach and affect Peter in quite the way, I suppose, people like me would expect and desire. At nine Peter is both young and quite old. At nine he is much wiser about many things than my sons will be at nine, and maybe nineteen. Peter has in fact taught me a lot about his neighborhood, about life on the streets, about survival: "*I get up when I get up, no special time. My mother has Alabama in her. She gets up with the sun, and she wants to go to bed when it gets dark. I try to tell her that up here things just get started in the night. But she gets mad. She wakes me up. If it weren't for her shaking me, I might sleep until noon. Sometimes we have a good breakfast, when the check comes. Later on, though, before it comes, it might just be some coffee and a slice of bread. She worries about food. She says we should eat what she gives us, but sometimes I'd rather go hungry. I was sick a long time ago, my stomach or something—maybe like my father, she says. So I don't like all the potatoes she pushes on us and cereal, all the time cereal. We're supposed to be lucky, because we get some food every day. Down South they can't be sure. That's what she says, and I guess she's right.*

"*Then I go to school. I eat what I can, and*

leave. I have two changes of clothes, one for everyday and one for Sunday. I wait on my friend Billy, and we're off by 8:15. He's from around here, and he's a year older. He knows everything. He can tell you if a woman is high on some stuff, or if she's been drinking, or she's off her mind about something. He knows. His brother has a convertible, a Buick. He pays off the police, but Billy won't say no more than that.

"In school we waste time until it's over. I do what I have to. I don't like the place. I feel like falling off all day, just putting my head down and saying goodbye to everyone until three. We're out then, and we sure wake up. I don't have to stop home first, not now. I go with Billy. We'll be in the alley, or we'll go to see them play pool. Then you know when it's time to go home. You hear someone say six o'clock, and you go in. I eat and I watch television. It must be around ten or eleven I'm in bed."

Peter sees rats all the time. He has been bitten by them. He has a big stick by his bed to use against them. They also claim the alley, even in the daytime. They are not large enough to be compared with cats, as some observers have insisted; they are simply large, confident, well-fed, unafraid rats. The garbage is theirs; the tenement is theirs; human flesh is theirs. When I first started visiting Peter's family, I wondered why they didn't do something to rid themselves of those rats, and the cockroaches, and the mosquitoes, and the flies, and the maggots, and the ants, and especially the garbage in the alley which attracts so much of all that "lower life." Eventually I began to see some of the reasons why. A large apartment building with many families has exactly two barrels in its basement. The halls of the building go unlighted. Many windows have no screens, and some windows are broken and boarded up. The stairs are dangerous; some of them have missing timber. ("We just jump over them," says Peter cheerfully.) And the landowner is no one in particular. Rent is collected by an agent, in the name of a "realty trust." Somewhere in City Hall there is a bureaucrat who unquestionably might be persuaded to prod someone in the "trust"; and one day I went with three of the tenants, including Peter's mother, to try that "approach." We waited and waited at City Hall. (I drove us there, clear across town, naturally.) Finally we met up with a man, a not very encouraging or inspiring or generous or friendly man. He told

us we would have to try yet another department and swear out a complaint; and that the "case" would have to be "studied," and that we would then be "notified of a decision." We went to the department down the hall, and waited some more, another hour and ten minutes. By then it was three o'clock, and the mothers wanted to go home. They weren't thinking of rats anymore, or poorly heated apartments, or garbage that had nowhere to go and often went uncollected for two weeks, not one. They were thinking of their children, who would be home from school and, in the case of two women, their husbands who would also soon be home. *"Maybe we should come back some other day,"* Peter's mother said. I noted she didn't say *tomorrow*, and I realized that I had read someplace that people like her aren't precisely "future-oriented."

Actually, both Peter and his mother have a very clear idea of what is ahead. For the mother it is *"more of the same."* One evening she was tired but unusually talkative, perhaps because a daughter of hers was sick: *"I'm glad to be speaking about all these things tonight. My little girl has a bad fever. I've been trying to cool her off all day. Maybe if there was a place near here, that we could go to, maybe I would have gone. But, like it is, I have to do the best I can and pray she'll be o.k."*

I asked whether she thought her children would find things different, and that's when she said it would be *"more of the same"* for them. Then she added a long afterthought: *"Maybe it'll be a little better for them. A mother has to have hope for her children, I guess. But I'm not too sure, I'll admit. Up here you know there's a lot more jobs around than in Alabama. We don't get them, but you know they're someplace near, and they tell you that if you go train for them, then you'll be eligible. So maybe Peter might someday have some real good steady work, and that would be something, yes sir it would. I keep telling him he should pay more attention to school, and put more of himself into the lessons they give there. But he says no, it's no good; it's a waste of time; they don't care what happens there, only if the kids don't keep quiet and mind themselves. Well, Peter has got to learn to mind himself, and not be fresh. He speaks back to me, these days. There'll be a time he won't even speak to me at all, I suppose. I used to blame it all on the city up here, city living. Back home we were always together, and there wasn't no place you could go, unless to Birmingham, and you couldn't do much for yourself there, we all knew. Of course, my momma, she knew how to make us behave. But I was thinking the other night, it wasn't so good back there either. Colored people, they'd beat on one another, and we had lot of people that liquor was eating away at them; they'd use wine by the gallon. All they'd do was work on the land, and then go back and kill themselves with wine. And then there'd be the next day—until they'd one evening go to sleep and never wake up. And we'd get the Bossman and he'd see to it they got buried.*

"Up here I think it's better, but don't ask me to tell you why. There's the welfare, that's for sure. And we get our water and if there isn't good heat, at least there's some. Yes, it's cold up here, but we had cold down there, too, only then we didn't have any heat, and we'd just die, some of us would, every winter with one of those freezing spells.

"And I do believe things are changing. On the television they talk to you, the colored man and all the others who aren't doing so good. My boy Peter, he says they're putting you on. That's all he sees, people "putting on" other people. But I think they all mean it, the white people. I never see them, except on television, when they say the white man wants good for the colored people. I think Peter could go and do better for himself later on, when he gets older, except for the fact that he just doesn't believe. He don't believe what they say, the teacher, or the man who says it's getting better for us—on television. I guess it's my fault. I never taught my children, any of them, to believe that kind of thing; because I never thought we'd ever have it any different, not in this life. So maybe I've failed Peter. I told him the other day, he should work hard, because of all the 'opportunity' they say is coming for us, and he said I was talking good, but where was my proof. So I went next door with him, to my neighbor's, and we asked her husband, and you know he sided with Peter. He said they were taking in a few here and a few there, and putting them in the front windows of all the big companies, but that all you have to do is look around at our block and you'd see all the young men, and they just haven't got a thing to do. Nothing."

Her son also looks to the future. Sometimes he talks—in his own words—"big." He'll one

day be a bombadier or *"something like that."* At other times he is less sure of things: *"I don't know what'll I'll be. Maybe nothing. I see the men sitting around, hiding from the welfare lady. They fool her. Maybe I'll fool her, too. I don't know what you can do. The teacher the other day said that if just one of us turned out o.k. she'd congratulate herself and call herself lucky."*

A while back a riot excited Peter and his mother, excited them and frightened them. The spectacle of the police being fought, of white-owned property being assaulted, stirred the boy a great deal: *"I figured the whole world might get changed around. I figured people would treat us better from now on. Only I don't think they will."* As for his mother, she was less hopeful, but even more apocalyptic: *"I told Peter we were going to pay for this good. I told him they wouldn't let us get away with it, not later on."* And in the midst of the trouble she was frightened as she had never before been: *"I saw them running around on the streets, the men and women, and they were talking about burning things down, and how there'd be nothing left when they got through. I sat there with my children and I thought we might die the way things are going, die right here. I didn't know what to do: if I should leave, in case they burn down the building, or if I should stay, so that the police don't arrest us, or we get mixed up with the crowd of people. I've never seen so many people, going in so many different directions. They were running and shouting and they didn't know what to do. They were so excited. My neighbor, she said they'd burn us all up, and then the white man would have himself one less of a headache. The colored man is a worse enemy to himself than the white. I mean, it's hard to know which is the worst."*

I find it as hard as she does to sort things out. When I think of her and the mothers like her I have worked with for years, when I think of Peter and his friends, I find myself caught between the contradictory observations I have made. Peter already seems a grim and unhappy child. He trusts no one white, not his white teacher, not the white policeman he sees, not the white welfare worker, not the white storekeeper, and not, I might add, me. There we are, the five of us from the 180,000,000 Americans who surround him and of course 20,000,000 others. Yet, Peter doesn't really trust his friends and neighbors, either. At nine he has learned to be careful, wary, guarded, doubtful, and calculating. His teacher may not know it, but Peter is a good sociologist, and a good political scientist, a good student of urban affairs. With devastating accuracy he can reveal how much of the "score" he knows; yes, and how fearful and sad and angry he is: *"This here city isn't for us. It's for the people downtown. We're here because, like my mother said, we had to come. If they could lock us up or sweep us away, they would. That's why I figure the only way you can stay ahead is get some kind of deal for yourself. If I had a choice I'd live someplace else, but I don't know where. It would be a place where they treated you right, and they didn't think you were some nuisance. But the only thing you can do is be careful of yourself; if not, you'll get killed somehow, like it happened to my father."*

His father died prematurely, and most probably, unnecessarily. Among the poor of our cities the grim medical statistics we all know about become terrible daily experiences. Among the black and white families I work with—in nearby but separate slums—disease and the pain that goes with it are taken for granted. When my children complain of an earache or demonstrate a skin rash I rush them to the doctor. When I have a headache, I take an aspirin; and if the headache is persistent, I can always get a medical check-up. Not so with Peter's mother and Peter; they have learned to live with sores and infections and poorly mended fractures and bad teeth and eyes that need but don't have the help of glasses. Yes, they can got to a city hospital and get free care; but again and again they don't. They come to the city without any previous experience as patients. They have never had the money to purchase a doctor's time. They have never had free medical care available. (I am speaking now of Appalachian whites as well as southern blacks.) It may comfort me to know that every American city provides some free medical services for its "indigent," but Peter's mother and thousands like her have quite a different view of things: *"I said to you the other time, I've tried there. It's like at City Hall, you wait and wait, and they pushes you and shove you and call your name, only to tell you to wait some more, and if you tell them you can't stay there all day, they'll say 'lady, go home, then.' You get sick just trying to get there. You have to give your children over to people or take*

them all with you; and the carfare is expensive. Why if we had a doctor around here, I could almost pay him with the carfare it takes to get there and back for all of us. And you know, they keep on having you come back and back, and they don't know what each other says. Each time they starts from scratch."

It so happens that recently I took Peter to a children's hospital and arranged for a series of evaluations which led to the following: a pair of glasses; a prolonged bout of dental work; antibiotic treatment for skin lesions; a thorough cardiac work-up, with the subsequent diagnosis of rheumatic heart disease, a conference between Peter's mother and a nutritionist, because the boy has been on a high-starch, low-protein, and low-vitamin diet all his life. He suffers from one attack of sinus trouble after another, from a succession of sore throats and earaches, from cold upon cold, even in the summer. A running nose is unsurprising to him—and so is chest pain and shortness of breath, due to a heart ailment, we now know.

At the same time Peter is tough. I have to emphasize again *how* tough and, yes, how "politic, cautious and meticulous," not in Prufrock's way, but in another way and for other reasons. Peter has learned to be wary as well as angry; tentative as well as extravagant; at times controlled and only under certain circumstances defiant: *"Most of the time, I think you have to watch your step. That's what I think. That's the difference between up here and down in the South. That's what my mother says, and she's right. I don't remember it down there, but I know she must be right. Here, you measure the next guy first and then make your move when you think it's a good time to."*

He was talking about *"how you get along"* when you leave school and go *"mix with the guys"* and start *"getting your deal."* He was telling me what an outrageous and unsafe world he has inherited and how very carefully he has made his appraisal of the future. Were I afflicted with some of his physical complaints, I would be fretful, annoyed, petulant, angry—and moved to do something, see someone, get a remedy, a pill, a promise of help. He has made his "adjustment" to the body's pain, and he has also learned to contend with the alley and the neighborhood and *us*, the world beyond: *"The cops come by here all the time. They drive up and down the street. They want to make sure everything is* o.k. to look at. They don't bother you, so long as you don't get in their way."

So, it is live and let live—except that families like Peter's have a tough time living, and of late have been troubling those cops, among others. Our cities have become not only battlegrounds, but places where all sorts of American problems and historical ironies have converged. Ailing, poorly fed, and proud Appalachian families have reluctantly left the hollows of eastern Kentucky and West Virginia for Chicago and Dayton and Cincinnati and Cleveland and Detroit, and even, I have found, Boston. They stick close together in all-white neighborhoods—or enclaves or sections or slums or ghettos or whatever. They wish to go home but can't, unless they are willing to be idle and hungry all the time. They confuse social workers and public officials of all kinds because they want and reject the city. Black families have also sought out cities and learned to feel frightened and disappointed.

I am a physician, and over the past ten years I have been asking myself how people like Peter and his mother survive in mind and body and spirit. And I have wanted to know what a twentieth-century American city "means" to them or "does" to them. People cannot be handed questionnaires and asked to answer such questions. They cannot be "interviewed" a few times and told to come across with a statement, a reply. But inside Peter and his brother and his sisters and his mother, and inside a number of Appalachian mothers and fathers and children I know, are feelings and thoughts and ideas —which, in my experience, come out casually or suddenly, by accident almost. After a year or two of talking, after experiences such as I have briefly described in a city hall, in a children's hospital, a lifetime of pent-up tensions and observation comes to blunt expression: "Down in Alabama we had to be careful about ourselves with the white man, but we had plenty of things we could do by ourselves. There was our side of town, and you could walk and run all over, and we had a garden you know. Up here they have you in a cage. There's no place to go, and all I do is stay in the building all day long and the night, too. I don't use my legs no more, hardly at all. I never see those trees, and my oldest girl, she misses planting time. It was bad down there. We had to leave. But it's no good here, too, I'll tell you. Once I woke up and I thought all the buildings on the block were fall-

ing down on me. And I was trying to climb out, but I couldn't. And then the next thing I knew, we were all back South, and I was standing near some sunflowers—you know, the tall ones that can shade you if you sit down.

"No, I don't dream much. I fall into a heavy sleep as soon as I touch the bed. The next thing I know I'm stirring myself to start in all over in the morning. It used to be the sun would wake me up, but now it's in my head, I guess. I know I've got to get the house going and off to school."

Her wistful, conscientious, law-abiding, devoutly Christian spirit hasn't completely escaped the notice of Peter, for all his hard-headed, cynical protestations: "If I had a chance, I'd like to get enough money to bring us all back to Alabama for a visit. Then I could prove it that it may be good down there, a little bit, even if it's no good, either. Like she says, we had to get out of there or we'd be dead by now. I hear say we all may get killed soon, it's so bad here; but I think we did right to get up here, and if we make them listen to us, the white man, maybe he will."

To which Peter's mother adds: "We've carried a lot of trouble in us, from way back in the beginning. I have these pains, and so does everyone around here. But you can't just die until you're ready to. And I do believe something is happening. I do believe I see that."

To which Peter adds: "Maybe it won't be that we'll win, but if we get killed, everyone will hear about it. Like the minister said, before we used to die real quiet, and no one stopped to pay notice."

Two years before Peter spoke those words he drew a picture for me, one of many he has done. When he was younger, and when I didn't know him so well as I think I do now, it was easier for us to have something tangible to do and then talk about. I used to visit the alley with him, as I still do, and one day I asked him to draw the alley. That was a good idea, he thought. (Not all of my suggestions were, however.) He started in, then stopped, and finally worked rather longer and harder than usual at the job. I busied myself with my own sketches, which from the start he insisted I do. Suddenly from across the table I heard him say he was through. Ordinarily he would slowly turn the drawing around for me to see; and I would get up and walk over to his side of the table, to see even better. But he didn't move his paper, and I didn't move myself. I saw what he had drawn, and he saw me looking. I was surprised and a bit stunned and more than a bit upset, and surely he saw my face and heard my utter silence. Often I would break the awkward moments when neither of us seemed to have anything to say, but this time it was his turn to do so: *"You know what it is?"* He knew that I liked us to talk about our work. I said no, I didn't—though in fact the vivid power of his black crayon had come right across to me. *"It's that hole we dug in the alley. I made it bigger here. If you fall into it, you can't get out. You die."*

He had drawn circles within circles, all of them black, and then a center, also black. He had imposed an X on the center. Nearby, strewn across the circles, were fragments of the human body—two faces, an arm, five legs. And after I had taken the scene in, I could only think to myself that I had been shown *"like it is in the alley"*—by an intelligent boy who knew what he saw around him, could give it expression, and, I am convinced, would respond to a different city, a city that is alive and breathing, one that is not for many of its citizens a virtual morgue.

12

GERALD D. SUTTLES

Anatomy of a Chicago Slum

Methodology: Gerald D. Suttles spent three years in the Near West Side of Chicago making a study of a multiethnic community that includes Italians, Mexicans, Negroes and Puerto Ricans. He took up residence in the area in the summer of 1963 and did not leave until almost three years later. It took him a year or more to acquire friends and enter the private worlds of families, social-athletic clubs and other groups. The findings of his study are published in *The Social Order of the Slum* from which *Trans*-action has taken excerpts —chiefly from materials on the Italian population. The book in its entirety shows that there are broad structural similarities between all the ethnic groups—Italian, Mexican, Negro and Puerto Rican, although this structure is more clearly developed among the Italians. The excerpts draw on some of Suttle's more general observations rather than his detailed empirical findings.

In its heyday, the Near West Side of Chicago was the stronghold of such men as Al (Scarface) Capone and Frank (The Enforcer) Nitti, and served as the kindergarten for several figures still active in the underworld. For convenience, I will call this part of Chicago the Addams area —after Jane Addams, who founded Hull House there. The name is artificial, since it is never used by the local residents.

The Addams area is one of the oldest slums in Chicago, and researchers have invaded it almost as often as new minority groups have. Like most slums, it remains something of a mystery. In some ways it is easiest to describe the neighborhood by describing how its residents deviate from the public standards of the wider community. The area has, for example, a high delinquency rate, numerous unwed mothers, and several adolescent "gangs." It is tempting to think that the residents are simply people suffering from cultural deprivation, unemployment, and a number of other urban ills. And if the residents insist upon the irrelevance of the standards of the wider community and the primacy of their own, this can be dismissed as sour grapes or an attempt to make of necessity a virtue.

Seen from the inside, however, Addams area residents require discipline and self-restraint in the same way as the wider community does. Conventional norms are not rejected but emphasized differently, or suspended for established reasons. The vast majority of the residents are quite conventional people. At the same time, those who remain in good standing are often exceptionally tolerant of and even encouraging to those who are "deviant."

Certainly the social practices of the residents are not just an inversion of those of the wider society, and the inhabitants would be outraged to hear as much. Nor is the neighborhood a cultural island with its own distinct and imported traditions. The area's internal structure features such commonplace distinctions as age, sex, territoriality, ethnicity, and personal identity. Taken out of context, many of the social arrangements of the Addams area may seem an illusory denial of the beliefs and values of the wider society. But actually the residents are bent on ordering local relations because the beliefs and evaluations of the wider society do not provide adequate guidelines for conduct.

In anthropology, territorial grouping has been a subject of continue interest. Most anthropological studies begin by focusing upon social groupings that can be defined by their areal distribution. In turn, many of the social units singled out for particular attention—the domestic unit, the homestead, the tribe, and so forth—frequently have locality as one of their principles of organization. And where locality and structural forms do not coincide, anthropologists have regarded this discrepancy as a distinct problem that raises a number of theoretical and methodological issues.

The most obvious reason for focusing on locality groups is that their members cannot simply ignore one another. People who routinely occupy the same place must either develop a moral order that includes all those present or fall into conflict. And because almost all societies create a public morality that exceeds the capabilities of some of its members, territorial groups are always faced with the prospect of people whose public character does not warrant trust. In the United States a very large percentage of our population fails to meet the public standards we set for measuring someone's merit, trustworthiness, and respectability.

Many groups have avoided compromising these ideals of public morality by territorial segregation. More exactly, they have simply retreated and left valuable portions of the inner city to those they distrust. Obviously, this practice has its limits—it tends to aggregate those who are poor, unsuccessful, and disreputable in the same slum neighborhoods. These people must compromise the ideals of public morality or remain permanently estranged from one another.

In slum neighborhoods, territorial aggregation usually comes before any common social framework for assuring orderly relations. After all, ethnic invasion, the encroachment of industry, and economic conditions constantly reshuffle slum residents and relocate them around new neighbors. Since the residents lack obvious grounds for assuming mutual trust, a combination of alternatives seems to offer the most promising course:

- Social relations can be restricted to only the safest ones. Families can withdraw to their households, where they see only close relatives. Segregation by age, sex, and ethnicity are maneuvers that will prevent at least the most unfair and most likely forms of conflict and exploitation. Remaining close to the household cuts down on the range of anonymity and reduces the number of social relations. The general pattern, then, should be a fan-shaped spatial arrangement, with women and children remaining close by the house while males move progressively outwards, depending on their age.
- Slum residents can assuage at least some of their apprehensions by a close inquiry into one another's personal character and past history. Communication, then, should be of an intimate character and aimed toward producing personal rather than formal relations. In turn, social relations will represent a sort of private compact in which particular loyalties replace impersonal standards of worth.

Neither of these patterns will immediately produce a comprehensive framework within which a large number of slum residents can safely negotiate with one another. The segregation by age, sex, and territorial groups, however, does provide a starting point from which face-to-face relations can grow and reach beyond each small territorial aggregation. The development of personal relations furnishes both a moral formula and a structural bridge between groups. Within each small, localized peer group, continuing face-to-face relations can eventually provide a personalistic order. Once these groups are established, a single personal relation between them can extend the range of such an order. Thus, with the acceptance of age-grading and territorial segregation, it becomes possible for slum neighborhoods to work out a moral order that includes most of their residents.

The Addams area actually consists of four dif

ferent sections, each occupied predominantly by Negroes, Italians, Puerto Ricans, and Mexicans. And each of these sections falls into a somewhat different stage in its development of a provincial order.

Despite this difference and others, all four ethnic sections share many characteristics and seem headed along the same social progression. The overall pattern is one in which age, sex, ethnic, and territorial units are fitted together like building blocks to create a larger structure. I have termed this pattern "ordered segmentation" to indicate two related features: (1) the orderly relationship between groups; and (2) the order in which groups combine in instances of conflict and opposition. This ordered segmentation is not equally developed in all ethnic sections but, in skeletal outline, it is the common framework within which groups are being formed and social relations are being cultivated.

My own experiences within the Addams area and the presentation of this volume are heavily influenced by the ordered segmentation of the neighborhood. I took up residence in the area in the summer of 1963 and left a little fewer than three years later.

As I acquired friends and close informants, my own ethnicity became a serious problem. A few people worked over my genealogy trying to find some trace that would allot me to a known ethnic group. After close inquiry, one old Italian lady announced with peals of laughter, "Geraldo, you're just an American." She did not mean it as a compliment, and I remember being depressed. In the Addams area, being without ethnicity means there is no one you can appeal to or claim as your own.

Only after a year or more in the Addams area was I able to penetrate the private world of its families, street-corner groups, and insular establishments. These are the groupings within which Addams area residents are least cautious and most likely to expose themselves. In large part my experience with these groups is limited to many adolescent male street-corner groups and my own adult friends, who formed a group of this type.

By far the most striking contrast is between the Negro and the Italian sections. For instance, almost all the Negroes live in public housing; the Italians usually control both their households and commercial establishments. The Negroes have very similar incomes and almost no political power; among the Italians, there *is* some internal differentiation of income and political power. Such differences draw the Italians and Negroes apart and generate radically different styles of life.

In most ways, the Puerto Rican section is the least complex of those in the Addams area. There are no more than 1100 Puerto Ricans in the section and, within broad age ranges, most of them know one another. Until 1965, no named groups had emerged among the Puerto Ricans.

The Mexicans are more numerous, and several named groups have developed among the teenagers. Unlike the Italians, however, the Mexican groups have not survived into adulthood. The Mexicans seem to have much in common with the Italians, and frequently their relationships are congenial. What gives the Mexicans pause is the occasional necessity to divide their loyalties between the Italians and the Negroes.

Although one must not overemphasize the extent of differences between all these ethnic sections, such differences as do occur loom large in the Addams area. The residents are actively looking for differences among themselves. The ethnic sections in the area constitute basic guidelines from which the residents of each section can expect certain forms of reciprocity, and anticipate the dangers that may be in store elsewhere.

The portion of the Addams area now controlled by the Italians is only a residue from the encroachments of the three other ethnic groups. But in total land space, it is the largest of any controlled by a single ethnic group. In population, it is not exceptionally big, though, and throughout the section an unusually high percentage of Mexicans have been accepted by the Italians as neighbors.

What the Italians lack in numbers, they often make up for by their reputation for using sheer force and for easy access to "influence" or "connections." It is said, for example, that many of the Italians are "Outfit people," and that many more could rely on mobsters if they needed help. Also, it is the general view that the Italians control both the vice and patronage of the First Ward, a political unit that includes the spoils of the Loop—downtown Chicago.

There are some very famous Italians in the Addams area, and they frequently get a spread in the city newspapers. There are many others not nearly so prominent but whose personal histories are still known in the neighborhood. At least five Italian policemen live in the area, and a few more who grew up there are assigned to the local district. The other ethnic groups have not a single resident or ex-resident policeman among them. Most of the precinct captains are also Italian; and, outside the projects, the Italians dominate those jobs provided by public funds. There are a number of Italian businessmen, each of whom controls a few jobs. It is also widely believed that they can "sponsor" a person into many of the industries of the city— the newsstands in the Loop, the city parks, the beauty-culture industry, a large printing company, and a number of clothing firms.

While there is some substance to this belief in Italian power and influence, it is actually quite exaggerated. Many of the Italian political figures seem to have little more than the privilege of announcing decisions that have been made by others. In most of the recent political actions that have affected the area, they have remained mute and docile. When the Medical Center was built and then extended, they said nothing. The Congress and the Dan Ryan Expressways were constructed with the local politicians hardly taking notice. Finally, when the University of Illinois was located at Congress Circle, the politicians, mobsters, and—indeed—all the male residents accepted it without even a show of resistance. In fact, only a group of Italian and Mexican housewives took up arms and sought to save some remnant of the neighborhood.

The Italians' notoriety for being in the rackets and having recourse to strong-arm methods is also a considerable exaggeration, or at least a misinterpretation. The majority of the local Italians are perfectly respectable people and gain nothing from organized crime. Yet, many of the common family names of the area have been sullied by some flagrant past episode by a relative. And in the area, family histories remain a basis for judging individual members and are extended to include all persons who share the same name. In another neighborhood, this information might be lost or ignored as improper; in the Addams area, it is almost impossible to keep family secrets, and they are kept alive in the constant round of rumor and gossip.

The local Italians themselves contribute to their reputation—because on many occasions they find it advantageous to intimate that they have connections with the Outfit. For example, outsiders are often flattered to think that they are in the confidence of someone who knows the underworld. Also, it is far more prestigious to have other people believe that one's background is buried in crime and violence than in public welfare. In America, organized crime has always received a certain respect, even when this respect had to be coerced. A recipient of public welfare is simply dismissed as unimportant. And during the Depression many of the Italians went on welfare.

"Right People" Can Protect Them

In addition, some of the Italians feel that a reputation of being in with the "right people" can in some circumstances ensure them against victimization. They often hint about their connections with the Outfit when facing the members of another ethnic group under uncertain odds, or when in an argument among themselves. Yet with friends and relatives, the Italians often complain bitterly of how they are maligned by the press and by their neighbors.

Ironically, the Italians are cautious in their dealings with one another; more than any other group, they are intimidated by the half-myth that is partly of their own creation. And indirectly this myth gives them considerable cohesion, and a certain freedom from the judgments and actions of the wider society. It is almost impossible to persuade one of them to make a complaint to the police, for instance, because of their fear of the Outfit; indeed, they shun all public sources of social control. They handle grievances, contracts, and exchanges in a very informal manner, usually limited to the immediate parties. If in need, they exact aid in the form of favors and generally ignore sources available to the general public. As a result, the Italians have been able to sustain among themselves the image of an independent, powerful, and self-confident people.

Behind the Scenes Bargaining

Yet the cohesion and solidarity of the Italians are very limited. They are based primarily on the suspicion that social arrangements are best made by private settlements. This suspicion, in turn, is based on the assumption that recourse to public means can do little more than excite retaliation and vengeance. These same suspicions and doubts undermine the possibilities of a unified and explicit stance by the Italians toward the wider community and political organization. First, very few of them believe that the others will cooperate in joint efforts unless it is to their personal advantage or they are under some dire threat. Second, the Italians simply fear that a united public stand will elicit a similar posture on the part of their adversaries and eliminate the opportunity for private negotiations. Accordingly, the Italians either shun public confrontations or slowly draw away, once so engaged. In retrospect, the spirit of *omerta* seems ineffectual when it confronts the explicit efforts of the wider community. (Literally, *omerta* means a conspiracy between thieves. The Italians use it to mean any private agreement that cannot be safely broached before the general public.)

The inability of the Italians to accept or engage in public appeals leaves them somewhat bewildered by the Negroes' civil-rights movement. By the Italians' standards, the Negroes are "making a federal case" out of something that should be handled by private agreement. Indeed, even those who accept the justice of the Negroes' cause remain perplexed by the Negroes' failure to approach *them* in some informal manner. Throughout the summer of 1964, when demonstrators were most active, the Italians always seemed aggrieved and surprised that the Negroes would "pull such a trick" without warning. The Negroes took this view as a "sham" and felt that the Italians had ample reason to anticipate their demands. To the Italians this was not the point. Of course, they knew that the Negroes had many long-standing demands and desires. What struck the Italians as unfair about the Negroes' demonstrations was their tactics: sudden public confrontations, without any chance for either side to retreat or compromise with grace.

Ultimately, both the Italians and Negroes did take their differences behind closed doors, and each settled for something less than their public demands. The main bone of contention was a local swimming pool dominated by the Italians and their Mexican guests.

In the background, of course, was the oppressive belief that the benefits of social life make up a fixed quantity and are already being used to the maximum. Thus, even the most liberal Italians assume that any gain to the Negroes must be their loss. On their own part, the Negroes make the same assumption and see no reason why the Italians should give way without a fight. Thus, whatever good intentions exist on either side are overruled by the seeming impracticality or lack of realism.

The Italians' career in the Addams area has been shaped by a traditional world view that relies heavily on a belief in "natural man." For example, it is felt to be "natural" for men to be sexual predators; for mothers to love their children, regardless of what their children do; for girls to connive at marriage; for boys to hate school; for a businessman to cheat strangers; and for anyone to choose pleasure in preference to discipline and duty. Implicit in the concept of natural man is the conviction that moral restraints have little real power in a situation in which they contradict man's natural impulses. Civilization is a mere gloss to hide man's true nature.

Often, although not always, man's natural impulses are at odds with his moral standards. Indeed, otherwise there would be no need for the church, the police, the government, and all other bodies of social control. But it is not always possible for these external bodies of social control to keep track of what people are doing. Inevitably, then, there will be occasions when people are free to choose between acting naturally and acting morally. For their own part, the Italians may have considerable conviction of their personal preferences for morality. In their dealings with other people, however, they have little faith in this thin thread of individual morality. Correspondingly, to them their own personal morality becomes utterly impractical and must be replaced by whatever amoral expedient seems necessary for self-defense.

The general outcome seems to be an overwhelming distrust of impersonal or "voluntary" relationships. The other side of the coin is an equally strong tendency to fall back on those relationships and identities where one's own welfare is guaranteed by "natural inclinations." For the most part these are kin relations, close friendship, common regional origins (*paesani*), joint residential unity, and sacred pledges like marriage, God, parenthood, etc. Thus, the Italians in the Addams area have tended to turn in upon themselves and become a provincial moral world.

Actually, many of the Italians are quite "Americanized." Frequently, though, these people lead something of a double life. During the daytime they leave the neighborhood and do their work without much thought of their ethnicity. When they come home in the evening, they are obliged to reassume their old world identity. This need not be so much a matter of taste as necessity. Other people are likely to already know their ethnicity, and evasions are likely to be interpreted as acts of snobbery or attempts at deception. Moreover, members of the other three ethnic groups refuse to accept such a person's Americanization, no matter how much it is stressed. To others, an attempt to minimize one's ethnicity is only a sly maneuver to escape responsibility for past wrongs or to gain admission into their confidence. Finally, there are still many old-timers in the neighborhood, and it would be very ill-mannered to parade one's Americanism before them. Thus, within the bounds of the local neighborhood, an Italian who plays at being an "American" runs the risk of being taken as a snob, phony, opportunist, coward, or fink.

Among the Italians themselves, notions of ethnicity are particularly well-elaborated. For the most part, these internal subdivisions are based on regional origins in Italy. By contrast, the other ethnic groups have very little internal differentiation. The Negroes make only a vague distinction between those raised in the South and those raised in the North. Among the former, Mississippians are sometimes singled out for special contempt. However, none of these divisions lead to cohesive social unities. But among the Italians their *paesani* (regional origins) take on great importance, and it remains the first perimeter beyond the family within which they look for aid or feel themselves in safe hands. Most *paesani* continue to hold their annual summer picnics and winter dance. Some have grown into full-scale organizations with elected officers, insurance plans, burial funds, and regular poker sessions.

Of all the ethnic groups in the Addams area, the Italians still have the richest ceremonial life.

Aside from the annual *paesani* dances and picnics, there are parades, *feste*, and several other occasions. In the summer, their church holds a carnival that duplicates much of the Italian *feste*. On Columbus Day there is a great parade in the Loop, exceeded in grandeur only by the one held by the Irish on St. Patrick's Day. During Lent there are several special religious events and afterwards a round of dances, parties, and feasts. Throughout the summer a local brass band periodically marches through the streets playing arias from Puccini and Verdi. Sidewalk vendors sell Italian lemonade, sausages, and beef sandwiches. Horsedrawn carts go about selling grapes during the fall winemaking season, tomatoes when they are ready to be turned to paste, and fruit and vegetables at almost any time of the year.

Communal Ceremonies and Festivities

Even weddings, communions, funerals, and wakes maintain some of their communal nature. Weddings are usually known of beforehand and often attract a number of onlookers as well as those invited. Afterwards the couple and their friends drive around the neighborhood in decorated cars, honking their horns at one another and whomever they recognize on the streets. Parochial-school children usually receive first communion as a group and attract a good deal of attention. Wakes are also open to almost anyone, and funeral processions often tour a portion of the neighborhood. On this sort of occasion, the Mexicans follow much the same practice, although they lack full control of a local church where they can carry out these affairs to the same extent as the Italians. Among the Negroes and Puerto Ricans, weddings, funerals, and religious events tend to be quite private affairs, open through invitation alone.

The Italians are also favored by the relatively long period over which many of them have been able to know one another and to decide upon whom they can or cannot trust. Over time, a considerable amount of information has been accumulated on many people, and this circulates in such a way as to be available to even a fairly recent resident. Moreover, the intertwining of social relations has become so extensive that contact with one person often opens passage to many others. In this sense, "getting acquainted" is almost unavoidable for a new resident.

The forms of social organization in the Italian section are far more extensive and complicated than those of the other ethnic groups. At the top are two groups, the "West Side Bloc" and the "Outfit," which share membership and whose participants are not all from the Addams area. The West Side Bloc is a group of Italian politicians whose constituency is much larger than the Addams area but which includes a definite wing in the area. Generally its members are assumed to belong to or to have connections with the Outfit. A good deal of power is attributed to them within the local neighborhood, city, state, and nation. The Outfit, more widely known as the Syndicate, includes many more people, but it is also assumed to reach beyond the Addams area. Locally, it is usually taken to include almost anyone who runs a tavern or a liquor store, or who relies on state licensing or city employment. A few other businessmen and local toughs are accredited with membership because of their notorious immunity to law enforcement or their reputed control of "favors."

Indirectly, the Outfit extends to a number of adult social-athletic clubs (s.a.c.'s). These clubs invariably have a storefront where the members spend their time in casual conversation or drink, or play cards. A few of their members belong to the Outfit, and a couple of these clubs are said to have a "regular game" for big stakes. Each group is fairly homogeneous in age, but collectively the groups range between the late 20s up to the late 60s.

Below these adult s.a.c's are a number of other s.a.c's that also have a clubhouse, but whose members are much younger. As a rule, they are somewhat beyond school age, but only a few are married, and practically none have children. To some degree, they are still involved in the extra-familial life that occupies teenagers. Occasionally they have dances, socials, and impromptu parties. On weekends they still roam around together, attending "socials" sponsored by other groups, looking for girls or for some kind of "action." Within each young man's s.a.c., the members' ages cover a narrow range. Together, all the groups range between about 19 and the late 20s. They form a distinct and well-recognized age grade in the neighborhood because of

their continuing involvement in those cross-sexual and recreational activities open to unmarried males.

Nevertheless, these young men's s.a.c.'s are somewhat outside the full round of activities that throw teenagers together. A good portion of their time is spent inside their clubhouse out of sight of their rivals or most bodies of social control. Most members are in their 20s and are able to openly enjoy routine forms of entertainment or excitement that the wider community provides and accepts. When they have a dance or party, it is usually restricted to those whom they invite. Being out of school, they are not forced each day to confront persons from beyond their neighborhood. Since many of them have cars, they need not trespass too much on someone else's domain.

These s.ac.'s are not assumed to have any active role in the Outfit. At most, it is expected that they might be able to gain a few exemptions from law enforcement and an occasional "favor," e.g., a job, a chance to run an illegal errand, a small loan, someone to sign for their clubhouse charter (required by law), and the purchase of stolen goods or of anything else the boys happen to have on hand. It is assumed that they could solicit help from the Outfit if they got into trouble with another group, but very rarely are they drawn into this type of conflict. Almost invariably the opponent is a much younger "street group" that has encroached on what the s.a.c. considers its "rights"—e.g., tried to crash one of their parties, insulted them on the streets, made noise nearby, or marked up their clubhouse. Even at these times, their actions seem designed to do little more than rid themselves of a temporary nuisance. Once rid of their tormentors, they usually do not pursue the issue further, and for good reason. To charter such a club requires three cosigners, and these people may withdraw their support if the group becomes too rowdy. Also, they have a landlord to contend with, and he can throw them out for the same reason. Finally, they cannot afford to make too many enemies; they have a piece of property, and it would be only too easy for their adversaries to get back at them. Unlike all the groups described in the other three sections, they have a stake in maintaining something like law and order.

All the remaining Italian groups include members who are of high-school age. While they too call themselves s.a.c.'s, none of them have a storefront. All of them do have an established "hangout," and they correspond to the usual image of a street-corner group.

While the street groups in this section of the area often express admiration for the adult s.a.c.'s, they seldom develop in an unbroken sequence into a full-fledged adult s.a.c. Usually when they grow old enough to rent a storefront they change their name, acquire new members from groups that have been their rivals, and lose a few of their long-term members. Some groups disband entirely, and their members are redistributed among the newly formed s.a.c.'s. Of the twelve young men's and adult s.a.c.'s, only one is said to have maintained the same name from the time it was a street-corner group. Even in this case some members have been added and others lost. Together, then, the Italian street-corner groups make up the population from which future young men's s.a.c.'s are drawn, but only a few street-corner groups form the nucleus of a s.a.c.

Conceptually, the Italian street groups and the older s.a.c.'s form a single unity. In the eyes of the boys, they are somewhat like the steps between grammar school and college. While there may be dropouts, breaks, and amalgamations, they still make up a series of steps through which one can advance with increasing age. Thus, each street group tends to see the adult s.a.c's as essentially an older and more perfect version of itself. What may be just as important is their equally strong sense of history. Locally, many of the members in the street groups can trace their group's genealogy back through the Taylor Dukes, the 40 game, the Genna Brothers, and the Capone mob. Actually, there is no clear idea of the exact order of this descent line; some people include groups that others leave out. Moreover, there is no widespread agreement on which specific group is the current successor to this lineage. Nonetheless, there is agreement that the groups on Taylor Street have illustrious progenitors. On some occasions this heritage may be something of a burden, and on others a source of pride. In any case, it is unavoidable, and usually the Italian street group prefaces its own name with the term "Taylor." Among the younger groups this is omitted only when their name is an amalgam made up from a specific street corner or block. Only the adult s.a.c.'s

regularly fail to acknowledge in their name the immediate territory within which they are situated.

Direct Line of Succession from the Outfit

Since they see themselves in a direct line of succession to groups reputed to be associated with the Outfit, these street-corner groups might be expected to have a strong criminal orientation. In the Addams area, however, the Italian groups are best known for their fighting prowess, and their official police records show no concentration on the more utilitarian forms of crime. The fact is that, like the other adolescent groups in the area, the Italian boys are not really free to choose their own goals and identities. Territorial arrangements juxtapose them against similar groups manned by Negro and Mexican boys. If the Italian street-corner groups fail to define themselves as fighting groups, their peers in the other ethnic groups are certainly going to assume as much.

There is also considerable rivalry between Italian street-corner groups of roughly the same age. Commonly they suspect each other of using force to establish their precedence. In turn, each group seems to think it must at least put on a tough exterior to avoid being "pushed around." Privately there is a great deal of talk among them about the Outfit and about criminal activities, but it is academic in the sense that there is no strong evidence that their behavior follows suit.

It is interesting that the adult s.a.c.'s that actually have members in the rackets avoid any conspicuous claims about their criminal activities or fighting abilities. Their names, for example, are quite tame, while those of the street groups tend to be rather menacing. And their dances, leisure-time activities, and interrelationships are quite private and unpretentious. Unlike the street groups, they never wear clothing that identifies their group membership. The older men in the s.a.c.'s make no apparent attempt to establish a publicly-known hierarchy among themselves. Other people occasionally attribute more respect to one than another of them, but there seems to be little consensus on this. On their own part, the older groups seem to pay little attention to their relative standing and to be on fairly good terms. During my three years in the area, I never heard of them fighting among themselves.

Unlike the Negro and Mexican ethnic sections, there are no female counterparts to the named Italian street-corner groups. A very few Italian girls belong to two Mexican girls' groups that "hung" in the Mexican section. This, in itself, was exceptional; almost always the minority members in a street group are from a lower-ranking ethnic group. The Italians girls, however, are under certain constraints that may be lacking for those in the other ethnic groups. Naturally, their parents disapprove of such a blatant display of feminine unity. The Italian parents may gain stature by their power and precedence in comparison to the Negro and Mexican adults. Yet what seems far more significant is the general form that boy-girl relationships take among the Italians. On either side, the slightest hint of interest in the other sex is likely to be taken in the most serious way; as either a rank insult or a final commitment. Thus, any explicit alliance between a boys' and girls' group can be interpreted in only one of two ways: (1) all the girls are "laying" for the boys, or (2) they are seriously attached to each other. Neither side seems quite willing to betray so much and, thus, they avoid such explicit alliances.

This dilemma was quite evident on many occasions while I was observing the Italian boys and girls. The girls seemed extraordinarily coy when they were in a "safe" position—with their parents, in church, etc. When alone and on their own they became equally cautious and noncommittal. On public occasions, the boys seemed almost to ignore the girls and even to snub them. On Taylor Street, for instance, an Italian boys' group and an Italian girls' group used to hang about 10 feet from each other. Almost invariably they would stand with their backs to each other, although there were many furtive glances back and forth. During almost two years of observation, I never saw them talk. Later, I was surprised to learn that everyone in each group was quite well-known to the other. For either of them to have acknowledged the other's presence openly, however, would have been too forward. The boys are quite aware of this dilemma and complain that the girls are not free enough to be convenient companions. This, they say, is one reason why they have to go elsewhere to date someone. At the same time, they perpetuate the old system by automatically assuming that the slightest sign of interest by a girl

makes her fair game. Out of self-defense, the girls are compelled to keep their distance. On private occasions, of course, there are many Italian boys and girls who sneak off to enjoy what others might consider an entirely conventional boy-girl relationship (petting, necking). In public, though, they studiously ignore each other. Throughout my time in the area I never saw a young Italian couple hold hands or walk together on the sidewalk.

The Barracudas were the first Mexican street-corner group to emerge in the Italian section. They first became a named group in the spring of 1964, and all members were Mexican.

Once established, the Barracudas installed themselves in the northwest corner of Sheridan Park. Virtually every Italian street group in the area makes use of this park, and several have their hangouts there. Other people in turn refer to the Italian groups collectively as "the guys from the Park." The park itself is partitioned into a finely graduated series of more or less private enclosures, with the most private hangout going to the reigning group and the least private to the weakest group. The northwest corner of the park is the most exposed of any portion, and this is where the Barracudas installed themselves. Even in this lowly spot, they were much resented by the other groups. To the Italians the Park was almost a sacred charge, and the Mexicans' intrusion was a ritual pollution. The Barracudas were harassed, ridiculed, and insulted. On their own part, they became belligerent and vaunted all sorts of outrageous claims about themselves. Soon the situation deteriorated and the Italian groups became extremely harsh with the Barracudas. Since the Barracudas were no match for even some of the younger Italian groups, they removed themselves to one member's house.

Their new hangout placed them in an anomalous position. Ethnically they were identified as a Mexican group. Yet they were located in a part of the area that had been conceded to the Puerto Ricans. And individually most of them continued to reside in the Italian section. The general result seems to have been that the Barracudas were isolated from any of the other group hierarchies and placed in opposition to every group in the area. Within a year every white group was their enemy, and the Negroes were not their friends. The Barracudas responded in kind and became even more truculent and boastful. More than any group in the area, they openly embraced the stance of a fighting group. They wrote their name all over the neighborhood and even on some of the other groups' hangouts. In the meantime, they made a clubhouse out of a lean-to adjacent to a building on Harrison Street. Inside they installed a shield on which they wrote "hate," "kill," and other violent words. Carrying a weapon became almost routine with them, and eventually they collected a small arsenal. In time they had several small-scale fights with both the Italians from the Park and the Mexicans around Polk and Laflin. In due course, they acquired so many enemies that they could hardly risk leaving the immediate area of their hangout. At the same time, some of them began to go to Eighteenth Street, where they had "connections"—relatives. This only brought them into conflict with other groups in this neighborhood. By the summer of 1965, the Barracudas were as isolated and resentful as ever.

"Incognitos" and the "Pica People"

There are two other groups in the Italian section, the Pica People and the Incognitos. The groups' names are themselves an expression of their isolation. The Incognitos self-consciously avoided comparison with the other groups: They did not hang in the Park, hold socials, or become involved in any of the local sidewalk confrontations. About the same age as the Contenders, the Incognitos were notably different in their exclusion from the local round of praise and recriminations.

"Pica People" is a derisive name meant as an insult for five young men about 19 to 25 years of age. Although these five individuals associate regularly, they claim no group identity and become angry when called the Pica People. Unlike the Incognitos, the Pica People are well-known and often accused of some predatory display. They do not fight for group honor, but there is friction between them and all the other street-corner groups in the Addams area.

It was impossible to determine how these two groups came into existence. (I talked only twice with the Incognitos, who simply said they "grew up together." Local people started calling the Pica People by that name after a movie in which the "Pica People" were sub-humans. I knew

some of the members of this group, but they became so angry at any mention of the name that I could not discuss it with them.) What is known of their composition may throw some light on why they were excluded from the structure of the other groups. All informants described the Incognitos as "good guys," still in school and no trouble to anyone. They were not considered college boys but, if asked, most informants said they thought some of them might go to college. Local youth agencies made no attempt to work with them, and the entire neighborhood seemed to feel they were not dangerous. Other street-corner groups in the Italian section did not look down on them, but they did exempt them from the ambitions that brought other groups into opposition.

The Pica People were just the opposite. All members were boastful of their alleged Outfit connections and their ability to intimidate other people. But the Pica People possessed so many personal flaws that they were rather useless to the Outfit. One member was slightly claustrophobic. Another was so weak that even much younger boys pushed him around. A third had an exceedingly unfortunate appearance. Under the circumstances, their pretensions became laughable.

Extremes of Street-Corner Groups

The Incognitos and the Pica People seem to represent the extremes of a range in which the street-corner group is considered the normal adolescent gathering. Modest and well-behaved youngsters are excluded as exceptions, as are criminally inclined but unsuccessful young men. Both of these groups fell outside the range considered normal by the local residents and were thereby dissociated from the total group hierarchy.

The social context of the Italian street groups is somewhat different from that of the street groups in the other three ethnic sections. Among the Italians, the major share of coercive power still remains in adult hands. The wider community may not be very pleased with the form *their* power takes, but it is the only case where the corporate power of the adolescents is tempered by that of the adults. Also, since many of the same adults have an active role in distributing some of the benefits that are held in store by the wider community, their power is augmented. Perhaps the most obvious result of the adults' ascendency is that the adolescents do not simply dismiss them or adulthood as unimportant. A more immediate consequence is to give many of the adults the prerogative of exacting considerable obedience from the local adolescents. It is not at all uncommon to see an Italian adult upbraid and humble one of the local youths. Not all adults have this privilege; but many do, and their example provides a distinct contrast to the other ethnic groups where similar efforts would be futile.

In the long run, the effectiveness of these coercive controls among the Italians may do little more than confirm their convictions that, outside of natural tendencies, there is no guarantee to moral conduct except economic and numerical strength. Within their own little world, however, such coercive measures constitute a fairly effective system of social control. Personal privacy and anonymity are almost impossible. In turn, each person's known or assumed connections dampen most chances at exploitation because of the fear of unknown consequences. Thus, the opportunities for immorality presented by transient relations and "fair game" are fairly rare. Within these limits, such an authoritarian system of social control will work. Outside their own section, of course, these conditions do not hold; and the Italian boys find themselves free to seize whatever advantages or opportunities present themselves. Among themselves, they are usually only a rowdy and boisterous crowd. With strangers or in other parts of the Addams area, they become particularly arrogant and unscrupulous.

With these qualifications, it appears that well-established adolescent street-corner groups are quite compatible with strong adult authority and influence. In fact, judging from the Italian section, these adolescent street-corner groups seem to be the building blocks out of which the older and more powerful groups have originated. The younger groups continue to replenish the older ones and help maintain the structure within which adults are shown deference.

Moreover, the total age-graded structure of groups in the Italian section relates youngsters to the wider society both instrumentally and conceptually. The Italian street groups see themselves as replacements in an age structure that becomes progressively less provincial. At the upper age level, groups even stop prefacing their name with the term "Taylor"; and a few of their members have a place in the wider society through the Outfit and West Side Bloc. The relationship between these age grades also provides a ladder down which favors and opportunities are distributed. The wider community may hesitate at accepting the legitimacy of these transactions, but they are mostly of a conventional form. The "Outfit" and the "West Side Bloc" have a strong interest in maintaining a degree of social order, and the sorts of wanton violence associated with gangs do not at all fit their taste.

In Conclusion

The Addams area is probably a more orderly slum than many others, and it departs sharply from the common image of an atomized and unruly urban rabble. For all its historical uniqueness, the neighborhood does establish the possibility of a moral order within its population. The recurrence of the circumstances that led to its organization is as uncertain as the future of the Addams area itself. In spite of all these uncertainties, the Addams area shows that slum residents are intent upon finding a moral order and are sometimes successful in doing so.

13

HERBERT J. GANS

Social Life: Suburban Homogeneity and Conformity

In part two, my focus shifts from Levittown to the Levittowners, and from a historical to a cross-sectional perspective—from the community to the people and the way they live at a specific point in time. Some critics charge that suburban life is socially, culturally, and emotionally destructive, and that the causes are to be found in the nature of suburbia and the move from the city. Testing their charges requires evaluation of the quality of Levittown life and measurement of Levittown's impact on its residents to determine what changes in behavior and attitudes have actually resulted from the move.

Many of the findings on Levittown's impact are based on interviews with two sets of Levittowners, one a nearly *random sample* of 45 buyers in Somerset Park, the first neighborhood to be settled, and the second, of 55 others in that neighborhood who had moved there from Philadelphia, here called the *Philadelphia* or *city sample*. The two samples were interviewed during 1960 and 1961, after they had lived in Levittown two to three years, and this determines the period on which the cross-sectional analysis is reporting. (The random sample was also interviewed just after its arrival in Levittown, thus providing data on the immediate impact of the move as well.) Both samples are small and not entirely random, so that the statistics cannot

supply the final scientific proof that statistics often imply, but they do illustrate what happened to people as a result of moving to Levittown.

THE QUALITY OF SOCIAL LIFE

Perhaps the most frequent indictment of suburban life has been leveled against the quality of social relationships. The critics charge that the suburbs are socially hyperactive and have made people so outgoing that they have little time or inclination for the development of personal autonomy. The pervasive homogeneity of the population has depressed the vitality of social life, and the absence of more heterogeneous neighbors and friends has imposed a **con**formity which further reduces the suburban**ite's** individuality. Indeed, studies showing the importance of physical propinquity in the choice of friends have been interpreted to suggest that physical layout, rather than people, determines the choice of friends. Because many suburbanites are Transients or Mobiles, they have been accused of wanting social companions only for the duration of their stay, disabling them for more intimate friendship.[1]

Evidence from Levittown suggests quite the opposite. People report an accelerated social life, and in fact looked forward to it before moving to Levittown. The major reason for the upswing is indeed homogeneity, but an equally appropriate term might be "compatibility." Propinquity may initiate social contact but it does not determine friendship. Many relationships are indeed transient, but this is no reflection on their intensity. Finally, conformity prevails, although less as malicious or passive copying than as sharing of useful ideas. In short, many of the *phenomena* identified by the critics occur in Levittown but their alleged *consequences* do not follow. Levittowners have not become outgoing, mindless conformers; they remain individuals, fulfilling the social aspirations with which they came. To be sure, social life in Levittown has its costs, but these seem minor compared to its rewards.

Neighboring[2]

About half the Levittowners interviewed said that they were visiting more with neighbors than in their former residence; about a quarter said less, and the remaining quarter reported no change.[3] The greatest increase was reported by the people who said they had wanted to do more visiting, particularly those who had had little opportunity for it in their previous residence. As one Philadelphian said, "We used to be with the in-laws and with my mother; we didn't bother with the neighbors before." Others had lacked compatible neighbors; people living in apartments had found few opportunities to get acquainted, and those in older or transitional areas had found their fellow residents unsuitable. This was as true of former suburbanites and small-town residents as of those from cities, and affected owners as well as renters. One home-owner explained, "Here in Levittown I have more in common; where we lived before, the neighbors were all my mother's age."

In addition to the desire to do more neighboring, the increase resulted initially from the newness of the community and the lack of shopping facilities and other places for daytime activities. But these reasons were mentioned far less often than the "friendliness" of the neighbors, and this in turn was a function of population homogeneity. One Levittowner, describing her next-door neighbor, said, "We see eye to eye on things, about raising kids, doing things together with your husband, living the same way; we have practically the same identical background." Conversely, the people who reported less neighboring were those who could not find compatible people on the block: older ones, some (but not all) people of highest and lowest status, and those who had difficulties in relating to neighbors, partic-

ularly second generation Jewish women from Philadelphia who were used to living among Jewish neighbors.[4] A handful wanted to continue spending their social life with relatives or preferred to have nothing to do with neighbors.

Of course, some friendliness was built into the neighbor relationship, for people needed each other for mutual aid. In a community far from the city, women are cut off from relatives and old friends—as well as from commuting husbands—so that readiness to provide mutual aid is the first criterion of being a good neighbor. This includes not only helping out in emergencies, but ameliorating periodic loneliness by being available for occasional coffee-klatsching and offering informal therapy by being willing to listen to another's troubles when necessary. Helping out also offers an opportunity—rare in everyday life—to practice the dictates of the Judeo-Christian ethic, and brings appropriate emotional rewards. The reciprocity engendered by mutual aid encourages—and allows—neighbors to keep a constant watch on each other, as they do in established neighborhoods everywhere. One night I drove out of my driveway at a slightly higher than usual speed, and my next-door neighbor came over to find out if anything was wrong, although later he wondered whether in his desire to be a good neighbor he had violated the norms of privacy and was being too nosy. The mutual observation that makes the block a goldfish bowl goes on mainly among adjacent neighbors, for with houses only ten feet apart, they see each other frequently and have to maintain friendly relations if that is at all possible. More distant neighbors could be ignored, however. Indeed, a Levittowner who had moved from a cohesive working class district said, "It's not like Philadelphia here. There you might know someone four blocks down the road as well as your next-door neighbor. Here you don't know people down the road." The block was a social unit only to assure a modicum of house and lawn care, beyond which there was no obligation for neighbors to associate.

Even propinquity did not require visiting. Although a number of studies have shown that social relationships are influenced and even determined by the site plan, this was not the case in Levittown.[5] Since Levittown was laid out with curved blocks, houses facing each other across front and back, there were relatively few neighbors with whom one had constant and in-

Table 1. *Visiting among Adjacent Neighbors, by Amount of Visiting*

Location of Neighbor	PERCENT REPORTING					
	Ranked Amount of Visiting					Not
	First	Second	Third	Fourth	All	Visited
Next door, right side	31	31	15	14	24	24
Next, door, left side	24	38	20	14	26	15
Across the street	36	22	23	23	26	4
Across the backyard	7	7	32	27	17	57
Other*	2	2	10	23	7	N.A.**
N	(45)	(42)	(40)	(22)	(149)	(26)

* This included other neighbors across the street or the backyard when a house faced or backed on two others.
** Not asked.

voluntary visual contact. Sometimes, even relationships with directly adjacent neighbors could be restricted to an exchange of hellos. For example, it took more than a year for me to meet the occupants of a house diagonally across the street from mine, even though we had been saying hello since the first weeks of occupancy. Another person told me he had never even met his next-door neighbor. Thus, despite a fairly high building density—five to six houses to the acre—there was no pressure to be sociable. Neighboring rarely extended more than three or four houses away in each direction, so that the "functional neighborhood" usually consisted of about ten to twelve houses at the most, although people did say hello to everyone on the block.[6] The boundaries of the functional neighborhood were delimited either by physical barriers or by social isolates who interrupted the flow of social relations.[7]

A more systematic test of the propinquity theory was made by asking interview respondents to rank the amount of visiting with their six most adjacent neighbors. If propinquity alone had determined visiting, one or two of the most adjacent neighbors, those on the right and left sides, should have been visited most often. As Table 1 indicates, however, about three quarters of *all* visiting was equally distributed between these two and the neighbor across the street, who was a little farther away, and the latter was actually visited most often. If people's first and second choices are combined, the data show that 31 percent chose right-hand neighbors, an equal

number left-hand ones, 29 percent those across the street, and the rest other adjacent ones. Thus, distance does not affect choice of the closest neighbors, although it does discourage visiting the less adjacent ones, and particularly backyard neighbors. Because of the 100-foot depths of the lots and the heat of the New Jersey summer, people made little use of the backyards, and the 200 feet between houses reduced visiting considerably.[8]

Some propinquity studies have found that visiting is affected by the location of the front door, and, among women, of the kitchen window from which they can see their neighbors while doing housework. This was not the case in Levittown. If the front door had been significant, owners of the Cape Cod and ranch houses should have chosen their right-hand and across-the-street neighbors most often; those of the Colonial houses should have chosen their left-hand and across-the-street neighbors. The data show that Cape Cod owners visited most often across the street, but equally between right- and left-hand neighbors; the ranch owners chose the left-hand neighbors twice as often as their other neighbors; and the Colonial owners showed a slight preference for left-hand neighbors.[9] In the "kitchen window test," the expected pattern was found only among Cape Cod house owners, but not the other two.[10] Had location been the prime determinant of friendship choice, neighbors should also have been mentioned as friends more than other Levittowners. Respondents said, however, that only 35 percent of the five couples they visited most frequently lived on their street, and 31 percent said that none of these favorite couples lived on their street.[11] Moreover, propinquity affected some types of social gatherings but not others; baby showers, cookouts, and barbecues drew only nearby neighbors; more formal parties involved mainly guests from other streets and neighborhoods.[12]

Since most of the interview questions were about adjacent neighbors, the findings are only a partial test of the propinquity theory. They suggest that a sizeable functional distance discourages visiting, but that among adjacent neighbors, people choose not the closest or the ones they see most often, but the ones they consider most compatible. Indeed, fully 82 percent of the respondents mentioned compatibility as the reason for choosing the neighbor they visited most frequently. If the site plan had forced some neighbors into constant visual contact—as do court or cul-de-sac schemes—they might have reacted by increased visiting (or intense enmity if they were incompatible), but the block layout gave Levittowners the opportunity for choice.

Neighbor relations among adults were also affected by the children, for children are neighbors too, and their mingling was determined almost entirely by age and propinquity.[13] The relatively traffic-free streets and the large supply of young children enabled mothers to limit their supervision of the children's outdoor play; and the overall compatibility, to give youngsters a free choice of playmates. But children were likely to quarrel, and when this led to fights and childish violence, their quarrels involved the parents. Half the random sample had heard of quarrels among neighbors on their block, and 81 percent of those were over the children. Adults quarreled most often when childish misbehavior required punishment and parents disagreed about methods. If the parents of fighting children agreed on discipline, each punished his child the same way and the incident was soon forgotten. If they disagreed, however, the parent who believed in harsh punishment often felt that the more permissive parent, not having punished "enough," was accusing the other child of having been at fault. A single parental disagreement might be forgiven, but if it happened repeatedly, an open break between neighbors could result. Of seventeen quarrels about which interview respondents were knowledgeable, nine had been concluded peacefully, but in the other eight cases,

parents were still not talking to each other. In one case, two neighbors finally came to blows and had to be placed on a peace bond by the municipal court.

Another type of adult quarrel involved physical disciplining of children by neighbors. Some people believe that only parents should spank their children; others, that neighbors have the right to do so if the child misbehaves out of sight of the parents. When a neighbor punishes another's child, he not only takes on a quasi-parental role but, by implication, accuses the parents of not raising and watching their children properly. In one such case, where a neighbor punished a little boy for sexual exhibitionism, the parent never spoke to him again.

Basically, differences over discipline reflect class differences in child-rearing. Middle class parents tend to be somewhat more permissive than working class ones, and when two children play together, the middle class child may be allowed to act in ways not permitted to the working class one. Also, working class parents administer physical punishment more freely, since this is not interpreted as a withdrawal of affection, whereas middle class families reserve spankings for extreme misbehavior. Then, as children get older, practices change. The working class child is given more freedom, and by comparison, the middle class child is given much less. He is expected to do his homework while his working class peers may be playing on the streets. Middle class people who observe this freedom, as well as the working class parents' tolerance of childish profanity, interpret it as neglect.

In some cases, middle class families even prohibit their children from playing with working class children. Prohibition is feasible if children are old enough to respect it or if parents supervise the children's play. Younger children cannot be prevented from playing with each other, however, and parental quarrels may result. If the working class children are older and in a minority, as they often are on the block, they may become outcasts, and since they are mobile, may look around for other, similarly discredited companions. Out of this may come a gang that vandalizes hostile middle class society.[14] People of low status experienced (or saw) the most quarrels, for 72 percent of blue collar respondents reported quarrels in their neighborhood, as compared to only 41 percent of the middle class.

The repetition of parental conflict over children's quarrels can lead to increasing estrangement, because other values and behavior patterns also differ between the classes. For example, in one case, what began as a series of minor disagreements about child-rearing was soon reinforced by critical comments on the part of the middle class people about the working class neighbor's laxity toward his lawn and his taste for expensive automobiles. All of these disagreements spiraled into considerable hostility over a year's time. Eventually, one of the feuding neighbors may move out—usually the middle class family which has greater resources to go elsewhere.

If the overall social climate of the block is good, other neighbors will try to patch up conflicts between parents. On one block, a child hit another with a toy, drawing blood and requiring a doctor. The mother of the injured youngster admitted it was his fault and suggested to the other mother that the two children be kept apart for a few days. However, she did not punish her child at once, and this was resented by the other mother (of working class background). She, in turn, forbade her child to see the guilty one, and both she and her husband broke off with his parents as well. After about a week, however, the feud ended. Each mother told other neighbors of what had happened, and the woman whose child had provoked the incident finally learned that the other mother thought he had not been properly punished. She thereupon let it be known among her neighbors that the child had in fact been punished on the day of the incident. In a few days the message reached its intended destination, whereupon the mother whose child had been hit invited her neighbor and another, neutral, neighbor to coffee. The coffee-klatsch resolved the differences, but only because the block's friendly climate had provided for the prior and circuitous communication that allowed the one mother to learn that the guilty child had indeed been punished. Had communication been poorer, other differences between the two neighbors might have been invoked to increase the conflict. Indeed, when the block's social climate is poor, the struggle will be limited to the involved parents, for no one wants to take sides. If a family becomes enmeshed in battles with a number of neighbors, however, that family is likely to be quickly ostracized, regardless of the social climate.

The importance of compatibility is extended also to relationships that do not involve children, and is underscored by the problems encountered by neighbors who differ significantly. One potential trouble spot was age. Although some elderly Levittowners were able to assume quasi-grandparental roles toward the street's children, others were lonely and uncomfortable among the young families, and enthusiastic gardeners were upset when children romped over flowerbeds and carefully tended lawns. The difficulty was exacerbated by the builder's prohibition of fences, a clause in the deed restriction that was later violated on a number of blocks and actually taken to court.

Class differences also expressed themselves in areas other than child-rearing.[15] Upper middle class women—whose concept of after-housework activity did not include coffee-klatsching, conversation about husbands, homes, and children, or gossiping about the neighbors—rejected and were rejected by the neighbors. So were women who were especially active in organizational life. Perhaps the major problems were faced by working class people who had been used to spending their free time with relatives or childhood friends and found it hard to become friendly with strangers (especially middle class ones). The change was particularly distressing to those who had spent all their lives in the neighborhood in which they grew up. If, when they moved to Levittown, they were sufficiently "open" to respond to friendly neighbors and found others of working class background nearby, they could adapt; if not, they were virtually isolated in their houses. For the latter, a small minority to be sure, life in Levittown was hard.[16] Ethnic differences were also a barrier between neighbors. Groups without a strong subcommunity were isolated, notably a handful of Japanese, Chinese, and Greek families. Some neighbors came with ethnic and racial prejudice, and anti-Semitism, though rare, could be justified by the old charge of Jewish clannishness[17] and by class differences resulting from generally higher incomes among Jews.[18]

A final barrier was sexual, and this affected the women whose husbands worked irregular schedules and might be home during the day. A woman neighbor did not visit another when her husband was home, partly because of the belief that a husband has first call on his wife's companionship, partly to prevent suspicion that her visit might be interpreted as a sexual interest in the husband. This practice is strongest among working class women, reflecting the traditional class norm that people of the opposite sex come together only for sexual reasons, and becomes weaker at higher class levels; in the upper middle class there are enough shared interests between men and women to discourage suspicion.[19] The sexual barrier sometimes inhibited neighbor relations among women whose husbands traveled as salesmen, pilots, or seamen, forcing their wives to associate with each other.

Couple Visiting[20]

Although 40 percent of the Levittowners reported more couple visiting than in their former residences, the change was not quite as great as for neighboring, requiring as it does the compatibility of four rather than two and more of a commitment toward friendship as well.[21] Like neighboring, the increase in couple visiting resulted principally from the supply of compatible people, although it was also encouraged significantly by organizational activity; members of voluntary associations and of the highly organized Jewish subcommunity reported the greatest increase.[22] Even the people who had not wanted to do more visiting before they moved to Levittown found themselves doing more if they were in organizations. Whether organizational membership encourages more visiting or vice versa is not clear; most likely, the same gregariousness that induces visiting also makes "joiners," for the latter have more friends in Levittown than the unaffiliated.

Couple visiting is governed by narrower criteria of compatibility than neighboring, for religiously mixed marriage partners reported more neighboring, but found themselves doing less couple visiting in Levittown.[23] Older people and people of lower status also reported decreases. Evidently, friendship choices were affected by religion, and people who straddled two had trouble finding friends. So did people who straddled the classes, for some Jewish women who had found Jewish organizations not to their liking, wanting more "cultural" activities but not being quite up to the civic programs of the cosmopolitans, reported that their social life suffered.

The patterns of couple visiting in Levittown question two features of the suburban critique —the superficiality of friendships and social hyperactivity. According to many critics of suburban life, the transience of the population induces transient relationships which end with departure from the community. Transient relationships undoubtedly exist; one Levittowner, who had gone back to visit old friends in her former community, returned to report that she no longer had much in common with them and that they had been, as she put it, "development friends." Other Transients established close friendships, however, and one family, temporarily transferred, returned to the block to be close to friends even though they would have preferred to move into one of Levitt's newer houses.

The criticism of "development" friendship harbors an implicit comparison with "bosom" friendship, assumed to have existed in the past, but there is no evidence that the comparison is empirically valid. Close friendships, I suspect, typically develop in childhood and adolescent peer groups, and can continue in a static society where people have as much in common in adulthood as in childhood. But in American society, and especially in the middle class, geographical and social mobility often separates people who have grown up together, so that shared interests among childhood friends are rare. Often, only nostalgia keeps the relationship going. Many Levittowners talk about close friends "at home," but they see them so rarely that the current strength of the friendship is never properly tested. Instead, they develop new friends at each stage of the life cycle or as they move up occupationally and develop new social and leisure interests. Closeness is not replaced by superficiality, but permanent friendships give way to new and perhaps shorter ones of similar closeness.[24]

Whether or not this relationship is desirable depends on one's values. People today, particularly the middle classes, are more gregarious than those of the past. The working class, restricted in social skills or content to range within a smaller, perhaps closer, network of relatives and childhood friends, comes nearest to retaining the traditional "bosom" friendship. But these people, in my research as in many other studies, report difficulties in making new friends as their life conditions change.[25]

The critics' charge that suburbanites indulge in hyperactive visiting to counteract boredom and loneliness brought on by the lack of urbanity in their communities is equally mistaken. Coming from academia where the weekend brought parties, and having just lived in an Italian working class neighborhood in Boston where people maintained an almost continual "open house," I was surprised at how little entertaining took place among Levittowners.[26] Although people often had visitors on Sunday afternoons, weekend evenings were not differentiated from the rest, a fact that should be obvious from the high ratings of television programs on the air at that time. I would guess that, on the average, Levittowners gathered informally not more than two or three times a month and gave formal parties about once a year, not counting those around Christmas and New Year's Eve. Social life in Levittown was not hyperactive by any stretch of the imagination, except perhaps in the first few months of putting out feelers. I suspect that the critics either confuse the early hyperactivity with the normal pattern once life has settled down, or they generalize from observations in upper middle class suburbs, where partying is a major leisure activity.

Admittedly, the critics could question my assumption that an increase in social life is equivalent to an improvement in its quality, and argue that it represents instead an escape from pervasive boredom. If the Levittowners had found their social life boring, however, they would either have cut it down or complained about greater boredom. The data indicate just the opposite, for those visiting more were less bored (and vice versa), and besides, if social life had been as dull as the critics claim, why would the interview respondents have been so enthusiastic about the friendliness of their fellow residents?

THE PROS AND CONS OF POPULATION HOMOGENEITY[27]

The suburban critique is quite emphatic on the subject of demographic homogeneity. For one thing, homogeneity violates the American Dream of a "balanced" community where people of diverse age, class, race, and religion live together. Allegedly, it creates dullness through sameness.

In addition, age homogeneity deprives children —and adults—of the wisdom of their elders, while class, racial, and religious homogeneity prevent children from learning how to live in our pluralistic society. Homogeneity is said to make people callous to the poor, intolerant of Negroes, and scornful of the aged. Finally, heterogeneity is said to allow upward mobility, encouraging working and lower class people to learn middle class ways from their more advantaged neighbors.[28]

There is no question that Levittown is quite homogeneous in age and income as compared to established cities and small towns, but such comparisons are in many ways irrelevant. People do not live in the political units we call "cities" or "small towns"; often their social life takes place in areas even smaller than a census tract. Many such areas in the city are about as homogeneous in class as Levittown, and slum and high-income areas, whether urban or suburban, are even more so. Small towns are notoriously rigid in their separation of rich and poor, and only appear to be more heterogeneous because individual neighborhoods are so small. All these considerations effectively question the belief that before the advent of modern suburbs Americans of all classes lived together. Admittedly, statistics compiled for cities and suburbs as a whole show that residential segregation by class and by race are on the increase, but these treands also reflect the breakdown of rigid class and caste systems in which low-status people "knew their place," and which made residential segregation unnecessary.

By ethnic and religious criteria, Lewittown is much less homogeneous than these other areas because people move in as individuals rather than as groups, and the enclaves found in some recently built urban neighborhoods, where 40 to 60 percent of the population comes from one ethnic or religious group, are absent. Nor is Levittown atypically homogeneous in age; new communities and subdivisions always attract young people, but over time, their populations "age" until the distribution resembles that of established communities.[29]

Finally, even class homogeneity is not as great as community-wide statistics would indicate. Of three families earning $7000 a year, one might be a skilled worker at the peak of his earning power and dependent on union activity for further raises; another, a white collar worker with some hope for a higher income; and the third, a young executive or professional at the start of his career. Their occupational and educational differences express themselves in many variations in life style, and if they are neighbors, each is likely to look elsewhere for companionship. Perhaps the best way to demonstrate that Levittown's homogeneity is more statistical than real is to describe my own nearby neighbors. Two were Anglo-Saxon Protestant couples from small towns, the breadwinners employed as engineers; one an agnostic and a golf buff, the other a skeptical Methodist who wanted to be a teacher. Across the backyard lived a Baptist white collar worker from Philadelphia and his Polish-American wife, who had brought her foreign-born mother with her to Levittown; and an Italian-American tractor operator (whose ambition was to own a junkyard) and his upwardly mobile wife, who restricted their social life to a brother down the street and a host of relatives who came regularly every Sunday in a fleet of Cadillacs. One of my next-door neighbors was a religious fundamentalist couple from the Deep South whose life revolved around the church; another was an equally religious Catholic blue collar worker and his wife, he originally a Viennese Jew, she a rural Protestant, who were politically liberal and as skeptical about middle class ways as any intellectual. Across the street, there was another Polish-American couple, highly mobile and conflicted over their obligations to the extended family; another engineer; and a retired Army officer. No wonder Levittowners were puzzled when a nationally known housing expert addressed them on the "pervasive homogeneity of suburban life."

Most Levittowners were pleased with the diversity they found among their neighbors, primarily because regional, ethnic, and religious differences are today almost innocuous and provide variety to spice the flow of conversation and the exchange of ideas. For example, my Southern neighbor discovered pizza at the home of the Italian-American neighbor and developed a passion for it, and I learned much about the personal rewards of Catholicism from my Catholic convert neighbors. At the same time, however, Levittowners wanted homogeneity of age and income—or rather, they wanted neighbors and friends with common interests and sufficient consensus of values to make for informal and uninhibited relations. Their reasons were motivated neither by antidemocratic feelings nor by an interest in conformity. Children need playmates of the same age, and because child-rearing problems vary with age, mothers like to be near women who have children of similar age. And because these problems also fluctuate with class, they want some similarity of that factor—not homogeneity of occupation and education so much as agreement on the ends and means of caring for child, husband, and home.

Income similarity is valued by the less affluent, not as an end in itself, but because people who must watch every penny cannot long be comfortable with more affluent neighbors, particularly when children come home demanding toys or clothes they have seen next door. Indeed, objective measures of class are not taken into account in people's associations at all, partly because they do not identify each other in these terms, but also because class differences are not the only criterion for association.[30] Sometimes neighbors of different backgrounds but with similar temperaments find themselves getting along nicely, especially if they learn to avoid activities and topics about which they disagree. For example, two women of diverse origins became good friends because they were both perfectionist housekeepers married to easy-going men, although they once quarreled bitterly over child-rearing values.

But Levittowners also want some homogeneity for themselves. As I noted before, cosmopolitans are impatient with locals, and vice versa; women who want to talk about cultural and civic matters are bored by conversations about home and family—and, again, vice versa; working class women who are used to the informal flow of talk with relatives need to find substitutes among neighbors with similar experience. Likewise, young people have little in common with older ones, and unless they want surrogate parents, prefer to socialize with neighbors and friends of similar age. Some Levittowners sought ethnic and religious homogeneity as well. Aside from the Jews and some of the Greeks, Japanese, and the foreign-born women of other nations, observant Catholics and fundamentalist Protestants sought "their own," the former because they were not entirely at ease with non-Catholic neighbors, the latter because their time-consuming church activity and their ascetic life styles set them apart from most other Levittowners. They mixed with their neighbors, of course, but their couple visiting was limited principally to the like-minded. Because of the diversity of ethnic and religious backgrounds, the Philadelphia sample was asked whether there had been any change in the amount of visiting with people of similar "national descent or religious preference"; 30 percent reported a decrease, but 20 percent reported an increase.[31] Those doing less such visiting in Levittown also said they were lonelier than in Philadelphia.

Most people had no difficulty finding the homogeneity they wanted in Levittown. Affluent and well-educated people could move into organizations or look for friends all over Levittown, but older people and people of lower income or poorly educated women were less able to move around either physically or socially. Women from these groups often did not have a car or did not know how to drive; many were reluctant to use baby-sitters for their children, only partly for financial reasons. Heterogeneity, then, may be a mixed blessing, particularly on the block, and something can be said for class and age homogeneity.

The alleged costs of homogeneity were also more unreal than the critics claim. It is probably true that Levittowners had less contact with old people than some urbanites (now rather rare) who still live in three-generation households. It is doubtful, however, that they had less contact with the older generation than urban and suburban residents of similar age and class, with the exception of the occupational Transients, who are far from home and may return only once a year. Whether or not this lack of contact with grandparents affects children negatively can only be discovered by systematic studies among them. My observations of children's relations with grandparents suggest that the older generation is strange to them and vice versa, less as a result of lack of contact than of the vastness of generational change.

This is also more or less true of adult relationships with the older generation. Social change in America has been so rapid that the ideas and experiences of the elderly are often anachronistic, especially so for young mobile Levittowners whose parents are first or second generation Americans. Philadelphia women who lived with their parents before they moved to Levittown complained at length about the difficulties of raising children and running a household under those conditions, even though some missed their mothers sorely after moving to Levittown. A few found surrogate mothers among friends or neighbors, but chose women only slightly older than themselves and rarely consulted elderly neighbors. As for the husbands, they were, to a man, glad they had moved away from parents and in-laws.

That suburban homogeneity deprives children of contact with urban pluralism and "reality" is also dubious.[ ] Critics assume that urban children experience heterogeneity, but middle class parents—and working class ones, too—try hard to shield them from contact with conditions and people of lower status. Upper middle class children may be taken on tours of the city, but to museums and shopping districts rather than to slums. Indeed, slum children, who are freer of parental supervision, probably see more of urban diversity than anyone else, although they do not often get into middle class areas.

The homogeneity of Levittown is not so pervasive that children are shielded from such unpleasant realities as alcoholism, mental illness, family strife, sexual aberration, or juvenile delinquency which exist everywhere. The one element missing on most Levittown blocks—though, of course, in many city neighborhoods too—is the presence of Negro families. Although young Negro women came from nearby Burlington to work as maids, there were only two Negro families in the three neighborhoods built before Levittown's integration, and about fifty in the three built since then. Most Levittown children are unlikely to see any Negroes around them and will not have real contact with them until they enter junior high school. But it is not at all certain that mere visual exposure—to Negroes or anyone else—encourages learning of pluralism and tolerance. Children pick up many of their attitudes from parents and peers, and these are not necessarily pluralistic. If visual exposure had the positive effects attributed to it, city children, who see more Negroes than suburban children do, should exhibit greater racial tolerance. In reality they do not; indeed, the middle class child growing up in a white suburb may be more opposed to segregation than one raised in an integrated city. This is not a justification for segregation, but a suggestion that visual exposure is no sure means to integration.

A generation of social research has demonstrated that racial and other forms of integration occur when diverse people can interact frequently in equal and noncompetitive situations.[ ]

Here the suburbs are at an advantage when it comes to religious and ethnic integration, but at a disadvantage for racial and class integration, for aside from residential segregation, suburban high schools bring together students from a narrower variety of residential areas than do urban ones. Again, mere diversity does not assure the kind of interaction that encourages integration, and a school with great diversity but sharp internal segregation may not be as desirable as one with less diversity but without internal segregation. Judging by life on the block in Levittown, maximal diversity and extreme heterogeneity encourage more conflict than integration, and while conflict can be desirable and even didactic, this is only true if it can be resolved in some way. People so different from each other in age or class that they cannot agree on anything are unlikely to derive much enrichment from heterogeneity.

A corollary of the belief in diversity as a stimulant to enrichment holds that working class and lower class people will benefit—and be improved—by living among middle class neighbors. Even if one overlooks the patronizing class bias implicit in this view, it is not at all certain that residential propinquity will produce the intended cultural change. In Levittown, working class families living alongside middle class ones went their own way most of the time. For mobile ones, heterogeneity is obviously desirable, provided middle class people are willing to teach them, but nonmobile ones will react negatively to force feedings of middle class culture. Neighbors are expected to treat each other as equals, and working class residents have enough difficulty paying the higher cost of living among middle class people, without being viewed as culturally deprived. When working class organizations used middle class Levittowners for technical and administrative services, they rejected those who looked down on them and constantly tested the others to make sure they measured up to the norms of working class culture. For example, at a VFW softball game, two middle class members were razzed unmercifully for their lack of athletic skill. Children are not yet fully aware of class, so that they can be with (and learn from) peers of other classes, and there is some evidence that in schools with a majority of middle-class children, working class children will adopt the formers' standards of school performance, and vice versa.[33]

By its very nature, demographic homogeneity is said to be incompatible with democracy, and advocates of diversity have emphasized that a democracy requires a heterogeneous community. However, as the description of Levittown's school and political conflict should indicate, bringing people with different interests together does not automatically result in the use of democratic procedures. Instead, it causes conflict, difficulties in decision-making, and attempts to sidestep democratic norms. If one group is threatened by another's demands, intolerance may even increase. Indeed, democratic procedure is often so fragile that it falls by the wayside under such stress, causing hysteria on the part of residents and the sort of panic on the part of the officials that I described. The fact is that the democratic process probably works more smoothly in a homogeneous population. Absence of conflict is of course a spurious goal, particularly in a pluralistic society, and cannot be used as an argument for homogeneity. On the other hand, unless conflict becomes an end in itself, heterogeneity is not a viable argument for greater democracy.

Critics of the suburbs also inveigh against physical homogeneity and mass-produced housing. Like much of the rest of the critique, this charge is a thinly veiled attack on the culture of working and lower middle class people, implying that mass-produced housing leads to mass-produced lives. The critics seem to forget that the town houses of the upper class in the nineteenth century were also physically homogeneous; that everyone, poor and rich alike, drives mass-produced, homogeneous cars without damage to their personalities; and that today, only the rich can afford custom-built housing. I heard no objection among the Levittowners about the similarity of their homes, nor the popular jokes about being unable to locate one's own house.[34] Esthetic diversity is preferred, however, and people talked about moving to a custom-built house in the future when they could afford it. Meanwhile, they made internal and external alterations in their Levitt house to reduce sameness and to place a personal stamp on their property.[35]

Block Homogeneity and Community Heterogeneity

Putting together all the arguments for and against homogeneity suggests that the optimum solution, at least in communities of homeowners who are raising small children, is *selective homogenity at the block level* and *heterogeneity at the community level*. Whereas a mixture of population types, and especially of rich and poor, is desirable in the community as a whole, heterogeneity on the block will not produce the intended tolerance, but will lead to conflict that is undesirable because it is essentially insoluble and thus becomes chronic. Selective homogeneity on the block will improve the tenor of neighbor relations, and will thus make it easier—although not easy—to realize heterogeneity at the community level.

By "block" I mean here an area in which frequent face-to-face relations take place, in most cases a *sub-block* of perhaps ten to twelve houses. Selective homogeneity requires enough consensus among neighbors to prevent insoluble conflict, to encourage positive although not necessarily intensive relationships between them, and to make visiting possible for those who want it in the immediate vicinity. If Levittown is at all typical, the crucial factors in homogeneity are age and class. The range of ages and classes that can live together is not so limited, however, as to require tenant selection programs. The voluntary selection pattern that now occurs on the basis of house price is more than sufficient, and as the ghettoization of the poor in public housing suggests, formal and involuntary selection has many serious disadvantages. Besides, it is questionable whether planners have the knowledge to go about planning other people's social relations, and even if they had the knowledge, it is doubtful that they have the right to do so.[36] Of course, selection through house price is also a form of planning, but since it is not directly related to tenants' specific characteristics, it leaves more room for choice.

The emphasis on voluntary selection also copes with another objection to homogeneity, that it crystallizes class divisions and makes people more aware of class differences. Implicit in this objection is the assumption that awareness of class differences is wrong, and that any attempt to use class as a separating criterion is undesirable. This assumption would be defensible if it were part of a larger program to eliminate or at least reduce economic inequities, but it is generally put forth by people who are uncomfortable about the existence of classes and want to solve the problem by avoiding it.

These observations have a number of implica-

tions for site planning. Given the boundaries within which neighboring takes place, the significant social unit in the community (at least, in one like Levittown) is the sub-block—which is not a physical unit. Conversely, the neighborhood of several hundred families which city planners have traditionally advocated is socially irrelevant, whatever virtues it may have in defining a catchment area for the elementary school or the neighborhood shopping center. In fact, in order to maximize community heterogeneity, it might be desirable to eliminate the neighborhood unit and plan for a heterogeneous array of homogeneous blocks, each block separated from the next by enough of a real or symbolic barrier to reassure those concerned with property values. This would encourage more heterogeneity in the elementary school and other neighborhood facilities, and would thus contribute significantly to community heterogeneity.[37]

Communities should be heterogeneous because they must reflect the pluralism of American society. Moreover, as long as local taxation is the main source of funds for community services, community homogeneity encourages undesirable inequalities. The high-income community can build modern schools and other high-quality facilities; the low-income community, which needs these facilities more urgently, lacks the tax base to support them. As a result, poor communities elect local governments which neglect public services and restrict the democratic process in the need to keep taxes minimal. Both financial inequity and its political consequences are eliminated more effectively by federal and state subsidy than by community heterogeneity, but so long as municipal services are financed locally, communities must include all income groups.

The criteria on which the advocacy of block homogeneity and community heterogeneity is based cannot justify racial homogeneity at either level. Experience with residential integration in many communities, including Levittown, indicates that it can be achieved without problems when the two races are similar in socioeconomic level and in the visible cultural aspects of class—provided, however, the whites are not beset by status fears. Indeed, the major barrier to effective integration is fear of status deprivation especially among white working class homeowners. The whites base their fears on the stereotype that nonwhite people are lower class, and make a hasty exodus that reduces not property values but the selling prices that can be obtained by the departing whites. When class differences between the races are great, the exodus is probably unavoidable, but where Negroes and whites have been of equal status, it can be prevented, at least in middle class areas. Yet even if this were not the case, homogeneity is only one value among many, and if any person chooses to move among people who differ in race—or age, income, religion, or any other background characteristic —he has the right to do so and the right to governmental support in his behalf. That such a move might wreak havoc with a block's social life or the community's consensus is of lower priority than the maintenance of such values as freedom of choice and equality. The advantages of residential homogeneity are not important enough to justify depriving anyone of access to housing and to educational and other opportunities.

CONFORMITY AND COMPETITION

The suburban critique is especially strident on the prevalence of conformity. It argues that relationships between neighbors and friends are regulated by the desire to copy each other to achieve uniformity. At the same time, the critics also see suburbanites as competitive, trying to keep up or down with the Joneses to satisfy the desire for status. Conforming (or copying) and competing are not the same—indeed, they are contradictory—but they are lumped together in the critique because they are based on the common assumption that, in the suburbs, behavior and opinion are determined by what the neighbors do and think, and individualism is found only in the city. Both competition and copying exist in Levittown, but not for the reasons suggested by the critics. They are ways of coping with heterogeneity and of retaining individuality while being part of the group. They exist in every group, but are more prevalent among homeowners and, because of the fascination with suburbia, more visible there. But this does not make them suburban phenomena.

Enough of the suburban critique has seeped into the reading matter of Levittowners to make "conformity" a pejorative term, and interview questions about it would have produced only denials. Competition is talked about in Levittown, however, and 60 percent of the random sample reported competition among their neighbors.[38] The examples they gave, however, not only included copying, but half the respondents described it positively. "I don't know what competition is," said one man. "Perhaps when we see the neighbors repairing the house, and we figure our own repairs would be a good idea." Another put it more enthusiastically: "Friends and neighbors ask me what I've done, and by our visiting different neighbors we get different ideas about fixing up the house—how we are going to paint. Instead of both of us buying an extension ladder, we go half and half."

In effect, diverging or deviant behavior can be seen as competition, conformity, or the chance to learn new ideas, depending on the observer. One who dislikes behavior common to several neighbors may accuse them of copying each other. If the behavior is dissimilar, it must be a result of competition: "keeping up with the Joneses" or "spending beyond one's means." When the behavior is approved, however, it is interpreted as sharing ideas. The observer's perspective is shaped principally by his relative class position, or by his estimate of his position. If the observer is of *higher* status than the observed, he will interpret the latter's attempt to share higher-status ideas as competing, and his sharing of lower status ways as copying. If the observer is of *lower* status than the observed, his ideas will not be shared, of course, but he will consider the more affluent life style of the higher-status neighbor as motivated by status-striving or "keeping up with the Joneses."[39] As one blue collar man put it, "There are some who act so darned important, as if they have so much, and I can't figure out what they are doing in Levittown when they have so much." Another blue collar man who had taught his neighbors about lawn care, and felt himself to be their equal, was not threatened: "One or two try to keep up with the Joneses, but generally people are not worried. If one gets ahead and another copies him, we laugh. Our attitude is, all the more power to him. When we can afford it, we make improvements too." In other words, when the observer feels he is equal to the observed, he will see competing and copying either as sharing or as friendly games. And socially mobile people tend to judge the ways of higher-status people positively, for they can look to their neighbors for guidance about how to live in the suburbs. "Everyone has fixed up their houses, but not to compete," a former city dweller reported. "At first none of us had anything and maybe you saw what others did and you copied it." Needless to say, those who are being copied may consider the mobile neighbor a competing upstart.

Status-striving is generally ascribed to people with more money, more education, and a different life style by those who cannot afford the style or prefer a different one. The same motive is inferred about social relations. Cliques of higher-status people are seen by lower-status observers as groups that coalesce for prestige reasons, and lower-status cliques are viewed by higher-status observers as groups that come together to conform. When relations among neighbors of unequal status deteriorate, the higher-status person explains it in terms of culturally or morally undesirable actions by the lower-class neighbor; the lower-status person ascribes the break to his neighbor's desire to be with more prestigious people. In reality, instances of over status-striving, carried out to show up the lower status of neighbors, are rare. "Keeping up" takes place, but mainly out of the need to maintain self-respect, to "put the best face forward" or not to be considered inferior and "fall behind." Serious status-striving is usually a desperate attempt by a socially isolated neighbor to salvage self-respect through material or symbolic displays of status, and is dismissed or scorned. One such neighbor was described as "trying to be the Joneses, and hoping people will follow him, but we don't pay any attention to him." Indeed, the social control norms of block life encourage "keeping down with the Joneses," and criticize displays of unusual affluence, so that people who can afford a higher standard of living than the rest and who show it publically are unpopular and are sometimes ostracized.[40]

Conforming and copying occur more frequently than competition, mostly to secure the proper appearance of the block to impress strangers. A pervasive system of social control develops to enforce standards of appearance on the block, mainly concerning lawn care.[41] Copying and some competition take place in this process, but neither the Levittowners nor the suburban critics would describe it in these terms. Everyone knows it is social control and accepts the need for it, although one year some of my neighbors and I wished we could pave our front lawns with green concrete to eliminate the endless watering and mowing and to forestall criticism of poor lawns.

The primary technique for social control is humor. Wisecracks are made to show up deviant behavior, and overt criticism surfaces only when the message behind the wisecracks does not get across. Humor is used to keep relations friendly and because people feel that demands for conformity are not entirely proper; they realize that such demands sometimes require a difficult compromise between individual and group standards. When it comes to lawn care, however, most people either have no hard-and-fast personal standards, or they value friendly relations more. Since the block norms and the compromises they require are usually worked out soon after the block is occupied—when everyone is striving to prove he will be a good neighbor—they are taken for granted by the time the block has settled down.

The demand for compromise is also reduced by limiting block standards to the exterior appearance of the front of the house and the front yard, the back being less visible to outsiders. Interiors, which involve the owner's ego more, are not subjected to criticism. People are praised for a nice-looking home, but there are no wisecracks about deviant taste in furnishings—at least, not to the owner. The same limitation holds for cars and other consumer goods purchased. Although I drove a 1952 Chevrolet, by far the oldest car on the block, no one ever joked with me about it,[42] but Levittowners who used trucks in their work and parked them on their streets at night, giving the block the image of a working class district, were criticized by middle class neighbors. The criticism was made behind their backs, however, because it affected the neighbors' source of livelihood. In this case, as in some others, social control was passed on to the township government, and eventually, it voted an ordinance prohibiting truck-parking on residential streets.

What people do inside their houses is considered their own affair, but loud parties, drunkenness, and any other noticeable activities that would give the block a bad reputation are criticized. So are parents who let their children run loose at all hours of the evening, not only because they publicly violate norms of good parenthood, but also because they make it harder for neighbors to put their own children to bed. Private deviant behavior is, of course, gossiped about with gusto, but only when it becomes visible, and repeatedly so, is gossip translated into overt criticism. Even visible deviance that affects block appearance is tolerated if it is minor and if the individual believes firmly in what he is doing. One Levittowner decided that he would buy a wooden screen door, rather than the popular but more expensive aluminum one. He decided, however, to maintain block uniformity by painting it with aluminum color. "People will think I'm cheap," he told me, "but I don't mind that. I know I'm thrifty." I do not know what people thought, but he was not criticized.

Copying also takes place without being impelled by conformity, and then becomes a group phenomenon that occurs in spurts. When one neighbor builds a patio or repaints his house, others are likely to follow his lead, but not automatically. On my block, for instance, one homeowner repainted his house in 1959 but no one imitated him. When another began to do it the next year, however, a rash of repainting occurred. If this had been simply a copying phenomenon, the painting should have started in 1959, especially since the first painter was a popular community leader. What happened in 1960 is easily explained. By that time, houses built in 1958 needed repainting, and when one man, who had an early vacation, devoted his two weeks to it, other men followed his example when they went on vacation.[43]

People also buy household items and plants they have seen at their neighbors', but only when the item is either widely desired or clearly useful. For example, early in Levittown's history, a rumor spread that the willow trees the builder had planted would eventually root into and crack the sewer pipes, and one man promptly took out his tree. Neighbors who were friends of his followed suit, but others refused to accept the rumor and kept their trees. On my block, the rumor was initiated by a Catholic leader, and within a week, the Catholics had taken out their willow trees, but the others had not followed suit. My own innovation, inexpensive bamboo shades to keep out the blazing sun, was not copied; people said they looked good, but no one imitated me.

COMPETITION, CONFORMITY, AND HETEROGENEITY

Both competition and conformity are ways of coping with heterogeneity, principally of class. When lower-status people are accused of copying and higher-status ones of living beyond their means to impress the neighbors, disapproval is put in terms of negative motives rather than class differences, for accusations of deviant behavior which blame individuals make it more difficult for the deviant to appeal to his group norms. Such accusations also enable people to ignore the existence of class differences. Class is a taboo subject, and the taboo is so pervasive, and so unconscious, that people rarely think in class terms.

Competition and conformity exist also because people are dependent on their neighbors. In working class or ethnic enclaves, where social life is concentrated among relatives, their criticism is feared more than the neighbors'. Upper middle class people, having less to do with neighbors, conform most closely to the demands of their friends. In Levittown, neighbors are an important reference group, not only for lower middle class people but for working class ones cut off from relatives. Even so, the prime cause of both competition and conformity is home ownership and the mutual need to preserve property and status values. Only 11 percent of former renters but 70 percent of former homeowners reported noticing competition in their former residence, but both observed it equally in Levittown. Moreover, whether they came from urban or suburban neighborhoods, they reported no more competition in Levittown than in the former residence. Consequently, competition is not distinctive either to Levittown or to the suburbs.

What, then, accounts for the critics' preoccupation with suburban conformity, and their tendency to see status competition as a dominant theme in suburban life? For one thing, many of these critics live in city apartments, where the concern for block status preservation is minimal. Also, they are largely upper middle class professionals, dedicated to cosmopolitan values and urban life and disdainful of the local and anti-urban values of lower middle class and working class people. Believing in the universality of these values, the critics refuse to acknowledge the existence of lower middle class or working class ways of living. Instead, they describe people as mindless conformers who would be cosmopolitans if they were not weak and allowed themselves to be swayed by builders, the mass media, and their neighbors.

The ascription of competitive behavior to the suburbs stems from another source. The upper middle class world, stressing as it does individuality, is a highly competitive one. In typically upper middle class occupations such as advertising, publishing, university teaching, law, and the arts, individual achievement is the main key to success, status, and security. The upper middle class is for this reason more competitive and more status-conscious than the other classes. Popular writers studying upper middle class suburbs have observed this competition and some have mistakenly ascribed it to suburbia, rather than to the criteria for success in the professions held by these particular suburbanites.[41] Those writing about lower-status suburbs have either drawn their information from upper middle class friends who have moved to lower middle class suburbs for financial reasons and found themselves a dissatisfied minority, or they have, like upper middle class people generally, viewed the lower-status people about whom they were writing as trying to compete with their betters.

Finally, the new suburbs, being more visible than other lower middle and working class residential areas, have become newsworthy, and during the 1950s they replaced "mass culture" as the scapegoat and most convenient target for the fear and distaste that upper middle class people feel for the rest of the population. Affluent suburbs have become false targets of dissatisfaction with the upper middle class's own status-consciousness and competition, the "rat-race" it experiences in career and social striving having been projected on life beyond the city limits.

The inaccuracy of the critique does not, of course, exclude the possibility that conforming and competing are undesirable or dangerous, or that too much of both take place in Levittown. I do not believe either to be the case. If one distinguishes between *wanted* conformity, as when neighbors learn from each other or share ideas; *tolerated* conformity, when they adjust their own standards in order to maintain friendly relations; and *unwanted* conformity, when they bow to pressure and give up their individuality, only the last is clearly undesirable, and in Levittown it is rare. Tolerated conformity requires some surrender of autonomy, but I can see why Levittowners feel it is more important to be friendly with ones' neighbors than to insist on individual but unpopular ways of fixing up the outside of the house. The amount of copying and conformity is hardly excessive, considering the heterogeneity on the block. Indeed,

given the random way in which Levittowners become neighbors, it is amazing that neighbor relations were so friendly and tolerant of individual differences. Of course, the working class and upper middle class minorities experience pressure for unwanted conformity, but the latter can get away from the block for social activities, and ultimately, only some of the former suffer. Ironically, their exposure to pressures for conformity is a result of the heterogeneity that the critics want to increase even further.

Notes

1. These charges can be found, for example, in Henderson, Allen, Keats, and Whyte (1956), Chaps. 25, 26.
2. Neighboring, or visiting with neighbors, was defined in the interview as "having coffee together, spending evenings together, or frequent conversations in or out of the house; anything more than saying hello or polite chatting about the weather." It was further defined as taking place among individuals rather than couples, and people were asked, "Are you, yourself, doing more visiting with neighbors than where you lived before, or less?"
3. Fifty-four per cent of the random sample was neighboring more than in the previous residence; 16 per cent, less; and 30 per cent, the same. Among Philadelphians, the percentages were 48, 19, and 33, respectively.
4. Thus, one third of the least educated in the random sample, and two thirds of the college-educated in the Philadelphia sample reported less neighboring. Jews from smaller towns who had already learned to live with non-Jewish neighbors, and third generation Jewish Philadelphians did not report less neighboring.
5. The principal post-World War II studies are Merton (1947a); Caplow and Foreman; Festinger, Schachter, and Back; Festinger; Dean (1953); Haeberle; Blake et al.; Whyte (1956), Chap. 25; and Wilmott (1963), Chap. 7. Critical analyses of these studies can be found in Gans (1961a), pp. 135–137 and Schorr, Chap. 1; of earlier ones, in Rosow.
6. Similar observations were reported in English new towns by Hole, pp. 164–167, and Willmott (1962), pp. 124–126. See also Willmott (1963), pp. 74–82.
7. The initial report on this phenomenon was by Whyte (1956), Chap. 25.
8. On narrower blocks, there was more interaction between backyard neighbors, however.
9. Among Cape Cod owners, 22 per cent visited

more often with the right- and left-hand neighbor, and 43 per cent, with the across-the-street neighbor. Among the ranch owners, the percentages were 46, 23, and 23, respectively; and among the Colonial ones, 30, 35, 30. The remaining visits were with yet other neighbors across the street or backyard.

10. If the location of the kitchen window had been significant, women in Cape Cod houses should have visited most often across the street, and 50 per cent did, as compared to 17 and 25 per cent with the right- and left-hand neighbor, respectively. Those in ranch houses should have visited most with the right-hand and backyard neighbors, but none chose the former, 17 per cent the latter, 33 per cent the left-hand neighbor, and 50 per cent the one across the street. Those in Colonial houses should also have chosen the backyard neighbor, but only 11 per cent did; 44 per cent preferred the right-hand one, and 22 per cent each the left-hand and the across-the-street neighbor.

11. Thirty-one per cent said more than two favorite couples lived on their street, and the remaining 38 per cent, less than two. As might be expected, college-educated respondents chose even fewer friends from their own street. Using street addresses actually overstated the role of propinquity, for not all people on the same street—especially if it was a long one—are neighbors, and several first met such couples in church or in a club. A study of an Irish new town reported 31 per cent of the best friends were neighbors. See Field and Desmond, p. 54.

12. Southworth.

13. This relationship varies with age, of course, and other children do not choose propinquitous playmates as often. Olsen's study of children's birthday parties reported in the Levittown newspaper showed that among three-year-olds, guests came from a median distance of 364 feet; 775 feet among four-year-olds, 1130 feet among seven-year-olds. The distance then remained fairly stable until it rose to about 2000 feet among twelve- and thirteen-year-olds.

14. A study of newcomers in an old suburb suggests that teenagers may even react to class conflict that is limited to parents. "If a family is scapegoated, the youngsters will soon turn up in some mischief or as delinquents." Thoma and Lindemann, p. 193.

15. Class conflicts among neighbors in Levittown, New York, are described by Dobriner (1963), pp. 107–108; in English new towns by Young and Willmott, Chap. 10, and by Willmott (1963), p. 114.

16. The social isolation of suburban working class women and better-educated ones with distinctive tastes is also reported by Gutman, pp. 174, 181–182. See also Haeberle, Chap. 7.

17. Although only 20 per cent of the random sample reported cliques on their blocks, all were Jewish ones, with one exception.

18. Jews often move into communities where the median income is lower than their own, partly because some prefer to spend a lower share of their income on housing, partly because they fear rejection from non-Jewish neighbors of similar income and education.

19. The sexual overtones did not affect my interviewing, because strangers were exempt. Women are permitted to have latent sexual interest in casual encounters—giving rise to jokes about the iceman and the milkman—and only neighbors' husbands are taboo.

20. People were asked about "the visiting you and your husband (wife) do with other couples, either among neighbors or anywhere else in Levittown."

21. Forty-four per cent of the random sample reported more couple visiting; 21 per cent, less; and 35 per cent, no change. Among the Philadelphians, the percentages were almost the same: 39, 22, and 39, respectively. In a new working class suburb, 38 per cent said "they entertain friends at home" more often than before, but 27 per cent reported less. See Berger (1960), p. 65.

22. Fifty per cent of organizational members and 27 per cent of non-members reported more couple visiting. So did 83 per cent of the Jews in the random sample, and 53 per cent in the city sample, as compared to 30 per cent and 17 per cent of the Protestants. The association between visiting and organizational activity was also found in Levittown, Pennsylvania by Jahoda et al., p. 107.

23. Among Philadelphians of mixed marriage, only 20 per cent reported an increase, and 60 per cent a decrease in couple visiting after leaving the city. Sixteen per cent in both samples were intermarriages, usually of Catholics with Protestants.

24. See, e.g., Whyte (1956), Chap. 21.

25. Low-status respondents have as many friends as middle- and high-status ones, but the former do less couple visiting than in the previous residence.

26. The neighbors I knew best in the West End of Boston had open house every Tuesday night, visited the open house of relatives every Friday night, and visited with yet other relatives and friends on Sundays.

27. Much of this section is taken from Gans (1961b).

28. For an incisive critique of the balanced community ideal, see Orlans, pp. 88–94.

29. For a description of this trend in the first Levittown, see Liell (1963). See also Willmott (1963), p. 23.
30. For similar findings in Fairless Hills, Pennsylvania, see Haeberle, p. 75.
31. Forty-four per cent said they had done "much" visiting with ethnic or religious peers in Philadelphia, and 52 per cent, "some." In Levittown, the percentages shifted slightly, to 37 and 66, respectively. Respondents were free to define what they considered "much" or "some." Jews and low-status people reported the most ethnic-religious visiting; Irish Catholics, the greatest increase after moving to Levittown.
32. See, e.g., Williams, pp. 437–447.
33. See, e.g., Wilson, but also the study by Sewell and Armer which questioned the impact of "neighborhood context" on educational aspirations. Of course, in school students are a captive audience, and school contacts among working and middle class students may evaporate after school hours.
34. A study of a Scottish new town reported that "only one-fifth of the tenants said they would prefer more variety and intermixture of house-types, while two-fifths regarded the row of identical buildings as a desirable feature," and that "a house which is one of many in a street can become personalized without much aid from the architect." See Hole, p. 169.
35. It is illuminating to compare the early popular writing about Levittown, New York, to more recent reports. Initially, the Long Island community was widely described (and decried) as a hideous example of mass-produced housing which would soon turn into a slum; twenty

years later, journalists report the diversity produced by the alteration of houses, and the charm created by the maturing of trees and shrubbery—and, of course, the demand for the houses, which now sell for about twice their original price.
36. Orlans, pp. 95–104, and Whyte (1956), pp. 348–349.
37. A similar solution has been proposed in England by Willmott (1963), pp. 117–18. See also Dean (1958).
38. People were asked, "What kind of competition have you noticed between the neighbors about such things as getting things for the house, fixing up the yard, or repainting the house?"
39. Forty-four per cent of the blue collar respondents reported "keeping up with the Joneses" among their neighbors, but only 31 per cent of the white collar and professional ones did so. In an English working class new town, 26 per cent made similar complaints, principally lower-income people about those with higher incomes. Willmott (1963), p. 98.
40. Whyte (1956), Chap. 24.
41. Meyersohn and Jackson, p. 281.
42. In fact, I was more often praised for having taken good care of the car, for my thrift, and for my good luck in possessing a better car than the more recent models.
43. Copying took place only when someone decided to paint his house another color. Since this violated a deed-restriction, people waited for someone to break the rules and then followed suit quickly—but they did not copy the initiator's color scheme.
44. See, e.g., Spectorsky.

14

ALBERT I. HERMALIN · REYNOLDS FARLEY

The Potential for Residential Integration in Cities and Suburbs: Implications for the Busing Controversy

The controversy over busing to effect school integration arises from the intersection of social trends and prevailing values. On the one hand, the legal, political, and value systems have been moving in the direction of expanding the civil rights of black citizens, with the focus on removing inequities in the educational system. Confronting these efforts has been the long standing residential segregation of blacks from whites, which limits the degree of school integration so long as neighborhoods remain the primary mode of student allocation.

To have both integrated and neighborhood schools one must have integrated neighborhoods. This paper examines the receptiveness to and economic potential for achieving higher levels of residential integration. Knowledge of the potential for residential integration may in itself affect public attitudes toward busing, schooling, and housing, and represents an important input to governmental decision-making. Particularly so,

since there is some evidence of ambiguity and misconception on this score. For example, in a 1968 study of fifteen cities, 56 percent of white respondents felt that Negro disadvantages in jobs, education, and housing were mainly due to "something about Negroes themselves" rather than mainly discrimination (Campbell, 1971:13). In the same study, 68 percent of the whites said that "many" or "some" Negroes "miss out on good housing because white owners won't rent or sell to them."

Assumptions about the causes and levels of residential segregation and its probable rate of change enter not only into popular arguments about busing but have figured prominently in several court decisions. In the years following Brown versus the Board of Education in 1954 which held that "racial discrimination in public education is unconstitutional," federal courts overturned those laws that prevented racial integration (*Brown* v. *Board of Education*, 349 U.S. 294, 1955). The Civil Rights Act of 1964, which included a provision to end de jure school segregation, led to further judicial and administrative action to remove the legal props bolstering racially segregated school systems. Despite such changes, school integration did not advance substantially from 1954 to 1967 (Farley and Taeuber, 1974; U.S. Bureau of the Census, 1971a, Tables 176 and 177). As a result, emphasis shifted from the de jure aspects of school segregation to so-called de facto reasons among which residential segregation by race received considerable attention.

Cases brought before the federal courts re-

From *American Sociological Review* 1973, Vol. 38 (October): 595–610. Reprinted by permission of the publisher and authors.

This paper is a revision of a draft presented at the annual meetings of the American Sociological Association in New Orleans, Louisiana, August 30, 1972. This research was supported, in part, by a grant from the Center for Population Research of the National Institutes of Child Health and Human Development, NIH-71-2210, "The Distribution and Differentiation of Population within Metropolitan Areas."

quired judges to consider the causes and nature of residential segregation in relation to school segregation to determine if a de jure pattern existed. Several important decisions resulted. Federal Judge Keith, hearing a case involving the Detroit suburb of Pontiac, Michigan, contended that a school board could not blithely observe the emergence of racially segregated neighborhoods, assign pupils to their neighborhood schools and then claim it bore no responsibility for the resulting school segregation. He ordered the busing of children in that suburb (*Davis* v. *School District of City of Pontiac*, 309 F. Supp., 1970). The Fourth Circuit similarly mandated busing to integrate schools in Mecklenburg County (Charlotte), North Carolina. The Supreme Court, in upholding this decision, noted the far reaching implications of the way school authorities constructed new schools and closed old ones. "People gravitate toward school facilities, just as schools are located in response to the needs of the people. The location of schools may thus influence the patterns of residential development of a metropolitan area and have important impact on composition of inner city neighborhoods" (*Swann* v. *Charlotte-Mecklenburg*, 402 U.S. 1, 1971). In these and other cases the courts recognized the long standing and pervasive nature of residential segregation, found this attributable in part to actions of school authorities, and held that, under certain circumstances, attendance zones which simply reflected the housing patterns were not acceptable.

In two recent cases federal courts took cognizance of the sharp differences in racial composition of cities and their suburbs. In many cities the majority of public school students are black; and even with busing, the racially integrated schools in these cities will be principally black. For instance, in the fall of 1970, in both Richmond, Virginia and Detroit, two-thirds of the public school pupils were Negroes (U.S. National Center for Educational Statistics, 1972: 655 and 1,496). In both areas, suits were filed to integrate the schools. Plaintiffs argued that local, state and federal policies resulted in out-migration of whites from the central cities, a piling up of blacks in the city and the general exclusion of blacks from the suburbs. Busing of students within these cities was seen as ineffective in eliminating racially segregated schools. This litigation led federal Judges Merhige in Richmond and Roth in Detroit to order cross-district busing to effect integration.

In this paper we focus on the actual and potential racial composition of central cities and their suburban rings. This topic is not only in keeping with the current attention to cross-district busing but has received less study than residential segregation in cities. Before turning to our analysis, we briefly review trends in white attitudes on the question of integrated schooling and housing; relevant black attitudes are reviewed in the final section of the paper.

WHITE ATTITUDES TOWARD SCHOOL AND RESIDENTIAL INTEGRATION

Since the early 1940's national and local surveys have sampled white respondents for their views on the racial situation. In Table 1, we present selected findings from several such studies.

At present there appears to be consensus among whites supporting integrated schools but major disagreement on busing. Greeley and Sheatsley (1971:14), tracing the results of NORC surveys, show that the proportion of whites favoring integrated schools increased from 30 percent in 1942, to 49 percent in 1956, 64 percent in 1963 and 75 percent in 1970 (Table 1, line 1). Concern about busing seems not to have altered this view. A *Detroit Free Press* survey, conducted shortly after Judge Roth's decision ordering cross-district busing, found that about 90 percent of the suburban and city whites in the Detroit area were against busing at the same time that 70 percent disagreed with the opinion that white and black children should go to separate schools (*Detroit Free Press*, May 7, 1972, p. C1).

Though whites strongly endorse the general goal of school integration, other responses suggest this is a highly tempered endorsement. Thus only about one-third of whites feel that blacks would be better educated in integrated classrooms; the proportion feeling that blacks are receiving an inferior education appeared to decline during the 1960's; and in the seven years following the landmark Supreme Court decision no more than a fourth of whites favored school integration in the near future. For many whites the disadvantages of busing may outweight the severity of the problem it is designed to ameliorate. Gallup polls in 1970 and 1971 found that 8 percent of the white respondents opposed the busing of white and black children from one district to another (Gallup, 1972: 2,243 and 2,329)

Propositions concerning busing appeared on the ballot in California and Florida in 1972, and a large majority of the voters in both states opposed busing (*New York Times*, March 16, 1972:30; November 12, 1972:38).

Panel B of Table 1 presents data for whites on attitudes related to residential integration. Line 1 here indicates that the receptivity of whites to having a black family with the same education and income move into their block has greatly increased over time and by 1972 was approved by four out of five respondents. It is worthwhile noting that whites have been as favorable to this posited situation of direct social contact as they have to the more generalized norm of school integration shown in line 1 of Panel A.

The other attitudes related to residential integration shown in Panel B—though showing lower proportions favorable—generally indicate growing receptivity during the 1960's (also see Pettigrew:1973). There is little direct comparability of the attitudes in Panels A and B. Line 3 of the former when compared with line 5 of the latter suggests that a circumstance in which whites are a minority is viewed no more adversely in the housing situation than in the school situation. We do not claim that these data show that whites are as receptive to residential integration as they are to school integration. Several scales designed to rank attitudes indicate they are not (Greeley and Sheatsley, 1971), though the matter requires further research into the structure of racial attitudes. The data do suggest that the receptiveness of whites to residential integration has grown over time and that differences in the two attitudes may be fairly small. Moreover, opposition to integrated housing appears less strong than opposition to busing; hence, it is worthwhile to explore the economic potential for residential integration, both in its own right and as an alternative means for achieving greater school integration. This is the focus of the next section.

RACIAL COMPOSITION OF CITIES AND SUBURBS

We begin by noting the trend in racial composition of urbanized areas. An urbanized area "consists of a central city, or cities, and surrounding closely settled territory" (U.S. Bureau of the Census, 1972, Appendix A); it permits a sharper comparison of central cities with their nearby densely settled suburban rings than does the Standard Metropolitan Statistical Area. Our analysis includes those urbanized areas included among the twenty-five largest in either 1950, 1960, or 1970—a criterion which encompasses the twenty-nine areas shown in Table 2. These twenty-nine areas, which contain thirty-nine central cities, include all those of one million or more in 1970; and they comprised almost 40 percent of the total U.S. population in that year (U.S. Bureau of the Census, 1952, Tables 6 and 17; 1961a, Tables 6 and 23; 1971b, Tables 1 and 21).

Table 2 presents the proportion black in 1950, 1960 and 1970 in each urbanized area, its central city (or cities), and its suburban ring—defined as the area lying outside the central city or cities.[1] In the twenty-nine urbanized areas, the black population grew faster than the white from 1960 to 1970, continuing a trend evident in the previous decade. This differential rate of growth was particularly marked in the central cities, with the proportion black there rising from 13 percent in 1950 to 26 percent in 1970.

The proportion of population black rose in each central city between 1950 and 1970. This is true of those central cities which annexed large surrounding areas such as Houston, Indianapolis and Dallas as well as of those whose boundaries remained fixed. By 1970 two of the areas—Washington and Atlanta—had central cities whose populations were predominantly black; and in four others—Detroit, St. Louis, Baltimore and New Orleans—the central city's population was in excess of 40 percent black.

Very different trends characterize suburban rings. The proportion black has remained at about 4 percent at all dates. In some areas black representation increased: from 4 to 6 percent in New York; from 2 to 5 percent in Los Angeles; and from 7 to 12 percent in Miami. In other areas, it decreased: from 6 to 4 percent in Detroit; from 12 to 6 percent in Kansas City; and from 14 to 10 percent in New Orleans. Some suburban rings, like those surrounding Milwaukee and Indianapolis, contained almost no blacks even though, at all dates, these central cities had large black populations.

The Commission on Civil Disorders, appointed by President Johnson following the riots of the 1960's, noted the continued in-migration of blacks to large cities and the out-migration of whites. They contended that current governmental pol-

Table 1. *White Attitudes toward School and Residential Integration*

	1942	1954	1956	1957	1958	1961	1963	1964	1965	1966	1968	1970	1971	1972
Panel A. School Integration														
1. % saying white & Negro students should attend same schools	30[a]		49[a]				63[a]	67[b]				75[a]		84[m]
1a. Southern whites only	2[a]		14[a]				30[a]	55[b]				47[a]		66[m]
2. % in favor of "immediate" school integration			18[d]	27[d]	27[d]	23[d]								
3. % with no objection to sending own children to a school with a majority of Negroes		41[e]			33[e]		25[e]		21[f]	28[f]	29[f,g]			42[m]
3a. Southern whites only		14[e]			11[e]		5[e]		16[f]	27[f]	26[f,g]			32[m]
4. % agreeing that Negroes receive an inferior education							48[h]			36[b]				
5. % agreeing that Negroes would be better educated in integrated classrooms										33[h,l]				35[c]
Panel B. Residential Integration														
1. % saying it would make no difference if Negro with same income and education moved into block	35[b]		51[b]				64[b]		68[b]					84[m]
1a. Detroit SMSA—not disturbed by stated event					<40[j]								68[j]	
2. % disagree slightly or strongly that whites have a right to keep Negroes out of their neighborhoods							44[a]					50[a]		55[m]
3. % saying Negroes have a right to live wherever they can afford to								53[x]			65[x]			
4. % saying they would not move if "colored people" came to live next door					55[l]		55[l]		65[l]	66[l]		67[x]		
5. % saying they would not move if "colored people" came to live in great numbers in neighborhood					20[l]		22[l]		31[l]	30[l]				

178

[a] National Opinion Research Center (NORC) surveys reported in Greeley and Sheatsley (1971: 13–14). For 1970 national figure, chart indicates 70%, text reports 75%.

[b] NORC survey reported in Sheatsley (1966: 222 and 235).

[c] Pertains to Detroit central city and suburbs, *Detroit Free Press* (May 7, 1972): C1.

[d] Gallup and Roper surveys reported in Schwartz (1967: 30). Questions are not exactly comparable, see source for details and meaning of "immediate."

[e] Gallup surveys reported in Schwartz (1967: 45–46 and 132). Questions not exactly comparable.

[f] Gallup surveys reported in Schwartz (1972: 1941, 2010 and 2211). National figures estimated from regional figures.

[g] Poll conducted in 1969.

[h] Harris survey reported in Brink and Harris (1966: 130).

[i] Date not clear from source. Inferred from text.

[j] Pertains to Detroit central city and suburbs. *The Detroit Area Study 1971 Report to Respondents*, Ann Arbor, Michigan: University of Michigan: University of Michigan, Detroit Area Study, Project 46822 (January 1972): 7.

[k] Institute for Social Research survey reported in Campbell (1971: 133).

[l] Gallup surveys reported in Schwartz (1967: 133) and in Gallup (1972: 1824, 1825, 1941, 1942 and 2022).

[m] NORC survey reported in NORC (1972).

Table 2. *Blacks as a Proportion of Total Population, 1950–1970*

Urbanized Area	Total Urbanized Area			Central City or Cities			Suburban Ring		
	1970	1960	1950	1970	1960	1950	1970	1960	1950
New York	14.9%	10.9%	8.1%	22.6%	14.9%	9.7%	5.9%	4.5%	3.9%
Los Angeles	9.2	7.1	5.4	16.5	12.2	7.9	4.8	3.2	2.3
Chicago	19.6	16.1	11.6	32.8	23.0	13.9	3.4	3.0	2.9
Philadelphia	19.8	17.3	14.8	33.6	26.4	18.1	6.9	6.1	6.7
Detroit	19.0	15.6	12.8	43.6	28.9	16.2	3.7	3.8	5.8
San Francisco	11.2	9.5	7.0	20.5	14.3	7.9	6.0	5.5	5.9
Boston	4.7	3.2	2.3	16.3	9.1	5.0	1.1	0.8	0.8
Washington	27.0	24.9	23.9	71.1	53.9	35.0	7.6	3.7	5.4
Cleveland	17.0	14.5	10.9	38.3	28.6	16.2	3.7	0.9	0.5
St. Louis	19.4	17.0	14.6	40.9	28.6	17.9	8.9	7.6	9.5
Pittsburgh	8.5	8.0	7.7	20.2	16.7	12.2	3.9	3.6	4.0
Minneapolis	1.9	1.5	1.3	4.0	2.5	1.5	0.2	0.1	0.1
Houston	20.4	20.7	19.4	25.7	22.9	20.9	5.8	10.5	10.7
Baltimore	28.0	24.1	20.6	46.4	34.6	23.4	3.2	3.5	8.1
Dallas	16.5	14.6	14.2	24.9	19.0	13.1	2.2	2.6	18.7
Milwaukee	8.5	5.5	2.6	14.7	8.4	3.4	0.2	0.2	0.1
Seattle	3.4	3.2	2.6	7.1	4.8	3.4	0.5	0.2	0.4
Miami	14.7	13.4	12.1	22.7	22.4	16.2	11.7	8.7	7.4
San Diego	5.0	4.3	3.7	7.9	6.0	4.5	1.4	0.7	1.3
Atlanta	25.1	27.1	28.1	51.3	38.3	36.6	5.8	7.6	12.1
Cincinnati	13.5	12.9	11.5	27.6	21.6	15.5	3.8	3.9	4.8
Kansas City	13.5	12.4	12.1	22.3	17.5	12.2	6.1	7.0	11.9
Buffalo	9.8	7.7	4.5	20.4	13.3	6.3	2.0	2.0	1.0
Denver	4.7	3.9	3.1	9.1	6.1	3.6	0.4	0.3	0.7
San Jose	1.7	0.7	0.5	2.5	1.0	0.6	1.2	0.5	0.3
New Orleans	32.0	31.2	29.4	45.0	37.2	31.9	10.9	14.0	13.9
Portland	2.8	2.5	2.1	8.3	4.4	2.6	0.3	0.3	0.8
Indianapolis	16.4	15.4	12.7	18.0	20.6	15.0	0.2	0.4	0.2
Providence	2.6	2.0	1.7	8.9	5.4	3.3	0.7	0.5	0.5
Total[a]	14.4	12.1	9.9	25.9	19.1	12.7	4.6	3.7	4.1

[a]Weighted by the size of the urbanized area.
Sources: U.S. Bureau of the Census, *Census of Population: 1970*, PC(1)-B, Table 23; *Census of Population: 1960*, PC(1)-B, Table 21; *Census of Population: 1950*, Vol. II, Table 34.

icies concerning housing, education and poverty were creating a situation wherein there would be in two decades: ". . . a white society principally located in suburbs, in smaller central cities, and in the peripheral parts of large central cities; and a Negro society largely concentrated within central cities" (U.S. National Advisory Commission on Civil Disorders, 1968:407).

The status of this prediction as of 1970 may be gauged in part from Table 2. In 1950, the proportion black in the central cities was not much different from the proportion black in the total urbanized area, 12.7 percent versus 9.9 percent, respectively. By 1970, the proportion black in central cities was 25.9 percent as against 14.4 percent for the total urbanized areas.

The dramatic effect of this pattern on the twenty-nine areas can be seen from the table on next page. Though the number of urbanized areas having a fifth or more of their population

Table 3. *Blacks or Nonwhites as a Proportion of Total Public Elementary School Enrollment; 1970 and 1960*[a]

Urbanized Area	Total Urbanized Area		Central City		Suburban Ring	
	1970	1960	1970	1960	1970	1960
New York	22.7%	16.5%	40.0%	26.1%	5.5%	6.1%
Los Angeles	12.2	10.3	23.6	19.1	6.8	5.2
Chicago	30.0	27.5	54.8	42.6	4.8	4.6
Philadelphia	31.5	29.6	61.1	50.1	10.5	10.0
Detroit	23.4	22.2	64.3	45.8	4.5	5.6
San Francisco	16.2	19.9	40.0	39.3	7.9	9.6
Boston	6.8	5.1	31.9	18.6	1.1	1.2
Washington	34.2	32.8	93.3	79.9	10.4	5.9
Cleveland	25.7	23.0	57.1	47.5	5.4	1.5
St. Louis	29.9	28.5	65.2	50.6	13.9	13.1
Pittsburgh	13.7	13.7	41.9	36.2	5.7	6.1
Minneapolis	2.4	2.6	7.6	5.3	0.2	0.4
Houston	24.8	23.3	32.1	26.5	7.1	11.5
Baltimore	40.6	36.1	66.8	52.5	4.2	5.6
Dallas	20.9	16.1	34.3	21.6	2.3	2.9
Milwaukee	14.3	11.0	27.7	18.0	0.2	0.4
Seattle	4.3	6.6	13.0	11.5	0.5	0.8
Miami	24.9	18.5	38.1	34.2	20.8	12.6
San Diego	7.1	7.1	11.7	10.4	1.4	1.8
Atlanta	29.7	31.1	65.2	45.5	7.6	9.8
Cincinnati	20.5	20.8	45.8	34.2	5.5	6.4
Kansas City	18.3	15.5	32.4	24.2	7.7	8.4
Buffalo	16.0	13.9	39.5	27.7	3.2	3.7
Denver	6.1	5.1	15.2	9.1	0.5	0.7
San Jose	2.2	2.8	3.2	3.0	1.4	2.7
New Orleans	48.5	48.0	68.6	57.7	18.8	24.4
Portland	3.9	4.7	9.8	8.7	0.3	0.8
Indianapolis	21.3	19.2	23.4	27.0	0.1	0.4
Providence	4.0	4.0	19.2	12.7	1.0	0.8
Total[b]	20.7	18.4	41.7	32.4	6.3	5.7

[a] Data for 1960 refer to nonwhites; for 1970, to blacks.

[b] Weighted by the size of the urbanized area.

Sources: U.S. Bureau of the Census, *Census of Population: 1960*, PC(1)-C, Tables 73 and 77; *Census of Population: 1970*, PC(1)-C, Tables 83 and 91.

black has changed little from 1950 to 1970, the number of central cities with this proportion has more than tripled. No suburban ring has one fifth of its population black and the number having a tenth or more of its population black has declined.

This city-suburban racial contrast is even more marked if the school age population is consid-ered. Table 3 shows the proportion black among public elementary school pupils living in these central cities and suburban rings. In this table, unlike Table 2, the data for 1960 refer to non-whites.

During the decade, the proportion of students black in these urbanized areas rose from 18 to 21 percent. In the central cities the gains were

*Number of Urbanized Areas, Central Cities, and
Suburban Rings with 20 Percent or More of the
Population Black in 1950, 1960, and 1970. (Based
on twenty-nine Urbanized Areas and thirty-nine
Central Cities)*

	1970	1960	1950
Number of urbanized areas with 20% or more of population black	5	5	4
Number of central cities with 20% or more of population black	23	16	6
Number of suburban rings:			
With 20% or more of population black	0	0	0
With 10% to 20% of population black	2	2	5

much more substantial—from 32 to 42 percent—
than in the suburban rings—a change from 5.7
to 6.3 percent black. In the central cities of
about half the twenty-nine areas, the proportion
black in the public elementary schools exceeds
40 percent. In nine of the thirty-nine central
cities—Atlanta, Baltimore, Detroit, Gary, Newark, New Orleans, Philadelphia, St. Louis and
Washington—at least three out of five students
were Negroes at the end of the decade.

In the suburban rings, there were few sharp
changes in the proportion of students black. In
some areas this proportion decreased, while in
others it increased, though in every case except
Miami by a smaller amount than the increase in
proportion black in the central city.

These changes in racial composition have been
recognized by the federal judges. In the decision
calling for cross-district busing in the Detroit
area, Judge Roth stated:

By the year 1960, the largest segment of the
city's white population was younger and of
child-bearing age. The population 0 to 15
years of age constituted 30 percent of the total
population of which 60 percent were white
and 40 percent were black. In 1970, the white
population was primarily aging while the
black population was younger and of child-
bearing age.

The percentage of black students in the Detroit public school system in 1975–76 will be 73
percent, in 1980–81, 81 percent and in 1992 it

will be virtually 100 percent if present trends
continue. (*Bradley* v. *Milliken*, Civ. Action
35257, F. Supp. 338, 585).

Judge Merhige, who wrote the decision ordering busing throughout the Richmond area contended:

Ever since the Brown versus Board of Education of Topeka ruling, population growth in
the Richmond metropolitan area has consisted mainly of the addition of whites to the
neighboring counties and blacks to the city.
In 1955, the Richmond city schools were 43
percent black and in the Chesterfield and
Henrico counties, about 15 percent black. In
1972, the city schools are 70 percent black and
the county schools, 8 percent black. (*Bradley* v. *Richmond*, Civ. Action 3353, F. Supp. 338,
90).

POTENTIAL REPRESENTATION OF BLACKS IN SUBURBAN RINGS

The proportion of population black is higher in
each of these central cities than in their suburban
rings and has been increasing more rapidly in
the cities than in the suburbs. In all these urbanized areas, the value of housing and the level
of family income is greater in the suburban ring
than in the central city. In addition, the average
black family income is lower than that of whites.
An obvious hypothesis is that the absence of
blacks from suburban rings may be largely accounted for by their economic status relative to
whites and the differential economic status of
city and suburban dwellers.

This hypothesis can be promptly rejected.
Blacks at all value levels of owned and rented
housing were overrepresented in the central
cities and underrepresented in the suburbs. The
same was true according to family income—at
each income level the proportion of blacks living
in the suburban ring tends to be much lower
than that of whites in the identical income
group. This led us to compute the racial distribution in urbanized areas that would be expected if blacks were distributed throughout
the urbanized area according to their own value
of housing or family income but were represented in the suburbs to the same extent as
whites at each economic level. For instance, we
took the observed distribution of black families
by income and at each income level applied the
appropriate income-specific proportion of whites

living in the suburban ring. Thus, if 60 percent of whites in the $10,000 to $15,000 income category of a given urbanized area lived in the suburban ring, we applied that proportion to the actual number of blacks with that income. This procedure estimated the number and proportion of blacks in the suburbs if blacks retained their own economic characteristics but had the suburban representation rates of the white population. In making this comparison, we dealt with the black and non-black populations. Since the majority of non-Negroes are whites, we designate this the white population.[2]

Table 4 presents results of this investigation. We indicate the actual proportion of the urbanized area's total black and white households living in the suburban ring. In 1970, for example, the proportion of black households living in the ring ranged from a low of less than one percent in Indianapolis to a high of 51 percent in Miami. The proportion of white households in the ring ranged from a minimum of 11 percent in Indianapolis to a peak of 84 percent in Washington. Data for families are available for both 1970 and 1960 and are included in Table 4; the actual proportions by family do not differ greatly from those by household.[3]

In comparison, the expected proportions of blacks in the suburban ring are then presented. In Detroit in 1970, 11 percent of the black and 70 percent of the white households in the urbanized area actually resided in the suburban ring. If black households retained their value-of-housing distributions—both owned and leased—but were represented in the suburbs in the same proportion as whites at each level, the overall proportion of black households found in the ring would rise to 48 percent. If Detroit area black families were represented in the suburbs to the same extent as whites with comparable incomes, 67 percent rather than the observed 12 percent of black families would have suburban residences.

Substantial changes in the racial distribution in urbanized areas would occur if the representation rates of blacks at every value of housing level equaled those of whites. In many areas roughly similar proportions of whites and blacks would be located in the suburban ring. Overall in 1970, the proportion of black households in the ring would increase from 16 to 43 percent, a proportion much nearer the white figure of 57 percent in the suburban ring.

When family income is the criterion, the racial gap would narrow even more. If there were no racial difference in representation rates, then the proportion of total whites and blacks found in the suburban ring would be about the same in Los Angeles, Washington, Houston, Seattle, San Diego, Kansas City, Indianapolis, San Jose, Portland, and Providence. Overall, 55 percent of the black families, not the observed 17 percent, would live in suburban rings. Similarly, when data for 1960 are examined, we discover that racial differences in population distributions would greatly decrease if blacks in each income category were as well represented in suburbia as whites.

Figures in Table 4 imply that economic factors do not account for much of the concentration of blacks in the central city. Merely changing the representation rates while holding constant the economic variables would greatly increase the proportion of blacks living in the suburbs. Nevertheless, we did observe that as economic levels increase, the proportion of population living in the ring tends to increase. This led us to further assess the relative importance of economic factors and representation rates in the areal distribution of blacks. Results of this analysis are contained in Table 5.

The first three columns present data concerning black family income and its relation to that of whites. These show that in 1970, average black family income was $8,000 or more in twenty of the twenty-nine urbanized areas. Between 1960 and 1970, the ratio of black to white mean income rose in a majority of the areas. These data probably understate the relative improvement of blacks since the ratios for 1960 compare nonwhite income to that of whites while the 1970 figures refer to Negroes.

The center and right hand columns of Table 5 measure components of black underrepresentation in the suburban ring. For every urbanized area we show the observed percentage point difference in the proportion of whites and blacks in the suburban ring. In the Philadelphia urbanized area in 1970, for example, 60 percent of the white and 18 percent of the black families lived in the suburban ring, yielding a difference of 42 percentage points (see Table 4). If blacks had their own family income distribution but the income-specific suburban representation rates of whites, 54 percent of the blacks would live in the suburbs. Thus, we can estimate that of the total

Table 4. *Actual Proportion of Urbanized Area Population in Suburban Ring by Race and Expected Proportion of Blacks in Ring on Basis of White Representation Rates*

Area Urbanized	Households—1970 Actual Proportion in Ring Black	White	Expected % of Blacks in Ring[a]	Families—1970 Actual Proportion in Ring Black	White	Expected % of Blacks in Ring[b]	Families—1960 Actual Proportion in Ring Nonwhite	White	Exp. % of Nonwhites in Ring[b]
New York	16%	47%	29%	17%	51%	43%	15%	41%	34%
Los Angeles	27	61	59	31	65	64	25	60	59
Chicago	7	51	30	8	54	46	6	39	32
Philadelphia	17	57	35	18	60	54	16	51	44
Detroit	11	70	48	12	73	67	12	59	53
San Francisco	32	62	53	34	70	66	29	58	55
Boston	16	77	71	16	80	76	19	74	70
Washington	17	84	75	20	91	90	10	75	70
Cleveland	13	71	35	14	72	64	3	59	50
St. Louis	31	73	46	31	76	68	25	61	50
Pittsburgh	32	74	67	33	77	73	29	70	67
Minneapolis	5	51	32	6	58	49	6	42	35
Houston	7	29	27	7	31	29	9	20	18
Baltimore	5	53	36	5	58	51	5	43	36
Dallas	5	39	34	5	43	39	5	30	27
Milwaukee	1	44	22	1	46	39	1	37	31
Seattle	7	52	44	8	59	56	5	37	35
Miami	51	73	56	56	76	71	42	69	63
San Diego	8	40	38	8	45	45	9	34	34
Atlanta	12	68	54	13	73	67	10	46	37
Cincinnati	15	62	50	17	66	62	14	55	50
Kansas City	25	56	45	26	60	57	27	51	46
Buffalo	11	62	37	11	63	56	13	52	45
Denver	3	46	35	3	53	49	6	40	37
San Jose	40	58	56	40	58	56	63	66	65
New Orleans	12	46	30	12	50	43	11	32	26
Portland	5	50	39	5	56	53	8	44	42
Indianapolis	<1	11	7	<1	12	11	1	30	25
Providence	19	77	67	19	79	76	16	70	65
Total[c]	16	57	43	17	60	55	14	50	44

[a] Expected on the basis of white suburban representation by value of housing.
[b] Expected on the basis of white suburban representation by family income.
[c] Weighted by the size of the urbanized area.
Source: See Table 5.

12 percentage-point difference, a proportion equal to 6 percentage points (that is, 60 minus 54) is attributable to racial differences in income distributions. We are, in effect, standardizing for representation rates to measure the effects of racial differences in income.

Similarly, we can assess the effect of racial differences in suburban representation rates by standardizing for income. That is, we can assume that the black income distribution changes and becomes identical to that of whites. We can then apply the blacks' own suburban representation rates to measure how the proportion of blacks in the suburban rings would be altered by raising the income level of blacks to that of whites. In Philadelphia, were this accomplished, the proportion of blacks in suburbia would be 19 percent, a discrepancy of 41 points (that is, 60 minus 19) from the observed proportion among whites. This discrepancy measures the effect of racial differences in suburban representation rates.

The observed and hypothetical discrepancies are presented in Table 5 for twenty-nine areas.

The two components do not necessarily sum to the total difference for there is an interaction component.

In each urbanized area in 1960 and 1970, the income component is smaller than the representation rate component; indeed in most urbanized areas it is much smaller than the representation component. Between 1960 and 1970, the income component changed very little in most areas; but the representation component increased. These figures indicate that if black incomes continue to increase more rapidly than those of whites, the representation of blacks in suburbia will change very little if the present income-specific representation rates persist. On the other hand, if the representation rates were changed, the proportion of blacks living in the suburban ring would rise sharply even if there were no change in income.

This pattern exists because the gap between black and white income tends to be smaller than the gap in white and black suburban representation. This is illustrated graphically in Figures 1A and 1B which pertain to the Detroit urban-

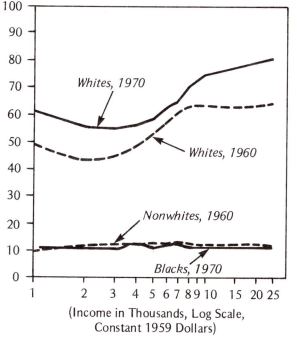

(Income in Thousands, Log Scale, Constant 1959 Dollars)

Figure 1A. *Proportion of Families in Each Income Level Living in the Suburban Ring, Detroit Urbanized Area.*

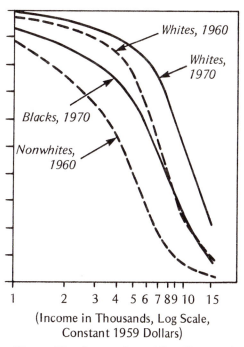

(Income in Thousands, Log Scale, Constant 1959 Dollars)

Figure 1B. *Proportion of Families Having Incomes of a Designated Amount or More, Detroit Urbanized Area*

Table 5. *Income of Black Families, 1970; Ratio of Black to White Family Income, 1970 and 1960; Racial Difference in Proportion of Urbanized Area Population in the Suburban Ring and Components of that Difference*

Urbanized Area	Family Income Data			Racial Difference (White minus Black) in Percentage of Urbanized Area Population in Suburban Ring					
	Mean Black Family Income 1970	Ratio of Black to White Mean Family Income		1970			1960[a]		
		1970	1960[a]	Total Difference	Attributable to Racial Differences in:		Total Difference	Attributable to Racial Differences in:	
					Income	Representation Rates		Income	Representation Rates
New York	$ 8,800	.60	.58	34	8	30	26	7	24
Los Angeles	8,900	.63	.66	34	1	31	35	1	33
Chicago	9,400	.61	.57	46	8	46	33	7	32
Philadelphia	8,600	.63	.57	42	6	41	35	7	34
Detroit	9,800	.64	.55	61	6	61	47	6	46
San Francisco	9,200	.62	.64	36	4	34	29	3	28
Boston	8,000	.57	.62	64	4	56	55	4	50
Washington	10,400	.59	.47	71	1	68	65	5	66
Cleveland	9,000	.61	.60	58	8	55	56	9	55
St. Louis	7,900	.57	.52	45	8	43	36	11	39
Pittsburgh	7,500	.60	.56	44	4	43	41	3	41

Minneapolis	9,200	.65	.65	52	9	48	36	7	32
Houston	7,300	.52	.47	24	2	24	11	2	12
Baltimore	8,600	.64	.60	53	7	51	38	7	37
Dallas	7,400	.51	.43	38	4	39	25	3	25
Milwaukee	8,500	.62	.64	45	7	44	36	6	35
Seattle	9,400	.66	.70	51	3	48	32	2	31
Miami	7,100	.55	.54	20	5	18	27	6	23
San Diego	8,500	.69	.64	37	0	37	25	0	25
Atlanta	7,600	.53	.43	60	6	61	36	9	39
Cincinnati	7,800	.60	.56	49	4	46	41	5	40
Kansas City	8,200	.62	.57	34	3	36	24	5	23
Buffalo	8,200	.66	.61	52	7	51	39	7	38
Denver	8,700	.67	.66	50	4	49	34	3	33
San Jose	11,400	.78	.86	18	2	19	3	1	3
New Orleans	6,100	.48	.47	38	7	38	21	6	22
Portland	8,100	.71	.67	51	3	50	36	2	35
Indianapolis	8,900	.65	.60	11	1	11	29	5	29
Providence	7,000	.60	.61	60	3	55	54	5	49
Total[b]	8,700	.61	.58	43	5	41	36	5	34

[a]Figures for 1960 are based upon data for nonwhites.

[b]Weighted average.

Sources: U.S. Bureau of the Census, Census of Population: 1960, PC(1)-C, Tables 76 and 78; Census of Population: 1970, PC(1)-B, Table 25; PC(1)-C, Tables 89 and 94.

187

ized area. The left hand panel shows the income-specific proportions of white and black families living in the suburban ring. At both dates, increments in income among whites were matched by increases in the percent living in the ring. Between 1960 and 1970, the share of whites living in suburbia rose at all income levels; and when the recent census was conducted, three out of four Detroit area whites reported a suburban address.

During this decade the income distribution of blacks improved as can be seen by examining the right hand panel, Figure 1B. Between 1960 and 1970, these curves shifted to the right—meaning higher real incomes and greater purchasing power—and the racial gap narrowed somewhat. By the end of the decade, more nonwhites were at those incomes at which a high proportion of whites live in the suburbs.

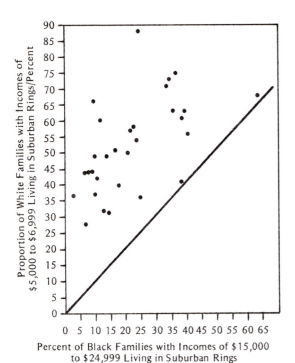

Percent of Black Families with Incomes of $15,000 to $24,999 Living in Suburban Rings

Figure 2. *Proportions of Black Families with Income of $15,000 to $24,999 and White Families with Income of $5,000 to $6,999 Living in Suburban Rings; Twenty-nine Urbanized Areas, 1970*
Source: See Table 5.

Despite rising income, 12 percent of Detroit area blacks lived in the suburbs at the beginning and end of the decade. The left hand side of Figure 1 indicates the reason. Among blacks, rises in income were not matched by increases in the proportion living in the suburbs. Furthermore, between 1960 and 1970, almost no change occurred in the proportion of blacks at any income level living in the suburban ring.

We examined analogous information for other urbanized areas, and the findings were similar. To be certain, the levels are not exactly the same in all areas and in certain areas the graphs contain particular wrinkles or indentations. Nevertheless, the overall pattern is clear. The increasing income of blacks has done little to reduce their concentration in central cities, and further rises in the income of blacks will not alter this pattern unless the representation rates change. In all areas, blacks in the higher income categories are less represented in suburbia than are whites in middle or low income brackets. Figure 2 illustrates this finding. It indicates the proportion of black families with incomes $15,000 to $24,999 in 1969 living in suburbs, plotted against the corresponding proportion of white families having incomes of $5,000 to $6,999. Points above the diagonal indicate that a higher proportion of the lower income white families are in the suburban ring than higher income black families. In every area, the proportion in the suburbs is much greater among the white families than among the black. Apparently a low income white family can obtain a suburban home or apartment more readily than a high income black family.

THE DISTRIBUTION OF THE BLACK POPULATION IN THE SUBURBAN RING

Although blacks comprise a small share of the suburban ring population, the actual number of blacks in the rings in 1970 ranged from a low of less than one hundred in Indianapolis to a high of almost 450,000 in New York and Los Angeles. We wished to determine whether these suburban blacks were distributed throughout the ring or concentrated in a few suburbs. The data for 1970 reveal that, in most suburban rings, the vast majority of blacks live in those few suburbs which have a large black population.

Table 6 presents findings for the Detroit urban

Table 6. *Actual Blacks in Detroit Suburbs and Blacks Expected on Basis of Value of Housing and Family Income; 1970 (Suburbs of 25,000 or More)*

Suburb	Occupied Housing Units	Value of Housing				Family Income	
		Number Occupied by Blacks		Prop. Occupied by Blacks		Prop. of Families Black	
		Act.	Exp.	Act.	Exp.	Act.	Exp.
Allen Park	11,489	1	856	<0.1%	7.5%	<0.1%	14.1%
Birmingham	8,636	3	494	<0.1	5.7	<0.1	12.4
Dearborn	34,614	2	4,670	<0.1	13.5	<0.1	15.9
Dearborn Heights	22,481	1	2,011	<0.1	8.9	<0.1	14.8
East Detroit	13,077	2	1,385	<0.1	10.6	<0.1	16.0
Ferndale	10,137	12	1,618	0.1	15.9	0.2	17.4
Garden City	10,482	2	1,076	<0.1	10.3	<0.1	15.1
Hamtramck	10,302	1,060	3,633	10.3	35.3	11.0	21.4
Highland Park	12,412	5,190	4,315	41.8	34.8	52.8	22.6
Inkster	10,443	4,443	1,870	42.5	17.9	42.8	18.3
Lincoln Park	15,999	1	2,363	<0.1	14.8	<0.1	16.5
Livonia	27,686	2	1,584	<0.1	5.7	<0.1	13.1
Madison Heights	10,963	4	1,154	<0.1	10.5	<0.1	15.7
Oak Park	10,940	14	712	0.1	6.5	0.1	14.5
Pontiac	25,581	5,784	5,221	22.6	20.4	23.9	20.7
Roseville	16,453	159	2,075	1.0	12.6	0.9	16.5
Royal Oak	27,451	8	2,649	<0.1	9.6	<0.1	15.0
St. Clair Shores	24,554	41	2,000	0.2	8.1	0.2	14.9
South Gate	9,148	2	957	<0.1	10.4	<0.1	15.1
Southfield	20,159	12	996	0.1	4.9	0.1	12.1
Sterling Heights	16,325	9	1,115	0.1	6.8	0.1	14.3
Taylor	18,498	4	2,384	<0.1	12.9	<0.1	16.6
Troy	12,195	7	850	0.1	7.0	<0.1	13.7
Warren	48,595	38	4,876	0.1	10.0	0.1	14.9
Westland	23,046	473	2,406	2.1	10.4	2.1	15.6
Wyandotte	12,922	5	2,530	<0.1	19.6	<0.1	18.0
Total	464,689	17,279	55,800	3.7	12.0	3.5	15.7

Sources: U.S. Bureau of the Census, *Census of Housing: 1970*, HC(1)-A24, Tables 8, 10, 11, 18, and 20; *Census of Population: 1970*, PC(1)-24B, Tables 26 and 29; PC(1)-24C, Tables 89, 94 and 107.

zed area. For each suburb of 25,000 or more, we indicate the total number of occupied dwelling units and the actual and expected units occupied by blacks. Looking at the actual numbers first, we see that more than 95 percent of the 17,000 Negro households in these twenty-six suburbs lived in four places—Hamtramck, Highland Park, Inkster and Pontiac. Twenty of the twenty-six suburbs contained fewer than fifty black households.

We determined what proportion of housing units in each economic category throughout the entire urbanized area was occupied by blacks. We next considered the distribution of owned and leased housing by value in each suburb and ascertained what number of blacks would be in that particular suburb were they present, at each value of housing, to the same extent that they are throughout the entire urbanized area. We show the actual and expected proportions black in Table 6. Similarly we ascertained what number of whites (non-Negroes) would be expected in each suburb if whites occupied homes there in each economic bracket to the same degree that they did throughout the entire urbanized area. The expected numbers of blacks and whites in each suburb sum to the total number of households located in that place.

For all twenty-six suburbs together, fewer than 4 percent of the total households are black; but the proportion expected on the basis of housing value is 12 percent. In nineteen of the twenty-six suburbs, one-tenth of one percent or less of the households are black, though five percent is the minimum expected. In most suburbs, the expected proportion black is between 9 and 18 percent. The actual proportion black falls within that range in only one suburb—Hamtramck.

Similar calculations were made using family income as the criterion. In the right hand columns of Table 6 we show the actual proportion of families black and the proportion black expected if each suburb had its own income distribution, but blacks at each income level were as well represented in that suburb as throughout the entire urbanized area. Using family income as the criterion, the discrepancy between the actual and expected proportions black is even greater.[4] In every suburb the expected proportion of families black is within the range of 12

to 23 percent. Yet, the actual proportion of families black is one-tenth of one percent or less in eighteen of the twenty-six suburbs.

The concentration of blacks in suburban rings was studied for seven urbanized areas and results are displayed in Table 7. We assembled data for all suburbs of 10,000 and over in 1970 in each suburban ring. First, the actual and expected proportions of households and families black are indicated for all suburbs together. In each case, the expected proportion black is much higher than the actual. In Washington, for instance, the actual proportion of families black is 5 percent; the expected proportion, 23 percent. In Cleveland, the actual is 2 percent; the expected, 12 percent. This illustrates further that economic factors do not account for the low proportion black in these suburban rings.[5]

To examine the distribution of blacks in these suburbs, segregation indices were calculated using individual suburbs as the units of analysis. The index of dissimilarity was the measure used to do this. A value of one hundred indicates complete segregation, and in such a case all suburbs would be exclusively black or white. A value of zero indicates complete integration— all suburbs would have identical racial compositions.[6] Segregation indices were calculated

Table 7. *Actual and Expected Proportions of Households and Families Black and Actual and Expected Residential Segregation Scores for Suburbs of 10,000 and Over, 1970*

| Urbanized Area | No. of Subs | Households | | | | Families | | | |
| | | Prop. of Households Headed by Blacks | | Residential Segregation Scores | | Prop. of Families Headed by Blacks | | Residential Segregation Scores | |
		Act.	Exp.[a]	Act.	Exp.[a]	Act.	Exp.[b]	Act.	Exp.[b]
Cleveland	38	4%	9%	77	21	4%	13%	77	5
Dallas	13	2	11	46	13	2	12	50	7
Detroit	46	4	12	86	22	4	16	87	6
Miami	15	3	8	66	12	3	11	65	8
St. Louis	30	9	12	77	27	9	15	78	10
San Fran.-Oakland	40	5	8	68	13	5	10	70	6
Washington	42	5	19	36	17	5	23	37	8

[a] Expected on the basis of value of housing occupied by blacks.

[b] Expected on the basis of black family income.

Sources: U.S. Bureau of the Census, *Census of Housing: 1970,* HC(1)-A, Tables 8, 10, 11, 18 and 20; *Census of Population: 1970,* PC(1)-B, Tables 26 and 29; PC(1)-C, Tables 89, 94 and 107.

twice. First we used the actual distributions of blacks and whites, and then we compared the expected distributions of blacks and whites. As shown in Table 7 in every case, the actual segregation score was at least double that expected on the basis of housing value. With regard to the distribution of families by income, the actual segregation scores were four or more times as large as the expected. This indicates that if blacks and whites were distributed throughout the suburban rings on the basis of the value of their housing or family income, there would be relatively little residential segregation by race on a suburb by suburb basis.

Lastly, we considered the level of residential segregation in central cities. Taeuber and Taeuber (1965) showed that there was a high degree of residential segregation in central cities in 1960 and that this had changed relatively little over the two previous decades. They furthermore demonstrated that the expected level of segregation, based on value of housing criteria similar to those used here, was much lower than that existing. Using census tracts as units, we calculated the actual index of segregation for a few central cities and found that segregation in 1970 was about at the same high level as in 1960.

Though expected indices cannot readily be calculated for 1970, other evidence strongly indicates that residential segregation in central cities in 1970 is far in excess of what would be expected on economic grounds alone.

CONCLUSION

This report corroborates and extends previous findings on racial changes in metropolitan areas and residential segregation. We find, first, a continuing growth of black population in these urbanized areas, particularly within the central cities. Second, economic criteria account for little of the observed concentration of blacks in central cities and their relative absence from the suburbs. Third, there is a high level of racial residential segregation within suburban rings which cannot be accounted for by economic criteria. In most instances, the majority of suburban blacks reside in a few suburbs, whatever their economic level. Fourth, based on scantier evidence, we believe that economic factors continue to account for little of the racial segregation of neighborhoods in central cities.

If one eliminates economic characteristics as the major source of residential segregation, then one must look to preference among blacks for residing in black neighborhoods or discrimination by whites, either explicit or covert, as the general causes. Recent surveys of the attitudes of urban blacks have found that they generally prefer racially mixed neighborhoods rather than the segregated neighborhoods in which they live, and they prefer to send their children to integrated public schools. The *Newsweek* polls found that the proportion of blacks indicating they wished to live in racially mixed neighborhoods increased during the 1960's reaching 67 percent toward the end of the decade. Seven of ten blacks claimed they wished to have their children attend schools with white youngsters (Brink and Harris, 1967:232–4). In the 1968 fifteen city study, only 13 percent of the blacks reported they preferred to live in an all or mostly Negro neighborhood; and only 6 percent held that black children should go to all or mostly Negro schools (Campbell and Schuman, 1968:15–16).

We believe then that the current level of residential segregation must be attributed largely to actions and attitudes, past and present, which have restricted the entry of blacks into predominately white neighborhoods. Our general conclusions are well captured by Judge Roth's findings in the Detroit case:

The city of Detroit is a community generally divided by racial lines. Residential segregation within the city and throughout the larger metropolitan areas is substantial, pervasive and of long standing. Black citizens are located in separate and distinct areas within the city and are not generally to be found in the suburbs. While the racially unrestricted choice of black persons and economic factors may have played some part in the development of this pattern of residential segregation, it is, in the main, the result of past and present practices and customs of racial discrimination, both public and private, which have and do restrict the housing opportunities of black people.

Governmental action and inaction at all levels: federal, state and local, have combined with those of private organizations, such as loaning institutions, real estate associations and brokerage firms to establish and maintain the patterns of residential segregation throughout the Detroit metropolitan area.

(*Bradley* v. *Milliken*, Civ. Action 35257. F. Supp. 338, 587).

A number of implications for policy and further research follow from these findings.

1. Increasing the proportion of blacks in white areas of the city or in the suburban ring does not require locating low income or subsidized housing in the suburbs, nor must residential integration await the further upgrading of black income. Policy makers should be made aware that this change does not require massive expenditures of federal, state or local money. Further steps to equalize the economic status of blacks and whites or to provide better housing to all low income people are indeed desirable on other grounds, but these steps need not delay the increased amount of residential integration already possible.

2. With the removal of explicit federal and state actions which hindered residential integration, such as Federal Housing Administration lending practices, the focus in removing existing impediments should be on what Amos Hawley has described as the "web of discrimination"— the real estate practices, the mortgage lending arrangements, the climate of opinion and the like—which deter blacks from obtaining the housing for which they are economically qualified (National Academy of Sciences, 1972:20–31; Hawley and Rock, 1973:19). Guidance in removing these impediments should be aided by research which further specifies the components of this "web" and their mode of operation as well as by research into regional and other factors associated with differing levels of residential integration by urbanized area.

3. It would be desirable to make widely known to policy makers and the population at large the considerable economic potential blacks now have to occupy housing at all value levels in the cities and suburbs. Glazer (1960:7) conjectured that the perceived socioeconomic distribution of a minority group affects the receptivity of white homeowners to having them as neighbors. If whites were made aware of the large middle class existing among blacks, their concern about racial residential integration might be lessened.

Further attitudinal research might well seek to determine how whites perceive the income distribution of blacks. In addition, surveys among both whites and blacks should obtain more precise measures of how each group defines an integrated neighborhood. It may well be that whites will typically consider a neighborhood integrated if it has 10 to 20 percent blacks, while blacks prefer to live in neighborhoods 30 to 40 percent black.

4. The bus is not the only vehicle for integrating schools. The economic potential exists to largely achieve both integrated schools and neighborhood schools through greater racial residential integration. Moreover, school integration achieved through greater residential integration may have different educational implications than that achieved through busing. Armor (1972) distinguishes "induced" school integration, as in a busing program, from "natural" school integration, which would arise from residential integration, and contends that "natural" school integration will promote a contact among blacks and whites of approximate socioeconomic equality that may better accomplish both educational goals and racial harmony.

However that may be, the available data demonstrate that the receptiveness and economic potential now exist for a high degree of residential integration. To the extent that this comes about, it will have far reaching implications for race relations; not the least important, in the context of current concern, is a form of school integration which is neighborhood based.

Notes

1. For each urbanized area, the same central city or cities were used at every date. They were those places defined as central cities in both the censuses of 1960 and 1970. If a city became a central city in 1970, it was not included. There were two exceptions to this rule: Clifton, New Jersey and Pawtucket, Rhode Island. They were excluded since data concerning their small black populations were not published by the Bureau of the Census in 1960.

2. In 1970, 1.6 percent of the non-Negro population consisted of nonwhites, that is, Orientals, Indians, Eskimoes and other races (U.S. Bureau of the Census, 1972, Table 60).

3. The 1960 data compare the white and non-white populations. At that date blacks comprised 92.1 percent of the nonwhite population (U.S. Bureau of the Census, 1961b, Table 44).

4. The method used to calculate the expected proportion here differs from that described in the previous section. Here we assume that the proportion of blacks found at a given economic level

for the entire urbanized area holds for each suburb; so that if black families account for 15 percent of all families in the $10,000 to $15,000 income category, we assume they account for this proportion of this income level in each suburb.

5. In a table not shown here we performed a similar calculation for the total suburban ring, including suburbs under 10,000, and total central city population of each of the twenty-nine urbanized areas. In every case, the expected proportion of the central city which is black was lower than actual; and the expected proportion of the suburban population black increased sharply. For the value of housing criterion, the expected proportion of households black in the suburban ring was at least double that actually found in twenty-two of the twenty-nine urbanized areas.

6. The size of the segregation index depends on the size of the areal units used. The smaller the sub-areas, the larger the index, so that an index value computed from suburbs as units will be less than if census tracts were used across the same geographic area.

Bibliography

Armor, David G. 1972. "The evidence on busing." The Public Interest 28 (Summer): 90–125.

Bradley v. Milliken, Civ. Action 35257 (E.D. Mich. 1971).

Bradley v. Richmond, Civ. Action 3353 (D.C. Va. 1972).

Brink, William and Louis Harris. 1967. Black and White. New York: Simon and Schuster.

Brown v. Board of Education, 349 U.S. 294 (1955).

Campbell, Angus. 1971. White Attitudes toward Black People. Ann Arbor: Institute for Social Research.

Campbell, Angus and Howard Schuman. 1968. Racial Attitudes in Fifteen Cities. Ann Arbor: Institute for Social Research.

Davis v. School District of City of Pontiac, 309 F. Supp. (1970).

Detroit Free Press. 1972. (May 7).

Farley, Reynolds and Alma F. Taeuber. Forthcoming. "Racial segregation in the public schools." American Journal of Sociology.

Gallup, George H. 1972. The Gallup Poll, New York: Random House.

Glazer, Nathan. 1960. "Introduction" in Nathan Glazer and Davis McEntire (eds.), Studies in Housing and Minority Groups, Berkeley: University of California Press.

Greeley, Andrew M. and Paul B. Sheatsley. 1971. "Attitudes toward integration." Scientific American 225 (December): 13–19.

Hawley, Amos H. and Vincent P. Rock (eds.). 1973. Segregation in Residential Areas. Washington: National Academy of Sciences.

National Academy of Sciences. 1972. Freedom of Choice in Housing. Washington: National Academy of Sciences.

National Opinion Research Center. 1972. National Data Program for the Social Sciences. Codebook for the Spring 1972 General Social Survey. Chicago: National Opinion Research Center, University of Chicago.

New York Times. 1972. (March 16 and November 12).

Pettigrew, Thomas F. 1973. "Attitudes on race and housing: a social-psychological view." Pp. 21–84 in Amos H. Hawley and Vincent P. Rock (eds.), Segregation in Residential Areas. Washington: National Academy of Sciences.

Schwartz, Mildred A. 1967. Trends in White Attitudes Toward Negroes. Chicago: National Opinion Research Center, University of Chicago.

Sheatsley, Paul B. 1966. "White attitudes toward the Negro." Daedalus 95 (Winter): 217–38.

Swann v. Charlotte-Mecklenburg, 402 U.S. 1 (1971).

Taeuber, Karl E. and Alma F. 1965. Negroes in Cities. Chicago: Aldine.

U.S. Bureau of the Census. 1952. Census of Population: 1950, P-A1. 1961a. Census of Population: 1960, Vol. I, Part A. 1961b. Census of Population: 1960, PC(1)-1B. 1971a. Statistical Abstract of the United States: 1971. 1971b. Census of Population: 1970, PC(1)-A1. 1972. Census of Population: 1970 PC(1)-B1.

U.S. National Advisory Commission on Civil Disorders. 1968. Report of the National Advisory Commission on Civil Disorders. New York: Bantam Books.

U.S. National Center for Educational Statistics. 1972. Directory of Public Elementary and Secondary Schools in Selected Districts, Enrollment and Staff by Racial-Ethnic Group. Fall 1970.

5
chapter

contents

emerging life styles

In the first explicit treatment of the master theme of this volume, cities in change, this chapter turns to emerging life styles. Here the selections provide less of a true cross-section than a selective spotlighting of some interesting, perhaps new, patterns of adaptation in the contemporary city. But, like the previous chapter, these pieces are intended to convey the rich variety of life styles that characterize different age, class, and ethnic groups.

Certainly a fundamental correlate of urbanization is bureaucratization, the tendency for ever greater areas of individual and community life to be regulated by dictates of large corporate and governmental organizations. Consequently, another current running through this section is how individuals and urban subcultures adapt to the encroachments of bureaucracy.

The first theme in Chapter 5 is "the city as tolerance and freedom," a theme quite current in social science thinking. A few years ago, theologian Harvey Cox suggested in *The Secular City* that the city represents freedom but also, ipso facto, responsibilities. He painted a picture of emerging urban man—secular, profane, pragmatic—whose city took shape not in physically delimited areas but in networks of interdependence and interest. But the essence of urban civility is another matter. Howard S. Becker and Irving L. Horowitz discuss San Franciscans' tolerance of an incredible range of life styles: beat, hippie, communal, pornographic; indeed, such styles give the city much of its distinctive flavor. Other American cities may follow suit to a lesser degree; but the reader should attempt to figure out what is unique about San Francisco—climate, occupational structure, leadership, history, ethnic composition—which puts it into the forefront of urban civility.

If San Francisco's civility is somewhat exceptional a more characteristic view of city life centers on the notion of overcrowding and the pathological consequences of high density. Studies of the aggressive behavior evidenced by white mice raised in overcrowded conditions have led some to the facile generalization that social space follows similar laws; that people living close together in densely populated ghettos or high-rise apartments manifest such pathological behavior as criminality, violence, drug and alcohol abuse, suicide, and so forth. So far there is little or no evidence to support this speculation. In order to explain why the "density-pathology" hypothesis may be wrong we have included Jacqueline Zito's paper which explores the life style of high-rise apartment dwellers. Interestingly, we discover that these living arrangements do, indeed, promote a kind of isolation and anonymity. Neighboring is characteristic only of those who are at home regularly or have children, a minority within the complex. But Zito goes on to explain this in ways that suggest an interpretation different from the easy connection between crowding and antisocial behavior. In the first place, most of these people are young professionals who have close ties to social and occupational groups in other areas of the city. They participate in social networks but not ones defined by location of residence. Second, anonymity within the high-rise complex provides a welcome form of privacy in what would otherwise be a difficult or "overload" situation, to use Milgram's term. The important point, of course, is that the urban dweller can symbolically define the physical environment and thereby avoid the pains inflicted on white mice.

The balance of the chapter deals, among other things, with the interplay between urbanism and bureaucracy in four very different urban subcultures. Considering, first, groups that are committed to urban life by choice or the absence of alternatives, two forms of coping are illustrated. In the case of the Blackstone Rangers, James McPherson shows how a turf-based street gang extended its hegemony, how politicians attempted to buy them off with federal funds, and how these funds were siphoned off to the gang and its members. If we regard this situation as neutrally as possible, the whole sequence of events represents a highly successful demonstration of "streetsmanship" combined with a certain bureaucratic finesse. Far from being cooled out by the city and federal establishment, this group succeeded temporarily in co-opting the bureaucracy itself. The article on singles in the city deals with the coping behavior of a different population; young unmarried, educated residents of the central city. While many of the friendship networks of these people stem from the bureaucratized occupational world, they tend to be dissatisfied with their work and seek affiliation with others in similar circumstances by choosing particular housing locations and visiting the singles bars.

By contrast to these groups, committed in some way to the city, the last two selections treat subcultures that have solved the bureaucratic threat by dropping out or never opting in. William Kornblum and Paul Lichter describe comparatively the intriguing case of urban gypsies. Here, like the Blackstone Rangers and doubtless other underclass groups, the gypsies maintain as much distance from the dominant culture as possible while at the same time attempting to manipulate it to their advantage—a practice they regard as perfectly justifiable. They are willing to live at the margins of urban society using its welfare system (in the case of Seattle) or its public services (in the Paris case) provided those contacts do not encroach on their own subculture and life style. Similarly William Erickson describes a well-established urban commune in which members earn their subsistence through various forms of contact with the larger society, but return their earnings to support the communal group. We see in this paper some of the highly structured mechanisms that are necessary to maintain a viable group that is within but not of the city.

This chapter can only begin to suggest the richly striated variety of changing urban life styles. To begin to fill in the picture the interested student might turn to the documentary reporting of Studs Terkel in *Division Street USA* or *Working*. Nevertheless, we would venture that the materials included here and similar descriptions of emerging urban life styles yield to certain general explanations. Urbanization and bureaucratization set the stage on which life styles emerge as mechanisms for coping with the environment. As these conditions change, become more cumbersome, so do life styles adapt. But such banalities are not the concern of social scientists.

Rather, we are concerned with explaining the nature of these changes and particularly their impact upon various social groups. In that vein we believe that urban life styles are to be explained by the interplay between the fundamental trend toward urbanization–bureaucratization and particularized responses that are fashioned by the exigencies of social class and subcultural values.

15

HOWARD S. BECKER · IRVING LOUIS HOROWITZ

The Culture of Civility:
San Francisco

Deviance and Democracy in "The City"

Deviants of many kinds live well in San Francisco —natives and tourists alike make that observation. The city's apparently casual and easygoing response to "sex, dope and cheap thrills" (to crib the suppressed full title of Janis Joplin's famous album—itself a San Francisco product) astounds visitors from other parts of the country who can scarcely credit either what they see happening or the way natives stroll by those same events unconcerned.

• Walking in the Tenderloin on a summer evening, a block from the Hilton, you hear a black whore cursing at a policeman: "I wasn't either blocking the sidewalk! Why don't you motherfucking fuzz mind your own goddam business!" The visiting New Yorker expects to see her arrested, if not shot, but the cop smiles good-naturedly and moves on, having got her back into the doorway where she is supposed to be.
• You enter one of the famous rock ballrooms and, as you stand getting used to the noise and lights, someone puts a lit joint of marijuana in your hand. The tourist looks for someplace to hide, not wishing to be caught in the mass arrest he expects to follow. No need to worry. The police will not come in, knowing that if they do they will have to arrest people and create disorder.
• Candidates for the city's Board of Supervisors make their pitch for the homosexual vote, esti-

mated by some at 90,000. They will not be run out of town; the candidates' remarks are dutifully reported in the daily paper, as are the evaluations of them by representatives of SIR, the Society for Individual Rights.
• The media report (tongue in cheek) the annual Halloween Drag Ball, for which hundreds of homosexuals turn out at one of the city's major hotels in full regalia, unharassed by police.
• One sees long-haired, bearded hippies all over the city, not just in a few preserves set aside for them. Straight citizens do not remark their presence, either by gawking, hostility or flight.
• Nudie movies, frank enough to satisfy anyone's curiosity, are exhibited in what must be the largest number of specialty movie houses per capita in the country. Periodic police attempts to close them down (one of the few occasions when repression has been attempted) fail.

The items can be multiplied indefinitely, and their multiplicity demands explanation. Most cities in the United States refuse to let deviants indulge themselves publicly, let alone tolerate candidates who seek their bloc votes. Quite the contrary. Other cities, New York and Chicago being good examples, would see events like these as signs of serious trouble, omens of a real breakdown in law enforcement and deviance control, the forerunner of saturnalia and barbarian takeover. Because its politicians and police allow and can live with activities that would freak out their opposite numbers elsewhere, San Francisco is a natural experiment in the consequences of tolerating deviance. We can see from its example what results when we ignore the warnings of the custodians of conventional morality. We can see too what lessons can be learned about the conditions under which problems that perhaps lie deeper than matters of morals or life style can be solved to the satisfaction of all the parties to them.

A Culture of Civility

We can summarize this low-key approach to deviance in the phrase "a culture of civility." What are its components, and how does it maintain itself?

San Francisco prides itself on its sophistication, on being the most European of American cities, on its picturesque cosmopolitanism. The picturesque quality, indeed the quaintness, rests in part on physical beauty. As the filling of the Bay and the destruction of the skyline by highrise buildings proceeds to destroy that beauty, the city has come to depend even more on the presence of undigested ethnic minorities. It is as though San Francisco did not wish its Italians, Chinese or Russians to assimilate and become standard Americans, preferring instead to maintain a panoply of ethnic differences: religious, cultural, and culinary (especially culinary). A sophisticated, livable city, on this view, contains people, colonies and societies of all kinds. Their differences create a mosaic of life styles, the very difference of whose sight and smell give pleasure.

Like ethnic minorities, deviant minorities create enclaves whose differences add to the pleasure of city life. Natives enjoy the presence of hippies and take tourists to see their areas, just as they take them to see the gay area of Polk Street. Deviance, like difference, is a civic resource, enjoyed by tourist and resident alike.

To enjoy deviance instead of fearing it requires a surrender of some commonsense notions about the world. Most people assume, when they see someone engaging in proscribed activity, that there is worse to come. "Anyone who would do that [take dope, dress in women's clothes, sell his body or whatever] would do anything" is the major premise of the syllogism. "If you break one law or convention, who knows where you'll stop." Common sense ignores the contrary cases around us everywhere: professional criminals often flourish a legionnaire's patriotism; housewives who are in every other respect conventional sometimes shoplift; homosexuals may be good family providers; some people, who habitually use the rings from poptop cans to work the parking meter, would not dream of taking dope, and vice versa. "Deviance," like conforming behavior, is highly selective. San Francisco's culture of civility, accepting that premise, assumes that if I know that you steal or take dope or peddle your ass, that is all I *know.* There may be more to know; then again, there may be nothing. The deviant may be perfectly decent in every other respect. We are often enjoined, in a generalization of therapeutic doctrine, to treat other people as individuals; that prescription comes nearer to being filled in San Francisco than in most places in the United States.

Because of that tolerance, deviants find it possible to live somewhat more openly in San Francisco than elsewhere. People do not try so hard to catch them at their deviant activities and are less likely to punish them when caught. Because they live more openly, what they do is more visible to straight members of the community. An established canon of social psychology tells us that we find it harder to maintain negative stereotypes when our personal experience belies them. We see more clearly and believe more deeply that hippies or homosexuals are not dangerous when we confront them on the street day after day or live alongside them and realize that beard plus long hair does not equal a drug-crazed maniac, that limp wrist plus lisp does not equal child-molester.

When such notions become embodied in a culture of civility, the citizenry begins to sense that "everyone" feels that way. We cannot say at what critical point a population senses that sophistication about deviance is the norm, rather than a liberal fad. But San Francisco clearly has that critical mass. To come on as an anti deviant, in a way that would probably win friends and influence voters in more parochial areas, risks being greeted by laughter and ridicule in San Francisco. Conservatives who believe in law and order are thus inclined to keep their beliefs to themselves. The more people keep moralistic notions to themselves, the more everyone believes that tolerance is widespread. The culture maintains itself by convincing the populace that it is indeed the culture.

It gets help from public pronouncements of civic officials, who enunciate what will be taken as the collective sentiment of the city. San Francisco officials occasionally angle for the conservative vote that disapproves licentiousness. But they more frequently take the side of liberty, if not license. When the police, several years ago, felt compelled to close the first of the "topless joints," the judge threw the case out. He reasoned that Supreme Court decisions required him to take into account contemporary community standards. In his judgment San Francisco was not a prudish community; the case was dismissed. The city's major paper, the *Chronicle*, approved. Few protested.

Similarly, when California's leading Yahoo, Superintendent of Public Instruction Max Rafferty, threatened to revoke the teaching credentials of any San Francisco teacher who used the obscene materials listed in the standard high school curriculum (Eldridge Cleaver's *Soul on Ice* and Le-Roi Jones' *Dutchman*), the City did not remove the offending books from its curriculum. Instead, it successfully sued to have Rafferty enjoined from interfering in its operation.

In short, San Franciscans know that they are supposed to be sophisticated and let that knowledge guide their public actions, whatever their private feelings. According to another well-known law of social psychology, their private feelings often come to resemble their public actions, and they learn to delight in what frightens citizens of less civil cities.

We do not suggest that all kinds of deviation are tolerated endlessly. The police try, in San Francisco as elsewhere, to stamp out some vices and keep a ceiling on others. Some deviance frightens San Franciscans too, because it seems to portend worse to come (most recently, users and purveyors of methedrine—"speed merchants" and "speed freaks"—whose drug use is popularly thought to result in violence and crime). But the line is drawn much farther over on the side of "toleration" in San Francisco than elsewhere. A vastly wider range of activities is publicly acceptable. Despite the wide range of visible freakiness, the citizenry takes it all in stride, without the fear and madness that permeates the conventional sectors of cities like Detroit, Chicago, New York, Washington, D.C. and similar centers of undaunted virtue.

Madames and Unionists

How does a culture of civility arise? Here we can only speculate, and then fragmentarily, since so few cities in the United States have one that we cannot make the comparisons that might un-cover the crucial conditions. San Francisco's history suggests a number of possibilities.

It has, for one thing, a Latin heritage. Always a major seaport, it has long tolerated the vice that caters to sailors typical of such ports. It grew at the time of the gold rush in an explosive way that burst through conventional social controls. It ceded to its ethnic minorities, particularly the Chinese, the right to engage in prostitution, gambling and other activities. Wickedness and high living form part of the prized past every "tourist" city constructs for itself; some minor downtown streets in San Francisco, for instance, are named for famous madames of the gold rush era.

Perhaps more important, a major potential source of repressive action—the working class—is in San Francisco more libertarian and politically sophisticated than one might expect. Harry Bridges' longshoremen act as bellwethers. It should be remembered that San Francisco is one of the few major American cities ever to experience a general strike. The event still reverberates, and working people who might support repression of others know by personal experience that the policeman may not be their friend. Trade unionism has a left-wing, honest base which gives the city a working-class democracy and even eccentricity, rather than the customary pattern of authoritarianism.

Finally, San Francisco is a town of single people. Whatever actual proportion of the adult population is married, the city's culture is oriented toward and organized for single people. As a consequence, citizens worry less about what public deviance will do to their children, for they don't have any and don't intend to, or they move from the city when they do. (Since there are, of course, plenty of families in the city, it may be more accurate to say that there are fewer white middle-class families, that being the stratum that would, if family-based, provide the greatest number of complaints about deviance. Black, chicano and oriental populations ordinarily have enough to worry about without becoming guardians of public morality.)

The Place To Live

San Francisco is known across the country as a haven for deviants. Good homosexuals hope to go to San Francisco to stay when they die, if not before. Indeed, one of the problems of deviant communities in San Francisco is coping with the periodic influx of a new generation of bohemians who have heard that it is the place to be: the beatnik migration of the late fifties and the hippie hordes of 1967. But those problems should not obscure what is more important: that there are stable communities of some size there to be disrupted. It is the stable homosexual community that promises politicians 90,000 votes and the stable bohemian communities of several vintages that provide both personnel and customers for some important local industries (developing, recording and distributing rock music is now a business of sizeable proportions).

Stable communities are stable because their members have found enough of what they want to stay where they are for a while. If where they were proved totally unsatisfying, they presumably would move elsewhere, unless restrained. But no one forces deviants to live in San Francisco. They stay there because it offers them, via the culture of civility, a place to live where they are not shunned as fearsome or disgusting, where agents of control (police and others) do not regard them as unfortunate excrescences to be excised at the first opportunity. Because they have a place to stay that does not harass them, they sink roots like more conventional citizens: find jobs, buy houses, make friends, vote and take part in political activities and all the other things that solid citizens do.

Sinking roots stabilizes deviants' lives, as it does the lives of conventional citizens. They find less need to act in the erratic ways deviants often behave elsewhere, less need to fulfill the prophecy that because they are deviant in one respect they will be deviant in other, more dangerous ways. San Francisco employers know that homosexuals make good employees. Why not? They are not likely to be blackmailed by enterprising hustlers. The police seldom haul them off to jail for little reason or beat them because they feel like pushing some "queers" around. Homosexuals fear none of this in San Francisco, or fear it much less than in most places, and so are less given to the overcompensatory "camping" that gets their fellows into trouble elsewhere.

Police and others do not harass deviants because they have found, though they may deny it for public relations purposes, that looking the other way is sometimes a good policy. It is easier, when a Be-In is going on, to turn your back on the sight of open marijuana smoking than it is to charge into the crowd and try to arrest people who will destroy the evidence before you get there, give you a hard time, make a fool of you and earn you a bad press—and have no conviction to show for it. At the same time, when you turn your back, nothing worse is likely to happen: no muggings, no thefts, no rapes, no riots. Police, more calculating than they seem, often choose to reach just this kind of accommodation with stable deviant communities.

The accommodation works in circular fashion. When deviants can live decent lives, they find it possible to behave decently. Furthermore, they acquire the kind of stake they are often denied elsewhere in the present and future structure of the community. That stake constrains them to behave in ways that will not outrage nondeviants, for they do not want to lose what they have. They thus curb their activities according to what they think the community will stand for.

The community in turn, and especially the police, will put up with more than they might otherwise, because they understand that nothing else is forthcoming, and because they find that what they are confronted with is not so bad after all. If homosexuals have a Halloween Drag Ball, the community discovers it can treat it as a good-natured joke; those who are offended discover that they needn't go near the Hilton while it is happening.

No doubt neither party to such a bargain gets quite what he would like. Straight members of the community presumably would prefer not to have whores walking the downtown streets, would prefer not to have gay bars operating openly. Deviants of all kinds presumably would prefer not to have to make any concessions to straight sensibilities. Each gives up something and gets something, and to that degree the arrangement becomes stable, the stability itself something both prize.

Deviance and Democracy

What we have just described verges on the idyllic, Peace and Harmony in Camelot forever. Such a dream of perfection does not exist in San Francisco, though more deviants there have more of the advantages of such a bargain, perhaps, than in any other city in the United States.

Nor is it clear that the system we described, even in its perfect form, would be such an idyll.

In San Francisco, as everywhere, the forces of decency and respectability draw the line somewhere and can be every bit as forceful and ruthless the other side of that line as the forces of decency and respectability anywhere else. When the Haight-Ashbury got "out of hand" with the overcrowded transiency of 1967, the city moved in the police Tactical Squad, the City Health Department and all the other bureaucratic weapons usually used to roust deviants. They did it again with the growth of violence in that area associated with the use and sale of methedrine. In general, the city has responded with great toughness to those deviants it believes will not be satisfied with something "reasonable." In particular, political dissent has sometimes been met with force, though San Francisco police have never indulged themselves on any large scale such as that which made Chicago police internationally detested.

The system has beauty only for those deviants who do not mind giving up some portion of their liberty, and then only if the portion they are willing to give up is the same as what the community wants given up. This no doubt is the reason an accommodative system works well with those whose deviant desires are narrowly circumscribed, and may have less utility with those whose wants can be accommodated only at the expense of others who will not easily give up their privileges. In fact, current political difficulties clearly result from the breakdown of accommodation.

These considerations indicate the more general importance of San Francisco's experiment in tolerating and accommodating to the minor forms of deviance encompassed in sex, dope and cheap thrills. How can a complex and differentiated society deal with variety and dissent and simultaneously with its own urges for centralized control? An accommodative relationship to difference, in which it is allowed to persist while it pays some minimal dues to the whole, is what San Francisco recommends to us, suggesting that the amount of the dues and the breadth of the license be set where both parties will, for the time being, stand still for it. The resulting working arrangement will be at least temporarily stable and provide for all concerned a tranquility that permits one to go about his business unarmed that many will find attractive.

But is this no more than a clever trick, a way of buying off deviant populations with minor freedoms while still keeping them enslaved? Beneath the rhetoric, the analysis is the same. The more radical statement adds only that the people who accept such a bargain ought not to, presumably because they have, if they only knew it, deeper and more important interests and desires which remain unsatisfied in the accommodative arrangements. So, of course, do those who hold them in check. Perhaps that is the ultimate lesson of San Francisco: the price of civilization, civility and living together peacefully is not getting everything you want.

Limits of Accommodation

It is tempting to think that an accommodation based on civility and mutual interest provides a model for settling the conflicts now wracking our urban areas. Our analysis suggests that this is a possibility, but no more than that. Peace can occur through accommodation, the example of the potheads and pimps tells us, only under certain not so easily attained conditions. Those conditions may not be present in the ethnic and political problems our major cities, San Francisco among them, are now experiencing.

Accommodation requires, as a first condition, that the parties involved prize peace and stability enough to give up some of what they want so that others may have their desires satisfied as well. But people take that point of view only when the accommodation leaves them enough of a share to want no more. Some urban groups no longer believe that they are getting that necessary minimum, either because they have learned to interpret their situation in a new light or because they have lost some advantages they once had.

Members of black communities may be no worse off than ever, but they are considerably worse off than whites and know it. For a variety of historical reasons, and as a matter of simple justice, some of them no longer regard the little they have as sufficient reason to keep the peace. All the discussion about how many blacks feel this way (is it 10 percent or 50 percent?) and how strongly they feel it (are they willing to fight?) is irrelevant to the main point: enough feel strongly enough to make a lot of trouble for the white community, thus changing the balance of costs to the whites and insisting on a new division of rights as the price of stability.

Some members of white communities probably are objectively worse off and may resent it sufficiently to give up peace and stability in an effort to raise the costs to others and thus minimize their losses. Many whites in civil service positions, in the skilled trades and in similar protected occupatonal positions have lost or are in danger of losing competitive job advantages as governments act to do something about the injustice that afflicts black communities. Without a general expansion of the economy, which is *not* what blacks demand, injustices inflicted on blacks can be remedied only by taking something away from more favorably situated whites. It may be possible to improve the education of poor black children, for instance, only by taking away some of the privileges of white teachers. It may be possible to give black youths a chance at apprenticeships in skilled trades only by removing the privileged access to those positions of the sons of present white union members. When whites lose those privileges, they may feel strongly enough to fracture the consensus of civility.

The deviant communities of San Francisco show us cases in which the parties involved agree in a way that leaves each enough. But that may only be possible when the interests to be accommodated involve morals and life styles. When those interests include substantial economic prizes, major forms of privilege and real political power, it may be that nothing less than a real-life assessment of relative intensities of desire and ability to inflict costs on others will suffice. That assessment takes place in the marketplace of conflict.

This suggests a second, more procedural condition for the achievement of urban peace through accommodation and civility. Mechanisms and procedures must exist by which the conflicting desires and resources for bargaining can be brought together to produce a temporarily stable working arrangement. The accommodations of enfocement officials and deviants typically occur in a host of minor bargaining situations. Hassles are settled by the people immediately involved, and settled "on their own merits"—which is to say, in a way that respects the strength of everyone's feelings and the amount of trouble each is prepared to make to have his way. The culture of civility works well because the myriad

of separate local bargains respect and reflect what most of the involved parties want or are willing to settle for.

We do not allow ourselves this extreme degree of decentralized decision-making with respect to many important problems (though many critics have suggested we should). Instead, we allow federal, state or city bureaucracies to make general policies that inhibit local accommodation. While government might well intervene when circumstances make bargaining positions unequal, we know now that it is not ordinarily well equipped to reach accommodative agreements that will work at the grass roots. Unable to know what the people who inhabit locally will want and settle for, officials turn to technocrats for solutions.

Thus, when we confront the problem of slums and urban renewal, we send for the planner and the bulldozer. But the lives of urban residents are not determined by the number or newness of buildings. The character of their relationships with one another and with the outside world does that. Planners and technocrats typically ignore those relationships, and their influence in shaping what people want, in constructing solutions. They define "slums" impersonally, using such impersonal criteria as density or deterioration, and fail to see how awakened group consciousness can turn a "slum" into a "ghetto," and a rise in moral repute turn a "ghetto" into a "neighborhood."

Too often, the search for "model cities" implies not so much a model as an ideology—a rationalistic vision of human interaction that implies a people whose consistency of behavior can nowhere be found. We already have "model cities": Brasilia at the bureaucratic end and Levittown at the residential end. And in both instances, the force of human impulses had to break through the web of formal models to make these places inhabitable. In Brasilia the rise of shantytown dwellings outside the federal buildings make the place "a city," whereas the Levittowners had to break the middle-class mode and pass through a generation of conformity before they could produce a decent living arrangement. To design a city in conformity to "community standards"—which turn out to be little more than the prejudices of building inspectors, housing designers and absentee landlords—only reinforces patterns of frustration, violence and antagonism that now characterize so many of

America's large cities. To think that the dismal failure of larger housing projects will be resolved by their dismal replacement of small housing projects is nonsense. Minibuildings are no more of a solution than maxibuildings are the problem.

In any event, centralized planning operating in this way does not produce a mechanism through which the mutual desires, claims and threats of interested groups can sort themselves out and allow a *modus vivendi*, if one exists, to uncover itself. The centralized body makes bargains for everyone under its influence, without knowing their circumstances or wants, and so makes it impossible for the people involved to reach a stable accommodation. But centralized planning still remains a major solution proffered for urban problems of every kind.

Accommodations reached through the mechanism of old-fashioned city political machines work little better, for contemporary machines typically fail to encompass all the people whose interests are at stake. Richard Daley demonstrated that when the Chicago ghetto, supposedly

solidly under his control, exploded and revealed some people his famed consensus had not included. Lyndon Johnson made the same discovery with respect to opponents of the Vietnam War. Insofar as centralized decision-making does not work, and interested parties are not allowed to make bargains at the local level, accommodative stability cannot occur.

So the example of San Francisco's handling of moral deviance may not provide the blueprint one would like for settling urban problems generally. Its requirements include a day-to-day working agreement among parties on the value of compromise and a procedure by which their immediate interests can be openly communicated and effectively adjusted. Those requirements are difficult to meet. Yet it may be that they are capable of being met in more places than we think, that even some of the knottier racial and political problems contain possibilities of accommodation, no more visible to us than the casual tolerance of deviance in San Francisco was thinkable to some of our prudish forebears.

16

JACQUELINE M. ZITO

Anonymity and Neighboring in an Urban, High-Rise Complex

A good deal has been written about such distinctive urban areas as the racial ghetto and the ethnic enclave but little attention has been paid to an equally distinctive urban living space—the high-rise, multi-building complex of "middle-class" apartment-dwellers. Non-residents tend to deplore the alleged anonymity and isolation of life in these places that supposedly combine minimum living space with maximum social distance. Big-city apartment dwellers are said not only not to know their neighbors, but not to care to know them.

This study attempts to ascertain the extent and nature of interaction among tenants in one such apartment complex. It finds that, in keeping with the prevailing cliches, social relations in this particular apartment complex were characterized by a high degree of anonymity and social isolation. There was also a pervasive ignorance about neighbors as well as little inclination to establish friendly relations with fellow residents.

In order to ascertain the nature of social relationships in such an apartment complex, one must seek answers to the following questions: How do people actually define "neighbor" and what is the ecology of a social "neighborhood" in a high-rise complex? Are neighborly and friendly relations sought and found among people within the project or found elsewhere? If they are sought among fellow residents, are these friendly relationships easily established? Furthermore, what is the nature of these neighborly relations and "neighboring patterns" in a high-rise complex? Does architecture help or hinder sociability, and to what extent does physical propinquity encourage or discourage social relations? Stated alternatively, the major areas of inquiry are: (1) the extent of anonymity and isolation within an urban high-rise complex; (2) the degree and nature of social contacts among residents, particularly within and outside the complex; (3) the nature of sociability among neighbors; (4) the ecology of social relations (that is, the definition of a social "neighborhood" in a high-rise complex); and (5) the influence of architecture on sociability and the effect of physical propinquity on social relations.

SETTING

The complex, here called Manhattan Towers, occupies four full city blocks. Its eight, 29-story buildings contain 4,000 apartments housing 12,000 residents. The buildings, identical in appearance, are not only tall, but also wide and narrow. On each floor, sixteen apartments open off a hall corridor running the width of each building.

Entering through the revolving doors centered in front of each building, one finds oneself in large, sparsely furnished lobby containing a scattering of potted plants. A carpeted area with low table and several chairs is set against a wall decorated with a mosaic or, in some buildings, mirror. The carpeted seating area often serves as a meeting place for residents, especially for elderly and retired tenants. Several doctor

Reprinted from *Urban Life and Culture* Vol. 3, No. 3 (Oct. 1974), pp. 243–263 by permission of the Publisher, Sage Publications, Inc.
Author's Note: I am grateful to Professor Herbert Gans for suggestions on conceptualization and for his interest in the study.

offices are on each main floor. In one building, there is also a beauty salon; in another, a boutique; in a third, an art gallery.

Manhattan Towers was completed eleven years ago, requiring two years of construction. It was one of the first such multi-building complexes constructed on the West Side of Manhattan. Confronted by financial problems even during construction, the owners not only offered lower rents than for comparable apartments on the more fashionable East Side, but, as further inducement, offered one month rent-free. Currently, the rents remain somewhat lower than equivalent-sized apartments on the East Side. However, apartments are now in demand, as indicated by a lengthy waiting list.

The apartments range in size from "studios" (combination living room and sleeping area) to three-bedroom. Balconies are part of some studio and one-bedroom units and most of the two- and three-bedroom apartments.

Manhattan Towers offers a tailor and cleaning service for each building, plus outdoor and indoor parking (garage), cable T.V., the usual laundry-room facilities and housekeeping services. Maintenance services—heating, air-conditioning, plumbing, and so forth—are rather efficiently and swiftly provided by management. A pre-school day center designed for children of working parents has recently been added and there is 24-hour doorman service for each building, as well as two security guards on duty around the clock. The neatly kept grounds around the complex include a mall, consisting of some trees and benches, as well as several playground areas.

Manhattan Towers' rental agents call it a "middle-class, high-rise residential community." The majority of tenants are middle-aged (between 40 and 65), married, and Jewish, their incomes ranging from $15,000 to $30,000. Approximately twenty-five percent earn over $30,000. Almost a third of those sampled were college professors, physicians, lawyers or corporate executives. About 80 percent of the tenants are married; another 15 percent are retired or widowed; the remaining 5 percent are single. Most of the married couples are either childless or their children are grown and no longer live with them. About one-fourth have children and about 50 percent of this group have small, pre-school age children. Most children go to private schools.

The dearth of teenagers in the building reflects the mobility pattern of tenants. Newly married, childless couples move in, live here while their children are young, then move away as their children get older (usually during their elementary-school years if they have not already done so before they begin school). The few such couples that do not depart are usually those whose profession and personal tastes require living in a large, cosmopolitan city.

Older married couples very often move in after their children are grown and remain here, thinking of Manhattan Towers as a permanent home. This is also true of older retired people. On the other hand, younger, single tenants are the most transient residents, usually moving after a few years.

During the day, maids are a common sight in elevators, mailrooms, laundry rooms and play areas. A fair number of the tenants are known to the general public, being writers, news commentators, and entertainers (musicians, actors, actresses, dancers, etc.) In addition, there are a large number of foreign residents: it is not uncommon to hear Chinese, French, German, or Hebrew spoken in elevators and public areas.

METHODOLOGY

This study employs three techniques of data collection: open-ended personal interviews, mail questionnaires, and participant observation. Originally, a personal interview was planned with a random sample of 50 residents but in pretesting, many obstacles were encountered. It was often difficult to elicit innocuous information, even when talking through a door; gaining entrance to apartments in order to interview tenants was almost impossible. Moreover, intervening circumstances made matters worse: a week after I began my study, a young woman was raped in her apartment. Several days later, a couple returning home late one evening surprised burglars; the wife was beaten and the husband murdered.

These events made tenants wary of strangers and unwilling to cooperate with personal interviewing. Having completed only 19 interviews, the personal interview schedule was then revised into a mail questionnaire. Using "apartment" as the sampling unit, 20 percent of the apartments in one building (that is, 90 apartments)

Table 1. *Reasons for Choosing To Live at Manhattan Towers*

	% Response (n = 85)
Apartment-Related Reasons:	
1. Value-"best buy for the rent"	52
2. Amount of space in apartments	3
3. Attractiveness of apartment and building	2
4. View from apartment	2
Subtotal	59
Location Reasons:	
5. Easy access to transportation	21
6. Proximity to job	9
7. Advantages of living close to a large cultural complex	5
8. Schools and facilities for children	0
9. Neighborhood	2
Subtotal	37
Other Reasons:	
Total %	100

were randomly sent questionnaires. The return rate was 73.3 percent. Income and educational levels appear to have had no effect on returns.

The third source of data was participant observation throughout the building complex and the immediate neighborhood, including elevators, laundry rooms, local stores, and so forth.

SATISFACTION AND SOCIAL COMPOSITION

Reasons for Choosing to Live at Manhattan Towers

"Security" and "convenience" (that is, doormen, maintenance service, available housekeeping services) are cited by over 95 percent of the respondents as major reasons for choosing to live in a high-rise complex. When asked why they specifically chose Manhattan Towers rather than another high-rise project, the majority (52 percent) mention "reasonable rent" and "value in terms of apartment size" as the prime determinants. Tenants generally feel they have the "best buy for the rent you pay." Locale is the second most often mentioned reason (37 percent) for choosing this particular complex; Man-

hattan Towers is near major lines of mass transit as well as a large cultural center. Table 1 describes in more detail reasons for choosing to live at Manhattan Towers.

Perceived Satisfaction with Living in Manhattan Towers

Tenants specify more advantages than disadvantages about living in the complex, with advantages outnumbering disadvantages by 5 to 1. The most often cited disadvantage is "lack of security" (33 percent). There are also a few complaints about elevator service, and a few younger couples believe the complex "is just too massive for any real communications between people." These complaints, however, are few in comparison to the positive comments reported. For example, while only 2 percent mention the "view" as a reason for moving in, over half report this as the major unanticipated advantage. The "view" includes a panoramic exposure to the Hudson River and the flow of river traffic—ocean liners, barges, tugboats, sailing vessels, and so forth.

The convenient location (for access to mass transit, work, cultural centers, shopping) an the spacious layout of the apartments are the next most often cited advantages. In addition, one-third of the respondents mention security and good service as positively perceived reasons for maintaining residence.

Using the number of perceived advantages and disadvantages mentioned by tenants as a measure of satisfaction and dissatisfaction with Manhattan Towers' living conditions, we may conclude that residents generally are quite satisfied.

Homogeneity among Residents

Residents view themselves as being similar to other tenants in terms of religion, cultural background, education and income level. However, they do not perceive similarity in terms of interests or leisure activities. (Another study of an urban high-rise also found that residents perceived homogeneity in terms of economic level, but not in terms of interests [Michelson 1973b: 18].) More than 60 percent of respondents name more ways in which they feel similar to other residents on their floor than ways in which they feel dissimilar. While other floor residents are perceived as "personally different sort of people than we are," when asked to describe similarities or differences in terms of interests, age, religious preference, cultural background, educational level, income level, and leisure activities, the results are as shown in Table 2.

Only 20 percent report similarity in terms of interests and only 37 percent in terms of age. No respondent under 40 feels he shares similar interests with his neighbors or that they are of a similar age. In fact, the under-40 group unani-

mously perceives other tenants as older. In contrast, tenants over 40 and under 65 years old uniformly feel they and their fellow residents are of similar ages and have similar interests.

The residents feel similar in religious preference (58 percent), cultural background (56 percent), education (58 percent), and income level (61 percent). Fifty-eight percent of the respondents perceive similar religious preferences. Every respondent who said he feels similar to other tenants in terms of religious preference is Jewish. Every non-Jewish respondent feels he has religious preferences different from other tenants. This may lead us to conclude that there is a perceived "Jewishness" to Manhattan Towers. In fact, most of the names on mailboxes are of Jewish origin, and almost three-fifths (58 percent) of the sample are apparently of Jewish origin.

Perception of educational homogeneity varies in terms of the education of the respondent (and/or spouse). In every case, those who perceive their educational level as similar to that of other tenants are college graduates (often, college-plus). On the other hand, those reporting dissimilar educational level do not have college degrees. The perceived norm for educational level in Manhattan Towers would appear to be college graduate or plus. In fact, 80 percent of those surveyed have received at least a college education.

Economic homogeneity is also perceived by residents. The majority (68 percent) of respondents believe their neighbors have an annual income between $15,000 and $30,000. In every case where the total family income was not within this $15,000 and $30,000 range, dissimilar income as compared with other tenants is reported.

Table 2. *Perceived Homogeneity among Residents*

| | % Respondents (n = 85) | | | |
Traits	Similar	Dissimilar	Don't Know	Total %
Interests	20	62	18	100
Age	37	57	6	100
Religious preference	58	36	6	100
Cultural background	56	30	14	100
Education	58	34	8	100
Income	61	24	15	100
Leisure activities	16	64	20	100

Conversely, respondents who have family incomes between $15,000 and $30,000 consistently perceive a similar income level with that of other residents.

In sum, there appears to be a shared perception by the majority of tenants as to what the average resident of Manhattan Towers is like: more than 40 years old, Jewish, a college graduate, with an annual income of between $15,000 and $30,000, and possessing professional status.

ANONYMITY AND ISOLATION

Life in a high-rise complex is often thought to be characterized by a high degree of anonymity and isolation. My findings suggest that this is true, at least for the middle-income, urban high-rise project studied.

One young, single psychologist reports not speaking to any other resident in the two years he lived in Manhattan Towers, but he may be an exception. Most people at least say "hello" or nod to some residents on their floor. However, only 8 percent of those surveyed "could recognize" everyone on their floor, and even fewer (2 percent) know the family names of every tenant on their floor. Furthermore, while more than half (56 percent) of the respondents can recognize at least half the people on their floor and say "hello" or nod when passing in the halls, or in elevators, the mailroom, lobby and sometimes in local stores, there appears to be a pervasive lack of specific knowledge about other tenants—not merely those in ones' own building, but also those on the same floor. That is, even tenants who have a "chatting relationship" are unlikely to know one another's occupations or life styles, except impressionistically. Although a high degree of anonymity and lack of specific knowledge about neighbors may appear to contradict the rather accurate perceptions of self-other similarities and differences reported above, this is only an apparent contradiction. Judging from their own rent, tenants have some idea of the income level necessary to live in Manhattan Towers. This income level also connotes educational level and life-style. Furthermore, residents see, overhear, and talk with other tenants in elevators, lobbies, and so forth; conversation, dress, deportment, and age all provide identity clues. Thus it is possible for tenants to have quite accurate self-other perceptions without actually knowing their neighbors.

Many residents are not interested in knowing their neighbors, nor do they especially care to establish even neighborly relationships with tenants on their floor, let alone within the building or the complex. This is especially true of working couples, childless couples, and unmarried men and women. Sixty-eight percent of the respondents report that they prefer to make friends outside the project. Except for nonworking wives with young children and older people, most residents appear to do their socializing elsewhere.

People do not move to Manhattan Towers to establish friendships within the complex or to meet new and interesting neighbors. Only 2 percent of the tenants surveyed say they moved to the complex because they had friends living there. No one claims to have moved in order to make new friends among other tenants. This does not mean residents are uninterested in establishing new friendships; they simply look for them elsewhere—in organizations, political clubs, the local synagogue or churches, or professional associations.

While some tenants (61 percent) report having one or a few (meaning two or three) friends living in the complex, an overwhelming majority—86 percent—of these friendships were established before moving to Manhattan Towers through contacts made outside the complex (in work or school, or organizations, clubs, church or synagogue) or through mutual acquaintances. Friendships were not usually established with neighbors or with other tenants in the complex. Neighbors do not usually become friends. While most respondents (62 percent) may say "hello" or even chat with neighbors, they do not consider them to be their "friends" and most prefer such social distance. When I inquired as to the reasons for this preference, the most frequent reply was the desire for a certain amount of anonymity, and the privacy and freedom it brings. As one tenants states "Cordial relations with my neighbors are all right, but friendships as such are strictly out."

Evidently, establishing friendship relations with one's neighbors bring obligations most residents neither desire nor have the time for. This is especially true for working couples, childless couples, and job-holding "singles." One professional couple suggested that their life-style and daily routines were simply not conducive to cultivating local friendships or even neighborly relations. "We work most of the day, often go out in the evening, have no children and go away often on weekends. When do we have time to *see* our neighbors, even if we did want to?"

Even if they desired to do so, there are few opportunities for residents to become acquainted. Although half of the respondents say they know someone from another building, these acquaintanceships arise in organizational settings (very often a political club), sometimes the P.T.A. or through a mutual acquaintance; or, if one has small children, from encounters at the play areas. However, if one is neither a joiner, extroverted nor possessed of children, it is quite difficult to become acquainted with tenants in other buildings. One potential "linkage" organization is the Tenant's Association; but it is ineffectual—only about 200 tenants belong to it.

New tenants have little opportunity to meet neighbors or other residents. Informal, get-acquainted gatherings are almost non-existent. Only one couple reported even attempting such an affair. A young physicist and his wife, several weeks after moving in, tried to become acquainted by inviting some neighbors over for Sunday brunch. Their "southern hospitality" was chilled when only two showed up.

Not only are informal gatherings almost non-existent, but knocking on a new neighbor's door to introduce oneself is also rare. It is not the norm for the new tenant, or the tenant already in residence to do this. Almost 90 percent of the respondents and almost everyone I have talked to say they met their neighbors in the halls or elevators or when coming into or leaving their apartments. However, new tenants may meet neighbors when a problem occurs, such as a complaint about a barking dog or an emergency.

The norm appears to be "benign neglect." Unless a tenant has indicated willingness to be friendly, even a self-introduction is considered a violation of privacy. Nevertheless, some residents are interested in establishing neighborly or friendly relations. Who they are, and how they go about establishing and maintaining such relationships, will be examined now.

LOCALIZED RESIDENTS

A minority of tenants are concerned to establish neighborly relations and make friends. These are the "localized residents," that is, tenants who are at home much of the day: non-working mothers, older people, and some non-working

wives without children. "Non-localized residents"—defined as those who are away most of the day, such as single working men and women, professionals, and working couples—comprise the majority of respondents (68 percent). The localized residents, especially the non-working mothers with preschool aged children, and older people, appear to have more need to find local friendships since they are the least mobile, socially and physically. Small children and old age are confining. However, even among this group, the desire for neighborly and/or friendly relations is limited and restricted to those in a similar situation (mothers with young children want to meet women in similar circumstances, old people want to meet other old people). Furthermore, while many such tenants desire more social contact, this should be interpreted in terms of desiring low-keyed companionship, not necessarily close friendship.

Non-working Mothers with Pre-school Age Children

For the non-working mother, especially with young children not yet attending school, meeting other tenants is not terribly difficult. About two-thirds of such mothers surveyed say they met most of their neighbors through their children. The playground areas are the meeting places for mothers. In the afternoon, weather permitting, one can usually find about a dozen or so in any one of three play areas.

Often, mothers meet through mutual acquaintances—who are also mothers. During warmer weather, they usually congregate several (2–4) times a week, meeting at the same playground area or in each other's apartment for coffee-klatsches, while the children play. In colder weather, they meet almost as frequently, but more often indoors, visiting in each other's apartment during the early afternoons. These coffee-klatsches usually consist of two or three mothers, rarely more.

It is difficult, however, to say how much of this type of interaction is perceived as "friendship" by the tenants. While these mothers do see a good deal of each other, the cementing factor in their relationship appears to be children. They rarely go places together (shopping, for example) or take children places together (for example, a museum). They rarely visit as couples and their husbands never get together by themselves. After their children begin school or they go back to work, such visiting and "coffee-klatsching" decreases.

When the children reach school age, they tend to seek out friends more on their own. Friends from school visit and they make friends with other children in the building. Certainly their parents guide their choices, and parents of school-age children may introduce their children to each other soon upon moving in. However, the quality and frequency of interaction among their mothers is slightly different from mothers with pre-school children. While the children may play together almost daily, usually outdoors in the playground, or in the lobbies, and frequently visit each other's apartment, their mothers see less of each other. This is evidently because being older, the need for supervising their play is reduced. While these children are rarely accompanied by an adult, mothers occasionally do take their children to another apartment to play but rarely stay to visit. They are seeking playmates for their children, not friendships with other parents (although this sometimes may occur).

Thus, the age and presence of children in a family is an important variable in determining the nature and frequency of neighboring among women. If their interests are similar, more enduring friendships will probably develop. Children, especially small children, may provide more of a need for social contacts among mothers and influence their frequency of interaction, but compatibility appears to determine whether more intense social relationships will develop (Gans, 1967: 155–6).

Older Residents

The older tenants want, and find, friendly relations, usually with other older people. They seem to prefer the companionship of those sharing their social position and condition—retired, living on limited incomes, usually having children and grandchildren who serve as topics of discussion. Apparently, a good many know other residents like themselves, perhaps having a relative living in the complex or in the surrounding area. Once in residence, they meet other older people, usually through a mutual acquaintance.

They seem not only to know many other older people in the building (they always seem to know each other when getting into the elevator) but they also know almost as much about what is happening in the building as the doorman. They tend to chat with anyone who will stop, but most often find mutual friendships among themselves.

Their main areas for meeting and socializing are outdoor benches, certain areas in the playground or in the rear of the buildings (usually the sunny areas), weather permitting. Weather not permitting, the lobbies and mail room substitute. Encounters usually occur several times a week and are devoted to chats and gossip about each other, the building, grandchildren and so forth. The women may do needlework; the men may play chess or checkers. Casual apartment visiting is rare, except among those who have been long-time friends.

Housewives without Children

Non-working housewives without children who remain at home also qualify as "localized residents." These women would like to have cordial relations with neighbors and have established some friendships with other tenants. Their need is not as great as that of residents with children who must find playmates for their offspring, or that of older people who are less mobile than they. They have more difficulty than either group in establishing friendly relations because of lack of opportunity to meet neighbors and the relatively small numbers of persons like themselves. Most childless wives work, even if only part-time, or involve themselves in clubs, organizations, or volunteer work.

In some such cases, husbands are brought together. If the foursome proves compatible, it may meet once every month or two. Such housewives usually get together with two or three women like themselves who are also home all day. This may happen on a weekly or biweekly basis. They visit in each other's apartments, go out for lunch, shop, or attend a movie or theater matinee.

A HIGH-RISE SOCIAL "NEIGHBORHOOD"

If you live in a four-block, eight-building, 4,000-apartment complex, whom do you consider your "neighbor"? The residents of Manhattan Towers define "neighbor" as much in terms of "friendliness" (that is, cordial relations) as in terms of physical propinquity. "Neighbor" is not, of course, defined uniformly by the residents. To some it means proximity—18 percent of the respondents say a "neighbor" is everyone on their floor; 15 percent say everyone on "their" side of the elevator (which includes half of the corridor). Most importantly, the majority (65 percent) of tenants surveyed define "neighbor" as someone living on their floor or within their building with whom they are friendly. "Friendliness" is defined as casual chatting in halls, elevator, laundry room, mailroom, lobby, in local stores, and public areas; but, not necessarily, visiting in each other's apartments.

Propinquity is important since residents are more exposed to residents living on their floor. Propinquity alone does not, however, determine if tenants occupying a particular location along the corridor will be considered "neighbors." Were location the prime determinant of friendly relations or the definition of "neighbor," those occupying apartments closest to the respondent should have been mentioned as neighbors or friends more than other tenants.

Although other studies have shown that social relationships are influenced, and even determined, by the site plan (Gans, 1967: 181; Merton, 1947; Caplow and Forman, 1950; Festinger et al., 1950) this does not appear to be true in Manhattan Towers. Respondents do not mention tenants in closer apartments or on the same floor more often than they mention tenants at the other end of the hall or on another floor; 54 percent of those surveyed deem as their neighbors tenants living on another floor within the building. Although about half the tenants deemed neighbors by fellow tenants live on the same floor, the proximity of their apartments varies. Hence, while proximity may facilitate social contacts, it does not appear to determine friendly relations or definition of others as "neighbor" (Gans, 1967: 154–9).

On the other hand, observation gives some support to the previous findings of propinquity studies (Merton, 1947; Caplow and Forman, 1950) which have stressed the impact of the "front door," in this case the apartment door. While tenants choose as neighbors residents who live nearby (across the hall, next door, and so forth) as often as they choose residents at the other end of the hall, or on another floor, they define as "neighbors" people living directly across the hall more often than those living in adjacent apartments. There appears to be more interaction with the occupants of apartments across the corridor. Almost three-fourths of the respondents report having "nothing to do with" (29 percent) or "minimal contact with" (43 percent) adjacent apartment dwellers. The "minimal contact" was restricted to "friendly greetings" if you encounter each other. But, about half the respondents report they are "friendly" and have more interaction with tenants living directly across the corridor.

The most frequent explanations for lack of contact between adjacent neighbors are dissimilar interests, age gap, or lack of interest in establishing neighborly contact. Only 8 percent of the respondents admit they are friendly with adjacent neighbors, and even this friendliness was mainly limited to "watering their plants, taking in their newspaper when they're away on vacations, or just chatting for a few minutes when we meet in the hall."

Such explanations do little to account for why residents are more neighborly with tenants in facing apartments. Tenants who *do* have neighborly relations with adjacent tenants and/or tenants living across from them, were asked why this is so. The most often stated reasons are "similar interests" and "compatibility." However, this is the prime determinant given for all their friendly and neighborly relations. They find the people living across the hall to be compatible twice as often as those living next door. Perhaps, the face-to-face aspect of the two doors being directly across from each other provides more opportunities for visual contact, making it more difficult to ignore the other. Such encounters may serve to impose more opportunities to become acquainted and more opportunities to discover mutual compatibility and shared interests.

NEIGHBORING PATTERNS

The frequency and intensity of social interaction among neighbors (that is, neighboring patterns) in Manhattan Towers vary depending on whether a tenant is a "localized resident" who is home most of the day or a "non-localized resident" away most of the day. Other important determinants of the nature of these social relationships are the presence of children in a family, and the age of the children.

Overall, there is relatively little neighboring in Manhattan Towers. Sixty-two percent of the tenants surveyed report they visit no neighbor regularly, even on a weekly or monthly basis. ("Visit" is defined as visiting inside other apartments.) For many, visiting means encountering a neighbor and being invited inside the apartment to chat, perhaps every two months or so. Of those who say they do visit neighbors regularly, more than half (58 percent) name only one neighbor (or family); 23 percent name two neighbors and 19 percent name three. None reports visiting more than three neighbors or families on a regular basis.

Localized Residents

"Localized Residents" are definitely in the minority of tenants surveyed, comprising 32 percent of the respondents. They visit with more neighbors, more often, than the non-localized tenants. Among them, mothers with pre-school age children regularly visit more neighbors, more often, than any other group of localized residents, usually about three neighbors, several (2–4) times a week. Non-working mothers with children in school, non-working childless mothers, and older people visit fewer tenants and less frequently. They usually visit two neighbors once or twice a week. The absence of children from the home during the day definitely decreases neighborly relations and sociability among tenants.

Non-Localized Residents

"Non-Localized Residents" visit far fewer neighbors and far less often than the "localized residents." Forty-two percent of these tenants say they visit with no neighbor as frequently as weekly or monthly. Visiting is usually haphazard, meeting a neighbor and being invited inside the apartment to chat, perhaps several times a year. (Unless couple visiting is involved; in which case, it is more planned.) Of those who do visit neighbors regularly, over half (64 percent) name only one neighbor or family with whom they do so; 20 percent name two neighbors; and 16 percent name three. No non-

localized resident reports visiting more than three neighbors (or families) on a regular basis. For the majority (78 percent) these regular visits are limited to once a month; for the remainder, visiting occurs every two months.

Visiting is rarest for the single working man and the working couple. They report visiting no one regularly. Most visiting among non-localized residents is among women, almost always among those who are married. Non-localized men, whether married or single, do not usually mingle, unless retired. Couple visiting (except for parties) is rare, especially if both spouses work. They visit neighbors on a much less regular basis. Furthermore, couple visiting involves more than neighboring: compatibility is required of four rather than two and more of a commitment toward friendship is needed. Couple visiting thus usually takes place when husbands work together or know each other, or when wives who are friendly introduce their husbands, who find themselves compatible.

SUMMARY AND CONCLUSIONS

A high degree of anonymity is found to exist within Manhattan Towers, a high-rise complex, although tenants are not actually unfriendly to each other. Most report chatting with and saying "hello" often to fellow tenants. But the desire for sociability and friendship among neighbors appears minimal.

Exceptions are the "localized residents," who have more need and opportunity for neighborly and friendly relations with other tenants. "Being home during the day" is apparently a significant determinant of sociability and neighborly relations. This conclusion is supportive of that of Gates et al. (1973) who find that "opportunity to meet neighbors," which is a result of "being home during the day" and "length of residency," is a more important determinant of "neighborly relations" than the "need for neighbors" or the existence of a sufficiently large pool of neighbors.

Neighborly relations, while not totally determined by proximity, are defined more in terms of cordiality and compatibility than in terms of "functional" friendship—defined as depending on people for mutual aid, sociability, companionship, solace, and so forth. Tenants look more toward friends living outside the complex rather than toward neighbors for such relationships.

Most neighbors call on each other only in emergencies.

The fact that friendships and socializing are concentrated away from the complex is a result not only of the desire for anonymity (and the privacy it brings) but also a result of life-styles in high-rise complexes. Many of the wives work; their friendship pattern is typical of working men—concentrated away from home, since they are not at home during the day.

Michelson found similar friendship patterns in his study of high-rise apartments in Toronto. "Perhaps as he suggests, this accounts for the anti-social image of high-rise apartments." Daily routines are conducive to non-local friendship formation (Michelson, 1973b: 19). Residents of a middle-class, high-rise, complex such as Manhattan Towers are generally highly educated; both husband and wife are more likely to be professionals. Hence, friendship patterns appear to be a function of the wife's employment and the general absence of children which combine to create a distinctive pattern of sociability and friendship formation.

Further, it is desirable to consider a latent function of anonymity in a high-rise complex. It permits privacy among the propinquitous. With 2,000 individuals residing in eight, 29-story buildings in a four-block square, privacy and psychological distance between people is difficult, if not impossible to obtain, without a high level of mutual anonymity. If lack of privacy and pressure for neighborliness prevails in such close and crowded quarters, the milieu might well be psychologically intolerable. In a chokingly close, urban environment, a high level of pervasive sociability could be psychically suffocating. Anonymity not only provides psychological distance, it also allows more freedom to come and go without interruption, thus permitting time-pressed residents to maintain their life routines and meet their preferred social obligations.

Finally, while the high degree of anonymity and isolation of life in this high-rise project has been documented, nothing has been said, on the other hand, about the quality of life, as perceived by the people living here. A high degree of satisfaction with their living conditions is reported by the tenants. Advantages outnumber disadvantages by five to one. Furthermore,

loneliness appears to be quite uncommon. When asked, "About how often do you get lonely living here?", all but two families (who had recently come from small towns) said "hardly ever" or "quite rarely." With the same two exceptions, no one feels lonelier in Manhattan Towers than where they had lived previously. About half of the sample do admit loneliness at times; however these respondents are more likely to have fewer ties outside of Manhattan Towers. With the exception of elderly widowers, marital status and age have far less relationship to loneliness than the number of social relationships a resident maintains outside the complex.

The narrative comments on the mail questionnaires and interviews give a general impression of satisfaction and pleasure. These are people, anonymity and local isolation notwithstanding, who are not especially lonely. Nor are they displeased with their manner of life in this urban, high-rise complex. Most lead busy lives. More important, they appear to be reasonably satisfied with their life-style.

References

Caplow, T. and R. Forman (1950) "Neighborhood interaction in a homogeneous community." Amer. Soc. Rev. 16 (June): 357–366.

Festinger, L. (1950) "Architecture and group membership." J. of Social Issues 7, 1 and 2: 152–163.

———, S. Schacter, and K. Back (1950) Social Pressures in Informal Groups. New York: Harper.

Gans, H. (1967) The Levittowners. New York: Pantheon.

Gates, A., H. Stevens, and B. Wellman (1973) "What makes a good neighbor?" Presented at the meetings of the American Sociological Association, New York City.

Merton, R. K. (1947) "The social psychology of housing," in W. Dennis (ed.) Current Trends in Social Psychology. Pittsburgh: Univ. of Pittsburgh Press.

Michelson, W. (1973a) "The reconciliation of 'subjective' and 'objective' data on physical environment in the community: the case of social contact in high-rise apartments." Presented at the meetings of the American Sociological Association, New York City.

———, (1973b) "Environmental change." University of Toronto Center for Urban and Community Studies. (mimeo)

17

JAMES ALAN McPHERSON

Inside the Blackstone Rangers

Sometime between 1961 and 1963, according to evidence presented to a Senate subcommittee chaired by John McClellan of Arkansas last July, an unknown number of black young men, who lived in the general area of Sixty-sixth Place and Blackstone Avenue in the Woodlawn area of Chicago's South Side ghetto, organized a street gang. Like most street gangs, it was formed to protect its members from intimidation by other gangs in the South Side area. The most formidable enemy of this new group was a gang called the Devil's Disciples, which claimed part of the neighboring Kenwood area. In the years which followed, the Disciples became the traditional enemies of the Woodlawn youths, who called themselves Blackstone Rangers.

At first the Rangers were interested only in protecting their territory and their membership from attacks and retaliations by the Disciples, but by 1965 there were an estimated 200 of them in the group, and they were breaking with traditional gang patterns. They were organizing in Woodlawn. And this organization caused some public concern, and even fear, because it began during a period of violent rivalry between the Rangers and the Disciples. During these formative stages the Blackstone Rangers seemed to have placed the running feud between the Disciples and themselves secondary to their primary goal: organization. Soon their influence in Woodlawn caused minor, less influential, less powerful gangs to join them. And they came from all over the South Side: the Maniacs, the Four Corners, the Lovers, the V.I.P.'s, the

Pythons, the Warlocks, the F.B.I., the Conservatives, the Pharaohs. At present there are anywhere from 3500 to 8000 boys and men who identify with the Blackstone Rangers and who have affixed the Ranger name to the names of their own gangs. Such is the organizational structure and size of the Blackstone Rangers today that they call themselves a Nation. The Ranger Nation is headed by a group of young men called the Main 21. Until 1968 the president of the organization was Eugene "Bull" Hairston, the vice president was Jeff Fort (also called "Angel" and "Black Prince"), and the warlord was George Rose (also called "Watusi" and "Mad Dog"). The Rangers' spiritual leader was Paul "The Preacher" Martin, and the rest of the Main 21 was made up of leaders of the minor gangs who had joined with the Rangers. Each individual gang, it seems, maintained its own organizational structure with its own officers; but collectively all of the gangs made up the Blackstone Nation, which is presently incorporated to do business under the laws of Illinois.

Since the emergence of the Ranger Nation, individual members have been charged with murder, robbery, rape, knifings, extortion of South Side merchants, traffic in narcotics, extortion and intimidation of young children, forced gang membership, and a general history of outright violence, especially against the Disciples who never joined the Rangers. On the other hand, the Ranger Nation has been credited with keeping the South Side of Chicago "cool" during the summer of 1967 and the spring of 1968, following the assassination of Dr. Martin Luther King. It has been said that they have kept drugs, alcoholics, prostitutes, and whites hunting for prostitutes out of their neighborhoods. They have also been credited with making genuine attempts to form lasting peace treaties be-

James Alan McPherson, "Inside the Blackstone Rangers, Part I," *The Atlantic Monthly*, vol. 223 (May 1969), pp. 74–84. Copyright © 1969, by The Atlantic Monthly Company, Boston, Mass. Reprinted with permission.

tween themselves and the Disciples in order to decrease the level of gang fighting on the South Side. They have been alternately praised and condemned by the national press, their community, the United States Senate, the local police, and Chicago youth organizations to such an extent that, if one depends on the news media for information, it is almost impossible to maintain a consistent opinion of the Blackstone Rangers.

Some of the Chicago papers have been quick to report any charges of violent activity against a Ranger. In newspaper accounts, the name of the gang takes precedence over the individual arrested and charged with crimes. Many of the charges are accurate; many of the young men who identify with the Rangers are guilty of various crimes. But much of the information passed on to the press is shown to have no substance upon investigation. Still, the adverse publicity serves to keep the Chicago communities, both black and white, in a state of apprehension over the Blackstone Ranger organization, as opposed to the individuals in it.

There has been, and presently still is, a cry for a massive police crackdown on the Rangers. To accomplish this, the Chicago Police Department, following a general order issued by former Chicago Superintendent of Police O. W. Wilson, formed the Gang Intelligence Unit in March of 1967 to learn more about the Rangers and to decrease forcibly the level of gang violence in all areas of Chicago generally, and in the South Side area in particular. The stated purpose of the Unit was to eliminate "the antisocial and criminal activities of groups of minors and young adults in the various communities within the city."

In early June of 1967, The Woodlawn Organization (T.W.O.), a grass roots community association made up of one hundred or so block clubs, and civic, religious, and business organizations in the Woodlawn area of the South Side, received a $957,000 grant from the Office of Economic Opportunity to set up a special kind of youth project in the Woodlawn area. The purpose of the program was to utilize the existing gang structures—the Blackstone Rangers and the Devil's Disciples—as a means of encouraging youth in the gangs as well as non-gang youth to become involved in a pre-employment orientation, motivational project. The project was to include eight hundred out-of-school unemployed youths. And the entire program was to operate through four job-training centers which were to be set up in the home territories of the Rangers and Disciples. Reverend Arthur Brazier, president of The Woodlawn Organization, was responsible for bringing the interest of OEO to the proposed program, which was admitted to be a "high-risk venture."

The money from OEO went directly to The Woodlawn Organization. It did not go through city agencies, although one of the conditions of the grant was that the mayor was to be "invited" to concur in the selection of a project director for the program. There is some opinion that the mayor's office was not pleased with this. In fact, the full operation of the program was delayed over two months because of the inability of the T.W.O. people and Mayor Richard J. Daley to come to an agreement on a director for the program. By the time the program officially began in September, a project director had not been hired, and the Rangers and Disciples had, apparently, lost much of their enthusiasm for the program.

In September of 1967, The Woodlawn Organization opened four training centers in the Woodlawn area: two for the Blackstone Rangers and two for the Devil's Disciples. One of the Ranger Centers was located in the First Presbyterian Church, a church in the Woodlawn area headed by Reverend John Fry, a white Presbyterian clergyman. The Xerox Corporation was hired to formulate the curriculum; the Chicago Urban League was hired to do job development; and Arthur Andersen & Company was hired to give T.W.O. monthly reviews. In addition, a Monitoring Unit with the Chicago police was set up to have two meetings a month with T.W.O. people and representatives from the two gangs, which had attempted to de-escalate the level of their violent rivalry since the new program had been announced.

The trainees were paid $45 a week to take five hours of instruction a day for five days a week, in addition to travel expenses. The instructors in the program, or Center Chiefs, were not professionals but gang leaders who were supposed to be under the supervision of professionals because, as Reverend Brazier stated before the McClellan Committee "many of these youth do not relate to professionals because the professionals with middle-class attitudes do not relate to them." Eugene Hairston, president of the Rangers, was hired as an assistant project director at a salary of $6500 a year. Jeff Fort, Ranger vice president, became a Center Chief and received $6000 a year. And many of the other members of the Main 21 occupied, at one time or another, salaried positions in the project. Apparently, there was not much public opposition to the hiring of gang leaders by the program. Rather, there seems to have been a reversal in public attitude toward the Rangers because of their performance in the year before the program began.

One of the activities which helped their public image was the production of a musical review called *Opportunity Please Knock*, which was sponsored by Oscar Brown, Jr., the jazz pianist, and performed by groups of Rangers and students from the Hyde Park High School. The show, which was eventually taken over by the Rangers, ran for six weeks in May and June of 1967. An estimated eight thousand people went to the First Presbyterian Church during the first weeks of its performance, and it received very favorable nationwide publicity. Subsequent performances were given in various suburban communities around Chicago, and parts of the show traveled to Watts to perform. Some members of the troupe appeared on the Smothers Brothers show, and *Ebony* featured a large color story of the production in its August 1967 issue.

A second instance of positive Ranger activity, which also gained them favorable publicity, was their willingness to be bused out of town on August 12, Bud Billiken Day (named for a mythical folk hero created by the Chicago *Daily Defender*, a black newspaper). All past major conflicts between the Rangers and the Disciples had taken place during the Bud Billiken Day Parade and picnic in the South Side's Washington Park. In 1966 the city of Chicago had financed an out-of-town picnic for the Rangers through the Boys' Club, although there is some evidence that it considered the picnic idea a kind of blackmail exacted by the Rangers. In 1967, however, The Woodlawn Organization requested from OEO permission to use $5000 of its funds to take six hundred Rangers to an out-of-town picnic at Valparaiso University. The Rangers made the decision to leave town, it is said, because of rumors of a brewing riot and the public expectation that they would cause or at least participate in it.

The Ranger vice president, Jeff Fort, had been jailed on July 30 for murder charges and was still in jail on Bud Billiken Day. There are con-

flicting statements about whether or not Fort threatened to start a riot. Policemen have testified that he stated that if he were arrested, "the city would burn," while other sources reported that he cautioned the Rangers, after his arrest, not to riot. In any case, he remained in jail until early September of 1967, and there was no riot. The Rangers attended their picnic, and there were few incidents during the day. Whether or not the Rangers and Disciples actively contributed to the calm remains an open question. But a safe assumption can be made that when the T.W.O. project began in September, the Blackstone Rangers were enjoying a good deal of favorable press coverage and community support.

A final incident in the fall of 1967 helped their image in the city. In the Kenwood district, which adjoins Woodlawn, the police dispersed a black-power rally on September 15. The crowd then moved to a local high school, where bottles were thrown and two shots were fired by a sniper. The situation seemed to have been too tense for the police, when Herbert Stevens, leader of the Four Corners Rangers and a member of the Main 21 (known as "Thunder"), was said to have stood before the crowd and said "All you who are willing to die, step up now. Otherwise, let's go home." And as he turned to leave he said, "When I come back, I don't want to see anybody on the streets. I want these streets cleared." When he returned in five minutes, the story goes, the crowd had broken up.

The Blackstone Rangers wanted to play a major role in determining how the OEO-Woodlawn project should be run, and there were meetings throughout the summer of 1967 between the gang leaders and representatives of T.W.O. to determine the extent of their voice in the project. These meetings were kept under surveillance by detectives from the Gang Intelligence Unit.

The public favor enjoyed by the Rangers during the summer of 1967 dropped off severely when the president and vice president were arrested in late September of 1967 for soliciting three juveniles—Marvin Martin, fifteen, Sander Martin, fourteen, and Dennis Jackson, also fourteen—to murder a narcotics dealer named Leo McClure. McClure was in fact one of three men who were shot. Though he was not, it emerged, the prime target, he was the only one of the three who died. Dennis Jackson was alleged to have done the actual shooting. Hairston, the Ranger president, was kept in jail without bond, and the newspapers printed so many stories about a Teen-Age Murder, Inc., and so many details of the case against Hairston, that the first courtroom case ended in a mistrial.

During the same period the activities of Reverend John Fry and the First Presbyterian Church, which served as one of the T.W.O. training centers, were called into question. The church was said to be an arsenal for the Rangers to store their guns and a place where they sold and smoked marijuana, had sexual activity, and held their secret gang meetings. Then Jeff Fort was arrested in October and charged with murdering a Disciple. Both his arrest and the earlier arrest of Hairston encouraged the press to give extensive adverse publicity to The Woodlawn Organization because of their employment by the project. Soon afterward, three of the Main leaders, also members of the T.W.O. staff, were indicted for rape. The detectives of the G.I.U. made extensive visits to the training centers and found, according to their reports, no actual training taking place, the falsification of time sheets, gambling, and evidence that marijuana was being smoked on the premises. Finally, a Disciple was shot in one of the two Disciple Centers with a shotgun. The shooting was said to have been an accident, but the G.I.U. detectives who investigated the shooting found evidence that "light narcotics" (Robitussin) were being used at the Disciple Center. It was about this time that Senator McClellan's Permanent Subcommittee on Investigations of the Committee on Government Operations began to gather evidence in its planned investigation of The Woodlawn Organization's "high-risk" project.

The investigation began on June 28, 1968, in Washington. There was nationwide television coverage as all those who had connections with the project, official or otherwise, testified before Senators Jacob Javits, Carl Curtis, Fred Harris, Edmund Muskie, Karl Mundt, and of course Chairman John McClellan, who asked most of the questions.

Reverend Arthur Brazier made a desperate attempt to defend his project, explaining how participation of gang members was necessary for its success and charging that harassment from the Gang Intelligence Unit and explosively adverse news publicity had made it almost impossible for the project to develop as anticipated. Members of the Gang Intelligence Unit testified that they had made extensive visits to the training centers during the period of their operation and had found very little, if any, instruction going on. They also testified to the long list of crimes said to have been committed by gang members while under the sponsorship of T.W.O., especially the murder which was said to have been solicited by Eugene Hairston and Jeff Fort.

Perhaps the most damaging testimony against the program, if not against the Rangers themselves, came from George Rose, a former warlord of the Rangers who had defected from the organization, and a Mrs. Annabelle Martin, a black mother of ten who claimed to have had a very close relationship with the gang. The two Martin boys allegedly solicited by Hairston to commit the murder of Leo McClure were her sons.

Rose testified that the Rangers were involved in the sale of narcotics; that trainees in the program were forced to kick back to the organization from $5 to $25 each week; that the Rangers, from the start, had no interest in job training and that the program was used only to increase the gang's membership and its treasury; and that the First Presbyterian Church and its people —Reverend John Fry, Charles Lapaglia, and Anne Schwalbach, all white—were attempting to control and direct the gang through influence over Jeff Fort.

According to Rose's testimony, Reverend Fry had actually written the proposal for the OEO grant and had turned it over to Reverend Brazier; the church was used for the sale of narcotics, the storage of guns, and a convenient place for the Rangers to engage in sexual activity. He also told the Commitee that Lapaglia had taken some of the Main 21 leaders on a trip to Michigan to purchase guns and on another trip to Philadelphia to attend a black-power conference where the murders of certain nonmilitant civil rights leaders were plotted. He said that the Rangers had made it known to Reverend Brazier that they considered the OEO money theirs and would not let outsiders—school dropouts who were not Rangers—into the program. And, according to his testimony, Brazier consented to this without informing OEO officials. Rose told the Committee that many of the gang leaders who had been hired as instructors or Center Chiefs had fifth- or sixth-grade educations and that Jeff Fort, who served as a Center Chief, could not read or write. Finally, he stated that students from regular schools were forced to drop out in order to join the program and the gang, and that those who refused were beaten, shot in the arms, forced to keep off the streets, or killed. In this way, he said, the Rangers induced "a couple hundred" students to leave public schools and join the program, and that it was a practice of the Rangers to solicit juveniles to commit murder because they received a lighter sentence if they were caught.

Of special interest was his testimony that the Rangers had offered to help the police, and, in fact, did outfit themselves in black uniforms, called themselves the police of the Blackstone Ranger Nation, policed their neighborhoods, and turned over to the police several non-Rangers in order to clear the name of their organization. He stated that the police accepted them at first, but then, "after we turned a couple of guys in and made it known that they weren't our guys, the police still started cracking our young fellows' heads, just because of the uniforms. They called us storm troopers because we had black jump boots, black pants tucked into the top of the boots. . . . They didn't like this at all. They called it mob action."

Rose also testified that after the Rangers were rejected by the police, Reverend John Fry advised them to begin extorting merchants. "Since we were being accused of it," he said, "there wasn't anything we could lose by doing it." Rose said that the Rangers got from $5000 to $8000 a week from tavern owners and various sums from shoe stores, clothing stores, food stores, and drugstores through threats of future violence against them.

Robert L. Pierson of the Chicago State's Attorney's Office told the Committee that the Rangers "are the beginning of a Black Mafia." He testified that the Rangers were, in fact, extorting merchants but that the merchants would not complain because of fear of retaliation from the gang. During the April days following the murder of Martin Luther King when the Rangers distributed signs to be displayed in the windows of neighborhood merchants, he said, they charged $50 for their protection.

Jeff Fort, who had assumed leadership of the gang after Hairston was convicted in May of 1968, was subpoenaed to testify before the Committee. He was sworn in but never sat down before Senator McClellan. Marshall Patner, Fort's lawyer, submitted a request that the Committee allow Fort to confront and cross-examine the witnesses who had testified against him. The request was refused by Senator McClellan under authority of the Committee Rules. After a heated exchange between Patner and Senator McClellan during which both the lawyer and Fort were reminded of the possibility of contempt charges if Fort refused to accept protection from the Fifth Amendment and proceed with his testimony, Marshall Patner turned to Fort, still standing beside him, and said: "We really must go." Then they walked out.

The Woodlawn, Kenwood, and parts of the Hyde Park areas of the South Side of Chicago are said to be Ranger territories. While the Rangers' presence in Hyde Park, especially in the area around the University of Chicago, is not very obvious to the casual observer, the walls of buildings in Woodlawn and Kenwood advertise their existence. It is impossible to pass a single block in Woodlawn without seeing the signs. Many of the buildings are being torn down, but most of the signs look fresh and bold and new; "Black P. Stone," "Stone Run It," "Almighty Black P. Stone Nation," "Don't Vote B.P.S." they read. The wind blows bits of dirt and plaster into the faces of the children who play among the bricks and rubbish in the lots where houses once stood.

Blackstone Rangers are shy these days. They do not talk to most strangers. Whenever Jeff Fort is arrested, and he has been arrested many times since the McClellan Committee hearings, the story is picked up by almost every major newspaper in the country. Perhaps it is because of determined harassment from the Gang Intelligence Unit that the Rangers have grown tight and uncommunicative. Whatever the cause, they are suspicious of strangers, and their meetings are held in secret. They no longer make use of the First Presbyterian Church; they may meet there from time to time, but not regularly. Possibly their only facility open to the public is the Black P. Stone Youth Center on the corner of Sixty-seventh and Blackstone, in the heart of the Woodlawn community. The building was once a Chinese laundry, and at another time it was a poolroom. Now it seems to serve as the central point for most Ranger activities. The building is windowless, and it is painted black. Few non-Rangers go into the building uninvited; only those who have dealings with the Nation seem to feel free to enter. And perhaps this is because of the large black-and-red "Almighty Black P. Stone" diamond-shaped symbol painted on the Blackstone Street side of the building. During the days adults hurry past the teen-age boys and men who may be standing outside the door. There is a bar a few doors away from the Center, and many of the older people who pass the building go in there to escape the wind, or into the barbecue house next to the bar, or else continue about whatever business they may have further down Sixty-seventh Street. The latch is broken, and the door is never really shut. Anyone can walk in, but for the most part only the children do.

Jeff Fort is the "Black Prince," the president, the "Chief" of the entire Blackstone operation. One cannot think of learning about the Nation without assuming that Jeff Fort is the key, the source of all information. To see Jeff, it is necessary to go to the Black P. Stone Youth Center and wait. It is necessary to wait a long time. Jeff Fort is extremely busy. Besides leading the Rangers, he is fighting a contempt of Congress conviction for walking out of the McClellan hearings last July (he was found guilty in November); awaiting certain cases pending against him in the Cook County courts; and, until he resigned in early December, working as a community organizer for the Kenwood-Oakland Community Organization (KOCO).

But waiting for Jeff Fort to come to the Center gives one the opportunity to observe some of the Rangers as they wander in and out of the smaller, first room of the place, which serves as an office. The room is painted black. There are two desks, a telephone, ancient magazines, a water cooler with no water, and a bulletin board. Tacked on the board are job announcements, pictures of Rangers who participated in *Opportunity Please Knock*, messages, and cartoons—including one by Jules Feiffer. It is not an impressive office, but the door never stops opening as the children come in. There is little in the office to suggest why they come, but sitting in the one big ragged chair in a dark corner of the office, one is able to observe a steady flow of children, boys and girls, ranging in age from seven to fourteen, walking in and out of the office as if in search of something.

Lamar Bell, the coordinator of the Black P. Stone Youth Center, does not mind my waiting. "The Chief is due here in a few hours," he always says. And he says it again, much later in the evening. It is obvious that he does not trust me. Finally he asks why I want to see the Chief. "I want to do a story on the Nation," I tell him. "I want to see how the Nation relates to the community and the police." Bell turns off completely. "Put *that* in your story!" he says, pushing a pink mimeographed sheet close to my face. "The trouble with Black Police in our community," it reads, "is not police brutality to blacks, it is that these men and women are afraid of the power structure. So they join it to save themselves from the misery of being Black and powerless. The only way they can prove themselves, to their Brother's and Sister's, your Mother and Father and my Mother and Father, and our children. If they weren't police they would be in the same shape as any other oppressed Black man, Woman, or Child. God help them," it went on, "for they know not what they do. To them, it's a job for money; to us it's our lives, home and children."

"This is just what I want to write about," I tell him.

Lamar Bell walks to the door between the office and the back room, which has been off limits to me during my past visits to the Center, and says, "You'll have to talk it over with the Chief. He'll be here in a couple of hours."

Every evening for at least three hours Lamar Bell and Carl Banks, one of the Center's teachers, conduct a percussion class for some of the younger boys who come there. Banks has been a Ranger for two years. He is twenty-one, and came to Chicago from New York two years ago. He wants to become a professional drummer and earns money from infrequent band engagements. The rest of his time he spends in the Center, teaching a percussion class for neighborhood children. He is friendly and talkative. "The kids are really interested in expressing themselves," he told me. "A lot of these kids are misunderstood. Drumming gives them a way to express themselves. If I had money for the course, I would get more equipment and books, take the kids to see other drummers perform. Try to work out a little drum and bugle corps."

From the chair where I sat in the office during my first visits to the Center, I could hear the music they made with their drums in the mysterious back room.

One Saturday night Bell informed me that there was an extra bongo drum and invited me to sit in on the session. He allowed me to enter the back room, a kind of auditorium with a small stage, and the three of us played drums, without speaking, for several hours. While we played, some of the older Rangers came in and watched us. They looked at me, and then at Bell, then at me again. It was obvious that I was not a Stone.

"You didn't give off the right vibrations," Art Richardson, the director of the Black P. Stone Youth Center, told me later that night. "That's why I was watching you. But you *could* be a Stone because you came into the Center and participated on *our* level. That's what Stone is all about."

Art Richardson believes in vibrations as a method of determining the sincerity of people. Although he grew up on the South Side of Chicago, he has been a Ranger for only two years. He is not a member of the Main 21, but because he is articulate and extremely intelligent, he has been made a "head" and director of the Black P. Stone Youth Center. He is twenty-eight, married, and has served in the Army. He was given an Undesirable Discharge in 1965 because, he says, "I was just exposed to prejudice and reacted to it in the only way I knew." He has a police record. He also has a way with people. He would rather ride a bus than a cab because, he says, "You can't get vibrations from peoples in a cab." He never says people; the word always comes out peoples, with enough warmth and emphasis to suggest sincerity.

The Englewood Urban Progress Center, located at 839 West Sixty-fourth Street in an area which is said to be Disciple territory, houses a concentration of community service agencies. The building itself is a Masonic Temple which has been converted into offices. Only the ground floor is used for official purposes; the upper floors are essentially unused, although the second floor has a fairly large auditorium with a stage and good seating capacity, and there are many other, smaller rooms, all quiet and waiting to be put into use. In one of the larger rooms on the second floor, the one with the stage, Darlene Blackburn, an accomplished black dancer of considerable reputation in Chicago, gives creative dance lessons to girls from the community. Waiting for her in the semilighted room are children, boys and girls, who come to participate in the class or to watch her dance. Art Richardson and I wait with them. Art wants to ask her to

dance at a Thanksgiving show he is organizing for the Black P. Stone Youth Center. While they wait, the children play at jumping off the stage and onto the floor, a distance of some three or four feet. Sometimes they fall on their faces, but they always laugh, and climb back onto the stage to jump again. It is a game.

"Look at that," Art told me.

A boy was dropping onto the stage from a trapdoor four or five feet above. He landed on his knees, unhurt, and climbed up to jump again.

"That's energy," Art said. "*We* can't do that anymore."

I agreed.

Art walked over to the stage and watched the boy jump again. This time he landed on his feet. "You know," he told me, coming back to where I was sitting, "the young brothers represent a form of energy just like any other energetic force in nature, just like the atom. If it could be channeled, if it could be turned to constructive directions just like the atom . . ." He began to walk about the room. "If I had a bigger place like this, I could bring more of the little brothers in and get that energy."

"What would you do with it?" I asked.

He looked up at the old Mason paintings on the walls and ceilings, half-hidden in the darkness. "I'd like to have job-training programs, arts and crafts workshops, adult workshops sort of like the P.T.A. to assemble adults just to get them to talk and maybe close the generation gap. Help them influence the kids in the necessary direction." He paused. "As a matter of fact, I would do exactly what the other organizations are trying to do. But only *I'd* do it. Most of the other organizations can't reach the kids. We can. We can give them something to relate to as theirs."

"What?" I asked him.

Art lowered his voice so that the children could not hear him. "Stone," he said softly. Most of Englewood, and whatever energy there is in it, still belongs to the Disciples.

No one really knows how many Rangers there now are in the South Side area. The Gang Intelligence Unit estimates that they claim a membership of from 1500 to 3000, while the Rangers themselves claim a membership of from 5000 to 8000. Perhaps the difficulty in estimating their number lies in the fact that the gang, if it can presently be called that, is not well organized. Aside from the Main 21, there seems to be very little perceptible formal organization or control by leaders over individual gang members. If anything, the Rangers seem to represent a certain spirit in their community, a spirit which is adopted by young people. But whether this adoption is voluntary or forced upon young people is one of the major controversial questions that concern the Woodlawn, Kenwood, Oakland, and Hyde Park communities.

During the McClellan hearings there was a good deal of testimony that small children were being forced to join the Rangers and pay protection money. There is some evidence, some opinion, that the Rangers are still recruiting. But few black people in the areas in which most of the intimidation is supposed to be going on seem willing to talk about it, especially to a black like myself who is not known to them. At the hearings, charges were also made that the Rangers were using The Woodlawn Organization's federal funds to line their own pockets. Few private black citizens have much to say about this either.

In the proposal for the Black P. Stone Youth Center the Rangers state that "above all things or ideas of personal materialistic gain, we intend to cultivate our people spiritually, mentally, physically, and economically. To construct and develop our ideal of a new method of existence and behavior." The proposed program is a plea for community support. At present, few adults come to the Center. "Our P.," the statement of intentions goes on, "stands for people, progress, and prosperity." There is no mention of power in the statement.

"We're only interested in trying to develop our community services," Art Richardson told me, "so that it becomes obvious to the peoples that we only have the community's interest at heart and the development of ourselves. We're interested in all peoples as long as they are interested in our philosophy."

The Rangers have scheduled weekly Saturday night meetings at the Center for adults. Some adults do come out, but they are few in number; and those who come wait around nervously for other adults to show and attempt to make conversation with the older Rangers. For the Rangers have a community relations problem. They lack the vocal support of the majority of adults in the areas in which they have an obvious influence over young people. Perhaps it is because many of the adults are unwilling to recognize the Rangers as a legitimate force in a community

crowded with "letter-name" organizations, all claiming a certain rapport with the grass roots.

Al Garrison, for example, is a twenty-five-year-old machinist. He is black, and he lives in the Woodlawn area. He grew up in Chicago, is divorced, and has two children. He is not so much concerned about the Rangers as he is about the present state of affairs in this country. He is afraid that his children will not live to reach his age. He believes that the country will not survive much longer, and he wonders why he continues to work every day. He believes that the Chicago police are corrupt beyond control. And he believes that the Mafia controls many members of the police force and the Blackstone Rangers.

"A friend of mine who used to be pretty big in the Rangers told me that white men run the gang," Garrison confides. "He said that they give the guys a new kind of dope that makes them want to kill people. They just go crazy when they take it," he says. "The whites are just using those boys."

Garrison is not bitter nor militant. In fact, he cannot understand militancy at this late stage in what he believes to be the decline of America from causes still unclear to him.

The Rangers do not appear to be militant either, at least not in the contemporary sense of the word. They have refused to make a coalition with the Black Panthers. They do not seem to have any political philosophy. If anything, they believe only in themselves and in their motto: "Stone Run It!" But they are waiting too. Whether it is for more federal funds or for their presence and power to be recognized by the black community through their influence over ghetto youth, they are waiting. And their energy is at work.

"Just don't *do* it, put some *soul* into it! *I* got more soul than International Shoe Company!" the man says. His name is just "Buzz." He is a highly skillful pool player: he has beaten the great Minnesota Fats. But he is also a Blackstone Ranger, and for three hours every Monday afternoon, from 3 p.m. until 6 p.m., he is a disc jockey for a music program called *Stone Thang,* sponsored by the University of Chicago's student-run WHPK-FM radio station and the Black P. Stone Nation. Buzz takes his work seriously: he keeps time with his fingers, he sings along with the records, he makes spontaneous, soulful comments, he sweats and smokes, and he enjoys himself. The Rangers take the program seriously too: at least three of them assist him, tight-lipped and silent, in the little studio on the second floor of the university's student activities building. "If you got any soul at all," he announces to his FM audience, "give old brother Buzz a call." And the telephone keeps ringing for three hours, and Buzz keeps talking.

The station's program director, Tom Jacobson, is a senior at the university. He observed that since *Stone Thang* began in October, there has been an increase in the station's audience, and, he believes, some improvements in communications between the Ranger community and the University of Chicago-Hyde Park white community. The station, however, is a low-power operation, and only reaches FM sets in the Woodlawn, Hyde Park, and South Side areas. The students hope to expand the station's operations to AM sets in order to reach more people, but, Jacobson said, present expansion is doubtful because of lack of funds.

"We've been trying to do this type of show for months," Jacobson commented. "Finally we got Chuck Lapaglia from the First Presbyterian Church and Jeff Fort to help us set it up. The object of the show is to make the Black P. Stone Nation a part of the community."

Buzz and the Rangers who assist him are volunteers. Their only visible compensation lies in the plentiful opportunities Buzz has to say, "This is a *Stone Thang* presented by the All Mighty Black P. Stone Nation!" The other Rangers in the studio look solemn whenever he says this.

"The kids dig Stone," Carl Banks told me. "But the older people aren't sincere enough to come down and give help. We'd like to get to older people through their kids. In a sense, we're babysitting here because a lot of parents aren't interested in their kids and a lot of them don't trust the Stones. That's why we passed out a list of our intentions—to let them know that it's a peaceful thing. Some people in the area are skeptical because of the past, but they ought to come in and see us now."

The Rangers want money. They want to expand the range of activities presently offered in their Center and set up other Centers in the South Side area. They believe that they have the people, or at least the younger people, with them. Now they want money to put their programs into operation. Lamar "Bob" Bell, a former member of the Main 21, estimates that the Nation needs about $259,000 a year to put its present plans into operation. While his estimate may be far from conservative, it is obvious that for whatever cultural programs the Rangers may have in mind, the Sixty-seventh Street Center will not provide adequate accommodations. At present they have three rooms: the outer room, which serves as an office; the back room, with a small stage; and a sort of kitchen area, with a small bathroom. All of these rooms are in poor repair. For equipment they have a percussion set, two bongo drums, a ping-pong table, and about twenty-four metal chairs.

The Rangers are attempting certain ventures in business. The newly formed Kenwood-Oakland Community Organization, funded by a $100,000 grant from the Community Renewal Society of Chicago and headed by Reverend Curtis Burrell, has loaned the Rangers $3000 to open a restaurant on South Woodlawn Avenue. But there is a feeling, an old one, going back to the days of the OEO grant and the sponsorship of the Rangers by The Woodlawn Organization and Reverend Arthur Brazier, that a supposedly legitimate organization is subsidizing gang activities and allowing an already uncontrollable force to grow even larger and more powerful.

In 1968 there were two incidents which increased public interest and, perhaps, concern for the Blackstone Rangers. The first was their attempt to control the violence on the South Side of Chicago in the uncertain days in April after the assassination of Dr. Martin Luther King by passing out to neighborhood merchants hand-painted signs which read: "Do Not Touch . . . Black P. Stone . . . Jeff." They are said to have also set up a riot-control center in the First Presbyterian Church, where they received calls from troubled areas and directed Ranger leaders to the scenes of potential riotous activity. Finally, the Rangers and the Disciples called a truce on the Sunday following the assassination, during which some 1500 Rangers and 400 Disciples marched through the Woodlawn area and met in a park near the University of Chicago to negotiate the end of violence, or at least the immediate hostility, between the traditionally enemy groups. The march was covered by the local press, and the Rangers were given credit for preventing a riot on the South Side.

And in August, while the police and hippies rioted in the hotel area and in Lincoln Park, the

outh Side remained calm. Whether or not the
angers were responsible for the calm remains
n open question. There is some evidence that
ne F.B.I. had investigated certain threats, some
f them alleged to have been made by Reverend
ohn Fry, that the Rangers were planning to riot
a the Loop, disrupt the Convention, and assassi-
ate Eugene McCarthy and Hubert Humphrey.
Captain Edward Buckney, head of the Chicago
olice Departmnt's Gang Intelligence Unit and
ne ninth black police captain in the history of
ne Chicago Police Department, does not believe
nat the Rangers were responsible for keeping
neir neighborhoods cool during the April riots.
Fry will tell you that they were responsible for
eeping things cool last April," he says, "but in
ur opinion that's a lot of hogwash. We just
on't believe that's so. We believe that idea was
 brand of hysteria created by the group to get
redit for something they didn't do."
As an example of the hysteria, Buckney related
nat in August of 1968, just after Jeff Fort was
uiled for probation violation and before the
emocratic Convention, Reverend Brazier and
ther community people requested a meeting
ith the superintendent of police. "Their basic
tch was 'We can't guarantee what will happen
ith Jeff in jail.' They were pressuring the po-
ce to release him on the implication of the pos-
bility of future violence. To me it's a means of
artering or dickering with the community for
eir own betterment," Buckney said. "There
ere no disturbances on the South Side, and the
ason was basically because the black commu-
ty did not want to become involved. If the
angers claim credit for it, that's some more hog-
ash."
"In April," he said, "there were about 5000
nited States troops, policemen, and many other
encies in the Kenwood-Woodlawn area. His-
rically, in Chicago there have never been riots
 the South Side; they have always been on the
est Side. The closest one was in April, and
ost of the damage there was done in Ranger-
isciple territory. Also, you have to consider the
ct that over in the Ranger end there is little
se to destroy because they have already de-
royed most of it."
Buckney was promoted to captain last No-
mber, just after the election. He senses that
s police position has made him unpopular in
rtain areas of the black community. But he
lieves that his role as a policeman is clearly

defined. "Our approach is the hard-line police
approach," he says. "We're not concerned with
sociological approaches. As long as they don't
violate the law, we don't concern ourselves with
them." And as a policeman Buckney is in fact
determined to break up the gang. He believes
that this can be accomplished if most of the
older members, possibly those who exert a bad
influence over the younger members, are taken
out of the area. He believes that 95 percent of
the young people in the gang are there because
they have no choice in the matter. "No one likes
to be continually shot at because he's not a member of the gang," he said. "If we could divorce
those who religiously believe in it from the community, the others would have a chance to get
out. If the courts deal severely with a considerable number of them, if the courts deal severely
in the cases pending against Jeff Fort and some
of the other Main leaders, I think the Rangers
could be broken up."
Like many other public officials in Chicago,
Captain Buckney blames overzealous clergymen
for the rapid growth of major gangs over the
past two years. During the McClellan investigation, and later, in the Chicago papers and on television, he criticized Reverend John Fry and Reverend Brazier for supporting the activities of the
Rangers and the Disciples. He was especially
critical of Burrell's subsequent hiring of Jeff
Fort as a community organizer. "From what we
have seen already," he stated, "we can tell what
kind of organizing he was doing. He used intimidation and fear to get young people to join the
gang." He blames Reverend Fry's First Presbyterian Church for luring these youths away from
the Boys' Clubs and into the church. Under
Fry's guidance, according to Captain Buckney,
the gang enjoyed a tremendous growth. He estimates the present membership of the Rangers
to be between 1500 and 3000 youths, but indicates
that Reverend Fry's estimation is closer to 4000.
"But I doubt if you could find any more than 300
hard-core Rangers," he remarked.
The captain believes that the most notable
achievement of the Rangers was the formation
of an entertainment troupe, a major part of
which was the "Blackstone Singers." "But you
have to look at that with a jaundiced eye too,"
he cautioned me. "Most of them were high
school kids, not hard-core Rangers." He feels
that too much attention is being given the gang
members to the exclusion of all the other poor

children in the Woodlawn community. "If people keep pushing the bad things under the rug, at the rate they're going now they soon will become untouchable because they've already done almost everything attributable to organized crime."

"I believe in giving credit where credit is due," he says of the Rangers, "but they don't do anything constructive. All they're interested in is money in their pockets. If you have any dealings with them, the question always is what can *you* do for *them*. You won't get much out of them for nothing."

Buckney has been criticized for what some Chicagoans call his persecution of the Rangers. He is aware of this, and seems to be able to live with his constant criticism from community-minded whites as well as from some of his fellow blacks. "I'm often accused of persecuting the black community," he admitted. "But when I look at these homicides"—he picked up a pile of papers from his desk and dropped them before continuing—"when I look at these and see a minimum of 95 percent to 97 percent of them coming out of the black community—well, I believe you have to concentrate your men where the problem is." In 1968, the captain disclosed, there have been more than ten killings in Woodlawn.

"If they were so sincere about doing something constructive for the community and if they have knowledge of crime, why don't they turn it over to the police?" the captain asked. "There've been other gangs who have turned members over to the police for doing some wrong. But the Rangers have rarely if ever cooperated with the police and probably never will. If one of them is locked up, they'll try anything possible to spring him—bribing witnesses, even intimidation. They have a complete disdain for the law. They won't even show up for court appearances."

This sort of suspicion is reciprocated: the chief witnesses against the T.W.O. project and the

Rangers before the McClellan Committee George Rose and Annabelle Martin, are rumored to have been bribed by the police to testify as they did. Rose had been arrested for a narcotics violation, but charges were never brought; and the two sons of Annabelle Martin had been previously arrested for the murder of Leo McClure and were the principal witnesses in the case against Eugene Hairston. The charges against both the boys were dropped. Both Mrs. Martin and George Rose moved out of Chicago. Captain Buckney denies the bribery allegations: "Bribery is, point-blank, not true. In the case of George Rose, we got word that the Rangers wanted him killed. We got to him first. All we wanted was inside information on the Rangers. Mrs. Martin certainly wasn't bribed. She was merely asked by the senators if she wanted to go to Washington, and she agreed. We just arranged for her transportation out of the city."

Since its formation in March of 1967, the Gang Intelligence Unit has grown in power and importance in the Chicago Police Department. In 1967 there were only thirty-eight policemen, mostly black, assigned to the Unit; but since the first part of November, plans have been made to increase its strength to two hundred men. "We're striving for 100 percent integration of the Unit," Captain Buckney told me. It is highly probable that members of the Unit have infiltrated the gang; Captain Buckney seems well informed of Ranger activities. But it is also just as probable that the Rangers know a good deal about the activities of the Unit.

Some non-G.I.U. policemen, like Field Commander William B. Griffin, have attempted to work with the Ranger organization rather than against it. "Griffin's problems are different from mine," Buckney says. "He may have to do what is best for the community, while I, if I were in his place, might do something different. But the general consensus in the police department is the hard-line police approach."

18

JOYCE R. STARR · DONALD E. CARNS

Singles in the City: Notes on Urban Adaptation

In the early part of this century, about the time of the first World War, the University of Chicago was establishing its preeminence in the field of sociology (not that it had much competition). Probably the major thrust of that effort concerned the sociology department's approach to the city, specifically to the city of Chicago. Beginning with Robert E. Park's seminal article in 1916, its later version, and the work of Thomas and Znaniecki, Burgess, Shaw, Wirth, and others, the school of "human ecology" attempted to consider the city as an analog to the ecology of all living things, i.e., the relationship between organisms, their physical and social environments, and their functionally interrelated network of associations. In large measure they were successful in focusing our attention on *processes* of social life in relation to areas of the city; that is, they conceptualized the city in terms of *both* turf and function and dealt with in such dynamic categories as assimilation, accommodation, conflict, and the like. At least three kinds of urban studies stemmed from this school of thought. Some analyzed Chicago and other cities in a comparative way, seeking to establish universal descriptions of land use in terms of an ecological model, i.e., the interrelationships between areas of the city. Building on this work, still others correlated incidence and prevalence of various social patterns (including social "pathologies") with areas of the city, attempting to demonstrate that aspects of land use—density, debilitation, familism or isolation, and so forth—play a major role in causing individual deviance, group deviant adaptations, physical and mental illness, family dissolution, or whatever. Still a third group paid close attention to the byproducts of industrialization: functional interdependence, identity and life style as reflecting the work role, the process of migration and urban acculturation, all of which Park had delineated as primary foci for an urban sociology. These researchers went into the city, studied its life styles, talked to its people, and frequently let them speak for themselves. They provided for us a portrait of both the underbelly of urban life and its higher orders—peculiar adaptations to the urban milieu and some of the personal and social costs and benefits which accrued. From *The Polish Peasant* through *The Jackroller*, *The Gold Coast and the Slum*, and *Brothers in Crime* to (among others) Becker's work on marijuana use and jazz musicians, a tradition of hitting the streets and talking to people has continued in American sociology.

In many important ways, Chicago and other cities have changed since those early days, but in certain fundamental aspects they are the same. Early Chicago was a city of rapid growth through immigration, especially by peoples from eastern and southern Europe. In more recent years, blacks, Southern whites, Spanish-Americans, and others have replicated this migration pattern to the city. Chicago is still segregated; there is still great competition for space and resources; and the processes of invasion and succession which produce neighborhood change continue unabated. Whether race and ethnicity as expressed in spatial use or socioeconomic position expressed in networks of interrelations is the criterion, nevertheless Chicago is still polyglot. It is on one particular social category that we wish to focus our attention in this essay: the educated, unmarried, urban young.

As much as in 1920, cities are still magnets today, for they maintain a virtual monopoly over access to the products and byproducts of an industrialized, mass-culture society. Even though colleges and universities are widely reputed to be marriage markets, channeling most students into legal marriages at or soon after graduation and thus ultimately into the suburbs, nevertheless large numbers of young college graduates migrate to the city each year, unmarried, more or less committed to a career, all sharing a fairly similar upbringing (in socioeconomic terms) and a virtually identical college experience. They do vary by gender and by sexual object preference (that is, most are straight but some are gay), by degree of career commitment, and by urbanity, to a certain extent.

This particular population is theoretically significant on a number of levels. In the first place, young, educated, single people constitute the focus of a considerable effort by advertisers and the media to create a "swinging" scene, whether it exists or not, or in what form it flourishes. In this sense, these singles are fully *au courant* as the "now" generation, the referent of much of our cultural fantasies about the good life: free and unrestricted, highly sexual and sensual, in short, *fun*. It is, of course, an empirical question: To what degree does the reality of urban single life approximate this media-generated fantasy? The question is significant in the same way any challenge to a stereotype is socially significant, whether it relates to blacks, women, students, communists, or whatever.

On a second level, young, educated, urban singles constitute the product of our advanced educational system, at least that segment which avoided marriage immediately after college. Although it shall not be a major focus of this paper, the degree that pre-urban socialization in school or at home prepared these people for the realities of urban living, or for its image, is a crucial question. It is crucial, of course, for it provides a partial test of the efficacy of these institutions, and it bears strongly on the adjustments these people make. Are they fulfilled, hopeful, nostalgic, sad, lonely, or what? These and other questions are being explored at length in other analyses currently under way.

And finally, this population will, in twenty years or so, be the married, middle-class suburbanites so well known to us all. To what degree do men and women anticipate this probable fu-

ture state? What are their attitudes toward marriage? Monogamy? Security? Responsibility?

Our general strategy in this paper shall involve a discussion of three major task areas, each of which must be solved in order for a successful adjustment to urban life to take place: finding and maintaining a place to live; finding, keeping, or changing jobs; and meeting friends, dates, and potential mates (whether legal or consensual).

THE SETTING

In rough descriptive terms, Chicago's North Side singles' community extends approximately eight miles north of the Loop, two and one-half miles to the West—depending upon how far north, and is bounded on the east by Lake Michigan. More accurately, however, this general area encompasses four fairly distinct subareas, each of which is home to a wide range of life styles. Closest to the Loop lies the Near North, a city planner's horror of twenty-story high-rise apartments seeded between renovated brownstones, providing a backdrop for a patchwork of standup style singles bars. Moving north, we find Chicago's Old Town, a subarea similarly characterized by aged brownstones, occasional duplexes, a few high-rises (being built at a feverish pace, therefore fundamentally altering the character of the neighborhoods), and Wells Street, a potpourri of fun houses, ice cream palaces, "head shops," and strip joints to which tourists and teenyboppers gravitate and which singles by and large avoid. Old Town merges into the Mid-North, a dense concentration of back-to-back high-rises and four-plus-ones (four-story apartment buildings, cheaply built, which took advantage of a loop-hole in Chicago's otherwise stringent building code; they are now illegal). this area, there is only a smattering of night spots and other retail establishments. At some point, debated, the Mid-North ends and New Town begins. This latter area managed without a specific name until the commercial boom began to move north along Broadway and Clark streets, giving rise to a profusion of easy-entry stores: boutiques, antiques, waterbeds, ethnic cuisine, sit-down bars ("that give you a chance to talk"), and a small sprinkling of Chicago's own "off-Broadway" and out-of-the-Loop theaters.

s also an area of mixed housing types: four-plus-
ones, brownstones, occasional high-rises nearer
o Lake Michigan; and it contains "homo-
neights," which is exactly what the name implies.

The proportion of young college graduates is
oy no means equally distributed in these areas
out tends to increase moving northward to the
Mid-North and New Town neighborhoods as
ents generally decrease. Moreover, despite the
overage the singles scene has received from fea-
ure sections of newspapers and from national
nagazines, other kinds of people living in these
reas undoubtedly outnumber the young un-
ttached graduates. Older persons, particularly
vidows, comprise a significant proportion of
his less newsworthy population. There is a mi-
ration pattern back to the city on the part of
uburban couples, with or without children, and
here are large numbers of young married people
nwilling to leave the city. Other residents in-
lude divorcees, bachelors over thirty, and stu-
ents. The common link between these groups
s neither age nor life style but rather an eye to
onvenience: proximity to the central business
istrict.

HE DATA

he discussion which follows is based on ap-
roximately seventy face-to-face interviews,
tructured but essentially open-ended, conducted
vith never-married college graduates of both
exes in their early to mid-twenties, who have not
one graduate work but have opted to come to
r remain in Chicago and work. Interviewing
as done during 1970 and the first half of 1971
nd, in fact, is still under way. No systematic
ampling method was considered feasible.
ather, a "snowball" technique of contacts plus
ttention to variability in occupations, living ar-
angements and locations, and other aspects of
fe style was used to recruit respondents.

ousing

espite the media's attention to the singles
:ene, the typical graduate arriving in Chicago
as minimal or nonexistent awareness of Chi-
ago's singles panorama, much less the purpose-

ful objective of peer segregation and subculture
participation. Similarly, the actual decision to
move to Chicago after finishing college is rarely
a function of *informed* expectations concerning
social life in the city. Rather, for the majority
of those who were themselves raised in Chicago
or its outlying areas, return is usually the result
of a choice no more considered than "it seemed
like the natural thing to do." On the part of
other in-migrant graduates, the decision appears
based on even more haphazard criteria: "I
wanted to get away from home and Chicago is
the nearest big city"; "A few of my close friends
from college were coming here, and I had no
place else to go so . . ."; "My boy friend had decided to move here"; "I figured the job market
would be better here than New York or San Francisco"; "The job I was offered just happened to
be based in this city." Female graduates typically offer one of the first three responses, while
males are more likely to respond with one of
the last two. Thus since the male's decision to
come to a particular city is work-related, while
his female counterpart's motive is more social,
it is frequently the case that a male will move
to a city where he has neither family nor friends
while a female moves to one only where friends
and/or family may serve whatever needs she has.
It follows from this that an in-migrant male to
Chicago is more likely to live alone when he first
comes into the city, while the out-of-town female
establishes living arrangements with one or two
friends from college. Also contributing to this
pattern, of course, is the fact that male graduates
earn higher salaries, thus are better able to
afford to live alone.

The data suggest that the typical in-migrant female does not have a car at her disposal, and
thus the first criterion she employs in looking
for a place to live is that it be close to transportation and within a reasonably short traveling distance from her place of work. A second major
concern is safety, both in terms of household integrity and area of residence. Thus many females often restrict their apartment hunt to
buildings equipped with doormen or buzzer systems and consequently are more likely than
males to move initially into a high-rise or four-
plus-one. By contrast, the typical male graduate
moving to Chicago is largely unconcerned with
safety and usually has a car as well. With entertainment expenses and automobile payments

(not to mention astronomical urban insurance costs) in mind, he typically prefers to do his economizing on rental costs and is therefore more likely to seek an older building. Moreover, because of these different considerations, males frequently seek apartments in blue-collar and migrant neighborhoods which border the area on the west.

Both men and women, however, soon encounter the inescapable fact that desirable apartments are at a premium. With seldom more than a weekend's time to complete their search, for most out-of-town graduates the decisive criterion in their choice of a building, and consequently a neighborhood, often turns out to be that "the apartment was available." In Chicago, at least, this is further confounded by the tradition of May to October leasing periods, which means that relatively fewer apartments are available at other times of the year. Furthermore, a significant proportion of in-migrant graduates never go through the apartment hunting process; they either move in with a friend, or a friend of a friend, who already has an apartment, or they let their roommate-to-be do the hunting and deciding.

Unlike California and some other states, there are few, if any, "singles only" buildings or complexes in Chicago, and none on the North Side in the area we are discussing. Chicago's North Side area does contain one mega-complex which rose from the rubble of a decaying area under the rubric and financing of "middle-income housing," but which has not served that population in any significant way. It houses about 6,000 people and bears a reputation as a miniature "swingle's city," but in actuality, the majority of its residents are neither under twenty-five nor single. More to the point, the data suggest that the majority of graduates, males in particular, prefer *not* to live in a building that fabricates and formalizes the meeting and dating process. To be sure, they have fond recollections of the communal-like living arrangements of their college years: "I knew 90 percent of the people living in my building; here I don't even know my next-door neighbor." But the key terms, and the kind of living situations these graduates seek, are exemplified by "spontaneous," "casual," and "not forced." The majority of those interviewed expressed discomfort if not disdain for any type of living arrangement that highlights and exploits their single status. After all, the city is supposed to permit freedom. It is probable, however, that where the climate permits year-round outdoor facilities, such as swimming pools and tennis courts, such housing complexes may in fact be more acceptable as "natural" settings to this population. This is in distinct contrast to "party rooms," "mixing lounges," and so forth that abound in cold-climate buildings bent on attracting single populations. This climate variable and all it entails is clearly a matter for future research.

It should be kept in mind that college students spend the bulk of their working day in classes or studying by themselves, alone. In classrooms even surrounded by peers, the student is not actually interacting with anyone in an active and meaningful sense. Nor does performance in college depend upon such interactions ever when they do occur. Although unlikely, it is quite possible to complete four years of college successfully and earn a bachelor's degree without ever speaking to a fellow student or, sad to say, a professor. This is very rarely the case in the world of work, where a great premium is placed on interpersonal skills no matter how high the level of technical proficiency. Graduates discover this fact of life very quickly. Ironically, when asked how, if at all, college prepared them for the experience of working, the typical response is "it taught me how to get along with people." It is not production as such, but rather the skills of performance that are essential in the work role, speaking of the modal case. And because the average working graduate in this sample finds himself or herself interacting with others eight or more hours per day, in pressure situations which could hardly be characterized as pure sociability, a great need for privacy results. The modal graduate laments the cold and unfriendly nature of the city, the lack of neighboring, and recalls his school days with considerable nostalgia. But the majority admit with some embarrassment that in fact they have put forth little effort to alter the situation, rarely making an overture and/or failing to act upon overtures made by others. Clearly one's house is a haven of privacy in an environment of functional and personal interaction.

Despite this, the fact remains that there is a strong concentration of homogeneous social types in these neighborhoods. From what the data indicate, this fact coupled with the home-as-haven concept leads us to seriously question whether concentrations of people with similar ages and educational backgrounds is a sufficient condition for meaningful social interaction. Focusing on the establishment of friendships and dating relationships, the data would suggest that neighborhood and housing based interactions are not significant access routes for the modal graduate in this sample.

When asked about this lack of neighborhood-based interaction, reasons vary. Some place the blame on themselves, but with little remorse. "I just never think about it"; "I know enough people." Others maintain it is due more to a lack of time than a lack of interest. But the majority attribute this infrequency of neighboring to the hostile and secondary nature of the big city milieu where "everyone is in a hurry," or is "concerned with making it," and is "so self-centered." Many decry Chicago's long dreary winters as a significant contributor to both their own unfriendliness in neighborhoods as well as the ill-tempered moods of others.

It follows that spring and summer seem to sweep in a moratorium on distrust and aloofness (and, ironically, along with it higher incidences of forcible rape, breaking and entering, and other acts also encouraged by warm weather). People emerge from indoors to bicycle through Chicago's extensive lakefront park system, meander through shops, take in the sun at the beach, go to outdoor concerts. Not only do the seasons have a bearing on actual behavior; they are very much a part of the consciousness of these graduates. Warm weather will be a time "when I'll find out who my neighbors are." Nonetheless, on the whole the data indicate that despite this dramatic seasonal shift in casual street behavior—from stares and averted eyes to smiles—it is still the rare encounter that develops beyond a quick "hi." Only one male respondent followed up a street meeting by asking the girl out, and in this instance both persons recognized each other as tenants of the same building. The few relationships that had evolved from casual neighborhood meetings in shops or laundromats or through a street encounter were viewed as eventful because they were so atypical. Quite unlike the college community, where it is implicitly taken for granted that socioeconomic background and social motives converge, in the city one has only the *appearance* of youth as a common bond, and even that may be highly suspect.

Making a Living

With reference to males, and in general cultural terms the concept of work, the preparations necessary for a life time work role and the behaviors essential for a successful performance in the occupational sphere are apparently well understood. These same things, however, are far more problematical for the educated woman. From data gathered from this sample, females may be placed in three categories, with some overlap: (1) the girl with a career obligation, one who has aspirations of developing her work role into a career, regardless of whether or not her particular college training was oriented to that end; (2) the female who views working as an "experience," who wants to gain satisfaction from her work and feel responsible, but who does not view this role as an end in itself or a lifetime career— likely to consider it as either temporary, until she marries, or as a definite secondary commitment to her primary future role as wife and mother (on the other hand, the career-committed girl tends to view the two roles as either comparable or complementary); (3) the girl who begrudges her work role, who would prefer not to have to work, either because she envisions herself as a wife and mother and not a worker, or simply because at this time in her life—and possibly for her entire lifetime—she is not ready to settle down to the responsibility of a job. In this category are girls who have not yet decided what they want to do with their lives. They may seek jobs that provide an extension to the moratorium on decision-making which characterized their college years; they may be, for example, waitresses or receptionists, working only to keep the body together.

Despite our claim that the work role for males is more culturally understood and accepted, nevertheless the males in this sample could also be placed into three categories with regard to their work orientation: (1) the conventional career-oriented male who seeks his successes within the corporate world or at least views success in traditional terms of prestige and financial gain; (2) the man who consciously rejects traditional work options and values and who works at temporary jobs—as a cab driver, in construction—with a concern primarily for minimal necessities, resembling, at this point, female type (3) above (also in this category are young men who attempt to gain satisfaction in non-middle class work situations, especially craftsmanship); (3) the male who straddles both worlds but belongs to neither. Typically craving material success, he lacks either talent or skill, or else his motivation to work—to conform to the exigencies of the corporate world—is low. Of the three types, this young graduate is most likely to find his work experiences highly frustrating, since it is unlikely that the type of job he is able to land or fulfill will, at the same time, satisfy his material cravings.

In a very real sense, however, the "straddler's" plight is shared, although to a lesser degree, by the typical graduate in the city, whether male or female. Some may be more, others less, concerned with the freedom only money can buy; but quite soon after graduation the majority confront what is perhaps one of this country's best-kept institutional secrets: a bachelor's degree is at best an admissions card to, not a guarantee of, upward mobility.

In *The Great Training Robbery*, Berger documents what the typical graduate objectively and subjectively experiences: the lack of fit between the proportion of educated persons in the United States and the number of jobs that call for such a background. It is not that certification in the form of a degree is without value but, that the elements of the certification process—socialization that encourages "creativity" and "responsibility" and unfolds within a relatively free and unstructured environment—do not in any significant way prepare the individual graduate for a work world in which creative and responsible positions are the exception rather than the rule, and where routinization prevails. While this reality both challenges and threatens the ego of the cream, it reveals above all the mediocrity of the crop. "Going to college" had previously been adequate testimony of personal worth; but simply "going to work" can soon provide evidence of abject failure.

Thus the typical graduate soon discovers that his or her job offers significantly less in the way of satisfaction or challenge than had been hoped for and, to a large extent, expected. In much the same way that personal associations have been documented as the major job satisfaction gained by blue-collar workers, so it is with these young urban graduates. And for the majority of the "contented-discontented," the status of young single and thus the necessary involvement in the meeting-mating process becomes an important

compensating factor, both as a measure of self-worth and as a competition for time and attention.

Friends and Dates

More than any other institution in the urban setting, the singles bar has received a disproportionate share of attention from the media. One has the image that young unmarried graduates rely almost solely upon the bar scene to establish the highly transitory relationships which seemingly form the underpinnings for the "sexual revolution": casual one-night stands in which females are sexually liberated to the point that their sexuality is that of the traditional male's. In Chicago such bars flourish in the Rush Street area in the first of the four residential areas discussed above.

From the data available, it appears that the typical graduate goes to singles bars only one or two nights a week, if then. These bars are, by and large, noisy; sitting is actively discouraged by an arrangement of narrow counters and a lack of seats; interaction is essentially nonverbal, especially at the point of attracting and initially establishing contact. But even this minimal contact with the stand-up bars would establish them as important settings in the singles panorama were it not for the fact that attendance at such places varies inversely with amount of time of residence in the city, and by the sixth month or so it is a fairly unusual woman who continues to frequent these places and establish her social contacts in this way. Certainly, by the time she is approaching the upper age point in this sample, twenty-five, the typical female has little use for this scene. Males may continue to go to swinging bars for a longer time. To understand this, it is merely necessary to differentiate between male and female sexual patterns and ignore the rhetoric of the sexual revolution. Males seek physical sex, or at least an environment which feeds their psychological fantasies, and since many high school educated females, e.g., secretaries, do frequent the swingers' bars, the age-old male pattern of having sex downward but marrying laterally or upward in the social spectrum is again played out in the urban setting. Using this same reasoning, male gay bars should and indeed do represent significant settings for meeting partners in the city, since a fair amount of the emphasis there is on the sexual side. There are a few lesbian-oriented bars in Chicago, but apparently far fewer than the number which cater to the male homosexual community. In summary, swinging bars are useful in the long run only if everyone is committed to swinging; or, in the case of upward-mobile women, they think that a certain proportion of sexual relationships which begin casually may well have a more permanent payoff.

Sit-down style bars, which abound in the more northerly parts of Chicago's North Side singles' area, get more of the long-term action, but it is a kind of action rarely mentioned in popular accounts of the single life style. In this sample, it is common to find women who frequent one or more of these bars, but they tend to define the crowd in terms of friends rather than potential dates. Thus, desiring conversation as they do, it is not uncommon to find young graduates in groups, with a date, or with a person of the same sex that they are interested in talking to.

Oue could argue that both styles of bars offer a nostalgic recreation of the college years in a peer-concentrated setting, but the payoff is more in terms of a feeling of security rather than actual dating relationships. In the case of the Rush Street bars, the security is apt to be hollow, since the scene tends to turn off these graduates with its contrived artificiality, the forced nature of the interaction patterns, and the highly strained and false conviviality so prevalent at most of them. Each bar has its following and thus its in-group which acts, for all intents and purposes, like a heterosexual fraternity. Since many of the regulars consist of persons with odd working hours—stewardesses, bartenders, waiters predominate—they are able to maintain this cliqueness in other settings, as, for example, having "their" section of Lake Michigan's Oak Street Beach for sunbathing during the week. However, most of the night-time regulars do not see each other outside of the bar setting. Most graduates, though, continuously refer to this scene as a "meat market" and the bar clientele as "plastic." For most persons are not aggressively or cosmetically suited for the kinds of interaction possible at these bars. Used to the informality of the college atmosphere, where "making it" just happened or involved only minimal effort, most graduates find the requirements for survival and success in the bar setting all the more repugnant.

If young urban graduates cannot establish dating relationships in the bars to any significant degree, where do they go? We have already discounted housing as a primary meeting-dating nexus. For a working person who spends his or her day at the office, interaction at home is likely to be restricted to the elevator or laundry room, the latter being the only facility in many buildings which could lend itself to this activity. But as one female graduate put it, recognizing that doing laundry is not one of the world's more delightful ways of spending an afternoon or evening, "I could go down there with all the beautiful people, but I like to get my laundry done in a hurry; I want to get it over with." Further, singles are a transient population and this fact reduces the probability of establishing lasting relationships in a building. But most significantly, a majority of graduates consider *home* as something private and inviolate. They do not like intrusions into their privacy; they do not wish to make the boundaries of their nest overly permeable. Thus many respondents reported that intrabuilding dating was "too close to home," that discontinued relationships could be awkward in such a setting. It was much more likely that graduates in this sample developed friends, rather than made dates, at or near their home bases.

Similarly, organizations do not appear to be significant sources of dating relationships in this sample. Other data indicate that persons in this age group are not volunteers to any great degree. Even those who were active in college find themselves unmotivated when it comes to seeking out organizations in the city. Comments such as "never get around to it" and "always seem to be busy" are common. Many do not perceive any great reward value from such associations, especially when compared to the payoffs from college associational involvement such as fraternities, student government, and the like. Comments indicating a kind of powerless alienation were also common; many felt they could have no significant effect on life through organizational activity in the city, whereas they had felt more intimately a part of the college community. More important, in college there was immediate recognition from peers that derived from such activities. In the city, where friends have scattered interests, there is no immediate and approving audience. Finally, formal voluntary organizations in a city like Chicago—for example, politics, antipollution groups, and those interested in the arts—tend to have a mixed membership including large numbers of married people. In short, they are not ideal ways to make dates and meet prospective mates.

But as places to meet dates, organizations fall short of the American ideal in the same way that buildings and bars do, for this ideal seems to stress *spontaneity* above all other values. The excitement which accompanies the American meeting-dating encounter seems to be centered on its accidental character. For the first twenty-one years of their lives, these graduates have been surrounded by their age peers and have rarely been forced to seek companionship. To do so now would involve a suspension of those values, and many are simply not prepared to take that step.

In passing, we should mention that parties are seldom cited by this sample as a vehicle for meeting dates. Partly this is because it takes time to establish enough contacts to guarantee invitations. Despite that, a majority of the graduates, even after having lived in the city for a period of time, either do not go to parties or find that they know most of the people at the parties they do attend. A number of comments to the effect that Chicago is a very clique-oriented city simply underscore the patterned nature of urban social interaction.

After eliminating most of the possible ways to meet dates, we are left with only one major alternative: the work situation. Among these respondents, work was the most frequently cited institutional setting for making friends and, indirectly, meeting persons of the opposite sex. And this should not be surprising, since it is at work that the average person spends most of his waking day; and due to the real requirements of the work role which were discussed previously, it is also the setting most likely to facilitate familiarity and emotional intimacy. By no means, however, does work automatically guarantee that a graduate will meet people. A necessary condition seems to be that the type of work bring the graduate into contact with persons who are not only close to him in age but also share his single status. Where the modal graduate finds himself in the exclusive company of fellow employees who are older or married, he is seldom able to develop close friendships. This fact, coupled with their odd working hours, may help explain the use of bars by many stewardesses

(and thus contributes to our understanding of their sexualized image in popular culture).

The relationship between work and dating is frequently a two-stage process. It is on the job that most graduates form friendships, much in line with the view of the city as a pattern of functionally, not spatially, interrelated people. They do not, by and large, date persons from the office for a number of reasons, among them, a lack of eligibles and the tendency to avoid social intimacy with persons one must face each day whether the relationship succeeded or failed. But through office friends, dates are arranged. It is, in short, a friend-of-a-friend pattern that provides the raw material out of which dating relationships are formed by the typical graduate in this sample.

Summary

Two predominant themes have emerged from this discussion of young, single college graduates in the city.

First, popular imagery, formed and reinforced by the media, is simply inaccurate in this case. There is little in the bars to attract these people, especially women. They are not leading (in most instances) a wildly free and sensual existence. Their apartment buildings are not re-creations of coeducational dormitories without housemothers. The graduates are people coping with the same problems we all face: finding a place to live, trying to get some satisfaction from a job, and seeking friends, dates, and ultimately mates in an environment for which they have been ill-prepared and which does not easily lend itself to stable human relationships. That they are coping is significant; that they are doing it as well as they are indicates a resiliency in the face of considerable odds. In short, our imagery should be reversed: these people are among those on the front-line of urban existence, combining as they do the usual goals of middle-class America—materialism, mating, and the like—without many of the usual institutional supports for their activities.

Second, we should reinforce something which has been a theme of urban studies for over a half-century but which has not captured its share of the literature or, especially, the methodology of urban studies: Turf, or place, or the housing environment is not a useful concept in undertanding the life styles of this large and growing rban subpopulation. To be sure, the retribalization or "new" pluralism used to describe urban minority actions during the past decade suggests that turf is still a viable concept, especially insofar as large and homogeneous urban subpopulations are residentially segregated and possess a similar consciousness. But the other side of Park, and of Durkheim and Simmel and many other urban students, should receive equal emphasis. For it is the way young graduates relate to the world of work, and the ways they form and dissolve friendships and establish associations out of work contexts, that does much to provide their stable anchors in the urban milieu. Perhaps Harvey Cox was being a bit hopeful when he proposed his two metaphors for the shape of *The Secular City:* "man at the giant switchboard" and "man at the cloverleaf"; but his basic point seems valid nonetheless. Emerging urban man must be studied as much in terms of his networks as his spaces. For these young graduates, at least, it is the former that provide his significant connections and form his sense of self and well-being, while the latter are becoming increasingly meaningless.

References

Becker, Howard S. *Outsiders.* New York: The Free Press, 1963.

Park, Robert. "The City: Suggestions for the Investigation of Human Behavior in the Urban Environment." *American Journal of Sociology* 32 (1926).

Park, Robert, Ernest W. Burgess, et al. *The City.* Chicago: University of Chicago Press, 1925.

Thomas, William I., and Florian Znaneicki. *The Polish Peasant in Europe and America.* Five volumes. Chicago: University of Chicago Press, 1918–1920.

Wirth, Louis. "Urbanism as a Way of Life." *American Journal of Sociology* 44 (1938).

Zorbaugh, Harvey W. *The Gold Coast and the Slum.* Chicago: University of Chicago Press, 1929.

19

WILLIAM KORNBLUM · PAUL LICHTER

Urban Gypsies and the Culture of Poverty

We need more studies of the social attitudes of criminals, of soldiers and sailors, of tavern life; and we should look at the evidence, not with a moralizing eye (Christ's poor were not always pretty), but with an eye for Brechtian values—the fatalism, the irony in the face of establishment homolies, the tenacity of self-preservation.

E. P. Thompson, *The Making of the English Working Class*

The remarkable achievement of the gypsies in Western societies is that they have maintained their traditional cultures and social structures despite all the pressures to assimilate which industrialized, urban societies bring to bear on foreigners. In the cities of Europe and America, where so many ethnic groups have struggled to win access to the social and material rewards of assimilation, the gypsies have resisted any temptation to compete for education, jobs, or rectitude in local communities. The gypsies continue to speak the language of the Rom, they maintain nomadic occupations, and they hold intact a patrimonial corporate family economy and a social structure based on endogamy. Unlike other diaspora peoples, the gypsies have never developed any but the most instrumental attachments to their host cultures. As nomads, wandering for centuries throughout Asia and Europe, the gypsies were never hunters or herdsmen who adapted to a difficult physical environment. Instead, they have been traders, tinkers, fortune-tellers, entertainers, and amiable conmen in a most human environment. This aspect of gypsy culture has been detailed in rural set-

tings, where gypsy families travelled throug the peasant lands of Central and Southern E rope, but in the city the gypsies are princes o the lumpenproletariat, and it is this special adaptation of gypsy culture which is our concer here.[1]

In general we do not support the theory tha there is a "culture of poverty" which organize the society of under-class urban people (Valen tine, 1968). Different groups adjust to povert with a wide range of adaptive strategies an world views, and no group values poverty itsel or makes it a desirable condition to wish upo its children. On the other hand, the gypsies ar an outstanding example of a people who hav spent generations in a milieu of great scarcit and whose culture allows them to survive an even flourish in relatively impoverished huma environments. In common with other unde class ethnic groups, the gypsy world view stresses values of individual and group surviva above all others. Among the recurring theme in gypsy thought are these: (1) the outside s ciety is corrupt and exploiting and should in tur be exploited whenever possible; (2) status pre tensions of group members and outsiders shoul be deflated, virtue cannot be maintained, an trust should be based on intimate knowledge personal biographies; (3) loyalty to the gyps

Reprinted from *Urban Life and Culture* Vol. 1, No. 3 (Oct. 1972), pp. 239–253 by permission of the Publisher, Sage Publications, Inc.

family must be maintained at all costs, for solidarity is essential to survival. Of course, in the gypsy world view, these themes are manifest in forms of expression and patterns of behavior which vary among culturally different gypsy subgroups in different urban situations. The present paper will describe how the main elements of the gypsy world view sustain gypsy society in the cities of France and the United States.

TWO GYPSY GROUPS:
THE BOYASH AND THE KALDERASH

The authors conducted field research in two settings: the first was among gypsies living on the industrial periphery of Paris; the second was among gypsies living in working-class neighborhoods of Seattle, Washington.[2] In the first case, the gypsies comprised a four-generation extended family, numbering approximately 87 persons. They made their base in a large, migrant shantytown, and although the family rarely moved en masse, it maintained a nomadic life style. Family members lived in their vehicles, and groups of them took frequent long trips through the French countryside. In the second case, in Seattle, the gypsies were more sedentary, although this is a matter of degree. The Seattle gypsies lived in private homes and tended to develop more prolonged attachments to some urban institutions than did the Parisian gypsies. On the other hand, the Seattle gypsies travelled widely throughout the West Coast states and could hardly be considered a sedentary people when compared to nongypsies.

The Parisian gypsies, whom the senior author was fortunate to meet and live with, are members of the Boyash group within the European Rom gypsies.[3] The Boyash are predominantly animal trainers and circus travellers who wander through Yugoslavia, Romania, and other Balkan countries. The Ivanovich family, the Boyash family with whom the senior author lived, included approximately 87 adults and children, almost all of whom were members of the extended family led by M. Ivanovich and his wife. Typical lodgings for the nuclear family units within the larger family were either traditional gypsy wagons or panel trucks and buses. These were grouped around separate courtyards which the family had appropriated in the migrant "bidonville." In addition to the actual gypsy family members, the Ivanoviches also offered their society and protection to a wide variety of hangers-on in the camp, including a number of superannuated prostitutes and French hobos (clochards). The latter were treated as servants who did much of the undesirable work around the camp, including cutting firewood for cooking stoves, and caring for the family's menagerie.

Animals are still the economic mainstay of the Boyash gypsies, and in large packing crates on the edge of their compound, the Ivanovich family housed a bear, two llamas, a pony, five monkeys, and assorted goats and dogs. Whenever money was needed, small groups of gypsy men and boys put on animal shows in the working-class market areas of Paris. In addition to these itinerant shows, family members also engaged in other economic activities, including some trade in gold, stolen auto parts, and used wagons. The Boyash women typically remain in the camp and do not go out to tell fortunes, as do the women of the Kalderash and other gypsy groups.

The Seattle gypsies, whom the junior author met as a welfare case worker, are members of the Kalderash group of Rom-speaking gypsies. The Kalderash are the largest of the Rom groups and comprise the majority of gypsies in cities of the United States. Perhaps the largest American gypsy colony is located in Brooklyn, N.Y., but other groups of Kalderash Rom live and travel in Chicago and Los Angeles and other large cities of the Southwest. The Seattle gypsies considered here belong to three extended families: the Stephens, the Millers, and the Georges. In Seattle, as elsewhere in the United States, the Kalderash gypsies do itinerant repair work on automobiles and some trading of autos.

Traditionally, the Kalderash were tinkers and repairers of metalware, and their ability to repair dented fenders is only one adaptation of this skill. In addition to metal-working, the Seattle Kalderash obtain much of their income by exploiting the welfare system. Since rather large numbers of related gypsies share the same name, it is easy to circulate children and otherwise claim larger benefits than are strictly due. Nevertheless, the Seattle gypsies live in one-family, rented houses and thus appear to their neighbors to conform to the American pattern of single-family dwelling and nuclear family organization. In reality, the gypsies associate exclusively with members of their extended family networks.

Neither the Parisian nor the Seattle gypsies

encourage their children to attend school at all, and the adults insist that gypsy language be spoken in the home. In consequence of this, most of the children and adolescents are illiterate. Like their parents, they must depend on a limited number of gypsy individuals in the families who can read. Of course illiteracy itself is not as important in creating dependence upon the extended family as is the fact that the children are rarely allowed to develop roles or peer relations in the outside community.

GYPSY WORLD VIEW AND THE LARGER SOCIETY: PARIS AND SEATTLE

Gypsies everywhere refer to nongypsies as "gadjé," a term similar in its nuances to "goy" or "ofay." The gadjé may be dangerous, they may be stupid, or they may be dangerously stupid, depending on their position in the larger society with respect to the gypsies. The world of the gadjo is a corrupt one, in which human exploitation is the rule, and the misery the gypsies have experienced is attributed to the exploitiveness of gadjo society. Beyond these common elements of the gypsy world view, the Boyash and Kalderash gypsies must deal with different urban institutions in metropolitan Paris and Seattle, and this necessity brings out contrasting modes of thought and behavior in the two groups. The Boyash gypsies most often deal with community political institutions, and they have developed to a fault the picaresque political style of under-class people. The Kalderash, on the other hand, are rarely visible in the urban communities where they live. On a regular basis, they deal only with the welfare system, and become extremely adept at working that system for their own benefit without becoming any more visible to the larger society.

In European cities, the Boyash gypsies are likely to live among other immigrant groups, particularly the Yugoslav, Algerian, and Spanish laborers who inhabit the migrant camps. The gypsies commonly travel between migrant camps, although they may make a more permanent base in a particular one. In consequence, the gypsies often find themselves considered part of a larger "social problem" in the urban communities where the camps are located. The gypsies and other migrants in the camps are often the subject of local ordinances and repressive actions by the police.[4] In reaction to hostile community officials, and given the difficulties of getting along with other nationality groups in a congested camp, Boyash gypsies place even greater stress on the need for internal solidarity than do the Kalderash. The Boyash gypsies often respond to repressive ordinances by becoming public figures, and by taking their case to sympathetic listeners in the press and in local government.

The situation of the American gypsies is quite different. As a group which exists in the proletarian backwaters of major cities, they have become less visible in the larger society just as the urban proletariat itself has receded into the background of American consciousness. Indeed, American gypsies have succeeded in becoming an almost secret culture. Even the most knowledgeable observers of the urban scene in Seattle are unaware of the existence of a gypsy community in the city. It is true that welfare officials notice gypsies who appear on the public assistance rolls. Most hospital personnel have also had experience with groups of gypsies who descend on the hospital to supervise the care of some important gypsy personage, usually claimed to be a king or queen of the gypsies.

In these instances, the gypsies use the outsiders' ignorance of their culture for instrumental purposes. For example, the claim that a hospitalized patients is a gypsy king or queen is usually sufficient to ensure that the patient receives special attention. In reality, however, the gypsies have no such monarchy, and the device is an elaborate public relations ploy designed to win concessions from local welfare institutions without making any concessions to the ethic of assimilation. In Europe, on the other hand, the conditions of gypsy life are still more difficult and it is often necessary for them actively to campaign for the right to maintain their traditional modes of existence.

The Boyash Style of Picaresque Politics

Since they lack power in urban communities, under-class groups develop political styles which rest on illusion and disarming attacks against conventional norms. To be "loud and wrong," to have "chutzpa," to "épater les bourgeois," and all statements of how to bluff and disarm the opposition when one is actually powerless. In the case of the Boyash gypsies, the politics of bluff and illusion are often carried to heights of the picaresque, as is apparent in the following episode from Parisian field notes:

The Boyash believe that they can train almost any animal, although their experience is limited to bears, goats, and monkeys, and their knowledge of other large animals is slim. Nevertheless, the elder Ivanovich convinced his sons and sons-in-law that they could add to their income and to the prestige of the family if they could procure and train an elephant. After mailing inquiries throughout their extensive network of contacts in European cities, they located a baby elephant for sale in Brussels. By calling in debts owed to them in the camp, and by selling some of their gold reserves, the family quickly raised the necessary cash. The senior Ivanovich and his three oldest sons left for Brussels at once to close the deal.

Once back at the camp on the edge of Paris, the elephant was installed in a large packing crate while the Ivanovich family congratulated themselves on the success of the venture. Other inhabitants of the bidonville—Algerians, Serbians, and Portuguese—flocked to the gypsy quarter to view this latest feat of the gypsies' ability to hustle and succeed. The elephant, along with the bear and other animals, was paraded through the camp regularly, and all other business came to a halt while the gypsies held center stage.

Three days later the elephant was dead, apparently the victim of careless worming by the former owner. Without delay the Ivanovich men armed themselves and rushed to Brussels to settle their debt. Before leaving, they and other members of the family dragged the elephant to an open space behind the camp. In their absence, it being the middle of a hot summer, the elephant began to cause serious concern among local health officials, who demanded that the gypsies bury the beast in a deep lime-filled pit. Since the adult men were gone, the gypsy women claimed that they would have to wait for their return, or else the township would have to dispose of the carcass. Four days passed, and this stalemate between the gypsy women and local officials continued. Photographers from *France-Soir* and other metropolitan newspapers brought the story to the attention of the larger city, while the mayor of the local township fumed and threatened to bulldoze the entire squatter settlement.

As the debate continued in the press and at the camp, the Ivanovich men made their second triumphal entrance, this time parading two adult llamas which they had accepted to make good on their loss. To inquiring reporters, the senior Ivanovich expressed concern that the township had not fulfilled its obligation to preserve the health of the community. He noted that he was in poor health and of advancing years. His eldest son had died the year before, leaving the family without its rightful heir, and his younger sons could not handle the job of digging a pit large enough to bury the carcass. All these interviews were conducted with a great deal of flourish and at such length as to make it difficult for township officials to speak with the gypsies alone. Usually the interviews climaxed with a parade of the new llamas, whose unique trait seemed to be a propensity to hiss and spit at admirers. By this time the story was being carried in "human interest" spots on the national television network, and the local officials were hardly in a position to carry out their threats.

In the end, the township sent a bulldozer to dig a large trench for the decaying elephant. The gypsies made a show of buying the lime and sprinkling it over the departed. It was only much later that M. Ivanovich discovered that his llamas were impossible to train for circus work. However, they did add another touch of the exotic for occasional parades.

The picaresque political style which the Ivanovich family has perfected seems necessary if their traditional corporate family economy is to remain intact. When travelling circuses were commonplace, the Boyash gypsies had little trouble showing their animals in city streets. Today, however, television and mass culture have made inroads into the audience for folk performances. More than ever before, the Boyash find it difficult to socialize their children into the traditional family occupations. Adolescent children feel shame at having to go into Paris with the older gypsy men to show the animals in the market places. They feel embarrassed at having to hold out a hat for donations and at being so often the object of laughter and scorn. But the Ivanovich world view reinforces their dependence on the extended gypsy family, and operates over time to bring the adolescents and young adults closer to the traditional gypsy values.

Within the family, shame and scorn are used to deflate illusions of personal status for the benefit of the entire group. For example, if a man or a woman is thought to be guilty of excessive pride, that person is upbraided in front of the entire family. If a protest is made, the common response from the senior Ivanovich couple is, for example, "Madame la Marquise, allez coucher dans ton chateau, ici nous sommes tous dans la misere"[5] (spoken in French rather than Rom for the added irony). This practice of using shame and cynicism to deflate illusions generalizes to all attitudes concerning the future. It is used in particular to describe the future of relations with the outside world, for family members believe the authorities will inevitably come to break up their camp, and therefore they must maintain their capacity to move out on short notice. They perceive the world of the gadjo as unstable and dependent for its order on arrangements among powerful actors. "Today we say vive le president," Madame Ivanovich explained. "Tomorrow we will say vive le roi, it's all the same to us."

Events in the gadjo world usually confirm the gypsies' cynicism and demonstrate to young gypsies the need to remain in the family. For example, during the abortive 1968 revolution in France, when Paris was crippled by general strikes and riots, the other migrant groups in the camp were forced to join the bread lines. The gypsies' major complain was the difficulty of obtaining cigarettes. Years of travel through the political states of Europe had prepared them for such events. They had only to call out their gold reserves and find sources of food through their wide-ranging contacts in the city in order to do quite well in this period of crisis in the gadjo society.

Kalderash Gypsies and Welfare Politics

The Seattle Kalderash strike a quite different stance with regard to the gadjo world. They place great emphasis on accumulating the trappings of material respectability, while making only the most minimal commitments to gadjo society. In part, this is possible because their traditional crafts more readily lend themselves to adaptation in American cities than would those of the Boyash gypsies. Also, opportunities abound in this society for the Kalderash gypsies to do well by seeming to the gadjé to do poorly.

Kalderash men engage in automobile body repairs, roofing, stove cleaning in restaurants, and other short-term jobs which do not result in any extensive personal or financial commitment between gypsy and employer. In almost all cases, the work is contracted and paid for by cash, so that the Seattle gypsy does not experience payroll deductions for Social Security or income tax, and no records of the transactions exist. This is particularly desirable for segments of the Kalderash families who are simultaneously receiving unemployment compensation or public assistance. Some Kalderash families also add to their level of living through the use or misuse of credit. If a family plans to move soon, they may have goods delivered to them at home under a false name, and large phone bills are accumulated in the process of communicating with far-flung kin. At times, it is possible to buy expensive items (color TVs, furniture and the like) on time under false names and abscond with them after making the down payment. Housing, too, can be had cheaply if the family makes a deposit, moves in, and pays no more rent until they are evicted and move some place else. These practices are not universal among Seattle's Kalderash gypsies; a large proportion pay their bills and conduct their business affairs quite conventionally. However, the instances of fraud cited here occur in a larger percentage of gypsy families than in most other ethnic groups. And it is the cultural premeditation of these activities which distinguishes gypsies from others who operate in terms of chance and opportunism.

These instances of conflict with gadjo society maintain the gypsy sense of community which, in turn, further isolates them from the respectable mainstream of American life. But the Kalderash do not perceive these situations as creating either personal or communal tension, for these are merely local adaptations of time-worn cultural practices. In the rural gypsy world view as described by Yoors (1967:34):

stealing from Gadjé was not really a misdeed as long as it was limited to the taking of basic necessities, and not in larger quantities than were needed at that moment. It was the intrusion of a sense of greed, in itself, that made stealing wrong, for it made men slaves to unnecessary appetites or to their desire for possessions. Gleaning a little dry wood for the fire, from the forest, was no misdeed. There was so much of it, and anyway if they did not take it it was left to rot. Putting a few horses to pasture overnight in someone's meadow was not that bad. Grass grew without the owner's active contribution or effort.

Urban gypsies in the United States often take an equivalent position with regard to the bountiful social environment created by American welfare institutions. In a forest of bureaus and branch offices, with so many transient gadjé who want to give help in such small amounts compared to the great riches elsewhere in the city, it is almost impossible to resist the temptation to glean supplementary incomes from the welfare institutions. The welfare system is grounded in principles of egalitarian liberalism and functions according to a bureaucratic methodology that is designed to treat all clients in a similar manner. But the Kalderash do not relate to established authority like "all clients." Their approach to the welfare system involves the creation of situations of quiet chaos for administrators and caseworkers. Since job turnover among these officials is quite high, it becomes almost impossible to sort out the record of aid to gypsies who do not have birth certificates, marriage certificates, or Social Security numbers, and yet maintain extremely large, extended families. The Kalderash gypsies' relation to the welfare system on the West Coast is evident in the following correspondence from the general manager of a large office of public assistance in California to the director of the Seattle-King County Central Office.

Dear Mr. M.—:
Enclosed please find Xeroxed copy of gypsy "family trees" recently compiled by this worker, who is presently responsible for all aid to Families with Dependent Children Gypsy families in —. It is believed this information may be useful to you and your Index office to forestall possible duplication of aid to these highly transient people.

Although almost all of the George families, underlined in red, are highly transient, worker is, at the moment, specifically concerned about the three children of Catherine George, presently sharing the same address. These are: Rachel (George) Mitchell, Case No. 533–038, mother of Jerry, date of birth 9/29/60: Tammy George, Case No. 624–152, mother of Baca, 9/29/60; Susie, 10/8/64; Peaches, 7/31/61; Ginny, 4/1/68; and Nana, 8/1/69; and Dina (Efram) Marks, Case No. 531–393, mother of Unda, 8/8/64.

The other families who have used the George residence temporarily while claiming aid, all of whom have left town within a week or two, are (see Xeroxed sheets), the Ruby George family, the Bobbie George family, the Lizzie Miller family, the Mary Miller family, the Rosie Miller family, the Steve and Ruby George family, the Tina George family and another Ruby George family. Actually almost all of the Miller-George families noted on the sheets attached, are, and have been highly transient. Please note, on page 9, the Steve and Majorie George family and the Ron and Ann Miller family placed out of order on page 6. They are somehow related to the Rita Miller family, bottom of page 8, who is reportedly receiving aid at the present in Portland, Oregon.

Worker has no doubt that if the families are, as reported, moving up and down the Western coast, applying for aid, they will be returning within a week or so claiming never to have left town.

Thank you for any assistance you can provide in this matter.

The family trees which "worker" compiled demonstrate the futility of attempting to trace the movements of Kalderash gypsies in the United States. The documents are crammed with page after page of names, birth dates, last known addresses, and suspected kin ties. In general, they are so confused as to make it impossible to have any confidence in the records, and the project itself becomes another instance of the effectiveness with which the gypsies manage their relationships with gadjé institutions. Also, there is no mention here of possible causes for Kalderash abuses of the welfare system. For their part, the Seattle gypsies often justify abuses of the welfare system on the grounds that laws making fortune-telling illegal in most cities deprive their women of their traditional means of earning a livelihood. And to make matters more difficult for welfare caseworkers, gypsy dealings with offices of public assistance tend to increase the amount of feuding which normally exists between large gypsy families.[6]

The Seattle gypsies often attempt to displace pressure from welfare officials onto other families with whom they are feuding. Such feuds are commonplace and may be due to quarrels over bride price, between competing fortune-telling shops, or other family rivalries. It is tempting to use the welfare system as a weapon in these quarrels by suggesting to caseworkers that another family may be abusing the system. These violations of in-group solidarity increase the level of bickering between gypsy families and in some instances act to increase dependence on the system itself. In general, the more the Kalderash gypsies struggle to retain their welfare benefits, the more they come to believe that the benefits are essential and must be maintained.

CONCLUSION

Of all the cultures which have encountered the assimilating pressures of modern, urban societies, the gypsy's has been perhaps the most self-sustaining. Rather than accept values from the dominant society, the tenacity of gypsy culture depends in large part on a specific rejection of those values. What Marcuse has called the "great refusal" of lumpenproletariat groups to become attached to the dominant institutions of the larger society has been a feature of gypsy culture for centuries. The Kalderash, the Boyash, the Lovara, and other Rom groups will continue to look with a cynical eye at the enticements Western societies offer to groups which assimilate. On the other hand, this research has demonstrated that the Boyash gypsies in France and the Kalderash gypsies in the United States must cope with quite different urban institutions. Although assimilation itself may be minimal for both gypsy groups, contrasting urban environments in Paris and Seattle call forth different adaptive strategies which themselves should have lasting effects on the survival of gypsy culture and the gypsy world view.

The Parisian gypsies' style of bluff and illusion in dealings with urban political institutions readily lends itself to further political organization among gypsies in general. As the Boyash take on public political roles, they also begin to select leaders who can represent more than one extended family. These are usually men and women who have had experiences such as described for the Ivanovich family, and whose advice in similar situations is sought after by other gypsy families in the city. It is not surprising, therefore, that in Paris and other European cities the gypsies have begun to organize ethnic political organizations whose activities are designed to win concessions which allow the gypsies to maintain their traditional life style. In contrast to the growng nationalism of European gypsies, gypsies in the United States are quite reluctant to assume public political roles or to do anything which draws attention to themselves. Thus Kalderash gypsies in Seattle attempt to limit their dealings with gadjo institutions to the welfare system, while remaining largely unknown as a people elsewhere in the city. The ease with which funds can be had from offices of public assistance, and the dependence the relationship fosters may eventually be inimical to the traditional mobility and independence of gypsy cultures.

Notes

1. The best general works on the gypsies, although they deal almost exclusively with rural, nomadic gypsies, are Clebert (1967) and Yoors (1967). Two journals chronicle the movement of European gypsies; they are *The Journal of the Gypsy Lore Society* (London), and *Etudes Tsiganes* (Bulletin de l'Association Des Etudes Tsiganes, Paris).

2. Kornblum lived with the Boyash gypsies in Paris for two months during 1968 and has conducted interviews with informants on gypsy cultures since that time. Lichter worked in Seattle as a volunteer caseworker for gypsy families during 1971.

3. Lang (1966) provides a good summary of materials on gypsy ethnicity.

4. One of the many ironies of this political conflict is the fact that the industrial suburbs of Paris, such as Saint Denis and La Courneuve, are often administered by elected officials of the French Communist Party. Debates within local party organizations over the treatment of gypsies and other migrant groups often are reduced to ideo-

logical conflict between Stalinist and Maoist factions in local governments.

5. "Your highness the Marquess, you go sleep in your castle, here the rest of us are down and out."

6. The subject of feuding among gypsy families deserves more attention than can be given to it in this paper. Solidarity among gypsy subgroups usually does not extend very far beyond the patrilocal extended families and long-standing feuds between gypsy families of different or the same subgroups are common.

References

Clebert, J. P. (1967) The Gypsies. Baltimore: Penguin.

Lang, F. (1966) "Tsiganes, gitanes, romanichels et autres distinctions." Etudes Tsiganes 6 (June): 11–22.

Valentine, C. A. (1968) Culture and Poverty. Chicago: Univ. of Chicago Press.

Yoors, J. (1967) The Gypsies. New York: Simon & Schuster.

20

WILLIAM ERICKSON

The Social Organization of an Urban Commune

The commune described in this account is one of the oldest, if not the oldest, urban commune in the United States. It is a religious commune located in a midwestern metropolis. Here it will be called Shalom,[1] not its real name, but indicative of the basic commitment to pacifism held by the group. What follows is a descriptive account of Shalom's basic features with regard to organizational structure and activities.

From a conventional sociological perspective, Shalom would be conceptualized as a sect, in the church-sect typology as conceived by E. Troeltsch, H. R. Niebuhr, B. Wilson, *et al.* Among other things, a sect displays characteristics of a closed social system. Indeed, any commune—sect or not—is likely to have the characteristics of a closed system. What emerges as sociologically interesting is not that Shalom *is* a sect but how sectarian commitment is maintained in the open environment of an urban area. Similarly, a basic sociological concern with all urban communes has to do with understanding how communal commitment is maintained in an open system environment. The following sketch of organizational structures and activities only begins to allude to this question of sectarian or communal identity maintenance. But it does show rather clearly that one particular sectarian commune

Reprinted from *Urban Life and Culture* Vol. 2, No. 2 (July 1973), pp. 231–256 by permission of the Publisher, Sage Publications, Inc.
AUTHOR'S NOTE: Materials reported here are drawn from my dissertation, *An Urban Commune As a Quasi-Kindred*, Department of Sociology, University of Illinois, Chicago Circle, 1971. Issues of identity maintenance alluded to in this article are treated in much greater detail in the larger study.

does operate as a closed system despite its members' daily and substantial interaction with the urban open system which surrounds them.

Before proceeding to actual description, a few preliminary comments of a methodological sort are appropriate. The data were collected as part of a larger field observation project. Field work was carried out over a nine-month period during which a number of techniques were employed—structured questionnaires, structured and non-structured interviews of an informant and respondent sort, structured and non-structured observation, and document content analyses. The description of committee structure and activities is based primarily on interview data. However, as the description turns to religious-cultural activities, the data are more dependent on observations, as I participated in many of those activities.

Since the present account does not include reports of systematic data quality controls, some general statements are in place. In any field observational research, the balance between ethnocentrism and "going native" is a major issue of data quality (for example, McCall and Simmons, 1969: 128–141). Frequently the resolution of this tension is idealized as some sort of mediation, balance or compromise. Realistically though, these opposing biases will be situational and persistent. Some observations will be biased one way and some the other. However, it appears that there is a curvilinear life-cycle for these biases. That is, early in a project, ethnocentrism is more likely; in mid-life, "going native" is more likely; and as the researcher comes to data collection closure and proceeds to his analysis he may return to ethnocentrism to maintain objectivity.

From the point of view of the native partici-
ants, a concurrent but converse pattern of re-
ctive effects probably occurs. That is, even
hough we usually think of reactive effects in
erms of the presence of the researcher it is the
erceptions of the natives that are at issue.
arly in the research they are likely to react to
he researcher as an ousider; in mid-life of the
roject they will have come to accept him; and
hen as closure approaches, they are likely to
eact as they had done earlier. In evaluation re-
earch, this last stage is most likely a conse-
uence of fears about the upcoming evaluative
eport. In the case of field work in an organiza-
on such as Shalom, it is more likely to be due
o mutual rejection, since a participant observer
, in some sense, a potential recruit. Whatever
he case, the mid-project data are the least biased
y reactive effects and most biased by "going
ative." "Going native" gains access to "back
age" regions but also may color the re-
archer's description. My account, as with any
hnographic account, will be more dependent on
he mid-cycle data than the early or late cycle.
his fact should be kept in mind by the reader,
irticularly as we proceed to description of the
isic features of religious life at Shalom.

THE HISTORICAL AND DEMOGRAPHIC
ACKGROUND OF SHALOM

lalom was established at its present metropoli-
n location in 1957 by a group of people who
ere disenchanted with their experiences with
ganized Christianity. As frequently happens
hen the source of discontent is perceived to
e structural as well as ideological, the future
lalomites and others formed small cells where
more personal sort of interaction could be
aintained. These "encounter groups" were
lled *koinonia* groups, *koinonia* being the word
ployed in the Greek New Testament for "fel-
wship." Among other things, the use of origi-
l terminology from the Early Christian comunity indicates an attempt to innovate their
urch infrastructurally by a return to "original"
rms rather than by radicalizing it. The koin-
ia groups included members of a town-gown
mmunity associated with a denominational
llege and seminary located in a small Mid-
estern town. One of the original Shalom mem-
rs had been a faculty member in the Theology

Department at the school. In the seminal period he seems to have been the initiative force,
but given the convention of consensual decision-
making, it would be simplistic to consider him
the initiator or *the* leader.

In the early years, effective recruitment was
primarily among those who had an Anabaptist religious background. All but one of the original
members were Mennonite. The members' dissent centered around their belief that the 16th
century Anabaptist spirit of social dissent—for
example, pacifism—and the literal view of "discipleship" had weakened in their Church bodies.[2]
Their original intent was to live out their beliefs
by providing a "Church home" for conscientious
military objectors doing alternative service at a
nearby hospital. They also felt it was possible
to have a "positive" stabilizing influence on a
physically deteriorating and racially changing urban neighborhood. They formed an economic
collective because they felt it not only was efficient, but was indeed the only way they could
avoid the organizational tendencies they were
protesting.

The original group included three married couples, two children and four unmarried adults.
They purchased a large house and lived collectively. Shortly thereafter they purchased a second home, as can be seen on the map (Figure
1). They continued to acquire buildings as their
numbers grew to over thirty adults and over
fifty children at the time of the study. In 1971
they also purchased a farm some two-three hours
distant from Shalom.

Like many inhabitants of today's metropolises,
the early Shalom members had rural and small
town backgrounds. But unlike many immigrants, they were highly educated. At the time
of my study, all adult members had at least a
high school education. In addition, nineteen of
these were college graduates and of these, eleven
had graduate degrees. The mean age of the
adults was thirty-five and a number of them were
fairly well established in occupational careers.[3]
Most were gainfully employed in occupations
outside of the commune, primarily in service occupations—teachers, social workers, mental
health workers and so on—and at the time of the
fieldwork three adult members had withdrawn
from the labor market and were pursuing full-
time studies. As with education level, the occupational prestige level of the employed members
was above average—more than 90% were in occu-

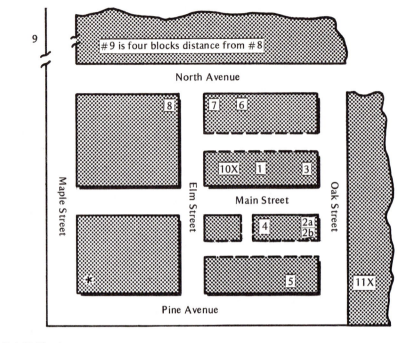

Unit Utilization

        1 = Meeting House, single females, Nursery
2a, 3, 4, 8 = Two Family Unit, Coffee House
       2b = PlayHouse (Renovated 4 car garage)
        5 = One Family Unit
        6 = One Family, single males
        7 = One Family, guest apartment, single males
        9 = Four Family Unit
      10X = Rental Unit for one family
      11X = Rented facility for record/book business

Designates functional
alleys traversed in
Shalom interaction

*What appears to be vacant land is not. This area is completely built up with houses and apartment buildings but to highlight Shalom facilities, other structures were left out of the map. Street names are fictitious.

Figure 1. *A Map of Shalom Property**

pations ranked above average on the Hodge "scale" (Hodge, et al.: 1964).

II. FORMAL STRUCTURE AND ORGANIZATION ACTIVITIES

Shalom continued its initial orientation to economic collectivism, and even after it began recruiting members from a variety of non-Anabaptist backgrounds, the original religious culture continued fairly intact. Obviously, many factor are involved in the maintenance of that cultur Selective recruitment criteria, along with drawn-out recruitment process allowing for su plemental socialization (if not resocializatio during "probation," partially explains such mai tenance success. The conservative influence consensual decision-making, which reduced th rate of innovation, could also be a factor. F present purposes, however, the maintenanc "success" of Shalom will merely be indicate through a description of the group's elaborated social organization. No systematic attempt to explain this success will be made.

The organizational complexity of Shalom can be inferred from Figure 1, the map of its housing units. No corporation, which Shalom legally is, could evolve as it has without developing considerable structure or patterned activity. For example, when the group began, it was small in number and owned only one building—No. 1 on the map. Some fifteen years later, Shalom had nine buildings, all but one of them suitable for multiple family occupancy. If nothing else, the financial arrangements associated with nine mortgages demanded formal organization that surely had not been envisioned in the early meetings of an encounter sort. Similarly, the diffusion of members geographically, concurrent with their growing numbers, required reorganization into submits where intensive interaction could be sustained. Originally, all members took all meals communally. At the time of the study this practice had been reduced to one weekly communal meal for the adults. The fact of geographic diffusion also makes clear that Shalom's closed system character is not due to ecological isolation in some sort of bounteried compound. If it is a closed system, it must be so in terms of interaction, not geography. All of these aspects, hinted at in the map, will become clearer as the actual arrangements are described.

Economics

One of the basic arrangements relevant to any corporation has to do with money: how it is obtained and how it is used, internally and externally. Shalom's basic income was provided by the eighteen employed adults who earned an estimated $150,000 a year or an individual average of about $8,000. In keeping with their system of total collectivity, wage-earners turned over their entire pay to the sub-unit to which they were attached.[4] From this fund, each family or single individual received a food and clothing subsidy, the specific amount being determined by the public welfare schedule used in their county of residence. The amounts were prorated according to the number of family members and the ages of the children. Thus, irrespective of actual earnings, each family lived on the same prorated income base.

Beyond these general allocation arrangements, there were some fairly complex aspects of fiscal distribution within the overall organization, which can be elaborated by reference to the flow of funds diagrammed in Figure 2 and to the description of interdependence contained in Figure 3. Once the subgroup received the member wages they were distributed as follows: The first portion, family allowance, remained constant except for adjustments for new offspring and changing ages. A second portion, incidental expenditures, varied from month to month, but most such expenditures were predetermined. For example, a medical expense did not require a group decision, it was automatically paid. Certain other types of emergency expenditures, however, were brought to the group's attention to be decided on a case by case basis. A third portion of the sub-group's fund was turned over to the "corporation" or Shalom as a whole. This portion was a constant amount which covered the cost of the "rent" for homes occupied by subgroup members and automobiles used by them. A fourth portion was turned over to the "Fellowship," their church. As was the corporation, the church was viewed as a distinct organizational entity. The amount allocated to the Fellowship was a set assessment analogous to an automatic tithe system. For the most part, then, the four types of allocation decisions were patterned. But the arrangements did involve considerable bookkeeping activity. Each sub-group had one or more persons involved in this task and even though it was a rationalized and/or routinized activity, it consumed a fair amount of time.

The above description can be clarified by describing economics from the perspective of the member. The basic material needs of the individual are exhaustively covered in the various arrangements. The resources for food, clothing, housing, transportation and medical care are provided systematically. Items such as furniture and appliances are also provided by, and owned by, the corporation. Television sets and musical instruments are not considered necessities, though widely found at Shalom, and are purchased out of personal food and clothing subsidies. The notion of necessity seems to be defined in terms of sustenance and responsibility. For example, a member who receives a traffic ticket pays for it himself. One who lives simply and carefully, has his needs met, but one who

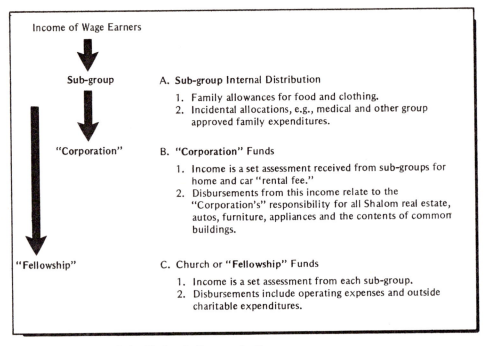

Figure 2. *The Flow of Funds in Shalom's Economic Structure*

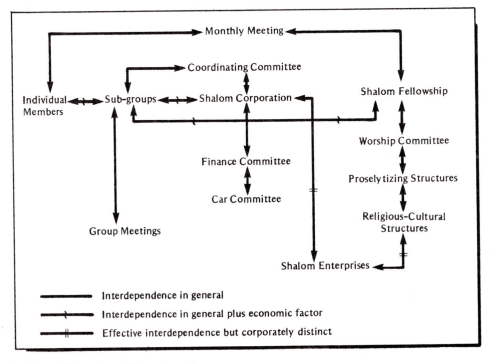

Figure 3. *Formal Structural Interdependence*

fails to avoid certain common contingencies of urban life, might indeed run into financial trouble. This is not to say that extraordinary expenditures or special circumstances are ignored by the sub-group. Each member has informal opportunity for presenting a financial appeal. In classic communistic fashion, the underlying rationale is "to each according to his need" rather than according to his contribution.

This description of economic arrangements might give the false impression that members' life-style was uniform. It is true that gross economic variation, say from abject poverty to opulence, did not exist. But there was no uniformity of dress, and there was no uniformity in food styles. Since usual factors, such as income, need and class variation, do not account for this lack of uniformity, the observed differences would appear to be consequences of variation in personal preference and in budgeting skills. Whatever the case, members themselves did not perceive one another in terms of relative class or stylistic differences. In many interview situations, I found that members simply had not been attentive to the symbols that had drawn my attention to differences among their lifestyles.

Economic Committee Structure

Both Figures 2 and 3 include references to the Shalom "Corporation." This entity held legal title to the real estate and to the automobiles shared by the members. These two types of property are reflected in the two committees under the corporation, the financial committee and the car committee respectively. In addition, economic activities were also carried on in the 'Fellowship' component of the organization but in that entity, the allocation of received monies was not handled by a separate committee. For the most part, the worship committee handled the monies and facilitated the decision-making relative to external charitable expenditures. Since there was no formal elaboration of economic structure under the Fellowship, only the finance and car committees of the corporation will be described here.

Finance Committee. As mentioned, the real estate holdings of Shalom are considerable. A conservative estimate of their worth would be $50,000.00. The percentage of equity obviously

varied, since some buildings were more recently obtained than others. The finances related to these mortgages and the maintenance of these properties were the concerns of the finance committee. This five-member committee was also responsible for numerous tasks associated with allocations not covered by sub-group disbursements. For example, committee members were responsible for keeping records for each family. The specific records involved were those used for income tax filing. Shalom members did not use their collectivism and incorporation as a nonprofit organization as a tax shelter. Therefore, they required meticulous records in order to avoid disadvantage in taxation. The finance committee also has partial involvement in a Coffee House and a day nursery run by Shalom, as well as in a record and book distributorship owned jointly by them and Fellowship Farm.[5] In these and other situations it was not a policy committee. Policy and major *ad hoc* decisions were referred to the entire membership at Monthly Meetings.

Car Committee. Ecologically concerned readers may be impressed by the fact that Shalom members pooled cars and had about two families per car rather than two cars per family. On the other hand, the sheer logistics of sharing automobiles may not seem so inviting. These logistics necessitated that a distinct car committee exist. The committee had two members, with responsibility for purchasing automobiles and deciding about and making arrangements for major maintenance and repairs. In addition, they had established a system for keeping track of member requests for extended use of autos. For example, during holiday periods, the requests for autos for extended trips could exceed availability. The committee not only received the requests but also adjudicated them. However, on a day-to-day basis, members made their car arrangements informally, as would be done in any family.

In brief, the economic arrangements at Shalom are complex. They clearly indicate a closed-system in their breadth and complexity, generating considerable formal organization both in terms of policy and committee structure. But the policies are primarily facilitative and subject to flexible interpretation. Similarly the structural aspects do not involve the existence of committees for their own sake or for some coopting purpose such as providing a "sense" of involvement. Committees do function to maintain member commitment but that is not their primary ostensible function. They are working rather than meeting groups and their labors are on-going activities, like the activities of the money handler(s) in any family. What meetings they do have are primarily concerned with developing their report to the Monthly Meeting. By reporting, they in a sense defer to that meeting. But with their considerable responsibility we would have to infer considerable power. In this respect, note should be made of the customary finding in organization analyses that responsibility and power are directly associated with length of membership. At the time of the field work, the mean length of membership in Shalom was 6.8 years, for the personnel of the finance committee, it was 8.3 years and for those on the car committee, 11 years.

Coordinating Arrangements

Originally the structure of Shalom was less complex, in that the total membership met together and made all decisions. With growth, certain functions continued to be allocated to existing committees. But when three sub-groups were formed, additional formal structure had to be elaborated if coordination were to continue. Part of the confusion in describing the formal structure is due to the fact that when these sub-groups were formed, the existing structure was expanded rather than reorganized. Thus, the way in which components interrelate is often confounded by the level of analysis, be it individual, sub-group, or the total organization.

The Coordinating Committee had two members from each of the three subgroups. The six met twice monthly and the representatives reported on the activities and concerns of their respective groups. In addition, other committees had access to and reported to the Coordinating Committee for purposes of establishing the agenda for the Monthly Meeting. The meeting of the Coordinating Committee was not closed to the general membership but such attendance was the exception.

An overall organizational chart of Shalom, as found in Figure 3, is a graphic display of the interdependence of the various formal structures and the intervening position of the Coordinating Committee. The mean length of tenure in Sha-

lom of the members of this commitee was 8.33 years, or, by member, 14, 12, 9, 8, 5 and 2 years. The committee's intervening location in the chart and the length of Shalom membership are indicators of the "power" of this group. Among other things, the Coordinating Committee was uniquely positioned to focus the Monthly Meeting. Even though decision-making by community consensus was the process ostensibly utilized, this process needs to be viewed in the light of overall formal structure. Paul Harrison, in an analysis of decision-making and power structures in a Free Church organization which emphasized autonomy of the local congregation, concluded that the effective power actually lay in the centralized church headquarters (1959). This finding and the small groups literature, generally, suggest that a similar analysis of Shalom might lead to the conclusion that while consensual decision-making is what is "believed," decisions may actually be being made by a smaller group, such as the Coordinating Committee.

Shalom Enterprises

Two additional structures are corporately distinct but not separate from Shalom, and relate to religious aspects of the commune that will be described in the next section. The first structure is the Shalom Day Nursery. This preschool nursery and day-care center was state licensed and authorized to care for 18 children. The Nursery was located on the first floor of the building that served as a meeting and worship facility. Space was rented from the Corporation at the rate of $150 per month, such payment reflecting the corporate separation. On the other hand, the Nursery Committee or the Board of the Nursery had three members, all Shalomites. Other member involvements included the Nursery bookkeeper who did this work gratis and who was also the "Corporation" bookkeeper. Social casework for establishing fees charged students' families was done—also gratis—by a social worker who was a Shalomite. Another member, a clinical psychologist, provided free consultation and occasional counseling to the clients. These interlocking involvements illustrate the informal ties that existed between the Corporation and the Day Nursery.

The actual operation of the nursery school was the responsibility of two female members of the commune. One of them had initiated the idea and established the program when she found herself occupationally unfulfilled. Other members had supported her in her decision to quit the job she disliked and facilitated the development of the nursery to fulfill her aspirations. Those aspirations are partially reflected in the Nursery's policy of charging the area's many economically troubled, one-parent families on an ability-to-pay basis rather than serving only those who could afford the set rate. The facilities were also available to member families who probably could not afford such service out of their food and clothing subsidy, the going rate in the area for such child-care facilities being $20–$25 per week, per full-day child.

One other member was employed "within" the overall Shalom organization. He worked half-time as a property manager, doing a variety of managing and maintenance tasks that are inevitable in nine buildings of some age. His other half-time job was that of manager of the phonograph record and book distributorship co-owned with Fellowship Farm. The "Farm" was founded by a Southern-Baptist theologian who attempted to protest the racism he found in Christian churches. It is located in the deep South and has been organized as a commune for over 30 years. Besides introducing scientific farming procedures to that area and establishing a racially integrated community, the founder also translated the New Testament from Greek to a 'folksy' English version entitled "The Cotton Patch Version of the New Testament." His books, recordings of his addresses, and a book written by the "initiator" of Shalom represent the sorts of materials distributed by the distributorship.

The business was neither a profit making nor a profit seeking enterprise. It was, rather, one of the means by which Shalom conveyed its message to outsiders. It had customers, including individuals and such institutions as churches, throughout Canada and the United States. In the view of the manager, economic profit or nonprofit was not an issue. He saw the cooperative effort with "Fellowship Farm" as a way of experiencing communalism with those outside of Shalom. Indeed, the Farm was one of the communes that comprised the network of communes with which Shalom identified and with which it made ongoing social exchanges. The substance of the published material expressed a perspective

that defined the basis of this network, frequently spoken of as "being the body of Christ." All of the materials involved some variation on this theme.

III. RELIGIOUS-CULTURAL ARRANGEMENTS

The centrality of religious matters at Shalom has already been indicated. Most simply put, religious activities were central to everyday life. As could be expected, some of these activities were structured or formalized and others were incidental to daily existence. From a Shalomite viewpoint, compartmentalization of activities or functional spheres is undesirable. From that viewpoint, nothing is only religious and everything is religiously imbued. Thus, a complete description of the group's religious life would be a total description of their total activity. Such, of course, is not possible. What follows is a description of the more patterned aspects of religion at Shalom. As such, it only begins to illuminate their culture.

Worship Committee

The basic formal religious structure revolved around the Worship Commitee. It had charge of all of the arrangements for worship activities at Shalom's Sunday morning meeting. Historically, it had designed the format of those meetings. On an ongoing basis, it determined the weekly content. The format observed during the period of the study had been established only a few years. A description of it is the best way to understand the tasks of the commitee and, at the same time, to gain insight into the religious culture of Shalom. The two to two-and-a-half hour Sunday morning meeting was comprised of three distinct sections. There was, first, a 20 to 30 minute period of singing. Three members tended to share the leadership of this section on a rotating basis. The leader for a particular week would select the songs and if necessary instruct the participants as well as lead them. The songbooks ordinarily used included a traditional hymnal of a non-liturgical Protestant denomination, a Roman Catholic folk-youth collection, and a Shalom Songbook, which included a variety of

Figure 4. *Types and Targets of Communicated Concerns*

	Self	PERSONAL Nuclear Fam.	Biol. Kin	Shalom	Supra Kindred	Other	Total
Petitional	0	0	4[a]	6	4	5	19
Informational	8	4	4	21	5	6	48
	8	4	8	27	9	11	67

[a] Two of these were offered by a third party.

religious songs focusing on decisions for radical commitment and simplicity of life-style.

The second section of the meeting involved the sharing of 'concerns and thanksgivings.' For the most part this was handled by three members. As with the songleading, the task was rotated but not in a patterned fashion. Ordinarily, one of them would move to the front or central area of the meeting and ask those present to express their 'concerns and thanksgivings.' Both members and visitors were invited to do so. Occasionally, a brief transitional address would precede the appeal for participation. 'Concerns and 'thanksgivings' took two basic forms. In Figure 4, the concerns I noted are divided into petitional and informational categories. Petitional items involve a request for a specific prayer or a request that the community 'be concerned' with something specific. Informational items take the form of announcements of some event or situation. Whether petitional or informational, the 'concerns and thanksgivings' further varied in terms of: (1) concern with issues personal to the speaker; (2) concern with Shalom; (3) concern with other communes in Shalom's network;[6] and (4) concern with other matters. The concrete concerns expressed involved illness, accidents, reasons for joy, meetings of people interested in radical Christianity, references to current events ranging from local to international matters, and so on. During my field work, each member shared information at least once and some did so virtually every week. Usually when no more participation seemed likely, the leader would summarize that day's items or key ones in the form of a prayer.

The third section of the "worship meeting" was more structured. Most Sundays it involved the

acting out of a drama. During the year of my fieldwork, the group traced the history of Western Christian radicalism in their dramas. In the previous two years, they had presented dramas depicting Old Testament and New Testament episodes. The dramas were written, directed and acted out by community members. The religious personages and movements depicted in the dramas are listed in Figure 5. They are categorized as sectarian or nonsectarian and scored for consistency (that is, for affirmation of sectarians and renunciation of nonsectarians) in terms of the general line taken in the script and post-presentation discussion. Even readers who have a good general historical knowledge will surely recognize less than a majority of the personages. The "obscurity" of many of them raises basic points about the maintenance of a radical identity. It seems plausible that, in this regard, the dramas performed a basic function. But for our present purposes, the relative "obscurity" indicates the elaborate research that must have gone into the development of these dramas. For the most part, they were written by two members who were theologically trained. Once completed, they were reproduced in sufficient copies for the number of parts to be played. Then the casting was coordinated by a member who was a highschool English instructor. The only rehearsal occurred about one hour before the actual meeting time. Following each presentation, there was a "study" or discussion period focusing on some aspect relevant to the historico-religious content of the drama. In no way was there a systematic attempt to integrate whatever had emerged in the previous sections, but occasionally such attempts would be made on an impromptu basis.

Figure 5. *Dramaturgical History*

Personage	Sectarian	Non-Sectarian	Affirmation	Renunciation	Mixed	Mixed	Consistency
Constantine		X		X			X
Eusebius		X		X			X
St. Francis of Assisi	X		X				X
St. Augustine		X	X[a]				0
Joan of Arc	X		X[b]				X
Bernard of Clairvoux	X		X				X
Peter of Bruys	X		X				X
Arnold of Brescia	X		X				X
Peter Waldo	X		X				X
John Huss	X		X				X
Martin Luther		X[c]		X[b]			X
Conrad Grebel	X		X				X
Ulrich Zwingli		X[c]			X		X
Hans Denk	X		X				X
Jacob Wideman	X		X				X
Peter Chelcicky	X		X				X
John Rokycarna		X			X		X
Oliver Cromwell		X[c]			X		X
Thomas Lurting	X		X				X
George Fox	X		X				X
Felix Manz	X		X				X
Niklaus Billeter		X		X			X
William Penn	X		X				X
John Wesley	X		X				X
John Woolman	X		X				X
Herman Francke	X		X				X
William Spener	X		X				X
Erasmus		X		X			X
Calvinist movement		X		X[b]			X
Counter Reformation Catholic movement		X		X[b]			X
Christopher Sower	X		X				X
James Logan	X			X			0
Total	21	11	21	8	3	0	30/32
% Sect. and Non-Sect. Personages and Movements	66%	34%					

[a] Augustine was affirmed because he gave up a life of "sexual promiscuity" and his churchliness was not at issue in the drama.

[b] Since a film was involved here, the scoring involves the post-film discussion only.

[c] These so-called reformers are classified in terms of their eventual position rather than in terms of initial breaks from the status quo of their day. In each of these cases this is how the Shalom presentation dealt with them.

This description of the three sections of the 'worship meeting' hopefully provides insight into the centrality of religion at Shalom as well as a better understanding of the kind of perspective found there. It also highlights the amount of community energy that necessarily was involved in planning and preparing such weekly events. In this respect, the Worship Commitee was similar to the previous committees discussed. However, their on-going activities also required the participation of most Shalom members at some time or another.

From the perspective of the community, the functions of the "worship meeting" were multiple. To some degree, the meeting involved external proselytizing, in that the public was welcome to attend, although no overt publicizing attempts were made. More centrally though, it functioned as an internal arrangement whereby the "worship and instruction" needs of the members were met. Indeed, this latter was the consistently verbalized purpose of the meeting. Simultaneously, it served as a vehicle for sharing internal information about sub-group phenomena or for circulating notice of external affairs of potential interest to members. Given members' geographic diffusion and separation into three sub-groups, this had obvious import for over-all solidarity. The content of the songs and dramas also expressed a solidarity that was acted out religiously and socially.

Sub-Group Meetings

Twice each week, members gathered together in their particular sub-groups. Attendance at these Sunday and Wednesday evening meetings was expected, if not "mandatory." The members, however, showed no sense of obligatory involvement. In this respect, the sub-group meetings were a basic opportunity for individual involvement in the community.

Sub-group meetings lasted about two hours. Sunday evening meetings were open to select visitors and to persons in a probationary status, called 'intentional neighbors'—people who had moved into the immediate area with the intent of considering and being considered for membership. Wednesday meetings were closed to all but actual members.

Sunday meetings in one of the two groups I attended involved group discussion led by a member who assumed a teacher-leader role. Two or three of the male participants assumed this role during my visits. The topics of discussion were always religious, specifically 'radical-Christian' in their content. Sometimes there was discussion of biblical themes, sometimes, of ethical issues. In the other observed group, the format was more or less a version of an encounter group. The convention was to gather in silence and wait for individuals to speak up, as in a Quaker meeting. Both sub-groups sang religious songs at every Sunday meeting and ordinarily, some time was provided for making announcements and sharing concerns which were beyond the focus of the given meeting. In extraordinary cases, sub-group business, too pressing to wait for Wednesday evening, was dealt with on Sundays. But even in the absence of pressing business, neither group's format was so rigid as to preclude situational inputs. There were no formal leaders in either group, but some emerged as such in the on-going interaction. Even so, no one was excluded from the topic initiation process and, indeed, all members participated to varying degrees.

As indicated, the Wednesday evening meetings were, without exception, closed to outsiders. Therefore, my information on them is based on informant interviews and on my reconstruction of references picked up in other settings, such as piecing together items that were raised at Sunday meetings but that referred to Wednesday meetings. A part of the Wednesday meetings seemed to be used for 'coming to clarity' on decisions about important issues, such as one sub-group's decision to buy a farm. Also, the ongoing business of the group was dealt with at this meeting. The culturally relevant activity of Wednesday, however, seemed to be "mutual criticism"[7] and encounter sessions. Shalom's culture specified that members who had grievances with other members, or mutual criticisms, were to follow a specific sequence, which, as they saw it, was outlined in the New Testament, Matthew 18. First, they were to talk with the individual. If resolution of the conflict was not forthcoming, they were then to bring it before the sub-group and if this did not resolve the issue, it was to be taken before the total community at the Monthly Meeting. Not only private grievances between individuals were handled in this way. A member who evidenced lack of solidarity with the group, for example, might be called to account for his behavior and asked to change it. The considerable amount of counseling that took place within the community was an adjunct to these group meetings. Counseling was not necessarily a sub-group activity, but did seem to be most closely tied to the purposes of

he sub-group meetings. Counseling variously
dealt with familial issues such as family interaction and child-rearing; personal issues such as
family interaction and child-rearing; personal
issues such as premarital and/or sexual phenomena or personal adjustment; and community
issues such as the reduction of commitment to
Shalom.

Theoretically, the sub-groups were fairly autonomous, in terms of both economic and re-
gious-cultural issues. But the emphasis on
community consensual decision-making constrained this theoretic autonomy, as did such
formal organizational structures as the Coordinating Committee.

Proselytizing Arrangements

Every ideological and/or religious organization
has arrangements for handling recruitment, public relations and the explanation of themselves
to outsiders. Shalom had a number of such arrangements, both formal and informal.

The weekly Coffee House was the clearest arrangement for telling outsiders about the group's
conception of community and religious faith.
Each Friday night, the basement and rear section
of one of the large homes were opened to the
public as a coffee house. The basement area was
furnished with a number of tables and lounging-
conversing settings. It was populated with numerous homemade candles of various shapes,
sizes and scents. Memorabilia of rural living
and traditional Americana were on the walls and
tables and hanging from the ceiling. From 9:00
p.m. to usually no later than 1:00 a.m., people
gathered for small group conversation in this
basement portion of the Coffee House. Around
:30 or so, an announcement was made that
entertainment was about to begin in the back of
the house—in the "Playhouse" (building No. 2
in the map). Some would leave the basement
and join those who had initially gathered in the
Playhouse, which also was set up with tables for
small groups. The combined attendance was 50–
0 persons per night.

The Coffee House was initiated and essentially
run by a couple who were deeply involved in performing music. They were assisted primarily
two other couples and a few of the community
managers. Those most intimately involved were
from one sub-group and even though the op-

erating budget was provided by the "Fellowship," the Coffee House was, in effect, a project
of this sub-group. Besides the entertainment,
there were numerous tasks associated with serving guests who were provided unlimited free
beverages (soda, coffee or tea), popcorn and a
variety of home-made sweets or baked goods.

Members were always on hand to talk with
visitors, whether strangers or acquaintances.
Particularly in the case of strangers, they engaged in information-imparting discussion. Always they had the eventual concern with 'where
the person is at' religiously. Some members
rarely, if ever, attended the Coffee House.
Others came basically when they had some non-
Shalom friends visiting, and yet others were always present. The main function of the Friday
night event, like Shalom life generally, was
clearly religious in nature. The songs were not
always religious and the conversations could
not all be characterized as having to do with
religion. But, as one member put it, "we don't
advertise the location of the coffee house because the type of people we are interested in are
more likely to find out by word of mouth." He
went on to explain that the "type of people" he
referred to were those who had basic religious
concerns.

The visitation program was another arrangement that involved recruitment and informational activities. People from a roughly thou-
sand-mile radius visited for periods of several
days to a week. These visitors were selected
according to their apparent religious sincerity
and their interest in communalism. In an interview with the member who was processing the
correspondence from prospective visitors, I
asked what he would do if one asked to visit
without making clear one's intentions. He said
he would write back for more information. I
then asked what would happen if a prospective
visitor indicated a non-religious basis for his interest in communalism. He replied that it would
be unlikely for the request to be granted.

After requests were processed by the Correspondence Officer and visitation was agreed to,
the details of housing and arrangements for
meals were turned over to one of the three sub-
groups. (Visitors were accommodated in a
guest apartment reserved for this purpose as
well as for accommodating friends.) Every
third week, one of the sub-groups was responsible for visitors. The actual mechanics were

often worked out by impromptu volunteers from a gathering such as a sub-group meeting. Beyond these basic amenities, informal arrangements were made in terms of who would spend time with the visitors and, often, to what end.

Similar in purpose to the above, but distinct, was a "program" of visitation by Shalom members to a myriad of communal conferences throughout the U.S. and Canada. (Here might also be included the speakers bureau function performed by Shalom representatives who occasionally spoke at local church organizations and social service agencies in their metropolitan area.) Again, most of these requests were processed initially by the Correspondence Officer. In distant and long-term trips the Financial Committee and the Car Committee were also involved.

In summary, the religious-cultural structures are somewhat more diffuse and difficult to specify than the economic arrangements. But they are elaborate, indeed, and in many ways fit the usual criteria of formality.

IV. AN ANALYTIC POSTSCRIPT

I have briefly described the economic, religious and cultural aspects of an urban commune. The description tends to emphasize structured and recurrent aspects and activities rather than day in and day out interaction among members. For all of the related shortcomings, such an account is necessary to sociological ethnography if comparison with existing sociological accounts is to be made. Many existing accounts of comparable organizations, such as families, churches and businesses, deal with their structures and recurrent activities. By comparison, Shalom is as complex as a small business, more complex than a similar size church and infinitely more complex than other family networks with a similar number of nuclear units—14 families and seven single adults.

Going beyond the present organizational description, it may be analytically relevant to conceive of Shalom as a kind of familial organization; specifically as a "quasi-kindred" (Farber, 1964), as an organization that performs many of the functions traditionally performed by biological kindred. For that matter, *most* urban communes may be seen as unique and specific responses to some of the oft-cited structural

changes associated with mobile and nucleated families. Many such communes go beyond nucleation to some form of group marriage or tribal family whereby conjugal unit are not retained. Shalom, however, represents a different sort of quasi-kindred, even though most of its members have experienced the geographic separation from biological kin. It has retained a very distinctive nuclear family unit and a very traditional value system with regard to marriage and family. Nonetheless, it is a quasi-kindred in that the total organization serves as a surrogate kindred for the component nuclear units.

Put another way, while members affirm traditional familial values, like many urban and mobile families, they do not sustain a high level of interaction with their extended biologic families. The parents of the adult members live an average of 650 miles from the commune. The reported exchange of visits amounts to only 1.2 visits per year. In the literature on kinship there is no clear data base line for visitation exchange rates. However, the findings consistently reflect higher rates than those found at Shalom. But in terms of their quasi-kindred—exchange with all fellow members—a wholly different exchange rate emerges. They are, indeed, in constant exchange with these "kindred." This is simply another way of indicating that Shalom is a closed network; that is, its members are relatively self-sufficient in terms of basic familial social "needs" as well as in terms of economic and religious "needs." The organizational account provided here describes the organizational means for maintaining such a closed system. Most newly emergent social forms in our urban society would undoubtedly involve less elaborated structure. But the account of Shalom reminds us that whenever new forms, counter forms, sects, communes, or quasi-kindred emerge, they persist if, and only if, the needs of the members are met. The payoff frequently will be in terms of informal or elementary social interaction (Homans, 1962). Such is the likely path to pursue if we want to obtain meaningful sociological understanding of the numerous urban enclaves where social change is occurring in our society.

Notes

1. The name Shalom and all other names in this article are pseudonyms.

2. The norm of "discipleship" adopted by the group is a literal interpretation of the Sermon on the Mount in the New Testament, Matthew 5–7.

3. That they are occupationally established is not true in the usual sociological sense of career commitment, because at Shalom, the community decides what a member will do occupationally and commitment to one's profession is viewed as negative and is informally but persistently discouraged. The members see commitments, such as professional ones, as inconsistent with total commitment to "radical Christianity" and to Shalom.

4. The offspring who earn money do not turn it over because they are not members. Similar to the Anabaptist emphasis on adult religious commitment, Shalom has deemed it inappropriate to consider offspring members by ascription. Since children cannot make a religious commitment, they cannot make a Shalom commitment and, therefore, are not subject to its economic collective rules with regard to their earnings. My references to "members" should always be read as referring to adults and not to children. The latter are involved in none of the activities described herein, except for part of the Sunday morning worship meeting.

5. Fellowship Farm is another long-term commune. It is referred to below.

6. Such as "Fellowship Farm."

7. In many ways Shalom handles internal conflict as did the Oneidans, who called their process "mutual criticism."

References

Farber, B. (1964) Family Organization and Interaction. San Francisco: Chandler.

Harrison, P. M. (1969) Authority and Power in the Free Church Tradition. Princeton: Princeton Univ. Press.

Hodge, R. W. and P. M. Seigel and P. Rossi (1964) "Occupational prestige in the United States, 1925–1963." Amer. J. of Sociology 70 (November): 286–302.

Homans, G. (1961) Social Behavior: Its Elementary Forms. New York: Harcourt, Brace & World.

McCall, G. J. and J. L. Simmons [eds.] (1969) Issues in Participant Observation. Reading, Mass.: Addison-Wesley.

Niebuhr, R. H. (1954) The Social Sources of Denominationalism. Hamden, Conn.: Shoe String.

Troeltsch, E. (1931) The Social Teaching of the Christian Churches (O. Wyan, trans.). London: George Allen & Unwin.

Wilson, B. R. (1959) "An analysis of sect development." Amer. Soc. Rev. 24 (February): 3–15.

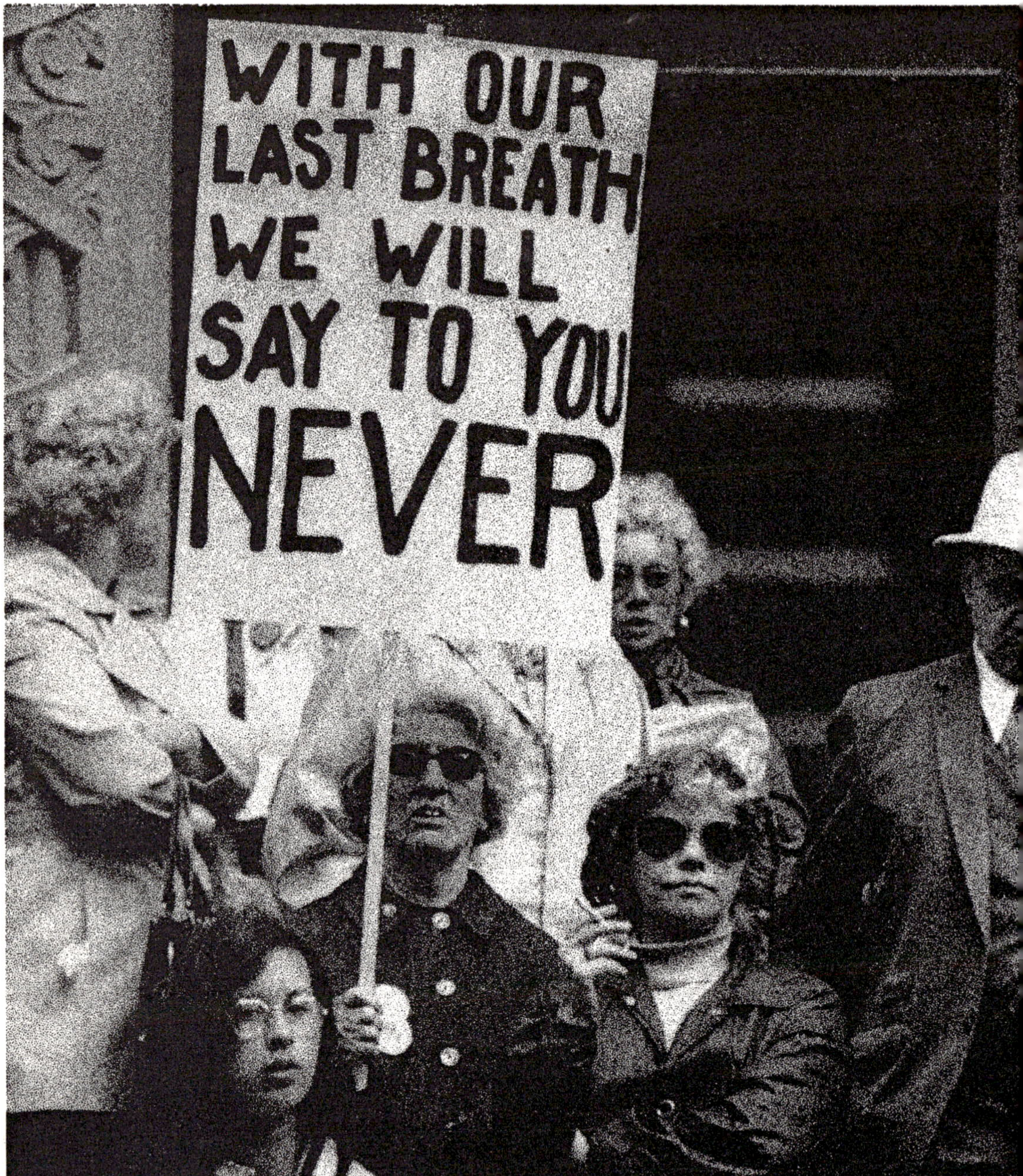
WITH OUR
LAST BREATH
WE WILL
SAY TO YOU
NEVER

contents

politics and control

the subject of urban politics constitutes another central theme in this volume. We have chosen politics as a key consideration because we believe, and hope to demonstrate, that urban problems such as education, segregation, collective violence, fiscal crises, and even the physical layout of cities are ultimately political questions. That is, they have their origins and take shape in conflicts among groups with divergent interests and differing amounts of power or the ability to realize their own will. This is not to say that the political process "determines all." On the contrary, patterns of urban politics are influenced by historical and legal characteristics of cities, their location and economic function, as well as the (racial or ethnic) composition of the population and the distinctive life styles that emerge from these influences. We would stress that the political process is more than a mere resultant of these forces, but a factor of equal importance interacting in complex ways with the themes we have considered thus far.

The chapter begins with two pieces on power and decision making which are paired contrasts. A long and lively debate has gone on over the structure of community power: whether U.S. cities should be described as "elitist" or "pluralist." The former position, expressed in Floyd Hunter's classic *Community Power Structure*, held that decision making power was held by a relatively small group of business and political leaders who exercised control over a variety of issue areas. By contrast, the award-winning book of Robert Dahl, *Who Governs*, and its proponents maintained that political influence in U.S. cities was broadly dispersed among citizen groups that formed shifting coalitions around different issues.

The two articles attempt to characterize this controversy and provide some answers to central questions. John Walton's original essay corrects many of the prevailing misconceptions about Hunter's pioneering work and, thereby, tries to show that much of the controversy involved attacks on straw men. He goes on to suggest certain points the two schools have in common and how these may illuminate the analysis of public issues. If Walton's essay is, in some sense, a defense of Hunter and the elitists, the article by Frank Munger puts the pluralist position in its best, nonpolemical, light. Munger explains that the myth of a tightly controlled urban elite breaks down as one begins to discover a variety of roles in the exercise of power and a variety of forms of political action. Once again it may be useful for the student to think about some of the ways these seemingly conflicting positions actually can complement one another.

In recent years the notion of "political culture" has been popular among political scientists. Exponents of this view argue that cities, like countries, have unique cultures or styles of doing things. Analyses of these styles, rather than of particular policy makers, is therefore a more definitive way of accounting for what gets done in the policy arena. James Q. Wilson's sparkling account of the political culture of Southern California is both good reading and good social science. Essentially he argues that to understand the often bizarre and unpredictable political behavior of this segment of the country, one must appreciate its ecological and social interaction patterns. In this piece we have a good example of the interplay between life styles and politics; how each influences the other. Further, it may be useful to compare and contrast Wilson's analysis with San Francisco's "culture of civility" as described by Becker and Horowitz in Chapter 5. How do these two California cities differ in their political cultures? Why? What difference does it seem to make?

Moving to another level of the political process, we take up next the participation of rank-and-file or grass-roots community groups. In the late 1960s "community control" became the rallying cry of many neighborhood and ghetto groups. Some felt that community control could encourage more democratic participation at the local level and, thereby, solve many urban problems. Focusing on the question of urban education, the most active area of community control strategies, we are able to portray citizen participation in some detail. Marilyn Gittell's article provides background to the movement for community control of schools as well as several case studies of how the strategy operated in experimental programs. Because these were short-lived and under constant political attack their effectiveness is hard to evaluate. Nevertheless, Gittell feels that they showed promise and deserve to be tried on a broader scale. But, apropos of this chapter's theme, such efforts encounter the resistance of politically powerful entrenched bureaucracies.

In a more radical analysis of the community control issue Stanley Aronowitz argues dialectically that the movement may encourage localism at the expense of broader alliances among neighborhoods and classes that are necessary to confront state and corporate centralization. Interestingly he suggests that issues like health care may be more effective vehicles for political mobilization than education.

So far we have dealt with groups that exhibit to some degree the ability to exercise influence in the urban political process. But this should not lead us to any false optimism about the power of urban residents to ameliorate social ills. The two concluding selections in the chapter demonstrate the powerlessness of groups drawn from very different positions of the social spectrum. Robert Blauner judiciously draws certain parallels between subjugated colonial peoples and the problems of American ghetto communities. While the similarities are far from precise, American ghettos are economically controlled by external interests; profits earned in ghetto business are extracted and invested elsewhere. Similarly political authority and key institutions, e.g., police and schools, are imposed and controlled from the outside. Blauner goes on to analyze ghetto rebellion, cultural nationalism, and community control movements as a response to the "colonial situation."

Finally, Harvey Molotch shows that the black, poor, and "colonized" are not the only victims of powerful economic and political interests. Following a disastrous oil spill on the beaches of Santa Barbara, California, a group of middle class concerned citizens and environmentalists organized to prevent further risky oil drilling offshore. Despite their political skills, organization, and access to technical specialists, their efforts were to no avail. Large corporations with high-level political support carried on as before.

Chapter 6 provides analyses of the process and consequences of urban decision making viewed from several perspectives. Certainly the conclusions to be drawn from these selections vary. They reflect, for example, cases of power structures more and less accessible to citizen influence, forms of grass-roots organization that are more and less effective at influencing public policy, and the kinds of issues or vested interests that are more and less implacable in the face of challenges for reform. For analytic purposes we would suggest that these dimensions—the power structure, the organization of reform groups, and the nature of the issues or stakes in the conflict—can be employed to characterize a variety of urban political struggles and their probable outcomes. The student might want to select a political conflict in some city he or she is acquainted with (e.g., a conflict over schools, zoning or new construction, highway construction, welfare, or whatever) and then consider how much can be said about the conflict, how much can be predicted about its outcome, just by filling in the information called for by these three dimensions. Assuming, as we must, that the exercise will not answer all of the important questions, one will then have a sense of the new avenues that need to be explored to improve our understanding of urban politics.

21

JOHN WALTON

The Bearing of Social Science Research on Public Issues: Floyd Hunter and the Study of Power

An issue of increasing importance in social science concerns the interrelationship of research and public policy. Although the issue is not entirely of recent origin, it has become particularly salient in the last few years as a result of the expanding scope of research endeavors and the advent of new opportunities for social scientists to examine, if not advise on, policy-related problems. As one observer has forcefully put it, "At long last, social science has come on center stage in American society."[1]

This change has been looked upon with mixed feelings. Optimistic appraisals view it as an opportunity to enlighten and rationalize public policy, while pessimistic assessments fear cooption by or the disingenuous use of research for the benefit of special political interests. Certain hardbitten "realists" seem to feel that both of these positions are naïve and that social research does not make a hell of a lot of difference one way or the other. The normative and empirical problems presented by these developments are extremely complex, and so far, our experience may be too limited to yield any generalizations. Thus, any discussion of the topic is well advised to limit its scope and deal with problems about which there is some relatively unambiguous information.[2]

The general topic of the interrelationship between research and public policy can be approached in three ways. The first concerns the question of how social science might influence policy: whether it can have some useful effect, how much effect, under what circumstances, and with what perils. A second, and perhaps more manageable approach, is how public policy

influences social science: from a sociology of knowledge standpoint, how policies affecting research grants or the availability of information help shape the content and orientation of social science. A third approach is to focus more specifically on the methods social scientists have actually used to examine public issues. Although less inclusive than the first-named approaches, this tack does allow one to get down to cases and assess the utility of current methods for generating some understanding of public issues.

The third approach is adopted in the present essay. One reason for that choice is that the questions it raises logically precede some of the other issues. That is, the question of how social science might influence policy must await an answer to the prior question, "Is social science ready?"[3] Is it, in specific areas, capable of generating understandings which the responsible social scientist would be willing to stand by as policy directives? It is one thing to decry willy-nilly policy-making that is uninformed by evidence concerning likely outcomes; it is quite another to presume that contemporary social science has a large stockpile of such evidence ready to deliver to any nonperverse policy-maker. In short, our first concern should be an assessment of specific research areas to determine whether the accumulated evidence suggests directives that bear on policy issues. Here it is reasonable to assume we shall encounter a good deal of variation. For example, we probably now possess more policy-related evidence on racial prejudice than on the consequences of rapid urbanization.

A second reason for adopting the present approach rests on substantive rather than logical considerations. Fortunately, there exists an extensive research literature devoted to the study of community power and decision-making.[4] An assessment of this field, particularly the cumulative contribution of a great many studies since 1953, when Floyd Hunter began this kind of work, will provide a unique and direct illustration of the bearing of social research on public issues.[5]

Floyd Hunter's Contribution

In 1953, Floyd Hunter published his classic work, *Community Power Structure: A Study of Decision Makers.*[6] A minimal yet interesting criterion of why this book can be called a classic is that it was Hunter who coined the term "power structure" which has now so thoroughly infused the vocabularies of social scientists and political activists.

There are, however, more compelling reasons for placing this work among a small handful of modern sociological classics, reasons which were never properly understood or which became obscured in the controversies that followed from Hunter's study. In the first place, it was a pioneering work, an original item. As Bonjean and Olson observe, "Prior to 1953 and the publication of Floyd Hunter's *Community Power Structure,* the question "Who governs?" was answered in much the same manner by both social scientists and the lay public.'"[7] With a true craftsman's skill, Hunter independently fashioned a set of research techniques that represented the first systematic approach to the study of power and that continued to undergird conemporary research designs.[8]

In its time, *Community Power Structure* was also a unique example of macrosociological research. Rather than focusing on a gang, a factory, or a prison, Hunter took on a major American city of half a million people.

The principal purpose of the book was also bold. Hunter's opening paragraph makes this clear:[9]

It has been evident to the writer for some years that policies on vital matters affecting community life seem to appear suddenly. They are acted upon; but with no precise knowledge on the part of the majority of citizens as to how these policies originated or by whom they are really sponsored. Much is done, but much is left undone. Some of the things done appear to be manipulated to the advantage of relatively few.

The purpose of the study, then, was to identify the leaders and patterns of power (i.e., leadership, groupings and methods of exercising power) that would explain how the policies just mentioned were decided upon and implemented.

Hunter's study of Atlanta, George, answers these questions in several fundamental themes. Because these findings have been so widely misunderstood or misinterpreted by subsequent critics, they will be succinctly put forth here.

1. Hunter employed a variety of specific techniques for identifying leaders and policy-making processes. The first involved questioning a panel of expert or knowledgeable community residents from a variety of institutional areas about who were the most important people in town when it came to getting things done. On the basis of these nominations, and for practical reasons, Hunter first arbitrarily took the top forty persons as policy-making leaders and examined their occupations, positions, and organizational affiliations. These leaders represented the following occupational categories: eleven commerce; seven banking, finance, or insurance; six professional (five were lawyers); five manufacturing and industry; five leisure (social leaders); four government; two labor. Six of the forty were women, concentrated mainly in leisure. Thus, as a first approximation of local leadership structure, Hunter concluded that business interests were most frequently represented; twenty-three of forty or, if lawyers are included, twenty-eight of forty, were from the business community. It is important to note at this stage that the judges making these selections were not themselves from business but represented a broad range of local organizations.

2. The next step in Hunter's method was to interview twenty-seven of the top forty leaders to determine their selections.[10] Answers to the simple question "Who is the biggest man in town?" and the request to rank the ten most important persons produced a rank-order of influence. The result was a high degree of consensus between procedures (1) and (2).

3. A third distinctive technique sought to de

ermine whether those persons listed actually onstituted social groups. To answer the quesion, Hunter employed three separate socioietric measures. First, leaders were asked, Who might best decide on a project?" This proiuced a clustering of mutual choices or "socioietric nets." The second index asked leaders ow well they knew other leaders. Third, a more bjective measure of interaction was employed iat ranked leaders on interlocking club memerships. The conclusion Hunter drew from iese separate measures was that the leaders did, ideed form social groups, they knew and interated with one another and, further, they also ormed among themselves smaller cliques or crowds." Finally, and most important, these ata showed that the leaders were organized ito "higher and lower limits groups" that played istinctive roles in the policy-making process, ie higher groups more respossible for policy ormulation and the lower for policy execution.
4. Rather than accepting these measures as efinitive, however, Hunter pressed further for formation on the policy-making process. In a iapter entitled "Projects, Issues and Policy," he :amined five specific issues to determine paterns of decision-making (the city's Plan of Delopment, traffic control, the sales tax question, ie Voter's Plan, and the Negro question). This stinctive method is often overlooked, perhaps ecause it appears after he had discussed the ineral structure of power. Nevertheless, it is ear that his study of actual issues informed at earlier discussion. For example, specific reference is made earlier to the Plan of Development as a prototypical policy decision.
5. From the use of these complementary ethods and a process of "triangulation," inter reached his major substantive conclusions. The leadership process is carried out by oups with differential power playing different les. A relatively small group of top policyakers, drawn largely from the business comunity, tend to formulate policy, while a much rger group of "understructure personnel" are arged with policy implementation. Across isies there is more "overlap" (multiple-issue rticipation) by top leaders than by understrucre personnel, who tend to be specialists coned to single-issue areas. Later, the same kinds distinctions are made using four levels of inence. Of fundamental importance, however, is : fact that the *same set* of leaders *do not* make policy decisions in all areas; they simply exhibit a greater degree of multiple-issue participation than lesser influentials. Hunter was most explicit about this when he talked of *multiple pyramids* of power with changing constituencies across issues. For example, he clearly states:[11]

. . . I doubt seriously that power forms a single pyramid with any nicety in a community the size of Regional City. There are *pyramids* of power in this community which seem more important to the present discussion than *a* pyramid.

and later:[12]

In the above illustration of structural action, the "men of independent decision" are a relatively small group. The "executors of policy" may run into the hundreds. This pattern of a relatively small decision-making group working through a larger under-structure is a reality, and if data were available, the total personnel involved in a major community project might possibly form a pyramid of power, but the constituency of the pyramid would change according to the project being acted upon.

As though to make the point incapable of misinterpretation Hunter goes on to provide several diagrams of how these constituencies and their leadership shift with issues.
6. In a final summary of the argument, Hunter endeavors to clarify the point that his leadership group is not to be confused with the entire business community or the upper classes:[13]

Each man mentioned as belonging to a crowd also belongs to a major business enterprise within the community—at least the clique leader does. His position within the bureaucratic structure of his business almost automatically makes him a community leader, if he wishes to become one. The test for admission to this circle of decision-makers is almost wholly a man's position in the business community in Reigonal City . . . Society prestige and deference to wealth are not among the primary criteria for admission to the upper ranks of the decision-makers according to the study of Regional City.

In short, the power of the leaders derives from their business organizational position, *not* from wealth or prestige, and leaders are those top business position occupants who *choose* to become involved in local decision-making.

7. In addition to these central themes, *Community Power Structure* uniquely explored several other areas. Given again that the study was conducted in the early 1950s, two of these were particularly prophetic: the study of the black subcommunity, and the state and national impact on local politics. These cannot be discussed in detail, but suffice it to say that a final virtue of Hunter's method was that it reached out upward and downward to identify constraints on and consequences of urban decision-making. In the case of the "Negro subcommunity," Hunter found that its top leaders knew and interacted with only second echelon decision-makers. He also saw this situation as changing:

The traditional methods of suppression and coercion are failing.[14]

The Negro citizenry is becoming increasingly organized, however, and the politicians are paying more attention to the demands of this group.[15]

In this instance policy formerly settled is being challenged by a group which is organized to a point where its voice must be heard, and the older methods of intimidation and coercion against this group are no longer effective. Many of the Negro leaders are relatively secure financially, and their own positions of leadership are threatened within their community if they remain subservient to the dominant group.[16]

Having produced this analysis prior to the emergence of Martin Luther King's organizational efforts in Atlanta, Hunter demonstrated perceptive and prophetic insights that are exceeding rare in social science. Once again, for this alone Floyd Hunter's work is classic.

Development of the Field

Perhaps the most relevant criterion for judging the importance of a contribution to social science is the amount of subsequent research it stimulates. In this respect Hunter's legacy is impressive. In the twenty years since *Community Power Structure* appeared, more than 500 books and articles have been written on the topic, some critical in commentary and some original studies of one or several communities and the literature continues to grow.[17] One would be hard pressed to cite comparable instances of research stimulation by a single work.

In the years immediately following Hunter's work, studies by Robert Agger, Delbert Miller, William D'Antonio, William Form, and others sought to replicate the Hunter technique in other cities and try out comparative designs. Frequently, these studies also involved certain methodological innovations. Generally, they found that by contrast to Atlanta, their cities exhibited less centralized and cohesive power arrangements. Often these differences were accounted for by reference to the characteristics of the cities, the special methods employed or the issues examined.

A major challenge to the Hunter approach was mounted by a group of Yale political scientists in the late 1950s led by Robert Dahl. Both the merits and the polemics of this challenge produced one of the most high-spirited debates in the recent history of American social science. Essentially, Dahl and the "pluralists" argued that Hunter and the "elitists" had produce a biased and wrongheaded interpretation of American urban politics. Much of the fault, it was claimed, lay in the Hunter "reputational" method of analysis which biased the results in favor of finding power elites as opposed to some alternative, more democratic arrangement. Specifically, the critics alleged that the method relied exclusively on reputations for influence rather than on actual influence, that it assumed an elite structure, and that it failed to deal with the actual decision-making process. The pluralists recommended a "decisional" or "event analysis" method that would reconstruct decision-making events to determine who actually participated and who influenced outcomes. The belief was, of course, that such a procedure would lead to a largely different interpretation of power and decision-making at the urban level.

In his study of New Haven, *Who Governs: Democracy and Power in an American City*, Dahl systematically advanced several new techniques, particularly historical analysis of the changing economic and ethnic backgrounds of city government officials and the analysis of three major issues: urban renewal, public education, and political campaigns. Case study analysis indicated the large pools of issue participants each. Next, Dahl developed lists of "social and economic notables," or the socially prominent and economically influential persons in New Haven. The *coup de grâce* of the analysis was to show, first, that a large number of varied individuals participated in these issues; and, second, that a rather small number of these participants were social or economic notables. Therefore, by implication, the Hunter thesis was to be rejected, for New Haven at least.

Unquestionably, Dahl produced a valuable book, and it is probably also true that the vigorous and protracted debate over elitism vs. pluralism had some beneficial consequences in the clarification of methods, assumptions and concepts. What is clearly incorrect, however, is the notion that Dahl's study tests Hunter's thesis or that Hunter committed the errors laid on his doorstep by the pluralists. On the first point, Dahl's test of the "elite dominance" notion through the use of lists of social and economic notables completely misses Hunter's point about the constituency of the top policy-making group.[20] As we saw in the quotation from Hunter, "society prestige and deference to wealth" were not the criteria that determined leadership status, rather it was business organizational position plus the choice to become involved. Second, as to the claim that Hunter did not study actual issues and issue participation, a careful reading of his book shows this to be a blatant oversight.

Just as Hunter attracted a group of followers, so did Dahl and the pluralists. Although the two camps appeared to differ markedly in their ideologies, their substantive results were often quite similar. Indeed, the only published comment by Floyd Hunter on the elitist-pluralist debate that raged for years around him was a generally supportive review of *Who Governs?* in which he noted:[21]

When he states, for example, that he finds little or no connection between economic dominance and processes of decision and reasons his way to a position of "political control" of affairs, whatever that is, I tend to fall off the cart. But I get back on when he finds connections between the mayor's official roles and his business roles. I have no trouble in understanding that "democratic pluralism" is at work in the upper reaches of the one-half of 1 percent of the policy-making array of New Haven. The fact that Dahl finds no connection between this narrow band of civic

democrats and the large body politic does not, as suggested, surprise anyone.

More important than a contrast between Dahl and Hunter is a broad review of the many studies that follow generally in this tradition. A paper of my own indicates specific propositions drawn from this literature about which there is more and less agreement.[22]

Robert Alford, a relatively objective student of the field, has indicated a series of points on which different studies agree. His analysis is quoted in detail because the general points are important to the subsequent discussion.[23]

Yet, the substantive findings of the community power studies are in remarkable agreement. The ideological disputes over method and terminology are due to a failure of both sides to recognize that the reputationalists are not concerned with the contemporary role of business leaders, bu rather with the long-range impact of economic and political activity of various status groups, and that the pluralists are not analyzing the nature of deeply embedded institutions, but rather the situational impact of many different factors affecting current decisions. Most studies share the following conclusions.

1. Public decision-making at any specific time occurs within a relatively narrow "agenda of alternatives" determined by constraints of political and economic structure and culture, deriving from the history of the nation, state, and local community.
2. The middle and upper classes provide most community leadership.
3. When working-class groups are organized into politically active unions, a base of opposition to the middle class is created which allows the raising of a variety of issues not usual when only the middle class is active.
4. In particular public decision-making situations, a variety of groups is likely to be active and the same persons are not likely to be found in all issue areas, except for certain public leaders like the mayor or the city manager.
5. At any specific point in time, distinctions concerning the proper boundaries between private and public actions establish the legitimacy of actions by government and public leaders.
6. As a corollary, many major decisions are

made autonomously by private economic leaders and are not subject to public control.

While the pluralists bent on repudiating Hunter committed their own errors, particularly in failing to analyze the community as a social structure rather than as a collection of autonomous individuals, they did contribute healthily to the expanding literature by developing alternative methods (e.g., issue analysis) and theoretical insights about democratic politics (e.g., Dahl's model of "dispersed inequalities," power resources and "slack systems"). That is, to some extent, a critical balance was struck. But once more some of the appearance of balance in the pluralists' writing stems from their misleading characterization of Hunter, who was just as concerned with issue analysis and democracy and power as was Dahl. Hunter begins and ends his book on these themes:

> The line of communication between the leaders and the people needs to be broadened and strengthened—and by more than a series of public relations and propaganda campaigns— else our concept of democracy is in danger of losing vitality in dealing with problems that affect all in common.[24]

> The task of social reconstruction may never be finished once and for all. It is a recurring task confronting each generation, which somehow manages to find courage to meet social issues as they arise. In spite of the limitations that confront the individual in relation to community participation on the level of policy decision, there is still room for him in this area. He may not find himself at the top; but, with proper attention given to structural arrangements of power in the community, he may find ways of having a voice in determining who should be at the top.[25]

Summarizing the development of this unique field since Hunter's initial study, two conclusions appear justified. First, despite differences in method and interpretation, there is a good deal of continuity in a large number of studies over a twenty-year period. Indeed, different researchers arrive at many common conclusions. In short, it is one distinct and relatively well-developed research tradition. Second, researchers of various persuasions share a common

interest in the question of participation and policy-making.

Contemporary Significance of the Field and Its Bearing on Public Issues

This essay began with the observation that the role of social science in public policy is an issue of increasing importance. Having gone some distance in characterizing a specific field where the study of policy-making is of central concern, we can now inquire into its bearing on the issue.

As was mentioned, the literature on community power runs to many hundreds of titles. Among these can be counted an impressive array of studies dealing with power and decision-making analyses of the following policy areas:

1. Urban renewal[26]
2. Social welfare[27]
3. General community or civic welfare[28]
4. Health and hospital services[29]
5. Community conflict[30]
6. Race relations[31]
7. Education[32]
8. Poverty programs[33]
9. Housing[34]
10. Ghetto violence[35]
11. Economic development[36]
12. Metropolitan government[37]
13. Absentee-owned corporations[38]
14. International border relations[39]

Within the scope of the present essay it would be impossible to generalize the particular results of these studies dealing in different ways with such disparate issues. Several of the studies do attempt their own theoretical explanation of differential success at policy implementation and are recommended as starting points for comparative generalizations.[40] What can be accomplished here is an interpretive synthesis of the principal themes in these studies and some suggestions for future applications.

Five general points appear to summarize the literature on power and public policy. First, these studies agree that the way power is distributed among leaders, participants, and the general population does make a difference in what gets done and what doesn't in a city. This is not to say that the power structure variable is the only or even the consistently most important factor in explaining community policy action. For example, the most progressive urban leadership groups may be frustrated in policy implementation due to legal and financial limitations or public indifference. To illustrate, progressive urban environmentalist groups may lack jurisdiction over nearby corporate polluters. Studies of fluoridation referenda indicate that the greater the voting turnout, the *less* likely are such beneficial, leadership-sponsored measures to be passed.[41] Conversely, even the most retrograde group of local leaders cannot stave off certain policy changes imposed from without. For example, public housing built with federal money must meet certain standards of integration, as must employment in federally sponsored construction, defense projects, and so forth. Within these limits, however, the structure and style of local decision-making is generally found to be one of the important factors in explanations of urban action or inaction.

No easy generalization is now possible concerning what specific power arrangements are likely to be associated with given policy outcomes or action vs. inaction. Several studies suggest that more decentralized power structures are associated with policy action although this plausible hypothesis needs greater specification and documentation.[42]

The second point of general agreement is that leadership structures can be reliably and validly identified through a combination of the techniques discussed earlier. It also appears that successive replications tend to converge on the generalization that American urban leadership structures represent a very small numerical proportion of the communities they serve and usually involve an alignment of top political and business positions; other interests may be represented in varying degrees, but this appears to be the baseline. This is not to infer that such power arrangements are necessarily close-knit or elitist; again we can expect variation there. That it does suggest is that the modal case reflects the disproportionate representation of political and economic interests of the middle and upper classes. Some studies suggest that this may be changing in the direction of more competitive arrangements as a result of increasing interdependence between urban and national institutions.[43]

A third suggestion, limited to more recent literature, is that the key variable in explaining power arrangements and policy outcomes may be the organizational structure of the city. Organizations, particularly public agencies, corporations, civic associations, civil rights and action groups, and the like, are to be understood as power resources and their interlinkages as "resource networks."[44] The greater the number of such resource networks (or what Mott[45] has suggestively termed "organizational interfaces"), the more likely is policy action. It should be noted that these power networks are not an automatic consequence of city size, but depend on historical factors and the nature of the organizations themselves.[46] Recent studies support the proposition and suggest intriguing possibilities for future studies of substantially greater explanatory significance.[47]

The fourth common theme represents somewhat of a paradox. Most of the literature concludes that numerous possibilities exist for intervention, organization, and policy-oriented social action, given an understanding of the power and decision-making process. Indeed, this was the larger point of Hunter's initial study and is eloquently elaborated in his concluding chapter when he discusses the differences between his approach and that of Saul Alinsky's community organization movement. Alinsky's point in *Reveille for Radicals*[48] was that conventional community action programs have been ineffective because of their piecemeal and nonstructural interpretation of the causes of local problems. This led him to the belief, which he acted upon, that effective change must rely on "people's organizations." While Hunter shares the same sympathies for needed change, he felt the Alinsky approach to be "politically utopian" and that more effective change could come from, first, a knowledge of the location of community (establishment) power and, second, more intensive participation in existing, functional organizations that are more likely of getting mass support. Nevertheless, Hunter was not unmindful of the paradoxical problem involved. In another prophetic passage, he noted,[49]

The leaders in the policy-making realm are not going to open the doors of participation with charitable graciousness. It has been noted that they may even use police power and the power of governmental machinery to keep back criticism and threatening political elements.

Yet he concludes more optimistically,[50]

Such tactics eventually will not win out if dissident groups are in earnest concerning a voice in the affairs of government or economic operations.

In short Hunter is arguing a tactical question which we may not be have the evidence for deciding. More likely is the possibility that he and Alinsky are both right, depending upon the issue at hand and the nature of existing organizations. The significance of the point in the present context is that power and decision-making research is generally in agreement with Hunter's cautious optimism and provides evidence of more and less successful policy-oriented action that may suggest some explanations. One such tentative explanation is that community action is more effective when it relies on power resources external to the community than when it relies on local grassroots resources.

A final theme about which there appears to be some agreement is that broader effective political participation on policy questions is by no means a romantic, unrealistic, or "disfunctional" prospect. This is particularly true of recent critiques of "elite pluralism" or "democratic elitism"—belief that elites are inevitable and good for you.[51] Some evidence is available, and more appears forthcoming, that broader participation in policy-making is both possible and beneficial.[52] Although the point may sound platitudinous, many "functionalist" social scientists have justified nonparticipation for its efficient and stabilizing consequences.

Reflecting on these summary points, it could be argued that they are not especially definitive and, therefore, no source of encouragement concerning the prospects of a public policy-oriented social science. This, of course, is largely a matter of interpretation; dim light is better than no light, but not terribly handy if you can't see where you are going. In this specific case, however, the summary points do suggest some directives as well as a large set of questions for more discriminating future research. This is no mean accomplishment, given the complexity of the problem. Clearly, we need more concrete and detailed analyses of problems like minority economic opportunities, welfare organization, health care, and alternative styles of urban living. Yet the social science heritage, from Floyd Hunter to the burgeoning contemporary concern with public policy and social action, indicates that social science is "ready" in the sense of possessing interest and experience to draw from. This is not to suggest that social scientists will make better policy-makers, an ambition of one of the founding fathers of sociology, August Comte, which (fortunately) was never taken seriously. What it does suggest is that in the hands of well-informed and unpretentious researchers, the tools and experience of social science can lead to more informed judgments on policy issues. The constraints on and consequences of such research are largely open questions.

Notes

1. Peter H. Rossi, "No Good Idea Goes Unpublished: Moynihan's Misunderstandings and the Proper Role of Social Science in Policy Making," *Social Science Quarterly*, 53 (December 1969) 469–479.

2. For some recent sources of such information see a special issue of the *Social Science Quarterly*, 53 (December 1969), on planned social intervention, and Dean Schooler, Jr., *Science, Scientists and Public Policy* (New York: The Free Press, 1971).

3. Cf. Joseph J. Spengler, "Is Social Science Ready?" *Social Science Quarterly*, 53 (December 1969), 449–468.

4. This literature is conveniently summarized in several sources that include extensive bibliographies: cf. Michael Aiken and Paul E. Mott (eds.) *The Structure of Community Power* (New York: Random House, 1970); Charles M. Bonjean, Terry N. Clark, and Robert Lineberry (eds.) *Community Politics: A Behavioral Approach* (New York: The Free Press, 1971); Frederick Wirt and Willis Hawley, *The Search for Community Power* (Englewood Cliffs: Prentice-Hall, Inc., 1968).

5. It should be recognized that we are treating here a unique topic in policy relevance. Many sociological interests (e.g., drug usage, racial prejudice, juvenile delinquency, etc.) have policy implications. Here we are dealing with research on policy making itself.

6. Floyd Hunter, *Community Power Structure: A Study of Decision Makers* (Chapel Hill: University of North Carolina Press, 1953).

7. Charles M. Bonjean and David M. Olson, "Community Leadership: Directions of Research," *Administrative Science Quarterly*, 3 (December 1964), 278–300.

8. Compare, for example, the methodological similarities between Hunter's work and such recent, important books as Robert E. Agger, Daniel Goldrich and Bert E. Swanson, *The Rulers and the Ruled* (New York: John Wiley & Sons, 1964); or Robert Presthus, *Men at the Top* (New York: Oxford University Press, 1964).

9. Hunter, *Community Power Service, op. cit.*, p. 1.

10. Though he doesn't say so, it is presumed that the other thirteen leaders were not available for interviews.

11. Hunter, *op. cit.*, p. 62.

12. *Ibid.*, p. 66.

13. *Ibid.*, pp. 78–79.

14. *Ibid.*, p. 149.

15. *Ibid.*, p. 250.

16. *Ibid.*, p. 217.

17. See note 4 above.

18. The debate and its protagonists' positions are described in the works mentioned in note 4 and in Terry N. Clark (ed.), *Community Structure and Decision Making: Comparative Analyses* (San Francisco: Chandler Publishing Co., 1968).

19. Robert Dahl, *Who Governs? Democracy and Power in an American City* (New Haven: Yale University Press, 1963).

20. On this error is predicated portions of Nelson W. Polsby's book, *Community Power and Political Theory* (New Haven: Yale University Press, 1963). Other portions of the book report further on the New Haven study in which Polsby and Raymond Wolfinger assisted Dahl.

21. Floyd Hunter, review of *Who Governs?* in *Administrative Science Quarterly*, 6 (March 1962), p. 518.

22. John Walton, "A Systematic Survey of Community Power Research," in Aiken and Mott, *The Structure of Community Power, op. cit.*, pp. 443–464.

23. Robert R. Alford, *Bureaucracy and Participation: Political Cultures in Four Wisconsin Cities* (Chicago: Rand McNally & Co., 1969), p. 194.

24. Hunter, *op. cit.*, p. 1.

25. *Ibid.*, p. 253.

26. Amos Hawley, "Community Power and Urban Renewal Success," *American Journal of Sociology*, 68 (January 1963), 422–431; Terry N. Clark, "Community Structure, Decision-Making, Budget Expenditures, and Urban Renewal in 51 American Communities," *American Sociological Review*, 33 (August 1968), 576–593; Michael Aiken and Robert R. Alford, "Community Structure and Innovation: The Case of Urban Renewal," *American Sociological Review*, 35 (August 1970), 650–665.

27. Floyd Hunter, Ruth C. Schaffer, and Cecil G. Sheps, *Community Organization: Action and Inaction* (Chapel Hill: University of North Carolina Press, 1956).

28. C. Wright Mills and Melville J. Ulmer, "Small Business and Civic Welfare," reprinted in Aiken and Mott, *The Structure of Community Power, op cit.*, 154–162; Irving A. Fowler, *Local Industrial Structures, Economic Power and Community Welfare: Thirty Small New York State Cities 1930–1950* (Totowa, New Jersey: Bedminster Press, 1964); William Kornhauser, "Power and Participation in the Local Community," *Health Education Monographs*, 6 (1959), 28–37.

29. Presthus, *op. cit.;* Ivan Belknap and John Steinle, *The Community and Its Hospitals* (Syracuse: Syracuse University Press, 1963).

30. James S. Coleman, *Community Conflict* (New York: The Free Press, 1957); William A. Gamson, "Rancorous Conflict in Community Politics," *American Sociological Review*, 31 (February 1966), 71–81; Herbert Danzger, "A Quantified Description of Community Conflict," *American Behavioral Scientist*, 12 (November–December 1968), 9–14.

31. Hunter, *op. cit.;* Danzger, *ibid.;* James McKee, "Community Power and Strategies in Race Relations," *Social Problems*, 6 (Winter 1958–1959), 41–51.

32. Dahl, *op. cit.;* Warner Bloomberg and Morris Sunshine, *Suburban Power Structures and Public Education: A Study of Values, Influence and Tax Effort* (Syracuse: Syracuse University Press, 1963); Ralph B. Kimbrough, *Political Power and Educational Decision Making* (Chicago: Rand McNally & Co., 1964).

33. Clark, *op. cit.;* Michael Aiken, "The Distribution of Community Power: Structural Bases and Social Consequences," in Aiken and Mott, *The Structure of Community Power, op. cit.;* Michael Aiken and Robert R. Alford, "Community Structure and The War on Poverty: Theoretical and Methodological Considerations," in Mattei Dogan (ed.), *Studies in Political Ecology* (in press).

34. Aiken, "The Distribution of Power," *op. cit.;* Floyd Hunter, *Housing Discrimination in Oakland, California*, A study prepared for the Mayor's Committee on Full Opportunity and the Council of Social Planning of Alameda County, 1964; Michael Aiken and Robert R. Alford, "Community Structure and Innovation: The Case of Public Housing," *American Political Science Review*, 64 (September 1970), 843–864.

35. Peter H. Rossi and Richard A. Berk, "Local Political Leadership and Popular Discontent in the Ghetto," *The Annals* of the American Academy

of Political and Social Science, 391 (September 1970), 111–127.

36. Presthus, op. cit.; John Walton, "Development Decision Making: A Comparative Study in Latin America," American Journal of Sociology, 75 (March 1970), 828–851.

37. Edward Sofen, "Problems of Metropolitan Leadership: The Miami Experience," Midwest Journal of Political Science, 5 (February 1961), 18–38; Edward Sofen, The Miami Metropolitan Experiment (Garden City: Doubleday–Anchor Books, 1966).

38. Roland J. Pellegrin and Charles H. Coates, "Absentee Owned Corporations and Community Power Structure," American Journal of Sociology, 61 (March 1956), 413–419; Robert O. Schulze, "The Bifurcation of Power in a Satellite City," in Morris Janowitz (ed.), Community Political Systems (Glencoe, Illinois: The Free Press, 1961).

39. William V. D'Antonio and William H. Form, Influentials in Two Border Cities: A Study in Community Decision Making (South Bend: University of Notre Dame, 1964).

40. Cf. Presthus, op. cit.; Aiken, "The Distribution of Power," op. cit.; Aiken and Alford, "The Case of Urban Renewal," op. cit.; Walton, "Development Decision Making," op. cit.

41. Kornhauser, op. cit.; William A. Gamson, "Community Issues and Their Outcome: How To Lose a Fluoridation Referendum," in Alvin W. Gouldner and S. M. Miller (eds.), Applied Sociology: Opportunities and Problems (New York: The Free Press, 1965).

42. Aiken, "The Distribution of Power," op. cit.; Clark, op. cit.

43. John Walton, "Differential Patterns of Community Power Structure: An Explanation Based on Interdependence," in Terry N. Clark (ed.), Community Structure, op. cit.

44. Cf. Robert Perrucci and Marc Pilisuk, "Leaders and Ruling Elites: The Interorganizational Bases of Community Power," American Sociological Review, 35 (December 1970), 1040–1057.

45. Paul E. Mott, "Configurations of Power," in Aiken and Mott, The Structure of Community Power, op. cit., 85–100.

46. Aiken, "The Distribution of Power," op. cit.; Walton, "Development Decision Making," op. cit.

47. Aiken and Alford, see the several articles cited above.

48. Saul Alinsky, Reveille for Radicals (Chicago: The University of Chicago Press, 1946).

49. I cannot resist the parenthetical comment that Hunter appears in this passage to be talking about the 1968 Democratic Party Convention, the Nixon Administration's policies toward the Black Panther Party, or publication of documents on U.S. involvement in Vietnam. It is a mark of the man's perceptivity and honesty that he dealt with these issues in a time when most sociology was banal and irrelevant to policy issues.

50. Hunter, Community Power Structure, 251–252.

51. Peter Bachrach, The Theory of Democratic Elitism: A Critique (Boston: Little, Brown and Company, 1967).

52. Carole Pateman, Participation and Democracy (New York: Oxford University Press, 1970).

22

FRANK J. MUNGER

Community Power and
Metropolitan Decision-Making

In these accounts of decision-making in the Syracuse metropolitan area we have reviewed some twenty-two cases or points of decision or action. Obviously they are not equal as regards breadth, depth, time span, importance of the participants, or significance of the issues; on the contrary, they vary greatly when appraised by these and other relevant criteria. They vary, too, in their pertinence to the subject and their contribution to achievement of the announced purpose of the study. Yet because of their common environment and subject-matter focus all contain suggestions for useful hypotheses. These may be examined under the dual headings of community power and metropolitan decision-making.

COMMUNITY POWER

The mythology of community power in Syracuse today is very clear. Any number of observers, including many knowledgeable in local affairs, will assert that a single man stands at the top (or, some might say, behind the top) of community affairs and runs things. This is Stewart F. Hancock, lawyer, banker, gentleman, spokesman for the old-line aristocracy, without whose consent, tacit or explicit, nothing of importance can be done. One writer refers to Hancock as "Mr. Syracuse."[1] Harking back to the categories ad-

vanced in Chapter I [of *Decisions in Syracuse*], Syracuse is commonly believed to have a slack, monolithic, pyramidal power structure with a businessman-attorney as its dominant figure. Many who hold this view concede that Hancock's power is now declining. The time spanned by this study, however, covers the period of his greatest reputed power, and the cases examined should demonstrate his leadership if in fact it possessed substance.

These analyses of actual decisions taken with respect to public problems in the Syracuse metropolitan area do not support an interpretation based on the concept of monolithic power. What is clear from the cases is that the pattern of decision-making in Syracuse has changed markedly over the last thirty years. The cases suggest that at one time the current myth had a solid foundation in fact, for earlier there was a high concentration of community authority in the hands of a single man, simultaneously a political leader and a public official. Expanding the already substantial powers vested in his predecessor as Republican county chairman, Rolland Marvin consolidated those powers with his authority as mayor to wield an unprecedented influence over public decisions. Moreover, he exercised his control with a minimum of public oversight. His ultimate rejection resulted partly from reaction against his autocratic methods, but more from the bitter opposition of Governor Thomas Dewey, still smarting over Marvin's support of Wendell Willkie at the 1940 Republican national convention.

After Marvin's defeat, a disintegration of political power took place. It was during this period that Stewart Hancock maximized his influence,

From Roscoe C. Martin et al., *Decisions in Syracuse* (Bloomington: Indiana University Press, 1961), chapter 14, pp. 317–347. Reprinted by permission. This chapter of Martin et al., was prepared by Frank J. Munger.

and community leadership passed from a combined political boss and elective public official to a lawyer-businessman with no pronounced inclination for public notice. In the process, a change occurred in the process of leadership itself. Partly in reaction to the tight control exercised by Marvin, partly perhaps as a result of the example set by the Post-War Planning Council, the circle of participants in community affairs broadened. Such a change was no doubt inevitable in any case in view of the steady growth in the size of the metropolitan community and the complexity of its interests; nevertheless it accompanied, perhaps as both cause and effect, a significant change in the pattern of leadership. Since more persons were involved in community affairs and more individuals therefore had to be consulted, no successor's influence could be unequivocally dominant as that of Marvin. Indeed, in the cases examined here Hancock appears only as one among several leaders.[2] A notable consequence of Marvin's fall was the collapse of central control over the Republican party organization. Lacking this essential part of Marvin's arsenal, subsequent community figures have never been able to force through measures over town opposition with Marvin's abandon. Whether the power system can at present be regarded as polylithic or whether it is in transition to monolithic control by some new individual leader is clearly an open question, although the fact that the change in the type of community leadership has accompanied changes in social forces would seem to suggest the former.

Even during the period of monolithic control, the case studies demonstrate the point that broad areas of public policy were left undirected by the dominant leaders of the community. That fact does not necessarily destroy the monolithic concept. As noted before, some distinction between major and minor policy must necessarily be made. So long as the top leaders continued to exercise tight control over such focal concerns as city and county budgets, they might properly be considered to be dominant even though they failed to assert control at all points of decision-making. The establishment of a children's court, for example, might be offered to interested citizens' groups as a minor concession which would not affect substantially the central financial concerns of local government.

Although this abdication of control over certain areas of policy-making may be accommo-

dated to a monolithic interpretation of the exercise of community power, it nevertheless has important consequences which are particularly evident within the real estate field. Chapters XI through XIII [of *Decisions in Syracuse*] make clear that in this area especially many lesser decisions are continually being made without reference to the power structure at its top levels. These decisions may be minimized as affecting only minor policy, but the fact remains that their cumulative impact has tremendous effect in shaping the course of development of the metropolitan area. The only recognized tool that might give the community leaders effective control over the accumulation of these decisions would be area-wide planning of land use, and either through tradition or through their own laissez-faire inclinations the leaders have been slow to grasp this weapon.

With respect to local-state relations, the cases clearly reveal the legislative advantages enjoyed by Syracuse and Onondaga County. By reason of their Republican affiliation both city and county are accorded a friendly reception in the perennially Republican legislature. When they ask for a special law, the legislature is quick to oblige. The only law sought from the state that provided any difficulty involved passage of the Alternative County Government law, a statute of general application. Two measures were indeed blocked, but both by gubernatorial vetoes.

The cases also demonstrate the difficulty of obtaining popular approval of a proposal for governmental reorganization. Three referenda were held on variations of this proposal. The first, supported by Democrats and opposed by Republicans, failed in both city and towns. The next, supported by neither party but opposed by neither, suffered a like fate. And even the third proposal (the county director plan), which was supported by both newspapers, a banner list of city leaders, and numerous party officials, failed to receive a county majority though carrying the city. The uniform lack of success of these efforts attests the conservatism of the electorate, the influence of the county bureaucracy, and the strong opposition of the towns (and more particularly their supervisors) to change.

Of the twenty-two cases examined, fourteen are found on examination to have involved decisions at the county level. Isolating these fourteen in order to obtain greater comparability through greater uniformity, it is possible to make n analysis of the effectiveness of exercise of power from an examination of the decisions reached. Robert Dahl has suggested a possible formula for such a calculation in his definition of community leader in terms of ability to (1) initiate proposals and carry them through, (2) override substantial opposition on behalf of a proposal, and (3) veto a proposal initiated by others. Making some rather arbitrary groupings of the interests involved in the cases at hand, the power demonstrated in these terms assumes the following pattern:

	Won	Lost	Did Not Participate
Republican Party	5	2	7
Democratic Party	1	3	10
Manufacturers Association	2	0	12
Chamber of Commerce—Governmental Research Bureau	2	2	10
CIO	0	1	13
Real estate interests	3	0	11
League of Women Voters	2	5	7
Community Chest/Council of Social Agencies/Onondaga County Health Association	2	2	10
Town government officials	5	2	7
Post-Standard	3	2	9
Herald-Journal	2	4	8
Village weekly newspapers	3	0	11

Such a listing, while of course not conclusive, nevertheless has high suggestive value. It demonstrates clearly that, in terms of community decision-making, the Democratic Party is not very important in Onondaga County; the lone Democratic victory represents the party's success in persuading Governor Lehman (Democrat) to veto a Republican county reorganization measure. The tabulation likewise shows that the League of Women Voters concerns itself with many problems, but is not very effective in winning acceptance for its proposals. The League's chief value obviously lies in the service it performs in calling problems up for consideration. The list also instances the ineffectiveness of organized labor in local decision-making. It indicates that labor does not lose; it simply fails to participate. Likewise less effective than might have been expected are the daily newspapers, which together lost oftener than they won. The group with what appears to be the best record of effective action is the Republican Party. In only two cases, however, can the party be said to have initiated the action it supported, and both of those involved Rolland Marvin as leader. The party organization therefore was rather a vehicle through which other interests sought to attain their goals. Success in obtaining party support usually guaranteed victory; but the party's own role was passive or instrumental, consisting in most cases of embracing decisions made elsewhere and seeing that the county government carried them out. The town officials were equally successful with, perhaps because often indistinguishable from, the Republican Party. The industrialists and the realtors had a low rate of participation, but were uniformly successful where they elected to commit their resources.

The most striking feature of the tabulation is the low level of participation in the decision-making process. No group tested its strength in a majority of the decisions, and most were involved in only a few cases. This warrants the conclusion that separate clusters of decision areas exist, each with its own distinct group of participants.[3] It effectively eliminates the notion of an all-sovereign wielder of community power, and it attacks (though it does not necessarily destroy) the concept of a monolithic power structure as applied to Syracuse. Under such circumstances it is meaningless to say that group A is more powerful than group B when A and B have never tested their strength against each other and because of their differing interests are not likely to.

The tabulation provides no clue concerning the problem of differential commitment, which as observed earlier is central to an appraisal of power and its exercise. The Chamber of Commerce, to illustrate, may take a mild interest in one measure and satisfy itself with a simple endorsement; in another case more tangibly related to the economic interest of its members, it may throw all its resources into a life-and-death struggle. It is manifestly unrealistic to regard the two commitments as being in any wise equal, for neither the rates nor the efficiencies of use of influence are comparable.

In summary, the decisions analyzed in this study afford no basis for easy generalizations about the structure and exercise of community power in the Syracuse metropolitan area. Only three overall conclusions seem warranted by the materials examined. First, the myth that significant decisions in Syracuse emanate from one source does not stand up under close scrutiny. Second, there tend to be as many decision centers as there are important decision areas, which means that the decision-making power is fragmented among the institutions, agencies, and individuals which cluster about these areas. Third, in reality there appear to be many kinds of community power, with one kind differing from another in so many fundamental ways as to make virtually impossible a meaningful comparison.

COMMUNITY POWER ROLES

The cases clearly indicate that a full model of the decision-making process would have to take into account the fact that decisions do not eventuate from single, individual choices but from a flow of choices. Who raised the issue and brought it to public attention? Who formulated the alternatives and marshaled the facts employed by the decision-makers in reaching their conclusions? To what extent were the decision-makers free to choose among these alternatives? A series of acts are involved in a decision to take or not to take a particular public action. It will prove useful to examine the process briefly. This may be done by identifying the roles involved in the exercise of community power.

The Initiators

Innumerable problems calling for remedial action can be identified within a metropolitan area for urban life is never perfect. Of these, however, only a limited number are—or in normal circumstances can be—brought forward for consideration. At times the process by which action is initiated may be almost automatic. Thus when an event occurs which sharply changes existing conditions to the detriment of a vocal group, a demand for action can be confidently expected. When the Big Sister and Big Brother programs were closed, the way was opened for creation of a county children's court. When a legislative act cut off child guidance funds to Onondaga County, establishment of a mental health board followed. The city's fiscal crisis of the late 1930s produced the county welfare consolidation. And so on.

More difficult to explain is the process by which action is initiated to remedy long-existent evils. Onondaga County's government structure is notoriously outdated; it has undergone no important change, much less anything approaching basic reorganization, for more than a century. As county agencies and functions have multiplied, the resulting problems have become steadily more severe. Only within comparatively recent years, however, did the League of Women Voters pick up the problem and make it an issue. What defines the point past which men (and women, too) are no longer disposed to endure?

The exercise of leadership by which action initiated has come most frequently from the professional members of the governmental agencies. State Health Department officials initiated consideration of a county health department; Richard Greene of the city probation office launched action looking toward a children's court; Serg Grimm, director of the City Planning Commission, inspired the Post-War Planning Council.

the psychiatry department of the State College of Medicine proposed the creation of the mental health clinic.

This fact in itself may not appear surprising; for a widely popular belief holds that governmental agencies continually seek to expand their powers and budgets, and this might appear to be evidence substantiating that view. But contrary evidence appears in the fact that the county, whose agencies were to be expanded, has most frequently resisted growth. County supervisors have shown little desire to engage in empire-building. They personify the town governments, and they prefer to keep county taxes low. An example is provided by the County Public Works Commission, which accepted only reluctantly operating responsibility for the metropolitan sewage treatment plant. State and city governmental officials have served as initiators of county action, but seldom have county spokesmen done so.

This undoubtedly is one factor in the difficulty of effecting a reorganization of the county government. If there were a county manager or other executive he might be expected to attempt to strengthen his own powers, much as the strong mayor seeks to grow stronger in the city. With no county executive to make a beginning, however, there is no place at which to begin; and leadership of the county reorganization movement therefore falls to such groups as the League of Women Voters.

The Experts

Providing an idea concerning something that needs to be done is, however, only the beginning. An idea may be sufficient to start the ball rolling, but sooner or later the central idea must be fleshed out into a plan for action. If the need is for county reorganization, a proposal in detail must be offered. If it is for sewage treatment, the response must be a carefully conceived scheme for meeting it. If the need is complex, so also will be the plan. This means that a need for technicians arises early and insistently in the decision-making process.

The most obvious source for expert assistance is the reservoir of local government employees. In practice this means the professional people in the various functional fields.[4] On occasion they may be the initiators of action themselves, but in any event they are likely soon to be consulted. Their availability is undoubtedly one reason why unifunctional changes are easier to accomplish than general reorganizations, a phenomenon often noted. In Onondaga County the most commonly employed source of expert assistance is quasi-governmental. The engineering firm of O'Brien and Gere provides professional advice on virtually every major public works project in the county.

There are limits, however, to the opportunities for utilizing governmental experts. If the public employees are inert, incompetent, or suspected of seeking opportunity to feather their own nests, an alternative source of expertise must be found. It is this dilemma that was responsible for the creation of the Governmental Research Bureau. In effect the business and industrial interests hired themselves a rival set of experts in whom they felt greater confidence.

Not all groups concerned with government problems can afford to hire their own experts. In this more normal situation several possibilities exist, any or all of which may be utilized. One alternative source of knowledge lies in the state administrative departments, which may find options that have been missed locally. In one sense this is what the state legislature attempts to accomplish in such a measure as the alternative government law. Options by themselves are not enough, however, and experts are needed to point out and facilitate their local applications. This function is performed by the state Health Department and the state Education Department, among others.

An additional source of professional assistance resides in Syracuse University and, to a lesser extent, LeMoyne College. The significance of the role played by the Syracuse University faculty lies particularly in the technical support it provides for programs outside the area of economic interest of the business and industrial communities, and in the assistance it gives to minority interests in the formulation of policy alternatives. In such fields as mental health, education, youth development, county planning, urban renewal, and, quite recently, metropolitan matters, university personnel are active participants. The agitation for county reorganization in the late 1930s was sparked by a Syracuse University faculty professor, and other faculty members have rendered expert assistance on all manner of community issues called up for public decision.

The Publicists

It is not enough, however, to have an idea—even an expertly prepared one—in order to have an issue. As the 1934 Bar Association plan for county reorganization demonstrated, a proposal must be known to the public to become an issue. This is peculiarly the province of the newspapers. In an objective measurement of community power the two Syracuse dailies would not rank particularly high; more often than not, as we have observed, the measures they support are defeated. But they are capable of forcing consideration of an issue. By reports of events, feature stories, and editorials they are able to push the decision-makers into hard choices on matters they might prefer to ignore. In other language, they can compel items to be placed on the community's public-action agenda. Television likewise plays an increasingly important role in this respect.

There are limits to the newspapers' freedom of choice, for certain groups and individuals by their position or prestige can force newspaper copy. High public officials, the Chamber of Commerce, the Medical Society can command newspaper coverage. Even here, however, the choice of the newspaper to report minimally or to "play up" a news event may make a good deal of difference. And newspaper publicity is likely to prove indispensable to the success of lesser causes.

The only serious rival to the newspaper in this respect is, curiously enough, the Democratic Party. Rarely does that party sit in the seat of power, and when it does nothing much may happen: the only Democratic mayor in three decades was ineffectual as a party spokesman. But the Democratic Party can force issues on the attention of the community. Ordinarily the party does not initiate issues, but rather chooses among those initiated by others. By offering resolutions and debating them within the Common Council and the Board of Supervisors, the Democrats command newspaper space since party conflict is good copy. Beyond this, through campaigns for office Democratic candidates mobilize other means of communication—television and radio time, advertising, rallies, word of mouth, etc.—to make issues of the matters chosen for discussion.

The Influentials

The nominal target of this publicity is the general public, which may indeed be the real target if an election for office or a referendum is at stake. More frequently, however, the proponents of a program address the public in order to attract the attention of a limited number of persons believed to hold the power of decision. The purpose is to convince them that something that affects them is at stake, and so to enlist their support. Key public officials are an obvious target of such a campaign. So also are the major economic groups with stakes in the community. Gathered together in the Chamber of Commerce and the Manufacturers Association they are important individually as well—Niagara Mohawk, General Electric, Carrier, the banks, etc.

Depending on the issue, the target also includes the major institutionalized social welfare and professional groups, such as the Community Chest, the Council of Social Agencies, and the Medical Society. Members of such groups may be drawn from the same social class as the leaders of the economic organizations, and indeed may sometimes be the same individuals; but their interest in social welfare, plus the effect of professional contracts, influences their behavior in different directions and makes them useful for different causes.

The struggle to win acceptance for a proposal may revolve largely around the effort to gain support among such groups without much attention to the formal governmental process, and defeat here may end the tale. This was the case with the postwar version of the county health department plan. When it failed to command the support of the Medical Society the proposal was dropped by the supervisors, who were only too glad to be relieved of the responsibility for making a decision.

The Brokers

As has been suggested, the core of the influentials consists of the economic groups with the most substantial stake in the community. The does not mean, however, that the heads of the corporations are themselves involved in the decision-making process. Normally they are hidden behind an intervening curtain of community representatives. These may be public relations men, or in the more recent jargon of General Electric, a "community relations team." But most frequently they are drawn from local law firms.

It is customary for a major corporation, though employing national legal advisors, to retain local counsel to represent it within the community. Similarly, if a real estate developer wants to rearrange or facilitate his relations with government, he goes to one of the principal law firms. And if a town government wants something, it too is likely to turn to a lawyer. In the cases examined in the previous chapters, the names of two law firms recurred frequently: Melvin and Melvin, and Bond, Schoeneck, and King. At least two others might be added, but, in so far as these cases reveal, they are not especially active in the negotiation of metropolitan decisions.

Community conflicts—and those involving economic interests in particular—are rarely fought out between the principals, but are handled by their legal representatives. And since it is the legal counsel who tells the principal what is possible and what is not, the latter's vision of political reality is shaped accordingly. In the process the lawyers, though brokers of power, wield substantial power themselves. And because the hostilities are conducted through intermediaries, community conflicts rarely erupt as open warfare but simmer along as protracted negotiations. Accommodation and compromise are emphasized in place of the all-or-nothing rewards of outright victory or complete defeat.

Less well-financed interests (that is, those of a noneconomic character) usually must serve the representative function themselves. As a result they may stumble, or suffer costly delays. As another result the decisions they seek are far more likely to be made in public, and to be couched in the extreme terms the skilled broker is able to avoid through negotiation and compromise.

The Transmitters of Power

Just as the true leaders of the economic interests are masked in the process of community deci-

sion-making by their representatives, so too are the final decision-makers, the governmental officials, concealed by a cover. Instead of dealing directly with, for example, the Board of Supervisors or its members, the representative of an economic group seeking action from the government is likely to go to the Republican party leader. And since both representative and leader are usually lawyers, the task may be no more complex than talking the matter over with his law partner. Under some circumstances, the representative may find himself as party leader. The New Process Gear case provides an illustration of the manner of operation of—and the results achieved by—the transmitters of power.

Republican party leaders ordinarily do not initiate action: in the cases presented above only Rolland Marvin could be said to have done so. But by possessing the capacity to issue orders to subordinates that will be obeyed, they enormously simplify the task of political contact for those with access to the party leadership. The clearest evidence of the effort and time they save is provided by the difficulties attending those groups—the League of Women Voters, for example—which have dealt with supervisors and the like on an individual basis, winning their support one by one.

The Authority of Government

Only the final step in the process of decision-making is the act of government itself, the approval or rejection of the proposal by the officials formally vested with the authority of office. Because the individual members of the Common Council or the Board of Supervisors are rarely persons of prominence in the community—customarily they consist of young men making their reputations and older men of long experience in the limited world of party affairs—it is conventional to minimize their role. When the time arrived for official action, Clarence King secured the votes he needed from them. With less persuasion and more power, Rolland Marvin did the same.

It is possible, however, to understate the role of the Common Council or the Board of Supervisors as well as to overstate it. The approval of the supervisors is essential since, for better or worse, they are the government of the county. Some supervisors, especially those from the rural towns, show a substantial capacity for independent action. Their resistance to change can be seen in the recurrent city-town struggles described in the cases above. Stubborn supervisors have at times delayed board approval for long periods, and when their own positions seem to them to be at stake, as in the case of a proposal for county governmental reorganization, they may exercise an effective veto over action. The role of the supervisors in decision-making is negative, but negative power may be as effective in its way as positive. Substantially the same may be said of the Common Council and its members.

Interrelationships among the Roles

The traditional approach to the study of community power has been to emphasize the role of the community influentials. Under the concept of power as a process, however, other roles became important. It is the argument of this analysis that isolation of the possessors of power from the participants in the flow and process of decision-making has little meaning. Power has value and substance only as it is used for something. The "powerful" community leader without idea men to suggest possibilities to him, or experts to package his program, or publicists to put wheels under it, or brokers to facilitate its consideration, or transmitters to bring it before the nominal decision-makers, can do little with his power. Community power is a network of action, not a locus of residence.

It is meaningless to try to measure these strands of community power against one another, to argue that the lawyer is more influential than the corporation executive, who in turn is more influential than the consulting engineer. Their power roles are not competitive, but complementary; they are links in a chain. When none of the partners to the process is expendable, none can truthfully be described as the inferior of any of the others.

The Environment and Freedom of Choice

One final aspect of the power process in relation to local decision-making remains to be considered: the degree of choice exercised within the community. The earliest studies of community power structure assumed a high measure of freedom for the individual community to choose its own course of action. A more recent line of inquiry, however, has opened the question of the degree to which decisions attributed to the local community are in fact determined by the unavoidable impact of such environmental factors as the population of the community, its resources, its taxable property, its ongoing commitments, its position vis-à-vis the state, etc. A striking part of Robert Wood's recent sudy of the governments in the New York City metropolitan area was an attempt to determine the extent to which local governmental expenditures in New Jersey are fixed by such factors, and to delimit the residual, unexplained variations in expenditures that might be attributed to the actual decisions of local governments. A similar study, concerned with expenditures for education, is now under way at Syracuse University.

In so far as these cases may be held to provide a guide, the realistic choices available to the Syracuse metropolitan community appear to be substantial. The size, growth pattern, and composition of the population would seem to offer no special problem. There is considerable unused or underused space within the city, with land to accommodate great growth outside; moreover there are no physical barriers to expansion either residential or industrial. The multiplicity of local governmental units serves as a complicating factor, but this is a normal obstacle to metropolitan action. The community's reserve resources are substantial, for while there are constitutional limits on both taxes and public debt, these have not usually proved to be a serious damper on government spending.[5] The state has embraced certain policies which have the effect of limiting local choice, but for the most part these have not been pursued rigorously. The most serious trammel is found in the native conservatism of the people, and even that yields before the blandishment (or the bludgeoning) of the Republican Party. In short, there are few environmental limitations on decision-making in the Syracuse metropolitan area which cannot be overridden where there is a combination of need and will.

In another sense, however, it is necessary to indicate a limit upon the conception of a decision as a free choice among alternatives by a determ nate set of decision-makers. This concerns what might be called the "inadvertence" of decisions. The cases make clear that many decisions are made partly by accident, that chance factors may play an important role, that sometimes a decision is the inevitable end product of past decisions that were made without anticipation of their consequences. Particularly in the real estate field this inadvertence of decision-making is evident. The Industrial Park was made possible by a confluence of seemingly unrelated past decisions—the forehanded accumulation of land, the provision of sewage facilities, the convenient location of a Thruway interchange, the laying of railroad trackage, etc. It might be argued that some of these decisions—as that of the Public Works Commission to provide sewerage—were taken in anticipation of some future industrial development, if not in foreknowledge of the Eagan project. This cannot be said, however, of Franklin's decision in the 1920s to obtain title to the lands involved. Yet without his action it is unlikely that an industrial park would have been created in this particular form or at this place. Industrial Park, then, was made possible by a series of individual actions taken over a period of thirty years without contemplation of any such eventuation as ultimately occurred. The cases examined here warrant the hypothesis that is characteristic of community decision-making in general.

METROPOLITAN COOPERATION AND ITS COMPONENTS

So far the analysis has been concerned with community power and the process of decision-making generally; it is now necessary to relate the subject to the metropolitan context of multiple governments. For many types of public decision within a metropolitan area it is necessary to secure favorable action from two or more governments, each subject to its own particular and peculiar combination of pressures. The schematic representation offered in Figure 1 will illustrate the point. There a hypothetical proposal that requires the support of three governments is presented, along with certain assumed combinations of pressures that admit of various courses of action. From the drawing, it is possible to identify three types of situations in which cooperative action becomes possible.

Parallel Action

The first and simplest of these is portrayed in diagrams A and B of Figure 1. A particular interest group seeks action from the three governments. So far as Government A is concerned, it may find that competing or conflicting interests are pushing in other directions, some favorable to action but of a modified character, others opposed to the program sought. Government B may present a somewhat different situation, with a new combination of interests playing upon the government officials and influencing their behavior, while Government C may involve a still different pattern. In diagram A the assumption is made that the interest group favoring action is sufficiently influential within each governmental jurisdiction to produce identical decisions among the three governments. In this instance metropolitan action is secured through the ability of a single interest (or coalition of interests) to bring pressure on each of the separate governments adequate to procure parallel action. Diagram B shows how a similar situation may produce contrary results. Although Governments B and C are responsive to the pressure from the group seeking action, the weight of the influences brought to bear upon Government A is such that it refuses to cooperate. Since the cooperation of all three is assumed to be necessary to adoption of the proposal, failure ensues.

All this may seem obvious, but the nature of the forces affecting the application of community power to governmental decision-making in a metropolitan context is ignored with astonishing frequency. When numerous governments exist within a metropolitan area, it is not realistic to assume that the same constellation of interests will exist or will exert equal weight in each. Consequently, when the cooperation of two or more governments is required differences are more to be expected than agreement, and deadlocks of the variety depicted in diagram B may easily develop. In this context it is wholly natural to expect that the influence of a particular community interest will vary with the nature and organization of the governmental unit called upon to act. The structure of government within the metropolitan area thus becomes a dynamic factor in the analysis of community power.

Situations requiring parallel action are particularly common in the field of real estate development. Ordinarily action or at least approval by

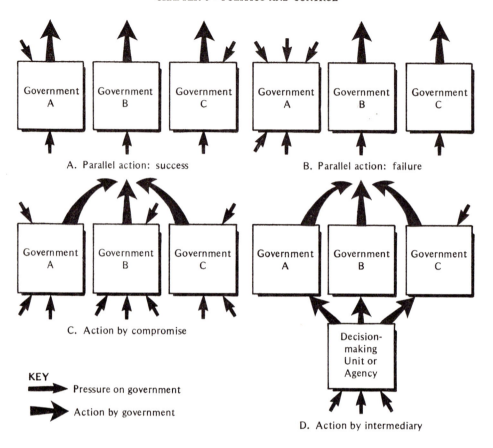

Figure 1. *Metropolitan decision-making: a schematic representation*

several governments and governmental agencies is required in advance of development. Frequently, however, there is no particular opposition to the proposal in any of the governmental units. A developer who lacks the necessary personal contacts may find it necessary to hire a representative to make the arrangements for him —mostly probably, as observed above, a legal firm with prior experience in this type of work— but once this is done the project is likely to proceed smoothly.

There are exceptions, of course. A shopping center, like that proposed in Fayetteville, may be adequately endowed with water supplies and sewerage and yet fail to win the necessary rezoning from a local government dominated by hostile interests. Faced by such an obstacle, the entrepreneur must choose between the alterna-

tives of abandoning his project or modifying it and trying again. And this is equally true whether the promotion is a real estate development or a new inter-town park or other metropolitan cooperative program.

The hostile forces that block action may originate with rival interests possessing superior influence or with the local government officials themselves. It would be a mistake to forget that governmental units—in the sense of their personnel—have lives of their own and are not always easily pushed about by the pressures brought to bear on them. Equally, of course, positive leadership in a cooperative undertaking may be provided by the public official, either because of his conviction that action is needed or because the bold and imaginative exercise of leadership is at times an effective political gambit. The argument has been advanced above that cooperative programs are often the result of the desires of public officials to head off pressures for governmental reorganization and consolidation. This is simply to restate the point made in Chapter 1, that public officials and governmental bureaucracies must themselves be regarded as participants in the contest over governmental decision-making.

Action by Compromise

A second type of situation also may produce cooperative action at the metropolitan level. This situation is portrayed in Figure 1-C. Again parallel action by three governments is regarded as essential to the success of the proposal. Again it is assumed that the influences brought to bear upon the three governments differ; these pressures, however, are so distributed as to produce a desire for action in each of the three governments, though action in differing forms. By negotiation and compromise an agreement is reached and parallel action is thus finally secured.

This type of cooperation seems to be relatively rare in the metropolitan area, and the reasons why this should be so are important to understanding the dynamics of the metropolitan power structure. It will already have become evident that this analysis of the means by which several governments can be brought into harmony on a common program is not necessarily peculiar to the metropolitan area. The same type of analysis can be applied to cooperation among the officials of a particular government. Each member of a city council is likely to be subject to different pressures: if a measure is to pass the council, it is necessary that agreement be reached among its members. The city council and the mayor in turn are subject to different pressures, and they must be brought into agreement. The same could be said of the president and the two houses of Congress on the national level.

There is, however, a difference. Cooperative action in the city and in Washington is continuous; the negotiating and bargaining never stop, and a concession on one issue can be balanced upon the next. But metropolitan bargaining involves the negotiation of agreement between two or more governments that have perhaps never cooperated before and may not again for years. Sayre and Kaufman have pointed out the sporadic and *ad hoc* character of both cooperative and competitive interrelationships between New York City and its neighbors.[9] It is clear from the case studies that the same can be said of relationships among the multiple governments of the Syracuse metropolitan area. In the absence of either a tradition of negotiation or diplomatic skills in bargaining, it is hardly surprising that agreements are reached but slowly and that insoluble deadlocks frequently block any action.

Action by Intermediary

In the absence of effective procedures for negotiated compromises, recourse must be had to some other device when powerful pressures for metropolitan action are blocked by one or more obstinate local governments. The third type of arrangement may be labeled action by intermediary. It may take the form of an appeal to some higher level of government, as the county or the state, for intercession when cooperation among towns, villages, and cities has failed. Or it may be found in an appeal to an extra-governmental organization capable of exercising control over the several local governments involved, as when the power of the political party is used to compel acquiescence in a decision. The common factor in both cases is that the issue is taken to some single, superior forum where the pressures for and against action can be assessed and a decision reached without the risk of veto within each of a series of local governments. A schematic representation of the direction of the pressures involved is suggested in Figure 1-D. Instances of both kinds of cooperative action by intermediary can be found in the cases above. Particularly interesting are the decisions in which the political party has been employed as a device to secure cooperation from governmental units that showed reluctance to act.

Within the Syracuse metropolitan area the Republican Party might be described as a kind of superstructure for decision-making which is called into action only on certain occasions. These include action on (1) issues that involve the party interest as such, e.g., nominations for office (not explored in this study), governmental reorganizations, etc.; and (2) issues that concern individuals in a position to ask the party's help.

Such individuals include the top industrial leaders who, it seems plausible to say, can secure party help when they need it regardless of the magnitude of the issue as measured, say, in dollars and cents. Presumably some relationship exists between the fact of access and campaign contributions to the party. Reversing this, it does not appear that the party leadership intervenes in an issue because it is big in thousands of dollars, but because it is big to persons who are important to the party.

Thus the Republican Party organization became the basic mechanism by which those interested in the relocation of the New Process Gear plant secured the cooperation of the local governmental officials. In an earlier quite similar case, not related in detail in this study, the Republican Party leadership intervened to prevent Solvay Process from moving when a zoning regulation by the Town of Camillus blocked the use of property for dumping sludge that the corporation considered essential for that purpose. In this case, which was remarkably similar to the New Process Gear incident, the initiative for action came from the Chamber of Commerce, whose leaders, working through party officials, arranged the complex intergovernmental trades necessary to persuade Camillus to rescind its zoning ordinance. On the other hand the establishment of the mental health board, involving very large expenditures, was determined without apparent intervention by the top political party leaders.

This last illustration is, of course, different in that it involved action by the Board of Supervisors rather than by several individual local governments. In an important sense, however, action by that body on intergovernmental issues may be regarded as metropolitan action, and has been so treated here. The members of the board actually are the heads of the significant local governments outside the City of Syracuse, the towns, and a major decision by the Board of Supervisors is therefore suggestive of group action by the towns. It is true that the institutional structure creates a somewhat different situation, since the rule of unanimity is replaced by one of majority vote; but in practice this has little effective meaning since all decisions are reached first in caucus and the Republican supervisors, who represent all or almost all of the towns, vote as a block.

This suggests that all actions of the Board of Supervisors might be termed action by intermediary, since all are taken through the Republican caucus. In a sense this is true, but there is an important distinction between two types of issues taken to caucus. Some groups with sufficient access to the top party leadership will take their case directly to these leaders, who will then convey orders through the caucus to the individual supervisors. Others will take their plea directly to the individual members of the government. They may do this because (1) they do not know any better; (2) they consider it more democratic to "contact everyone" (and boast that they do); or (3) they are unable to gain access to the superstructure. Ordinarily their requests will necessitate party action too, since the party caucus is dominant in decision-making; but the caucus in the latter case will play the role of a decision-making unit rather than a vehicle to convey orders from the top.

Emphasis on the role of the political party as an intermediary in reaching metropolitan decisions should not becloud recognition of the fact that the state government often performs the same role. A common thread running through the cases is the ease with which problems of local cooperation within Onondaga County have been resolved when necessary by special legislation. Time and again when the provisions of the General County Government Law do not fit the perceived needs of the county, or when a local agency (e.g., the Public Works Commission) is to be created, or whatever the need may be, the legislature has smoothed the way by a special act.

This role played by the legislature is not, however, unrelated to the political party considerations treated above. Both phenomena result from the same cause: that Onondaga County differs from the usual image of metropolitan area in that the central city, its surrounding suburbs, the county, and the state legislature all are Republican. It is highly significant that this identity of partisan affiliation exists in a state in which party names are not nominal (as they might be in the South with reversed party labels), but in which instead party organizations are relatively tightly structured and capable of exercising discipline over their members. It is this concurrence of party membership that makes it possible for a Republican mayor of Syracuse, who is also Republican county chair-

an, to integrate welfare functions in the
ounty, as Marvin did in the 1930s, and it is this
concurrence further that makes the Republican
gislative leadership so readily responsive to
e wishes of Onondaga County. It is not meant
suggest that such coincidence uniformly
akes for metropolitan action, for legislative re-
onsiveness may be to a negative as well as to
positive stimulus.

The reverse of this proposition also is valid.
report for Utica (in Oneida County) suggests
at the absence of partisan identity between
e central city administration and the county
oard—a far more frequent occurrence than in
racuse, since Utica is more often Democratic
an not—has produced conflicts that have some-
mes acted as barriers to metropolitan cooper-
ion.[7] That partisan differences between the
ntral city and the surrounding areas, as well
between the city and the legislature, hamper
e resolution of problems in the New York City
etropolitan area is so evident as hardly to re-
ire documentation.[8]

The conclusion seems inescapable therefore
at one of the potent forces encouraging and
cilitating metropolitan action in the Syracuse
etropolitan area has been the existence of a
iversal and disciplined party allegiance that
s united central city, suburban governments,
unty government, and state legislature in com-
on cause.

ETROPOLITAN DECISION-MAKING
ND INSTITUTIONAL CHANGE

Chapter I [of *Decisions in Syracuse*] a model
metropolitan decision-making was presented;
e ingredient was missing from that model,
wever, which is included in the pattern of
cision-making described by Sayre and Kauf-
n. In their model the contest over the con-
ol of governmental action occurs within an in-
tutional framework characterized as the
les of the game." These consist partly of
les laid down by law determining the struc-
es and jurisdictions of governments, partly of
es emanating from social consensus. The
les of the game are not unvarying, but are sub-
t to change.

study of metropolitan governmental reorgani-
ion consists in essence of an examination of

the circumstances under which the rules of the
game in the metropolitan contest over decision-
making actually do change. In general two
kinds of circumstances can be identified under
which changes are made in that part of the rules
of the game consisting of formal governmental
institutions. In the first place, an institutional
change may occur as the result of an effort by one
of the contestants in the decision-making struggle to secure an advantage for himself. An individual or group may seek advantage by tinker-
ing with the governmental institutions, by using
control over some of the powers of government
to introduce changes in order to make easier control over other parts of the government. This
sort of maneuver occurs constantly in government, particularly with respect to the rules affecting the selection of government personnel.
Election laws are altered, election dates changed,
electoral districts reapportioned, changes made
in terms of administrative officials, etc.

"Reform" movements of this sort are likely
initially to possess only a narrow basis of support; if they were strong, they would not need
to seek such advantages. The permanence of
such a change, therefore, is likely to depend upon
its effectiveness. If the strategy succeeds in securing a monopolistic power position for the con-
testant who profits by it, then the change will be
retained. On the other hand, there may be circumstances in which the change has unexpected
consequences and groups that feared they would
be injured come to approve it. Sayre and Kaufman suggest that the creation of the City of
Greater New York in the 1890s occurred somewhat in this fashion. One of the prime movers
in the consolidation of the cities of Brooklyn
and New York, the greatest metropolitan governmental reorganization in American history, was
Thomas C. Platt, Republican leader in New
York State, who anticipated that the position of
the regular Republicans in the combined municipality would be improved. He was wrong, but
the new system proved sufficiently flexible to
accommodate itself to the interests of other
groups who, initially opposed, ultimately came to
support it.

The rules of the game can be changed for a
second reason also, namely that the contestants
agree generally that the existing institutions are
incapable of producing solutions to the problems
of society. Explanation of what is meant will

require consideration of a model different from that which views decision-making as a contest. For while governmental policy-making may legitimately be regarded as a contest, government at the same time must be recognized as a social institution with a social purpose. Its purpose is the solving of problems of conflict among groups within the society, and its efficacy in accomplishing that purpose depends in considerable part upon its internal organization. If the institutions of government are hopelessly disorganized, they may fail completely in the solving of problems. In the language of the contest previously used as a model, no major group will find it possible to achieve a significant innovation in governmental policy, and as new problems arise the failure to find solutions will produce a steady accumulation of tensions. This is the precise charge leveled against the government of the Fourth Republic in France, which was generally characterized by the term *immobilisme*. *Immobilisme* is not, however, a national disease that can be suffered only by Frenchmen; it can also affect other governments, including those of metropolitan areas within the United States.

Such a formulation suggests the existence of three variables which determine the likelihood of substantial governmental reorganization: (1) the number of problems facing the society; (2) the expectations of its members as to how many of their problems should be resolved through the instrumentality of government; and (3) the capacity of the governmental institutions to resolve problems. Variation in any one of the three factors or any combination of the three may generate demands for reorganization. A movement for reform may therefore result from: (1) new problems introduced by technological developments; (2) demands by substantial parts of the population for higher levels of governmental service; (3) a relative decline in the efficiency of government (for whatever reason); or (4) some combination of these factors. Reform movements of this kind are distinguished from those aimed at creating advantages for one of the parties to the contest both by the generality of the support they receive and by the greater durability of any changes they may bring about.[9]

It is commonplace to cite the role of crisis in encouraging experimentation with governmental institutions. A flood that leads to creation of a flood control district is an obvious illustration. Or the crisis may be felt secondhand: John Gaus

has called attention to the effects of the disastrous Cocoanut Grove fire in Boston in tightening fire regulations generally across the country. The fatal school fire in Chicago in the late 1950s had something of the same effect, at least so far as school buildings were concerned. In the present context, a crisis may be defined as a rapid multiplication of the problems faced by government. Although a slow accumulation of problems of similar magnitude eventually may produce much the same overloading of the problem-solving capacity of the governmental institutions, it appears that a rapid decline in governmental ability to meet public expectations produces a greater psychological readiness to make changes in the institutions themselves.

This analysis has relevance to the Syracuse metropolitan area. If Onondaga County faced crisis, more incentive for change might be found, but the metropolitan area has not experienced a real disaster and there is no reason to expect that it will. A breakdown in government could provide the occasion for drastic reorganization, but no such event has occurred. If the governments of Syracuse and Onondaga County are not spectacularly good, neither are they dramatically bad; and there has been no public evidence of gross mismanagement or other emergency to provoke significant structural change. The physical environment has been the source of only minor annoyances. Onondaga Creek, which runs through the heart of the city's central business district, overflowed its banks for century but the largest flood of record caused damage of no more than $100,000. This is not the stuff of which governmental reorganizations are made. Rather, the floods led to a succession of minor ameliorative measures—the straightening and deepening of the channel in 1868, extensions of the improved channel from time to time —and finally to a federally financed $4,252,2◌ flood control project in 1950. The only stringency that might have forced any sort of governmental reorganization was the cost of the 19◌ project, and the assumption of responsibility by the federal government eliminated even the mild compulsion.[10]

Today the disaster most likely to precipitate substantial governmental action would be a major exodus in industry. Both exodus and drastic action, however, seem highly unlikely eventualities. Individual industries have moved or threatened to move from the city, but public reactio◌

to such threats has been for the most part sporadic and piecemeal. As individual problems, such as sewage or water, have emerged, they have been dealt with on an *ad hoc* basis. Little enthusiasm has been shown for the creation of new governmental institutions to deal on an area-wide basis with the multiplicity of metropolitan problems.

In this Syracuse deviates little from the national norm, for it is universally observed that multi-functional reform, that is, general governmental reorganization, is far more difficult to secure than a redistribution of individual functions among existing governments. Probably the most significant reason for this lies in the character of the different interest groups involved. Elevation of a single program to the metropolitan level is ordinarily sought by an economic interest group which finds a new governmental service necessary to its economic well-being. In the standard situation, this means that local industry has been brought face to face with the problem of a shortage of water, an oversupply of pollution, an undersupply of transportation, or whatever, and demands—successfully—that government take a hand in the matter. Although economic interests may be alleged to be at stake in government reorganizations (which are often sold as moves to have money by eliminating "waste"), the monetary gains involved are more diffuse, less certain, and often suspect. The industrialist or businessman may fear that a rejuvenated government, even if more efficient in its use of tax moneys, might seek to justify itself by embarking on new and more expensive programs. The cause of metropolitan reorganization is therefore likely to be supported only by individuals attracted by its rational simplicity, but without either an established position of influence within the community or the kind of economic commitment that will produce vigorous action.

An additional factor which encourages the piecemeal approach to metropolitan problems in the Syracuse area is the coincidence of the county boundary with what has long been regarded as the metropolitan area. On the positive side this has facilitated the handling of metropolitan problems by their transfer to the county government, a procedure frequently employed. Solution of individual problems in this way, however, relieves the pressure for a more general reorganization. On a limited scale this

phenomenon was encountered in the proposal for a county health department. Because the most serious of the rural health needs have been met by state programs, private action, the county mental health program, etc., insufficient incentive has been found to support a drastic change. In words appropriate to a formula proposed above it may be said that, although both the number of problems and the expectations of what government should do about them have been increasing in the Syracuse metropolitan area, the existence of a county with a metropolitan jurisdiction has made possible a problem-solving process effective enough to head off serious metropolitan governmental proposals.

The build-up of functions at the county level has in turn created a further problem by making more serious the consequences of the failure to reorganize the county government. There seems little reason to doubt that Onondaga County will follow the other metropolitan counties of the state within the next few years and reorganize.[11] If we are to learn from history this will entail the creation of a county executive, who will immediately become the center of a move for expanding the county government's powers. County reorganization thus will result in a growth in county authority, and in the relaxation and ultimate abandonment of the tradition of minimal local government.

In the long run, the most effective practical argument for the transfer of urban governmental functions to the county is likely to emphasize not the increase in the problem-solving capacity of government but the preservation of party advantage. Syracuse has long been a citadel of Republicanism. It seems improbable, however, that the Republican Party can do more than delay the partisan realignment likely to occur within the city as a result of popualtion change. In local elections in the past the Republicans have succeeded in maintaining their hold on the Negro vote. By national standards such a situation is unnatural, and the vote of the rapidly increasing Negro population may be expected eventually to tip the balance within the city to the Democratic Party. Another prospective development pointing in that direction is the growth in the political strength of labor. The approach of equality and the threat of superiority in the city by the Democrats is likely to encourage a rapid transfer of functions to the county by the Republican leaders, secure in the conviction the county government constitutes a stronghold from which they cannot easily be routed. If such a transfer does not take place, indeed, it is logical to anticipate a steady accumulation of metropolitan conflicts as the unifying force of Republicanism relaxes its grip. In such a twilight of the *Pax Republicana*, the resulting tensions would erupt in violent party warfare. He would be rash who would prophesy the outcome in terms of possible solutions to metropolitan problems.

Notes

1. Wayne Hodges, *Company and Community: Case Studies in Industry-City Relationships* (New York: Harper and Brothers, 1958).
2. It is worth reiteration that the cases studied center on governmental decision-making. It is quite possible that an examination of decisions taken in the private sector, as in private charity or cultural affairs, would provide convincing evidence of Stewart Hancock's power in those areas. Similarly, an analysis of day-to-day decision-making–action on zoning variances, the choice of government personnel, the letting of contracts, etc.—might produce different conclusions from those recorded here.
3. This conclusion corroborates the findings of another contemporary study of community leadership in Syracuse. See Linton C. Freeman and others, *Local Community Leadership* (Syracuse: University College of Syracuse University, 1960).
4. The creation in recent years of the Department of Research and Development and the Regional Planning Board suggests that the county is conscious of the need for developing sources of its own for general staff assistance.
5. A recent report states that the unused borrowing capacity of the local governments in Onondaga County (including city and county) totals $143,500,000. Metropolitan Development Association, *A Profile of Onondaga County*, pp. 16–18.
6. Wallace S. Sayre and Herbert Kaufman, *Governing New York City* (New York: Russell Sage Foundation, 1960), p. 562.
7. State of New York, Special Legislative Committee on Revision and Simplification of the Constitution, *Staff Report on Metropolitan Utica-Rome* (Report 6, May 1958). The report specifically makes this point.
8. See Sayre and Kaufman, *op. cit.*, p. 562.
9. The author is indebted to Coleman Woodbury for suggesting this line of reasoning. The concept of ineffective problem-solving may provide a substitute for the normative framework ordinarily used to justify metropolitan reorganization, which in effect simply states that a metropolitan government would be more sensible. To the extent that the reports pleading for the creation of new metropolitan governments written within this normative framework are effective, it would seem probable that they produce their impact by changing the expectations of the population as to what government service levels should be. It seems plausible that they might be still more effective if they were aimed deliberately at that objective.
10. Jonathan B. Pollard, "The Effects of the 195_ Flood Control Project upon Utilization of the Onondaga Valley Flood Plain, New York" (unpublished M.A. thesis, Syracuse University, July 1960).
11. Some see hope for early and perhaps significant action in the work of the county charter commission appointed late in 1960. See Chapter IX for a brief comment on recent developments respecting county reorganization.

23

JAMES Q. WILSON

A Guide to Reagan Country: The Political Culture of Southern California

A person like myself, who grew up in Southern California, finds it increasingly difficult to understand people who say they understand California. "Explaining California," especially Southern California, has always been a favorite pastime or New Yorkers and Bostonians who have changed planes in Los Angeles, or made a two-day trip to the RAND Corporation, or just speculated on what kind of state could be responsible or Hollywood. Nor need one be an Easterner to play the game; living in San Francisco carries with it a permanent license not only to explain but to explain away (*far away*) Los Angeles.

This game might have been regarded as an amusing (though to me, irritating) diversion so long as what was being explained or "understood" was Hollywood and Vine, or orange-juice stands shaped like oranges, or Aimee Semple McPherson, or the Great I Am, or traffic on the Los Angeles freeways. It became a little less amusing when the same "explanations" thought appropriate for Aimee and the poor orange-juice vendors (most of whom, by the way, have disappeared) were applied to the John Birch Society and other manifestations of the Far Right. Anybody crazy enough to buy orange juice at such places or to drive on those freeways must be crazy enough to be a Bircher. Let two Birch-e loudmouths pop off anywhere else in the coun-

try and we rush to our sociology texts to see whether it is alienation or the decline of the small entrepreneur that is the cause; let two of them say the same thing in Los Angeles, and we just smile knowingly and murmur, "It figures."

Even this systematic application of the double standard was harmless enough before Ronald Reagan. Now a striking conservative personality has become governor of the largest state in the union by an election plurality of over a million votes, most of which he picked up in Southern California. This Hollywood-actor-turned-politician ("it figures") has, to the amazement of many, made a rather considerable impression, not only on the voters of his state but on Republicans around the country including, apparently, a group of presumably toughminded fellow governors. From now at least through the 1968 convention we have to take Reagan quite seriously, and even if he fails to go the distance we must, I think, take Reaganism seriously. It will be with us for a long time under one guise or another. We will not take it seriously by trying explain it away as if it were something sold at one of those orange-juice stands or preached from the pulpit at some cultist church.

I grew up in Reagan country—not Hollywood, but the lower-middle-class suburbs of Los Angeles. It was a distinctive way of life. I think I could still recognize another person who grew up there no matter where I should meet him, just as surely as an Italian can spot a person from his village or region even though they are both now in Queens. I am under no illusion that anyone has the slightest interest in my boyhood (I have next to no interest in it myself), but I do suspect

James Q. Wilson, "A Guide to Reagan Country: The Political Culture of Southern California," *Commentary*, vol. 43 (May 1967), pp. 37–45. Reprinted from *Commentary*, by permission; copyright © 1967 by the American Jewish Committee.

that it may be useful to try to explain what it was like at least in general terms, and how what it was like is relevant to what is happening there today. Though I grew up and went to school there, I left a long time ago in order to acquire some expensive Eastern postgraduate degrees and a political outlook that would now make me vote against Reagan if I had the chance. I do not intend here to write an apology for Reagan; even if I thought like that, which I don't, I would never write it down anywhere my colleagues at Harvard might read it.

I

The important thing to know about Southern California is that the people who live there, who grew up there, love it. Not just the way one has an attachment to a hometown, any hometown, but the way people love the realization that they have found the right mode of life. People who live in Southern California are not richer or better educated than those who live in New York; the significant point about them is that they don't live in New York, and don't want to. If they did, they—the average Los Angeleno (my family, for example)—would have lived most of their lives in a walkup flat in, say, the Yorkville section of Manhattan or not far off Flatbush Avenue in Brooklyn. Given their income in 1930, life would have been crowded, noisy, cold, threatening—in short, *urban*. In Long Beach or Inglewood or Huntington Park or Bellflower, by contrast, life was carried on in a detached house with a lawn in front and a car in the garage, part of a quiet neighborhood, with no crime (except kids racing noisy cars), no cold, no smells, no congestion. The monthly payments on that bungalow—one or two bedrooms, one bath, a miniscule dining room, and never enough closets—would have been no more than the rent on the walkup flat in Brooklyn or Yorkville. In 1940, with the Depression still in force, *over half the population* of Los Angeles lived in single-family homes. Only about half of these were owner-occupied, but even to rent a house was such a vast improvement over renting an apartment that nobody looked back; they only looked ahead to the time they could pick up their own mortgage. San Francisco in the same year was another matter. Only a third of the population

lived in single-family homes there, the reason being that there were almost no *houses* to rent; if you wanted a house, you had to buy it, and not many people in 1940 could afford to buy.

There has been a good deal of loose talk about "radical" politics (which I suppose means anything to the Right of Earl Warren) developing out of a rootless, highly mobile population with no sense of *place*, of continuity, of stability. That may explain radical politics somewhere, but not in Los Angeles. The people who voted for Reagan have lived for years, in many cases decades, in Southern California. And they have lived in houses, not anonymous, impersonal apartment buildings.

Indeed, it was during the period of Los Angeles's greatest population growth that it voted over and over again, for Earl Warren—the very embodiment (then) of moderation. The explanation, I believe, is quite simple: truly rootless mobile people are more likely to vote the way established institutions—newspapers, churches, labor unions, business firms—tell them to vote. Revolutions are never made by the last man to get off the train; they are made by those who got off a long time ago and, having put down roots and formed their own assessment of matters, have the confidence, the long-nurtured discontent, and the knowledge of how to get things done sufficient to support independent political action. (Radical politics, I suspect, follows the same pattern as Negro riots: contrary to what the McCone Commission asserted but did not prove, the Negroes who rioted in Watts—or at least those who rioted violently enough to get themselves arrested—were Negroes who had been in Watts for a long time. Over half the teenage Negroes arrested had been *born* in California; over three-fourths had lived there for more than five years.)

In any case, it is a mistake to try to explain a particular election by underlying social trends. Elections, after all, are choices, and how they come out depends on who the voters have to choose between. That Reagan won last year does not mean that *last year* some ineluctable social force finally surfaced and carried the day. A vote for Reaganism was always possible in Southern California (and had revealed itself in countless congressional and local elections). The point I wish to make is that there has for long time been a "Reagan point of view" in the Southern California electorate, that this point of view was powerfully shaped by the kinds of people who went to California and the conditions of life there.

The people who in 1940 lived in those hundreds of thousands of detached and semi-detached homes came from all over the country, but primarily they came from the Midwest, the border states, and the "near South." Almost none came from Europe: about 6 percent, to be exact, had been born in Italy, Ireland, Germany, France, Sweden, or Russia; another 2½ percent had been born in Mexico. (In San Francisco, the proportion of foreign born was twice as large.) But 28 percent had been born in the American heartland—the dustbowl states (Texas, Oklahoma, Arkansas, Louisiana, Kansas, Nebraska), or the border states (Indiana, Missouri, Tennessee, Kentucky) and the upper plains (Iowa, Wisconsin, Minnesota, the Dakotas). If you add in the nearby mountain and Southwestern states (Colorado, Utah, Arizona, New Mexico, Nevada), the total proportion rises to over a third. And if you add in the persons whose parents had been born in these states, the proportion no doubt (there are no figures) exceeds a half. Again, San Francisco is a contrast—only about a tenth of its people in 1940 were from the heartland states. Between 1920 and 1940, during the Depression, over 400,000 persons born in the heartland moved to Los Angeles. *Less than a tenth* as many moved to San Francisco.

Except for Arkansas, Louisiana, and Texas, no Southern states are included in these migration figures. This is important to bear in mind—such conservatism as Southern California displays was not imported from the Deep South. In fact, even those who came from Southern states were likely to be from places like West Texas, where Confederate sentiment was never very strong.

These migrants were rural and small-town people. And here, of course, another popular explanation of Southern California politics takes the stage. These voters are supposed to yearn for the simpler life and the small-town virtues that they left behind. They are reactionary, it is claimed, in the precise sense: seeking to turn back the clock to a day when life was easier, virtues less complicated, and the Ten Commandments a sufficient guide. Perhaps so—there is no doubt some truth in this. But it flies in the face of the fact that these are people who *left* small-town and rural America (millions more stayed behind, after all)—and left it for jobs in big defense plants and large office buildings. I was never aware of any effort to re-create small-town America in Southern California, unless you put in that category the Victory Gardens people planted to raise vegetables during the war. On the contrary, they adopted rather quickly a suburban style of life, with its attendant devotion to the growing of a decent lawn (how many farms have you ever seen with a good lawn?). Furthermore, it is not the migrants themselves who on the whole have voted for Reaganism, but their children. The migrants voted for Roosevelt and Upton Sinclair and looked on disapprovingly as their children began to adopt the hedonistic mores of Southern California teenage life. There was as much intergenerational conflict among the Okies and Arkies in California as among the Italians and the Irish in Boston or New York. And yet it was these youngsters who grew up, married, moved out to Orange County or to Lakewood, and voted for Reagan and castigated Pat Brown, the last of the New Deal-Fair Deal Democrats. (To be completely accurate, a lot of the older people voted for Reagan, too, but they, I imagine, found it much harder to let go of their traditional attachment to Franklin Roosevelt and Earl Warren; the young people had no trouble at all.)

This is not to say that the migrants brought nothing with them. On the contrary, they brought an essential ingredient of Southern California life—fundamentalist Protestant individualism. We like to think of the store-front church as being a Negro invention; not so. I remember scores of white store-front churches—mostly of small Pentecostal and Adventist sects—lining the main streets of Long Beach. Most people, of course, went to established churches, but these were only bigger and slightly more orthodox versions of the same thing—Baptists, Methodists, Mormons, Brethren, Church of God, and so on. Church was a very important part of life, but hardly any two people belonged to the same one. We were Catholics, and we had to drive out into the dairy farming county (I will never forget the way Sunday morning smelled—incense and cow manure, in equal portions) where there were enough Mexican farmhands and Dutch Catholic dairymen to make up a parish. All my friends sang hymns and listened to "preachin'." And the preaching was evangelical, fundamentalist, and preoccupied with the obligation of the *individual* to find and enter into a right relationship with God, with no sacraments, rituals, covenants, or grace to make it easy.

The religious character of San Francisco was strikingly different. In 1936 (the last time the government took a census of church organizations), 70 percent of the reported church membership of San Francisco, but only 40 percent of that in Los Angeles, was Catholic. And of the claimed members of Protestant sects, 40 percent in San Francisco, but only 26 percent in Los Angeles, belonged to the high-status, nonfundamentalist churches—Congregational, Episcopalian, Unitarian, and Universalist. Both cities had about the same proportion of Jews, but, as will be argued in a moment, the leadership, at least, of the two Jewish communities was rather different. Los Angeles, and even more its middle-class suburbs, was Protestant and fundamentalist Protestant at that.

The social structure did nothing to change the individualistic orientation of life. People had no identities except their personal identities, no obvious group affiliations to make possible any reference to them by collective nouns. I never heard the phrase "ethnic group" until I was in graduate school. I never knew there were Irishmen (I was amazed many years later to learn that, at least on my mother's side, I had been one all along) or Italians (except funny organ grinders in the movies, all of whom looked like Chico Marx). We knew there were Negroes (but none within miles of where we lived) and Jews (they ran Hollywood and New York, we knew, but not many of us had ever met one). Nobody ever even pointed out to me that I was a Catholic (except once, when a friend explained that that was probably the reason I wouldn't join the Order of De Molay, a young people's Masonic group).

The absence of such group identities and of neighborhoods associated with those identities may be one reason for the enormous emphasis on "personality." Teenagers everywhere, of course, place great stock in this, mostly, I suppose, because they feel such an urgent need to establish an identity and to be liked by others. But in Southern California, it went far beyond that—there was a cult of personality that dominated every aspect of life. Everybody was compared in terms of his or her personality; contests for student-body office were based on it. To be "popular" and "sincere" was vital. In a New York high school, by contrast, personality would have to share importance in such contests with a

certain amount of bloc voting among the Irish, Italians, and Jews, or between "project" people and brownstone people, or even between leftists and far leftists.

Perhaps because of the absence of ethnic and religious blocs which in turn are associated with certain political positions, perhaps because Southern California (then) was very remote from those urban centers where "The Future of Socialism" was being earnestly debated, student life in and around Los Angeles was remarkably apolitical. Most people were vaguely for Roosevelt, though there was a substantial (and growing) group that announced defiantly that while their parents had voted for FDR in '32, and perhaps even in '36, they weren't going to do *that* anymore. Registered Democrats who voted Republican were commonplace, but after noting that fact there wasn't, politically, much left to be said. (It was different in downtown Los Angeles where the Jews lived; L.A. High, and later Los Angeles State College, were very political. A considerable Wallace movement flourished in 1948. Many of those people are now in the Democratic club movement.)

Politics for these people came to mean, in later years, expressing directly one's individual political preferences and expecting them to be added up by a kind of political algebra into a general statement of the public interest. "Bloc voting" and group preferences were unheard of and, when heard of, unthinkable. And the idea that political parties ought to do anything besides help add up preferences was most heterodox—the worst thing that could be said about it was that it was "Eastern." The well-known institutional features of California's political system—weak parties, the extensive use of the referendum to decide policy issues, nonpartisanship—were perfectly matched to the political mentality that was nurtured in Southern California.

That nurturing was distinctive but hard to describe. Rural Anglo-Saxon Protestants have lived in lots of states, but they haven't produced the Southern California style of politics anywhere else. One reason is to be found in what it was like, and to a considerable extent is still like, to grow up in Southern California. Everybody, as I have already noted, lived in a single-family house. There was no public transportation to speak of, so that the movement of people within the city followed no set corridors. People moved about freely and in so doing saw how

everybody lived. That movement was institutionalized in the Sunday Afternoon Drive—not to
the beach or an amusement park, but just
"around" to look at homes, call on friends, or
visit distant relatives. A house was, as a Catholic might put it, the outward and visible sign of
inward grace. There was no anonymity provided
by apartment buildings or tenements or
projects. Each family had a house; there it was,
for all to see and inspect. With a practiced
glance, one could tell how much it cost, how well
it was cared for, how good a lawn had been
coaxed into uncertain life, and how tastefully
plants and shrubs had been set out.

A strong, socially reinforced commitment to
property was thus developed, evident in how
people treat those homes today. An enormous
amount of energy and money is devoted to repairing, improving, remodeling, extending, and
landscaping. Even in areas with fairly low incomes, such as those where the elderly and the
retired live, houses are not on the whole allowed
to deteriorate. A family might buy a house for
six or seven thousand dollars with, for the period, a big mortgage, and then spend several
times that over a generation or two in home improvements. Those who could not afford it substituted labor for capital. People were practicing
do-it-yourself in Southern California long before anybody in the advertising business thought
to give it a name. Year-round warm weather
made year-round outdoor labor possible—and, of
course, year-round outdoor inspection by one's
critical neighbors.

Much of this labor was cooperative. The
Southern California equivalent of the Eastern
uncle who could "get it for you wholesale" was
the Los Angeles brother-in-law who would help
you put on a new roof, or paint the garage, or
lend you (and show you how to use) his power
saw. A vast, informally organized labor exchange permeated the region, with occasional
trades of great complexity running through several intermediaries—the friend who would ask
his brother, the plumber, to help you if you
would ask your uncle with the mixer to lay the
concrete in front of somebody's sister's home.
Saturday saw people driving all over the county
carrying out these assignments.

Driving. Driving everywhere, over great distances, with scarcely any thought to the enormous mileages they were logging. A car was the
absolutely essential piece of social overhead

capital. With it, you could get a job, meet a
girl, hang around with the boys, go to a drive-in,
see football games away from home, take in the
beach parties at Laguna or Corona del Mar, or
go to the Palladium ballroom in Hollywood. To
have a car meant being somebody; to have to
borrow a car meant knowing somebody; to have
no car at all, owned or borrowed, was to be left
out—way out.

Those cars led parents and professional moral-
ists to speak of "teenagers and their jalopies."
They were not jalopies—not to us, anyway. The
oldest, most careworn Ford Model A was a thing
of beauty. To be sure, the beauty often had to
be coaxed out; yet what was life for but to do
the coaxing and take credit for the beauty?
Beauty, of course, meant different things to different boys. For some, it was speed and power;
and so they would drop a V-8 block into the "A"
chassis and then carefully, lovingly, bore it out,
stroke it, port it, and put two barrels or four barrels on it. For others, beauty was in the body,
not the engine, and their energies would go into
customizing the car—dropping the rear end,
chopping down the top, leading in the fenders,
stripping off the chrome (it took Detroit decades
to recognize the merits of these changes and
then to mass-produce them), and above all painting, sanding, rubbing, painting, sanding, rubbing
—for ten or fifteen or twenty coats, usually of
metallic paint. Again, warm weather made it
easier—you could work outside year round and
if you ran out of money before the job was finished (which was most of the time), you could
drive around in the unfinished product with no
top, primed but not painted, and no hood over
the engine. Of late, Mr. Tom Wolfe of *New York*
magazine has discovered car customizing and
decided it is a folk art. It wasn't folk art in the
'40s; it was life.

The sense of property developed by this activity has never been measured and perhaps
never can be; I am convinced it was enormous
and fundamental. After marriage, devoting energy to the improvement of a house was simply
a grown-up extension of what, as a juvenile, one
had done with cars. There is, of course, a paradox here: the car was used in great part to get
girls. It was a hand-polished, custom-made rolling bedroom, or so its creators hoped. (In this
they were as often disappointed as a Harvard
man taking a Radcliffe girl into his house rooms
during parietal hours; every girl likes to be *seen*

in such places, but a distressingly small proportion are inclined to *do* anything there.) But the hedonistic purposes to which the car might be put did not detract from its power to create and sustain a very conventional and bourgeois sense of property and responsibility, for in the last analysis the car was not a means to an end but an end in itself. Shocked parents never got that point: they saw the excess that the car permitted, they did not see the intensely middle-class values that it instilled.

Low-density, single-family homes, a lack of public transportation, the absence of ethnic neighborhoods, and the use of cars combined to prevent the formation of streetcorner gangs, except in very central portions of Los Angeles and one or two older cities. The principal after-school occupation of a teenage Eastern boy from a working-class family is to "hang out" at the corner candystore, the ice-cream parlor, or in front of the drugstore with class and ethnic compatriots. Having a "corner" of your own—or having "turf," in the case of the ambitious and imperialistic—would have made no sense to an equivalent group of young men in Southern California. The Eastern life-style produced a feeling of *territory*, the Western life-style a feeling of *property*. Teenagers in Southern California hung out together, to be sure, but not in any fixed spot, and where they did hang out tended to be a place reached by a car, with lots of free parking for other cars. The drive-in restaurant was the premier institution catering to this need. But it was also a very democratic institution, since it was not (and because of its location some distance from one's home, could not become) the "turf" of any particular gang. Rich and poor, Protestant and Catholic, anybody with a car could get there and, barring a losing fight over a girl, stay there. There were rivalries, but like modern warfare they tended to be between large, heterogeneous, and impersonal rivals—one high school against another, not one ethnic group against another.

Can all this explain why Southern California is so different, politically, from Northern California—why it, so much more than the Bay Area, supported Goldwater and Reagan? Perhaps not entirely. And yet I believe the kind of people living there and their life-styles are very important, much more important than, say, the presumed influence of the conservative Los Angeles *Times*. The Oakland *Tribune* is even more con-

servative, but the East Bay region it serves is more "liberal" in its voting than L.A. And the very liberal McClatchey newspapers in the Central Valley do not seem to have turned back the Reagan tide. On the other hand, San Francisco has Southern-California-style suburbs as well, with bungalows and cars and the like, and the people there are not as conservative as their counterparts in the South. But as we have seen, the people who migrated to San Francisco in the '30s and '40s were different from those who settled in Los Angeles. And once the different life-styles of the two cities became apparent, non-Californians must have begun deciding to move to the Bay Area or to Los Angeles on the basis, in part, of what they had heard about those styles. A small but visible difference in the beginning thus became a very large difference in the end.

II

The political institutions and economic character of Southern California reinforced the life style and gave it expression. Politics, as I have said, was non-partisan, free-swinging, slightly populistic—a direct appeal to the people was to be made on all issues. The major parties for decades were virtually moribund and therefore never performed their customary (and to my thinking, desirable) task of aggregating interests, blurring issues, strengthening party loyalties, and finding moderate candidates. Not that the people wanted immoderate candidates. So long, at least, as the issues were not very grave—before civil rights, and welfare, and Berkeley, and crime—they wanted honest, competent administrators who favored change but in an orderly manner. In Earl Warren they got such a man and he made sure the regular Republican party, whose fat cats were on the whole considerably to his Right, would not have a chance to replace him. He built a personal following outside the regular, and cumbersome, party apparatus. Like most personal followings, however, it made no provision for a transfer of power. The obvious Warren protégé—Thomas Kuchel—was in the Senate, Warren's personal following in the state could not be handed to another man, and the party was in no shape to find a candidate of its own. Any man with money and a good smile

ould take a crack at capturing the nomination
on his own, and many did.

Such organization as existed tended to be in the
North, rather than the South. San Francisco
and Alameda County across the bay had more in
the way of party machinery, financed on a
steady basis, than the South had, at least until
the emergence of the California Democratic
Clubs. A little organization goes a long way in
an organizational vacuum, and the North exercised a disproportionate influence in California
politics for some time. The Northern Democrats had some old families—many Jewish—who
helped pay the party's bills during the long, lean
years.

The South had few such persons—or more accurately, it had some very rich, self-made men
from the oil business and from the vast agricultural enterprises of the Imperial Valley who
were conservative Democrats in the (by now)
well-documented tradition of the American
Southwest. They may be more visible in Texas
today, but twenty years ago they were more influential in California.

Why? There were Jews in Southern California, tens of thousands of them in and around
Los Angeles. (Yet looking back on my high-
school days, I can think of only one Jew I was
personally acquainted with, and he went to another high school across town. Jews were Hollywood, we all knew.) Many of them were in the
movie industry and in command of wealth and
great resources for publicity. Why didn't they
help to finance and lead the Southern California
Democratic party? Some did—or tried—at least
for a while. A high point of that influence was
the 1950 senatorial campaign of the liberal Helen
Gahagan Douglas, the movie actress. It wasn't
George Murphy or Ronald Reagan who put Hollywood into politics, it was Mrs. Douglas, who lost
to Richard Nixon. Two years before, many of
her supporters had turned, in frustration, to
third-party politics and become important figures in the 1948 campaign of Henry Wallace. It
was a disaster. Bolting the party nationally was
a far more serious thing than bolting it locally,
where it could hardly be said to exist. The Tru-
man Democrats took control in California and,
when Communist party influence in the Wallace
movement became too obvious to be denied
(Wallace himself was to admit it later), they
were in a position to treat the Douglas and Wallace Democrats as thoroughly discredited in the

eyes of the voters. Shortly thereafter, the era of
McCarthyism descended upon the country, and
Hollywood involvement in politics was for
the time being finished. What Mrs. Douglas had
begun, Henry Wallace and Joe McCarthy succeeded in ending.

But it was not only that Hollywood Jews had
lost power, it was also that Hollywood Jews
were different from those in other urban centers. The social and economic heights of Hollywood were commanded, not by German Jews,
but by East Europeans; not by old families but
by immigrants; not by Wall Street smoothness
but by *nouveau riche* entrepreneurship. Such
Hollywood money as went into politics was used
much as money was then used in the movie industry—impulsively, by dictatorial men used to
having their own way, and on behalf of "stars."
If the star system worked on the movie lots, why
couldn't it work in politics? Thus, a glamorous
figure, a big name and occasionally a conspicuous
nut could get *personal* backing for a campaign,
but there was little or no money for organization,
for routine affairs, or for professional (and necessarily bureaucratic) leadership.

Anyway, the voter wasn't much interested in
liberalism even if it could be financed. Los Angeles was prosperous, and even greater prosperity seemed just around the corner. The aircraft plants and shipyards had taken tens of
thousands of families and given every member,
including the mother, a job, thereby putting
them, in four years' time, in a wholly different
and higher economic bracket. A generation of
slow gain was compressed into a few years;
progress wasn't around the corner, or something
you hoped for for your kids, it was right here
and now. War prosperity affected the whole
country, but it had a special effect on Southern
California—there was more of it, because there
was more war industry located there, and it
benefited people who only a few years before
had been fighting for survival on a dust-swept
farm in the Texas panhandle. John Steinbeck
has told us how those farmers and sharecroppers
saw California as the Promised Land. But they
had only been promised relief checks from the
Farm Security Administration; instead, they
found overtime checks from Lockheed.

Next to the kind of people who live there, the
rate of economic growth of Southern California
—and today, of the whole Southwest—is the
main key to its political life. Visiting scholars

make much of the business domination of Dallas, or the presumed influence of the Los Angeles *Times* in Southern California, or the "Chamber of Commerce mentality" of San Diego. The important thing to understand is that these have not been alien influences imposed from above on the populace—they are merely the more obvious indicators of the fact that business values are widely shared. (Not business *control;* voters are as quick to resent that, when it is pointed out to them, in Los Angeles as anywhere. Sam Yorty became mayor by running against the *Times* and other "downtown interests," and he is still very popular in his city, however much ridicule he may take from Robert Kennedy in Washington.) Business values are here meant in the widest sense—a desire for expansion and growth, a high rate of increase in property values, finding and developing mass markets, and keeping capital moving and labor productive.

No one was immune from this psychology. How could he be? Everyone was buying, or intended to buy, his own home. Many factory workers and salesmen speculated in real estate on the side. A favorite topic of conversation at our dinner table, and I am sure at thousands of dinner tables just like it, was the latest story about the fantastic price a certain parcel had just been sold for and what a shame it was that we passed up the chance to buy it two years ago for peanuts. (We never seemed to have enough peanuts around at the right time.) The purpose of government was to facilitate this growth—open up new land, bring in water, make credit easy, keep the defense plants rolling. Government was not there to keep painfully-acquired positions secure by paying out benefits or legislating new regulations. Government was there to help bring in the future, not protect the past.

Not everyone felt this way, of course. Elderly people who came to California to retire had a different view. They wanted pensions, benefits, regulations. They were numerous and visible, but though they come quickly to mind when one thinks back on the shuffleboard and croquet courts at Lincoln Park in Long Beach or on the soapbox orators and bench-sitters in Pershing Square in Los Angeles, they were never representative of the local political ethos. They were the butt of countless jokes and the target for much political criticism: they wanted to hold back tomorrow (it was believed), cash their relief checks, and lie in the sun. That was *wrong,*

most working families thought. The Negro, who today is the victim of the anti-welfare sentiment, was actually the second victim; the first was the old folks. They were attacked for moving to California "just to get a pension," told to "go back where they came from," and fought against in countless welfare issues. (About the only thing they were spared were allegations that they constituted a sexual threat. I cannot recall my father, no paragon of tolerance, ever trying to clinch an argument against a liberal by asking him how he would like it if his daughter grew up and married an old man.)

The old folks fought back, but in California it was a *protest* movement. George McLain organized the old folks (nobody ever called them "senior citizens"; they didn't even call themselves that) and made them a potent force in state politics, but it was a force directed *against* the two major parties and their candidates. He won concessions for his followers and now they may be so secure as to be accepted as a political fact of life; what they wanted, however, was never accepted.

Southern California's political culture, including but not limited to what might be called Reaganism, is one which I suspect is characteristic of areas experiencing rapid economic growth and general prosperity, especially if there are few institutions—political parties, churches, labor unions—to frame the issues and blunt popular instincts. People there are concerned about the growth in the size of the economic pie, not (except for the elderly) in preserving the size of their present slice. The attributes in a person to be admired are those which indicate his ability to enhance his position and expand his resources, not conserve his position and maintain his resources. If I had to cite only one way in which Southwestern politics differ from Northeastern politics, it would be this: the former region is developmental, future-oriented, and growth-conscious; the latter is conserving, past or present-oriented, and security-conscious. Note that I say "conserving," not conservative; there is a difference. The Northeast by some measures is less "conservative" than the Southwest, though it is easy to exaggerate the difference. A conserva*tive* is usually thought of as a person who favors limited government, minimized administrative involvement in private affairs, maximum free choice. A conserver, on the other hand, needs *more* government in order to protect present stakes from change, from threats posed by other groups, and from competition.

Before we get carried away with the difference, some qualifications are in order. There are conserving forces at work in Southern California. One is the elderly. Another is the slowly emerging labor movement. For years Los Angeles was a tough city in which to be a trade unionist. There are still people who remember with horror the bombing of the Los Angeles *Times*. But unions are making headway. One is the Retail Clerks, which is organizing in the supermarkets and dime stores; another is the Machinists, active in aircraft and auto assembly plants. And the region's economic growth has not unleashed anything like the hysteria of the Florida land boom.

Even more important as a challenge to the general political culture of the region, with its concern for property, propriety, individual responsibility, economic growth, and limited government, is ideological liberalism. By the time McCarthyism was ending and the blacklists were beginning to lose their grip on Hollywood (perhaps because faced with the competition from television and European producers, Hollywood could no longer afford the luxury of a blacklist), Adlai Stevenson was making his appearance as a force in the Democratic party. The enormous outpouring of support for him in Southern California has been oft remarked upon, as has the vigorous club movement that grew up in the aftermath of his 1952 and 1956 Presidential campaigns. The movement activated a wholly new generation of political enthusiasts and provided a new base of operations for some of the leftovers from older forms of liberal and radical politics.

These clubs did not recruit the people I have been describing in earlier pages, nor have they taken hold in the areas in which these people live. The clubs grew up on the northern and eastern periphery of the region—the Hollywood Hills, Santa Monica, Beverly Hills, Pacific Palisades, and out into the college towns, such as Pomona, in the interior. Young Jews, young intellectuals, persons transplanted to Los Angeles from the East (by 1940, about 10 percent of the population had been born in New England, New Jersey, or Pennsylvania), and older California radicals flocked into the clubs. But the clubs never really took root among the working-class

and middle-class bungalows of Long Beach, Inglewood, or Redondo Beach, to say nothing of Orange County to the Southeast. The Democratic clubs initially had little interest in Southern California; they were interested in national and international issues. (The civil-rights movement has changed that; the clubs are now deeply involved in such matters locally.) They had, at the outset, no real program for California (though they had one for just about everything else), and thus there was no necessary conflict between what they wanted and what those who later voted for Reagan wanted—no necessary conflict, perhaps, but conflict nonetheless. And the most intense kind of conflict, for what was at stake were large and symbolic issues—Red China, capital punishment, world peace, and civil liberties. The Southern California electorate quickly became deeply polarized.

The polarization is not immediately evident in voting statistics. In the aggregate, Southern California elects a mixture of liberals and conservatives much like any other region, and on many of its famous referenda votes for and against public expenditures about like other areas. But these aggregate figures conceal the real symptoms of polarization—several Democrats (not all) are as far to the Left of their party as possible; several Republicans (not all) are as far to the Right of their party as possible. And on referenda issues—especially those involving such matters as open occupancy in housing—the returns and the polls suggest that Southern California has both the most intense proponents and the most intense opponents (the latter outnumbering the former: the region as a whole was against fair housing by a considerable margin; in San Francisco, the vote was both less lopsided and, I suspect, based on less intensely polarized views). This is *not* the same thing as saying that Southern California is more "bigoted" than the Bay Area. Because of the way the issue was framed, people were asked to vote *for the right* to sell their property to whomever they chose. In Southern California, property rights are vital and freedom in their exercise staunchly defended. There have been, I would guess, fewer attacks on Negro families seeking homes in white neighborhoods in Southern California than in say, Pennsylvania, Ohio, or Illinois. The housing issue was fought out at a more general level—not over whether one was for or against Negroes, but over alternative conceptions of what freedom requires. And the polarization of opinion on this issue, as on most, was most intense among persons of higher status. The educated, affluent Easterners and intellectuals (who work in law firms or the communications media or the universities) are more inclined than their less well-off fellows to support the Democratic clubs and liberalism; the educated, affluent sons and daughters of the Midwestern migrants (who now work as engineers and accountants in aerospace and petroleum industries) are more inclined than their less well-off fellows to support Goldwater and Reagan.

III

Is Southern California's political culture unique? Not really—it is but the earliest, most publicized, and most heavily populated example of a pattern now to be found throughout much of the Southwest. It appeared first in Southern California because more people went there and because California's political institutions gave almost immediate expression to it. In other states, the party structure constrained its free expression for a time; the ambitions of rival politicians and factions in Texas and Arizona made the ideology less evident, at least for a while. Goldwater's easy victory at the 1964 Republican convention indicates how widespread are certain aspects of that culture—in fact, it overstates it, because Goldwater himself overstated many features of that culture. The Southern Californians about whom I have written want limited government, personal responsibility, "basic" education, a resurgence of patriotism, an end to "chiseling," and a more restrained Supreme Court. They are not quite so certain that they want an adventurous foreign policy or a high-risk international confrontation with Communism. No doubt the militant Goldwater enthusiasts wanted such a policy, but they must have mistaken what the rank-and-file would support. Reagan has not yet made the same mistake—he took Goldwater's views, stripped away the foreign policy (except for very general statements) and references to turning back the clock on Social Security (after all, he wanted a coalition between the elderly and the young).

But Goldwater, however badly-managed his campaign, won the convention and won it by methods and with supporters which, in whatever state they were found, could very easily have been found in Southern California. Amateur political clubs, impassioned volunteers, appeals to highly moral and symbolic issues—the Republican party professionals had, to their profound irritation, to put up with all of it, just as party professionals in California, Democrats and Republicans alike, have been putting up with it since the early 1950s.

The Southern California political style is spreading; it seems to be, at least in the Western part of the United States, the concomitant of the American success story. There, millions of people are realizing their ambitions. They are not "rootless" or yearning for "small-town simplicity" or profoundly irritated by all the hustle and bustle; they are acquiring security, education, living space, and a life style that is based in its day-to-day routine on gentility, courtesy, hospitality, virtue. Why then, are they so discontent? It is not with their lot that they are discontent, it is with the lot of the nation. *The very virtue they have and practice are, in their eyes, conspicuously absent from society as a whole.* Politics is corrupt—not in the petty sense, though there is that—but in the large sense; to these people, it consists of "deals," of the catering to selfish interests, of cynical manipulation and doubletalk. The universities are corrupt—children don't act as if they appreciate what is being given them, they don't work hard, and they are lectured to by devious and wrongheaded professors. And above all, everywhere they look somebody is trying to get "something for nothing," and succeeding.

These views may not be confined only to the political culture in which they are now articulated. Surveys I have taken, and others I have read, indicate that the single most widespread concern of middle-class Americans is over the "decay of values"—evidenced by "crime in the streets," juvenile delinquency, public lewdness and the like, but going much beyond these manifestations to include everything that suggests that people no longer act in accordance with decent values and right reason. In many places, especially in the Northeast, our political institutions (happily) do not allow such views to play much part in elections. Parties, led by professionals, instinctively shun such issues, feeling somehow that public debate over virtue is irrelevant (what can government do about it?) and dangerous (nobody can agree on what virtue s or that your party has more of it). Powerful nonpolitical institutions tend, also, to keep such issues out of politics or to insist that they be matters of private conscience. For one, the Catholic Church, which draws the religious and moral interests of its followers inward, toward the sacraments and the educational and religious facilities of the Church which must be maintained and served. For another, large labor unions which have never mistaken a "stamp out smut" campaign for a fifty-cent increase in the minimum wage. And a self-conscious intelligentsia with common ties to prestigious centers of liberal-arts education has, in many regions, especially the East and the Bay Area, an important role to play among local elites. They use their access to the mass media and to officialdom to make certain that other, non-moral issues pre-

dominate—after all, the major function of the schools they went to was to induce them to rebel against the "middle-class morality" which, in the modern parlance, is a hangup.

Regional differences will never disappear entirely, and thus the political culture of Southern California will never be *the* political culture of our society. But the strength of all those institutions which resist it is waning, and thus we are likely to have more of it in more places in the future. I happen to think that morality is important and that those concerned about it are decent people (after all, I'm related to a sizable number of them). But I fear for the time when politics is seized with the issue. Our system of government cannot handle matters of that sort (can any democratic system?) and it may be torn apart by the effort.

24

MARILYN GITTELL

Decentralization and Citizen Participation in Education

The major arena in which decentralization and citizen control have been contested is in urban public education. It is appropriate, therefore, to use this experience to understand the complexities of social change demonstrated by that struggle.

During 70 years of American public school education, citizen participation has periodically played an important part in shaping educational policies. Civic groups at the turn of the century were especially active in supporting highly innovative programs for the new immigrant population. The arrival of these groups placed a tremendous burden on the schools, particularly because of the need to acculturate large numbers of non-English-speaking students (2). Almost immediately, citizen groups were formed to apply pressure for new educational programs. They actively campaigned for such innovations as kindergarten classes, first established for German-speaking children in Wisconsin. Subsequently, many city school systems incorporated kindergarten classes into the lower-school programs, and still others provided visiting teachers to work with children in their homes to supplant school programs (2). Colin Greer's recent study (44), however, indicates that these efforts fall short of success and that the immigrant poor were never effectively dealt with by the public education system.

Indirectly, the expanding school population was also a force in restructuring the school system. School board membership, administrative posts, and teaching positions had been traditionally distributed as political patronage (19). As the inadequacies of patronage in education were exposed, civic groups moved to bring professionalism into school systems (8)(18). There developed two systems of education: one urban based on civil service and in many ways politically unaccountable; the other suburban and rural, with some measure of accountability through formal elected boards with control over policy (1) (60). A combination of the civic reform movement and scientific management provided the rationale for major changes in school organization in the first part of the 20th century. One of the major groups organized for this purpose, the Public Education Association (14), acted through its branches in several cities to depoliticize school systems and secure structural reorganization. The citizen groups which provided the thrust for urban reform were largely middle class or upper middle class, and their commitment was more paternalistic than democratic. The local board of education was designed to be the primary means of citizen participation in school policy making. In keeping with the strong reform tradition, local boards of education were to be independent of city government, thus separating education from city functions with which it might compete for resources and removing it from direct political control (25 (48). Periodically, recommendations emerged, particularly from academic sources, to abolish boards of education and establish the education function as a division or department of city government under the mayor. These suggestions were rarely taken seriously because of strong opposition from the professional educators who wanted to insulate the educational system from intruders (21) (39).

The Local School Board

Members of boards of education recruited from the middle and upper classes were generally established community leaders who had demonstrated some prior role in educational circles. According to a study by the U.S. Office of Education, these boards were comprised of professionals and business-management people (85). Seldom were board members blue-collar workers, teachers, small businessmen, or lower-management people. In more recent years large-city boards included some minority group representation, but their general character remained the same, whether elected or appointed. Thus, in 1964, Goldhammer concluded in his study of school boards ". . . school board members are predominantly conservative . . . because of the extent to which they represent values harmonious with the most influential elements of the community" (40).

As the chief policy-making organ of the school system, the school board is theoretically responsible for outlining policies to be implemented by the professional staff. Because boards seldom have any appreciable staff of their own, they must rely heavily on the superintendent and other school professionals for information and policy recommendations. The power of school boards may vary somewhat from city to city, but generally, studies of school boards indicate they are preoccupied with details and not policy issues. One author, a former Chicago school board member, noted the frustrations that school board members experience in the face of overwhelming problems and the lack of time and resources to deal with those problems. He notes in particular their inability to deal with important policy matters (70).

The Expansion of Professionalism

With the expansion of professionalization and school bureaucracies in the last three decades, civic groups have tended to become more supportive and less critical of school professionals and city school systems (23). They see their task largely as one of securing ever-expanding fiscal support for education from federal, state, and city governments (1) (9). Parent groups in the schools, on the other hand, concern themselves more with individual school needs and pay little attention to city or systemwide issues (42) (57).

Over the years, schoolmen have successfully convinced consumers and public officials that their professional expertise qualifies them to control all aspects of educational policy. Budgets, determination of curriculum, personnel, and pupil policy are considered matters of internal school policy, not to be encumbered by what is described as outside "political interference."

Social science research and support for scientific management further bolstered the trend toward increasing the power of bureaucrats and reducing the role of public groups and elected officials. The measurement of policy output was determined always in terms other than discrete public benefit. Total expenditures, gross amounts allocated, or simple per capita calculations ignored the inequity of social programs and policies. The common assumption of researchers and professionals was that increased use of professionals in a program as indicated in higher costs would result in an improved delivery of service (64) (65) (66).

Vast changes in the character of the urban school population in the 1950's and the 1960's (88) served as a catalyst for heightened concerns about the viability of these entrenched and highly bureaucratized professional school systems. Earlier failures with educating an immigrant poor population could no longer be covered by a labor market receptive to blue-collar, unskilled workers. The expansion of credentialing and the shrinkage in jobs caused by automation placed an added burden on the poor and in turn increased their expectations and demands on city school systems. Higher drop-out rates and low reading scores and skills development in ghetto schools became a rallying point for those who challenged the effectiveness of those systems (37) (50) (54) (55).

The Failure of Integration

The first thrust for the new education reform movement in the 1950's was for integration. The reasoning suggested that in integrated schools overt discrimination against blacks, Puerto Ricans, Chicanos, and lower-class groups could not be maintained (6). National, state, and city civil rights groups such as the NAACP, Urban League, and CORE took on the struggle for educational improvement through school integration. Local ad hoc groups also organized around particular integration proposals (35) (74). On the spearhead of integration, the battle for educational reform was forged. The recognition that the politics of education was a reflection of the institutional politics of the society as a whole was immediately impressed upon those who were advocating some adjustment in the system (10). There was almost immediate recognition that professional defense of the system as it was suggested the lack of widely claimed "objective" criteria for educational policy making. First subtly, and then more overtly and directly, the schoolmen and their middle-class public counterparts demonstrated their commitment to preserving a system which served their needs. Even those who saw gradual changes or adjustments in the schools as reasonable approaches to fulfilling the court directives on integration were faced with strong resistance. City school boards across the country adopted general policies committed to integration, and looked to their administrative staffs for implementation (17) (74). Little was forthcoming. In several instances, school professionals themselves were the source for inaction. Racism was a good part of the story; however, the issue proved even more complex. It was also a matter of power—the power of the professional to control his own setting (16) (39). Teachers and supervisors who had only recently organized in the large cities were reaping new benefits as a strong political force in the city community. Union contracts and work agreements set the framework for general school policy; personnel requirements and increased salaries established a high percentage of mandatory costs in education budgets. Class size, student-teacher ratios, special personnel requirements, and increased expenditures were defined by these groups as synonymous with better education (4). Although the Coleman Report (15) went a long way in undermining these, by now accepted standards of educational quality, it did not demolish them sufficiently to prevent continued argument for their support. Organized professional groups continued to use these

criteria for evaluating education output and continued to assert that increased school expenditures would produce better education. Mounting evidence contradicted these assumptions (51). As education costs spiraled in the 1950's and 1960's, educational achievement declined, particularly in the cities and particularly in the poor and minority group neighborhoods (13) (30) (79).

More than ten years of integration proposals, including paired schools, open enrollment, busing, intermediate schools, etc., fell by the wayside (81). All of the large cities showed increased residential segregation each year and increased school segregation as well (83). With minor exceptions, in most large- and middle-sized cities, the integration effort was a total failure (3) (37) (84). Public and professional resistance increased as successive proposals were announced, although plans were seldom implemented.

By the 1960's, a decade of activity in attempts to reform urban schools brought a new level of sophistication to the reformers. The civil rights groups had forced city school systems to reveal for the first time reading scores; which showed massive failure (88). People began to look more closely at student achievement as integral to educational output. The professionals' argument that the socioeconomic background of the student determined his success or failure in school appeared to eschew institutional responsibility for output. As integrationists looked at the educational product more closely, they began to question even more directly the role of school professionals and school systems. Could one accept that lower-class children were not educable, as the professionals seemed to suggest, or was it the responsibility of schools to educate children regardless of background? Should they not adjust institutions, policies, and programs to the educational needs of the consumers, or were they to remain middle-class institutions serving only a middle-class clientele (7) (33) (47) (75)?

The Emergence of Community Control

Recognition of a constantly declining education quality and lack of success in achieving integration in the 1950's and 1960's led to the emergence of the decentralization-community control concept as a new thrust for school reform (11) (29).

This was predicated on the realization that the political environment of school decision making was the determinant of quality education. So long as the schools in the ghetto were controlled by people removed from the needs of minority children (and often by those who viewed lower-class children as uneducable) quality education would not or could not be achieved. It was a concept born in IS 201, in New York City, among a group of parent activists who had struggled hard and long for an integrated school (86). Their argument was basic. If they were to be denied integration, they should at least control their own schools and develop the means to quality education. Although dissatisfaction with the schools was based on educational failure, these demands also reflected a general and continuing alienation by the black community from those who ran the system, and a heightened frustration with their inability to influence those institutions which shaped their lives and the lives of their children (11). Although one would assume from the rhetoric that our experience with decentralization is widespread, in fact, it is rather limited. A plethora of government programs starting with OEO called for public participation, but few, outside education, involved restructuring the institutions to allow for engagement of citizens in decision making.

In the 1950's Kenneth Clark presciently confronted the political as well as the educational issue in his study of Harlem, appropriately titled, "Powerlessness in the Ghetto." The target was the centralized bureaucratic structure of a large-city school system (11). The power holders were the professional staff and the teachers union who in concert monopolized decision making in the system. The consumers, parents and children, were nonparticipants. A variety of studies over a decade identified this pattern of power in urban school systems in America. The evidence suggested why the opposition was mounting and strenuous efforts at reform within the local community were growing.

Earlier studies (13) (46) (67) had intermittently identified the problem of large-scale bureaucracies which were not responsive to local needs; however, those studies were more concerned with the need for *administrative* decentralization of the school system. They did not view the failure of the schools as in any way connected to the lack of client involvement. This distinction between administrative decentralization and community control becomes particularly important to later developments in the school reform movement.

In the summer of 1966, having failed to achieve their goal, the IS 201 parents demanded that the New York City Board of Education give them a direct voice in the operation of their school (29). They provided the major impetus for the creation of the three "demonstration districts" in New York City. They used the phrase "community control" of those districts in their negotiations with the mayor and the superintendent of schools. Many of these community activists and parents in Harlem were trained in Community Action Programs funded by Office of Economic Opportunity and were familiar with the concept of community participation. Recognizing the limits of non-policy-making participatory roles for community people, they advanced that concept to one of community control. More middle-class and professional reformers joined them in their struggle, espousing the need for decentralization of city school systems to make them more responsive to community interests (82). This new reform movement was not abandoning integration as a cause, it merely established a prior claim for quality education and accepted the reality of a declining opportunity for integration to serve as a means to that end. What they did not fully perceive was that both efforts, integration and decentralization-community control, attacked the same institutional core—a status-oriented school system devised to protect middle-class professional interests. Both reforms tampered with the distribution of power which concentrated control in the hands of school professionals who were threatened by any change in the structure. It was not an accident that the alignment of forces on both issues was the same. Those who opposed integration opposed decentralization; those who long supported integration were in the forefront of the movement for local neighborhood control of the schools.

In the fall of 1967, a plan for community participation and school decentralization emerged from the Bundy Plan (62) prepared for the New York City public school system. Important elements of this plan were largely contained in legislation recommended by the New York State Board of Regents in the 1968 legislative session.

Both the Bundy and the Regents' plans called for the election of *local* boards of education in districts throughout New York City (the Bundy Plan called for 30–45 districts; the Regents' legislation, 10 large and 20 smaller special districts) which would have some budget, personnel, and curriculum powers. Both plans provided for retention of a central-city education agency to set standards, control capital budget expenditures, and provide other central services. The City Board of Examiners, the Board's professional credentialing agent, would be eliminated, making appointment and promotion procedures more flexible.

The Bundy Plan

Recommendations dealt with four main problems: the nature of community voice in educational policy, the composition and selection of community boards of education, relations between community boards and higher authorities, and reform of the personnel system.

To guarantee that community school districts would have flexibility in the way they spent their funds, the panel proposed that they receive lump-sum allocations from the board of education. This would eliminate line-item restrictions, so that the community boards could determine their own priorities. Only through lump-sum allocation would community school boards have effective power to make their own decisions on pupil-teacher ratios, the functions of personnel, the number and kinds of books and other instructional materials, the conduct of experimental programs, and a host of other needs and educational strategies.

To ensure that districts with special needs would receive their fair share, the panel proposed that these lump sums be allocated by a formula that would go beyond per-capita allotment and take into account such factors as income levels, unemployment rates, and the presence, in particular districts, of either non-English-speaking children or gifted children. To ensure against misuse of funds, the panel outlined a number of auditing and reporting procedures and other safeguards.

The choices open to the Bundy Panel in the difficult decisions regarding composition of community boards included communitywide representation, parent-only representation, and arrangements that would include professional representation. The panel decided on a parent-based system, which, it felt, would be most responsive to the needs and interests of children attending the public schools and would prevent a takeover by organized party or church interests.

Seeking to encourage maximum parent participation in the selection process, the Panel recommended that a prescribed proportion of eligible parents—"at a level sufficiently substantial to constitute an effective participatory process"—be established, below which elections would not be valid. In such cases, it proposed that a new election or alternative methods of obtaining parental representation should be employed. (The legislation passed in 1969 carried no such provisions, and, as it turns out, only 15 percent of the eligible voters participated in the initial elections in March 1970.)

The Panel proposed a two-stage process for selection of the parent members: Representatives of individual schools would be chosen by an assembly of parents; these representatives, in turn, would select board members on a basis proportionate to the pupil population of each school.

In fixing on a parent-only majority, the Panel sought to avoid the danger that these local boards might be dominated by political clubs, by majorities of residents who were not parents, or by sectarian groups that might not hold the interest of public education uppermost. (The 1969 decentralization law did not limit voting to parents, and in the first elections fears that such organized interests as sectarian groups, the UFT and political parties would prevail were borne out in many districts.)

The Panel leavened its recommendations favoring parents, however, with a provision that five of the 11 community board members be appointed by the mayor. This provision reflected a concern for minorities within districts marked by a strong racial or ethnic character—particularly Puerto Ricans in largely Negro neighborhoods. Thus, the reports declared,

It is a real possibility, especially in the early years of the reorganized school system, that a parentally chosen district panel might wholly exclude representatives of minority groups in that district. While we do not hold with proportional representation on Commu-

nity School Boards, we do believe that total
exclusion of minority representation would
violate the spirit of community participation
in the educational process.

The Panel decided on the mayor as the agent
or choosing the centrally selected members be-
ause of his citywide purview and his prior re-
ponsibility for the city's schools, notably in the
location of the school budget from the total
unicipal budget. Another consideration was to
elp insure a broadly based representation. Rec-
gnizing that this decision would unleash
arges of political domination (such charges
d develop), the Panel nonetheless argued that
ere were now strong reasons for breaking
own the supposed wall between a city's highest
olitical office and its public school system.
ationwide recognition of the urban crisis and
s educational component was growing, and tra-
tional strictures maintaining a separation be-
een political and educational authority were
eakening.
Both by admitting parents to a more active
le in the educational process and by building
closer link to elected government, the Panel
ught responsibility and accountability—a
hool system so organized as to be more re-
onsive to the needs of the citizens. It was
so hoped that, through closer ties with city gov-
nment, the schools would be able to coordinate
eir programs with other city agencies, such as
60 existing planning districts and its recrea-
on, health, and antipoverty efforts.
Without diluting the essential independence
d decision making of the community boards,
e Panel proposed that the community boards
ve a number of ties with the central education
ency (the NYC Board of Education). These
s would include the latter's authority over pu-
l transfers (to ensure optimum utilization of
hool buildings throughout the city), over nego-
tions of the union contract, and—of crucial
portance—over integration policy.
Anticipating charges that a federated school
stem might lead to sectarian pockets—black
wer districts on the one hand, or ultraconserv-
ive or segregationist districts on the other—the
nel proposed that the central agency be em-
wered to overrule any actions by a community
hool board "that are judged to be inimical to a

free and open society." But the Panel said this
power ought to follow guidelines established by
the state commissioner of education. It further
cautioned that the central power to curb parochi-
alism or sectarianism should not be interpreted
to exclude a reasonable curricular emphasis
upon the cultural background of groups that
were a large element in a given school—an obvious reference to frequent demands in the ghettos
for attention to Negro history and Hispanic and
Afro-American studies. Personnel power which
was to be delegated to the community boards
would include the right to hire a community superintendent of schools. While preserving tenure and centralized collective bargaining, the
Panel proposed to place hiring and the granting
of tenure at the community level. Its single
most important—and controversial—personnel
recommendation called for elimination of the
central citywide examination system and its venerable Board of Examiners, established in 1898.

This recommendation was intended to ensure a
wider pool for recruitment of personnel and a
more flexible promotion system. In New York
State, only two school systems, New York City's
and Buffalo's, required examinations for teacher
certification beyond the state standards. The
centralized examinations, they considered, con-
flicted with the requirements of effective decentralization. The examination system had also
produced an inbred leadership structure that discouraged flexibility and change. The Panel
called, instead, for "a broadening of the concept
of merit and qualification leadership, opening
the system to more talents and ability, both
from within and without the system."
New York City schoolmen were alarmed by the
prospects of these changes. The president of
the Board of Education, the sole dissenting member of the Bundy Panel, sharply criticized the
Bundy report: "Serious problems must arise in
re-casting, in one single stroke, the largest educational system in the world." The professional
groups joined in the charge of a "balkanization"
of the city system, arguing that the plan would
also impede school integration and would be a
substitute for needed government spending in
the schools. Neither the union nor its new col-
league, the CSA (Council of Supervisory Associations), spared expense in their attempts to defeat the passage of a decentralization bill based
on the Bundy Plan.

The Ocean Hill-Brownsville Experiment

Since the fall of 1968, school reformers throughout the United States preface their commitment to educational change with the qualifying phrase, "but we don't want another Ocean Hill-Brownsville." (Ocean Hill-Brownsville was one of three demonstration districts created by the New York City Board of Education in 1967.) This is not unlike the historical search of philosophers and social scientists for a theory of institutional change which is gradual and nondisruptive. As much as they profess change, their priority is stability, and, on balance, there are few changes worthy of an open confrontation with the system. Although the circumstances of the confrontation in Ocean Hill-Brownsville, surprisingly, did not involve violence during a 36-day strike of the city school system, it did openly challenge the power and vested interests of the system sufficiently to be judged by some as revolutionary.

In fact, community control (and the IS 201 and Ocean Hill-Brownsville experiments as forerunners in that struggle) is true to the reformist tradition of urban movements. The concept of community control represents an effort to work within the system, adjusting it to new circumstances and needs. It seeks a balance between public or citizen participation with professional roles in the policy process. It prescribes shared responsibility. It is reformist and not revolutionary in that it does not seek the destruction of the system. The experience of the New York City demonstration districts is particularly relevant, therefore, to any consideration of the potential for community participation as a vehicle for institutional change in urban school systems.

Some of the participants in the particular setting of the Ocean Hill-Brownsville controversy obviously saw the impact of the demands of this experimental school district as a possible catalyst to a major transformation of public education systems over a period of time. At first glance this may seem extraordinary: that a single school district of eight schools and less than 8,000 students should threaten the whole fabric of public education not only in New York City but throughout the country. Certainly the creation of the district on an experimental basis and the reluctant delegation of minimum authority to it by a central lay board of education in the spring of 1967 did not foreshadow the deep implications of that gesture.

None of the community leaders involved had any illusions about the fact that they were being placated by the creation of demonstration districts. They were not offered integrated schools and they were not offered citywide reform. It was merely a question of how much they could get, and was the package worth agreement.

The negotiations and determination of final plans for the creation of the districts were conducted in the winter of 1966, continuing into the spring of 1967. By April the plans were set. The districts created as experiments by the New York City Board of Education were to test the concept of community participation (36).

In the fall of 1967 the Ocean Hill-Brownsville district's planning board changed the circumstances of the experiment (63). The district took immediate action in running off an official election; it appointed a unit administrator and stated its commitment to seek appointment of a special category of demonstration school principal. Clearly the local leadership was bent on confronting the system at its core. They were not willing to accept the traditional personnel selection system. They had begun to translate community participation into community control. It was a natural evolution. It is not certain that the community leadership seriously planned a strategy of confrontation politics, or whether they conceived their efforts in those terms, but that was the impact (26) (61).

At first, the mayor and Ford Foundation officials (Ford funded some of the district's new programs) viewed the districts and their plans as a reasonable adjustment in the system, which it must be said, cost them nothing in the way of power. What they failed to appreciate and what quickly became evident was their own lack of power in this particular political subsystem (the school system) and their inability to force compromises of any kind from those who held power—the school professionals. The circumstances reflected, again in microcosm, the diminishing power of the traditional city leadership and their ineffectiveness in achieving an adjustment in the system. Ultimately, the reality forced both the mayor and the foundation to back down when challenged by the teacher union and professional power, thus abandoning support for the districts and the experiment.

How fundamental was this effort at institutional change? At a minimum it attacked the structure on the delivery of services and the allocation of resources. At a maximum it potentially challenged the institutionalization of racism in America. It seriously challenged the "merit" civil service system which had become the mainstay of the American bureaucratic structure. It raised the issue of accountability of public service professionals and pointed to the distribution of power in the system and the inequities of the policy output of that structure. In a short three years, the Ocean Hill-Brownsville districts and IS 201, through such seemingly simple acts as hiring their own principals, allocating larger sums of money for the use of paraprofessionals, transferring or dismissing teachers, and adopting a variety of new educational programs, had brought all of these issues into the forefront of the political arena. If these seemingly simple acts had not been such a serious threat to the system, it would be unlikely that they would produce such a strong and immediate response (36).

Anti-Semitism and Racism

Perhaps the most disturbing effect of the strike was the polarization of black and white, in particular, black and Jew. Most studies indicate less anti-Semitism among black than among whites, but the strike significantly increased black hostility to the Jewish community. It did not create black anti-Semitism but crystallized it in New York. As Jews have increasingly gained acceptance in American society, their reformism has tended to diminish. Black resentment at the lessening of the traditional reformism of their Jewish allies has been growing stronger for some time. Only half the city's Jews supported the proposed civilian review board, and some Jews opposed the building of low-income housing for blacks in Jewish neighborhoods. Still Jewish reformism persists; a recent poll revealed that Jews are the largest white group supporting school decentralization in New York.

In part, the racial tension can be viewed merely as the result of an out-group's resentment of those in power. In New York, both the teaching and the supervisory staffs are predominantly Jewish. Their interest in maintaining the status quo was seized upon by black extremists who produced leaflets attacking not the staff or teachers but the Jews. In turn, the UFT and the CSA distributed copies of those leaflets in an attempt to gather support for their own positions. At this point, the leadership of the Jewish community overreacted.

Black anti-Semitism was not the product of community control. The Ocean Hill board and unit administrator clearly disavowed anti-Semitism, and the board pointedly noted that it hired a predominantly white, predominantly Jewish teaching staff to fill the classrooms of striking teachers. These new teachers, estranged from the union because of the decentralization issue, eventually took a newspaper advertisement in order to deny publicly the existence of anti-Semitism in the district's schools.

The racial antagonisms unleashed by the strike made it the most racially polarizing event in the city's history. The extent of black anti-Semitism and anti-white feeling is an indication that urban school reform efforts to transfer power face hard-core opposition (35) (86). So long as community roles were supportive of the system they could be countenanced; this was true of the traditional parent association roles and even the efforts of the citizen education interest groups. Effective community action, oriented to institutional change, was another matter. If decentralization involved a redistribution of power, the resistance would be immediately manifest.

Evaluating Decentralization and Community Control

Further experience with citywide decentralization plans in New York City, Detroit, Philadelphia, Boston, and Los Angeles supports the conclusion that any effort to reorder school systems through a change in the distribution of power, giving local communities control over school policy, would be met by a coalition of opposition in city and state legislatures. Most noteworthy was the failure of the Bundy Plan in New York City which called for rather fundamental change in the role of parents in the policy process (29).

From 1967 to date, the urban school reform movement has been concentrated on increasing community control of the schools through expanded citizen participation in the decision process combined with a breaking down of large-city school systems to the local neighborhood level. The extent of local power sought for neighborhood school boards varies according to particular plans (34, 68). The rhetoric, however, far exceeds action, and we have few models of effective decentralization and community control. It is easy to espouse support for the concept of decentralization, as many do, while at the same time denying the concept of local control. In fact, at least six large cities adopted what they describe as school decentralization plans—they are arrangement for administrative decentralization, but make no provision for increased local community roles. They do not seek to include any new public voice in the policy process to balance professional control of the system. The plans call for dividing the city into districts and assigning district superintendents to field positions. In some cities even these field superintendents are maintained at headquarters and have little contact with the local community.

In 1969-70 two large cities adopted citywide decentralization plans under state legislation. In Detroit and New York City the school decentralization plans called for election of local school boards which had the power to choose their own superintendents under traditionally prescribed standards for qualification. In both cities the size of the districts, boundaries, and election procedures reduced the effective role of local communities under the plan. The results of local board elections in both cities are reflective of this. See Tables 1 and 2). Minority representation on local boards in both cities has been minimal—less than it had been on citywide boards. The intended goal of local election of local boards—increased representation of the minority population—was successfully thwarted by how boundaries were set and election procedures. There are some who, now pointing to these results, argue against the effectiveness of decentralization, ignoring that the content of the plans produced the undesired results (72). Election of local boards is not a guarantee there will be a distribution of power. Local elections with well-planned districting can easily maintain the existing power structure, as it did in New York City and Detroit. Large districts and complex election procedures are useful tools in controlling results.

The New York law gave the semblance of de-

centralizing education decision making, but essentially preserved the status quo. It denied local boards any substantial authority over personnel, budget, and educational programs (36)

But if the law was a setback to those groups seeking a voice in making school policy, the elections themselves proved a further disaster. The Institute for Community Studies conducted a one-year study of the elections and the election procedures. It found that the proportional representation system had a "built-in tendency to pit well-organized groups against those that are less organized" (24). The board members elected from these elections were the opposite of that intended. The typical board member was a white male Catholic, professionally trained, with two children, and living in his district for about nine years with his children in parochial school.

The study showed that 63.8 per cent of these new board members are middle-class professionals. And, most importantly, 53.2 per cent of these board members have children in parochial and not in public schools. This in a school system that is 57.2 per cent black and Puerto Rican, many of whom are children of a client poor. Of 279 members elected, only 47 are black (16. per cent) and 30 are Puerto Rican (10.8 per cent). Of 12 districts with 85 per cent of their pupils black or Puerto Rican, there are six which have boards with a majority of black and Puerto Rican members. And it is on these six boards that 44 of 87 citywide minority members sit. Ten districts elected all-white boards in areas where the black and Puerto Rican school population ranged from 11 to 66 per cent. The Institute study concluded: "To achieve political effectiveness by activating large numbers of people, especially lower-class citizens, necessitates a substantial command of time, manpower, publicity, organization, legitimacy, know-how and the ingredient that often determines the availability of others, money" (24).

The New York experience was duplicated in Detroit, the other major city to institute school decentralization. Although Detroit created only eight regional boards instead of New York's 3 only 30 per cent of their members are black in city whose school population is 63 per cent black. Moreover, 61.3 per cent of the local board members are middle-class professionals.

Critics of decentralization have also pointed the low voter turnout in the New York City local board elections as evidence of its failure to s

Table 1. *Comparative Profile of Local School Board Members (Averages)*

Area Represented	OCCUPATION						EDUCATION			% Public School Parents
	% of Board Members in Professional, Technical, or Managerial Positions	% of Board Members Employed as Paraprofessionals or by Poverty Agencies	% of Members in the Clergy	% of Members Who Are Housewives	% of Members Who Are Laborers or Mechanics	Other	% H.S. or Grade School	% B.A. or M.A.	% Professional	
NYC Under Decentralization (1970)	63.8	10.3	5.3	16.6	4.0	10.0	33	56	23	46.8
Detroit Under Decentralization	61.3	—	3.2	12.9	22.6	—	50	44.1	5.9	67.6
Demonstration Districts NYC	16	44	9	22	3.3	6	78	6	15	85

Table 2. *Comparison of Ethnic Backgrounds of Local School Board Members (Averages)*

Area Represented	% Pupil Population Non-White	% School Board Members Non-White
NYC Under Decentralization (1970)	34.4	17
Detroit Under Decentralization	63	30
Demonstration Districts NYC (Lay Members)	56	61

cure participation. A black and Puerto Rican boycott of the election, dissatisfaction with the plan, as well as the complexities of proportional representation voting are a partial explanation of the limited turnout; but more important is the recognition that change cannot be expected to occur immediately. A more accurate measure will be the extent of participation in local communities over the next several years and in succeeding elections.

Can school decentralization be judged a failure based on experiences in these cities? Not exactly. First, as has been noted, procedures forced the results, and these can be adjusted to secure more meaningful representation. Second, even with minimal legislative mandate, local school boards may expand their roles by broad interpretation of their powers. In a two-year evaluation of the New York City districts it is evident that about one-fourth of the local boards are moving towards increased policy roles (77), and pressure has been brought to bear on the legislature to revise the law, to further expand local board powers.

Further evidence must be developed in evaluating New York City and Detroit before final judgments are made. In the evaluation of the New York City experience, several conclusions are relevant to an appreciation of the basic issues likely to arise in any effort to achieve effective decentralization.

Most community school board members interviewed in New York City identified personnel as one of the most important issues with which they deal. Their judgment affirms the projection of several of the analysts of decentralization, that "the effectiveness of the local school board in changing the schools will depend to a great extent on the cooperation and proficiency of the school staff in carrying out such charges" (77). One can argue, furthermore, that "if the local district is bound by existing personnel practices [that is, central examination and assignment of staff] . . . it will not have broadened its own power base in the vital area of control over jobs" (particularly in the districts with low achievement). Thus, some districts have sought to gain power in the area of personnel by hiring acting principals. Doing so enables them to bypass the civil service requirements for principals. They have done so in the belief that civil service examinations are predicated not on performance but on conformity to professional standards (77).

Only recently has the validity of those examinations been challenged. In a recent court decision in New York City, a federal judge (Mansfield) noted that the examination procedure for selection of principals of the New York City Board of Education has never been validated. He noted that the Board of Examiners (the credentialing agent of the Board of Education) has never even attempted to prove that their examination selects the best performers. He argued further that the criteria for principals' performance could not be efficiently translated into a written examination (12).

The local boards in New York City have been able to develop new procedures for the selection of principals under this decision. Noteworthy is the fact that those districts having the greatest parent participation not only experienced the greatest change in personnel selection methods, they also seemed to differ from their counterparts in the types of people chosen and preferred. These districts generally sought to hire and maintain a level of minority personnel more closely related to the composition of the pupil population of the district. This would suggest that even under a plan which did not call for direct community roles, local boards can effectively delegate their powers to parent groups in schools and achieve more direct participation

It further suggests that where increased participation is encouraged, more changes in procedures and policies are likely to occur.

The New York City experience over the last two years demonstrates that pressure for increasing local roles comes primarily in the lower-class neighborhood, but several middle-class areas have also developed procedures for encouraging parent involvement and are seeking broader delegations of power from the central board and/or revised legislation. Although there has been little progress in the area of local discretion over school budgets, particularly because of the mandatory expenditures which result from the union contact, some signs of pressure in this area are also developing. Greater local involvement in the determination of Title I expenditures has been achieved in a majority of the 31 districts and some reallocation of expenditures and priorities have been made in several districts. Experimentation with new educational programs seems to be more accepted by the local boards, although results cannot be measured. This rundown suggests that progress has been made in the local school districts and, given adjustments in the law, more can be anticipated.

Another source of evaluation of community control relates back to the experience with the demonstration school districts in New York City from 1967 to 1969, although they were abolished under the 1969 legislation. These experiments were closer to concepts of local control although their powers were never clearly defined.

For one thing, the three districts enlisted new participants, board members who were black or Puerto Rican, many poor, who were dedicated to school reform. The typical community school board member was a poor, black female with some poverty program experience and with children in the public school. More than 25 per cent of the normally apathetic community people voted in these elections compared with the average 10 per cent voting in the citywide decentralization election of 1970. Most of these board members with children in the schools had felt that public schools had failed and that something had to be done to improve the schools. They were reform-minded, seeking visible and immediate change in the schools (36).

These members affected personnel policy. They brought in more minority supervisors, the first black, Puerto Rican, and Chinese principals; the first black community superintendents. They enlisted more energetic and dedicated teachers in the slums. And they created a highly innovative education climate. In Ocean Hill-Brownsville the alienation between parents and urban schools was reduced. A study of parents showed that 36 per cent of those sampled belonged to a Parent Association and an overwhelming 86 per cent of the parents visited a school. Four-fifths of the parents believed that they had more influence in the running of the schools, and three-fifths felt their schools were better or the same. And although they felt they had some influence they wanted more (41).

There were more experimental programs adopted by these boards composed of the urban poor than the most affluent educational districts in the country. Ocean Hill had many programs, including a British Open Integrated Day, the teaching of reading first in Spanish, then in English, a Montessori school, a Bereiter-Englemann school, and on and on. The sheer variety of programs attested to the educational principal that each child is different and learns at different paces and in different methods.

In IS 201, study shows the pupils did better academically than the rest of the city in percentage terms; they improved at a time when the rest of the city pupils declined because of the long strike. In one school where a new experimental method was employed, the Caleb Gattegno method, the results were dramatic. The 1970 test score results produced at least a one-year advance in reading scores. And the study links that academic success with feelings of efficacy and self-control that these Harlem pupils experienced in a true locally controlled urban school district (45).

The experiment was too short to appraise the long-range educational effects of the program; most important, these besieged districts were under constant attack from professional school interests. Nevertheless, there is sufficient indication to suggest the educational promise of a truly decentralized school system (87). Some commentators have looked at low reading score results in later years, after the districts were abolished, and conclude that the educational output was negative (72, 49). Certainly there is no hard evidence that reading scores will improve under community control. Such evidence would only be available if some experiment over time allowed for such an evaluation to be made.

Urban School Reform in the 1970's

More along the lines of the demonstration districts, alternate community schools and districts within city school systems have been established in several cities, and they continue to gain support. The Adams-Morgan School and the Anacostia District in Washington, D.C., were experiments of that kind. More recently, the city of Newark has announced the creation of an Experimental School System with financial support from the Office of Education. Under the program, community groups and parent organizations in the city will design, develop, and operate schools for 5,000 students from kindergarten through high school. The plan will permit a Federation Community Schools with independent operation in many areas currently under control of the Board of Education. Essential to the program is community and parental participation (58).

Support is growing outside of school circles for decentralization of the large-city systems and balancing professional bureaucratic roles with parent, student, and community participation. Many of the peripheral groups have also sensed the movement and see in it greater advantage to themselves in a setting unfettered by bureaucratic constraints. Plans call for citywide arrangements and/or optional experimental plans for special districts or community schools within the system.

Administrative decentralization must be distinguished from political decentralization particularly because compromise arrangements often call for administrative decentralization as if it could answer the demands of those seeking an increased community role in school decision making. Administrative decentralization means a shuffling of the bureaucratic and professional staff to provide for more direct field contact— this may involve the creation of field offices or merely the creation of field titles. Political decentralization, on the other hand, requires a shift in power from professionals to the community.

Often administrative decentralization attempts to forestall real local control or compromises between community pressure for policy control and professional defense of the status quo. In Los Angeles, the school board and the professionals twice defeated state legislation for a study of effective decentralization of the Watts district and instead encouraged administrative decentralization of the school system. In other cities mounting community interest and pressure for local control was responded to with plans which call for dividing the city school system into districts or regions and assigning district superintendents to these field positions. None of these plans include a new role for the community or a balancing of professional power with citizen participation.

In Philadelphia, Boston, and Los Angeles the professional school associations and/or the union were instrumental in defeating efforts to move toward delegation of policy-making powers to the local communities. In several cities like Houston and Milwaukee, administrative decentralization was a reaction to pressure from local community groups. Neither plan provided for increased community participation. State studies of political decentralization have been conducted in California and Massachusetts, and currently studies are underway in Illinois and Wisconsin, but there appears to be little evidence that professional pressures opposing political decentralization can be avoided even at the state level. The results in California and Massachusetts suggest that the outcome in most states is more likely to be a plan for administrative decentralization of the city school system.

Reform of the school system from the top, through its administrative structure, has been suggested by some reformers as a desirable alternative to immediate plans for local control. This usually involves bringing in a superintendent committed to rehauling the system. Philadelphia was a good example of an all-out central reform effort; it had the full support of the Ford Foundation and the Office of Education in extensive new funding. Two recent books on the Philadelphia system written by people involved in that struggle have labeled it a failure. In a Philadelphia decentralization study which was prepared in 1970 by a commission on which the various school interests were represented, agreement could not be reached to delegate any power to local boards. The union and supervisory representatives dissented from even minimal proposals for decentralization of decision making. Management and financial studies and plans adopted based on these studies which were to modernize school reporting and increase public accountability have also fallen far short of their goals. Experimental programs widely publicized have since been abandoned. These were programs imposed from the central office.

Washington, D.C., is another city in which central reform and circulation of top leadership have been touted as the means for change. Some effort was made under a special projects division to establish some policy power in local boards in Anacostia and in the Adams-Morgan School. The Adams-Morgan School experiment was one of the earliest efforts to establish a local board to run its school. All early evaluations of Adams-Morgan were very positive, although the lack of board control over budget was viewed as a major problem. The Anacostia district, set up with OE support, fell far short of its goal of community control and got bogged down in District politics. Some attribute the failure of Anacostia to minimum funding and limited support.

If the evidence of the vital role of teacher and student attitudes as the major input to educational output is seriously regarded, then minimal programs and/or central system adjustments can never work. Long-range programs and more selective staff recruitment are essential. Changing attitudes can only come from a major shift in the political and social environment of the schools—genuine community control might achieve such results if it were given a chance.

In any plan for decentralization which is committed to go beyond administrative restructuring, the extent of community participation in policy development can be viewed in several stages. The first consideration is the preparation of the plan; this is probably the most crucial and the most difficult stage at which to involve the public. The planning phase is generally viewed by professionals as solely theirs, and dependent upon professional expertise. There may also be concern that early public participation can endanger or cause undue delay. There is increasing awareness, however, that the early involvement of community representatives is likely to result in the development of more realistic plans, supported by the community at critical stages. Early public participation can also be an effective means of broadening the base of participation in subsequent implementation. Engagement in the process of planning assures fuller appreciation of the intricacies of a

function. In the Fort Lincoln project and Anacostia district in Washington, D.C., community groups were involved in the planning period (28).

The content of plans for decentralization provides another basis for evaluation of community roles and potentially provides the measure for its effectiveness. The extent of balancing of community and professional roles, and central and local power are the key issues. The major policy questions in any plan will be the setting of local boundaries, the system of representation and governance for the local agency, and the division of personnel and budget power between the central and local agency. Clearly, the size of districts and their constituency can influence the extent and character of community participation, as evidenced in the New York City and Detroit plans.

The division of responsibility for policy between the central and local boards relating to personnel and budget will directly affect the extent to which new local units with new participants can achieve institutional change. If civil service, contract and/or budget constraints so completely delimit local policy roles as to make them nonfunctional, there is little reason to anticipate meaningful local participation. Much of the evidence suggests that if a central authority is retained close to its previous roles and new local decentralization units have little or no power, there will be no inducement to participation. The citizenry will quickly measure the investment of time in terms of ability to effect policy.

If the purpose of decentralization is to effect institutional change, shared responsibility between professionals and clients requires a redistribution of power. The division of responsibility between central and local agencies and the extent of control of local representative bodies, as well as the mechanism for broad participation as reflected in the plan, will determine the potential for these results. When central agencies are abolished or diminished in size, these can be indications of significant potential shifts in roles beyond the specific delegations of power to local agencies. Such provision can be included in legislation or formal plans.

The final stage for evaluation of decentralization would be in the implementation of a plan. Even a limited delegation of power can be broadened in practice as indicated by the experience in

Ocean Hill-Brownsville. Conversely, broad grants of power may not be fully utilized for various reasons. In the case of the three demonstration school districts in New York City, no specific power was delegated, but local strategies used harassment, pressure, and open confrontation to broaden their roles. The greater the direct involvement of community in the two earlier stages, the more likely it will be that local units will take on policy roles in the implementation. The broader the base of participation, the more highly organized the community is, the more probable that concern will be with local control over policy. The output of policy change is also more likely to result under the above circumstances. On the other hand, those programs centrally established, with very limited or no local community participation, will generally produce little community interest or involvement at any stage. Needless to say, the chances for institutional or policy changes are also nil.

Alternative Schools

Even in the light of what appears to be some promising developments in the decentralization of urban school systems, there are a large number of people who consider these too gradual and too minimal to warrant optimism or support.

Another phase of the movement for community schools has developed outside and as an alternative to the public school system. It reflects the frustration encountered by those who have attempted to reform the public system without success. In Boston and Milwaukee, federations of community schools have been developed. In both cities these schools are in ghetto communities servicing their needs; they are run by local parent boards. In other cities, individual community schools have been established. Although they are faced with constant financial crisis, alternative community schools can avoid the hard-core problems attached to trying to change an established system. They can develop their own personnel policies under broad state requirements and they have full control over their budgets, determining their own priorities in the allocation of resources. These are relatively new experiments and their impact on educational output cannot yet be judged. All that can be observed is the greater sensitivity and

interest in achieving quality education, the willingness to experiment with new educational ideas, and an openness with children, parents, and residents which suggests a more positive attitude toward schooling. In these schools there has been a considerable community involvement in the selection of personnel (56).

A National Association of Community Schools was organized in 1970 to bring together the wide variety of community school districts and individual schools which are cropping up around the country and share common problems and interests. One of the primary efforts of the Association is to devise more satisfactory means of funding these alternatives to the public school system.

Community-controlled schools which are mushrooming throughout America have demonstrated in their short lifetimes that the various communities can be effectively involved in the development of a positive educational environment. Although small in number, they are the source of significant experimentation and have as a group adopted a more humanistic approach to learning. They have challenged the kind of professionalism which internalized school politics and closed off the views of those who may have the most to offer in the way of educational change. They have rejected conformity and are dedicated to meeting the needs of their consumers through a balance of interest.

Conclusion

Reconstructing the governance of American education offers the possibility of creating an environment in which priorities can be reordered and responsiveness to the various communities of interest assured. The dynamic of a viable social system, if it is to be functional, requires a constant reappraisal and adjustment of its institutions.

Those who control the schools have been unable to produce acceptable results; they have excluded the public and the students from a meaningful role in the policy process. The structure of schools must be adjusted to encourage the involvement of all interested parties and to give the community greater control over educational institutions (59). Participation in itself provides an involvement with the system which can diminish alienation and also serve to stimu

te educational change; it is itself an educa-
onal experience. This new role for the comunity is not conceived as an abandonment of
rofessionalism, but rather an effort to achieve
proper balance between professionalism and
ublic participation in the policy process (69).
ommunity control implies a redistribution of
ower within the educational subsystem. The
efinition of "community" includes not only
arents of school children, but also segments of
ne public which have been excluded from a role
i public education. It is directed toward achiev-
ig a mechanism for a participatory system
hich can deal with the political failure of edu-
ation systems. Community control is intended
o create an environment in which more mean-
igful educational policies can be developed and
wide variety of alternate solutions and tech-
ques can be experimented with. It also seeks
 achieve a more equitable allocation of re-
ources as a result of the redistribution of power.
seems plausible to assume that a school sys-
m devoted to community needs, which serve as
a agent of community interests, will provide a
ore conductive environment in which children
n learn. This conclusion is based on the find-
g of education research that child and teacher
titudes are the major influence in education
rformance. In the community school environ-
ent there is a far better opportunity to achieve
e more positive and sympathetic attitudes
hich will lead to a better performance and ed-
ational achievement.
Properly instituted, community control is an
strument of social change. The redistribution
power is in itself an aspect of that change. If
lequate provision is made for the technical
sources to carry out this new role, community
rticipation has the potential for providing
w insights into our concept of professionalism
well as our general theories of educational
pertise. If community boards have the re-
urces to engage a variety of professionals in
e policy process, institutional changes of all
nds can be anticipated.
In Crozier's study of The Bureaucratic Phe-
menon, he identifies the need to check the
wer of the experts and the pseudo-experts (20).
 concludes that a dynamic equilibrium system
far more favorable to change, but recognizes
at public bureaucracies tend to be static rather
an dynamic. The former describes a system in
ich management is closed and narrow in its

perspective, with little bargaining between
groups. The dynamic model involves constant
shifting in the bargaining, possible only in a
bureaucratic structure in which subordinates
participate in the decision-making process. Urban school bureaucracies are of the static variety, and decentralization and participation in the
policy process provide the only opportunity to
move toward a more dynamic model.

Quality public education without the involvement and participation of the consumers is a
contradiction in terms. Basic reform of a public
institution does not simply consist of apparent
improvements in the quality of its professional
functions; it depends on the strength of the process through which the institution is governed
and its responsiveness to education needs (53).
It depends on the variety of sources which can
make contributions to that system. A closed
structure is by its nature static. The failure or
short life of many purely pedagogical reform
movements in public education in America may
in fact be traced to the absence of participation
by parents and the larger community. The potential for finding solutions to educational problems can only be enhanced by the broader range
of alternatives offered by laymen and nonschool
professionals.

References

1. Stephen K. Bailey *et al.*, *Schoolmen and Politics: A Study of State Aid to Education in the
   Northeast* (Syracuse: Syracuse University Press,
   1962).
2. Selma Berrol, "The Schools of New York in
   Transition: 1898–1914," *The Urban Review*, Vol.
   1 (December 1966), pp. 15–20.
3. Maurice R. Berube, "White Liberals, Black
   Schools," *Commonweal* (ct., 966).
4. ———, "Problems of Teacher Unionism," *New
   Politics*, Vol. IV (Fall 1965), pp. 37–42.
5. Maurice R. Berube and Marilyn Gittell, *Confrontation at Ocean Hill-Brownsville* (New York:
   Frederick A. Praeger, 1969).
6. *Brown v. Board of Education of Topeka*, 347
   U.S. 483 (1954).
7. Jerome Bruner, "Culture, Politics and Pedagogy,"
   Saturday Review, Vol. 51 (May 18, 1968).
8. Raymond E. Callahan, *Education and the Cult
   of Efficiency: A Study of the Social Forces That
   Have Shaped the Administration of Public
   Schools* (Chicago: University of Chicago Press,
   1962).

9. Ronald F. Campbell, Luvern L. Cunningham, and R. F. McPhee, *The Organization and Control of American Schools* (Columbus: Charles E. Merrill, 1965).

10. Stokely Carmichael and Charles Hamilton, *Black Power: The Politics of Liberation in America* (New York: Vantage Books, 1967).

11. Kenneth B. Clark, *Dark Ghetto* (New York: Harper and Row, 1965).

12. *Boston M. Chance and Louis C. Mercado v. The Board of Examiners and the Board of Education of the City of New York*, 70 civ. 4141 United States District Court Southern District of New York, 1971 (mimeo).

13. Citizens' Advisory Committee on School Needs, *Findings and Recommendations* (abridged) (Detroit: the Committee, 1958).

14. Sol Cohen, *Progressives and Urban School Reforms* (New York: Bureau of Publications, Teachers College, Columbia University, 1964).

15. James Coleman, *et al.*, *Equality of Educational Opportunity*, U.S. Office of Education (Washington, D.C.: Government Printing Office, 1966).

16. James Conant, *Slums and Suburbs: A Commentary on Schools in Metropolitan Areas* (New York: McGraw Hill, 1961).

17. Robert L. Crain and David Street, "School Desegregation & School Decision Making," in Marilyn Gittell (ed.), *Educating an Urban Population* (Beverly Hills, Calif.: Sage Publications, 1967).

18. Lawrence A. Cremen, *The Transformation of the School* (New York: Vintage Books, 1961).

19. Joseph M. Cronin, *The Board of Education in the Great Cities, 1890–1964*, doctoral dissertation (Palo Alto: Stanford University, 1965).

20. Michel Crozier, *The Bureaucratic Phenomenon* (Chicago: Phoenix Books, University of Chicago Press, 1967).

21. Ellwood Cubberly, *Public Education in the United States*, revised edition (Boston, 1934).

22. Luvern L. Cunningham, "A School District and City Government," *The American School Board Journal*, Vol. 141, No. 6 (December 1960), pp. 9–11, 37.

23. Robert A. Dahl, *Who Governs? Democracy and Power in an American City* (New Haven: Yale University Press, 1961).

24. Boulton H. Demas, *The School Elections: A Critique of the 1969 N.Y.C. School Decentralization*.

25. Thomas H. Elliot, "Towards an Understanding of Public School Politics," *Teachers College Record*, Vol. LXII (November 1960), pp. 118–132.

26. Jason Epstein, "The Real McCoy," A Review of the Teachers Strike by Martin Mayer, *New York Review of Books*, Vol. 12, No. 5 (March 12, 1969).

27. *Equal Educational Opportunity—1971*, Hearing Before the Select Committee on Equal Educational Opportunity of the United States Senate, 92nd Congress, Washington, D.C. (December 1, 2, 3, 1971).

28. Mario D. Fantini, Milton A. Young and Frieda Douglas, *A Design for a New & Relevant System of Education for Fort Lincoln New Town* (Washington, D.C.: School District, 1968).

29. ———, Marilyn Gittell, and Richard Magat, *Community Control and the Urban School* (New York: Praeger Publishers, 1971).

30. ——— and Gerald Weinstein, *The Disadvantage Challenge to Education* (New York: Harper & Row, 1968).

31. Joseph Featherstone, "A New Kind of Schooling," *New Republic*, Vol. 58 (March 2, 1968).

32. David J. Fox, *Expansion of the More Effective School Program* (Center for Urban Education September 1967).

33. Edgar Z. Friedenberg, "Requiem for the Urban School," *Saturday Review*, Vol. 50 (November 1, 1967).

34. Marilyn Gittell, "School Decentralization Today," *Community Issues*, Vol. 3, No. 1 (Flushing, N.Y.: Institute for Community Studies Queens College, November 1971).

35. ——— and T. Edward Hollander, *Six Urban School Districts: A Comparative Study of Institutional Response* (New York: Praeger, 1968).

36. ———, *et al.*, *Local Control in Education: Three Demonstration School Districts in New York City* (New York: Praeger Publishers, 1972).

37. ——— and Alan G. Hevesi (eds.), *The Politics of Urban Education* (New York: Frederick A. Praeger, 1969).

38. ——— (ed.), *Educating an Urban Population* (Beverly Hills, Calif.: Sage Publications, 1967).

39. ———, *Participants and Participation: A Study of School Policy in New York City* (New York: Praeger Publishers, 1968).

40. Keith Goldhammer, *The School Board* (New York: The Center for Applied Research in Education, Inc. 1964), p. 97.

41. Frances Gottfried, "A Survey of Parental Views of the Ocean Hill-Brownsville Experiment *Community Issues*, Vol. 2, No. 5 (Flushing, N.Y. Institute for Community Studies, Queens College, October 1970).

42. Grace Graham, *The Public School in the American Community* (New York: Harper & Row 1963).

43. William R. Grant, "Community Control v School Integration in Detroit," *The Public Interest*, Vol. 24 (Summer 1971), pp. 62–79.

44. Colin Greer, *The Great School Legend* (New York: Basic Books, 1972).

45. Marie Guttentag, unpublished manuscript, available at Harlem Research Center of the City University of New York.

46. Robert J. Havighurst, *The Public Schools*

Chicago (Chicago: The Board of Education of the City of Chicago, 1964).

47. ——, *Education in Metropolitan Areas* (Boston: Allyn & Bacon, 1966).

48. Nelson B. Henry and Jerome G. Kerwin, *School and City Government* (Chicago: The University of Chicago Press, 1938).

49. Nat Hentoff, "Mugging A Corpse," *The Village Voice*, March 2, 1972.

50. ——, *Our Children Are Dying* (New York: The Viking Press, Inc., 1966).

51. *High School*, film produced by Frederick Wiseman (1969), available on rental basis from Zipporah Films, Inc., 54 Lewis Wharf, Boston, Mass. Mass. 02110.

52. Lawrence Iannaconne, *Politics in Education* (New York: The Center in Applied Research in Education, Inc., 1967).

53. Michael B. Katz, *Class Bureaucracy and Schools: The Illusion of Educational Change in America* (New York: Praeger Publishers, 1971).

54. Herbert Kohl, *36 Children* (New York: New American Library, 1967).

55. Jonathan Kozol, *Death at an Early Age* (New York: Bantam Books, Inc., 1968).

56. ——, *Free Schools* (New York: Houghton Mifflin, 1972).

57. William C. Kvaraceus, "P.T.A. The Irrelevant Giant," *The Nation* (October 5, 1963), pp. 200–201.

58. Henry M. Levin (ed.), *Community Control of Schools* (Washington, D.C.: The Brookings Institution, 1970), p. 289.

59. Rod Lewis, "Indian Education Legislation," *Inequality in Education*, Vol. 10 (December 1971), pp. 19–21; Dan Rosenfelt, "New Regulations for Federal Indian Funds," *Inequality in Education*, Vol. 10 (December 1971), pp. 21–25.

60. Roscoe Martin, *Government and the Suburban School* (Syracuse: Syracuse University Press, 1962).

61. Martin Mayer, *The Teachers Strike* (New York: Harper and Row, 1969).

62. Mayor's Advisory Panel on Decentralization of the New York City Schools, *Reconnection for Learning: A Community School System for New York City* (New York: Praeger Publishers, 1969).

63. Rhody A. McCoy, "The Formation of a Community Controlled School District," in Henry M. Levin (ed.), *Community Control of Schools* (Washington, D.C.: The Brookings Institution, 1970).

64. Jerry Miner, *Social and Economic Factors in Spending for Public Education*, The Economics & Politics of Education Series (Syracuse: Syracuse University Press, 1963).

65. Paul R. Mort, "Cost-Quality Relationships in Education," in R. L. Johns and E. L. Morphet (eds.), *Problems and Issues in Public School Finance* (National Conference of Professors of Educational Administration, 1952).

66. ——, *Fiscal Readiness for the Stress of Change* (Pittsburgh: University of Pittsburgh, 1957).

67. William R. Odell, "Educational Survey Report for the Philadelphia Board of Education" (Philadelphia: The Board of Public Education, 1965).

68. Tim Parsons, "The Community School Movement," *Community Issues*, Vol. 2, No. 6 (December 1970), Institute for Community Studies, Queens College, City University of New York.

69. Harry A. Passow, *Towards Creating A Model Urban School System: A Study of the Washington, D.C., Public Schools* (New York: Teachers College, Columbia University, 1967).

70. Joseph Pois, *The School Board Crisis: A Chicago Case Study* (Chicago: Educational Methods, Inc., 1964).

71. Public Education Association, *The Status of Negro and Puerto Rican Children and Youth in the Public Schools* (New York: The Association, 1955).

72. Diane Ravitch "Community Control Revisited," *Commentary*, Vol. 53, No. 2 (February 1972), pp. 69–74.

73. Donald H. Ross, *Administration For Adaptability* (New York: Metropolitan School Study Council, Teachers College, Columbia University, 1951).

74. David Rogers, *110 Livingston Street: Politics and Bureaucracy in the New York City School System* (New York: Random House, 1968).

75. Robert Rosenthal and Lenore Jacobson, *Pygmalion in the Classroom: Teacher Expectation and Pupil Intellectual Development* (New York: Holt, Rinehart & Winston, 1968).

76. Robert H. Salisbury et al., *State Politics & The Public Schools* (New York: Knopf, 1964).

77. *School Decentralization and School Policy in New York City*, a Report for the New York State Commission on the Quality, Cost and Financing of Elementary and Secondary Education (Flushing, N.Y.: Institute for Community Studies, 1971).

78. Scope (School & Community Organized for Partnership in Education), *Bulletin* (New York, 1969).

79. Patricia Cayo Sexton, *Education & Income* (New York: The Viking Press, Inc., 1961).

80. Albert Shanker, "Where We Stand," *New York Times*, February 13, 1972.

81. Eleanor B. Sheldon and Raymond A. Glazer, *Pupils and Schools in New York City; A Fact Book* (New York: Russell Sage Foundation, 1965).

82. Adele Spier, "The Two Bridges Model School District," *Community Issues*, Vol. 1, No. 3 (Feb-

ruary 1969), Institute for Community Studies, Queens College, City University of New York.

83. Karl E. Taeuber and Alma F. Taeuber, *Negroes in Cities* (Chicago: Aldine Publishing Co., 1965).

84. Urban League of Greater New York, *A Study of the Problems of Integration in New York City Public Schools Since 1955* (New York: Urban League of Greater New York, 1963).

85. Alpheus L. White, "An Analysis of School Board Organization: Trends and Developments in School Board Organizations and Practices in Cities with a Population of 100,000 or More," *American School Board Journal*, Vol. CXLVI

(April 1963), pp. 7–8; *Characteristics of Local School Board Policy*, Manuals (Washington, D.C.: U.S. Department of Health, Education, and Welfare, Office of Education, 1959); *Local School Boards: Organization and Practice* (Washington, D.C.: U.S. Government Printing Office, 1962).

86. Miriam Wasserman, "The I.S. 201 Story," *Urban Review*, Vol. 11 (June 1969), pp. 3–15.

87. Charles Wilson, "Beginning of a Miracle," *Interim Report* (August 1969).

88. Roger R. Woock and Harry L. Miller, *Social Foundations of Urban Education* (Illinois: The Dryden Press, Inc., 1970).

25

STANLEY ARONOWITZ

The Dialectics of Community Control

The Black movement seeks more than a piece of the white man's pie served at the white man's table. The movement today, unlike the traditional civil rights movement, is oriented toward power.

The advance from integration to Black power and community control has reversed the century-old strategy of the civil rights movement, which sought an alliance of white liberals with the Black middle class, generally under paternalistic white leadership, to achieve democratic rights for all. While the assertion of independence from white domination and the emphasis on community control represent a necessary step in the struggle for liberation, experience suggests that it is not sufficient for fundamental social change. To win its objectives, the movement for community control and Black power needs a new conception of alliances, and even a redefinition of the objectives themselves.

The replacement of the demand for equality of opportunity with that of community control reflects the failure of the struggle for integration to achieve its stated goals, despite its blessing of legal and judicial legitimacy. Though well aware of the demographic, economic and political barriers to the integration of schools, health facilities, and employment, Blacks understand the failure of integration in another dimension: racism. Whatever the causes for the failure of

integration, the distress and despair at white society's determined refusal to open the doors of opportunity compelled a new strategy.

With the shift to community control, the piece-of-the-pie philosophy was not actually abandoned—rather it was reinterpreted. Black people still want to share American affluence, but are not content to receive it within the framework of white-dominated institutions. They are now asking for their share within a new context—Black control of Black communities and their institutions. But unless this struggle is broadened into a general struggle for popular, democratic control over all aspects of economic, political and social life, community control is certain to be absorbed by what Richard Cloward calls "corporate imperialism in the ghetto," a new domestic colonialism.

Conservative and Radical Tendencies

Inherent in the concept of community control are both conservative and radical tendencies which, in the long run, may prove irreconcilable. On one hand, the political and economic thrust of the demand remains conservative: i.e., it does not challenge the present means of allocating resources among the various elements of the political economy. To a large degree, the emphasis on community control has turned Black politics away from issues of national power and thus, in part, represents a step backwards. In struggling for a redistribution of local resources, Blacks come into conflict with white working-class and middle-class communities, rather than the national government and the corporate institutions which control it. The working as-

Reprinted with permission from *Social Policy*, May/June 1970. Copyright 1970. All rights reserved.

STANLEY ARONOWITZ, formerly a trade union organizer, now works in the social welfare field. He is a columnist for the radical weekly, *The Guardian*.

sumption of much of the Black movement is that residents of white neighborhoods are their competitors for the available funds for education, health, housing and other essential services. In this paradigm, the large corporate employers and foundations appear as the allies of the Black community and the trade unions and blue-collar workers as their enemies.

On the other hand, the demand for community control raises the fundamental issue of power in a dramatic and radical fashion. The language of urban renewal legislation of the 1950s and the Economic Opportunity Act of 1964, with the terms *citizens' participation* and *maximum feasible participation of the poor*, promised the Black and poor communities a voice in decisions affecting their localities. But it was assumed that whatever new structures were created would be part of, and clearly subordinate within, the existing government bureaucracies. Instead, community control is challenging the prerogatives of the centralized bureaucracies to make basic policy determinations affecting local areas and represents a step in the ongoing struggle to wrest power from bureaucratic and hierarchical institutions of government and industry. It attempts to redefine the democratic process by rejecting the efficacy of representative institutions, such as the national and local legislative bodies, to reflect popular aspirations.

Community control is analogous, at least in embryo, to the demand for self-determination raised by colonial peoples in Africa, Asia and Latin America. Historically, community control has its roots in the French Revolution's ideal of mass democracy, according to which individuals delegate their prerogatives to no one, but make all essential decisions of policy themselves through popular assemblies, councils, town meetings, etc. The move toward decentralization, therefore, goes deeper than distrust of central institutions of power. Potentially, it implies an alternative model of government and social decision-making.

Objectives of Community Control

After four years of struggle for community control and Black power, we can begin to assess both the possibilities and limitations of this approach for achieving a series of stated objectives. Generally, these objectives have been: (a) to achieve quality services under indigenous leadership within geographic communities; (b) to secure a more favorable allocation of resources by city, state and federal governments to improve service delivery systems; (c) to develop a cadre of political and social leadership within the Black community capable of reflecting the community's aspirations and helping to deliver quality services; and (d) to gain some measure of control of the ghetto community.

There are serious limitations to the demand for community control:

1. It is based upon a narrow conception of power.
2. By limiting objectives to the local community, it fails to define, either implicitly or explicitly, the real obstacles to their achievement.
3. The goals themselves ignore the problem of national economic power.

To the extent that there is a movement for Black political power it is confined within the two-party system and defines politics as electoral politics. Working within the system Blacks have succeeded in electing nine members of Congress, many state legislators and several hundred municipal officials. But such officials possess little genuine power, especially in the era of the military-industrial complex. The ghetto community is far from the commanding heights of national corporate power where the essential political as well as economic decisions are made.

Only the Black Panther Party and other smaller radical groups have attempted to change the goal of Black and Third World power on national and international canvas. These groups, however, remain on the margin of political leadership in ghetto communities and government repression may limit, if not smother, whatever influence and political outreach they do possess.

The False Hope of Black Capitalism

Most community control advocates accept some concept of economic self-determination. This aspiration has been expressed largely in the rejection of white-owned small businesses within the ghetto, although the alternative proposed more Black individual or cooperative ownership of marginal businesses. Such economic development programs must rely on primary support from white-controlled corporations or government in the form of seed capital, woking capital and guaranteed markets and can survive only at the mercy of white corporate finance.

The Black capitalist program is really an integration program which attempts to develop a new set of managers for white-controlled businesses in the ghetto, if control is understood in its financial meaning. Only a few of the Black economic development efforts recognize this danger, but an answer to the perplexing problem of capital formation is not easy to come by. The best that has been proposed is a system of producer consumer cooperatives or nonprofit community development corporations, neither of which can avoid the private money market or the tax system for procuring capital. The facts of national economic life, that is, the existence of central market mechanisms and capital scarcity for small business, militate against a solution to the problem within the framework of Black capitalism.

With the demands for community control of social service institutions within the ghetto, similar drawbacks emerge. White working-class and middle-class resistance to Black claims for expanded services is inevitable unless the obstacles are clearly defined and surmounted. Few community control advocates have been willing to raise the problem of national priorities, namely, that 80 percent of the federal budget, directly and indirectly, is spent on war and related activities. Nor has the tax structure of state and local government been challenged. Right now more than two-thirds of local services are provided out of nonfederal taxes. The major responsibility for schools, sanitation, health and other social expenditures rests on state and local government. The primary sources of revenue for these services are regressive excise taxes, taxes on small property and on wages or salaries. Add to this the fact that 85 percent of federal revenue is derived from the first $8,000 of income, and it becomes clear that the tax burden on working-class and middle-class people, white and Black, is so heavy that demands for increased services from any sector of the population are likely to be opposed as long as war remains the nation's major priority and large corporations which benefit from it are exempt from paying most of the costs of government and social programs.

In short, the incipient alliance of the Black poor with the large corporations and foundations against white and Black wage and salary earners is self-defeating. It does not have the social weight to win its limited objectives. More important, it puts the poor in the unseemly position of attempting to forge a coalition with their oppressors. An alternate strategy would be joint struggles of those segments of the white and Black communities who suffer equally from deteriorating services, a polluted environment and declining real wages against the corporations which manipulate the government to serve their particular interests.

Localism: Strengths and Weaknesses

While localistic organization has prevented the development of political clout by these groups. one of the strengths of the movement for popular power has been its revival of the concept of community against the atomization and alienation of mass society. In a period of urban decay and the loosening of traditional ties of ethnicity and geography, the strong sense of solidarity engendered by welfare recipients and health rights organizations fighting to control the conditions of their own lives has provided an important antidote to the larger trends of population dispersal and consequent anomie. However, the inchoate development of community consciousness, a strength of the community control movement, has so far prevented the forging of broad alliances to achieve even the united goal of community control of specific institutions.

In New York City, where the struggle for community control has reached the highest and most intense level in the nation, the geographic community as the focus of political organization is most apparent. Not only is there little communication and a great deal of distrust among the numerous ghetto and slum communities within the city, but groups within the same neighborhood fighting for local control of different institutions are isolated from one another.

The slogan "community control" is a rubric covering many fragmented and disconnected movements. And usually it is defined differently in each case. For example, some groups seek control over the money, hiring policies and curriculum of a single school or school district. Others are content to demand any one of these prerogatives without considering their right to determine policies governing the other. Underlying the fragmentation is the proprietary aspiration of parents or health consumers who have been unable to recognize their community of interest with those functioning in another geographic area or within the same neighborhood. Contributing to this fragmentation was the way in which the community control concept was tested in New York City public schools.

The New York City School Struggle

The Ford Foundation made grants to three experimental school districts in Manhattan and Brooklyn, encouraging parents and teachers to participate in the decision-making process. The central Board of Education, however, retained its control over all major areas of policy, including teacher qualifications, curriculum and allocation of educational resources. The parents and allied community groups were invited to administer schools within the district, but were forced to operate within the constraints of the guidelines astutely set up by the central bureaucracy of the Board of Education. It was community "control" defined as management. The Janus-faced policy of the central Board of Education evoked a hostile response from the community, but local groups soon discovered that they were hemmed in, not only by the Board but by the state legislature as well.

The experimental districts possessed neither the vision nor the clout to impress their demands on those who hold the real power in the schools. The requisite vision and political strength could only be obtained if the experimental districts were capable of calling upon disgruntled parents around the city to make similar demands on the Board of Education and, at the same time, to support the broadening of community power in the experimental school districts.

To a certain extent the administrative quality of the experimental districts prevented the development of a citywide strategy. Parents and teachers alike were caught in a tug-of-war with the central Board of Education and among themselves. This fight on two fronts was abetted by the spotlight of local and national publicity and thwarted any possibility of developing a citywide

movement of parents, students and sympathetic teachers against the Board. Implicit in the method of struggle adopted by the experimental districts was the conflict between their need to protect their severely limited and ill-defined authority and the need to expand the fight beyond the geographic limits of the districts themselves.

From the beginning, the rules of the game were determined by the administrative hierarchy of the Board of Education, which easily convinced the teachers that their real enemy was the Black parents and the Black community in general. The leadership of the United Federation of Teachers decided that the central Board was the lesser of two evils and used the political weight of the union's 55,000 members to extract sufficient economic concessions and veto power over the decentralization plans to convince the Board that they could become a reliable reactionary mass base.

The working teachers, historically oppressed by the central Board of Education, were easily victimized by their own leadership. In the end, they won their 40 pieces of silver, but their long-standing grievances over class size and the overload of administrative responsibility, as well as chronic lack of job security, remain.

Despite some efforts toward broadening support and including teachers in a common struggle, the community control forces were unable to mount an effective counterattack. The Board of Education adroitly manipulated and divided the teachers and parents, and the Ford Foundation leadership prevented the emergence of anything more than a localistic movement for community control.

A New Front Opens: Health Services

The struggle for popular control of health services is just beginning, but it may offer more promising opportunities for the development of interracial and interclass links than has the area of education. The unique feature of the deterioration of health services is that it affects large sections of the middle-class and working-class white population as well as the Black poor. Most union health insurance plans have been outstripped by the astronomical rise in costs of hospital services: coverage rarely extends to the full cost of illness. Recent increases in health insurance costs have been geared to maintain the present level of coverage rather than to broaden it. Overcrowding of hospitals is becoming endemic—even many voluntary hospitals have long patient waiting lists—as building and service funds have been restricted by the fiscal crisis of local and state governments.

There are two strategic aspects of the struggle for popular control of health institutions. First, it is becoming a fight to prevent municipal governments from turning over public property to the voluntary hospitals and to the doctors who control them. The appearance of new hospital corporations in New York and Detroit is the harbinger of a general pattern of health care. Tax monies will now be used to finance the provision of medical services by private agencies not really accountable to either the community or even the municipal government. This way of providing public service is already widespread in the transportation industry, where the creation of public corporations, sometimes called bridge, tunnel or transportation authorities, has had the effect of turning over a major public utility to the banks and to other investors. The rationale for this move is often the need for efficient and quality service at low cost. However, costs have continued to rise and services to deteriorate. There is no apparent gain in efficiency when the private sector controls essential services. The proposals for new hospital corporations are nothing more than a giveaway program.

The second aspect of popular control in the health industry is the new concept that the consumer of health services should have the power to determine the shape and content of the service delivery system. The concept of the health consumer transcends both geographic limitations and the limitations of relying entirely on the poor or the underclass for a constituency. Health movements have embraced a particular spectrum of dissatisfied persons which crosses class boundaries, although it is apparent that the poor, the working-class and lower middle-class consumers suffer disproportionately.

Once again, however, there is contention between the demand for control over a particular institution and the need for a broader concept of community control. The powers in health institutions are the doctors and the larger corporate philanthropics. Most boards of directors of community-based hospitals read like a sociological study of community power structure, for they are the very groups which hold economic, political and institutional power in most areas of community life. Unless the connection is made between control over health, education and welfare on one hand and economic and political power on the other, the contest over any individual institution remains unequal and frustrating.

Beyond the Corporate Framework

The basic assumption behind the fragmented struggle for community control is the pluralistic model of political power, according to which control of such institutions as schools can be divorced from control in other areas of social and economic life. Most militant advocates of local control adhere to this model in assuming that it is possible actually to transform the quality of human service institutions by taking decisive power over their administration and pressuring existing government funding agencies for a reordering of fiscal priorities. They believe that the question of power can be reduced to pressure-group politics. They are ready to march, sit in and employ a wide variety of pressure tactics to achieve their aims. But they are not prepared to make a radical critique of national power, either in class or economic terms.

A radical analysis of power in America reveals the interlocking character of control over all institutions in a pyramid fashion, with the pinnacle of power in most local institutions held by the same groups of corporations and their professional servants in government or human service bureaucracies. This analysis implies the need for a generalized concept of popular control of all public institutions and the economy which can appeal not only to Black and poor but also to working-class and most middle-class people—to all who are deprived of a significant voice in the institutions which determine our lives. It requires that the movement for popular control search out societal alternatives beyond the confines of the corporate capitalist framework.

Other Titles of Interest:

Alston, Jon P. and K. Imogene Dean. Socioeconomic Factors Associated with Attitudes toward Welfare Recipients and the Causes of Poverty.

Burns, Eveline M. Social Security in Evolution: Toward What?

Frieden, Bernard J. The Changing Prospects for Social Planning.

Gilbert, Neil. Assessing Service Delivery Methods: Some Unsettled Questions.

Hayek, Friedrich A. Planning and Democracy.

Herzog, Elizabeth and Cecelia E. Sudia. Fatherless Homes: A Review of the Research.

Hoshino, George. Britain's Debate on Universal or Selective Social Services: Lessons for America.

Lipsky, Michael. Rent Strikes: Poor Man's Weapon.

Lockard, Duane, Russell D. Murphy, Arthur Naftalin and Edward C. Banfield. Banfield's Unheavenly City: A Symposium and Response.

Maluccio, Anthony N. and Wilma D. Marlow. Residential Treatment of Emotionally Disturbed Children: A Review of the Literature.

Mileski, Maureen. Courtroom Encounters—An Observation of a Lower Criminal Court.

Schick, Allen. The Cybernetic State.

Simpson, Richard L. Beyond Rational Bureaucracy: Changing Values and Social Integration in Post-Industrial Society.

Stegman, Michael. The New Mythology of Housing.

Weiner, Norman L. and Charles V. Willie. Decisions by Juvenile Officers.

Weisman, Irving. Drug Abuse: Some Practical Dilemmas.

Wolins, Martin. Societal Function of Social Welfare.

26

ROBERT BLAUNER

Internal Colonialism and Ghetto Revolt[1]

is becoming almost fashionable to analyze merican racial conflict today in terms of the ·lonial analogy. I shall argue in this paper that e utility of this perspective depends upon a stinction between colonization as a process and ·lonialism as a social, economic, and political stem. It is the experience of colonization that 'ro-Americans share with many of the nonwhite ople of the world. But this subjugation has ken place in a societal context that differs in portant respects from the situation of "classi- l colonialism." In the body of this essay I shall ok at some major developments in black pro- st—the urban riots, cultural nationalism, and e movement for ghetto control—as collective sponses to colonized status. Viewing our do- estic situation as a special form of coloniza- on outside a context of a colonial system will lp explain some of the dilemmas and the am- uities within these movements.

The present crisis in American life has brought out changes in social perspectives and the estioning of long accepted frameworks. Intel- tuals and social scientists have been forced the pressure of events to look at old defini- ns of the character of our society, the role of ism, and the workings of basic institutions. e depth and volatility of contemporary racial flict challenge sociologists in particular to estion the adequacy of theoretical models by ich we have explained American race relations the past.

For a long time the distinctiveness of the Negro situation among the ethnic minorities was placed in terms of color, and the systematic dis- crimination that follows from our deep-seated racial prejudices. This was sometimes called the caste theory, and while provocative, it missed essential and dynamic features of American race relations. In the past ten years there has been a tendency to view Afro-Americans as another eth- nic group not basically different in experience from previous ethnics and whose "immigration" condition in the North would in time follow their upward course. The inadequacy of this model is now clear—even the Kerner Report devotes a chapter to criticizing this analogy. A more re- cent (though hardly new) approach views the es- sence of racial subordination in economic class terms: Black people as an underclass are to a degree specially exploited and to a degree eco- nomically dispensable in an automating society. Important as are economic factors, the power of race and racism in America cannot be sufficiently explained through class analysis. Into this the- ory vacuum steps the model of internal colonial- ism. Problematic and imprecise as it is, it gives hope of becoming a framework that can inte- grate the insights of caste and racism, ethnicity, culture, and economic exploitation into an over- all conceptual scheme. At the same time, the danger of the colonial model is the imposition of an artificial analogy which might keep us from facing up to the fact (to quote Harold Cruse) that "the American black and white social phe- nomenon is a uniquely new world thing."[2]

During the late 1950s, identification with Afri- can nations and other colonial or formerly colo- nized peoples grew in importance among black militants.[3] As a result the U.S. was increasingly

---

bert Blauner, "Internal Colonialism and etto Revolt," *Social Problems*, vol. 16, no. 4 ·ring 1969), pp. 393–408. Reprinted by permis- n of the author and the Society for the Study Social Problems.

seen as a colonial power and the concept of domestic colonialism was introduced into the political analysis and rhetoric of militant nationalists. During the same period black social theorists began developing this frame of reference for explaining American realities. As early as 1962, Cruse characterized race relations in this country as "domestic colonialism."[4] Three years later in *Dark Ghetto*, Kenneth Clark demonstrated how the political, economic, and social structure of Harlem was essentially that of a colony.[5] Finally in 1967, a full-blown elaboration of "internal colonialism" provided the theoretical framework for Carmichael and Hamilton's widely read *Black Power*.[6] The following year the colonial analogy gained currency and new "respectability" when Senator McCarthy habitually referred to black Americans as a colonized people during his campaign. While the rhetoric of internal colonialism was catching on, other social scientists began to raise questions about its appropriateness as a scheme of analysis.

The colonial analysis has been rejected as obscurantist and misleading by scholars who point to the significant differences in history and social-political conditions between our domestic patterns and what took place in Africa and India. Colonialism traditionally refers to the establishment of domination over a geographically external political unit, most often inhabited by people of a different race and culture, where this domination is political and economic, and the colony exists subordinated to and dependent upon the mother country. Typically the colonizers exploit the land, the raw materials, the labor, and other resources of the colonized nation; in addition a formal recognition is given to the difference in power, autonomy, and political status, and various agencies are set up to maintain this subordination. Seemingly the analogy must be stretched beyond usefulness if the American version is to be forced into this model. For here we are talking about group relations within a society; the mother country—colony separation in geography is absent. Though whites certainly colonized the territory of the original Americas, internal colonization of Afro-Americans did not involve the settlement of whites in any land that was unequivocally black. And unlike the colonial situation, there has been no formal recognition of differing power since slavery was abolished outside the South. Classic colonialism involved the control and exploitation of the majority of a nation by a minority of outsiders, whereas in America the people who are oppressed were themselves originally outsiders and are a numerical minority.

The conventional critique of "internal colonialism" is useful in pointing to the differences between our domestic patterns and the overseas situation. But in its bold attack it tends to lose sight of common experiences that have been historically shared by the most subjugated racial minorities in America and non-white peoples in some other parts of the world. For understanding the most dramatic recent developments on the race scene, this common core element—which I shall call colonization—may be more important than the undeniable divergences between the two contexts.

The common features ultimately relate to the fact that the classical colonialism of the imperialist era and American racism developed out of the same historical situation and reflected common world economic and power stratification. The slave trade for the most part preceded the imperialist partition and economic exploitation of Africa, and in fact may have been a necessary prerequisite for colonial conquest—since helped deplete and pacify Africa, undermining the resistance to direct occupation. Slavery contributed one of the basic raw materials for the textile industry which provided much of the capital for the West's industrial development and need for economic expansionism. The essential condition for both American slavery and European colonialism was the power domination and the technological superiority of the Western world in its relation to peoples of non-Western and nonwhite origins. This objective supremacy in technology and military power buttressed the West's sense of cultural superiority, laying the basis for racist ideologies that were elaborated to justify control and exploitation of nonwhite people. Thus because classical colonialism and America's internal version developed out of similar balance of technological, cultural, and power relations, a common *process* of social oppression characterized the racial patterns in the two contexts—despite the variation in political and social structure.

There appear to be four basic components of the colonization complex. The first refers to how the racial group enters into the dominant society (whether colonial power or not). Color zation begins with a forced, involuntary entry. Second, there is an impact on the culture and social organization of the colonized people which is more than just a result of such "natural" processes as contact and acculturation. The colonizing power carries out a policy which constrains, transforms, or destroys indigenous values, orientations, and ways of life. Third, colonization involves a relationship by which members of the colonized group tend to be administered by representatives of the dominant power. There is an experience of being managed and manipulated by outsiders in terms of ethnic status.

A final fundament of colonization is racism. Racism is a principle of social domination by which a group seen as inferior or different in terms of alleged biological characteristics is exploited, controlled, and oppressed socially and psychically by a superordinate group. Except for the marginal case of Japanese imperialism, the major examples of colonialism have involved the subjugation of nonwhite Asian, African, and Latin American peoples by white European powers. Thus racism has generally accompanied colonialism. Race prejudice can exist without colonization—the experience of Asian-American minorities is a case in point—but racism as a system of domination is part of the complex of colonization.

The concept of colonization stresses the enormous fatefulness of the historical factor, namely the manner in which a minority group becomes a part of the dominant society.[7] The crucial difference between the colonized Americans and the ethnic immigrant minorities is that the latter have always been able to operate fairly competitively within that relatively open section of the social and economic order because these groups came voluntarily in search of a better life, because their movements in society were not administratively controlled, and because they transformed their culture at their own pace—giving up ethnic values and institutions when it was seen as a desirable exchange for improvements in social position.

In present-day America, a major device of black colonization is the powerless ghetto. As Kenneth Clark describes the situation:

Ghettoes are the consequence of the imposition of external power and the institutionali-

zation of powerlessness. In this respect, they are in fact social, political, educational, and above all—economic colonies. Those confined within the ghetto walls are subject peoples. They are victims of the greed, cruelty, insensitivity, guilt and fear of their masters . . .

The community can best be described in terms of the analogy of a powerless colony. Its political leadership is divided, and all but one or two of its political leaders are shortsighted and dependent upon the larger political power structure. Its social agencies are financially precarious and dependent upon sources of support outside the community. Its churches are isolated or dependent. Its economy is dominated by small businesses which are largely owned by absentee owners, and its tenements and other real property are also owned by absentee landlords.

Under a system of centralization, Harlem's schools are controlled by forces outside of the community. Programs and policies are supervised and determined by individuals who do not live in the community . . .[8]

Of course many ethnic groups in America have lived in ghettoes. What make the black ghettoes an expression of colonized status are three special features. First, the ethnic ghettoes arose more from voluntary choice, both in the sense of the choice to immigrate to America and the decision to live among one's fellow ethnics. Second, the immigrant ghettoes tended to be a one and two generation phenomenon; they were actually way-stations in the process of acculturation and assimilation. When they continue to persist as in the case of San Francisco's Chinatown, it is because they are big business for the ethnics themselves and there is a new stream of immigrants. The black ghetto on the other hand has been a more permanent phenomenon, although some individuals do escape it. But most relevant is the third point. European ethnic groups like the Poles, Italians, and Jews generally only experienced a brief period, often less than a generation, during which their residential buildings, commercial stores, and other enterprises were owned by outsiders. The Chinese and Japanese faced handicaps of color prejudice that were almost as strong as the blacks faced, but very soon gained control of their internal communities, because their traditional ethnic culture and social organization had not been destroyed by slavery and internal colonization.

But Afro-Americans are distinct in the extent to which their segregated communities have remained controlled economically, politically, and administratively from the outside. One indicator of this difference is the estimate that the "income of Chinese-Americans from Chinese-owned businesses is in proportion to their numbers 45 times as great as the income of Negroes from Negro owned business."[9] But what is true of business is also true for the other social institutions that operate within the ghetto. The educators, policemen, social workers, politicians, and others who administer the affairs of ghetto residents are typically whites who live outside the black community. Thus the ghetto plays a strategic role as the focus for the administration by outsiders which is also essential to the structure of overseas colonialism.[10]

The colonial status of the Negro community goes beyond the issue of ownership and decision-making within black neighborhoods. The Afro-American population in most cities has very little influence on the power structure and institutions of the larger metropolis, despite the fact that in numerical terms, blacks tend to be the most sizeable of the various interest groups. A recent analysis of policy-making in Chicago estimates that "Negroes really hold less than 1 percent of the effective power in the Chicago metropolitan area. [Negroes are 20 percent of Cook County's population.] Realistically the power structure of Chicago is hardly less white than that of Mississippi."[11]

Colonization outside of a traditional colonial structure has its own special conditions. The group culture and social structure of the colonized in America is less developed; it is also less autonomous. In addition, the colonized are a numerical minority, and furthermore they are ghettoized more totally and are more dispersed than people under classic colonialism. Though these realities affect the magnitude and direction of response, it is my basic thesis that the most important expressions of protest in the black community during the recent years reflect the colonized status of Afro-America. Riots, programs of separation, politics of community control, the black revolutionary movements, and cultural nationalism each represent a different strategy of attack on domestic colonialism in America. Let us now examine some of these movements.

Riot or Revolt?

The so-called riots are being increasingly recognized as a preliminary if primitive form of mass rebellion against a colonial status. There is still a tendency to absorb their meaning within the conventional scope of assimilation-integration politics: some commentators stress the material motives involved in looting as a sign that the rioters want to join America's middle class affluence just like everyone else. That motives are mixed and often unconscious, that black people want good furniture and television sets like whites is beside the point. The guiding impulse in most major outbreaks has not been integration with American society, but an attempt to stake out a sphere of control by moving against that society and destroying the symbols of its oppression.

In my critique of the McCone report I observed that the rioters were asserting a claim to territoriality, an unorganized and rather inchoate attempt to gain control over their community or "turf."[12] In succeeding disorders also the thrust of the action has been the attempt to clear out an alien presence, white men and officials rather than a drive to kill whites as in a conventional race riot. The main attacks have been directed at the property of white businessmen and at the police who operate in the black community "like an army of occupation" protecting the interests of outside exploiters and maintaining the domination over the ghetto by the central metropolitan power structure.[13] The Kerner Report misleads when it attempts to explain riots in terms of integration: "What the rioters appear to be seeking was fuller participation in the social order and the material benefits enjoyed by the majority of American citizens. Rather than rejecting the American system, they were anxious to obtain a place for themselves in it." More accurately, the revolts pointed to alienation from this system on the part of many poor and also not-so-poor blacks. The sacredness of private property, that unconsciously accepted bulwark of our social arrangements, was rejected; people who looted apparently without guilt generally remarked that they were taking things that "really belonged" to them anyway. Obviously the society's bases of legitimacy and authority have been attacked. Law and order has long been viewed as the white man's law and order by Afro-Americans; but now this perspective characteristic of a colonized people is out in the open. And the Kerner Report's own data question how well ghetto rebels are buying the system: In Newark only 33 percent of self-reported rioters said they thought this country was worth fighting for in the event of a major war; in the Detroit sample the figure was 55 percent.[16]

One of the most significant consequences of the process of colonization is a weakening of the colonized's individual and collective will to resist his oppression. It has been easier to contain and control black ghettoes because communal bonds and group solidarity have been weakened through divisions among leadership, failures of organization, and a general disspiritment that accompanies social oppression. The riots are a signal that the will to resist has broken the mold of accommodation. In some cities as in Watts they also represented nascent movements toward community identity. In several riot-torn ghettoes the outbursts have stimulated new organizations and movements. If it is true that the riot phenomenon of 1964–68 has passed its peak, its historical import may be more for the "internal" organizing momentum generated than for any profound "external" response of the larger society facing up to underlying causes.

Despite the appeal of Frantz Fanon to young black revolutionaries, America is not Algeria. It is difficult to foresee how riots in our cities can play a role equivalent to rioting in the colonial situation as an integral phase in a movement for national liberation. In 1968 some militant groups (for example, the Black Panther Party in Oakland) had concluded that ghetto riots were self-defeating of the lives and interests of black people in the present balance of organization and manpower, though they had served a role to stimulate both black consciousness and white awareness of the depths of racial crisis. Such militants have been influential in "cooling" their communities during periods of high riot potential. Theoretically oriented black radicals see riots as spontaneous mass behavior which must be replaced by a revolutionary organization and consciousness. But despite the differences in objective conditions, the violence of the 1960s seems to serve the same psychic function, assertions of dignity and manhood for young blacks in urban

ghettoes, as it did for the colonized of North Africa described by Fanon and Memmi.[17]

Cultural Nationalism

Cultural conflict is generic to the colonial relation because colonization involves the domination of Western technological values over the more communal cultures of non-Western peoples. Colonialism played havoc with the national integrity of the peoples it brought under its sway. Of course, all traditional cultures are threatened by industrialism, the city, and modernization in communication, transportation, health, and education. What is special are the political and administrative decisions of colonizers in managing and controlling colonized peoples. The boundaries of African colonies, for example, were drawn to suit the political conveniences of the European nations without regard to the social organization and cultures of African tribes and kingdoms. Thus Nigeria as blocked out by the British included the Yorubas and the Ibos, whose civil war today is a residuum of the colonialist's disrespect for the integrity of indigenous cultures.

The most total destruction of culture in the colonization process took place not in traditional colonialism but in America. As Frazier stressed, the integral cultures of the diverse African peoples who furnished the slave trade were destroyed because slaves from different tribes, kingdoms, and linguistic groups were purposely separated to maximize domination and control. Thus language, religion, and national loyalties were lost in North America much more completely than in the Caribbean and Brazil where slavery developed somewhat differently. Thus on this key point America's internal colonization has been more total and extreme than situations of classic colonialism. For the British in India and the European powers in Africa were not able —as outnumbered minorities—to destroy the national and tribal cultures of the colonized. Recall that American slavery lasted 250 years and its racist aftermath another 100. Colonial dependency in the case of British Kenya and French Algeria lasted only 77 and 125 years respectively. In the wake of this more drastic uprooting and destruction of culture and social organization, much more powerful agencies of social, political, and psychological domination developed in the American case.

Colonial control of many peoples inhabiting the colonies was more a goal than a fact, and at Independence there were undoubtedly fairly large numbers of Africans who had never seen a colonial administrator. The gradual process of extension of control from the administrative center on the African coast contrasts sharply with the total uprooting involved in the slave trade and the totalitarian aspects of slavery in the United States. Whether or not Elkins is correct in treating slavery as a total institution, it undoubtedly had a far more radical and pervasive impact on American slaves than did colonialism on the vast majority of Africans.[18]

Yet a similar cultural process unfolds in both contexts of colonialism. To the extent that they are involved in the larger society and economy, the colonized are caught up in a conflict between two cultures. Fanon has described how the assimilation-oriented schools of Martinique taught him to reject his own culture and blackness in favor of Westernized, French, and white values.[19] Both the colonized elites under traditional colonialism and perhaps the majority of Afro-Americans today experience a parallel split in identity, cultural loyalty, and political orientation.[20]

The colonizers use their culture to socialize the colonized elites (intellectuals, politicians, and middle class) into an identification with the colonial system. Because Western culture has the prestige, the power, and the key to open the limited opportunity that a minority of the colonized may achieve, the first reaction seems to be an acceptance of the dominant values. Call it brainwashing as the Black Muslims put it; call it identifying with the aggressor if you prefer Freudian terminology; call it a natural response to the hope and belief that integration and democratization can really take place if you favor a more commonsense explanation, this initial acceptance in time crumbles on the realities of racism and colonialism. The colonized, seeing that his success within colonialism is at the expense of his group and his own inner identity, moves radically toward a rejection of the Western culture and develops a nationalist outlook that celebrates his people and their traditions. As Memmi describes it:

Assimilation being abandoned, the colonized's liberation must be carried out through a recovery of self and of autonomous dignity. Attempts at imitating the colonizer required self-denial; the colonizer's rejection is the indispensable prelude to self-discovery. That accusing and annihilating image must be shaken off; oppression must be attacked boldly since it is impossible to go around it. After having been rejected for so long by the colonizer, the day has come when it is the colonized who must refuse the colonizer.[21]

Memmi's book, *The Colonizer and the Colonized*, is based on his experience as a Tunisian Jew in a marginal position between the French and the colonized Arab majority. The uncanny parallels between the North African situation he describes and the course of black-white relations in our society is the best impressionist argument I know for the thesis that we have a colonized group and a colonizing system in America. His discussion of why even the most radical French anticolonialist cannot participate in the struggle of the colonized is directly applicable to the situation of the white liberal and radical vis-à-vis the black movement. His portrait of the colonized is as good an analysis of the psychology behind Black Power and black nationalism as anything that has been written in the U.S. Consider for example:

Considered *en bloc* as *them*, *they*, or *those*, different from every point of view, homogeneous in a radical heterogeneity, the colonized reacts by rejecting all the colonizers *en bloc*. The distinction between deed and intent has no great significance in the colonial situation. In the eyes of the colonized, all Europeans in the colonies are de facto colonizers, and whether they want to be or not, they are colonizers in some ways. By their privileged economic position, by belonging to the political system of oppression, or by participating in an effectively negative complex toward the colonized, they are colonizers ... They are supporters or at least unconscious accomplices of that great collective aggression of Europe.[22]

The same passion which made him admire and absorb Europe shall make him assert his differences; since those differences, after all, are within him and correctly constitute his true self.[23]

The important thing now is to rebuild his people, whatever be their authentic nature; to reforge their unity, communicate with it, and to feel that they belong.[24]

Cultural revitalization movements play a key role in anti-colonial movements. They follow an inner necessity and logic of their own that comes from the consequences of colonialism on groups and personal identities; they are also essential to provide the solidarity which the political or military phase of the anticolonial revolution requires. In the U.S. an Afro-American culture has been developing since slavery out of the ingredients of African worldviews, the experience of bondage, Southern values and customs, migration and the Northern lower-class ghettoes, and most importantly, the political history of the black population in its struggle against racism.[25] That Afro-Americans are moving toward cultural nationalism in a period when ethnic loyalties tend to be weak (and perhaps on the decline) in this country is another confirmation of the unique colonized position of the black group. (A similar nationalism seems to be growing among American Indians and Mexican-Americans.)

The Movement for Ghetto Control

The call for Black Power unites a number of varied movements and tendencies.[26] Though no clear-cut program has yet emerged, the most important emphasis seems to be the movement for control of the ghetto. Black leaders and organizations are increasingly concerned with owning and controlling those institutions that exist within or impinge upon their community. The colonial model provides a key to the understanding of this movement, and indeed ghetto control advocates have increasingly invoked the language of colonialism in pressing for local home rule. The framework of anticolonialism explains why the struggle for poor people's or community control of poverty programs has been more central in many cities than the content of these programs and why it has been crucial to exclude whites from leadership positions in black organizations.

The key institutions that anticolonialists want to take over or control are business, social services, schools, and the police. Though many spokesmen have advocated the exclusion of white landlords and small businessmen from the ghetto, this program has evidently not struck fire with the black population and little concrete movement toward economic expropriation has yet developed. Welfare recipients have organized in many cities to protect their rights and gain a greater voice in the decisions that affect them, but whole communities have not yet been able to mount direct action against welfare colonialism. Thus schools and the police seem now to be the burning issues of ghetto control politics.

During the past few years there has been a dramatic shift from educational integration as the primary goal to that of community control of the schools. Afro-Americans are demanding their own school boards, with the power to hire and fire principals and teachers and to construct a curriculum which would be relevant to the special needs and culture style of ghetto youth. Especially active in high schools and colleges have been black students, whose protests have centered on the incorporation of Black Power and black culture into the educational system. Consider how similar is the spirit behind these developments to the attitude of the colonized North African toward European education:

He will prefer a long period of educational mistakes to the continuance of the colonizer's school organization. He will choose institutional disorder in order to destroy the institutions built by the colonizer as soon as possible. There we will see, indeed a reactive drive of profound protest. He will no longer owe anything to the colonizer and will have definitely broken with him.[27]

Protest and institutional disorder over the issue of school control came to a head in 1968 in New York City. The procrastination in the Albany State legislature, the several crippling strikes called by the teachers union, and the almost frenzied response of Jewish organizations makes it clear that decolonization of education faces the resistance of powerful vested interests.[28] The situation is too dynamic at present to assess probable future results. However, it can be safely predicted that some form of school decentralization will be institutionalized in New York, and the movement for community control of education will spread to more cities.

This movement reflects some of the problems and ambiguities that stem from the situation of colonization outside an immediate colonial context. The Afro-American community is not parallel in structure to the communities of colonized nations under traditional colonialism. The significant difference here is the lack of fully developed indigenous institutions besides the church. Outside of some areas of the South there is really no black economy, and most Afro-Americans are inevitably caught up in the larger society's structure of occupations, education, and mass communication. Thus the ethnic nationalist orientation which reflects the reality of colonization exists alongside an integrationist orientation which corresponds to the reality that the institutions of the larger society are much more developed than those of the incipient nation.[29] As would be expected the movement for school control reflects both tendencies. The militant leaders who spearhead such local movements may be primarily motivated by the desire to gain control over the community's institutions—they are anticolonialists first and foremost. Many parents who support them may share this goal also, but the majority are probably more concerned about creating a new education that will enable their children to "make it" in the society and the economy as a whole—they know that the present school system fails ghetto children and does not prepare them for participation in American life.

There is a growing recognition that the police are the most crucial institution maintaining the colonized status of black Americans. And of all establishment institutions, police departments probably include the highest proportion of individual racists. This is no accident since central to the workings of racism (an essential component of colonization) are attacks on the humanity and dignity of the subject group. Through their normal routines, the police constrict Afro-Americans to black neighborhoods by harassing and questioning them when found outside the ghetto; they break up groups of youth congregating on corners or in cars without any provocation; and they continue to use offensive and racist language no matter how many intergroup understanding seminars have been built into the police academy. They also shoot to kill ghetto residents for alleged crimes such as car thefts and running from police officers.[30]

Police are key agents in the power equation as well as the drama of dehumanization. In the final analysis they do the dirty work for the larger system by restricting the striking back of black rebels to skirmishes inside the ghetto, thus deflecting energies and attacks from the communities and institutions of the larger power structure. In a historical review, Gary Marx notes that since the French revolution, police and other authorities have killed large numbers of demonstrators and rioters; the rebellious "rabble" rarely destroys human life. The same pattern has been repeated in America's recent revolts.[31] Journalistic accounts appearing in the press recently suggest that police see themselves as defending the interests of white people against a tide of black insurgence; furthermore the majority of whites appear to view "blue power" in this light. There is probably no other opinion on which the races are as far apart today as they are on the question of attitudes toward the police.

In many cases set off by a confrontation between a policeman and a black citizen, the ghetto uprisings have dramatized the role of law enforcement and the issue of police brutality. In their aftermath, movements have arisen to contain police activity. One of the first was the Community Alert Patrol in Los Angeles, a method of policing the police in order to keep them honest and constrain their violations of personal dignity. This was the first tactic of the Black Panther Party which originated in Oakland, perhaps the most significant group to challenge the police role in maintaining the ghetto as a colony. The Panthers' later policy of openly carrying guns (a legally protected right) and their intention of defending themselves against police aggression has brought on a series of confrontations with the Oakland police department. All indications are that the authorities intend to destroy the Panthers by shooting, framing up, or legally harassing their leadership—diverting the group's energies away from its primary purpose of self-defense and organization of the black community to that of legal defense and gaining support in the white community.

There are three major approaches to "police colonialism" that correspond to reformist and revolutionary readings of the situation. The most elementary and also superficial sees colonialism in the fact that ghettoes are overwhelmingly patrolled by white rather than by black officers. The proposal—supported today by many police departments—to increase the number of blacks on local forces to something like their distribution in the city would then make it possible to reduce the use of white cops in the ghetto. This reform should be supported, for a variety of obvious reasons, but it does not get to the heart of the police role as agents of colonization.

The Kerner Report documents the fact that in some cases black policemen can be as brutal as their white counterparts. The Report does not tell us who polices the ghetto, but they have compiled the proportion of Negroes on the forces of the major cities. In some cities the disparity is so striking that white police inevitably dominate ghetto patrols. (In Oakland 31 percent of the population and only 4 percent of the police are black; in Detroit the figures are 39 percent and 5 percent; and in New Orleans 41 and 4.) In other cities, however, the proportion of black cops is approaching the distribution in the city: Philadelphia 29 percent and 20 percent; Chicago 27 percent and 17 percent.[32] These figures also suggest that both the extent and the pattern of colonization may vary from one city to another. It would be useful to study how black communities differ in degree of control over internal institutions as well as in economic and political power in the metropolitan area.

A second demand which gets more to the issue is that police should live in the communities they patrol. The idea here is that black cops who lived in the ghetto would have to be accountable to the community; if they came on like white cops then "the brothers would take care of business" and make their lives miserable. The third or maximalist position is based on the premise that the police play no positive role in the ghettoes. It calls for the withdrawal of metropolitan officers from black communities and the substitution of an autonomous indigenous force that would maintain order without oppressing the population. The precise relationship between such an independent police, the city and county law enforcement agencies, a ghetto governing body that would supervise and finance it, and especially the law itself is yet unclear. It is unlikely that we will soon face these problems directly as they have arisen in the case of New York's schools. Of all the programs of decolonization, police autonomy will be most resisted. It gets to the heart of how the state functions to control and contain the black community through delegating the legitimate use of violence to police authority.

The various Black Power programs that are aimed at gaining control of individual ghettoes—buying up property and businesses, running the schools through community boards, taking over antipoverty programs and other social agencies, diminishing the arbitrary power of the police—can serve to revitalize the institutions of the ghetto and build up an economic, professional, and political power base. These programs seem limited; we do not know at present if they are enough in themselves to end colonized status.[33] But they are certainly a necessary first step.

The Role of Whites

What makes the Kerner Report a less-than-radical document is its superficial treatment of racism and its reluctance to confront the colonized relationship between black people and the larger society. The Report emphasizes the attitudes and feelings that make up white racism, rather than the system of privilege and control which is the heart of the matter.[34] With all its discussion of the ghetto and its problems, it never faces the question of the stake that white Americans have in racism and ghettoization.

This is not a simple question, but this paper should not end with the impression that police are the major villains. All white Americans gain some privileges and advantage from the colonization of black communities.[35] The majority of whites also lose something from this oppression and division in society. Serious research should be directed to the ways in which white individuals and institutions are tied into the ghetto. In closing let me suggest some possible parameters.

1. It is my guess that only a small minority of whites make a direct economic profit from ghetto colonization. This is hopeful in that the ouster of white businessmen may become politically feasible. Much more significant, however, are the private and corporate interests in the land and residential property of the black community; their holdings and influence on urban decision-making must be exposed and combated.

2. A much larger minority have occupational and professional interests in the present arrangements. The Kerner Commission reports that 1.3 million nonwhite men would have to be upgraded occupationally in order to make the black job distribution roughly similar to the white. They advocate this without mentioning that 1.3

million specially privileged white workers would lose in the bargain.[30] In addition there are those professionals who carry out what Lee Rainwater has called the "dirty work" of administering the lives of the ghetto poor: the social workers, the school teachers, the urban development people, and of course the police.[37] The social problems of the black community will ultimately be solved only by people and organizations from that community; thus the emphasis within these professions must shift toward training such a cadre of minority personnel. Social scientists who teach and study problems of race and poverty likewise have an obligation to replace themselves by bringing into the graduate schools and college faculties men of color who will become the future experts in these areas. For cultural and intellectual imperialism is as real as welfare colonialism, though it is currently screened behind such unassailable shibboleths as universalism and the objectivity of scientific inquiry.

3. Without downgrading the vested interests of profit and profession, the real nitty-gritty elements of the white stake are political power and bureaucratic security. Whereas few whites have much understanding of the realities of race relations and ghetto life, I think most give tacit or at least subconscious support for the containment and control of the black population. Whereas most whites have extremely distorted images of black power, many—if not most—would still be frightened by actual black political power. Racial groups and identities are real in American life; white Americans sense they are on top, and they fear possible reprisals or disruptions were power to be more equalized. There seems to be a paranoid fear in the white psyche of black dominance; the belief that black autonomy would mean unbridled license is so ingrained that such reasonable outcomes as black political majorities and independent black police forces will be bitterly resisted.

On this level the major mass bulwark of colonization is the administrative need for bureaucratic security so that the middle classes can go about their life and business in peace and quiet. The black militant movement is a threat to the orderly procedures by which bureaucracies and suburbs manage their existence, and I think today there are more people who feel a stake in conventional procedures than there are those who gain directly from racism. For in their fight for institutional control, the colonized will not play by the white rules of the game. These administrative rules have kept them down and out of the system; therefore they have no necessary intention of running institutions in the image of the white middle class.

The liberal, humanist value that violence is the worst sin cannot be defended today if one is committed squarely against racism and for self-determination. For some violence is almost inevitable in the decolonization process; unfortunately racism in America has been so effective that the greatest power Afro-Americans (and perhaps also Mexican-Americans) wield today is the power to disrupt. If we are going to swing with these revolutionary times and at least respond positively to the anticolonial movement, we will have to learn to live with conflict, confrontation, constant change, and what may be real or apparent chaos and disorder.

A positive response from the white majority needs to be in two major directions at the same time. First, community liberation movements should be supported in every way by pulling out white instruments of direct control and exploitation and substituting technical assistance to the community when this is asked for. But it is not enough to relate affirmatively to the nationalist movement for ghetto control without at the same time radically opening doors for full participation in the institutions of the mainstream. Otherwise the liberal and radical position is little different than the tradtional segregationist. Freedom in the special conditions of American colonization means that the colonized must have the choice between participation in the larger society and in their own independent structures.

Notes

1. This is a revised version of a paper delivered at the University of California Centennial Program, "Studies in Violence," Los Angeles, June 1, 1968. For criticisms and ideas that have improved an earlier draft, I am indebted to Robert Wood, Lincoln Bergman, and Gary Marx. As a good colonialist I have probably restated (read: stolen) more ideas from the writings of Kenneth Clark, Stokely Carmichael, Franz Fanon and especially such contributors to the Black Panther Party (Oakland) newspaper as Huey Newton, Bobby Seale, Eldridge Cleaver, and Kathleen Cleaver than I have appropriately

credited or generated myself. In self-defense I should state that I began working somewhat independently on a colonial analysis of American race relations in the fall of 1965; see my "Whitewash Over Watts: The Failure of the McCone Report," Transaction, 3 (March–April 1966), pp. 3–9, 54.

Harold Cruse, Rebellion or Revolution, New York: 1968, p. 214.

Nationalism, including an orientation toward Africa, is no new development. It has been a constant tendency within Afro-American politics. See Cruse, ibid., esp. chaps. 5–7.

This was six years before the publication of The Crisis of the Negro Intellectual, New York: Morrow, 1968, which brought Cruse into prominence. Thus the 1962 article was not widely read until its reprinting in Cruse's essays, Rebellion or Revolution, op. cit.

Kenneth Clark, Dark Ghetto, New York: Harper and Row, 1965. Clark's analysis first appeared a year earlier in Youth in the Ghetto, New York: Haryou Associates, 1964.

Stokely Carmichael and Charles Hamilton, Black Power, New York: Random, 1967.

As Eldridge Cleaver reminds us, "Black people are a stolen people held in a colonial status on stolen land, and any analysis which does not acknowledge the colonial status of black people cannot hope to deal with the real problem," "The Land Question," Ramparts, 6 (May 1968), p. 51.

Youth in the Ghetto, op. cit., pp. 10–11; 79–80.

N. Glazer and D. P. Moynihan, Beyond the Melting Pot, Cambridge, Mass.: M.I.T., 1963, p. 37.

"When we speak of Negro social disabilities under capitalism, . . . we refer to the fact that he does not own anything—even what is ownable in his own community. Thus to fight for black liberation is to fight for his right to own. The Negro is politically compromised today because he owns nothing. He has little voice in the affairs of state because he owns nothing. The fundamental reason why the Negro bourgeois-democratic revolution has been aborted is because American capitalism has prevented the development of a black class of capitalist owners of institutions and economic tools. To take one crucial example, Negro radicals today are severely hampered in their task of educating the black masses on political issues because Negroes do not own any of the necessary means of propaganda and communication. The Negro owns no printing presses, he has no stake in the networks of the means of communication. Inside his own communities he does not own the house he lives in, the property he lives on, nor the wholesale and retail sources from which he buys his commodities. He does not own the edifices in which he enjoys culture and entertainment or in which he socializes. In capitalist society, an individual or group that does not own anything is powerless." H. Cruse, "Behind the Black Power Slogan," in Cruse, Rebellion or Revolution, op. cit., pp. 238–39.

11. Harold M. Baron, "Black Powerlessness in Chicago," Transaction, 6 (Nov., 1968), pp. 27–33.

12. R. Blauner, "Whitewash Over Watts," op. cit.

13. "The police function to support and enforce the interests of the dominant political, social, and economic interests of the town" is a statement made by a former police scholar and official, according to A. Neiderhoffer, Behind the Shield, New York: Doubleday, 1967 as cited by Gary T. Marx, "Civil Disorder and the Agents of Control," Journal of Social Issues, forthcoming.

14. Report of the National Advisory Commission on Civil Disorders, N.Y.: Bantam, March 1968, p. 7.

15. This kind of attitude has a long history among American Negroes. During slavery, Blacks used the same rationalization to justify stealing from their masters. Appropriating things from the master was viewed as "taking part of his property for the benefit of another part; whereas stealing referred to appropriating something from another slave, an offense that was not condoned." Kenneth Stampp, The Peculiar Institution, Vintage, 1956, p. 127.

16. Report of the National Advisory Commission on Civil Disorders, op. cit., p. 178.

17. Franz Fanon, Wretched of the Earth, New York: Grove, 1963; Albert Memmi, The Colonizer and the Colonized, Boston: Beacon, 1967.

18. Robert Wood, "Colonialism in Africa and America: Some Conceptual Considerations," December 1967, unpublished paper.

19. F. Fanon, Black Skins, White Masks, New York: Grove, 1967.

20. Harold Cruse has described how these two themes of integration with the larger society and identification with ethnic nationality have struggled within the political and cultural movements of Negro Americans. The Crisis of the Negro Intellectual, op. cit.

21. Memmi, op. cit., p. 128.

22. Ibid., p. 130.

23. Ibid., p. 132.

24. Ibid., p. 134.

25. In another essay, I argue against the standard sociological position that denies the existence of an ethnic Afro-American culture and I expand on the above themes. The concept of "Soul" is astonishingly parallel in content to the mystique of "Negritude" in Africa; the Pan-African culture movement has its parallel in the

burgeoning Black culture mood in Afro-American communities. See "Black Culture: Myth or Reality" in Peter Rose, editor, *Americans From Africa*, Atherton, 1969.

26. Scholars and social commentators, black and white alike, disagree in interpreting the contemporary Black Power movement. The issues concern whether this is a new development in black protest or an old tendency revised; whether the movement is radical, revolutionary, reformist, or conservative; and whether this orientation is unique to Afro-Americans or essentially a black parallel to other ethnic group strategies for collective mobility. For an interesting discussion of Black Power as a modernized version of Booker T. Washington's separatism and economism, see Harold Cruse, *Rebellion or Revolution, op. cit.*, pp. 193–258.

27. Memmi, *op. cit.*, pp. 137–138.

28. For the New York school conflict see Jason Epstein, "The Politics of School Decentralization," *New York Review of Books*, June 6, 1968, pp. 26–32; and "The New York City School Revolt," *ibid.*, 11, no. 6, pp. 37–41.

29. This dual split in the politics and psyche of the Black American was poetically described by Du Bois in his *Souls of Black Folk*, and more recently has been insightfully analyzed by Harold Cruse in *The Crisis of the Negro Intellectual, op. cit.* Cruse has also characterized the problem of the black community as that of underdevelopment.

30. A recent survey of police finds "that in the predominantly Negro areas of several large cities, many of the police perceive the residents as basically hostile, especially the youth and adolescents. A lack of public support—from citizens, from courts, and from laws—is the policeman's major complaint. But some of the public criticism can be traced to the activities in which he engages day by day, and perhaps to the tone in which he enforces the "law" in the Negro neighborhoods. Most frequently he is 'called upon' to intervene in domestic quarrels and break up loitering groups. He stops and frisks two or three times as many people as are carrying dangerous weapons or are actual criminals, and almost half of these don't wish to cooperate with the policeman's efforts." Peter Rossi *et al.*, "Between Black and White—The Faces of American Institutions and the Ghetto," in Supplemental Studies for The National Advisory Commission on Civil Disorders, July 1968, p. 114.

31. "In the Gordon Riots of 1780 demonstrators destroyed property and freed prisoners, but did not seem to kill anyone, while authorities killed several hundred rioters and hung an additional 25. In the Rebellion Riots of the French Revolution, 'though several hundred rioters were killed, they killed no one. Up to the end of the summer of 1967, this pattern had clearly been repeated, as police, not rioters, were responsible for most of the more than 100 deaths that have occurred. Similarly, in a related context, the more than 100 civil rights murders of recent years have been matched by almost no murders of racist whites." G. Marx, "Civil Disorders and the Agents of Social Control," *op. cit.*

32. Report of the National Advisory Commission on Civil Disorders, *op. cit.*, p. 321. That black officers nevertheless would make a difference is suggested by data from one of the supplemental studies to the Kerner Report. They found Negro policemen working in the ghettoes considerably more sympathetic to the community and its social problems than their white counterparts. Peter Rossi *et al.*, "Between Black and White—The Faces of American Institutions in the Ghetto," *op. cit.*, chap. 6.

33. Eldridge Cleaver has called this first stage of the anticolonial movement *community liberation* in contrast to a more long-range goal of *national* liberation. E. Cleaver, "Community Imperialism," Black Panther Party newspaper, (May 18, 1968).

34. For a discussion of this failure to deal with racism, see Gary T. Marx, "Report of the National Commission: The Analysis of Disorder or Disorderly Analysis," 1968, unpublished paper.

35. Such a statement is easier to assert than to document but I am attempting the latter in a forthcoming book tentatively titled *White Racism, Black Culture*, to be published by Little Brown, 1970.

36. Report of the National Advisory Commission on Civil Disorders, *op. cit.*, pp. 253–256.

37. Lee Rainwater, "The Revolt of the Dirty Workers," *Trans*action, 5 (1967), pp. 2, 64.

27

HARVEY MOLOTCH

Oil in Santa Barbara and Power in America

More than oil leaked from Union Oil's Platform A in the Santa Barbara Channel—a bit of truth about power in America spilled out along with it. It is the thesis of this paper that this tech-nological "accident," like all accidents, provides clues to the realities of social structure (in this instance, power arrangements) not otherwise available to the outside observer. Further, it is argued, the response of the aggrieved popula-tion (the citizenry of Santa Barbara) provides insight into the more general process which shapes disillusionment and frustration among those who come to closely examine and be in-jured by existing power arrangements.

A few historical details concerning the case under examination are in order. For over fif-teen years, Santa Barbara's political leaders had attempted to prevent despoilation of their coast-line by oil drilling on adjacent federal waters. Although they were unsuccessful in blocking eventual oil leasing (in February 1968) of *federal* waters beyond the three-mile limit, they were able to establish a sanctuary within *state* waters

Harvey Molotch, "Oil in Santa Barbara and Power in America," *Sociological Inquiry*, vol. 40 (Winter 1970), pp. 131–144. Reprinted by permis-sion.

This paper was written as Working Paper No. Community and Organization Research Insti-tute, University of California, Santa Barbara. It was delivered at the 1969 Annual Meeting of the American Sociological Association, San Fran-cisco. A shorter version has been published in *Ramparts*, November 1969. The author wishes to thank his wife, Linda Molotch, for her active col-laboration, and Robert Sollen, reporter for the Santa Barbara *News-Press*, for his cooperation and critical comments on an early draft.

(thus foregoing the extraordinary revenues which leases in such areas bring to adjacent lo-calities—e.g., the riches of Long Beach). It was therefore a great irony that the one city which voluntarily exchanged revenue for a pure envi-ronment should find itself faced, on January 28, 1969, with a massive eruption of crude oil—an eruption which was, in the end, to cover the entire city coastline (as well as much of Ventura and Santa Barbara County coastline as well) with a thick coat of crude oil. The air was soured for many hundreds of feet inland and the traditional economic base of the region (tour-ism) was under threat. After ten days of un-successful attempts, the runaway well was brought under control, only to be followed by a second eruption on February 12. This fissure was closed on March 3, but was followed by a sustained "seepage" of oil—a leakage which con-tinues, at this writing, to pollute the sea, the air, and the famed local beaches. The oil companies had paid $603,000,000 for their lease rights and neither they nor the federal government bear any significant legal responsibility toward the locali-ties which these lease rights might endanger.

If the big spill had occurred almost anywhere else (e.g., Lima, Ohio; Lompoc, California), it is likely that the current research opportunity would not have developed. But Santa Barbara is different. Of its 70,000 residents, a dispropor-tionate number are upper class and upper mid-dle class. They are persons who, having a wide choice of where in the world they might live, have chosen Santa Barbara for its ideal climate, gentle beauty, and sophisticated "culture." Thus a large number of worldly, rich, well-educated persons—individuals with resources, spare time, and contacts with national and international elites—found themselves with a commonly shared disagreeable situation: the pollution of their otherwise near-perfect environment. Santa Barbarans thus possessed none of the "problems" which otherwise are said to inhibit effective community response to external threat: they are not urban villagers (cf. Gans, 1962); they are not internally divided and parochial like the Springdalers (cf. Vidich & Bensman, 1960); nor emaciated with self-doubt and organizational naiveté as is supposed of the ghetto dwellers. With moral indignation and high self-confidence, they set out to right the wrong so obviously done them.

Their response was immediate. The stodgy *Santa Barbara News-Press* inaugurated a series of editorials, unique in uncompromising stridency. Under the leadership of a former state senator and a local corporate executive, a community organization was established called "GOO" (Get Oil Out!) which took a militant stand against any and all oil activity in the Channel.

In a petition to President Nixon (eventually to gain 110,000 signatures), GOO's position was clearly stated:

> . . . With the seabed filled with fissures in this area, similar disastrous oil operation accidents may be expected. And with one of the largest faults centered in the channel waters, one sizeable earthquake could mean possible disaster for the entire channel area . . .

> Therefore, we the undersigned do call upon the state of California and the Federal Government to promote conservation by:
> 1. Taking immediate action to have present off-shore oil operations cease and desist at once.
> 2. Issuing no further leases in the Santa Barbara Channel.
> 3. Having all oil platforms and rigs removed from this area at the earliest possible date.

The same theme emerged in the hundreds of letters published by the *News-Press* in the weeks to follow and in the positions taken by virtually every local civic and government body. Both in terms of its volume (372 letters published in February alone) and the intensity of the revealed opinions, the flow of letters was hailed by the *News-Press* as "unprecedented." Rallies were held at the beach; GOO petitions were circulated at local shopping centers and sent to friends around the country; a fund-raising dramatic spoof of the oil industry was produced at a local high school. Local artists, playwrights, advertising men, retired executives and academic specialists from the local campus of the University of California (UCSB) executed special projects appropriate to their areas of expertise.

A GOO strategy emerged for a two-front attack. Local indignation, producing the petition to the President and thousands of letters to key members of Congress and the executive would lead to appropriate legislation. Legal action in the courts against the oil companies and the federal government would have the double effect of recouping some of the financial losses certain to be endured by the local tourist and fishing industries while at the same time serving notice that drilling would be a much less profitable operation than it was supposed to be. Legislation to ban drilling was introduced by Cranston in the U.S. Senate and Teague in the House of Representatives. Joint suits by the city and County of Santa Barbara (later joined by the state) for $1 billion in damages was filed against the oil companies and the federal government.

All of these activities—petitions, rallies, court action, and legislative lobbying—were significant for their similarity in revealing faith in "the system." The tendency was to blame the oil companies. There was a muckraking tone to the Santa Barbara response: oil and the profit-crazy executives of Union Oil were ruining Santa Barbara—but once our national and state leaders became aware of what was going on, and were provided with the "facts" of the case, justice would be done.

Indeed, there was good reason for hope. The quick and enthusiastic responses of Teague and Cranston represented a consensus of men otherwise polar opposites in their political behavior. Democrat Cranston was a charter member of the liberal California Democratic Council; Republican Teague was a staunch fiscal and moral conservative (e.g., a strong Vietnam hawk and unrelenting harrasser of the local Center for the Study of Democratic Institutions). The bills, for which there was great optimism, would have had the consequence of effecting a "permanent" ban on drilling in the Channel.

But from other quarters there was silence. Santa Barbara's representatives in the state legislature either said nothing or (in later stages offered minimal support. It took several months for Senator Murphy to introduce Congressional legislation (for which he admitted to having little hope) which would have had the consequence of exchanging the oil companies' leases in the Channel for comparable leases in the under-exploited Elk Hills oil reserve in California's Kern County. Most disappointing of all to Santa Barbarans, Governor Reagan withheld support or proposals which would end the drilling.

As subsequent events unfolded, this seemingly inexplicable silence of the democratically elected representatives began to fall into place as part of a more general problem. American democracy came to be seen as a much more complicated affair than a system in which government officials actuate the desires of the "people who elected them" once those desires came to be known. Instead, increasing recognition came to be given to the "all-powerful oil lobby," to legislators "in the pockets of Oil," to academicians "bought" by Oil, and to regulatory agencies which lobby for those they are supposed to regulate. In other words, Santa Barbarans became increasingly *ideological*, increasingly *sociological*, and in the words of some observers, increasingly *"radical."*[1] Writing from his lodgings in the area's most exclusive hotel (the Santa Barbara Biltmore), and irate citizen penned these words in his published letter to the *News-Press*:

We the people can protest and protest and it means nothing because the industrial and military junta are the country. They tell us, the People, what is good for the oil companies is good for the People. To that I say, Like Hell!

Profit is their language and the proof of all this is their history (*SBNP*,[2] Feb. 26, 1969, p. A-6).

As time wore on, the editorials and letters continued in their bitterness.

The Executive Branch and the Regulatory Agencies: Disillusionment

From the start, Secretary Hickel's actions were regarded with suspicion. His publicized associations with Alaskan Oil interests did his reputation no good in Santa Barbara. When, after a halt to drilling (for "review" of procedures) immediately after the initial eruption, Hickel one day later ordered a resumption of drilling and production (even as the oil continued to gush into the channel), the government's response was seen as unbelievingly consistent with conservationists' worst fears. That he backed down within 48 hours and ordered a halt to drilling and production was taken as a response to the massive nationwide media play then being given to the Santa Barbara plight and to the citizens' mass outcry just then beginning to reach Washington.

Disenchantment with Hickel and the executive branch also came through less spectacular, less specific, but nevertheless genuine activity. First of all, Hickel's failure to support any of the legislation introduced to halt drilling was seen as an *action* favoring Oil. His remarks on the subject, while often expressing sympathy with Santa Barbarans[3] (and for a while placating local sentiment) were revealed as hypocritical in light of the action not taken. Of further note was the constant attempt by the Interior Department to minimize the extent of damage in Santa Barbara or to hint at possible "compromises" which were seen locally as near-total capitulation to the oil companies.

Volume of Oil Spillage. Many specific examples might be cited. An early (and continuing) issue in the oil spill was the *volume* of oil spilling into the Channel. The U.S. Geological Survey (administered by Interior), when queried by reporters, broke its silence on the subject with estimates which struck as incredible in Santa Barbara. One of the extraordinary attributes of the Santa Barbara locale is the presence of a technology establishment among the most sophisticated in the country. Several officials of the General Research Corporation (a local R & D firm with experience in marine technology) initiated studies of the oil outflow and announced findings of pollution volume at a "minimum" of tenfold the Interior estimate. Further, General Research provided (and the *News-Press* published) a detailed account of the methods used in making the estimate (cf. Allan, 1969). Despite repeated challenges from the press, Interior both refused to alter its estimate or to reveal its method for making estimates. Throughout the crisis, the divergence of the estimates remained at about tenfold.

The "seepage" was estimated by the Geological Survey to have been reduced from 1,260 gallons per day to about 630 gallons. General Research, however, estimated the leakage at the rate of 8,400 gallons per day at the same point in time as Interior's 630 gallon estimate. The lowest estimate of all was provided by an official of the Western Oil and Gas Association, in a letter to the *Wall Street Journal*. His estimate: "Probably less than 100 gallons a day" (*SBNP*, August 5, 1969: A-1).

Damage to Beaches. Still another point of contention was the state of the beaches at varying points in time. The oil companies, through various public relations officials, constantly minimized the actual amount of damage and maximized the effect of Union Oil's cleanup activity. What surprised (and most irritated) the locals was the fact that Interior statements implied the same goal. Thus Hickel referred at a press conference to the "recent" oil spill, providing the impression that the oil spill was over, at a time when freshly erupting oil was continuing to stain local beaches. President Nixon appeared locally to "inspect" the damage to beaches, and Interior arranged for him to land his helicopter on a city beach which had been cleaned thoroughly in the days just before, but spared him a close-up of much of the rest of the county shoreline which continued to be covered with a thick coat of crude oil. (The beach visited by Nixon has been oil stained on many occasions subsequent to the President's departure.) Secret servicemen kept the placards and shouts of several hundred demonstrators safely out of Presidential viewing or hearing distance.

Continuously, the Oil and Interior combine implied the beaches to be restored when Santa Barbarans knew that even a beach which looked clean was by no means restored. The *News-Press*, through a comprehensive series of interviews with local and national experts on wildlife and geology, made the following points clear:

1. As long as oil remained on the water and oil continued to leak from beneath the sands, all Santa Barbara beaches were subject to continuous doses of oil—subject only to the vagaries of wind change. Indeed, all through the spill and up to the present point in time, a beach walk is likely to result in tar on the feet. On "bad days" the beaches are unapproachable.

2. The damage to the "ecological chain" (a concept which has become a household phrase in Santa Barbara) is of unknown proportions. Much study will be necessary to learn the extent of damage.

3. The continuous alternating natural erosion and building up of beach sands means that "clean" beaches contain layers of oil at various sublevels under the mounting sands, layers which will once again be exposed when the cycle reverses itself and erosion begins anew. Thus, it will take many years for the beaches of Santa Barbara to be completely restored, even if the present seepage is halted and no additional pollution occurs.

Damage to Wildlife. Oil on feathers is ingested by birds; continuous preening thus leads to death. In what local and national authorities called a hopeless task, two bird-cleaning centers were established to cleanse feathers and otherwise administer to damaged wildfowl. (Oil money helped to establish and supply these centers.) Both spokesmen from Oil and the federal government then adopted these centers as sources of "data" on the extent of damage to wildfowl. Thus, the number of dead birds due to pollution was computed on the basis of number of fatalities at the wildfowl centers.[4] This of course is preposterous, given the fact that dying birds are provided with very inefficient means of propelling themselves to such designated places. The obviousness of this dramatic understatement of fatalities was never acknowledged by either Oil or Interior—although noted in Santa Barbara.

At least those birds in the hands of local ornithologists could be confirmed as dead—and this fact could not be disputed by either Oil or Interior. Not so, however, with species whose corpses are more difficult to produce on command. Several observers at the Channel Islands (a national wildlife preserve containing one of the country's largest colonies of sea animals) reported sighting unusually large numbers of dead sea-lion pups—on the oil-stained shores of one of the islands. Statement and counter-statement followed, with Oil's defenders arguing that the animals were not dead at all—but only appeared inert because they were sleeping. Despite the testimony of staff experts of the local Museum of Natural History and the Museum Scientist of UCSB's Biological Sciences Department that the number of "inert" sea-lion pups was far larger than normal and that field trips had confirmed the deaths, the position of Oil, as also expressed by the Department of the Navy (which administers the stricken island), remained adamant that the sea animals were only sleeping (cf. *Life*, June 13, 1969; July 4, 1969). The dramatic beaching of an unusually large number of dead whales on the beaches of Northern California—whales which had just completed their migration through the Santa Barbara Channel—was acknowledged, but held not to be caused by oil pollution. No direct linkage (or non-linkage) with oil could be demonstrated by investigating scientists (cf. *San Francisco Chronicle*, March 12, 1969: 1–3).

In the end, it was not simply Interior, its U.S. Geological Survey and the President which either supported or tacitly accepted Oil's public relations tactics. The regulatory agencies at both national and state level, by action, inaction, and implication had the consequence of defending Oil at virtually every turn. Thus, at the outset of the first big blow, as the ocean churned with bubbling oil and gas, the U.S. Coast Guard (which patrols Channel waters regularly) failed to notify local officials of the pollution threat because, in the words of the local commander, "the seriousness of the situation was not apparent until late in the day Tuesday and it was difficult to reach officials after business hours" (*SBNP*, January 30, 1969: A-1, 4). Officials ended up hearing of the spill from the *News-Press*.

The Army Corps of Engineers must approve all structures placed on the ocean floor and thus had the discretion to hold public hearings on each application for a permit to build a drilling platform. With the exception of a single *pro forma* ceremony held on a platform erected in 1967, requests for such hearings were never granted. In its most recent handling of these matters (at a point long after the initial eruption and as oil still leaks into the ocean) the Corps changed its criteria for public hearings by restricting written objections to new drilling to "the effects of the proposed exploratory drilling on *navigation or national defense*" (*SBNP*, August 17, 1969: A-1, 4). Prior to the spill, effects on *fish and wildlife* were specified by the Army as possible grounds for objection, but at that time such objections, when raised, were more easily dismissed as unfounded.

The Federal Water Pollution Control Administration consistently attempted to understate the amount of damage done to waterfowl by quoting the "hospital dead" as though a reasonable assessment of the net damage. State agencies followed the same pattern. The charge of "Industry domination" of state conservation boards was levelled by the State Deputy Attorney General, Charles O'Brien (*SBNP*, February 9, 1969: A-6). Thomas Gaines, a Union Oil executive, actually sits as a member on the State Agency Board most directly connected with the control of pollution in Channel waters. In correspondence with complaining citizens, N. B. Livermore, Jr., of the Resources Agency of California, refers to the continuing oil spill as "minor seepage" with "no major long-term effect on the marine ecology." The letter adopts the perspective of Interior and Oil, even though the state was in no way being held culpable for the spill (letter, undated to Joseph Keefe, citizen, University of California, Santa Barbara Library, on file).

With these details under their belts, Santa Barbarans were in a position to understand the sweeping condemnation of the regulatory system as contained in a *News-Press* front page, banner-headlined interview with Rep. Richard D. Ottinger (D–NY), quoted as follows: "And so on down the line. Each agency has a tendency to become the captive of the industry that it is to regulate" (*SBNP*, March 1, 1969: A-1).

The Congress: Disillusionment

Irritations with Interior were paralleled by frustrations encountered in dealing with the Congressional establishment which had the responsibility of holding hearings on ameliorative legislation. A delegation of Santa Barbarans was scheduled to testify in Washington on the Cranston bill. From the questions which Congressmen asked of them, and the manner in which they were "handled," the delegation could only conclude that the Committee was "in the pockets of Oil." As one of the returning delegates put it, the presentation bespoke of "total futility."

At this writing, six months after their introduction, both the Cranston and Teague bills lie buried in committee with little prospect of surfacing. Cranston has softened his bill significantly—requiring only that new drilling be suspended until Congress is convinced that sufficient technological safeguards exist. But to no avail.

Science and Technology: Disillusionment

From the start, part of the shock of the oil spill was that such a thing could happen in a country with such sophisticated technology. The much overworked phrase, "If we can send a man to the moon . . ." was even more overworked in Santa Barbara. When, in years previous, Santa Barbara's elected officials had attempted to halt the original sale of leases, "assurances" were given from Interior that such an "accident" could not occur, given the highly developed state of the art. Not only did it occur, but the original gusher of oil spewed forth completely out of control for ten days, and the continuing "seepage" which followed it remains uncontrolled to the present moment, seven months later. That the government would embark upon so massive a drilling program with such unsophisticated technologies, was striking indeed.

Further, not only were the technologies inadequate and the plans for stopping a leak, should it occur, nonexistent, but the area in which the drilling took place was known to be ultra-hazardous from the outset. That is, drilling was occurring on an ocean bottom known for its extraordinary geological circumstances—porous sands lacking a bedrock "ceiling" capable of containing runaway oil and gas. Thus the continuing leakage through the sands at various points above the oil reservoir is unstoppable, and could have been anticipated with the data *known to all parties involved.*

Another peculiarity of the Channel is the fact that it is located in the heart of earthquake activity in that region of the country which, among all regions, is among the very most earthquake prone.[5] Santa Barbarans are now asking what might occur in an earthquake: if pipes on the ocean floor and casings through the ocean bottom should be sheared, the damage done by the Channel's *thousands* of potential producing wells would be devastating to the entire coast of Southern California.[6]

Recurrent attempts have been made to ameliorate the continuing seep by placing floating booms around an area of leakage and then having workboats skim off the leakage from within the demarcated area.[7] Chemical dispersants, of various varieties, have also been tried. But the oil bounces over the sea booms in the choppy waters; the work boats suck up only a drop in the bucket and the dispersants are effective only

when used in quantities which constitute a graver pollution threat than the oil they are designed to eliminate. Cement is poured into suspected fissures in an attempt to seal them up. Oil on beaches is periodically cleaned by dumping straw over the sands and then raking up the straw along with the oil it absorbs.

This striking contrast between the sophistication of the means used to locate and extract oil compared to the primitiveness of the means to control and clean it up was widely noted in Santa Barbara. It is the result of a system which promotes research and development which leads to strategic profitability rather than to social utility. The common sight of men throwing straw on miles of beaches within sight of complex drilling rigs capable of exploiting resources thousands of feet below the ocean's surface, made the point clear.

The futility of the cleanup and control efforts was widely noted in Santa Barbara. Secretary Hickel's announcement that the Interior Department was generating new "tough" regulations to control off-shore drilling was thus met with great skepticism. The Santa Barbara County Board of Supervisors was invited to "review" these new regulations—and refused to do so in the belief that such participation would be used to provide the fraudulent impression of democratic responsiveness—when, in fact, the relevant decisions had been already made. In previous years when they were fighting against the leasing of the Channel, the Supervisors had been assured of technological safeguards; now, as the emergency continued, they could witness for themselves the dearth of any means for ending the leakage in the Channel. They had also heard the testimony of a high-ranking Interior engineer who, when asked if such safeguards could positively prevent future spills, explained that "no prudent engineer would ever make such a claim" (*SBNP*, February 19, 1969: A-1). They also had the testimony of Donald Solanas, a regional supervisor of Interior's U.S. Geological Survey, who had said about the Union Platform eruption:

I could have had an engineer on that platform 24 hours a day, 7 days a week and he couldn't have prevented the accident.

His "explanation" of the cause of the "accident": "Mother earth broke down on us" (*SBNP*, February 28, 1969: C-12).

Given these facts, as contained in the remarks of Interior's own spokesmen, combined with testimony and information received from non-Interior personnel, Interior's new regulations, and the invitation to the County to participate in making them, could only be a ruse to preface a resumption of drilling. In initiating the County's policy of not responding to Interior's "invitation," a County Supervisor explained: "I think we may be falling into a trap" (*SBNP*, April 1, 1969).

The very next day, the Supervisors' suspicions were confirmed. Interior announced a selective resumption of drilling "to relieve pressures." (*News-Press* letter writers asked if the "pressure" was geological or political.) The new tough regulations were themselves seriously flawed by the fact that most of their provisions specified those measures, such as buoyant booms around platforms, availability of chemical dispersants, etc., which had proven almost totally useless in the current emergency. They fell far short of minimum safety requirements as enumerated by UC Santa Barbara geologist Robert Curry who criticized a previous version of the same regulations as "relatively trivial" and "toothless"[8] (*SBNP*, March 5, 1969: C-9).

On the other hand, the new regulations did specify that oil companies would henceforth be financially responsible for damages resulting from pollution mishaps. (This had been the *de facto* reality in the Union case; the company had assumed responsibility for the cleanup, and advised stockholders that such costs were covered by "more than adequate" insurance.[9]) The liability requirement has been vociferously condemned by the oil companies—particularly by those firms which have failed to make significant strikes on their Channel leases (*SBNP*, March 14, 1969). Several of these companies have now entered suit (supported by the ACLU) against the federal government charging that the arbitrary changing of lease conditions renders Channel exploitation "economically and practically impossible," thus depriving them of rights of due process (*SBNP*, April 10, 1969: A-1).

The weaknesses of the new regulations came not as a surprise to people who had already adapted to thinking of Oil and the Interior Department as the same source. There was much less preparation for the results of the Presidential Committee of "distinguished" scientists and engineers (the DuBridge Panel) which was to

recommend means of eliminating the seepage under Platform A. Given the half-hearted, inexpensive and primitive attempts by Union Oil to deal with the seepage, feeling ran high that at last the technological sophistication of the nation would be harnessed to solve this particular vexing problem. Instead, the panel—after a two-day session and after hearing testimony from no one not connected with either Oil or Interior—recommended the "solution" of drilling an additional fifty wells under Platform A in order to pump the area dry as quickly as possible. The process would require ten to twenty years, one member of the panel estimated.[10]

The recommendation was severely terse, requiring no more than one and a half pages of type. Despite an immediate local clamor, Interior refused to make public the data on the reasoning behind the recommendations. The information on Channel geological conditions was provided by the oil companies; the Geological Survey routinely depends upon the oil industry for the data upon which it makes its "regulatory" decisions. The data, being proprietary, could thus not be released. Totally inexplicable, in light of this "explanation," is Interior's continuing refusal to immediately provide the information given a recent clearance by Union Oil for public release of all the data. Santa Barbara's local experts have thus been thwarted by the counter-arguments of Oil-Interior that "if you had the information we have, you would agree with us."

Science was also having its non-neutral consequences on the other battlefront being waged by Santa Barbarans. The chief Deputy Attorney General of California, in his April 7 speech to the blue-ribbon Channel City Club of Santa Barbara, complained that the oil industry

is preventing oil drilling experts from aiding the Attorney General's office in its lawsuits over the Santa Barbara oil spill (*SBNP*, Aug. 8, 1969).

Complaining that his office has been unable to get assistance from petroleum experts at California universities, the Deputy Attorney General further stated:

The university experts all seem to be working on grants from the oil industry. There is an atmosphere of fear. The experts are afraid that if they assist us in our case on behalf of the people of California, they will lose their oil industry grants.

At the Santa Barbara Campus of the University, there is little Oil money in evidence and few, if any, faculty members have entered into proprietary research arrangements with Oil. Petroleum geology and engineering is simply not a local specialty. Yet it is a fact that Oil interests did contact several Santa Barbara faculty members with offers of funds for studies of the ecological effects of the oil spill, with publication rights stipulated by Oil.[11] It is also the case that the Federal Water Pollution Control Administration explicitly requested a UC Santa Barbara botanist to withhold the findings of his study, funded by that Agency, on the ecological consequences of the spill (*SBNP*, July 29, 1969: A-3).

Except for the Deputy Attorney General's complaint, none of these revelations received any publicity outside of Santa Barbara. But the Attorney's allegation became something of a statewide issue. A professor at the Berkeley campus, in his attempt to refute the allegation, actually confirmed it. Wilbur H. Somerton, Professor of petroleum engineering, indicated he could not testify against Oil

because my work depends on good relations with the petroleum industry. My interest is serving the petroleum industry. I view my obligation to the community as supplying it with well-trained petroleum engineers. We train the industry's engineers and they help us. (*SBNP*, April 12, 1969, as quoted from a *San Francisco Chronicle* interview.)

Santa Barbara's leaders were incredulous about the whole affair. The question—one which is more often asked by the downtrodden sectors of the society—was asked: "Whose University is this, anyway?" A local executive and GOO leader asked, "If the truth isn't in the universities, where is it?" A conservative member of the State Legislature, in a move reminiscent of SDS demands, went so far as to ask an end to all faculty "moonlighting" for industry. In Santa Barbara, the only place where all of this publicity was occurring, there was thus an opportunity for insight into the linkages between knowledge, the University, government, and Oil and the resultant non-neutrality of science. The

backgrounds of many members of the DuBridge Panel were linked publicly to the oil industry. In a line of reasoning usually the handiwork of groups like SDS, a *News-Press* letter writer labeled Dr. DuBridge as a servant of Oil interests because, as a past President of Cal Tech, he would have had to defer to Oil in generating the massive funding which that institution requires. In fact, the relationship was quite direct. Not only has Union Oil been a contributor to Cal Tech, but Fred Hartley (Union's President) is a Cal Tech trustee. The impropriety of such a man as DuBridge serving as the key "scientist" in determining the Santa Barbara outcome seemed more and more obvious.

Taxation and Patriotism: Disillusionment

From Engler's detailed study of the politics of Oil, we learn that the oil companies combat local resistance with arguments that hurt: taxation and patriotism (cf. Engler, 1961). They threaten to take their operations elsewhere, thus depriving the locality of taxes and jobs. The more grandiose argument is made that oil is necessary for the national defense; hence, any weakening of "incentives" to discover and produce oil plays into the hands of the enemy.

Santa Barbara, needing money less than most locales and valuing environment more, learned enough to know better. Santa Barbara wanted oil to leave, but oil would not. Because the oil is produced in federal waters, only a tiny proportion of Santa Barbara County's budget indirectly comes from oil, and virtually none of the city of Santa Barbara's budget comes from oil. *News-Press* letters and articles disposed of the defense argument with these points: (1) oil companies deliberately limit oil production under geographical quota restrictions designed to maintain the high price of oil by regulating supply; (2) the federal oil import quota (also sponsored by the oil industry) which restricts imports from abroad, weakens the country's defense posture by forcing the nation to exhaust its own finite supply while the Soviets rely on the Middle East; (3) most oil imported into the U.S. comes from relatively dependable sources in South America which foreign wars would not endanger (4) the next major war will be a nuclear holocaust with possible oil shortages a very low level problem.

Just as an attempt to answer the national defense argument led to conclusions the very opposite of Oil's position, so did a closer examination of the tax argument. For not only did Oil
not pay very much in local taxes, Oil also paid
very little in *federal* taxes. In another of its
front-page editorials the *News-Press* made the
facts clear. The combination of the output restrictions, extraordinary tax write-off privileges
for drilling expenses, the import quota, and the
7.5 percent depletion allowance, all created an
artificially high price of U.S. oil—a price almost
double the world market price for the comparable product delivered to comparable U.S.
destinations.[12] The combination of incentives
available creates a situation where some oil companies pay no taxes whatever during extraordinarily profitable years. In the years 1962–1966,
Standard of New Jersey paid less than 4 percent
of profits in taxes, Standard of California, less
than 3 percent, and twenty-two of the largest oil
companies paid slightly more than 6 percent
(*SBNP*, February 16, 1969: A-1). It was pointed
out, again and again to Santa Barbarans, that it
was this system of subsidy which made the relatively high cost deep-sea exploration and drilling
of the Channel profitable in the first place. Thus,
the citizens of Santa Barbara, as federal taxpayers and fleeced consumers were subsidizing
their own demise. The consequence of such a
revelation can only be *infuriating*.

The Mobilization of Bias

The actions of Oil and Interior and the contexts
in which such actions took place can be reexam-
ined in terms of their function in diffusing local
opposition, disorienting dissenters, and otherwise limiting the scope of issues which are potentially part of public controversies. E. E. Schattschneider (1960: 71) has noted:

All forms of political organization have a bias
in favor of the exploitation of some kinds of
conflict and the suppression of others because
organization is the mobilization of bias.
Some issues are organized into politics while
others are organized out.

Expanding the notion slightly, certain techniques shaping the "mobilization of bias" can
be said to have been revealed by the present case
study.

1. *The pseudo-event.* Boorstin (1962) has described the use of the pseudo-event in a large
variety of task accomplishment situations. A
pseudo-event occurs when men arrange conditions to simulate a certain kind of event, such
that certain prearranged consequences follow as
though the actual event had taken place. Several pseudo-events may be cited. *Local participation in decision making.* From the outset, it
was obvious that national actions vis-à-vis Oil in
Santa Barbara had as their strategy the freezing
out of any local participation in decisions affecting the Channel. Thus, when in 1968 the federal
government first called for bids on a Channel
lease, local officials were not even informed.
When subsequently queried about the matter,
federal officials indicated that the lease which
was advertised for bid was just a corrective measure to prevent drainage of a "little old oil pool"
on federal property adjacent to a state lease producing for Standard and Humble. This "little
old pool" was to draw a high bonus bid of
$21,189,000 from a syndicate headed by Phillips
(*SBNP*, February 9, 1969: A-17). Further, local
officials were not notified by any government
agency in the case of the original oil spill, nor
(except after the spill was already widely
known) in the case of any of the previous or subsequent more "minor" spills. Perhaps the
thrust of the federal government's colonialist attitude toward the local community was contained in an Interior Department engineer's
memo written to J. Cordell Moore, Assistant Secretary of Interior, explaining the policy of refusing public hearings prefatory to drilling: "We
preferred not to stir up the natives any more
than possible."[13] (The memo was released by
Senator Cranston and excerpted on page 1 of the
News-Press.)

Given this known history, the Santa Barbara
County Board of Supervisors refused the call
for "participation" in drawing up new "tougher"
drilling regulations, precisely because they
knew the government had no intention of creating "safe" drilling regulations. They refused to
take part in the pseudo-event and thus refused to
let the consequences (in this case the appearance
of democratic decision-making and local assent)
of a pseudo-event occur.

Other attempts at the staging of pseudo-events
may be cited. Nixon's "inspection" of the Santa
Barbara beachfront was an obvious one. Another series of pseudo-events were the Congres-

sional hearings staged by legislators who were, in the words of a local well-to-do lady leader of GOO, "kept men." The locals blew off steam—but the hearing of arguments and the proposing of appropriate legislation based on those arguments (the presumed essence of the Congressional hearing as a former event) certainly did not come off. Many Santa Barbarans had a similar impression of the court hearings regarding the various legal maneuvers against oil drilling; legal proceedings came to be similarly seen as ceremonious arrangements for the accomplishing of tasks not revealed by their formally-stated properties.

2. *The creeping event.* A creeping event is, in a sense, the opposite of a pseudo-event. It occurs when something is actually taking place, but when the manifest signs of the event are arranged to occur at an inconspicuously gradual and piecemeal pace, thus eliminating some of the consequences which would otherwise follow from the event if it were to be perceived all-at-once to be occurring. Two major creeping events were arranged for the Santa Barbara Channel. Although the great bulk of the bidding for leases in the Channel occurred simultaneously, the first lease was, as was made clear earlier, advertised for bid prior to the others and prior to any public announcement of the leasing of the Channel. The federal waters' virginity was thus ended up with only a whimper. A more salient example of the creeping event is the resumption of production and drilling after Hickel's second moratorium. Authorization to resume *production* on different specific groups of wells occurred on these dates in 1969: February 17; February 21; February 22; and March 3. Authorization to resume *drilling* of various groups of new wells was announced by Interior on these dates in 1969: April 1, June 12, July 2, August 2, and August 16. (This is being written on August 20.) Each time, the resumption was announced as a safety precaution to relieve pressures, until finally on the most recent resumption date, the word "deplete" was used for the first time as the reason for granting permission to drill. There is thus no *particular* point in time in which production and drilling was re-authorized for the Channel—and full resumption has still not been officially authorized.

A creeping event has the consequences of diffusing resistance to the event by holding back

what journalists call a "time peg" on which to hang "the story." Even if the aggrieved party should get wind that "something is going on," strenuous reaction is inhibited. Non-routine activity has as its prerequisite the crossing of a certain threshold point of input; the dribbling out of an event has the consequence of making each of the revealed inputs fall below the threshold level necessary for non-routine activity. By the time it becomes quite clear that "something is going on" both the aggrieved and the sponsor of the creeping event can ask why there should be a response "*now*" when there was none previously to the very same kind of stimulus. In such manner, the aggrieved has resort only to frustration and a gnawing feeling that "events are sweeping him by."

3. *The "neutrality" of science and the "knowledge" producers.* I have already dealt at some length with the disillusionment of Santa Barbarans with the "experts" and the University. After learning for themselves of the collusion between government and Oil and the use of secret science as a prop to that collusion, Santa Barbarans found themselves in the unenviable position of having to demonstrate that science and knowledge were, in fact, not neutral arbiters. They had to demonstrate, by themselves, that the continued drilling was not safe, that the "experts" who said it was safe were the hirelings directly or indirectly of Oil interests and that the report of the DuBridge Panel recommending massive drilling was a fraudulent document. They had to document that the University *petroleum* geologists were themselves in league with their adversaries and that knowledge unfavorable to the Oil interests was systematically withheld by virtue of the very structure of the knowledge industry. As the SDS has learned in other contexts, this is no small task. It is a long story to tell, a complicated story to tell, and one which pits lay persons (and a few academic renegades) against a profession and patrons of a profession. An illustration of the difficulties involved may be drawn from very recent history. Seventeen Santa Barbara plaintiffs, represented by the ACLU, sought a temporary injunction against additional Channel drilling at least until the information utilized by the DuBridge Panel was made public and a hearing could be held. The injunction was not granted and, in the end, the presiding federal judge ruled in favor of what

he termed the "expert" opinions available to the Secretary of the Interior. It was a function of limited time for rebuttal, the disorienting confusions of courtroom procedures, and also perhaps the desire to not offend the Court, that the ACLU lawyer could not make his subtle, complex, and highly controversial case that the "experts" were partisans and that their scientific "findings" follow from that partisanship.

4. Constraints of communication media. Just as the courtroom setting was not amenable to a full reproduction of the details surrounding the basis for the ACLU case, so the media in general—through restrictions of time and style—prevent a full airing of the details of the case. A more cynical analysis of the media's inability to make known the Santa Barbara "problem" in its full fidelity might hinge on an allegation that the media are constrained by fear of "pressures" from Oil and its allies; Metromedia, for example, sent a team to Santa Barbara which spent several days documenting, interviewing and filming for an hour-long program—only to suddenly drop the whole matter due to what is reported by locals in touch with the network to have been "pressures" from Oil. Such blatant interventions aside, however, the problem of full reproduction of the Santa Barbara "news" would remain problematic nonetheless.

News media are notorious for the anecdotal nature of their reporting; even so-called "think pieces" rarely go beyond a stringing together of proximate "events." There are no analyses of the "mobilization of bias" or linkages of men's actions and their pecuniary interests. Science and learning are assumed to be neutral; regulatory agencies are assumed to function as "watchdogs" for the public. Information to the contrary of these assumptions is treated as exotic exception; in the manner of Drew Pearson columns, exception piles upon exception without intellectual combination, analysis or ideological synthesis. The complexity of the situation to be reported, the wealth of details needed to support such analyses require more time and effort than journalists have at their command. Their recitation would produce long stories not consistent with space requirements and make-up preferences of newspapers and analogous constraints of the other media. A full telling of the whole story would tax the reader/viewer and would risk boring him.

For these reasons, the rather extensive media coverage of the oil spill centered on a few dramatic moments in its history (e.g., the initial gusher of oil) and a few simple-to-tell "human interest" aspects such as the pathetic deaths of the sea birds struggling along the oil-covered sands. With increasing temporal and geographical distance from the initial spill, national coverage became increasingly rare and increasingly sloppy. Interior statements on the state of the "crisis" were reported without local rejoinders as the newsmen who would have gathered them began leaving the scene. It is to be kept in mind that, relative to other local events, the Santa Barbara spill received extraordinarily extensive national coverage.[14] The point is that this coverage is nevertheless inadequate in both its quality and quantity to adequately inform the American public.

5. The routinization of evil. An oft quoted American cliché is that the news media cover only the "bad" things; the everyday world of people going about their business in conformity with American ideals loses out to the coverage of student and ghetto "riots," wars and crime, corruption and sin. The grain of truth in this cliché should not obfuscate the fact that there are *certain kinds of evil* which, partially for reasons cited in the preceding paragraphs, also lose their place in the public media and the public mind. Pollution of the Santa Barbara Channel is now routine; the issue is not whether or not the Channel is polluted, but *how much* it is polluted. A recent oil slick discovered off a Phillips Platform in the Channel was dismissed by an oil company official as a "routine" drilling byproduct which was not viewed as "obnoxious." That "about half" of the current oil seeping into the Channel is allegedly being recovered is taken as an improvement sufficient to preclude the "outrage" that a big national story would require.

Similarly, the pollution of the "moral environment" becomes routine; politicians are, of course, on the take, in the pockets of Oil, etc. The depletion allowance issue becomes not whether or not such special benefits should exist at all, but rather whether it should be at the level of 20 or 27.5 percent. "Compromises" emerge such as the 24 percent depletion allowance and the new "tough" drilling regulations, which are already being hailed as "victories" for the reformers (cf. *Los Angeles Times,* July 14,

1969:17). Like the oil spill itself, the depletion allowance debate becomes buried in its own disorienting detail, its ceremonious pseudo-events and in the triviality of the "solutions" which ultimately come to be considered as the "real" options. Evil is both banal and complicated; both of these attributes contribute to its durability.[15]

The Struggle for the Means to Power

It should (although it does not) go without saying that the parties competing to shape decision making on oil in Santa Barbara do not have equal access to the means of "mobilizing bias" which this paper has discussed. The same social structural characteristics which Michels has asserted make for an "iron law of oligarchy" make for, in this case, a series of extraordinary advantages for the Oil-government combine. The ability to create pseudo-events such as Nixon's Santa Barbara inspection or controls necessary to bring off well-timed creeping events are not evenly distributed throughout the social structure. Lacking such ready access to media, lacking the ability to stage events at will, lacking a well-integrated system of arrangements for goal attainment (at least in comparison to their adversaries) Santa Barbara's leaders have met with repeated frustrations.

Their response to their relative powerlessness has been analogous to other groups and individuals who, from a similar vantage point, come to see the system up close. They become willing to expand their repertoire of means of influence as their cynicism and bitterness increase concomitantly. Letter writing gives way to demonstrations, demonstrations to civil disobedience. People refuse to participate in "democratic procedures" which are a part of the opposition's event-management strategy. Confrontation politics arise as a means of countering with "events" of one's own, thus providing the media with "stories" which can be simply and energetically told. The lesson is learned that "the power to make a reportable event is . . . the power to make experience" (Boorstin, 1962:10).

Rallies were held at local beaches; Congressmen and state and national officials were greeted by demonstrations. (Fred Hartley, of Union Oil, inadvertently landed his plane in the midst of one such demonstration, causing a rather ugly name-calling scene to ensue.) A "sail-in" was held one Sunday with a flotilla of local pleasure boats forming a circle around Platform A, each craft bearing large anti-oil banners. (Months earlier boats coming near the platforms were sprayed by oil personnel with fire hoses.) City hall meetings were packed with citizens reciting "demands" for immediate and forceful local action.

A City Council election in the midst of the crisis resulted in the landslide election of the Council's bitterest critic and the defeat of a veteran Councilman suspected of having "oil interests." In a rare action, the *News-Press* condemned the local Chamber of Commerce for accepting oil money for a fraudulent tourist advertising campaign which touted Santa Barbara (including its beaches) as restored to its former beauty. (In the end, references to the beaches were removed from subsequent advertisements but the oil-financed campaign continued briefly.

In the meantime, as a *Wall Street Journal* reporter was to observe, "a current of gloom and despair" ran through the ranks of Santa Barbara's militants. The president of Sloan Instruments Corporation, an international R & D firm with headquarters in Santa Barbara, came to comment:

> We are so God-damned frustrated. The whole democratic process seems to be falling apart. Nobody responds to us, and we end up doing things progressively less reasonable. This town is going to blow up if there isn't some reasonable attitude expressed by the Federal Government—nothing seems to happen except that we lose.

Similarly, a well-to-do widow, during a legal proceeding in Federal District Court in which Santa Barbara was once again "losing," whispered in the author's ear:

> Now I understand why those young people at the University go around throwing things . . . The individual has no rights at all.

One possible grand strategy for Santa Barbara was outlined by a local public relations man and GOO worker:

> We've got to run the oil men out. The city owns the wharf and the harbor that the company has to use. The city has got to deny its facilities to oil traffic, service boats, cranes

348

and the like. If the city contravenes some federal navigation laws (which such actions would unquestionably involve), to hell with it.

The only hope to save Santa Barbara is to awaken the nation to the ravishment. That will take public officials who are willing to block oil traffic with their bodies and with police hoses, if necessary. Then federal marshals or federal troops would have to come in. This would pull in the national news media (*SBNP*, July 6, 1969, p. 7).

This scenario has thus far not occurred in Santa Barbara, although the use of the wharf by the oil industries has led to certain militant actions. A picket was maintained at the wharf for two weeks, protesting the conversion of the pier from a recreation and tourist facility to a heavy industrial plant for the use of the oil companies.[16] A boycott of other wharf businesses (e.g., two restaurants) was urged. The picket line was led by white, middle-class adults—one of whom had almost won the mayorality of Santa Barbara in a previous election. Hardly a "radical" or a "militant," this same man was several months later representing his neighborhood protective association in its opposition to the presence of a "Free School" described by this man (somewhat ambivalently) as a "hippie hotel."

Prior to the picketing, a dramatic Easter Sunday confrontation (involving approximately 500 persons) took place between demonstrators and city police. Unexpectedly, as a wharf rally was breaking up, an oil service truck began driving up the pier to make delivery of casing supplies for oil drilling. There was a spontaneous sit-down in front of the truck. For the first time since the Ku Klux Klan folded in the 1930s, a group of Santa Barbarans (some young, some "hippie," but many hard-working middle-class adults), was publicly taking the law into its own hands. After much lengthy discussion between police, the truck driver and the demonstrators, the truck was ordered away and the demonstrators remained to rejoice their victory. The following day's *News-Press* editorial, while not supportive of such tactics, found much to excuse—noteworthy given the paper's long standing bitter opposition to similar tactics when exercised by dissident Northern blacks or student radicals. A companion demonstration on the water failed to materialize; a group of Santa Barbarans was to sail to the Union platform and "take it"; choppy seas, however, precluded a landing, caus-

ing the would-be conquerors to return to port in failure.

It would be difficult to speculate at this writing what forms Santa Barbara's resistance might take in the future. The veteran *News-Press* reporter who has covered the important oil stories has publicly stated that if the government fails to eliminate both the pollution and its causes, "there will, at best be civil disobedience in Santa Barbara and at worst, violence." In fact, talk of "blowing up" the ugly platforms has been recurrent—and is heard in all social circles.

But just as this kind of talk is not completely serious, it is difficult to know the degree to which the other kinds of militant statements are serious. Despite frequent observations of the "radicalization"[17] of Santa Barbara, it is difficult to determine the extent to which the authentic grievances against Oil have generalized to a radical analysis of American society. Certainly an SDS membership campaign among Santa Barbara adults would be a dismal failure. But that is too severe a test. People, especially basically contented people, change their world-view only very slowly, if at all. Most Santa Barbarans go about their comfortable lives in the ways they always did; they may even help Ronald Reagan to another term in the statehouse. But I do conclude that large numbers of persons have been moved, and that they have been moved in the directions of the radical left. They have gained insights into the structure of power in America not possessed by similarly situated persons in other parts of the country. The claim is thus that some Santa Barbarans, especially those with most interest and most information about the oil spill and its surrounding circumstances, have come to view power in America more intellectually, more analytically, more sociologically— more *radically*—then they did before.

I hold this to be a general sociological response to a series of concomitant circumstances, which can be simply enumerated (*again!*) as follows:

1. *Injustice.* The powerful are operating in a manner inconsistent with the normatively sanctioned expectations of an aggrieved population. The aggrieved population is deprived of certain felt needs as a result.
2. *Information.* Those who are unjustly treated are provided with rather complete information regarding this disparity between expectations and actual perform-

ances of the powerful. In the present case, that information has been provided to Santa Barbarans (and only to Santa Barbarans) by virtue of their own observations of local physical conditions and by virtue of the unrelenting coverage of the city's newspaper. Hardly a day has gone by since the initial spill that the front page has not carried an oil story; everything the paper can gets its hands on is printed. It carries analyses; it makes the connections As an appropriate result, Oil officials have condemned the paper as a "lousy" and "distorted" publication of "lies."[18]

3. *Literacy and Leisure.* In order for the information relevant to the injustice to be assimilated in all its infuriating complexity, the aggrieved parties must be, in the larger sense of the terms, literate and leisured. They must have the ability and the time to read, to ponder and to get upset.

My perspective thus differs from those who would regard the radical response as appropriate to some form or another of social or psychological freak. Radicalism is not a subtle form of mental illness (cf. recent statements of such as Bettelheim) caused by "rapid technological change," or increasing "impersonality" in the modern world; radicals are neither "immature," "under-disciplined," nor "anti-intellectual." Quite the reverse. They are persons who most clearly live under the conditions specified above and who make the most rational (and moral) response, given those circumstances. Thus radical movements draw their membership disproportionately from the most leisured, intelligent, and informed of the white youth (cf. Flacks, 1967), and from the young blacks whose situations are most analogous to these white counterparts.

The Accident as a Research Methodology

If the present research effort has had as its strategy anything pretentious enough to be termed a "methodology," it is the methodology of what could be called "accident research." I define an "accident" as an occasion in which miscalculation leads to the breakdown of customary order. It has as its central characteristic the fact that an event occurs which is, to some large degree, unanticipated by those whose actions caused it

to occur. As an event, an accident is thus crucially dissimilar both from the pseudo-event and the creeping event. It differs from the pseudo event in that it bespeaks of an authentic and an unplanned happening; it differs from the creeping event in its suddenness, its sensation, in the fact that it brings to light a series of preconditions, actions and consequences all at once. It is "news"—often sensational news. Thresholds are reached; attentions are held.

The accident thus tends to have consequences which are the very opposite of events which are pseudo or creeping. Instead of being a deliberately planned contribution to a purposely developed "social structure" (or, in the jargon of the relevant sociological literature, "decisional outcome"), it has as its consequence the revelation of features of a social system, or of individuals' actions and personalities, which are otherwise deliberately obfuscated by those with the resources to create pseudo- and creeping events. A resultant convenience is that the media, at the point of accident, may come to function as able and persistent research assistants.

At the level of everyday individual behavior the accident is an important lay methodological resource of gossipers—especially for learning about those possessing the personality and physical resources to shield their private lives from public view. It is thus that the recent Ted Kennedy accident functioned so well for the purpose (perhaps useless) of gaining access to that individual's private routines and private dispositions. An accident such as the recent unprovoked police shooting of a deaf mute on the streets of Los Angeles provides analogous insights into routine police behavior which official records could never reveal. The massive and unprecedented Santa Barbara oil spill has similarly led to important revelations about the structure of power. An accident is thus an important instrument for learning about the lives of the powerful and the features of the social system which they deliberately and quasi-deliberately create. It is available as a research focus for those seeking a comprehensive understanding of the structure of power in America.

Finale

Bachrach and Baratz (1962) have pointed to the plight of the pluralist students of community power who lack any criteria for the inevitable *selecting* of the "key political decisions" which serve as the basis for their research conclusions. I offer accident as a criterion. An accident is not a decision, but it does provide a basis for insight into whole series of decisons and non-decisions, events and pseudo-events which, taken together, might provide an explanation of the structure of power. Even though the local community is notorious for the increasing triviality of the decisions which occur within it (cf. Schulze, 1961; Vidich and Bensman, 1958; Mills, 1956), accident research at the local level might serve as "micro"-analyses capable of revealing the "second face of power" (Bachrach and Baratz), ordinarily left faceless by traditional community studies which fail to concern themselves with the processes by which bias is mobilized and thus how "issues" rise and fall.

The present effort has been the relatively more difficult one of learning not about community power, but about national power—and the relationship between national and local power. The "findings" highlight the extraordinary intransigence of national institutions in the face of local dissent, but more importantly, point to the processes and tactics which undermine that dissent and frustraate and radicalize the dissenters.

The leadership described between Oil, government, and the knowledge industry does not constitute a unique pattern of power in America. All major sectors of the industrial economy lend themselves to the same kind of analysis as Oil in Santa Barbara. Where such analyses have been carried out, the results are analogous in their content and analogous in the outrage which they cause. The nation's defeat in Vietnam, in a sense an accident, has led to analogous revelations about the arms industry and the manner in which American foreign policy is waged.[19] Comparable scrutinies of the agriculture industry, the banking industry, etc., would, in my opinion, lead to the same infuriating findings as the Vietnam defeat and the oil spill.

The national media dwell upon only a few accidents at a time. But across the country, in various localities, accidents routinely occur—accidents which can tell much not only about local power, but about national power as well. Community power studies typically have resulted in revelations of the "pluralistic" squabbles among local sub-elites which are stimulated by exogenous interventions (cf. Walton, 1968). Accident

research at the local level might bring to light the larger societal arrangements which structure the parameters of such local debate. Research at the local level could thus serve as an avenue to knowledge about *national* power. Sociologists should be ready when an accident hits in their neighborhood, and then go to work.

Notes

1. See the report of Morton Mintz in the June 29, 1969, *Washington Post*. The conjunction of these three attributes is not, in my opinion, coincidental.

2. *SBNP* will be used to denote *Santa Barbara News-Press* throughout this paper.

3. Hickel publicly stated and wrote (personal communication) that the original leasing was a mistake and that he was doing all within discretionary power to solve this problem.

4. In a February 7 letter to Union Oil shareholders, Fred Hartley informed them that the bird refuge centers had been "very successful in their efforts." In fact, by April 30, 1969, only 150 birds (of thousands treated) had been returned to the natural habitat as "fully recovered," and the survival rate of birds treated was estimated as a miraculously high (in light of previous experience) 20 percent (cf. *SBNP*, April 30, 1969: F-3).

5. Cf. "Damaging Earthquakes of the United States through 1966," Fig. 2, National Earthquake Information Center, Environmental Science Services Administration, Coast and Geodetic Survey.

6. See Interview with Donald Weaver, Professor or Geology, UCSB, *SBNP*, Feb. 21, 1969, p. A-1, 6. (Also, remarks by Professor Donald Runnells, UCSB geologist, *SBNP*, Feb. 23, 1969, p. B-2.) Both stress the dangers of faults in the Channel, and potential earthquakes.

7. More recently plastic tents have been placed on the ocean floor to trap seeping oil; it is being claimed that half the runaway oil is now being trapped in these tents.

8. Curry's criticism is as follows:
   "These new regulations make no mention at all about in-pipe safety valves to prevent blowouts, or to shut off the flow of oil deep in the well should the oil and gas escape from the drill hole region into a natural fissure at some depth below the wellhead blowout preventers. There is also no requirement for a backup valve in case the required preventer fails to work. Remember, the runaway well on Union Platform A was equipped with a wellhead blowout

preventer. The blowout occurred some 200 feet below that device.

"Only one of the new guidelines seems to recognize the possible calamitous results of earthquakes which are inevitable on the western offshore leases. None of the regulations require the minimization of pollution hazards during drilling that may result from a moderate-magnitude, nearby shallow-focus earthquake, seismic sea wave (tsunami) or submarine landslide which could shear off wells below the surface.

"None of the regulations state anything at all about onshore oil and gas storage facilities liable to release their contents into the oceans upon rupture due to an earthquake or seismic seawave.

"None of the new regulations stipulate that wells must be cased to below a level of geologic hazard, or below a depth of possible open fissures or porous sands, and, as such, none of these changes would have helped the present situation in the Santa Barbara Channel or the almost continuous blowout that has been going on since last year in the Bass Straits off Tasmania, where one also finds porous sands extending all the way up to the sea floor in a tectonically active region—exactly the situation we have here."

9. Letter from Fred Hartley, President of Union Oil, to "all shareholders," dated February 7, 1969.

10. Robert Curry of the geography department of the University of California, Santa Barbara, warned that such a tactic might in fact accelerate leakage. If, as he thought, the oil reservoirs under the Channel are linked, accelerated development of one such reservoir would, through erosion of subterranean linkage channels, accelerate the flow of oil into the reservoir under Platform A, thus adding to the uncontrolled flow of oil through the sands and into the ocean. Curry was not asked to testify by the Du Bridge Panel.

11. Verbal communication from one of the faculty members involved. The kind of "studies" which oil enjoys is typified by a research conclusion by Professor Wheeler J. North of Cal Tech, who after performing a one-week study of the Channel ecology under Western Oil and Gas Association sponsorship, determined that it was the California winter floods which caused most of the evident disturbance and that (as quoted from the Association Journal) "Santa Barbara beaches and marine life should be back to normal by summer with no adverse impact on tourism." Summer came with oil on the beaches, birds unreturned, and beach motels with unprecedented vacancies.

12. Cf. Walter J. Mead, "The Economics of Depletion Allowance," testimony presented to Assembly Revenue and Taxation Committee, California Legislature, June 10, 1969, mimeo; "The System of Government Subsidies to the Oil Industry," testimony presented to the U.S. Senate Subcommittee on Antitrust and Monopoly, March 11, 1969. The ostensible purpose of the depletion allowance is to encourage oil companies to explore for new oil reserves. A report to the Treasury Department by Consad Research Corp. concluded that *elimination* of the depletion allowance would decrease oil reserves by only 3 percent. The report advised that more efficient means could be found than a system which causes the government to pay $10 for every $1 in oil added to reserves. (Cf. Leo Rennert, "Oil Industry's Favors," *SBNP*, April 27, 1969, pp. A-14, 15, as reprinted from the *Sacramento Bee*.)

13. Cranston publicly confronted the staff engineer, Eugene Standley, who stated that he could neither confirm or deny writing the memo. (Cf. *SBNP*, March 11, 1969, p. A-1).

14. Major magazine coverage occurred in these (and other) national publications: *Time* (Feb. 14, 1969); *Newsweek* (March 3, 1969); *Life* (June 13, 1969); *Saturday Review* (May 10, 1969); *Sierra Club Bulletin*; *Sports Illustrated* (April 10, 1969). The last three articles cited were written by Santa Barbarans.

15. The notion of the banality of evil is adapted from the usage of Arendt, 1963.

16. As a result of local opposition, Union Oil was to subsequently move its operations from the Santa Barbara wharf to a more distant port in Ventura County.

17. Cf. Morton Mintz, "Oil Spill 'Radicalizes' a Conservative West Coast City," *Washington Post*, June 29, 1969, pp. C-1, 5.

18. Union Oil's public relations director stated: "In all my long career, I have never seen such distorted coverage of a news event as the *Santa Barbara News-Press* has foisted on its readers. It's a lousy newspaper." (*SBNP*, May 28, 1969, p. A-1).

19. I have in mind the exhaustively documented series of articles by I. F. Stone in the *New York Review of Books* over the course of 1968 and 1969, a series made possible, in part, by the outrage of Senator Fulbright and others at the *mistake* of Vietnam.

References

Allen, Allan A. 1969. "Santa Barbara Oil Spill." Statement presented to the U.S. Senate Interior

Committee, Subcommittee on Minerals, Materials and Fuels, May 20, 1969.

Arendt, Hannah. 1963. *Eichmann in Jerusalem: A Report on the Banality of Evil.* New York: The Viking Press.

Bachrach, Peter, and Morton Baratz. 1962. "The Two Faces of Power." *American Political Science Review,* 57 (December), 947–952.

Boorstin, Daniel J. 1961. *The Image.* New York: Atheneum Press.

Engler, Robert. 1961. *The Politics of Oil.* New York: Macmillan.

Flacks, Richard. 1967. "The Liberated Generation." *Journal of Social Issues,* 22 (December), 521–543.

Gans, Herbert. 1962. *The Urban Villagers.* New York: The Free Press of Glencoe.

Mills, C. Wright. 1956. *The Power Elite.* New York: Oxford University Press.

Schattschneider, E. E. 1960. *The Semisovereign People.* New York: Holt, Rinehart & Winston.

Schulze, Robert O. 1961. "The Bifurcation of Power in a Satellite City." Pp. 19–81 in Morris Janowitz (ed.), *Community Political Systems.* New York: The Free Press of Glencoe.

Vidich, Arthur, and Joseph Bensman. 1958. *Small Town in Mass Society.* Princeton: Princeton University Press.

Walton, John. 1968. "The Vertical Axis of Community Organization and the Structure of Power." Pp. 353–367 in Willis D. Hawley and Frederick M. Wirt (eds.), *The Search for Community Power.* Englewood Cliffs, N.J.: Prentice-Hall.

7
chapter

contents

the changing character
of urban politics

this section deals with social change and what we may be able to expect for the future of urban political systems. As recent discussions in the media and the councils of government indicate, the problems are immense. Schools, health care, pollution, ghettoes, housing, welfare, declining tax bases, and overcrowding only begin to suggest the range of problems which some analysts estimate would require a cool trillion-dollar commitment of public and private resources for even short-term solutions. The selections that follow suggest some of the more and less optimistic views of alternative futures for the city and its political institutions.

Henry Cohen's paper on governing the "megacentropolis" provides a systematic beginning statement of many of the problems dealt with in the selections that follow. Cohen lists twelve important constraints of effective city governance and discusses each in some detail. His emphasis is mainly on political or managerial difficulties. Indeed, he concludes that money alone will not solve urban problems and goes on to offer four recommendations for improved delivery of urban services.

Given this different view on whether and under what conditions the city may be governable, the next reading provides some indication of changing patterns of political control. Edward Greer's study of Gary, Indiana, suggests the massive problems facing the type of cities in which blacks have been able to gain control of the mayor's office. Not only had the huge corporations in the city, the steel mills, ignored any civic responsibility for years, but Richard Hatcher's new administration was also the object of deliberate sabotage from whites who had lost the political fight or were fearful of losing their city jobs.

The next three articles provide selective case studies of change in institutional arrangements; that is, how older ways of organizational behavior are changing in response to new urban conditions. In an original essay for this volume Leonard Rubinowitz discusses many of the blatant and subtle ways in which segregated housing has been perpetuated in American cities and suburbs through the complicity of private developers, mortgage lenders, and the federal government. The important point to stress here is that segregated housing is a result of more than individual prejudice; it provides a classic example of institutional racism. On a somewhat more optimistic note Rubinowitz goes on to indicate a number of new legal strategies that are being employed to "open up the suburbs."

Since many of us work and reside, at least for a period of several years, in a university setting, the original essay by Andrew Gordon and associates has particular relevance. Gordon suggests that the time is past when universities and urban researchers may assume the role of disinterested observers of the city, dropping in to collect data and returning to some sanctuary where research results are circulated among a small group of like-minded academics. Since this is the case, Gordon asks what are some of the ways in which the university and its unique resources may be responsibly involved in the struggles of urban communities. Drawing on a fund of experiences from the work of Northwestern University's Center for Urban Affairs the essay discusses many of the possibilities and pitfalls of university-community involvement. For the student who justifiably asks "what use is social science" or "what can it contribute to the solution of urban problems," this discussion provides some answers, not always satisfying or definitive.

Finally, the article by Francis Fox Piven evaluates many of the myths about who benefitted from the Great Society programs of the late 1960s and about the roots of the current fiscal crisis of the cities. Piven shows that federal funds then flowing into the cities did not go mainly to welfare mothers and black or brown urban migrants as is usually believed. Rather, it went largely to "organized provider groups": social workers, teachers, police, sanitation workers, and other unionized public employees. This discussion provides an important foundation for several of the arguments presented in the following chapter.

The chapter concludes with two absorbing accounts of new forms of political participation. You will recall that Chapter 6 ended with two discussions of powerless groups, ghetto dwellers and environmentalists. In this chapter on change the discussions of Blauner and Molotch are neatly paralleled and contrasted. In his elegant and moving account of Chicago's Contract Buyers League, James McPherson tells the story of two ghetto communities that were able to organize themselves to resist the cruel exploitation of powerful real estate interests. In addition to tracing the complicated history of this movement, McPherson provides a wealth of insights into questions such as the role of the church in black community politics, the tenuous alliances between blacks, Jews, and other white liberals, and the sources of division within the black community. Implicit in McPherson's case study is a view of the future somewhat different from Blauner's. Finally, Allan Schnaiberg's original essay on participation in the environmental movement rounds out the study by Molotch. Schnaiberg distinguishes four types of movement participants according to how environmental problems are defined and what actions follow from such conceptions. His "radicals" seem to correspond to the group Molotch studied, but there are other kinds of participants too, the cosmetologists, meliorists, and reformists. Most important in this essay, however, is Schnaiberg's cost-benefit analysis of environmental programs and their impact on various social classes. Illustratively, he argues that schemes for improving environmental quality may entail heavy costs to the upper class (in terms of plant improvements and reduced profits) and the lower class (in regressive taxation), yet yield relatively small incremental benefits to all. Such circumstances could lead to upper-lower class alliances to defeat reform efforts of middle class political groups. Whatever the outcomes—and he suggests alternatives—the key point is that serious reforms intrinsically involve conflicts of class interests.

Several articles in this chapter dovetail neatly with companion pieces while others are selective examinations of prominent events or institutions. Taken together, however, they cover a broad range of the changing character of urban politics. For the most part the mood of these essays is critical, but it also reflects a tempered optimism. Social scientists, like most of the general public, are optimists at heart. And perhaps this is commendable. But the careful reader should continue to pose the question of whether such sanguine appraisals are justified. Given all the evidence presented: "are cities governable even with some form of community control?"; "can segregated housing patterns be turned around with legal methods?"; "can universities really help solve urban problems?"; "do black communities or environmental groups really have a chance in the face of powerful institutional and class interests?" Obviously none of these questions yield to a yes or no answer. Social science, at best, can only answer them in terms of a greater or lesser likelihood under certain conditions. But these are the urban questions which we can now begin to attempt answers for with the evidence at hand.

28

HENRY COHEN

Governing Megacentropolis:
The Constraints

The difficulties of governing our large metropolitan cities are manifested in the increasingly severe survival problems of large-city mayors, the struggle to maintain service standards in a number of traditional municipal activities such as sanitation, the extension of blight despite sizable renewal and housing programs in many communities, and the inability to respond effectively to demands for changes in programs and services. The disgovernance syndrome (as distinct from non-, mal-, and un-) has developed during a decade when municipal governments as a group have broadened their responsibilities, have attempted to do more and better, and have in fact been more responsive to problems of human welfare than ever before. We may expect during the '70s and '80s that municipal governments as a group will further broaden their responsibility, and that they will try to do more rather than less with respect to the social and economic well-being of their citizens. In order to consider what changes are needed to enable them to broaden their efforts and be more effective, it is essential to examine the ingredients of the disgovernance syndrome.

Some of these factors are those of scale and expanse. Some are primarily political, and some administrative and managerial. Others are more clearly sociological or cultural in character. All are, however, many-sided and so interrelated with one another that they become difficult to group into a typology. Individually, the factors might be dealt with; it is their simultaneous oc-

currence which creates the disgovernance syndrome.

Twelve factors, by no means a complete list, contribute significantly to current difficulties in mega-urban management.

1. The size of the metropolitan cities
2. The increasing bureaucratization and professionalism of municipal services
3. The growing distance between central decision and points of impact
4. The explosion in public demand and expectation
5. The complexities of federal-state-local arrangements
6. The increasing breakdown of formal political machinery at the local level
7. The scale and character of the postwar migration
8. The interdependency in urban living
9. The metropolitanization of many urban problems
10. The inadequacy of the arrangements for sheltering the municipal chief executive
11. The inability to renew the older sections of the large cities
12. The pervasiveness of a mood of alienation and powerlessness

1. The size of the metropolitan cities. The largeness of the metropolis has many beneficial qualities. Administratively, it provides a basis for stimulating specialization and achieving efficiencies and economies which are difficult to obtain in small units. Economically, it offers a diversified labor force, concentrated markets, and opportunities for creativity that lead to growth, high levels of productivity, better paid workers, and possibilities for higher standards of living for more people. Socially, it provides

Henry Cohen, "The Constraints," from "Governing the Megacentropolis: A Symposium," *Public Administration Review*, vol. 30 (September/October 1970), pp. 488–497. Reprinted by permission.

diversity, stimulation, greater opportunities for the exchange of ideas. In many ways, because of this, it contributes to the liberation of man. On the one hand it provides greater opportunities for privacy and thereby freedom from the more crushing and repressive features of parochial communities, and on the other hand it provides an environment in which rigid thought and value systems (parochial rigidities) are difficult to sustain because of their constant exposure to fresh ideas and perspectives.

However, the very largeness of the city contributes to the development of many problems which cannot be easily dispelled by concentration alone on the "benefit" side of the equation. In order that the large city function, many aspects of operation must become systematized and reduced to regularity. The regularities themselves frequently become automatic and rigid, and therefore not easy to change. These new "systems" rigidities become difficult to deal with, and if they persist long enough in the face of complaint, opposition, and "reason," they are felt to be as oppressive as the "parochial" rigidities. As we shall see, the consequences of the systems rigidities are clearly observable in the increasing bureaucratization of municipal services, and the growing distance between central decision and local impact.

Students of municipal government who concentrate on efficiency and management principles are sanguine over the size issue. They tend to overlook or minimize the deeper political and sociological consequences of many of the traditional political or administrative reforms.

2. The increasing bureaucratization and professionalization of municipal services. The bureaucratization and professionalization of municipal services have many positive aspects, more than can here be recited. For example, without ignoring many valid current concerns over a variety of environmental conditions, it is nothing short of remarkable that so much is right about big-city public health. Water supplies are generally safe to drink, milk is uncontaminated, and most communicable disease is under control. The anxieties of plague and pestilence have largely been dispelled for urban dwellers in the United States. Despite some breakdowns in recent years due to increases in utilization and overload, most urban dwellers take rapid transit

services, the provision of gas, electricity, and telephone services for granted. These positive achievements are in great measure the function of technological advancement on the one hand and the invention and management of large service delivery systems.

While cities were growing and expanding, and new technologies were arising, the systems rigidities had little time to crystallize or were less noticeable and offensive than today. Progressively however, the bureaucratic and professional systems have become more and more impervious to review and change. What started at first as efforts to define criteria to assure technical and professional competence have become closed systems to protect a class. What started as a means of assuring a community objective—high quality of service—has become a small group objective-protection of role and status. The functionaries who manage and operate the city system develop a stake in the "system," and over time consider changes in the system from their point of view rather than from the point of view and interest of the consumer. As the functionaries organize and become the primary factors in defining the elements, practices, and character of the particular system, political leadership and the receivers and consumers of the public services becomes less capable of influencing the systems of public service. The public sector, more than the private sector, becomes increasingly unresponsive to consumer demand. Not only do the functionaries vote, but because they are highly organized, they are able to have a disproportionate influence on elections by virtue of their ability to funnel campaign contributions and provide cadres of workers. In addition, since they are sophisticated in managing the system, they appreciate the significance of voting in primary elections where turnouts are typically low.

This displacement of objectives has contributed to crisis conditions in many large cities. Increasing expenditures are matched only by increasing public dissatisfaction. Its most serious overt form is evidenced in the barriers to program changes and involvement that the prevailing rules and practices present to the newcomer groups—the Negroes, Puerto Ricans, and Mexican-Americans. However, the rigidities are serious, apart from the racial factor. For example, the high costs of providing medical care under

Medicare and Medicaid are not primarily a function of the presence in the cities of the ethnic poor, they are more significantly a function of the practices and arrangements for providing medical care.

3. *The growing distance between central decision and points of impact.* The largeness of the city and the growth of large service systems through which to carry out the public business have contributed substantially to the sense of alienation of the receiver of services from the systems which serve him. The receivers of service feel they are not getting what they want, when they want it, and how they want it. The receivers of services who have begun to look upon themselves as citizens with rights do not want to be treated as clients on the dole. They seek a new citizen-customer relationship to the system which is difficult to develop without the realities of currency transactions, competition, and the incentives of profit. Central decision makers laying out rules, patterns of service, and personnel policies are frustrated over their inability to translate intent into practice. The systems over which they preside do not deliver the services as they would like those services to be delivered.

The enormous variations from neighborhood to neighborhood in the need for different types of services, and in the character of the services provided, cannot easily be coped with in the face of the "system" rigidities. Decentralization, so appealing a solution, cannot easily overcome the differences in resource availability, area by area, nor the function of the center in resources allocation.

The need to systematize activities, procedures, and methods in the large metropolis tends to leave less discretion to the individual public servant, and tends to make public services less responsive to individual or localized needs and conditions.

The levers of change from the point of view of the receiver of service are remote. In the public sector, in contrast to the private sector, there are few incentives for the renderer of service in the field to satisfy the customer. The electoral process offers the voter little relief from the impersonal and impervious administrative structures of the large city. The resulting alienation is not confined to the blacks, Puerto Ricans, and Mexican-Americans; it is endemic among many groups in the large city.

4. *The explosion in public demand and expectations.* The rapidity of change since World War II—the change in character of the civil rights quest, the increased unionization of public employees, and the radicalization of large portions of the youth population—have severely weakened the ability of local political and administrative leadership to cope with problems by resorting to incremental strategies. Incrementalism has become a devalued currency. It is still in use, in fact there may be no alternative to it, but it enjoys no public confidence. During the '50s, the northern and western cities attempted to deal with the increased migration from the South and from Puerto Rico with incremental strategies. The problem of absorption would be solved, it was thought, if a few more remedial reading teachers were added, foster care services expanded, casework services more effectively coordinated, and additional public housing units constructed. The large cities were being hit by a tidal wave, but their informed leadership—in and out of government—was tilting with windmills. By the early 1960s, more than half of black America, for the first time, lived outside the states of the old confederacy, and growing numbers of black youth born and raised in the freer environment of the northern and western cities were coming of age. Their demand was not for incremental improvement, but for parity—freedom now. Incremental strategies were based on assumed relationships and program targets which were no longer acceptable. Though parity could not be achieved overnight, the "reasonable" objectives of the old incremental strategies became passé. The '60s was a decade in which new targets and objectives were defined and negotiated. Their achievement was clearly beyond the means and capability of municipal leadership. This explosion in expectation was not limited to the blacks. Comparable revolutions in the patterns of demand erupted among public employees, the young, and other interest groups.

Public leadership, caught in the crossfire of demands, is overwhelmed. Raising tax revenues is not easier and bureaucratic resistance to change is if anything greater than heretofore. At a deeper level, the knowledge base needed for problem solving is not keeping up with the multiplication and intensification of the problems. The demand for radical change and improvement has become universal. While municipal governments try to do more, the limits to improvement and resistance to change become formidable. There seems to be no way to break away from incrementalism which we may not want to live with but without which we cannot survive.

5. *The complexity of federal-state-local arrangements.* The intergovernmental system of the United States is unsymmetrical. Different federal programs involve the locality through a variety of arrangements. Similarly, the states do not have uniform responsibilities, and the patterns of state-city relationships are varied. The character, scope, and structure of municipal and county governments is also extremely variegated. This infinitely varied system is a product of regional and historical differences in the country. This lack of symmetry in the intergovernmental system has had many advantages in preserving flexibility in the arrangements by which the system operates over the American continent. Nevertheless, the difficulties for localities in managing the federal system are immense. For one thing, responsibility and power are diffused. One need but examine any number of programs which are intergovernmental in character, such as welfare, manpower, and model cities, to appreciate how difficult it is to assess accountability, and how even more difficult it is for local leadership (which is the target of popular wrath) to affect the programs substantially. The administrative and political hazards of managing many of the New Frontier programs in the face of erratic congressional funding have driven many mayors to distraction.

The lack of accountability which flows from these complex intergovernmental arrangements contributes to the difficulties local government faces in broadening its responsibilities to its citizens in the absence of sufficient locally generated tax revenues.

6. *The increasing breakdown of formal political machinery at the local level.* Local political machines have come into increasing disrepute over the past hundred years. Civic reform, going back to the muckraking period late in the last century, has steadily eroded the strength of local political structures. The reforms took many forms: nonpartisan government, the city manager system, the civil service system, and competitive bidding, among others. Reform came on the heels of scandals, widespread corruption, and incompetence. Whatever its weaknesses, and it had many, the system of local politics had many benefits for which we have not yet provided effective substitutes.

At the ward or district level, the leader or captain, in contact with his constituents, was able to mediate within the governmental system for them. He could overcome rules and bypass the chain of command. He preserved some flexibility in a system which size, technology, and bureaucracy was beginning to make increasingly rigid.

At the citywide level, the political system functioned to get things done. It might exact a price, but subways would get built, roads paved, and aqueducts constructed. Dissidents would be quieted, bought off, or removed. Legislators from districts with competing claims would be permitted to represent their districts, but others would be kept in line, not free to express their moral qualms. With the political machine, the balance in decision making was more towards doing things and doing things faster. The public system had some of the aspects of the private system—particularly money incentive. Since the machine in one manner or another took a cut, the premium was on high-volume turnover. The more that was done, the greater the profit.

The emphasis in civic reform was in substituting technocracy and professionalism for politics. The mediating role that the political machine played was lost or largely reduced. Local citizens in need of service had to cope with the bureaucracy directly, with its rigidities untempered by the softening influence of politics. With no controlling group in the system having a stake in getting things done, projects and decisions were left to the mercy of elongated administrative and consultative processes where the veto dominates and the decisive act is a rarity. With no relatively coherent political machine, every legislator feels freer to play for the most parochial advantage. The executive is left to manage as best he can, without the disciplining, mediating, and humanizing properties of the political machine.

7. The scale and character of the postwar migration. Since World War II, Negro migration to the North and West has changed the character of white-black relations in the nation as a whole, and has created some of the most difficult problems confronting the medium and large cities. In New York City alone, almost two and a quarter million blacks and Puerto Ricans have migrated or been born in the last twenty-five years. This largest of the nation's cities had to accommodate and absorb a preindustrial population equal to over one-quarter of the population which resided in the city over this period. In most of the other large cities the proportion to be absorbed has been even greater. The demands on resources, talent, knowledge, and political skill have taxed municipal government and municipal leadership.

The recent migration has focused on certain deficiencies in the pattern of municipal services which until recently were all but ignored. The bulk of municipal services are provided on what can be described as a self-service basis. The potential user of the service must recognize his need for the service and seek it out. This applies to most welfare and social services, health services, and library service. It applies also to education, even though here state laws establish schooling as compulsory. In the other than the human resource area, the self-service system applies to certain aspects of zoning, and to a variety of licensing and other regulatory matters. Thus, the local service system contains an assortment of services or requirements with respect to which the individual citizen must make his own decisions as to need or applicability. He must then exercise the initiative to secure the service, license, or approval. Historically, the bulk of the service system has never successfully coped with the problems of providing services for people or groups who are incapable of brokering the system themselves. Only for situations where there is a clear and present danger (public safety, public health, or other potential catastrophe) have the municipal services been organized for intervention. The new migration pointed up the inadequacy of the assumptions underlying the municipal service patterns, and created the political imperatives which made it essential to deal with these inadequacies. The new migrants were unfamiliar with the service systems, and, in many instances, they had difficulty with the language.

They were unable to broker the system for themselves or their children. In comparison to the migrants in earlier years, the new migrants were U.S. citizens, and the levels of expectations of the public service systems were higher. Thus, the municipal services suddenly came under attack because of the inadequacy of their outreach capability, and municipal workers who had been working conscientiously under one set of assumptions were suddenly under attack because the rules were changed. Stemming from the migration, the demand to modify services, enrich services, extend services, and create new services has added to the pressures of limited financial resources. One need not detail here the riots and other dramatic forms of conflict, to underscore how the new migration has attributed to the added burdens of managing the cities.

8. The interdependency in urban living. The highly technical system essential for maintaining life and activity in the city creates a high degree of interdependency. The technical system, broken at any point, creates friction and enormous inconvenience. Relatively small numbers of individuals can thus tie up the system. Strikes among public employees can bring to a halt major subsystems of activity—transportation, sanitation services, hospitals, and others. Demonstrators and sit-ins can consume executive energy, so that general planning, program development, and management are neglected. Priorities are distorted in favor of those who are employed in activities, the curtailment of which makes the community at large most vulnerable, or of those whose tactics, regardless of purpose, are most dramatic or appealing. Traditional systems of voicing concern—in meetings, conferences, and public hearings—lose their value. The escalation of demands, and extremeness of expression, and the disruption of daily life have become the norm.

9. The metropolitanization of many urban problems. The increasing interdependency in urban living extends beyond the central city boundaries to the assorted jurisdictions surrounding the city. Many of the residents of these outer zones are former central city dwellers who have moved outward in search of less dense residential areas. Partly the outward movement reflects a desire to escape some of the social and financial burdens of central-city living, including the problems of crime and delinquency. It is natural, therefore, to expect suburbanites to resist those metropolitan approaches which will transfer some of the central-city burdens to them. Beyond the crucial physical and economic development concerns, such as transportation, water supply, and water pollution, are a series of regional problems which defy easy solution. For example, fiscal inequities arise from the variations in the regional distribution of business properties, commuter population, and low-income population. Some communities, including most of the central cities, carry disproportionate costs in meeting the requirements of business and industry from which the whole region benefits and in meeting the needs of low-income people who concentrate in the cities. The demographic equation in most central cities, because it creates such a concentrated burden on the center, requires a regional strategy for the redistribution of low-income population throughout the region. The economic well-being of all in the region depends on preventing the central cities from being crushed by the overload of problems. Yet, most suburbanites will not willingly share the burden. Unless the state governments intervene strongly, which is unlikely, the cities will thus continue to live with intolerable problems for at least the next generation or two.

10. The inadequacy of arrangements for sheltering the municipal chief executive. In strong mayor cities, where the political machine has been weakened, mayors are left with relatively little shelter from the all-consuming crossfires of municipal life. They are also deprived of the out-reach capability and intelligence network which a political machine in touch with ordinary citizens can provide. In the city manager cities, the city council, to which the manager reports, does provide to some extent both shelter for the manager and a corrective balance that keeps government in touch with the people. In the larger cities, the mayors have little strength for dealing with the bureaucracies when they attempt to make them more responsive to constituency demands and winds of change. These mayoralty difficulties are exacerbated by the growth of intergovernmental programs which are usually administered by vertical bureaucracies in which the professionals and administra-

tors within each program track at every level of government mutually reinforce one another against intrusion from political executives or generalist administrators. Few federal programs are designed to strengthen the mayor's capability to cope with complex local issues and relations. Unlike the council-manager system or the collegial system which exists in many European cities, the mayor alone in American big-city government bears performance responsibility. With performance becoming more and more difficult, the mayor's job has become exposed and dangerous.

11. The inability to renew the older sections of the large cities. Building on vacant land, though it has its problems, is not comparable to the difficulties confronting built-up cities with substantial sections of decay. The difficulties in tenant relocation and the increased militancy of neighborhood groups have made urban renewal all but impossible. In addition to the problems arising from the large substandard housing stock, others arise from the lack of an adequate system of public facilities. Despite the enormous need for modern schools, hospitals and other health facilities, community centers and libraries, and for space for a growing array of community activities, formidable obstacles lay in the way of constructing public facilities in the ghetto. The community consultation process, essential as it may be, nevertheless causes lengthy delays in the processing of projects from conception to completion. Not only do these delays lead to significant increases in costs of construction, but they impede progress in dealing with deep problems because of the inadequacy of existing facilities. Municipal government is constantly caught between the Scylla of insufficient attention to community interest, and the Charybdis of slow action and delay. We can expect this problem to become worse, not easier.

12. The pervasiveness of a mood of alienation and powerlessness. Feelings of alienation and powerlessness are not confined to the blacks, the Puerto Ricans, and the Mexican-Americans. These feelings are present among many young people, and among many others of all ages caught in the web of complex public and private organizational systems, and of dense urban neighborhoods.

The changing social structure of urban family life has drastically modified the living style of the aged, who nationally represent 10 percent of central city population. Social Security and Medicare may improve some of the conditions of living, but they do not deal with the psychosocial rupture between the aged and others in the urban setting.

The failure to cope adequately with the large migrations from the South and Puerto Rico, and the failure to date to integrate the blacks and the browns into our social and economic life, have contributed to rises in crime and delinquency which create fear and anxiety among all groups in the population, and add to the tensions among the races.

The city, among other things, is a competitive arena, where men and women compete for improved opportunity, status, and recognition. In the bigger cities the competition is heightened, for the stakes and the rewards are potentially greater. Even for those who achieve relative rates of affluence, life in the city is like a slippery slope.

While there are, obviously, differences in the degree and character of alienation and powerlessness or helplessness among different groups, it is important to recognize how pervasive these phenomena are.

The interdependency of modern living, while it assures freedom in some ways, limits it in others. Mounting dissatisfaction and frustration erupts in attacks on existing organizational arrangements and procedures. Some of the protest is directed at overcoming inequity and injustice, while other protest is directed at the apparent senselessness of so much bureaucratic behavior and anachronistic practice. The distance between the individual and the amorphous forces which affect him contributes on the one hand to a state of helplessness, and on the other to attacks on the faceless establishment in which all power appears to reside. The difficulty is further seen in the anomaly of our progress. We know by the indicators that most measurable conditions are getting better, but most immeasurable things are also getting worse. For the minorities, even to the extent that conditions have become somewhat better, the gap seldom narrows and the pain deepens. As the decibel count of protest rises, it becomes more and more difficult to do anything in public life, yet the demands for accomplishment go up, not down.

Not only are the people alienated and powerless, but so are the organization men, and the political leadership. So, alienation and powerlessness are pervasive and cannot be relieved simply by improving this or that service, or satisfying this or that constituency.

Can Cities Assume Ultimate Responsibility for Human Welfare?

Considering the difficulties in organizing communal existence to deal with already defined responsibilities, it is rather mystical to hold out hope that cities can organize themselves to assume ultimate responsibility for human welfare, even if ultimate responsibility could be defined.

An examination of the intergovernmental system shows how elusive a pastime it would be for city governments to attempt to assume ultimate responsibility.

Though increased financial resources would help the cities cope with some of their problems, it should be clear from the above discussion that money alone will not be sufficient. Similarly, managerial improvements to deliver services more effectively would help, but will not be sufficient. What is needed are changes in a variety of political arrangements. The following notions are intended to suggest only a few directions we may have to pursue.

1. Intergovernmental arrangements must be simplified so that it becomes easier for local political and executive leadership to organize programs and to define the relationships among programs. The existing system of categorical grants places too much of the balance of power into the vertical bureaucracies, vis-à-vis the city political leadership. It also places too much power into the hands of state government, where the political equation is different from that of city governments. The intervention of state bureaucracies merely adds delays and complications. Building on the bloc grant principle embodied in model cities legislation, big-city mayors would be strengthened in their efforts to cope with city problems and with the wide array of conflicting interest groups.

2. Because of the growing power of the bureaucrats and professionals, steps need to be taken to strengthen the role and participation of consumers and receivers of services in the decision-making process. Most of the experimenta-

tion with community action programs in the last seven years has been somewhat to the side of the regular governmental and political structure. It is perhaps time to begin efforts to regularize these activities in a number of ways, such as holding elections to community and neighborhood boards on days when municipal voting normally takes place.

In addition, changes in the structure of local legislative bodies should be considered. In large cities we should perhaps reverse the trend towards smaller councils and begin to enlarge the councils in a number of ways. The doubling of wards or districts would provide representation responsive to smaller constituencies. The addition of more at-large seats would provide representation for interest groups which are not geographically concentrated. The introduction of proportional representation in at-large elections would assure participation of an assortment of citywide interests. Such measures should be accompanied by a strengthening of council committee structure which should be provided with funds for adequate staffing. Larger councils, while more unwieldy than smaller bodies, would at least concentrate more of the furious conflict within the legislative bodies where in the end, decisions must be made, budgets approved, and taxing policy set. By channeling more of the demands and frustrations into the legislative arena, the bargaining should hopefully become more realistic and the expectations more realizable. There is great educational value in investing groups with performance responsibility. While in the short run, such new legislative bodies might make the life of the mayor and executive agencies more miserable, in the long run it should help them. It would regularize some of the random conflict and organize it around real choices. Much of the conflict would be within the legislative bodies among different interest groups, and not directed as much at the executive. Furthermore, as the executive agencies became more sensitive to consumer demand, the areas of conflict should lessen.

3. There has been much discussion in recent years about the delegation of certain local government functions to community groups. Actually, there is a long history of contracting out certain functions to private health, welfare, and recreation agencies. There are also substantial precedents in which local governments purchas services from other governments. Recentl some of the discussion has centered around th development of two-tier governmental arrang ments within big cities, following the Londo pattern. Some of the reviews of the London bo ough system indicate that this system does no produce more efficient, effective, or responsiv service. Apparently, citizen involvement is no increased, and the bureaucratic rigidities tha plague the large-city systems exist in the boroug governments. Nevertheless, the distrust i American cities of the large government agencie cannot be ignored. There are benefits that coul accrue from a pluralistic system of service de livery in the large cities. It can stimulate nev leadership and new ideas, and by introducin competition into the system, it could keep every one on his toes. We should be searching fo ways to delegate certain functions, recognizin that each such effort will have hazards and draw backs. Certain recreation functions can be del gated to local groups; who do central agencie have to run programs in local schools or parks Certain housing functions can be delegated; wh can local groups not be given responsibilities fo some housing inspection functions? Why nc delegate some of the local sanitation services Why not delegate some of the responsibilities fo standing traffic violations? This list could b lengthened. The New York experience wit school decentralization should be observed car fully; it may provide some insight into ways c moving towards a two-tier system of local go ernment in the U.S.

4. Local governments need to expand the coordinative capabilities at the neighborhoo level, and improve the information and referra services for individual citizens. A large varie of efforts have been undertaken along thes lines: the Citizens Advice Bureau in Englan the neighborhood multiservice centers in a nur ber of American cities, and the model cities pr grams among others. None is yet so successf a model that we can extend it rapidly. Recer attempts in New York and Boston to extend tl mayoralty outreach into neighborhoods, in di tinction to a functional department outreac bear watching. The expansion of services, whi important, is no substitute for improvement methods of linking people to services and ma ing services more responsive to individual need

Conclusion

The disgovernance syndrome in the big cities embodies political and sociological factors more than it does managerial and administrative factors. It represents matters of mood and feeling which are not easily quantifiable. It represents a sense of malaise with things as they are, despite the social and economic improvements in life for so many. It also represents some of the consequences of America's unresolved racial problems. For cities to deal with these problems will require more funds, a strengthening of the central executive vis-à-vis the governmental bureaucracies, a strengthening of consumer groups vis-à-vis the providers of the public services, the invention of new political mechanisms which bring the competing interests more effectively into the decision-making system, and the creation of administrative mechanisms which assist citizens in getting more nearly what they need and what is their right. If we can resolve more effectively these political and administrative issues, then cities will be able to serve their citizens better. If we cannot, then people will have to look elsewhere.

29

EDWARD GREER

The "Liberation" of Gary, Indiana

In silhouette, the skyline of Gary, Indiana, could serve as the perfect emblem of America's industrial might—or its industrial pollution. In the half-century since they were built, the great mills of the United States Steel Corporation—once the largest steel complex on earth—have produced more than a quarter-trillion tons of steel. They have also produced one of the highest air pollution rates on earth. Day and night the tall stacks belch out a ruddy smoke that newcomers to the city find almost intolerable.

Apart from its appalling physical presence, the most striking thing about Gary is the very narrow compass in which the people of the city lead their lives. Three-quarters of the total work force is directly employed by the United States Steel Corporation. About 75 percent of all male employment is in durable goods manufacture and in the wholesale-retail trades, and a majority of this labor force is blue-collar. This means that the cultural tone of the city is solidly working-class.

But not poor. Most Gary workers own their own homes, and the city's median income is 10 percent above the national average. The lives of these people, however, are parochial, circumscribed, on a tight focus. With the exception of the ethnic clubs, the union and the Catholic church, the outstanding social edifices in Gary are its bars, gambling joints and whorehouses.

Company Town

The city of Gary was the largest of all company towns in America. The United States Steel Cor-

poration began construction in 1905, after assembling the necessary parcel of land on the Lake Michigan shore front. Within two years over $40 million had been invested in the project; by now the figure must be well into the billions.

Gary was built practically from scratch. Swamps had to be dredged and dunes leveled a belt-line railroad to Chicago had to be constructed, as well as a port for ore ships and of course a vast complex of manufacturing facilities including coke ovens, blast furnaces and an independent electrical power plant. The city was laid out by corporation architects and engineers and largely developed by the corporation-owned Gary Land Company, which did not sell off most of its holdings until the thirties. Even though the original city plan included locations for a variety of civic, cultural and commercial uses (though woefully little for park land), an eminent critic, John W. Reps, points out that "failed sadly in its attempt to produce a community pattern noticeably different or better than elsewhere."

The corporation planned more than the physical nature of the city. It also had agents advertise in Europe and the South to bring in workers from as many different backgrounds as possible to build the mills and work in them. Today over fifty ethnic groups are represented in the population.

This imported labor was cheap, and it was hoped that cultural differences and language barriers would curtail the growth of a socialist labor movement. The tough pioneer character of the city and the fact that many of the immigrant workers' families had not yet joined them in this country combined to create a lawless and vice-ridden atmosphere which the corporation did little to curtail. In much more than its genesis and name, then, Gary is indelibly stamped in the mold of its corporate creators.

Labor and the Left

During the course of the First World War, government and vigilante repression broke the back of the Socialist party in small-town America, though it was not very strong to begin with. Simultaneously, however, the Left grew rapidly as a political force among the foreign-born in large urban centers. As the war continued, labor peace was kept by a combination of prosperity (full employment and overtime), pressures for production in the "national interest," and Wilsonian and corporate promises of an extension of democracy in the workplace after the war was over. The promises of a change in priorities proved empty, and in 1919 the long-suppressed grievances of the steelworkers broke forth. Especially among the unskilled immigrant workers, demands for an industrial union, a reduction of the workday from twelve to eight hours and better pay and working conditions sparked a spontaneous movement for an industry-wide strike.

For a time it appeared that the workers would win the Great Steel Strike of 1919, but despite the capable leadership of William Z. Foster the strike was broken. The native white skilled-labor aristocracy refused to support it, and the corporation imported blacks from the South to scab in the mills. This defeat helped set back the prospect of militant industrial trade unionism for almost a generation. And meanwhile, racism, a consumer-oriented culture (especially the automobile and relaxed sexual mores) and reforms from above (by the mid-twenties the eight-hour day had been voluntarily granted in the mills) combined to prevent the Left from recovering as a significant social force.

It was in this period between World War I and the Depression that a substantial black population came to Gary. Before the war only a handful of black families lived there, and few of them worked in the mills. During World War I, when immigration from abroad was choked off, blacks were encouraged to move to Gary to make up for the labor shortage caused by expanding production. After the war this policy was continued, most spectacularly during the strike, but rather consistently throughout the twenties. In 1920 blacks made up 9.6 percent of the population; in 1930 they were 17.8 percent—and they were proportionately represented in the steel industry work force.

When the CIO was organized during the depression, an interracial alliance was absolutely essential to the task. In Gary a disproportionate number of the union organizers were black; the Communist party's slogan of "black and white unite and fight" proved useful as an organizing tactic. Nevertheless, it was only during World War II (and not as the result of the radicals' efforts) that black workers made a substantial structural advance in the economy. Demography, wartime full employment and labor shortages proved more important to the lot of black workers than their own efforts and those of their allies.

As after the First World War, so after the second, there came a repression to counter the growth of the Left. The Communist component of the trade union movement was wiped out, and in the general atmosphere of the early cold war black people, too, found themselves on the defensive. At the local level in Gary, the remaining trade union leaders made their peace with the corporation (as well as the local racketeers and Democratic party politicians), while various campaigns in the forties to racially integrate the schools and parks failed utterly.

Finally, in the early fifties, the inherently limited nature of the trade union when organized as a purely defensive institution of the working class—and one moreover that fully accepts capitalist property and legal norms—stood fully revealed. The Steelworkers Union gave up its right to strike over local grievances, which the Left had made a key part of its organizing policy, in return for binding arbitration, which better suited the needs and tempers of the emerging labor bureaucrats.

Corporate Racism

The corporation thus regained effective full control over the work process. As a result, the corporation could increase the amount of profit realized per worker. It could also intensify the special oppression of the black workers; foremen could now assign them discriminatorily to the worst tasks without real union opposition. This corporate racism had the additional benefit of weakening the workers' solidarity. For its part, the union abolished shop stewards, replacing them with one full-time elected "griever." This of course further attenuated rank-and-file control over the union bureaucracy, aided in depoliticizing the workers and gave further rein to the union's inclination to mediate worker/employer differences at the point of production, rather than sharpen the lines of struggle in the political economy as a whole.

The corporate and union elites justified this process by substantial wage increases, together with other benefits such as improved pension and welfare plans. For these gains a price was paid. Higher product prices, inflation and a rising tax burden on the workers all ensued from the union's passive acceptance of corporate priorities.

There were extremely important racial consequences as well. For as the union leadership was drawn further and further into complicity with corporate goals, a large segment of the industrial working class found itself in the apparently contradictory position of opposing the needs of the poorest workers for increased social welfare services. A large part of the material basis for white working-class racism originates here. Gary steelworkres, struggling to meet their home mortgage payments, are loath to permit increased assessments for additional municipal services which they view as mostly benefitting black people.

United States Steel

Needless to say, the corporation helped to develop, promote and protect the Gary working class's new ways of viewing itself and its world.

In the mill, the corporation systematically gave the black workers the dirtiest jobs (in the coke plants, for example) and bypassed them for promotion—especially for the key skilled jobs and as foremen. Nor has that policy changed. Although about a third of the employees in the Gary Works are black, and many of them have high seniority, and although virtually all the foremen are promoted directly from the ranks without needing any special qualifications, there are almost no black (or Spanish-speaking) foremen. According to figures submitted by the United States Steel Corporation to the Gary Human Relations Commission, as of 31 March 1968, out of a total of 1,011 first-line supervisors (foremen) only 22 were black.

The corporation not only practices racism directly, it also encourages it indirectly by supporting other discriminatory institutions in Gary. Except for some free professionals and small business, the entire business community is a de facto fief of the corporation. The Gary Chamber of Commerce has never to my knowledge differed from the corporation on any matter of substance, though it was often in its economic self-interest to do so. This has been true even with regard to raising the corporation's property assessment, which would directly benefit local business financially. And in its hiring and sales practices, as well as in its social roles, this group is a leading force for both institutional racism and racist attitudes in the community. For instance, it is well known that the local banks are very reluctant to advance mortgage money in black areas of town, thus assuring their physical decline. White workers then draw the reasonable conclusion that the movement of blacks into their neighborhoods will be at the expense of the value of their homes and react accordingly. The local media, completely dependent financially on the local business community, can fairly be described as overtly racist. The story of the voting fraud conspiracy to prevent the election of the present mayor, Richard Hatcher, a black man, didn't get into the local paper until days after it made the front page of the *New York Times*.

The newspaper publisher is very close to the national Catholic hierarchy and the local bishop who in turn is closely linked to the local banks. The church is rhetorically moderately liberal at the diocesan level, but among the ethnic parishes the clergy are often overtly racist.

Political Considerations

While the United States Steel Corporation has an annual budget of $5 billion, the city of Gary operates on some $10 million annually. (This figure applied only to municipal government functions; it excludes expenditures by the school, welfare authorities, the Sanitary Board and the Redevelopment Commission.)

And the power of the city government, as is

usually the case in this country, is highly fragmented. Its legal and financial authority is inadequate to carry out the public functions for which it bears responsibility. The power of the mayor is particularly limited. State civil service laws insulate school, welfare, fire, and police personnel from the control of City Hall. Administrative agencies control key functions such as urban renewal, the low-income housing authority, sanitation, the park system and the board of health. Appointive boards, with long and staggered terms of tenure, hire the administrators of these agencies; and although in the long run a skillful mayor can obtain substantial control over their operations, in the short run (especially if there are sharp policy differences) his power may well be marginal.

Two other structural factors set the context in which local government in Gary—and in America generally—is forced to operate. First, key municipal functions increasingly depend upon federal aid; such is the case with the poverty program, urban renewal, low-income housing and, to a substantial degree, welfare, education, and even police and sanitation. Thus, the priorities of the federal government increasingly shape the alternatives and options open to local officials, and their real independence is attenuated.

Second, the tax resources of local governments —resting for the most part on comparatively static real estate levies—are less and less able to meet the sharply rising costs of municipal services and operations. These costs reflect the increased social costs of production and welfare, costs that corporations are able to pass on to the general public.

This problem is particularly acute in Gary because of the ability of the corporation to remain grossly underassessed. As a result, there are implacable pressures to resist expansion of municipal services, even if the need for them is critical. In particular, since funds go to maintain existing services, it is virtually impossible for a local government to initiate any substantive innovations unless prior funding is assured. In this context, a sustained response to the urban crisis is prevented not only by a fragmentation of power but also by a lack of economic resources on a scale necessary to obtain significant results.

For the city of Gary, until the election of Mayor Hatcher, it was academic to talk about such considerations as the limits of local government as an instrument of social change and improvement of the general welfare. Before him, municipal government had been more or less content simply to mediate between the rackets on the one hand and the ethnic groups and business community on the other.

The Democratic Party, structured through the Lake County machine, was the mechanism for accomplishing a division of spoils and for maintaining at least a formal legitimacy for a government that provided a minimum return to its citizenry. Left alone by the corporation, which subscribed to an inspired policy of live and let live where municipal politics were concerned, this political coalition governed Gary as it saw fit.

In return for the benevolent neutrality of the corporation toward its junior partner, the governing coalition refrained from attempting to raise the corporation's tax assessments or to otherwise insinuate itself into the absolute sovereignty of the corporation over the Gary Works. Air pollution activities were subjected only to token inspection and control, and in the entire history of the city the Building Department never sent an inspector into the mill. (These and other assertions about illegal or shady activities are based on reports from reliable informants and were usually verified by a second source. I served under Mayor Hatcher as director of the Office of Program Coordination until February 1969.)

In this setting—particularly in the absence of a large middle class interested in "good government" reform—politics was little more than a racket, with the city government as the chief spoils. An informal custom grew up that representatives of different ethnic minorities would each hold the mayor's office for one term. The mayor then, in association with the county officials, would supervise the organized crime (mostly gambling, liquor, and prostitution) within the community. In effect, the police force and the prosecutor's office were used to erect and centralize a protection racket with the mayor as its director and organized crime as its client. Very large sums of money were involved, as indicated by the fact that one recent mayor was described by Internal Revenue officials as having an estimated annual income while in office of $1.5 million.

Besides the racket of protecting criminal activity, other sources of funds contributed to the large illicit incomes of city officials. There were almost 1,000 patronage jobs to distribute to supporters or sell to friends. There were proceeds from a myriad of business transactions and contracts carried out under municipal authority. Every aspect of municipal activity was drawn into the cash nexus.

For instance, by local ordinance one had to pass an examination and pay a $150 fee for a contractor's license to do repair or construction work within city limits. The licensing statute was enacted to maintain reasonable standards of performance and thus protect the public. In reality, as late as 1967, passing the exam required few skills, except the ability to come up with $1,200 for the relevant officials, or $1,500 if the recipient was unfortunate enough to have black skin.

Gary municipal affairs also had a racist quality. The black population continued to rise until in the early sixties it composed an absolute majority. Yet the benefits of the system just outlined were restricted to the less scrupulous of the leaders of other ethnic groups, which constituted altogether only 40 percent of the population. The spoils came from all; they were distributed only among whites.

And this was true not only for illegal spoils and patronage but also for legitimate municipal services. As one example, after Hatcher became mayor, one of the major complaints of the white citizenry concerned the sharp decline in the frequency of garbage collection. This resulted, not from a drop in efficiency of the General Services division, as was often charged, but from the fact that the garbage routes were finally equalized between white and black areas.

In short, the city government was itself just another aspect of the institutionalized structure of racism in Gary. To assure the acquiescence of Gary's blacks to the system, traditional mechanisms of repression were used: bought black politicians and ward leaders, token jobs, the threat of violence against rebels and the spreading of a sense of impotence and despair. For instance, it was a Gary tradition for the Democratic machine to contribute $1,500 each week to a black ministers' alliance for them to distribute to needy parishioners—with the tacit understanding that when elections came around they would help deliver the vote.

Hatcher's Campaign

The successful insurgency of Richard Gordon Hatcher destroyed the core of this entire relationship.

Hatcher developed what can best be described as a black united front, inasmuch as it embraced all sectors of the black community by social class, occupation, ideology, and temperament. The basis of this united front was a commonly held view that black people as a racial group were discriminated against by the politically dominant forces. Creating it required that Hatcher bridge existing divisions in the black community, which he did by refusing to be drawn into a disavowel of any sector of the black movement either to his left or right—except for those local black politicians who were lackeys of the Democratic machine. Despite immense public pressure, for example, Hatcher refused to condemn Stokely Carmichael, even though scurrilous right-wing literature was widely circulated calling him a tool of Carmichael and Fidel Castro. Actually, the rumor that hurt Hatcher the most was the false assertion that he was secretly engaged to a white campaign worker—and it was so damaging in the black community that special pains had to be taken to overcome it.

Muhammed Ali was brought to the city to campaign for Hatcher, but Hubert Humphrey was not invited because of the bitter opposition of white antiwar elements within his campaign committee. It is worth noting that a substantial portion of Hatcher's financial and technical assistance came from a very small group of white liberals and radicals, who, while they played a role disproportionate to their numbers, suffered significant hostility from their white neighbors for involving themselves openly with Hatcher. Their support, however, made it possible for the campaign to appeal, at least rhetorically, to all the citizens on an interracial basis.

Of course, this support in the white community did not translate into votes. When the count was complete in the general election, only 13 percent of Gary's overwhelmingly Democratic white voters failed to bolt to the Republicans; and if one omits the Jewish professional and business section of town, that percentage falls to 6 percent (in blue-collar Glen Park)—a figure more explicable by polling booth error than goodwill.

Even in the Democratic primary against the incumbent mayor, Hatcher barely won, although he had the support of a large majority of the Spanish-speaking vote and overwhelming support (over 90 percent) of the black vote. His victory was possible, moreover, only because the white vote was split almost down the middle due to the entry of an insurgent and popular "backlash" candidate.

Hatcher's primary victory was particularly impressive given the obstacles he had to face. First, his entire primary campaign was run on less than $50,000, while the machine spent an estimated $500,000 in cash on buying black votes alone. Second, the media was openly hostile to Hatcher. And third, efforts were made to physically intimidate the candidate and his supporters. Death threats were common, and many beatings occurred. Without a doubt, the unprecedented action of the Hatcher organization in forming its own self-defense squads was essential in preventing mass intimidation. It was even necessary on primary day for armed groups to force open polls in black areas that would otherwise have remained inoperative.

These extraordinary methods demonstrated both how tenuous are the democratic rights of black people and what amazing organization and determination are necessary to enforce them when real shifts of power appear to be at stake. When the primary results came in, thousands of black citizens in Gary literally danced in the streets with joy; and everyone believed that the old Gary was gone forever.

Hatcher's Temptations

Immediately after the primary victory, the local alignment of forces was to some degree overshadowed by the rapid interposition of national ones. Until Hatcher won the primary, he was left to sink or swim by himself; after he established his own independent base of power, a new and more complex political process began: his reintegration into the national political system.

The county Democratic machine offered Hatcher a bargain: its support and $100,000 for the general election campaign in return for naming the chief of police, corporation counsel, and controller. Naturally, Hatcher refused to accept a deal that would have made him a puppet of the corrupt elements he was determined to oust from power. Thereupon the county ma-

chine (and the subdistrict director of the Steelworkers Union) declared itself for, and campaigned for, the Republican.

But the question was not left there. To allow the Democratic Party to desert a candidate solely because he was black would make a shambles of its appeal to black America. And dominant liberal forces within the Democratic Party clearly had other positive interests in seeing Hatcher elected. Most dramatically, the Kennedy wing of the Democratic party moved rapidly to adopt Hatcher, offering him sorely needed political support, financial backing, and technical assistance, without any strings attached. By doing this, it both solidified its already strong support from the black community and made it more reasonable for blacks to continue to place their faith in the Democratic Party and in the political system as a whole.

As a necessary response to this development (although it might have happened anyway), the Johnson-Humphrey wing of the Democratic Party also offered support. And this meant that the governor of Indiana and the Indiana state Democratic Party endorsed Hatcher as well—despite the opposition of the powerful Lake County machine. Thus Hatcher achieved legitimacy within the political system—a legitimacy that he would need when it came to blocking a serious voting fraud plot to prevent his winning the election.

Despite clear evidence of what was happening, the Justice Department nevertheless refused to intervene against this plot until Hatcher's campaign committee sent telegrams to key federal officials warning them that failure to do so would result in a massive race riot for which the federal officials would be held publicly responsible. Only by this unorthodox maneuver, whose credibility rested on Hatcher's known independent appeal and constituency, was the federal executive branch persuaded to enforce the law. Its intervention, striking 5,000 phony names from the voter rolls, guaranteed a Hatcher victory instead of a Hatcher defeat.

The refusal of the Justice Department to move except under what amounted to blackmail indicated that the Johnson-Humphrey wing of the party was not enthusiastic about Hatcher, whose iconoclastic and often radical behavior did not assure that he would behave appropriately after he was in power. But its decision finally to act, together with the readiness of the Kennedy forces to fully back Hatcher, suggests that there was a national strategy into which the Hatcher insurgency could perhaps be fitted.

My own view of that national strategy is that the federal government and the Democratic party were attempting to accommodate themselves to rising black insurgency, and especially electoral insurgency, so as to contain it within the two-party system. This strategy necessitated sacrificing, at least to a degree, vested parochial interests such as entrenched and corrupt machines.

Furthermore, black insurgency from below is potentially a force to rationalize obsolete local governments. The long-term crisis of the cities, itself reflecting a contradiction between public gain and private interest, has called forth the best reform efforts of the corporate liberal elite. Centered in the federal government, with its penumbra of foundations, law firms, and universities, the political forces associated with this rationalizing process were most clearly predominant in the Kennedy wing of the Democratic Party.

The economic forces whose interests are served by this process are first the banks, insurance companies, and other sections of large capital heavily invested in urban property and, more generally, the interests of corporate capital as a whole—whose continued long-range profit and security rest on a stable, integrated, and loyal population.

Thus the support given to Hatcher was rational to the system as a whole and not at all peculiar, even though it potentially implied economic and political loss for the corporation, United States Steel, whose operations on the spot might become more difficult. The interests of the governing class as a whole and of particular parts of it often diverge; this gap made it possible for Hatcher to achieve some power within the system. How these national factors would shape the amount and forms of power Hatcher actually obtained became quite evident within his first year of office.

Mosaic of Black Power

When I arrived in the city five months after the inauguration, my first task was to aid in the process of bringing a semblance of order out of what can fairly be described as administrative chaos.

When the new administration took over City Hall in January 1968, it found itself without the keys to offices, with many vital records missing (for example, the file on the United States Steel Corporation in the controller's office) and with a large part of the city government's movable equipment stolen. The police force, for example, had so scavenged the patrol cars for tires and batteries that about 90 percent of them were inoperable. This sort of thing is hardly what one thinks of as a normal process of American government. It seems more appropriate to a bitter ex-colonial power. It is, in fact, exactly what happened as the French left Sekou Toure's Guinea.

There were no funds available. This was because the city council had sharply cut the municipal budget the previous summer in anticipation of a Hatcher victory. It intended, if he lost, to legislate a supplemental appropriation. But when he won without bringing in a council majority with him, its action assured that he would be especially badly crippled in his efforts to run the city government with a modicum of efficiency. Moreover, whenever something went wrong, the media could and did blame the mayor for his lack of concern or ability.

Not only did Richard Hatcher find his position sabotaged by the previous administration even before he arrived, but holdovers, until they were removed from their positions, continued to circumvent his authority by design or accident. And this comparatively unfavorable situation extended to every possible sphere of municipal activities.

Another problem was that the new administrators had to take over the management of a large, unwieldly and obsolete municipal system without the slightest prior executive experience. That there were no black people in Gary with such experience in spite of the high degree of education and intelligence in the black community is explicable only in terms of institutionalized racism—blacks in Gary were never permitted such experiences and occupational roles. Hatcher staffed his key positions with black men who had been schoolteachers, the professional role most closely analogous to running a government bureaucracy. Although several of these men were, in my view, of outstanding ability, they still had to learn everything by tria

nd error, an arduous and painful way to main-
ain a complex institution.

Furthermore, this learning process was not
1ade any easier by the unusually heavy demands
laced on the time of the mayor and his top
ides by the national news media, maneuvering
actions of the Democratc Party, a multiplicity
f civil rights organizations, universities and vol-
ntary associations, and others who viewed the
1ayor as a celebrity to be importuned, exploited,
nd displayed. This outpouring of national in-
·rest in a small, parochial city came on top of
1d was almost equal to the already heavy work-
·ad of the mayor.

Nor were there even clerical personnel to an-
ver the mail and phone calls, let alone ration-
ly respond to the deluge. The municipal bud-
·t provided the mayor with a single secretary;
took most of the first summer to make the nec-
sary arrangements to pay for another two sectaries for the mayor's own needs. One result
as that as late as June 1968 there was still a
vo-month backlog of personal mail, which was
1ally answered by much overtime work.

In addition to these problems, there were
hers, not as common to American politics, such
the threat of violence, which had to be faced
an aspect of daily life. The problem of se-
rity was debilitating, especially after the King
d Kennedy assassinations. In view of the
ayor's aggressive drive against local organized
ime, the race hatred whipped up during and
ter the campaign by the right wing, and the
story of violence in the steel town, this con-
rn with security was not excessive, and main-
ining it was a problem. Since the police were
·sely linked with the local Right, it was neces-
ry to provide the mayor with private body-
ards. The presence of this armed and fore-
ding staff impaired efficiency without improv-
; safety, especially since the mayor shrugged
the danger and refused to cooperate with
·se security efforts.

n addition, the tremendous amounts of aid
were offered by foundations, universities, and
leral officials proved to be a mixed blessing.
e time needed to oversee existing processes
s preempted by the complex negotiations sur-
unding the development and implementation
a panoply of new federal programs. There
l never been a Concentrated Employment Pro-
1m in Gary, nor a Model Cities Program, nor
l the poverty program been locally controlled.

Some of these programs weren't only new to
Gary, they hadn't been implemented anywhere
else either. The municipal bureaucracy, which
under previous administrations had deliberately
spared itself the embarrassment of federal au-
dits, didn't have the slightest idea as to how to
utilize or run these complex federal programs.
Moreover, none of the experts who brought this
largesse to Gary had a clear understanding of
how it was to be integrated into the existing
municipal system and social structure. These
new federal programs sprang up overnight—new
bureaucracies, ossified at birth—and their actual
purposes and effects bore little relation to the
legislative purposes of the congressional statutes
that authorized them.

Needless to say, ordinary municipal employees
experienced this outside assistance as a source
of confusion and additional demoralization, and
their efficiency declined further. Even the new
leadership was often overwhelmed by, and defensive before, the sophisticated eastern federal
bureaucrats and private consultants who clearly
wanted only to help out America's first black
mayor. The gifts, in other words, carried a fearful price.

Bureaucratic Enemies

Except for the uniformed officials and the
schools, which were largely outside the mayor's
control, the standing city bureaucracy was a key
dilemma for Mayor Hatcher.

The mayor had run on a reform program. His
official campaign platform placed "good government" first, ahead of even tax reform and civil
rights. Hatcher was deeply committed to eliminating graft and corruption, improving the efficiency of municipal government—especially the
delivery of services to those sectors of the citizenry that had been most deprived—and he did
not view his regime as merely the substitution
of black faces for white ones in positions of
power.

But he also had a particular historic injustice
to rectify: the gross under-representation of
blacks in the city government, and their complete exclusion from policy-making positions.
Moreover, implicit in his campaign was a promise to reward his followers, who were mostly
black. (At least most participants in the cam-

paign assumed such a promise; Hatcher himself never spoke about the matter.)

Consequently, there was tremendous pressure from below to kick out everyone not covered by civil service protection and substitute all black personnel in their places. But to do so would have deepened the hostility of the white population and probably weakened Hatcher's potential leverage in the national Democratic Party. He resisted this pressure, asserting that he believed in an interracial administration. However, in addition to this belief (which, as far as I could determine, was genuine), there were other circumstances that dictated his course of action in this matter.

To begin with, it was always a premise of the administration that vital municipal services (police and fire protection, garbage collection, education, public health measures) had to be continued—both because the people of Gary absolutely needed them and because the failure to maintain them would represent a setback for black struggles throughout the country.

It also appeared that with a wholesale and abrupt transition to a totally new work force it would be impossible to continue these services, particularly because of a lack of the necessary skills and experiences among the black population—especially at the level of administration and skilled technical personnel. In this respect Hatcher faced the classic problem faced by all social revolutions and nationalist movements of recent times: after the seizure of power, how is it possible to run a complex society when those who traditionally ran it are now enemies?

The strategy Hatcher employed to meet this problem was the following. The bulk of the old personnel was retained. At the top level of the administration (personal staff, corporation counsel, chief of police, controller) new, trustworthy individuals were brought in. Then, gradually, new department heads were chosen, and new rank-and-file people included. If they had the skill already, they came at the beginning; if they didn't, they were brought in at a rate slow enough to provide for on-the-job training from the holdovers, without disrupting the ongoing functions of the particular department.

The main weakness of this gradualist strategy was that it permitted the old bureaucracy to survive—its institutional base was not destroyed.

The result was that the new political priorities of the administration could not be implemented with any degree of effectiveness in a new municipal political practice. City government remained remarkably like what it had been in the past, at least from the perspective of the average citizen in the community. While the political leadership was tied up with the kinds of problems I noted earlier, the bureaucracy proceeded on its own course, which was basically one of passive resistance. There were two aspects to this: bureaucratic inertia, a sullen rejection of any changes in established routine that might cause conflicts and difficulties for the employees, and active opposition based on politics and racism, to new methods and goals advocated by the mayor.

To cite just one example, the mayor decided to give a very high priority to enforcement of the housing codes, which had never been seriously implemented by preceding administrations. After much hard work, the Building Department was revamped to engage in aggressive inspection work. Cases stopped being "lost," and the number of inspections was increased by 4,000 percent while their quality was improved and standardized. Then it was discovered that cases prepared for legal enforcement were being tabled by the Legal Department on grounds of technical defects.

I personally ascertained that the alleged legal defects were simply untrue. I then assumed that the reason for the legal staff's behavior was that they were overburdened with work. Conferences were held to explain to them the mayor's priorities so they could rearrange their work schedule. Instead, a series of bitter personal fights resulted, culminating in my removal from that area of work since the staff attorneys threatened to resign if there were continued interference with their professional responsibility. In the course of these disputes, both black and white attorneys expressed the opinion that they did not consider themselves a legal aid bureau for Gary's poor, and furthermore the root of the city's housing problem was the indolent and malicious behavior of the tenants. In their view, it was therefore unjust to vigorously enforce the existing statutes against the landlords. Thus, despite the administration's pledge, black ghetto residents did not find their lives ameliorated in that respect.

Gradually, then, the promise of vast change after the new mayor took office came to be seen as illusory. Indeed, what actually occurred was much like an African neocolonial entity: new faces, new rhetoric and people whose lives were scarcely affected except in their feelings towards their government.

The outcome was not due to a failure of good faith on the part of the Hatcher administration. Nor does it prove the fallacious maximalist proposition that no amelioration of the people's conditions of life is possible prior to a revolution. Instead, it was due to the decline of the local mass base of the Hatcher administration and the array of national political forces confronting it.

Most black people in Gary were neither prepared nor able to take upon themselves the functions performed for them by specialized bureaucracies. They relied upon the government for education, welfare, public health, police and fire protection, enforcement of the building codes and other standards, maintenance of the public roads, and the like. Unable to develop alternative popularly based community institutions to carry on these functions by democratic self-government, the new administration was forced to rely upon the city bureaucracy—forced to pursue the option that could only result in minor changes.

Aborted Liberation

The most significant consequence of the Hatcher administration's failure to transcend the structural terrain on which it functioned was political, the erosion of popular support after the successful mobilization of energies involved in the campaign. The decline of mass participation in the political process contributed in turn to the tendency of the new regime to solve its dilemmas by bureaucratic means or by relying on outside support from the federal government.

The decline in mass support ought not to be confused with a loss of votes in an election. Indeed, Hatcher is now probably as secure politically as the average big city mayor. The point is that the mass of the black population is not actively involved in helping to run the city. Thus, their political experiences are not enlarged, their understanding of the larger society and how it functions has not improved, and they are not being trained to better organize for their own interests. In short, the liberating process of the struggle for office was aborted after the initial goal was achieved—and before it could even begin to confront the profound problems faced by the mass of urban black Americans.

For example, after the inauguration, old supporters found themselves on the outside looking in. For the most part, since there was no organized effort to continue to involve them (and indeed to do so could not but conflict with the dominant strategy of the administration), they had to be content to remain passive onlookers. Moreover, the average citizen put a lot of faith in the mayor and wanted to give him an opportunity to do his job without intruding on the process.

Even among the most politicized rank-and-file elements there was a fear of interfering. Painfully conscious of their lack of training and experience, they were afraid of "blowing it." Instead they maintained a benevolent watchfulness, an attitude reinforced by the sense that Hatcher was unique, that his performance was some kind of test of black people as a race. (Whites were not the only people encouraged by the media to think in these terms.) There were of course some old supporters who were frankly disillusioned: they did not receive the patronage or other assistance they had expected: they were treated rudely by a bureaucratic holdover or were merely unable to reach the ear of a leader who was once accessible as a friend.

The ebbing away of popular participation could be seen most markedly in the Spanish-speaking community, which could not reassure itself with the symbolic satisfaction of having a member of its group in the national spotlight. With even less education and prior opportunity than the blacks, they found that the qualifications barrier to municipal government left them with even less patronage than they felt to be their due reward. This feeling of betrayal was actively supported by the former machine politicians and criminal elements, who consciously evoked ethnic prejudices to isolate the mayor and weaken his popular support.

What happened in the first year of the new administration, then, was a contradiction between efficiency and ethnic solidarity. At each point the mayor felt he had to rely upon the expert bureaucracy, even at the cost of increasing his distance from his mass base. And this conflict manifested itself in a series of inexorable political events (the appointment of outside advisors, for example), each of which further contributed to eroding the popular base of the still new leadership.

As Antonio Gramsci pointed out, beneath this contradiction lies a deeper one: a historic class deprivation—inflicted on the oppressed by the very structure of the existing society—which barred the underclass from access to the skills necessary for it to run the society directly in its own interests and according to its own standard of civilization. Unless an oppressed social group is able to constitute itself as what Gramsci characterizes as a counterhegemonic social bloc, its conquest of state power cannot be much more than a change in leaders. Given the overall relation of forces in the country at large, such an undertaking was beyond the power of the black community in Gary in 1968. Therefore, dominant national political forces were able quickly to reconstitute their overall control.

National Power

What happened to Richard Hatcher in Gary in his first year as mayor raises important questions—questions that might be of only theoretical interest if he were indeed in a unique position. He is not. Carl Stokes, a black, is mayor of Cleveland. Charles Evers, a black, is mayor of Fayette, Mississippi. Thomas Bradley, a black, very nearly became mayor of Los Angeles. Kenneth Gibson, a black, is now mayor of Newark. The list will grow, and with it the question of how we are to understand the mass participation of blacks in electoral policies in this country and the future of their movement.

I believe that until new concepts are worked out, the best way of understanding this process is by analogy with certain national liberation movements in colonial or neocolonial countries. Of course, the participants—in Gary as in Newark—are Americans, and they aren't calling for a UN plebiscite. But they were clearly conscious of themselves as using elections as a tool, as a step toward a much larger (though admittedly ill-defined) ultimate goal—a goal whose key elements of economic change, political power, dignity, defense of a "new" culture and so forth are very close to those of colonial peoples. It is because Hatcher embraced these larger objectives (without, of course, using precisely the rhetoric) that his campaign can be thought of as part of a nationalist process that has a trajectory quite similar to that of anticolonial liberation movements.

In its weakened local posture, the Hatcher administration was unable to resist successfully a large degree of cooptation by the national political authorities. Despite a brave vote at the Democratic National Convention for Reverend Channing Philips, Hatcher was essentially forced to cooperate with the national government and Democratic Party—even to the extent of calling on the sheriff of Cook County to send deputies to reinforce the local police when a "mini-riot" occurred in the black ghetto.

Without either a nationally coordinated movement or an autonomous base of local insurgency—one capable of carrying out on a mass scale government functions outside the official structure—Hatcher's insurgency was contained within the existing national political system. Or to express it somewhat differently, the attempt by black forces to use the electoral process to further their national liberation was aborted by a countervailing process of neocolonialism carried out by the federal government. Bluntly speaking, the piecemeal achievement of power through parliamentary means is a fraud—at least as far as black Americans are concerned.

The process by which the national power maintained itself, and even forced the new administration to aid it in doing so, was relatively simple. As the gap between the popular constituency and the new government widened, like many another administration, Hatcher's found itself increasingly forced to rely upon its "accomplishments" to maintain its popularity and to fulfill its deeply held obligation to aid the community.

Lacking adequate autonomous financial resources—the mill remained in private hands, and it still proved impossible to assess it for tax purposes as its true value—accomplishments were necessarily dependent upon obtaining outside funds. In this case, the funds had to come from the federal government, preferably in the form of quick performance projects to maintain popular support and to enable everyone to appear to be doing something to improve matters.

These new programs injected a flow of cash into the community, and they created many new jobs. In his first year in office, the mayor obtained in cash or pledges more federal funds than his entire local budget. Hopes began to b engendered that these programs were the key to solving local problems, while the time spent on preparing them completed the isolation of the leadership from the people.

Then, too, the stress of this forced and artificial growth created endless opportunities for nepotism and even thievery. Men who had never earned a decent living before found themselves as high-paid executives under no requirement to produce any tangible results. Indeed, federal authorities seemed glad to dispense the funds without exercising adequate controls over their expenditures. A situation arose in which those who boasted of how they were hustling the system became prisoners of its largesse.

Even the most honest and courageous leader, such as Mayor Hatcher, could not help but be trapped by the aid offered him by the federal authorities. After all, how can any elected local executive turn down millions of dollars to dispense with as he sees fit to help precisely those people he was elected to aid? The acceptance of the help guaranteed the continuation of bonds of dependence. For without any real autonomous power base, and with new vested interests and expectations created by the flow of funds into the community, and with no available alternative path of development, the relation of power between the local leader and the national state was necessarily and decisively weighted toward the latter.

In Gary, Indiana, within one year after the most prodigious feat in the history of its black population—the conquest of local political power —their insurgency has been almost totally contained. It is indeed difficult to see how the existing administration can extricate itself from its comparative impasse in the absence of fresh national developments, or of a new, more politically coherent popular upsurge from below.

There is, however, no doubt that the struggle waged by the black people of Gary, Indiana, is a landmark on their road to freedom; for the experiences of life and struggle have become another part of their heritage—and thus a promise for us all.

30

LEONARD S. RUBINOWITZ

The Problem of Metropolitan Housing Choice: Who Gets to Live Where?

INTRODUCTION: AMERICAN APARTHEID

In 1968, the Presidential Commission which was established to determine the causes of the urban riots of the 1960s warned that:

> ... The nation is rapidly moving toward two increasingly separate Americas. Within two decades, this division could be so deep that it would be almost impossible to unite: a white society principally located in suburbs, in smaller central cities, and in the peripheral parts of large central cities, and a Negro society largely concentrated within large central cities. The Negro society will be permanently relegated to its current status, possibly even if we expend great amounts of money and effort in trying to "gild" the ghetto. In the long run, continuation and expansion of such a permanent division threatens us with two perils. The first is the danger of sustained violence in our cities ... The second is the danger of a conclusive repudiation of the traditional American ideals of individual dignity, freedom, and equality of opportunity. We will not be able to espouse these ideals meaningfully to the rest of the world, to ourselves, to our children. They may still recite the Pledge of Allegiance and say "one nation . . . indivisible." But they will be learning cynicism, not patriotism. We cannot escape responsibility for choosing the future of our metropolitan areas and the human relations which develop within them. It is a responsibility so critical that even an unconscious choice to continue present policies has the gravest implications ... We must choose. Indeed, we are choosing.[1]

And the results of the 1970 census indicate that we are continuing to choose the path of racial segregation in this country. The metropolitan patterns of segregation that were pointed out in 1968 were reconfirmed by the 1970 census. The black population in major cities continued to grow very substantially, while the black population in the suburbs remained almost constant. What little growth in black population in the suburbs took place was largely in pre-existing pockets of black concentrations. Meanwhile, the white exodus from the cities to the suburbs was of enormous proportions. During the 1960s the white population in the suburbs increased by 15.5 million.

In overall terms, the black population increased at double the rate of the white population. But the black growth was concentrated in the central cities. The black percentage of central city population increased from 16 to 21 percent in the space of one decade.[2]

The outlook for the future, if present trends are not reversed, is for metropolitan residential apartheid. Projections indicate that by the year 2000, whites will make up only 25 percent of the population of our central cities and blacks will comprise 75 percent of that population.[3]

Although economic segregation is not as pervasive as racial segregation, low and moderate income people tend to live in central cities rather than the suburbs of metropolitan areas. Th

The author wishes to express his appreciation to John Walton and Erica Pascal for their helpful comments on an earlier draft of this paper.

tendency becomes stronger towards the lower end of the income scale:

In 1969 one-fifth of all central city families had incomes below $5,000, or 1.7 times the proportion of such families in suburbia.[4]

In 1970 central cities contained 8.2 million people below the poverty line (12.9 percent of the population), while suburbs had 5.4 million people in this category (7.1 percent of the population). Thus, the absolute number of poor persons was 1.5 times as large in central cities as in suburbs in 1970. The percentage of total population defined as poor was 1.8 times as large in central cities as in suburbs.

Thus, it is clear that lower-income people and racial minorities are denied equal access to suburbia. This pattern poses critical problems for these groups and for society at large, problems that cannot be solved within the boundaries of central cities.

IMPACT OF
METROPOLITAN SEGREGATION

Continuing the present pattern of the separation of the races and classes would be extremely costly, both in social and dollar terms. The costs are imposed not only on those excluded from the suburbs, but on the central city itself and even many suburban interests. First is the "jobs-housing mismatch," the disastrous geographical disparity between the jobs and housing opportunities for people needed to fill them. Because of these increasing distances between the job sites and the places where low-income people and minorities are able to live, central city workers are often unaware of suburban job openings. These openings are often communicated by informal methods, such as word of mouth or signs posted at the plant, which do not reach inner city residents. The suburban employers pay the price, too, as jobs go unfilled and turnover and absenteeism among unskilled and semi-skilled workers remain at a high level. The country pays an enormous price for this mismatch because of the wasteful use it involves of our limited energy resources. For those who can find suburban jobs and can afford to commute from the city, the trip must usually be made by car because the suburban job sites are decentralized and the mass transit systems are not generally designed to serve the "reverse commuter," causing inordinate costs in time and money. The outbound traffic on major expressways is as heavy as the inbound traffic during rush hour in many major cities. If housing was available for these suburban employees near their jobs, the costs for the workers, the employers, and the country as a whole would be significantly reduced.

In addition to the "jobs-housing mismatch," suburban exclusion perpetuates the great disparities in educational opportunities between races and classes. Suburban public schools are generally considered to be superior to those in the central cities. Achieving the national objective of equality of educational opportunity requires that all income and recial groups have access to quality public schools through residential mobility as well as other methods. Indeed there would be little need to debate the highly controversial issue of bussing if housing opportunities for racial and economic minorities were available in suburbia.

Finally, the exclusionary pattern of suburban development is intimately related to the decline of older neighborhoods in the central city and inner ring suburbs. The key private sector actors in the real estate process (institutional investors, developers, etc.) have engaged in a practice referred to as "disinvestment." They have chosen not to invest their resources in older neighborhoods, but instead to develop new housing for middle and upper-income whites on the suburban fringe. They appeal to people's "preference" rather than to any basic "need" for a "decent home and a suitable living environment," the goal articulated by Congress for all Americans. These actors seek to encourage primarily white, middle-income people to move out of their decent homes and suitable living environments in the city or older suburbs to "preferred" homes and environments in the fringe suburbs.

The investment decisions have highly significant consequences for older neighborhoods in the central cities and close-in suburbs. These areas are left without an adequate supply of "conventional" mortgage credit. They are "redlined." This means that lenders are unwilling to make mortgage loans available in the area unless they are protected against loss by federal insurance or guarantees. Thus, people seeking to buy houses or make home repairs in those neighborhoods must rely on federally insured loans, primarily through the Federal Housing Administration (FHA). Because of the FHA insurance, the lender does not have the same incentive as the "conventional" lender (one without federal insurance or guarantees) to exercise care in assessing the risks involved in lending money on a particular house to a particular buyer. In addition to this structural problem, there have been serious administrative abuses. Since FHA began insuring large numbers of mortgages in older neighborhoods in the late 1960s, there has been significant maladministration and fraud in these programs. The result has been a high level of foreclosure and abandonment in neighborhoods where FHA loans are concentrated, generally the "redlined" neighborhoods. Thus, as these loans are concentrated in older neighborhoods, the neighborhoods tend to decline. In short, the private investor's decision to invest in the exclusionary suburbs and disinvest from the older neighborhoods decreases the chances for the urban neighborhoods to remain viable.

BARRIERS TO ENTRY

The exclusion of the poor and minorities from suburbia has deep historical roots in overtly discriminatory practices by individuals, the real estate industry, and government at all levels. The roots of the problem also are buried, in a significant way, in the land use regulatory processes of local government. The exclusionary vehicles have become more subtle, but none the less effective, in recent years.

Racial Discrimination

The history of exclusion of racial minorities from the suburbs involves a variety of public and private institutions and individuals in a direct, overt way. Sellers and landlords in white areas simply would not sell or rent to blacks or other minorities. In the sale of housing, restrictive covenants were used to formalize this process. These covenants committed the owner of a house *not* to sell his or her house to specified minorities. If the person disregarded the covenant, the state courts would hold the seller legally liable

and prohibit the sale of the house and/or require the payment of damages. It was not until 1948 that the Supreme Court decided that it was unconstitutional for state courts to enforce restrictive covenants.[5]

The real estate industry was a partner in this practice of discrimination. Realtors would not show blacks homes in white suburbia. Lenders, such as banks and savings and loan associations, generally would not make loans to blacks seeking to buy a house in a white neighborhood.

Public policy supported these discriminatory practices. Some municipalities adopted explicit racial zoning ordinances, which defined the blocks on which blacks could and could not live. The United States Supreme Court held this type of ordinance unconstitutional in 1917.[6]

In a more recent period, the state of California enacted a constitutional provision which, in effect, prevented the state and municipalities from prohibiting racial discrimination in housing. In 1967, the Supreme Court held this provision unconstitutional under the federal constitution.[7]

The federal government has been perhaps the worst governmental offender. It has played a significant role in the housing market since the 1930s and for much of that period operated its programs on an explicitly racially discriminatory basis. The earliest of the major programs was the Federal Housing Administration (FHA) mortgage insurance program which was enacted during the depression to encourage banks to make mortgage loans, by insuring the lenders against any loss on these loans. FHA mortgage insurance helped to bring about the flowering of the tract developments in the suburbs in the postwar period, but those federally assisted developments were essentially closed to blacks. The FHA manual prohibited insuring a mortgage of a black buyer moving into a white neighborhood, on the assumption that the family would lower property values and make the loan an unacceptable risk. At the same time, the FHA would not insure loans in the inner city, where the housing was older and where most blacks lived. In addition, the FHA encouraged the use of restrictive covenants and did not cease doing so until two years after the Supreme Court decision rendering these provisions unenforceable. The result of FHA policies and practices was that there was virtually no participation by blacks in the agency's mortgage insurance programs through the 1950s.

During the 1930s, the federal government also enacted the public housing program to build and subsidize housing for low-income people. In many cities, the program was operated on a segregated basis. Separate waiting lists were maintained for whites and blacks and the tenants were assigned to public housing projects built in areas predominantly of their own race. This "separate but equal" method of operating the public housing program continued well beyond the Supreme Court's decision in 1954 that the "separate but equal" approach to public education was unconstitutional.

In short, overt racial discrimination in housing was common until very recently, including the active participation of many sectors of the real estate industry and the cooperation, or at least acquiescence, of government at all levels. As these practices have been challenged, the forms of discrimination have become more subtle. For example, some realtors engage in "steering": showing homes in white areas to prospective white purchasers and homes in black and racially changing areas to prospective black purchasers. In the inner city, brokers have engaged in "blockbusting," or encouraging middle-income white people to move to the suburbs, using racial fears to panic the residents to move out because of the alleged in-migration of blacks.

Economic Exclusion

In addition to the various forms of racial discrimination, minorities and lower-income people generally have been excluded from the suburbs by the "entry fee." The cost of housing in much of suburbia is too high for lower-income people and minorities to afford.

Traditionally, suburbs have used their power to regulate the use of land within their borders in ways that prevent the construction of housing within the means of low and moderate-income people. The requirements imposed on housing developments by zoning ordinances forced the price of the housing up beyond the means of those groups. For example, most suburbs prohibit mobile home developments through their zoning ordinance, thus excluding the one form of new housing that may be affordable by lower-income people without public subsidies. Many suburbs prohibit or severely limit the development of apartments, which can generally be pro-

vided less expensively than single family homes. Even with regard to single family homes, many communities require that they be of certain minimum size or on a lot of a specified minimum size, which escalates the cost of the house. Even if the zoning ordinance permits apartments or modest homes to be built, it may require that any developer wishing to do so have his plans approved by the zoning boiard. Approval of developments for families with modest incomes may never be forthcoming.

In recent years, suburbs have turned also to growth control and timed development ordinances which limit the pace of development within the community. These ordinances may also have the effect of driving up the cost of the housing that is built beyond prices which lower-income people can afford, even with subsidies. They reduce the amount of land available for development at any given time, thus increasing the price of that land.

In addition to land use controls which have been in the hands of local governments since the early part of the twentieth century, legislation creating many of the federal subsidized housing programs has given communities either an explicit or implicit veto over the use of the programs within its borders. For example, the original public housing program could not be utilized in a community unless there was a public agency to administer it and the local governing body had entered into an agreement to cooperate with that agency. Non-action by the locality was sufficient to prevent the operation of the program. Even the modified version of that program enacted in 1974 permits the local government a significant voice in whether and where any subsidized housing is to go in the community. If the community opposes a particular development, the federal government must respect that position unless there is a sound reason for doing otherwise.

STRATEGIES FOR OPENING THE SUBURBS

Anti-Discrimination Strategies

Until the late 1960s, the response to racially discriminatory practices consisted largely of local and state fair housing ordinances which depended on the filing of complaints by victims of discrimination and often did not contain effective sanctions when discrimination was found.

In 1968, in the aftermath of the assassination of Martin Luther King, Congress enacted the federal fair housing law, which supplemented the local and state open housing legislation and put the federal government explicitly on the side of non-discrimination in housing.[8] The law prohibits discrimination on the basis of race, creed, color, or national origin in the sale or rental of most of the country's housing. The law exempts certain transactions from its coverage, such as most home sales without a real estate broker. People who feel they have been discriminated against under the terms of this law can seek assistance from the federal Department of Housing and Urban Development (HUD) in conciliating their complaint. If HUD believes that the complaint has merit, the agency will try to bring the parties together together and work out an agreement, which may include making the house or apartment available to the minority person, payment of damages, and/or a commitment on the part of the person or company against whom the complaint was made to take steps to carry out a program of non-discrimination. This approach has had limited success because of the voluntary nature of the process and the long delays caused by the lack of staff available to carry out the investigation and conciliation process.

If HUD is unable to resolve the complaint through concilliation, it can refer the matter to the Justice Department for prosecution in court. Generally, the Justice Department can sue if there is a "pattern or practice" of discrimination involved or if the case raises questions of general public importance.

Alternatively, a person who believes he or she was discriminated against can go directly to federal court under the 1968 law. In some metropolitan areas, there are voluntary organizations which represent such clients. In Chicago, for example, the Leadership Council for Metropolitan Open Communities has been highly successful in gaining the house or apartment for its clients through judicial decisions or out-of-court settlements, which frequently involve financial awards as well.

The 1968 fair housing law is buttressed by a Supreme Court decision which came shortly after its passage.[9] In *Jones v. Mayer*, the Court interpreted a century-old civil rights act to prohibit discrimination based on race in the sale or rental of *any* housing. Some of the gaps in coverage left by Congress in 1968 were filled by the Supreme Court in its interpretation of the earlier statute.

The legal strategy of suing landlords, realtors, sellers, and other private sector actors under the 1866 and 1968 laws is an important means of increasing suburban housing opportunities for minorities. For example, both steering and blockbusting are illegal under federal law and many state and local laws, but the practices persist. One of the strategies used to combat steering is the "audit," a systematic way of detecting steering by realtors. Black and white couples independently make contact with a realtor and seek the same kind of housing in the same kind of area. The listings and the areas to which the respective couples are referred by the realtor are compared. If the black couples are referred to predominantly black or integrated areas and the white couples are shown housing in white areas, there may be grounds for legal action. Some lawsuits have been filed on this basis and others are likely to follow, since steering represents an important but subtle obstacle to the movement of minorities to the suburbs.

Beyond Non-Discrimination: Affirmative Efforts

Even if the strategies to prevent racial discrimination are used aggressively and effectively, there is an additional task around which strategies are evolving. The history of racial residential discrimination and the continuation of such practices in new and more subtle forms has left an indelible imprint in the minds of most minority group members. Although these discriminatory tactics persist, there are predominantly white suburban communities where blacks can move in without harrassment or where they may even be welcomed. But the history of discrimination and hostility pervades the mind set of most blacks, and the lack of information about suburban communities which are "open" leads most black prospective buyers or renters to consider only the inner city as a potential place to live.

Public policy and private organizations have recognized the need to move beyond prevention of discrimination in order to open up suburban ousing opportunities to minorities. In the federal fair housing law, Congress mandated the ecretary of HUD to administer all of the gency's programs "affirmatively" to further the olicy of fair housing.[10] As part of its effort to arry out this affirmative responsibility, HUD sued "affirmative Marketing" regulations in 972.[11] The regulations required housing de-elopers who were seeking assistance under HUD rograms to develop and implement a plan to ttract tenants or buyers of racial groups who ould not generally apply. For suburban de-elopments, this usually meant blacks and other acial minorities were to be actively solicited arough advertising, contacts with community rganizations, and other means devised by the eveloper. Although these regulations seemed hold promise for attracting minorities to the aburbs, the evidence to date indicates that UD has not vigorously enforced them.[12] In-lequate plans are approved by HUD frequently id little effort is made to determine whether en these minimal plans are implemented. The nited evidence also indicates that the affirma-ve marketing process has done little to attract inorities to federally assisted suburban hous-g developments.

While the federal government has made halt-g steps toward moving beyond efforts to pre-nt discrimination, private fair housing organi-tions in some areas have made vigorous efforts inform inner city residents of the housing portunities in the suburbs and to provide unselling services. The counselling attempts identify communities where minorities are ely to be welcome and sympathetic realtors assist them. These counselling services are lvertised on television and in newspapers to ach the widest possible audience within the inority community. However, the resources ailable for such efforts are very limited and ust be expanded if such programs are to be rried out at the scale needed.

ducing the Cost of Suburban Housing

assortment of exclusionary devices have pre-nted development of housing for low and mod-ate-income people in suburbia. In response these obstacles, strategies have been devel-ed, particularly in the last ten years, to bring

about "inclusionary" results. One commentator has suggested that the distinguishing mark of an inclusionary land use program is the application of local government's regulatory powers over land to facilitate the development of new housing for low-and moderate-income families.[13] Although local officials could adopt such a program based on an enlightened self-interest or a belief in the goal, that has not been the pattern to date.

Efforts to lower suburban exclusionary barriers have come instead largely from: (1) public bodies with a multi-jurisdictional responsibility, through legislation, administrative actions and planning activities; and (2) private individuals and organizations using legal strategies for "opening the suburbs."[14]

1. Public Strategies: Local, Regional and State. Attempts by public bodies to bring about suburban acceptance of low and moderate-income housing have taken place at the county, regional, state, and federal levels. Some of these approaches have directly challenged the land use regulations which escalate the cost of housing, but most have focused on identifying an affirmative obligation or seeking a specific commitment from the community to permit development of needed housing for low and moderate-income people.

At the county level, two suburban counties in the Washington, D.C. area have passed ordinances which require housing developments of fifty or more units to include a component of low and moderate-income housing.[15] Fifteen percent of the housing units must be priced within the means of low and moderate-income people. Although the Fairfax County, Virginia, ordinance was held invalid by the courts of that state, the Montgomery County, Maryland ordinance still stands.[16] Montgomery County is adjacent to Washington and is the site of several major government installations as well as an increasing number of private employers. Many of the employees cannot afford the housing that is currently available in Montgomery County, and the result has been serious problems of job vacancies, turnover, and absenteeism. Some corporate employers have even told county officials that if they had anticipated these problems, they would not have moved their operations to the county.[17] This kind of pressure helped to facilitate the passage of the ordinance requiring developers to make provision for lower-income people.

Beyond actions by counties with an inclusionary thrust, the early 1970s witnessed a growing involvement of metropolitan and regional bodies in housing issues. The most significant effort has been the development of "allocation" or "fair share" plans, which identify where the needed low and moderate-income housing should be located. They do not usually designate specific sites for the housing. Instead, "subareas" or planning areas are defined (these may be local communities) within which specific quantities of low and moderate-income housing should be provided or which should receive a particular level of priority for subsidized housing.

The first housing allocation plan to be developed was the Miami Valley Regional Planning Commission's *Housing Plan for the Miami Valley Region*. In 1970, the Commission identified a serious shortage of low and moderate-income housing in the Dayton, Ohio, region and proposed that each community assume responsibility for a proportionate share of that housing.

In the period immediately following the adoption of the Miami Valley plan, there was a very substantial increase in the rate of production of federally subsidized housing nationwide. This coincidence makes it difficult to evaluate the impact of the plan and the commission's implementation efforts. It is impossible to know how much subsidized housing would have been built in the Dayton region and where it would have been located in the absence of the allocation plan. Evaluation is made even more difficult because of the moratorium imposed by the national administration early in 1973, which virtually shut off new activity under the subsidized housing programs.

However, there are some indications that the Miami Valley plan has stimulated acceptance of low and moderate-income housing in more Dayton suburbs than would have happened without the plan. Between 1970 and 1973, there were over 3,000 low and moderate-income housing units produced in the region, with another 2,500 units scheduled for completion by 1975. Several of the suburban areas had achieved a high percentage of the units allocated to them. Although the bulk of the new subsidized housing has continued to be built in Dayton, development has expanded into many suburban areas of the region.

Allocation plans have become an accepted part of the planner's role. Agencies in the Washington, D.C., Minneapolis-St. Paul, San Bernardino, California, and Denver areas, among others, have followed the general approach initiated by the Miami Valley Regional Planning Commission, with the goal of encouraging suburban communities to accept a share of the region's housing needs.

While the regional agencies have begun to use the tools at their disposal for lowering suburban exclusionary barriers, several states have also developed techniques for achieving this purpose. One of the best known models is the Massachusetts Anti-Snob Zoning Law.[19] The law generally prohibits communities from excluding housing developments for lower-income people until 1 percent of the locality's housing is for such people. Then the community may deny any subsequent request to permit development of such housing. The community has the same discretion if, at any point, low and moderate-income housing occupies 1.5 percent of the land zoned for residential, commercial, or industrial uses. Before that time, denial is permitted only in special circumstances.

In addition, the Massachusetts law establishes a state appeals process, in case a locality turns down a proposed housing development for lower-income people. If the state appeals committee finds that the proposed development is consistent with the locality's needs, the committee may direct the locality to issue the necessary permits to allow construction. The locality can appeal that decision in court, however. Communities have delayed the construction of subsidized housing by using the procedures in the law, in the hope of preventing them from ever being built.

In New York, the legislature enacted a more streamlined procedure, which enabled the state Urban Development Corporation to ignore local zoning requirements if the agency felt that was necessary in order to develop housing for low and moderate-income people. The agency kept this power in reserve for several years, but in 1972 threatened to use it to develop a modest amount of housing in nine suburbs of New York City. Before the agency was able to proceed, the legislature rescinded its authority to override local zoning and, instead, provided town with an explicit veto power over any housing proposed by the Urban Development Corporation.

In Pennsylvania, the state urban affairs agency determined that it could make grants of recreational funds to previously exclusionary communities only if they lowered their barriers. The agency informed several communities which had applied for grants that they could not receive the state funds unless they took steps to become "inclusionary." The communities challenged the state agency in court, as going beyond its authority in denying them funds. The communities won the initial legal battles.

Thus, although several states have attempted to increase access to the suburbs, these legislative and administrative efforts take place within serious political constraints. Suburbs hold the balance of power in most of the large urban state legislatures and their representatives can usually block efforts to lower the suburban barriers.

2. Public Strategies: Federal. Although similar political dynamics are operating in Congress, the 1974 Housing and Community Development Act indicates a degree of commitment at the federal level to increasing geographical choices of lower-income people. Congress explicitly tied the receipt of federal funds by localities to the development of local housing plans. Communities are eligible to apply for federal funds to be used for a wide range of community development purposes, such as street repairs, rehabilitation of housing, and purchase of park land. In order to receive these federal funds, however, the community must submit a housing plan. These plans include an analysis of: (1) the housing conditions in the community; (2) the housing needs of people living in the community as well as nonresidents who would be expected to reside there if housing was made available; (3) an annual goal for the low and moderate-income housing to be provided; and (4) the general areas where the housing is to be located.

Even before the enactment of the Housing and Community Development Act of 1974, the federal government had a number of tools available for opening the suburbs. For example, HUD administers the Section 701 planning program, which provides funds for planning agencies to carry out comprehensive planning. Without federal funds, many regional and metropolitan planning agencies could not exist. To be eligible for these funds, the agencies must undertake a "housing element" to insure that "the housing needs of both the region and the local communities studied in the planning will be adequately covered in terms of existing and prospective immigrant population growth."[20]

In administering this requirement, HUD can condition planning funds on the development of an action-oriented housing plan such as the "fair share" plans discussed earlier. In one case, HUD held up planning funds for the Southeastern Wisconsin Regional Planning Commission (SEWRPC) because of "its lack of a short term action plan or strategy" for housing.[21] HUD suggested that the regional agency develop an allocation plan for the seven-county region. SEWRPC accepted these conditions, received its funding, and undertook an allocation plan for the region, for 2,000 units of low and moderate-income housing.

A second planning tool at HUD's disposal is the A-95 review process, named after a circular issued by the Office of Management and Budget. The circular provides that local applications for federal assistance under a variety of programs are to be reviewed by regional and state agencies. These agencies are to see to it that the applications are consistent with regional and state plans as well as federal civil rights requirements. This circular meshes with the "housing element" requirement. The regional agency which carries out A-95 reviews is often the same agency which receives 701 planning funds and therefore must develop a "housing element." When the regional agency reviews applications for federal assistance from communities in its jurisdiction, it can inquire whether the community is acting in a manner consistent with the "housing element." For example, a community whose zoning bars the construction of housing for low and moderate-income people may be acting inconsistently with the housing element. When this community applies for a HUD grant, the regional agency can recommend that the grant not be approved by HUD unless the community takes affirmative steps to facilitate the development of needed housing. That recommendation is then forwarded to HUD, which can honor it (although it is not bound to do so) and refuse to approve the grant unless the community takes appropriate action in the housing area. In two instances in Connecticut, the A-95 process was used to block sewer grants to exclusionary suburban communities until pledges to revise local zoning in an inclusionary direction were made.[22]

HUD is not the only federal agency with potential for opening the suburbs. For example, the General Services Administration (GSA) has a mandate in this area. GSA is the landlord for most federal agencies. It controls over 10,000 facilities across the country. These facilities represent very substantial financial resources for the communities in which they are located.

In 1970, Executive Order 11512 was issued. It required that, in selecting sites for federal facilities, GSA should study the availability of housing for the federal employees, along with about twenty other factors. GSA then signed an agreement with HUD, under which HUD would assist in providing housing needed for these purposes. Initially, a study was to be made of the available housing in the area and if there was a shortage, an "affirmative action plan" was to be developed. In the first several years after the executive order, no such plans were developed.

The Equal Employment Opportunity Commission (EEOC) is still another federal agency which has leverage in suburbia. The EEOC has the responsibility for enforcing the employment discrimination provisions of Title VII of the 1964 Civil Rights Act. The agency's potential involvement in suburbia arises out of the movement of corporate facilities to suburbia. Many of these corporate move-outs from the central cities have extremely adverse effects on the minorities in the company's work force, who are locked in to inner city housing. A 1971 memorandum prepared by the EEOC general counsel's office suggested that such relocations may constitute employment discrimination under the statute:

> The transfer of an employer's facilities constitutes a *prima facie* violation of Title VII if (1) the community from which an employer moves has a higher percentage of minority workers than the community to which he moves, or (2) the transfer affects the employment situation of the employer's minority workers more adversely than it affects his remaining workers, and (3) the employer fails to take measures to correct such disparate effects.[23]

In spite of this opinion of the EEOC legal office, the agency has not responded to several complaints that have been filed challenging proposed corporate relocations on the grounds of their disparate impact on minority workers. The EEOC has taken no public position on this issue, although it has the potential through its powers of publicity and its ability to file discrimination suits to influence the course of corporate relocations, perhaps delaying them until adequate housing opportunities are provided.

Thus, the federal laws, executive orders, and policies constitute a potentially potent array of tools for increasing housing opportunities of the poor and minorities. Among HUD, the Justice Department, GSA, the EEOC and other federal agencies, there is substantial leverage available.

3. *Litigation as an Inclusionary Strategy.* In addition to legislative, administrative, and planning approaches, litigation has been an important strategy for lowering the suburban exclusionary barriers. The courts in several states have been sympathetic to challenges to local zoning schemes which make impossible the construction of housing for lower-income people. In the most advanced case in this area, the Mount Laurel case, the New Jersey Supreme Court said that communities have an affirmative responsibility to use their zoning power to see to it that land is available for housing for lower-income people.[24] This obligation, according to the court means that enough appropriately zoned land must be available for development of a community's proportionate share of the region's need for low and moderate-income housing. Although the court did not say that the municipality has a further duty to see to it that the housing is actually provided on that land, the decision is a significant step forward in overcoming the legal barriers to building housing for lower-income people in suburbia. This decision is not binding on the courts of any other states, but it may encourage courts in other state to remove the legal impediments to needed construction.

Another legal approach to "opening the suburbs" began with a challenge to the placement of low-income housing within a central city. In *Gautreaux v. Chicago Housing Authority,* the federal court found that the public housing program in Chicago had been operated on a segregated basis, with most of the housing being built in black neighborhoods and occupied by blacks and the small amount of housing which was located outside of the ghetto being occupied largely by whites.[25] The court of appeals said that in order to remedy this situation, public housing had to be built not only in white areas of the city but in the suburbs as well, since the city was becoming increasingly black. The Supreme Court agreed to decide whether metropolitan relief was necessary and appropriate in these circumstances.

FUTURE PROSPECTS

The Problems

The emergence of a "movement" to open the suburbs to blacks and low and moderate-income people generally came about only in the late 1960s. The effort is still in its early stages and the progress has been limited. The opponents are numerous and varied. They include not only people who object to the in-migration of racial minorities and poor people, but protectors of the environment who wish to stop or slow the growth of their communities and people who are concerned about the fiscal impacts of housing for lower-income people. Not only are the motives varied, but so are the techniques available to frustrate the efforts of advocates of opening the suburbs. Even when the legislatures or the courts take positive actions, their decisions are not self-executing. Obstruction is possible in many forms and at the least, the opponents of change are often able to cause long delays. Frequently, they are able to entirely block the efforts at change. To make the picture somewhat bleaker, legislatures and courts are often on the side of maintaining the exclusionary patterns.

The examples of frustration of the mandate of the law in this area are plentiful. For example, when a Pennsylvania court ruled that a community could not prohibit apartment developments entirely, the municipality zoned a rock quarry for multi-family housing.[26] And when HUD conditioned funding to a Detroit suburb on the implementation of an open housing program, the residents voted to reject the federal funds.[27]

The Housing and Community Development Act of 1974 provides another example of the principle that the law and the reality may be very different in this area of increasing housing choice. This statute requires that communities seeking community development funds include a housing assistance plan for meeting the needs of residents and non-residents who would be likely to seek housing within their borders. However, the housing plan need say nothing about how the applicant is going to achieve the goals stated in the plan. Indeed, there is no explicit requirement that the community take any steps whatsoever to see to it that the housing becomes a reality. Nor is there any stipulation that if the housing plan is not implemented, the community will lose future funding under the community development program. The subsidies that are necessary to carry out most of these plans and make housing available for lower-income people are provided through Section 8 of the same statute. But the Section 8 program relies primarily on private parties and local housing agencies for the initiative bringing subsidized housing into existence. If no private developers or landlords or local housing agencies come forward to participate in the program, the community may continue to receive community development funds, and the housing plan may join the heap of well-intentioned plans that have not been implemented.

Finally, the courts and legislatures are by no means uniformly supportive of the efforts to open the suburbs. On the contrary, they are often major obstacles on the road to suburbia. For example, the U.S. Supreme Court has handed down several recent decisions which are likely to impede progress. In *James v. Valtierra*, the Court held that it was constitutional for the state of California to provide for a referendum on low-income public housing.[28] The case arose after public housing projects were excluded through referenda. The Court held that the state had a long tradition of having referenda on various subjects and this was simply an exercise of the democratic process. Other communities around the country have begun to pass ordinances requiring referenda before any subsidized housing developments can be built. Where there is no tradition of referenda and where the purpose of the ordinance is clearly to keep out minorities, the courts may strike down these ordinances. But at the very least, the Supreme Court has given the suburbs another means of delay.

In *Belle Terre v. Boraas*, the Supreme Court held that the community could use its zoning ordinance to prohibit communes, because communities are entitled to take action to protect their environment.[29] Although the case did not involve poor people or racial minorities specifically, it opened the way for communities to argue that prohibitions on apartments and provisions for large minimum lot sizes are measures designed to protect the physical and social environment of the community, within the meaning of the Supreme Court's decision in the *Belle Terre* case.

In 1975, the Supreme Court decided the case of *Warth v. Seldin*, in which it held that people who were not residents of a community had no legal standing to challenge the community's zoning ordinance.[30] The plaintiffs in the case were residents of the inner city of Rochester, who were challenging the exclusionary nature of the zoning ordinance of the suburb of Penfield. These plaintiffs are exactly the kinds of people whose interests the open suburbs advocates are seeking to advance. But the Supreme Court said that you have to live in the community already in order to have a sufficient stake in the consequences of its zoning actions to be able to challenge them.

These unfavorable decisions by the Supreme Court have led many lawyers involved in exclusionary zoning litigation to conclude that their battles must be fought in the state courts, since the federal courts have been helpful only where a racially discriminaory motive has been demonstrated. Even in the state judicial arena, however, the majority of the states' courts have not shown any particular receptivity to the claims of those excluded from the suburbs.

Legislatures have been similarly unenthusiastic about taking action to open the suburbs. The legislative efforts discussed earlier do not represent the tip of an iceberg. They constitute most of the iceberg. Many efforts to enact legislation in this field have died because of the powerful influence of suburban interests. (This is, of course, one of the reasons that open suburbs advocates turned to the courts in the first place.) For example, a bill proposed by the governor of New Jersey in 1972 to involve the state in encouraging voluntary "fair share" planning could not even attract a sponsor willing to introduce it in the legislature.

The Promise

In spite of all of these problems, the efforts to open the suburbs have borne some fruit in a relatively short time and hold promise for making significant progress in the future. Several approaches seem to have particular potential. One of these is the cluster of strategies linking suburban housing opportunities to suburban jobs. The crucial need of employers and employees alike to have housing in proximity to suburban job sites has prompted the introduction of legislation (the Workers Residential Rights Act in Illinois), the initiation of litigation in Detroit against the Michigan Automobile Club and efforts by corporations to apply their leverage.[31] For many communities, the corporate facilities represent important tax resources and the threat of the loss of such income may move them to take inclusionary steps. Evidence of the growing support for job-related housing measures is the response to the Workers' Residential Rights Act in the Illinois legislature. The bill would require communities that experience substantial employment growth to make provision for an amount of housing for low and moderate income workers in proportion to the scale of the expansion in jobs. The bill received the overwhelming support of those voting in the general assembly in 1973. The speaker determined that the bill intruded on home rule powers and therefore needed a three-fifths vote of the entire chamber under the state constitution. Although the bill did not pass, the strong showing indicated the viability of linking jobs and housing in order to open the suburbs. The variety of vehicles available for making this linkage should encourage both private groups and public bodies to pursue these strategies.

A second approach which should be useful in the future is litigation designed to bring about inclusionary actions by the suburbs. Even with all the difficulties inherent in trying to bring about complex social changes through the courts, the judicial process remains one of the best strategies available. In the federal courts, challenges are most likely to succeed when it is possible to establish a racial motivation for the exclusionary practice. Federal court litigation might also focus on forcing the federal agencies to carry out their mandates and use the leverage available to them. For example, a lawsuit was brought to prod the General Services Administration to meet its obligations under the 197_ executive order.[32] The case involved a $25 million Internal Revenue Center in Brookhaven, New York, which was designed to house 4,000 employees. The federal court found that there was not adequate housing in the community for these employees, as well as the entire population of the area, and that the GSA had violated the executive order by not taking steps to assure the availability of such housing. Instead of holding up construction of the facility, which was well advanced at the time, the court required the GSA to use 220 units of surplus housing at a nearby air base for low-income residents of the county. Similar cases have been filed to prevent HUD and other federal agencies from making grants to exclusionary communities.

In addition to the federal courts, there are promising approaches to be used in the state courts. The courts of New Jersey, Pennsylvania, Connecticut, and other states have focused on the problem of economic exclusion and begun to provide remedies in this area.

At the other end of the "voluntary-compulsory" spectrum from litigation is the regional planning process. The regional agencies in some parts of the country are becoming deeply involved in opening up suburban housing opportunities. These organizations are moving from a traditionally passive stance on housing into developing and attempting to implement allocation plans. These plans do not, in themselves, alter zoning patterns or remove other impediments which may price lower-income housing out of an area. However, they do focus public attention on the issue, define an affirmative responsibility of municipalities, and provide a political context within which local officials can be moved to respond favorably to subsidized housing proposals which come before them.

Finally, although the Housing and Community Development Act of 1974 has all the pitfalls discussed in the last section, it also contains significant potential. In addition to the explicit "carrot and stick" approach of conditioning the granting of community development funds on development of a housing assistance plan, the statute contains a new subsidized housing program.

It is critical that public subsidies be available to bring housing within the means of lower-income people. Without subsidies, even housing built under the least restrictive land use regulations will be too expensive for lower-income people. The cost of land, materials, labor, and financing has reached the point that the majority of American families cannot afford new housing without the aid of some form of subsidy. The problem is particularly acute for lower-income families seeking housing in the suburbs.

In January, 1973, the administration imposed a moratorium on all of the federally subsidized housing programs which were then in existence. The subsidies which had facilitated a record rate of construction of housing for low and moderate-income people since the programs were initiated in 1968 were suspended and construction under these programs virtually came to a halt. It was not until the Housing and Community Development Act of 1974 was passed that the potential was renewed for providing a significant amount of housing in the suburbs for people in need of subsidies.

The subsidized housing program enacted in 1974 consolidated many of the pre-existing programs. It provides rental subsidies for low and moderate-income people in new, existing, or rehabilitated housing. The housing can be provided by public agencies, private profit or nonprofit developers or landlords of existing rental units. Although suburbs retain a voice in determining where this housing is to be located, they do not have the absolute veto which existed under some of the earlier subsidized housing programs.

5. Conclusion: The Rocky Road to Suburbia. There is a long history of exclusion of the poor and the minorities from the suburbs of this country. The methods of exclusion have changed, but racial and economic segregation persist. In the last decade, diverse methods have been developed by government and voluntary organizations to lower the barriers and increase the opportunity for lower-income people and minorities to move into suburban communities. Litigation, legislation, and political and planning strategies have all played a significant role in this effort and will continue to do so in the future.

Future strategies for increasing the access of lower-income people and minorities to the suburbs are likely to include provision of public subsidies, efforts to bring about "inclusionary" land use measures by suburban communities, continued enforcement of local, state and federal fair housing and related laws, and affirmative programs to inform and counsel minority families with regard to the housing opportunities open to them in the suburbs.

In short, although progress has been made, the road to the suburbs is still not a smooth one for low-income people and minorities. It is a very long road, with pitfalls and detours throughout the route. The trip is far from being finished. The greater part of the task remains ahead.

Notes

1. Report of the National Advisory Commission on Civil Disorders (Washington, D.C.: 1969), pp. 407–408.
2. U.S. Bureau of the Census, "United States Summary, Final Report, General Demographic Trends for Metropolitan Areas, 1960 to 1970," PHC (2)-1, pp. 4–5.
3. United States Commission on Civil Rights, *Equal Opportunity in Suburbia* (1974), p. 4.
4. "Barriers to Minority Suburban Access," Statement by George H. Brown, Director, Bureau of the Census, U.S. Department of Commerce, *Hearings of the United States Commission on Civil Rights* (Washington, D.C., Government Printing Office, 1971), pp. 523–65.
5. Shelley v. Kraemer, 334 U.S. 1 (1948).
6. Buchanan v. Warley, 245 U.S. 60 (1917).
7. Reitman v. Mulkey, 387 U.S. 369 (1967).
8. Title VIII, Civil Rights Act of 1968, 42 U.S.C. §3608 (a) et. seq.
9. Jones v. Mayer, 392 U.S. 409 (1968).
10. 42 U.S.C. § 3608 (d) (5).
11. 37 Fed. Reg. 2 (January 5, 1972).
12. Leonard Rubinowitz, Joel Greenfield, and Jay Harris, *Affirmative Marketing of Federally Assisted Housing: Implementation in the Chicago Metropolitan Area* (Evanston: Center for Urban Affairs, Northwestern University, 1975).
13. Herbert M. Franklin, David Falk, and Arthur J. Levin, *In-Zoning, A Guide for Policy-Makers on Inclusionary Land Use Programs* (Washington, D.C.: The Potomac Institute, Inc., 1975), p. 1.
14. See Leonard S. Rubinowitz, *Low-Income Housing: Suburban Strategies* (Cambridge: Ballinger Publishing Company, 1974), Richard F. Babcock and Fred P. Bosselman, *Exclusionary Zoning, Land Use Regulation and Housing in the 1970's* (New York: Praeger Publishers, 1973),

Mary Brooks, *Lower-Income Housing: The Planners' Response* (Chicago: American Society of Planning Officials-Planning Advisory Service, 1972), Herbert M. Franklin, David Falk, and Arthur J. Levin, op. cit.
15. Fairfax County, Va., Code § 30-2.2.2(2)(a); Montgomery County, Md., Code, Chap. 25A, "Housing, Moderately Priced".
16. Board of Supervisors of Fairfax County v. De-Groff Enterprises, 214 Va. 235(1973).
17. Statement by Ida Garrott, *Hearings of the United States Commission on Civil Rights* (Washington, D.C.: Government Printing Office, 1971), p. 73.
18. Franklin, *op. cit.*, p. 166.
19. 40 B. Mass. Gen. Laws Ann. §§ 20–23.
20. 40 U.S.C. § 461(a) (1970).
21. Letter from Edward M. Levin, Jr., Acting Assistant Regional Administrator for Metropolitan Planning and Development, Chicago Regional Office of HUD, to George Berteau, Chairman, Southeastern Wisconsin Regional Planning Commission, March 31, 1971.
22. I. Sikorsky, "A-95: Deterrent to Discriminatory Zoning," *Civil Rights Digest* (August 1972), p. 19.
23. This document, dated July 7, 1971, reached the press without public announcement by the Equal Employment Opportunity Commission.
24. Southern Burlington N.A.A.C.P. v. Township of Mount Laurel, —— N.J. —— (1975).
25. Gautreaux v. Chicago Housing Authority, 296 F. Supp. 907 (N.D. Ill. 1969).
26. Appeal of Girsh, 437 Pa. 237, 263 A. 2d 395 (1970).
27. Leonard S. Rubinowitz, *Low-Income Housing: Suburban Strategies* (Cambrige: Ballinger Publishing Company, 1974), pp. 149–152.
28. James v. Valtierra, 402 U.S. 137 (1971).
29. Village of Belle Terre v. Boraas, 42 U.S.L.W 4475 (U.S. April 1, 1974).
30. Warth v. Seldin, —— U.S. —— (1975).
31. H.B. 709, State of Illinois (1973); Bell v. Automobile Club of Michigan, cited in Potomac Institute Memorandum 73-1 (January 2, 1973), p. 4.
32. Brookhaven Housing Coalition, et. al. v. Robert L. Kunzig, Administrator, General Services Administration, Civil No. 71-C-1001 (E.D.N.Y., April 19, 1972).

ANDREW GORDON · MALCOLM BUSH · JUDITH WITTNER

Experiences and Perspectives on University-Community Relations

Introduction

Studies of contemporary problems, of public and private bureaucracies, of social services, or of the poor have been traditional for academicians; their approach to this research, however, has not been impartial. For example, scholarly research on corporations has often been at the request of the organization, perhaps for a consultant's fee. Studies of urban problems are frequently undertaken for government agencies. The poor, or social service recipients, or delinquents, have been scrutinized for purely theoretical reasons, or for the benefit of a social agency which mediates academic contact with program recipients. Findings which imply action on political consequences usually have been relegated to scholarly journals, where they are read by a limited, elitist audience.

The "ivory tower" nature of academic pursuits is largely overemphasized. University personnel have a well-documented history of involvement in applied research, but the application has usually served the interests of the powerful. The distinction is not in the nature of the research: academicians have cooperated fully in advancing the machinery of war, as well as the efficiency of factory work. These efforts have been justified on the grounds of their potential theoretical impact, or perhaps undertaken with minimal academic justification. Academic research

is contracted, paid for, and delivered to identifiable clientele.

The Center for Urban Affairs at Northwestern University is struggling to modify the predominating imbalance which normally exists in extra-university research relationships. Rather than implementing research which is designed to inform our own methods and theories, and which gives little priority to the immediate relevance of the outcome to respondents, due consideration is given to the inclusion of information which is expected to benefit the traditional subjects of social science.

We have, in effect, attempted to implement a stance of *mutuality*, within which, for example, government service recipients are treated as co-investigators. The research undertaken contains a mix, both theoretical and pragmatic in appeal. These attempts have involved new priorities and strategies, and have thrown us into relationships with professional and nonprofessional personnel outside the university, relationships for which we were unprepared.

We believe that reflective thought and experience can lead to the development of skills which will facilitate research which is socially useful as well as intellectually enlightening. The intent of this paper is to explore some areas of difficulty that we have encountered in our serious attempt to implement this revised academic stance, and to suggest some new directions for the future.

An outline of representative studies conducted through the Center will provide a framework for the observations which follow. These studies illustrate the range of experiences in which the Center has been involved, and will be referred to throughout the rest of the paper.

This article was written for *Cities in Change*, edited by John Walton and Donald Carns (2nd edition; Allyn and Bacon, 1976) and is a revision and update of an article from the first edition.

Contract Buying

In the late 1960's the Contract Buyer's League (CBL) was established in Chicago to identify, inform, and serve black persons who had purchased homes on contract. Contract buying, common throughout the Midwest, is more costly and more hazardous than mortgage buying. A contract buyer normally needs only a small down payment, but builds no equity in his home until it is fully paid for—often thirty years or longer—or until the contract is converted to a mortgage.

On behalf of thousands of blacks for whom it was argued that the racially discriminatory character of the housing market forced "unconscionable" contract arrangements, a class suit was initiated in federal court, with contract sellers, savings and loan associations, and federal housing agencies as defendants. The plaintiffs include but are not limited to, the members of the Contract Buyers League. Legal services on behalf of the plaintiffs, who otherwise could not afford adequate representation, have been donated by a prestigious Chicago firm. The lawyer-client relationship has provided a unique experience for the lawyers: many of the plaintiffs have withheld contract payments or resisted eviction against the advice of counsel. The definition of the plaintiff class ensures the inclusion of contract buyers who may never have heard of the case. The extent and nature of the data exceed the normal experience of law firms.

Academicians have been involved in the collection and analysis of the data, the design and rationale of a sample of the universe of buyers contracts, and the design and administration of a questionnaire for securing legally valid data from the plaintiff sample. In addition, personnel at the Center have explored solutions to the methodological and theoretical difficulties imposed by real-world constraints (e.g., selectively missing data, unreachable contract buyers) on the initial sample.

We were involved for nearly two years. During that time we worked with the community organization, its leadership, and the voluntary legal staff. Out-of-court settlements by the defendant-sellers already have resulted in a $2 million saving to contract buyers. But the cases are still entangled in federal courts, and the outcome is therefore yet to be determined.

Community Self-Determination

The Kenwood-Oakland Community Organization (KOCO), located in a particularly blighted and ignored area of Chicago, received a five-year grant for business and social development. The Community Renewal Society (CRS), a church-related Chicago organization, was to encourage business, foundations, and religious institutions to invest unrestricted funds in an effort to demonstrate that strict community self-determination could be efficacious. The corporate donors were being asked to give their funds under at least two unusual conditions. First, they were to invest in a high-risk venture whose payoff would not be easily measurable. Second, it was said that they were to have limited control over the use of the funds.

The relations between the CRS and KOCO were formalized in a covenant of agreement. Through its component agencies KOCO was to employ the guaranteed funds to develop housing, business and social services in a neighborhood with powerful youth nations, and with few established businesses and lacking critical public services.

The covenant between KOCO and the CRS obligated the parties to an independent evaluation which would identify the strengths and weaknesses of the organization's efforts. The evaluation was to be used for possible modification of the organization and for the benefit of future organization efforts elsewhere. A small staff at the Center attempted to implement that evaluation. Our best attempts were met with difficulties for which we were unprepared. Some of these problems are explored in this paper.

Access to Public Information

Throughout the nation there are statutes which outline the public right to information held by public agencies. The laws often liberally interpret the citizen's right to know. We have completed a large-scale project to explore in some detail the critical determinants of one's access to public information. In the process of implementing our research, we encountered striking and often unexpected resistance from public information sources, and other investigators have reported similar problems. By means of field experimental design and subsequent observation we have ascertained some of the variables which affect the actual availability of public information, including the nature and reputation of the inquirer, the nature of the source-agency from whom it is requested, the labor necessary to extract, and more generally, the anticipated impact of release on the source-agency (Gordon, Divorski, Gordon, & Heinz, 1973).

Social Service Delivery

Woodlawn Service Program. One of the initial projects of the Illinois Institute for Social Policy under Republican governor Richard Olgivie was the Woodlawn Service Program (WSP). The governor's office guaranteed WSP administrative control over state social services in Woodlawn, a predominantly black neighborhood near the University of Chicago. The task of the program was to design and administer a comprehensive, integrated program for the delivery of state social services, a delivery responsive to the needs of the community and sufficiently evaluated so that successful strategies could be implemented statewide.

We at the Center served in an advisory capacity to the administrators, suggesting how, with minimal embarrassment to program recipients, one might gauge community needs and thereby begin to provide a service package which was acceptable to the community and capable of being evaluated. Our task was not to advise on the content of the program, but merely on the forms of data collection which would yield comprehensive and useful information.

There has been a staffing turnover at the IISP, and our advisory capacity has been terminated, due largely to difficulties of the kind which are explored in this paper. We have attempted to broaden our experience in this area, and have continued to develop models for the systematic inclusion of data from recipients of agency services (Gordon and Campbell, 1971; Campbell, 1973).

Deinstitutionalization

In recent years there has been a trend toward the elimination of large residential institutions for the care and treatment of mental patients, the aged, the chronically ill, prisoners, and neglected, dependent and delinquent minors. Since 1973, Center staff have had the opportunity to study this process at first hand through their involvement with the program of deinstitutionalization of dependent and neglected children in the State of Illinois. When the Democratic Governor Daniel Walker appointed Jerome Miller, the former Director of the Dept. of Youth Services in Massachusetts who was responsible for closing juvenile correctional institutions in that state, to be director of the Illinois Dept. of Children and Family Services, the specific mandate was to develop and implement a similar program for dependent and neglected children. Miller, who in Massachusetts had worked closely with Harvard's Center for Criminal Justice, approached the CUA staff with a request for assistance in developing innovative information systems for DCFS, including new case planning forms which would make institutional placement of children more difficult and would assure that child and family perspectives on their problems were the central focus of all service and placement decisions.

In large part because of this experience in the early stages of the deinstitutionalization process, and because our cooperation with DCFS had assured us easy access at all levels of departmental operations, the Center was selected by the Office of Child Development, United States Department of Health, Education and Welfare, to conduct a study of alternative placements for dependent and neglected children. The purpose of this research was to develop guidelines for deinstitutionalization which could be used in states where such programs were under consideration.

Shortly after the Center had begun the OCD study, political events took an unexpected turn. Child care agency administrators had reacted strongly to the deinstitutionalization efforts of the Dept. and to its director, calling for his resignation in legislative hearings, public meetings, before the press, and in appeals to the governor. This activity culminated in the summer of 1974 with the appointment of a Director of DCFS less identified with the policy of eliminating institutions for children. As a result, the Department no longer projects an explicit anti-institutional bias, although there are still strong pressures on workers to keep children in their own homes, or in homelike settings.

In spite of the vagaries of the political situation, the Center has been able to continue research under the terms of the OCD grant. This is in part because the range of alternative placements for state-supported children has remained largely unchanged. More important, however, is the fact that we have been able to retain the original central focus of our research: interviews with the clients themselves (children and their families) in order to determine their opinions about their own placement experiences and to develop, if possible, strategies of effective client participation in future placement decisions.

Delinquency Intervention

One of Director Miller's attempts to restructure services to juveniles in Illinois drew directly on his experience with juvenile justice in Massachusetts. Within the Department of Children and Family Services he set up a demonstration project for alternatives to incarceration for juveniles. This project, called the Unified Delinquency Intervention Services (UDIS), was entrusted to Paul DeMuro, an aide of Miller's in Massachusetts with a lively commitment to juvenile justice reforms. The UDIS model departs significantly from most in its two-tiered approach: UDIS personnel are explicitly *case managers* rather than direct service workers. Services for juveniles who would, in theory, otherwise be incarcerated in penal institutions are purchased from long standing and newly established alternatives, often community based, which span the spectrum from minimal advocacy intervention to relatively closed residential settings, and include foster homes, wilderness programs, and family counseling, among many others. The responsibility of the case manager is actively to track and advocate for every case, rather than only for those clients whose crises are obvious, and to certify that service agencies are accountable to service delivery, deadlines, so on. This explicit responsibility for up-to-date monitoring required an information system advanced beyond that available in DCFS. Encouraged by our efforts with DCFS, DeMuro contracted with the Center for Urban Affairs to create and experiment with an information system which would provide up-to-date background, tracking and placement data on UDIS youth and service providers. DeMuro regarded both the reality and the appearance of a accountability as an important contrast to most programs which provide innovative services. An important recipient of the data is a Juvenile Justice Policy Board of the Illinois directors of relevant departments (Corrections, Children and Family Services, etc.) to whom an accounting is made at monthly meetings. Working with the multiple constituenties of UDIS, including the staff, clients, policy board, and service providers, has been frustrating, inspiring, and always illuminating.

Minority Business

The Opportunity Funding Corporation (OFC) is a private agency largely funded by the Office of Economic Opportunity (OEO). The task of the OFC is to leverage investment in, and support for, minority businessmen. They are attempting to implement a range of programs, including deposit guarantees and interest subsidies to minority banks, and credit support for minority contractors.

Before programs will be approved for funding it must be demonstrated that they can be evaluated to OEO's satisfaction. The OFC is primarily concerned with success as a demonstration program, but also wishes to influence the infusion of funds into poverty-area businesses. Answerable formally or informally to many groups, OFC is immeshed in an intricate web of interested parties. A team from Northwestern consulted in the designing of evaluations of these programs for OFC.

Public School Discrimination

The Center undertook an investigation of the distribution of staffing expenditures by race and class in the Chicago Public Schools, with the expectation that the funding allocations might discriminate against predominately black schools. Most of the data were readily available in public documents, and the Chicago Board of Education cooperated when asked. The data were consistent with expectations. From one point of view, the bulk of the discrepancy could be explained by the voluntary placement of senior faculty

ulty in predominately white schools, and with respect to that analysis, the onus falls on the teachers' union rather than on the Board of Education. Careful revision in expenditures was proposed by the Board of Education soon after the publication of these data. This revision balances the allocations as measured by our indices while, in the opinion of many, preserving the fundamental inequities in the schools. Center staff are continuing to monitor adjustments in the allocation of monies (Berk, Mack, and McKnight, 1971).

The Law-Enforcement Study Group

The Law Enforcement Study Group (LESG) is a broadly sponsored organization which is attempting to determine whether public officials are administering the criminal law on a nondiscriminatory basis. Most of their research is conducted through the Center of Urban Affairs. These studies have involved us in a broad range of experiences, some of which are briefly described below.

Court Reform

There had developed in Evanston, Illinois, a persistent but undocumented belief that the local court bonding practices and availability of counsel were unfair. A mayor's committee was established in response to the death in jail of a young Evanston citizen. For that committee, a team of lawyers and social scientist associated with the Center undertook a systematic analysis, largely based on readily available court and legal records, of counsel and bonding practices in the Evanston courts in 1970. The report and committee recommendations (Mercer, Gordon, and Fahey, 1971), largely critical of present practices, were submitted to the mayor, who expressed great enthusiasm for the findings and recommendations. Some proposals, such as ticketing for misdemeanors, have been implemented. Others, including far-reaching court reforms, are under consideration by City Council committees.

Other LESG reports which also have sparked controversy include an investigation of the Chicago coroner's office which suggests that the office merely ratifies police judgments about the nature and cause of deaths; and a report on the juvenile court which illustrates local anachronisms in the treatment of juveniles as adult offenders. All these studies have been undertaken largely with publically available data, and each has been widely discussed.

The Center staff is regularly contacted by established or nascent community organizations who, because it has been required of them or because they wish to know, are seeking advice and support for surrveys of the needs and interest of persons in the Chicago area.

The research briefly outlined above is a sampling of the studies undertaken through the Center for Urban Affairs. They are a varied lot, and form the experiential basis for the discussion which follows. This is a preliminary statement, and reflects our belief that a thorough airing of these issues may benefit others who are attempting to implement a revised university-community relationship. The details of these studies and others are available in papers issued through the Center.

The following discussion is organized around four major themes, though the dividing lines between them are nebulous. First, we shall briefly discuss some reasons why the academic community might advantageously accept these new strategies. Next, we shall focus on issues regarding access to the community organizations with whom we attempt to work. Then, we shall explore ways in which findings are distributed, internally and externally. In a brief summary, we attempt to suggest possible revisions through which these relationships might be more easily facilitated.

A. Within the University

There are many sound reasons why academicians, particularly academic social scientists, should welcome a new stance with regard to what constitutes appropriate research. These reasons include: theoretical and methodological concerns. Theory building should integrate many diverse viewpoints, while traditional procedures have represented community opinions only through biased intermediaries. Particularistic methodologies should give way to others which recognize inherent biases and attempt to overcome them through a variety of approaches (e.g., the triangulation of deliberately diverse measures [Campbell and Fiske, 1959]). Our support for new directions for academic research should also be motivated by pragmatic concerns. Organized community interests actively shun research which does not involve some benefit to them. Students rebel at an uninvolved or self-serving social science in an era of pressing social concerns. Finally, there is the concern for democratic principles. The systematic exclusion or misrepresentation of legitimate interests in a society which supports academic pursuits is inconsistent with genuine democracy. As institutions of a free society, universities, too, should strive to balance these interests.

Methodological issues. A major objection to academic research on social problems has been the lack of methodological sophistication (Evans, 1969). There is some validity to this point of view, though much criticism of the imprecision of field-implemented research may come from an inflated notion of the precision of "laboratory" or "pure" academic research. Whenever a concept or theory is translated into a measurable index, respondent confusion about the meaning of a question, deliberate fabrication, equipment error, the complexity of the information borne by physiological channels, the trivializing of a complex concept with a simple index-all of these and more plague the laboratory or armchair theorist; the same is true in the field.

Recent literature reflects attempts to refine measurement and conceptualization, and emphasizes that no single measure will ever suffice and that global measures are often uninterpretable. This recognition has prompted the deliberate inclusion of multiple measures, each imperfect and misleading. The best measures are chosen to minimize correlated error, in order to triangulate on the concept of interest.

Just as laboratory work suffers from inexactness, so do field studies; they add some errors and eliminate others. For example, field settings are realistic where the laboratory is not. The solutions to the methodological and theoretical problems which originate in laboratories are of certain principal types, but the exact solutions are idiosyncratic. The same is true in nonlaboratory research, or in the analysis of data generated for purposes other than research.

The field implementation of rigorous research is difficult and often frustrating. Since studies of the nature discussed here are likely to have important policy implications, it is critical that they be conducted with particular care. Grievous errors can be committed in even the most expensive field research. Despite the heavy investment in the well-documented Ohio-Westinghouse evaluation of Headstart (Williams and Evans, 1969), for example, it has been persuasively demonstrated that the "controls" for Headstart recipients were predestined to achieve better than the Headstart pupils and therefore to underestimate the success of the program (Campbell and Erlebacher, 1970). No single control would have sufficed, and precision could only be approached with a more complex design. The design chosen, however, guaranteed seriously misleading results which had the effect of reflecting erroneously and disadvantageously on Headstart.

Another widely publicized study of an entirely different kind is Heussenstamm's demonstration of police harrassment of students whose cars bore Black Panther bumper stickers (Heussenstamm, 1970). Fifteen students who had not had any traffic violations during the preceding twelve months attached Black Panther bumper stickers to their cars. Within seventeen days they had received a total of thirty-three traffic violations and at least $500 in fines. The shock value of the results is not disputed, but there are some unfortunate methodological difficulties which render the data difficult to interpret, and certainly weaken its efficacy for legal action. For example, the students knew when their cars bore the stickers, and had they wished, they could have deliberately provoked the police. Heussenstamm acknowledges that the study was only intended as a pilot, but has had trouble getting funds for replication.

It appears to us that social science studies of controversial issues must be as rigorous as possible. Our response to a request to advise on a tighter demonstration of this differential treatment had difficulties of its own (Gordon and Myers, 1970). The original study was cheap; the more precise replication is expensive, for example. In addition, we faced the unresolved legal issue of whether the project involved entrapment of the police. (See Divorski, Gordon, and Heinz, 1973, for a commentary on this issue. We abandoned our design when we were convinced that experimental participants wer potentially in mortal danger, so deep was the animosity between the police and the Black Panthers. We are continuing to investigate alternative designs, however, because of legal assurance that the documentation of alleged harrassment would be a valuable contribution.

Many field studies in applied social research have encountered important methodological problems. It would be foolish to expect rigorous field work without the experience of failure. We need careful documentation of those experiences and serious attempts to reflect on and learn from the failures.

Achieving clear results. The clarity achievable in the laboratory manipulation of variables, imprecise as it is, is intellectually satisfying, and this clarity provides a model for which to strive in nonlaboratory, field experimental or quasi-experimental situations. But is also often true that clarity is achieved at great expense. The artificial simplicity of controlled manipulation may skirt the complex interactions which bear the true explanation of an effect. Further, the unreality imposed in the laboratory may more severely affect behavior than the intrusion of a social scientist in a field setting, where the researcher is relatively unimportant (Becker, 1970).

In their search for precision, researchers have too long shunned situations where precision is more difficult and have thereby foreclosed efforts to bring precision to the more realistic field setting. Because they are slow to consider an hypothesis validated, academicians often refuse to commit themselves to the validity of field findings. Lawyers, politicians, and community leaders who are not so protective of scientific pretension demand a right to know, now, and the scientist often cannot respond. Time is frequently a critical factor for the community organization that may be trying to fulfill a pressing need, or for the government agency responding to a legislative deadline. The academic demand for time to tool up before researchers feel fully prepared to engage in research; the academic rhythm which makes university researchers available in some seasons but not in others; and the demand for time to consider all aspects of research findings may considerably erode the potential usefulness of academicians. Academicians need a revised procedure which either allows a quicker, if attenuated faith, in

research findings, or a willingness to proceed along a course of action which may be subject to a revised evaluation when firmer results become available. The community organization leader and the politician must respond to the immediate needs or demands of the community, or of the funding agency, or of corporate donors. Organization leaders or the political sponsors of a program want evaluations to praise chosen procedures and to avoid any focus on failures—a situation that poses many dilemmas for the committed social scientist.

Political naivete. The credential prerequisite to a university appointment, and the "other worldliness" which is normally necessary to gain that credential, assures that relatively little political savvy will creep into academe. The rarefied nature of academic theory and empirical research have been justified by the need to guarantee precision of measurement and analysis. But these prerequisites, too, have buffered academicians from political realities, and have had the consequence of squelching serious efforts to develop inclusive theoretical and methodological schemes. Recently, for example, methodologies have been available for credible evaluative research, but we lack the skills and understanding to implement them. To a large extent our design attempts flounder because they still make demands exceeding real-world realities. Clients, community or governmental, openly refuse to cooperate, or they conceal data. Critical methodological suggestions, acknowledged as such, are never operationalized. Staff members with direct responsibility for research are swamped by "more pressing" tasks. And so it goes.

Naivete is best modified by experience, and the appropriate experiences frequently cannot be brought to the campus. Some have suggested systematic placement of academicians in government agencies for real-world exposure (Cowhig, 1971). We have developed a voucher system through which community organizations can purchase university services of their own choosing, a strategy designed to ensure consideration of the mutual needs of both parties (Epperson, 1971). This will receive further consideration later in this paper.

Students and research. Adjustments in research and dissemination of results may prove also to be effective remedies for some of the student dissent and disenchantment with academia. Students are justifiably concerned about their lack of a voice in university affairs; if they shared with faculty the opportunity to submit minority reports, and if there were a fuller disclosure of research decisions, much of this criticism would be answered. Students issue demands for relevance, and scholars mistake their unease for laziness of thought or action, assuming that students are inventing excuses for inactivity. Some of this is surely the case; some students are so fully disenchanted that total escapism can overtake them. Professors who modify their teaching should be warned by those students who are soon disillusioned with classes which emphasize relevance at the expense of scientific merit—a panacea sought by some teachers. But honest intellectual pursuit which at the same time explores pressing social issues, with the same academic intensity which is associated with "purer" stuff, kindles interest and energy which many of us have been encouraged to witness returning to the campuses. Students are the clients of academics, and are an important party in the relationship between the university and the community. It has been the Center's experience that students involved in community research often find it to be one of the most valuable experiences of their university careers. The combination of research activities which take them into the day to day life of the community and which have a day to day relevance, and the examination of those activities by the standards of inquiry they have been taught, prove a fruitful mix.

The Center, which gained from the students involvement in the deinstitutionalization project, found that student interviewers of children and their parents displayed a persistence, enthusiasm and sensitivity which elicited in the vast majority of cases a warm and open response. We doubt whether the interviewing staff of a large opinion testing organization would have produced as much valuable data with a clientele that was difficult to find, hostile to official intervention, and suspicious of the consequences of research done supposedly on their behalf.

The one disadvantage of student involvement sometimes came where students and professional child care workers met. Initially in some cases, and persistently in others, some of the professionals resisted the entire research on the grounds that the day to day researchers were students without qualifications, skills or experience. Our feeling was that this response sometimes occurred where the professionals were, students apart, opposed to the direction the research was taking or were suffering from a dose of evaluation apprehension.

B. Access

Trust. Outsiders are viewed with alarm in many of the governmental and community organizations which interest us. Academicians are hardly immune from this lack of trust. Resources are often limited, and any new commitment, especially one with a distant payoff, is viewed as a potential drain on those resources. Universities, often located in or near ghettos, have frequently advanced their own interests at the expense of the community. The universities in Woodlawn (Chicago) and in Morningside Heights (New York), for example, have been considered by some to be among the most powerful and amoral community adversaries.

Specific experience with university researchers has not always mollified this portrait, even when there has been academic interaction with community organizations, social services recipients, and the poor. Academicians have frequently entered the community, asked embarrassing questions, and promised some vague and future benefit from the research. Frequently these research efforts provide no immediate payoff for the host organization, and often these projects are undertaken at the expense of short-range community goals. Epperson and Detzel (1971) systematically surveyed the experience of university personnel with urban clients. Among those professionals who acknowledged any involvement with the community, interviews revealed that the vast majority of their contacts had been at the behest of and to the advantage of an intermediary, government or private agency, and not with regard to priorities determined by the community. Of the very few academicians who even attempted direct communication with the community, all considered their ventures to be failures, and the difficulties often included the denial of client trust and cooperation.

In the climate of apprehension, which frequently accompanies academic-community cooperative efforts, unwelcome turns of events may bear useful side effects. In the case of contract buying, for example, the lawyers decided that questions which could not be strongly argued as essential to the court case would have to be dropped. Items about the buyer's attitudes, which represented a major theoretical benefit from our cooperation, were eliminated. A major component of the data from an academic perspective was therefore eviscerated, though important methodological issues remained. Our relationship to the organization was probably strengthened, however, for our continuing cooperation balanced the nagging suspicion that our efforts were only self-serving.

Because of the historical university stance, the academician is seriously mistrusted by the street researcher. When the academician attempts to cooperate in ameliorative efforts, he frequently becomes the least protected representative of establishment interest. A large measure of his task may be to modify that opinion, and to learn its subtle truth.

Overpromise or inerpreted overpromise. The heady enthusiasm which carries the day when real-world research is undertaken sometimes gives way to gloom and disillusion when the results are in. There are several reasons why these occur. One of the most frequently encountered reasons is the lack of understanding about how much careful work is involved in creditable field research. Often the research team is not prepared for the difficulties which arise in persuading the organization to remain accountable to the researchers. For numerous reasons, a researcher who has involved himself in cooperative research may feel certain that appropriate methodological advice will produce data which will serve the organizations' purposes. However, once the data collection is under way it may become clear that problems encountered in the process of data collection are formidable, perhaps insurmountable in the immediate instance, and that as a result the data are no longer as clear or supportive as he envisioned they would be. There even may be deliberate deceit on one side or the other where, for example, the researcher has promised supportive results in order to gain access, or where the community organizer has promised access in order to gain the cover, legitimacy, and publicity which the cooperation with a university normally provides.

Center personnel have sometimes found that once a research team has demonstrated faith in the organization's work by accepting a cooperative role, the organization will expect the researchers to operate as committed advocates, rather than as researchers. The organization may expect the research team, for example, to participate in the irregular manipulation or misleading presentation of data. Refusal to do so may be regarded as betrayal.

Often, in large part because of their lack of experience, researchers expect that scrupulous research will be far more advantageous to the organization than it actually is. Many organizations contend with such huge difficulties, and the problems they intend to ameliorate are so vast, that their relatively trivial tactics and political pressures stand no chance of making major inroads. The involvement of academicians with community organizations in the theory or methodology of an intervention has often led to disappointment on all sides, either because the potential political thrust has been misinterpreted or because their enthusiasm led researchers to promise more than they could deliver.

Given the present state of the art of evaluation, for example, it is usually guaranteed that when researchers seem to receive full evaluative cooperation, one of two things is happening: (1) crucial and potentially damaging data are being subverted; or (2) the cooperative agency knows very well in advance what the proper analysis of their data will reveal, and want to ensure credibility by having the analysis done by an independent source. In the latter case, the data may be intended for partisan political source. In the latter case, the data may be intended for partisan political purposes, with which the researcher may or may not have sympathy. When the data for a critical examination of the Evanston courts were made readily available by the courtroom officers, it was because they recognized the dissolution of the court system and felt that only the publicity which would accompany an analysis would produce the changes they desired (Mercer, Gordon, and Fahey, 1971). When the Chicago Board of Education was fully cooperative with a study which demonstrated a racial disparity in school expenditures (Berk, Mack, and McKnight, 1971), they knew that the differential was accounted for by the requested placement of senior teachers in white neighborhoods. The Board, too, suffered from the union-supported seniority privileges, and was seeking the publicity which would accompany the disclosure of these data.

Even when the community groups are prepared to let the results of the research suggest what they may, the research may still be blinkered for another reason. When academicians are invited to participate in the research at its inception the sponsoring agency will have defined the problem they want investigated. Very often there will be a professional literature and accepted sense about the nature of the problem and the proper terms within which the debate should be conducted. If the academician is to serve the interests of the agency's clients as well as those of the agency, for example, he should not assume consensus between the agency and the client on the nature of the "problem" to be solved. The choice of criteria to measure the success of a program or an agency's work is very often a political decision, not one wholly determined by the logic of the situation. The OCD project illuminates the problem. Child care professionals who write about child care (practitioners sometimes have different views) suggest that the emotional health of a child removed from home is the key problem and that behind all practical problems of child care and family life lie lurking a range of psychoses. Therefore, they ask for emotional health indicators as measures of success. Politicians, in contrast, are concerned about the relationship between broken homes and crime, delinquency and the acquistion of employment skills. Meanwhile the client in the system, the child removed from his home, may be most concerned that he has a place to live in which he feels reasonably comfortable and that he knows at least one person whom he trusts and who is sympathetic and understanding about *his* concerns. Quite possibly the client's criteria are critical determinants of how his life turns out. The academicians must be aware of the differences between these criteria and should realize that the decision to choose one set over another is also a decision to align the research primarily with the interests and concerns of the group whose criteria they have chosen to adopt. There is another related problem with independent measures. In child care the debate about treatment has traditionally been one contrasting institutionalized care *versus* foster care. More recently the debate has been extended to include those two options plus ways of serving children in their own homes.

But the two traditional options were developed for political and economic reasons in the mid-nineteenth century before the notions of therapy developed. The attachment of therapeutic significance to both seems more in the nature of a modern justification for them than a decision that given any options, they are the best in the light of present knowledge. In these circumstances the academicians should ask whether the terms in which the debate has traditionally been conducted are the most enlightening. In the OCD research project we decided to add to our inquiry questions which would get at the issues of whether there are standards of good and appropriate caretaking for children which cut across types of placement for children—criteria which avoid the traditional assumptions but what may nevertheless turn out to be the most important variables.

Another issue is too infrequently considered. Child care commentaries often recommend seemingly minor palliatives for major problems. Academicians should ask themselves whether the treatment whose effect is to be examined is in the light of past research and informed common sense, trivial and not likely to affect the outcome. It may be a waste of everyone's time for example to spend much energy investigating the question of whether an hour's therapy a week can on its own solve major economic, urban, familial and personal problems.

Even when the treatments are major, as for example the massive infusion of money into programs or direct aid, one should not necessarily measure the success of that infusion only against measurable changes in the client's life. It may be—to note Christopher Jenck's point (Jencks, 1972)—that even though differences in the measurable material standards of schools do not explain a great deal of the differences in the students academic success, that the material standards are worth maintaining for their own sake; that is, that since a student spends so much of his life in school it is better that the walls be painted, the broken windows be mended and the library be full of books than that the reverse be true even if we cannot demonstrate the connection between those factors and first academic success and then later earning ability.

There is another, more radical criticism which those who advocate restructured university-community relations must recognize. However these modified strategies are implemented, the interaction is to serve the public good through thorough and interpretable disclosure of information. The premise underlying these projects is that genuine improvement will accompany careful research and the accumulation of rigorous data. But from one point of view, all these tactics are not "ameliorative", but *"merely ameliorative"* at best, for they are rooted in a mistaken analysis. From this perspective, genuine structural change through such efforts is impossible, for the preservation of the poor and disenfranchised is too functional for the un-poor, both the slightly better off and the truly rich (Gans, 1971). It is, by this analysis, misleading to offer even high-powered services to organizations so poorly placed that their efforts are futile. From this point of view, clients of public service agencies are ultimately impotent with or without minor efforts on their behalf, and attempts to include the impoverished in the decision-making process will never receive more than lip service. By this analysis, even the most well intentioned surveys of need, or improved information systems or sound evaluations ultimately serve to forestall effective action, and often further exacerbate existing disparities of power. The clients of systems and other persons with whom we speak of cooperating are so impotent or trivially financed compared to others in the systems we seek to alter that rigorous methods can only more fully document failure, destroy illusions, and aggravate frustrations. Though this brief statement may caricature this critical perspective, it implies a resistance to our research efforts which parallels many of our actual experiences. It is a perspective which we must keep in mind, and which we will comment on again later in this paper.

C. Implementation

Overcommitment. Because the skills which are critical to the success of competent research are diverse, and because there are relatively few people engaged in this kind of work, field- and community-oriented academicians find themselves spread thin. They are expected to represent a wide variety of interests and skills, rather than to reflect the far narrower abilities and training that they possess. The pressure to comment and advise on everything academic absorbs time and energy which, if fully dedicated

to the skills they actually can bring to a problem area, might result in more meaningful programs. Researchers are often asked, essentially, to pretend or to develop renaissance skills. Succumbing to these pressures can instead lead to efforts which are shallow, corrupt, and useless.

We can predict dilettantism from those who try to master several skills, however critical those skills may be. Since we collectively lack some essential skills, particularly political ones, perhaps we should develop structural encouragements for specialists, whose expertise links established disciplines. An enlightened university hiring and recognition policy which incorporates the resources of nonacademicians who can provide necessary linkages with extra-university constituencies is an important step in this direction. This suggestion is developed later in this paper.

Process vs. outcome. There is a distinction frequently encountered in the literature on research—between studies of *process* (i.e., the various techniques and components of community or governmental action) and studies of *outcome* (i.e., the eventual results of such action). The distinction is often misleading, conceptually and empirically. Researchers are frequently called in after programs are fully developed, under the assumption that outcomes can be studied quite apart from process, and after data collection. Usually, however, it is no longer possible to recover the preprogram information against which change can be measured. The intuitive indices which sometimes exist are often too global to be useful, and there is insufficient knowledge about extra-organizational pressures or seasonal or secular trends to provide a context for interpreting whatever change may have occurred as a result of the program. The solutions to these difficulties are of the same genre whether the research focuses on the effects of specific program components, or attempts to illustrate and evaluate the efficacy of the overall program. The emphasis here has been on futile attempts to recoup errors resulting from belated attention to research requirements. But even where the data needs of researchers have been entertained from the onset, the research is often so low in program priority that it is eviscerated through resource allocation. The priorities of community organizations rarely emphasize theoretical payoff to academicians. To guarantee that their interests mesh with those of the community, university personnel may willingly accept reduced resources for research. In the short run this may be reasonable, even necessary, to ensure a continuing relationship. In the long run, it may be costly.

Organizational persistence. The pace and priorities of traditional scholarly work are disruptive of the routine activities of most extra-university organizations. Community organizations focus on local issues and, with few resources to spare, cooperate in the research effort, mostly out of a conviction that such cooperation will in the end serve their own purposes. The viability of a community organization is tied to the achievement of local victories, apparent or real, which support energy and enthusiasm. Human and financial resources must be directed toward the solution of immediate problems. As one community leader told us when we seemed to be imposing on his time, "We are not in the business of producing Ph.D.'s." Similarly, political agencies, hoping to influence governmental appropriation by demonstrated success, insist that researchers produce clear findings which will be persuasive in Congress, and sometimes force premature closure, or definitive analysis before the definitive data exist. If researchers can cooperate in these publicity efforts without prostituting themselves, for instance by presenting existing data in the most graphic, least obscure manner, the efforts should be made. If instead, the demand is for the falsification or selective elimination of data, then, at least, in the long-range interests of these efforts, such support must be denied.

Staff ineptitude. Trained and sensitive talent in community organizations is often so scarce that the talented quickly move to the top; those who have the time and responsibility for liaison with researchers are often underskilled for the task. In governmental agencies, researchers often deal with bureaucrats whose dedication or training is not sufficient to ensure effective cooperation. Evaluation research, for instance, has only recently become academically respectable. Persons hired for their background in this area may impose a research framework which is harmful rather than valuable to the organization. Academicians, on the other hand, may possess the technical skills to design an appropriate evaluation, but have neither the time nor the ties to the organization which are necessary to implement their plans. Their too-direct intervention may appear to be a lack of confidence in the skills of the organizational researchers, which may result in the loss of future cooperation.

Lack of client cooperation. Some of the strongest arguments which have been mounted against university involvement in political and extra-university affairs have involved the impracticality of securing the data this research demands. No matter how skillfully nonreactive techniques are utilized, much of the fundamental data must come from persons who have come to view the university as exploitative. As an example of how those prejudices can compromise research, consider the outspoken leader of the Kenwood-Oakland community organization who was arrested for murder and held for several months without trial and unavailable for comment. Just as surely as the organization knew he was innocent, they knew that on the basis of some unrevealed information he had been arrested and held, and they knew we were present, asking questions whose immediate purpose was unclear. It was **no** surprise to us that cooperation flagged, and that data which we considered critical to an even-handed process study were no longer available. After the leader had spent six months in jail, the judge threw out the state's case as completely without foundation, a bitter organization victory, but irretrievably late to recover our original research purposes.

Problems of comparability. Normally, an irreducible necessity for proper research is some basis for comparison. If, for example, an attempt at social amelioration is introduced, it is impossible appropriately to evaluate the effect of the program in most instances without comparative information from similarly situated others who are *not* recipients of the program. There are infrequent situations in which these comparisons are unnecessary, e.g., programs in which a massive program departs so drastically from previous policy that the effects are obvious. These occurrences are extremely rare.

Far more common is the initiation of a local and relatively meager program, in one or a limited number of locations. Limited resources

r reform guarantee that across-the-board re-
rms are unlikely. Necessarily limited pro-
ams should therefore be implemented in the
ost evaluable way, and this includes systematic
ocation so that nonrecipients approximate
ue controls (Campbell, 1969). Any control or
mparison group is necessarily inexact. In the
st designs there must be several control-
oups, each comprised of people who either re-
ive no amelioration or one that is vastly differ-
t (weaker, less diversified, etc.) from the one
out which the program planners were un-
ubtedly enthusiastic. In our child care re-
arch, where it was impossible and improper
randomly assign children to different types of
acement, we used four methods to gain com-
rative information. We selected a compari-
n group from among school children who lived
the same geographic areas as our sample but
no had never been in contact with the child
re agency, and a comparison group from chil-
en whose families had applied to the Depart-
ent for help but whom the Department had de-
led not to place. We also asked children who
d experienced multiple placements to make
mparisons across their own placements. Fi-
lly, we purposely selected children into our in-
tutional sample from institutions that were
d to represent the range from good to bad in-
tutions and which contained children who
nged from those said to have very few, if
y problems, to those said to have many. In
s way we hoped to capture a variety of opin-
ns about the range of experiences in the uni-
se our sample was supposed to represent and
examine any particular findings from a num-
· of different vantage points. In addition, the
ne and similar questions about the experi-
:es and outcomes of caretaking were asked of
children and a variety of adults—profes-
nals, parents, foster parents.

he logic of comparative information included
m the onset of a program is straightforward,
experience with planned comparison groups
social reform is meager. In structuring an
perimental state social service program in
oria, the staff of the Illinois Institute for Social
icy (IISP) has given serious thought to in-
oretable comparisons. Though the financial
mmunity is notoriously resistant to evaluation,
· suggestions for an information system for
Opportunity Funding Corporation which
uld maximize interpretability met little re-

sistance, once it was designed to be as undis-
ruptive as possible.

Administrative staffs have assumed—and it is
an assumption which has defeated several otherwise creditable evaluations—that even if the staff
understood the logic of comparative information, program recipients would clearly balk at
the blatant exploitation: data collection without
remuneration and without a noticeable change
in their lives.

Our suspicions have paralleled those of the
administrators. At best, we have expected differential dropout rates between program recipients and the imperfect controls, which create
difficulties of interpretation. When the community has been asked directly, however, rather
than through administrative intermediaries, for
their reactions to these design niceties, the experience has been that they are far more understanding than professionals expect. Such
innocent misrepresentation of client feelings by
service worker intermediaries is not unusual and
is, in fact, one of the strongest reasons we argue
for systematic and direct feedback from all constituencies, most especially, program recipients.
In the New Jersey Negative Income Tax Experiment, the design was tighter than most because
of enormous planning, and the availability of
"control" individuals who received no subsidy,
beyond $10 per month for filling out question-
naires. Many fewer of the controls than expected balked at this procedure, and those who
did were easily persuaded that chance decisions
about program inclusion were quite lottery-like
and reasonable—the luck of the draw. Some differential dropout rates occurred, but not enough
to ruin the data. In short, we fear a misplaced
liberalism among program administrators as
well as among academicians, which distorts the
opinions of program recipients. It is frequently
the administrator and not the clients who say
the client won't understand and won't cooperate.

The following case provides a concrete example of the possible misrepresentation of community attitudes by program administrators. In
our advisory capacity to the Woodlawn program
for the improved delivery of social services, the
inherited arrangement meant that the administrators had to receive program approval fom
a community board. We were told that if we
had proposals for gauging community opinions
of and experiences with social services, those

forms would have to be revised and approved by that board. We were advised that the board would have to be carefully handled, for they would find academic procedures obscure and inappropriate. We viewed our appearance before the board as an opportunity rather than a threat. We wished to explain the strategies we had developed, to gain their advice on the most comprehensible wording of the items, to incorporate those they wished to include, and to be advised on the best local strategy for implementing the pretest. The community board was in fact cautious; they were fed up with academic surveys, and had already rejected one which was typically embarrassing and cumbersome. We thought our presentation was successful and that the board was highly receptive. To our surprise, strong dissention came the next day from the program administrator who felt we had provided the board with too much potential leverage, so much so that the administration would not be able to function without community scrutiny.

Resources. As mentioned above in another context, community agencies and government bureaus are often strapped for funds. With some forethought a reasonable evaluation often costs no more than a sloppy one, but the funds may be committed for neither. Instead, an organization may construct a public relations piece out of whole cloth, or ignore evaluation altogether. Prerequisite "evaluation" agreements often accompany government or corporate grants, but they do not guarantee an adequate evaluation, and sometimes they only produce corruption. Some projects cannot be evaluated in the present climate, or with the present skills and tools, and such a prerequisite may only ensure fabrication. So long as it is known that the refunding of an agency or the position of an administrator rests on the narrowly defined "success" of his program, administrators cannot afford to cooperate in even-handed evaluation research (Campbell, 1969).

When collection of intellectually or methodologically satisfying data is beyond the financial means of fringe or extra-establishment organizations, or when research would so drain the limited resources that funds would be better spent in other ways, university-based research advisors whose interests are aligned with the organizations may donate their time for the methodological and practical experience. But the

residual research costs may still be insurmoun[t]able. It would be a new and terrible immorali[ty] if, for the sake of expensive methodologies, aca[d]emicians interfered with the intent of comm[u]nity activists. When precision is within th[e] means of such groups, it should be demande[d.] Careful evaluation is unusual, but it is consi[s]tent with recent government policy statement[s.] When serious evaluation would therefore in itse[lf] be an effective means for advancing a group's i[n]terests or for soliciting financial support, th[is] should be made clear at the policy level. If th[e] evaluation cannot be done on a shoestring, a[nd] only a shoestring is available, the long-range be[n]efit to precise evaluation will only be gained b[y] the social scientist's refusing to cooperate in th[e] effort.

Starr (1970) has described an alternative [re]search strategy. The method was developed wi[th] an ad hoc community organization which wa[s] attempting to affect bail reform in Chicago. Th[e] Chicago courts had not been influenced by th[e] Vera Foundation (Ares, et al., 1963) demonstr[a]tion that persons with ties in the community, r[e]leased on their own recognizance, are as like[ly] to appear in court as those on bond. The ear[ly] attempts to contact officers of the court we[re] frustrated. Rather than being receptive to t[he] study of procedures which had ameliorat[ed] bonding situations elsewhere, an importa[nt] judge responded: "Who gave you the authori[ty] to do this? All you want to do is let murdere[rs] and rapists on the streets." With this and t[he] temperance advised by other organizations wh[o] were trying (unsuccessfully) to reform the ba[il] system, the ad hoc committee found it difficult [to] sustain enthusiasm. Further, it was clear th[at] the colorless documentation of specific pr[o]cedures in Chicago would have no satisfacto[ry] local impact. Starr described the evaluation [as] a research strategy with enormous publici[ty] value: Up to fifty concerned citizens at once [in]undate the court room, all are bent on objective[ly] recording the information which would doc[u]ment the bond-related procedures in Chicago a[nd] provide the data for alternatives. The proble[ms] here are enormous, methodologically and othe[r]wise, but in this instance the courts respond[ed] to the publicity as they never have to other pre[s]sures, and have modified their bail procedure[s.] Participatio[n] in this study revivified the comm[u]nity organization as well. These alternative ta[c]tics deserve exploration for the lessons they be[ar] and for the problems alleviated as well as those introduced.

Inadequately prepared research strategies have undesirable repercussions for further research. Normal politeness, a respect for the lives of the researched which exceeds the traditional lot of the laboratory subject, is to be exercised. During one academic period the Uptown community of Chicago was deluged by large numbers of enthusiastic and unprepared undergraduates in a hastily planned research project. The hostile community reaction resulted in the threat of public interest class action enjoining academicians from any further disruptive activity in that area. Surely this unfortunate experience renders any future thoughtful and concerned research activity more difficult.

The strategy described by Starr, which involved concerned citizens as co-data-gatherers, is a better model. The publicity value of their court attendance en masse forced the legal remedy demanded. However, publicity value is likely to decrease with repeated instances, and it is also likely to be less valuable in those instances where the desires of the target are not aligned with the research cause.

D. Dissemination

Lack of communication channels. It would be foolish to expect scholars to refine the skills which would produce truly effective commentary on policy, without experience accumulated from many such attempts. But the standards and prerequisites which govern the selection of articles for respected academic journals virtually guarantee that the experience gained cannot be passed through normal channels. Research is judged by its precision, often according to irrelevant criteria; priority is granted to studies whose findings appear clearcut and relatively unambiguous. At the present stage of development even the best field-oriented work is not likely to produce such findings. Admissions of difficulties are normally excised from a manuscript or consigned to footnotes. Yet only through the detailed communication of these difficulties and attempted solutions, with difficulties *emphasized* rather than elided or obscured, can researchers in varied settings begin to discern patterns and possible avenues toward their amelioration.

Scientific advancement has been secured through the fullest revelation of data, and the alternative analyses and interpretations of others within the community of scholars who reject a certain point of view. The same general rules may apply in a rigorously applied social science. Those who disagree with analyses and demand the opportunity to reanalyze our data should have it.

Communication to organization. Since it is unlikely that some community organizations will ever be able to fully trust academic personnel, perhaps one of the most effective ways to provide academic support for such efforts would be to prepare a handbook which demythologizes the research process, and circulates the basic information organizations need to perform their *own* research, either for internal purposes, or for presentation to others. We can count on this strategy to produce another sieve through which only seemingly successful research strategies or supportive results reach the public. This may only place community organizations on a par with public agencies, who selectively declare "confidential" any findings that are embarrassing or shoddy. But at least we'll all know where we stand. No one can be expected, particularly in the pursuit of a defined goal, to recognize and equally weigh everyone's interests. An approximation of that mix of interests would be a broad availability of the capacity to do persuasive research, and an acceptance of, if not an enthusiasm for, the advocate reanalysis of controversial findings.

Becoming public relations. No matter how openly an organization may have entertained the notion of honest evaluation, the final report is likely to be buried and uninfluential if it is not an enthusiastic endorsement rather than an equivocal evaluation. This possibility is bound to provoke despair among honest researchers and may seem sufficient reason for retreating to the purity of the laboratory or inapplicable theoretical stances. Our "solution" in one instance where rumors and realities of governmental infiltration and harassment of a community organization had rendered certain data simply unobtainable, and a realistic evaluation therefore impossible, was to attempt to construct an "interim report" which said nothing untrue, but which so painfully hedged with careful sentences that it could be described at best, as it was by an insider, as "a masterful piece of tight-rope walking." Though some organization members were clearly pleased with an honest, equivocal evaluation, we also understood that no better cooperation was forthcoming, and that we would continue to dishonestly fulfill the role of "objective" evaluators required by the donors. We terminated our relationship as comfortably as possible.

Later, our equivocal interim report was publicized as entirely "favorable." Writing it brought to mind problems of a critic of a wishy-washy movie who cautiously words his review so no choice phrases can be lifted out of context and used for publicity. But our best writing efforts were unsuccessful; excerpts from our piece became a cornerstone for future fundraising. For the sake of our future research in this content area, and for the sake of our integrity as social scientists, we felt we had to sever our ties with the organization.

In this instance, the likely and erroneous interpretation is that we left in disgust, because of a lack of cooperation. Instead, we felt that the project, however laudable, simply could not be evaluated in the present political climate. This decision was not an easy one, for our faith in the possible benefits of an even-handed evaluation remained. Some of the organization's best efforts were stymied, we felt, by entrenched and powerful political interests greater than the organization and beyond its control, and we believe that a critical evaluation of that position would be a useful service. But it was clear that because of internal and external strife the organization could not entrust researchers with the data which might have supported this case, and we also felt that we would not be privy to the data which would allow an effective intra-organizational study (Gordon and Mack, 1971).

Reporting complex data. Community and governmental personnel with whom researchers work are often frustrated by the ways in which complex data are presented. Their pragmatic situation often requires a clear-cut and practical answer to a research question—an answer which allows them to make a choice between competing alternatives. In our study of deinstitutionalization, for example, federal officials might find it easier to effect policy from findings which unequivocally supported foster homes *vs* group homes, or community-based *vs* community-removed settings as alternatives to institutions for dependent and neglected children. But on that matter our data are clear-cut: the situation is too complex for us responsibly to provide such straightforward choices. Without a doubt some foster homes are preferable to some group homes, for example, and some group homes to other foster homes. Moreover, any specific recommendations for placement alternatives which we made from our data would apply to *present* realities. We can document both the shifting effectiveness of various alternatives fashioned to meet the needs of children, and the negative impact of persisting with a policy based on out-dated recommendations.

In this regard, statistics can be as much a burden as an advantage. Statistics are important and influential for their utility in summarizing volumes of information. At the same time, summaries by definition ignore individual distinctions, and these distinctions can be particularly critical in areas of social service. For example, it is apparent that foster homes are *on the average* seen to be preferred to placement in large institutions. The present policy momentum away from institutions is in part a response to the sense practitioners have of this apparent advantage of foster homes. In the course of our research, however, we encountered numerous individual clients, in specific contrast to statistical summary, who were better off in institutional placement than in foster homes. Sometimes this was due to high quality institutions, sometimes to the individual situation of the child. The important point here is that appropriate placement determination in these cases demanded a sensitivity to individual differences which summary statistics tend to cancel.

We see our responsibility as reporters and interpreters of complex data to resist strongly any pressure to settle for misleading and individually destructive simple summaries.

But minutely correct presentation can sometimes intimidate, overwhelm, and confuse any of us, including community and political audiences so that carefully hedged findings may ultimately have no impact whatsoever. Our experience has been that critical cautions are often ignored even if the summaries are not, and that even complex arguments must be made simple and straightforward.

This is a problem with which we must constantly deal. One avenue would be to sidestep these kinds of research involvements in order to preserve academic purity—a conclusion we will not accept. But significant effort must be put into developing forms of presentation which preserve appropriate methodological and theoretical cautions while nevertheless having some practical utility.

Data confidentiality. Because of whatever trust that has been established, we have in several organizations, within and without the government, been privy to critical data which, if interpreted out of context, could be fundamentally damaging, or could provoke litigation against the organization or individuals within. In legal actions, since we have collected much of our data from the files of defendants, we have been required to sign agreements which enjoin us to obey established laws of discovery. That agreement restricts what can be revealed or published without the permission of the court.

One moral dilemma is clear. Academic pursuit at its best involves the free and open pursuit of knowledge, unfettered by the political necessities which necessarily are of paramount concern to activists. Our bias insists that no data should be confidential, beyond the protection of the personal lives of the "subjects" interviewed. Rarely has the issue come up, for rarely has social science data been of any interest to outsiders. Those concerned with re-analysis had no interest in the identity of individual respondents.

In more directly relevant research, the data unearthed through the research process, or indirectly discovered because of the access which the research relationship made possible, may be of crucial legal and/or political relevance to outsiders. We have frequently encountered this set of circumstances. Doctor-patient and lawyer-client relationships are legally confidential, but the social researcher enjoys no such privileges. It appears that the present state of the legal situation is such that academic research records are fully subpoenable.

The press has had its right to protect its sources reaffirmed by the courts, but we cannot assume that this vital protection applies to sources in action-oriented research. We feel certain that many honest and exacting researchers are naively holding on to data which they do not realize could be demanded through legal action. Researchers should acknowledge this clearly and in advance to those from whom they collect information. The researcher could, for example, either state that he cannot guarantee the protection of whatever confidential information the source might provide, or give personal, extra-legal assurances. Proposals have been advanced about various technical precautions, for example, scrambling data so they are uninterpretable to the uninitiated, or aggregating data so that individuals cannot be identified (Boruch, 1971); nevertheless, existing law is such that a researcher could be asked to provide his tactics for data-scrambling.

Even if data could be fully protected, what is the academician's responsibility about data revelation? Poor analyses have been the norm, and faults are often uncovered only through independent re-analysis. If we are to enter into such research, particularly at this crucial time when the appropriate skills are only now being developed, for the sake of free inquiry and technical advancement, re-analysis must be received enthusiastically for the sake of free inquiry and technical advancement.

Once one has agreed to cooperate with an organization in a research venture the results of which are crucially important, where lies the moral choice between breaking the promise made to protect discovered information, and being true to what seem to be larger interests? The dilemma is not new, and the choices are never easy. Daniel Ellsberg was privy, through his capacity with the Rand Corporation, to documents the revelations of which he believed would end the war in Vietnam. He argued that the authors of those documents and of government policy were the victims of a policy created by predecessors from which they could not extract themselves. After futile attempts to reveal the information through channels, he broke laws and trusts by making his extraordinary revelations (Ellsberg, 1971).

Reporters became aware that because of established practices which forbid them to cite verbatim or for attribution information available through government "backgrounders", they had become tools for the manipulation of news rather than representatives of a free press. Similar instances on a more mundane scale may easily occur when the access made available through promises of confidentiality to an organization leads to the discovery of information which is more vital than it at first appeared.

Conclusion

It is a fact well worth repeating that academic research has not been antagonistic to the needs of powerful social and political interests. The policy sciences especially have often failed to challenge existing relations of inequality or have contributed to their maintenance by assuming such relations to be inevitable. Yet there are policy-oriented academicians who reject these positions and who see their work ideally to be a way in which reason can be brought to bear on important and urgent social problems. Their disciplines, they hope, are a means to understand the world as a precondition to changing it.

The Center for Urban Affairs is a community of faculty and students for the most part committed to this latter model of academic work. Most of the projects undertaken at the Center could be described as seeking to identify the interests and improve the lot of the traditionally powerless subjects of academic research. We have had a broad array of illuminating experiences in our attempts to implement a revised university-community relationship. Our experiences have taught us much, and there is much more to learn. We are attempting to incorporate our new understandings into theoretical and methodological models which will move us further along, and efforts in which we have cooperated thus far have produced some very real benefits such as, for example, the concrete financial gains to the buyers of homes on contract in Chicago.

For all of these efforts and the strategies proposed below, however, an important question remains unanswered. Can an institution such as the Center be instrumental in the development of strategies which effect more fundamental changes than those described in this paper? An easy response is that if only we try harder, or develop better methods of research, or better arguments for transforming institutions, then we will be more successful. Sometimes the problem seems to be "unreasonable" organizational self-interest which must be overcome, or the unreachability of powerful political figures.

Possibly, however, the problems we seek to eliminate are ones that lie beyond a greater commitment to the task, or to experiments with methods of data collection, or even the inclusion of client populations in their own life decisions. As an example of this dilemma, voucher systems on a grand scale are currently in favor as client-empowering devices. They have been suggested as remedies for a range of problems from urban education to mental health. The presupposition on which these systems are based is that the free operation of the market allows the consumers to "vote" with their money for the products and services which they alone determine are necessary, thus providing a built-in check on the growth of superfluous or inadequate programs. The market, then, represents the ultimate form of democracy. Yet this faith in the benevolent operation of the free market flies in the face of what we have come to understand to be the impotence of consumers excluded from fundamental decisions about production (the range of choices offered) or distribution (those who command more money, command more resources). When one adds to this the stigma and moral opprobrium attached to public services in this society, these may be programs which are bound to fail.

Any "real-world" research which engages the resources and energies of a number of people and groups inevitably has a political component. Our work on the deinstitutionalization project, for example, has taken place in the context of many important political cross-pressures. Political influence was used to prevent the closing of children's institutions; the Director of the agency, who had given us free access to conduct the study, was removed from his post; and efforts to construct instruments to insure client input in agency decisions ran afoul of on-line workers threatened by what they saw as increased paper work, as well as higher-level administrators tentative about decision-making inputs from "non-professionals". It is possible, however, that these are rear-guard actions, and that those who are in favor of deinstitutionalization may finally win the day, but not because of the moral force of their cause. It is too expensive to maintain large institutional structures, and often too obviously brutal to lock people up in them. Given such modern inventions as drug therapy and behavior modification, it may be unnecessary. There is the distinct possibility, then, that our work will contribute little to the lives of the people affected by this reform. At best, we would hope that closing institutions for children, and allowing them and their families to choose among a range of alternatives of care, will provide these clients with a greater measure of control over their personal lives than before. Poor families, or those in distress, will have more to say about the disposition of their children; poor children, or those in trouble, will have more to say about what kind of family setting they grow up in. It is not our intention to minimize this gain in personal freedom, especially among those who by virtue of their class, age, and poverty have so little, but to suggest that we may be caught in an impossible contradiction. While we go about changing some aspects of the system for the better (or what we take to be the better), we may at the same time be helping to reproduce the very inequalities which our research was undertaken to eliminate. For many years the concentration on and glorification of personal life has been a powerful centrifugal force, an ideology which encourages the denial of social connections beyond the individual and his family, and a withdrawal from arenas of collective struggle. As we undertake our work at the Center to enhance the range of choice available to these families and to help to eliminate the worst abuses of the system, we fail to challenge this long-standing antagonism between the personal and the social. Indeed, when we focus our attention and our hope on the *individual* choices of the clients, we reinforce the notion that there may be individual solutions to these social problems. To the extent that we fail to grapple with this serious and difficult issue, by uncovering and challenging many of the assumptions on which our well-intentioned efforts rest, we, too, must be counted as part of the problem. We must consider as well the implications for us of Barbara Wonton's statement that "we prefer today to analyze the infected individual rather than rid the infection from the environment."

Some of us did hope that our concern to elicit the opinions of clients would encourage the children to begin to act toward the system in a united way on their own behalf. On the one hand, those of us who voiced this possibility seriously underestimated the degree to which the children had already developed strategies for survival. On the other hand, we seriously over-estimated our impact, and the degree to which change was possible and likely within an institution characterized by complex and reciprocal relations with the rest of society. Yet these problems are structured into our position as policy researchers focused on planned change within one institution.

On the face of it then it may be impossible to develop partial solutions which leave intact material and social inequalities which are the main components of a class system. People who must turn to social service agencies are often isolated from their family and their community. Their plight is the result of their failures in other areas —principally in the scramble for jobs and scarce resources into which most of us are thrown and which many of us do not survive. Unless these patterns of inequality themselves are subjected to attack, we are only putting bandages on the institutions designed to deal with its residue. The system of public child care functions in many respects as a separate institution for the most vulnerable of the working class. Unless we wish to resurrect the disreputable idea of "separate but equal", it is hard to imagine any changes inside the system that will not maintain the inequalities we deplore.

The alternative, we hope, is not to wait for a total, systemic transformation, but to begin where we are, with awareness of our limitations as academics, to work toward that goal. Correcting the most blatant abuses that take place in institutions and alternate settings, providing information about institutional practices, offering the facilities of the university to the less-well endowed community, these can all be important and unique functions of policy research centers. But it may be misleading to those who make use of our skills, and to ourselves, if we were to expect our efforts alone to lead to a new state of affairs.

Outlined below are some proposals to maximize the mutual gain to the scholar and the community with explicit recognition of the limitations expressed above, but recognizing as well the mutual value of efforts which have occurred thus far. These proposals build upon our research and thinking, and have in common the attempt to develop mechanisms (1) for short-circuiting some of the academic problems which have occurred, and (2) for creating situations for the continuing growth both of the academic and the extra-university personnel, without sacrificing scholarship.

Handbook

Many of the difficulties we have encountered in our new relationships with non-university persons might be alleviated with a simple and honest document, e.g., a handbook, which communicates our capacities and our skills. The handbook could explore the frequent misconceptions both of the scholar and of the community personnel with whom he has worked, and should comment on the limits of such involvements. The document should detail the extent to which confidentiality can be guaranteed. It should be specific about the cooperation which we have learned is necessary in order for the research to be of any mutual advantage and it should comment on the kinds of cooperation any research arrangement will necessitate.

Enhanced Experience

We should continue to work toward institutional structures which maximize the exposure of our students to areas of social and political concern, in a manner which allows them to reflect on what they are learning in the classroom. Academic standards should not be sacrificed; the aim is a program which emphasizes action *and* reflection. We should give academicians who have an interest in applying their skills to these areas of concern an opportunity to expose themselves systematically to extra-academic influences which confront this research, e.g., through placement in a government agency. It is the *combination* of exposure and opportunity for reflection which is vital here.

Likewise, we should encourage and offer opportunities for the training of personnel. In disadvantaged organizations these skills are most clearly lacking. The training would have the effect, not of creating an imbalance, but of distributing necessary skills more democratically.

Client Feedback

Because it would correct another crucial imbalance, we should continue to support attempts to encourage the systematic feedback from the recipients of social service programs. Such feedback must include their opinions of the nature of their experience with the governmental or private agency. Frequently recipients have been asked how badly off they are, though in no way has an evaluation scheme followed which allowed them to comment on whether governmental programs run on their behalf were making a difference. Our experiences have forcefully demonstrated that often they are *the experts* on the impact of social services. These feedback systems should be designed to maximize the likelihood that the information will be responded to, so that the recipients can evaluate the nature of the response (Gordon and Campbell, 1971).

Vouchers

There has been a prevalent hierarchy of interests when universities and community groups have worked together. Normally, university personnel offer whatever it is they wish to provide (e.g., theoretical input, sociological skills, surveys) and the community group has at most the choice of taking what is offered, or taking nothing at all. The offer may be gratefully accepted, since any resource may be of benefit, but given some greater choice from among the vast resources of universities, community groups might make far different choices.

Through the Center, Epperson (1971) initiated a proposal for this voucher relationship between community groups and universities. The proposal resulted in a state funded project through which less-advantaged community groups can purchase services of their choice at participating universities. The plan allows for the purchase of definitional, strategic or any other university services in such a way that maximum information about the universities' capacity to respond is gauged, as is the organizations' ability to utilize the services. Most importantly, through the vouchers community groups are encouraged to engage university facilities in research which they determine to be necessary, and on their own terms. By assuring that the research be undertaken for a different master—the community—the project is designed to produce efforts more responsive to community needs. Equally important from the university perspective the early research on this project (Pitts, 1975) has demonstrated unequivocally that this modified form of working with the community provides valuable and unanticipated perspectives on the world the university seeks to study. We need to build on this experience with various clients, consumers and community groups to redress the academic biases which the universities' more common relationship to the community have promoted.

There are no panaceas presented here. Our experiences teaches us all too well that specifying the ground rules for some of the proposed realignments, such as the vouchers for services, is very difficult and time consuming, and implementation even more so. Attempts to build in legitimate mechanisms for client evaluations of services received meet incredible challenges and opposition. But our proposals are based on the urgency of the need, and we are better able to anticipate and overcome many of these difficulties now, with the benefit of the experiences we have had. What we are proposing are more opportunities for experience, experience which will further the responsible involvement of the university in community affairs.

References

Ares, C., A. Rankin, and H. Sturz. "The Manhattan Bail Project: An interim report on the use of pretrial parole." *New York University Law Review* 38: 67–95.

Becker, Howard S. 1970. "Field Work Evidence." Pp. 39–62 in Becker, *Sociological Work*. Chicago: Aldine Publishing Company.

Berk, R., R. Mack, and J. McKnight. 1971. *Race and Class Differences in Per Pupil Expenditures in Chicago, 1969–1970.* Evanston: Northwestern University, Center for Urban Affairs.

Boruch, R. 1971. "Assuring Confidentiality of Response: A note on strategies." *The American Sociologist* (November).

Campbell, D. T. 1969. "Reforms as Experiments." *American Psychologist* 24 (4).

Campbell, D. T. 1973. "Methods for the Experimenting Society." Unpublished manuscript.

Campbell, D. T., and A. Erlebacher. 1970. "How regression artifacts in quasi-experimental evaluations can mistakenly make compensatory education look harmful." Pp. 185–210 in J. Hellmuth (ed.), *Compensatory Education: A National Debate.* New York: Brunner/Mazel, Inc.

Campbell, D. T., and D. Fiske. 1959. "Convergent and discriminant validation by the multitrait-multimethod matrix." *Psych. Bulletin* 56: 81–105.

Cowhig, James. 1971. "Federal grant-supported social research and 'relevance': Some reservations." *American Sociologist* (June): 65–68.

Divorski, S., A. Gordon, and J. Heinz. 1973. "Public access to government information: A field experiment." *Northwestern University Law Review*, May-June, Pp. 240–279.

Ellsberg, Daniel. 1971. Comments on the ABC Television Network.

Evans, John. 1969. "Evaluating social action programs." *Social Science Quarterly* 50 (3): 4–22.

Epperson, David. 1971. *The Scholar's Response to Urban Discontent.* Evanston: Northwestern University, Center for Urban Affairs.

Epperson, David, and D. Detzel. 1971. *The Scholar in Urban Problem Solving: Rhetoric, Reality, Remedies and Recommendations.* Evanston: Northwestern University, Center for Urban Affairs.

Gans, Herbert. 1971. "The uses of poverty: The poor pay all." *Social Policy* (July/August): 20–24.

Gordon, A., and D. T. Campbell. 1971. "Recommended accounting procedures for the evaluation of improvements in the delivery of state social services." Report to the Illinois Institute for Social Policy. Evanston: Northwestern University, Center for Urban Affairs. 51 pp.

Gordon, A., S. Divorski, M. Gordon, and J. Heinz. 1973. "Public information and public access: A sociological interpretation." *Northwestern University Law Review*, pp. 280–308.

Gordon, A., and R. Mack. 1971. *The Kenwood-Oakland Community Organization and Toward Responsible Freedom.* Evanston: Northwestern University, Center for Urban Affairs.

Gordon, A., and J. Meyers. 1970. *Methodological Recommendations for Extensions of the Heussenstamm Bumper Sticker Study.* Evanston: Northwestern University, Center for Urban Affairs (September).

Jencks, C. 1972. *Inequality: A Reassessment of the Effect of Schooling in America.* New York: Basic Books, Inc.

Mercer, S., A. Gordon, and R. Fahey. 1971. *Release on Bond and Legal Representatives of Criminal Defendants Arrested in Evanston, Illinois, in 1970.* Evanston: Northwestern University, Center for Urban Affairs.

Pitts, J. 1975. "The community service voucher program: An experiment in community access to university resources." Society for the Study of Social Problems, annual meeting.

Reissman, Frank. 1969. "Community control and human services." New York University (mimeo).

Rossi, Peter. 1969. "Practice, method and theory in evaluating social action programs." In D. Moynihan (ed.), *On Understanding Poverty: Per-*

spectives from the Social Sciences. New York: Basic Books, Inc.

Starr, Joyce. 1971. *Taking Research Out of Academia and Into the Street.* Evanston: Northwestern University, Department of Sociology.

Weiss, R., and M. Rein. 1969. "The evaluation of broad-aim programs: A cautionary case and a moral." *The Annals* of the American Academy of Political and Social Science, September: 133–142.

32

FRANCIS FOX PIVEN

The Urban Crisis: Who Got What and Why?

For quite a while, complaints about the urban fiscal crisis have been droning on, becoming as familiar as complaints about big government, or big bureaucracy, or high taxes—and almost as boring as well. Now suddenly the crisis seems indeed to be upon us: School closings are threatened, library services are curtailed, subway trains go unrepaired, welfare grants are cut, all because big-city costs have escalated to the point where local governments can no longer foot the bill. Yet for all the talk, and all the complaints, there has been no convincing explanation of just how it happened that, quite suddenly in the 1960s, the whole municipal housekeeping system seemed to become virtually unmanageable. This is especially odd because, not long ago, the study of city politics and city services was a favorite among American political scientists, and one subject they had gone far to illuminate. Now, with everything knocked askew, they seem to have very little to say that could stand as political analysis.

To be sure, there is a widely accepted explanation. The big cities are said to be in trouble because of the "needs" of blacks for services—a view given authority by the professionals who run the service agencies and echoed by the politicians who depend upon these agencies. Service "needs," the argument goes, have been increasing at a much faster rate than local revenues. The alleged reason is demographic: The

large number of impoverished black southern migrants to the cities presumably requires far greater investments in services, including more elaborate educational programs, more frequent garbage collection, more intensive policing, if the city is to be maintained at accustomed levels of civil decency and order. Thus, city agencies have been forced to expand and elaborate their activities. However, the necessary expansion is presumably constricted for lack of local revenues, particularly since the better-off taxpaying residents and businesses have been leaving the city (hastened on their way by the black migration).[1] To this standard explanation of the crisis, there is also a standard remedy: namely, to increase municipal revenues, whether by enlarging federal and state aid to the cities or by redrawing jurisdictional boundaries to recapture suburban taxpayers.[2]

It is true, of course, that black children who receive little in the way of skills or motivation at home may require more effort from the schools; that densely packed slums require more garbage collection; that disorganized neighborhoods require more policing. For instance, the New York City Fire Department reports a 300 percent increase in fires the last twenty years. But fires and similar calamities that threaten a wide public are one thing; welfare, education and health services, which account for by far the largest portion of big-city budgets, quite another. And while by any objective measure the new residents of the city have greater needs for such services, there are several reasons to doubt that the urban crisis is the simple result of rising needs and declining revenues.

For one thing, the trend in service budgets suggests otherwise. Blacks began to pour into the cities in very large numbers after World War II, but costs did not rise precipitously until the mid-1960s.[3] *In other words, the needs of the black poor were not recognized for two decades.* For another, any scrutiny of agency budgets shows that, except for public welfare, *the expansion of services to the poor, as such, does not account for a very large proportion of increased expenditures.* It was other groups, *mainly organized provider groups,* who reaped the lion's share of the swollen budgets. The notion that services are being strained to respond to the needs of the new urban poor, in short, takes little account either of when the strains occurred or of the groups who actually benefited from increased expenditures.

These two facts should lead us to look beyond the "rising needs—declining revenues" theory for an explanation of urban troubles. And once we do, perhaps some political common sense can emerge. School administrators and sanitation commissioners may describe their agencies as ruled by professional standards and as shaped by disinterested commitments to the public good, and thus define rising costs as a direct and proper response to the needs of people. But schools and sanitation departments are, after all, agencies of local government, substructures of the local political apparatus, and are managed in response to local political forces. The mere fact that people are poor or that the poor need special services has never led government to respond. Service agencies are political agencies, administered to deal with political problems, not service problems.

Now this view is not especially novel. Indeed, if there is any aspect of the American political system that was persuasively analyzed in the past, it was the political uses of municipal services in promoting allegiance and muting conflict. Public jobs, contracts and services were dispensed by city bosses to maintain loyal cadres and loyal followers among the heterogeneous groups of the city. Somehow political analysts have forgotten this in their accounts of the contemporary urban crisis, testimony perhaps to the extent to which the doublethink of professional bureaucrats has befogged the common sense of us all. That is, we are confused by changes in the style of urban-service politics, failing to see that although the style has changed, the function has not. In the era of the big-city machine, municipal authorities managed to maintain a degree of consensus and allegiance among diverse groups by distributing public goods in the form of private favors. Today public goods are distributed through the service bureaucracies. With that change, the process of dispensing public goods has become more formalized, the struggles between groups more public, and the language of city politics more professional. As I will try to explain a little later, these changes were in some ways crucial in the development of what we call the urban crisis. My main point for now, however, is that while we may refer to the schools or the sanitation department as if they are politically neutral, these agencies yield up a whole variety of benefits, and it is by distributing, redistributing and adapting these payoffs of the city agencies that urban political leaders manage to keep peace and build allegiances among the diverse groups in the city. In other words, the jobs, contracts, perquisites, as well as the actual services of the municipal housekeeping agencies, are just as much the substance of urban politics as they ever were.

All of which is to say that when there is a severe disturbance in the administration and financing of municipal services, the underlying cause is likely to be a fundamental disturbance in political relations. To account for the service "crisis" we should look at the changing relationship between political forces—at rising group conflict and weakening allegiances—and the way in which these disturbances set off an avalanche of new demands. To cope with these strains political leaders expanded and proliferated the benefits of the city agencies. What I shall argue, in sum, is that the urban crisis is not a crisis of rising needs but a crisis of rising demands.

Any number of circumstances may disturb existing political relationships, with the result that political leaders are less capable of restraining the demands of various groups. Severe economic dislocations may activate groups that previously asked little of government, as in the 1930s. Or groups may rise in the economic structure, acquiring political force and pressing new demands as a result. Or large-scale migration may alter the balance between groups. Any of these situations may generate sharp antagonism among groups, and as some new groups acquire a measure of influence, they may undermine established political relationships. In the period of uncertainty that ensues, discontent is likely to spread, political alignments may shift, and all giances to a political leadership may become insecure. In the context of this general unrest, political leaders, unsure of their footing, are far more likely to respond to the specific demands of specific groups for enlarged benefits or new "rights." Periods of political instability, in other words, nurture new claims and claimants. This is what happened in the cities in the 1960s, and it happened at a time when the urban political system was uniquely ill equipped to curb the spiral of rising demands that resulted.

The Political Disturbances That Led to Rising Demands

If the service needs of the black poor do not account for the troubles in the cities, the political impact of the black migration probably does. Massive shifts of population are almost always disturbing to a political system, for new relations have to be formed between a political leadership and constituent groups. The migration of large numbers of blacks from the rural South to a few core cities during and after World War II, leading many middle-class white constituents to leave for the suburbs, posed just this challenge to the existing political organization of the cities. But for a long time local governments resisted responding to the newcomers with the services, symbols and benefits that might have won the allegiance of these newcomers, just as the allegiance of other groups had previously been won.

The task of political integration was made difficult by at least four circumstances. One was the very magnitude of the influx. Between 1940 and 1960, nearly 4 million blacks left the land and, for the most part, settled in big northern cities. Consequently, by 1960 at least one in five residents of our fifty largest cities was a black, and in the biggest cities the propositions were much greater. It is no exaggeration to say that the cities were inundated by sheer numbers.

Second, these large numbers were mainly lower-class blacks, whose presence aroused ferocious race and class hatreds, especially among white ethnics who lived in neighborhoods bordering the ghettos and who felt their homes and school endangered. As ghetto numbers enlarged, race and class polarities worsened, and political leaders, still firmly tied to the traditional inhabitants of the cities, were in no position to give concessions to the black poor.

Not only was race pitted against race, class against class, but the changing style of urban politics made concessions to conflicting groups a very treacherous matter. Just because the jobs, services and contracts that fueled the urban political organization were no longer dispensed covertly, in the form of private favors, but rather as matters of public policy, each concession was destined to become a subject of open political conflict. As a result, mayors found it very difficult to finesse their traditional constituents: New public housing for blacks, for example, could not be concealed, and every project threatened to arouse a storm of controversy. Despite their growing numbers and their obvious needs, therefore, blacks got very little in the way of municipal benefits throughout the 1940s and 1950s. Chicago, where the machine style was still entrenched, gave a little more; the Cook County AFDC rolls, for example, rose by eighty percent in the 1950s, and blacks were given some political jobs. But in most cities the local service agencies resisted the newcomers. In New York City and Los Angeles, for example, the AFDC rolls remained virtually unchanged in the 1950s. In many places public housing was brought to a halt; urban renewal generally became the instrument of black removal; and half the major southern cities (which also received large numbers of black migrants from rural areas) actually managed to reduce their welfare rolls, often by as much as half.[4]

Finally, when blacks entered the cities they were confronted by a relatively new development in city politics: namely, the existence of large associations of public employees, whether teachers, policemen, sanitation men or the like. The provider groups not only had a very large stake in the design and operation of public programs—for there is hardly any aspect of public policy that does not impinge on matters of working conditions, job security or fringe benefits—but they had become numerous enough, organized enough and independent enough to wield substantial influence in matters affecting their interests.

The development of large, well-organized and independent provider groups has been going on for many years, probably beginning with the emergence of the civil-service merit system at the turn of the century (a development usually credited to the efforts of reformers who sought to improve the quality of municipal services, to eliminate graft and to dislodge machine leaders).[5] But although the civil service originated in the struggle between party leaders and reformers, it launched municipal employees as an independent force. As city services expanded, the enlarging numbers of public employees began to form associations. Often these originated as benevolent societies, such as New York City's Patrolmen's Benevolent Association, which formed in the 1890s. Protected by the merit system, these associations gradually gained some influence in their own right, and they exerted that influence at both the municipal and the state level to shape legislation and to monitor personnel policies so as to protect and advance their occupational interests.

The result was that, over time, many groups of public employees managed to win substantial control over numerous matters affecting their jobs and their agencies: entrance requirements, tenure guarantees, working conditions, job prerogatives, promotion criteria, retirement benefits. Except where wages were concerned, other groups in the cities rarely became sufficiently aroused to block efforts by public employees to advance their interests. But all of this also meant that when blacks arrived in the cities, local political leaders did not control the jobs— and, in cases where job prerogatives had been precisely specified by regulation, did not even control the services—that might have been given as concessions to the black newcomers.

Under the best of circumstances, of course, the task of integrating a new and uprooted rural population into local political structures would have taken time and would have been difficult. But for all of the reasons given, local government was showing little taste for the task. As a result, a large population that had been set loose from southern feudal institutions was not absorbed into the regulating political institutions (or economic institutions, for they were also resisted there) of the city. Eventually that dislocated population became volatile, both in the streets and at the polls. By 1960 that volatility forced the federal government to take an unprecedented role in urban politics.[6]

Urban blacks, who had been loyal Democrats for almost three decades, had begun to defect even as their numbers grew, signaling the failure of the municipal political machinery. New ways to reach and reward the urban black voter were needed. Accordingly, administration analysts began to explore strategies to cement the allegiance of the urban black vote to the national party. What emerged, not all at once but over a number of years, was a series of federal service programs directed to the ghetto. The first appropriations were small, as with the Juvenile Delinquency and Youth Offenses Control Act of 1961, but each program enlarged upon the other, up until the model-cities legislation of 1966. Some of the new programs—in manpower development, in education, in health—were relatively straightforward. All they did was give new funds to local agencies to be used to provide jobs or services for the poor. Thus, funds appropriated under Title I of the Elementary and Secondary Education Act of 1965 were earmarked for educational facilities for poor children; the medicaid program enacted in 1965 reimbursed health agencies and physicians for treating the poor; and manpower agencies were funded specifically to provide jobs or job training for the poor.

Other of the new federal programs were neither so simple nor so straightforward, and these were the ones that became the hallmark of the Great Society. The federal memoranda describing them were studded with terms like "inner city," "institutional change" and "maximum feasible participation." But if this language was often confusing, the programs themselves ought not to have been. The "inner city," after all, was a euphemism for the ghetto, and activities funded under such titles as delinquency prevention, mental health, antipoverty or model cities turned out, in the streets of the cities, to look very much alike. What they looked like was nothing less than the old political machine.

Federal funds were used to create new storefront-style agencies in the ghettos, staffed with professionals who helped local people find jobs, obtain welfare or deal with school officials. Neighborhood leaders were also hired, named community workers, neighborhood aides or whatever, but in fact close kin to the old ward heelers, for they drew larger numbers of people into the new programs, spreading the federal spoils.

But federal spoils were not enough, for there were not many of them. If blacks were to wrapped into the political organization of the cities, the traditional agencies of local government, which controlled the bulk of federal, state and local appropriations, had to be reoriented. Municipal agencies had to be made to respond to blacks.

Various tactics to produce such reform were tried, at first under the guise of experiments in "institutional change," but the experiments got little cooperation from local bureaucrats. Therefore, as turbulence spread in the northern ghettos, the federal officials began to try another way to promote institutional change—"maximum feasible participation of residents of the areas and members of the groups served." Under that slogan the Great Society programs gave money to ghetto organizations, which then used the money to harrass city agencies. Community workers were hired to badger housing inspectors and to pry loose welfare payments. Lawyers on the federal payroll took municipal agencies to court on behalf of ghetto clients. Later the new programs helped organize the ghetto poor to picket the welfare department or to boycott the school system.

In these various ways, then, the federal government intervened in local politics and forced local government to do what it had earlier failed to do. Federal dollars and federal authority were used to resuscitate the functions of the political machine, on the one hand *by spurring local service agencies to respond to the black newcomers,* and on the other *by spurring blacks to make demands upon city services.*

As it turned out, blacks made their largest tangible gains from this process through the public-welfare system. Total national welfare costs rose from about $4 billion in 1960 to nearly $15 billion in 1970. Big cities that received the largest numbers of black and Spanish-speaking migrants and that were most shaken by the political reverberations of that migration also experienced the largest welfare-budget rises. In New York, Los Angeles and Baltimore, for example, the AFDC rolls quadrupled, and costs rose even faster. In some cities, moreover, welfare costs were absorbing an ever-larger share of the local budget, a bigger piece of the public pie. In New York City, for example, welfare costs absorbed about twelve percent of the city's budget in the '50s; but by 1970, the share going to welfare had grown to about twenty-five percent (of a much larger budget), mainly because the proportion of the city's population on Aid to Families of Dependent Children increased from 2.6 percent in 1960 to 11.0 percent in 1970.[7] In other words, the blacks who triggered the disturbances received their biggest payoffs from welfare,[8] mainly because other groups were not competing within the welfare system for a share of relief benefits.[9]

But if blacks got welfare, that was just about all they got. Less obvious than the emergence of black demands—but much more important in accounting for increasing service costs—was the reaction of organized whites to these political developments, particularly the groups who had direct material stakes in the running of the local services. If the new upthrust of black claims threatened and jostled many groups in the city, none were so alert or so shrill as those who had traditionally gotten the main benefits of the municipal services. These were the people who depended, directly or indirectly, on the city treasury for their livelihood: They worked in the municipal agencies, in agencies that were publicly funded (e.g., voluntary hospitals), in professional services that were publicly reimbursed (e.g., doctors) or in businesses that depended on city contracts (e.g., contractors and construction workers). Partly they were incited by black claims that seemed to threaten their traditional preserves. Partly they were no longer held in check by stable relationships with political leaders, for these relations had weakened or become uncertain or even turned to enmity: Indeed, in some cases, the leaders themselves had been toppled, shaken loose by the conflict and instability of the times. In effect, the groups who worked for or profited from city government had become unleashed, at the same time that newcomers were snapping at their heels.

The result was that the provider groups reacted with a rush of new demands. And these groups had considerable muscle to back up their claims. Not only were they unusually numerous and well organized, but they were allied to broader constituencies by their class and ethnic ties and by their union affiliations. Moreover, their demands for increased benefits, whether higher salaries or lower work load or greater autonomy, were always couched in terms of protecting the professional standards of the city services, a posture that helped win them broad public support. As a result, even when the organized providers backed up their demands by closing the schools, or stopping the subways, or letting the garbage pile up, many people were ready to blame the inconveniences on political officials.

Local political leaders, their ties to their constituencies undermined by population shifts and spreading discontent, were in a poor position to resist or temper these escalating demands, especially the demands of groups with the power to halt the services on which a broader constituency depended. Instead, to maintain their position they tried to expand and elaborate the benefits—the payrolls, the contracts, the perquisites and the services—of the municipal agencies.

Nor, as had been true in the era of the machine, was it easy to use these concessions to restore stable relationships. Where once political leaders had been able to anticipate or allay the claims of various groups, dealing with them one by one, now each concession was public, precipitating rival claims from other groups, each demand ricocheting against the other in an upward spiral. Not only did public concessions excite rivalry, but political officials lost the ability to held groups in check in another way as well; unlike their machine predecessors, they could attach few conditions to the concessions they made. Each job offered, each wage increase conceded, each job prerogative granted was now ensconced in civil-service regulations or union contracts and, thus firmly secured, could not be withdrawn. Political leaders had lost any leverage in their dealings; each concession simply became the launching pad for higher demands. Instead of regular exchange relationships, open conflict and uncertainty became the rule. The result was a virtual run upon the city treasury by a host of organized groups in the city, each competing with the other for a larger share of municipal benefits. Benefits multiplied and budgets soared—and so did the discontent of various groups with the schools, or police, or housing, or welfare, or health. To illustrate, we need to examine the fiscal impact of mounting political claims in greater detail.

Rising Demands and the Fiscal Crisis

Education is a good example, for it is the single largest service run by localities, accounting for forty percent of the outlays of state and local government in 1968, up from thirty percent in 1948.[10] The huge expenditures involved in running the schools are also potential benefits—jobs for teachers, contracts for maintenance and construction, and educational services for children—all things to be gained by different groups in the local community. Accordingly, the educational system became a leading target of black demands,[11] at first mainly in the form of the struggle for integrated schools. Later, worn down by local resistance to integration and guided by the Great Society programs that provided staff, meeting rooms, mimeograph machines, and lawyers to ghetto groups,[12] the difficult demands for integration were transformed into demands for "citizen participation," which meant a share of the jobs, contracts and status positions that the school system yields up.[13]

Blacks made some gains. Boards of education began hiring more black teachers, and some cities instituted schemes for "community control" that ensconced local black leaders in the lower echelons of the school hierarchy.[14] But the organized producer groups, whose salaries account for an estimated eighty percent of rising school costs,[15] made far larger gains. Incited by black claims that seemed to challenge their traditional preserves, and emboldened by a weak and conciliatory city government, the groups who depend on school budgets began rapidly to enlarge and entrench their stakes. Most evident in the scramble were teaching and supervisory personnel, who were numerous and well organized and became ever more strident—so much so that the opening of each school year is now signaled by news of teacher strikes in cities throughout the country. And threatened city officials strained to respond by expanding the salaries, jobs, programs and privileges they had to offer. One result was that average salaries in New York City, Chicago, Los Angeles, Philadelphia, Washington, D.C., and San Francisco topped the $10,000 mark by 1969, *in most instances having doubled* in the decade. Nationally, teachers' salaries have risen about eight percent each year since 1965.[16] Not only did the teachers win rapid increases in salaries but, often prompted by new black demands, they exploited contract negotiations and intensive lobbying to win new guarantees of job security, increased pensions and "improvements" in educational policy that have had the effect of increasing their own ranks—all of which drove up school budgets, especially in the big cities where blacks were concentrated.[17] In Baltimore, where the black population has reached forty-seven percent, the school budget increased from $57 million in 1961 to $184 million in 1971; in New Orleans from $28.5 million to $73.9 million in 1971; in Boston school costs rose from $35.4 million in 1961 to $95.7 million in 1971.[18] Total national educational costs, which in 1957 amounted to $12 billion, topped $40 billion by 1968,[19] and the U.S. Office of Education expects costs to continue to rise, by at least thirty-seven percent by 1975. In this process, blacks may have triggered the flood of new demands on the schools, but organized whites turned out to be the main beneficiaries.

What happened in education happened in other services as well. Costs rose precipitously across the board as mayors tried to extend the benefits of the service agencies to quiet the discordant and clamoring groups in the city. One way was to expand the number of jobs, often by creating new agencies, so that there was more to go around. Hence, in New York City the municipal payroll expanded by over 145,000 jobs in the 1960s, and the rate of increase doubled after Mayor John V. Lindsay took office in 1965.[20] By 1971, 381,000 people were on the municipal payroll. Some 34,000 of these new employees were black and Puerto Rican "paraprofessionals," according to the city's personnel director. Others were Lindsay supporters, put on the payroll as part of his effort to build a new political organization out of the turmoil.[21] Most of the rest were new teachers, policemen and social workers, some hired to compensate for reduced work loads won by existing employees (teachers won reduced class sizes, patrolmen the right to work in pairs), others hired to staff an actual expansion that had taken place in some services to appease claimant groups who were demanding more welfare, safer streets or better snow removal.[22] As a result, total state and local governmental employment in the city rose from 8.2 percent of the total labor force in 1960 to 14 percent in 1970. A similar trend of expanded public employment took place in other big cities. In Detroit state and local employment rose from 9 percent of the labor force in 1960 to 12.2 percent in 1970; in Philadelphia from 6.9 percent to 9.8 percent; in Los Angeles from 9.8 percent to 12.0 percent; in San Francisco from 12.2 percent in 1960 to 15.2 percent in 1970.[23]

Another way to try to deal with the clamor was to concede larger and larger salaries and more liberal pensions to existing employees who were pressing new demands, and pressing hard, with transit, or garbage, or police strikes (or sick-outs or slow-downs) that paralyzed whole cities.[24] In Detroit, garbage collectors allowed refuse to accumulate in the streets when the city offered them only a six-percent wage increase after the police won an eleven-percent increase.[25] In Cincinnati, municipal laborers and garbage collectors threatened a "massive civil-disobedience campaign" when they were offered less than the $945 annual raise won by policemen and firemen.[26] In Philadelphia, garbage collectors engaged in a slowdown when a policeman was appointed to head their department.[27] A San Francisco strike by 7500 city workers shut down the schools and the transit system and disrupted several other services simultaneously.[28] An unprecedented wildcat strike by New York City's policemen, already the highest-paid police force in the world, would have cost the city an estimated $56,936 a year for every policeman (and $56,214 for every fireman) if demands for salaries, pensions, fringe benefits and reduced work time had been conceded.[29] If these demands were perhaps a bit theatrical, the pay raises for city employees in New York City did average twelve percent each year in 1967, 1968 and 1969. Meanwhile, the U.S. Bureau of Labor Statistics reported that the earnings of health professionals in the city rose by eighty percent in the decade, at least double the increase in factory wages. In other cities across the country similar groups were making similar gains; municipal salaries rose by seven to ten percent in both 1968 and 1969, or about twice as fast as the Consumer Price Index.[30]

The pattern of crazily rising municipal budgets is the direct result of these diverse and pyramiding claims on city services, claims triggered by political instability.[31] Accordingly, budget trends followed political trends. New York City, for example, received about 1.25 million blacks and Puerto Ricans in the years between 1950 and 1965, while about 1.5 million whites left the city. The political reverberations of these shifts weakened the Democratic party organization and resulted in the Lindsay victory on a fusion ticket in 1965. But the Lindsay government was extremely unstable, without ties to established constituents, virtually without a political organization and extremely vulnerable to the demands of the different groups, including the ghetto groups whose support it was trying to cultivate. New

York also had very strong and staunch provider groups, as everyone knows from the transit, garbage, teacher and police strikes, each of which in turn threatened municipal calamity. The subsequent escalation of demands by blacks and Puerto Ricans on the one hand, and municipal provider groups on the other, produced the much-publicized turmoil and conflict that wracked the city.

To deal with these troubles, city officials made concessions, with the result that the municipal budget almost quadrupled in the last decade. And as the turmoil rose, so did city costs: An annual budget rise of 6 percent in the 1950s and 8.5 percent in the early 1960s became an annual rise of 15 percent after 1965.[32] New York now spends half again as much per capita as other cities over a million (excluding educational costs), twice as much per capita as cities between 500,000 and a million, and three times as much as the other 288 cities.[33]

A few cities where the existing political organization was firmly entrenched and machine-style politics still strong were spared. Chicago is the notable example, and Chicago's political organization shows in lower welfare costs, in per-pupil expenditures that are half that of New York City, in garbage-collection costs of $22 a ton compared to $49 in New York City. Mayor Daley never lost his grip. With the white wards firmly in tow, he made modest concessions to blacks earlier and without fear of setting off a chain reaction of demands by other groups. And so he never gave as much, either to blacks or to organized whites. But most other large cities show a pattern of escalating discontent and escalating service budgets more like New York City than Chicago.[34] By 1970 the total costs of local government had risen about 350 percent over 1950.

The cities are unable to raise revenues commensurate with these expenditures; and they are unable to resist the claims that underlie rising expenditures. And that is what the fiscal crisis is all about. Cities exist only by state decree, and depend entirely on the state governments for their taxing powers.[35] Concretely this has meant that the states have taken for themselves the preferred taxes[36] leaving the localities to depend primarily on the property tax (which accounts for seventy percent of revenues raised by local governments),[37] supplemented by a local sales tax in many places, user charges (e.g., sewer and water fees) and, in some places, a local income tax.[38] The big cities have had little choice but to drive up these local taxes to which they are limited, but at serious costs.[39] New York City, for example, taxes property at rates twice the national average, yielding a property-tax roll three times as large as any other city. New York City also has an income tax, which is rising rapidly. Newark, plagued by racial conflict, ranks second in the nation in its rate of property tax.[40]

The exploitation of any of these taxes is fraught with dilemmas for localities. By raising either property or sale taxes excessively, they risk driving out the business and industry on which their tax rolls eventually depend, and risk also the political ire of their constituents. For instance, it was estimated that a one-percent increase in the New York City sales tax had the effect of driving six percent of all clothing and household-furnishing sales out beyond the city line, along with thousands of jobs.[41] A New York property-tax rate of four percent of true value on new improvements is thought by many to have acted as a brake on most new construction, excepting the very high-yielding office buildings and luxury apartments. Boston's six percent of true-value property tax brought private construction to a halt until the law was changed so that new improvements were taxed only half as heavily as existing buildings.[42] Increases in either sales- or property-tax rates thus entail the serious danger of diminishing revenues by eroding the tax base. To make matters worse, with the beginning of recession in 1969, revenues from sales and income taxes began to fall off, while the interest the cities had to pay for borrowing rose, at a time when local governments were going more and more into hock.[43]

Fiscal Constraints and Political Turmoil

In the face of fiscal constraints, demands on city halls do not simply stop. Indeed, a number of frustrated claimants seem ready for rebellion. When pension concessions to some employees in New York City were thwarted by the state legislature, the enraged municipal unions closed the bridges to the city and closed the sewage plants, while the president of Local 237 intoned that "Governor Rockefeller needs to be reminded that the teamsters are made of sterner stuff than the people of Czechoslovakia and Austria who caved in so easily to Hitler three decades ago.''[44] If most groups were less dramatic in pressing their demands, it is probably because they were more quickly conciliated than these workers, many of whom were black and Puerto Rican. The political instability, which escalating demands both signify and exacerbate, rocked one city government after another. Indeed, many big-city mayors simply quit the job, something that does not happen very often in politics.

The reason they give is money—money to appease the anarchic demands of urban groups. Joseph Barr, former mayor of Pittsburgh and a past president of the United States Conference of Mayors, explained that "the main problem of any mayor of any city of any size is money . . . we are just choked by the taxes. The middle classes are fleeing to the suburbs and the tax base is going down and down . . . if the mayors don't get relief from the legislatures, God help them! . . . Any mayor who is not frustrated is not thinking." Arthur Naftalin, former mayor of Minneapolis and also a past president of the United States Conference of Mayors, said that the "most difficult and most important problem [is that the city] can't reach the resources. The states have kept the cities on a leash, tying them to the property tax—which is regressive. Old people and low-income people live in the city, and they catch the burden increasingly." Thomas C. Tarrington, mayor of Denver 1963–1968, when he resigned in midterm, said when he left:

I hope to heaven the cities are not ungovernable . . . [but] with perhaps few if any exceptions, the financial and organizational structures of most large cities are hardly up to the needs of 1969 or 1970. Our cities were structured financially when we were a rural nation and our structures of government are such that the mayors lack not only the financial resources but the authority to do the job.

Ivan Allen, Jr., mayor of Atlanta since 1962: "At my age I question whether I would have been physically able to continue for another four years in the face of the constant pressure, the innumerable crises, and the confrontations that have occurred in the cities." A. D. Sillingson, mayor of Omaha from 1965: "I've gone through three and a half tough years in this racial business, and could just stand so much." And the country's first black mayor, Carl B. Stokes of Cleveland, interviewed before he was reelected by the slim-

mest of margins in 1969, announced that the biggest challenge facing someone in his position was "obtaining the necessary money with which to meet the necessary needs of a big city."[45] Mr. Stokes declined to run again in 1971, leaving Cleveland politics fragmented among eleven different candidates. The list of prominent mayors who threw in the sponge includes such celebrated urban reformers as Jerome P. Cavanaugh of Detroit and Richard C. Lee of New Haven. Nearly half the United States Conference of Mayors Executive Committee and Advisory Council have retired or announced their intentions of retiring after their present term, an "unprecedented" number according to a conference spokesman.

Whether the candidates were new aspirants moving in to fill the vacuum or older hands sticking it out, by 1969 big-city elections throughout the country reflected the instability of the times. Mayor Lindsay was reelected, but with only forty-two percent of the vote. The same year two Democrats ran against each other in Detroit. In Pittsburgh Peter F. Flaherty, an insurgent Democrat, won only to promptly repudiate the ward chairman who turned out the vote for him; in Youngstown, a solidly Democratic city, a Republican was elected; in Philadelphia, where registration is heavily Democratic, the Democratic party was unable to block a Republican sweep headed by District Attorney Arlen Specter, putting him in line for a try at the mayor's office. Of 156 Connecticut towns and cities that held elections in 1969, forty-six municipalities switched parties. And an assembly of eighty-five representatives of federal, state and local governments, labor and religious leaders, editors and educators, meeting at Arden House in 1969, pronounced:

America is in the midst of an urban crisis demonstrating an inadequacy and incompetency of basic policies, programs and institutions and presenting a crisis of confidence. These failures affect every public service—education, housing, welfare, health, and hospitals, transportation, pollution control, the administration of criminal justice, and a host of others—producing daily deterioration in the quality of life. Although most visible in the large cities, that deterioration spreads to suburbia, exurbia, and beyond. Frustration rises as government fails to respond.[46]

This pronouncement came not from a radical caucus but from a gathering of the most prestigious representatives of American institutions.

Those who for the time survived the turmoil were even shriller in sounding the alarm. Mayor Joseph Alioto of San Francisco said simply: "The sky's falling in on the cities; it really is. We've had six cops killed in San Francisco since I took office. We need jobs and money for the poor and haven't money for either. . . . We can't go on like this. Even the capitalistic system's not going to survive the way we're going." Kenneth Gibson, the black mayor of Newark: "Wherever the cities are going, Newark's going to get there first. . . . If we had a bubonic plague in Newark everybody would try to help, but we really have a worse plague and nobody notices." Mayor Wesley Uhlman of Seattle said he was so busy putting out fires he had no time to think about anything else. Moon Candrieu, the mayor of New Orleans: "We've taxed everything that moves and everything that stands still, and if anything moves again, we tax that too. . . . The cities are going down the pipe and if we're going to save them we'd better do it now; three years from now will be too late." "Boston," said Mayor Kevin White, "is a tinderbox. . . . The fact is, it's an armed camp. One out of every five people in Boston is on welfare. Look, we raise 70 percent of our money with the property tax, but half our property is untaxable and 20 percent of our people are bankrupt. Could you run a business that way?" And Mayor Lindsay of New York proclaimed: "The cities of America are in a battle for survival. . . . Frankly, even with help in Washington, I'm not sure we can pull out the urban crisis in time."[47] (Not long afterwards, Governor Rockefeller suggested that perhaps New York City's government, at least, ought not to survive, that it might be a good idea to abolish the present city structure and begin all over.)[48]

The mayors speak of the twin troubles of scarce revenues and racial confrontation. And it is no accident that the troubles occur together and are most severe in the biggest cities. It was the biggest cities that experienced the most serious disturbance of traditional political relations as a result of the influx of blacks and the outflux of many whites. In this context, demands by black newcomers triggered a rush of new demands by whites, especially the large and well-organized provider groups that flourished in the big cities. The weakened and vulnerable mayors responded; they gave more and more of the jobs, salaries, contracts and services that had always worked to win and hold the allegiance of diverse groups. The eventual inability of the cities to garner the vastly increased revenues needed to fuel this process helped bring the urban political process to a point of crisis. The fiscal crisis is indeed real—not because of mounting "needs" for services but because of mounting demands for the benefits associated with the municipal bureaucracies. To block the responses of the bureaucracies to these demands for lack of revenues is to block a process of political accommodation in the largest population centers of the nation. The defection of the mayors was another sign of how deep the disturbances were, not in health agencies or welfare agencies, but in the urban political structure.

Federalism as a Constraining Influence

If mayors cannot resist the demands of contending groups in the cities, there are signs that the state and federal governments can, and will. The fiscal interrelations that undergird the federal system and leave the cities dependent on state and federal grants for an increasing portion of their funds are also a mechanism by which state and federal politics come to intervene in and control city politics. This is happening most clearly and directly through changes in state expenditures for the cities.

With their own taxing powers constricted from the outset, the mayors had little recourse but to turn to the states for enlarged grants-in-aid, trying to pass upward the political pressures they felt, usually summoning the press and the urban pressure groups to help. Since governors and legislators were not entirely immune to pressures from the city constituencies, the urban states increased their aid to the big cities.[49] Metropolises like New York City and Los Angeles now get roughly a quarter of their revenues from the state.

Accordingly, state budgets also escalated, and state taxes rose.[50] All in all, at least twenty-one states imposed new taxes or increased old taxes in 1968, and thirty-seven states in 1969, usually as a result of protracted struggle.[51] North Carolina enacted the largest program of new or increased taxes in its history; Illinois and Maine introduced an income tax, bringing to thirty-eight the number of states imposing some form of income tax;

outh Carolina passed its first major tax increase
1 a decade. Even Ohio moved to change its
radition of low-tax and low-service policies that
ad forced thirteen school districts in the state
> close. Overall, state and local taxes rose from
ve percent of the Gross National Product in 1946
> more than eight percent of the GNP in 1969.
mericans paid an average of $380 in state and
>cal taxes in the fiscal year 1968, $42 more per
erson than the previous year, and more than
ouble the fiscal year 1967. The rate tended to
e highest in urban states: In New York the
er-person tax burden was $576; in California,
540; in Massachusetts, $453. The low was in
rkansas, with a tax rate of $221.[52]

But raising taxes in Albany or Sacramento to
ay for politics in New York City or Los Angeles
 no simple matter, for the state capitals are
ot nearly as vulnerable as city halls to urban
ressure groups, but are very vulnerable indeed
> the suburbs and small towns that are antago-
ized by both higher taxes and city troubles. Be-
des, the mass of urban voters also resent taxes,
pecially when taxes are used to pay off the or-
nized interests in the service systems, without
elding visibly better services.[53] Accordingly,
en while taxes are raised, state grants to the
ties are cut anyway. Thus, the New York State
gislature reduced grant-in-aid formulas in wel-
re and medicaid (programs that go mainly to
e central cities and mainly to blacks in those
ties) in 1969[54] and again in 1971 (1970 was an
ection year and so the governor proposed in-
reased aid to the cities without tax increases).
ach time, the cuts were effected in all-night
arathon sessions of the legislature, replete with
ramatic denouncements by Democratic legis-
tors from the cities and cries of betrayal from
e mayors. Despite the cuts, anticipated state
ending still rose by $878 million in 1969, the
ghest for any single year excepting the previous
cal year in which the rise had been $890 mil-
on. By 1970, when the proposed budget had
ached $8.45 billion, requiring $1.1 billion in new
xes, the outcry was so terrific that the gov-
nor reversed his proposals and led the legisla-
re in a budget-slashing session, with welfare
d medicaid programs the main targets.

When Governor Ronald Reagan, a self-pro-
aimed fiscal conservative, nevertheless submit-
d a record-breaking $6.37-billion budget for
e 1969–1970 fiscal year, he met a storm of polit-
al protest that threatened a legislative im-

passe, leaving California without a budget. The
next year Reagan proposed to solve the state's
"fiscal crisis" by cutting welfare and medicaid
expenditures by $800 million; even so, he sub-
mitted another record budget of $6.7 billion.
When the long legislative battle that ensued was
over, the governor signed an unbalanced budget
of $7.3 billion, with substantial cuts in welfare
and medicaid nevertheless.

Pennsylvania's former Republican Governor
Raymond P. Shafer, in his short two years in
office, managed to win the opposition of all but
twenty-three percent of Pennsylvania voters as
he and the legislature fought about how to raise
$500 million in new revenues. At the beginning
of his term in 1967 the governor was forced to
raise state sales taxes to six percent, despite his
campaign pledge of no new taxes, and early in
1969, with the budget $200 million short, he pro-
posed that state's first income tax. When Shafer
left office the income tax was enacted by his successor, Democratic Governor Milton Shapp,
only to be voided by the Pennsylvania Supreme
Court in 1971. A modified income-tax law was
finally passed, but by that time the state legislature was also making spending reductions, including a fifty-percent cut in state education appropriations for ghetto districts.[55]

When Connecticut's 1969 biannual state budget
proposal required a $700-million tax increase de-
spite cuts in the welfare budget, the Democratic-
controlled General Assembly rebelled, forcing a
hectic special session of the state legislature to
hammer out a new budget and tax program. In
the tumultuous weeks that followed, a compromise package presumably agreed upon by the
Democratic governor and the Democratic majority in both houses was repeatedly thrown into
doubt. When the session was over, Connecticut
had passed the largest tax program in its history,
had borrowed $32.5 million, and Governor John
N. Dempsey had announced he would not seek
reelection. Two years later Republican Governor Thomas J. Meskill engaged the legislature
in battle again over another record budget that
the governor proposed to pay for with a seven-
percent sales tax—the highest in the country.
Not only the legislature, but the insurance industries, the mayor of Hartford and 5000 marchers
took part in the protest that ensued, leading to a
compromise tax package that replaced the sales-
tax increase with a new state income tax, together with more borrowing and new welfare

cuts as well. A few short months later, after new public protests, the income tax was repealed, the sales-tax increase was restored, and more spending cuts were made, mainly in state grants to municipalities and in welfare appropriations.

The New Jersey legislature, at a special session called by Democratic Governor Richard Hughes in 1969 to plead for added revenues for urban areas, rejected a new tax on banks and lending institutions—this despite the urging of the governor, who called the cities of the state "sick" and its largest city, Newark, "sick unto death," and despite the clamor of New Jersey's mayors. The legislature eventually agreed to redirect some existing urban-aid funds to pay for increased police and fire salaries—a measure made particularly urgent after Newark's firemen went on strike, forcing the city to make emergency salary arrangements. When Republican Governor William T. Cahill took office later that year he signed a measure raising the New Jersey sales tax to five percent, claiming he faced a "major state fiscal crisis" of a $300-million deficit.

Other state governments are locked in similar fiscal and political battles. Michigan began the 1972 fiscal year without authorization to spend money after the legislature had been virtually paralyzed by a six-month struggle over the $2-billion budget, which the governor had proposed to finance with a thirty-eight percent increase in the state income tax. Wisconsin cut welfare and urban-aid expenditures over Governor Ody J. Fish's protest and, having enacted a new and broadened sales tax, precipitated a march on the capital by Milwaukee poor. Not long afterward, Governor Fish resigned, imperiling the Wisconsin Republican party. In Rhode Island, Democratic Governor Frank E. Licht promised no new taxes in his reelection campaign in 1970 and two months later recommended an income tax, amidst loud voter protest. When Texas, having passed the largest tax bill in its history in 1969, faced a deficit of $400 million in 1971, Governor Preston E. Smith vetoed the entire second year of a two-year budget, which totaled $7.1 billion.

In brief, pressures from the big cities were channeled upward to the state capitals, with some response. At least in the big urbanized states, governors and legislatures moved toward bailing out the cities, with the result that state expenditures and state taxes skyrocketed. But the reaction is setting in; the taxpayers' revolt is being felt in state legislatures across the coun-

try. And as raucous legislative battles continue a trend is emerging: The states are turning out to be a restraining influence on city politics, and especially on ghetto politics.

While, in the main, grants-in-aid were not actually reduced, they were not increased enough to cover rising city costs either, and the toll is being taken. Some municipalities began to cut payroll and services. By 1971 vacancies were going unfilled in New York City, Baltimore, Denver and Kansas City. San Diego and Cleveland reduced rubbish collection; Dallas cut capital improvements; Kansas City let its elm trees die.[57] Detroit started closing park toilets. And some city employees were actually being dismissed in Los Angeles, Cleveland, Detroit, Kansas City, Cincinnati, Indianapolis, Pittsburgh and New York City. "This is the first time since the Depression that I have participated in this kind of cutback of education," said Cincinnati's superintendent of schools.[57] "You run as far as you can, but when you run out of gas you've got to stop," said Baltimore's Mayor Thomas J. D'Alesandro.

But the biggest cuts imposed by the states were in the programs from which blacks had gained the most as a result of their emergence as a force in the cities. Special state appropriations for health and education in ghetto districts were being cut; nine states cut back their medicaid programs;[58] and most important, at least nineteen states reduced welfare benefits by mid-1971 according to a *New York Times* survey. Moreover, new state measures to root out "welfare fraud," or to reinstitute residence restrictions, or to force recipients into work programs threatened far more drastic erosion of black gains in the near future.

There are signs that the federal government has also become a restraining influence on city politics. In the early 1960s the national Democratic administration had used its grants to the cities to intervene in city politics, encouraging ghetto groups to demand more from city hall and forcing recalcitrant mayors to be more responsive to the enlarging and volatile ghetto whose allegiance had become critical to the national Democratic party. But a Republican administration was not nearly so oriented to the big cities, least of all to the ghettos of the big cities. Accordingly, the directions of the Great Society programs that the Nixon administration had inherited were shifted; bit by bit the new federal poverty agencies were scattered among the old line federal bureaucracies, and the local agencies that had been set up in the ghettos were given to understand that confrontation tactics had to be halted. By now the Great Society looks much like traditional grant-in-aid programs; the federal fuel for ghetto agitation has been cut off. And new administration proposals for revenue sharing would give state and local governments firm control of the use of federal grants, unhampered by the "maximum feasible participation" provisions that helped to stir ghetto demands in the 1960s.

There are other signs as well. The wage freeze stopped, at least temporarily, the escalation of municipal salaries, and this despite the outcry of teachers across the country. Finally, and perhaps most portentous for blacks, the administration's proposal for "welfare reform" would give the federal government a much larger role in welfare policy, lifting the struggle for who gets what outside of the arena of city politics where blacks had developed some power and had gotten some welfare.

Nor is it likely, were the Democrats to regain the presidency and thus regain the initiative in federal legislation, that the pattern of federal restraint would be entirely reversed. The conditions that made the ghettos a political force for a brief space of time seem to have changed. For one thing, there is not much action, either in the streets or in the voting booths. The protests and marches and riots have subsided, at least partly because the most aggressive people in the black population were absorbed; it was they who got the jobs and honorary positions yielded to blacks during the turmoil. These concessions, together with the Great Society programs that helped produce them, seem to have done their work, not only in restoring a degree of order to the streets but in restoring ghetto voters to Democratic columns.

In any case, it was not ghetto insurgency of itself that gave blacks some political force in the 1960s. Rather it was that the insurgents were concentrated in the big cities, and the big cities played a very large role in Democratic politics. That also is changing; the cities are losing ground to the suburbs, even in Democratic calculations, and trouble in the cities is not likely to carry the same weight with Democratic presidents that it once did.

To be sure, a Democratic administration might be readier than a Republican one to refuel local

services, to fund a grand new cornucopia of social programs. The pressures are mounting, and they come from several sources. One is the cities themselves, for to say that the cities are no longer as important as they once were is not to say Democratic leaders will want the cities to go under. Moreover, the inflated costs of the city are spreading to the suburbs and beyond, and these communities are also pressing for federal aid. Finally, there is the force of the organized producers themselves, who have become very significant indeed in national politics; the education lobby and the health lobby already wield substantial influence in Washington, and they are growing rapidly. But while these pressures suggest that new federal funds will be forthcoming, the rise of the suburbs and the parallel rise of the professional lobbies indicate that it is these groups who are likely to be the main beneficiaries.

The future expansion of the federal role in local services has another, perhaps more profound, significance. It means that the decline of the local political unit in the American political structure, already far advanced, will continue. No matter how much talk we may hear about a "new American revolution," through which the federal government will return revenues and power to the people, enlarged federal grants mean enlarged federal power, for grants are a means of influencing local political developments, not only by benefiting some groups and not others but through federally imposed conditions that come with the new moneys. These conditions, by curbing the discretion of local political leaders, also erode the power of local pressure groups. As localities lose their political autonomy, the forces that remain viable will be those capable of exerting national political influence. Some may view this change as an advance, for in the past local communities have been notoriously oligarchical. But for blacks it is not an advance; it is in the local politics of the big cities that they have gained what influence they have.

The general truths to be drawn from this tale of the cities seem clear enough and familiar enough, for what happened in the 1960s has happened before in history. The lower classes made the trouble, and other groups made the gains. In the United States in the 1960s, it was urban blacks who made the trouble, and it was the organized producer groups in the cities who made the largest gains. Those of the working and middle classes who were not among the organized producers got little enough themselves, and they were made to pay with their tax moneys for gains granted to others. Their resentments grew. Now, to appease them, the small gains that blacks did make in the course of the disturbances are being whittled away.

There is, I think, an even more important truth, though one perhaps not so quickly recognized. These were the events of a political struggle, of groups pitted against each other and against officialdom. But every stage of that struggle was shaped and limited by the structures in which these groups were enmeshed. A local service apparatus, which at the outset benefited some and not others, set the stage for group struggle. Service structures that offered only certain kinds of benefits determined the agenda of group struggle. And a fiscal structure that limited the contest mainly to benefits paid for by state and local taxes largely succeeded in keeping the struggle confined within the lower and middle strata of American society. School teachers turned against the ghetto, taxpayers against both, but no one turned against the concentrations of individual and corporate wealth in America. Local government, in short, is important, less for the issues it decides than for the issues it keeps submerged. Of the issues submerged by the events of the urban crisis, not the least is the more equitable distribution of wealth in America.

Notes

1. This view of the urban problem was given official status by the "Riot Commission." According to the commission:

   [The] fourfold dilemma of the American city [is]: Fewer tax dollars come in, as large numbers of middle-income tax payers move out of central cities and property values and business decline; More tax dollars are required, to provide essential public services and facilities, and to meet the needs of expanding lower-income groups; Each tax dollar buys less, because of increasing costs. Citizen dissatisfaction with municipal services grows as needs, expectations and standards of living increase throughout the community [*Report of the National Advisory Commission on Civil Disorders* (New York: Bantam, 1968), p. 389].

   Similarly, Alan K. Campbell and Donna E. Shalala write: "Most of the substantive problems flow, at least in part, from . . . the fact that the central cities have been left with segments of the population most in need of expensive services, and the redistribution of economic activities has reduced the relative ability of these areas to support such services" ["Problems Unsolved, Solutions Untried: The Urban Crisis," in *The States and the Urban Crisis* (Englewood Cliffs, N.J.: Prentice-Hall, 1970), p. 7]. The conventional wisdom is again echoed by the U.S. Advisory Commission on Intergovernmental Relations:

   The large central cities are in the throes of a deepening fiscal crisis. On the one hand, they are confronted with the need to satisfy rapidly growing expenditure requirements triggered by the rising number of "high cost" citizens. On the other hand, their tax resources are growing at a decreasing rate (and in some cases actually declining), a reflection of the *exodus of middle and high income families and business firms from the central city to suburbia* [italics in original] [*Fiscal Balance in the American Federal System: Metropolitan Fiscal Disparities* (Washington, D.C.: Government Printing Office, 1967). Vol II p. 5].

   Politicians share this view. "In the last 1[?] years, 200,000 middle-class whites have moved out of St. Louis," said Mayor A. J. Cervantes, "and 100,000 blacks, many of them poor, have moved in. It costs us *eight times as much* to provide city services to the poor as to the middle-class" [italics in original] [the *New York Times*, May 22, 1970].

2. As a matter of fact, city revenues have not declined at all, but have risen astronomically, although not as astronomically as costs. Presumably, if the city had been able to hold or attract better-off residents and businesses, revenues would have risen even faster, and the fiscal aspect of the urban crisis would not have developed.

3. It should be made clear at the outset that the costs of government generally rose steadily in the years after World War II. This is the subject of James O'Connor's analysis in "The Fiscal Crisis of the State," *Socialist Revolution* 1, 1 (January/February 1970), 12–54; 1, 2 (March/April 1970), 34–94. But while all government budgets expanded, state and local costs rose much faster, and costs in the central cities rose the most rapidly of all, especially after 196[?]. Thus, according to the Citizens' Budget Commission, New York City's budget increased almost eight times as fast in the five fiscal years between 1964 and 1969 as during the postwar years 1949 to 1954. From an average annual

increase of 5.5 percent in 1954, budget costs jumped to 9.1 percent in 1964 and to 14.2 percent in 1969 (the *New York Times*, January 11, 1960). It is with this exceptional rise that this article is concerned.

4. For a discussion of the uses of welfare in resisting black migrants, see Frances Fox Piven and Richard A. Cloward, *Regulating the Poor: The Functions of Public Welfare* (New York: Pantheon, 1971), Chapters 7 and 8.

5. At least some of the employees in all cities with more than 500,000 inhabitants are now under civil service; in about half of these cities, virtually all employees have such protections.

6. See Piven and Cloward, *op. cit.*, Chapters 9 and 10, on the impact of the black migration on the Democratic administration of the 1960s.

7. *Changing Patterns of Prices, Pay, Workers, and Work on the New York Scene*, U.S. Department of Labor, Bureau of Labor Statistics (New York: Middle Atlantic Regional Office, May 1971), Regional Reports No. 20, p. 36.

8. The dole, needless to say, is a very different sort of concession from the higher salaries, pensions and on-the-job prerogatives won by other groups. For one thing, the dole means continued poverty and low status. For another, it is easier to take away, for recipients remain relatively weak and unorganized.

9. That poor minorities made large gains through the welfare "crisis" and other groups did not is important to understanding the furious opposition that soaring welfare budgets arouse. Organized welfare-agency workers were competing for the welfare dollar, of course, but were not nearly so successful as the workers in other services, for they were not in a position to take much advantage of political turmoil. They were not nearly so numerous or well organized as teachers, policemen or firemen, and they could not use the threat of withholding services to exact concessions nearly so effectively. Unlike schoolteachers or garbage men, their services were of importance only to the very poor.

10. See *State and Local Finances: Significant Features 1967–1970*, U.S. Advisory Commission on Intergovernmental Relations (Washington, D.C.: Government Printing Office, 1969), Figure 6, p. 39.

11. Conflict and competition over the schools have been further heightened because the proportion of blacks in the schools has increased even more rapidly than the proportion of blacks in the population, owing to the youthfulness of blacks and the flight of whites to private schools. In Washington, blacks constituted fifty-four percent of the local population in 1965, but ninety percent of the school children; in St. Louis blacks were twenty-seven percent of the

population, but sixty-three percent of the school population; in Chicago, they were twenty-three percent of the general population, but fifty-three percent of the school population; in New York City, where blacks and Puerto Ricans make up about twenty-seven percent of the population, fifty-two percent of the children in the schools were black or Puerto Rican. Of the twenty-eight target cities in the nation, seventeen had black majorities in the school system by 1965. See *Racial Isolation in the Public School*, U.S. Commission on Civil Rights (Washington, D.C.: Government Printing Office, February 20, 1967), Table II–2.

12. The federal government was also providing direct funds to improve the education of the "disadvantaged" under Title I of the Elementary and Secondary Education Act of 1965. However, although in four years following the passage of the act, $4.3 billion was appropriated for Title I, it was widely charged that these funds were misused and diverted from the poor by many local school boards.

13. A series of training guides to such efforts, prepared with federal funds by a local poverty program known as United Bronx Parents, included a kit on "How to Evaluate Your School" and a series of leaflets on such matters as "The Expense Budget—Where Does all the Money Go?" "The Construction Budget—When the Community Controls Construction We Will Have the Schools We Need," as well as an all-purpose handbook on parents' rights vis-à-vis the schools. Not surprisingly, Albert Shanker, president of the teachers union in New York City, charged there was "an organized effort to bring about rule in the schools by violence," involving the use of flying squads of disrupters who went from school to school and who, he said, had been trained with government (i.e., poverty program) funds (the *New York Times*, November 16, 1970, p. 2).

14. See Urban America, Inc., and the Urban Coalition, *One Year Later: An Assessment of the Nation's Response to the Crisis Described by the National Advisory Commission on Civil Disorders* (New York: Praeger, 1969), pp. 34–35. See also Naomi Levine with Richard Cohen, *Ocean-hill-Brownsville: A Case History of Schools in Crisis* (New York: Popular Library, 1969), pp. 127–128.

15. This estimate was reported by Fred Hechinger, the *New York Times*, August 29, 1971.

16. Averaging $9200 in 1970–1971, according to the National Education Association.

17. State averages reflect the political troubles in big cities. Thus, in an urban state like New York, $1251 was spent per pupil in 1969–1970, and New Jersey, California, Connecticut and Massachusetts were not far behind. This rep-

resented an increase of about eighty percent in per-pupil expenditures since 1965–1966.

18. Educational costs have also risen sharply outside the central cities, particularly in the adjacent suburban school districts. These rises are a direct reverberation of troubles in the cities. Suburban school boards must remain competitive with the rising salary levels of educational personnel in the central cities, particularly considering the high priority placed on education by the middle-class suburbs. For example, between 1958 and 1959, enrollment in the Westchester, New York, schools increased by 1.5 percent, and the operating budget by 12 percent. In Fairfield, Connecticut, enrollment increased by 5.2 percent, the budget by 13.2 percent. In Suffolk County, New York, enrollment increased by 6.6 percent, the budget by 11.6 percent. In Monmouth, New Jersey, enrollment increased by 4.4 percent, the budget by 19 percent. Moreover, there are also increasing numbers of blacks in some of the older suburbs, with the result that these towns are experiencing political disturbances very similar to those of the big cities.

19. *State and Local Finances, op. cit.*, p. 39.

20. *Changing Patterns of Prices, Pay, Workers, and Work, op. cit.*, pp. 7–8.

21. Some 25,000 of the new jobs were noncompetitive (the *New York Times*, May 28, 1971). Not surprisingly, the governor suggested that the mayor economize by cutting these, instead of always talking about cutting the number of policemen and firemen.

22. Welfare is the main example of an actual expansion of services, for the number of welfare employees increased largely as a reflection of increasing case loads. But so were new policemen hired to appease a broad constituency concerned about rising crime, sanitation men to answer demands for cleaner streets, and so forth.

23. *Changing Patterns of Prices, Pay, Workers, and Work, op. cit.*, p. 9. Moreover, big payrolls were a big city phenomenon. A study showed that, in three states studied in detail, the ratio of public employment per 100 population varied sharply by city size, more so in New Jersey and Ohio, less markedly in Texas. See *Urban and Rural America: Policies for Future Growth*, U.S. Advisory Commission on Intergovernmental Relations (Washington, D.C.: Government Printing Office, April 1968), pp. 47–49.

24. According to Harold Rubin:

Time lost by state and local government employees due to work stoppages climbed from 7,510 man-days in 1958 to 2,535,000 man-days in 1968, according to the U.S. Bureau of Labor Statistics. Such strikes have not been limited to those performing "nonessential duties." For example, during the first half of 1970 there have been strikes by prison guards (New Jersey), sanitation men (Cincinnati, Ohio; Phoenix, Arizona; Atlanta, Georgia; Seattle, Washington; and Charlotte, North Carolina), teachers (Youngstown, Ohio; Minneapolis, Minnesota; Butte, Montana; Tulsa, Oklahoma; Boston, Massachusetts; Newark and Jersey City, New Jersey; and Los Angeles, California, to list only some of the larger school systems involved), bus drivers (Cleveland, Ohio; Tacoma, Washington; and San Diego, California) hospital employees (State of New Jersey; Detroit, Michigan), policemen (Newport, Kentucky; Livonia, Michigan; and Winthrop, Massachusetts), and firemen (Newark, Ohio, and Racine, Wisconsin) ["Labor Relations in State and Local Governments," in Robert A. Connery and William V. Farr (eds.), *Unionization of Municipal Employees* (New York: Columbia University, The Academy of Political Science, 1971), pp. 20–21.]

25. The *New York Times*, June 13, 1971.

26. The *New York Times*, January 31, 1970.

27. The *New York Times*, February 26, 1970.

28. The *New York Times*, March 17, 1970.

29. The *New York Times*, March 15, 1971. These estimates were given to the press by the city's budget director.

30. Rising wages and pension benefits among municipal employees are frequently attributed to unionization, which has indeed spread in the 1960s, rather than to changes in city politics. Membership in the American Federation of State, County, and Municipal employees increased from 180,000 to 425,000 in one decade. The American Federation of Teachers enlarged its ranks from 60,000 members in 1961 to 175,000 in 1969. But to point to unionization as a cause simply diverts the argument, since the spread and militancy of unionism among city employees in the 1960s must itself be explained. In any case, a Brookings Institution study of nineteen local governments showed no conclusive differences between unionized and nonunionized wages; both had risen substantially. See David Stanley, "The Effect of Unions on Local Governments," Connery and Farr (ed.), *op. cit.*, p. 47.

31. Norton Long and others have argued that the city's economic problems are largely the result of efforts by city employees to keep up with pay scales in the private sector, despite the absence of productivity increases in public-service jobs comparable to those that justify wage increases in the private sector ("The City as Reservation," *The Public Interest*, No. 25 [Fall 1971]). This argument, however, presumes that

430

city pay scales lag behind private scales and that city workers are merely straining to catch up. Quite the opposite has come to be true in some big cities. A 1970 study by the Middle Atlantic Bureau of Labor Statistics of pay rates in the New York metropolitan area found city pay rates to be much higher than private-industry rates. For example, carpenters, electricians and plumbers who worked for the city earned fully sixty percent more than those in private industry; painters and automobile mechanics earned thirty-six percent more; even messengers, typists, switchboard operators and janitors were substantially better off when they worked for the city. Moreover, *city workers also received far better holiday, vacation, health insurance and pension benefits.* It should also be noted that all but the last grouping were also much better paid in the city than in the suburbs. And so were patrolmen, firemen, sanitation man and social workers substantially better paid in the city than in the suburbs. A similar conclusion was reached by Bennett Harrison, who compared mean weekly earnings in the public and private sector of twelve metropolitan areas, using 1966 data. His calculations reveal a sharp disparity between public and private earnings in the central cities (although in 1966 some categories of suburban earnings were higher than the central city). See his *Public Employment and Urban Poverty* (Washington, D.C.: The Urban Institute, 1971), p. 30.

32. Put another way the average annual increase in New York City's expense budget during the last five years was $582 million, or eight times as high as the $71-million annual average increase from fiscal 1949 to fiscal 1954.

33. "Report on Financing Our Urban Needs," *Our Nation's Cities* (Washington, D.C.: Government Printing Office, March 1969), p. 21.

34. According to *Fiscal Balance in the American Federal System:*

National aggregates for 1957 and 1962 and more restricted data for 1964–65 indicate that local government in the metropolitan areas spends more and taxes more per person than in the remainder of the country . . . there is a striking contrast in non-educational expenditures—which include all the public welfare, health, hospital, public safety and other public services essential to the well-being of citizens. These general government costs are two-thirds higher in the metropolitan areas than they are in the rest of the country [*op. cit.*, Vol. II, p. 59].

Specifically, per-capita expenditures during 1964–1965 averaged $301.20 in the thirty-seven largest metropolitan areas, compared to $218.31

in small or nonmetropolitan areas (*ibid.*, Table 16, p. 60). As for the central cities themselves, "central cities contained 18.6 percent of the population (in 1964–65), but accounted for almost 25 percent of all local expenditure." In per-capita terms, local government expenditure in the large central cities "was 21 percent higher than in their outside regions, and almost two-thirds above that for the rest of the nation" (*ibid.*, p. 62). Moreover, when educational costs are omitted (suburban communities spend a great deal on education), the thirty-seven largest central cities "had an outlay of $232 per capita in 1965—$100 greater than their suburban counterparts" (*ibid.*, p. 6). By 1966–1967, the disparity had become more dramatic in many cities. Per-capita general expenditures, *including* education costs, was $475 in Washington, D.C., compared to $224 in the Washington suburban ring; $324 in Baltimore, compared to $210 in the suburban ring; $441 in Newark, compared to $271 in the suburban ring; $335 in Boston, compared to $224 in the suburban ring; $267 in St. Louis, and $187 in the suburbs (*State and Local Finances, op. cit.*, p. 70). Similarly, a study of fifty-five local governments in the San Francisco–Oakland metropolitan area showed that both the property-tax rate and the level of per-capita expenditures were higher in the central city. In dormitory suburbs, per-capita expenditures were only fifty-eight percent of those in the central city. See Julius Margolis, "Municipal Fiscal Structure in a Metropolitan Region," *Journal of Political Economy*, 65 (June 1957), p. 232.

35. The New York State Constitution, for example, specifies that:

It shall be the duty of the Legislature, subject to the provisions of this Constitution, to restrict the power of taxation, assessment, borrowing money, contracting indebtedness, and loaning the credit of countries, cities, towns and villages, so as to prevent abuses in taxation and assessments and in contracting of indebtedness by them. Nothing in this article shall be construed to prevent the Legislature from further restricting the powers herein specified (Article VIII, Section 12).

Traditionally the states have granted powers of taxation to the localities only very reluctantly.

36. Not only do states limit the taxing powers of localities, but they have the authority to mandate local expenditures (e.g., salary increases for police and firemen) with or without adjusting local taxing powers to pay for them. They also have the authority to vote tax exemptions at local expense for favored groups. State legis-

latures are given to doing exactly that, exacerbating the financial plight of local governments.

37. This was $27 billion out of $40 billion that localities raised in revenues from their own sources in 1967–1968 (*State and Local Finances, op. cit.,* Table 8, p. 31). It should be noted that property taxes are declining relative to other sources of local revenue. At the turn of the century about eighty percent of state and local budgets were financed by the property tax. Today the states hardly rely on it at all. Nevertheless, local governments still finance about half their budgets with property taxes.

38. The first city income tax was levied in Philadelphia, in 1939, when the city was on the verge of bankruptcy. The use of the income tax by big cities spread in the 1960s, with Akron and Detroit adopting it in 1962, Kansas City in 1964, Baltimore and New York City in 1966 and Cleveland in 1967. See *City Income Taxes* (New York: Tax Foundation, Inc., 1967), Research Publication No. 12, pp. 7–9. City income taxes must, of course, also be approved by the state, an approval that is not always forthcoming.

39. By 1964–65, per-capita local taxes in the central cities of the thirty-seven largest metropolitan areas had risen to $200 per capita. In Washington, D.C., taxes were $291 per capita; in New York City $279; and in Newark $273. Overall, central-city residents were paying seven percent of their income in local taxes and in the biggest cities ten percent (*Fiscal Balance in the American Federal System, op. cit.,* Vol. II, pp. 75–79).

40. By 1968 official statistics for the nation as a whole showed local property taxes totaling $27.8 billion. The annual rise since then is estimated at between $1 and $3 billion.

41. *Our Nation's Cities, op. cit.,* p. 24.

42. *Our Nation's Cities, op. cit.,* pp. 36–37. To understand the full impact of property taxes, one must remember that these are taxes on capital value, and not on income yielded. Thus, a three percent-of-true-value tax on improvements can easily tax away seventy-five percent of the net income that a new building would otherwise earn—a loss, economists generally agree, that tends to be passed on to the consumers. See, for example, Dick Netzer, *Economics of the Property Tax* (Washington, D.C.: The Brookings Institute, 1966), pp. 40–62.

43. Local tax collections increased by 500 percent between World War II and 1967, but costs have risen ten percent faster, and the bigger the city, the tighter the squeeze. If the process were to continue, and today's growth rate of city spending vs. city revenues to continue, a recent study commissioned by the National League of Cities estimates a gap of $262 billion by 1980 (*Our Nation's Cities, op. cit.,* p. 22). Measured another way, state and local indebtedness combined rose by 400 percent since 1948, while the federal debt rose by only twenty-six percent (*U.S. Fiscal Balance in the American Federal System, op. cit.,* Vol. I, p. 55). In the thirty-six large central cities alone, the cumulative tax gap could reach $25 to $30 billion by 1975 (*ibid.,* Vol. II, p. 91). A special Commission on the Cities in the Seventies, established by the National Urban Coalition, concluded that by 1980 most cities will be "totally bankrupt" (the *New York Times,* September 24, 1971).

44. The statement went on to say "that which is good enough for white cops and firemen is good enough for black and Puerto Rican employees of New York City" (the *New York Times,* June 8, 1971). According to city officials, the annual cost of pension benefits, which had been $215 million in 1960, was projected to reach $1.3 billion in the next ten years (the *New York Times,* June 9, 1971).

45. The *Christian Science Monitor,* September 4, 1969.

46. The *States and the Urban Crisis,* Report of the Thirty-Sixth American Assembly (Harriman, N.Y.: Arden House, October 30–November 2, 1969). The Report went on, not surprisingly, to recommend increased state and federal aid for the cities.

47. James Reston, "The President and the Mayors," the *New York Times,* March 24, 1971. In another column on April 21, 1971, Reston summarized the reports of the big-city mayors as: "First, they felt the crisis of the cities was the major threat to the security of the nation—more serious than Vietnam or anything else. Second, they felt that the bankruptcy and anarchy were underestimated. . . . They sound like communiques from a battlefield. . . . They have got beyond all the questions of race or party and are looking for power and leadership to deal with the urban problem."

48. The governor said he had in mind a new structure like the London County Council. City political leaders, for their part, had been proposing to abolish city-state relations by declaring New York City a separate state.

49. By 1966–1967, per-capita intergovernmental aid was substantially higher for the central cities than suburban localities (contrary to popular impression). Per-capita aid to Washington, D.C., was $181, compared to $81 in the outlying suburbs; $174 to Baltimore, and $101 to the suburbs; $179 to Boston, and $74 to the suburbs; $220 to New York City, and $163 to the suburbs; $144 to Newark, and $53 to the sub-

urbs; $70 to Philadelphia, and $61 to the suburbs; $88 to Chicago, and $55 to the suburbs; $126 to Detroit, and $115 to the suburbs (*State and Local Finances, op. cit.,* Table 29, p. 69).

50. Arthur Levitt, controller of the state of New York, recently released figures showing that state spending had increased from $1.3 billion in 1956 to $3.9 billion in 1964, to approximately $8 billion in 1968. In the four years ending in 1968, state spending rose by an annual average of $875 million, or 18.7 percent. In 1968 the spending increase was $1.4 billion, or 22.1 percent over the previous year (the *New York Times,* April 2, 1969–July 7, 1969). During this same five-year period, state revenues from taxes and federal aid increased from $3.7 billion to $7.2 billion. In other words, spending exceeded revenues, and by greater margins in each of the successive years. The total deficit for the five-year period amounted to $2.5 billion, which, of course, had to be borrowed. A large part of this rise in New York State's budget reflects aid to localities, which increased from $622 million in fiscal 1955 to $1.04 billion in fiscal 1960, to $1.67 billion in 1965, and $3.23 billion in fiscal year 1969. State spending for aid to education has doubled in the last six years, and the state share of welfare and medicaid costs doubled in only four years.

51. By 1971 the estimated difference between revenues and outlays were in excess of $500 million in New York, California and Texas. Florida was short $120 million; New Jersey $100 million; Connecticut $200 million (the *New York Times,* January 3, 1971). A handful of rural states, however, were considering tax cuts.

52. Data provided by the Commerce Clearing House, as reported in the *New York Times,* September 27, 1970.

53. A Gallup poll in 1969 showed that forty-nine percent would not vote for more money to pay for schools if additional taxes were sought, against forty-five percent who would (the *New York Times,* August 17, 1969). Another key fact in understanding the populist character of the tax revolt is that state and local taxes consist mainly in sales and property taxes and various user charges, all of which tend to be relatively regressive. Even the state income tax, when it is used, is usually imposed as a fixed percentage of income (unlike the graduated federal income tax, which takes more from those who have more, at least in principle). In any case, fully two-thirds of state revenues were raised from sales and gross receipt taxes. [*State and Government Finances in 1967,* U.S. Bureau of the Census (Washington, D.C.: Government Printing Office, 1968), Table I, p. 7]. Consequently, the new taxes have had a severe impact on the working and middle classes, who are paying a larger and larger percentage of personal income to state and local government. In New York, state and local taxes now absorb over thirteen percent of personal income; in California, over twelve percent; in Illinois and Ohio over eight percent. As a result of rising state and local taxes (and price inflation), per-capita disposable personal income fell considerably between 1965 and 1969. See Paul M. Schwab, "Two Measures of Purchasing Power Contrasted," *Monthly Labor Review* (April 1971). By contrast, federal taxes declined as a percent of Gross National Product between 1948–1968, during which period state and local taxes rose from about five percent to eight percent of GNP (*State and Local Finances, op. cit.,* Figure 5, p. 29). The "tax revolt" in the states should be no surprise.

54. Most of the 1969 welfare cuts were restored within a short time, but the 1971 cuts were not.

55. The *New York Times,* February 16, 1971; June 9, 17, 19, 25, 1971; and July 2, 1971.

56. The *New York Times,* August 30, 1970; November 27, 1970; and May 25, 1971.

57. Nationally, the annual rise in teacher salaries slumped to only 5.5 percent, after rising by about 8 percent each year for several years.

58. Usually by limiting eligibility, or limiting the types of services covered, or requiring co-payments by patients. See *Health Law Newsletter* (Los Angeles: National Legal Program on Health Problems of the Poor, June 1971), p. 2.

JAMES ALAN McPHERSON

In My Father's House There Are Many Mansions–And I'm Going to Get Me Some of Them Too: The Story of the Contract Buyers League

THE STORY OF THE CONTRACT BUYERS LEAGUE

". . . every human being's life in this world is inevitably mixed with every other life and, no matter what laws we pass, no matter what precautions we take, unless the people we meet are kindly and decent and human and liberty-loving, then there is no liberty. Freedom comes from human beings, rather than from laws and institutions."

—Clarence Darrow

Summation to jury in the trial of Henry Sweet, Detroit, 1926

I People and Houses

The way to Lawndale, on Chicago's West Side, is by el: a twenty-minute ride from the Loop to Pulaski Road, a twenty-minute ride back. In the early morning, and again in the evening, the cars running between the two sections of the city are packed with black workers. Airport attendants, maids, waitresses, janitors, truck drivers, factory workers: a cross section of the unskilled. These are people conditioned by urban living: nothing surprises them. In the rattling cars there is little laughter or talk, nor is there much complaining.

The community itself, Lawndale, is very much like any other black section of a major American

city. About 180,000 people crowd into its 12 square miles. Whether it is called a ghetto or a community, the visible symbols remain the same: the sense of Elizabethan vitality and ferment painfully contrasting with the physical reality of spiritually dead loafers in colorful habits decorating the fronts of bars and stores and barbershops; children darting in and out of these shops or playing in gutters; mothers hauling plastic sacks of clothes to and from the laundromats, young women looking vacantly nowhere. The radio music which keeps it all alive blares into the street, sometimes overpowered by bull-voiced disc jockeys hawking cars and clothes and color televisions. Older women look down on the street, watching the children and just watching; a repossession notice, from downtown, floats along the pavement on the wind. The stylized movements of eyes and fingers and feet; the screaming colors; the pictures and posters of this year's politicians sloppily pasted over those

Reprinted by permission of William Morris Agency, Inc. and The Atlantic Monthly Company, Boston, Mass. Copyright © 1972 by James Alan McPherson.

om last year; the bourbon billboards; the un-
eared lots and falling houses bearing the graffiti
f resident groups—Vice Lords, Conservative
ice Lords, Disciples, Black Panthers. The store-
ront churches; the other houses struggling to
rvive; the sense of having seen it all or of hav-
g read about it all someplace before.

But something new and positive has started
re that makes Lawndale more than just an-
her ghetto. Along the streets intersecting Pu-
ski Road are hundreds of old, but solidly con-
ructed two- and three-flat houses which many
the residents hope to rehabilitate eventually.
all, shabby, weatherworn brick structures, they
ggest a stability that is foreign to the idea of a
etto. Yet these houses, and the fight of Lawn-
le people to save them, are what make this par-
cular ghetto a community and a symbol of na-
nal significance.

Sometime this year, amid the hoopla and glit-
r of the two national political conventions, the
surrection there of suppressed issues and the
vish promises for dealing with them, the fate
these people and their houses will be decided
the United States District Court for the Nor-
ern District of Illinois. Two court cases ar-
ed by white lawyers, *Baker* v. *F & F Invest-
ent* and *Clark* v. *Universal Builders*, represent
ur years of cooperative activity by the people
Lawndale on the West Side of Chicago, joined
other black families from the South Side of
icago. The cases bind over three thousand
ack families and their homes to a difficult ques-
n which must eventually be answered by the
urts: has a businessman the legal right to
ake a profit from a market created by racial
scrimination where the buyer has no other
ace to deal?

e problem is common to every American
etto. What has happened in Chicago has hap-
ned in other cities. But a popular movement
do something about it began in Chicago, and
icago is the central stage on which the result-
t drama is now coming to a climax.

Chicago is perhaps the most residentially seg-
gated city in the country. Its reputation is
sed on a strong tradition of neighborhood
vns or "ethnic states." Their people—Bohe-
ans, Germans, Irish, Italians, Jews, Lithua-
ans, Poles—tended to settle together and de-
d their customs and their borders against
wcomers. Black people were the ultimate

newcomers. Lured up from the South by stories
of higher wages, political freedom, the good life,
they settled on the South Side and began testing
borders.

By the end of World War I their own borders
had been erected for them. Jim Crow ordinances
and restrictive covenants were used to control
any expansion. Specifically, the Chicago Real
Estate Board's Code of Ethics cautioned: "A realtor should never be instrumental in introducing
into a neighborhood . . . members of any race or
nationality or any individual whose presence
would be clearly detrimental to property values
in that neighborhood." But the black influx
continued, and by the 1940s the South Side could
no longer accommodate the migrants. Sub-
scribers to the American Dream, they wanted the
stability symbolized by home ownership. Some
jumped the borders and spilled over into wherever housing was available: East Chicago, Chicago Heights. Some went as far as Gary, Indiana, and sat waiting for a chance to move back.
At the same time, many whites were moving
into the suburbs.

In 1948 the United States Supreme Court ruled
racially restrictive covenants judicially unenforceable. In 1950 the Real Estate Board
dropped the words "race" and "nationality" from
its code, but the policy remained the same. In
the mid-1950s when urban renewal began its
demolition and removal program in black slum
areas, a number of "panic peddlers" seized on
the U.S. Supreme Court's 1948 ruling to "open
up" and "turn" white residential neighborhoods
over to eager black buyers. For most poor black
families uprooted by urban renewal, as well as
for those seeking to get out of other overcrowded black communities, the choice was a
simple one: accept segregated public housing,
challenge segregationist practices in white ethnic neighborhoods and depend on police protection, or attempt to buy one of the solidly constructed homes rapidly becoming available
through a combination of panic peddling and
the exodus of white ethnics to the suburbs.
Many poor black families, like those in Lawndale, chose to follow the blockbusters.

Between 1958 and 1961, most of the southern
part of Lawndale passed from white to black
occupancy, with little enough push from the
blockbusters. Some merely hired black women
to walk their children through white neighborhoods, or paid black men to drive noisy cars

through an area a few times a day. Sometimes it was a telephone call for "Johnnie Mae." Another caller might simply say, "They're coming." The whites sold, many at prices far below the appraised value of their homes. And very shortly, sometimes within the same week, the houses would be resold to eager black families at inflated prices and at very high interest rates on installment purchase contracts. These contracts differ radically from the mortgages with which most Americans buy their homes. They are like a department store "easy-payment" plan.

The terms of the contracts (standard forms were approved by the Chicago Bar) allow the purchaser to take immediate possession of the property, but give him no equity or title until the full contract price is paid. The purchaser is obliged to pay specified installments on the purchase price over a period of years, the deed and title to the property to be delivered upon completion of such payments. Also, like the restrictive terms of a conditional sales contract, the seller has the right to reclaim the property and to keep all past payments if a single payment is missed. Since the buyer's equity in the property does not build up, he cannot obtain a mortgage unless a specific mortgage provision is written into the contract. And while the buyer is obliged to pay for insurance, taxes, and all repairs on the property, the seller usually selects the insurance company and can collect all claims for damages to the property. Most policies cover only the seller's mortgage interest, and not the contract value for which the property was sold. In many respects the contract buyer's rights are as minimal as those of a renter. (In some cases, less: at least in a landlord-tenant situation, the landlord is responsible for the upkeep of the building.) Besides the contractual advantages, many sellers were permitted under Illinois law to conceal their identities through the device of the land trust. While a title and trust company kept record titles, the beneficiaries, identified only by trust numbers, maintained complete control of the property. An additional advantage was provided by the swift remedies of the Illinois eviction law.

Most realtors who purchased the homes from fleeing whites could get mortgage financing from the banks. But for purchasers like the Howell Collins family there was no such advantage. Mr. and Mrs. Collins, an elderly black couple, contracted to buy their duplex home in Lawndale

on September 26, 1960. The seller had purchased the place one month earlier from a white family for about $14,500, but sold it to the Collins family for $25,500. The seller obtained a mortgage for $12,000. The Collins family paid $1500 down and signed a contract to pay the $24,000 balance in monthly installments of $191 (plus monthly deposits for insurance and taxes) at an interest rate of 7 percent for 19 years. Under the contract, they will pay a total of approximately $45,000 for the building, including over $19,000 in interest. If the Collinses had been able to get a mortgage and terms similar to those the realtor got, they would have paid a total of about $20,000 for the home over a shorter period of time.*

But the roots of the situation go much deeper than panic peddling. These black families were forced to buy on contract because they were excluded from Federal Housing Administration mortgage backing—in contrast to the availability of FHA mortgages for some blacks in some neighborhoods that have been black all along. From the FHA's creation in the 1930s, its policies, like those of the Chicago Real Estate Board, reflected a belief that property value in a residential area decreased when the residents were not of the same social, economic, and racial group. Besides including a sample restrictive covenant, the FHA underwriting manual of 1938 advised that "if a neighborhood is to retain stability, it is necessary that properties shall continue to be occupied by the same social and racial groups." Despite token reforms in this policy between 1947 and 1954, builders and leaders still remained free to make their own decisions. The agency requirement that a building be judged "economically sound" before mortgage backing could be given favored new houses and not the used residential properties usually bought by black families. Finally, an FHA administrative procedure of "red-lining" black or changing areas of a city as "high-risk" placed another, circular restriction on potential black home purchasers: as soon as more than a token number of them moved into an area, the neighborhood could be labeled "high

---

*These estimates are based on information provided by Collins in testimony before the Public Welfare Committee of the Illinois House of Representatives, and on the records of the Contract Buyers League.

risk" or "changing," and FHA backing of mortgages might terminate. Banks, savings and loan associations, the major homeowners' insurance companies—even the Veterans Administration—usually followed FHA guidelines.

Thus, besides being virtually restricted from the broader housing market, many black home buyers could not expect FHA backing of a mortgage if the purchased homes were not judged "economically sound" or if they were in areas designated "changing" or "high-risk." Despite the number of studies, beginning with Luigi Laurenti's *Property Values and Race*, which challenged the popular idea that "black people lower property value," these latter FHA policies did not change until after the 1967 riots, when FHA offices were instructed to consider all buildings in riot or riot-threatened areas as "acceptable risk." However, between 1938 and 1967 countless numbers of black home buyers who were unable to meet FHA requirements were obliged to rely on the use of installment purchase contracts.

Many Lawndale families, on the advice of lawyers, had signed contracts which would bind them to the houses without benefit of equity or ownership until the early 1980s. To meet the monthly payments some husbands worked two and sometimes three jobs. Many wives were also forced to work, resulting in the destruction of their family life. Unsupervised children drifted into the street gangs in the area. In addition to the monthly payments, many buyers were forced to pay for costly repairs on their homes as soon as the contracts were signed. One couple, it is reported, had been told by a seller that the building they purchased was free of building-code violations. Three weeks after the family moved in, a building inspector appeared and required them to spend another $2500 to correct code violations.

In the period 1958–1961 more than one half the homes in Lawndale were purchased on contract. Chicago is not by any means the only city where black people have bought homes on contract. Situations similar to Chicago's exist in every major American city where the black population has been shut off from the broader housing market and excluded from FHA-backed mortgages. Baltimore is one; Washington, D.C. is another; Cincinnati is a third. In Baltimore, a grass-roots movement challenging similar practices sprang up about the same time the people of Lawndale began to organize. But the Chicago movement has gone the furthest, and the legal cases that have come to the point of resolution in Chicago are now the test cases for the ocuntry.

One day in early 1968, Mrs. Ruth Wells, a soft-spoken, attractive black woman in her mid-thirties, got up enough courage to go into a contract seller's office and ask why the sum of $1500 had been added on to her contract balance for insurance. Three years later, her voice no longer soft, Mrs. Wells sat in the comfortably furnished living room of her home in Lawndale, and told a story that has now become fixed in black American folk history. "Before I left home that morning," she said, "I was very concerned over whether I was right or wrong. This has always been a problem with me: being afraid to really step out because I was afraid to be wrong. So I prayed a prayer before I left home that morning. I am not a real religious fanatic, but I do believe wholeheartedly in God because I feel that I would not have made it this far if not for a true and living God. That morning I went into my closet and closed the door and shut out everything. I asked the Lord to show me that day where I was wrong between the time I left this house and returned. I said, 'If I'm wrong in expecting this man to do something, then I won't bother him anymore. But if I'm right, I want You to show me and I'll fight on.'

"When I got down there I asked to see the insurance policy. I said, 'You must have *forgot!* I don't live on North Shore Drive [an affluent white neighborhood]. I live in *Lawndale*. We don't have any mansions out there to be paying $1500 for insurance. You don't even pay that much a year in far better neighborhoods. I may be *living* here, but my *mind* didn't stop working after I started living here!' So the seller called the secretary and had her bring the policy. But when he went to pass the policy across the desk, his hand actually just trembled so until the paper was fluttering in the wind. And for him to shake so, not just from being nervous, this *had* to be something. I had forgot about the prayer, but the minute I saw his hand I *knew* I was right. It's as though someone had told me, 'Look!' I *felt so good!* When he offered to cancel the $1500 I told him I had *changed my mind!* I got more *faith* sitting there in that man's office because I knew he was wrong and *he* knew he was wrong. I thought, 'Somebody done touched him and let him know. He's feeling something he's never felt before: *guilt!*' He's all trembling and shaking, really upset. And I thought to myself, 'I didn't upset him, but I know *who* did.'"

Mr. and Mrs. Wells bought the duplex for $23,000 in 1959 from a real estate company. They paid $3000 down and signed a contract which required them to pay the $20,000 balance over a 15-year, 10-month period and which allowed them the option of obtaining a mortgage after 50 percent of the principal had been paid. This was done by late 1967. Mr. and Mrs. Wells then hired a black lawyer to negotiate the mortgage for them; but instead, he reported back that the seller would agree to the mortgage only after an additional $1500 had been paid. "I asked him what the $1500 was for," Mrs. Wells recalls. "He said he didn't know. Later he called back and said it was for insurance. Now, my contract itemizes my payments each month: insurance, taxes, principal, interest, and my total payment: $201.40. Now, if I'm paying insurance in with the rest each month, I'm *not* in arrears with my payments. I was always before then normally a quiet person who wouldn't talk, especially to a stranger. But something just got in me and I was just fed up and tired. I don't care how hard I worked, how many hours I put in, I was still in the same boat."

Mrs. Wells was not alone when she went into the contract seller's office. More than six months before the confrontation, John Redmond Macnamara, a thirty-year-old white Jesuit seminarian, and twelve white students had moved into Lawndale. Macnamara, a native of Skokie, Illinois, and then a student at the Bellarmine School of Theology, had spent most of the previous year in the community on a one-day-a-week basis as a member of a service project sponsored by the Presentation Roman Catholic Church of Lawndale. The community-service project was started by Monsignor John J. Egan, the new pastor of Presentation Church and then director of the Office of Urban Affairs of the Roman Catholic Archdiocese of Chicago. Macnamara and the other Catholic students moved into an old apartment on South Independence, a few blocks away from the Wells home, and began to walk the streets of Lawndale. They had no program to present. Instead, following Saul Alinsky's example, they listened to the people with only three ideas in mind: to discover what problems were facing the community, to provide services for bringing people together, and once the machin-

ery for an organized and developing community was set up, to move on.

During the summer of 1967, despite harassment and intimidation by young black men in the neighborhood, the young whites visited all the families in a twelve-block area and listened to what the people said. There were many complaints against exploitation by merchants, high tax payments, the absence of city services, the lack of play lots for community children, and a general disinterest on the part of the mayor's office in reports of building-code violations.

As an initial project, the whites enlisted the help of young black people from the area to stage public demonstrations. On one occasion nine full cans of uncollected garbage from Lawndale were "dumped" on the plaza of the downtown Civic Center; during the first three days of July, children from the area were taken to a public park in Bridgeport—home of Chicago's Mayor Richard J. Daley—and allowed to play. There were a few fines for littering, and some Bridgeport adults threw rocks and bottles at the white students and Lawndale children. But afterwards the city began regular garbage collections and constructed one children's play lot in Lawndale. But by September, when most of the students were returning to college, the project had accomplished little else.

Father Egan introduced Mrs. Ruth Wells to Jack Macnamara. An outspoken priest rigidly dedicated to serving the Lawndale community, Father Egan had helped Mrs. Wells on past occasions. "I called him," Mrs. Wells says, "and asked if he could recommend a lawyer I could trust. I wanted to find out what steps I could take because I knew that something was wrong. I told him, 'If this man could just put $1500 on my bill out of the sky like this, I'll *never* finish paying. It's just like blackmail, only I don't know what I've been blackmailed for. If I pay this, he could add anything else he wanted. My own lawyer didn't even question the $1500. He just *arranged* how I could pay it.' I told Father Egan, 'If I let him get away with this, I'll be paying for the rest of my life for *nothing*! I don't have anything, and I'm steady paying.'"

That same day Father Egan sent Macnamara and Sister Andrew, who had ten years of real estate experience before becoming a nun, to see Mrs. Wells. Already somewhat knowledgeable about the contract sales pattern in Lawndale they advised her to invest $45 in an FHA appraisal of the house. The estimate came back at $14,750. Between the time the family bought the house for $23,000 and early 1968, they had had the bathroom modernized, redone the kitchen, built new back porches for both apartments and had them enclosed, rewired the entire house, put on a new roof, and put in new front steps and a sidewalk. The students did a title search of the property and found that the seller had paid about $14,000 for it. They encouraged Mrs. Wells to talk with the contract seller. After several attempts to telephone him at his office and home, Father Egan, Macnamara, and Sister Andrew accompanied Mr. and Mrs. Wells to the seller's office. There they stood in the background and allowed Mrs. Wells to do the talking. "I let him know how much I had found out about the property," Mrs. Wells says. "And I told him that I knew he paid less than the amount of [the official mortgage] stamps on the deed. He is a smart man. I don't mean smart because he outsmarted me, because I don't feel that I'm smart."

Mrs. Wells says the seller explained that insurance had gone up over a period of years. She asked why she had not been informed before. "He said he didn't want to *worry* me," she says. "I got more angry then than I was before I went down there. See, he's clapping me on the back with one hand and picking my pocket with the other. He had decided to add this $1500 on when he saw that we hadn't faltered and were going to get the building on mortgage. I asked him how he slept at night. He said he slept very well except when he had worked a little too hard at the office." Mrs. Wells pauses to laugh. "I'm sure he does," she goes on. "He's getting checks in the mail every month, educating his kids, and if you're ragged and hungry that's *your* business! But I told him *why* I thought he slept pretty good. He said when he got ready for spiritual advice he definitely would not come to me. I thanked him, and told him I wouldn't go to him either."

Then Mrs. Wells asked to see the policy.

Official records show that title to the Wells house was held by a local bank under a trust number. The couple paid $3000 down and contracted to pay the $20,000 balance in monthly installments of $175 for 15 years with a 7 percent interest rate on the unpaid balance, the maximum under Illinois law. The seller had purchased the property a little more than one month before by obtaining a mortgage for $10,000 and paying the former owner $3500 in cash. Two years later, after Mr. and Mrs. Wells had made improvements on the property, the seller refinanced and obtained a second mortgage for $12,000. Although only about $14,000 was originally paid for the property, and its appraised value in 1968 was only $14,750, Mr. and Mrs. Wells will pay a total of $36,250 for their home. Macnamara estimates that if they had been able to purchase the building on mortgage for $14,000 and had made the same monthly payments at the same interest rates, they would have paid approximately $21,000.

"We conducted about six weeks of research down at the Chicago Title and Trust Company," Macnamara says, "and discovered that about 50 percent of the buildings were being bought on contract by black people and that the prices of all these buildings were approximately the same, and that the sellers had picked these buildings up for $10,000 to $15,000 less than what they were being sold to black families for. What we did with this information was to go to people's homes to see if it was really an issue with them. We'd say, 'Did you know that the guy who sold you this house only paid $13,000 for it?' "

But even if the buyers did not know, few of them would respond to Macnamara and the students. There is a stigma attached to contract buying, a certain implication of helplessness and ignorance. Public meetings were organized in the basement of Presentation Church, with twenty to twenty-five people in attendance. But they were silent. Few people wanted to expose their scars to a tall, blond white man with piercing blue eyes, surrounded by white helpers. "Jack would come by my house before every meeting on Wednesday nights," Mrs. Wells recalls of the early days, "but he wouldn't say anything. So I said to my husband, 'There's something he wants, but he won't say it.' My husband said, 'What do you think it is?' I said, 'He wants one of *us* to get up and talk.' He said, 'Well, what good would that do?' I said, 'The people don't trust them because they're white. But we're black and we're *in* it, and I feel sure all these other people might be in the same boat. But they won't say anything. They just sit there and *look!*' I didn't even know them then," she admits. "I didn't even know my next-door neighbor." Finally, Mrs. Wells volunteered to tell the people her story. At the next meeting she stood, held on to the back of a chair, and told them about her own contract situation and about her confrontation with the seller. "I said that the money for the appraisal was the best forty-five dollars I ever spent," she says, "and asked if any of them was in the same boat. Immediately practically every hand in the room went up with a question. And *that's* when the thing got started. So then I would get up every Wednesday night and I would tell it: 'Tell your family and your friends, your neighbors, the people you work with, if they bought on contract they should come out!'"

"Each Wednesday night thereafter we got more and more people. On some nights we didn't even have standing room. That's when I found out that up until a few years ago most of our sisters and brothers, not only in Chicago but in many major cities in the United States, bought on contract and were being cheated. I'm not talking about people with eighth-grade educations either. I'm talking about black people with *degrees!*"

The Contract Buyers League of Lawndale began in January, 1968, as part of the interaction between the meetings in the basement of Presentation Church and sessions in Macnamara's sparsely furnished apartment on South Independence Boulevard. Getting the estimated 3000 Lawndale contracts renegotiated became the issue for which the Presentation Church workers had been searching. The students set up filing systems in the apartment, and slowly gathered information. Other Jesuits and white college students passed through the apartment, and spread word of the organization. Contributions began to come in. At one Eastern girls' college the students gave up their lunch money for the League.

Young black men from the neighborhood, some of them gang members and others just curious, eased into the apartment, freeloading, disrupting, "raiding," threatening the whites. At one point gang members issued a deadline for the whites to be out of the community. The deadline came and passed, and the whites stayed on. During the riots following Martin Luther King's assassination, Macnamara's life was threatened, and one young black man did beat him severely. But when angry black people summoned the police, Macnamara refused to identify the attacker.

Thirty lawyers whose opinions were asked advised the League that nothing could be done. But the people made their own decision: they decided to picket the offices and suburban homes of the sellers and pressure them to renegotiate the contracts. The students traced the trust numbers on the deeds to the beneficiaries. Once an identity was discovered, twelve or so people —Jesuits, nuns, students, and contract buyers— would picket the front of his office, or a few would go to his neighborhood and pass out leaflets to his neighbors explaining CBL grievances. In some instances they even met commuter trains as they rolled into suburban stations, carrying signs which told all passengers that their fellow commuter, Mr. X, was a slumlord.

Because they always informed the Chicago Police Department and the press before each picket attempt, there were no incidents of violence. The pickets were prepared to follow all orders from policemen and later submit any complaints to the Department's Human Relations Section. On a few occasions Chicago policemen accepted their leaflets. One very active white supporter likes to tell about the instance when one of the sellers threatened violence against the pickets. "The police came and the people had the experience that the law worked for them," he points out, "because the police told the realtor that they were there to protect the pickets and that he would be arrested if he continued to threaten them." The pickets also had the support of church and human relations groups, and a number of lawyers who advised them on the legal limitations of picketing. At one point, thanks to the presence of several FBI agents ordered to the scene by Thomas Foran, U.S. Attorney for the Northern District of Illinois, they were even able to picket outside the General Federal Savings and Loan office in Cicero, Illinois. According to an article in the Chicago *Defender* entitled "The Day Cicero Didn't Riot," some of the Cicero citizens even accepted their flyer and wished them luck.

In the spring of 1968 the major publicity began. Soon after one seller made a tentative agreement to renegotiate three hundred of his contracts, the Chicago *Sun-Times* ran a small story called "Money Miracle in a Chicago Ghetto." And although the seller later refused to renegotiate, the publicity continued. The *Daily News*, giving an example of what Father Egan had termed "a vile race tax," ran a long story on the troubles of a family of buyers named Peeler, and the $16,000 house that will eventually cost them $46,780 in principal and interest. In early July, Macnamara, Mr. Howell Collins, and several other contract buyers testified before the Illinois House of Representatives' Public Welfare Committee, receiving extensive publicity. There was talk of federal indictments being brought against officials of ten defunct savings and loan associations for "possible misapplication of federally insured funds"; there was talk of drafting a bill which would require the identities of land trust beneficiaries to be made public; there were suggestions of a link between contract selling and the crime syndicate, and urgings to require the sellers and savings and loan officials to testify before the Welfare Committee. But the political publicity, some of which was prompted by the heat of that election year, died down. The buyers took a new step. They began pressuring the Chicago FHA office, denouncing its policies as the basic cause of their housing difficulties and demanding that it intervene in the conflict. The Chicago office, headed by Ernest Stevens, was apparently embarrassed by the FHA's role in encouraging segregated housing. In the mid-sixties it had discontinued the "red-lining" policies. Just at the time the conflict broke, a campaigning Richard Nixon had guardedly criticized the role played by FHA in creating black slums. "The FHA is largely limited today to safe mortgages," he said. "It should be turned in the direction of taking greater mortgage risks so that it can function effectively in slum areas where now it does little."

Pressured by the buyers, the Chicago FHA office expressed a willingness to grant mortgages to the buyers based on the current appraised value of the houses. But the CBL rejected the offer because it allowed the sellers to receive the full contract balances. According to Macnamara, the FHA offer protected the seller by "allowing him to get out of the deal and receive immediate cash after he has had the benefit of raking off the highest interest profits which come at the early stages of the installment contract." With the help of lawyers, CBL worked out its own "fair-price formula" based on the price paid by the seller for the property plus 15 percent of the cost, supposedly representing the amount of profit he should have received. But few of the sellers would agree to this method. Most were opposed to high settlements and what they termed the "shameful harassment" of them by the CBL.

Most of the men who hold the Lawndale contracts are Jewish real estate salesmen or assignees who regard contract selling as a legitimate business. Like most white merchants in black communities, many of them remained behind in Lawndale after the other whites left. The sellers take pride in their ability to read the contract sales market, and many regard themselves as suppliers of homes for people who were shut out of the broader housing market. Ironically, many of them enjoyed close relationships with their buyers, and occasionally "carried" families that fell behind in payments. The emotional and psychological depths of the seller-buyer relationship might have been touched by one of the first sellers who agreed to renegotiate. "I like the people on the West Side," he says. "I was good to them. I lent them money, did them favors, and acted as a father-confessor to them. I didn't know I was doing any harm to them. My office wasn't hit during the rioting because they knew I was all right. When this CBL thing started, they went to another seller first. I never figured they would come to me because I didn't think I had done anything wrong. But they did. I couldn't believe it when they said I had cheated people. I went home to my wife and said, 'Isn't this the American system, where we make as much profit as we can?' She said, 'Yes, you're right.' Two days later she said, 'No, *you're* wrong and *they're* right.' And pretty soon I said to myself, 'No, you're wrong.'"

There are three classes of businessmen involved in the Lawndale contract sales situation: those who actually negotiated contracts and receive all the profits, those whose real estate offices act as agents for investors in contract sales, and those in investment firms who bought contracts from sellers at discount. It is unknown how many contract sellers were actually engaged in blockbusting. Of the thirty or forty known sellers and trust beneficiaries, only a few have large numbers of contracts. Most have three hundred or less. And while most were able to get mortgage financing and refinancing of their initial purchases, a few paid cash out of their own pockets. Some of them attempt to justify the markup in prices before resale to black families by insisting that they spent considerable money rehabilitating the houses; and some complain that the tendency of black families to wreck the houses or abandon them after short habitation periods added a high-risk element to the business. Some are lawyers. All the sellers insist that they sold, or would have sold, homes on equal contract terms to both black and white people. And like the buyers, most of them denounce banks and the FHA as the real villains.

II Religion and Race

To understand the evolution of the Contract Buyers League, one must be aware of the religious configurations and people which surrounded it. The initial impression is of a coalition made up of blacks and Catholics fighting Jewish contract sellers. But there have been black and Catholic contract sellers and slumlords in Chicago, just as there have always been black, Catholic, and Jewish people who have opposed them. Indeed, the democratic and selfless interaction among the three groups during the life of the League was itself a dramatization of the best moments, and the best moral impulses, of the old civil rights movement.

The Roman Catholic Archbishop of Chicago, John Cardinal Cody, never endorsed or supported the CBL. The fact that the organization was born in a Catholic Church and drew a large measure of support from Catholic lawyers, students, suburbanites, and Jesuits probably resulted from Jack Macnamara's own Catholic background and connections. But beyond that was his personal magnetism. Tall, pensive, seemingly soft-spoken, but sharp-tempered, with frighteningly direct blue eyes, he brought to the League a special genius for organization and a gift for inspiring confidence in people.

Following high school he entered the Jesuit Seminary; after two years of study he dropped out and worked his way through Loyola College as an airport night-clerk; after one year of law school at the University of Chicago he went back to the seminary, and left again to teach high school in Cincinnati. He once said of himself: "When I was in college, I was the kind of person who would say, 'If I can make it, everybody else

can too.'" But after deciding to live in Lawndale, he received permission to postpone two additional years of seminary study. A quietly intense worker with his own ideas, he nevertheless encouraged the contract buyers to make their own decisions; and he advised all volunteers, lawyers included, to do the same. The black people respected him for this. When his church superiors asked him to leave Lawndale and resume his theological studies, CBL leaders responded with an appeal to the Society of Jesus in Rome, requesting that Macnamara be ordained as a Jesuit without further study so that he could remain in the community. "There was a man sent from God named John," the appeal stated, "to bear witness to the light. Jack is such a man. Some have compared him to Moses, who received his commission directly from God and who went to the Pharaoh, as Jack goes to the centers of power for us today, to say, 'Let my people go.'"

Not only are most of the contract sellers Jewish; many of the Lawndale houses eventually sold on contract were purchased from Jewish families. As it happens, a few years before Macnamara came to Lawndale the Chicago Jewish Council on Urban Affairs had become interested in the contract sales problem. In 1964 it financed a study project, an amalgam of black Baptists, Catholics, and Jews, called the Lawndale Peoples' Planning and Action Council. Under its director, Lew Kreinberg, the council began researching the estate of a Jewish realtor who left hundreds of contracts after his death. Rabbi Robert J. Marx, former president of the Jewish Council on Urban Affairs, was instrumental in getting the council started; and when the contract sales problem became an issue, he attempted to rally the support of the Jewish community behind the buyers. He attended several CBL meetings, invited contract buyers to speak at his suburban synagogue, raised funds for the buyers, and attempted to pressure the sellers morally into renegotiating their contracts. As chairman of a newly formed Joint-Jewish Committee on Urban Problems, an amalgam of the Anti-Defamation League, the Jewish Federation, and the American Jewish Committee, he condemned the West Side contract sales. Additional support for the buyers came from other members of the Chicago Jewish community, such as Gordon Sherman, then president of the Midas-International Corporation. (Sherman subsequently lost control of

Midas to his father in a proxy fight, and now devotes most of his energies to a group called Businessmen for the Public Interest. But while head of Midas he made an initial contribution to CBL of $5000 of his own money, and pledged the Midas-International Foundation to contribute $25,000 for a two-year period.) A number of Jewish lawyers, accountants, and workers also volunteered their help.

But beyond the opportunity to give money, service, and moral support to the buyers, Rabbi Marx saw an opportunity to explore the causes of the frictions which, in the past decade, have developed between lower-class black people and Jewish merchants in their communities. The question he was trying to answer was the one posed by Professor Victor Rosenblum of Northwestern Law School, who examined the CBL movement in his Law and Social Change seminar. "Blacks and Jews have in the past been very close on the question of the civil rights movement." Professor Rosenblum observes. "These ties have been rich and deep and real. [But] a good deal of the business relationship, that has not been a good relationship at all, has been a Jewish relationship. . . . Are there explanations which enter the realm of sociology?"

In a speech entitled "The People In Between," prompted by his work on the contract sales issue, Rabbi Marx argues that, historically, the Jewish merchant or landlord in a diaspora community plays a middle role: neither part of the masses nor part of the power structure, in the context of the community he is nevertheless seen by the masses as a marginal and highly visible symbol of the power structure. "The slum landlord, the contract seller, the ghetto merchant, the Jewish politician in an all-black area," he said, "may be the marginal remainders of what was once a proud Jewish community. Their presence in slum areas is a reality to which we cannot close our eyes. These are the men who play the interstitial role with the most heavy hand. They are in a position where they emerge not as marginal, but as characteristic. It is doubtful whether anyone will ever question how a telephone company exploits poor people by tempting them to spend more money than they should on fancy telephones or long-distance calls. The Jewish ghetto merchant, however, despite his own conceptualization of his role, is almost invariably placed in a position where his business ethics will be questioned because of the prices or interest he charges or because of the temptations he places before his customers."

Despite Rabbi Marx's sympathy for both sides in the conflict, both the sellers and their own supporters within the Jewish community were displeased with his support of the buyers. On occasion some sellers had attempted to raise anti-Semitism as an issue, making charges against both the contract buyers and some of their supporters. When the attitude of most Jewish community leaders remained unchanged, a group of the sellers sued all the CBL leaders, Macnamara, Father Egan, Rabbi Marx, and Gordon Sherman, charging the disruption of their business and claiming $1 million in damages from each. Then, in a further attempt to rally Jewish solidarity behind them and give the appearance of a Jewish-black issue, the sellers dropped both Rabbi Marx and Gordon Sherman from the suit. "We fought being dismissed," Rabbi Marx explains in his Highland Park home, "because we wanted a Jewish commitment on the buyers' side."

Rabbi Marx talks candidly about his involvement: "We would bring in the contract sellers and try to talk to them about renegotiating their contracts," he recalls. "I remember one seller who came into my office. He said, 'Rabbi, I have to talk with you. I have to do something. I can't live with myself. My conscience can't take any more.' Now that man has renegotiated. The Jewish Council on Urban Affairs has not been in a position to say we've done this, becasue our whole emphasis has been to put resources into the communities in which we work, and they're black and white."

Rabbi Marx suspects that he has been made to pay for his involvement. In mid-1971 he resigned as president of the Jewish Council on Urban Affairs and was subsequently invited to head the Union of American Hebrew Congregations in New York. According to him, the decision to move was not entirely his own. "In many ways I'm going to New York because of this issue," he says. "When we fought them [the sellers], some of the people in high places got very angry at me. So that when New York says to me, 'We need you here—we want your talent and besides we think that there are a couple of key enemies that you have in Chicago that would make it uncomfortable for you to stay there,' that's because of the contract sales issue. That's how involved we were, fighting within the Jewish community. Now, you don't like to be a rabbi fighting Jews. Martin Luther King taught me one thing: If you're a black man, you don't fight other black men; you fight the enemy. I don't like fighting Jews, but I want the Jewish community to see how a couple of guys have been hurting them."

Like Rabbi Marx, Gordon Sherman found that support of the CBL caused many sellers to view him with suspicion. "There were always the insinuations," he recalls, "that mine was a double defection: that as a capitalist I was on the wrong side, and that as a Jew, how could I make anything conspicuous that might be held up in a negative light by non-Jews? The sellers must have seen me as an enemy, but they also saw me as some kind of nut. They'd say, **'He's one of us, and he should be on our side!'** People in this society," he says, "are used to being on the *right* side, not because of what we believe but because of where life has put us. **When** they saw me spoiling for trouble on the *other* side and using my *means*—because the whole game is based on denying some people the means to fight back and so if someone *lends* them the means, it's like shipping arms to Russia—they didn't like it. I didn't have much contact, but the feedback I got implied that I was doing something very wrong and, secretly, that I was some kind of well-meaning nut."

Despite the efforts of some sellers to distort the issues, there was never any visible bias against them as Jews. Jack Macnamara is convinced that the mode of operation of the CBL prevented the emergence of any such conflict. "The black people never made an issue of it," he notes. "But the Real Estate Investors' Association tried to call it an anti-Semitic movement. However, the involvement of Gordon Sherman and Rabbi Marx and the support of the Jewish Council on Urban Affairs and Jewish people in the suburbs showed that the charge was superficial."

Among the black contract buyers one can hear very few references to the ethnic identities of the sellers. Indeed, some buyers praise, in retrospect, the "smart Jew lawyer" who advised them against contract buying years before. Very few of the Lawndale people make distinctions between Jewish and other white Americans. This point was made, with some sly humor, by Clyde Ross, the CBL co-chairman, when his deposition was being taken by a lawyer for the sellers. Ac-

cording to Ross, he was asked whether he had ever spoken about the CBL at a synagogue. "I said, 'Hell no!'" Ross relates. "He said, 'Well, I happen to know that you made a speech in Highland Park at a Jewish synagogue.' I said, 'You see, all of y'all look alike to me.' I said, 'I don't know a Jew from a Polish or a Italian or a Irish. I don't know *who* I was speaking to down there. Only thing I know is that all y'all was *white*.' I said, 'You can call it what you want.' He got very angry, because he thought I should know what a Jew was. I don't know nothin' about no Jew. I thought it was a religion. **A**nd he's white. So he's a *white* man as far as **I**'m concerned." Ross pauses a bit before adding: "He got very angry because I put him down with the Polish."

"I think that when you get off on race you lose your point and your goal," Mrs. Ruth Wells says.

But there is an additional religious dimension involved, which may explain why a group of Northern, inner-city black people were able to maintain an organization as complex as the CBL for over four years. The Lawndale people are primarily Baptist. Most are middle-aged, and most are migrants from Alabama, Arkansas, and Mississippi. The structure of their Wednesday night meetings resembles that of a Baptist church service. In a sense, the CBL people have abstracted the form of Sunday morning storefront church meetings and reassembled it around an economic issue, in much the same way that Martin Luther King managed to reassemble the religious convictions of Southern black church people around political and economic issues during the early sixties.

Every Wednesday night during the first three years of the CBL, Mrs. Luceal Johnson and other Lawndale women would cook a communion dinner in Jack Macnamara's apartment. The atmosphere would be relaxed and gossipy, with contract buyers and white lawyers sitting down to plates of fried chicken. Then they would walk the few blocks to Martin Luther King Hall, in the basement of Presentation Church, for the meeting.

A long prayer, in the rhythmic, singsong idiom of a fundamentalist black minister, usually precedes each meeting. All prayers are spontaneous, asking God for guidance, offering thanks for the progress of the League, and usually including references to the sellers, judges, and recent incidents, involving the League. The people it silently with heads bowed during the prayers, but afterwards a hymn or spiritual might be sung by the entire audience. Then a progress report is given by either Charles Baker, the CBL chairman, or Clyde Ross, the co-chairman. Ross's deliveries, more free-wheeling than Baker's, usually weave in reports of CBL progress and failures with inspirational asides and references to the Old Testament. Besides a mastery of the evangelical idiom, Ross is able to evoke the mood of a black church sermon: the call and response, the repetition of certain patterns of words known by each member of the audience since childhood church services, the question-and-answer dialogue between minister and audience, the building of his speeches to an emotional epiphany which provides a cathartic sense of union between speaker and audience. He has talked of Moses delivering the people across the Red Sea, of Ezekiel looking down into the Valley of Dry Bones (both references are to Macnamara), and of Pharaoh's Army (the sheriff's deputies and security guards who eventually evicted a number of people from their homes). Easygoing, introspective ,and more than a little concerned over his lack of formal education, Ross nonetheless undergoes an almost complete change of personality when addressing the CBL members.

At one point, Ross offered the following speech at a Wednesday night meeting:

Let me tell you a story that I experienced when I was quite young. One of my chores around the family home in the South was to graze the cow. We had no pasture, so we had to graze the cow wherever we could find grassy areas. So we would put a chain around the cow's foot, and we would lock it down real tight, and then we would drive an iron peg down and fasten the other end of the chain onto this peg. The cow would go around in this circle and nibble all the grass she could nibble in this circle until there was no more. But one day I came back to water her and the chain was *off*, and she could have got away. But she was still going round in this circle because she was afraid of the pinch of the chain. That's the way some of us are right today. We can get *out! We can get out now!* But we *still* marching round in the *slave circle* because we don't want to be hurt by society's slave chain. We still feel it. We still feel it on our legs. We're *loose! We are loose!* Move *out!* Move out *a little bit further! Nip* the

grass out there because it's *pretty! Just move!* The chain is gone. It's only *you* that think it's there. *Move out!* And stop these men from *robbing* you! And stop these men from *persecuting* you! Move out! And *get* some of this land that was *yours* from the start! The chain is off.

After a short speech by Baker, Macnamara, Mrs. Wells, or one of the lawyers, the people are expected to stand up and talk about their own experiences with contract buying, the situation of their own cases in the courts, or any contract with "their" seller. Even the white lawyers and workers are expected to do this. The testimonies are much like "witnessing," a process through which individuals share with other congregants the story of their journey from "sin" to salvation. But in the case of the CBL people, contract buying has been identified with sin, renegotiation with salvation, and the League itself as God's instrument of salvation. The shameless identification of oneself as a victim or "sucker," which was virtually impossible before the CBL started, is now a common occurrence. For example, one nervous, middle-aged black woman who was not even a League member was moved to make the following statement after sitting through one of the meetings:

Good evening ladies and gentlemen. The best thing you can do is git you a lawyer who'll mean you some good and not the other man some good. We bought some property. The lot was $650. The seller put us up a house and on the bill of sale it said " a complete house." We carried it to our lawyer and he said, "Well, he says a complete house." He didn't give us no gutters, no yard, or nothing. We went back over there and I said, "There ain't no gutters, the water's just running on down into our house." He comes back out, puts the gutters in and levels the yard and charges us $6000 for that. I went back to the lawyer and he say, "He can charge you what he want for his work. He *did* give you a complete house." That's why I say git you a lawyer that's go'n do *you* some good and not the other fellow. So he can read all that fine writing that you not educated to read. And then you can git somewhere. Don't, they gonna beat you regardless of what you go by. Then he come tellin' me to sign a *quick deed* [quitclaim deed] after all that money we done paid.

On the other hand, some of the people whose contracts were favorably renegotiated after the lawsuits were filed returned to the meetings to state their respect for the instrument of their salvation.

Some part of this pattern reoccurs in all the meetings: a fragment of a larger ritual as old as the Black American Church. Participation in it involves a special kind of discipline, requiring a willed perspective on good and bad, maintained not because of an unawareness of political realities or even because of fear of retaliation, but because of a fierce determination to preserve one's own humanity and one's own belief in the ultimate perfectability of man through the sometimes mysterious ways of God. The buyers, in their unity, do not see the sellers in racial terms. What they do see is that the sellers, as an outside force, have inadvertently provided them with an opportunity to assert their sense of community and of morality. In such a context, the positive force of black unity is more important than racial or religious bitterness.

But far beyond the specific economic and social issues, the CBL raises the question of the relationship between the rituals of the Black Church and black grass-roots political activity. How can one account for the appeal, among millions of black Americans, of the evangelical idiom used by Martin Luther King, or the modified and modernized use of that same idiom currently being used by Jesse Jackson? Or the apocalyptic impulses behind so much of militant black protest during the sixties? While some critics say that King paid too little attention to the possibilities of moral outcry as a means of achieving political goals far removed from Christian idealism, others note that many of those committed to achieving strictly political goals, unlike King, pay too little attention to moral outcry as an effective technique for reaching grass-roots black people. The difficulty arises from a failure to recognize one of the most powerful legacies of black slaves to their generations.

On one level this legacy is essentially moral. It involves a system of beliefs concerning the conception of God and His power as demonstrated in the myths of the Old Testament. Black slaves incorporated these Jewish folk dramas into their definitions of themselves centuries ago. As part of the group psyche they were passed along, mainly within the churches, from one generation to the next. Some historians

and social critics have dismissed this intense identification with Old Testament personalities and myths as no more than an escape mechanism with which slaves protected themselves from having to face the brutal realities of their lives. But it was more than this. Slaves took on a sense of morality which allowed, or almost required, them to make judgments about the people and institutions which held them captive. A sense of optimism came with the religion which helped them to survive and which still functions in a secular context, in spirituals and jazz and blues. The identification provided an almost omnipotent perspective, which made biblical codes the ultimate moral standards, and a sense of history and reality that was sometimes sharper than that of whites.

This is part of what was passed along within the churches. And the minister's responsibility, especially in the more fundamentalist churches, was not so much to be a moral example for his people as it was to reinforce this perspective every Sunday morning by spinning out, and relating to their present situation, one of the moral dramas from the pages of the Old Testament: good versus evil, right versus wrong, God's will versus man's. The result of this has been the creation of a broad level of black society that retains abstract moral codes which are sometimes in conflict with certain capitalistic freedoms and political restrictions allowed by American society. Traditional American standards of morality have never been adequate to define the values of black people who are on this level. But they are the ones who followed King the Christian, who called him Moses, and who now keep pictures of him on their mantels. They will walk out of their churches for any politician or leader—Nat Turner, Adam Clayton Powell, Martin Luther King, Jesse Jackson—who knows their style and who can converse with them in their idiom. Under the care of the right leader the appeal becomes political.

Charles Baker, the CBL chairman, takes all this for granted without really understanding the causes. "Most of our people are church people and nonviolent," he says. "They studied to be religious. You have to push them into a fight. Ninety-eight percent of them were born in the South. But I'll tell you something: there's nobody in the world more violent than these people if you make them mad. And I'll tell you something else: there's nobody in the world who wants peace more than these people, and they'd bend over backwards to get it. This kind of fellow's been taught all his life, 'Thou shalt not kill.' And he'd just hate to do something like that. But it hurts him when somebody misuses him."

A person who symbolizes both the grievances and the convictions of most West Side CBL members is Mrs. Luceal Johnson. A stout, handsome woman in her late fifties, she migrated to Chicago from Natchez, Mississippi, in 1940. When she and her husband bought their home on contract, they were led to believe that they would be allowed a mortgage after 50 percent of the principal had been paid. In point of fact, they did receive a mortgage; the seller simply allowed them to assume his own mortgage obligation and reduced their monthly contract payments. But when they attempted to borrow money on it to get their back porch repaired, the same lawyer who had advised them that they were getting a "good deal" on the contract sale informed them that the mortgage was worthless. He did, however, arrange another "deal" for them. Under its terms, they received a loan of $1300 to pay off certain bills, and the lawyer "arranged" for a contractor to repair and enclose the porch. In return, the Johnsons will have to pay $6000 for the loan and repairs. Mrs. Johnson has been a domestic for over thirty years.

"I makes my living scrubbing floors," she declares. "And I ain't ashamed to tell it because I makes it *honestly*. I makes an honest dollar. I'm still doing it, and it feel *good!* That's all I ever know to do. My parents weren't able to give me an education, but they did teach me to work. And they taught me all about being honest. And I work for real rich peoples that have been more than nice to me. They know all about the unjust things that go on in America, and they're in the fight too. Because they see America falling, and they're going to suffer too."

To Mrs. Johnson, the racial and economic implications of her involvement has been negated by larger religious and spiritual considerations. "I wasn't such a fool," she says, "that when I bought the house I didn't have a mouthpiece with me. But the bad part of the thing is that we just don't have what we need in our lives to go out and do something, white or black; we just don't have *love*. And this is the key point to everything. CBL just made a *step* in correcting it.

We stepped out on God's word. We couldn't have man to depend on because man had let us down. We stepped out on *faith* that we *could* do something about this thing when God heard our cry. Because everytime we get ready to spend a dollar we got to go by a man with no justice in his heart. We wouldn't have these problems if we recognized just a little of God's word. But now, we just like the Children of Israel: both sides, black and white. We're just the spit [spitting image] of them. And God will punish you when you walk away from Him too far. And we can't make the journey without Him. I don't care *who* says we can. And I don't care who you are or where you come from; you just as well stay in your pants, because God ain't go'n let you go too far. And this is the onliest thing I got to rely on; I don't put my trust in *no man no more!* Education is fine; all of these peoples that we're buying our houses from, they're overequipped with education. But there ain't no God-life in them, because if they *had* it they wouldn't be doing the things that they are doing. We're just lacking love in our hearts for one another. And the onliest way we'll win is we've got to have faith that we're fighting for the right thing. And then we can't pack no hate along with us in this fight. Can't get *mad* with the man. Just feel *sorry* for him!"

How did the CBL get started?

"God kept sending peoples to warn, just like He's doing today. He sent Amos, Hosea, He sent other men to warn the Children of Israel of their wrongdoings. Just like today every once in a while somebody springs up from somewhere. I had never heard of a Martin Luther King, but all of a sudden he jumped up out of the middle of nowhere and started telling America about the wrongdoing. And what did they do? They killed him because they didn't want to hear the truth. But you can't kill the truth. *You cannot kill the word of God!* So I think that prayer accounted for the organization of the League. Going on my job each day, I pray, 'Lord, keep me and help me to come up from under these burdens.' "

How do you know God caused the CBL to get started?

"You ask me if I believe God had something to do with CBL getting started? *Who else* had anything to do with it?! You can *rest assured* that *man* didn't! What happened in CBL happened *through* man! So I feel, and I'm sure that

I'm right, that God heard our cry. You've got to give God the credit for these people who've come in here and put their lives on the line to work in this. This ain't no two- or three-dollar deal we messing with here. This is *millions* of dollars! And peoples will kill you about money; that's *all* they'll kill you about, *money!* So God heard our cry in Lawndale. Jack Macnamara come in and laid his life on the line, warned the peoples and told the peoples in figures and facts that they're being cheated. Then God blessed him with a whole lot of more peoples to come in and surround him to help in the fight. See, God will bail you out. He's bailing *us* out. But this ain't no situation to get hung up on color; getting hung up on some of *God's love* will bail us out."

What part of the Bible would you say is closest to what has happened in the CBL?

"I think of 'Love one another,' and the Commandments'. If we love the Lord our God with all our hearts and all our souls and minds, and love our neighbors as ourselves, we done covered them Commandments. And 'Let not your heart be troubled; he that believes in God believes also in me.' And I think of 'In my Father's House there are many mansions,' *and I'm going to get me some of them too!* If I didn't believe these passages of the. Scriptures, I would get right out there and raise hell with the rest of the peoples. But I'm not mad and angry. God blessed me with health to keep on working. . . . And if the laws and the judges and the peoples in the high places can't find no justice for me, I'm getting mine through Christ Jesus. I don't worry about it anymore. If I don't get *nothing* back, if I can just pay for the house and get a clear title, I'll be just as happy as if they come and give me a lot of money. 'Cause I'm gonna spend it anyway."

Some CBL people mythmake as they go along; thus, Jack Macnamara as Moses, or Ezekiel. He smiles with what may be embarrassment when questioned about his reactions to these biblical references. Some suspect that he subtly encouraged the people to view the conflict in a moral perspective. Macnamara denies this. "My own thinking," he says, "is that a truly religious act is usually also a political act, and a social act, and maybe even a legal act. I've always felt that there is a religious element in what's going on here which was really taught to me by the people themselves, while at the same time there are

some things from my religious background which I have imparted to them. . . .

"The other side of it," he continues, "is that the churches have really duped black people through the years. They teach a religious faith that Jesus will fix things if you wait long enough. I remember going to a black church a while back, and the thing that stands out most in my mind is the hymn they sang in the middle of the service: 'Jesus Will Fix It, After A While.' This really did violence to me personally because it seems to me the truly believing person believes that God will work but also that we have to do our part in it. Faith is really faith in ourselves and God being able to accomplish something together rather than simply faith that God will take care of everything if you wait long enough. But two things have impressed me. One is the attitude of the people toward the sellers. It's not one of bitterness and hatred. The other is—particularly at the beginning; it's not as strong now—there were people who turned down fantastic settlements $10,000 and $12,000 settlements, until the seller would agree to renegotiate everybody's contract on the same basis. When I see that happening, then I see God, really alive, and can believe."

III The Law

Once CBL members began demanding renegotiation of contracts, most of the sellers joined together and organized the Real Estate Investors Association. They hired lawyers, and each seller put approximately $5000 into a fund in preparation for possible legal action.

But the CBL was also reorganizing.

From the South Side of Chicago, in late 1968 came hundreds of young middle-class black people who had purchased newly constructed single family homes from ten small companies doing joint-venture business under the collective name Universal Builders. Between 1960 and 1968, Universal had built and the ten companies had sold more than 1000 homes to black families, mostly on contract, and salesmen for the ten companies are said to have insisted, even to a family with a $10,000 down payment, that contract terms were better than those allowed by a conventional mortgage. The South Side buyers had heard about the West Side CBL through the news media and through the oral communications network which links all black communities. The South Siders saw themselves at a similar economic disadvantage, despite their relatively higher incomes, better educations, and newer homes. And indeed, the financial practices of the companies were similar to those on the West Side.

The CBL expanded to accommodate the newcomers from the South Side. The word "Lawndale," which had been in its original title, was dropped, and it became simply the Contract Buyers League. Toward the end of 1968 it moved from Macnamara's apartment into an office on South Pulaski Road, the West Side's main avenue. The white workers and supporters formed the Gamaliel Foundation, a nonprofit "advisory" offspring of the Presentation Church Project, which solicited and contributed money for the support of the CBL. To ensure that the black contract buyers would maintain full control of the organization, four of them were hired to run the new office: Mrs. Ruth Wells, who had been actively involved all along; Mrs. Henrietta Banks, a sharp, gregarious middle-aged contract buyer; Charles Baker, an even-tempered buyer who was granted leave from the Campbell Soup Company's Chicago factory so that he could become a full-time worker as CBL chairman; and co-chairman Clyde Ross, a brooding man who was also granted leave by the Campbell Soup Company. But both organizations, the black buyers and their white allies, used the same office.

Money came from many sources. Besides the contributions from Gordon Sherman, Jesuits across the country, Catholic students, private citizens, and small foundations gave financial support.

But the most important contribution to the CBL resulted from the interest of Harold W. Sullivan, presiding judge of the Circuit Court of Cook County. Irish Catholic like Macnamara, and also a native of Skokie, Judge Sullivan responded immediately to Macnamara's request for lawyers. He organized a Lawyers Committee, and persuaded forty to fifty Chicago lawyers to attend a dinner meeting at which Macnamara and several contract buyers explained the situation. As honorary chairman, Judge Sullivan advised the lawyers that "the legal profession has an outstanding opportunity to demonstrate its social conscience simply by aiding in the renegotiation of these contracts."

The most extensive commitment of free lawyer services came from Albert E. Jenner, senior partner of Jenner & Block, a leading law firm in Chicago. Although called politically conservative, Jenner & Block had a few years before permitted some of its younger lawyers to take on gratis criminal defense work, and had been considering the possibility of opening a free legal services office in a black area of the city. Albert Jenner has served as Chief Counsel for the Warren Commission and as a member of the President's Commission on Civil Disorders. Among the lawyers from Jenner & Block who volunteered were Thomas P. Sullivan, a hard-driving middle-aged trial lawyer with an excellent reputation, John G. Stiller, John C. Tucker, Richard T. Franch, and David Roston, all young and aggressive junior members of the firm.

Another volunteer was Thomas Boodell, Jr., a young, soft-spoken Harvard Law School graduate. After four years of work in his father's small but prestigious firm, Boodell, Sears, Sugrue & Crowley, Tom Boodell decided to go on his own for a while. He tried his hand at magazine editing, spent some time camping out and thinking, and then heard about the contract sales effort. As a child in the suburbs, he had heard his father condemning contract selling at the dinner table. During the summer of 1968 he walked into Lawndale, attended the Wednesday night dinners and meetings, and got acquainted with the people. In the fall, he wrote a proposal to the Adlai Stevenson Institute of International Affairs at the University of Chicago, asking that he be accepted as a Stevenson Fellow and allowed to begin research on contract selling. Boodell was accepted that same fall and received fellowships from both the Institute and the American Bar Foundation. "I had no idea of where it was heading at that time," Tom Boodell admits three years later. "One thing I observed when I first went out to Lawndale was that they didn't trust lawyers. But from the facts they showed me I felt there had to be some aspect of the problem that could be framed legally and taken into a courtroom setting, if they wanted that. So I just started think about it. I went to some of the meetings and sort of plodded along."

The CBL people, however, did not intend to plod along. In late November of 1968, after ten months of picketing, the sellers had not agreed to more than seven renegotiations. Charles

Baker announced a payment-withholding strike. Since most of the sellers had to meet their own monthly mortgage, tax, and insurance payments on the buildings with part of the contract money they collected, the CBL's payment strike was calculated to apply economic pressures. Each month the League would collect money orders for the monthly payments, which each buyer would make out to himself, and put them in escrow. Those West Side buyers who had rented out flats in their buildings promised their tenants a 25 percent reduction in rents after renegotiation if they agreed not to pay them to the sellers. Charles Baker, speaking for most members of the strike, vowed that if the sellers repossessed the buildings, CBL would discourage other black families from buying them. "The speculators need not fear that the buildings will burn down," he said. "We don't want them to collect money on the insurance we have paid over the years."

The strike lasted five months, despite threats of mass evictions. By the middle of January, 1969, 60 families had been sued for possession under the sellers' old protection, the eviction law. But more and more people joined the strike. By late March, 595 families had joined, withholding over $250,000. At each Wednesday night meeting Charles Baker would announce the total amount withheld, and the people would cheer. "If you see a lot of these sellers leaving town," Baker said at one point while reading off the total, "*this is why!*"

Like the creation of the CBL, *Clark* v. *Universal Builders* and *Baker* v. *F & F Investment* result from the collision of two previously unconnected events: the payment-withholding strike by black contract buyers in December, 1968, and the U.S. Supreme Court's *Jones* v. *Mayer* ruling in June, 1968, which resurrected a section of the 1866 Civil Rights Act (p. 69), and said abolition of "badges of slavery" required that a dollar in the hands of a black man must have the same economic power as a dollar in the hands of a white man. Tom Sullivan, the Jenner & Block trial lawyer, and Robert Ming, a black lawyer who is a veteran of civil rights litigation, were the men who tied the Supreme Court's *Jones* v. *Mayer* ruling to the CBL's lawsuits. A slim, reserved Irish Catholic, Sullivan takes care to explain exactly how he came to file the suits. "Judge Harold Sullivan called and said there was a big emergency with possible evictions coming up," Sullivan (no relation to the judge) recalls.

"I told him to have the CBL people come into my office. In late November they came in. I met Jack Macnamara and some of the others for the first time. They explained the problem, and said the lawyers had told them there was nothing that could be done. I said, 'Well, I don't agree with that. I would be surprised if there were nothing that could be done.' At that time the *Jones* v. *Mayer* case had just come down and everyone was very much aware of the old 1866 Civil Rights Act. So I said I would look into it, with the idea of eventually filing some lawsuits. Shortly after that I got in touch with Bob Ming and asked if he would join me in the case. He said he would. So during December, Bob Ming, John Stifler, Tom Boodell, and I evolved what is now the basic lawsuit. And on January 6, 1969, we filed the West Side suit [*Baker*]; and a couple of weeks after, we filed the South Side suit [*Clark*]."

Both suits were filed in the United States District Court for the Northern District of Illinois. The West Side suit joined three classes of defendants: contract sellers, lending institutions which granted them mortgages, and the assignees of both the sellers and the lenders. Besides conspiracy and the alleged violations of civil rights, the defendants were charged with blockbusting, violations of federal antitrust and securities laws, unconscionability, usury, and fraud.

In the South Side suit, the ten companies and Universal Builders were charged with conspiracy, civil rights and federal securities violations, unconscionability, usury, and fraud. In both cases the statement of facts was essentially the same as was the charge that both classes of sellers had exploited customs and usage of residential segregation and the artificial scarcity of housing for their own financial benefit.

Lawyers for both sets of sellers immediately filed motions that the cases be dismissed, charging that no claim upon which relief could be granted had been stated by the complaints. CBL lawyers filed memoranda in opposition to the motions. And in late March the Justice Department intervened, filing a small "friend-of-the-court" brief in support of the civil rights count of the West Side complaint.

For some time before its intervention in March, the Justice Department had been petitioned to enter the case. According to Jack Macnamara, Chicago supporters of the CBL had made several attempts to convince outgoing At torney General Ramsey Clark to bring the weight of the Justice Department behind the buyers. Thomas Foran, United States Attorney for the Northern District of Illinois, for example, had supported the CBL from its beginning. Foran encouraged Thomas Todd, a young black Assistant U.S. Attorney, to get involved on the side of the buyers. Another government supporter was

THE LAW AND THE COURTS—A Chronology

• 1827—The Illinois Forcible Entry and Detainer Act—the state's eviction law—was passed as a speedy remedy for landlords against trespassing tenants, but amended in 1861 to include contract buying. Delinquent buyers could be sued for possession after being served with a thirty-day warning notice of demand for payment and intent to start forcible proceedings, with the further warning that the contract would be terminated and tax payments forfeited. Procedures in circuit court have been concerned with "issue of possession"; defendants' response has been limited to whether notice was received and whether money was owed. To appeal an eviction judgment and raise defenses, defendant must post, within five days of judgment, a full amount appeal bond covering all delinquencies and all payments to become due during time of the appeal (usually one to one and a half years). Most contracts required buyers to pay sellers' fees and costs in the event of these proceedings.

• 1866—United States Congress passes the nation's first Civil Rights Act under authority of section II of the Thirteenth Amendment. Section I of the 1866 Act, now codified as 42 United States Code, section 1982, states that:

All citizens of the United States shall have the same right, in every State and Territory, as is enjoyed by white citizens thereof to inherit, purchase, lease, sell, hold, and convey real and personal property.

In arguing that Congress had power under the Thirteenth Amendment to pass such a law, Illinois Senator Lyman Trumbull, sponsor of the Civil Rights Act, noted: "I have no doubt that under this provision . . . we may destroy all these discrimina-

tions in civil rights against the black man; and if we cannot, our constitutional amendment amounts to nothing."
From 1866 until 1968, section 1982 was interpreted to prevent states, and not the private actions of individuals, from violating the civil rights of blacks.

• 1948—United States Supreme Court, in *Shelley* v. *Kraemer* and companion cases, held that judicial enforcement of racially restrictive covenants violated the equal protection clause of the Fourteenth Amendment. Section 1982, considered in a companion case, was still noted to be applicable only against state action.

• 1968—United States Supreme Court, in *Jones* v. *Alfred H. Mayer Co.*, dropped the legal and technical requirements and simply applied the constitutionality of section 1982 to bar *all* racial discrimination, private as well as public, in the sale or rental of property. The statute was construed as a valid exercise of the power of Congress to enforce the Thirteenth Amendment. Justice Potter Stewart: "At the very least, the freedom that Congress is empowered to secure under the Thirteenth Amendment includes the freedom to buy whatever a white man can buy, the right to live wherever a white man can live. If Congress cannot say that being a free man means at least this much, then the Thirteenth Amendment made a promise the nation cannot keep."

• 1969—Hubert L. Will, Federal District Judge for the Northern District of Illinois, denying a motion to dismiss two class actions brought by the Contract Buyers League against private parties, held that a cause of action had been stated under section 1982, as the 1866 Civil Rights Act was interpreted in *Jones* v. *Mayer*.

John McKnight, former director of the Midwestern Office of the Civil Rights Commission.

Foran and Todd had sent a copy of the two complaints to Ramsey Clark during the last days of the Johnson Administration, trying to get a commitment. But even telegrams and petitions from sympathetic congressmen were ineffective. Finally, in January, 1969, during the very first days of the Nixon Administration, Jerris Leonard, Assistant Attorney General in charge of the Justice Department's Civil Rights Division, agreed to see Macnamara, Todd, and McKnight. They immediately flew to Washington. "One of the points I kept stressing to Leonard," Macnamara recalls, "was that kids in the neighborhood believed that going through the law wouldn't work, and the only thing that would work would be bombing the real estate people; and that it seemed important for an Administration concerned about violence to do its part in helping to prove to the people that justice can be obtained by going through the courts. At the end of the conference Mr. Leonard said to me, 'If we do come into this case you have a grave obligation to let the people know that we did come in.' I said, 'I have a grave obligation to let the people know if you do decide to come in or if you decide not to come in.' Mr. Leonard threw up his hands and said, 'All right. You've got me!'"

The Justice Department, as a federal agency, was caught between the pressures on it to intervene and the probability that CBL lawyers would eventually join, as co-defendants in the lawsuits, the Federal Housing Administration, the Veterans Administration, and the Federal Savings and Loan Insurance Corporation. To prevent immediate embarrassment, a deal was made between the Department and CBL lawyers: if CBL would refrain for the time being from making the three federal agencies co-defendants, the government would intervene on behalf of the buyers. Thomas Todd wrote an initial forty-three-page draft of a government brief, of which ten pages were "really scathing about the FHA." But just before arguments on the motion to dismiss were to be heard and Todd was preparing to fly to Washington to get Justice Department approval of the brief, he received a call from Jerris Leonard. According to Todd, Leonard indicated that while the Justice Department was not opposed to the CBL issues, there was no money for the trip. "I asked whether he would

see me if I came," Todd recalls. "And he said yes."

Thomas Foran contributed $50, Todd paid $50, and $50 more came from other sources. Thomas Todd flew to Washington. "Were they surprised to see *me!*" Thomas Todd says. "I stormed around and demanded that they see me. At last one of Leonard's assistants came out and said that he would look at the brief. I have no doubt that he was a brilliant young law graduate, but in two hours he had cut my forty-three-page brief down to seven and there was nothing left of it. The ten pages I had on the FHA had been dismissed in a sentence. I am a gentle person, normally, but I called him everything I could think of and accused him of having a robot mind and a computerized attitude. Now, the Justice Department in Washington is very quiet; everybody there is either sleeping or dead. But in the middle of it all I cursed him in the best street language. He said that we would rework it then. And we did. All night. The result was an eleven-page brief which said almost nothing. This was Leonard's doing. I flew back to Chicago on Thursday night. We had already sent out notices that we would be looking to intervene on Friday morning. Well, despite the reluctance of the Justice Department to get in, they had the press releases ready in Washington. And although we were not before the judge until 10:30 A.M., they had releases out saying we had been in at 9:30 A.M. They said this was an indication of what the Administration was going to do to help black people. But the brief said absolutely nothing. It got them a million dollars' worth of publicity."

The Justice Department's press release contained Attorney General John Mitchell's statement that the brief was "the federal government's first effort to break massive Northern housing segregation under the Supreme Court's ruling in *Jones* v. *Mayer*." Jerris Leonard noted at a Washington press conference that this was the first time the federal government had entered a housing suit, brought by private parties, at the district court level; and that it was also the first attack by the Justice Department on sales terms which are more onerous to blacks than to whites. He called the overcharges a "race tax," and indicated that the federal government was considering attacks on similar speculation in other cities, Detroit among them. "Anyone who rakes off a profit based on racial discrimination should have to pay it back with interest," he told the press.

In late May, after an initial ruling that the cases could be filed as class actions,* Judge Hubert L. Will of the federal district court delivered his opinion on the sellers' motion to dismiss. A brilliant, forceful judge, he had been under tremendous pressures from both sides since being assigned to the cases. Besides the publicity, the strike, the intervention of the Justice Department, heated outbursts in his court, and charges by West Side sellers that he was anti-Semitic, he was also to be criticized by local groups, including the Urban League, for proceeding with the cases too slowly. On the most crucial issue, the applicability of the 1866 Civil Rights Act as interpreted in *Jones* v. *Mayer*, he ruled that the buyers had stated a case:

What was true in *Jones* is true here also—the defendants call "revolutionary" what is simply a denial of their assumption that there is a necessary sanctity in the *status quo*. Defendants present the discredited claim that it is necessarily right for businessmen to secure profits wherever profit is available, arguing specifically with respect to this case that they did not create the system of *de facto* segregation which was the condition for the alleged discriminatory profit. But the law in the United States has grown to define certain economic bonds and ethical limits of business enterprise. . . . So we are hearing an old and obsolete lament. For it is now understood that under section 1982 [of the 1866 Civil Rights Act] as interpreted in *Jones* v. *Alfred H. Mayer Co.*, there cannot in this country be markets or profits based on the color of a man's skin.

In ruling that a civil rights claim had been stated and in answer to the defendants' contention that the claim alleged "hypothetical" discrimination, Judge Will noted that "defendants' position elaborated is that if property is sold to a negro above what can be demonstrated to be

the usual market price, there is no discrimination unless the same seller actually sells to whites at a lower price. It should be clear that in law the result would be obnoxious. In logic, it is ridiculous. It would mean that the 1866 Civil Rights Act, which was created to be an instrument for the abolition of discrimination, allows an injustice so long as it is visited entirely on negroes."

He dismissed the charged violations of securities laws, as well as charges of unconscionability, fraud, and usury. But he refused to dismiss the savings and loan associations as defendant-lenders.

Over a year after Judge Will's opinion, Sullivan and Ming amended their complaint to join as defendants the Federal Housing Administration, the Veterans Administration, and the Federal Savings and Loan Insurance Corporation. Both the FHA and the VA were charged with complicity and discriminatory practices in the backing of mortgages. The FSLIC was charged with taking over a number of savings and loan associations, which had folded because of alleged backing of speculators, and holding over 800 mortgages on properties sold to black people on contracts which were still being administered at the same inflated prices. This time the federal government filed a motion claiming immunity and asking to be dismissed. So far, this level of the litigation has not been resolved.

That is how the two CBL lawsuits, *Baker* v. *F. & F. Investment* and *Clark* v. *Universal Builders*, got into federal court.

The buyers' payment-withholding strike had been ended by two agreements following the filing of *Baker* v. *F. & F. Investment* and *Clark* v. *Universal Builders*. The South Side agreement, made on March 4, 1969, required South Side buyers to continue making payments "without prejudice" directly to Universal Builders. The West Side agreement, made on April 3, 1969, required all striking buyers to continue making payments and required all sellers to deposit a portion of the monthly payments in escrow each month pending outcome of *Baker*. Because they were negotiated by lawyers and entered as court orders, the agreements bound a young, highly energetic black grass-roots movement and a small group of mostly white, relatively moderate lawyers to the same goal. The marriage was sometimes a strained one; the priorities were different. Few buyers wanted to continue making di-

* A class action is a suit in which representatives of a specific group of people file a lawsuit, on behalf of all those similarly situated, but too numerous to bring before a court, in which common questions of the law and fact predominate over individual questions. The resolution of the lawsuit settles the interest of all parties similarly situated.

rect payments to the sellers, and favored mass confrontation tactics and economic pressure to achieve renegotiation. The lawyers confined their efforts to the legal arena, to winning the two cases. The differences in approach created tension, discord, sometimes mistrust. But there were even more fundamental problems.

One was the relationship between the black and white CBL workers and the young people of the West Side, which had been tense all along. Lawndale, with its resident street gangs, has one of the highest crime rates in Chicago. The gang members did not actively support the organization; some of them harassed white CBL workers, but they did not try to impede the CBL's progress. Charles Baker believes that CBL's presence has been responsible for a decrease in Lawndale gang activity. He attributes this to the fact that CBL is "working with the parents of the so-called gangs," and takes pride in pointing out that the CBL office window is the only one on Pulaski Road without an iron grating protecting it. In the window is a large sign listing the names and amounts of renegotiated savings of CBL families.

And there was tension in the loose alliance between West and South Side people. The alliance endured from late 1968 through early 1970. But there were growing differences. Besides dissimilarities in age and education, many of the South Side people, as occupants of newer homes, considered themselves removed from the original ghettos. All were committed to peaceful mass confrontation tactics. But some South Siders were embarrassed by the revivalist overtones of the West Side meetings. Most viewed their problem in strictly economic terms, and others were suspicious of the whites who surrounded, and possibly influenced, the lower-class West Side members. The South Side people held their own meetings in their own area of the city, but most of the decision-making seems to have been confined to the West Side office. The differences were further compounded by the semi-autonomous roles and styles of the two sets of leaders. Both Charles Baker and Clyde Ross of the West Side were former factory workers, both were from the same town in Mississippi, and both were paid employees of the Gamaliel Foundation. Relatively easygoing and cautious, they suggest the kind of participatory leadership common in the early days of the civil rights movement. Sidney Clark and Arthur Green, the two South Side leaders, were not employed by the Foundation; rather their involvement and speaking ability tended to project them as spokesmen. Clark, the buyer in whose name the South Side class action was brought, was the most vocal spokesman.

But there were also many areas of agreement between the two groups. Both mistrusted the legal process. Both worried that the involvement of lawyers might redirect or neutralize the energy of the organization. While most buyers were pleased by the filing of *Baker* and *Clark*, they did not feel that the two lawsuits were the only way of getting the contracts renegotiated, and they resented the end of the strike and the resumption of payments directly to the sellers. Some buyers say that the West Side sellers stopped discussing renegotiation of the contracts as soon as the strike ended, and also that they used offers of high settlements to the leaders in an attempt to undermine group solidarity, and offers of small settlements to encourage rank-and-file buyers to sign out of the plaintiff classes. In addition, a number of buyers with "permissive delinquencies" who had been "carried" by their sellers (many at good rates of interest) prior to the strike were now being required to pay up in full. Although the court-order agreement ending the strike had stated that delinquencies were to be amortized "over a reasonable period," the phrase was never clarified to the satisfaction of either side.

And so, over the objections of their lawyers, the buyers started a second payment strike. Of the numerous reasons now given by the buyers in justification of the second strike, three stand out:

A second strike would resume the economic pressure on the sellers while the pretrial process dragged on, and perhaps force them to renegotiate.

Second, once the suits had been filed and the first strike had ended, there was little the CBL could do to maintain its cohesiveness. Limited as it was to a single issue, the grass-roots movement was threatened with extinction once the lawyers moved the conflict into the courts. Most members lacked the time and skill to participate in the legal discovery work. Furthermore, the sellers' lawyers fought the buyers' having access to information obtained for purposes of the lawsuit. It was being used in CBL propaganda, they charged. Many buyers were bitter

ver the inequality of remedies available to the
wo sides, and they believed that without direct
ressure on the sellers, both negotiation and the
ases would fail.

Finally, the buyers wanted to use mass evic-
on publicity pressures to attack the state's
viction law. In 1968 an estimated 42,000 fami-
es, both renters and contract buyers, had been
ued for possession under authority of this evic-
on law. One reporter estimated that in the
rst six months of 1969, 21,751 more eviction ac-
ons had been started. In August, 1969, a Chi-
ago paper printed a story charging that the
irst Municipal District Court was an "eviction
ill," with one judge sometimes ordering evic-
ons at the rate of twenty a minute as land-
rds, their lawyers, or secretaries yelled "plain-
ff" when defendants were called. Public atten-
on was directed to the eviction courts.

The buyers had an additional reason for want-
ig to test the eviction law. In early 1969, Mar-
all Patner, an energetic, reform-minded lawyer
ho was then executive director of Businessmen
r the Public Interest, had taken the case of a
outh Side family ordered evicted during the
rst strike. Since his days with Chicago Legal
id, Patner had been slowly formulating argu-
ents against the defense-and-appeal bond pro-
sions of the statute; and during the eviction
roceedings brought against Mr. and Mrs. Ches-
r Fisher by Rosewood Corporation (one of the
n companies under Universal's name) he had
tempted to raise the sales terms and condi-
ons of their contract as a defense. The testi-
ony was ruled "not germane to the issue of
ossession" and excluded. Patner then argued
at the inability of the buyers to raise equitable
fenses was a denial of due process and equal
otection. Then with a $5000 appeal bond con-
ibuted to the Fishers from private sources, he
ok their case, *Rosewood*, to the Illinois Su-
eme Court. "Even before my work with Legal
d," Marshall Patner says, "I was interested in
e forcible entry. I was doing some commer-
al work for a real estate firm under the evic-
on law. Most were hardship cases, but I did
t into evictions eventually. I got to know the
w much better than most people who would
rmally get in on the other side. From then
I was waiting for a chance to challenge it."
us, when the CBL made its decision to call a
cond strike, Macnamara and a few of the CBL
ders were aware that *Rosewood*, directly chal-

lenging the eviction law, was pending before the
court.

The co-counsels, Sullivan and Ming, were
strongly opposed to the second payment strike.
When informed of the plan, they held a hurried
series of meetings with the buyers and attempted
to discourage it by describing in detail the remedies available to the sellers under the eviction
law, and expressing concern over the possibility
of violence during the evictions. Some South
Side CBL members also opposed the strike, and
objected to having to risk their own homes for
people who were delinquent in their contract
payments. But both sets of leaders and both sets
of buyers voted to risk mass evictions in order
to carry out the strike.

The second withholding strike began on July 19,
1969. The procedure was the same as before:
each month the leaders would collect money orders for contract payments, which each striker
would make out to himself, and place them in
escrow. Any buyer who saved his own money
was not considered part of the official strike.
Many were fearful of going against the court order that had ended the first strike; nevertheless,
they withheld the money. By the end of the summer, eviction proceedings had been brought
against 261 of the 552 striking families. The hearings were summary: Under the eviction law, the
sellers' lawyers simply alleged that each buyer
had been notified of his delinquency, and the
buyer's response was limited to two responses;
whether he had received notice and whether he
owed money. Bonds for those who wanted to
appeal the judgments were set on the average of
$4000, but some were as high as $7500. At first
the cases were being handled by a number of
volunteer lawyers and law students, some of
whom attempted to raise the contract terms as
defenses. But most of the lawyers eventually
withdraw from representing the strikers either
because they felt the strikers were wrong to live
in the houses without paying or because they felt
that the strikers had not been overcharged in
the first place, or because they felt the futility of
trying to break the eviction pattern. Most of the
law students withdrew because of this same futility, and because of the pressures from the
judges. Subsequently, many buyers began representing themselves before the judges, and
raised questions far beyond the scope of the issue
of possession. One judge, in telling a woman
that his hands were tied because the law required

her to pay up or get out, said, "Young lady, I'm sorry to say this but somebody has led you down the wrong path and has misled you. And I know who." "You're right, your honor," the woman replied. "They misled me in Mississippi. I came up here to get a better place to raise my family. I was misled in Mississippi, but I was misled worse here because there they don't hide their hands. I came here to get justice and you are sitting up there agreeing with me and at the end you are going to shake your head and say, 'There is nothing I can do. My hands are tied.' I am being misled *here*!"

Jesuits from all over the country raised $250,000 to be used as a lump-sum appeal bond, but the court would not permit this, and the money was returned to the donors.

The strikers began preparing for the evictions. In early December, 1969, former Cook County Sheriff Joseph Woods began the ordered evictions of South Side strikers. But as soon as his men had evicted Mrs. Elizabeth Nelson and nine children from their home and left the scene, a large crowd of CBL members, nuns, priests, rabbis, and other supporters moved the furniture back into the house. Sheriff Woods (a Republican who was then running for president of the County Board and who might have feared creating an issue which would allow the Democrats to mobilize black voters) then announced a moratorium on evictions until after Christmas. He also announced a policy of suspending future evictions when the temperature went below twenty degrees.

However, on January 5, twenty-five deputies attempted to evict another South Side family. This time more than two hundred CBL members and supporters were crammed inside the house when the deputies arrived. The deputies moved off and attempted a third eviction in another area. But again CBL members and supporters aborted the attempt by crowding into and surrounding the house.

Many CBL people take pride in disclosing the "map strategy" they used against Woods. Actually, both the sheriff's office and the CBL were involved in a ritual calculated to prevent violence on the eviction scenes. In fact, many CBL members believe that the evictions began on the more stable South Side because of the lesser danger of a confrontation between deputies and gang members there than in the West Side neighborhoods. The CBL office would be warned beforehand, by "friends" inside the

sheriff's office, of scheduled eviction sites. Word would go out to members and supporters by telephone that "Pharaoh is riding." Watchers would be posted to report the gathering and movements of the deputies to the group, which would be waiting on standby at 4 A.M. As soon as the intended house was known, buyers and supporters would rush to the house and surround it.

When the eviction party arrived at a house, one of the deputies would walk through the crowd expecting to be blocked at the door. There would be some words exchanged about "obstructing a process of law," names would be taken, and the buyer would be cited for criminal trespass. The deputies would then leave the scene, and the cited striker would later surrender on his own and post bail. On one occasion a deputy was overheard telling a buyer who was blocking the door to his home: "Make it look good." It was a practical solution to a volatile situation, as demonstrated by the next eviction attempt.

On January 29, 1970, Sheriff Woods brought along two hundred deputies and Chicago Task Force Policemen. The movers were able to pick the lock, cut telephone wires, and put the furniture into the snow before CBL people could arrive on the scene. Sixteen security guards, hired by Universal Builders, were posted inside the house to prevent its reoccupation. But after the deputies and police had gone, CBL members and supporters trapped the guards inside the house. The guards fired some shots. Joseph Gibson, a South Side member of the strike, probably prevented the development of a more explosive situation by calming the crowd and then assuring the guards that they would not be harmed if they came out. The guards left the house. The crowd moved the furniture back. Soon after this attempt, Sheriff Woods announced that he would never again send two hundred men and spend $25,000 of the taxpayers' money for a twenty-minute eviction, and ordered a halt to all eviction attempts until the courts had ruled in the cases of those families charged with criminal trespass. Universal Builders immediately sued Woods for $7 million, and the circuit court threatened contempt citations.

In early February, 1970, two federal judges heard Tom Sullivan's arguments against the eviction law, but decided to abstain from passing on it because of Marshall Patner's case *Rosewood*, which raised the same question about the statute and was then pending before the Illinois Supreme Court. Then, in a remarkable display of legal red-tape cutting, Tom Sullivan managed to have a number of eviction cases transferred from the circuit courts and consolidated with *Rosewood*. The court scheduled arguments in *Rosewood* for early March of that year.

There was also activity on another level. In early April, 1970, Chicago Mayor Richard J. Daley agreed to intervene in the dispute. He had been petitioned to intervene once before, in early February. At that time an agreement had been worked out by lawyers for Universal Builders and Sullivan's group. But the South Side strikers, who were the ones under most imminent threat of eviction, had rejected the agreement because of the alleged political influence behind it and the fact that it did not mention renegotiation of the contracts. There were rumors that there were connecions between high officials in Universal Builders and the Democratic organization, and some South Side people noted that before Mayor Daley came into the conflict, Universal Builders had not been in the mood for compromise. But it is just as probable that both Mayor Daley and Universal officials were concerned over the tension and potential racial conflict that the evictions might cause. Both Robert Ming and Tom Sullivan were equally concerned. When they presented the February agreement to the South Side strikers, tempers were high. And they were being criticized by both Judge Will and other lawyers for not keeping the people in line. Only about fifty South Side strikers accepted the first agreement.

There were additional reasons for them to request Mayor Daley to mediate a second agreement. By late February, Sheriff Woods had departed from the sham eviction ritual and gotten down to the serious business of actually clearing the houses. During the early morning two hundred deputies and policemen would arrive in buses, close off an entire South Side block to prevent CBL members and supporters from entering, and evict all striking families on the block. Each eviction took less than an hour; while the deputies and policemen closed off the street, professional movers went in and cleared the houses; then the deputies and officers moved back into the buses and drove off to the next eviction site, leaving at the houses security guards armed with shotguns. During the last few weeks of March and until the halt called by Mayor Da-

ley before the second mediation session, Woods successfully evicted twenty-one striking families. Even while five hundred CBL members and supporters were downtown petitioning Mayor Daley to re-enter the dispute, Woods was evicting four more striking families.

On April 7 the sessions began in Mayor Daley's office. Buyers, sellers, and lawyers for both sides held separate meetings. Mayor Daley announced on television, "What is now on the streets will be brought to the bargaining table, and settled there with the buyers and sellers sitting around it." The sessions were long. Reports from inside the office called them "fine meetings," "productive." The City Council passed a resolution endorsing the mayor's intervention. One CBL leader remarked: "I'd like to say something in favor of the mayor, this great mayor. He doesn't want anyone to leave these meetings, and he just keeps on hollering at you until you get an agreement."

Rumors went around: Mayor Daley was in contact with judges of the Illinois Supreme Court who were about to deliver their opinion in *Rosewood;* Mayor Daley was considering revoking the building license of Universal Builders if the latter did not call off the evictions; Mayor Daley would order Sheriff Woods to hold off the evictions until after the *Rosewood* decision had been handed down. Many buyers who engaged in this speculation were forgetting that Universal was no longer building houses, and that Sheriff Woods, a Republican and a county official, was acting under court orders. Many believed in the mayor's power to "control" the sellers, even if the courts could not. The faith that many lower-class Chicago black people have in Daley is one of his major political assets.

On April 8, after two sessions, Mayor Daley announced a solution that was "fair to all." Even the CBL leaders, walking out of his office, called it a "very good" settlement. Both Sidney Clark and Arthur Green signed it. The press called it "A Nice Day's Work for the Mayor," and hoped that the buyers would accept and tensions ease. Since the agreement was between Universal Builders and the South Side buyers, Mayor Daley arranged a meeting between them at the Sherman House. Again Sullivan and Ming urged the strikers to accept. There was a one-week deadline.

The April agreement to end the payment-withholding strike was almost the same as the previous agreement. The strikers were to pay all withheld money and all future installments di-rectly to Universal. In return, Universal would deposit $50,000 in an account and claim it and all eviction costs only if the Illinois Supreme Court upheld the constitutionality of the evic-tion law. If the court struck down the law, the $50,000 would remain in the account, subject to court orders pending the outcome of *Clark* v. *Universal Builders*, and the striking buyers would not have to pay eviction costs. All con-tract sales would be reinstated, all eviction judg-ments vacated, and Universal would not charge penalty interest rates for past defaults in pay-ment. (This second agreement differed from the first in that Universal also promised to put aside an additional $500 each month pending out-come of *Clark*, and indicated that it might con-sider refinancing some or all of the contracts.)

A number of South Side strikers rejected the agreement because it contained no specific pro-vision for renegotiation of the contracts. Both Clark and Green were criticized for signing the agreement, and soon joined other strikers in de-nouncing it. "I think the South Side people *lost* in the mayor's office," one participant observes, "by not insisting that they were in there not to stop the evictions but to renegotiate."

Two days before the agreement deadline, the Illinois Supreme Court handed down its deci-sion in *Rosewood*. Avoiding the constitutional questions, the court reinterpreted the state evic-tion law to allow contract buyers to raise equit-able defenses in eviction proceedings. The court did not pass on the appeal bond provisions of the act, and only the few buyers who had posted appeal bonds could take advantage of the de-cision.

The strike was never officially ended. But most of the South Side strikers finally accepted the proposed agreement, turned their escrow money over to Universal, and waited for the out-come of *Clark* v. *Universal Builders* in the fed-eral courts.

In Lawndale a number of families continued to withhold, but the back of the group effort was broken. Sheriff Woods handled the West Side evictions carefully, moving only a few families at a time. But some CBL members and sup-porters continued to move families back into the houses. Most strikers agreed to pay, how-ever, when Judge Will, before resigning from the two class actions, announced that he would dis-miss all strikers as plaintiffs from the lawsuit.

The seventy-to-eighty South Side buyers who rejected the agreement reached in Mayor Daley's office were eventually evicted by Sheriff Woods and his successor. Some moved back in and were evicted again, and again. The tension that had been building between the two sides of the organization now exploded into hostility and charges of "selling out." The core of South Side people who opposed ending the strike against Universal broke with the CBL and began their own organization, led by Sidney Clark and Ar-thur Green. This splinter group drew support from independent politicians, white students, and some vocal South Side businessmen. Nei-ther Clark nor Green will discuss the grievances of the group or his own involvement, but it is clear that the mood was bitter. South Side buy-ers sympathetic to the West Side people were ex-cluded from the splinter group's meetings, and attempts were made to produce some sense of vindication for its members. At one point a group of them "sat in" at the governor's office to protest Universal's policies; on another occa-sion they "evicted" the head of the Chicago FHA office. Once, when some of those living in their houses under criminal trespass charges were or-dered jailed for a few days, supporters from Jesse Jackson's Operation Breadbasket de-manded to be locked in the cells with them. Sid-ney Clark expressed the mood of the group dur-ing a public meeting. "We are not in the business of compromising," he said. "We are not com-promising on anything. You people have strug-gled too long and too much. If anybody got any Uncle Tom ideas about sneaking in and messing up, you better just stay out of the way because this is a *for-real* movement here. Universal is *going* to renegotiate these contracts. Universal is *not* going to make the money it made before."

The group's bitterness and mistrust were ac-centuated by the intervention of another outside influence. In the summer of 1970 Sherman Skol-nick, a white legal researcher who chaired an or-ganization called the Citizens' Committee to Clean Up Corruption in the Courts, was invited to address one of the meetings. Skolnick brought along "fact sheets" bearing the title "Who Represents Who In the Contract Buyers League?" which were passed out to the audi-ence. The sheets denounced a number of judges, among them was the name of Federal Judge J. Sam Perry, who had been assigned to hear *Clark* v. *Universal Builders* following Judge Will's re ease of it. Skolnick also listed Albert Jenner as a bank director and charged his law firm with torpedoing civil rights cases in the past. Skolnick alleged that Jenner's firm had volunteered its services to the CBL in order to turn the thrust of the grass-roots movement into the courts where it could be killed off, and that the possibility of having to renegotiate "25,000 contracts in the city of Chicago" threatened a number of banks holding mortgages from the sellers. "If they couldn't turn this grass-roots movement around, their banks would go under. They need this blood money to exist on," he told the group, and suggested that the Catholic Church and the Democratic Party were also involved in the attempt to "sell out" the movement. A class action, he said, was "the work of the devil" because of its binding nature on those not immediately involved in bringing the action, and suggested that both *Clark* and *Baker* were "sellout" cases. You think that some lawyer like Jenner, who makes $2500 a day as a bank director, is going to get up feeling for poor working people who work two and three jobs to make their payments?" he said. "The first thing that'll happen if you win is that his bank will go under. So which side is he on? . . . What the hell do they give a damn about *your constitutional rights?* You've got to deal with first things first. Get this picture: A *bank director* went to court in our name, *Jenner,* and the case went to other *bank directors* who sit in robes and call themselves judges, and they sit next to the flag and tell you about the Constitution and all that bullshit! The only ones who are not bank directors are *you!"*

What is most significant about this meeting is that the people seemed to *want* to believe him. In late August, 1970, nine South Side buyers, including Sidney Clark and Arthur Green, filed a complain in the Cook County Circuit Court. They named as defendants Jack Macnamara, Albert Jenner, Tom Sullivan, Robert Ming, John Stifler, Charles Baker, a Catholic bishop of Chicago, the Archbishop of Chicago, the Gamaliel Foundation, Gordon Sherman, and several of the white workers. Sherman Skolnick drafted the complaint.

The allegations attacked every level that had contributed to the Contract Buyers League. The Catholic bishop was charged with being the beneficial owner of contracts through a connection with one of Universal's ten companies; the Gamaliel Foundation was charged with having an interest in safeguarding the relationship between the Catholic bishop and Universal, funneling money to the lawyers disguised as "litigation costs," and with financing the CBL in order to ensure that the organization did not get out of hand; Baker was charged with being an agent for the lawyers, who allegedly used him to solicit employment from Clark, Green, and other South Side buyers; Jenner, Sullivan, Stifler, and Ming were alleged to have falsely and maliciously purported to be the attorneys for South Side buyers during the negotiations in Mayor Daley's office, and were charged with failing to carry out their instructions; Gordon Sherman was accused of funneling money through the Gamaliel Foundation to the lawyers. The list of damages claimed by the plaintiffs included the interference with their rights to seek redress of their own grievances; blockading of their rights to solicit their own lawyers; the alleged compromising of their rights and destinies through control of the lawsuit; and personal claims for public humiliation and the disruption of their property and family lives. They asked $5 million in exemplary damages, $5 million in actual damages, and costs.

The filing of this case in 1970 was not only symbolic of the growing mistrust of white motives which continues to isolate blacks and whites. It was a renunciation of three years of dedication, sacrifice, and personal pain on the part of both black contract buyers and the people who supported them. The breach between the two classes of black people was widened. Ironically, the people with fewer middle-class pretensions—the West Siders—retained their perspective. The lawyers were hurt and irritated. Sullivan, Ming, Stifler, and Jenner immediately withdrew from handling the nine plaintiffs, but continued to represent the eighty other South Side buyers who had been evicted but who did not join in the suit. But they requested an injunction to prevent the nine buyers and Skolnick from interfering with their preparation of the two major lawsuits. They also requested a hearing to determine whether they had properly and adequately represented the class of plaintiffs. At the hearing it was determined that they had. Subsequently, charges against Gordon Sherman and the Catholic bishop were dropped, but the charges against all the others remain unchanged. They denied the charges but did not move for dismissal, in order to avoid providing the plaintiffs with additional ammunition. The case is still pending.

IV   How It Ends

Despite the bitter split that threatened the CBL, the entire experience has been a successful one. Speculation on the outcome of either of the two federal court cases would be premature, but it is worthwhile to define some of the legal difficulties which Sullivan and the other lawyers are likely to face.

In doing so, one might consider the statement of one of the South Side buyers who joined in the suit against Sullivan. "There are enough laws on the book now to protect adequately all the people in this country," he said. "You don't *have* to go into court and start begging and pleading about rights and all that." But in point of fact, there are relatively few laws on the books that can provide meaningful remedies for contract buyers. A tenet of American law is that courts are extremely reluctant to interfere in contractual relationships. This is probably the reason why the early volunteer lawyers eventually decided that nothing could be done for the buyers. Most lawyers recognize that only a radical reconsideration of the policy reasons and values that support the inviolability of contracts can help the buyers.

Both *Clark* v. *Universal Builders* and *Baker* v. *F & F Investment* are challenging the federal courts to make such a reconsideration. But the fact that an essentially commercial appeal has been made within the context of a civil rights complaint charging racial discrimination tends to make the problem even more complex. Beyond the reluctance of courts to interfere in commercial areas there is a fundamental weakness in the two CBL cases based on the Supreme Court's decision in *Jones* v. *Mayer* in 1968. The discrimination alleged in the two cases does not fit the conceptual model on which *Jones* was decided. In the usual civil rights case, as in *Jones*, a black plaintiff alleges that a white defendant's treatment of him was not equal to that which was actually given to whites. But in the two CBL cases no such allegations were possible because of a lack of evidence that the sellers had ever made more favorable contract sales to whites. And in ruling that the CBL complaints had stated a claim under Section I of the 1866 Civil Rights Act, Judge Will raised the point that may well symbolize the real significance of the CBL experience:

> Defendants contend that this holding would mean that every non-white citizen has a cause of action . . . to either rescind or reform . . . a purchase or leasing of either *real* or *personal* property by the simple allegation that he was charged more than a white person *would have been charged* or that he received less favorable terms and conditions than would have been given a white person.

The essential words are "would have been charged." In the absence of evidence that the sellers actually charged or would have charged whites less for similar property, the conduct does not seem to fit the traditional conceptual model. Moreover, Judge Will's analysis assumes that property in a changing neighborhood would have some value in a white market. These ambiguities could result in the CBL's losing the two lawsuits. On the other hand, as one commentator suggests, Judge Will could have been moving toward a new theory of liability, merging both civil rights and commercial law, and dispensing with the old conceptual model.

There is already considerable pressure on the federal courts to develop some approach to commercial discrimination. In Baltimore, where a grass-roots movement similar to the CBL has grown up, a civil rights complaint, *Montebello Community Association* v. *Goldseker*, was filed about a year after the Chicago lawsuits. Besides *Montebello*, similar sales practices are being challenged in Washington, D.C., and the CBL office has received calls and visitors from many other cities.

Many people are convinced that without the two strikes and the evictions the courts would never have moved as far as they have in *Clark, Baker, Rosewood,* and related cases. Jack Macnamara is convinced of that much. "Everybody knows it," he says; "if they deny it, they're *blind. Nothing* would have happened if it hadn't been for the activities of the people! The people themselves created a situation which forced people to respond on a somewhat part-time basis." And Tom Sullivan says almost the same thing. "Repeatedly," he says, "lawyers have been forced to improvise and to push beyond the frontier, so to speak, *not* because of their own ingenuity or anything that they started, but rather despite themselves and over their objections that it couldn't be done, because the people said, "Well, screw it, we're going to do it this way anyhow.' "

Among the buyers there is absolute certainty that nothing would have been done if they had not acted. In fact, many of the people who continued to withhold their payments after the major part of the strike was over did so because they did not believe that any relief would come through the courts.

The Contract Buyers League survived the strike, but it is not the same organization. One reason is that Jack Macnamara has left. During the evictions he had to be hospitalized for exhaustion. In late 1970 he asked to be released from his Jesuit vows. In June, 1971, he married Peggy O'Connor, a CBL volunteer. It was a Catholic wedding, but Mrs. Luceal Johnson was asked to stand beside the priest and speak. The young black man who once beat Macnamara also attended. A few months after the wedding Macnamara took a job with Applied Resources Incorporated in New York, and left Lawndale. His leaving was in accordance with the original goals of the old Presentation Church Project: "To move on, once the machinery for an organized and developing community was set up, and leave the people to function on their own." During the three years of his involvement he had remained in the background, requiring the black members to make their own decisions. Macnamara's departure was probably an extension of this same determination to make the black people aware of their own potential to fight for themselves. In fact, he said as much to them before leaving. "All kinds of credit is given at CBL meetings," he told them. "People talk about all that white people are doing in supporting what you people are doing. They couldn't have done a thing without you. The real heroes of the CBL are not the white men, and it's about time that black people stopped saying thank you to white men, except in a very general way, and started saying, 'It's about time you gave us what we had coming.' A lot of people have said that I have done a lot for the people. I think the real thing is that the people have done a lot for me. And I'd like to thank them."

But the people have also done a lot for themselves. Almost 200 buyers have saved close to $2 million in principal and interest from renegotiated contracts. Some families have had their balances reduced by as much as $40,000 under the CBL's "fair-price formula." Others have accepted smaller settlements from the Federal Savings and Loan Insurance Corporation, which took over a number of bankrupt savings and loan associations that had granted mortgages to speculators. Quite a number of other families have accepted smaller settlements from their sellers in return' for signing out of the lawsuits. In many instances, according to CBL leaders, the sellers will also pay to patch up the outsides of the houses. An estimated 150 to 200 West Side people have announced themselves renegotiated and have dropped all contact with the CBL. Nothing within the power of the leaders has been able to make them disclose the amounts of their settlements. In some cases, Clyde Ross says, a family is told by the seller to remain silent because it is getting a better deal than all the others. The longer the West Side case is delayed, the fewer buyers there may be in the plaintiff class. In fact, when *Baker* is finally scheduled for trial, there might not be a plaintiff class.

Aside from their uncertain situations as plaintiffs, however, the CBL people have made a number of commercial accomplishments. The First National Bank of Chicago is now allowing Lawndale homeowners conventional mortgages at reasonable interest rates. And several insurance companies have been convinced by Clyde Ross that the underwriting of homeowners' policies in "high-risk" areas can be profitable. Although the coverage is still not available to all black families in Chicago, as of January, 1972, more than three hundred CBL families had obtained new policies with broader coverage at an average savings of $100 in annual premiums. There is also some talk of receiving rehabilitation money from the Department of Housing and Urban Development. But despite over three years of meetings with HUD and city officials, nothing substantial has developed. "I don't know what will come of it," Charles Baker admits, "but the government has already approved the loan. The only problem is getting it by the city. But if they do let it by, we'll have $100,000, and a lot of these people who have already been renegotiated might show up again."

Although the CBL is still functioning, it is questionable how much longer it will be able to exert the influence it once had. Through 1971 it was more an administrative than a mass activity organization. In the small office on Pulaski Road, Clyde Ross, Charles Baker, Henrietta

Banks, Ruth Wells, and a few white workers helped the people who wanted to apply for mortgages or insurance. At the peak of its appeal, in early 1970, the Wednesday night meetings could draw up to six hundred members and supporters on a subzero Chicago night. Budding politicians, sensing the arrival of a strong grass-roots organization, would attend the meetings with leaflets and encouraging speeches. By the next winter, however, the meetings seldom drew more than one hundred people. And few politicians. In June, 1971, when CBL held its third annual benefit at Presentation Church, fewer than three hundred members and supporters were present. By the end of last summer the meetings drew only thirty to forty members.

But Charles Baker believes that the CBL is just as effective now as it was several years ago. "We're still serving our purpose," he says. "Our purpose was to get the people relief from the contracts. Even though some of them are doing it on their own, they wouldn't have done it if it hadn't been for us."

There is also the matter of the practical knowledge the people have gained from their experience. "The good part about it," says Mrs. Luceal Johnson, who will not receive anything even if *Baker* is successful, "is that nobody will ever cheat me again *the longest day I live!* Nobody will ever sit back on his fanny and say, '*Here comes a sucker. Let's get her!*' Won't get me no *more!* I'm *through* being cheated. They got to get up and live off the sweat of their *own* brows. And I'm so sure they ain't g'on cheat me no more until I'll move into a *tent* before I buy another house and get it *unjustly.* I'll move into a *pup-tent!* And I'm going to teach my children to don't buy one the way I bought it."

Both Charles Baker and Clyde Ross, former factory workers, now understand the fine points about contracts, mortgages, insurance, and interest. So do a number of the others. Charles Baker, speaking of his hopes for the eventual rehabilitation of Lawndale, says, "Talk about *freedom?* Since I've been in this I've seen the perfect way you can get freedom: with *this!*" and points to his head. The lessons are not lost. A policy at the meetings is that when there are no further questions from the audience, one of the leaders will ask the audience questions:

"What would be the first step if you were going to buy another house to keep from getting gypped like you did last time?"

"Have it *appraised!*" is the collective response. The lessons are not lost.

The circle widens. A group of Chicago lawyers, following Tom Sullivan's suggestion, has started a fund that will supply scholarships for black students who want to pursue careers in law. By the end of 1971 there was more than $900,000 in the fund, and twenty black students were enrolled in Chicago area law schools. Ten more will enter in the fall of 1972. Sidney Clark, the former South Side leader, is already attending law school at night, on his own.

On another level there is the matter of the whites who volunteered their help and support to the organization. Most of them were new to both experiences: the inner city and black people. Most of the Presentation Project workers had some initial difficulties with young black people in the Lawndale area, but all seem to have gained clearer perspectives on the nature of the many levels of tension between the two groups. One young man, Mike Gecan, a recent Yale graduate whose family lives in a "changing" area of Chicago's far West Side, has been trying to develop a white grass-roots organization to combat the fears aroused by the blockbusters who are said to be operating in the area. And one elderly white couple, regular attenders of all CBL meetings, say in response to the question, Why?, "It's the only thing left in the country that we know about where there's still a chance to see justice demonstrated." There are at least one hundred whites who no longer fear walking through the Lawndale community.

There is also the question of the money: the $2 million in renegotiated savings and the inestimable amount that might result from the two lawsuits. Many of the people want to rehabilitate the houses and create businesses that will employ, and perhaps also rehabilitate, the young people of the community. "*Don't* tell me we can't operate our own businesses," Charles Baker says. "We've been operating the white man's businesses all our lives. You have to put your *own* business in your *own* neighborhood. People say they want Lawndale to be the best place in Chicago to live. There's nothing nice here now, but you've got a lot of vacant lots, and sooner or later somebody's going to start building. We got the best chance in the world to start out right, if we get citizen participation like we have in CBL." To implement this plan, the leaders have announced a project to buy some of the three hundred vacant lots in the area before urban renewal buys them and begins "relocating" the community.

Beyond the political and economic goals of the four-year struggle, the effort symbolized a conflict, for many of those involved, between the determined assertions of themselves and institutions that had kept them physically and psychically "in their place." To all of them the many orders to continue payments *directly* to the sellers ignored what was essentially an issue of human dignity. As Tom Boodell says, "The main difficulty most strikers had was the emotional problem of paying money to the sellers. CBL people were willing to pay anyone but the sellers, and almost on the basis that 'we don't care what happens to it afterwards.'" Many have had an opportunity to test the strength of these institutions on a number of levels. The contract has made some cynical and bitter. Many still believe that the two class actions are "sell-out" cases. One black woman, who bought a house vacated by an evicted South Side striker, laughs resignedly when asked about the two cases, "Is *that* still going on?" she asks. "It's a *joke!* We just have to learn there's no justice for the Negro. We have to learn to accept what they let us have." But many others have taken quite an opposite point of view. They are silently waiting for the trials to begin, and end.

In the late fall of 1971, Federal District Judge J. Sam Perry announced that trial of *Clark* v. *Universal Builders* would begin in early 1972. Until that time Maureen MacDonald and other white Gamaliel Foundation workers had been concentrating on researching West Side contract sales situations. They immediately dropped work on *Baker* v. *F & F Investment* and began compiling building cost comparisons and interviews in preparation for *Clark*, before Judge Perry ordered an end to discovery work.

Sullivan, Boodell, Stifler, and the other lawyers began going out to the Wednesday night meetings regularly; each week one of them would be present to explain the last steps in the trial preparation to CBL members, and to urge them to

bring all South Side buyers still in the *Clark* plaintiff class to the meetings so that their depositions could be taken. In an attempt to bring the two factions together again, one of the lawyers told the few South Side people in the audience that the depositions had to be completed as fast as possible, and encouraged them to spread the word on the South Side. "Tell them we are prepared to meet with them anyplace they want," the lawyer said. "The meetings will be over here," Charles Baker said.

The South Side people began coming over to the West Side meetings. On some Wednesday nights there would be fifty of them present; on other nights almost one hundred. They were quiet, and settled a bit uneasily into the chairs among the West Side people. Some members of the splinter group attended, and brushed off questions about its past. "I have nothing to say that's important," one man said, smiling with timidity. Others asked polite questions about *Clark*, wanting to know what was expected of them. Some had lost their homes during the evictions; some had not; some had never been involved in CBL. All of them were urged by the lawyers to tell other South Side families about the trial date and the necessary interviews. "Even if you hate *me*," Clyde Ross told them, his voice straining with the effort, "even if you can't stand your neighbor and don't want to talk to him, at least stop hating him long enough to tell him about the trial. This is no *trick!* Tell them we *are* going to trial."

Much, much more than the complaints of thirty-five hundred Chicago contract buyers has been joined into the two class actions. The implications are wide and deep. Countless black people in all parts of the country are watching Chicago and waiting for the outcome of the two CBL cases.

The two cases represent, as Clarence Darrow said in a 1926 trial involving other black people who tried to buy property, a "cross-section of human history." They represent, he said, "the future, and the hope of some of us that the future shall be better than the past."

34

ALLAN SCHNAIBERG

Politics, Participation and Pollution: The "Environmental Movement"

The city dweller of the early 1960s who thought that American urban problems had reached their zenith with the pressures generated by the civil rights movement was an optimist, as things have subsequently turned out. Not only did the 1960–1970 period produce an urban-based "war on poverty" and an anti-Vietnam war movement, but in the last years there emerged still another problem-oriented social movement—the "environmental movement."

But, like the other major social and political problems that had been imposed on the consciousness (and conscience) of urban Americans, environmental issues became ever more complex and solutions appeared farther and farther on the horizon. Short-term solutions were often unworkable and even more frequently inadequate to *halt* the continuing degradation of the environment. They were still more inadequate to *reverse* the cumulative degradation of decades and even centuries that existed in the urban (and rural) American environment.

However, what was accomplished by the end of the decade was the creation of a large-scale social movement of "environmentalists." If success is defined in the American context in terms of size and rate of growth, it is clear that the environmental movement is far more successful than its predecessors, such as the civil rights movement. Organizations like the Sierra Club and Environmental Action have compiled lists of the many thousands of organizations that have

been involved in some form of environmental action, and a recent list for Illinois alone produced some 250 names.[1] Likewise, it is an indisputable fact that mass media awareness of the dimensions of the environmental problem has *grown* in the United States,[2] whether one measures this is in terms of column-inches, numbers of stories (a six-fold increase from 1955 to 1963)[3] or editorials. And finally, the distribution of concern about pollution and environmental degradation is distributed throughout the United States,[4] not being confined initially to one segments of the country, as the early civil rights movement was concentrated on the South.

Yet, in spite of this phenomenal "success" in educating the public and creating a viable organization, the degree to which the environmental movement has accomplished its stated goal, that of improving environmental quality, is at best extremely limited. Although some short-term actions, such as limited glass and paper recycling, have had some beneficial environmental impacts, it is not at all clear that any major workable long-term solutions have been given a firm foothold. In order to comprehend why this has happened, the environmental movement must be placed in its proper historical and sociopolitical setting. The central question to be posed is: Given the universal approval to improving our (universal) environment, why is it that the environmental movement has had limited success, and has, in the process, generated substantial community conflict which threatens the future viability of the movement? How is it that in a period of perhaps three to five years we have moved from a focus on environment as the

This article is original to this book. The assistance of the Center for Urban Affairs, Northwestern University, is gratefully acknowledged.

neans for achieving national unity to a position, by the Chairman of the Board of Directors of General Motors, attacking some environmentalists as seeking to destroy the American way of life?

. . . the short term political advantage offered by spectacular but unsound consumer legislation can do lasting *damage* to the very consumers it purports to help. The consumer is the loser when *irresponsible* criticism and *ill-conceived* legislation break down faith in our economic system, when *harassment* distracts us from our modern challenge, when the very idea of free enterprise is diminished in the eyes of the young people who must one day manage our businesses. Corporate responsibility is a catchword of the *adversary* culture that is so evident today. If something is wrong with American society, *blame* business . . . The dull cloud of *pessimism* and *distrust* which some have cast over free enterprise is impairing the ability of business to meet its basic economic responsibilities—not to mention its capacity to take on newer ones[5] [emphasis mine].

Historical Basis

In an attempt to either discredit or justify the environmental "bandwagon" effect, a number of authors have cited the long history of environmental degradation that existed in England and other societies early in the Industrial Revolution.[6] Furthermore, they have cited the "alarmists" or "Jeremiahs" of these periods, warning of the imminent decline of cities, and indeed of civilizations, if environmental problems were not solved. At the very least, this indicated merely that history, like Scripture, can be quoted by the evil for his own purposes.

Let us grant the long history of the degradation of the environment; the question arises as to why a *movement* emerged in the late 1960s, aimed at confrontation with the forces leading to such degradation. The most common explanation is that a consciousness or awareness of the quality of the environment did not emerge until then. But this merely begs the question: if the degradation has been occurring for at least a century why did this awareness emerge only in the late 1960s?[7] One possible answer is that the scientific basis for evaluating the degradation was nonexistent until this point: a glance at

the volumes of any major scientific publication, any major engineering or planning journal or the like will surely dispel such a naïve assumption. Technical information, whether on water quality, the effects of pesticides on animal food chains, air pollution, or water resources, mineral resources, etc., have all been available in some form for several decades, at the very least.

Clearly, then, it was neither a sudden crisis nor a totally new type of information that created the preconditions for the environmental movement. Two components, I will argue, were necessary and sufficient to provide the impetus. The first is the precedent set by the two major movements of young Americans, the more important of which was the civil rights movement, which spanned the late 1950s and the early 1960s. It might not be misleading to cite the uniqueness of this movement, involving massive numbers of individuals struggling in a cause that went beyond their immediate economic concerns (unlike many other earlier social movements in the United States), and a confrontation with various levels of the power structure. It was the first social movement to capure the energies of subsantial numbers of the college population, shifting their concerns from private to public goals. And it was the first to extend and develop new techniques of *participation* in resistance to existing social forces, using sit-ins, mass demonstratons, marches, picketing, leafletting and media contact for *public* interests (unlike labor unions, which had used some of these, but largely for the private ends of the membership).[8] The second movement, the anti-Vietnam-war organization, served to further develop some of these techniques and to build a base for an ecology movement to a limited extent (along with providing a competitive movement in the later 1960s).[9] The Vietnam movement indicated that the civil rights techniques could be applied to other public issues, thereby generalizing the process of *participatory mobilization*[10] around social issues.

Both these major social movements shared one additional quality, which was transmitted to the environmental movement, as we shall see. Whether in civil rights or antiwar causes, the evaluation of *success* proved to be extremely difficult, even though "equality" or "peace" had some intuitive and simple appeal at the start of the movements. The questions that nagged leaders of both movements were centered around the adequacy of public awareness or arousal about the issues, legislation, litigation, limited enforcement, and the like. In other words, though there was initial acceptance of common *ultimate* goals, there emerged a proliferation of intermediate organizational goals (which were themselves means to the achievement of the ultimate goal). Faced with these dilemmas of self-evaluation, many groups responded in the classical sociological mold: the growth of their organization became the measure of their success. This particular type of "goal displacement"[11] appears to have disseminated to the environmental movement as well, as we shall presently observe.

I have said that there was a second major precondition for the ecology movement: this was the emergence of a popularized perspective on environmental problems. It would appear likely that this honor falls to Rachel Carson, whose *The Silent Spring*, published in 1962,[12] became the touchstone of the ecology movement. Why, it may be asked, was this popularized work necessary for the creation of a movement, when the evidence of pollution existed much earlier in the form of smog and the like in metropolises like Los Angeles and New York, and water pollution in virtually every major body of water? One possible interpretation is that Carson's book provided a much more sinister worldview, one in which the forces undermining the ecosystem operated much less dramatically but with greater impact than any lay observer could appreciate. Furthermore, Carson's work exposed some of the social and economic *and* scientific infrastructure that had *knowingly* permitted ecological degradation to occur. Put in other terms, Rachel Carson provided convincing evidence for a lack of a constituency that supported environmental systems, and an eloquent plea for the creation of such a constituency. The validation of the thesis that no substantial constituency existed is contained in the fact that it was approximately eight years before a "National Environmental Teach-In" was organized. In those eight years, a large proportion of the educated and general population made do with the convenient rationalizations that "someone else was the expert in charge," as David Miller[13] has put it. To a great extent, as we shall see, many of these rationalizations continue today, within the environmental movement, as well as in the general population.

Several caveats should be noted at this point,

concerning the above observations. In the first instance, there have been organizations devoted to preserving some portions of our environment for some considerable period in America, ranging from conservation (and conservative)[14] groups to organic farming proponents and organic food advocates.[15] But few of these, in spite of public rhetoric to the contrary, were actively concerned about the total environmental system, and fewer still were acting to prevent what they believed was an imminent apocalypse of environmental collapse. Correspondingly, none of these movements ever captured the attention of large numbers of people, nor did they mount the political campaigns to convince the political and economic elites of the seriousness of the situation. That is, the present movement is unique in its scope and intensity.

A second caveat is that of multiple causation. I have discussed two central factors in the emergence of the movement, one dealing with techniques and the other dealing with goals and mobilizing ideologies. Yet there were many other influences that led to the emergence as well. Among these might be the growing interest in wilderness recreation and camping,[16] in part a reflection of continued metropolitan decay and the expansion of urbanized areas (with suburbs effectively removing a green or "natural" belt around the central cities, thus further removing urbanites from contact with nature). The growth of camping and natural-area recreation had a variety of impacts; for one thing, they placed tremendous pressures on existing facilities, leading to a national concern about the present inadequacy and future paucity of recreational areas; in addition, they exposed the degradation of many of these areas through the "multiple-use" by logging and ranching and mining interests, approved in the name of the people of the United States by the Department of the Interior and its subsidiaries.[17] In addition to this pressure, numerous other pressures mounted in the period before and during the movement's emergence to reinforce and expand the urgency associated with environmental preservation, many of these associated with particular population groups and/or particular regions of the country.[18] A full discussion of these factors is beyond the scope of this work.

The final caveat which should be noted here is that the prime movers in the creation of the movement differed for groups of participants

While some substantial segment of the action groups emerged from direct experience with the civil rights movement, the "war on poverty," or the antiwar movement, this is by no means true of all the groups (a simple observation of the age of many young environmentalists would suffice to show that they were too young to have acted in the civil rights movement, for example). Thus the movement consisted of the "veterans" of prior social action, as well as the new environmental "recruits," many of whom had totally different social backgrounds and ideologies, and an interest only in the preservation of the "environment." This diversity of backgrounds, as we shall presently observe, is an important aspect of the movement.

Definitions of the Problem and Concomitant Actions

The scope of the environment, and consequently the scope of environmental problems, is both the strength and weakness of the ecology movement. The strength lies in the fact that every citizen is in some way touched by environmental quality, and thus everyone is a potential activist in the "cause." Furthermore, as was stated repeatedly in the early days of the movement, no one could deny the *ultimate* goal of environmental preservation, i.e., it was a universal objective. In this sense it differed considerably from its predecessors, the civil rights, antipoverty and antiwar movements. Yet the differences, as I will demonstrate, were only in degree. The very breadth of the environmental problems that exist permitted, indeed required, some degree of specialization among the participants, since no group could mount sufficient social and political pressures on all environmental fronts, given a general lack of resources. Furthermore, the fact that environmental problems touched every citizen was in part a corollary of the fact that every citizen's activities in turn *affected* the environment.

At the outset, there was some attempt (Machiavellian or otherwise) to stress the *universal* contribution to environmental problems, as a rallying cry for massive participation in environmental improvement.[19] But this universality was clearly a double-edged sword: if everyone's actions contributed to environmental decay, then environmental improvement programs were bound to have an impact upon everyone's *actions* ultimately. A trivial statement perhaps, yet the possible profundity of this observation has escaped the consciousness of many of the current and past participants, although it has likely influenced the *non*participation of many citizens! That is, it may be precisely the expectation of such consequences that has deterred some segments of the population from participation in environmental groups. Put most simply, the message here is a variant of the Black Panther perspective: If you're part of the problem, then you are affected by the solution.

What precisely do we mean when we link "actions" to environmental problems? One simple view is the classification of actions into *consumption* and *production;* insofar as we consume and/or produce, our action has some environmental consequences. In every such action, material is transformed in some fashion, and always involving some energy loss (the Second Law of Thermodynamics), which we might term depletion of energy resources.[20] In addition to the energy loss, there are frequently byproducts of the consumption/production processes, such that new materials are formed, which are discharged into the environment; these might properly be called pollution, which in turn is a special case of the general problem of depletion of *usable* resources. Material, unlike energy, is conserved, so that we transform by combustion a usable resource such as coal into a nonusable (at some level) byproduct or "pollutant" like sulfur dioxide or dust particles. Thus pollution and resource usability depletion are part of the same process, and are intimately linked to *every* act of consumption or production in a society. Again, once stated, this principle appears to border on the trivial, yet only a handful of the ecology movement participants, I would claim, fully appreciate this set of linkages between the economic sphere and the ecological. Everyone involved sees a part, has a "piece of the action," yet few recognize the wholistic and *universal* applicability of these principles. The evidence for this statement lies in the public outcries of many ecologcal activists for a "technological" solution to environmental degradation;[21] any good physicist could tell them that this is equivalent to asking for a perpetual motion machine which would negate the Second Law of Thermodynamics, a privilege which is not accorded even to the most powerful nation in the world. Technological proposals such as the catalytic auto muffler, cooling towers for nuclear power plants, larger urban sewage treatment plants, and so on, all have *resource* costs associated with their production and use, and thus all have some negative environmental impact along with their obvious positive functions.

If few environmentalists see the whole picture, what "pieces" do they perceive, and what types of corrective actions are proposed by or engaged in by the several groups? On a simple level, we can outline four major types of "movement" participants, recognizing that this is merely a first approximation to describing the various approaches currently being attempted. These types are (a) cosmetologists, (b) meliorists, (c) reformists, and (d) radicals.[22] Each of these types, which will presently be described, has operationalized its "piece of the action" on either or both of two planes: the individual level of action and the collective level. What follows is a brief description of the definition of *the* environmental problem modally used by the group, and the concomitant solutions or actions proposed by the group.

(a) *Cosmetologists.* For this group, the prime mover is the most immediate sense perception of the group. In the urban areas, one of the most conspicuous consequences of consumption is waste of various types, discarded in both public and private locales. The generic concept for such waste is "litter," so that the cosmetologists are primarily engaged in an "anti-litter" campaign of one or another types. This might be termed a "postconsumption" level of action, since it deals only with the byproducts of consumption, basically consumer goods packaging. It should be stressed that this type is neither concerned directly about consumption nor about production functions. Their primary concern is with the *disposal* process; a typical successful environmental action would be collection of paper and other wastes from public places (or vacant lots, etc.) and transporting it to city incinerators or sanitary land fills. What happens to the solid wastes after this point is of no direct concern to these groups, by their criterion of success.

It would not be unfair to state that these groups are the most naïve environmentalists, for a variety of reasons. In the first place, they ignore the fundamental social and economic behaviors which cause "litter," thus engaging in a never-ending (recurrent expenditure, in economic terms) struggle. They neither criticize the consumption habits of the population, which engages in waste production of various types, including litter, nor do they criticize the production behavior, which engages in an ever-increasing proliferation of disposable packaging, thus perpetuating the problem. And finally, they fail to recognize the ecological facts of life, in that the materials they aggregate may merely increase concentrated air and water and land pollution or degradation, through municipal waste-disposal procedures.

The fact that their definition of the problem is an immediate sense perception (visual litter) is correlative of the backgrounds of these environmentalists. Typical civic groups of this type are Boy Scout groups, ladies' Garden Clubs, PTA groups, and the like. Most of the participants were unaffiliated with any prior sociopolitical movement, like the civil rights campaign, and indeed may be precisely from the lower-middle or upper-middle classes which strongly opposed such movements. In other words, these are groups which have been drawn into the environmental movement *de novo*, and view the environmental problem as isolated from most other major social issues. They are thus the groups most likely to be supported by industrialists engaged in the creation of the problem, e.g., soft drink bottlers, glass producers, paper companies, and to be totally insensitive to the environmental impact of these latter groups.

In terms of individual pro-environment actions, participants in this group engage in careful disposal of solid wastes (though not necessarily of liquid wastes, since this is not as visible a form of pollution). On a collective or group action basis, they may form clean-up committees, particularly in poor neighborhoods, or public urban places such as parks and playgrounds they may also sponsor anti-litter advertising, circulate litterbags, provide additional litter containers in public places, and so on.

In many ways, the cosmetologists represent one pole of environmental awareness, and perhaps are most representative of the American population in terms of consciousness of processes leading to environmental decay, as well as of the nature and extent of this decay. They have also become one of the "straw men" for critiques by more sensitive environmentalists especially the radical groups.

(b) *Meliorists.* Like the cosmetologists, this group focuses primarily on consumption-related activities. In many other ways, they are similar to the cosmetologists, in terms of perspective on the socioeconomic origins of environmental problems. But there is a greater knowledge of the extent of environmental problems, and the physical processes that directly affect the urban environment. For example, a prime example of their activity would be glass, paper, or aluminum can recycling. Unlike the cosmetologists, these participants understand that incineration or compacting or sludge dispersal is not the "final" solution for waste disposal. Indeed, many of them recognize that concentration of such waste often exacerbates the problem, since this may mean an overload on the local water system, air flows, or open land quality and availability. They recognize the potential in the application of the Law of Conservation of Matter (and Energy) through the social organization of recycling programs. Thus the aim is to transform "waste" into "usable material," rather than merely disposing of waste into an environmental "sink," and accepting the *social* definition of waste.[23]

Unfortunately, they share with the cosmetologists a great deal of naïveté and limited worldviews. They do not attempt to locate the source of the waste in the areas of production, or at a later stage, in the realm of consumer preferences (and lack of consumer sovereignty). Programs are organized on a local basis, with no carryover to regional or national groups, in many cases. Moreover, they often fail to appreciate the economics of recycling, thereby permitting (indeed, encouraging) producers to gain excessive profits from recycling procedures, e.g., using volunteer community labor to man recycling stations, and perhaps even to transport the recycled material directly (or through municipal agencies) to the packaging factory. Though some municipal agencies have utilized producer payments for support of costs of transportation and allocation of space for recycling material storage, there has been little or no attempt to evaluate objectively the profit margins of producers in resale of the recycled material. Furthermore, many of these meliorist action groups are in part supported by these same producers, a point which critics frequently stress.[24]

On an individual level, participants engage in directing their own waste products (glass bottles and jars, aluminum drink containers, old newspapers) to recycling areas. At the collective level, they may help to set up such recycling stations, contacting producers or other purchasers of recyclable material, engaging in negotiations for sites, manning these sites, and providing community publicity for such activities. Most communities now have such "Citizens for a Better Environment" types of organization, usually created for such specific recycling types of activity.

The cosmetologists and the meliorists may both be placed in the laissez-faire, grassroots, or populist sociopolitical orientation. They share a faith in aggregated *voluntary* action, both on their own part and on the part of the local citizenry. At the upper limit, they may attempt to negotiate with local elites (political and economic) to gain support for their advertising or recycling programs, but with only the vaguest self-definition of an "interest group." By and large their self-view is one of interlocuter, attempting to *coordinate* or *organize* the *preexisting* proto-environmental orientations of the population. There is some differentiation made by many of these groups on a social class basis, but this is mainly of the superficial type. For example, cosmetologists may observe that the poor "litter" more, in that they observe greater waste in poor areas (never questioning the differentials in sanitary department service in poor and affluent areas of the city). Likewise, the meliorists may reason that a greater effort is required to recycle disposable materials from poorer areas, because of communication barriers, lack of auto transportation, etc. (again, never probing beyond this level of observation for alternative explanations of poverty, other than lack of skills, etc.). It is likely that prior movement experiences have been quite limited for much of this group, although the objectives of civil rights and other movements may have been supported.

(c) *Reformists.* This is the first group which begins to consider both the consumption and production aspects of environmental decay. In addition, they are generally more knowledgable about the physical-biological aspects of environmental processes, as contrasted with the cosmetologists and many of the meliorists. For example, in considering a glass recycling program, such groups may question the environmental economics (as well as the standard economics), on an environmental-social cost-benefit basis.

CHAPTER 7 · THE CHANGING CHARACTER OF URBAN POLITICS

That is, they might weigh the energy costs of melting silica for glass, distributing the glass, then crushing the glass and remelting it for a second use, as against the multiple-use of returnable bottles (which may make twenty to twenty-five trips) from a single melting operation. Obviously, the information required to make such assessments is detailed and requires considerable expertise and organizational skill to use and obtain. Yet this is clearly the direction in which societies will ultimately have to go, to maximize the protection of the environment.[25]

In addition to gathering and analyzing such detailed environmental and production data, however, such reformist groups engage quite self-consciously in a variety of lobbying activities, as special-interest groups.[26] They tend to be the groups that attend public hearings at local, state, and even national levels. They mount the campaigns against particular producers, or classes of producers, that provide products which are degrading of the environment in their production stage and/or their final-use stage. And finally, they also engage in consumer education campaigns. Perhaps the most notable success such groups have had is in the phosphate-detergent campaign. Taking as a starting point the evidence that high phosphate levels of water promote the rapid growth of algae, which subsequently die and absorb a lake's oxygen supply (eutrophication process), they have engaged in a multi-tiered environmental action. This has included the chemical analysis of major detergents (often with findings quite different from manufacturers' analyses), the publication of findings and circulation to the public newspapers, supermarket shopping areas, etc. And simultaneously, they have brought pressure to bear on local political administrations to ban high-phosphate detergents, with success in at least two states. They have argued with city officials on a hard economic basis, rather than simply playing the "moral environmentalist" role, and have varied their level of arguments according to the various audiences they have approached. Similar kinds of activities have taken shape in the areas of auto pollution, highway construction, land fill operations, construction of nuclear power facilities, and so on. Many of these are activities that are properly termed "participatory technology,"[27] emphasizing the use of technology in the production phase of economic activity.

Unlike the cosmetologists and the meliorists,

the reformists have not restricted themselves to a grassroots movement, arousing consumer ire and changing their buying behavior. Rather, they have recognized that in many areas, there is in fact little "consumer sovereignty" in terms of environmentally benign alternative products. Hence their public and political pressures on the major producers (e.g., Campaign GM),[28] along with the somewhat less effective consumer boycotts. Along with the greater appreciation for the "web of nature" (which they share with the meliorists), they have developed the beginnings of a similar appreciation for the "web of society," which intersects with the former. In part this stems from the high level of professional and technical skills possessed by this group, and very likely from the prior movement experiences of many of the participants. This joint grassroots-elitist strategy is highly reminiscent of the civil rights campaigns as well as the later antiwar and antipoverty campaigns, reflecting such movement experiences and conventional local political experience for some participants. In the Chicago area, the most prominent experienced group is the "Businessmen for the Public Interest," but other inexperienced groups such as "Northwestern Students for a Better Environment" have been equally active and effective.

On an individual level, many participants attempt to reduce some elements of consumption (e.g., substituting bicycles for auto transport, buying unleaded gasoline, low-phosphate detergents, etc.), in addition to proselytizing for particular campaigns and a wider environmental worldview of colleagues, friends, voluntary associations, etc. At the collective level, strategies vary widely, from simple media advertising to major journalistic efforts, creation of new action organizations, provision of technical expertise, Congressional and local lobbying activities, etc. Clearly the most conspicuous representative of this movement is Ralph Nader, whose background is *consumer* protection, rather than *environmental* protection activity. Others in this area include Barry Commoner and Paul Ehrlich, though none of these individuals can be adequately classified in the present scheme.

(d) *Radicals*. The differences between radicals and reformers may be termed differences of degree, or of kind, depending on the observer. Whereas reformists stress the need for control and revision, radical environmentalists aim at total restructuring of the social and especially the economic system. This varies from a direct attack on capitalist economic systems per se, to a rather more wide-reaching critique of industrial society in general (although with a heavy emphasis on the United States). This is the only group which ever engages in an *international* scale of analysis, in large part because the backgrounds of many of these participants is in the antiwar movement, with its internationalist "Third World" orientation, and thus links resource utilization in the United States to an economic imperialism which systematically depletes resources of most underdeveloped countries.

One major difference between reformists and radicals is the former's emphasis on *means* of achieving environmental quality, or procedures for implementing goals, whereas radical environmentalists concentrate on the social-philosophical goals of a society in adaptation to the natural environment, and the necessary major value shifts required in America to move in this direction. A harsher evaluation might be that radical actions are utopian, unlike the more pragmatic reformist directives. But the radical perspective also indicates the fundamental incompatability of an expansive industrial society with the preservation of environmental quality. The role of government (including regulatory agencies) is viewed differently by the two groups as well: whereas reformists see government as the major lever of environmental change, imperfect as governmental organization may be, radicals see little opportunity for mediation by the government. What is interesting about this contrast is that it reflects a very different orientation, on the part of the two groups, to the degree of "representativeness" of government (urban, state, and national): reformists see governments as insufficiently representative of the "public interest," whereas radicals see governments as all to representative of the "false consciousness" of the producers and consumers in America. Hence the stronger emphasis on grassroots participation on the reformists' part, as contrasted with the cynicism of the radical environmentalists, who view themselves as a handful of "true believers."[29]

Because of the emphasis on goals rather than means, the radical environmental movement is highly fractionated. On an individual level, the range is from "alternative life styles," involving low levels of material consumption, concentrating on a Zen- or Maoist-like discipline and concentration on environmental impact, to a much more active political strategy (a range not unlike that among blacks, from "cultural nationalism" to civil rights activism).[30] At a collective level, there is a similar range, from urban and rural communes to direct and disruptive strategies at the political and economic level.[31] Groups such as the Council on Economic Priorities attempt to gather heretofore secret company data on pollution, along with data on other major social problems. For the radicals, there is little meaning in separating environmental problems from the "corporate" or "industrial state," and the inequalities therein. Although there may be periodic cooperation with reformist groups, by and large radical environmentalists presume that such groups share the "false consciousness" of the bulk of American society, and that their efforts are bound to have little impact.[32] Where such cooperation has occurred, the results have often been important: the reformists maintain their demands, while remaining "negotiable," and the pressures created by radical tactics often drive industrialists or politicians into serious negotiation with reformist groups. In part, the suspicion of "Establishment politics" derives from the considerable experience many of the radicals have had in the anti-Vietnam movement (and some civil rights experience).

Some Consequences of Environmental Actions

One of the major criticism leveled at "environmentalists" by radical political groups is the political and social naïveté of the former. Since the movement developed at precisely the peak of the anti-Vietnam movement, there has been deep suspicion that this "unifying" movement was a distraction (although this conveniently ignores the rise of environmental movements in most European societies not directly involved in the war), created with the connivance of politicians and major industrialists. Unfortunately, the activities of several of the groups listed appear supportive of such a claim; in particular, cosmetologists and meliorists generally engage in activities at least cosponsored by major industries (or local political administrations). And politicians at all levels have used such actions and concerns to distract attention from issues like the Vietnam war, in fact. Although the direct effects of such activity may be positive and highly visible, this very visibility has much greater side-effects, runs the radical argument. It provides some direct evidence that "things are getting better," thereby increasing the public's receptivity to the "eco-pornography" of the major producers.[33] In particular, the cosmetologists and meliorists themselves are most susceptible to this perception, both by predisposition and by the fact that the "success" of their activity has resulted from the cooperative nature of the major producers (and politicians). From this, it follows that there is a reinforcement of a perception that "we're all part of the problem, and will all work together for a solution."

It would thus not be unfair to state that cosmetologists and meliorists find their expectations *confirmed* by their environmental action. That is, they continue to believe that environmental problems are solvable, that they are capable of solution at minor costs and minor inconvenience, and that there is no opposition in this country to environmental improvement. Whether this is viewed as a Machiavellian manipulation of such groups by economic elites, or merely a self-fulfilling prophecy depends on one's perspective.

Turning to reformist groups, a rather different picture appears to emerge. For those who have emerged from considerable experience in the civil rights, antiwar, or antipoverty programs and movements, the environmental problem arena is seen as a resultant of the same processes as have been observed previously, at least among the major elite groups. Venality, shortsightedness, corruption, self-interest—all of these operate in the environmental impact area as well as for other major social issues. However, for those with little or no background in direct political action, the environmental area is fraught with new social learning. For social inequalities enter into environmental effects, in spite of the early reductionist perspective of our "one environment, shared by all." Indeed, the question for many sensitive reformists has become "who owns the environment?" Who is the "public" for whom the "public interest" is being served by current political and economic policies?

At the very least, the discoveries of many reformists include the following: (a) a new awareness of the complexity of society, and the corresponding complexity of the ecosystem—on the one hand, a new insight into the meaning of the "division of labor in society" (without the necessary integration, at many points), and its consequences for the "web of nature"; (b) discovery of the power, and powerlessness, of grassroots organizations—a painful awareness of the efforts required to mobilize citizenry, and the limits on responsiveness of elites even to a mobilized group; (c) a recognition of the close interrelationships (power elite) among key economic and political elites in most metropolitan areas, so that the analytic distinction between economic and political power becomes highly blurred; (d) a growth in awareness of social inequalities in the socioeconomic structure, and therefore of some of the causes of the resulting differentials in the evaluation of environmental problems; (e) institutional control—the degree to which the current economic and political policies have been reinforced by a variety of institutions, from educational to religious, raises the question as to where the control of the major social institutions in America *in fact* rests.[34] Some of these issues will be discussed below in greater detail.

Finally, for the radical groups, their activity has tended to reinforce their worldview, concerning the basic materialism and undemocratic nature of American society.[35] Since their concentration has been on ends, not means, this is both understandable and comforting for such groups. The response may in many cases simply be a form of retreatism, into a communal (often rural rather than urban) life style, and a separation from the degraded environment—or at least, a perception of such isolationism.

On the basis of the above formulation, it appears to be the reformists that have been transformed most markedly in the environmental action field. These are the "liberals" of the environmental action movement, and like the many liberal political groups in other social arenas, they have been most affected, and most bifurcated, by their experiences. For many, it has led to intense politicization and a Marxist socioeconomic worldview, while for others the response has been a form of retreatism, similar to the radical response, with one difference: the liberal retreatism is more often a return to the status quo, not to an alternative life style.[36]

Some Causes of Nonparticipation in the Environmental Movement

Thus far, the analysis of the environmental movement has been phrased in terms of the major participants in the movement. Clearly, such a frame of reference is highly limited, since it ignores the vast numbers of Americans who have not directly participated in any movement actions. Since the majority of participants in the movement appear to be middle class,[37] it would appear that the most significant social groups here are the poor (or at least the less affluent), and the most affluent classes. Although participation in any voluntary association has repeatedly been demonstrated to be strongly associated with the social class of the individual,[38] the environmental movement appears to be somewhat of an exception to this sociological rule of thumb. For there appears to be an underrepresentation of the rich in the movement, along with the "normal" low levels of participation of the poor (and most conspicuously, the black poor).[39] What are the likely explanations for this distribution?

In order to approach an explanation, the social and economic realities of environmental degradation need to be clarified. Some approach to this has been made in the discussion of reformist and radical environmental groups, but the issues need to be clarified further. We need to start by first differentiating between the total impact of a social group on the environment, and the "per capita" or individual contribution. The latter appears most appropriate here, since we are concerned with the reasons why *individuals* of a given social class are more likely not to participate in the environmental movement, rather than explaining the distribution of total environmental impact of a social *class*.

If we discuss environmental impacts from and on individuals of a given social class, one useful framework is a general "cost-benefit" approach, a standard tool of economists and increasingly used for a variety of evaluation schemes. At the outset of the environmental movement, a serious attempt was made by a variety of politicians and industrialists to infuse the movement with the following assumption: Regardless of what the net costs of environmental degradation are, this same net cost is borne equally by all citizens. And strange as it may seem, this element of social and political propaganda held sway for some considerable period in the movement—and still does, for the cosmetologists and the meliorists at the very least. Why intelligent and cynical observers of social reality ever seriously adhered to such a preposterous position is a question which cannot be readily answered here. Among

other postulated explanations, the most important one appears to be the extreme division of American society at the start of the movement, and the widespread quest for the elusive "national unity" via a new "national purpose" (especially one that was "constructive," unlike the Vietnam war).

Given that no social scientist, on the basis of decades of evidence of social inequalities in the United States, could accept the equality of citizens of various social classes with regard to any issue, what were (and are) the underlying realities? If we turn to costs of environmental degradation, the following appears to be an accurate statement: regardless of the particular cost dimension examined, environmental costs to the individual are consistently higher for the poor than for the more affluent. Whether in terms of air pollution (higher in central city areas, where high concentrations of poor reside), water pollution (more severe in high-density areas, again where the poor reside), or land pollution (impact of DDT spraying is most severe for migrant farm laborers, for example), the poor are in a position of entrapment.[40] That is, they generally have little freedom to move away from areas of highest pollution which have, in part at least, *become* undesirable because of pollution. This is true for the familiar reasons of economic and racial discrimination, leading to a poor (and in many cases black) central city, with middle- and upper-class white suburban rings surrounding it. Though it is by no means universally true that all types of environmental decay are most severe in the central city, it is certainly true that the poor suffer from whatever metropolitan-area-wide degradation exists to a greater extent than do the more affluent suburbanites. Even if we were to discount the differential possibility of relocating within the metropolitan area as irrelevant, the more affluent still possess considerably more resources to seek recreation, a second home, health resorts, and other amenities to alleviate the persistent effects of environmental decay. And, if we project current environmental decay to the apocalypse that many forecast, one would have to be incredibly naïve to believe that such a catastrophe would strike uniformly across social lines. If air deteriorates, oxygen is available to the more affluent; if water deteriorates, water purifiers or bottle water will go to the highest bidders; and the choicest land already belongs to the corporate elite![41] Short of massive civil in-surrection and the revolt of the military against the "military-industrial" complex, in other words, the environmental decay will continue to strike hardest against the least affluent.[42]

Turning to the *benefits* that have accrued over the years from systematic free use of the environmental resources of air and water, again we find significant differentiation. It is true that producers produce for the consumers in a society, but it is equally true that in a society with unequal income distribution the levels of consumption differ markedly. Thus the most affluent, the economic elite of America, have benefitted in a twofold manner from such systematic environmental exploitation: in terms of their roles as producers (and major stockholders),[43] they have reaped enormous profit levels from industrial and related enterprises. And second, as the largest consumers, they have benefitted from the lower costs of consumer goods to a substantially greater extent than those with lower levels of consumption.[44]

If we view our society in a simple-minded tripartite division of lower, middle and upper classes, the following cost-benefit picture emerges. The lower classes have maximum costs and minimum benefits from environmental decay. The upper classes have minimum cost and maximum benefits. It may be assumed that the middle classes are intermediate on both issues: they incur moderate levels of cost (although some might argue that their costs are closer to those of the lower classes than to the upper), and moderate levels of benefit (although again, their level may be somewhat closer to the lower than the upper classes). The middle-class position may be closer to that of the poor than the rich because of the similar dependence of each on labor market situations, and the much smaller differentials in income and tax burdens in the former comparison. In terms of *net* cost-benefit, then, the lower classes have maximal *net* costs, and the upper classes have minimal *net* costs (or maximal net benefits, put more directly), with the middle classes intermediate.

Accepting the above as a rough indication of the ordering of the major social classes, the reason for the nonparticipation of the upper classes is clear: they are merely acting so as to maximize their net benefits, by continuing to use environmental systems for profit maximization. Yet on the basis of the above, we have failed to account for the low participation of the poor or lower

classes in the movement, in addition to the middle class component of the movement. One element is needed to complete this explanation: the control over social and economic organization of the United States by the urban-industrial elites.

Whether we examine environmental improvement suggestions, from one or another movement (especially reformist) and nonmovement groups, the one commonality is the element of cost incurred. This is true whether the path to pollution abatement[45] is through legislation—via tax credits, fines, direct subsidies; or through litigation—fines, delays in construction, shut-downs, etc. In the case of "carrot" (positive) incentives, some group of taxpayers and/or consumers ultimately foots the bill, in the form of taxes paid, or increased prices. For "stick" (disincentive) actions, increased prices and decreased employment are frequently the concomitants. Given the power of the industrial elite to influence the legislative processes at every level, from gathering of information[46] to directing campaign contributions for "sensitive" candidates, it is clear that legislation will have the most pro-elite orientation that money can purchase—and even more so, in the case of enforcement.[47] The legal powers of the corporation are wide enough to discourage and delay enforcement of environmental legislation interminably, as reformists have been painfully learning over the past five years.[48] Yet the costs of fines, legal costs, abatement equipment, etc., must ultimately be borne by some group. And it is here that the lower classes are apprehensive, and rightfully so, to a considerable extent. Whether as consumer, taxpayer (including every level of tax from municipal to federal), aid recipient, or employee, they already bear an economically regressive burden; there is little reason for them not to expect the anticipated environmental improvement costs to fall disproportionately on their shoulders.[49]

Indeed, it should be stressed, the realities have been demonstrated even at this early date. For example, the increased electricity rates granted one Illinois power company recently, which were contingent on the company's installing substantially improved air pollution abatement equipment, have had this impact. Any price increase in a necessary consumer good like electricity provides a disproportionately large impact on the poor—a standard inflationary situation. As environmental groups successfully take on other industrial titans, similar inflationary effects will be felt, and their impact on the poor has been well documented by economists.

Hence the resistance of the poor to the environmental movement,[50] along with resistance of the rich. Is this the answer to our earlier hypothetical question "who owns the environment?" Furthermore, what does this suggest for the future of the environmental movement? One gloomy, though by no means unlikely, prospect is for the emergence of a coalition between the poor and the rich, to sabotage the environmental activists. Indeed, the reactions of the Chairman of the Board of General Motors bears a striking similarity to those of many of the leaders of the poor. . . . Can it be that a new "war on poverty" rhetoric will emerge, with the casuality of the war being the environment? (And with poverty left undiminished, to serve as a rallying cry in future threats to the elite?) Can it really be that the tangible and intangible environment of the United States is so differently perceived by these several social classes that such a result is possible? One need merely to contrast the recent coverage of environmental problems by the editors of *Fortune*, on the one (and upper-class) hand, and those of *Ramparts*,[51] on the other. A search of the *Fortune* reports reveals very little assessment of differential benefits from environmental degradation, and equally little concern with differential allocation of costs of environmental improvement. The *Ramparts* approach focuses almost exclusively on precisely these differentials, and the related issues of social justice and environmental control. It continuously confronts and attacks the simplistic (and self-serving) view of *Fortune* that environmental control be conceived of as a "national mission," arguing that the differential control and concern *within* the nation" is the crucial lever for environmental change.

Looking Forward

We have seen that there are very different answers to the question "where do we go from here?" Recent environmental events have, in fact, largely ignored the crucial social dimensions of this question. What legislation has been enacted has been relatively weak either in its legislative form or in the actual enforcement of such legislation. Yet there have been *some* important

environmental controls initiated nonetheless, which have short and long term effects, e.g., in sulfur dioxide emissions from coal, some detergent phosphate reductions.

But, what is virtually universally true of current legislation is that it ignores the questions of social justice that have been raised. There is no provision in such legislation for apportioning costs of environmental improvement on any basis other than the "market," in spite of a growing awareness among some environmentalists of the social-class differentials in the cost-benefit parameters. If we project into the future the legislative trends of the past four to five years, two things become apparent: (1) there will be no provision whatsoever for allocating pollution costs on the basis of *cumulative* benefits derived by the upper classes from environmental decay; and (2) it is almost as unlikely that such costs will be allocated without the upper classes deriving *present* and *future* benefits from environmental improvement.

This second point requires some clarification. If an automobile manufacturer installs pollution emission equipment on an auto, then the manufacturing cost of such equipment is certain to be passed on to the consumer. However, it is also likely that the "normal" margin of profit the company (especially the major stockholders) obtains will be applied to this equipment, as well as the rest of the auto. Thus the company in fact makes an additional profit on the pollution equipment. Here industrialists might be expected to show less reluctance to change (although with a careful eye on demand curves), since they will profit from pollution abatement as they profited from pollution! But consumers, especially lower income groups, will be more likely to be adverse to such courses of environmental improvement, for the major beneficiaries of such action are the upper classes, and those bearing the costs are middle and lower classes.

An even more subtle example is that of "regulated utilities," e.g., electric and gas companies. Here companies apply for a higher rate, in order to install new plant pollution abatement equipment. But this new equipment is now part of the company's *capital*, which is thereby increased, and at the next rate hearing, another rate increase is likely to be approved so that the "fair rate of return" (i.e., profit divided by *capital*) allowed the utility by law will be maintained. Thus consumers, and especially the poor, will have borne a double burden by this "normal" process of rate regulation, all in the name of environmental quality, but largely benefiting the major shareholders of utilities.

These examples and projections afford a gloomy outlook, as well as an explanation for the current lack of substantial environmental improvement. The major controllers of industry are already maximizing their net benefits from the environment, and have little to gain; the middle and especially the lower classes can expect to bear the main costs of environmental improvement. Hence, aside from the most active environmentalists, there is little constituency for environmental improvement. What changes have occurred and will occur are going to increase the burdens on the middle and lower classes, while permitting a continuation of profit maximization by the upper classes. Thus the likely outcome, at best, is a substitution of social exploitation for environmental exploitation . . . Only a well-organized, politically skilled environmental movement that will devote its resources to informing the larger public of these threats can intercede in this "normal market process" occurring.

An Alternative Scenario

Lest we end on a Jeremaic note,[52] some alternative paths to environmental quality should be noted. If we accept as a premise that the reformist group holds the greatest pragmatic promise for improving the environment of the over-two-hundred-million in the United States, then what changes need to occur to prevent the success of the possible anti-environmental coalition of rich and poor cited above or the substitution of social for environmental exploitation? At the outset, the harsh socioeconomic realities underlying the nonparticipation of these two groups must be recognized and dealt with, seriously and consistently. On the one side, the likely and powerful opposition of the elite to any "meaningful" program of action should be anticipated, and planned for. By "meaningful," I mean a program for environmental improvement which will not be paid for disproportionately (or even proportionately, for that matter) by the poor. Industrialists may overcome their natural inertia and accept programs which lay the burdens on the door of the middle class and poor—but that cannot be construed as a "meaningful" environmental program, since the resulting *social environmental* degradation may far outweigh any gain in the *physical* environment, and the "quality of life" may suffer irreparable damages.

Therefore, any proposal for environmental action must clearly incorporate the elements of social justice, and there must be a commitment of the middle-class proponents to *explicitly* build in such considerations. This is a political necessity, as well as a moral prerequisite, since the coalition of rich and poor is sufficent to doom any proposal. But the coalition of the poor and the middle class *may* sufficiently offset the existing political imbalance to provide passage of significant proposals.[53]

One example, in closing, neatly illustrates the potential involved in a meaningful environmental movement. In the Chicago area, a program for paper recycling was recently established.[54] This involved the collection of newspapers from middle- and upper-class white suburban areas and the transportation of the newsprint to a black community development organization in Chicago, which packages and sells the newsprint to paper companies for recycling. Here is a situation in which the environmental movement had provided the impetus for newspaper transport on the part of middle- and upper-class individuals, to a point where lower-class groups benefitted from the operation. On one level, one can dismiss this cynically as a trivial operation—yet it contains all the elements of a meaningful environmental movement. For this action represents a form of income transfer from more to less affluent groups,[55] while contributing to the preservation of trees and lowering water pollution (in newspaper production).

How many such scenarios can we write? We will only discover this through trying; the stakes certainly merit the effort.

Notes

1. Among other sources, environmental action groups are listed in the *Guide to Organized Environmental Efforts* (Washington, D.C.: Environmental Resources, Inc., 1971). A brief list and references also appear in *Earth Day—the Beginning* (New York: Arno Press/New York Times, 1970), edited by the National Staff of Environmental Action. The Illinois List was compiled for the Illinois Science Related Info

mation Center (ISRIC), an affiliate of the national Scientists' Institute for Public Information (SIPI).

2. A summary of public opinion polls from the 1960–70 period supports this contention: see Cecile Trop and Leslie L. Roos, Jr., "Public Opinion and the Environment," pp. 52–63 in Leslie L. Roos, Jr. (ed.), *The Politics of Ecosuiside* (New York: Holt, Rinehart & Winston, Inc., 1971).

3. *Ibid.*; and John C. Maloney and Lynn Slovonsky, "The Pollution Issue: A Survey of Editional Judgments" (p. 64), in Roos (ed.), *op. cit.*

4. Trop and Roos, *op. cit.*

5. This address by James M. Roche to the Executive Club of Chicago is excerpted in "Defending Big Business," *The New York Times*, April 21, 1971 (p. 47).

6. For England, an interesting history of pollution and its opponents is contained in Jack Bregman and Sergei Lenormand, *The Pollution Paradox* (New York: Spartan Books, 1966), chapter 1; and William Wise, *Killer Smog* (New York: Audubon/Ballantine, 1968), pp. 8–63. A cynical interpretation is provided by Alexander King, "The Environmental Bandwagon, And Some Other Matters Concerning the Future of the Human Race," pp. 189–201 in Clifton Fadiman and Jean White, *Ecocide . . . And Thoughts Toward Survival* (Palo Alto, California: James F. Freel and Associates, 1971).

7. Some discussion of the peaks and troughs of environmental concern is found (for England) in Wise, *op. cit.*, and more recently (for the U.S.) in Trop and Roos, *op. cit.*

8. Although many activists, in their truncated sense of history, conveniently forget this, there was considerable precedence in the 1950s for nonviolent protest. Not only labor unions, but a variety of interest groups, including the unemployed, had used most of the *techniques* of the civil rights movement earlier (and examples abound in other societies, such as India, France, Italy), with the possible exception of the sit-in (and there had earlier been similar union activity in plants). What was unique about the movement was the *goal*—a societal, humanitarian objective, not the self-interested activity of earlier periods.

9. For example, note the decline in *New York Times* coverage of the environment, Trop and Roos, *op. cit.*, p. 57. A succinct statement on this is I. F. Stone, "Con Games," in Environmental Action Staff (ed.), *Earth Day—The Beginning, op. cit.*

10. The classic statement on "social mobilization" is Karl Deutsch, "Social Mobilization and Political Development," *American Political Science Review* 55 (September 1961), 493–511. "Participatory mobilization" here refers to the self-conscious pattern of action involved in social movements, a special form of mobilization process.

11. This concept emerged in David Sills, "The Succession of Goals," pp. 146–59 in Amitai Etzioni (ed.), *Complex Organizations: A Sociological Reader* (New York: Holt, Rinehart & Winston, Inc., 1960). [The larger study, from which this was drawn, is *The Volunteers* (Glencoe, Illinois: The Free Press, 1957)]. In situations like this, the survival of the organization becomes transformed from an instrumental objective to a consummatory one—and the organizational leadership frequently devises a new set of "goals" to rationalize the continuation of the organization.

12. Rachel Carson, *The Silent Spring* (Boston: Houghton Mifflin Company, 1962).

13. David C. Miller, "Ecology—The Last Fad," pp. 303–310 in Fred Carvell and Max Tadlock (eds.), *It's Not Too Late . . .* (Beverly Hills: Glencoe Press, 1971). Miller lists six rationalizations (p. 304) for "choosing not to be an active agent" in the formation of the future.

14. Groups like the Sierra Club, whose broader interests in environmental (as opposed to simply *wilderness*) preservation has expanded its membership phenomenally in recent years, from 15,000 in 1960 to over 85,000 in 1970 [*Congressional Quarterly Almanac* (Washington, D.C.: Congressional Quarterly Service, January 30, 1970), p. 282]. Part of the recent success of such groups has been their coalition with other active environmental interest groups, as suggested by Daniel R. Grant, "Carrots, Sticks, and Consensus," in Lynton K. Caldwell (ed.), *Environmental Studies—Papers on the Politics of Public Administration of Man-Environment Relationships* (Bloomington: Institute of Public Administration, Indiana University, 1967). A brief history of the government's role in conservation is David C. Coyle, *Conservation: An American Story of Conflict and Accomplishment* (New Brunswick: Rutgers University Press, 1957).

15. The most notable example being the late J. I. Rodale, author of the standard American works on organic gardening and farming, and publisher in recent years of such environmental journals as the *Environmental Action Bulletin* and its predecessor, the *Eco-Bulletin*.

16. See, for example, the growth in membership of organizations like the Sierra Club (note 14).

17. One of the many examples is the U.S. Forest Service: see Luther J. Carter, "Timber Management: Improvement Implies New Land-Use Policies," *Science* 170 (December 25, 1970), 1387–1390.

18. Numerous examples have been treated: see, for example, Jeremy Main, "Conservationists at the Barricades," pp. 167–180; and Judson Gooding, "Victory on San Francisco Bay," pp. 181–188, both in *The Environment: A National Mission for the Seventies* (New York: Perennial Library/Harper and Row, 1969), by the editors of *Fortune*.

19. Characteristic of this position is the recent statement of President Nixon, pp. 11–13 in *The Environment: . . . (Fortune* editors), *op. cit.*

20. A simple and readable explanation of these principles is provided in Kenneth E. Boulding, "The Economics of the Coming Spaceship Earth," in Henry Jarrett (ed.), *Environmental Quality in a Growing Economy* (Baltimore: The Johns Hopkins Press, 1966).

21. One pessimistic critique of such demands is Beryl L. Crowe, "The Tragedy of the Commons Revisited," *Science* 166 (November 28, 1969), pp. 1103–1107.

22. This typology draws in part on a much earlier classification by Robert K. Merton, "Social Structure and Anomie," chapter IV in his *Social Theory and Social Structure* (New York: The Free Press, 1957), revised edition.

23. For an interesting contrast of the U.S. and China on the uses of waste, see Leon A. Orleans and R. P. Suttmeier, "The Mao Ethic and Environmental Quality," *Science* 170 (December 11, 1970), pp. 1173–1176.

24. A brief example from the *Washington Post* of April 23, 1970, is reprinted (p. 33) in Environmental Action's *Earth Day—The Beginning, op. cit.*

25. Some general overviews on this are contained in Boulding, *op. cit.*; Eugene P. Odum, "The Strategy of Ecosystem Development," *Science* 164 (April 18, 1969), 262–270; and J. Alan Wagar, "Growth vs. the Quality of Life," *Science* 168 June 5, 1970), 1179–1184, among others.

26. David Brower, who left the leadership of the Sierra Club to found Friends of the Earth, was one of the long-time conservationists who recognized the need for such direct political action— and thus formed the Friends as a non-tax-exempt organization in order to carry out such lobbying activity in a direct (and hopefully) effective manner.

27. This term was used by James D. Carroll ["Participatory Technology," *Science* 171 (February 19, 1971), 647–653] to describe recent activist efforts, as well as to advocate future movements. The strained (and tangential) relationships of ecologists to technology are discussed in William Murdoch and Joseph Connell, "The Ecologist's Role and the Non-solution of Technology," pp. 47–62 in Fadiman and White, *op. cit.*

28. A brief summary of "Campaign GM" and its pressures on universities (and other institutions) appears in Luther J. Carter, "Campaign GM: Corporation Critics Seek Support of Universities," *Science* 168 (April 24, 1970), 452–455.

29. A representative statement by the Berkeley Ecology Center, entitled "Four Changes," is reprinted in Garrett de Bell (ed.), *The Environmental Handbook* (New York: Ballantine Books, 1970), pp. 323–333. See also Katherine Barkley and Steve Weissman, "The Eco-Establishment," pp. 15–24 in *Eco-Catastrophe* (San Francisco: Canfield Press, 1970), edited by *Ramparts* staff.

30. *Ibid.*

31. A variety of "underground" ecology periodicals (such as *Clear Creek*) provide a sense of this range of action, as does the editorial by the *Ramparts* editors, pp. vi–xii in *Eco-Catastrophe, op. cit.*, and the report by Sol Stern, "Rural Renewal: Trouble in Paradise," pp. 146–158 in *ibid.*, citing the conflict between radical environmentalists and the "consumer society."

32. Barkley and Weissman, *op. cit.*, among others. For a counterview, see Kenneth E. F. Watt, "Whole Earth," pp. 5–25 in Environmental Action, *Earth Day—The Beginning, op. cit.*

33. Jerry Mander (*sic*), "The Media and Environmental Awareness," (pp. 253–262), and Thomas Turner, "Eco-Pornography, or How To Spot an Ecological Phony," (pp. 263–267), both in *The Environmental Handbook, op. cit.*, deal with this.

34. Some of the reasons for the lack of awareness of many of these social structural inequalities are discussed in Norbert Wiley, "America's Unique Class Politics: The Interplay of the Labor, Credit and Commodity Markets," *American Sociological Review* 32 (August 1967): 525–541. An example of the new awareness is in Harvey Molotch, "Santa Barbara: Oil in the Velvet Playground," pp. 84–105 in *Eco-Catastrophe, op. cit.*

35. One reductionist approach has been the attribution of the problem to "cultural" values, specifically the Judeo-Christian ethic [Lynn White, Jr. "The Historical Roots of Our Ecologic Crisis," *Science* 155 (March 10, 1967), 1203–1207]. An attack on this position and some of the simplistic radical critiques is found in Lewis W. Moncrief, "The Cultural Basis for Our Environmental Crisis," *Science* 170 (October 30, 1970), 508–512.

36. Many of these differences in responses have been predicted—Marx discusses the outcome and strategies of scientists, but his observations are applicable to the entire environmental movement. Leo Marx, "American Institutions and Ecological Ideals," *Science* 170 (November 27 1970): 945–952.

37. Though no systematic inventory of the activist exists, the results of many public opinion polls point to the middle class as having the greatest

concern for environmental degradation. For a national report, see Trop and Roos, "Public Opinion . . .", *loc. cit.;* a recent survey of the Chicago area supports this—see Calvin P. Bradford, *et al.,* "Public Attitudes and Social Trends in Chicago: An Annual Inventory," Center for Urban Affairs, Northwestern University (April 1971), especially pp. 11–15.

38. A summary of such findings appears in Arnold M. Rose, *Sociology: The Study of Human Relations,* second edition (New York: Alfred A. Knopf, 1965), chapter 10.

39. See, among many others, Harold Sprout, "The Environmental Crisis in the Context of American Politics," Center for International Studies, Princeton University (March 1970).

40. A point stressed by many participants in "Earth Day." See the brief (but pointed) observations by Freddie Mae Brown *et al.,* Adam Walinsky, Charles A. Hayes, and others, in *Earth Day—The Beginning, op. cit.*

41. Peter Barnes, "Land Reform in America," *The New Republic* (June 5, 12, and 19, 1971).

42. Yet it is the more affluent, or better educated, respondents (though not necessarily the economic elite) who indicate a greater impact of environmental decay on their lives. See Trop and Roos, *op. cit.,* pp. 53, 58–59; and *The United States Public Considers Its Environment* (Princeton: American Institute of Public Opinion, February 1969).

43. This is one of the repeated findings in consumer finance surveys: see James N. Morgan, "Contributions of Survey Research to Economics," in Charles Y. Block (ed.), *Survey Research in the Social Sciences* (New York: Russell Sage Foundation, 1967), especially p. 224.

44. Although it should be noted that consumption of material goods is not perfectly correlated with income, i.e., lower income elasticity of demand at higher income levels.

45. The economics of environmental control have been discussed in many places: for example, Neil H. Jacoby, "Corporations, Government and the Environment: Policy Approaches to a Better Urban America," pp. 169–188 in Fadiman and White, *op. cit.;* Harold Sprout, *op. cit.;* Sanford Rose, "The Economics of Environmental Quality," pp. 65–87 in *The Environment* (Fortune), *op. cit.* A radical critique of the underlying social equity issues is in Martin Gellen, "The Making of a Pollution-Industrial Complex," pp. 73–83 in *Eco-Catastrophe, op. cit.*

46. The extent of industrialists' control over environmental data-collection has recently been indicated: see Vic Reinemer, "Budget Bureau: Do Advisory Panels Have an Industry Bias?" *Science* 169 (July 3, 1970), 36–39.

47. The failure of federal regulatory agencies is a long and sordid history. One recent example is

in: Luther J. Carter, "Timber Management: Improvement Implies New Land-Use Policies," *Science* 170 (December 25, 1970): 1387–1390.

48. As reported in Michael Kitzmiller, "Environment and the Law," pp. 149–168 in Fadiman and White, *op. cit.;* and Victor J. Yannacone, "Sue the Bastards," pp. 179–195 in *Earth Day—The Beginning, op. cit.*

49. The most simple and eloquent statement of this position was by the head of the National Welfare Rights Organization: George Wiley, "Ecology and the Poor," pp. 213–216 in *Earth Day—The Beginning, op. cit.* Evidence of public attitudes on taxation and transfer of environmental funds from other areas is found in Trop and Roos, *op. cit.;* and the attitudes (and behavior) of major industrialists are reported in Robert S. Diamond, "What Business Thinks About Its Environment," pp. 55–64 in *The Environment* (Fortune), *op. cit.*

50. Clearly, this is not the only factor for their underpresentation. Rather, it is a serious compounding effect, over and above the "normal" problems of creating action organizations among the poor. Furthermore, the "failure" of the poor to perceive their pressing environmental problems also contribute to this low participation. Whether this is a perceptual problem (due to lack of contact with particular media sources, etc.) or merely represents the greater press of problems of health, unemployment, security, etc., on their consciousness is not clear. Bradford *et al., op. cit.,* indicate in their recent survey of the Chicago metropolitan area that for all the *non*environmental problem issues, it is the poor (and/or the black) who perceive the problem is most severe.

51. *The Environment* (Fortune), *op. cit.; Eco-Catastrophe, op. cit.* Industrial-oriented authors frequently cite the need for *growth* to solve environmental *and* social equity problems (Rose, *op. cit.;* Jacoby, *op. cit.*), whereas few radical (or committed reformist) authors take this position. One of the few sociologists taking a stance similar to the *Fortune* perspective is Samuel Z. Klausner, *On Man in His Environment* (San Francisco: Jossey-Bass, Inc., 1971).

52. Akin to that of Anthony d'Amato, "The Politics of Ecosuicide," pp. 10–28 in Roos, *op. cit.,* or Crowe, *op. cit.*

53. A point stressed by Sprout, *op. cit.*

54. This is the STEP (*Save Trees, Eliminate Pollution*) program.

55. A more pessimistic scenario is contained in Arthur Simon, "Battle of Beaufort," *The New Republic* (May 23, 1970); all of the major themes above are represented, and the outcome led to the poor (and black) residents paying for conservation and water quality. The dilemma of community development vs. environmental qual-

ity is further illustrated by taking proposals for decentralization of urban power (e.g., Irving Louis Horowitz, " 'Separate But Equal': Revolution and Counter-Revolution in the American City," *Social Problems* 17, no. 3 (Winter 1970): 294–312; and projecting the urban environmental outcomes of such proposals.

8
chapter

contents

cities and the future

et us begin by agreeing upon the obvious: no one knows what the future will bring in any area of life. All we can hope to do, in relation to cities of the future, is study trends which appear in past and present cities and do our best to extend them into the future. Variation occurs, of course, in which trends one selects for attention and what kind of model is used to extend the present—linear, dialectic, curvilinear, or other.

The first decision, one concerning substantive matters (and also to a certain extent, the change model itself), is usually a value judgment, which in turn is closely related to the sort of training a person has received or, if an activist or utopian, the vision of the future most congenial to his ideology. Thus, for example, many science fiction writers create utopian or dystopian cities in their fiction, depending upon whether the positive or negative mode is dominant in their writing style. But both creations reflect what is usually a common underlying theme: a desire for simplification, for a return to an unalienated state of mankind in which work and living are more closely tied to total units and experiences. They seek the small group, the individually hand-crafted product, nature, and so forth. An example of a negative utopia (dystopia) may be found in Kurt Vonnegut's *Player Piano*, a terrifying view of a totally automated society, specifically an automated city, the mythical "Ilium," New York. Positive utopias abound in the works of men like Robert Heinlein: the noble quest, individual success against the forces of society, the role of good citizen in societies of the future, and so forth.

Insofar as possible, we have tried to gather readings for this final chapter which reflect *realistic* thinking about the future of cities. We do not mean to disparage other kinds of projections as necessarily unrealistic; in fact the world of *Player Piano* could, under certain circumstances, be one of the future cities which H. Wentworth Eldredge discusses in the first article of this chapter. But we sense that predictions or proposals about the future city will be more useful to the student if they are intimately grounded in known or suspected trends in cities of today—the 1970s—especially those in the developed West.

Eldredge offers us some fifteen alternative views of the future city, particularly as regards its physical form, ranging from the more likely to the more "futuristic" or bizarre (by contemporary standards). Midway between these poles he also provides some discussion of new towns, a topic treated only by Gans (Chapter 4) in this volume and deserving of this additional comment. Perhaps most intriguing is Eldredge's description of "the water city" and "the wired city." Recalling the descriptions of early cities from Chapter 2, and considering the relatively short span of historical time that has brought us to complex contemporary urban forms, some of these extrapolations do not tax the imagination. But, to emphasize once more that these are realistic, not fanciful, images of the future, you should consult the references following this article and note that serious plans have been developed for many of these alternatives, e.g., "the water city" as a solution to Tokyo's overcrowding.

The second selection in this chapter, Jane Jacob's "Some Patterns of Future Development," is an excellent illustration of this kind of approach: a direct and imaginative extrapolation of trends coupled with her views of the potential health of cities which do or do not correspond to the patterns she predicts. Briefly stated, she argues that manufacturing is inevitably diversifying; that is, moving away from a strictly mass-market concept. To the extent that a city is fixed in a decaying form of production (e.g., mass production of tractors), it is at the same time part of the establishment (that is, it possesses power currently) and is becoming increasingly irrelevant and possibly unproductive in terms of total growth and change in the economy of the society. At the same time, cities in the forefront because they have newer industries catering to newer, more diversified and specialized markets, especially in the service rather than strictly production orientation toward consumers, will show more positive signs of future economic health. But at the same time, these are less powerful than the older, mass-production cities. The real power struggles of the future, according to Jacobs, will be between entrenched and emerging concepts of the economy. At the same time, Jacob's view is a critique of the mass-society technocrats who have been predicting for so long the eventual elimination of most jobs, including white-collar ones, through automation. Jacobs actually predicts a proliferation of types of work in newer societies which become founded on diversified services and limited production concepts, a trend fully in line with the post-industrial society idea and the apparent development of an incredible array of life styles and specialized needs among the young and, increasingly, their elders.

It is significant that the Nixon administration secured governmental subsidies to shore up the ailing Lockheed Corporation; monies were allocated in 1970 for the Penn Central Railroad. By definition, both industries are powerful, for their economic utility is founded on a technology that has been around for a relatively long time. These companies and industries have intimate ties with the polity and, perhaps more importantly, with American cultural values as they modally exist today. Such activities will be retained long past their economic usefulness because of the companies' power, while newer, more risk-prone industries will try and fail, and perhaps eventually succeed. But in that way the entire economic system will change imperceptibly as more and more risk-takers venture forth.

Thus Jacobs provides for us an analysis of the basic underpinnings of all modern Western cities—the economic process—and by showing how changes are occurring in that base, she enables us to imagine which cities will survive in what ways and, perhaps more importantly, what kind of jobs and social roles we can expect in cities of the future.

Anthony Downs' paper on alternatives for the American ghetto touches on some of the themes found in previous selections (e.g., Coles, Suttles, Hermalin and Farley, McPherson, Blauner) and is included here for additional reasons. First, it concerns the overarching problem of separation and inequality in cities. Second, Downs attacks the problem not at the level of policy or program, but by examining several alternative *strategies* for urban ghetto change, alternatives which encompass the broad range of real possibilities and rise above patchwork tactics of the past several years. Finally, the paper complements many of the specific policies Moynihan spells out below and, thereby, sharpens the contrasting perspectives that close this chapter.

A short and admittedly topical piece follows by Richard Reeves on the fiscal crisis of New York City in 1975. A not uncommon belief in the U.S. is that New York reflects the imminent future of the nation and its cities. We doubt this is universally true, but it is true in enough cases to take this brief characterization as a model of the political and economic failures which may soon describe the major urban problem of the 1970s and 1980s. Stated differently, *either* this fiscal crisis will be the major urban problem of the next decade, *or* some broader national solution will be developed. The Reeves article, then, provides a dramatic case study against which we can evaluate the two contrasting perspectives that follow on what happened and where we go from here.

"Toward a National Urban Policy," by Daniel P. Moynihan, is a ten-point policy statement about American cities which, if adopted, would at least provide both a focus for and a unifying codification of present federal, state, and local efforts to change and improve urban areas. Note that Moynihan's first and most pressing point concerns the poverty and social isolation of American urban minorities, especially blacks. One suspects that if this alone became the overriding urban policy statement for the United States, and if in ten years it could be dealt with substantially, then most other urban problems would become more manageable. Not that other things do not need to be done, but Moynihan's article is less a program statement than a plea for policy and statement of values. Thus, he notes that existing programs and quasi-policies, which inhibit rather than encourage solutions to urban problems, should be changed immediately, for they are incongruent with long-term planning for change. Among these are programs that encourage an imbalance of power in cities, not only among elements of the private sector, but also among the divisions of local government and its services. Thus, many proposed plans for metropolitan government which have been soundly defeated at the polls by suburban residents might stand a better chance if federal and state policies provided strong economic encouragements. After reading Moynihan, one undoubtedly will wonder how cities manage to exist today at all; the answer is that they all exist, but few function well. But we have here the start toward future solutions, written by a man formerly close to the top of the pyramid of power in this society.

As we started out saying, no one knows or can know the future until he experiences it. But the articles in Chapter 8 represent some of the best attempts to understand future trends, both from the point of view of prediction and from the perspective of influencing what will happen. For it is our ability to knowledgeably understand urban dynamics that will give rise to our capability to control, and thus to improve, the quality of urban life in the future.

Finally, John Mollenkopf provides a detailed and explicit challenge to liberal views of the urban future found in Downs, Moynihan, and even Jacobs. His fundamental theme is that since World War II the economic function of the U.S. city has been changing from one of production to another of consumption. Moreover, the locus of economic activities has shifted with production moving to the suburbs and the city increasingly becoming the center of a less productive service economy. Federal government policies have helped promote these changes (cf. Rubinowitz) and the result has been a fragmentation of local government, most recently of "progrowth" coalitions. In short, many of the urban problems documented in this volume result from deeper causes in a changing economy and opportunistic political strategies to atune to these changes. The implications of Mollenkopf's analysis are easily drawn. Without changing the nature of the economic forces that play upon capitalist cities the solutions offered by Downs, Moynihan, and others will always be piecemeal, partial holding actions. Is socialist organization an answer as Mollenkopf suggests? We can scarcely answer that question since, despite pretenses of scientific objectivity, these questions have not been given due attention in American urban studies.

If we cannot reliably chart the future, we should be able to frankly admit the plausibility and researchability of these alternative explanations and then get down to the business of discovering which account for the urban condition. As we started out saying, no one knows or can know the future until he experiences it. But the articles in Chapter 8 represent some of the best attempts to understand future trends, both from the point of view of prediction and from the perspective of influencing what will happen. For it is our ability to understand urban dynamics that will give rise to our capability to control, and thus to improve, the quality of urban life in the future.

35

H. WENTWORTH ELDREDGE

Alternative Possible Urban Futures

The twenty-first century will witness a considerable variety of urban forms in the West, in the socialist bloc and in developing countries. Multi-group, multi-valued societies should and will offer options in both societal and physical urban living. A spectrum of experimental urban types is developing all over the world and there is much to be learned from these types in their continuous refinement. The author surveys existing and emerging types: those which offer "more of the same" in a surprise-free future, the new towns or cities which provide innovative life styles, and the extreme and intriguing variants which may feed back into the more normal forms. At present the first type looks most likely to persist.

Given the multi-group society of the present USA with widely divergent value systems, over-riding democratic values with heavy égalitarian overtones preclude any reductionism to *one national pattern* for societal/physical urbanism. Such a naive, crude, cruel and simplistic perception of "human nature" is not remotely feasible in modern Western nations even though there is a tendency to approach it in totalitaria. The enormous powers of the intellectual, technical, even behavioural and organisation technologies make it possible to "have diversity, choice and to meet human needs" for the first time in history.[1] Undoubtedly, we do have some options for our urben futures, despite the energy crunch.

In the "post-industrial society" with its heavy emphasis on the knowledge industry, there is bound to be a multiplicity of variants on patterns already visible in the 1970s. To select a few representative searches for options: *Futures Conditional*,[2] guided by that lively ex-engineer turned socio-economist Robert Theobald, is an attempt to imagine various future scenarios for the next thirty years. Paul Goodman early saw *Seeds of Liberation*[3] in new thought patterns that would free humanity for building, first better societal futures and later physical structures. The American Institute of Planners launched in 1966 a massive enquiry directed by William R. Ewald Jr into the next fifty years, budgeting over $1.25 million from a variety of public and private sources. This was a hefty attempt to illumine American (and the world's) professional city planners as to the rich variety of the feasible roads ahead.[4] An amazing variety of authors —many exceptionally perceptive—from a wide spectrum of doers and thinkers at least concur to form the clear message that bumbling along with "more of the same" would be hopelessly inadequate. Urban design student Kevin Lynch in "The Possible City"[5] stresses that "mobility, access and communication are indeed the essential qualities of an urbanised region—its reason for being". This has been echoed by transportation specialist Wilfred Owen who emphasises the fact that access to activity nodes—jobs, dwellings and recreation—is the key to civilised community development. He glimpses the developing inter changeability of communication (movement of ideas) with transportation (movement of people and goods) which is bound to affect life territory and life styles shortly.[6] Even a hard-headed urban administrator, Roger Starr, Executive Director of New York's Citizens' Housing and Planning Council, bewailing the incessant critical attacks on "the city" by Utopian types such as Lewis Mumford, Jane Jacobs, Herbert Gans, Victor Gruen, *et al* knows that the balancing of the

This article was originally published in FUTURES, The Journal of Forecasting and Planning (IPC Science and Technology Press Ltd.) Vol. 6, No. 1, February 1974, pp. 26–41.

multiplicity of values (held by divergent groups *now*) is already an almost impossible task;[7] it is bound to be worse in the future as groups multiply and pathways further divide. *Mass society* as "one dead level" seems less likely in the 1970s than it did in the 1950s.

If market choices are to be largely replaced by designed options under a National Urban Policy (NUP), then widespread societal/physical alternative possibilities must be built for multiple present and future life styles. Minimum standards can probably be set; egalitarianism, heavily reinforced—and resisted—by increasingly scarce resources, will be quite likely to create iron maxima, but within these very wide parameters an NUP can offer the citizenry a great variety for numerous versions of an existence of "style and quality". There undoubtedly will be both monetary and societal costs involved in making large numbers of available options, but the resultant stunting of society's rich fabric by dull sameness suggests immediate high societal costs and potential high monetary-costs for the failure to provide such options. Inadequate life styles are a "shaped charge" aimed at urban viability—a rather complex way of stating that insistent frustration leads to tension resulting in the possibility of grim revolution (a most costly societal exercise).

Thus it would appear that one of the most overwhelming tasks of NUP planners is to make readily available rewarding, feasible options in diverse physical and societal forms and combinations thereof.

Traditionally planners have tended to think in terms of multi-purpose or multi-functional cities; this seems a rather narrow conclusion to induce from a long human experience drawn from governmental, religious, recreational, learning, trading and industrial types of cities. The future would see specialised cities with clues elaborated from the above simple list of existent forms with such revised types as: (a) the ceremonial city (Washington, Islamabad), (b) the university city (Oxford as it was), (c) the research city (Novosibirsk), (d) the artistic city (Aspen, Colorado), (e) the fun city or Hedonopolis (Cannes, Miami Beach), (f) communication or media city (see option 14 below), (g) the museum city (Bruges, Williamsburg, Nara) including Museums of the future (Mesa City of Soleri), (h) experimental cities of varied types (health, new social relations, communal economic developments), (i)

any combination of the above! In fact each venture could be considered as an experiment,[8] and so treated. Actually, sharply differentiated satellite cities in a metropolitan area or sectors or communities within a core city could offer rewarding variations.

Here is a realistic catalogue of feasible, relatively "surprise-free" urban options ahead; it assumes that no major economic, military or ecological catastrophe will befall the world and its cities in the next three decades. Given multigroup society with divergent life styles and values, holistic planners must offer a wide spectrum of choice. Despite both physical and societal utopianists, it is more than likely that in the year 2000 AD, post-industrial society will be surprisingly like the present only—hopefully—"better". These fifteen options,[9] all pretty standard, are not mutually exclusive and much overlapping is evident; within options there are clearly various sub-options which are not pursued here. Further, the emphasis tends to be on the physical/spatial framework and on location (especially under Type A) which together do not remotely determine societal structuring. Much social diversity is possible within similar man-made physical environments as within similar natural physical environments; the relationship between design and behaviour is not one-to-one. These options are grouped under two categories: Type A—almost certain to continue; and Type B—generally far-out potential environments; no attempt is made to weigh formally the importance of the various options. Certain options clearly occur within the territory of larger urban forms —others are relatively free-standing entities or activity centres. What effects a widespread appreciation of the energy crisis will have on all this is not yet clear.

Type A: Almost Certain to Continue

Option 1. Megalopolis or urban region. This is modern society's fate. Most of the post-industrial urban population (80%?) will dwell in Options 1, 2 and 3. THE PACIFIC BELT (Japan), BOSWASH (Boston to Washington) and RANDSTAD (Holland) are already here. Can such sprawling territorial giantism be redeveloped by opening up "density breaks" (similar to "fire breaks" in a forest) and by the creation of varied activity nodes to restructure interaction and upgrade the Quality of Life (QOL) in such vast agglomerations? These have been defined as "man heaps" by Lewis Mumford, "conurbations" by the English. Obviously there is a multitude of life styles possible and existent in megalopolis.

Option 2. Metropolitan Central City (500,000 and up), as a high activity area with "cosmopolitan" sophisticated recreation, jobs and living. The French regional *métropoles d'équilibre* fit this pattern; high-rise, vertically-zoned buildings could serve as an experiment. Both "straight" and "counter" cultures can find room here. This is the locus of high pressure private and public development in the USA as "the city fights back" to lure middle-class population into returning from the suburbs to live and to interact. It means modern office buildings, pedestrian malls and pediment (or higher) walkways with interesting and diverse shops, recreational and cultural facilities—in short the lure of the bazaar which has given variety to urban life. "New Towns in Town" (NTIT) belong here most certainly in an attempt to divide the city into some semblance of meaningful communities (at least at the level of simple services); social development planning will be a must in large sectors of central city. The *metropolis* shades into:

Option 3. Smaller central city (50,000 to 500,000), similar qualities but on a less national and more regional scale. The possibility exists of creating an *entire* community spirit. Town housing, vertically-zoned buildings with possible class and ethnic mixtures. Somewhere between a 250,000 and 500,000 population seems to be presently the critical mass for the full spectrum of city functions. QOL efforts would pay off richly here. The 1970 US Census indicates that cities in this group have continued to grow where Metropolitan Central Cities (Option 2) are levelling off.

Option 4. Small central city or town (up to 50,000), still less national/regional interaction and more on a localised scale. Local realities adjusted more clearly to varied natural environments and with specific functions, such as: the research city; shore city; recreation city; university/learning/information city; mountain city.

Option 5. Satellite cities for Options 2 and 3 to gain the putative benefits of Option 4; closely linked with new communities, but could be upgraded existent towns or cities.

Option 6. Inner suburbs (a subset) for all three major city types (2, 3, 4) must be divided into "communities" (NTIT again) serving various life styles according to economic class, vocational and/or leisure interests, religion, ethnicity, race, etc.—high-rise and low-rise (town houses/cluster housing). There should be a great variety of suburban types to suit various life styles. The USA has its special problem in white/black antagonisms and unless adequate optional suburban space (both integrated or non-integrated) is made available for blacks to leave central city, the ghetto problem will continue. Undoubtedly sub-options whether to integrate or not must be made available to face the hard reality of continuing prejudice. Patently this applies also to outer suburbs and to new towns. Here derelict land can be used as new green space for recreation and relief.

Option 7. Outer suburbs, similar but of a less "urban" character. Varied life styles are stressed by design both physical and societal; a greater attempt through cluster housing to create "community." Some high-rise buildings in open settings are inevitable.

Option 8. Exurbia. Quasi-rural existence of a scattered grain but due to advanced transportation "urbanistic" in quality; not unrelated to "the wired city" and the 1-day work week. Made possible by the electric pump, septic tank and four-wheeled drive vehicle; haunt of "hill-billy" types and seclusive "intellectuals". This is high cost scatteration, but an immensely rewarding option for certain personality types—who may be either incompetent, truly creative, or merely hiding from the horrid urban world.[10] Increasingly the haunt of the counter-culture and very suitable for new experimental family/community variants. Alpine recreational resorts possibly fit this category; the seashore has been pretty generally usurped by sprawl.

Option 9. New Towns (or latterly *New Communities*). Building cities *de novo* has held a great attraction for mankind; "leave the messy clutter behind and start afresh" might even be traced back to mobile hunters striking the befouled en campment to move on to virgin areas. New towns are simply dwellings, jobs, recreation, a wide spectrum of services and *controlled* size. Most certainly the current fervor about new cities/towns/communities indicates a deep-seated dissatisfaction with existent urban forms. This is unquestionably the area for widespread experimentation both with physical forms and with societal structure; and a means of ascertaining and developing client desires or choices. Somewhat oversold as a universal panacea at the moment, the enormous costs for the needed infrastructure of a massive new cities programme to cope with a significant percentage of the expected 80 to 100 million new Americans (35,000,000 new households ±) by the twenty-first century boggles the imagination. To build for 25% only (20 to 25 million persons) would require 2,000 towns for 100,000 inhabitants, each costing between $2–5 thousand million in public and private investment, leading to an over-all cost of $10,000,000 million at least.[11] While undoubtedly much will of necessity be spent in any case to house, amuse and provide jobs for the expected hordes, it is most unlikely that exploiting the vast existing urban infrastructure would even approach such costs—though the possible benefits of thousands of new towns might be of extraordinary magnitude.[12]

Examples of New Towns

Before proceeding further it should be stressed that new towns can consist of

- free-standing independent communities (Brasilia and Novosibirsk Academic City)
- groups of related free-standing functionally divergent communities (Lewis Mumford's ideal)
- satellite communities with high self-employment (London ring new towns)
- extensions of cities; really glorified, quasi-independent suburbs (Long Island Levittowns and Stockholm's semi-satellite cities)
- "New Towns in Town" (NTIT), live tissue grafts to existing internal city structure (Fort Lincoln, Washington, DC).[13]

Minnesota Experimental City (MXC), brainchild of oceanographer, physicist, meteorologist, Athelstan Spilhaus, aided by, among others, Buckminster Fuller, urbanologist Harvey Perloff, economist Walter Heller, was to be built by private financing on 50,000 acres, 10 miles north of Minneapolis with a maximum population of 250,000.[14] This is perhaps the most obviously experimental effort to date both physically and societally: downtown will be roofed over; the municipal power plant is to be partially fuelled by garbage; cable TV will approximate "the wired city" (Option 15); farms and factories will be mixed; while people will be housed in megastructures complete with waterless toilets, people-movers and universal computer-managed charge accounts. New city Vaudreuil to house and provide jobs for 150,000 residents is to be built by the French government in the Basse-Seine region outside Paris. It will have the world's first urban centre without noise or pollution (?) and all green zones in the general area are to be preserved, as was announced by President Pompidou. The city's traffic will flow underground; factory smoke is to be carried off by underground conduits—gases being burned at the source; apartments and business buildings to be sound-proofed; with all refuse moved through underground conduits to be used in adding to the city's requirements for central heating. These are merely the most "advanced" examples of a new communities world movement (milennia old) which includes the architecturally striking Brasilia and Chandigarh—and the older Washington, Canberra and New Delhi (the British imperial city stage). The thirty-odd British New Towns are globally renowned; by 1963 probably well over one thousand new towns of various shapes and sizes had been identified.[15] There is a recent 1973 report that there are already 1,000 in the USSR alone.[16] The best known US examples: Columbia (Maryland), Reston (Virginia), Flower Mound (Texas), Jonathan (Minnesota), and Irvine (California)—all privately financed—are in varying degrees innovative socially and physically—primarily in amenities. The semi-satellite cities coupled to the public urban transit system of Stockholm (they do not provide jobs for more than half the resident population) have also attracted world attention concentrating especially on the town centres so reminiscent of American shopping centres without that ugly, naked parking necklace of automobiles. The Dutch have done a splended job in reclaiming the Zuider Zee for new town development. Tapiola, a tiny gem for only 17,000 persons using adroitly both green and blue (water)

491

space, has cheered the world with the realisation that pleasant urban living is possible. Japan with characteristic zeal plans to dot the hinterland of Tokyo with quasi-new towns composed of rather barren, high-density dwellings. Tama New Town to house 410,000 on 7,500 acres is the prime example. (Incidentally this is the same acreage as Reston which is designed to house 75,000 with high recreational amenities.) At Tama, tenants, generally middle income, are to be selected by lot and divided into "neighbourhoods", generally convenience-oriented, of 15 000 people. Most dwellers are expected to commute to Shinjuku (New Town in Town) or through it to central Tokyo for work.[17] India is planning a "New Bombay" for a potential population of two million;[18] whether it will be built is another question.

As is well known, Israel has constructed a variety of new towns/new communities: larger ones for port or industrial purposes; smaller for agricultural development often connected with defence[19] under an urban settlement hierarchy system based on Christaller. Connected with the physical siting of population are the renowned versions of communal settlements: the *kibbutz* and *mashav*. Thus the twin experimental functions of new communities are exhibited there: technological virtuosity and fresh social patterning. Noteworthy in new community development worldwide is the great variety of fresh governmental authorities or public corporations invented to get on with the job—where traditional government has been obviously too wooden to do so.

While, for example, the original or Mark I postwar British new towns were aimed in the London region at decanting the central city population, new towns or massively developed old towns both in Britain and elsewhere are now perceived as potentially powerful development nodes furthering national urbanisation policy with high technology, industry, high education, and population distribution.[20] Even Herbert Gans, égalitarian sociologist, believes that treated delicately new communities might possibly make positive contributions to the nasty desegregation muddle here,[21] as will perhaps "Soul City", the Black New Town in North Carolina near Raleigh-Durham under the leadership of Floyd B. McKissick with a planned eventual population of 50,000.[22] Finally, the United States Government is officially dedicated to sponsoring

new communities in the Housing Acts of 1970 and 1972. Up to now the action has hardly been impressive; there is no remotely visible over-all strategy for siting or the scale of the total effort.

Option 10. A rural/agricultural setting could now be brought more easily into "urbanistic" living patterns by transportation and telecommunication. European agricultural life has long been town/village centred, contrary to the US mode of isolated homesteads. Clearly an increasing humankind will need more and more food while a (declining) proportion of the population will continue to opt for an agricultural life style. Of course, for some very considerable period there will be islands of "backward" rural culture preserved in Asia, Africa, Latin America and possibly portions of North America. Such areas could offer a rewarding life style for the actual inhabitants and "museums for living" (small residual forms throughout the world) for the denizens of more urbanised habitats.

Type B. Far-Out Potential Environments

These could be either physical or societal—or more likely some combination of both; they might serve as temporary experiences for the many or for the permanent life style of a few.

Option 11. Mega-structures or "mini-cities" have fascinated men at least since the Tower of Babel.[23] Characteristically, there is a Disneyland project copyrighted in 1960 "The Community of Tomorrow" which will be a whole *enclosed* model town for 20,000 persons on fifty acres *only*, to be part of the Florida Disney World. Paolo Soleri has had the greatest visibility recently as a highly successful youth-guru with his concepts of giant supra-terrestrial human hives housing up to hundreds of thousands of persons.[24] Soleri has fuzzy, complicated, intuitive, communalistic notions about group life joined to his often cantilevered bridge-like structures which allies him to far-out commune options as well.[25] It will be interesting to see the clients his constructions attract once scale has been attained.

Apparently the term mega- (giant) structure was the invention of Fumihiko Maki of the Japanese Metabolist Group in 1964. *Habitat* by the Israeli architect, Moshe Safdie, prepared for Expo 1967 in Montreal, while financially an initial disaster, has become a much publicised example of this sort of "plug-in", "clip-on" structure;[26] for the record it is turning out to be both a financial and a societal success. Taby, satellite community outside Stockholm, houses 5,000 people in one group of vast, curved structures, flanked by eight tower blocks containing another 3,000; while in Denmark "at Gladsaxe about 15 miles from Copenhagen, five 16-storey slabs, each 300 feet long, extend in tandem". This latter construct seems to negate the warm humanism of Danish planning; the buildings are factory-made prefabs, site assembled: "These slabs are aligned with formal, rigid, relentless horizontality."[27]

Even mega-structures (human hives) directly in town have been flirted with by responsible officials. In 1966 Governor Rockefeller of New York State proposed a futuristic design for Battery Park City of massive towers for the lower tip of Manhattan, high connective bridges, dozens of apartments with a high pedestrian mall surrounded by other rabbit-warren dwellings on a large land fill totalling 90 plus acres. After lengthy negotiations with the New York City fathers, the plan was realistically toned down into a less grandiose format[28] and is still being re-thought.

In effect though, vertically-zoned buildings with garages and services below ground, retail trade at ground level rising to business offices, to schools and finally to varied dwellings topped by the inevitable penthouse (the higher you go the more it costs?) give promise of things to come. Many of these mega-structures are theoretically capable of infinite expansion or contraction, an eternal meccano set which might be one partial answer to an increasingly mobile society.

Option 12. The Water City Scarcity of usable shore land and possibly usable shallow water (what happens to the ecological balance?) have led recently to large-scale "futuristic" designs for enormous activity nodes on reclaimed land or on stilts in shallow water. Buckminster Fuller advocated this for Japan in Tokyo Bay using his newly-beloved tetrahedron shape as piles.[29] Given oriental population densities and typical minimal family space, the water city/megastructure idea does not seem out of place now and may be a necessity in the future. Fuller carried his ideas further in the Triton Floating Community of 30,000 persons with structures up to

twenty storeys; these ferro/concrete platforms could be built in shipyards and towed to usable places just offshore of existing coastal cities to be "anchored" in water up to twenty or thirty feet in depth.[30] This project was financed by the US Department of Housing and Urban Development; a trial construction nearly came to fruition in Baltimore harbour. There is a present scheme afloat to develop an artificial island off Tokyo; Kenzo Tange had explored brilliantly the Tokyo Bay project earlier in his *Tokyo 1960* plan.[31] There have been, of course, precursor water cities: Swiss Neolithic Lake Dwellings, Bangkok's *klongs* (canal life); Hong Kong's sampan colony at Victoria; Borneo and New Guinea stilt villages and even Fort Lauderdale. After all, most of the southern tip of Manhattan Island was once under water. Tange's plan called for a reconstruction of the central city and for a huge expansion in mega-structure form into Tokyo Bay—both linear in form—to take care of a 1980 estimated population of 20,000,000 for the metropolitan area of the Japanese capital!

As a matter of fact, based on research conducted at the Athens Center of Ekistics on the "City of the Future Project", John G. Papaioannou concluded "that floating settlements on the oceans are expected to be considerably less costly than settlements on different land (mountains, swamps, deserts, frozen soil, etc)[32] some seventy to one hundred years hence with the earth trending toward one world city, Doxiadis' Ecumenopolis.

Option 13. Underwater, underground and space habitations on a scale large enough to be significant. Jacques Cousteau collaborated in the design of a floating island to be built off the coast of Monaco which would have undersea features: ". . . more comfortable dwelling quarters may be floating stably a hundred feet or so below the surface where any wave motion is so damped out as to be unnoticeable."[33]

The habitation-cum-fortress underground house is something new, although underground factories were well known in Nazi Germany and the United Kingdom during World War II as well as the ill-fated Maginot Line. The salubrious atmosphere of huge salt mine caverns could conceivably serve for community experimentation. *Sousterrain* dwellings could have temperature control and construction savings immediately applicable, especially in hot desert areas and quite possibly in sub-Arctic regions. Certainly in central city, burying certain structures and services below ground is already in progress with multi-storey underground parking garages in many cities (Paris, for example) and the increasing use of sub-surface delivery roadways and shopping areas.

The Committee for the Future has as its avowed (and partially endowed) purpose the development of extra-terrestrial space to ease the environmental burden and "the opening of the solar system for humanity beginning with the establishment of a lunar community available to people of all nations". Unlikely as some of these science fiction solutions may appear today, at least they may in time offer recreational locations for future persons searching for new experience.[34]

Option 14. Communes and other societal innovations. Recent new societies in the USA with presumed behavioural innovations are generally the efflorescence of the counter-culture; they are largely and consciously simplistic in technology and are the *nouvelle vague* in societal structuring. Chinese communist "communes" with heavy overtones of directed "togetherness" are quite another thing! Even elementary contact with anthropology and history would suggest that middle class, capitalist, nationalist, habitaions/life styles with certain economic, political, religious, familial, recreational institutions hardly exhaust the possbilities for human arrangements. Nor does a minimal connection with the long story of Utopian schemes and real Utopian communities lead one to assume that it all began with *Walden Two.*[35]

Despite the often jejune aspects of such experimental communal Utopias and the relatively few persons involved in any groups that approach a quasi-organised effort, the present impact is felt no matter how faintly—by a whole generation of American youth (and their foreign imitators) who see an appealing alternative life style to modern traditional Western civilisation. In short, a counterpoint theme, no matter how unsubstantial, has been established; it is already "out there".

Physical communes are in a sense concrete expressions of Utopia, the no-place ideal world, to which the forefathers of most Americans emigrated from their assorted homelands. Once arrived they and their descendants continued to pursue the dream across the wide and once beauteous continent until everything stopped in 1893 (the end of the frontier) on the shores of the Pacific. More extreme seekers for the perfect/ideal life probably founded more Utopian colonies in the New World than elsewhere (although Robert Owen was English and Charles Fourier was French). A catalogue of better known nineteenth-century ventures here would include the celibate New England Shakers (so-called because of their curious dancing/shuffling worship) who early preached "the careful craftsmen"; the Owenites at New Harmony in Indiana, a socialist/communist community; Brook Farm, a poetic Phalanx with high-minded pretensions in almost anarchist interaction dedicated to "the honesty of a life of labor and the beauty of a life of humanity".[36] The Oneida community believing in "Free Love and Bible Communism" was started in 1847, and still continues in altered form as Oneida Ltd.—successful silver manufacturers. The general theme running through such nineteenth-century experiments sounds familiar enough today in their search for "freedom", "love" and the escape from crude materialism to production "for use rather than profit". America's penchant for revivalist religious movements such as the Seventh Day Adventists and the Mormons has produced somewhat similar far-out societal design. Patently youth culture, unhappily extended well past sexual potency by the lumbering contemporary educational process (and the probable need to keep the masses of young off the job-market in capitalist culture) has become enshrined in the whole counter-culture movement of which the encyclopedic *Whole Earth Catalog*[37] gives some clue of the myriad forms of this "romantic" reaction to industrialism and the search for a "new freedom". The Hippie communes both urban and rural (both benign and evil as some of the murderous, dehumanised monster groups show) possibly number 3,000 in the USA. If each group is comprised of a population of ten (a serious study for environmental purposes found in the Minneapolis area that the twelve communes investigated there had a total of 116 members)[38] the total population of American communes would thus be 30,000 in a nation of 210,000,000 which hardly heralds the Revolution! Even if there were 100,000 such communes, upset is not yet upon us.

Hippie core-values as the extreme example of these minimum physical planning/maximum societal planning variants are an interesting summary of the counter-culture: [39] free, sensually expressive (anti-intellectual), immediate, natural, colourful/baroque, spontaneous, primitive, mystical, égalitarian, communal.

This largely societal option has been introduced here since it is clearly "innovative" and "revolutionary" (often in puerile ways) in its implications for standard society and in its messages to developing lands about the "failures" of industrial society. It could be, however, only the tip of the iceberg of dissatisfaction with the industrial culture of Western society. Minimal space seems to be the *only* physical planning expense involved; the commune people make their own societal plans. Such exotics must not be crushed—even if someone else has "to tend store". The affluent West affords millions of the idle rich, non-producing youngsters, idling oldsters and millions of unemployed; it most certainly can afford a few tens of thousands of experimenters seeking a better life on earth. [40] They might even have something!

Communes, as here defined, obviously do not exhaust possibilities for societal innovation in urban places. A creative systems approach to housing, largely economic, has been sketched, [41] including (a) an executive, professional, intellectual housing centre, (b) new, non-competitive shared-value orientation, (c) "housing as a self-renewing function which adjusts and develops as individuals, opportunities and communities evolve" (no on-site maintenance!), (d) multiple consumer choices, (e) creation of new credit sources due to housing as a "containerised unit—with registered, computerised bonded and insured controlled units", (f) "Mutual Insurance fund" to include youth participation and leisure time home-building as inputs with, finally (g) registered bankable certificates of the units for "house complex" easily exchangeable as a restless population moves above.

ption 15. "The Wired City." With the phenomenal growth of cable television (potentially capable of two-way transmission) added to the almost infinite potentialities of multi-channel electronic interaction through "people's satellites", [42] a non-territorial, high-intensity participatory community fitted to the "post-civilised" or "information society", could await us. [43] Despite

piecemeal research, very considerable argumentation, a few limited experiments, [44] and a galloping electronic technology, it seems unlikely that the multiplicity of ordinary (and creative new) functions, which should be possible at considerable energy saving, will be much in operation in even the most sophisticated nations before the commencement of the twenty-first century. The bits of the picture puzzle are slowly being fitted together but they still do not form a whole. It appears that the basic scenario will be a national [45] cable/micro-wave grid of metropolitan networks reinforced or supplanted with satellite connections and eventually lasers; computers serving both as storage facilities and as analysts with display capabilities will be at the centre of this intellectual technology. [46] In the UK consideration is already being given to setting up a national computer grid. In "the wired city" every dwelling will have its typewriter-like keyboard with print-out capabilities and display screen in the home information recreation/business centre (additional home terminals are naturally possible). This equipment will not be cheap and some trained intelligence will be needed to operate such sophisticated gadgetry thus bringing up future questions of equity, égalitarianism and the massive financing and maintenance of such "public services".

Here are some of the bits yet to be assembled in a potential non-territorial, electronic society, partially substituting the transmission of ideas for the transportation of people and goods, and freed to a certain extent from spatial considerations. [47] As transportation expert Wilfred Owen has pointed out: [48]

> The significance of communications as a substitute for transport derives from the fact that while the unit costs of transportation continue to rise as quality declines, telecommunications tend to increase in quality and decline in cost. Distance is important in transportation, but with communication satellites distance is almost irrelevant.

Here is a portion of what "the wired city" might provide:

• *Information storage available by computer/TV*
national data bank on the total society (with all the safeguards of privacy)
national library
national music library

national theatre/cinema library

national health records and diagnostic information

scientific information service

crime information

credit information

- *Home service facilities*
  all banking and transactions ("the end of money")
  shopping (plus delivery)
  recreation (passive and active—"anyone for chess?")
  crime prevention
  education in the home for children *and* adults
  automatised cooking
  visiting via video-phone
  print-out news (*The New York Times* nationwide)
  "mail" delivery electronically

- *Advanced societal innovations*
  public opinion surveys
  sampling to replace voting
  "participatory democracy"[49]
  TV surveillance of public (and private!) places
  new industrial/business locations
  new employment patterns (4-day, 3-day, even 2-day work week in a *work place* away from the dwelling)
  new population distribution
  "home visits" by the doctor and specialist
  increased physical and societal design capabilities
  new and powerful techniques for mass behaviour, control and surveillance
  systems design and guided social change[50]

All is clearly not sweetness and light in this future city. What if evil "philosopher kings" should occupy central positions in the national/international network? If "euphoria" characterised the initial reaction to the two-way television, coaxial cable, computer, peoples satellite syndrome, one already sees signs of *alarm* prior hopefully to advanced *protective action* (including active *ombudsman* functions) before the need arises.[51] Finally, for the loyal fans of central city as "the place where the action is", "the wired city" is already posing quite a problem as "people stay away in droves" from downtown especially for evening recreation with simpleminded, existent TV as one reason.

The US Department of Housing and Urban Development has commissioned a study on the impacts of advanced telecommunications technology on American cities during the next twelve years[52] which concludes significantly that:

- The advent of telecommunications technology (TCT), while highly beneficial to some segments of society, will prove detrimental to others.
- The positive impacts of TCT will be felt primarily in the middle class suburbs, while the negative impacts will be concentrated in the central cities.
- TCT will not play a highly visible role in the major urban developments of the next 12 years. Unless specifically anticipated by federal and local planning, impacts will not be properly understood and regulated until considerable damage has been done.
- The primary urban impact of TCT will be to reduce the economic viability of the central city by accelerating (though not directly causing) the delocalisation of business and commerce.
- The social impacts of TCT are to be found at least as much in the indirect effects of TCT on the fiscal strength of cities, as in the direct effects of new gadgets on the life styles of individuals.
- The sector most affected by TCT is the service sector, in which processes involving paper transactions are particularly sensitive to technological substitution.
- It is unlikely that the central city population will derive much benefit, in the next 12 years, from such "luxury" applications of TCT as shopping or working at home.
- The most important *positive* impacts of TCT in central cities will be in the areas of technical education (expecially in programmes designed to develop job skills among inner-city residents), and routine city services (especially in transit systems, police and fire protection, etc) and remote medical or diagnostic services.

Having explored at some length goals for a good "society" and a rather considerable number of alternative possible urban futures, one is driven to the realisation that quite probably "more of the same" will be the lot of Western urbanism for the rest of this century and probably well on into the next. "Peripheral sprawl will undoubtedly be the dominant form of future urban growth throughout the US"[53] and the Western world. This will probably be true for the socialist nations as well; a degree of urban chaos is predictable for the developing countries as a "geniu forecast".[54] It is most likely that there will be no urban systems-break; far-out options will oc cur only here and there. The standard world projection of *one spread city*,[55] slopping untidily into the next, is all too likely for those nations incapable of the act of will, the intellectual effort, and the *real Politik* ability to direct their growth, as well as sufficient consensus and capital resources to bring about actively planned, alternative rewarding large-scale variations of the human condition. Superior "intentional societies and ordered environments" still seem just beyond our grasp.[56]

References and Notes

1. Leonard Duhl, "Teaching and Social Policy", *The Bulletin of the Association of Collegiate Schools of Planning*, Winter 1971, pages 4–10.
2. New York: The Bobbs-Merrill Co., 1972. *Teg's 1984* (Chicago, The Swallow Press 1972), a participatory, experimental book on new societal/physical forms by Theobald and J. M. Scott, where, it is claimed, "ego can involve the reader".
3. Paul Goodman (ed.), *Seeds of Liberation* (New York, George Braziller, 1964).
4. *The Next Fifty Years* series commemorated the 50th anniversary of the founding of the American Institute of Planners. Published by the University of Indiana Press (Bloomington, Illinois), it consists of three volumes: Vol. I *Environment and Man* (1967), Vol. II *Environment and Change* (1968), Vol. III *Environment and Policy* (1968).
5. *Ibid.*, Vol. III, page 145.
6. Wilfred Owen, "Telecommunication and Life Styles", *The Accessible City* (Washington, The Brookings Institution, 1972), pages 132–133.
7. Roger Starr, *Urban Choices: The City and Its Critics* (Baltimore, Penguin Books, 1967).
8. John McHale, *Future Cities: Notes on a Typology* (unpublished draft).
9. The urban future could be sliced differently. Cf. Anthony Downs, "Alternate Forms of Future Urban Growth in the United States", *Journal of the American Institute of Planners*, January 1970, page 4. Incidentally, using ten key variables involved in urban development (with several arbitrarily chosen values for each), Downs indicates the logical possibility of 93 312 potential forms of future urban growth! (page 3).
10. Satirised some years ago by A. C. Spectorsky, *The Exurbanites* (New York, Berkeley Publishing Co., 1955).
11. Extrapolated loosely from Walter K. Vinett, *Paper Number Three, The Scenario for Minnesota's Experimental City* (Minneapolis, University of Minnesota, Office for Applied Social Science and the Future, 1972).
12. "Non-metropolitan new cities or expanded communities are not likely to capture any significant fraction of the nation's [USA] future urban growth in spite of their current vogue in planning literature." Anthony Downs, *op. cit.*, page 11.
13. Harvey S. Perloff, *New Towns in Town* (Washington, D.C., Resources for the Future, 1966), reprint.
14. *Time*, February 26, 1973. Sadly abandoned in April 1973—funds ran out.
15. F. J. Osborn and Arnold Whittick, *The New Towns: The Answer to Megalopolis* (New York, McGraw-Hill, 1963), pages 141–148.
16. According to the Department of Housing and Urban Development (*The New York Times*, April 26, 1973).
17. *Information Series* 20, *HUD International*, U.S. Department of Housing and Urban Development, January 15, 1973.
18. Dena Kaye, "Across the Gateway and Into the Curry," *Saturday Review/World*, September 11, 1973.
19. Ann Louis Strong, *Planned Urban Environments* (Baltimore, Md., The Johns Hopkins University Press, 1971), pages 170–173.
20. Cf. Lawrence Susskind and Gary Hack, "New Communities in a National Urban Growth Strategy," *Technology Review* (February 1972), pages 30–42; also "New Communities," An American Institute of Planners Background Paper, No. 2, 1968.
21. Revised version of a paper presented for the Symposium on "The Human Dimensions of Planning," UCLA, June, 1972.
22. "The Planning Process for New Town Development: Soul City," A Planning Studio Course, Fall 1969, Department of City and Regional Planning, University of North Carolina, Chapel Hill, under David Godschalk.
23. A visually striking book on mega-structures is Justus Dahinden's *Urban Structures for the Future* (New York, Praeger, 1972).
24. Paolo Soleri, *Arcology—The City in the Image of Man* (Cambridge, MIT Press, 1969), in the tradition of "design utopias".
25. See Ralph Wilcoxen, *Paolo Soleri: A Bibliography* (Monticello, Illinois, Council of Planning Librarians Exchange Bibliography, No. 88, June, 1969). According to the *New York Times* (Nov. 4, 1973), Soleri stated, "The only way to keep autos out of the city is to build a city without streets."
26. Cf. William Zuk and Roger H. Clark, *Kinetic Architecture* (New York, Van Nostrand Reinhold, 1970). To quote the blurb, "Exciting open-

ended planning: proposed and actual structures that are *replaceable, deformable, incremental, expandable, reversible*—even *disposable.*" Italics the editor. Cf. also Peter Cook (ed.), *Archigram* (New York, Praeger, 1973).

27. *The New York Times*, December 2, 1965.

28. *The New York Times*, November 22, 1970.

29. *Playboy*, December 1967.

30. *The New York Times*, November 3, 1968.

31. Kenzo Tange Team, *A Plan for Tokyo*, 1960 (Tokyo), drawn largely from the April 1961 issue (in English) of the *Japanese Architect*.

32. "Future Urbanization Patterns: A Long-Range World Wide View," paper prepared for presentation at the Second International Future Research Conference, Kyoto, Japan, 1970, page 17.

33. *Congressional Record*, November 15, 1965, "Extention of Remarks of Hon. Claiborne Pell, October 22, 1965".

34. 130 Spruce Street, Philadelphia, Pa. 19106. SYNCON is their elaborate physical and intellectual system to relate varied disciplines in a holistic effort to solve primarily urban problems. *Unibutz: Out of this World* (an interplanetary, international kibbutz) was explored at some length in the World Institute Council's *Fields Within Fields* by various intellectuals in 1971 (Vol. 40, No. 1).

35. B. F. Skinner, *Walden Two* (New York, The Macmillan Co., 1948). Cf. W. H. G. Armytage, *Yesterday's Tomorrows: A Historical Survey of Future Societies* (Toronto, University of Toronto Press, 1968).

36. *The Complete Works of Ralph Waldo Emerson*, edited by E. W. Emerson (Boston, Houghton Mifflin & Co., 1904), Vol. 10, 359–360, quoted in Peyton E. Richter (ed.), *Utopias: Social Ideals and Communal Experiments* (Boston, Holbrook Press, 1971), page 129. The examples cited here were drawn from this work.

37. *The Last Whole Earth Catalog* (New York, Random House, 1971).

38. Michael Carr and Dan MacLeon, "Getting It Together," *Environment*, Vol. 14, No. 5 (November 1972). The study was conducted under the auspices of the American Association for the Advancement of Science.

39. Drawn from Fred Davis, *On Youth Sub-Cultures: The Hippie Variant* (New York, General Learning Press, 1971—module).

40. This most certainly is not to encourage elaborate planning provisions for odd groups searching for instant Nirvana through Drug Utopias—a not inconsiderable subset or variant of existant communal experimentation. Cf. Richard Blum, *Utopiates: The Use and Users of LSD-25* (New York, Dodd, Mead & Company, 1963).

41. Julius Stulman, "Creative Systems in Housing," *The World Institute Council*, Vol. 4, No. 2, 1971.

42. For example, ANIK, the Canadian internal satellite.

43. Sloan Commission on Cable Television, *On the Cable: The Television of Abundance* (New York, McGraw-Hill, 1971) is a fairly straight line projection of more-of-the-same TV pattern only with more choice up to the turn of the century. More imaginative alternative potentials could have been rewardingly explored; the societal planning lead time is shorter than one thinks to cope with the wired city.

44. Jonathan New Town, Minneapolis, Minn.; Tama New Town, Japan; and Washington New Town, County Durham, England.

45. This, of course, could be international as Eurovision has already accomplished for one-way television.

46. James Martin and Adrian R. D. Norman, *The Computerized Society* (Englewood Cliffs, N.J., Prentice-Hall, 1970), page 66.

47. Cf. Melvin M. Webber an Carolyn C. Webber, "Culture, Territoriality and the Elastic Mile," in H. Wentworth Eldredge, (ed.), *Taming Megalopolis* (New York, Anchor-Doubleday, 1967), Vol. I, pages 35–54, which considers the existant professional non-territorial community.

48. Wilfred Owens, *The Accessible City* (Washington, D.C., The Brookings Institution, 1972), page 132. Cf. the hyper-optimistic "30 Services That Two-Way Television Can Provide" by Paul Baran in *The Futurist*, Vol. III, No. 5 (October 1973).

49. *Project Minerva* (Electronic Town Hall Project) has already carried out preliminary exercises in some 803 households of a middle-income high rise housing complex in one of the nation's largest cities ". . . in the comfort of their own homes recently, and aired their views about their security problems during an electronic town hall meeting." Amitai Etzioni, who is conducting the experiment, believes he could carry this out with 40,000 persons. Center for Policy Research, Inc., 475 Riverside Drive, New York, *Newsletter* No. 8, January, **1973**, and *Behavior Today*, Vol. 4, No. 10, March **5**, 1973.

50. Robert Boguslaw, *The New Utopians: A Study of System Designs and Social Change* (Englewood Cliffs, N.J., Prentice-Hall, 1965). As well as explaining latent capabilities for powerful symbiotic man/machine interaction, Boguslaw wisely explores paranoid possibilities in Chapter 8, "The Power of Systems and Systems of Power."

51. These terms are the main headings for portions of the Martin/Norman book, *op. cit.*

52. Marvin Cetron, *An Analysis of the Impact of Ac*

vanced *Telecommunications Technology on the American City* (Washington, D.C./Arlington, Va., Forecasting International Ltd., 1973), quoted from the "Executive Summary," pages iv–v.

53. Anthony Downs, *op. cit.*, page 11.

54. Marvin Cetron's terms.

55. *Spread City: Projection of Development Trends and the Issues They Pose: The Tri-State New York Metropolitan Region*, 1960–1985 (New York Regional Plan Association, Bulletin 100, September 1962).

56. Paul Reed, *Intentional Societies and Ordered Environments* (Monticello, Illinois, Council of Planning Librarians Exchange Bibliography No. 320, 1972).

36

JANE JACOBS

Some Patterns of Future Development

We now have in hand all the major processes at work in a growing city economy. First, the city finds in an older city or cities an expanding market for its initial export work, and it builds up a collection of numerous local businesses to supply producers' goods and services to the initial export work. Second, some of the local suppliers of producers' goods and services export their own work. The city builds up an additional collection of local businesses to supply producers' goods and services to the new export work. Some of these new local suppliers take to exporting their own work. The city builds up more local business to supply producers' goods and services to them, and so on. The city earns a growing volume and growing diversity of imports.

Third, many of the imports the city has been earning are replaced by goods and services produced locally, a process that causes explosive city growth. The city, at the same time, shifts the composition of its imports. Its local economy grows large (and diverse) in proportion to the volume of the city's exports and imports. Owing to the powerful multiplier effect of the replacement process, the local economy contains room for entirely new kinds of goods and services, that is, goods and services formerly neither imported nor locally produced. Among these can be unprecedented goods and services. The replacement of imports causes total economic activity to expand rapidly. Fourth, the city's greatly enlarged and greatly diversified local economy becomes a potential source of numerous and diversified exports, including many consumer goods and services as well as producers' goods and services, and still other exports built upon local goods and services. The city's exporting organizations arise by (a) adding the export work to other people's local work; (b) adding the export work to different local work of their own; and (c) exporting their own local work. By generating new exports, the city earns more imports. But many of the new exports merely compensate for older exports the city loses through obsolescence of older exports, transplants of some exporting organizations into the rural world, and replacement of its exports by local production in former customer cities.

Fifth, from this time on, the city continues to generate new exports and earn imports; replace imports with local production; generate new exports and earn imports; replace imports with local production, and so on.

All of these processes, taken together, compose two interlocking, reciprocating systems; the first triggers off the second. (A diagram correlating the two reciprocating systems appears in Section IV of the Appendix.) If any one process fails, the entire system fails and the city stagnates economically.

Among the producers' goods and services that form in the course of these events are those that supply capital to new goods and services that are forming and growing, as well as to older goods and services. The root process is the adding of new work to older divisions of labor, thus multiplying the divisions of labor, to some of which still newer activities can be added. This underlying process, which I have symbolized as $D + A \rightarrow nD$, makes possible all the others.

The Emergence of Differentiated Production

These processes and the systems they compose are old and predictable, though the goods and services they cast up change and are not necessarily predictable. As the new goods and services emerge, certain dominant patterns of economic organization also change. These are large, gradual and cumulative movements. For example, the dominant form of manufacturing used to be craftwork. This has been succeeded in currently advanced economies by mass production, a sequence, incidentally, which occurs in ancient as well as modern times. Mohenjodaro and Harappā had their mass-production industries, and cities of the Roman Empire developed mass-produced lamps, pottery, and other utensils. Machines developed in the industrial revolution of the nineteenth century have been strikingly successful means of carrying out mass production, but the concept and practice are older. Is mass production the ultimate type of manufacturing? Or is there a more advanced type?

Before touching on that question, let us notice another large pattern that has changed over time: organizational work. Merchants used to organize manufacturing; in the main, the type of manufacturing they organized was craftwork. Trade was not only the work of arranging exchanges of goods, it was also the activity that organized other economic activities. Manufacturers used to aspire to become merchants because merchants were the organizers. But now we do not find automobile manufacturers, say, aspiring to become dealers. Manufacturing now tends to be the economic activity around which other activities center, including many forms of trade and services. Manufacturing has become not only the work of making things, but also an activity that organizes other economic activities. This change has corresponded, in time, with the rise of mass-production manufacturing. For those who would like to see these movements shown schematically, a little diagram appears in Section V of the Appendix.

When Adam Smith looked at England, the most advanced economy of the eighteenth century, he found clues to future patterns of economic development. Mass production was not then the dominant form of manufacturing, but nevertheless Smith saw it as a coming thing. I think, from the symptoms to be observed, that the economy of the United States is in process of stagnating.* Nevertheless, it is still the most advanced economy to be found. Therefore, no matter what its own future may be, it is a suitable economy in which to look for clues to patterns that may be found in more highly developed economies of the future—wherever those economies may prove to be.

Garment making, I think, affords an interesting clue to future manufacturing because it exemplifies manufacturing of three distinctly different kinds. The oldest is craftwork, the method of hand tailors and seamstresses. It persists to this day in fine custom tailoring and in the work of couturiers. The second is mass production. This is the method used for making overalls, army uniforms, men's popularly priced shirts, most socks, nylon stockings, and many standard items of underclothing. Mass-production manufacturing of garments in the United States began in the 1860s. At that time, it would have appeared that garment manufacturing was to be done in a few very large organizations turning out highly standardized products. One of the first successes, described by Ishbel Ross in *Crusades and Crinolines*, was a small hoop skirt turned out in the factory of Ellen Demorest, a remarkable innovator of many developments in garment manufacturing, pattern manufacturing, and fashion journalism. The skirt she massproduced was "one of the wonders of the crinoline age and achieved immense popularity and distribution." A writer of the time, quoted by Miss Ross, said, "Madame Demorest deserves grateful remembrance for being the first to introduce a really excellent, cheap hoop skirt; and so popular did they immediately become, that other manufacturers were compelled to reduce their prices, although none have ever pretended to vie with these in cost, quality of material used, and amount of labor expended upon them." It was these skirts to which *Fortune* was referring in a survey of the New York garment industry almost

---

* I would not venture to prophesy how decisive this stagnation is. If it proves to be profound and unremitting, it could be comparable to that of the later Roman Empire or to that of many another economy in which revitalization, if it has occurred at all, has followed only upon revolution. If stagnation is still reversible in the United States, then by definition vigorous city-development processes not only can, but will, start into motion again.

a century later, when it noted that one-third of all those employed in the industry in New York in the 1860s worked in one establishment that made hoop skirts, "certainly the closest approach that there has even been to a General Motors in the [women's] clothing trade." While no one organization did come to dominate the mass-production clothing industry, the greatest successes in mass-produced garments were made by firms that concentrated upon finding large common denominators in the clothing market.

The third method of garment manufacturing has arisen chiefly during this century, has grown much more rapidly than the other two, and has become the dominant form. For lack of any present generic name, let us call it differentiated production. This method produces relatively modest amounts of each item as compared with mass production, yet it is not craft manufacturing either. In some ways it resembles mass-production work more than it resembles craft-work. Thanks to this third kind of garment making, one can look at a crowd of thousands of persons in a large city park on a fine day or gathered to watch a parade, and be hard put to find two women or two children dressed in identical outfits. One also sees in the same crowd more variety in men's clothing than one would have found a generation ago. This is the kind of garment manufacturing that used to amaze visiting Europeans; they took back the extraordinary news that even shopgirls and factory girls in the United States were fashionably clothed in a dazzling variety of dresses. Europeans now use this kind of manufacturing themselves. In America it is this manufacturing that renders the poor deceptively invisible, as Michael Harrington has pointed out. They do not wear a uniform of the poor, nor do they dress in rags. Because of their clothing, they look more prosperous than they are, an amazing economic achievement on the part of the garment industry.

The salient distinction between mass production and differentiated production is in the way the manufacturers look at the market—or, if one prefers, at the need for garments. A mass-production manufacturer seeks common denominators in the market; he exploits similar needs. A differentiated-production manufacturer depends on differences to be found in the market. He deliberately exploits the fact that people have differing tastes in styles, fabrics, and colors, differing clothing budgets and, as individuals, reasons for needing diverse clothing (e.g., garments for going to parties, lounging, sports, work, city activities, country activities). The two different approaches to the market give rise to other distinctions between mass production and differentiated production. Mass production churns out far greater numbers of identical items than does differentiated production. Much more design and development work goes into differentiated production than into mass production, in proportion to the volume of output.

Mass-production manufacturing introduces variations into total output only if great expansion in volume justifies variations which can also be produced in large volumes. A producer of black socks may devote part of his expanding volume to production of brown socks, much as automobile makers have introduced new models when their markets expanded. But the variations thus introduced in mass production are almost invariably superficial and they too are calculated to satisfy major common denominators in the potential market. The variations created through differentiated production are precisely what permit this production at all; *variations are not a result of expanded volume in differentiated production*, they are primary.

Consider, in this light, what has been happening to newspapers in the United States. The mass-production city dailies, aimed at common denominators in the market for newspapers, seem to have passed their heyday. They have declined steeply in number; many of those remaining have declined in circulation. In the meantime, city and suburban weekly newspapers have been growing rapidly both in number and circulation. The new weeklies aim at differences within the city newspaper markets. They carry news and features which are of vital importance or of interest to people in this or that district, but may be of little importance or interest elsewhere. Some cut across geography to aim at special communities of interest. These weeklies are not a return to the old-fashioned country and small-town weeklies run off on hand presses by their editors. In their production methods, the new papers are more like the mass-production newspapers. Nor are they, as a rule, culturally backward. Some make the mass-production newspapers seem old-fashioned in their writing, layouts, photography and subject matter. The weeklies are doing a job that was left undone, and that must inherently be left undone, in mass production. The reason the mass-production dailies are declining is not, however, that there are no significant similarities in a city's total market for news, but that the job once done by mass-production newspapers has been largely duplicated by television and radio news and feature programs, and by the mass-production weekly news magazines.

Also, there is a market for standard agricultural tractors and their accessories which are aimed at widespread similarities of needs among farmers, though this is no longer the kind of farm-equipment business that is growing appreciably. As far back as 1961, *Fortune* reported that the giant, mass-production farm-equipment manufacturers were in economic trouble. Their business was static or declining, and they were saddled with huge factories working below capacity and numerous retail outlets that no longer paid their way. The rapidly growing farm-equipment business was going disproportionately to more than a thousand small manufacturers who were aiming precisely at differences within the market. The big companies had stayed too long with "the mass concept," *Fortune* commented. "Less of [the farmers'] equipment money goes for the standard items . . . Today a small company can manufacture a highly specialized item of equipment just as easily as a large firm, and often at a better profit." Again, the relatively small-scale differentiated equipment production is not a return to craft methods.

In *The Silent Spring*, Rachel Carson attacked the practice of applying chemical pesticides wholesale—the mass-production approach to pest infestations. Instead, she advocated differentiated production based upon sophisticated biological controls of varying kinds, according to circumstances. This is a far cry from depending on the barnyard cat and the fly swatter, and resigning oneself to watching the locusts consume the year's work. It is a far more advanced approach than indiscriminate, wholesale use of chemicals. Miss Carson also advocated differentiation of crops within geographical localities, pointing out that mass production in farming itself—great factory farms devoted to one kind of cash crop—leads inherently to drastic imbalances of natural life and tends to increase the potential ravages of plant diseases and pests. (It also, I might add, can be economically disastrous to a rural region and often has been. A rural economy with all its eggs in one basket is bound

to lose out from changes in markets.) As we might expect, Miss Carson's point has been heeded first in cities. Not many years ago, for instance, New York City was using the mass-production approach to street-tree planting. All the trees planted were London planes which were raised in great mass-production tree nurseries. As Robert Nichols, a landscape architect, had been pointing out, some twenty different varieties of trees do quite as well as London planes on the city streets; but the city had been committed, under a powerful administrator, Robert Moses, to mass production in this as in all things affecting parks or supervised by the parks department. Now, realizing the wholesale disaster that a London plane tree blight would bring, the city has begun differentiated planting of street trees.

I have brought trees and agricultural equipment into this discussion not only because they illustrate that there is more reason to produce for differences than variations of whims or tastes, but also to show that differentiated production is not a luxury and another term for "custom made." Differentiated production, in spite of its disproportionate requirements for design and development work, is not an extravagance. In real life, real and important differences abound, whether in nature or in a market, whether in the resistance of trees to diseases or in the information about current events needed by people in differing districts. And with economic development all kinds of differentiations increase; they do not diminish.

For some economic needs, mass production is superb. The common denominators are valid and enduring. Mass production is well suited, for example, to brick manufacturing, making screwdrivers, bed sheets, paper, electric light bulbs, and telephones. I am not proposing that mass production will disappear from economic life. Farmers still need their standard tractors; people still need standard denim pants or their equivalents. The point is that for some goods, mass production is a makeshift. It represents only an early stage of development and is valid only as an inadequate expedient until more advanced differentiated production has been developed. Consider transportation. The automobile is overdepended upon as an expedient for replacing the still less adequate horse; it is largely a makeshift in lieu of still undeveloped types of vehicles and methods of surface transportation for short and long distance. Still, it is unlikely that the automobile will be supplanted by some other mass-produced vehicle. Rather, it will be supplanted by many different kinds of vehicles and many new kinds of transportation services based not upon crude common denominators of moving people and goods, but on differentiations. Nor will the automobile be wholly supplanted. It will be valid for some of these needs, although no doubt it will be radically changed and also more differentiated. Other vehicles will be completely different from automobiles. New forms of swift and smooth water travel will almost surely be developed, possibly making use of hydrofoils of many designs and sizes. These will first be used on waterways for express transportation within cities and between cities. Their manufacture will most likely begin in cities where they are used first.

In still other kinds of manufacturing, mass production is so unsuitable that it cannot be used even as an expedient. In such cases, if the industry is to develop at all, it must be based on differentiated production from the beginning. The electronics industries are an illustration of this kind of manufacturing. Many business analysts have pointed out that electronics manufacturing has developed differently from automobile manufacturing in which hundreds of enterprises were reduced to very few as the industry grew. The hundreds of early electronics enterprises did not reduce to a few huge mass-production companies. Instead, the hundreds increased to thousands and most have remained relatively small. The radical difference is not accidental. Electronics manufacturing is based only slightly on similarities of needs for electronic devices; it must satisfy immense numbers of diverse needs within the total market.

The construction industries have emerged only rather recently from the craft-manufacturing stage, of which many vestiges linger. As mass production became predominant in many other types of manufacturing, construction was a case of arrested development. Now construction seems to be arrested in the mass-production stage, although mass-production building is clearly a makeshift. For example, back in 1961 New York City proposed rebuilding the neighborhood in which I lived. The idea was to wipe out virtually every structure that occupied the land and mass-produce a new "neighborhood," formed for the most part of large, identical build-

ings. Even if the plan had been to construct identical small buildings it would have been the same approach in essence. The idea was to build for similarities of need, similarities of use and, by means of clearance, to impose similarities of sites that could accommodate mass-production construction. The project was to have cost an estimated $35,000,000. Because of the wholesale destruction of more than seven hundred already existing dwellings, the expenditure would have resulted in a net gain of about 300 dwelling units and a net loss of 156 businesses that employed about 2,500 persons. Some of these businesses might have relocated elsewhere, at additional economic costs not included in the $35,000,000, but most would have represented a total loss. They would have disappeared from the economy.

This scheme was defeated. Residents and property owners in the neighborhood, through their civic organization, the West Village Committee, then hired a firm of architects and planners and instructed them to work out a wholly different scheme. New buildings, gardens and public sidewalk plazas were to be added in already vacant sites, abandoned plots, and makeshift parking lots, without destroying a single existing dwelling or requiring the removal of any business, other than the random and usually illegal parking. The architects met these requirements by working out designs for three different sizes of relatively small buildings (most, of ten apartments each) that could be fitted into existing vacant and abandoned sites individually and in combinations. The buildings themselves were capable of many differentiations, not only into apartments of differing sizes, but also of differing uses such as retail stores and workshops. This scheme, costing an estimated $8,700,000 instead of $35,000,00 (both at 1964 prices), provided a net increase of 475 dwelling units, instead of 300, and destroyed no businesses. This second plan was a far cry from the old craft manufacturing of dwellings; indeed, it was designed to use a number of building techniques and materials more advanced than those being currently employed by mass-production builders. But it is a long way from mass-producing a neighborhood.*

---

* Apparently it was too advanced. Although the differentiated-production plan was prepared in 1962, and building could have begun that year

With growth of differentiated production in developing economies of the future, we may expect to find other changes in economic life. The average size of manufacturing enterprises will be smaller than at present. But the numbers of manufacturing enterprises will greatly increase and so will the total volume of manufactured goods. Most mass-production enterprises that have not been made obsolete by differentiated production—and many will remain—will have been transplanted to the countryside and into inert towns. There, with their low requirements of labor, their large requirements of space, and their relative self-sufficiency, these industries can operate more efficiently than in cities. Mass-production manufacturing will no longer be regarded as city work. Cities will manufacture even more goods than they do today, but these will be almost wholly differentiated production goods, made in relatively small, or very small, organizations.

Manufacturing work will, I think, no longer be the chief activity around which other economic activities are organized, as it is today and as the work of merchants once was. Instead, services will become the predominant organizational work, the instigators of other economic activities, including manufacturing. For an obvious example, consider what has been happening in the case of office machines. The older sorts—typewriters, dictating machines, adding machines and so on—are bought simply as machines. If a service is also bought along with them, it is a minor appendage: maintenance checking and repair, brief instructions to users of the machines, a trade-in service when a new machine is bought to replace an old one. But some of the new kinds of office machines are not

bought in this way, Rather, what is bought is first and foremost a service: the service of analyzing and programming the work of an office, such as billing, payroll preparation, and sales and inventory analyzing. The machines are bought as an appendage to accommodate the system prescribed by the analytical service. Sometimes the machines are not even bought. Instead, an office may buy services from a computer or data-processing center, and it will be the service organization that buys or leases the necessary machines. In either case, service work is the organizing activity for the other work, including the manufacturing of the machines.

It is not likely that manufacturers of vehicles will organize the transportation of the future, as they do now, to a considerable extent. The organizing forces, rather, will be transportation services, including even the services of renting differentiated automobiles for different purposes to individual users. The manufacturing will be done specifically to meet needs of these various services. When I was conjecturing, in Chapter Three [of Jacob's *The Economy of Cities*] how waste recycling systems might be organized in developing economies of the future, I suggested that services would be the key work in such industries, and that the service organizations would be customers for many kinds of waste-collecting equipment. This conjecture was based upon the logic of the work, but it corresponds to what I suspect is the coming trend in economic organization generally. Service organizations in developing economies of the future are likely to draw upon products made by many different manufacturers, and are likely to be larger than manufacturing organizations. Even so, they will begin as small businesses and expand as they add innovations.

No doubt, to English-speaking people of the future, especially if they happen to live in developing and highly advanced economies, it will seem quaint that "service" carries a connotation of servants' work, and even quainter that these economically important and awesomely large organizations should, in many cases, have sprung from such menial work as cleaning, minor maintenance, or chauffeuring. The case will seem, no doubt, as quaint as it seems to us that manufacturing arose upon servants' work, or that merchants originated from vagabonds and beggars

---

the city bureaucracies—whose philosophy and also rules and regulations were all shaped by the mass-production approach to construction and planning—opposed it adamantly until 1967, when they at last permitted it to begin inching its way through red tape, a process still under way as this is written. In the meantime, mass-production construction has continued, and vast amounts of money have of course been spent for an amazingly small yield of improved housing accommodations; the shortage of habitable housing has thus been increasing, not diminishing, as deterioration has outrun net construction.

who were even lowlier than the manorial servants of their time.

Economic Conflict

There is no point in pretending that economic development is in everyone's interest. Development of petroleum for lamp fuel was not good for the American whaling industry nor for those whose economic and social power were bound up with that industry. Development of new forms of public transit would not be good for today's petroleum industry or highway builders or automobile manufacturers, nor for anyone whose economic or social power is bound up with those industries. Development of economically important new goods and services by blacks would not be to the interests, as they see them, of white racists, including unconscious racists and paternalists.

In developing economies, even the well-established activities that are not directly affected adversely by new goods and services are indirectly affected, and so are the people whose economic and social power are tied up with those established activities. It is a question of sharing power. As an economy grows, its older, well-established economic interests grow less important and less powerful as a part of the whole. Furthermore, the most meteoric rises (starting at almost nothing) occur in new activities. The older activities do not necessarily decline in absolute size and wealth—indeed, they or their changing derivatives often expand in response to the general expansion—but they suffer at least a relative decline. And so do the people who derive their social and economic power from them. In Çatal Hüyük it is unlikely that the huntsmen ruled the roost as they must have at an earlier, remote time when there was no trading in the ancestral society and no way of getting food and craft materials other than hunting. The malapportioned state legislatures of the United States, elected by votes disproportionately weighted in favor of rural areas, small towns, and little stagnant cities, were an anachronism. But they were an accurate picture of political, social and economic power at the time apportionments were first made. And then they were clung to by precisely the groups in American life —the farmers, the people in inert towns—whose importance in the whole had declined as the rest of the economy developed more swiftly. In short, economic development, no matter when or where it occurs, is profoundly subversive of the status quo.

Marx thought that the principal conflict to be found in economic life, at any rate in industrialized countries, was the deep disparity of interests between owners and employees, but this is a secondary kind of conflict. If one accepts Marx's conception, then revolution should occur (as indeed he expected) in the most industrialized societies, rather than in economically backward and stagnant countries. Also, if one accepts his conception, much of the behavior of labor unions becomes impossible to understand. In real life, unions, once they have become institutionalized, can successfully deal with employers; and the interests of the two, to a large extent, then coincide. It is to the interests of construction workers that a great deal of construction be undertaken, and if this hurts other workers by wiping out the businesses to which their jobs are attached, so much the worse for them. It is also in the interests of labor unions that their industries should not change technologically; this, of course, often puts unions in conflict with employers—but even more so, in conflict with the interests of industries (and workers in those industries) that produce new technological devices. The inherent solidarity of the working class is an economic fiction.

Nor do the interests of already well-organized workers inherently correspond with the interests of those who have no well-established work to pursue, who are "redundant" in a stagnant economy, and thus short-changed on the goods and services they receive. Should the creativity of such people be allowed to flourish, it must change things as they are, upset the status quo, make some well-established activities obsolete and reduce the relative importance of others. Of course, the creativity of "redundant" people would make the economy develop, prosper and expand; but it is also a threat to all those workers and employers attached to activities potentially threatened by development. It is no accident that demands by blacks for control of ghetto education are desperately opposed not only by school boards (employers) but also by associations of school principals and by teachers' unions (employees); if anything, more inplacably by the latter than the former. That the change may be to the benefit of children, and might result in significant development of education, is beside the point to those threatened. To be sure, when almost no workers in an economy believe they are becoming better off, and almost all are coming to hate the status quo, they may join in an attack upon it. But an economy must already have become profoundly flawed before this occurs, especially if the assault is to succeed.

The primary economic conflict, I think, is between people whose interests are with already well-established economic activities, and those whose interests are with the emergence of new economic activities. This is a conflict that can never be put to rest except by economic stagnation. For the new economic activities of today are the well-established activities of tomorrow which will be threatened in turn by further economic development. In this conflict, other things being equal, the well-established activities and those whose interests are attached to them, must win. They are, by definition, the stronger. The only possible way to keep open the economic opportunities for new activities is for a "third force" to protect their weak and still incipient interests. Only governments can play this economic role. And sometimes, for pitifully brief intervals, they do. But because development subverts the status quo, the status quo soon subverts governments. When development has proceeded for a bit, and has cast up strong new activities, governments come to derive their power from those already well-established interests, and not from still incipient organizations, activities and interests.

In human history, most people in most places most of the time have existed miserably in stagnant economies. Developing economies have been the exceptions, and their histories, as developing economies, have been brief. Now here, now there, a group of cities grows vigorously by the processes I have been describing in this book and then lapses into stagnation for the benefit of people who have already become powerful. I am not one who believes that flying saucers carry creatures from other solar systems who poke curiously into our earthly affairs. But if such beings were to arrive, with their marvelously advanced contrivances, we may be sure we would be agog to learn how their tech-

nology worked. The important question however, would be something quite different: What kinds of governments had they invented which had succeeded in keeping open the opportunities for economic and technological development instead of closing them off? Without helpful advice from outer space, this remains one of the most pressing and least regarded problems.

Provided that some groups on earth continue either muddling or revolutionizing themselves into periods of economic development, we can be absolutely sure of a few things about future cities. The cities will not be smaller, simpler or more specialized than cities of today. Rather, they will be more intricate, comprehensive, diversified, and larger than today's, and will have even more complicated jumbles of old and new things than ours do. The bureaucratized, simplified cities, so dear to present-day city planners and urban designers, and familiar also to readers of science fiction and utopian proposals, run counter to the processes of city growth and economic development. Conformity and monotony, even when they are embellished with a froth of novelty, are not attributes of developing and economically vigorous cities. They are attributes of stagnant settlements. To some people, the vision of a future in which life is simpler than it is now, and work has become so routine as to be scarcely noticeable, is an exhilarating vision. To other people, it is depressing. But no matter. The vision is irrelevant for developing and influential economies of the future. In highly developed future economies, there will be more kinds of work to do than today, not fewer. And many people in great, growing cities of the future will be engaged in the unroutine business of economic trial and error. They will be faced with acute practical problems which we cannot now imagine. They will add new work to older work.

APPENDIX

IV. The two reciprocating systems of city growth

The various processes that have been diagramed operate as two major reciprocating systems. The first system is the process of simple export generating in a young city. Producers' goods and services become exports. The export multiplier increases the numbers and varieties of producers' goods and services. More producers' goods and services become exports, and so on, the process sustaining itself as indicated by the curved arrows. Simultaneously, the city's earned imports grow in volume and variety:

The second system is set in motion. Imports, having grown, are replaced. The versatile export generating of a large city becomes possible. So do subsequent episodes of import replacing:

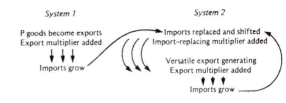

V. Changing patterns of economic activities

As suggested . . . , the predominant methods of manufacturing change as an economy develops. So do the kinds of activities around which—and also by which—other economic activities are organized. Let us correlate these changes, and also relate them to the situation in currently highly developed economies:

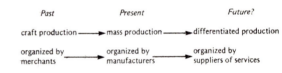

37

ANTHONY DOWNS

Alternative Futures for the American Ghetto

In the past few years, the so-called "ghetto" areas of large American cities have emerged as one of the major focal points of national and local concern. Yet there have been very few attempts to develop a comprehensive, long-run strategy for dealing with the complex forces that have created our explosive ghetto problems.

Historically, the word "ghetto" meant an area in which a certain identifiable group was compelled to live. The word retains this meaning of geographic constraint, but now refers to two different kinds of constraining forces. In its *racial* sense, a ghetto is an area to which members of an ethnic minority, particularly Negroes, are residentially restricted by social, economic, and physical pressures from the rest of society. In this meaning, a ghetto can contain wealthy and middle-income residents as well as poor ones. In its *economic* sense, a ghetto is an area in which poor people are compelled to live because they cannot afford better accommodations. In this meaning, a ghetto contains mainly poor people, regardless of race or color.

Considerable confusion arises from failure to distinguish clearly between these different meanings of the word "ghetto." In the remainder of this analysis, I will use the word in its racial sense unless otherwise noted.[1]

The Population of Ghettos

In March 1966, there were 12.5 million nonwhites living in all U.S. central cities, of whom 12.1 mil-

lion were Negroes. Since the Negroes were highly segregated residentially, this number serves as a good estimate of the 1966 ghetto population in the racial sense. Approximately 39 percent of these racial ghetto residents had incomes below the "poverty level" (the equivalent of $3,300 per year for a four-person household), based upon data for 1964 (the latest available).[2]

On the other hand, in 1964 the total number of persons with incomes below the "poverty level" in all U.S. central cities was about 10.1 million. Approximately 56 percent of these persons were white and 44 percent were nonwhite.[3] Since there were about 11.3 million nonwhites altogether in central cities in 1964, the ghetto in its purely economic sense contained about 11 percent fewer people than in its racial sense. Moreover, about 4.4 million persons were doubly ghetto residents in 1964—they were central-city citizens who were both poor and nonwhite.[4]

No matter which ghetto definition is used, it is clear that the population of ghettos is a small fraction of total U.S. population—less than 7 percent. Moreover, future growth in the ghetto population will be dwarfed by future growth in the suburbs of metropolitan areas, which are predominantly white. From 1960 through 1980, those suburbs will gain about 40.9 million persons.[5] Thus the *growth* of suburban population in this period will be almost twice as large as the *total size* of all U.S. ghettos by 1980.

Any policies designed to cope with the ghetto must recognize that the concentrations of Negro population in our central cities are growing rapidly. In 1950, there were 6.5 million Negroes in central cities. In 1960, there were 9.7 million. This represents an increase of 49.2 percent, or an average of 320,000 persons per year. In the same

Anthony Downs, "Alternative Futures for the American Ghetto," *Daedalus*, vol. 97, no. 4 (Fall 68), pp. 1331–1378. Reprinted by permission.

decade, the white population of central cities went from 45.5 million to 47.7 million, an increase of 2.2 million, or 4.8 percent. However, in the largest central cities, the white population actually declined while the Negro population rose sharply.[6]

Since 1960, the growth of nonwhite population in central cities has continued unabated. White population growth in all those cities taken together has, however, ceased entirely. In 1966 the total Negro population of all central cities was about 12.1 million. This is a gain of 2.4 million since 1960, or about 400,000 persons per year. Thus the *absolute* rate of growth of ghettos per year has gone up to its highest level in history. In contrast, the white population of central cities in 1965 was 46.4 million, or 1.3 million *less* than in 1960. So for all 224 central cities considered as a whole, all population growth now consists of gains in Negro population.[7]

Moreover, nearly all Negro population growth is now occurring in ghettos, rather than in suburbs or rural areas. From 1960 to 1966, 89 percent of all nonwhite population growth was in central cities, and 11 percent was in suburbs. Nonmetropolitan areas (including the rural South) actually *lost* nonwhite population. This indicates that heavy out-migration from rural areas to cities is still going on.[8]

Future Ghetto Growth
If Present Policies Continue

All evidence points to the conclusion that future nonwhite population growth will continue to be concentrated in central cities unless major changes in public policies are made. Not one single significant program of any federal, state, or local government is aimed at altering this tendency or is likely to have the unintended effect of doing so.[9] Moreover, although nonwhite fertility rates have declined since 1957 along with white fertility rates, ghetto growth is likely to remain rapid because of continued in-migration, as well as natural increase.

Recent estimates made by the National Advisory Commission on Civil Disorders indicate that the central-city Negro population for the whole U.S. will be about 13.6 million in 1970 and could rise to as high as 20.3 million by 1985. These estimates assume continued nonwhite in-migration at about the same rate as prevailed from 1960 to 1966. But even if net in-migration

is reduced to zero, the 1985 central-city Negro population would be about 17.3 million.[10]

Within individual cities, rapid expansion of segregated ghetto areas will undoubtedly continue. Our 1967 field surveys in Chicago show that about 2.9 city blocks *per week* are shifting from predominantly white to nonwhite occupancy, mainly on the edge of already nonwhite areas. This is somewhat lower than the 3.5 blocks-per-week average from 1960 to 1966, but above the average of 2.6 from 1950 to 1960.[11] If such "peripheral spread" of central-city ghettos continues at nearly the same rate—and there is no present reason to believe it will not—then a number of major central cities will become over 50 percent Negro in total population by 1985. These cities include Chicago, Philadelphia, St. Louis, Detroit, Cleveland, Oakland, Baltimore, New Orleans, Richmond, and Jacksonville. Washington, D.C., Newark, and Gary are already over 50 percent Negro. The proportion of nonwhites in the public school systems in most of these cities now exceeds 50 percent. It will probably be approaching 90 percent by 1983—unless major changes in school programs and districting are adopted before then.[12]

This future growth has critical implications for a great many policy objectives connected with ghettos. For example, it has been suggested that school district boundaries within central cities should be manipulated so as to counteract *de facto* segregation by creating districts in which many Negroes and many whites will jointly reside. This solution is practical over the long run only when there is reasonable stability in the total size of these two groups. But when one group is rapidly expanding in a city where there is no vacant land to build additional housing, then the other group must contract. The only alternative is sharp rises in density which are now occurring. Therefore, as the Negro population expands in such cities, the white population inevitably falls. So possibilities for ending *de facto* segregation in this manner inexorably shrink as time passes. For this and other reasons, no policy toward ghettos can afford to ignore this rapid expansion of the Negro population.

The Complexity of the Ghetto
Population and Ghetto Problems

To be accurate, every analysis of ghettos and their problems must avoid two tempting oversimplifications. The first is conceiving of the ghetto population as a single homogeneous group, all of whose members have similar characteristics, attitudes, and desires. Thus, because many ghetto residents are unemployed or "underemployed" in low-paying, transient jobs, it is easy—but false—to think of all ghetto households as plagued by unemployment. Similarly, because some ghetto residents have carried out riots and looting, whites frequently talk as though *all* ghetto dwellers hate whites, are prone to violence, or are likely to behave irresponsibly. Yet all careful studies of recent riots show that only a small minority of ghetto residents participated in any way, a majority disapprove of such activity, and most would like to have more contact with whites and more integration.[13]

In reality, each racial ghetto contains a tremendous variety of persons who exhibit widely differing attitudes toward almost every question. Many are very poor, but just as many are not. Many have radical views—especially young people; many others are quite conservative—especially the older people. Many are "on welfare," but many more are steadily employed.

This diversity means that public policy concerning any given ghetto problem cannot be successful if it is aimed at or based upon the attitudes and desires of only one group of persons affected by that problem. For example, take unemployment. Programs providing job training for young people could, if expanded enough, affect a large proportion of ghetto dwellers. But the inability of many adult ghetto men to obtain and keep steady, well-paying jobs is also a critical ghetto problem.[14] Also, many women with children cannot work because no adequate day-care facilities are available. Thus, public policy concerning every ghetto problems must have many complex facets in order to work well.

A second widely prevalent oversimplification of ghetto problems is concentration of remedial action upon a single substandard condition. For instance, improving the deplorable housing conditions in many slums would not in itself eliminate most of the dehumanizing forces which operate there. In fact, no single category of programs can possibly be adequate to cope with the tangled problems that exist in ghettos. Any effective ghetto-improvement strategy must concern itself with at least jobs and employment, education, housing, health, personal safety, crime prevention, and income maintenance for dependent persons. A number of other programs

could be added, but I believe these are the most critical.[15]

The Location of New Jobs

Most new employment opportunities are being created in the suburban portions of our metropolitan areas, not anywhere near central-city ghettos.[16] Furthermore, this trend is likely to continue indefinitely into the future. It is true that downtown office-space concentrations in a few large cities have created additional jobs near ghettos. But the outflow of manufacturing and retailing jobs has normally offset this addition significantly—and in many cases has caused a net loss of jobs in central cities.

If we are going to provide jobs for the rapidly expanding ghetto population, particularly jobs that do not call for high levels of skills, we must somehow bring these potential workers closer to the locations of new employment opportunities. This can be done in three ways: by moving job locations so new jobs are created in the ghetto, by moving ghetto residents so they live nearer the new jobs, or by creating better transportation between the ghetto and the locations of new jobs. The first alternative—creating new jobs in the ghetto—will not occur in the future under normal free-market conditions, in my opinion.

That nearly all *new* job opportunities will be located in suburbs does not mean that central cities cannot provide *any* employment to their Negro residents. There are still millions of jobs located in central cities. Just the turnover in workers regarding those jobs will open up a great many potential positions for Negro central-city residents in the future—if employers and other workers cease racial discrimination in their hiring and promotion practices. Nevertheless, as the total numbers of Negro central-city job-seekers steadily rises, the need to link them with emerging sources of new employment in the suburbs will become more and more urgent as a means of reducing unemployment in Negro neighborhoods.

Recently, a number of proposals have been advanced to create public subsidies or guaranteed profits encouraging free enterprise to locate new jobs in ghettos.[17] It is possible that they might work to some extent if the promised profits are high enough to offset the risks and disadvantages involved. Any ghetto improvement strategy must, however, face the problem of linking up persons who need employment with those firms which can provide it or those public agencies assigned to create it.

The Future "Cost Squeeze" on Local Governments

Traditionally, individual productivity has risen faster in the manufacturing, mining, construction, and agricultural sectors of our economy than in sectors where personal services are dominant—such as finance, insurance, and real estate; retailing; services; and government. The ability to employ larger amounts of capital per worker, coupled with technological change, has caused much larger increases in hourly output-per-worker in the former sectors than in the latter.

All sectors compete with one another for talent and personnel, and all use many of the same products as basic inputs. This means that wages and salaries in the service-dominated sectors must generally keep up with those in the capital-dominated sectors. This tends to place a "squeeze" on the cost of those activities for which individual productivity is hard to increase.

A recent analysis of the performing arts by economists William Baumol and William Bowen highlighted this type of "cost squeeze" as the major reason why it is so difficult to sustain theaters, opera, symphonies, and ballet companies on a self-supporting basis.[18] A pianist cannot perform Chopin's Minute Waltz in 30 seconds, or spend half as much time learning how to play it, to improve efficiency. Yet his salary and the salaries of all the electricians, accompanists, administrators, and others needed for the performing arts are constantly raised to keep their living standards comparable with those of people in the sectors where wage gains can be offset by productivity increases.

Baumol has argued that a similar "cost squeeze" is one of the reasons why state and local expenditures have risen so fast in the postwar period. They increased 257 percent from 1950 to 1966, as compared to 159 percent for Gross National Product and 206 percent for federal expenditures.[19] Moreover, Baumol believes that this pressure to increase service-oriented wages and salaries faster than real output-per-man-hour in the service-oriented sectors will generate an even bigger "explosion" of local and state government costs in the future. For one thing, a higher fraction of society is now and will be employed in public activities than ever before. So there is a steady increase in the proportion of persons whose compensation tends to rise faster than their real output. This reflects both rapid automation in non-service-oriented sectors and an increasing shift of consumer demand toward such services as education, entertainment, and government activities of all types.

The resulting upward pressure on local and state government costs—and tax needs—will undoubtedly be offset to some extent by two forces. The first is greater automation of services themselves through use of computers, closed-circuit TV, duplicating machines, and other devices. The second is the partial substitution of semi-skilled and low-skilled assistants for highly-skilled professionals. For example, teachers' aids could relieve professional teachers of immense amounts of administration and paperwork, thereby freeing the latter for more effective use of their time.

Nevertheless, the huge future growth of suburban population will almost certainly force a continuance of the trend toward rising local and state taxes that has now gone on for twenty years. Similar upward pressure on revenue needs will be felt even more strongly by central-city governments. Center cities will contain ever higher proportions of low-income residents who need more services per capita than wealthier suburbanites.

This future "cost squeeze" is important to our analysis because of its impact upon the willingness of suburban taxpayers to help finance any large-scale programs aimed at improving ghetto conditions. Such programs would almost certainly require significant income redistribution from the relatively wealthy suburban population to the relatively poor central-city population. Yet suburbanites will be experiencing steadily rising local and state tax burdens to pay for the services they need themselves.

The "Law of Dominance"

The achievement of stable racial integration of both whites and nonwhites in housing or public schools is a rare phenomenon in large American cities. Contrary to the views of many, this is *not* because whites are unwilling to share schools or residential neighborhoods with nonwhites. A vast majority of whites of all income groups would be willing to send their children to integrated schools or live in integrated neighborhoods, *as long as they were sure that the white group concerned would remain in the majority* in those facilities or areas.

The residential and educational objectives of these whites are not dependent upon their maintaining any kind of "ethnic purity" in their neighborhoods or schools. Rather, those objectives depend upon their maintaining a certain degree of "cultural dominance" therein.[20] These whites—like most other middle-class citizens of any race—want to be sure that the social, cultural, and economic milieu and values of their own group dominate their own residential environment and the educational environment of their children. This desire in turn springs from the typical middle-class belief of all racial groups that everyday life should be primarily a *value-reinforcing* experience for both adults and children, rather than primarily a *value-altering* one. The best way to ensure that this will happen is to isolate somewhat oneself and one's children in an everyday environment dominated by—but not necessarily exclusively comprised of—other families and children whose social, economic, cultural, and even religious views and attitudes are approximately the same as one's own.

There is no intrinsic reason why race or color should be perceived as a factor relevant to attaining such relative homogeneity. Clearly, race and color have no necessary linkage with the kinds of social, cultural, economic, or religious characteristics and values that can have a true functional impact upon adults and children. Yet I believe a majority of middle-class white Americans still perceive race and color as relevant factors in their assessment of the kind of homogeneity they seek to attain. Moreover, this false perception is reinforced by their lack of everyday experience and contact with Negroes who are, in fact, like them in all important respects. Therefore, in deciding whether a given neighborhood or a given school exhibits the kind of environment in which "their own" traits are and will remain dominant, they consider Negroes as members of "another" group.

It is true that some people want themselves and their children to be immersed in a wide variety of viewpoints, values, and types of people, rather than a relatively homogeneous group.[21] This desire is particularly strong among the intellectuals who dominate the urban planning profession. They are also the strongest supporters of big-city life and the most vitriolic critics of suburbia. Yet I believe their viewpoint—though dominant in recent public discussions of urban problems—is actually shared by only a tiny minority of Americans of any racial group. Almost everyone favors at least some exposure to a wide variety of viewpoints. But experience in our own society and most others shows that the overwhelming majority of middle-class families choose residential locations and schools precisely in order to provide the kind of value-reinforcing experience described above. This is why most Jews live in predominantly Jewish neighborhoods, even in suburbs; why Catholic parents continue to support separate school systems; and partly why so few middle-class Negro families have been willing to risk moving to all-white suburbs even where there is almost no threat of any harassment.

However demeaning this phenomenon may be to Negroes, it must be recognized if we are to understand why residential segregation has persisted so strongly in the United States, and what conditions are necessary to create viable racial integration. The expansion of nonwhite residential areas has led to "massive transition" from white to nonwhite occupancy mainly because there has been no mechanism that could assure the whites in any given area that they would remain in the majority after nonwhites once began entering. Normal population turnover causes about 20 percent of the residents of the average U.S. neighborhood to move out every year because of income changes, job transfers, shifts in life-cycle position, or deaths. In order for a neighborhood to retain any given character, the persons who moved in to occupy the resulting vacancies must be similar to those who have departed.

But once Negroes begin entering an all-white neighborhood near the ghetto, most other white families become convinced that the area will eventually become all Negro, mainly because this has happened so often before. Hence it is difficult to persuade whites not now living there to move in and occupy vacancies. They are only willing to move into neighborhoods where whites are now the dominant majority and seem likely to remain so. Hence the whites who would otherwise have moved in from elsewhere stop doing so.[22] This means that almost all vacancies are eventually occupied by nonwhites, and the neighborhood inexorably shifts toward a heavy nonwhite majority. Once this happens, the remaining whites also seek to leave, since they do not wish to remain in an area where they have lost their culturally dominant position.

As a result, whites who would be quite satisfied—even delighted—to live in an integrated neighborhood *as members of the majority* are never given the opportunity to do so. Instead, for reasons beyond the control of each individual, they are forced to choose between complete segregation or living in an area heavily dominated by members of what they consider "another group." Given their values, they choose the former.

Many—especially Negroes—may deplore the racially prejudiced desire of most white middle-class citizens to live in neighborhoods and use schools where other white middle-class households are dominant. Nevertheless, this desire seems to be firmly entrenched among most whites at present. Hence public policy cannot ignore this desire if it hopes to be effective. Moreover, this attitude does not preclude the development of racial integration, as long as whites are in the majority and believe they will remain so. The problem is convincing them that their majority status will persist in mixed areas in the face of past experience to the contrary. Even more difficult, the people who must be persuaded are not those now living in a mixed area, but those who must keep moving in from elsewhere to maintain racial balance as vacancies occur through normal population turnover.

Clearly, the dynamic processes related to this "Law of Dominance" are critical to any strategy concerning the future of American ghettos. They are especially relevant to strategies which seek to achieve stable residential or educational integration of whites and nonwhites, instead of the "massive transition" and "massive segregation" which have dominated the spatial patterns of non-white population growth in the past twenty years. Such stable integration will occur in most areas only if there is some way to guarantee the white majority that it will remain the "dominant" majority. This implies some form of "quotas" concerning the proportion of nonwhites in the facility or area concerned—even legally supported "quotas."

Unless some such "balancing devices" are *explicitly* used and reinforced by public policies

and laws to establish their credibility, whites will continue to withdrew from—or, more crucially, fail to keep entering—any facility or area into which significant numbers of nonwhites are entering. This means a continuation of *de facto* segregation and a reinforcement of the white belief that any nonwhite entry inevitably leads to "massive transition." Even more importantly, it means continued failure to eliminate white perception of race as a critical factor by encouraging whites and nonwhites to live together in conditions of stability. Thus, in my opinion, the only way to destroy the racial prejudice at the root of the "Law of Cultural Dominance" is to shape current public policy in recognition of that "Law" so as to encourage widespread experience that will undermine it.[23]

The Concept of Social Strategy

Americans typically do not attempt to solve social problems by means of behavior patterns that could reasonably be considered "strategies." The concept of strategy implies development of a single comprehensive, long-range plan to cope with some significant social problem. But U.S. decision-making concerning domestic issues is too fragmented and diffused to permit the formulation of any such long-range plan regarding a given problem. Instead, we approach most social problems through a process which has been aptly labeled "disjointed incrementalism."[24] Each decision-maker or actor makes whatever choices seem to him to be the most appropriate at that moment, in light of his own interests and his own view of the public welfare. For two reasons, he pays little attention to most of the consequences of his action upon others—especially the long-run consequences. First, no one has the detailed knowledge and foresight necessary to comprehend all those consequences. Second, no one has the time nor the energy to negotiate in advance with all others likely to be affected by his actions. So instead he acts "blindly" and waits for those who are hurt to complain or those who are benefited to applaud.

A process of mutual adjustment ensues. Those who are unduly harmed by each decision supposedly recoup their losses by exercising whatever economic, moral, or political powers are available to them. Those who benefit use their powers to encourage more of the same. Presiding over this melee is a set of mainly "reactive" governments and other public agencies. They keep altering the "rules of the game" and their own programs and behavior so as to correct any grievous imbalances that appear.

There is no guarantee that the checks and balances built into this uncoordinated process will effectively counteract every destructive condition or trend that emerges from it. It is certainly possible that each individual will be motivated by the incentives facing him to take actions that, when combined with those taken by others acting in a similar individualistic fashion, will lead to collective disaster.

So far in history, the system has been remarkably effective at avoiding such outcomes. Part of this success undoubtedly results from society's ability to generate in most of its citizens a single set of basic values and even broad policy objectives that exert a cohesive influence on their supposedly individualistic decisions. But another important ingredient in the system's success is the ability of enough signficant actors in it to perceive threatening trends in time to formulate and carry out ameliorating policies.

This means they must accurately forecast any potentially dire outcome of current trends. They must also visualize alternative outcomes that would be preferable and are within the capabilities of society. Finally, they must devise policies and programs that will shift individual incentives so one of those alternatives will occur. In some cases, the ongoing trends that threaten society are strongly entrenched in its institutional structure. If so, alternatives that avoid the pending threats may not be attainable without fundamental changes in institutions. Those changes in turn may be possible only if a preponderance of powerful people in society share at least a broad concept of the need for change and the kinds of objectives motivating it. This concept closely resembles a social strategy. It visualizes a certain desired outcome, implies a wide range of policies by various actors necessary to attain that outcome, and serves as a "hidden coordinator" of seemingly individualistic behavior. The above reasoning implies two conclusions crucial to this analysis. First, strategic thinking about social problems can play a vital role in stimulating social change even where decision-making is dominated by disjointed incrementalism. Second, the alternative outcomes conceived such thinking can usefully include some which

could not be achieved without major changes in existing institutions or values. For example, some of the strategies discussed herein require a highly coordinated set of policy decisions. Such coordination is unlikely to occur in the presently fragmentalized governmental structures of our metropolitan areas unless major changes in the incentives facing these governments are created.

I will therefore formulate several alternative strategies for coping with the problems posed by future ghetto growth, even though carrying out some of them would require a far more consciously coordinated development of social change than has been typical of America in the past.

Formulation of Major Alternative Strategies

Because of the immense complexity of our society, an infinite number of alternative future strategies regarding ghettos could conceivably be designed. But for purposes of practical consideration, this number must be narrowed drastically to a few that highlight the major choices facing us. Selecting these few is inescapably arbitrary—there is no "scientific" way to do it. I believe, however, that the narrowing of alternative ghetto futures can best be accomplished by focusing upon the major choices relating to the following three questions:

- To what extent should future nonwhite population growth be concentrated within the central cities, as it has been in the past twenty years?
- To what extent should our white and nonwhite populations be residentially segregated from each other in the future?
- To what extent should society redistribute income to relatively depressed urban areas or population groups in society in a process of "enrichment"?

Each of these questions can be answered with any one of a whole spectrum of responses from one extreme to the other. But for purposes of analysis, I believe we can usefully narrow these answers down to just two points on the spectrum for each question. This allows us to reduce the alternatives to the following:

Degree-of-Concentration Alternatives
1. Continue to concentrate nonwhite population growth in central cities or perhaps in a few

older suburbs next to central cities. (*Concentration*)

2. Disperse nonwhite population growth widely throughout all parts of metropolitan areas. (*Dispersal*)

Degree-of-Segregation Alternatives

1. Continue to cluster whites and nonwhites in residentially segregated neighborhoods, regardless of where they are within the metropolitan area. (*Segregation*)
2. Scatter the nonwhite population, or at least a significant fraction of it, "randomly" among white residential areas to achieve at least partial residential integration. (*Integration*)

Degree-of-Enrichment Alternatives

1. Continue to provide relatively low-level welfare, educational, housing, job-training, and other support to the most deprived groups in the population—both those who are incapable of working, such as the vast majority of public-aid recipients, and those who might possibly work, but are unemployed because of lack of skills, discrimination, lack of desire, or any other reason. (*Non-enrichment*)
2. Greatly raise the level of support to welfare, educational, housing, job-training, and other programs for the most deprived groups, largely through federally aided programs. (*Enrichment*)

Even narrowing the alternatives in this fashion leaves a logical possibility of eight different combinations. A number of these can, however, be ruled out as internally inconsistent in practice. For example, I believe it is extremely unlikely that any strategy of dispersing the nonwhite population throughout metropolitan areas could be accomplished without provision of substantially greater incentives to both nonwhites (to get them to move) and whites (to increase their willingness to accept large numbers of nonwhite in-migrants without strong resistance). Thus no combination of both dispersal and non-enrichment need be considered.

Similarly, in the very long run, concentration of future nonwhite population growth within central cities is probably inconsistent with integration. Many of those cities will become so preponderantly nonwhite that integration within their borders will be impossible. Admittedly, it may take two or more decades for this to occur in some central cities, and it might never occur in others. Nevertheless, some types of integration (such as in the public schools) will become

impossible long before that if a concentration policy is followed. For these reasons, I will consider only one special combination containing both concentration and integration. This consists of continued concentration, but a build-up of a gradually expanding inner-city core of fully integrated housing and public facilities created through massive urban renewal. For reasons explained below, this strategy would require a significant enrichment program too.

This whole process of elimination leaves five basic alternative strategies relevant to future development of ghettos. For convenience, each has been assigned a short name to be used throughout the remainder of this article. These strategies can be summarized as follows:

1. *Present Policies:* concentration, segregation, non-enrichment.
2. *Enrichment Only:* concentration, segregation, enrichment.
3. *Integrated Core:* concentration, integration (in the center only), enrichment.
4. *Segregated Dispersal:* dispersal, segregation, enrichment.
5. *Integrated Dispersal:* dispersal, integration, enrichment.

Before these strategies are examined in detail two things about them should be emphasized.

First, they apply to individual metropolitan areas. Therefore, it would be at least theoretically impossible to adopt different strategies toward the ghetto in different metropolitan areas. There are, in fact, some convincing reasons why this would be an excellent idea.

Second, these strategies are formed from relatively extreme points on the relevant ranges of possibilities. Hence they could actually be adopted in various mixtures, rather than in the "pure" forms set forth above. This further strengthens the case for using a variety of approaches across the country. For purposes of analysis, however, it is fruitful to examine each of these strategies initially as though it were to be the sole instrument for coping with ghetto problems in all metropolitan areas.

The Present-Policies Strategy

In order to carry out this strategy, we need merely do nothing more than we do now. Even existing federal programs aimed at aiding cities

—such as the Model Cities Program—will continue or accelerate concentration, segregation, and non-enrichment, unless those programs are colossally expanded.

I do not wish to imply that present federal and local efforts in the anti-poverty program, the public housing program, the urban renewal program, health programs, educational programs, and many others are not of significant benefit to residents of ghettos. They are. Nevertheless, as both recent investigations and recent violence have emphasized, existing programs have succeeded neither in stemming the various adverse trends operating in ghetto areas nor in substantially eliminating the deplorable conditions there. Therefore, the strategy of continuing our present policies and our present level of effort is essentially not going to alter current conditions in ghettos.

This may make it seem silly to label continuation of present policies as a specific antighetto strategy. Yet failure to adopt effective policies is still a strategy. It may not be a successful one, but it nevertheless is an expression of society's current commitment and attitude toward the ghetto.

Thus, if we maintain our current programs and policies, segregated areas of residence in our central cities will continue to expand rapidly and to suffer from all the difficult problems inherent in both racial and economic ghettos.

The Enrichment-Only Strategy

The second fundamental ghetto future strategy I call "enrichment only." This approach is aimed at dramatically improving the quality of life within the confines of present ghetto areas and those nearby areas into which ghettos will expand in the future if concentration continues. I presume that any such policy would apply to the poverty meaning of ghetto more than the racial one—that is, any enrichment strategy would aim at upgrading the lowest-income and most disadvantagd citizens of our central cities, regardless of race. Nevertheless, a sizable proportion of such persons are nonwhites. Moreover, programs aimed at reducing racial discrimination in employment and in the quality of public services would form an important part of any strategy aimed at upgrading the most deprived groups. So the enrichment-only strategy would still concentrate upon the same areas as if it were to follow a racial policy.

The basic idea underlying the enrichment-only strategy (and part of every other strategy involving enrichment) is to develop federally financed programs that would greatly improve the education, housing, incomes, employment and job-training, and social services received by ghetto residents. This would involve vastly expanding the scale of present programs, changing the nature of many of them because they are now ineffective or would be if operated at a much larger scale, and creating incentives for a much greater participation of private capital in ghetto activities. Such incentives could include tax credits for investments made in designated ghetto areas, wage subsidies (connected with on-the-job training but lasting longer than such training so as to induce employers to hire unskilled ghetto residents), rent or ownership supplements for poor families, enabling them to rent or buy housing created by private capital, and others.[25]

It is important to realize that the enrichment-only strategy would end neither racial segregation nor the concentration of nonwhites in central cities (and some older adjoining suburbs). It would help many Negroes attain middle-class status and thus make it easier for them to leave the ghetto if they wanted to. Undoubtedly many would. But, by making life in central-city ghettos more attractive without creating any strong pressures for integration or dispersal of the nonwhite population, such a policy would increase the in-migration of nonwhites into central cities. This would speed up the expansion of racially segregated areas in central cities, thereby accelerating the process of "massive transition" of whole neighborhoods from white to nonwhite occupancy.

The Integrated-Core Strategy

This strategy is similar to the enrichment-only strategy because both would attempt to upgrade the quality of life in central-city ghettos through massive federally assisted programs. The integrated-core strategy would also seek, however, to eliminate racial segregation in an ever expanding core of the city by creating a socially, economically, and racially integrated community there. This integrated core would be built up through large-scale urban renewal programs, with the land re-uses including scattered-site public housing, middle-income housing suitable for families with children, and high-quality public services—especially schools.

All of these re-uses would be based upon "managed integration"—that is, deliberate achievement of a racial balance containing a majority of whites but a significant minority of Negroes. Thus, the integrated-core strategy could be carried out only if deliberate racial discrimination aimed at avoiding *de facto* segregation becomes recognized by the Supreme Court as a legitimate tactic for public agencies. In fact, such recognition will probably be a necessity for any strategy involving a significant degree of integration in public schools, public housing, or even private residential areas. This conclusion was recently recognized by the Chicago Board of Education, its staff, and its consultants, who all recommended the use of quotas in schools located in racially changing neighborhoods to promote stable integration.[26]

The integrated-core strategy essentially represents a compromise between an ideal condition and two harsh realities. The ideal condition is development of a fully integrated society in which whites and Negroes live together harmoniously and the race of each individual is not recognized by anyone as a significant factor in any public or private decisions.

The first harsh reality is that the present desire of most whites to dominate their own environment means that integration can only be achieved through deliberate management and through the willingness of some Negroes to share schools and residences as a minority. The second harsh reality is the assumption that it will be impossible to disperse the massive Negro ghettos of major central cities fast enough to prevent many of those cities from eventually becoming predominantly, or even almost exclusively, Negro in population. The development of predominantly Negro central cities, with high proportions of low-income residents, ringed by predominantly white suburbs with much wealthier residents, might lead to a shattering polarization that would split society along both racial and spatial lines.

This strategy seeks to avoid any such polarization by building an integrated core of white and nonwhites in central cities, including many leaders of both races in politics, business, and civic affairs. Negro leadership will properly assume the dominant position in central-city politics in many major cities after Negroes have become a majority of the municipal electorates there. By that time, integration of leadership within those cities will, it is to be hoped, have become a sufficient reality so that leaders of both races can work together in utilizing the central city's great economic assets, rather than fighting one another for control over them.

Thus, the integrated-core strategy postulates that a significant movement toward racial integration is essential to keep American society from "exploding" as a result of a combined racial-spatial confrontation of central cities vs. suburbs in many large metropolitan areas. It also postulates that development of integration in the suburbs through massive dispersal cannot occur fast enough to avoid such a confrontation. Therefore, integration must be developed on an "inside-out" basis, starting in the core of the central city, rather than in the suburbs.

The Concept of Dispersal

The two dispersal strategies concerning the future of ghettos are both based upon a single key assumption: that the problems of ghettos cannot be solved so long as millions of Negroes, particular those with low incomes and other significant disadvantages, are required or persuaded to live together in segregated ghetto areas within our central cities. These strategies contend that large numbers of Negroes should be given strong incentives to move voluntarily from central cities into suburban areas, including those in which no Negroes presently reside.

To illustrate what "large numbers" really means, let us postulate one version of dispersal which I call the "constant-size ghetto strategy." This strictly hypothetical strategy aims at stopping the growth of existing central-city ghettos by dispersing enough Negroes from central cities to the suburbs (or to peripheral central-city areas) to offset potential future increases in that growth. Taking the period from 1970 through 1975, estimates made by the National Advisory Commission on Civil Disorders show that the nonwhite population of all U.S. central cities taken as a whole would, in the absence of any dispersal strategy, expand from about 13.6 million to about 15.5 million.[27] Thus, if dispersal of nonwhites were to take place at a scale larg enough to keep central-city racial ghettos at their 1970 level during the five subsequent years, there would have to be an out-movement of 1.9 million Negroes into the suburbs. This amounts to 380,000 per year.

From 1950 to 1960, the suburban Negro population of all U.S. metropolitan areas grew a total of only 60,000 per year. In that decade, the white population of suburban portions of our metropolitan areas (the so-called "urban fringe") increased by about 1,720,000 persons per year. Thus, 96.6 percent of all suburban population growth consisted of whites. From 1960 to 1966, the Negro population growth in all suburban areas declined sharply to a rate of 33,300 per year. In fact, there was actually in-migration of Negroes from suburbs to central cities. But the white population in all suburbs went up an average of 1,750,000 per year. Thus the proportion of suburban growth made up of whites climbed to 98.1 percent—an even higher fraction than in the decade from 1950 to 1960.[28] Undoubtedly, some of this white population increase was caused by an exodus of whites from central cities in response to the growth therein. If future Negro population growth in central cities were stopped by a large-scale dispersion policy, then white population growth in the suburbs would be definitely smaller than it was from 1950 through 1966. The size of the resulting decline would depend upon the fraction of white exodus from central cities that occurs in response to Negro growth, as opposed to such other factors as rising incomes, the aging central-city housing stock, and shifts in life-cycle position. If whites leave central cities in a one-to-one ratio with the expansion of Negro population therein, then a cessation of Negro ghetto growth would result in a large drop in white suburban growth. In that case, future suburban population increases would consist of about 23 percent Negroes (based on very rough calculations). This contrasts with proportions of less than 5 percent from 1950 through 1960 and less than 3 percent from 1960 through 1966.

Clearly, such dispersal would represent a radical change in existing trends. Not only would it stop the expansion of Negro ghettos in central cities, but it would also inject a significant Negro population into many presently all-white suburban areas. It is true that policies of dispersal would not necessarily have to be at this large scale. Dispersal aimed not at stopping ghetto growth, but merely at slowing it down somewhat could be carried out at a much lower scale. Yet even such policies would represent a marked departure from past U.S. practice.

Such a sharp break with the past would be necessary for any significant dispersal of Negroes. Merely providing the *opportunity* for Negroes to move out of ghettos would, at least in the short run, not result in many moving. Even adoption of a vigorously enforced nationwide open-occupancy law applying to *all* residences would not greatly speed up the present snail's-pace rate of dispersion. Experience in those states that have open-occupancy ordinances decisively proves this conclusion.

Hence, positive incentives for dispersion would have to be created in order to speed up the rate at which Negroes voluntarily move from central cities and settle in suburban areas. (Certainly no policy involving *involuntary* movement of either whites or Negroes should ever be considered.) Such incentives could include rent supplements, ownership supplements, special school-support bonus payments linked to the education of children moving out from ghettos, and other devices which essentially attach a subsidy to a person. Then, when the person moves, he and the community into which he goes get credit for that subsidy. This creates incentives both for him to move and for the community to accept him gladly. Both of the strategies involving dispersal would thus represent radical changes in existing practices.

Segregated vs. Integrated Dispersal

One of the fundamental purposes of any dispersal strategy is providing Negro Americans with real freedom of choice concerning housing and school accommodations. The experience of other ethnic groups indicates that Negroes would exercise that choice in suburban areas in a combination of two ways. Some individual Negro households would become scattered "randomly" in largely white residential areas. But other Negro households—probably a larger number—would voluntarily cluster together. This would create primarily Negro neighborhoods, or even primarily Negro suburban communities. Such a combination of both *scattering* and *clustering* would occur even if Negro households had absolutely no fears of hostility or antagonism from white neighbors. It is unrealistic to suppose, however, that *all* prejudice against Negro neighbors can be eliminated from presently all-white suburbs in the immediate future. As a result, even if a dispersal strategy is carried out, there will still be some external pressure against Negro newcomers. This will encourage an even higher proportion of incoming Negro households to cluster together than would do so in the absence of all fears and antagonism. Moreover, public policies to accomplish dispersion might include deliberate creation of some moderate sized clusters of Negro families, as in scattered-site public housing developments.

Once all-Negro clusters appear in previously all-white suburbs, there is a high probability that they turn into "ghetto-lets" or "mini-ghettos." The same forces that produced ghettos in central cities are likely to repeat themselves in suburbs, though in a much less pathological form. Those pressures are a rapidly expanding Negro population, the "Law of Cultural Dominance" among whites, and at least some restriction of Negro choice in areas far removed from existing all-Negro neighborhoods. Therefore, once a Negro cluster becomes large enough so that Negro children dominate a local elementary school, the typical phenomenon of white withdrawal from the local residential real-estate market is likely to occur. This has already taken place regarding Jews and gentiles in many suburban areas. Thus, any dispersal strategy that does not explicitly aim at preventing segregation, too, will probably create new segregated neighborhoods in the suburbs.

This new form of *de facto* segregation will, however, have far less damaging effects upon Negroes than existing segregation concentrated in central cities. In the first place, if Negro clusters are deliberately created in almost all parts of the metropolitan area at once, whites will be unable to flee to "completely safe" suburbs without accepting impractically long commuting journeys. This will strongly reduce the white propensity to abandon an area after Negroes begin entering it. Moreover, the presence of some Negroes in all parts of suburbia will also make it far easier for individual Negro families to move into all-white neighborhoods on a scattered basis. Thus any dispersal policy that really disperses Negroes in the suburbs will immediately create an enormous improvement in the real freedom of residential choice enjoyed by individual Negro families. This will be true even if most of those families actually choose to remain in Negro clusters.

Second, any dispersal strategy would presumably be accompanied by strongly enforced open-occupancy laws applying to all housing. At present, these laws do not lead to scattering, but they would in the climate of a dispersal strategy. Then Negro willingness to move into all-white areas would rise sharply, and white antagonism toward such move-ins would stop.

Third, *de facto* residential segregation need not lead to segregated suburban schools. In relatively small communities, such as most suburbs, it is easy to bus students to achieve stable racial balance. Thus, the formation of clustered Negro housing would not have to cause the quality-of-education problems that now exist in central-city ghettos. True, if a given suburb became predominantly Negro, its schools might become quite segregated. In that case, school systems in adjoining suburbs might have to merge or at least work out student exchange procedures with the segregated community in order to counteract segregation. This may be difficult to accomplish (though in the climate of a dispersal strategy, it would be at least thinkable). Hence it is possible that some segregated school systems might appear in suburban areas. But Negro families would still have far more opportunities than they do now to move to areas with integrated schools.

A dispersal strategy that did not succeed in initially placing Negro households in almost all parts of the metropolitan area would be more likely to generate "ghetto-lets." Hence, if dispersal tactics call for initially concentrating or dispersion only to a few suburbs, it is quite possible that segregated dispersal would result. This implies that integrated dispersal could be attained in only two ways. Either the initial dispersal strategy must place Negroes in almost all suburban communities, or specific integration-furthering mechanisms—such as school and residential quotas—must be adopted.

The speculative nature of the above discussion illustrates that society needs to do much more thinking about what dispersal really means, how it might be achieved, what alternative forms it might take, and what its consequences would be.

In an article of this length, it is impossible to present an adequate analysis of each of the strategies described above. Certain factors will, however, have a crucial influence on which strategy actually prevails. These factors should be at least briefly mentioned here.

The Possibility of a Spatial-Racial "Confrontation"

Society's existing policies toward the ghetto are, by definition, those called for by the present policies strategy. Yet there are strong reasons to believe that maintenance of these policies in ghettos is not possible. The striking increase in violence in big-city ghettos is probably related to a combination of higher aspirations, reduced sanctions against the use of violence, and continued deplorable slum conditions. If so, persistence of the present-policies strategy may continue to spawn incidents, riots, and perhaps guerrilla warfare. Then existing local police forces might have to be supplemented with para-military forces on continuous alert. Thus, the present-policies strategy might lead to further polarization of whites and Negroes and even to the creation of semi-martial law in big cities.

Moreover, when Negroes become the dominant political force in many large central cities, they may understandably demand radical changes in present policies. At the same time, major private capital investment in those cities might virtually cease if white-dominated firms and industries decided the risks of involvement there were too great. In light of recent disorders, this seems very likely. Such withdrawal of private capital has already occurred in almost every single ghetto area in the U.S. Even if private investment continues, big cities containing high proportions of low-income Negroes would need substantial income transfers from the federal government to meet the demands of their electorates for improved services and living conditions.

But by that time, Congress will be more heavily influenced by representatives of the suburban electorate. The suburbs will comprise 41 percent of our total population by 1985, as opposed to 33 percent in 1960. Central cities will decline from 31 percent to 27 percent.[29] Under a present-policies strategy, this influential suburban electorate will be over 95 percent white, whereas the central-city population in all metropolitan areas together will be slightly over 60 percent white. The suburban electorate will be much wealthier than the central-city population,

which will consist mainly of Negroes and older whites. Yet even the suburbs will be feeling the squeeze of higher local government costs generated by rising service salaries. Hence the federal government may refuse to approve the massive income transfers from suburbs to central cities that the mayors of the latter will desperately need in order to placate their relatively deprived electorates. After all, many big-city mayors are already beseeching the federal government for massive aid—including [former] Republicans like John Lindsay—and their electorates are not yet dominated by low-income Negroes.

Thus the present-policies strategy, if pursued for any long period of time, might lead to a simultaneous political and economic "confrontation" in many metropolitan areas. Such a "confrontation" would involve mainly Negro, mainly poor, and fiscally bankrupt larger central cities on the one hand, and mainly white, much wealthier, but highly taxed suburbs on the other hand. Some older suburbs will also have become Negro by that time, but the vast majority of suburbs will still be "lily white." A few metropolitan areas may seek to avoid the political aspects of such a confrontation by shifting to some form of metropolitan government designed to prevent Negroes from gaining political control of central cities. Yet such a move will hardly eliminate the basic segregation and relative poverty generating hostility in the urban Negro population. In fact, it might increase that population's sense of frustration and alienation.

In my opinion, there is a serious question whether American society in its present form could survive such a confrontation. If the Negro population felt itself wrongly "penned in" and discriminated against, as seems likely, many of its members might be driven to supporting the kind of irrational rebellion now being preached by a tiny minority. Considering the level of violence we have encountered already, it is hard to believe that the conditions that might emanate from a prolonged present-policies strategy would not generate much more. Yet the Negro community cannot hope to defeat the white community in a pitched battle. It is outnumbered 9 to 1 in population and vastly more than that in resources. Thus any massive resort to violence by Negroes would probably bring even more massive retaliation by whites. This could lead to a kind of urban *apartheid*, with martial law in cities, enforced residence of Negroes in segregated areas, and a drastic reduction in personal freedom for both groups, especially Negroes.

Such an outcome would obviously violate all American traditions of individual liberty and Constitutional law. It would destroy "the American dream" of freedom and equal opportunity for all. Therefore, to many observers this result is unthinkable. They believe that we would somehow "change things" before they occurred. This must mean that either the present-policies strategy would not lead to the kind of confrontation I have described, or we would abandon that strategy before the confrontation occurred.

Can the Present-Policies Strategy Avoid "Confrontation"?

What outcomes from a present-policies strategy might prevent this kind of confrontation? For one thing, if incomes in the Negro community rise rapidly without any additional programs, the Negro population of central cities may enter the middle class at a fast rate. If so, the Negro electorate that comes to dominate many major central cities politically by 1985 under the present-policies strategy may consist largely of stable, well-to-do citizens capable of supporting an effective local government.

To test this possibility, we have done some projections of incomes in the nonwhite population on a rough basis through 1983, assuming a present-policies strategy. These indicate that about two-thirds of the nonwhite population at that time will have incomes *above* the existing poverty level—about the same fraction as at present. Since nonwhites will then form a much larger share of total central-city population, however, the percentage of *total* central-city population below the present poverty level might actually *rise* slightly. It is possible that nonwhite incomes might increase faster than in this forecast. Yet it is almost certain that the substitution of a relatively poor nonwhite group for a middle-income white group in central cities under a status-quo strategy will counterbalance likely increases in the incomes of nonwhites.

As a result, the electorate that will exist in major cities when Negroes become a majority will probably be just as poor as it is now (in real income terms). In contrast, the population in surrounding suburbs will be much wealthier than it is now. Thus, even if nonwhite incomes rise rapidly, there is still likely to be a significant "gap" between central-city and suburban income levels at that time—probably larger than at present.

Yet even under *present* conditions, many large central cities are critically short of revenue. Furthermore, in a generally wealthier society, it is highly probable that most central-city electorates will demand higher-than-existing levels of public service. Finally, the general cost of all government services will have risen sharply because of the productivity trends explained earlier. Hence, future central-city governments will have much higher costs, but not much greater resources than they do now. So rising incomes among nonwhites will not remove the fiscal pressure on central-city governments that is a key ingredient in the "confrontation" described above.

Moreover, the population group most responsible for violence and disturbances in central cities appears to consist of young Negro men between fifteen and twenty-four years of age. A high proportion of these people are unemployed because they lack skills (many are high school dropouts) and elementary training and motivation. This group will undoubtedly grow larger through natural increase and in-migration. Its problems are not likely to be solved under a status-quo strategy. Hence, even if the vast majority of nonwhites in central cities have increasing reason to abhor violence and riots, the *absolute size* of this more alienated group in 1975 will be 40 percent larger than in 1966, and even larger by 1985.[30] This implies that at least part of this group might start actions forcing the kind of "confrontation" I have described.

Most of the other possible developments under a non-enrichment strategy that would avoid any major "confrontation" involve abandoning concentration of Negroes in central cities. Thus, some observers argue that members of the Negro middle class will increasingly move out to suburban communities as their incomes rise with no further encouragement from public programs. In this way, Negroes would be following the precedent of other ethnic groups. Up to now, there is no evidence that this has started to occur, even though a large Negro middle class already exists. But if such a pattern did evolve, it would amount to dispersal rather than the concentration implicit in the present-policies strategy.

Can Present Policies Be Sustained?

In any event, there appears to be significant probability—which I subjectively judge to be at least 25 percent and perhaps as high as 75 percent—that the present-policies strategy will prove unsustainable. If adopted, it would probably generate major repercussions that would force it to be abandoned. Society would be compelled either to suspend traditional individual rights and adopt martial law in cities or to institute major programs to improve ghetto conditions or to move toward wider dispersal of the Negro population, or some combination of these. Admittedly, there is no certainty that the present-policies strategy will lead to these outcomes. Nevertheless, I believe the probability that it will is high enough to make this strategy essentially self-defeating. Modern life is too dynamic for the status quo to be preserved for long.

Yet the present-policies strategy is the one society has so far chosen. Almost all current public policies tend to further concentration, segregation, and non-enrichment, as mentioned earlier. The few supposedly anti-concentration devices adopted, such as open-occupancy laws, have proved almost totally ineffective. All we have to do to confirm our choice of that strategy is to continue existing policies. In fact, avoiding this strategy will be difficult, because doing so will require major changes in present attitudes as well as in existing resource allocations.

The "Black Power" Case for the Enrichment-Only Strategy

The enrichment-only strategy is consistent with a current ideology that has come to be called the "Black Power" viewpoint. This viewpoint has been criticized by many, and some of its proponents have misused it to incite violence. Yet it is certainly an intellectually respectable and defensible position containing some persuasive elements.

The "Black Power" argument states that the Negro American population needs to overcome its feelings of powerlessness and lack of self-respect before it can assume its proper role in society. It can do so only by exerting power over the decisions that directly affect its own members. According to this view, a fully integrated society is not really possible until the Negro minority has developed its own internal strength. Therefore, the ideal society in which race itself is not an important factor can only come much later. It could exist only after Negroes had gained power and self-respect by remaining in concentrated areas over which they could assume political and economic control and direction. Hence this view contends that a future in which central cities become primarily Negro and suburbs almost entirely white would be an advantage rather than a disadvantage.

The "Black Power" view has several notable strong points. First, such assumption of local power would be fully consistent with the behavior of previous nationality groups, such as the Irish in New York and Boston. They, too, came up from the bottom of the social and economic ladder, where they had been insulted and discriminated against. And they did it by gaining political and economic control over the areas in which they lived.

Second, it is unquestionably true that one of the two most important factors providing Negroes with all their recent gains in legal rights and actual welfare has been their own forceful presentation of grievances and demands. (The other factor has been high-level prosperity in the economy in general.) Negro-originated marches, demonstrations, protests, and even riots have had immensely more impact in improving their actual power, income, and opportunities than all the "purely voluntary" actions of whites combined—including those of white liberals.

Third, time is on the side of the "Black Power" argument if current population growth and location trends continue. As pointed out earlier, Negroes are likely to become a majority of the electorate in many large American cities within the next fifteen years, unless radically new policies are adopted. By giving Negroes political control over these cities, this trend would provide them with a powerful bargaining position in dealing with the rest of society—a tool they now sorely lack.

Fourth, the "Black Power" viewpoint provides many key ideological supports for Negro self-development. It stresses the need for Negroes to become proud of their color and their history, more conscious of their own strengths. It also focuses their attention on the need for organizing themselves economically and politically. Hence it could provide a focal point for arousing and channeling the largely untapped self-development energies of the Negro American population. One of the greatest difficulties in improving ghettos is discovering effective ways in which the lowest-income and most deprived residents can develop their own capabilities by participating more fully in the decisions and activities that affect them. Such "learning by doing" is, in my opinion, a vital part of the process of bringing deprived people into the main stream of American society. Insofar as "Black Power" proponents could develop such mechanisms, they would immensely benefit American society.

There are, however, also significant flaws in the "Black Power" argument. First, Negroes do not in fact have much power in the U.S. Nor is it clear just how they can obtain power solely through their own efforts, particularly in the near future. "Black Power" advocates constantly talk about "taking what is rightfully theirs" because they are dissatisfied with what "whitey" is willing to turn over to them voluntarily. They also reject the condescension inherent in whites' "giving" Negroes anything, including more power. But what bargaining power can Negroes use to compel whites to yield greater control over the economic and political decisions that affect them?

There are two possible answers. First, they could organize themselves so cohesively that they would become a potent political and economic force through highly disciplined but fully legal action. Examples would be block voting and economic boycotts. So far, nearly all efforts at such internal organization have foundered on the solid rocks of apathy, lack of funds, internal dissension, and disbelief that anything could be accomplished.

Second, Negroes could launch direct action—such as demonstrations and marches—that would morally, economically, or physically threaten the white community. This approach has so far proved to be the most successful. But many Negroes believe it has not improved their situation as fast as is necessary. Hence, there is a tendency to shift the form of threat employed to more and more violent action in order to get faster and more profound results. This tendency need only influence a small minority of Negroes in order to cause a significant escalation of violence. Yet such an escalation might result in massive retaliation by the white community that would worsen the Negroes' position. What is needed is enough of a threat to cause the white

community to start changing its own attitudes and allocation of resources in ways far more favorable to Negroes, but not so much of a threat as to cause withdrawal of all white cooperation and sympathy.

This conclusion points up the second flaw in the "Black Power" case: Ultimately, U.S. Negroes cannot solve their own problems in isolation, because they are fully enmeshed in a society dominated by whites. The solution to Negro problems lies as much in the white community as in the Negro community. This is especially true because whites control the economic resources needed to provide Negroes with meaningful equality of opportunity. Hence, any strategy of action by Negro leaders that totally alienates the white community is doomed to failure.

Yet "Black Power" advocates are probably correct in arguing that Negroes must develop an ideology that focuses upon self-determination and therefore has some "anti-white" tinges. They need an "enemy" against which to organize the Negro community. History proves that organization *against* a concrete opponent is far more effective than one *for* some abstract goal. They also need an abrasive ideology that threatens whites enough to open their eyes to the Negroes' plight and their own need to do something significant to improve it. The question is how they can accomplish these goals without going too far and thereby creating violent anti-white hostility among Negroes and equally violent anti-Negro sentiment among whites.

In the past few years, many Negro Americans—including prominent community leaders—have shifted their sights away from direct racial integration as a goal. Instead they have focused upon other goals more consistent with the "Black Power" viewpoint. They want better housing, better schools, better jobs, and better personal security within all-Negro areas—and a much stronger Negro voice in controlling all these things. These enrichment-only objectives have apparently eclipsed their desire for greater ability to enter directly into white-dominated portions of the society. This rather dramatic change in values appears to rule out much possibility of Negroes' accepting either dispersal strategy.

In my opinion, the main cause of this shift in objectives is the failure of white society to offer any real hope for large-scale integration. After years of seeking equality under the law, Negro leaders have discovered that even removal of legal barriers is not producing much progress toward a true sharing in the life of white-dominated society. Why should they keep knocking on the door if no one will answer? Why not turn instead to existing all-Negro communities and try to improve conditions there? Indeed, I believe continued white refusal to engage in meaningful, large-scale integration will make it impossible for any self-respecting Negroes to avoid espousing some version of the "Black Power" viewpoint. Understandably, they will not be able to accept the conclusion that most of the millions of Negroes whom whites force to live racially segregated lives must therefore be condemned to inferior educations, housing, culture, or anything else.

Rather, they will reason, there must be some way to make the quality of life in all-Negro portions of a racially segregated society just as good as it is in the all-white portions. And if equality in terms of the indices of desirability accepted by whites cannot be achieved, then some of these "Black Power" advocates will be willing to attain at least nominal equality by denouncing those indicators as specious. They will further claim —with some justification—that life in all-white portions of society cannot be better and may be morally worse because whites suffer from racial blindness.

The reason why this argument is and will be advanced so strongly is certainly understandable. Those who advance it would hardly be human if they were not at least tempted to do so. As long as present white attitudes and behavior persist, adopting any other view amounts to despairing of any chance at equality for most Negroes.

Can the Enrichment-Only Strategy Create "Separate but Equal" Societies?[31]

The "Black Power" viewpoint essentially argues that racially separate societies in America can provide equal opportunities for all their members if Negroes are able to control their own affairs. Yet there is a great deal of evidence that this argument is false.

Certainly concerning employment, equality of opportunity for Negroes cannot possibly be attained in a segregated labor market. Negroes must be provided with full freedom and equality regarding entry into and advancement within

the white-dominated enterprises that are overwhelmingly preponderant in our economy. Only in this way can they have any hope of achieving an occupational equality with whites.

In education, the evidence is far more ambiguous. The recent reports of the Office of Education and the Civil Rights Commission contend that both racial and economic integration are essential to the attainment of educational equality for Negroes.[32] Yet critics of these reports point out that many types of enrichment programs were not tested in the studies conducted by the authors. Unfortunately, most alternative approaches have not yet been tried on a scale large enough to determine whether any of them will work. Yet one conclusion does seem reasonable: Any real improvement in the quality of education in low-income, all-Negro areas will cost a great deal more money than is now being spent there, and perhaps more than is being spent per pupil anywhere.

Thus, society may face a choice between three fundamental alternatives: providing Negroes with good-quality education through massive integration in schools (which would require considerably more spending per pupil than now exists), providing Negroes with good-quality education through large-scale and extremely expensive enrichment programs, or continuing to relegate many Negroes to inferior educations that severely limit their lifetime opportunities. The third alternative is what we are now choosing. Whether or not the second choice—improving schools in all-Negro areas—will really work is not yet known. The enrichment alternative is based upon the as-yet-unproven premise that it will work.

Regarding housing, the enrichment-only strategy could undoubtedly greatly improve the quantity, variety, and environment of decent housing units available to the disadvantaged population of central cities. Nevertheless, it could not in itself provide Negroes of *any* economic level with the same freedom and range of choice as whites with equal incomes have. Clearly, in this field "separate but equal" does not mean *really* equal. Undoubtedly, all-white suburban areas provide a far greater range and variety of housing and environmental settings than can possibly be found in central cities or all-Negro suburbs alone.

Moreover, there is an acute scarcity of vacant land in many of our largest central cities. Therefore, greatly expanding the supply of decent housing for low-income families in those cities at a rapid rate requires creating many new units for them in the suburbs too.

Thus, if society adopts one of the many possible versions of the enrichment-only strategy, it may face the prospect of perpetuating two separate societies—one white and one Negro—similar to those that would develop under the present-policies strategy. If the enrichment programs carried out proved highly effective, then the gap between these two societies in income, education, housing, and other qualities of life would be nowhere near so great as under the present-policies strategy. Hence, the possibility of a potentially catastrophic "confrontation" between these two societies sometime in the next twenty years would be greatly reduced.

Nevertheless, I do not believe it will really be possible to create two separate societies that are truly equal. Therefore, even if the enrichment-only strategy proved extraordinarily successful at improving the lot of disadvantaged central-city residents of all races and colors (which is by no means a certainty), it would still leave a significant gap in opportunity and achievement between the separate white and Negro societies which would continue to emerge over the next twenty years. This gap would remain a powerful source of tension that might lead to violence, for experience proves that men seeking equality are not placated by even very great absolute progress when they perceive that a significant gap remains between themselves and others in society who are no more deserving of success then they. And that would be precisely the situation twenty years from now under the enrichment-only strategy—whether linked to "Black Power" concepts or not.

Why Dispersal Should Be Seriously Considered

As pointed out earlier, either of the two dispersal strategies would require radical changes in current trends and policies concerning the location of Negro population growth. Moreover, it is likely that massive dispersal would at present be opposed by *both* suburban whites and central-city Negroes. Many of the former would object to an influx of Negroes, and many of the latter would prefer to live together in a highly urbanized environment. Why should we even consider a strategy that is not only socially disruptive, but likely to please almost nobody?

In my opinion, there are five reasons why we should give enrichment plus dispersal serious consideration. First, future job-creation is going to be primarily in suburban area, but the unskilled population is going to be more and more concentrated in central-city ghettos unless some dispersion occurs. Such an increasing divergence between where the workers are and where the jobs are will make it ever more difficult to create anything like full employment in decent jobs for ghetto residents. In contrast, if those residents were to move into suburban areas, they would be exposed to more knowledge of job opportunities and would have to make much shorter trips to reach them. Hence they would have a far better chance of getting decent employment.

Second, the recent U.S. Office of Education and U.S. Civil Rights Commission reports on equality of achievement in education reach a *tentative* conclusion that it is necessary to end the clustering of lower-income Negro students together in segregated schools in order to improve their education significantly.[33] As I understand these reports, they imply that the most significant factor in the quality of education of any student is the atmosphere provided by his home and by his fellow students both in and out of the classroom. When this atmosphere is dominated by members of deprived families, the quality of education is inescapably reduced—at least within the ranges of class size and pupil-teacher ratios that have been tried on a large scale. Therefore, if we are to provide effective educational opportunities for the most deprived groups in our society to improve themselves significantly, we must somehow expose them to members of other social classes in their educational experience. But there are not enough members of the Negro middle class "to go around," so to speak. Hence this means some intermingling of children from the deprived groups with those from not-so-deprived white groups, at least in schools. Because of the difficulties of bussing large numbers of student from the hearts of central cities to suburban areas, it makes sense to accomplish this objective through some residential dispersal. This consideration tends to support the integrated dispersal strategy to some extent, even though these reports have received significant criticism as noted above.

Third, development of an adequate housing supply for low-income and middle-income families and provision of true freedom of choice in housing for Negroes of all income levels will require out-movement of large numbers of both groups from central cities to suburbs. I do not believe that such an out-movement will occur "spontaneously" merely as a result of increasing prosperity among Negroes in central cities. Even the recently passed national open-occupancy law is unlikely to generate it. Rather, a program of positive incentives and of actual construction of new housing in suburban areas will be necessary.

Fourth, continued concentration of large numbers of Negroes under relatively impoverished conditions in ghettos may lead to unacceptably high levels of crime and violence in central cities. The outbreak of riots and disorders in mostly nonwhite areas in our central cities in the past few years is unprecedented in American history. As the report of the National Advisory Commission on Civil Disorders indicates, continuing to concentrate masses of the nonwhite population in ghettos dominated by poverty and permeated with an atmosphere of deprivation and hopelessness is likely to perpetuate or intensify these disorders. This could lead to the disastrous outcome already discussed in connection with the present-policies strategy.

Fifth, a continuation of ghetto growth will, over the next three or four decades, produce a society more racially segregated than any in our history. We will have older, blighted central cities occupied almost solely by millions of Negroes, and newer, more modern suburban areas occupied almost solely by whites. Prospects for moving from that situation to a truly integrated society in which race is not a factor in key human decisions are not encouraging. In fact, by that time we will be faced with a fantastically more massive dispersal problem than the present one if we really want to achieve a society integrated in more than just words.

Thus, only the two enrichment-plus-dispersal strategies explicitly seek to create a single society rather than accepting our present perpetuation of two separate societies: one white and one Negro. Dispersal would involve specific policies and programs at least starting us toward reversal of the profoundly divisive trend now so evident in our metropolitan areas. It may seem extraordinarily difficult to begin such a reversal.

But however difficult it may be now, it will be vastly more difficult in twenty years if the number of Negroes segregated in central cities is 8 million larger than it is today.

The Difficulty of Gaining Acceptance for Dispersal

I am fully aware that any strategy involving significant dispersal may now seem wholly impractical to responsible politicians and social leaders. The voluntary movement of large numbers of Negroes from ghettos to the suburbs encouraged by federal programs presupposes radical changes in existing attitudes among both suburban whites and central-city Negroes.

In spite of our social mobility, Americans are extremely sensitive to class differentiations. We have deliberately developed class-stratified suburban areas. Residents of each suburb use zoning, tax rates, lot-size requirements, and other devices to exclude persons considered farther down the ladder of social and economic prominance. As each group and each family moves upward in our mobile society, they become more concerned about creating social distance between themselves and those now below them—including those who were once equal to them.

I certainly do not deplore the historic traditions of self-improvement and protection of amenities and privileges that have been won through hard work and perseverance. These traditions should and will continue in some form, because it is proper for successful people to enjoy the fruits of their efforts.

Nevertheless, it is at least possible that the social objective of upgrading the lowest and most deprived groups in our society cannot be accomplished if we simultaneously insist upon excluding those groups from nearly all daily contact with other more fortunate people—as we do now—by maintaining extremely rigid class distinctions by geographic area. Thus, the best dispersal policy might be one that promoted day-to-day interclass and interracial experiences without changing the dominant socioeconomic character of the receiving suburban areas. This would allow persons moving out from the inner city to benefit from the existing character of those suburbs. Such a policy implies that the newcomers would comprise a minority in each area into which they went. This means that an integrated-dispersal strategy might ultimately provide the most desirable form of dispersal. It would enable the group that was already there to maintain nearly intact their conception of the proper standards for that community, while sharing the benefits of those standards with others.

Even this change in attitude, however, presupposes a shift in values of profound magnitude among white middle-class Americans. Furthermore, I doubt that most Negroes today want to live in white communities in which they would be relatively isolated from other Negroes. Hence they might prefer a segregated-dispersal strategy, if they were willing to accept dispersal at all. Yet, since most suburban areas are already incorporated into predominantly white communities, where and how could such a strategy be initiated?

Some Tactical Mechanisms for
Encouraging Dispersal

Any attempt to achieve dispersal must involve specific answers to two basic questions:

1. What *mechanisms* can be designed to encourage voluntary out-movement of large numbers of Negroes into the suburbs and their peaceful acceptance and welcome by whites there?
2. What *incentives* can be developed leading particular interest groups in society to press politically for—or at least support—employment of those mechanisms?

Let us consider the mechanisms first. Americans have always used one basic approach to get people to overcome inertia and make voluntarily some socially desirable change. It consists of providing a significant economic or other reward for persons who behave in the desired manner. That reward might be free land (as for homesteaders and railroads in the nineteenth century), or tax reductions (as for homeowners or investors in equipment in the past few years), or direct payments (as for farmers), or services and income supplements tied to participation in specific programs (as for users of the G.I. Bill in education).

In the case of dispersion, I believe the system of rewards used should probably have the following characteristics:[34]

1. Advantages should accrue both to the Negro households moving out from central cities and to the suburban households into whose communities the newcomers move.
2. Whenever possible, these advantages should consist of rewards administered under metropolitan-area-wide organizations specifically set up for such a purpose. These organizations could be quasi-private bodies able to cooperate directly with existing local governments and other geographically limited organizations. Hence they would *not* be metropolitan governments.
3. Advantages to out-moving households might include the following:

   a. The possibility of sending their children to top-quality schools that receive special grants because of participation in programs involving out-moving children.
   b. Home-buying or renting financial aids available only to out-moving families or at least with assigned proportions of their total funding available only to such families.
   c. Top-priority access to special programs concerning employment and on-the-job training in suburban industrial and other firms. In my opinion, such programs might be effectively built around the self-selection principle embodied in the G.I. Bill—that is, eligible persons would be given certificates enabling those firms who hire them to receive special benefits to compensate for their lower productivity or training costs. Such benefits might include tax credits or direct payments. The persons receiving these certificates would then make their own choice of employers among firms participating in such programs. This would preserve maximum individual choice among program participants.

4. Advantages to households already living in the receiving areas might include:

   a. Special aid to schools receiving children of out-moving Negro families. Such aid should consist of funds linked to the students in such families (as Title I funding under the Elementary and Secondary Education Act is now linked to low-income families). But the per-student amount of aid given should greatly exceed the added direct cost of teaching each out-moving student. Hence the school district concerned would have a positive incentive to accept such students because of the financial "bonuses" they would bring with them. Those bonuses could be used to upgrade the entire receiving school or cut locally-borne costs therein.

b. "Bonus" community financing to participating suburban local governments. Again, the payments involved should significantly exceed the added costs of servicing in-coming families, so that each participating community would be able to improve other services too.

c. Giving higher priority in other federal programs to communities participating in out-movement programs than to those refusing to participate. These related programs could include sewer and water financing, planning aid, and selection as locations for federal installations.

5. Benefits available for out-moving families and receiving areas could be restricted by geographic area to avoid either paying people discriminately by race or wasting funds paying families who would move out anyway. A precedent for giving residents of certain neighborhoods special benefits already exists in the urban renewal and Model Cities programs. Thus, specific ghetto neighborhoods could be designated "origination" areas and largely white suburban communities designated "receiving" areas. Benefits would accrue only to persons moving from the former to the latter or to residents of the latter participating in reception programs.

6. If these programs were part of an integrated-dispersal strategy, they could be linked to quota systems concerning newcomers to each school or community involved. Thus, the special bonus aids would be available only up to a certain fraction of the total school enrollment or residential population of a given receiving community. This restriction would be aimed at retaining in the schools or communities concerned the dominance of the groups originally residing there. It is to be hoped that the result would be suburban integration, rather than a shift of massive neighborhood transition from central cities to suburbs.

The above suggestions are highly tentative and exploratory. Yet I hope they at least indicate that practical mechanisms can be created that might achieve a substantial amount of peaceful Negro out-movement—if they were adopted in a general atmosphere of social encouragement of dispersal.

Some aspects of the basic approach described above may seem terribly unjust. In particular,

this approach rewards the advantaged (those already living in suburbs) as well as the disadvantaged (those moving out of deprived areas into suburbs) in order to get the former to accept the latter. Yet that is a key mechanism, one which free-enterprise systems have always employed when they seek to attain high-priority ends through voluntary action. Our society abounds with arrangements that provide special economic advantages to those who are already privileged, presumably in order to evoke socially desired behavior from them. Examples are oil depletion allowances, stock option plans for top executives, profitable contracts for defense firms, lower tax rates on capital gains, and subsidy payments to wealthy farmers. I am defending neither the equity nor the effectiveness of these particular examples. Yet they illustrate that we often adopt public policies that pay the rich to undertake behavior which presumably benefits society as a whole.

A second aspect of the approach to dispersal I have described which might seem harsh is that no benefits apparently accrue to disadvantaged persons who fail to move out to the suburbs. As stated earlier, however, I believe dispersal programs should only be undertaken simultaneously with large-scale ghetto enrichment programs. The latter would provide comparable, or even greater, benefits for those "left behind" in central cities—who will undoubtedly comprise the vast majority of Negroes in our metropolitan areas for many years to come.

Developing Political Support for Dispersal

The concept of dispersal will remain nothing but an empty theory unless a significant number of Americans decide their best interests lie in politically supporting specific dispersal mechanisms. It is conceivable that such support might result from a massive "change of heart" among white suburbanites. They might view dispersal as a way to "purge themselves" of the kind of "white racism" which the National Advisory Commission on Civil Disorders described. I do not think this will occur. In fact, I believe recent urban violence has tended to make white suburbanites more hostile than ever to the idea of having Negroes live next door to them.

Yet, on the other hand, several specific groups in society are beginning to realize that dispersal might benefit them immensely. The motivation of persons in these groups varies widely, from pure moral guilt to sheer self-interest. But almost all significant social change in the United States has occurred because a wide variety of different types of people with diverse motives have formed a coalition to accomplish something. In my opinion, only through that kind of process will any of the basic strategies I have described (except the present-policies strategy) ever be achieved.

I believe the groups favorable to dispersal now include, or soon will include the following:

1. Suburban industrialists. In many metropolitan areas, they are experiencing acute labor shortages, particularly of unskilled workers. They will soon be willing to provide open and powerful political support for the construction of low-income and moderate-income housing for Negro workers and their families in current all-white suburbs.

2. Downtown-oriented retailers, bankers, restaurant operators, hotel operators, and other businessmen in our larger cities. In cities where disorders have penetrated into central business districts (such as Milwaukee and Washington), many former patrons have stopped visiting these areas altogether—especially at night. If disorders in these areas get worse, the impact upon both consumer patronage and future capital investment in big-city downtowns could be catastrophic. Those whose enterprises are "locked in" such areas will soon realize they must vigorously support both stronger law enforcement and positive programs aimed at alleviating Negro discontent. At first, these programs will consist primarily of ghetto enrichment, but these groups will soon begin to support dispersal too.

3. Home builders. They would benefit from any large-scale programs of housing construction. But the delays and difficulties of carrying out such programs within central cities are much greater than they are on vacant suburban land. Hence they will eventually exert at least low-level support for dispersal if it means large-scale subsidy of privately built homes.

4. White central-city politicians in large cities. As the populations of their cities shift toward Negro majorities, they will be more and more willing to support some dispersal policies, as well as the enrichment programs they now espouse.

5. Businessmen in general with plants, offices,

or other facilities "locked in" large central cities. An increasing number of such persons will realize that they will emerge losers from any major "confrontation" between black-dominated central cities and white-dominated suburbs, as described earlier.

6. Persons of all types whose consciences influence them to accept the National Advisory Commission's conclusion that dispersal of some kind is the only way to avoid perpetuating two separate societies, with the Negro one forever denied equality.

Since these groups now constitute a small minority of Americans a great many other Americans must change their existing values considerably if large-scale dispersal is ever to occur. Yet the alternatives to such a strategy—especially the one we are now pursuing—could conceivably lead us to equally grave changes in values. For example, if there is an extremely significant increase in violence in Negro ghettos which spills over into all-white areas, the white population might react with harshly repressive measures that would significantly restrict individual freedoms, as noted above. This, too, would call for a basic shift in our values. But it is a shift which I regard with much more alarm than the one required by a dispersal strategy. In fact, in this age of rapid technological change, it is naïve to suppose that there will not in the future be significant alterations in attitudes that we presently take for granted.

The Scale of Efforts Required

The foregoing discussion emphasizes that any strategy likely to have a significant impact upon ghettos will require a very much larger effort than we are now devoting to this problem. Even a "pure" ghetto-enrichment strategy, which does not eliminate or even slow down the growth of the racial ghetto, would require a significantly greater allocation of financial and manpower resources to coping with the problems of the urban poor. A dispersal strategy that addresses itself to breaking up or at least slowing down the growth of the racial ghetto would also require even more profound changes in values and attitudes. Only the first strategy—that of continuing our present activities—requires no immediate change in effort or values. But it may eventually result in significant value changes to

—and perhaps far less desirable ones than are required by the other two alternatives.

Thus, there is simply no easy way to cope with this problem. In my opinion, past federal programs and many currently suggested approaches have suffered from the desire to find a cheap solution to what is an extremely expensive problem. The problem is expensive in terms not only of money, but also of our national talents and our willingness to change our basic values. In one way or another, we must and will accommodate ourselves to this problem. We cannot evade it.

Creating the Programs and Incentives Necessary to Achieve Any Desired Ghetto Future

Each strategy contains two basic parts: a desired outcome and a set of actions designed to achieve that outcome. I have not placed equal emphasis on these two parts in discussing each of the five strategies concerning ghetto futures. For example, the present-policies strategy as I have described it is essentially a set of actions— the continuation of present policies. Hence it does not emphasize a desired outcome. In fact, I have pointed out several reasons why its outcome might be quite undesirable. Conversely, my discussion of the enrichment-only strategy has focused upon its outcome. Hence I have not made any suggestions about how that outcome might be brought about. Similar emphasis upon the outcome rather than the means of attaining it also marks the discussion of the integrated-core strategy. Even my tentative analysis of how dispersal might be carried out hardly represents a complete blueprint for action.

Any strategy is really just wishful thinking until it links the outcome it envisions with some feasible means of attaining that outcome. This is especially true regarding several of the ghetto futures I have described, since they embody such radical changes in society. They are likely to remain largely fantasies, rather than real alternatives, until specific programs for achieving them can be defined. I have made some program suggestions in connection with dispersal strategies in order to prove that dispersal is not totally unrealistic. Unfortunately, the complexity of developing similar suggestions for the other strategies involving social change prevents my attempting to do so in this article.

Nevertheless, there are five basic principles crucial to formulating such programs.

1. No proposed "solution" to ghetto problems that is not eventually supported by the majority of the white middle class can possibly succeed.[35]

2. The actions designed to bring about any desired outcome must be linked to incentives that will appeal both to the self-interest of all groups concerned and to their consciences. In fact, the most difficult part of implementing any strategy (other than the present-policies strategy) will be providing effective incentives for the relatively well-off white majority. This group must be persuaded to expand many resources, and alter its own traditional behavior, in order to produce outcomes that appear to benefit mainly a small minority of the population. As indicated in the discussion of dispersal, each segment of the white majority (such as business, labor, suburbanites, senior citizens, farmers, and so forth) must be presented with arguments and incentives which appeal specifically to its interests. An example is the argument that business suffers great losses of potential profits and output because of the failure of poor Negroes to engage in high-level consumption and the inability of poorly educated Negro workers to help meet high demands for skilled labor.

3. Any program designed to achieve a given outcome should involve significant action by the private sector. Otherwise, society may relegate ghettos to a position of dependency upon government that is inconsistent with full equality in American life. On the other hand, it is naïve to suppose that the private sector can or will bear the huge expense of coping with ghetto problems unaided. Society as a whole must pay the extra costs of on-the-job training programs, new factories located in ghettos, union training of unskilled Negro apprentices, and other actions aimed at helping the unskilled or otherwise "left out" enter the mainstream of our economy. These actions must be carried out by nongovernmental organizations, but financed by the government through direct payments, tax credits or other means.

4. No program involving ghettos can be effective unless it involves a high degree of meaningful participation by ghetto residents, and significant exercise of power and authority by them. We must realize that ghettos cannot be drawn into the mainstream of American life without

some redistribution of authority and power, as well as income, for equality in America means exercise of significant self-determination. Admittedly, lack of skill and experience may cause that exercise to be disorderly, inefficient, and even corrupt at first—as it was among the Irish, Italians, Jews, and others in the past. Therefore, turning over more power in ghetto areas to local residents may actually cause a short-run decline in the professional quality of government there —whether in schools, the police, or local government in general. Yet it will greatly alter the attitudes of residents toward those institutions and begin to draw them into the real functioning of our society. So it should and must come.

5. The more benefits that most ghetto residents receive through programs aimed at helping them, the more dissatisfied and vocally discontent certain small parts of the ghetto community are likely to become. This makes the problem of persuading the white majority to support large-scale aid programs doubly difficult. It also means that socioeconomic programs will have to be accompanied by greatly enlarged and improved law-enforcement efforts, particularly those in which ghetto leaders themselves play significant roles. Yet emphasis on improving law enforcement alone, without massively trying to meet the other needs of ghetto residents, will probably prove disastrous. Such one-sided emphasis on "law and order" could easily provoke steadily rising violence shifting in form toward guerrilla warfare. The need to avoid this outcome further emphasises the importance of relying more and more on ghetto communities to develop their own internal controls of violence, with outside aid, as is consistent with the preceding principle of greater self-determination.

Merely stated these principles emphasizes how far we are from having designed practical programs to achieve most of the outcomes set forth in this article. In my opinion, one of the most important tasks facing us is the formulation and public discussion of the specific ingredients needed for such programs. But even that cannot be done until we have recognized more explicitly the various possible futures of American ghettoes and weighed their relative advantages and disadvantages.

At present, most public discussion and thought about racial and ghetto problems in America

suffer from a failure to define or even to consider explicit possible long-range outcomes of public policy. This is one reason why such discussion seems so confused, inchoate, and frustrating. I hope that the ideas set forth in this article can serve as a nucleus for more fruitful public discussion of this crucial topic, for the future of American ghettos will determine to a large extent the future of America itself.

References

1. The first draft of this article was written in the early summer of 1967. Subsequently, the author became the consultant to the National Advisory Commission on Civil Disorders. In that capacity, he wrote the rough drafts of several chapters in the Commission's final report. One of these (Chapter 16) contains many of the ideas set forth in this article. Nevertheless, there are sufficient differences between the contents and presentation of Chapter 16 in the Commission's Report and this article to warrant separate publication of the latter. The contents of this article express the thoughts of its author only and do not necessarily represent the views of either the National Advisory Commission on Civil Disorder or Real Estate Research Corporation.
2. Data from the Social Security Administration.
3. *Report of the National Advisory Commission on Civil Disorders* (Washington, D.C.: March 1, 1968), p. 127. This document will hereafter be referred to as the *NACCD Report*.
4. *Ibid.*, pp. 121, 127.
5. Based upon the Census Bureau's Series D projections of future population—the ones assuming the lowest of the four levels of future fertility used by the Census Bureau. See U.S. Bureau of the Census, *Statistical Abstracts of the United States, 1967* (88th Edition; Washington, D.C., 1967), pp. 8–10.
6. *NACCD Report*, p. 121.
7. *Ibid.*
8. *Ibid.*
9. Open-occupancy legislation appears to be aimed at shifting the location of some future nonwhite growth to presently all-white areas. Experience in those states which have had open-occupancy ordinances for some time indicates, however, that they have little, if any, impact in altering the distribution of nonwhite population growth.
10. *NACCD Report*, p. 227.
11. Surveys conducted annually by Real Estate Research Corporation, results unpublished.
12. *NACCD Report*, p. 216.

13. See Raymond J. Murphy and James M. Watson, *The Structure of Discontent*, Mimeographed, Los Angeles: University of California at Los Angeles, June 1, 1967.

14. *NACCD Report*, pp. 123–131.

15. Specific recommendations concerning these subjects are set forth in the *NACCD Report*, Chapter 17.

16. See John F. Kain, "The Distribution and Movement of Jobs and Industry," in *The Metropolitan Enigma*, ed. James Q. Wilson (Washington, D.C., 1967).

17. These include legislative proposals made by Senator Javits, the late Senator Robert Kennedy, and Senator Percy.

18. William Baumol and William Bowen, *The Performing Arts: The Economic Dilemma* (New York: 20th Century Fund).

19. *NACCD Report*, p. 217.

20. Insofar as I know, this principle was first formulated by my father, James C. Downs, Jr.

21. Two well-known urban specialists with such views are Jane Jacobs and Victor Gruen. See Jane Jacobs, *The Life and Death of Great American Cities* (New York, 1961), and Victor Gruen, *The Heart of Our Cities* (New York, 1964).

22. This phenomenon explains why it is so difficult to halt "massive transition" from white to nonwhite occupancy once it begins. It tends to continue even when whites originally living in the area concerned do not "panic" at all. As long as normal turnover continues to produce vacancies, and only nonwhites fill them, such transition is inescapable. The key persons whose behavior must be affected to stop transition are not the whites living in the area at the outset, but those living scattered elsewhere in the metropolitan area or even other parts of the nation. They are the persons who must move into the areas as vacancies appear in order to maintain racial balance therein. Thus, attempts to organize existing white residents so as to prevent them from fleeing almost always fail to halt transition. Organizers can rarely identify "the whites who aren't there yet," so they cannot influence the decisions of these potential future occupants, and transition continues relentlessly.

23. The U.S. Supreme Court will soon have to face up to the consequences of this "Law." In order to attack *de facto* segregation effectivly, it must recognize racial discrimination in the form of school quotas as Constitutional. At present, our society cannot achieve integration or end segregation without deliberate and explicit racial discrimination by public authorities. This is true in relation to other public facilities besides schools, including hospitals and housing.

24. This term and usage were coined by Charles E. Lindblom. See Lindblom and David Braybrooke, *The Strategy of Decision* (New York, 1963).

25. See the *NACCD Report*, Chapter 17.

26. See their statements as quoted in the Chicago *Daily News*, August 25, 1967.

27. *NACCD Report*, p. 227.

28. *Ibid.*, p. 121.

29. These figures are based upon the Census Bureau's Series D population projections. If higher fertility projections are used, the suburbs would contain slightly higher proportions of total population in 1985. See the reference cited in footnote 5.

30. *NACCD Report*, pp. 216–217.

31. This section of the article was written after Chapter 16 of the *NACCD Report* had been completed and closely parallels the contents of certain parts of that chapter.

32. See James Coleman *et al.*, *Equality of Educational Opportunity* (Washington, D.C., 1966), and the U.S. Civil Rights Commission, *Racial Isolation in the Public Schools* (Washington, D.C., 1967).

33. *Ibid.*

34. Many of the programs described in this section have been recommended by the National Advisory Commission on Civil Disorders. See the *NACCD Report*, Chapter 17.

35. This fact is recognized by most Negro leaders not committed to zealously militant separatism. For example, see Kenneth Clark, *Dark Ghetto* (New York, 1965), p. 222.

38

RICHARD REEVES

How Democracy Died in New York

There was a serious attempt two weeks ago to persuade Governor Hugh Carey to remove Mayor Abraham Beame from office. The discussion ended when it was agreed—as they say, at the highest levels—that City Council President Paul O'Dwyer would be even worse than Beame as the city's chief executive.

That is very informed opinion on the quality of leadership in New York City. The people of New York have no political leader.

"*You* are the mayor of New York," I said one day last week to Felix Rohatyn, an investment banker who is the most visible representative of Big MAC, the Municipal Assistance Corporation formed to sell New York's municipal bonds because the city has run out of credit and credibility.

That is the state of self-government, or democracy, in New York City. The city is, in effect, being effectively run by an unelected board of investment bankers, academics, an accountant, and corporate executives—a New Yorker who had been away for a few months might think there had been a coup d'état.

In Manhattan, four lawyers in Rockefeller Center have been ordered by the governor's office to draft a federal bankruptcy statute, a proposed law to allow New York City to become the first municipal unit to go into general indebtedness bankruptcy since Medley, Florida, a town of 350 people, went under in 1968. In Albany, contingency planning has begun for mobilizing the National Guard if widespread rioting results from the inability to distribute welfare checks because of bankruptcy or a general strike of municipal employees.

That is the state of New York City. In three weeks it might collapse or explode if Big MAC cannot borrow enough money to meet payrolls and bille due in mid-August.

The system broke down, make no mistake about that. Elected leadership has not and apparently will not lead—politicians deceive the public and, perhaps, themselves into a crisis they seem incapable of managing, or even understanding. The watchdogs did not see. Newspapers, civic groups, and banks, too, ignored or misunderstood what was happening until it was too late.

And **things** are going to get a lot worse before they get better—if they ever do get better. The immediate credit crisis will be resolved with some unpleasantness, but it is only a beginning of New York's future problems. Borrowing a few billion dollars is not going to save or renew the city, only preserve it as an eroding monument to the cruelties of history.

New York's problem is not credit, it is income—the people of the city can no longer support themselves and will no longer be allowed to govern themselves. Blame pathetic Abe Beame and arrogant John Lindsay, blame the good old American greed of the municipal unions and the sanctimonious myopia of the New York *Times* and the banks. All of them, particularly the politicians, deserve anything that can be said about them, but the long-range problems of New York go further back, back to a day when Thomas Jefferson wrote a letter to James Madison saying: "I think our governments will remain virtuous for centuries as long as they are chiefly agricultural, and this will continue as long as there shall be vacant lands in any part of America. When they get piled upon one another in large cities as in Europe, they will become corrupt as in Europe."

New York's government, unfortunately, has been anything but virtuous and has gotten itself into a bind that will have to be resolved through negotiation, bankruptcy, or federal intervention —in that order of probability.

In a negotiation scenario, the "end" of the crisis would probably come in some kind of all-night session like the ones that sometimes prevented subway strikes a few years ago. Mayor Beame and his confused cronies, the leaders of the municipal unions, and representatives of the city's largest banks will be locked off in three separate rooms with officers of Big MAC and aides of Governor Carey shuttling between them. Actually, the shuttling will be mostly between the unions and the banks—Beame has become irrelevant, "the people" will have no voice—with the Big MACers trying to get the unions to agree to pay cuts and new work rules in return for some kind of job security and the banks to accept the union concessions as fiscally virtuous incentives to buy and market Big MAC bonds over, say, the next three years.

The bankruptcy scenario would result from a failure of negotiations. New York, like little Medley, Florida, would file a petition of financial adjustments with state courts or with federal courts under Chapter IX of the federal bankruptcy laws, probably the latter. A judge would then approve a plan for satisfying the city's creditors. The creditors will not be solely the holders of "defaulted" municipal bonds, they will be the bond holders plus city employees, vendors, and the recipients of welfare and other mandated municipal benefits. Or, the judge could delegate jurisdiction for the plan to receivers or trustees —the most likely candidates for that job would be the board of directors of Big MAC or some other group of appointed, elite, and responsible citizens.

Nothing as big as New York has ever gone bust in the United States, which is why Big MAC lawyers are trying to draft new legislation— Chapter IX may be inadequate for the task of establishing the priority of claims against the assets of New York City. Do the bond holders have unquestioned first call on city revenues and property? Should City Hall be mortgaged? Should Central Park be sold to developers? Do you pay cops first, or send out welfare checks? Someone has to decide, and the possibility of delayed decision is striking terror in some well-informed hearts. "There could be chaos," said a key figure in the city's immediate future. "What if people march from Harlem and Brooklyn because there are no welfare checks, or the police go on strike and use force to prevent the checks from being delivered?"

A federal-intervention scenario centers around Federal Reserve Board Chairman Arthur Burns and Secretary of the Treasury William Simon and is now being considered in Washington, not because they love New York, but because they are concerned about the stability of the city's big banks and the nation's governmental bond market. Direct federal aid to the city is probably out of the question, but the Federal Reserve Bank could make a lot of bankers and traders happy—and make Big MAC borrowing possible— by allowing banks to use the bonds as par value collateral for Federal Reserve loans. In other words, the banks would get federal credit in the amount of untrusted city promises.

So, something called "New York City" will be around after this crisis. But what will it be? It will be a lot of people, most of them pretty poor, living under circumstances dictated to them by an unelected board of their fiscally responsible betters. Self-government will be denied residents of the city for years, possibly forever—Jefferson, Burns, and Simon and other antiurban Americans always thought it would come to this. Ten years is probably the minimum term of the city's subjugation to Big MAC or unelected trustees of some kind. That was how long Fall River, Massachusetts, was controlled by the Fall River board of finance after it collapsed in 1931 under conditions quite similar to New York's in 1975. Substituting a few words—"recession" for "depression," for instance—and taking into account that New York has a multitude of exiting industries and businesses, the Big Apple is just a big Fall River, as the Massachusetts city's story was recounted in 1973 by the federal government's Advisory Commission on Intergovernmental Relations:

"Although the beginning of the 1929 Depression may have been responsible for the timing of Fall River's default, there had been a gradual build-up of fiscal problems over the preceding decade. The basic causes were the departure of a substantial number of textile factories . . . the failure of Fall River to take any steps to adjust to its declining economic base, and the continuation by the city of unsound financial management. . . .

"A sharp drop in revenues occurred. Failure to make a corresponding reduction in expenditures led to large revenue-expenditure imbalances for Fall River in the late 1920's . . . [and] borrowing in anticipation of taxes. . . . By November, 1930, as the impact of the Depression was felt, the banks financing these notes were forced to examine applications for renewals more carefully, and the dangerous situation in Fall River reached a crisis. . . .

"[The Massachusetts] legislature responded [to the crisis] by appointing a board of finance consisting of three members (one a resident of Fall River) that took over management of Fall River's government on February 19, 1931. The legislation created a virtual receivership for a ten-year period, with absolute power to control and manage all appropriations and expenditures of the city and to establish a definite fiscal policy that would restore the city's vanished credit."

In case you haven't noticed it lately, Fall River ain't what it used to be. New York won't be either. Politicians there refused to deal with the reality that the closing of the textile mills meant local government had to change its goals and operations, just as politicians here refuse to face the reality that a national economy decentralized by jet planes, superhighways, and instant communications meant local government had to adjust.

Neither Lindsay nor Beame, our democratically elected leaders, was willing or able to face the reality of a New York reduced by economic trends. There are serious questions about whether Beame understands even now. Two weeks ago he called reporters into his City Hall office to inform the city that the worst was over, the crisis had passed. That was when Big MAC board members began petitioning Carey for the mayor's removal from office.

"We were pleading with Beame to go on television and let the people know how bad things really were and he did precisely the opposite," said one board member. "The man is dangerous."

Foolish perhaps, but no longer dangerous. The mayor has been stripped of power, credibility, and dignity. When he was asked ten days ago if the city's situation was grave, Beame's first answer was: "If big MAC says it is. . . ." He still thinks he can avoid involvement, that he can somehow survive politically by shifting responsibility and attention to Big MAC or Felix Rohatyn,

to somebody, anybody. And Hugh Carey is not all that different. Although the governor moved rather effectively in creating and supporting Big MAC, he has also energetically dodged explaining to an unrepresented and, I think, largely uncomprehending public what is happening and what is going to happen to them. Our leaders, and, thus, our democracy, have failed—they have abdicated, turning their power over to private boards, bankers, and union leaders. (Giving away power—and *responsibility*—has become a standard strategy of New York politicians as city problems become more complex. After the 1966 subway strike, Lindsay turned the transit system over to a state agency, the Metropolitan Transportation Authority. After a teachers' strike, the school system was decentralized to the point where no one seemed to be in charge.)

But elected leaders were hardly alone in this failure. Donna Shalala, a political scientist on the Big MAC board, put it this way: "The whole system broke down. Government hid big deficits each year and got away with it because there were no outside checks—business, the press, civic groups failed."

I failed. I was the City Hall bureau chief of the New York *Times* in 1967 and 1968, when Lindsay began playing some of the tricks—"budget gimmicks"—that led inevitably to the credit crisis. We, if I can use that word for myself and the *Times*, spotted some things, particularly Lindsay's Panglossian rhetoric and phony statistics about the rate of the city's economic decline and the overloading of future pension obligations to municipal employees. Other things went by us—the significance of the shifting of salaries and other operating expenses into the city's capital budget as a way of sneaking into deficit financing and escalating debt, and the deceptive numbers that were being pushed out by City Hall and the unions to hide the real cost of labor settlements. I don't blame the unions for being greedy—that is their nature and function—as much as I blame Lindsay for buying labor peace at any price, and then lying about the price.

The press also managed to ignore the few voices of reality heard around town, particularly Dean Dick Netzer of New York University, Howard Samuels, and the Citizens Budget Commission. Netzer seemed too academic, Samuels too ambitious, and CBC too suspect because it cried "Wolf!" at any hint of higher taxes on its business-oriented membership. I can remember in portant New Yorkers laughing at Samuels two years ago when he predicted almost to the day when the money would run out. Besides, the sounds of warning never matched the thunder of nonsense, like Bella Abzug advocating that the city become the fifty-first state.

And the banks! If they take a loss on city bonds and notes, they have only themselves to blame. Two years ago, the Advisory Commission on Intergovernmental Relations formally warned them: "Private agencies such as banks, bond attorneys, and rating firms should show more concern for the misuse of short-term operating debt by cities because such debt carried beyond the end of the fiscal year is a threat to the financial solvency of a city." But, however blame is finally distributed, the current credit crisis is a symptom, perhaps a small itch, in the continuing decline of America's older cities. The basic problem of New York and Detroit and Newark is that they are no longer needed—at least, needed by the rest of America in the way they once were. New York as a communications, cultural, and, ironically, financial capital is more vital to the United States than Newark, but most of the old cities have to be classified with telegrams and the Twentieth Century Limited. Their time has passed. New York City is no longer the manufacturing center and distribution hub of the eastern United States. Its functions have been decentralized to a thousand smaller places.

Perhaps it had to come to this—it was certainly meant to. The United States has always been an antiurban country, fostered by gentlemen farmers, raised in the log-cabin tradition. In America there has always been something suspect about anyone born on the Lower East Side of anywhere. The first important public policy of the republic—the Northwest Ordinance of 1785—provided cheap land for rural settlers and free land for their public schools. The children of New York City and Philadelphia did not have public schools for another 50 years, and they waited 100 years more for any federal assistance in building them.

And antiurbanism didn't end when the West was won. Federal legislation of the twentieth century, whatever it was designed to do, has helped to destroy New York and other older cities. The Agricultural Adjustment Act of the 1930's mechanized our farms and started pushing an unskilled rural underclass onto the welfare rolls of northern cities. The Federal Housing Acts of the 1930's and 1940's guaranteed the financing of the suburbs, subsidizing the exodus of the taxpaying middle class out of the cities. The National Defense Highway Act of the 1950's not only saved us from the Russians, but provided a $50-billion suburban transportation system, so that commerce and industry could follow workers into the greener pastures. It was an expensive business, financed by taxes paid in the cities—New York, for one, sent anywhere from $10 to $20 in income taxes to Washington for every dollar that came back in federal aid. All that began to change in the 1960's, largely because urban areas gained political representation with the Supreme Court's landmark "one man, one vote" ruling.

But the 1960's were too late for New York; by then the mortgaging of its future had begun. And so had the breakdown of the nation's greatest city—it happened to us just as it had happened to the city-states of Athens and Florence when they no longer dominated the countryside. Writing of sixteenth-century city-states, Robert Crowley, using the word *meed* to mean "profit," said 200 years ago:

"And this is a city/In name, but in deed/It is a pack of people/That seek after meed/For officers and all/Do seek their own gain,/But for the wealth of the Commons/Not one taketh pain./And hell without order/I may it well call/Where every man is for himself/And no man for all."

39

DANIEL P. MOYNIHAN

Toward a National Urban Policy

In the spring of 1969, President Nixon met in the Cabinet room with ten mayors of American cities. They were nothing if not a variegated lot, mixing party, religion, race, region in the fine confusion of American politics. They had been chosen to be representative in this respect, and were unrepresentative only in qualities of energy and intelligence that would have set them apart in any company. What was more notable about them, however, was that in the interval between the invitation from the White House and the meeting with the President, four had announced they would not run again. The mayor of Detroit who, at the last minute, could not attend, announced *his* noncandidacy in June.

Their decisions were not a complete surprise. More and more, for the men charged with governance of our cities, politics has become the art of the impossible. It is not to be wondered that they flee. But we, in a sense, are left behind. And are in trouble.

At a time of great anxiety—a time that one of the nation's leading news magazines now routinely describes as "the most serious domestic crisis since the Civil War," a time when Richard Rovere, writing of the 1972 elections, can add parenthetically, "assuming that democracy in America survives that long"—these personal decisions may seem of small consequence; yet one suspects they are not.

All agree that the tumult of the time arises, in essence, from a crisis of authority. The institutions that shaped conduct and behavior in the past are being challenged or, worse, ignored. It is in the nature of authority, as Robert A. Nisbet continues to remind us, that it is consensual, that it is not coercive. When authority systems collapse, they are replaced by power systems that *are* coercive.* Our vocabulary rather fails us here: the term "authority" is an unloved one with its connotations of "authoritarianism," but there appears to be no substitute. Happily, public opinion is not so dependent on political vocabulary, certainly not on the vocabulary of political science, as some assume. For all the ambiguity of the public rhetoric of the moment, the desire of the great mass of our people is clear. They sense the advent of a power-based society and they fear it. They seek peace. They look to the restoration of legitimacy, if not in existing institutions, then in new or modified ones. They look for a lessening of violent confrontations at home and, in great numbers, for an end to war abroad. Concern for personal safety on the part of city dwellers has become a live *political* fact, while the reappearance—what, praise God, did we do to bring this upon ourselves?—of a Stalinoid rhetoric of apocalyptic abuse on the left, and its echoes on the right, have created a public atmosphere of anxiety and portent that would seem to have touched us all. It is with every good reason that the nation gropes for some means to weather the storm of unreason that has broken upon us.

It would also seem that Americans at this moment are much preoccupied with the issue of freedom—or, rather, with new, meaningful ways

Daniel P. Moynihan, "Toward a National Urban Policy," *The Public Interest*, no. 17 (Fall 1969), pp. 3–20. Copyright © National Affairs, Inc., 1969. This article is Chapter 1 in Moynihan's book, *Toward a National Urban Policy* (New York: Basic Books, Inc., Publishers, © 1970). Reprinted by permission of National Affairs, Inc., and Daniel P. Moynihan.

* "The Twilight of Authority," *The Public Interest*, no. 15, Spring 1969.

in which freedom is seen to be expanded or constrained. We are, for example, beginning to evolve some sense of the meaning of group freedom. This comes after a century of preoccupation with individual rights of a kind which were seen as somehow opposed to, and even threatened by, group identities and anything so dubious in conception as *group* rights.

The Civil Rights Act of 1964 was the culmination of the political energies generated by that earlier period. The provisions which forbade employers, universities, governments, or whatever to have any knowledge of the race, religion, or national origin of individuals with which they dealt marked in some ways the high-water mark of Social Darwinism in America; its assumption that "equality" meant *only* equal opportunity did not long stand unopposed. Indeed, by 1965 the federal government had already, as best one can tell, begun to require ethnic and racial census of its own employees, and also of federal contractors and research grant recipients. To do so violated the spirit if not the letter of the Civil Rights Act, with its implicit model of the lone individual locked in equal—and remorseless—competition in the marketplace, but very much in harmony with the emerging sense of the 1960s that groups have identities and entitlements as well as do individuals. This view is diffusing rapidly. In Massachusetts, for example, legislation of the Civil Rights Act period, which declared any public school with more than 50 percent black pupils to be racially "imbalanced" and in consequence illegal, is already being challenged—by precisely those who supported it in the first instance. Insofar as these demands have been most in evidence among black Americans, there is not the least reason to doubt that they will now diffuse to other groups, defined in various ways, and that new institutions will arise to respond to this new understanding of the nature of community.

In sum, two tendencies would appear to dominate the period. The *sense of general community is eroding*, and with it the authority of existing relationships; simultaneously, a powerful *quest for specific community is emerging* in the form of ever more intensive assertions of racial and ethnic identities. Although this is reported in the media largely in terms of black nationalism, it is just as reasonable to identify emergent attitudes in the "white working class" as part of the same phenomenon. The singular quality of these two tendencies is that they are at once com-

plementary and opposed. While the ideas are harmonious, the practices that would seem to support one interest are typically seen as opposing the other. Thus, one need not be a moral philosopher or a social psychologist to see that much of the "crisis of the cities" arises from the interaction of these intense new demands, and the relative inability of the urban social system to respond to them.

Programs Do Not a Policy Make

Rightly or otherwise—and one is no longer sure of this—it is our tradition in such circumstances to look to government. Social responses to changed social requirements take the form, in industrial democracies, of changed government policies. This has led, in the present situation, to a reasonably inventive spate of program proposals of the kind the New Deal more or less began and which flourished most notably in the period between the presidential elections of 1960 and 1968, when the number of domestic programs of the federal government increased from 45 to 435. Understandably, however, there has been a diminution of the confidence with which such proposals were formerly regarded. To say the least, there has been a certain nonlinearity in the relationship between the number of categorical aid programs issuing forth from Washington and the degree of social satisfaction that has ensued.

Hence the issue arises as to whether the demands of the time are not to be met in terms of *policy*, as well as program. It has been said of urban planners that they have been traumatized by the realization that everything relates to everything. But this is so, and need paralyze no one; the perception of this truth can provide a powerful analytic tool.

Our problems in the area of social peace and individual or group freedom occur in urban settings. Can it be that our difficulties in coping with these problems originate, in some measure, from the inadequacies of the setting in which they arise? Crime on the streets and campus violence may mark the onset of a native nihilism: but in the first instance they represent nothing more complex than the failure of law enforcement. Black rage and white resistance, "Third World" separatism, and restricted neighborhoods all may define a collapse in the integuments of the social contract: but, again, in the first instance they represent for the most part simply the failure of urban arrangements to meet the expectations of the urban population in the areas of jobs, schools, housing, transportation, public health, administrative responsiveness, and political flexibility. If all these are related, one to the other, and if in combination they do not seem to be working well, the question arises whether the society ought not to attempt a more coherent response. In a word: ought not a national urban crisis to be met with something like a national urban policy? Ought not the vast efforts to control the situation of the present be at least informed by some sense of goals for the future?

The United States does not now have an urban policy. The idea that there might be such is new. So also is the Urban Affairs Council, established by President Nixon on January 23, 1969, as the first official act of his administration, to "advise and assist" with respect to urban affairs, specifically "in the development of a national urban policy, having regard both to immediate and to long-range concerns, and to priorities among them."

What Happened

The central circumstance, as stated, is that America is an urban nation, and has been for half a century.

This is not to say Americans live in *big* cities. They do not. In 1960 only 9.8 percent of the population lived in cities of one million or more. Ninety-eight percent of the units of local government have fewer than 50,000 persons. In terms of the 1960 census, only somewhat more than a quarter of congressmen represented districts in which a majority of residents lived in central city areas. The 1970 census will show that the majority of Americans in metropolitan areas in fact live in suburbs, while a great many more live in urban settlements of quite modest size. But they are not the less urban for that reason, providing conditions of living and problems of government profoundly different from that of the agricultural, small town past.

The essentials of the present "urban crisis" are simple enough to relate. Until about World War II, the growth of the city, as Otto Eckstein argues, was "a logical, economic development." At

least it was such in the northeastern quadrant of the United States, where most urban troubles are supposed to exist. The political jurisdiction of the city more or less defined the area of intensive economic development, that in turn more or less defined the area of intensive settlement. Thereafter, however, economic incentives and social desires combined to produce a fractionating process that made it ever more difficult to collect enough power in any one place to provide the rudiments of effective government. As a result of or as a part of this process, the central area ceased to grow and began to decline. The core began to rot.

Two special circumstances compounded this problem. First, the extraordinary migration of the rural southern Negro to the northern city. Second, a postwar population explosion (90 million babies were born between 1946 and 1968) that placed immense pressures on municipal services, and drove many whites to the suburbs seeking relief. (Both these influences are now somewhat attenuating, but their effects will be present for at least several decades, and indeed a new baby boom may be in the offing.) As a result, the problems of economic stagnation of the central city became desperately exacerbated by those of racial tension. In the course of the 1960s tension turned into open racial strife.

City governments began to respond to the onset of economic obsolescence and social rigidity a generation or more ago, but quickly found their fiscal resources strained near to the limit. State governments became involved, and much the same process ensued. Starting in the postwar period, the federal government itself became increasingly caught up with urban problems. In recent years resources on a fairly considerable scale have flowed from Washington to the cities of the land, and will clearly continue to do so However, in the evolution of a national urban policy, more is involved than merely the question of programs and their funding. Too many programs have produced too few results simply to accept a more or less straightforward extrapolation of past and present practices into an oversized but familiar future. *The question of method has become as salient as that of goals themselves.*

As yet, the federal government, no more than state or local government, has not found an effective *incentive* system—comparable to profit in private enterprise, prestige in intellectual activi ity, rank in military organization—whereby to shape the forces at work in urban areas in such a way that urban goals, whatever they may be, are in fact attained. This search for incentives, and the realization that present procedures such as categorical grant-in-aid programs do not seem to provide sufficiently powerful ones, must accompany and suffuse the effort to establish goals as such. We must seek, not just policy, but policy allied to a vigorous strategy for obtaining results from it.

Finally, the federal establishment must develop a much heightened sensitivity to its "hidden" urban policies. There is hardly a department or agency of the national government whose programs do not in some way have important consequences for the life of cities, and those who live in them. Frequently—one is tempted to say normally!—the political appointees and career executives concerned do *not* see themselves as involved with, much less responsible for the urban consequences of their programs and policies. They are, to their minds, simply building highways, guaranteeing mortgages, advancing agriculture, or whatever. No one has made clear to them that they are simultaneously redistributing employment opportunities, segregating or desegregating neighborhoods, depopulating the countryside and filling up the slums, etc.: all these things as second and third order consequences of nominally unrelated programs. Already this institutional naïveté has become cause for suspicion; in the future it simply must not be tolerated. Indeed, in the future, a primary mark of competence in a federal official should be the ability to see the interconnections between programs immediately at hand and the urban problems that pervade the larger society.

The Fundaments of Urban Policy

It having been long established that, with respect to general codes of behavior, eleven precepts are too many and nine too few, ten points of urban policy may be set forth, scaled roughly to correspond to a combined measure of urgency and importance.

1. The poverty and social isolation of minority groups in central cities is the single most serious problem of the American city today. It must be attacked with urgency, with a greater commit-

ment of resources than has heretofore been the case, and with programs designed especially for this purpose.

The 1960s have seen enormous economic advances among minority groups, especially Negroes. Outside the south, 37 percent of Negro families earn $8,000 per year or more, that being approximately the national median income. In cities in the largest metropolitan areas, 20 percent of Negro families in 1967 reported family incomes of $10,000 or over. The earnings of *young* married black couples are approaching parity with whites.

Nonetheless, certain forms of social disorganization and dependency appear to be increasing among the urban poor. Recently, Conrad Taeuber, associate director of the Bureau of the Census, reported that in the largest metropolitan areas—those with one million or more inhabitants—"the number of black families with a woman as head increased by 83 percent since 1960; the number of black families with a man as head increased by only 15 percent during the same period." Disorganization, isolation, and discrimination seemingly have led to violence, and this violence has in turn been increasingly politicized by those seeking a "confrontation" with "white" society.

Urban policy must have as its first goal the transformation of the urban lower class into a stable community based on dependable and adequate income flows, social equality, and social mobility. Efforts to improve the conditions of life in the present caste-created slums must never take precedence over efforts to enable the slum population to disperse throughout the metropolitan areas involved. Urban policy accepts the reality of ethnic neighborhoods based on free choice, but asserts that the active intervention of government is called for to enable free choice to include integrated living as a normal option.

It is impossible to comprehend the situation of the black urban poor without first seeing that they have experienced not merely a major migration in the past generation, but also that they now live in a state almost of demographic siege as a result of population growth. What demographers call the "dependency ratio"—the number of children per thousand adult males—for blacks is nearly twice that for whites, and the gap widened sharply in the 1960s.

It is this factor, surely, that accounts for much of the present distress of the black urban slums.

At the same time, it is fairly clear that the sharp escalation in the number of births that characterized the past twenty-five years has more or less come to an end. The number of Negro females under age five is now exactly the number aged five to nine. Thus the 1980s will see a slackening of the present severe demands on the earning power of adult Negroes, and also on the public institutions that provide services for children. But for the decade immediately ahead, those demands will continue to rise—especially for central city blacks, whose median age is a bit more than ten years below that for whites—and will clearly have a priority claim on public resources.

2. *Economic and social forces in urban areas are not self-balancing. Imbalances in industry, transportation, housing, social services, and similar elements of urban life frequently tend to become more rather than less pronounced, and this tendency is often abetted by public policies. A concept of urban balance may be tentatively set forth: a social condition in which forces tending to produce imbalance induce counterforces that simultaneously admit change while maintaining equilibrium. It must be the constant object to federal officials whose programs affect urban areas—and there are few whose do not—to seek such equilibrium.*

The evidence is considerable that many federal programs have induced sharp imbalances in the "ecology" of urban areas—the highway program, for example, is frequently charged with this, and there is wide agreement that other, specifically city-oriented programs such as urban renewal have frequently accomplished just the opposite of their nominal objectives. The reasons are increasingly evident. Cities are complex social systems. Interventions that, intentionally or not, affect one component of the system almost invariably affect second, third, and fourth components as well, and these in turn affect the first component, often in ways quite opposite to the direction of the initial intervention. Most

federal urban programs have assumed fairly simple cause and effect relationships that do not exist in the complex real world. Moreover, they have typically been based on "common sense" rather than research in an area where common sense can be notoriously misleading. In the words of Jay W. Forrester, "With a high degree of confidence we can say that the intuitive solution to the problems of complex social systems will be wrong most of the time."

This doubtless is true, but it need not be a traumatizing truth. As Lee Rainwater argues, the logic of mutlivariate analysis, and experience with it, suggest that some components of a complex system are always vastly more important than others, so that when (if) these are accurately identified a process of analysis that begins with the assertion of chaos can in fact end by producing quite concise and purposeful social strategies.

3. *At least part of the relative ineffectiveness of the efforts of urban government to respond to urban problems derives from the fragmented and obsolescent structure of urban government itself. The federal government should constantly encourage and provide incentives for the reorganization of local government in response to the reality of metropolitan conditions. The objective of the federal government should be that local government be stronger and more effective, more visible, accessible, and meaningful to local inhabitants. To this end the federal government should discourage the creation of paragovernments designed to deal with special problems by evading or avoiding the jurisdiction of established local authorities, and should encourage effective decentralization.*

Although the "quality" of local government, especially in large cities, has been seen to improve of late, there appears to have been a decline in the vitality of local political systems, and an almost total disappearance of serious effort to reorganize metropolitan areas into new and more rational governmental jurisdictions. Federal efforts to recreate the ethnic-neighborhood-based community organization, as in the poverty program, or to induce metropolitan area planning as in various urban development programs, have had a measure of success, but nothing like that hoped for. Meanwhile the middle-class norm of "participation" has diffused downward

Table 1. *Children per 1000 adult males*

	1960	1966
White	1,365	1,406
Negro	1,922	2,216

and outward, so that federal urban programs now routinely require citizen participation in the planning process and beyond; yet somehow this does not seem to have led to more competent communities. In some instances it appears rather to have escalated the level of stalemate.

It may be we have not been entirely candid with ourselves in this area. Citizen participation, as Elliott A. Krause has pointed out, is in practice a "bureaucratic ideology," a device whereby public officials induce nonpublic individuals to act in a way the officials desire. Although the putative object may be, indeed almost always is, to improve the lot of the citizen, it is not settled that the actual consequences are anything like that. The ways of the officials, of course, are often not those of the elected representatives of the people, and the "citizens" may become a rope in the tug-of-war between bureaucrat and representative. Especially in a federal system, "citizen participation" easily becomes a device whereby the far-off federal bureaucracy acquires a weapon with which to battle the elected officials of local government. Whatever the nominal intent, the normal outcome is federal support for those who would dinimish the legitimacy of local government. But it is not clear that the federal purposes are typically advanced through this process. To the contrary, an all-round diminishment rather than enhancement of energies seems to occur.

This would appear especially true when "citizen participation" has in effect meant putting indignant citizens on the payroll. However much these citizens may continue to "protest," the action acquires a certain hollow ring. Something like this has already happened to groups that have been openly or covertly supported by the federal government, seeking to influence public opinion on matters of public policy. This stratagem is a new practice in American democracy. It began in the field of foreign affairs, and has now spread to the domestic area. To a quite astonishing degree it will be found that those groups that nominally are pressing for social change and development in the poverty field, for example, are in fact subsidized by federal funds. This occurs in protean ways—research grants, training contracts, or whatever—and is done with the best of intentions. But, again, with what results is far from clear. Can this development, for example, account for the curious fact that there seems to be so much protest in the streets of the nation, but so little, as it were, in its legislatures? Is it the case, in other words, that the process of public subsidy is subtly debilitating?

Whatever the truth of this judgment, it is nevertheless clear that a national urban policy must look first to the vitality of the elected governments of the urban areas, and must seek to increase their capacity for independent, effective, and creative action. This suggests an effort to find some way out of the present fragmentation, and a certain restraint on the creation of federally financed "competitive governments."

Nathan Glazer has made the useful observation that in London and Tokyo comprehensive metropolitan government is combined with a complex system of "subgovernments"—the London Boroughs—representing units of 200,000–250,000 persons. These are "real" governments, with important powers in areas such as education, welfare, and housing. In England, at all events, they are governed through an electoral system involving the national political parties in essentially their national postures. (Indeed, the boroughs make up the basic units of the parties' urban structure.) It may well be there is need for social inventions of this kind in the great American cities, especially with respect to power over matters such as welfare, education, and housing that are now subject to intense debates concerning "local control." The demand for "local control" is altogether to be welcomed. In some degree it can be seen to arise from the bureaucratic barbarities of the highway programs of the 1950s, for example. But in the largest degree it reflects the processes of democracy catching up with the content of contemporary government. As government more and more involves itself in matters that very much touch on the lives of individual citizens, those individuals seek a greater voice in the programs concerned. In the hands of ideologues or dimwits, this demand can lead to an utter paralysis of government. It has already done so in dozens of urban development situations. But approached with a measure of sensitivity—and patience—it can lead to a considerable revitalization of urban government.

4. A primary object of federal urban policy must be to restore the fiscal vitality of urban government, with the particular object of ensuring that local governments normally have enough resources on hand or available to make local initiative in public affairs a reality.

For all the rise in actual amounts, federal aid to state and local government has increased only from 12 percent of state-local revenue in 1958 to 17 percent in 1967. Increasingly, state and local governments that try to meet their responsibilities lurch from one fiscal crisis to another. In such circumstances, the capacity for creative local government becomes least in precisely those jurisdictions where it might most be expected. As much as any other single factor, this condition may be judged to account for the malaise of city government, and especially for the reluctance of the more self-sufficient suburbs to associate themselves with the nearly bankrupt central cities. Surviving from one fiscal deadline to another, the central cities commonly adopt policies which only compound their ultimate difficulties. Yet their options are so few. As James Q. Wilson writes, "The great bulk of any city's budget is, in effect, a fixed charge the mayor is powerless to alter more than trivially." The basic equation, as it were, of American political economy is that for each one percent increase in the Gross National Product, the income of the federal government increases one and one-half percent, while the normal income of city governments rises half to three-quarters of a point at most. Hence both a clear opportunity and a no less manifest necessity exist for the federal government to adopt as a deliberate policy an increase in its aid to urban governments. This should be done in part through revenue sharing, in part through an increase in categorical assistance, hopefully in much more consolidated forms than now exist, and through credit assistance.

It may not be expected that this process will occur rapidly. The prospects for an enormous "peace and growth dividend" to follow the cessation of hostilities in Vietnam are far less bright than they were painted. But the fact is that as a nation we grow steadily richer, not poorer, and we can afford the government we need. This means, among our very first priorities, an increase in the resources available to city governments.

A clear opportunity exists for the federal government to adopt as a deliberate policy an increase in its aid to state and local governments in the aftermath of the Vietnam War. Much analysis is in order, but in approximate terms it may be argued that the present proportion of aid should be about doubled, with the immediate objective that the federal government contribution constitute one-third of state and local revenue.

5. *Federal urban policy should seek to equalize the provision of public services as among different jurisdictions in metropolitan areas.*

Although the standard depiction of the (black) residents of central cities as grossly deprived with respect to schools and other social services, when compared with their suburban (white) neighbors, requires endless qualification, the essential truth is that life for the well-to-do is better than life for the poor, and that these populations tend to be separated by artificial government boundaries within metropolitan areas. (The people in between may live on either side of the boundaries, and are typically overlooked altogether.) At a minimum, federal policy should seek a dollar-for-dollar equivalence in the provision of social services having most to do with economic and social opportunity. This includes, at the top of the list, public education and public safety. (Obviously there will always be some relatively small jurisdictions—"the Scarsdale school system"—that spend a great deal more than others, being richer; but there can be national or regional norms and no central city should be allowed to operate below them.)

Beyond the provision of equal resources lies the troubled and elusive question of equal results. Should equality of educational opportunity extend to equality of educational achievement (as between one group of children and another)? Should equality of police protection extend to equality of risks of criminal victimization? That is to say, should there be not only as many police, but also as few crimes in one area of the city as in another? These are hardly simple questions, but as they are increasingly posed it is increasingly evident that we shall have to try to find answers.

The area of housing is one of special and immediate urgency. In America, housing is not regarded as a public utility (and a scarce one!) as it is in many of the industrial democracies of Europe, but there can hardly be any remaining doubt that the strong and regular production of housing is nearly a public necessity. We shall not solve the problem of racial isolation without it. Housing must not only be open, *it must be available.* The process of filtration out from dense center city slums can only take place if the housing perimeter, as it were, is sufficiently porous. For too long now, the production of housing has been a function, not of the need for housing as such but rather of the need to increase or decrease the money supply, or whatever. Somehow a greater regularity of effective demand must be provided the housing industry, and its level of production must be increased.

6. *The federal government must assert a specific interest in the movement of people, displaced by technology or driven by poverty, from rural to urban areas, and also in the movement from densely populated central cities to suburban areas.*

Much of the present urban crisis derives from the almost total absence of any provision for an orderly movement of persons off the countryside and into the city. The federal government made extraordinary, and extraordinarily successful, efforts to provide for the resettlement of Hungarian refugees in the 1950s and Cuban refugees in the 1960s. But almost nothing has been done for Americans driven from their homes by forces no less imperious.

Rural to urban migration has not stopped, and will not for some time. Increasingly, it is possible to predict where it will occur, and in what time sequence. (In 1968, for example, testing of mechanical tobacco harvesting began on the east coast and the first mechanical grape pickers were used on the west coast.) Hence, it is possible to prepare for it, both by training those who leave, and providing for them where they arrive. Doubtless the United States will remain a nation of exceptionally mobile persons, but the completely unassisted processes of the past need not continue with respect to the migration of impoverished rural populations.

There are increasing indications that the dramatic movement of Negro Americans to central city areas may be slackening, and that a counter movement to surrounding suburban areas may have begun. This process is to be encouraged in every way, especially by the maintenance of a flexible and open housing market. But it remains the case that in the next thirty years we will add 100 million persons to our population. Knowing that, it is impossible to have no policy with respect to where they will be located. *For to let nature take its course is a policy.* To consider what might be best for all concerned and

to seek to provide it is surely a more acceptable goal.

7. *State government has an indispensable role in the management of urban affairs, and must be supported and encouraged by the federal government in the performance of this role.*

This fact, being all but self-evident, tends to be overlooked. Indeed, the trend of recent legislative measures almost invariably prompted by executive initiatives has been to establish a direct federal-city relationship. States have been bypassed, and doubtless some have used this as an excuse to avoid their responsibilities of providing the legal and governmental conditions under which urban problems can be effectively confronted.

It has, of course, been a tradition of social reform in America that city government is bad and that, if anything, state government is worse. This is neither true as a generalization nor useful as a principle. But it is true that, by and large, state governments (with an occasional exception such as New York) have *not* involved themselves with urban problems, and are readily enough seen by mayors as the real enemy. But this helps neither. States *must* become involved. City governments, without exception, are creatures of state governments. City boundaries, jurisdictions, and powers are given and taken away by state governments. It is surely time the federal establishment sought to lend a sense of coherence and a measure of progressivism to this fundamental process.

The role of state government in urban affairs cannot easily be overlooked (though it may be deliberately ignored on political or ideological grounds). By contrast, it is relatively easy to overlook county government, and possibly an even more serious mistake to do so. In a steadily increasing number of metropolitan areas, it is the county rather than the original core city that has become the only unit of government which makes any geographical sense. That is to say, the only unit whose boundaries contain most or all of the actual urban settlement. The powers of county government have typically lagged well behind its potential, but it may also be noted that in the few—the very few—instances of urban reorganization to take place since World War II, county government has assumed a principal, even primary role in the new arrangement.

8. *The federal government must develop and put into practice far more effective incentive systems than now exist whereby state and local governments, and private interests too, can be led to achieve the goals of federal programs.*

The typical federal grant-in-aid program provides its recipients with an immediate reward for promising to work toward some specified goal—raising the education achievement of minority children, providing medical care for the poor, cleaning up the air, reviving the downtown business district. But there is almost no reward for actually achieving such goals—and rarely any punishment for failing to do so.

There is a growing consensus that the federal government should provide market competition for public programs, or devise ways to imitate market conditions. In particular, it is increasingly agreed that federal aid should be given directly to the consumers of the programs concerned—individuals included—thus enabling them to choose among competing suppliers of the goods or services that the program is designed to provide. Probably no single development would more enliven and energize the role of government in urban affairs than a move from the *monopoly service* strategy of the grant-in-aid programs to a *market* strategy of providing the most reward to those suppliers that survive competition.

In this precise sense, it is evident that federal programs designed to assist those city-dwelling groups that are least well off, least mobile, and least able to fend for themselves must in many areas move beyond a *services* strategy to an approach that provides inducements to move from a dependent and deficient status to one of independence and sufficiency. Essentially, this is an *income* strategy, based fundamentally on the provision of incentives to increase the earnings and to expand the property base of the poorest groups.

Urban policy should in general be directed to raising the level of political activity and concentrating it in the electoral process. It is nonetheless possible and useful to be alert for areas of intense but unproductive political conflict and to devise ways to avoid such conflict through market strategies. Thus conflicts over "control" of public education systems have frequently of late taken on the aspect of disputes over control of a monopoly service, a sole source of a needed good. Clearly some of the ferocity that ensues

can be avoided through free choice arrangements that, in effect, eliminate monopoly control. If we move in this direction, difficult "minimum standard" regulation problems will almost certainly arise, and must be anticipated. No arrangement meets every need, and a good deal of change is primarily to be justified on grounds that certain systems need change for their own sake. (Small school districts, controlled by locally elected boards may be just the thing for New York City. However, in Phoenix, Arizona, where they have just that, consolidation and centralization would appear to be the desire of educational reformers.) But either way, a measure of market competition can surely improve the provision of public services, much as it has proved an efficient way to obtain various public paraphernalia, from bolt-action rifles to lunar landing vehicles.

Here as elsewhere, it is essential to pursue and to identify the *hidden* urban policies of government. These are nowhere more central to the issue than in the matter of incentives. Thus, for better than half a century now, city governments with the encouragement of state and federal authorities have been seeking to direct urban investment and development in accordance with principles embodied in zoning codes, and not infrequently in accord with precise city plans. However, during this same time the tax laws have provided the utmost incentive to pursue just the opposite objectives of those incorporated in the codes and the plans. It has, for example, been estimated that returns from land speculation based on zoning code changes or average incur half the tax load of returns from investment in physical improvements. Inevitably, energy and capital have diverted *away* from pursuing the plan and *toward* subverting it. It little avails for government to deplore the evasion of its purposes in such areas. Government has in fact established two sets of purposes, and provided vastly greater inducements to pursue the implicit rather than the avowed ones. Until public authorities, and the public itself, learn to be much more alert to these situations, and far more open in discussing and managing them, we must expect the present pattern of self-defeating contradictions to continue.

9. *The federal government must provide more and better information concerning urban affairs and should sponsor extensive and sustained research into urban problems.*

Much of the social progress of recent years derives from the increasing quality and quantity of government-generated statistics and government-supported research. However, there is general agreement that the time is at hand when a general consolidation is in order, bringing a measure of symmetry to the now widely dispersed (and somewhat uneven) data-collecting and research-supporting activities. Such consolidation should not be limited to urban problems, but it must surely include attention to urban questions.

The federal government should, in particular, recognize that most of the issues that appear most critical just now do so in large measure because they are so little understood. This is perhaps especially so with respect to issues of minority group education, but generally applies to all the truly difficult and elusive issues of the moment. More and better inquiry is called for. In particular, the federal government must begin to sponsor longitudinal research, i.e., research designed to follow individual and communal development over long periods of time. It should also consider providing demographic and economic projections for political subdivisions as a routine service, much as the weather and the economy are forecast. Thus, Karl Taeuber has shown how seemingly unrelated policies of local governments can increase the degree of racial and economic differentiation between political jurisdictions, especially between cities and suburbs.

Similarly, the extraordinary inquiry into the educational system begun by the U.S. Office of Education under the direction of James S. Coleman should somehow be established on an ongoing basis. It is now perfectly clear that little is known about the processes whereby publicly-provided resources affect educational outcomes. The great mass of those involved in education, and of that portion of the public that interests itself in educational matters, continue undisturbed in its old beliefs. But the bases of their beliefs are already thoroughly undermined and the whole structure is likely to collapse in a panic of disillusion and despair unless something like new knowledge is developed to replace the old. Here again, longitudinal inquiries are essential. And here also, it should be insisted that however little the new understandings may have diffused beyond the academic research centers in which they originated, the American public is accustomed to the idea that understandings do change and, especially in the field of education, is quite open to experimentation and innovation.

Much of the methodology of contemporary social science originated in clinical psychology, and perhaps for that reason tends to be "deficiency-oriented." Social scientists raise social *problems*, the study of which can become a social problem in its own right if it is never balanced by the identification and analysis of social *successes*. We are not an unsuccessful country. To the contrary, few societies work as hard at their problems, solve as many, and in the process stumble on more unexpected and fulsome opportunities. The cry of the decent householder who asks why the social science profession (and the news media which increasingly follow the profession) must be ever preoccupied with juvenile delinquency and never with juvenile decency deserves to be heard. Social science like medical science has been preoccupied with pathology, with pain. A measure of inquiry into the sources of health and pleasure is overdue, and is properly a subject of federal support.

10. The federal government, by its own example, and by incentives, should seek the development of a far heightened sense of the finite resources of the natural environment, and the fundamental importance of aesthetics in successful urban growth.

The process of "uglification" may first have developed in Europe; but, as with much else, the technological breakthroughs have taken place in the United States. American cities have grown to be as ugly as they are, not as a consequence of the failure of design, but rather because of the success of a certain interaction of economic, technological, and cultural forces. It is economically efficient to exploit the natural resources of land, and air, and water by technological means that the culture does not reject, albeit that the result is an increasingly despoiled, debilitated, and now even dangerous urban environment.

It is not clear how this is to change, and so the matter which the twenty-second century, say, will almost certainly see as having been the primary urban issue of the twentieth century is ranked last in the public priorities of the moment. But there *are* signs that the culture is changing, that the frontier sense of a natural environment of unlimited resources, all but impervious to human harm, is being replaced by an acute awareness that serious, possibly irreparable harm is being done to the environment, and that somehow the process must be reversed. This *could* lead to a new, nonexploitive technology, and thence to a new structure of economic incentives.

The federal establishment is showing signs that this cultural change is affecting its actions, and so do state and city governments. But the process needs to be raised to the level of a conscious pursuit of policy. The quality of the urban environment, a measure deriving from a humane and understanding use of the natural resources together with the creative use of design in architecture and in the distribution of activities and people, must become a proclaimed concern of government. And here the federal government can lead. It must seek out its hidden policies. (The design of public housing projects, for example, surely has had the consequence of manipulating the lives of those who inhabit them. By and large the federal government set the conditions that have determined the disastrous designs of the past two decades. It is thus responsible for the results, and should force itself to realize that.) And it must be acutely aware of the force of its own example. If scientists (as we are told) in the Manhattan Project were prepared to dismiss the problem of longlived radioactive wastes as one that could be solved merely by ocean dumping, there are few grounds for amazement that business executives in Detroit for so long manufactured automobiles that emitted poison gases into the atmosphere. Both patterns of decision evolved from the primacy of economic concerns in the context of the exploitation of the natural environment in ways the culture did not forbid. There are, however, increasing signs that we are beginning to change in this respect. We may before long evolve into a society in which the understanding of and concern about environmental pollution, and the

general uglification of American life, will be both culturally vibrant and politically potent.

Social peace is a primary objective of social policy. To the extent that this derives from a shared sense of the aesthetic value and historical significance of the public places of the city, the federal government has a direct interest in encouraging such qualities.

Daniel J. Elazar has observed that while Americans have been willing to become urbanized, they have adamantly resisted becoming "citified." Yet a measure of "citification" is needed. There are perhaps half a dozen cities in America whose disappearance would, apart from the inconvenience, cause any real regret. To lose one of those six would plunge much of the nation and almost all the immediate inhabitants into genuine grief. Something of value in our lives would have been lost, and we would know it. The difference between these cities that would be missed and the rest that would not, resides fundamentally in the combination of architectural beauty, social amenity, and cultural vigor that sets them apart. It has ever been such. To create such a city and to preserve it was the great ideal of the Greek civilization, and it may yet become ours as we step back ever so cautiously from the worship of the nation-state with its barbarous modernity and impotent might. We might well consider the claims for a different life asserted in the oath of the Aethenian city-state:

We will ever strive for the ideals and sacred things of the city, both alone and with many;
We will uncreasingly seek to quicken the sense of public duty;
We will revere and obey the city's laws;
We will transmit this city not only not less, but greater, better and more beautiful than it was transmitted to us.

40

JOHN H. MOLLENKOPF

The Post-War Politics of Urban Development

During the 1960s, a dual political crisis unfolded in America's big cities.* One aspect of this crisis involved what Daniel Bell and Virginia Held called "The Community Revolution."[1] Across the country, neighborhood groups mounted campaigns to halt urban renewal, provide decent housing for themselves, and reclaim the public institutions which so strongly influence urban life. These groups squatted in vacant housing, stormed public hearings, mobilized thousands for marches and mass meetings, sat in front of bulldozers, and generally made life miserable for public officials. Starting in 1964, a series of ghetto rebellions swept from Cleveland, Watts, Newark, Detroit and Washington to dozens of other cities, generalizing this community-based political crisis. To make matters worse, the national government found itself increasingly unable to sustain support for imperialism abroad and liberal myths at home. The revolt of the neighborhoods thus became an important part of a widespread, though ill-defined political culture of insurgency.

While these waves were beating against City Hall, pressures from *within* the realm of orthodox city politics also began to undermine the mayoral coalitions which had structured urban politics since the mid-1950s. Increasingly organized and militant civil servants pressed for higher pay and better working conditions.

Neighborhood merchants and property owners insisted on improved services at lower tax cost, igniting what some saw as a "taxpayer's revolt." Reformist critics from professions like law and planning meanwhile took well-aimed potshots at the customary ways of doing city business. Mayors found their habitual solutions to such conflicts, namely increased federal funding, increased taxes, reduced services, and stimulated economic growth, to no avail, for these were the very practices being bitterly attacked. Together with external attacks, these internal difficulties caused severe fracture lines in many progrowth political coalitions, and caused some to crumble.

Big city mayorships were never as secure as other electoral offices, and certainly did not provide an easy path to higher positions, but in 1969 alone such prominent mayors as Lee (New Haven), Cavanagh (Detroit), Naftalin (Minneapolis), and Allen (Atlanta) left office.[2] Since then many others, such as Lindsay, Tate, and Barr, have departed, and remaining stalwarts like Alioto, Daley, and White may meet the same fate. A few retired voluntarily and others retired in order to avoid losing battles, but some were forcibly succeeded by "law and order" candidates, anti-renewal conservatives, blacks, and even a few self-proclaimed radicals. The prominence alone of those deposed suggests that the late '60s were a time of growing instability in city politics.

Why did these two developments take place? What is their significance? Were they merely summer lightning? Urban violence and protest generated much "instant research" but few convincing explanations. In the main, prevailing arguments involved notions about the influence of the civil rights movement, OEO's "stirring up

---

* October 1, 1975

Overuse has made the term "crisis" an imprecise word. Here it denotes circumstances under which an institution or social system has serious difficulties in reproducing itself. Mere conflict or antagonism may attend a crisis, but does not constitute one.

trouble," and the like. Riot analysts reached into their sociological trick bag and came up with "alienation," "frustrated expectations," "pervasive racism," and similar attitudinal arguments about why people rioted. And the destabilization of city political coalitions was, by and large, attributed to white ethnic reaction to black neighborhoods' transgressions of tacit boundary lines.[3] Far fewer thoughts were advanced concerning the impact of these frequently-lamented events.

Such views are both incomplete and conceptually and empirically inadequate. Why did people develop these ideas and attitudes? What specific mechanisms propelled them to act in the mid-Sixties, rather than ten years earlier or later? Why did they act against the specific targets they chose? How can the level of urban white ethnic activity, which was by no means primarily anti-black in its aims, be explained? Was, as Bell and Held argue, this activity merely an overheating of the democratic cauldron? Orthodox explanations have no response.

In order to answer these questions, a larger causal context must be established. It is the thesis of this paper that the dual political breakdown of the 1960s was part of a larger dialectic between local government's attempt to solve a central city land value and revenue crisis, and its striving to manage the unanticipated, but nevertheless sharp, political consequences of the "solution" chosen. In short, the dual political crisis grew out of a class-based struggle over the nature of urban development. It is argued here that politics and the activities of local government played a central role in determining the outcome of this struggle, but were also strongly shaped by it in turn.

It is important to examine the period between 1945 and the present with great care. First, this was a period of unparalleled urban violence and political activity. Though comparisons are not easy, even the urban upheavals of the industrial revolution apparently did not throw city politics into such a state of uproar and mass disaffection. Second, this was a period not only of great and qualitatively new metropolitan growth, particularly suburban growth, but of a major reconstitution of central city and land use patterns. Finally, it illustrates the central role which politics and the state play in what many, both on the left and the right, have viewed as a matter principally of economics.

I. A FRAMEWORK FOR UNDERSTANDING URBAN POLITICS

First and foremost, the city must be analyzed as the main physical location in which production, distribution, and the accumulation of wealth take place. These processes strongly color the nature of urban institutions. In turn, these institutions (principally large corporations, financial intermediaries, institutionalized political competition, local government programs, and production and distribution technology) exert their own particularizing influence on urban economic activity.

Even the physical layout of cities reflects, albeit in a complex and incomplete manner, the requirements of efficient production and exchange. Some cities, such as Gary, Indiana, or Pullman, Illinois, were laid out with such ideas specifically in mind. The principal impact of the city planning profession, however partial given the dreams of visionaries like Le Corbusier, has been to reduce economically "irrational" elements of older, more haphazardly-developed cities.[4]

But cities are more than networks of streets sidewalks, office buildings, and other public and private investments designed to produce maximum returns. The people who live in them inevitably express their human needs and pleasures in cultural, social, and geographic ways. By turning their environments to human as well as economic ends, they develop a sense of communal enjoyment which however fragmented, often exercises great sway. It is frequently likely, now to say necessary, that such communal feelings collide with the demands of production. The neighborhood saloon, with its time-honored rowdiness, clashed with the orderly, sober work habits desired in the factory. In another nineteenth century example, early volunteer fire departments evidently devoted as much time to battling each other as they did fighting fires. In the midwest, an entire corporate-based urban reform movement was launched to "Americanize immigrant workers into more reliable ways. Such conflicts have frequently arisen over neighborhood turf (the battle to control Pullman led to a nationwide rail strike in 1894). As circumstances dictated that cities become not only fashioned but refashioned in the period after World War II, such struggles became increasingly prominent.

Of the many institutions which mediate between the economic, accumulation-oriented side of urban life and its communal, human need-oriented side, none is more important than politics and the organization of local government. On the whole, local politics has functioned to enhance accumulation and control the ebullient and sometimes explosive aspect of urban life. Machine politics in the nineteenth century, for example, exerted its control through saloons, fraternal organizations, the straw boss work system, and even criminal activities, while the Catholic Church also exerted a strong restraining influence.[6] Yet local government's controlling influence has never operated smoothly nor with complete effect. U.S. urban history contains a large catalog of urban protest movements which plagued local politics and in turn made the process of economic growth at the very least more costly. Indeed, some scholars have viewed political reform movements of the late nineteenth and early twentieth centuries as an attempt by business interests to reduce these costs and gain more complete control over production and its environment, particularly its political environment.[7] Urban politics, in other words, plays a difficult, and often contradictory role in the unfolding of economic growth, but nevertheless a centrally important one. In particular, it must be viewed in terms of four interacting tendencies:

1. The changing character of the accumulation process, with its consequent impact on the composition and relations between social strata.
2. In particular, the resulting spatial differentiation of economic activities across different regions and cities, and within cities themselves.
3. The conflicting demands on government, national as well as local, which call for it to "solve" irresolvable trade-offs between accumulation and human needs.
4. A resulting long-term trend towards fragmentation and depoliticization of local government (linked to growing segmentation in the class structure and consequently in political expression).

Each of the last three tendencies derives from the first, but each also has exerted its own distinct and relatively independent effect on urban politics. To elaborate briefly on each point, a society's mode of production clearly determines the broad outlines of its city life. Weber, in his classic monograph on *The City*, discussed the role of religious, military, and market modes of producing and accumulating wealth on preindustrial urban life, a theme repeated in Mumford's magnificent *City in History*. The transition from mercantile to industrial capitalism, for example, shaped the composition, form, and political antagonisms of U.S. cities between 1790 and 1890. One need only compare colonial Boston's life as a port city with that of its latter day industrial satellites (Lowell, Lawrence) or turn-of-the-century Chicago to appreciate the profound truth of this proposition. Machine politics, the characteristic late nineteenth century urban political form, functioned not only to put in place key public works and services, but as a great engine of social peace amidst divisive clangor of a newly formed urban industrial working class. It grew in response to two incipient crises, one of production needs and one of class conflict.

Between 1945 and the present, in advanced countries, cities experienced an equally significant transition from industrial to post-industrial capitalism. James O'Connor has described this as a shift from accumulationist to disaccumulationist capitalism; the orthodox economist Victor Fuchs called it "the service revolution"; and Manuel Castells and David Harvey have spoken of the city's shift from an environment designed for production to one designed to promote consumption.[8] But no matter which terms one chooses to describe this transition, it has had a thorough-going impact on the national and international hierarchy of cities, the relationships between central cities and suburbs, and the spatial, social, and political relations within cities.

The key aspect of this change has been to convert the central city from a location for industrial work to one in which office-based command and control activities occur. Big cities have become key locations for nonproductive but nevertheless central business and government activities. This tendency has been reinforced by uneven development within the U.S. and internationally as well. As Cohen has pointed out, a series of world cities has emerged which may oversee production not only in the suburbs or hinterlands, but in the third world as well.[9] This tendency in the world economy undercuts the urban blue collar work force, underdevelops rural parts of the U.S. (particularly the South) and transfers the fruits of third world development to U.S. metropolitan centers. Collateral aspects of empire, such as the arms industry, also influence cities like Los Angeles.[10]

These forces have introduced many new factions into city politics, and have exacerbated the urban fiscal crisis as well. In subsequent pages these matters will be developed further; from an overall perspective, however, it seems clear that the modern corporate-based central city requires many more city services (i.e., transportation, traffic management, utilities, economic development and manpower training among others) than its nineteenth century counterpart.

A second tendency involves the city as what Harvey has called a "built environment" for economic activity.[11] This term is perhaps too narrow, for the city institutionalizes social as well as physical relationships through the investment in productive capital, housing, transportation, and so forth. But this said, it is clear that the metropolitan location of residences and economic activities has changed substantially since 1945. "Suburbanization," a cover term for a host of related trends, has reshaped the urban political arena, stimulated new political conflicts, and posed unexpected difficulties for metropolitan economies. Migration of rural, poor minorities to the central city, the dispersion of manufacturing, warehousing, and sales activities to the metropolitan periphery, and the relatively declining central city tax base have all played a part in the 1960's community mobilization and political instability.[12]

Third, local and national government actively promoted many of these contradictory changes. By setting up the Federal National Mortgage Association, the Home Loan Bank Board, and the FHA and VA loan programs, as well as subsidizing home ownership through the tax laws, the federal government provided a capital pool to finance these changes and provided individuals with a strong incentive to undertake them.[13] Direct expenditures on urban renewal, urban freeways, and mass transit provided much of the social capital required for these developments. But these policies jeopardized central city property values and helped to precipitate a chronic central city fiscal crisis.

This left the cities and the federal government the task of reinforcing downtown development, bridging the central city revenue gap, and simultaneously paying the costs of sustaining or restoring central city social peace. Among the resulting measures were urban renewal, urban

mass transit aid, the War on Poverty, and Model Cities. Given the requirements of the 1975 national economic crisis for austerity and energy conservation, some of these programs have become contradictory and difficult, to say the least. Certainly since 1946, federal intervention has elevated local politics to a matter of national concern and set a local political price tag on national policy aims.

The fourth and final tendency concerns the fragmented nature of local governance and its depoliticization, and the class segmentation with which they are associated. Political scientists have often noted that city governments are functionally decentralized, that political conflict has an interest group character, and that within the metropolis, government is highly fragmented. What they often miss is that these characteristics grew out of a long history of struggle for control over local government. This struggle would not have occurred if government were not both central to the urban economy and relatively autonomous from any given social stratum—that is, if it were not for the state's dual but contradictory role as guarantor both of accumulation and social peace. Middle and upper class political responses in the nineteenth century removed many elements of local government activity from the public arena by establishing nonpartisan, businesslike city charters, appointed commissions, suburban self-government, and the like. Devices like the independent, appointive authority (e.g., redevelopment authorities, port authorities, and transit authorities), proliferated in the period after 1930.[14] While such devices removed much activity from public debate and scrutiny, it also made coherent overall policy much more difficult to achieve.

The increasing segmentation within the class structure complicated matters. O'Connor has distinguished three sectors within the economy: the monopoly sector, the state sector, and the competitive sector.[15] Each has a specific set of interests and labor-capital conflicts, and each has a distinct relationship to state activity.[16] Large monopoly corporations require heavy government investments in social capital (roads, sewage facilities, research, educating a sophisticated labor force, etc.) and particularly seek to have them financed by the central city property tax, to which they are relatively invulnerable. Monopoly sector workers, both blue and white collar, have benefitted from industry-wide bargaining and high wage gains in return for giving up control over new technology; they have in large measure made up the new wave of post-World War II urban and suburban homeowners. As such, they tend to oppose spending on social services and upward movements in the property tax.

Competitive sector capital is composed of such firms as retailers, restaurants, real estate developers, construction firms, and the service sector generally. Because the firms are competitive, their profit margins are lower and their labor poorly paid. As a result, these firms often seek out local government as a protected market for construction contracts, supplies, insurance, etc. Most competitive firms favor expenditures which increase the volume of trade, but they nearly uniformly oppose reliance on the property tax and spending on social services. Competitive sector labor, on the other hand, tends to be located in the central city, heavily third world, and tenants rather than homeowners. They depended on government social services rather than union contracts for non-wage benefits. Though regressive taxes hit them hardest, they are also strong supporters of the welfare state.

The state sector by definition operates outside private sector market constraints. City government managers, firms under contract to the city, and city employees are necessarily highly political in the pursuit of their economic ends. City workers have developed extensive political power as the organizing role of urban political parties has declined. Civil service regulations and union strength make work discipline hard to enforce and, together with bureaucratic autonomy, encourage political alliances between agencies and elements of the private sector which benefit from agency activity. The relationship between the construction trades, real estate developers, and planning departments, urban renewal authorities, and public works departments is an outstanding case in point. Management and labor in the public sector, and their private sector contractors and beneficiaries, jointly favor increased local spending, especially for growth-oriented projects. Politically, they are a powerful force in favor of such spending. Since many city workers live outside the central city, they are not particularly sensitive to tax policies.

The interests of these sectors lead to some natural" political alliances. Monopoly firms, competitive labor, and state labor favor growing local expenditures, while competitive capital and monopoly labor oppose them. On the issue of growth, competitive firms like real estate owners and developers, construction firms, and their suppliers join the alliance, while competitive sector labor, which bears many hidden costs of growth, tends to drop away.

This latter alliance (large corporations, real estate developers and contractors, the building trades, and some government employees) gains significance because local government has long occupied a decisive position in the space economy. Beginning with the first urban services (water and streets), and extending through franchised utilities (streetcars, electricity, telephones) to zoning, urban renewal, mass transit, and urban freeways, local government has decisively influenced land use and land values.[17] Those with the largest stakes in land use have reciprocally found local government, from its earliest days, a bountiful vineyard in which to labor. Indeed, this private influence on public works investments and subsequent costs imposed on the public goes a long way towards explaining the dynamics of corruption and reform in American urban politics.

Fragmented government and a segmented class structure, then, heighten the importance of public labor and the amount of class conflict not only against but *within* local government. Clients of and workers within bureaucracies which are tightly entwined with property values (police, fire, planning, renewal, public works, etc.) push for accumulation-oriented spending and resist outside influence. Not so peacefully, they coexist with bureaucracies designed to incorporate dissident competitive sector labor seeking social spending (e.g., Model Cities, Community Action Programs, "emergency" federally-funded job programs). While certain aspects of this situation conform to traditional pluralist descriptions, the result is far from equalitarian or responsive.[18]

The interaction of these four tendencies suggests many contradictions. The state of the national accumulation process, for example, seems to necessitate recessionary measures which challenge some basic suppositions of post-war urban development. Or one might examine the internally antagonistic policies by which the federal government encourages dispersal and central city development simultaneously.

This paper, however, will concentrate on the way these factors influenced big city political stability, and hence urban development. It argues, in broadest outline, that local government's role in stimulating central city development contradicted its role as the guarantor of social peace and political cohesion. To put the matter schematically, (1) national changes in the accumulation process, changes in the spatial structure of economic activities, and federal policies aimed at converting the city from a device for production to one of consumption precipitated a crisis in central city real estate values shortly after the second world war. This was, of course, a period of suburban boom. This crisis involved what was then called "the cancerous effect of the slums"* on the central business district, relatively and even absolutely declining property values, and hence a central city fiscal crisis.

This development set the stage for (2) an alliance of central city politicians, a new breed of bureaucrats, large corporations, central business district real estate and merchant interests, and the construction trades. This pro-growth coalition pushed nationally for a strong urban renewal and highway program, and locally for downtown redevelopment. Strong, innovative mayors like Richard Daley, Richard Lee, Kevin White, and Joseph Alioto, and equally strong, not to say dictatorial renewal administrators like Robert Moses, Edward Logue, and M. Justin Herman forged sufficiently strong local coalitions to change the skylines of every major city.

Unfortunately for these figures, (3) their very successes undermined their position. By doing its part to reinforce the command and control functions of the central city over the metropolitan area, the surrounding region, and even overseas territories, the pro-growth imposed tremendous costs on central city residents. Growth generally and state intervention specifically displaced stable communities, exacerbated racial tensions, imposed heavy tax on those least able to pay, and proliferated burdens like commuting time, congestion, and pollution. It is thus to the local consequences of growth that the dual crisis of the 1960s can be traced.

At present, (4) the situation remains undecided. In some cities the pro-growth coalition has cleverly succeeded in reconciling incompatibles

through the generous application of jobs, program money, and other slices of pie. Others have skillfully exploited social divisions. But where conflicts have forced mayors to choose between support from the traditional bureaucracies and support from minority neighborhoods, or between growth beneficiaries and growth sufferers (taxpayers, displacees, transitional neighborhoods), alternative but usually transitory coalitions have sometimes emerged. The diversity of those opposed to growth has hampered the forging of an alternative program, particularly one which includes rank-and-file workers in city bureaucracies. While the current crisis has diverted attention towards survival, and has exacerbated social cleavages, it has also cut deeply into central city neighborhoods, and may yet provide the basis for an alternative.

The remainder of this paper will analyze and illustrate these four stages in the central city politics of post-World War II urban development using four case study cities: Boston, Cambridge, San Francisco, and Berkeley. These two metropolitan areas typify Cohen's world cities: they are centers of finance, high technology industry, high-level service activities, and corporate headquarters which influence national and international regions. The satellite cities of Berkeley and Cambridge house major centers of research and development and, to varying degrees, share a legacy of factory work and ethnic diversity. These cities thus typify a broad range of large, old, ethnic metropolitan areas. Though a distinction between them and the newer, rapidly growing cities of the South and Southwest (e.g., Albuquerque, Phoenix, Dallas) and between them and smaller regional cities (e.g., Louisville or Omaha) must be drawn, nevertheless they adequately represent the dozen or so largest and most important American cities.

II. THE CENTRAL CITY FROM 1940–1956: CRISIS AND RESPONSE

A. The Crisis

Nothing so neatly illustrates the rise and subsequent destabilization of growth-oriented urban politics as the changing meaning of the term "urban crisis." In 1950, the term included the central city's loss of population to the suburbs

---

* In this period, slums as a whole were declining in population. Black and other minority ghettos were growing, however, and the term thus has distinctly racist overtones.

ts growing minority population, expanding black slums, and threatened property values. It was generally conceived as a crisis. By 1970, the term covered not only social problems like racism, poverty, crime, and poor housing, but seeming political chaos and growing doubts about whether cities could overcome "negative externalities" like traffic congestion, pollution, and real estate disinvestment.[19] It was, in short, a crisis not of revenues but of political *demands*. Having once reflected mainly the economic travails of the central business district, the term came to cover the whole society's social and political conflicts.[20]

Central city property values—and tax roles—generally reached a peak about 1930, only to be knocked down during the Depression. Total local revenues declined considerably between 1930 and 1934, but picked up with greater economic activity and higher tax rates during World War II. Nevertheless, central city mayors, the bondholding institutions which had narrowly averted total defaults during the Depression by forcing city expenditure cutbacks, and downtown business interests were sorely worried about the post-war future of the central city.[21] They had ample reason.

During the 1940s and 1950s, central cities experienced a growing expenditure revenue gap. A 1952 study of New York City's prospects concluded that, given then current trends in revenues and expenditures, a $165 million gap would develop by 1953, burgeoning to $300 million by 1955.[22] This was a period, one must remember, before the advent of urban renewal and other

substantial state and federal transfers to central cities. Mayors of other big cities faced similar problems. In Boston, for example, to finance moderately rising expenditures for existing services and compensate for a declining tax base, the city administration boosted assessment rates on commercial and industrial property to "the unheard-of rates of 100 percent of true value" and the tax rate reached $86 per $1000, a point at which the business community could complain with some justice that an increase much "beyond this level will spell disaster."[23]

Table 1 illustrates these trends for the four cities under consideration. It shows that all four reached a peak in the tax base about 1930 which was not recovered until much later: Boston has never recovered; Cambridge did so in the late 1940's, but has recently experienced a decline owing to a militant tenant's movement; San Francisco recovered in the late fifties, and subsequently showed the strong gains; while Berkeley, which is more suburban and residential in character, suffered least and has made the strongest long term showing. While some of these cities made small gains during the 1950s, assessed values did not turn sharply upwards until the late 1960s.

The main point is that immediately after the war, all four cities faced a limited tax base and slowly growing (occasionally falling) land values at a time when costs for city budgets, both for services and capital investment, were rising. As a result, tax rates in all four cities rose sharply. As we shall see, such trends produced a political response in each of the cities.

Table 1. *Total Assessed Value of All Real Property Subject to Tax**

(in millions of dollars)

	1930	1940	1950	1960	1970	1974
Boston	$1,828	1,362	1,430	1,338	1,459	1,557
Cambridge	174	160	191	213	280	276
San Francisco	1,201	984	818	1,482	1,924	2,540
Berkeley	108	93	127	167	274	338

* These figures can only be taken as suggestive, given differing and politically sensitive methods of arriving at assessments. All are supposedly based on full market values.

Source: Assessor's Offices, Boston, Cambridge, San Francisco, Berkeley, and Alameda County.

B. The Federal Response

According to contemporary analyses, the causes of this fiscal and central city property value crisis were two-fold: on the one hand, the metropolitan dispersion of economic activity meant that central city revenues were declining relative to suburban fiscal capacity. On the other, growing poor black and other minority neighborhoods required expenditures over and above their revenue contributions and "threatened" neighboring property values.[24] Contributing to the problem were increases in tax exempt land (e.g., for new highways), limited tax mechanisms, and difficulties in raising public sector productivity. The appropriate policy seemed clear: eliminate "blighting" slums, stimulate investment in the central business district, and provide the transportation infrastructure necessary to keep the CBD "viable." And the only source of this policy, it seemed equally clear, was the federal government.[25]

The result of this consensus was pressure for federally-assisted efforts at slum clearance and urban renewal, culminating first in passage of the 1949 Housing Act and then in 1954 amendments which improved its central city impact. Litigation, the Korean War, and defects in the legislation, together with long planning lead times prevented urban renewal from having a substantial impact before about 1960, but when it arrived, it did so with great clamor on all sides.[26] As Table 2 suggests, the investment in urban renewal areas burgeoned rapidly after 1960. As a matter of comparison, total residential mortgages outstanding in 1970 were $334 billion, and in 1970 $26.5 billion was raised on *all* commercial property mortgages and corporate and foreign bonds.[27] Urban renewal thus involved an important part of all non-residential urban investment.

In his testimony before the House Banking and Currency Committee on the 1949 Act, Housing and Home Finance Agency Director Raymond Foley clearly stated the reason urban renewal should be enacted:

The mayors and other city officials daily face the problem of heavy municipal expenditures for essential municipal services in slum areas which far exceed the taxes derived from those areas. As new building is forced to the periphery of cities and the tax base in cities and the

Table 2. *Yearly Preliminary Loans for Urban Renewal*

(in millions of dollars)

1970	$3,833
1968	2,812
1966	1,806
1964	1,474
1962	1,118
1960	706
1958	239
1956	94
1954	44

Source: The Bond Buyer, "Statistics on State and Local Government Finance," May, 1971, p. 17. Total outstanding notes, 1954–1970, was $22.547 billion.

tax base in the central city areas decreases, they face the problem of constantly increasing municipal outlays for capital improvements and additions required to serve the newly developed areas. They do not have access to the financial resources required to absorb the full costs of the necessary write down in anything approaching the volume that is required for effective slum clearance operation.[28]

Urban renewal was to throw a wall around a creeping "blight," that is, the growing social problem of the minority urban poor, in order to preserve and enhance central city land values and contain poor neighborhoods' influence.* I was no wonder that the program was executed with frequent racist overtones.

A somewhat different coalition forged the second principal link in the national urban policy chain. Late in September, 1954, President Eisenhower appointed a five person Advisory Committee on a National Highway Program. The Committee included Lucius Clay, a former army general then chairman of Continental Can's board of directors (who had also been associated with

---

* To some extent the official argument was fallacious and self-serving because slums were being depopulated by whites' departures, not withstanding the growing numbers. Thanks to Bill Tabb and Larry Sawers for reminding me of this point. Blacks' arrival may have been caused more by declining land values than the reverse.

Goldman, Sachs, and Marine Midland Trust); David Beck, then Teamsters president; S. Sloan Coalt, Bankers Trust Company president and Morgan Bank director; William Roberts, president of Allis-Chalmers, road equipment manufacturer; and Stephen D. Bechtel, president of Bechtel Engineering, father of the Bay Area Rapid Transit District, and builder of numerous public works projects. Their report, "A Ten-Year National Highway Program," led to the passage of the $56 billion Interstate and National Defense Highway Act in 1956.[29]

Though this program was largely administered through State Highway Departments, rather than municipal governments, planning for urban freeway construction was by all accounts a highly political affair. Not only were congressmen and local political officials influential in helping to determine route and interchange locations, but big city chambers of commerce were made a formal part of the highway planning process. Together with auto-oil-highway construction-trucking interests in the national economy, they formed a formidable alliance for the construction of urban freeways.[30]

To varying degrees, as we shall see, all four case study cities embraced these two programs. But in so doing, it was not at all clear that these cities were taking doses of the right medicine. However effective these programs might be for real estate owners, it is highly doubtful that a physical approach could resolve problems like crime, delinquency, or the demand for social services.

III. THE DEEPER ROOTS OF THE POST-WAR URBAN CRISIS

The underlying causes of the central city land value fiscal crisis go far beyond the negative externalities and public expenditure requirements of urban slums. At least four factors played a part: (A) the national shift from an industrial to a service sector-office activity economy; (B) strong metropolitan dispersion trends (driven by political and labor-capital struggles as well as economic and technological considerations); (C) an associated internal migration; and (D) the contradictory role of local government and its general fragmentation and weakness.

A. National Economic Trends and the Central City

In the immediate post war years, a major economic tide had shifted against the central cities. By the end of the 1950s definitive academic studies had clearly established the parameters of this sea change. As Raymond Vernon reported in 1959,

> Office activities . . . will continue to expand. This activity aside, one sees only a growing obsolescence in the rest of the central city beyond its central business district.[31]

John Kain, another leading urban economist, reached similar conclusions. "Most central parts of metropolitan areas are losing employment to outlying areas and this process is, if anything, accelerating," he wrote in the early 1960s.[32]

These analysts give principally technological and market-oriented reasons for central city decline: improved transportation, the growing suburban retail market, the cheapness of suburban land, new production technologies requiring linear organization of work, and the piling up of "agglomeration diseconomies" like inner city congestion. And no doubt these factors worked towards making central cities a less important locus of manufacturing and retailing.

The positive side of this analysis stressed the continuing role of the central business district, if not the central city, as a home for corporate headquarters and related service activities. The hearts of big cities provide an "unduplicatable resource for firms requiring quick and efficient communication in persons as well as minimization of transportation of their supplies and output."[33] As such, they were still a natural location for markets of information, capital, expertise, and for corporate decision-making.

Table 3 suggests that central city employment markets conformed quite closely in the 1958–1963 period to Vernon's and Kain's prediction of absolute losses, while the more recent period does not. Cohen and James have suggested that the more recent central city gains were due to the overheated war economy of the mid-1960s and indeed, owing to the mid-1970s recession and widespread political opposition, the office building boom has slowed. Nevertheless, it must be admitted that service, govern-

Table 3. *Job Location Trends (11 Largest SMSAs)*

	(thousands)			(percentage)			1958 BASE (thousands)	
	Central City	Suburbs	Metro	Central City	Suburbs	Metro	Central City	Suburbs
Gain in Jobs 1958–1963								
Manufacturing	−125	130	005	− 7.9%	12.2%	.3%	1,952	1,178
Trade (R & W)	− 30	226	186	− 1.8%	22.6%	16.6%	1,704	710
Finance and RE	56	42	98	8.1%	32.6%	12.9%	686	129
Services	133	215	348	10.8%	37.7%	19.3%	1,230	570
Government	76	138	214	6.4%	29.7%	12.9%	1,191	466
Total Employment	84	806	890	1.1%	22.5%	11.3%	7,826	3,578
							1967 ENDPOINT (thousands)	
Gain in Jobs 1963–1967								
Manufacturing	− 23	129	106	− 1.3%	9.9%	3.3%	1,804	1,473
Trade (R & W)	51	236	287	3.1%	33.2%	11.0%	1,725	1,162
Finance and RE	38	28	66	5.1%	12.2%	7.2%	780	199
Services	175	201	376	12.8%	25.6%	17.4%	1,538	986
Government	175	178	353	13.8%	29.5%	18.9%	1,442	772
Total Employment	430	840	1270	5.5%	19.2%	10.3%	8,340	5,224

Source: Alexander Ganz, *Our Large Cities: New Light on Their Recent Transformation* (Cambridge: MIT Lab for Environmental Studies, 1972), Table II–8 and Appendix Table II–1.

ment, real estate, finance, and similar office-type functions showed unpredicted strength during the 1960s and remain strong in many cities today.[34] Particularly in Boston and San Francisco, major new buildings are in execution, and in Cambridge the skyline along Massachusetts Avenue was transformed between 1972 and 1975. The employment changes and the previously noted improvement in central city tax bases, both of which are quite real, must be traced to factors over and above strictly economic conditions: namely, the impact of the pro-growth coalition.

Tables 4 and 5 illustrate the impact of the changing character of the national economy on the four central cities.

Both Boston and San Francisco, and their satellites Cambridge and to some extent Berkeley, must be regarded as older central cities, long-developed. (Berkeley is a partial exception because it contains a large student and professional population, but it also contains industrial areas similar to Oakland and has a large black population.) Cities of this type were hit hardest by the national shift from production to services,

and these tables starkly etch the loss of central city holders of construction, manufacturing, transportation, and sales jobs, particularly during the 1950s.[35]

But Boston and San Francisco are major capital markets, each providing a home for numerous large corporations, banks, and insurance companies. Similarly, Cambridge and Berkeley contain large educational, technology, and research and development establishments. Tables 4 and 5 therefore also reflect how the economy's shift made possible strong employment gains in clerical work, government, and professional occupations, as well as in finance and real estate (not shown). This was especially true of the 1960s. Again these trends were not accidental: such gains were quite deliberately focused, as we shall see, in the central cities through the plans of the pre-growth coalitions.

B. Metropolitan Dispersion

The Vernon-Kain orthodoxy, often repeated by Chambers of Commerce, holds, as has been pointed out, that purely technological and transportation forces dictated suburban development. Urban historians, making the same argument, have traced the forces of suburbanization to streetcar line extensions, speculative home building, and the decline of annexations in the late nineteenth century.[36]

These forces are undoubtedly real, but the Vernon-Kain analysis has serious shortcomings because it fails to show why and how technological changes, such as improved transportation, were introduced. As it turns out, the technological innovation process, as Marx originally argued, grows out of struggles over production and profit. Not just the firm's search for comparative advantage over its competitors, but its owners' search for comparative advantage over its workforce and their milieu drives the technology innovation process.[37] In the urban context, the rise of suburban housing developments, relocation of manufacturing establishments outside the tense and dangerous central city, and the development of politically autonomous suburban communities can all be traced back to the capitalist struggle to control the productive process.[38] This fact has evidently characterized metropolitan dispersion since the mid-nineteenth century, but it seems to have accelerated in the period after World War II. By failing to see this relationship, the standard analysis also fails to see that technologies are inherently political, that is to say bound up with state activity and the political relations of classes.

While the evidence is at best fragmentary and the issue sorely needs further research, it seems that suburban housing and suburban production facilities answered a dual problem sharply posed during World War II. On the one hand, without something to absorb the productive capacity developed during the war, many business commentators and policy-makers evidently feared a return to the Depression.[39] On the other, the black migration to such war industry cities as Detroit had created very serious labor problems.[40] Some aspects are well known—overcrowded housing, pent-up housing demand, racial antagonisms—but others were equally sharp. The vulnerable location of large manufacturing es-

Table 4. *Boston-Cambridge 1950–1960–1970 Employment Trends (male and female)*

(numbers in thousands)

Occupation	1950 Bos	1950 Cam	1960 Bos	1960 Cam	1950–1960 change Bos	1950–1960 change Cam	1970 Bos	1970 Cam	1960–1970 change Bos	1960–1970 change Cam
Prof., tech., kindred	32.5	7.3	43.5	9.9	+33.8%	+35.6%	44.9	16.0	+ 3.2%	+61.8%
Mgrs., offs.	23.8	3.1	17.6	2.2	−26.1	−29.1	15.0	2.5	−14.8	+13.6
Clerical	60.6	7.8	59.0	9.3	− 2.7	+19.2	71.7	10.8	+21.5	+16.1
Sales	26.0	3.0	18.4	1.8	−29.3	−40.0	15.0	1.0	−18.5	+ 5.3
Craftsmen	42.0	5.9	32.4	4.1	−22.0	−30.5	27.2	3.4	−16.1	−17.1
Operatives	61.2	10.0	52.2	7.9	−14.7	−21.0	27.9	4.1	−46.5	−48.1
Pr. houseworkers	5.1	1.0	3.6	0.9	−29.4	−10.0	2.0	.5	−44.5	−44.4
Service workers	39.9	5.3	34.5	3.6	−13.8	−32.1	42.7	5.5	+23.8	+52.8
Laborers	17.7	2.6	12.0	1.5	−32.2	−23.1	11.0	1.1	− 8.3	−36.3
Industry										
Construction	15.4	2.0	12.4	1.2	−19.5	−40.0	11.7	1.2	− 5.6	0.0
Manufacturing	73.8	13.8	70.3	12.1	− 4.7	−12.3	46.7	8.0	−29.3	−33.9
Transportation	31.3	4.7	14.3	1.5	−54.4	−68.0	10.6	1.0	−23.1	−33.3
Wholesale & retail	75.8	8.9	53.5	6.3	−34.3	−29.4	51.7	5.9	− 3.4	− 6.3
Personal services	21.5	2.8	11.4	1.0	−46.9	−64.3	13.6	1.9	+19.3	+90.0
Selected professional services	35.0	8.6	43.1	12.9	+23.1	+50.0	67.8	20.8	+57.3	+61.2
Public administration	23.2	2.7	19.3	2.4	−16.7	−11.1	19.4	2.4	+ .5	0.0
Total Population	801	120	697	108	− 8.7	− 9.0	641	100	− 8.0	− 7.4

Table 5. *Berkeley-San Francisco 1950–1960–1970 Employment Trends* (male and female)*

(numbers in thousands)

Occupation	1950 SF	1950 Berk	1960 SF	1960 Berk	1950–1960 change SF	1950–1960 change Berk	1970 SF	1970 Berk	1960–1970 change SF	1960–1970 change Berk
Prof., Tech., kindred	35.9	11.2	40.5	13.2	+12.8%	+17.9%	55.9	18.5	+38.0%	+24.8%
Mgrs., offs., & props.	36.9	5.2	28.9	3.7	−21.7	−28.8	25.3	3.2	−12.1	−15.6
Clerical	72.8	9.0	79.3	9.2	+ 8.9	+ 2.2	92.2	11.2	+16.3	+21.7
Sales	30.4	4.1	25.2	3.0	−17.1	−22.0	22.7	2.7	− 9.0	−10.0
Craftsmen	40.8	4.6	32.8	3.5	−19.6	−23.9	26.9	3.0	−18.0	−14.3
Operatives	44.4	4.8	38.2	3.7	−14.0	−22.9	23.3	2.5	−39.0	−32.5
Private household workers	6.9	1.6	7.0	1.6	+ 1.5	0.0	5.1	1.2	−27.3	−25.0
Service workers	40.3	4.5	39.3	4.1	+ 2.4	− 8.9	45.4	5.2	+15.6	+26.8
Laborers	17.6	2.2	14.5	1.9	−16.5	− 9.1	11.5	1.9	−20.7	−36.8
Industry										
Construction	18.7	2.3	14.1	1.5	−24.6	−34.7	12.2	1.4	−13.5	− 6.7
Manufacturing	55.9	7.8	54.5	6.4	− 2.5	−18.0	37.3	4.9	−31.6	−23.4
Transportation	38.6	3.6	24.4	1.8	−36.7	−50.0	20.8	1.3	−14.8	−27.7
Wholesale & retail	80.2	8.2	67.9	6.1	−15.3	−25.6	64.7	6.6	− 4.7	+ 8.2
Personal services	26.0	4.5	23.8	2.6	− 8.5	−42.2	24.2	3.3	+ 1.7	+26.9
Selected professional services†	32.4	11.0	43.4	14.8	+33.0	+34.6	74.7	22.2	+72.1	+74.3
Public administration	25.1	4.1	23.0	3.8	− 8.4	− 7.3	25.3	3.7	+ 9.7	− 2.6
Total population	775	114	740	111	− 4.5	− 2.6	716	118	− 3.2	+ 6.3

* U.S. Department of Commerce, Bureau of Census, Census of Housing, 1950, 1960, 1970, Cal P-C5, PC(1)-137 and PC(1)-C6.

† Health and hospital, education and legal, engineering, and miscellaneous services.

tablishments in the midst of working class neighborhoods, themselves beset by all manner of problems, evidently spurred corporations to set up new small plants in safer suburban locations. By doing so, corporations could solve both problems at once: stimulate demand (through the suburban military-industrial and auto-oil-highway complexes), and restore social control to the production environment.

That the latter was a serious factor in postwar suburban expansion is suggested by a 1948 debate published by San Francisco's Commonwealth Club, a businessman's association. Chaired by a community developer and ex-president of the National Association of Home Builders, this session discussed the reasons for urban decentralization. While technological explanations were given, as the vice president of the American Trust Company stated:

Labor developments in the last decade may well be the chief contributing factor in speeding regional dispersion of industry, and have an important part in the nationwide tendency toward industrial decentralization. In this period good employee relations have become a number one goal. Labor costs have expanded markedly. Conditions under which employees live, as well as work, vitally influence management-labor relations. Generally, large aggregations of labor in one big [central city] plant are more subject to outside disrupting influences, and have less happy relations with management, than in smaller [suburban] plants.[41]

The report goes on to quote the California Stat Reconstruction and Re-employment Commis sion's 1946 report "New Factories for Californi Communities": "Workers could own their ow homes and enjoy contentment, leisure, lower living costs, and better health. . . . The managers of many large and small plants which have located in Santa Clara County testify that their employees are more loyal, more cooperative, and more productive workers than those they have had in the big cities."

The Commonwealth Club session cited Santa Clara manufacturers with similar urban and suburban plants, who claimed that the suburban locations had lower turnover rates, less absence, fewer disputes, and more productivity. Another manufacturer said even five hundred employees was too many to have in one place. "We are going to get away from tenements, traffic jams, high taxes, crowded streetcars, and transient labor, with all the economic waste and irritation those things involve." The session concluded with a vote of 101 to 2 that dispersal improved workers' health and 51 to 37 that dispersal, in general, increased profits.[42]

Boston Metropolitan development responded to similar pressures after the war. Although it does not seem to have been planned with public sponsorship in quite the same way as the San Francisco Peninsula's electronics and aircraft industries, Cabot Cabot and Forbes quite effectively stimulated development of the electronics industry along Boston's Route 128.[43] The nature of interlocking directorates, financing, and the presence of old Brahmin families in some of these firms suggests this development was planned quite consciously by Boston's corporate establishment.[44] In other words, dispersion resulted not just from the imperatives of competition, but also from a reasonably clear understanding of the social control aspects of plant location.

C. Internal Migration

Americans have always been an extremely mobile people geographically, if not economically. A national sample in 1968 showed that about half the population had made a substantial move, including one fifth who had moved from the countryside to the large metropolitan areas. Of the 40 million people living in the larger cities, fully half were born in small towns or rural areas. For non-whites, this relationship is even more striking.[45]

The changing nature of the national economy since 1940 was accompanied by an equally significant internal migration. It was triggered partly by the very development of war time productive capacity in large cities, and partly by the capitalization of agriculture and other aspects of uneven development in the rural South, Puerto Rico and Mexico. Black migration to the urban north began around 1920, with the forced abatement of European migration. By 1968, blacks were *more* urbanized than whites and formed an increasingly large component, along with other minority populations, of the central city citizenry.

During the 1940s 1.6 million blacks migrated cityward, more than the total of the previous thirty years, in response to wartime labor demands. Then in the 1950s mechanized agriculture forced even more blacks towards the north. Between 1949 and 1952 alone, the demand for unskilled agricultural labor in the Mississippi Delta counties dropped by 72 percent.[46]

This post-1940s migration first inserted blacks into the northern urban economy, and then, in the post-war period, steadily deprived them of jobs and housing as veterans returned. The 1950s were thus a time when northern urban blacks struggled to establish a sense of community, elaborate communal institutions, and carve out an economic niche. This effort, as we have seen, was viewed by whites as a menacing, "blighting" development. Yet as Table 6 shows, blacks made steady numerical gains in the four cities under consideration. Other minority ethnic groups follow similar patterns.

Recent arrivals joined already established black neighborhoods in each of these cities, and by the 1960s their number was expanding more by natural increase than migration. By the time that the influence of the pro-growth was most devastatingly felt, these black communities had passed a generation at least from its conservative Southern roots, had begun to establish a more independent, community-based leadership.

D. The Central City Political Vacuum and Contradictory Demands on City Government

A final factor also underlay the central city land value and fiscal crisis: the absence of strong leadership possessed of a clear program. As

Table 6. *Black Population*

(Thousands: Percent of City Population)

	1950		1960		1970	
	No.	Percent	No.	Percent	No.	Percent
Boston	40	5	63	9	105	16
Cambridge	6	5	7	7	9	9
San Francisco	43	6	74	10	96	13
Berkeley	13	12	22	20	28	24

Source: 1950, 1960, and 1970 Census of Population. These figures are undoubtedly low.

Raymond Wolfinger has rightly pointed out, the only way we really know that machine politics is really dead is because we have killed it so often.[47] The years immediately after World War II provided one such demise, and perhaps one of the more spectacular ones. In 1949, Mayor James Michael Curley of Boston failed to win re-election, and the Hague Machine in Jersey City also suffered a severe electoral setback. In Chicago, the regular party organization entered a period of relative decline, from which Richard Daley later resurrected it with years of careful work.[48] Elsewhere, though machine politics remained alive and well (in cities like Philadelphia, Pittsburgh, New Haven, Providence and St. Louis), it was bereft of any winning program. Nor did regular machine mayors appear attractive to the potential allies they would need were they to address adequately the central city property value and fiscal crisis.[49] In short, local government did not seem likely to live up to the demands being placed on it. Instead, big cities seemed dominated by haphazardly corrupt, functionally isolated bureaucracies with no particular goal except muddling through the deepening crisis.

The stage was thus fully set for a new turn in city politics. Deep forces within the national economy and metropolitan social structures had precipitated a crisis within the central city. National government policy, owing to its need to stimulate the economy as a whole and regulate labor-capital relations, had exacerbated this problem, yet it had responded to specifically central business district needs by 1956 with two key tools: urban renewal and freeways. Though central city-based banks, corporations, real es-

tate, and retailing interests were increasingly well organized and aware of the need for action, they had not made connections with big city mayors. It was in this period, between the mid-1950s and the mid-1960s, that the pro-growth coalition emerged with full force.

IV. THE RISE OF THE PRO-GROWTH COALITIONS, 1955–1970

At different rates and in numerous local variants, big city politicians and businessmen forged a new alliance around central city development in the years between 1955 and 1970. In an important but not widely emulated 1964 article, Robert Salisbury argued that a "new convergance of power" was developing in city politics, based on "an executive-centered coalition" of businessmen, progressive mayors, and planning-oriented technocrats.[50]

Sometimes this coalition was led by a bureaucratically based machine mayor, albeit one with reform overtones like Chicago's Daley or Pittsburgh's Lawrence. Sometimes it stood apart, in uneasy coexistence with machine organizations, as in Neward. And sometimes it defeated a machine organization and stood in an essentially antagonistic relationship to mainline city bureaucracies, at least at the outset, as in Boston under Collins. While Salisbury never expanded his analysis in this way, certain dimensions seem present in almost every situation.[51]

One element proved to be strong leadership from renewal executives, who learned how to use the urban renewal program like a political panzer division, massing forces in secret and then launching lightning attacks on the chosen territory. Robert Moses, as Robert Caro's widely-heralded biography shows, invented the basic techniques in this process, the independent authority, secret planning, well-timed deadline manipulation, and good Washington contacts.[52] Edward Logue, first renewal director under Lee in New Haven, then under Collins in Boston, and finally director of New York's Urban Development Corporation, refined and endowed with political sophistication most of these techniques. In the process he trained a bevy of administrators who went on to direct renewal in such other cities as Washington, D.C., Miami, New York, and Cleveland, or to work for such corporations as James Scheuer (a developer), R. H. Macy, and the United Nations Development Corporation.[53] At the same time, large new bureaucracies commanding money, technical expertise, and large manpower pools were developed to back up these leaders.

A second element involves more or less direct corporate sponsorship of the renewal process. As Roger Friedland has shown, nearly every major city developed, during the 1950s, a corporate-based planning body interested in urban development. More often than not, these groups included high executives in the city's largest corporations; many were able to raise sufficient funds to hire staff members and conduct studies of "proper" urban development patterns.[54] Their activities essentially fit the mold outlined by Kolko's, Weinstein's, and Domhoff's studies of corporate liberalism; that is, these business planning groups first developed their ideas *in camera*, subsequently developed a wider business consensus around them, and then ultimately promoted them by various political means, including most especially connections with growth-oriented mayors. Even where corporations designated to finance or undertake redevelopment were outsiders to a given city, they seem to have had strong local backers or partners. (This is an area, however, where further research would be well repaid.)

Pittsbugh provides a classic example of how high-level corporate interests developed and implemented renewal plans. R. K. Mellon, heir to a fortune which included Koppers, Pittsburgh Consolidation Coal, the Mellon Bank, and Gulf Oil, established the Allegheny Conference on Community Development in 1943 because, it seemed, Pittsburgh was "on the brink of disaster."[55] Mel-

lon pulled together a group of young, innovative executives (many of whom he had appointed), appointed an executive director, and proceeded to develop plans for what became the Golden Triangle, Pittsburgh's new central business district. The ACCD also developed plans to reduce steel—and coal—related pollution, in order to make Pittsburgh a less unattractive place to live.

In what one commentator called a "reverse welfare state," Mellon, the ACCD, and its corporate cohorts forged an alliance with David Lawrence and the city's Democratic machine, and proceeded to reshape Pittsburgh.[56] It did so, of course, in part because it could create a wide consensus around this program. Because Lawrence and his organization could unite Republican corporate leaders, merchant and real estate interests, the construction trades, and the Democratic party around the divisible benefits so plentifully derived from renewal, the corporate program became what was for a long while an unstoppable public program.[57]

The third element in this alliance proved to be a new generation of growth-oriented mayors. Daley was first elected mayor of Chicago in 1955, after the weak, interim Kennelly administration. Though firmly in control of the Cook County Democratic Party, Daley was stung by charges of bossism and set out to recruit backing from the Chicago business community. Too, as Mike Royko points out, "the fastest way to show people that something is happening is to build things." And build Daley did.[58] By the mid-1960s, he had the solid backing of Chicago's business and real estate communities.

Similarly, New Haven's Mayor Lee was elected in 1953 on a campaign of modernizing the city. He too succeeded a relatively weak mayor, and managed to forge decent working relations with the city's Democratic organization. Lee, a former Yale and Chamber of Commerce public relations officer, subsequently piled up larger election margins upon putting renewal into action.[59] Similarly, in numerous other cities innovative, growth-minded mayors, with strong professional and business backing, reached office in the period between 1955 and 1965. Among the best known are those mentioned earlier: the Lindsays, Aliotos, Collinses, Whites, Cavanaghs, Uhlmans, and the rest.

Though no careful, comparative survey of these mayors has been done, it appears that they share certain characteristics. They generally have a liberal, technocratic outlook, come from professional careers, and have strong ties to the local business community. Yet at the same time they also tend to come from ethnic backgrounds, and to one degree or another can replicate the appeal upon which ethnic machine candidates usually bank. Almost without exception they are Democrats, and if they begin their careers without the support of old-line city bureaucracies and regular party organizations, they have usually been able, towards the maturity of their careers, to build ties with them. In general, they have been management-oriented, introducing new techniques like program budgeting, program planning, and computerized management systems. They have skillfully shaken the federal money tree for free resources with which to build their own parallel bureaucracies, often outside of city civil service, as a political base.[60]

There are other elements within this coalition too: city labor councils and construction trades councils, regular party organizations, realty interests, good government groups, and others. Their participation, however, was both more variable and of less decisive importance. Of more significance was the fact that, in the late 1950s and early 1960s, at least, a growth platform could be touted as a panacea. Since the negative consequences had not yet fully emerged, attention could be focused on prospective rising tax bases, construction jobs and contracts, new housing, expanded central city institutions and the like. While neighborhoods were not aware of the consequences for them, local business could see clearly the wide range of benefits which would accrue. Renewal, therefore, commanded, for a time, a working if not general, consensus.

The two metropolitan areas under study, and the four central cities, embraced fully the pro-growth coalition during the late 1950s. The specific patterns differed somewhat because the nature of local corporate interests and their connection to local machine politics (where it existed) differed, but the general outline holds for each.

Boston's first pro-growth mayor was John Hynes, who defeated James Michael Curley in 1951 with the aid of the New Boston Committee, a business-based reform group. Faced with a deepening fiscal crisis, Hynes attempted in 1957 to secure loans for city operations, and city bankers forced him to cut back city employees

by 5 percent in eighteen months. In an attempt to reverse tax base declines, Hynes initiated the now-infamous West End Project, one of the first massive slum clearance projects in the country. It displaced over 2,600 families.[61] He also put together the Prudential Center project—he compared it to the rolling away of the stone in front of Jesus' tomb—with support from George Oakes, a Brahmin vice president of R. M. Bradley, one of Boston's leading real estate firms; Cardinal Cushing; and Charles Coolidge, Brahmin partner in Ropes and Gray, perhaps Boston's most prestigious law firm.[62]

In 1959, a second important election occurred. One candidate, machine Democrat John E. Powers, appeared to be in the lead and threatened, if elected, to declare city bankruptcy in order to get the city out of its fiscal jam. This naturally threw shivers down the spines of the city's Brahmin bond-holders, and a business group, soon dubbed "The Vault," organized to put John Collins into the mayoralty. Originally conceived as receiver should the city default on its obligations, the group raised a substantial amount of money to back Irish Democrat Collins. He won.

Among the Vault's members were Gerald Blakely (prime mover behind Route 128 for Cabot, Cabot and Forbes), Coolidge, Ralph Lowell (retired Chairman of the Boston Safety Deposit and Trust Co. and director of numerous Boston corporations), Carl Gilbert (chairman at Gillette and Raytheon director), Lloyd Brace (chairman of the First National Bank of Boston), and various other Brahmin bankers, insurance company executives, retailers, and utility company executives. With their backing, Collins improved city administration, used their money to hire consultants, and trimmed 1,200 more employees from the payroll. But most of all, he hired Ed Logue as redevelopment director and initiated the "New Boston" renewal program that ultimately subjected 10 percent of the city's land area to redevelopment.

In Cambridge, the universities and their high-technology industrial allies provided the corporate organization for urban renewal.[63] In a coalition less focused on any single political figure, the city's ethnic politicians pushed MIT's plans to develop Tech Square and Kendall Square in an effort to "Blitz the slums," as then-mayor Edward Crane put it. The universities provided technical assistance for renewal applications, jointly set up a nonprofit corporation to spur housing development and undertook their own very substantial development programs. The net result was to reshape Cambridge's entire composition by the end of the 1960s. Most of the industrial plants, including Riverside Press, Simplex Wire, Biltrite Rubber, and the like, were bought by the universities as these firms departed, and developed for new university and high-technology research and development uses. As a result, not only were many families and small businesses displaced, but incredible stresses were placed on the working class housing stock.

San Francisco's Mayor Joseph Alioto was a comparatively late arrival, having been first elected in 1967, but had done duty as chairman of the redevelopment agency in the late 1950s. Alioto put together a political coalition based on big labor, big real estate, and big corporations, with substantial minority neighborhood support for good measure. This alliance gave strong backing to renewal during the mid-1960s, but it is necessary to go back much further to establish the essentially non-partisan sources of San Francisco's pro-growth coalition.[64]

In 1945, leaders of the region's major corporations founded the Bay Area Council, upon which membership was open only to chief executives, including those of the Bank of America, American Trust Company, Standard Oil of California, Pacific Gas and Electric, etc. The BAC concentrated primarily on two issues: regional transportation, which had been in a shambles during World War II, and industrial location, including urban renewal. It issued a number of important studies, and developed business consensus most importantly for the development of the Bay Area Rapid Transit District, or BART. BART's impact on the Bay Area is a complex story of government action at corporate behest all of its own. BART's $1.6 billion dollar capital investment will influence Bay Area development for decades alone, and strongly reinforces the San Francisco CBD.

Some of its San Francisco members founded a second committee in 1956, the Blythe-Zellerbach committee, to back urban renewal.[65] It in turn set up a broader group, S. F. Planning and Urban Renewal Association (SPUR), to build support largely among the city's professionals for urban renewal. In the late 1950s B-Z gave money for renewal related studies to the City Planning Department, and in the early 1960s, SPUR was designated the official citizen participation unit for renewal in San Francisco.

As a result of these business initiatives and the resulting alliance they forged with Mayor Alioto and his two predecessors, San Francisco, like Boston and Cambridge, launched into massive urban renewal efforts. During all three administrations, M. Justin Herman, previously a HHFA official responsible for overseeing renewal in the western regions, provided strong leadership for renewal. Indeed, community spokesmen often berated him as a dictator, a charge Herman's usual response did little to disprove. With backing from B-Z, SPUR, major city property owners, and most trade unions and subsequently from Alioto and his organized political strength, Herman undertook to redevelop large areas adjacent to the central business district, the city's produce market, its Japanese neighborhood, its major black neighborhood, and a variety of other sites. Though community opposition prevented entry into the Mission District, San Francisco's Latino neighborhood, in 1967, these other projects seem destined for ultimate completion.[66]

Berkeley established yet another variant of the pro-growth orientation, in keeping with that city's hothouse politics. Unlike the other three cities, Berkeley is neither the center of much corporate activity nor of extensive banking. It is, rather, an odd combination of middle class suburbs, working class black suburb, and university "ghetto." Berkeley has the most "professionalized" and least politicized bureaucracy of all four cities, and undoubtedly the most ideologically charged electoral politics. A city manager city with a strong progressive history, there were no machine politicians in Berkeley to build a corporate-ethnic alliance in behalf of renewal. Instead, Berkeley had for most of the 1960s a self-made millionaire engineer for a mayor. This official, Wallace Johnson, stood slightly to the right of Barry Goldwater and espoused non-political, business-like administration. He achieved office during a highly-divisive 1963 campaign concerning open house (which Berkeley defeated). During the student riots in the late 1960s he advocated "riot wardens" drawn from the city's more responsible classes to keep order.

As a manufacturer and vigorous opponent of Berkeley radicalism, Johnson strongly backed private enterprise and renewal. He provided political support for the controversial West Berkeley Industrial Park, which would have displaced a number of black families, and a bayshore shopping center and marina, strongly opposed by environmentalists. More importantly, however, Johnson spearheaded a campaign in the early 1960s to bury BART lines in Berkeley rather than have them run on elevated structures. This campaign, which won by 83 percent, resulted in a large cut-and-cover operation which displaced substantial amounts of housing; BART itself, of course, proved to be a major spur to Berkeley highrise development. Johnson and his allies on the Berkeley Real Estate Board proved to be among the strongest supporters of BART in concept, if not always in execution.[67]

As in Cambridge, the university also acted as a principal stimulant to development through its rapid post war expansion. Under Clark Kerr, University enrollments rose rapidly after World War II. With them came large scale university construction, student pressure on the housing market, and a shift in merchandising to attract the student market. Like Cambridge, the university promoted high-technology and research and development firms. And as in Cambridge, Lawrence Radiation Laboratory and other university efforts were linked with military-industrial activities. Unlike the other cities, however, and owing to the weakness of corporate influence, no full-blown pro-growth coalition ever developed.

These cities suggest certain basic themes. One is the rather clear corporate planning initiative, which develops the basic renewal scheme, often with corporate resources, and then sells it to the right bureaucratic and political figures. It may even recruit the executives to operate the renewal program. The second theme is the emergence of growth-oriented mayors, who seize the corporate-inspired development plans as a program on which they can create a strong organization. Even in Berkeley, where corporate activity is least evident, some of these tendencies were weakly present. The developers and central business district interests who benefitted most directly from urban renewal proved to be the largest campaign contributors to the growth-oriented politicians in each city. But more was involved than a simple graft relationship—pro-growth mayors were able, as long as the costs remained confined, to build a much broader base of support for their regimes. Renewal provided manpower, benefits, resources, and latent political support, for any mayor audacious enough to reach for them.[68]

The initiative for the pro-growth coalition thus came from two sides: corporate planning interests on the one, dynamic and aggressive politicians on the other. The extent to which these two jelled in a coalition determined how massively a city moved into renewal. And three of the four cities under consideration produced a solid coalition indeed. Boston, Cambridge, and San Francisco rank 4th, 7th and 10th nationally after New Haven, in terms of renewal funds per capita.[69] Boston and San Francisco contain the two largest residential renewal projects in the country. These cities, as we have seen, were governed after the mid-1950s by a strong pro-growth coalition. In Berkeley, where the material conditions for such a coalition were weaker, the thrust for renewal was weaker, but not absent.

V. THE CHICKENS COME HOME TO ROOST

Urban Struggles Against the Consequences of Growth, 1965–1975

A. The Consequences of the Pro-Growth Coalition

As time passed, the seamy side of urban development started to seep out from under its glossy covering rationalization. As a sign on the side of a vacant lot created by renewal in Cambridge said,

> No War Declared,
> No Storm Had Flared
> No Sudden Bomb So Cruel,
> Just a Need for Land,
> A Greedy Hand
> And A Sign
> That Said,
> "Urban Renewal"[70]

Though Boston's West End residents failed to mobilize against that city's first massive clearance, they banded together afterward and became symbols, in the many neighborhoods to which they were displaced, of the destruction renewal portended for working class neighborhoods. It was a pattern which was to recur in most places where the pro-growth coalition was strong.

The pro-growth coalition engineered a massive allocation of private and social resources. Since 1949, the federal government has committed over $8.2 billion in direct outlays and more than $22.5 billion in bonded debt. By 1968 private investors had sunk an estimated additional $35.3 billion into 524 renewal projects across the country. In addition, some $70 billion has been expended on interstate highways, a substantial portion of which went to high-cost urban areas. As a result of these investments, more than a quarter of a million families have been displaced each year. They have received only $34.8 million in relocation payments, or less than 1 percent of the direct federal outlay![71]

Even those who defend the renewal program on other grounds admit that it is upwardly redistributive. "The result is a regressive income redistribution," wrote one analyst, "with lower-income groups who consume at the lower end of the housing stock suffering the most."[72] A glance at some national figures indicates the extent of this effect. (See Table 7.) As these figures show, more than one million people per year were being displaced in the late 1960s, notwithstanding a drop in highway displacements forced by urban freeway opponents. Assuming an equal chance for everyone, and no one displaced twice, this means that in a ten-year period, fully 6.3 percent of the urban population was displaced. Of course chances are not equal, so residents of poor neighborhoods near central business dis-

tricts probably are three or four times more likely to suffer.

Displacement of this kind carries many costs: out of pocket expenses, higher rents, psychic trauma, sundered friendships, more crowded low rent housing, and on and on. Downs identified twenty-two separate costs borne by those displaced, though he believes only ten should be wholly or partly compensated (others are important, he argues, but impossible to price).[73] For those costs he is willing to estimate, he believes renewal imposes (and he underestimates substantially the number displaced), "unfair . . . costs of at least $156.5 to $232 million per year upon approximately 237,000 displaced persons and at least another 237,000 non-displaced persons." In other words renewal costs displaced families, who average $4,000 a year in income, fully $1,000![74]

Much of this damage has been done in the cities under examination. Boston has thirty-four renewal projects with almost a quarter of a billion dollars' worth of authorized spending. Cambridge has eight projects with $28 million authorized, holding up well comparatively. San Francisco has fifteen projects, with $165 million authorized including the single biggest residential renewal project in its black Western Addition neighborhood. Berkeley trails with $6.4 million authorized.

The impact has fallen squarely on poor neighborhoods. The Western Addition A-1 and A-2 projects involve $100 million in public money, and have displaced eight thousand people; the Yerba Buena convention center has also displaced thousands. And this seems unlikely to

Table 7. *Urban Renewal and Highway Displacements, Compensatory Payments*

(thousands)

	1964	1965	1966	1967	1968	1969	1970
Urban Renewal*	636	712	780	851	915	1001	1035
Interstate Highways	97	94	99	90	87	62	59
Average Payment†	$73	$75	$76	$79	$82	$91	$95

* Assumes average family size is 3.0 individuals.

† Weighted average of payments to renters displaced. No comparison was made to highway displacees until 1969.

Source: See note 71.

be anything but a drain on San Francisco's revenues.[75] Boston's South End redevelopment area, rated at $37 million in public money, ranks among the top three residential projects, and has also displaced thousands of people. In Berkeley BART's construction has displaced about a thousand low income families. In all of these areas renewal and highway construction demolished far more low rent housing units than were ever replaced.

Equally important to consider are the re-uses to which the cleared land was put. While no careful comparative studies of this question appear to have been done, the evidence of the cities under consideration suggest that re-uses were by and large in direct service to the central business district and dominant government and educational institutions.

In Boston, renewal in the South End was designed to produce "maximum upgrading," to use Edward Logue's words, in a housing stock adjacent to the CBD, a hospital complex, and the newer office developments in the Back Bay. Other large Boston renewal projects cleared land near Massachusetts General Hospital, for a new Government Center office complex, and for the Prudential Life Insurance Company.

In San Francisco, renewal made possible the Golden Gateway Center, upgraded housing near City Hall, and a large-scale convention and sports center/office building complex. Similarly, renewal in Cambridge cleared away white ethnic working class neighborhoods to make way for office building complexes sponsored by M.I.T. and Cabot, Cabot and Forbes. In Berkeley, renewal removed low-rent housing in West Berkeley for an industrial park.

The class nature of renewal, in other words, finds clear expression not only in the distribution of costs and benefits, which all observers acknowledge is highly regressive. The class purpose emerges in the shift of land's very function from low rent housing for relatively stable working class neighborhoods to luxury housing for the middle class, office buildings for corporations and government, and transportation facilities to serve them.

This shift of territorial organization triggered a whole chain of disruptive consequences for the central city, most of which fell upon poor neighborhoods or pitted newer minority areas against older ethnic communities. Thus not only did growth mobilize those directly and adversely af-

fected, but it stimulated racial antagonisms as displacees sought housing in other areas. As minority neighborhoods became more influential, this racial turf battle extended to city bureaucracies and other politically sensitive employment areas as well.[76]

B. The Neighborhood Response

Though one would not learn it from the existing literature on community mobilization, in almost every instance the roots of mobilization may be found in struggles over growth. Most of the community turbulence of the 1960s was firmly directed against urban renewal, highway construction, the declining availability of decent, inexpensive housing, expansion of dominant institutions, and city bureaucracies tightly dominated by ethnic groups being displaced in the urban population by minority newcomers.

The four cities demonstrate this point quite firmly. In Boston, major community protests involved urban renewal, construction of the Inner Belt highway, the inadequacy of housing, hospital expansion, and rent control. In Cambridge, the issues were largely the same, coupled with opposition to Harvard's and M.I.T.'s expansion. In San Francisco, protests emerged against urban renewal in the Western Addition and the Mission, against housing quality, in favor of community control over housing development, and against racism in the education and law enforcement bureaucracies, and in various firms' hiring practices. Finally, in Berkeley movements developed against renewal, displacement from BART, community control over development of areas around BART, police brutality, and political control of the city as a whole (with students and blacks pitted against suburbanites).[77]

Some of the same basic causes contributed to the wave of riots across urban America between 1964 and 1968. Virtually all of the riot areas were sites of major renewal efforts; quite frequently struggles over the nature of renewal lurked behind the riots as an implicit issue, as in the case of Newark's planned new medical school. On a city-by-city basis, the simple correlation between city expenditures for renewal and the occurrence of riots between 1964–1968 for 100 large cities was .352.[78] While this is an admittedly crude measurement, since other factors might lessen or strengthen this relationship it is nonetheless suggestive. And, where riotous violence occurred in the four cities (with the exception of Berkeley), it was in neighborhoods strongly affected by urban renewal. The most significant riots occurred in Boston's black Roxbury and black/Puerto Rican South End, both subjected to large-scale renewal.

One of the outstanding characteristics of these movements, which are fully described elsewhere,[70] is their alternative conception of how urban development might occur, at least within their neighborhoods. Although this conception never completely jelled, either within any given neighborhood or nationally, it always tended to have the same elements. Opposition to market allocation of private housing, opposition to planning for businesses rather than people, desire for community control of major government services, calls for rent control and government-subsidized housing, and experimentation with local self-development were repeated in all the cities examined. In the process of battling development, new neighborhood-oriented institutions like tenant unions, advocacy planning bodies, tenant self-management corporations, and social service advocacy organizations grew up. Though many of these institutions failed or were drawn into the mechanics of traditional city bureaucracies, many retained an important role in the neighborhood and modestly yet obviously pointed towards how a whole society might be organized along alternative lines.

C. The Breakdown of the Pro-Growth Coalitions

The second part of the mid-1960's dual political crisis, namely the internal breakdown of the pro-growth coalition's network of alliances, is a complex matter which cannot be treated fully here. It has three basic parts. First, neighborhood mobilization slowed down government decision making and threatened electoral consequences. In response, mayors, realizing they needed a more sophisticated approach, began to allow groups a mostly symbolic part in the policy process,[80] and to set up parallel but for the most part powerless bureaucracies like Model Cities. This introduced discordant elements into city hall. Worse, they were well-paid discordant elements, and their example suggested to other city employees (especially uniformed services

and craft workers) that only by growing more uncooperative would their own rewards be maximized. The growing external pressure on the coalition made this strategy all the more effective.[81]

Second, as growth costs became apparent, constituencies which previously supported growth began to swing into opposition. Fiscally conservative elected officials urged that commuters be taxed more fully for the costs of growth, while urban upper middle class professionals opposed the transformation of "their" cities and mixed neighborhoods. The climate of public opinion, once unified, became divided. Middle class blacks in Boston, Harvard liberals in Cambridge, and ecology-oriented activist professionals in Berkeley and San Francisco all mounted anti-growth campaigns.

Finally, both business and labor drew back from full-scale support from the pro-growth coalition because both disfavor, and to some extent fear, the politicization of their activities. Neither wished to accept the forms of public control, ranging from hearings, to environmental impact reports, to neighborhood vetos, to affirmative action programs which were emerging from the battles against growth.

Overlaying this set of frictions was a central city fiscal and social crisis which was, as has been argued, deepened not only by growth policies but by the growing overall differentiation between workplace and dwelling place, low-productivity central city service functions, and suburban tax protection. The political fight against growth, the burgeoning central city fiscal needs, and the international plight of American empire joined together to throw old policies and political alliances into question.[82] It did so not only on an electoral level, but on the level of policy adequacy or viability. At a national level, as we shall see, policy changed toward austerity and retrenchment in social spending (which further undermined local mayoral efforts to hide the differences between growth beneficiaries and growth sufferers under a plush patronage carpet), and towards a policy of growth without constraint from labor or neighborhoods. In all, conservative policy makers had decided that the old approaches to growth had simply become too costly.[83]

From 1969 onward, these forces clearly sapped local pro-growth electoral coalitions. In general, they have survived only where the negative consequences were relatively slight (perhaps because development was more sophisticated politically), or where pro-growth mayors have demonstrated exceedingly clever political skills.[54]

Simply to mention some of the more famous cases, "cop" mayors took over in Minneapolis, St. Paul, and Philadelphia, and law-and-order candidates came close to winning in Newark (Anthony Imperiale), Boston (Louise Day Hicks), and New York (Mario Procaciono), to name a few. In a number of cases these candidates either beat or lost narrowly to black candidates. Blacks, of course, managed to win office in Gary, Cleveland, Newark, and most recently in Los Angeles and Atlanta. Shrewd pro-growth mayors, particularly Alioto in San Francisco, White in Boston, Uhlman in Seattle, and Landieu in New Orleans, managed to reconcile opposing sides and avert losses to either blacks, middle class anti-growth exponents, or law-and-order advocates, but they often did so by the skin of their teeth. (Uhlman, for example, was faced with recall when he adopted a hard stand against pay increases for Seattle firemen.)

Both White and Alioto employed Model Cities, OEO, job programs, and similar federal patronage resources to sustain minority community support while acting tough on disorder and boosting growth. They employed their federal resources all the more shrewdly by allowing "community control," rather than exercising tight oversight over funds and employees. But they knew when to call in their debts. In the last analysis, however, their staying power remains in doubt. Alioto retires in 1975, White must stand for re-election in racially troubled times, and the Daley regime, to mention another example, has been challenged by scandal, black opposition, and white middle class reformism.

In a few cities, particularly Cambridge and Berkeley, an alliance of poor neighborhoods radical students, and a fraction of the middle class appalled by the depredations of growth, united to elect "radical" mayors and city councillors. Similar tendencies occurred in Madison, Wisconsin, where the socialist Wisconsin Alliance scored some gains, and to a lesser extent in other Wisconsin and Massachusetts cities.

Another interesting variant includes New Haven and Pittsburgh, veritable progenitors of the pro-growth coalition. In these cities candidates strongly oriented towards white ethnic neighborhoods (Bart Guida in New Haven, Peter Fla-

herty in Pittsburgh) won mayoral elections. Both are conservative Democrats who have been relative mavericks as far as the local party organizations were concerned, although Guida received support from New Haven Democratic leader Barbieri. Both, finally, have cut city payrolls, taxes, and opposed renewal efforts.

What are the consequences of this declining potency of the pro-growth coalition? Aside from the fact that city politics has been opened up to all manner of electoral ventures, and that opportunist politicians have had a field day in exploiting sometimes legitimate grievances in a thoroughly racist manner, *the main consequence has been to throw up barriers against growth.* In Berkeley, this influence has accomplished this quite concretely, as it were, by building barriers across many of the city's streets.

In response to neighborhood protest in the mid-1960s, federal policy and local practice with respect to renewal changed substantially. Relocation rights were strengthened, neighborhood advisory committees required, the amount of subsidized housing increased, affirmative action hiring propounded, and many renewal projects delayed, restructured, or killed altogether. New zoning and other impediments to development were thrown up in various neighborhoods in the cities under consideration. To summarize the matter, quite real and serious obstacles were developed to thwart some of the worst consequences of growth. While many of them were designed simply to "buy off" neighborhood opposition and allow the realization of corporate ends, others have proven to be substantial impediments.

It is in this light that recent federal policy towards the cities can be understood. Under President Nixon, the urban renewal program as understood up until 1974 was entirely dismantled. In its place the administration initiated "community development revenue sharing," which allowed localities to use money as they saw fit, subject only to broad guidelines. This new policy has four chief aspects: (a) it substitutes a *smaller* total amount of money for a host of federal categorical grants (ranging from renewal to Model Cities) which had fallen under the influence of both neighborhood and real estate industry interest groups; (b) because the money is spent by localities rather than the federal government, the procedural rights built up under the old renewal program are negated; (c) it helps restore mayoral power against hard-to-control bureaucracies and others competing for influence over the course of urban development; and (d) it gutted subsidized housing programs for the poor.[85]

Some have interpreted these changes as signalling that growth itself has become economically exhausted. Actually, the reverse is true: growth policies of the 1960s became politically exhausted, and as their strength waned, the costs of bringing along a sufficiently sizeable constituency mounted. The current Nixon-Ford administration is attempting, in areas ranging from redevelopment to manpower training to welfare, to eliminate just these politically-driven costs. It is seeking, through the general application of austerity measures, to re-start the growth process on its own terms: that is, it is seeking to restore "natural" and automatic moral authority to growth.

VI. TENDENCIES WITHIN THE CURRENT POLITICAL INSTABILITY

The conditions pushing pro-growth coalitions towards breakdown—neighborhood protest, constraints on the growth process, loss of mass legitimacy, independence of public employees, and serious divisions among growth supporters— have not operated uniformly over all cities. Nor have they, for given classes of cities, led consistently to an alternative political coalition for the future. Nevertheless, some broad patterns can be discerned.

A. The Strength of Growth

The pro-growth coalition took on its most public role in cities where state action was most necessary to promote the large-scale urban changes which have occurred since World War II. These cities are primarily large, old, highly ethnic and blue collar, with large but worn capital investments which needed to be replaced rather than developed *de novo*. Heterogeneity provides one of the hallmarks for such cities, thus making a well-worked out political alliance network all the more necessary.

By contrast, newer, fast-growing cities of the South and Southwest, and smaller cities generally, could undertake most of the needed invest-

ments on a purely private basis. No outmoded built environment (in both the social and physical senses) needed to be dismantled. Countertendencies to corporate strength, such as unions and well-organized minorities, proved infrequent. Without such requirements for political action, the standard devices of zoning and public works proved sufficient for a rapid spurt of growth over the last several decades. In such cities, with Phoenix, Houston, Los Angeles, and San Jose, and to a lesser extent Dallas/Ft. Worth and Atlanta, growth interests needed only an efficient, business minded city government, and not even a particularly powerful one at that. Alliances among major corporations, banks, and developers proved in the main to be all that was needed, and they could operate largely outside public scrutiny. In these cities, then, growth-oriented mayors tended to survive much more easily than their Northeastern colleagues.[86]

In the cities where pressures against growth exerted themselves most severely, a variety of equally temporary outcomes seems to have appeared. In some cities, mayors managed, through political adroitness, to paper over some of the divisions between growth proponents, neighborhoods suffering from growth, and unruly public workers. Mayors like Alioto, White, Cavanaugh, Ivan Allen, and Moon Ladrieu had good connections with business and development interests, provided professionally oriented and innovative leadership, and at the same time drew minority support on the basis of large scale "citizen participation" and social welfare-oriented programs. To varying degrees, each was successful in exerting enough political control over civil service employees to mount a strong campaign apparatus, perhaps the principal fact in accounting for Daley's strength in Chicago. Yet each of these mayors found their grip on public office uncertain to say the least.

In a number of cases conservative, white ethnic, small property-owning candidates propelled themselves into office on the basis of a revolt against rising taxes, neighborhood disruption, and growing black influence. While these candidates have links to regular Democratic organizations, they are often hostile to civil service employees and the professional planning apparatus lodged in city hall. These "law and order" and "anti-busing" candidates, such as Stenvig in Minneapolis, McCarty in St. Paul, Flaherty in Pittsburgh, Guida in New Haven, Rizzo in Philadelphia, Imperiale in Newark, and Louise Day Hicks in Boston, have made an important but not lasting imprint on urban politics. In general, they have had no understanding of the forces which have created the plight against which they are reacting, and therefore no program for dealing with them. In the main, they have ultimately succumbed to the forces of the better organized growth-politics-as-usual.

A third tendency includes black mayors who, having foregone support from (white) regular organizations, must find it in roughly the same platform as their pro-growth predecessors no matter how violently black neighborhoods might oppose renewal *per se*. When all is said and done, renewal can be used as an important source of patronage for black elites, particularly under the Housing and Community Development Act of 1974. Black mayors in Newark, Detroit, Cleveland, Atlanta, Gary, and Los Angeles have found it necessary to elicit support from liberal wings of their business communities, if only to keep firms from leaving the city. Inability to control growing and powerful black populations may be an important contributing factor in business relocation out of such central cities as Detroit and St. Louis.[87] Thus though black mayors have generally opposed the depredations of renewal and resistance from white ethnic-dominated bureaucracies, their abilities have been strictly circumscribed.

The fourth tendency rejects both growth and reliance on orthodox local political organization based on public employees: so-called radical candidates. Aside from the university-dominated cities mentioned, in some instances environmentalists have joined with threatened neighborhoods to overcome both business and bureaucracy. In Somerville and Lynn, Massachusetts, renewal and highway developments which threatened major areas and which were backed by patently nepotistic and corrupt city governments triggered election of strongly liberal reform slates. Because they were not rooted in the patronage structure of the cities' bureaucracies, however, these candidates also found themselves unable to substantially change the course of local government. At most they could veto widely opposed projects; positive achievements were another matter altogether.

None of these alternatives have established a hammerlock on the future. Pre-growth coalitions are still at bay. Law and order regimes have been discredited (Rizzo and police corrup-

tion) or undercut by pro-growth coalitions anxious to get back in business (Minneapolis and St. Paul). Black mayors appear to be holding their own, by and large, but in the end may not turn out much different than pro-growth coalitions simply manned by black people. This seems particularly likely given the ideology of institution-building and patronage accumulation current within the black community. Finally, none of the "radical" coalitions have distinguished themselves either by being particularly principled (backsliding has been endemic in both Berkeley and Cambridge) or by developing a hold outside student strongholds. In short, the situation remains unsettled. While the current economic crisis and market-oriented federal austerity policies may rekindle pre-growth policies for a time, it seems unlikely that they will be able to overcome permanently the opposition which is sure to arise.

VII. CONCLUSIONS AND SPECULATIONS

Orthodox political science and economics have attempted to explain metropolitan decentralization and the content of urban politics with what are in essence market models. For both economists and political scientists, departure for the suburbs simply constituted a choice individuals made about lifestyles given a range of means and opportunities. For Edward Banfield, growing personal incomes, improved transportation technology, rising populations, and internal migrations lead "naturally" to suburbanization.[88] For economist Charles Tiebout, the number of metropolitan political jurisdictions and the various political outcomes in each reflect merely a market competition among governments selling different public policy packages for different tax prices. For the urban economics literature as a whole, transportation and production techniques, and the way they exert their influence through competition, determined not only metropolitan dispersion but land use intensities within the central city.[89] One firm discovers the truck and the space-extensive suburban plant layout, and by its newfound efficiency forces all other to adopt the same methods. Within the city, an entrepreneur captures benefits from the general urban growth by finding better uses for a given piece of land; if previous social patterns are disrupted, only the market is to blame.

Economists have great difficulty in analyzing and evaluating the content of urban policy, and tend to think markets would do a better job (alas, if they could only be introduced!). Political scientists understand more clearly that public policies must be marketed through bureaucratic and electoral mechanisms which utilize the divisible nature of policy *inputs* for strength, not their collective and uncontrollable outputs. But even here they employ market notions of political completion; to recall once more Bell and Held's views, they explain the protest of the 1960s in terms of inflated and necessarily impossible expectations from government.

This paper has rejected such views on two counts: first, market explanations remain essentially circular unless the context in which the market operates are specified. In this case, markets function in the midst of a basic conflict over the direction and purpose of urban life, namely the conflict between urban form for human purposes and urban form for efficient capitalist production. New transportation technologies or plant locations are introduced not merely to reduce marginal marketing costs, but to increase production's social control over the entire environment of work. The upgrading of inner city neighborhoods occurs not simply because young lawyers and businesspeople find them quaint, but because the city economic system as a whole is predicated on concentrating command functions in the central city and making it possible for a workforce to have ready access to it.

Secondly, market explanations deny or mystify the central yet contradictory role of the state. Of all the contextual factors that structure markets, the state is the most important. Land use patterns are inherently collective, public matters. They cannot be set up without government actions ranging from roads and sewers to police and fire protection to government constraints on how owners use their property. As a result, land use questions (always subject to the fundamental tension described above) inevitably tend to become political. How the politics of land use are organized, and therefore contained, provides perhaps the central theme of U.S. urban political history.

The view presented here holds that urban land use policies are at the center of a vortex of forces. In order to promote growth of land values and central city revenues (problems which were themselves in part the result of other government policies), business, government, and to a lesser extent organized labor forged a pro-growth alliance. The consequence of this alliance was an important class-based transformation of land uses, which in turn triggered severe tensions both within and outside the growth alliance. The consequent political breakdown involved placing steadily increasing costs and impediments to growth which the Federal government is presently attempting, without a great deal of success, to throw off. This move has shifted some aspects of the battle over land use into a battle over the composition of city budgets. The situation remains fluid.

Although it has as yet not materialized, the current situation provides an important opening for a new, more progressive coalition within city politics. During the dual political breakdown of the 1960s, neighborhoods and city workers tended to ignore each other when not being downright antagonistic. Yet for both parties, this was a shortsighted, if unsurprising course, Neighborhoods made their greatest gains when they gathered support from within city bureaucracies, while conservative political forces can isolate public employees with ease if they fail to build strong constituencies within neighborhoods and client groups. But on what grounds could such an alliance be effected?

The missing link, to this point, has been a political movement explicitly based on putting in place new city spending priorities and land use patterns rather than merely redistributing patronage. Such a party of public service producers and consumers would encourage means to make them directly responsive to each other rather than insulated by a layer of brokerage-oriented politics. It would seek to change the framework of decision making and the values implicit within it rather than simply reducing police expenditures here and increasing welfare expenditures there. Whether such an alliance can emerge remains to be seen, but when all is said and done, this remains the task of city dwellers who would like to live in a truly humane city.

Acknowledgments

This paper was stimulated and influenced by discussions within the Bay Area *Kapitalistate* Group (in particular with Jim O'Connor), the *Common Sense* city bureau (Dan Feshbach, Chester Hartman, and Jim Shock), and by the work of David Gordon, David Harvey, and Claus Offe. An earlier version was presented to the Conference on Urban Political Economy, New School for Social Research on February 16, 1975. Roger Friedland, Bob Heifetz, Judith Lamare, Margaret Levi, Ann Markusen, Jon Pynoos, faculty members of the San Francisco State Urban Studies program, Larry Sauers, Phil Singerman, Bill Tabb, and Peter Williams shared their nearly overwhelming criticisms with me, and though likely none of them will be totally satisfied with my response, the paper is stronger for their efforts. Neither Professor James Q. Wilson nor Professor Raymond Wolfinger was won over by my argument, but I am grateful to both for showing me some of its weaknesses. Finally, though some parts of the paper may remain in error, I thank all of those who told me it was useful to them and gave me the courage to go on with it.

References

1. Daniel Bell and Virginia Held, "The Community Revolution," *The Public Interest* 16 (Summer, 1969), pp. 142–177. For a full account of this development, see John Mollenkopf, "Community Organization and City Politics" (Ph.D. dissertation, Harvard University, 1973).

2. Fred Powledge, "The Flight from City Hall," *Harper's Magazine* (November, 1969) and James Q. Wilson and Harold Wilde, "The Urban Mood," *Commentary* (October, 1969). Lee and Barr (Pittsburgh) were replaced by conservative, maverick Democrats opposed to urban renewal, Naftalin and Tate by cop mayors, Allen by a black, and others by more machine-oriented candidates.

3. See the previously cited articles by Wilson and Wilde and Bell and Held, as well as D. P. Moynihan, *Maximum Feasible Misunderstanding* (New York: Free Press, 1969), for explanations of this type about community mobilization and city politics. On riots, see the *Report of the National Advisory Commission on Civil Disorders* (New York: Bantam, 1968), especially pp. 1–2, 8–11. Political science did an incredibly poor job on this subject. It failed to anticipate riots, failed to anticipate their winding down, and now, despite the fact that significant urban rioting continues, it fails to pay any attention to it. Evidently the subject is no longer "policy relevant."

4. LeCorbusier, *The City of Tomorrow* (Cambridge: MIT Press, [1929] 1971), suggests what the efficient city might look like. The conclusion is drawn from Alan Altshuler, *The City Planning Process*, (Ithaca: Cornell University Press, 1965).

5. See Eric Hobsbawm, *Labouring Men* (London: Weidenfeld and Nicolson, 1964) and Allan Silver, "The Demand for Order in Civil Society," in David Bordua, ed., *The Police* (New York: John Wiley, 1967) for discussions of the clash between working class cultural traits and work.

6. Among the most vivid portrayals of this phenomenon in the literature on machine politics are Lincoln Steffens, *Autobiography* (New York: Harcourt, Brace, 1931), and Upton Sinclair, *The Jungle.* (New York: Harper, 1951). Marc Karson, *American Labor Unions and Politics* (Carbondale: So. Illinois Press, 1958) describes the Catholic Church's influence.

7. This view has been most boldly stated by David Gordon in his unpublished work on urban history. See also S. P. Hayes, "The Politics of Reform in Municipal Government in the Progressive Era," in Daniel Gordon, ed., *Social Change and Urban Politics* (Englewood Cliffs: Prentice-Hall, 1973).

8. James O'Connor, *The Class Struggle* (manuscript), Chapters 1 and 2. Victor Fuchs, *The Service Economy* (New York: Columbia University Press for NBER, 1968). David Harvey, "The Political Economy of Urbanization in Advanced Capitalist Societies, the Case of the United States" (Johns Hopkins University Center for Metropolitan Planning and Research, 1974), Manuel Castells, "Neo-Capitalism, Collective Consumption and Urban Contradictions: New Sources of Inequality and New Models for Change" (Centre D'Etude des Mouvements Sociales, Ecole Practique des Hautes Etudes, Paris, 1973).

9. Robert B. Cohen, "Urban Effects of the Internationalization of Capital and Labor," (unpublished paper, Human Resources Project, Columbia University, 1975).

10. Judith Lamare, Jim Shock, and Terry Karl have stressed this point to me. The effects of imperialism and internationalization of capital and labor clearly require much more research attention than they have received to date.

11. Harvey, *op. cit.*, and *Social Justice and the City* (Baltimore: Johns Hopkins University Press, 1973), especially pp. 261–274.

12. For a politically enlightening debate on the consequences of these trends, see George Sternleib, "The City as Sandbox," and Norton Long, "The City as Reservation," *The Public Interest* 25 (Fall, 1971); Alexander Ganz, "The City—Sandbox, Reservation, or Dynamo?" *Public Policy* 21 (Winter, 1973), pp. 107–123, and Franklin James, "The City: Sandbox, Reservation, or Dynamo? A Reply," *Public Policy* 22 (Winter, 1974), pp. 39–52.

13. Harvey, "The Political Economy of Urbanization," op. cit. Michael Stone, "Federal Housing Policy: A Political-Economic Analysis," in J. Pynoos, R. Schafer, and C. Hartman, eds., Housing Urban America (Chicago: Aldine, 1973), pp. 423–433. Describes the state's role in rationalizing and stimulating housing finance, and therefore promoting land development. See also Henry J. Aaron, Shelter and Subsidies (Washington, D.C.: Brookings Institution, 1972) for an analysis of the regressive distribution of housing subsidies.

14. Robert Caro, The Power Broker, op. cit., richly treats the way the fortunes of the inventor of such devices rose along with those of his creation.

15. James R. O'Connor, The Fiscal Crisis of the State (New York: St. Martin's Press, 1973). My debt to O'Connor is obvious. See also Claus Offe, "The Abolition of Market Control and the Problem of Legitimacy," Kapitalistate 1,2 (1973, 1974).

16. In addition to O'Connor's work, the next six paragraphs also draw heavily on Dan Feshbach, "Nibbling at the Bullet: Origins of the Urban Fiscal Crisis," (work in progress, 1975).

17. Sam Bass Warner, Jr., provides a useful history of local government influence over land use in The Urban Wilderness (New York: Harper, 1972), pp. 15–54, "Saving Yesterday's Property."

18. Ira Katznelson, "The Crisis of the Capitalist City: Urban Politics and Social Control," (manuscript, 1974), has emphasized the absorbtive functions of local bureaucracies.

19. John Kain has wondered, for example, whether federal investments should be made in the central city. ". . . I know of no good statement," he wrote, "of why these trends should be reversed." He continued, "attempting to reverse a massive, nationwide social and economic movement (that is suburbanization) strikes me as the most costly method—and the one least likely to succeed—of helping pay for needed central city services." John M. Kain, "The Distribution and Movement of Jobs and Industry," in J. Q. Wilson, ed., The Metropolitan Enigma (Cambridge: Harvard University Press, 1968), p. 37.

20. For an orthodox cataloging of urban crises, circa 1970, see Barbara Bergeman, "The Urban Crisis," American Economic Review (September, 1969), p. 639, or the previously cited Kerner Commission report.

21. Revenue figures come from "Statistics on State and Local Government Finance," The Bond Buyer 9 (May, 1971), p. 40. Douglas Ludeman, The Investment Merits of Big City Bonds (Boston: Financial Publishing Company, 1973), discusses the history of municipal finances, the defaults of the 1930s, and the current prospects for defaults.

22. The Report was Financial Problems of New York, reported in Carl Shoup, "New York City's Financial Situation and the Transit Fare," National Tax Journal 5 (September, 1952), pp. 218–226.

23. Robert Wood, Suburbia (Boston: Houghton Mifflin, 1958), p. 72. Wood was evidently quoting a comment in the Boston Municipal Research Bureau Bulletin when he described impending disaster.

24. Ibid., p. 71–72. Wood reports that slums occupied 20 percent of Boston's non-business land, required 45 percent of its expenditures, but contributed only 6 percent of its revenue. Similar figures were widely reported by other mayors in testimony favoring passage of the 1949 Housing and Urban Renewal Act. See also "Downtown Woes," Business Week 1309 (October 2, 1954), p. 64, which reports the first meeting of executives from twenty-seven downtown associations "to discuss ways of combatting the threat to downtown property values and store sales." They decided to push for improved downtown parking, freeways, better mass transit, and "improvement projects to reduce blight areas." Public Management, the National Municipal Review, American City, carried frequent articles on this general subject.

25. Shoup, Ludeman, op. cit. Dick Netzer, "Toll Roads and the Crisis in Highway Finance," National Tax Journal 5 (June, 1952), pp. 107–119, argued that existing policy favored rural areas, that urban highways were desperately needed, and that they could not be self-financing through tolls. He thus made one of the earliest arguments for federally-financed urban freeways. Similarly, Harlan Cleveland, "Are the Cities Broke," National Civic Review 50 (March, 1961), pp. 126–130, pointed out that there was sufficient wealth in urban areas, but paradoxically no way for localities to tax it; he called as a result for further federal involvement.

26. The 1954 amendments allowed 10 percent of renewal funds to be applied to projects neither primarily residential before or after renewal, liberalized the treatment of projects aiding universities and hospitals, and streamlined the application procedures. The Senate Subcommittee on Housing study "The Central City Problem," previously cited, provides an excellent legislative history of the program's administration, pp. 39–67. As yet no full scale study of the origins and social support for the 1949 housing act has been undertaken; I have relied on the brief description given in Lawrence Friedman, Government and Slum Housing (Chicago: Rand McNally, 1968), pp. 102–113, 148–155.

27. David Harvey, "The Political Economy of Urbanization in Advanced Capitalist Societies—the Case of the United States," (unpublished manuscript, Johns Hopkins University, Geography Department, 1975), tables 6 and 7.

28. Raymond Moley, testimony to the House Banking and Currency Committee Hearings on the 1949 Housing Act, p. 26. Baltimore mayor D'Alesandro echoed these sentiments (p. 528–530). He claimed that locally financed efforts had proven insufficient for renewal, and that assessments in Baltimore's growing slums had declined over $10 million between 1938 and 1948. He also filed several dozen letters from other big city mayors making claims of the same general type.

29. President's Advisory Committee on a National Highway Program, "A Ten Year National Highway Program," (Washington, D.C., January, 1955). Robert Goodman, *After the Planners* (New York: Simon and Schuster, 1971), pp. 69–84, "The Highway Gravy Train."

30. Helen Leavitt, *Superhighway Superhoax* (Garden City: Doubleday, 1970), Ben Kelley, *The Pavers and the Paved* (New York: Donald Brown, 1971), David Hapgood, "The Highwaymen," *Washington Monthly* (March, 1969).

31. Raymond Vernon, "The Changing Economic Function of the Central City," in J. Q. Wilson, ed., *Urban Renewal* (Cambridge: MIT Press, 1967), pp. 22–23. His statements were based on an exhaustive study of post war New York City.

32. Kain, "Distribution and Movement," *op. cit.*, p. 29.

33. House Subcommittee on Urban Affairs, "Central City Problem and Urban Renewal Policy," (93rd Congress, February, 1973), p. 24. Beverly Duncan and Stanley Lieberson, *Metropolis and Region in Transition* (Beverly Hills: Sage, 1970) give evidence based on banking transactions to show how central cities not only maintained but enhanced their financial dominance over subordinate regional cities. Although they do not argue the point, this trend clearly includes overseas as well as U.S. hinterland investments.

34. Benjamin Cohen, "Trends in Negro Employment within Large Metropolitan Areas," *Public Policy* 19 (Fall, 1971), pp. 611–620, and Franklin James, "The City: Sandbox, Reservation, or Dynamo?—A Reply," *op. cit.* See also Bennett Harrison, *Urban Economic Development* (Washington, D.C.: Urban Institute, 1974), Chapter 2, for the most up-to-date and comprehensive restatement of these arguments.

35. These tables show the occupations of central city residents, rather than the location of jobs. The overlap is strong, however.

36. Sam Bass Warner, Jr., *Urban Wilderness, op. cit.*

37. Steven Marglin, "What Do Bosses Do?" and Kathy Stone, "The Origins of Job Structures in the Steel Industry," *Review of Radical Political Economics* 6 (Summer, 1974), pp. 60–112, 113–173.

38. David Gordon, "Stages of Capital Accumulation and Urban Development in the U.S.," (New School for Social Research, February, 1974), Dan Feshbach, "Class Struggle and the Postwar Suburban Expansion," (forthcoming), and Marc Weiss and Martin Gellen, "The Rise and Fall of the Cold War Consensus," in Judith Carnoy and Marc Weiss, eds., *A House Divided* (Boston: Little, Brown, 1973), pp. 14–37.

39. Meyerson and Banfield, *Politics, Planning, op. cit.*, p. 19.

40. Hariette Arnow, *The Dollmaker* (New York: Avon, 1972, originally published in 1954) presents a searing case study of the ironies of "modernization" as experienced by an Appalachian family which moves to war-time Detroit.

41. "Should-Must Cities Decentralize?" *The Commonwealth* 24 (May 31, 1948). Previously the report stated that technology now allowed smaller plants. But instead of giving a naive determinism, it states, "This fact makes possible small factories in suburban or rural areas, where some of the problems attendant upon production in congested urban centers are less apparent or even non-existent. These related directly or indirectly to labor." p. 13.

42. Most of those attending were San Francisco businessmen, and the speakers were not, by all accounts, trying to sell anyone real estate. They were discussing what they obviously felt was a serious issue. It was the same sort of concern—and wartime experience—with poor transportation that led to the business consensus to build the Bay Area Rapid Transit System, subject of another Commonwealth Club forum.

43. "After the Cabots—Jerry Blakely," *Fortune* (November, 1960).

44. "Two, Three, Many Tech Squares," (MIT chapter of SDS, 1969); "The Promised Land Use," (Grass Roots, Palo Alto, n.d.), discusses Stanford University's role in generating war-related aircraft and electronics industry in Santa Clara county. Particularly important was the founding of Stanford Research Institute in 1946.

45. U.S. Bureau of the Census, *Current Population Reports*, Series P-23, No. 25, "Lifetime Migration Histories of the American People," p. 87.

46. *Ibid.*, No. 38, "The Social and Economic Status of Negroes in the U.S., 1970," p. 11. R. H. Day, "Technological Change and the Sharecropper," *American Economic Review* 57 (June, 1967), pp. 427–449.

47. Raymond Wolfinger, "Why Political Machines Have Not Withered Away and Other Revisionist Thoughts," *Journal of Politics* 34 (May, 1972),

pp. 365–398; also *The Politics of Progress* (Englewood Cliffs, N.J.: Prentice-Hall, 1974), Chapter 4. This excellent discussion is an important corrective to the notion that machine-type politics has passed from the urban scene.

48. Edward Banfield and James Q. Wilson, *City Politics* (New York: Vintage, 1963), pp. 123–124.

49. George Sternleib, "Is Business Abandoning the Big City," *Harvard Business Review* 39 (January/February, 1961), pp. 6–14 reports results from a survey of 2,200 executives conducted in the late 1950s. Only about a third of them, predominantly utility and retail executives, thought the situation was "serious" or "critical" and in general businessmen were leery of being drawn into ward politics. The same is reported in Harold Kaplan, *Urban Renewal Politics* (New York: Columbia University Press, 1963), p. 72 with respect to insurance executives in Newark.

50. Robert Salisbury, "Urban Politics: The New Convergence of Power," *Journal of Politics* 26 (November, 1964), pp. 775–797.

51. Wolfinger's previously cited book, *Politics of Progress*, is an important and useful case study of the development of this coalition in New Haven, but it is also a running polemic against the views about to be expressed. Two points can be made: first, like Berkeley, New Haven is not the locus of important corporate interests, aside from Yale, and one can therefore understand why corporate influence is less strong than in other cities. More importantly, however, Wolfinger systematically underrates Yale's influence by paying too much attention to Mayor Lee's supposed anti-Yale actions. In a city like New Haven or Cambridge any smart politician would make more or less rhetorical stands because of strong anti-university sentiment within the electorate. An objective assessment of urban renewal's impact on New Haven, like renewal's impact around the University of Chicago, shows that it strongly favored long term university interests.

52. Robert Caro, *The Power Broker: Robert Moses and the Fall of New York* (New York: Knopf, 1974).

53. Wolfinger, *Politics of Progress, op. cit.*, p. 275n.

54. Roger Friedland, "Corporations and Urban Renewal: Conditions, Consequences, and Participation," (unpublished paper, University of Wisconsin, 1974). Friedland gives example for Detroit, where auto manufacturers sponsored urban renewal, Hartford, where insurance companies formed Greater Hartford Progress, Inc., Houston, where oil companies were actively involved, DuPont's role in Wilmington, Delaware, and numerous others. See also Matthew Edel, "Urban Land Use Conflicts," *RRPE* 3 (Summer, 1971), pp. 76–89, which discusses the role of a corporate dominated citizen's committee on Detroit's renewal.

55. Roy Lubove, *Twentieth Century Pittsburgh: Government, Business, and Environmental Change* (New York: John Wiley, 1969).

56. The comment was by Lubove, p. 107.

57. Frank Hawkins, "Lawrence of Pittsburgh: Boss of the Mellon Patch," *Harper's Magazine* (August, 1956), and Arnold Auerbach, "Power and Progress in Pittsburgh," *Transaction* 2 (September/October, 1965), pp. 15–20.

58. Mike Royko, *Boss* (New York: Signet, 1971), p. 97. Pp. 96–106 describe how Daley got the backing of the Loop, the University of Chicago, etc., through the use of urban renewal.

59. Raymond Wolfinger, *Politics of Progress, op. cit.*, pp. 157–179.

60. Admittedly this collective portrait is impressionistic and undoubtedly fails to account for important variations among pro-growth mayors. Nevertheless, I believe it touches the important themes, particularly with respect to the use of federal money and the attendant technicians as a political base. Logue, for example, was a key factor in setting up community action agencies in New Haven and Boston, and the latter agency, together with the Little City Hall Program, provided Mayor White with electoral manpower and expertise.

61. Much of this material is based upon John Mendeloff, "The Business Elite and the Politics of Boston with a Focus on the Issue of Urban Renewal," (unpublished senior honors thesis, Harvard College, 1969).

62. *Ibid.*, p. 14. Coolidge and Oakes sat on the boards of numerous Boston corporations, including Eastern Gas and Fuel, H. P. Hood, and Mitre as well as the Chamber of Commerce and Committee for the Central Business District. Comparison with Jesus comes from "How Hynes Steered the Pru to Boston," *Boston Sunday Globe*, January 11, 1970, p. A-25. To get the building Massachusetts added Article 121A to its constitution, allowing negotiated property tax rates in such developments.

63. See the previously cited pamphlet, "Two, Three, Many Tech Squares," as well as John Mollenkopf and Jon Pynoos, "Property, Politics, and Local Housing Policy," *Politics and Society* 2 (Summer, 1972), pp. 407–432, for a more extended discussion of political relationships within Cambridge.

64. Chester Hartman, *Yerba Buena: Land Grab and Community Resistance in San Francisco* (San Francisco: Glide Publications, 330 Ellis Street, 1974) provides the best overall view of these developments, particularly in chapters 1 and 2. The reader is urged to turn to this book for a fuller statement. See also Fred Wirt, *Power in*

the City (Berkeley: University of California Press, 1974), pp. 161–274; *Pacific Research and World Empire Telegram* 4 (November-December, 1972) special issue on regionalism, containing articles on BART, the Bay Area Council, and housing development; Bruce Brugmann and Greggar Sletteland, eds., *The Ultimate Highrise* (San Francisco: The Bay Guardian, 1971); and Danny Beagle et al., "Turf Power and the Tax Man," *Leviathan* 1 (April, 1969), pp. 3–11.

65. Hartman, *op. cit.*, pp. 34–35. The Blythe-Zellerbach committee included Charles Blythe, a prominent stockbroker and director of Hewlett-Packard electronics in Palo Alto, and J. D. Zellerbach, toilet paper magnate and *de facto* owner of Bogalusa, Alabama, as well as other prominent San Franciscans like the Stanford board chairman, the Bank of America president, and Stephen Bechtel of Bechtel Engineering. Bechtel, it should be recalled, was instrumental in setting up the interstate highway system. He planned and built BART, and strongly pushed downtown San Francisco's redevelopment, not least by building a massive new corporate headquarters there.

66. *The National Journal*, September 18, 1971, quoted one HUD official as saying Herman was "one of the men responsible for getting urban renewal named 'the federal bulldozer' and 'negro removal.'"

67. John Mollenkopf, "Community Organization," *op. cit.*, chapter 5.

68. Moses to the contrary, the same cannot always be said for renewal officials. When Logue ran for Mayor of Boston in 1967, despite widespread business and professional support, Kevin White beat him soundly in the primary.

69. Per capita renewal expenditures can only approximate the actual importance of renewal, given varying land costs, etc. Very large cities, too, tend to receive proportionately less funds. Here are the figures:

Large Cities Ranked by
Renewal Dollars per Capita

	Population (Thousands)	Renewal $ (millions)	$ per cap.
New Haven	138	$171	$1,239
Newark	382	212	555
(Boston)	(641)	(314)	(490)
Hartford	158	069	437
Rochester	296	125	370
(Cambridge)	(101)	(036)	(356)
Washington, D.C.	757	258	341
Cincinnati	452	323	323
(San Francisco)	(716)	(229)	(320)

	Population (Thousands)	Renewal $ (millions)	$ Per cap.
Baltimore	906	220	243
Philadelphia	1949	433	222
***			
Detroit	1511	192	127
Chicago	3363	238	071
New York City	7895	471	059
(Berkeley)	(117)	(006)	(051)
Los Angeles	2816	130	046
Dallas	844	008	009
Phoenix	582	003	003
Houston	1232	000	000

Sources: 1970 Census of Population, 1973 HUD *Urban Renewal Directory*

The ranking nevertheless demonstrates that cities known to have strong growth-oriented establishments also received high per capital amounts of renewal money. Large cities received absolutely large amounts of money. The only exceptions to this rule appear to be the fast-growing but very new cities of the South and Southwest, particularly Houston, which required very little *re*development.

70. Depicted in Goodman, *After the Planners, op. cit.*, p. 62.

71. Department of Housing and Urban Development, *Urban Renewal Directory* June 30, 1971, p. 1; Department of Transportation, "1971 Annual Report on Highway Relocation Assistance," House Committee on Public Works, April, 1971, p. 8; "Urban Renewal: A Statistical Profile," *Journal of Housing* (September, 1970), p. 429.

72. Jerome Rothenberg, *An Economic Evaluation of Urban Renewal* (Washington: Brookings Institution, 1967), p. 15.

73. Anthony Downs, "Losses Imposed on Urban Households by Uncompensated Highway and Renewal Costs," in *Urban Problems and Prospects* (Chicago: Markham, 1970), pp. 192–229. See also Chester Hartman, "Displaced Persons," *Society* 9 (July/August, 1972), pp. 53–65.

74. Downs, *op. cit.*, p. 232.

75. Hartman, *Yerba Buena, op. cit.*, Chapter 6.

76. A full analysis of the direct and indirect negative consequences has yet to be undertaken. Most benefit cost studies ignore distributional issues, and those which do not generally limit their attention to quantifiable costs. In order to stimulate further thinking, the following list of consequences of growth (by no means complete) is offered:

1. Individual Effects
   shift of tax burden from CBD to tenants and homeowners

upward pressure on land uses, rents, rent/income ratios

individual monetary and psychic costs

restriction of housing and employment choices; "crowding"

2. Neighborhood Effects

market failure, disinvestment, abandonment of non-designated neighborhoods

"reverse blockbusting" in potentially valuable neighborhoods

destruction of social ties and cultural institutions

lags in bureaucratic response to newly arrived populations

social conflict generated by neighborhood invasions

exacerbated inequality in neighborhood distribution of services

3. City-Wide Effects

aggravation of fiscal crisis owing to created needs, developments with unfavorable cost/revenue ratios

suburban exploitation of central city services

concentration of low wage service industries in central cities; internal colonialism

4. Metropolitan Effects

conflict over distribution of tax burden (Serrano Case)

conflict over distribution of schooling (Richmond Case)

conflict over distribution of public housing (Gatreaux Case)

conflict over distribution of jobs (affirmative action)

further fragmentation of authority

conflict between ecological and job development movements

social waste (in added commuting time, pollution, congestion, etc.)

77. For an exhaustive account of community mobilization in these cities, see Mollenkopf, "Community Organization and City Politics," *op. cit.* Chapter 8 of this work gives an account of why the strength of community response varied from place to place.

78. *Ibid.*, Appendix IV, p. 1.

79. *Ibid.*

80. Michael Lipsky, "Protest as a Political Resource," *American Political Science Review* 62 (December, 1968) pp. 1144–58 and David Olson and Michael Lipsky, *Riot Commission Politics* (New Brunswick: Transaction Books, 1975).

81. Frances Fox Piven, "The Urban Crisis: Who Got What and Why," in Robert Paul Wolff, ed., *1984 Revisited* (New York: Knopf, 1973).

82. For a discussion of these problems in a national context, see Bay Area Kapitalistate Group, "Watergate, or The Eighteenth Brumaire of Richard Nixon," *Kapitalistate* 3 (1975), pp. 3–24.

83. For a thorough-going analysis of the current crisis' impact on the cities, see "Cities in Crisis," URPE packet on the current crisis, 1975.

84. Unattributed statements about city political trends come mainly from reading the *New York Times Index* and selected issues of the *Times* itself.

85. Richard T. Legates and Mary Morgan, "The Perils of Special Revenue Sharing for Community Development," *AIP Journal* (July, 1973), pp. 254–264.

86. Carl Susman, "Moving the City Slickers Out," *Southern Exposure* (Fall, 1974), pp. 99–107, discusses the rise of "the new South." Robert Alford, *Bureaucracy and Participation* (Chicago: Rand McNally, 1969) suggests the manner in which economic structure influences political culture, while Alex Hicks, Roger Friedland, and Ed Johnson have shown that region, presence of corporate capital, and strength of organized labor influence welfare expenditures across states, "The Political Economy of Redistribution in the American States," paper presented to the 1975 American Sociological Association meetings. By inference one might conclude that labor's strength and diversity, and capital's strength and hegemony would each influence renewal and other urban spending policies, though the matter requires much further work. See also Cohen, *op. cit.* and Michael Reich, "The Economics of Racism," in Edwards, Reich, and Weisskopf, eds., *The Capitalist System* (Englewood Cliffs, N.J.: Prentice-Hall, 1972), pp. 313–322. Reich shows that black-white wage differentials are strongly related to income inequality among whites, thus suggesting that southern cities have particularly powerful and effective business communities.

87. This point was suggested to me by Rick Hill, and deserves exploration.

88. Edward Banfield, *The Unheavenly City* (Boston: Little, Brown, 1973), Chapter 2.

89. Charles Tiebout, "A Pure Theory of Local Expenditures," *Journal of Political Economy* 64 (October, 1956), pp. 416–424. As for dispersion, see the previously cited Kain article and virtually any standard urban economics text.

toward a synthesis of studies on the urban condition

∂ s we come to the conclusion of this volume some questions may linger in the minds of many readers: "What does it all add up to?" "How do these numerous ideas and points of view fit together in some comprehensive understanding of the city?" These are fair questions and we shall attempt an answer in these closing remarks. But, first, a few provisos should be entered.

What we have referred to in these pages as the "urban condition" is an immensely complex topic, in some ways indistinguishable from the condition of contemporary society as a whole. To ask for a neat and packaged overview of such a topic is to ask for something the youthful social sciences cannot deliver and should not promise. For that reason, as we indicated in Chapter 1, our decision in this volume has been to treat *selectively* certain issues which we believe to be fundamental but by no means definitive of the urban condition. Basic concepts and processes, life styles, politics, change, and the future are themes that provide *one* way of organizing the field, but they necessarily exclude other interesting topics. The point is that since we have begun with a limited set of concerns, our integration of them will itself be limited. Yet, this seems the wise and prudent course. On the one hand, it is manifestly impossible to treat all of the issues and topics in the study of cities in one place. On the other, any premature integration of the field would likely prove a disservice by luring us into an incomplete or superficial understanding. Serious social scientists must practice what the psychologists call a "tolerance for ambiguity" or a frank recognition of the lack of closure at any given point. Otherwise they run the graver risk of exaggerating what they do know and failing to recognize what they do not. Consequently, what follows here is one attempt to integrate the field, based on the ideas developed earlier.

Understanding both the necessary and prudential bases for cautious generalization, let us now return to some of the fundamental themes of this volume in an effort to assess what we do know and where we go from here.

1. The Origins of Cities. Cities as we know them today (i.e., large-scale agglomerations of people concentrated in social space for the accomplishment of economic and administrative functions) are a relatively recent development in human history. Above all their creation was the result of changes in the economic organization of modern society, particularly the advent of industrial capitalism which required, on the one hand, a concentration of labor and productive facilities and, on the other, the commercialization of agriculture which forced many small farmers off the land. Yet, if industrialization was a fundamental cause of urbanization, it was by no means the only one. As Weber pointed out, the political and administrative

---

This conclusion was written by John Walton especially for the second edition.

apparatus of the nation state both required and contributed to consolidation of the urban population. Note here we are not saying that cities were absent in pre-industrial, pre-capitalist, or pre-nation state societies. Rather, it was the combination of those influences that gave rise to accelerated urbanization, a new role for the city within the larger society, and, hence, the city as we know it today.

2. Accelerated Urbanization. While cities are relatively recent in terms of the scope of human history, the more important fact is that the world's urban population is increasing at an exponential rate. By 1980 estimates are that slightly more than one-half of the world's population will still be rural dwellersr, but that fraction has been reduced enormously since 1920. Moreover, when we look at the more developed countries as well as the location of human and productive resources in less developed countries, it becomes clear that the world's key resources are overwhelmingly concentrated in large cities. This fact has fundamental implications for global social organization. Increasingly we must speak of "urban societies" or "an urban world" stratified to serve the interests of cities at the expense of other areas.

3. The Process of Urbanization. When we turn from the cold statistics of accelerated urbanization to the social process of migration which (in addition to natural increase) contribute to it, we discover some unexpected results. People migrate to the city largely for economic reasons: declining sources of employment in the countryside and the possibilitiy of jobs in the city. Yet, there are other motives for migration, such as the education of children, albeit of lesser importance. Most important, however, the new urban life does not appear especially traumatic or conducive of social disorganization as armchair theorists had once speculated. Migration and adaptation to the city are supported by family and friendship ties; migrants are housed and assisted in finding jobs by relatives or persons from their home town. Often they settle in neighborhoods that recreate the village of origin in the interstices of the metropolis.

4. Social Differentiation. Another myth that collapses under examination is the notion that large and growing cities are composed of teeming masses or rootless strangers adrift in a disorganized and alien world. On the contrary, cities embrace a complex social and spatial patchwork of subcommunities variously organized according to the bonds of ethnicity, nationality, occupation, social class, life styles, and subcultural values. As we shall stress momentarily, they are also organized according to influences "external" to the subcommunities themselves; influences such as political power and economic interest that shape patterns of land use. For the moment, however, we would stress that cities are highly differentiated social and spatial environments. Classical models of urban ecology attempted, with some success, to explain the nature of that differentiation while "social area analysis" and "factorial ecology" have continued the effort. When these techniques are coupled with historical and political influences intelligible portraits of urban structure begin to emerge.

5. Social Organization and Life Style. The foregoing influences (ethnicity, class, political power, etc.) not only give rise to differentiated urban sub-communities, but these socio-spatial environments take on characteristic forms of social organization. While the bases of this organization vary, most of the communities are nonetheless organized—not anomic, anarchic, individualistic, or chaotic. Illustratively we suggested that slums may find their organization based upon the exigencies of territory, ethnicity, and poverty while suburbs are structured around social class, occupation, racial homogeneity, and the enactment of certain values. or life styles. But, more important is the idea that the bases upon which communities are organized produce characteristic consequences. They shape the social environment and, thereby, the experience of the individual. Moreover, as research continues we are increasingly able to predict or explain the individual life consequences of various forms of community organization; e.g., compare the life styles of slum, high rise, and suburb dwellers.

6. Social Segregation. The bulk of the available evidence suggests that American, and likely other, cities are becoming increasingly segregated by race, education, occupation, income, and social status as they become older and larger. The moral and political implications of this fact are awesome and will continue to define the "American Dilemma" in years to come. As we have seen, a number of strategies are afoot to alter this condition; but the trend continues. Recent evidence seems to suggest that black migration to large, northern cities has leveled off which may mean that the trend will not continue to exacerbate. But neither will it be reserved by population shifts alone. And the continuing influx of Spanish-speaking migrants suggests that even-tempered optimism may not be warranted.

7. Bureaucratization. We have noted and documented considerable variation in urban life styles and community organization as a function of the "culture" of particular cities as well as the familiar influences of race, class, ethnicity, and other factors. Yet, one pervasive feature of urban life is the role of large corporate and governmental bureaucracies, themselves increasingly interdependent. The consequences of bureaucratization are reflected in at least two areas treated in this volume.

With respect to life styles, bureaucracy encroaches on the daily routines of groups as far apart as young singles and street gang members. Methods of coping with the alienation engendered vary widely. Some, like the young singles, adapt to an uneasy and unsatisfying compromise between their personal lives and the exigencies of the occupational world. Others, like the gypsies and black ghetto youth who have less to lose and, therefore, less reason to adapt, attempt to manipulate bureaucracy to their own advantage. And still others, like the residents of urban communes, attempt to organize alternative nonbureaucratized communities but discover, ironically, that their maintenance requires a good deal of formal structure. Perhaps we have here some sort of continuum on which different social groups assume different places according to their stake in conventional society. But the larger truth is that no segment of the urban population, however conventional or exotic, can escape the influence of bureaucracy.

Second, bureaucratization poses a similar dilemma with respect to politics. The post-World War II years have witnessed a growing alliance between big business and big government in the pursuit of "urban development." The "organized provider groups" have benefitted from this alliance through the political pressure they have been able to exercise while the urban poor have borne extraordinary costs for the continued "smooth" functioning of the urban economy. Now the coalition seems to be falling apart from within and as a result of the anti-bureaucratic response of the community control movement from without. Once again, the point is that urban questions cannot be understood apart from the interplay between individuals or citizen groups and bureaucracy.

8. *Power and Powerlessness*. Our materials demonstrate several things concerning the structure of control in cities. Though it may be simplistic we must begin with two observations. First, cities vary with respect to the centralization of decision making. In some, like Richard Daley's Chicago, power is tightly organized and its holders are capable of effective action in most of those areas in which they choose to act. In others, like New York or Los Angeles, power is diffuse, resulting in elaborate coalition-building in order to accomplish anything. Second, despite this variation, the vast majority of cities are "elitist" in the sense that however many participate or compete in the decision-making process, they are always a small minority of the population and typically represent the higher reaches of the socio-economic status ladder, the business community, and the voluntary associations of the white upper middle class. Less simplistic was the demonstration that enough research has now been done on the topic to suggest a set of variables that may predict and help explain this modal pattern and various configurations of power.

Our materials also suggest that power is "situational and mercurial." Contrary to some expectations, well-organized middle-class citizen groups possessing resources and political skills, such as the Santa Barbara environmentalists, may be completely frustrated in their efforts to change policy; while seemingly powerless groups like Chicago's contract buyers achieve relatively substantial gains. Recognizing the complexity of the problem and the many questions it includes, we have suggested that the first steps toward an explanation may be taken by considering the interplay between the characteristics of the dominant power structure, the organizational features of contesting groups, and the nature of the stakes involved in the conflict.

9. *Inequality and Mobilization*. Urban politics and the institutional arrangements through which they are manifest have undergone metamorphic change in the last decade or so. With a few exceptions big city machine politics are a thing of the past, but so, it seems, are reformist politics and the smooth running, if inegalitarian, coalitional politics of the post-World War II era. Today, the urban political process is characterized by two complemen-

tary poles of conflict: inequality and mobilization. Social inequality in the city has increased, not abated, in the last few decades and this trend includes but goes beyond the forms of segregation already discussed. Illustratively, black income is declining as a proportion of white income. The share of taxes borne by central city residents for municipal services has increased at a higher rate than that of suburbanites (who often use those services as commuters) while the quality of services have declined. Urban neighborhood banks invest their depositors' savings in suburban housing developments and shopping centers while denying loans (or requiring much more stringent repayment terms) in the communities where the savings were generated. Meanwhile businesses and jobs take flight from the city and governments respond to the mess that is left with increased police power.

Largely as a consequence of these and related developments the 1970s have witnessed the emergence of a new kind of "mobilization politics" (to borrow a phrase from Gideon Sjoberg), a style of politics that has dissolved and moved beyond the old alignments based on electoral politics. By mobilization politics we do not mean "pluralism." Rather, we refer to the increasing politicization of groups threatened in one way or another by increasing inequality and the new alignments produced by these conflicts. This volume has documented a number of instances of mobilization politics in the cases of the community control and environmental movements, black community organization and municipal unions, or the community alliances of lawyers and university researchers. We do not presume to know where this movement may be headed. Various alternatives present themselves ranging from a more civil and democratized urban politics dedicated to the *redistribution* of resources to oppressive counter-measures by those who have benefitted from the process of increasing inequality. Suffice it to say that these distributional issues (in housing, schools, services, jobs, etc.) will define the urban politics of the foreseeable future.

In summary it may not be collectively immodest to suggest that studies of the urban condition have advanced our understanding in certain key respects. Obviously much remains to be done but, at a minimum, we are now better equipped to identify what it is that needs to be done. As we pen these lines the city, so long described in the language of "crisis," is entering a new and different crisis or, perhaps, the culmination of many earlier ones. While this is presently termed the fiscal crisis, its roots are much deeper, stemming from the progressive unfolding of a system of racial, social, and economic inequality. In this volume you will find explanations of how that came about. Regrettably, you will not find any easy solution. Reformist efforts to shore up the city economically while leaving the mechanisms producing social inequality untouched may buy a little time but they will soon fail as they have in the past, bringing us to the present impasse.